The New York Times Film Reviews 1977-1978

The New York Times Film Reviews 1977-1978

The New York Times & Arno Press/New York 1979

Library of Congress Catalog Card Number: 70-112777

ISBN 0-405-12760-X

Manufactured in the United States of America by Arno Press Inc.

Contents

Foreword

In 1970, THE NEW YORK TIMES FILM REVIEWS (1913-1968) was published. It was a five-volume set, containing over 18,000 film reviews exactly as they first appeared in The Times.

The collection was accompanied by a sixth volume, an 1,100 page computer-generated index, which afforded ready access to the material by film titles, by producing and distributing companies, and by the names of all actors, directors and other persons listed in the credits.

Further volumes appeared in 1971, 1973, 1975 and 1977 reproducing the reviews that were printed in The Times during the years 1969-1970, 1971-1972, 1973-1974 and 1975-1976; the present volume carries the collection through 1978. The index as originally conceived was incorporated into the 1969-1970, 1971-1972, 1973-1974, 1975-1976 volumes and the present volume.

New compilations will by published periodically to keep the collection constantly updated.

BEST FILMS

Articles listing the best and award-winning films published in The Times appear at the end of each year's reviews. These include the awards of the Academy of Motion Picture Arts and Sciences and the "best films" selections of The New York Times and the New York Film Critics.

The New York Times
Film Reviews
1977

1977

FILM VIEW

RICHARD EDER

Hollywood's Affair With the Anti-Hero

When King Kong, searching for his tiny morsel of comfort, upends an elevated train, fishes out a blonde, sees that she isn't the right one, and throws her away—fatally—the audience laughs and applauds. When he bats down a helicopter they cheer. When he dies they groan. The movie is unreservedly pro-ape.

Or is it simply anti-human? The sympathies of the audience are curiously maneuvered. Most of them, presumably, are people who grow surly when the garbage isn't picked up and furious when there is a mugging on their street. How can they be on the side of this 50-foot urban blight who squashes people whenever he takes a step? Can the authorities really be made out to be fools and villains for trying to get rid of him? Would the pro-Kong audience want to live in a city where giant apes are allowed to roam around, and to get into movie theaters free by stepping on them?

There has been a recent horde of American films in which values are stood right on their heads. These movies are distinguished not just by an abundance of villainy and a virtual lack of heroes but by a lack of any virtuous context whatever. Their image of the world is that of a chaos whose evil is apportioned between that which is visible and plainly marked and that which is disguised as goodness. The rulers are all corrupt but so are the ruled; there is no point of contrast. The protagonist is neither hero nor anti-hero; he is simply someone who discovers the general disease and tries not so much to fight it as stay afloat in it. If there is some kind of hero it is a totem, existing not for its own sake but to point up the evil around it. It may be a madman—as with Howard Beale, the newscaster turned oracle in "Network" or . . . a giant ape. In no case is it human.

The examples come to hand almost too easily. From "Three Days of the Condor" to Peckinpah's "Killer Elite" to "Marathon Man" to "The Next Man" we get remarkably similar situations. The central character—often not much more than a nice shrug and a pleasant way of wearing his clothes—is pitted against a web of evil. He cuts it; behind the web is a bigger web, and so on. All the powers are tainted, but that's not all: if it were, the films would stand, I suppose, as some kind of political or sociological commentary. The taint goes down as well as up; ordinary people are stupid, selfish, venal, inept and foolish. The protagonist—even a relatively vigorous one such as Dustin Hoffman in "Marathon Man"—is ultimately struggling for nothing but himself and maybe his girl (until he is obliged to shoot her).

As for "King Kong," time has changed its values even more than its technology. The original film created a monster whose fearfulness was real though there was a ghost of charm behind it. The new monster is positively smarmy in its winsomeness. But the chief difference is that the new, expensive version of the story comes preserved in a chemical misanthropy; fashionable enough, and leaving the kind of burning aftertaste associated with cheap doughnuts. Its human species, unlike that of the original, is malevolent.

The impulse to explore, to discover, to bring back what you've discovered, that we find in the first "King Kong" is now replaced by simple greed—the greed of the oil company representative, Fred Wilson, to find a gusher; his greed in trying to convert King Kong into a gusher of a different sort. The greedy curiosity of the swarming crowds: humanity as an anthill or a carcass full of maggots.

Despite some fatty talk about "King Kong" being concerned with the environment, the intellectual content of the film is more on the order of a reflex than a thought. Perhaps there's no reason to take it with any seriousness—though perhaps there is: a great many more people will end up seeing it than Ophuls's "Memory of Justice"—except that a reflex does reflect conditioning and the conditioning may be worth looking at.

Take the treatment of masses of people. The gatherings that used to hoist the hero up on their shoulders in the old Frank Capra films are scarcely a memory. The crowds have turned mean. For example, there was the voracious and totally overdrawn mob scene in "Day of the Locust." The movie wasn't able to preserve the nightmare feeling of the book. All it could do was reproduce, in a heavily literal manner, the grotesque figures that peopled the nightmare. The film's mob was not so much an erupting force as a costume party where everyone was told to come ugly.

At least the image had some freshness at the time. But even then its nausea was suspect. I remember coming out of "Locust" at the 1975 Cannes Festival. There, appropriately, was the crowd waiting to see the stars come out. It was hot, and people pushed and shoved with a decided urgency. It was uncomfortable but innocent, and rather funny. It may not have been humanity at its best, but there was not the slightest doubt that it was humanity and not the locusts of the film.

By now this ugly mob, symbol of the human race, is a cliché. It is shot loftily from above, a scurrying mass of lewd urgency, in "King Kong." In "Two-Minute Warning" the football crowd that is supposed to be the victim of a mad sniper goes berserk and vicious when he starts shooting. There is nothing to hang the film upon. The sniper is evil, the police are incompetent or brutal, and the mob is a mass of murderously flailing feet and contorted faces. It is like filming Noah's Ark from the point of view of the Flood; "Jaws" from the point of view of the shark.

Even in "Network," a far better though eventually foolish film, the masses are sheep. All of New York sticks its head out of the window and shouts when Howard Beales orders it to; the crowds flock docilely into the studio to watch him rave. True, Paddy Chayefsky's intention is satirical but he is too much saddled with realism to quite make it. The true satirist must be winged enough to hold up the cesspool without spilling it.

This current view of the crowd is not simply a new exploration of the likelihood that the individual may be right and the masses wrong. Nobody is right; there is no rightness. There is simply, perhaps, somebody who hasn't yet been initiated into wrongness but probably will be soon. (No doubt Dustin Hoffman will eventually go to work for the same people that employed the dentist; and William Holden will be back any day as a summer replacement for Barbara Walters.) It is like "An Enemy of the People" in which Dr. Stockmann is the first to propose burning his evidence that the town springs are contaminated.

'There has been a recent horde of films in which values are stood right on their heads.'

For thousands of years the notion of weightlessness, of being able to float free of gravity was a human fantasy. Over the past 20 years or so, with space travel and its simulations, it has been experienced, described and analyzed. The reality is almost the exact opposite of the fantasy. It means a painful reinvention of every slightest move; a loss, not a gain, in freedom and spontaneity. Putting on a slipper can be a catastrophe, and drinking through a straw the step-by-step reconstruction of hydrodynamics. Gravity, depleting and occasionally fatal though it may be, seems essential to our being and well being. It is the precondition for the joy as well as the fear of flying.

Nihilism is the moral equivalent of weightlessness. In small doses it can be of some use: to deflate a ponderous argument or make some temporary breathing-space in an overly rigid and encrusted political or esthetic system. Generally speaking, though, it makes as poor art as it does politics. And it makes terrible movies. (I am talking about nihilism; not anarchy, which, of course, is something quite different.)

By introducing a consistently malevolent and valueless quality into films—no doubt from faddishness or an effort to capitalize on a fashionable post-Vietnam, post-Watergate aimlessness—it deadens them. Denunciation is part of life but it isn't the same as life. From their physical nature movies are inert things—unlike actors on a stage, who can excite us simply by standing there—and life must be put into them.

I am not arguing that movies cannot be denunciatory or angry. Many of the best ones are. But this denunciation is achieved in a uniquely indirect manner.

In a word, we hate by loving. Denunciation comes not by denouncing evil but first, by giving life to, and, second, by making us love the life in, things that are injured by evil. The tremendous attack upon war in Renoir's "Grand Illusion" comes about because we have seen the marvelous living humanity of the characters who are shattered by war. "Four Hundred Blows" makes its very painful points by means of the bruises we see upon the loveliness of the boy Doinel. "Grapes of Wrath" doesn't get its power from creating evil characters but from the luminous Joads as played by Henry Fonda and his fellow actors.

Now it is quite artificial, and totally obtuse to say that what is wrong with so many American movies today is that they are negative. "Rocky" seems to me to be quite a good movie, but it is not good because its message is positive. It is good insofar as it has as many as three characters who are frequently and unpredictably alive. One can imagine the wave of perfectly dreadful movies, spilling over with sweetness and decency, that is likely to follow upon the success of a "Rocky" and upon what I suspect may develop into a campaign for more uplift.

The basic defect in the movies I have been talking about isn't their lack of real heroes. A movie can do without heroes, though a movie that tries to say anything of any weight must be able to suggest that heroism is at least a theoretical possibility, that it exists even if only as a vacancy. Anti-heroes are fine in movies — Bogart, among

'Effective films denounce by making us love the life in things injured by evil'

others, was good at them—but their anti-heroism was a personal option, not a universal statement. Movies should not be totalitarian: they can be about three monsters in a cave, but they should be able to suggest that this cave exists in a countryside where there is a possibility that real cows are giving milk and that, apart from selling this milk, people may also drink it, and sometimes—who knows?—give it away.

The nihilism—and the deadening effect—of many recent films—lies partly in the fact that everything is colored the same color as the main characters. If they are hopeless, so is the world. But there is something more.

These movies not only lack heroes; more seriously, they lack villains. They have all kinds of execrable characters in them, but they are not real. They are caricatures; badly drawn in the case of a "King Kong" or a "Two-Minute Warning," well drawn in "Network." But is it really credible, after a couple of thousand years of playwriting, that a movie with even slightly serious pretensions should assume that because a character is villainous he or she must lack humanity as well?

Perhaps the example is trivial, but then so is the movie: Clint Eastwood's latest Dirty Harry film, "The Enforcer," has a whole collection of corrupt or soft-headed types who interfere with Inspector Harry Callahan's efforts to wipe out crime. He gets rid of them one by one, but they topple like so many cardboard ducks in a shooting gallery. As entertainment — forget about art—they would be a lot more interesting if they had characters.

In "Network" the cardboard ducks simply have better things to say. But though their manias are well-parodied, none of them have any real life—as against liveliness — except William Holden, and he is about as interesting as one gray sock.

Now make a ludicrous comparison: "King Kong" with the lovely Russian film "Solaris." Both, in a sense, are about mankind despoiling the mysteries of nature. In "King Kong" it is the ape and his island; in "Solaris" it is a strange planet.

King Kong's despoiler is Fred Wilson. He is played as a leer and a sneer by Charles Grodin; he is greed and nothing else. He tells us nothing about ourselves. After all, none of us are Platonic archtypes, not even of the vices. In "Solaris" the despoilers—actual or potential—are complex, tortured figures acting for understandable, even noble reasons. We see ourselves in them and because we do, we can see their evil in us.

If our movies are to achieve this kind of insight; if they are to keep any life in the depiction of crass, violent or dangerous human beings they must find ways of presenting evil as the affliction of these human beings, not as their definitions. It isn't a question of removing the evil but of leaving in the humanity. ■

1977 Ja 2, II:11:1

FILM VIEW

VINCENT CANBY

In Memory of Some Forgettable Films

Talk to any producer long enough and he'll eventually tell you that nobody ever sets out to make a bad film. Which means that no producer ever sets out to lose money. In Hollywood, good films are the ones that make money and lousy films are the ones that flop at the box office. The terms "good" and "bad" have nothing to do with artistic expression and everything to do with economics, which is why film producers are genuinely, sincerely puzzled by whatever it is that critics think that critics should do. Who needs critics when there are plenty of certified public accountants around? Theirs is the only criticism that means anything.

This is why I've tried to pick some of the worst films that were also the most successful financially. It's a matter of principle to shake up the community. Why kick a movie that not many people have seen anyway? This year it hasn't been easy. Heaven knows I've tried, but some of the worst films were also box office disasters. Could it be a happy trend? I doubt it.

Here's my list:

"The Blue Bird." This first American-Soviet coproduction is so bad you might suspect that the Chinese Communists made it, but no. It was directed by George Cukor, starred Elizabeth Taylor, Jane Fonda, Ava Gardner and other reputable English-speaking actors, as well as Russian actors, and it's based on the Maeterlinck classic that had its world premiere under Stanislavsky's direction at the Moscow Art Theater in 1908. Perhaps if the Russians had been left alone they might have made a pretty little dance film out of the mystical, moral fable about happiness being a pigeon dyed blue in your own back yard. The Russians weren't left alone, though. The result looks like a mad doctor's transplant of a goose's head onto the body of a chicken. Nothing fits. Worse, it is a bore that cuts cleanly across all age brackets.

"Drum." This sequel to the financially successful "Mandingo" continues in serial style the story of the nasty, lascivious, sadistic, mean, rude, evil, and supposedly erotic goings-on down on the old Louisiana slave-breeding plantation whose name gave the first film its title. Steve Carver directed it as if he were making a multi-million-dollar porn film devoted to the activities of what the trade calls "mixed combos." It may give you some idea of how bad it is to know that Dino De Laurentis ("King Kong") took his name off it.

"Gable and Lombard." Clark Gable and Carole Lombard were star-crossed stars. After a long and ardent affair they were finally legally free to marry, only to be parted by Carole's premature death in a plane crash. With Jill Clayburgh playing Carole, and James Brolin playing Clark in what looks to be a Clark Gable party mask, "Gable and Lombard" makes their True-Life romance seem slightly less momentous than the Debbie Reynolds-Eddie Fisher marriage.

"The Incredible Sarah." Who says nobody ever sets out to make a lousy movie? This ridiculous biography of the life and career of the young Sarah Bernhardt, played by the not-so-young Glenda Jackson, gives the whole thing away. The movie makers put in long hours to come up with something as consistently poor as this. Helen M. Strauss, the producer, first optioned Ruth Wolff's screenplay, which, as filmed, appears to have been a series of talking tableaux about the trials of being an actress, and then she hired Richard Fleischer to direct it, apparently on the promise that every scene would contain either a cliché or a non-sequitur. Fleischer delivered the goods as ordered and got from Miss Jackson a performance that could have been pasted-together out-takes from "Hedda," "The Maids," "The Devil Is A Woman," plus a few days' worth of shooting of new material. Like good filmmaking, bad filmmaking is work, work, work.

"Lifeguard." This film about the frustrations of a southern California lifeguard who finds himself obsolete at 32 isn't terribly important but how can one resist a movie that asks, in effect, whether such a fellow should take a job selling Porsches, stay on with the Parks Department emptying litter baskets, or shoot himself? California movie critics treated this with all of the solemnity that movie critics elsewhere reserve for "controversial" problem pictures about coal miners, capital punishment and the Bomb. This country may not be as homogenized as the watching of television can lead us to think.

"Lipstick." When I reviewed "Lipstick" last April I described it as a glamour film about rape. Now I suspect it may have been the world's longest theatrical film trailer for a television ad campaign. The film stars Margaux Hemingway as a high-fashion model who has a terrible time after being raped by a psychopathic composer of avant garde music. Miss Hemingway was terrible in the film but looks suitably wet-lipped, frosty, large-eyed and healthy as "Babe," the smashing looking young woman now identified with the Revlon firm's cosmetics of that name. Was the title of the film (another Dino De Laurentiis presentation) simply a coincidence?

• • •

"Midway." The special effects and trick photography in the new "King Kong" are almost enough fun to make up for chutzpah that led to the remake. The special effects and trick photography in "Midway," which attempts to dramatize the events leading up to the great Pacific naval battle of 1942, demonstrate that such technical wizardry is not easy. The "Midway" material is as tacky as the direction (by Jack Smight), the screenplay (by Donald S. Sanford) and the performances by a cast of male stars who look as if they'd been in mothballs for 30 years.

"The Next Man." Sean Connery plays a visionary Saudi Arabian minister of state, a fellow who has a strangely Scots-sounding accent, and Cornelia Sharpe plays a rich American girl who wants to assassinate him before he can bring peace to the Middle East. The film, directed by Richard C. Sarafian, means to be a suspense thriller but it's really a contest between the senses of duty of the Arab and the American. Guess who wins? The news is not all bad. If the film loses enough money it may persuade pro-

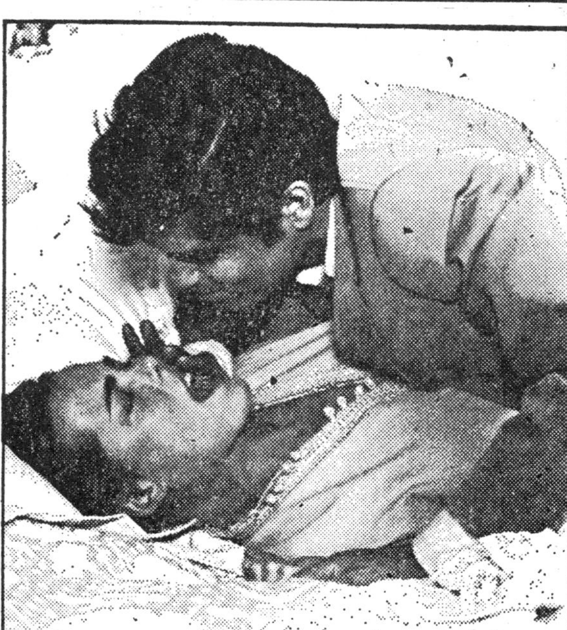

Among those who flunked in 1976 were Gregory Peck and Harvey Stephens in "The Omen"; Harry Andrews in "The Blue Bird"; Glenda Jackson in "The Incredible Sarah"; and Margaux Hemingway and Chris Sarandon in "Lipstick."

ducers to declare a moratorium on further feather-brained suspense thrillers for a while.

• • •

"The Omen." The box office success of this sloppily made but stern exercise in satanism has slopped over into book-publishing, which found a best-seller in David Selzer's paperback novelization of his screenplay. Gregory Peck, in a role that befits his station in Hollywood society, plays an American ambassador to the Court of St. James who is instrumental in making Satan's latest coming a huge success. It would have been a film to warm the heart of the late Sen. Joseph McCarthy, who always suspected the State Department was up to no good.

• • •

"A Star Is Born." Barbra Streisand is the star, executive producer, designer of "musical concepts," contributor of her own wardrobe, and a collaborator on two of the film's songs. There are other people in this nervy remake of the great George Cukor-Moss Hart-Judy Garland film (itself a remake), including Kris Kristofferson, but they cannot disguise the fact that the new "Star Is Born" is a one-woman show starring a talented singer in love with a hand-mike. Some of the songs are good but the movie, about the rock music industry and its stars, is a lightweight, transistorized portrait of vanity for anyone who's less than totally committed to Streisand.

1977 Ja 2, II:1:1

CORRECTION: In my Jan. 2 piece, "In Memory of Some Forgettable Films," I gave Revlon the credit for the high-powered "Babe" advertising campaign that features Margaux Hemingway. I made a mistake. I should have known that Babe is a Fabergé fragrance, but I forgot.

1977 Ja 16, II:18:2

SPECIAL DELIVERY, directed by Paul Wendkos; screenplay by Don Gazzaniga; produced by Richard Berg; Charles A. Pratt, executive producer; director of photography, Harry Stradling Jr.; music, Lalo Schifrin; editor, Houseley Stevenson; a BCP production, distributed by American International Pictures. Running time: 99 minutes. At neighborhood theaters. This film has been rated PG.

Jack Murdock .... Bo Svenson
Mary Jane .... Cybill Shepherd
Zabelski .... Tom Atkins
Hubert Zane .... Sorrell Booke
Swivot .... Gerrit Graham
Carl Graff .... Michael C. Gwynne
Snake .... Jeff Goldblum
Mr. Chu .... Robert Ito
Wyatt .... Vic Tayback

By VINCENT CANBY

"Special Delivery," which opened at neighborhood theaters yesterday, is a comic melodrama about a bank holdup and the subsequent efforts of several different parties to put their hands on the loot. It stars Bo Svenson, as an ex-Marine sergeant who masterminds the caper, and Cybill Shepherd, as a smart-talking innocent who cuts herself in on the job for the fun of it. They are pleasant company if you are accidentally trapped with them.

Michael C. Gwynne has some good moments as a junkie, but neither Paul Wendkos, who directed the film, nor Don Gazzaniga, who wrote it, is very adept at melodrama and action. The film ends in a car chase of the sort that makes you realize that the screeching of tires has become the most overused and boring sound in movies today.

•

"Special Delivery," which has been rated PG ("Parental Guidance Suggested"), possibly offers some clues as to how a potential R film gets upgraded to PG. Although a character in "Special Delivery" has obviously been filmed saying "goddamn," the "god" has been bleeped from the soundtrack. The film also includes some violence of a not very brutal kind.

1977 Ja 13, 47:2

Lonely Madness

THE GOALIE'S ANXIETY AT THE PENALTY KICK, directed by Wim Wenders; screenplay (German with English subtitles) by Mr. Wenders and Peter Handke, based on the novel by Mr. Handke; director of photography, Robbie Muller; editor, Peter Przygodda; music, Jurgen Knieper; distributed by Bauer International. Running time: 101 minutes. At the Film Forum, 1 Vandam Street. This film has not been rated.

Josef Bloch .... Arthur Brauss
Hertha Gabler .... Kai Fischer
Gloria T. .... Erika Pluhar
Anna .... Libgart Schwarz
Maria .... Marie Bardischewski
Salesman .... Michael Toost
Girl .... Edda Koch
Idiot .... Rudiger Vogler

By VINCENT CANBY

WHEN WE FIRST see Josef Bloch (Arthur Brauss), the goalie, he is isolated in a long shot at the far end of the soccer field. The frantic activity of the game at the other end of the field has no apparent relation to him. He walks around impatiently. He wipes his hands. He is a lean man, all tendons that have been tense so long that even the most ordinary gesture seems to be a kind of tic.

Suddenly the game closes in on him and Josef Bloch, who has been waiting for this moment, fails to prevent the score. He displays no impatience with himself, no bitterness, no visible emotion whatsoever. For, as we learn in Wim Wenders's superlative screen version of Peter Handke's novel "The

Goalie's Anxiety at the Penalty Kick," Josef Bloch has been disconnected.

This precise and beautiful German film, directed by Mr. Wenders and written by him and Mr. Handke, was originally shown in New York at the Museum of Modern Art's 1972 New Directors/New Films series, but it is only now having its commercial premiere at the Film Forum, where it opened yesterday. It will be seen there at 7:30 P.M. today through Sunday, and at the same time next weekend, Thursday through Sunday.

•

Like the Handke novel, the film will be described—incorrectly, I think—as dispassionate, which is not to see the film, or the book for its style, which is about as self-effacing as a style can be without disappearing entirely. However, "The Goalie's Anxiety at the Penalty Kick" is seething with feelings that are so ambiguous, so terrifying, that like Josef Bloch, the film can recognize them only obliquely, as if trying to put a good face on things by refusing to make a fuss.

"The Goalie's Anxiety at the Penalty Kick" is a carefully composed, unhysterical record of one man's coming-apart. At the end of his last game, Josef Bloch wanders aimlessly around a Vienna that is both familiar to him and as strange as the inside of a beehive. He drinks. He plays the jukebox. He sleeps. He gets mugged. He picks up a girl and goes to her apartment at the edge of an airfield. They make love. The next morning they have breakfast. He thinks he sees ants in the teapot. He strangles her. He leaves. He buys a newspaper and gets on a bus. . . .

Those sentences suggest the tempo of the film, but not its impact on the viewer who, by being required to fill in explanations the film makers resolutely refuse to give, becomes drawn into Josef Bloch's madness in a way that leaves one breathless and high. It's as exciting as any conventionally successful and high suspense film.

Mr. Handke's novels—he is perhaps better known here as a playwright—has been associated with France's nouveau roman and the work of Alain Robbe-Grillet. The methods are similar, but there is a major, crucial difference. Mr. Robbe-Grillet's novels and films seem bent on demonstrating the boredom of alienated man by turning their backs on the reader and boring him into a stupor. "The Goalie's Anxiety" is also about disconnection, but the novelist's impulse is furious, rather than bored. His work has the vigor of a revolutionist.

Since "The Goalie's Anxiety" was first shown in New York, Mr. Wenders has been represented by two later films seen at the New York Film Festival, "Alice in the Cities" and "Kings of the Road," but because neither has had the force and cool beauty of this film, I would assume he needs a collaborator of Mr. Handke's discipline and intellectual enthusiasm.

"The Goalie's Anxiety" doesn't contain one redundant shot or unnecessary camera movement. For the most part, the camera seldom moves. It is content to record the actors walking into and out of a frame, more or less in the passive manner of Josef Bloch as he regards the odd behavior of himself and of the strangers in the world around him.

•

This simplicity, as opposed to the fancy photography and the modish fragmentation of time and image favored by Mr. Robbe-Grillet ("L'Immortelle," "The Man Who Lies"), has the effect of making us see people, objects and bits of action with a clarity so stunning that they come to have for us as much menace and mystery as they have for the mad Josef Bloch.

"The Goalie's Anxiety at the Penalty Kick" is a remarkable, fascinating film, one that suggests, among many other things, that the nouveau film, if indeed there is to be such a thing, will be plain, unadorned, direct, not an accumulation of fashionable mannerisms.

1977 Ja 14, C4:4

Arthur Brauss in "The Goalie's Anxiety at the Penalty Kick"

FILM VIEW

VINCENT CANBY

What Are We To Make Of Remakes?

"King Kong" and "A Star Is Born," two of the season's most expensive and most highly publicized productions, are inaugurating Hollywood's newest remake trend with something less than transcendental excitement while raising serious questions about the mental health of an industry that, when in doubt if not panic, begins dabbling in resurrection.

"King Kong" is not really a failure. It is, rather, a $25,000,000 so-what. It's the Merian C. Cooper-Ernest B. Schoedsack "King Kong," originally made in 1933, updated with references to "Deep Throat," the World Trade Center and the energy crisis. This is, I suppose, Hollywood's equivalent of one of those Broadway revivals that attempts to give new relevancy to "Hamlet" by shifting the location from a Denmark of the Dark Ages to 20th-century Las Vegas. But King Kong is not Hamlet. He's not even Sherlock Holmes or Robin Hood or Tom Sawyer, infinitely adaptable characters who have an ability to speak to each new generation while never losing touch with their own.

When Cooper and Schoedsack made their "King Kong" 44 years ago, they made what amounted to a definitive version, meaning there really wasn't much more that anyone could do with this living comic strip except, as Dino De Laurentiis, the producer of the new film, and John Guillermin and Lorenzo Semple, Jr., its director and writer, respectively, have shown, add color and contemporary wisecracks. It's not worth the effort. "King Kong" is an artifact of the American thirties. To update it is as foolish and thankless an endeavor as attempting to resurrect Little Orphan Annie in a series of confrontations with Symbionese Liberation Army.

"King Kong" is harmless and not all that difficult to sit through. "A Star Is Born" is something else. An almost measurably unpleasant demonstration of a voracious ego gobbling up a nice old chestnut that was first made in 1937 by William Wellman and again in 1954 by George Cukor, Moss Hart and most especially Judy Garland.

Barbra Streisand, the executive producer, star, part-time songwriter and designer of the film's "musical concepts," apparently thought that she would have a sure-thing by remaking this story about the tragic love affair between a new star and an old star on his way down by simply shifting the background from Hollywood and movie-making to today's rock music scene. There was, after all, the apparently durable, four-hankie love story that twice before had moved two quite disparate generations of film-goers, plus the show-biz background that would allow her to sing her head off without wrenching reality around.

The only things she didn't reckon on were her own inability to act in any plausible fashion an unknown singer, especially when the camera apotheosizes her from start to finish, and the nature of the rock industry and its people. If Streisand spends most of her time in "A Star Is Born" more or less presenting herself to us rather than acting, Kris Kristofferson, as the has-been rock star who loves her so much he makes the ultimate sacrifice, is just as bad in a role that makes no sense anyway.

It's not Kristofferson's fault that the film is so arranged and set up that we never hear him sing. Barbra is the only one who comes through loud and clear (and endlessly) on the soundtrack. It is his fault that he accepted an impossible assignment. The sort of character he plays might well die of an overdose of something, or in an auto accident, but suicide has nothing to do with the nature of the fellow we see on the screen. But then it looks as if the basic material of "A Star Is Born," which is admittedly soapy, was only looked upon as a convenience to be used to reach the greater goal: to get Barbra on-screen at some length. If you look upon this "Star Is Born" as a photographed personal appearance by Streisand, then the film's lack of genuine feeling and common sense makes no difference.

One doesn't have to believe that the original "King Kong" and the earlier versions of "A Star Is Born" are classics to be worried about the paltriness of the ambitions and the hopes represented by these two new films, and by the whole remake trend in general.

Unlike a stage production, a movie does not disappear after its last screening. It goes into a can and it continues to exist for as long as film stock can survive. Why, then, do so many people, including some talented film-makers, want to remake films that have already been done about as well as they will ever be?

Economics, I suspect, is the major reason. Moviemakers love to get their hands on what they call the "pre-sold" property, which is usually a best-selling book or a hit play, something that the paying public already has heard of in advance of the film version. In the current market, with the gap between the hit films and the flops growing wider every day, the pre-sold property is at a premium—as close as anything can be to a sure thing—and how better pre-sold could a property be than by having already been a hit film?

There is also the consideration that a remake of an earlier hit film will contain those mysterious components that will attract an audience even if the producer of the remake does not emphasize or publicize in any way the relationship of the new to the old. The producers of the new "King Kong" and "A Star Is Born" make no bones about what they're up to, hoping that a certain familiarity will create interest.

On the other hand, it's the content that seems to have interested William Friedkin, who is currently finishing production of his remake of Henri-Georges Clouzot's French classic, "The Wages of Fear." The new picture will not be called "The Wages of Fear" but "Sorcerer," thus to call attention, I'm sure, to the fact that Friedkin's last film was the immensely successful "The Exorcist." The Hollywood remake of Lina Wertmuller's recently successful comedy, "The Seduction of Mimi," will be called "Which

Culver

"A Star Is Born" (1937)—Janet Gaynor, Fredric March and a cop

"A Star Is Born" (1954)—Judy Garland, James Mason and Oscar

Bettmann Archives

"A Star Is Born" (1977)—Kris Kristofferson, Barbra Streisand . . . and Barbra Streisand

Way Is Up?" and will star Richard Pryor as a radicalized grapepicker, a role based on the one played by Giancarlo Giannini in the Italian film.

Some of the other remakes on the schedule include new versions of "Kind Hearts and Coronets," to be done by Melvin Frank; "Here Comes Mr. Jordan," which Elaine May is writing for Warren Beatty with the title of "Heaven Can Wait" (but not to be confused with Ernst Lubitsch's 1943 comedy with the same title); a "Prisoner of Zenda" with Peter Sellers playing two roles; "The Cat and The Canary," to be directed by Radley Metzger, whose most recent films have been pornos; and "The Hurricane," to be produced by Dino DeLaurentiis, the man who brought us "King Kong" the second time.

Why should anyone seriously want to remake films like "Casablanca" and "Notorious" when the originals are still so vivid? Is there any director in his right mind who believes that he could top the Alfred Hitchcock "Notorious?" A novelist who told his publisher that he was working on an updated version of "A Farewell to Arms" would be immediately packed off to the bin. But not in Hollywood. He'd get a contract. I assume that Melvin Frank really believes that he can bring something new and original to his version of "Kind Hearts and Coronets," something that was missing from the original that starred Alec Guinness, but as a clever, successful screenwriter and director, wouldn't it be more fun (and less suicidal) to work on a new property that wouldn't be measured against an existing classic?

On second thought, perhaps Hitchcock might be able to improve "Notorious" in a remake. One of the few remakes I can remember that was better than the original was Hitchcock's 1956 version of his own 1935 "The Man Who Knew Too Much," but that was in the manner of a novelist or playwright reworking his own material, something that few filmmakers ever have the opportunity to do. The most spectacular — and rewarding — example of this rare feat is Abel Gance's "Bonaparte and The Revolution," which Gance made originally in 1927 (as "Napoléon Vu Par Abel Gance") and then reworked and reedited over the years, adding sound, among other things, until, as "Bonaparte and The Revolution," it became virtually the sum of the director's career, over 40 years in the making.

The most peculiar aspect of this remake trend is that although it seems the result of highly conservative, bet-hedging policies on the part of movie producers, the majority of remakes of classic films have been disasters, financially and artistically. John Ford's "Mogambo," a 1953 remake of Victor Fleming's 1932 "Red Dust," is an exception, but does anyone remember the name of the man who directed the idiotic 1966 remake of John Ford's 1939 "Stagecoach"? (Gordon Douglas). Or even want to know who had the temerity to remake Hitchcock's "The 39 Steps" in 1960? (That was Ralph Thomas.)

One might argue that only filmmakers of limited vision and sensitivity, to say nothing of talent, could allow themselves to become involved in redoing a classic film, which would explain why most of them aren't very good. But there's another consideration particular to movies. That is that all films, even the classics, are especially reflective of the popular culture of the time in which they're created. For all of the clever special effects in the new "King Kong," the film's essential fantasy is still rooted in an earlier, pre-bomb, pre-satellite era when our imaginations had a freedom denied us today.

Movies can't easily be updated, modernized without looking like old men with dyed hair. Movie audiences, however, are capable of responding to a classic film no matter how far removed in time the film is. Since we can enter—go back to—the world of a classic film, isn't it asking too much that it be able to adapt itself to our time in a remake?

If you check Variety's latest list of the all-time box-office hits, you'll see that of the first 20 films, only two could be classified as remakes, Cecil B. DeMille's 1956 "The Ten Commandments" and William Wyler's 1959 "Ben-Hur," and both of these were new versions of films that had been made originally as silents many years earlier. In addition to having a kind of suffocating effect on the imaginations of the people who make them, as well as on the film industry as a whole, remakes don't even make business sense.

1977 Ja 16, II:1:5

GET CHARLIE TULLY, directed by Cliff Owen, written by John Warren and John Singer; photographed by Ernest Steward; produced by E. M. Smedley Aston. At the Fine Arts Theater, East 58th Street. Running time: 97 minutes. This film has been rated PG.

Charlie Tully .... Dick Emery
Sid Sabbath .... Derren Nesbit
Reggie Campbell Peek .... Ronald Fraser
Libby Niven .... Pat Coombs
Arnold Van Cleef .... William Franklyn
Jo Mason .... Cheryl Kennedy

By RICHARD EDER

Underwear and bottoms. They are the underpinnings for generations of British music-hall humor. The pound has shrunk but not the poundage—to judge, at least, by the new British movie "Get Charlie Tully."

This offering of ponderous jokes and broad acting, which opened yesterday at the Fine Arts Theater, has a sneaky appeal. It is not camp. The jokes are often old and corny, but we are not asked to laugh on the grounds that they are old and corny. We are asked to laugh on the ground that they are funny.

•

It is refreshing. It is—maybe sentimentality is involved—touching, like a parade of Chelsea pensioners. And some of the jokes, in fact, *are* funny.

At the start, the arch con man, Charlie Tully, is sitting in a Buckingham Palace office—never mind how—selling a gullible Italian industrialist the hand of Princess Anne for a consideration of several hundred thousand pounds. At the end, Charlie Tully is dressed as a monsignor and selling the Sistine Chapel to a pair of American tourists.

In between, he is pursued by the law, by a gang of rough London gangsters and by a Mafia detachment seeking to avenge the Italian industrialist. Apart from these diversionary incidents, Tully's main concern is finding the Swiss bank number that harbors the Princess Anne bridal money. It was deposited there by an associate on whom a wall fell before he could disclose the number.

As it happens, the number is tattooed, in sections, on the bottoms of four young women with whom the associate was on friendly terms. A lot of dressing and undressing takes place.

As Tully, Dick Emery is energetic and sometimes funny, though his timing and mugging are such that you get the feeling that a cheering audience has been placed behind the camera. Far better is Ronald Fraser as the associate. Mr. Fraser has two owl eyes, a ginger mustache, a long nose stuffed full of adenoids and a lovely faith that things will turn out well. Unfortunately there's that wall.

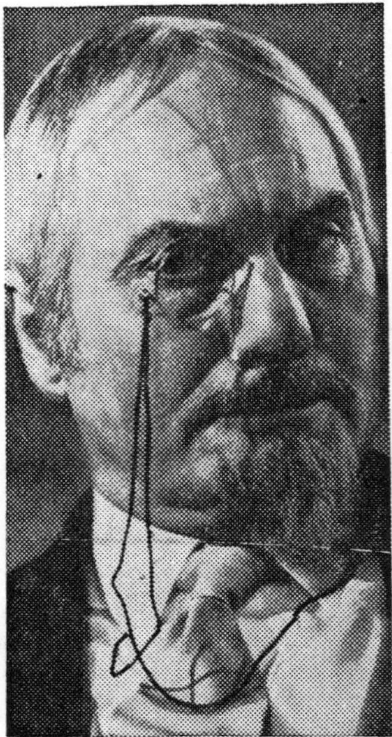

Dick Emery
Energetic and funny

•

The movie is rated PG ("Parental Guidance Suggested"). Children in particular are likely to be delighted by the film's abundant use of posterior disclosure.

1977 Ja 17, 32:1

Bulging Mystique

PUMPING IRON, directed by George Butler and Robert Fiore, from the book by Charles Gaines and Mr. Butler; produced by Mr. Fiore and Mr. Butler; photographed by Mr. Fiore; edited by Larry Silk and Geof Bartz. Distributed by Cinema 5. At the Plaza Theater. Running time: 85 minutes. This film has been rated PG.

WITH: Arnold Schwarzenegger, Louis Ferrigno, Matty and Victoria Ferrignor, Mike Katz, Franco Columbu and others.

By RICHARD EDER

LIKE THE HUGE LIPS grown by Ubangi women, the startlingly overdeveloped musculature of professional body-builders is apt to seem more of a deformity than an achievement to outsiders.

At the least, the body-building mystique as well as its physical results have a good deal of the bizarre about them. As Arnold Schwarzenegger, the best-known of the champions, puts it, "Some people look at you and think it's kind of strange."

Mr. Schwarzenegger is the central figure in "Pumping Iron," an interesting, rather slick and excessively long documentary about the small but intensely competitive world of body-building. It opened yesterday at the Plaza Theater.

In the picture's first section we see Mr. Schwarzenegger, a handsome man with a body as knotted as an especially lumpy vegetable soup, training, giving exhibitions and talking about his profession.

•

As they practice swelling their muscles and striking poses—all the time looking at themselves—the body-builders have the self-absorbed look of fashion models. In some cases—particularly with one contender, Louis Ferrigno—the mournful expression peering out of all those deltoids, triceps and latissima dorsi calls up an image that skitters around a while before it is pinned down.

George Butler

Arnold Schwarzenegger displays his physique in "Pumping Iron."

It is, in fact, that of the 90-pound weakling to whom the body-building ads were directed. It is not so much as if the body-builders had become muscular, but as if they had put on great muscle overcoats. The hungry face protrudes from the collar.

Or, in the case of Mr. Schwarzenegger, the pleased face. The Austrian-born athlete has become rich from his profession and its spin-offs, is perpetually surrounded by beautiful women, and to cap it all, is a witty if not always convincing exponent of the body-building philosophy.

•

The first thing the outsider realizes, watching the film, is that the object of all that weight-lifting is neither strength nor prowess, but appearance. Mr. Schwarzenegger calls himself a sculptor of his own body. "You look in the mirror and see you need a little more deltoids to make symmetry. So you exercise and put more deltoid on. A sculptor will slap stuff on."

The second part of the film is about the world championship contest, held in South Africa, to choose Mr. Olympia. It concentrates particularly on Mr. Schwarzenegger, the titleholder, and Mr. Ferrigno, a principal challenger.

The desperate intensity of Mr. Ferrigno, drilled with ferocious concentration by his father, contrasts with the more urbane attitude of the Austrian champion. At one point, Mr. Schwarzenegger practices weightlifting, using two women as barbells.

But the appearance is deceptive. Mr. Schwarienegger explains with a candor that seems more appealing than it really is—once you think about it—how he "messes up his opponents." He talks to them. He uses the guarded camaraderie that precedes the competition to play all kinds of one-up games.

One of his stories is about the advice he gave to a novice who was competing with him at Munich. He told him that

"PUMPING IRON"—Franco Columbu primes himself for a series of upside-down sit-ups, much to the amusement of Arnold Schwarzenegger and friends.

the judges set great store by a theatrical delivery. He suggested that the man scream while doing his poses. Higher screams when the arms were raised. Deep screams when they were lowered.

"After about four poses they dragged him off," Mr. Schwarzenegger recalls, laughing.

Obviously, in the body-building trade it is a question of mind over muscles.

•

The movie is rated PG ("Parental Guidance Suggested"). There is an occasional expression of the kind one might expect to hear in a weight-lifter's training camp or practically anywhere else.

1977 Ja 19, C20:1

THE HOLES, directed by Pierre Tchernia; screenplay (French with English subtitles) by Mr. Tchernia; produced by Saul Cooper; director of photography, Jean Tournier; music, Gerard Calvi; distributed by Burbank International Films. Running time: 94 minutes. At tehe Eastside Cinema, Third Avenue at 55th Street, and other theaters. This film has been rated PG.

Gaspard de Montfermeil	Philippe Noiret
Public Works Minister	Charles Denner
Jean-Paul Rondin	Michel Serrault
Commissioner Lalatte	Michel Galabru
Postman	Gerard Depardieu
Mariet-Helene	Chantal Goya
Ginette Lalatte	Annie Cordy
Pamela Pendleton-Pumkin	Prudence Harrington

"The Holes," the 1974 French movie that opened at the Eastside Cinema and other theaters yesterday, is a comedy that pretends to defend individualism and eccentricity even though it seems clearly designed for people who eat junk food while watching sit-coms on television.

It's a facetious tale about a nutty aristocrat (Philippe Noiret) who lives in the catacombs of Paris and the ravages of modernization going on upstairs. His adversary is the progress-obsessed Minister of Public Works (Charles Denner), who, among other things, plans to relieve traffic congestion by paving over the Seine and painting a white line down the middle.

Pierre Tchernia, reported to be something of a French television personality, wrote the screenplay and directed the cast that includes Gérard Depardieu in the small role of a mailman. It's one of those films the French don't usually export, for very good reason.

•

"The Holes" has been rated PG (Parental Guidance Suggested"), though the only possibly offensive thing about it is a failure of imagination.

VINCENT CANBY

1977 Ja 20, 45:1

SHOOT, directed by Harvey Hart; screenplay by Dick Berg, based on the novel by Douglas Fairbairn; produced by Harve Sherman; executive producer, Mr. Berg; music, Doug Riley; editors, Ron Wisman and Peter Shatalow; director of photography, Zale Magder; distributed by Avco Embassy Pictures. Running time: 94 minutes. At the Cinerama 2 Theater, Broadway at 47th Street, and other theaters. This film has been rated R.

Rex	Cliff Robertson
Lou	Ernest Borgnine
Zeke	Henry Silva
Pete	James Blendick
Bob	Larry Reynolds
Jim	Les Carlson
Paula	Helen Shaver
Ellen	Gloria Chetwynd
Mrs. Graham	Kate Reid

By VINCENT CANBY

One wintry afternoon, when Rex Jeanette (Cliff Robertson), a well-to-do appliance merchant, and several of his friends are out hunting unsuccessfully, they come upon another party of hunters who emerge from the woods just across a small river. "It's funny," says a colleague of Rex's "they look just like us." Suddenly one of the strangers shoots at Rex's group, whose members return the fire and apparently kill one of the attackers. Both parties retire from the field.

Does anyone call the police or get a doctor or do anything rational? Of course not. If anyone had, there would be no movie called "Shoot," the mini-minded, bloodthirsty, supposedly anti-gun movie that opened yesterday at the Cinerama 2 and other theaters.

"Shoot," a Canadian film directed by Harvey Hart, written by Dick Berg and based on a novel by Douglas Fairbairn, apparently hopes to be making a statement about the mayhem that can be caused by easy access to weaponry, but most of the time the film doesn't believe in itself. When one character says to another, "I can't believe it really happened," it's as if the film makers were trying to disassociate themselves from the melodramatic nonsense they've concocted.

Rex and his pals, including Lou (Ernest Borgnine), are portrayed as right-wing gun nuts. You can tell this because they have American flags in their dens, tell dirty stories and treat their wives badly. When Rex prepares to go hunting, he gets great pleasure slowly lubricating the barrel of his shotgun. Rex has problems all right, but passing a gun-control law isn't going to solve them.

•

It's the conceit of this film that instead of reporting the riverside confrontation, Rex and his friends, as well as their unknown enemies, would decide to fight it out in earnest the following weekend with high-powered rifles, machine guns and bazookas, all borrowed from the National Guard. "We're trying to prevent a slaughter," says Rex, "not to start one," which is meant to identify Rex with various ludicrous foreign-policy statements.

The overstuffed point of the film is that certain men need to fight to express themselves and that in this need there's a lesson for mankind. Perhaps, but it's a very simplistic point and a drearily foolish movie in which everyone does badly, including Kate Reid, who has a briefly embarrassing scene as the whisky-soaked, sex-starved widow of the murdered hunter.

1977 Ja 20, 46:6

MADAME KITTY, directed by Tinto Brass; screenplay by Ennio De Concini, Maria Pia Fusco and Mr. Brass; executive producer, Carla Cipriani; produced by Giulio Sbarigia and Ermanno Donati; director of photography, Silvano Ippoliti; editor, Mr. Brass; music, Fiorenzo Carpi; distributed by Trans-American Pictures. Running time: 111 minutes. At the Cinerama 2 and other theaters. This film has been rated X.

Wallenberg	Helmut Berger
Kitty	Ingrid Thulin
Margherita	Teresa Ann Savoy
Hans	Bekim Fehmiu
Biondo	John Steiner
Dino	Stefano Satta Flores
Rauss	Dan Van Husen
Cliff	John Ireland
Herta Wallenberg	Tina Aumont

By VINCENT CANBY

Tinto Brass, an Italian director of little demonstrable talent and a great deal of self-esteem, apparently made "Madame Kitty" as a sort of finger exercise in preparation of his forthcoming production of "Gore Vidal's Caligula."

"Madame Kitty" is a ludicrously straight-faced, elegantly over-designed (by Ken Adam), soft-core porn epic about a little-known chapter in Nazi depravity at the beginning of World War II.

Those beastly Nazis would do absolutely anything, Mr. Brass reveals in "Madame Kitty," even bug the rooms of Berlin's fanciest whorehouse and staff it with beautiful informers. It's Mr. Brass's point, I think, that such people certainly wouldn't hesitate to build concentration camps.

Ingrid Thulin, who once made some excellent films for Ingmar Bergman, plays Madame Kitty as a sort of good-hearted, bisexual counselor of camp, a lady who who sings a lot of naughty songs and is shocked down to her garter belt when she learns that her house has been infiltrated by the Nazis. Helmut Berger, who's beginning to act more decadent than is really necessary, plays a sadistic Nazi officer, and Teresa Ann Savoy, an English actress, is cast as an ardent National Socialist, an enthusiastic recruit to Madame Kitty's house, who, toward the end, must say, "I feel as if I'm waking from a nightmare."

I assume she says it, though I can't be sure, because much of the dialogue seems to have been post-synchronized. The style of the film alternates between gross realism and an equally gross expressionism that indicates that Mr. Brass has his own delusions of grandeur. There's a good deal of nudity and simulated licentiousness, including the almost constant sipping of Rhine wine and a lot of mirthless laughter.

1977 Ja 22, 13:1

HARLAN COUNTY, U.S.A., documentary film directed and produced by Barbara Kopple; photographed by Hart Perry, Kevin Keating, Phil Parmet, Flip McCarthy and Tom Hurwitz; edited by Nancy Baker, Mary Lampson, Lora Hays and Mirra Bank; music by Hazel Dickens, Merle Travis and others. At the Cinema II Theater, Third Avenue and 60th Street. Running time: 103 minutes. This film is rated PG.

"Harlan County" was shown at the last New York Film Festival. The following is an excerpt from Richard Eder's review, which appeared Oct. 15. The film begins today at the Cinema II Theater.

Coal miners are a permanent underground in more than the literal sense. They trouble any society they support: like feet, the more they are weighed down by their owners the more pain they give.

"Harlan County, U.S.A.," is a full-length documentary of the year-long strike carried on by the miners at the Brookside works in eastern Kentucky. It has flaws, some of them considerable, but it is a fascinating and moving work. Its strength lies chiefly in its ability to illuminate the peculiar frightfulness and valor of coal-mining, and make it clear just why coal miners can never be rightly treated as less than a very special case.

•

Barbara Kopple and her photographers have got right inside the life of the miners and their families in their long struggle against the operators of the Brookside mine and its parent company, the Duke Power Company. It is a brilliantly detailed report from one side of a battle that caused one death, several shootings and a flood of violent bitterness; and that brought back to Harlan County memories of the much-bloodier coal strikes of the early 1930's.

•

The film shows the picketing, the use of state troopers to keep the road open for nonstrikers, the confrontations, a shooting, the efforts of the strikers and their families to remain organized and united through the long year. It intercuts old footage from the 1931 strike, where five miners were killed. It also details the successful battle of reformers to oust the old national leadership of the U.M.W.; and the support given to the Harlan County strike by the new leadership under Arnold R. Miller.

Some of the thematic interweaving is awkward, but this is more than made up for by the extraordinary intimacy Miss Kopple has achieved with the strikers and with the bitter life of the strike. There is an old miner, lungs torn by coal dust, who makes our chests hurt as he talks. There are frightening scenes of tight-lipped strikebreakers, guns openly displayed, pushing through the pickets. There is a terrifying night scene where shots are fired and we see the leader of the strikebreakers brandishing a pistol in the cab of his pick-up truck. There is a heartbreaking scene where the mother of the slain miner collapses at his wake. There is much more, equally good.

The film is entirely partisan. Considering that the company's refusal to sign a contract was condemned by the National Labor Relations Board as a pretext not to recognize the union and considering that the film itself is forthrightly an effort to see the struggle through the miners' own eyes, this is no real drawback.

More serious are the sometimes questionable ways in which the film advances its message: that the Harlan strike is only part of a struggle, and that the miners must go on struggling and striking. The instance I am thinking of comes in its suggestion that the reformist leadership of the U.M.W. may have sold out in 1974—after the Harlan County strike was over—by recommending acceptance of a national mine contract that curtails local strikes.

•

The film does not call this a sell-out —it uses no narration at all and conveys its message by its editing—but all reactions of individual miners that it shows before the vote are negative. Yet the membership ratified the contract by 44,000 to 34,000. The film states this, to be sure; yet somehow all the faces we have learned to admire during the long Harlan County struggle seem to push us to feel toward Mr. Miller the same way we felt toward the recalcitrant mine owners.

•

This film has been rated PG ("Parental Guidance suggested"). Possibly it is because of the occasional atmosphere of violence and the rough things people say because of it.

1977 Ja 24, 18:3

THE DAY THAT SHOOK THE WORLD, directed by Veljko Bulajic; screenplay by Paul Jarrico; cinematographer, Jan Curik; editor, Roger Dwyre; music by Juan Carlos Calderon and Libus Fiser; an Oliver A. Unger Presentation of a Mundo Film Production; released by American International Pictures. Running time: 111 minutes. This film is rated R. At the Festival Theater, Fifth Avenue at 57th Street.

Archduke Ferdinand .... Christopher Plummer
Duchess Sophie .... Florinda Bolkan
Djuro Sarac .... Maximilian Schell
Gavrilo Princip .... Irfan Mensur

By A. H. WEILER

Despite an awesome title, "The Day That Shook the World," which arrived at the Festival yesterday, is more quaint than explosive. As a dramatization of the fulminating events leading up to and including the royal murders that triggered World War I, it is a fragmented revival of the past that evolves largely as a picturesque adventure rather than portentous, persuasive history.

Filmed well over a year ago on authentic Yugoslav locations, this "Day That Shook the World" appears to have been cut somewhat confusingly, for all of the obviously good, serious intentions of its little-known director, Veljko Bulajic, and his American scenarist, Paul Jarrico.

Although they focus in captivating color on the June 1914 assassination in Sarajevo of Archduke Franz Ferdinand, heir to the Austro-Hungarian throne, and his morganatic wife, Sophie, their plotters, the burning nationalistic issues and the regal machinations that led to that fateful day are touched on in a succession of brief, fuzzy intrigues. The hatred of Bosnian, Serbian, Muslim and other nationalities of Hapsburg dominance is merely indicated. And the backgrounds of the seemingly educated, mostly youthful student-conspirators are also glossed over.

If memory serves, photographs of the Archduke and his spouse were portraits of a rather heavy-set, mature couple, but in the persons of Christopher Plummer and Florinda Bolkan they are a strikingly photogenic, regal and loving pair. Mr. Plummer not only adores the equally loving, stately, brunette Miss Bolkan and their three children but also carries off official duties at military maneuvers and dinners with the same brashness he evinces in a mild clash with Franz Joseph, the irascible, octogenarian emperor.

Maximilian Schell plays the role of the tortured, eventually ill-fated, bearded revolutionary who trains the callow assassins, with simple, glum determination. Among the largely Yugoslav supporting cast, Irfan Mensur plays Gavrilo Princip, the young conspirator who fired the fatal shots. Like his colleagues, he is simply a harried type more involved in a series of escapes from detection by the police than in character delineation.

In guiding his fairly large cast, Mr. Bulajic has succeeded in creating a good deal of melodrama, some tension and a few tepid romantic interludes. And Jan Curik, his cinematographer, has captured the scenic charms of an operetta-like countryside and the visual qualities of vintage automobiles, colorful uniforms and sham battles with toy-like soldiers in maneuvers. Unfortunately, their "Day That Shook the World" is a footnote to history that is rarely moving.

1977 Ja 24, 18:6

LES GALETTES DE PONT AVEN (The Cookies of Pont Aven), directed and written by Joel Seria; edited by Marcel Combes; music by Philippe Sarde. Released by PRO Films. At the 68th Street Playhouse. Running time: 100 minutes. This film has not been rated.

Henri Serin .... Jean-Pierre Marielle
Marie .... Jeanne Goupil
Angela .... Dolores MacDonough
Le Cure .... Romain Bouteille

By RICHARD EDER

"Les Galettes de Pont Aven" is said to have been commercially successful in France. Maybe it broke on the trip over. What we see, as shown at the 68th Street Playhouse, is in pieces, and pretty shoddy ones.

It starts out as the story of a sex-obsessed umbrella salesman with a frigid wife and warm clients. Then, for no very compelling reason, the salesman becomes a naïf painter, still sex-obsessed. Then he becomes a drunk. Then, after a pretty chambermaid takes him up, he turns to selling refreshments on a Brittany beach. There are some inexplicable insertions involving a dead boar and two maniacal hermits.

As the protagonist, Jean-Pierre Marielle is comically dignified as long as he is selling umbrellas and seducing the wives of umbrella-store owners; after that, he is out of his depth and the movie drowns.

1977 Ja 24, 19:1

CORRECTION

The film "Les Galettes de Pont Aven," which was reviewed yesterday, did not open at the 68th Street Playhouse, which is showing "The Marquise of O . . ." indefinitely. "Les Galettes," which The Times's critic saw at a preview, may open at a later date.

1977 Ja 25, 37:6

Fake Feathers

PROVIDENCE, directed by Alain Resnais; screenplay by David Mercer; produced by Yves Gasser and Klaus Hellwig for Action Films; director of photography, Ricardo Aronovich; music, Miklos Rozsa; editor, Albert Jurgenson; distributed by Cinema 5 Films. Running time: 104 minutes. At the Cinema 3 Theater, 59th Street west of Fifth Avenue. This film has been rated R.

Sonia Langham .... Ellen Burstyn
Claud Langham .... Dirk Bogarde
Clive Langham .... John Gielgud
Kevin Woodford .... David Warner
Helen Wiener/Molly Langham .... Elaine Stritch
Dave Woodford .... Denis Lawson
Dr. Mark Eddington .... Cyril Luckham
Miss Boon .... Kathryn Leigh-Scott
Mr. Jenner .... Milo Sperber
Karen .... Anna Wing
Nils .... Peter Arne

By VINCENT CANBY

IT IS DARK but the moon is stage-bright. The camera moves elegantly through very expensive foliage —even oak leaves shine like gardenia plants. We could be back in "Rebecca" on the road to Manderley, but no such luck. That might be fun. We are in the drunken, anxiety-ridden fantasies of Clive Langham (John Gielgud), a second-rate, 78-year-old English novelist who is having a bad night while thinking he is dying and jotting down a few notes for his next book.

We are also at the start of Alain Resnais's disastrously ill-chosen comedy, "Providence," the French director's first film in English that yesterday opened at—and opened—Rugoff Theaters' beautiful new Cinema 3 on the lower level of the Plaza Hotel. Cinema 3, which has been done entirely in soft golds, beiges and grays, and is so comfortable one would like to nap there, Cinema 3 would be an unqualified smash without the picture.

"Providence" is based on an original screenplay by David Mercer, the English writer ("Morgan: A Suitable Case for Treatment") who is better known as a playwright, and, indeed, in spite of all of the film's brisk, desperate cutting around among old Clive Langham's fantasies, the film has the static manner of an easily mountable but fatally empty play script.

The shock of "Providence" is how Mr. Resnais ("Hiroshima, Mon Amour," "La Guerre Est Finie," etc.) could have fallen for such windy pretensions. Is it because English is not his first language or could it be that he's echoing a statement made within the film by Clive Langham to the effect that "style is feeling"?

•

If so, the feeling of "Providence" is the kind of cold chic that can be easily purchased by hiring the right cameraman, set designer, composer and actors who, in addition to Mr. Gielgud, include Dirk Bogarde, Ellen Burstyn, David Warner and Elaine Stritch.

To say that they are miscast would be to suggest that other people might do better, which I doubt. Each performance is as bereft of real style (meaning, point) as the material.

This material is what may have you swatting an innocent Cinema 3 usher as you leave. Most of the film is composed of old Clive's "notes" for his new novel, which involves his son (Mr. Bogarde) who is a priggish barrister, his long-suffering daughter-in-law (Miss Burstyn), another young man (Mr. Warner) and his son's mistress (Miss Stritch), a character created out of whole cloth by Clive in the image of his own dead wife, who committed suicide.

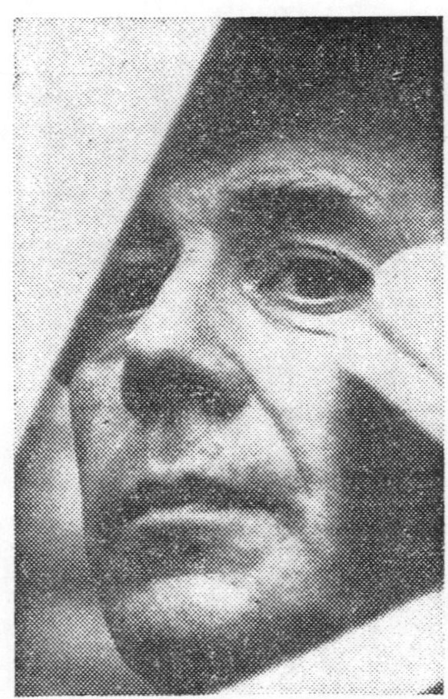

Dick Bogarde in "Providence," a film bereft of any real style.

"PROVIDENCE"—John Gielgud and Ellen Burstyn play a neurotic novelist and his daughter-in-law in Alain Resnais's film.

As the old man tosses and turns in his bed, drinking white wine and complaining of pains in his rectum, we se his "characters" as he imagines them and as they sometimes refuse to do his bidding. The old man, it's soon obvious, has imposed on these perfectly decent folk all of his own fears and guilts about a lifetime spent in philandering, selfishness, disinterest in his family, while he enjoyed a reputation as a writer he never really deserved. The structure is complicated but sadly uncomplex.

The setting of Clive's "novel" is one of those unidentified countries that, in meaning to be anywhere, is actually nowhere. Clive wants his daughter-in-law to have an affair with Mr. Warner, but she balks. The country they inhabit seems to be in a stage of seige, which could be a cheap reference to Allende's Chile, or to the death that Clive awaits.

There are so many references to other films in "Providence" ("Rebecca," werewolf movies, Terence Rattigan-potboilers, Hollywood films, good and bad, for which Miklos Rozsa, the composer for "Providence," also did the score), that one suspects that Mr. Renais and Mr. Mercer might have some thoughts about the state of popular entertainment, though nothing emerges except a dreary demonstration.

At one point, Clive says of his fantasies, "Oh, well, if one has led a fatuous life, one might as well have fatuous nightmares," but the movie makers can't sidestep their own responsibilities so easily. Aside from the true feeling and intelligence that Mr. Gielgud, a magician as well as a great actor, occasionally can bring to a line, Mr. Mercer's method is to have his characters toss wanly sardonic aphorisms back and forth, while Mr. Resnais's is to make everything look alternately menacing and posh. "Providence' 'is a lot of fuss and fake feathers about nothing.

1977 Ja 26, C17:3

Childhood Animated

THE CANADIAN ANIMATOR Caroline Leaf has devised a technique in which lines have a dreamy smudginess and seem to float out of one another. The effect is half comical, half poetic, and Miss Leaf used it triumphantly in a short film about the love of an owl for a duck, shown last year at the Film Forum.

Her new piece, "The Street," is less original but it is still a lovely work. It is the best thing in a pleasant but rather modest collection of five shorts about childhood that opened at the Forum yesterday.

In effect, Miss Leaf's piece is an animated illustration of a story by Mordechai Richler in which a boy tells of the painfully prolonged death of his grandmother.

•

His voice relates, with childlike terseness, the strains and sorrows caused by the long dying. The boy's mother is worn out with the burden of caring for the old woman; his father suffers quietly but philosophically at seeing his wife age in such service. The boy talks with his sister and with friends about death; he wonders if he will get the grandmother's room when she dies.

A mournful but comical series of faces accompany the account. In her silvery, cloudy way, Miss Leaf is not far from drawing thought itself.

The other pieces are of varying interest. There is a photographic essay about the delivery of a baby by a French doctor who believes that the initial trauma of birth is unnecessary. When the baby comes out, instead of spanking it, he fondles it, holds it, floats it gently in the water. The baby looks pleased and unfolds like a water lily but—who knows? Whatever the practice does or does not do for babies, it could do something for the humanity of doctors.

•

The other pieces are feebler. There is a brief, not particularly clever, animated cartoon about a kindergarten class. There is a mildly amusing, though thin, fantasy about a teen-ager who falls in love with Fidel Castro. And there is the piece which gives the title to the series, "Sweet Sounds." It is, I am afraid, a remarkably pedestrian account of small children being taught music at the Mannes School.

The program runs through Sunday, and has a second run from Feb. 3 through 6.

RICHARD EDER

1977 Ja 28, C8:6

FREAKY FRIDAY, directed by Gary Nelson; screenplay by Mary Rodgers, based on her book of the same name; edited by Cotton Warburton; music by Al Kasha and Joel Hirschhorn; director of photography, Charles F. Wheeler; produced by Ron Miller; released by Buena Vista Distribution Co. At the Guild Theater, at Rockefeller Plaza; 86th Street Twin I, at Lexington Avenue; Loews 83d Street Triplex 2, on Broadway and neighborhood theaters. Running time: 95 minutes. This film is rated G.

Ellen Andrews .... Barbara Harris
Annabel .... Jodie Foster
Mr. Andrews .... John Astin
Mrs. Schmauss .... Patsy Kelly

By RICHAR EDER

There is a surefire way to tell a picture put out by the Walt Disney organization. At some point a dog will be shown cocking its head wisely. If the dog is omitted, it makes little difference; the movie does the head-cocking.

These films, a kind of unemployment-relief program for good actors — "Freaky Friday," which opened yesterday at theaters around town, has Jodie Foster and Barbara Harris—are merchandised as harmless fun. I suppose they are harmless, but they give the sensation that every red corpuscle in one's blood is being replaced by a red jelly-bean. That doesn't feel healthy.

In "Freaky Friday" a mother (Miss Harris) and a daughter (Miss Foster) find themselves wishing they were in each other's shoes after a morning of mutual bickering about such things as eating a proper breakfast and tidying the bedroom.

They promptly do become each other. Miss Foster is obliged to do the housework and cater a buffet for her father's business associates. Miss Harris has to cope with field hockey, marching bands and rum-raisin banana splits. By day's end each is reconciled to her original situation.

Toward the end there are some amusing car-chase scenes. Elsewhere the humor is clotted by the feeling that the jokes are chasing the reactions, instead of the other way around.

1977 Ja 29, 11:1

FROM NOON TIL THREE, directed by Frank D. Gilroy; screenplay by Mr. Gilroy, based on his novel; produced by M. J. Frankovich and William Self; director of photography, Lucien Ballard; music, Elmer Bernstein; editor, Maury Winetrobe; distributed by United Artists. Runnnig time: 99 minutes. At the Mark 2 Theater, Seventh Avenue at 47th Street, and other theaters. This film has been rated PG.

Graham Dorsey .... Charles Bronson
Amanda Starbuck .... Jill Ireland
Buck Powers .... Douglas V. Fowley
Ape .... Stan Haze
Boy .... Damon Douglas
Mexican .... Hector Morales
Sheriff .... Bert Williams
Rev. Cabot .... William Lantreau
Edna .... Betty Cole
Sam .... Davis Roberts
Postmaster Hall .... Fred Franklyn
Dr. Finger .... Sonny Jones
Deke .... Hoke Howell
Mr. Foster .... Howard Brunner

By VINCENT CANBY

As Graham Dorsey (Charles Bronson) and his associates ride single-file into the small Western town, intent on robbing the bank on the far end of Main Street, they are made uneasy by the absence of people. There's not a person or an animal in sight. The place seems to be the Marie Celeste of frontier villages, a vessel abandoned by its crew and passengers for no particular reason. Once in the bank, their worries are forgotten as they stuff their bags, pockets and shirts with money. On the way out, however, the gang is ambushed. One by one, the bandits are picked off by the furious citizens until Graham Dorsey wakes up screaming. He's been having a nightmare.

Frank D. Gilroy's witty, discreetly composed "From Noon Till Three," which opened yesterday at the Mark 2 and other theaters, is about the fateful events that take place on the day after Graham Dorsey's nightmare. To get out of the long-planned holdup he has been dreading, he arranges to miss it by having to hide out in the prairie-gothic mansion of a beautiful, rich, quite looney widow, Amanda Starbuck (Jill Ireland), whom he seduces, more or less to pass the time, only to unlock forces far more devastating than those of any ordinary posse.

"From Noon Till Three" is neither a conventionally comic Western nor a conventional comedy, and it certainly isn't a conventional Bronson film. More than anything else, I suppose, it is an ebulliently

Charles Bronson
Remarkably attractive performance

cheerful satire of contemporary myth-making and celebrity, cast as a fable of the Old West.

Not all of it is equally successful, and it takes its time making certain points, which, being made, are made again; yet its intelligence and its narrative shape are immensely satisfying.

Graham Dorsey's seduction of the rich widow turns out to be as much of a nightmare trap as the one he dreamed of just before the bank job. When all of his associates are caught during the holdup and hanged, and when he also is thought to have been executed, the romantically liberated widow tells her story to the world via book and song.

She and her supposedly dead lover, who lived a lifetime of love between noon and three, become objects of national adoration. The frontier town is turned into a hustling tourist center, the mansion a shrine, and Amanda herself into the keeper of the flame.

Under such circumstances, it's no surprise that she greets Graham Dorsey's eventual return with something less than enthusiasm. A large part of the world refuses to allow the destructoin of the legend. Does anyone want to believe that John Dillinger is alive and well and selling Pontiacs in Scranton?

Mr. Gilroy, who not only directed the film but also wrote the screenplay based on his own novel, has a nice, light way with irony that prevents "From Noon Till Three" from tripping over its own rather large intentions. He's also obtained two remarkably attractive, absolutely straight performances from Mr. Bronson, who is funny without ever lunging at a laugh (as Burt Reynolds often does under similar circumstances) and from Miss Ireland, whose cool, somewhat steely beauty are perfectly suited to the widow who manages almost immediately to transform a real-life experience into mass-media material with plenty of spin-offs.

Mr. Gilroy, the Pulitzer Prize-winning playwright ("The Subject Was Roses") and a director of talent and taste ("Desperate Characters"), has made a film of unusual beauty, with the help of Lucien Ballard, te cameraman, and Robert Clatworthy, the production designer.

It was especially irritating then that, when I saw the film at the first showing at the Mark 2 yesterday, the print was in such poor shape it looked as if a cat had been scratching its claws on it. Further, it seemed to be out of focus about half the time while the music of Led Zeppelin, in "The Song Remains the Same" in the adjoining theater, was audible throughout. People who pay admission should not have to put up with such sloppiness.

•

"From Noon Till Three," which has been rated PG ("Parental Guidance Suggested"), contains some vulgar language and a couple of bedroom scenes that are less steamy than comic.

1977 Ja 29, 11:1

Labor Double Bill

UNION MAIDS, a documentary film directed and produced by Julia Reichert, James Klein and Miles Mogulescu; editors, Mr. Klein and Miss Reichert; directors of photography, Sherry Novick and Tony Heriza; distributed by New Day Films and Distribution Co-op. Running time: 55 minutes.
ON THE LINE, a documentary film directed and produced by Barbara N. Weiss; narrator, Rip Torn; Barrow and Marc N. Weiss; narrator, Rip Torn; production and editing by Carol Anshien, Miss Barrow, Affonso Beato, Ted Churchill, James Klein, Michael Levine, Robert Machover, Miss Margolis, Julie Reichert, Karen Sellars, Ceevah Sobel, Rhody Streeter and Mr. Weiss; distributed by Distribution Co-op. Running time: 60 minutes. At the Elgin Theater, Eighth Avenue at 9th Street.

By VINCENT CANBY

"UNION MAIDS" is 55 minutes long. It's a documentary, photographed in black-and-white and, I suspect, it's designed principally for television; but it's one of the more moving, more cheering theatrical experiences available in New York this weekend.

It can be seen at noon tomorrow and Sunday, this weekend and next, at the Elgin Theater, on a double bill with "On the Line," a more elaborate—in color and longer by five minutes—documentary that, like "Union Maids," deals with cooperative social action, which is sometimes but not always trade-unionism.

"Union Maids" is very much about trade-unionism but it's even more about three extraordinary women, Kate Hyndman, Stella Nowicki and Sylvia Woods who, in the course of three separate interviews, which are intercut with each other and with period newsreel footage, recall their lives as women laborers and union organizers in Chicago in the late 20's and 30's.

It was a sometimes brutal, bitter, mingy time for all labor and especially for women who didn't believe their places were necessarily in the home. Yet it was also a time of terrific hope, when one could believe in social and political progress and measure it by the concessions won through group action.

Kate, who appears to be the oldest of the three, has the face of an elderly schoolmistress whose seeming severity is constantly denied by her comic self-appraisals and by the warmth and the passion with which she recalls her life as a labor militant and feminist. That didn't always go down too well with the labor militants who were male.

A scene from Barbara Margolis's documentary "On the Line" at the Elgin

Stella grew up on a farm in Michigan and, as a young woman, moved to Chicago to work in the stockyards. Sylvia, a black woman who was born and bred in New Orleans, also moved to Chicago at an early age. There, she was active in organizing the laundry workers who, as she remembers with biting humor, were mostly women who worked seven days a week and had to provide written explanations to their bosses when they were absent.

Largely because of Sylvia this requirement was eventually dropped. Her ploy: to persuade every woman to give as the reason for her absenteeism, "just tired."

Julia Reichert, James Klein and Miles Mogulescu, who jointly directed and produced "Union Maids," never get in the way of their subjects and never put words in their mouths. They don't have to. Sylvia, Stella and Kate are three naturals, characters whose hearts and minds leap off the screen with a kind of grace and nobility I haven't seen in a documentary since Jerry Bruck's "I.F. Stone's Weekly."

"On the Line," directed and produced by Barbara Margolis, has no comparable focal points and, indeed, I'm not quite sure if it has any focal point at all. It looks rather like a documentary whose material failed to provide the film maker with the kind of drama and narrative shape that Barbara Koppel found in her "Harlan County, U.S.A." Its material includes interviews with workers at the Ford Motor Company in Mahwah, N.J., with rent-striking residents at Co-op City in the Bronx, an engineer at an RCA plant who feels the company no longer values him and with a Medicaid worker.

Their common complaint is that contemporary America is running amok with rising prices, unemployment, and a generally heedless attitude on the part of the people who might be able to control the economy.

There's nothing especially wrong with the vision the film presents, but the vision is too diffuse to have much impact on the screen. The film maker wants it to say more than she does, to which end, I suppose, Miss Margolis uses an off-screen narrator (Rip Torn), which gives "On the Line" the feeling of an industrial film. The best, most effective, documentaries tend to speak for themselves, not through off-screen mouthpieces.

1977 F 4, C8:3

EARLY SWEDISH MOVIES AT THE MODERN

By RICHARD EDER

Ingmar Bergman's father was a clergyman. On Sundays after the service he would show movies, generally Swedish ones.

Predestination is hardly necessary with a background like that. Bergman's films are modern sermons, plotted in an empty church and shaped—more than most of us realize—by the shadow and light, the bleak revelry, the sense of ghosts in the land and the mind contained the early Swedish films shown on those Sunday afternoons.

This weekend, and lasting until early April, the Museum of Modern Art will be showing some of Bergman's Sunday afternoons: a collection of the best surviving examples of the Swedish silent film.

Not that the program is set up that way. The show, organized by the Museum's Film Department with the help of the Swedish Film Institute (which is supplying the prints), sets out to present a body of work with a value of its own; one little known in this country. The show centers mainly around the work of two major directors, Victor Sjostrom and Mauritz Stiller.

Yet take Sjostrom's "The Phantom Chariot." (March 5 and 7). It is framed in blackness, as if the light were dark and the highlights were fugitive shadows. It starts with a wild drunken brawl in a churchyard. The protagonist, played by Sjostrom himself—who so many years later would play the old rememberer in Bergman's "Wild Strawberries"—is knocked on the head. The rest of the picture is a mixture of delusion and reality: fantasies about a chariot sent to collect the souls of the dead, interwoven with flashbacks of the protagonist's own life and loves.

Complex, savage and with a half-fraudulent mystery. Coarse, half-rustic figures propelled or led on by a ghostly illumination. It is a film Bergman particularly remembered being impressed by; and it is impossible to see it now without getting a new perspective upon the harsh originality of "The Seventh Seal."

Sjostrom organized his films with the entrances and exits, the playing to a motionless camera, that is clearly derived from the theater. The plays, furthermore, are melodramas, and the acting has all the eye-rolling and underlined gesture common to films made between 1910 and 1920.

The figures scurry and posture in a fashion that is too obsolete to be interesting. But there is something more. In "Terje Vigen," which is playing on Sunday, the movement is more poetic than dramatic. It is, in fact, the recreation of a poem by Ibsen; the legend of a man who lives by the sea and loses wife and child in a famine.

The reality in this still and moving film is not the plot, but the landscapes. The landscape of rock and water, and of the gray unchanging sky. The landscape of Terje Vigen's face. Suffering is as unmovable on that face as the seams on the rocks or the waves—which move but are replaced—on the sea. The motionless camera stretches out time in such a fashion that none of these things are static but simply proceed at the speed of the earth.

In contrast with the work of Sjostrom is the more agile and witty style of Mauritz Stiller, a director who inspired Lubitsch, for example. In "Love and Journalism," also playing Sunday, the plot cavorts suitably as farce. A handsome explorer returns home. A woman reporter, barred from an interview, gets a job as a pretty incompetent maid. Pretty and incompetent, that is. Love strikes, etc., etc.

The real movement is not in the plot, though, but in the faces and stances of the lovers. It is a dialogue of gesture; Karin Molander as the journalist has a face that is an epigram, a body—relaxing and going taut—that is a retort.

Another Stiller comedy, considerably more sophisticated, is his "Erotikon, (March 3 and 5); a witty, perhaps ambiguous mockery of the rich, it tells of a series of shifting relationships, among a professor, his wife, a sculptor who loves her, and others. Temptation is a game more than a reality. The mind dabbles in it; what the bodies do is almost beside the point.

The more dramatic side of Stiller's work is also shown. "The Treasure of Arne" (Feb. 20 and 22) is an elaborate epic tragedy, taking place in the 16th century, and based on a novel by Selma Lagerlof. Snowbound landscapes and the sea are used to frame the small figures and their struggles.

The balance of the program includes other works by Sjostrom and Stiller, and some by lesser-known directors. In particular, there is "The Prisoner of Karlsten's Fortress," which was shown yesterday. It is a knotty and silly melodrama about a man who steals a scientist's secret formula for making explosives, and hides the professor's daughter in a castle. The film—appropriately, by the Hasselblad Studios, which in those days made films as well as cameras—is mainly about deep focus.

One short film, "Peter the Tramp," (March 12 and 18) used Greta Garbo when she was still known as Greta Gustaffson.

At every conceivable opportunity people are photographed through doorways, down passages and on the other side of windows, in order to show off the technique. It is an early example of technological folly—we have the movie for the sake of the camera instead of vice versa.

For programs and times on the day of a show, call 956-7078. For advance information, call 956-7284. Tickets are $2, $1.25 for students and 75 cents for the elderly and children.

1977 F 4, C8:3

FILM VIEW

VINCENT CANBY

From Mining Coal to 'Pumping Iron'

Great themes like war and peace and social and political change don't necessarily make great fiction films. They tend to get in the way of the creative imagination, to intimidate the filmmaker into adopting the sort of piety and uplift that once marked the work of Stanley Kramer when he was busy solving the problems of race relations and saving the world from the horrors of nuclear holocaust. In such films characters who should be people tend, instead, to become fixed positions, predetermined points on society's compass, mouthpieces that say all those things that are expected of them as if they were actors in a commercial for God.

Good fiction, however, can ennoble any subject no matter how small, frivolous, mean or unpleasant it may be. The same is occasionally true of good documentary films as the Maysles brothers demonstrated in "Salesman," that sad and funny portrait of a hustling, door-to-door Bible salesman who is approaching the end of his rope. Yet, for reasons I'm not quite sure of, great themes are generally more accessible to the makers of documentaries. It may be that the themes, accurately identified by the filmmakers, then describe the films that are made. It's not an automatic process by any means, but it helps the filmmaker to have a subject worth exploring.

These thoughts are prompted by four films, each the work of new, young filmmakers:

Barbara Kopple's moving, passionately observed "Harlan County, U.S.A.," a report on the bitter, eventually violent, 13-month strike of Kentucky coal miners who believed they had the right to be represented by the United Mine Workers of America, now at Cinema II;

"Union Maids," a stirring recollection of the labor movement in Chicago in the 1930s, told in the faces and the words of three women who fought the battles in the shops and on the picket lines, a film made by James Klein, Julia Reichert and Miles Mogelscu;

"On The Line," an equally passionate though none too subtle cry for collective action to fight the injustices of an impersonal capitalism, produced and directed by Barbara Margolis; and

"Pumping Iron," the loving and anything but critical examination of male body-building in America (and around the world) today, which the film identifies as a spectator sport, but it's a spectator sport more or less the way watching the Miss America pageants is a spectator sport, directed by George Butler and Robert Fiore, and now playing at the Plaza.

"Pumping Iron" is a slickly made film as completely committed to its subject as "Harlan County, U.S.A." is committed to its Kentucky coal miners, and I suppose the two films shouldn't be made to compete; yet Miss Kopple's documentary is an important film and "Pumping Iron" is to movie-going what junk food is to meat, potatoes and a green vegetable. It's not even successful at accomplishing what I take to have been its modest goal, that is, to render comprehensible the very special world of the full-time body-builder. Perhaps the person who made the trailer for "Pumping Iron" really knew what he was up to when he wrote of body-building: "It's more than a sport. It's a philosophy . . . it's an obsession." In that progression of importance, I fear.

The distinguishing feature of "Harlan County, U.S.A.," as it is of all great documentaries, is the sense it conveys

"Harlan County, U.S.A." records a strike in coal country.

of the complexity, the mystery, the contradictions and the great possibilities of the human condition. It's this quality that made Marcel Ophuls's "The Memory of Justice" so spell-binding for almost five hours, and which ultimately rendered academic arguments about the extent to which Ophuls himself believes, in the complicity of all citizens everywhere in any nation's crimes, be it Hitler or Vietnam.

No matter how you interpret Ophuls, in "The Memory of Justice" or "The Sorrow and The Pity," you cannot misinterpret the pieces of his jigsaw puzzles—the dozens of people he interviews, and whose lives pour off the screen in an extravagant profusion of feelings that have the effect reminding all of us of our potential for both good and evil.

On a much smaller scale this is what "Harlan County, U.S.A." accomplishes as Miss Kopple and her crew follow the lives of the miners and their families in a crucial labor struggle of the sort that seems almost prehistoric to us today. By living in the mining community, by sharing its commitment, and by expressing an obvious sympathy, the filmmaker was able to record an exalting if not unique chapter in American social history.

Miss Kopple was lucky to the extent that the events of the Harlan County strike gave her film a natural narrative shape, which builds to the violence that helped bring the strike to an end and which includes the revolt of the U.M.W. rank-and-file against the administration of W. A. ("Tony") Boyle.

That shape, perhaps, makes the film somewhat more satisfying than it might otherwise be, but the film's force is not in narrative shape but in the lives we see on screen—the old man who's dying of the black-lung disease, the young striker who bristles at some bit of cautionary advice from the union lawyer ("Lawyers are made for getting you out of trouble after you get in, not for keeping you out of it. . . ."), a miner's wife who says, "If I get shot, they can't shoot the union out of me," and the wide-bottomed, gun-toting chief of the strike-breakers who's a more outrageous villain than any Hollywood producer would have the nerve to cast in a fiction film.

Does Miss Kopple stack the cards in favor of the strikers? It's difficult to see how she could avoid it if that means she's pro-union, but the issues are clearly stated and never for a moment does she pretend to any sort of neutrality, which is, I suspect, a largely over-rated virtue in this sort of journalism when the journalist's position is never in doubt.

Though "Union Maids," which is a 55-minute feature, is being shown on a special double-bill on weekends at the Elgin Theater with the 60-minute "On The Line," it would make a much better companion piece to "Harlan County, U.S.A." "Union Maids" is a deceptively simple looking film, being composed mostly of separate, face-to-face interviews with three extraordinary women, each of whom recalls the trials of being an unskilled woman laborer in Chicago in the thirties, as well as being a labor organizer. Their recollections and their comments on the contemporary scene are made especially affecting by the double-view they share with us. They remember the enthusiasm, faith, excitement and trust that trade unionism once represented. This is then coupled with the awareness of what has happened today to so many trade unions whose wealth makes them conservative and at times corrupt, as is illustrated so dramatically in "Harlan County" in the physical deterioration we see in W. A. Boyle in the course of the film.

"Union Maids" looks simple but it is a beautifully composed little film, making extremely effective use of fine, rousing old trade union songs as well as of newsreel footage of the period.

Much less effective is "On The Line," which employs a narrator (Rip Torn) and interviews a number of people who behave as if they'd been programmed to say what they say. It almost sounds like an industrial film on behalf of socialism, and while there's nothing wrong with the sentiments expressed relating to the depressed state of the economy, rising living costs and unemployment, the film never once works as a film. It just sort of pokes a finger in your shoulder and preaches. The people have no lives of their own.

In "The Night of The Iguana" Tennessee Williams has one of his characters say something to the effect that "nothing human disgusts me," which has always struck me as a most arrogant bit of reverse self-esteem. One must, I think, have reached a certain, very elevated state of grace to be able to make such a statement and mean it. The line came back to me as I watched some of the body-building displays in "Pumping Iron." I remember in particular a sequence in which Arnold Schwartzenegger, who has been Mr. World, Mr. Olympia and Mr. Universe, turns away from the camera and flexes his back muscles in such a way that it seems as if we could be watching an especially lumpy Hungarian goulash move through the intestines. By the end of the film, I must admit, I'd gotten used to the sight of the pumped-up, inflated physiques so that they didn't seem quite so grotesque, but the film still comes across as a kind of cheerful hype, a movie that goes on a carefully-guided, scenic tour of the world of body-building, allowing some of the fellows to look a little foolish and simple-minded, of course, but generally sharing. Schwaftzenegger's high opinion of himself and his profession, which he chooses to think of as an art on the order of sculpture (only, you see, he uses his body instead of clay). A little later the movie allows Schwartzenegger to describe the feeling as he pumps up his muscles before an exhibition as being a lot like an orgasm. Which may provide the key to this sort of body-building.

Whatever it is, the film does not answer a lot of questions that the uninitiated might have liked to ask. What happens to the muscles when a fellow gets old? How much money do the professionals make? (Schwartzenegger refers to his "secretary," which suggests big money and show-biz.) Do body builders ever fail, make mistakes and over-develop the wrong muscles? Do they get hernias? Doesn't this sort of narcissism suggest a rather greater incidence of homosexuality than anyone in the film acknowledges? Or maybe asexuality? Do those bulging blood vessels ever pop? Instead of "Pumping Iron" the movie could have easily been titled "Varicose Vanities."

"Pumping Iron" is about physically large people with small goals. "Harlan County, U.S.A.," where everyone looks as if he smoked too much, didn't get the right food and needed six months in the sun, is the opposite. Documentaries, no matter how carefully photographed and edited to shape the truth, measure lives as accurately as they measure bodies.

1977 F 6, II:1:1

'Twilight's Last Gleaming': No Star

"Twilight's Last Gleaming" is Robert Aldrich's deadly solemn, gadgety suspense-melodrama about a disgruntled, liberal-thinking United States general, a Vietnam veteran whose out-spoken antiwar views got him railroaded to prison on a trumped-up murder charge.

The general, played by Burt Lancaster, breaks out of the slammer with three other Death-Row prisoners to take possession of a Titan missile base in Montana. With his finger on the button, the renegade general demands $10-million in unmarked bills, the use of Air Force One to take him and his associates to the country of their choice, the President of the United States as hostage and, most important, a full disclosure of "the facts" about the war.

These "facts," unfortunately, are fully disclosed in the course of "Twilight's Last Gleaming" and immediately ridicule the movie's claims to importance contained in its publicity. Instead, the facts suggest that Mr. Aldrich, who directed the film, and Ronald M. Cohen and Edward Huebsch, who wrote the screenplay, set in 1981, haven't yet caught up even to 1975.

"TWILIGHT'S LAST GLEAMING"—Burt Lancaster and Paul Winfield seize Charles Durning, the President, in Robert Aldrich's film.

The Cast

TWILIGHT'S LAST GLEAMING, directed by Robert Aldrich; screenplay by Ronald M. Cohen and Edward Huebsch, based on the novel, "Viper Three," by Walter Wager; produced by Merv Adelson; executive producer, Helmut Jedele; music, Jerry Goldsmith; director of cinematography, Robert Hauser, editor, Michael Luciano; a Lorimar-Bavaria presentation, distributed by Allied Artists. Running time: 144 minutes. At Loew's State 2, Broadway at 45 Street, UA Eastside Cinema, Third Avenue at 55th Street, and Loew's Orpheum, 86th Street near Third Avenue. This film has been rated R.

Lawrence Dell .... Burt Lancaster
Gen. MacKenzie .... Richard Widmark
President Stevens .... Charles Durning
Defense Secretary Guthrie .... Melvyn Douglas
Powell .... Paul Winfield
Garvas .... Burt Young
State Secretary Renfrew .... Joseph Cotten
James Forrest .... Roscoe Lee Browne
Gen. O'Rourke .... Gerald S. O'Loughlin
Capt. Towne .... Richard Jaeckel
Attorney-General Klinger .... William Marshall
Col. Bernstein .... Charles Aidman
C.I.A. Director Whittaker .... Leif Erickson
Gen. Crane .... Charles McGraw

The facts are contained in a Top Secret memo reporting that a former President of the United States agreed to continue the Vietnam War at the insistence of his military advisers and cabinet members who argued that the senseless slaughter was the only way the Soviets would understand that the United States meant business. Good grief! All of the characters in the film, whose minds are so tiny they've totally forgotten the Pentagon Papers and Watergate, are convinced that such a move toward "open" government would result in the collapse of the American way of life and death.

In "Twilight's Last Gleaming," this memo is what Alfred Hitchcock likes to call the "McGuffin," the secret thing or information that heroes and villains battle for in any Hitchcock espionage film. Mr. Hitchcock knows enough never to tell us what the McGuffin is, since nothing can seem as important as it's been built up to be. I've gone into it at some length here because the McGuffin of "Twilight's Last Gleaming" is a measure of the movie's wooly-headedness.

Otherwise, the film has the appearance of a rather classy television show in which people are forever picking up and putting down telephones, buzzing secretaries, and getting into and out of various means of transportation—automobiles, jet airplanes, helicopters and elevators.

Mr. Aldrich obtains a good deal of suspense from idiotic material, though his use of the split-screen doesn't double suspense as often as it cuts it in half. There also are two decently straight performances by Mr. Lancaster and Charles Durning, who plays the President as the sort of man who has adequacy thrust upon him.

The other actors are mostly terrible, including some who look as if they'd passed through old age and gone on to the embalming room.

I suppose that "Twilight's Last Gleaming," which opened at three theaters yesterday, might also claim to be important in pointing out how close nuclear destruction always is, but this is important the way that a sign, "Don't Walk On The Tracks," is important as literature.

VINCENT CANBY

1977 F 10, 48:1

FUN WITH DICK AND JANE, directed by Ted Kotcheff; screenplay by David Giler, Jerry Belson and Mordecai Richler, based on a story by Gerald Gaiser; produced by Peter Bart and Max Pavlevsky; director of cinematography, Fred J. Koenekamp; music, Ernest Gold; editor, Danford B. Greene; distributed by Columbia Pictures. Running time: 95 minutes. At Loews State 1, Broadway at 45th Street, and Loews Tower East, Third Avenue near 72d Street. This film has been rated PG.

Dick Harper	George Segal
Jane Harper	Jane Fonda
Charlie Blanchard	Ed McMahon
Doctor Will	Dick Gautier
Loan company manager	Allan Miller
Raoul Esteban	Hank Garcia
Jane's father	John Dehner
Mr. Weeks	Walter Brooke
Jane's mother	Mary Jackson
Immigration officer	James Jeter
Charlie's secretary	Maxine Stuart
Bob	Fred Willard

By VINCENT CANBY

When Dick Harper (George Segal) loses his job as a Los Angeles aerospace engineer, he and his wife Jane (Jane Fonda) find themselves in the classic bind of the once-upwardly mobile. They have no bank balance, owe $72,000 on their house and have already borrowed the limit on their life insurance. Their swimming pool is still an ugly hole in the ground Jane hopes they can finish it and then economize by not heating it. When they are two months in arrears, the landscape company sends around a crew to remove their plants and trees, and, while they're at it, to roll up the lawn. What to do?

•

Dick and Jane take to crime, which is the point at which you have every right to expect that "Fun With Dick and Jane" is going to stumble over the cuteness of the gimmick that, from the opening credits, has been shadowing the film like a gloomy bill collector. The good news is that it doesn't. "Fun With Dick and Jane," written by David Giler, Jerry Belson and Mordecai Richler, and directed by Ted Kotcheff, is a deceptively sunny, sometimes uproariously funny comedy about the bad taste, vulgarity and awful aimlessness of a certain kind of middle-class American affluence.

Buried not very deeply within the film, there is a small flaw. We are asked to like and to sympathize with Dick and Jane, played by Mr. Segal and Miss Fonda with a fine, earnest kind of intensity I associate with good schewball comedy of the past, and we do like them enormously, even though the characters are completely dedicated to maintaining all-wrong values. In this respect, the film seems to want to stand on both sides of the fence at once, to take credit for having a social conscience while not really honoring it. It's not enough for us to be told that Dick and Jane are really ripping off the system. They aren't that believably cynical.

This may be taking the film more seriously than anyone intended, though I doubt it. Mr. Kotcheff and the men who wrote "Fun With Dick and Jane" are so aware of what it's about that they haven't hesitated to employ bad taste in their attack on it. There is no other way to explain, for example, a throwaway comedy bit that features a man whose vocal chords have been removed and who must talk through a transistorized amplifier. On the surface this has nothing to do with social satire and everything to do with callousness, but then it may be argued that "Fun With Dick and Jane" is about the callousness of the system. I'm not convinced it works.

•

What does work are the series of scenes that are virtually blackout sketches that define, first, the degradation to which Dick and Jane are brought by their poverty, and, second, their criminal escapades, whether holding up the telephone company—while all the legitimate customers cheer—or stealing the offering at a church whose pastor preaches the profit motive —"Remember," he tells his flock, "the cross is a plus sign."

I never have trouble remembering that Miss Fonda is a fine dramatic actress but I'm surprised all over again every time I see her do comedy with the mixture of comic intelligence and abandon she shows here. One sequence in particular, in which she makes a botch of an attempt at fashion modeling in a crowded restaurant at lunchtime, is a nearly priceless piece of modern slapstick. Another is Dick's brief appearance as a supernumerary in the opera chorus. Old stuff and still good.

The members of the supporting cast, headed by Ed McMahon as Dick's alternately smarmy and sozzled former employer, are excellent. Among those who come to mind first are John Dehner and Mary Jackson, as Jane's rich parents who, when Dick loses his job, congratulate her on the opportunity life has provided to demonstrate her self-reliance. "Oh," says mom, tears in her eyes, "I'm so happy for you!"

•

"Fun With Dick and Jane," which has been rated PG ("Parental Guidance Suggested"), includes a lot of vulgar language and gestures that are perfectly in keeping with the point and method of the movie.

1977 F 10, 48:1

George Segal and Jane Fonda
Likable characters

Cassandra Crossing' Doomed By Silly Premise, Miscasting

By RICHARD EDER

THE CASSANDRA CROSSING, directed by George Pan Cosmatos; written by Tom Mankiewicz, Robert Katz and Mr. Cosmâtos; produced by Carlo Ponti; director of photography, Enio Guarnieri; edited by Francois Bonnot and Roberto Silvi; music by Jerry Goldsmith; presented by Sir Lew Grade and Mr. Ponti. Released by Avco Embassy. At Loews Astor Plaza and other theaters. Running time: 125 minutes. This film has been rated R.

Jennifer	Sophia Loren
Chamberlain	Richard Harris
Nicole	Ava Gardner
Mackenzie	Burt Lancaster
Navarro	Martin Sheen
Elena	Ingrid Thulin
Kaplan	Lee Strasberg
Stack	John Phillip Law
Susan	Ann Turkel
Father Haley	O. J. Simpson

It would be paranoid—as paranoid as the film itself—to see in "The Cassandra Crossing" some covert and kinky attempt at anti-American propaganda. Stupidity can be kinkier than propaganda, and this movie is profoundly, offensively stupid.

The United States dirty-tricks people, it tells us, have secreted a whole laboratory full of pneumonic plague germs inside the World Health Organization headquarters in Geneva. Terrorists try to steal it and are shot—what are United States Marine guards doing inside the W.H.O.?—but one escapes to hide in the Geneva-Stockholm Express.

•

Gray and sweaty, the terrorist goes through the train, breathing in the passengers' faces and retching over the rice in the galley. Burt Lancaster, the United States Army Intelligence chief in Geneva, learns he has a problem. Instead of getting the Swiss authorities to stop the train and quarantine everyone, he manages in some unexplained fashion to have the train sealed and dispatched to Poland.

(Questions: Why doesn't he want to tell the Swiss authorities? Embarrassment? Why is it less embarrassing to tell the Polish authorities? And how does an Army Intelligence colonel manage to reroute a train without getting the national railroad officials to help?)

But the border-crossing bridge is known to be fatally deficient. The conductor knows it, and so do the 1,000 passengers on board. They try to reach the engineer and tell him to stop the train. They engage in a wild machine-gun battle with American soldiers placed on the train to prevent this.

(Questions: Would American soldiers really shoot down passengers so they could all go over a worm-eaten bridge together? If the conductor knows the bridge is rotten wouldn't the engineer know, too? Why doesn't the conductor simply pull the emergency signal? Why . . . oh, never mind.)

Except for the photography, which is rather good, the film, which opened yesterday at Loews Astor Plaza and other theaters, carries out its ridiculous premises with uniform incompetence.

Burt Lancaster bears his totally incomprehensible role as if it were a toothache. His jaw is clamped so tight that it looks swollen.

Ingrid Thulin and Lee Strasberg are adequate in awful roles. Ava Gardner is awful in an awful role.

Sophia Loren is totally miscast as a bright, quirky writer who is pursuing her divorced husband. Richard Harris, the husband, is vacuous as the neurosurgeon charged with trying to handle a pneumonic plague epidemic.

The plague germs rapidly mutate into something harmless, like a cold. The film never mutates: It just goes on, becoming more and more lethal.

1977 F 10, 48:2

"THE CASSANDRA CROSSING"—Richard Harris and Fausta Avelli are caught up in a shoot-out in George Cosmato's thriller.

Art Carney and Lily Tomlin in Robert Benton's "The Late Show"

Fading Private Eye

THE LATE SHOW, directed and written by Robert Benton; produced by Robert Altman; director of photography, Chuck Rosher; editors, Lou Lombardo and Peter Appleton; music, Ken Wannberg; distributed By Warner Bros. Running time: 94 minutes. At the Sutton Theater, 57th Street near Third Avenue. This film has been rated PG.

Ira Wells	Art Carney
Margo	Lily Tomlin
Charlie Hatter	Bill Macy
Ron Birdwell	Eugene Roche
Laura Birdwell	Joanna Cassidy
Lamar	John Considine
Mrs. Schmidt	Ruth Nelson
Sergeant Dayton	John Davey
Harry Regan	Howard Duff

By VINCENT CANBY

A CLASSIC, 1950's-type of Los Angeles private eye grows old like anyone else. He doesn't fade away poetically or go out in a blaze of bullets.. He slows down like an ancient alarm clock. He also gets thick around the middle and begins to lose his hearing. His wife, necessary in his youth, has left him, but he never saw much of her anyway. What the hell—that's life. He has given up the two-bit office with the filing cabinet—no clients—and moved out of his apartment into a rooming house. On good days he visits the track. Once a week he hauls his laundry to and from the laundromat.

He remains scrupulously honest and, for reasons he wouldn't understand, becomes increasingly neat and tidy about his person. This is the way of some old people for whom immaculate grooming is a kind of disguise for the decay taking place within. He isn't bitter. Life was never a bowl of cherries. It's enough now if his ulcer shuts up.

This is Ira Wells, one-time contemporary of Sam Spade and Philip Marlowe, as characterized by the incomparable Art Carney in Robert Benton's wise and witty new film, "The Late Show." The movie, which opened yesterday at the Sutton, is a comedy-melodrama that employs the devices of old private-eye fiction to create an entertainment that is completely up-to-date and as full of resonances as its title.

As Mr. Benton, who both wrote and directed "The Late Show," spins out the details of the caper that overtakes Ira Wells so late in life, he is also paying his respects to all those earlier films that still can keep us up to the cold hours of the morning on television. Jean-Luc Godard once said the only adequate way to review one film is by making another. Mr. Benton's is a funny, tightly constructed, knowledgeable, affectionate rave that all of us can share.

It begins in accepted fashion, late at night, when Ira answers a knock at his door to greet his old pal Harry Regan (Howard Duff). Ira is delighted and invites Harry in, at which point Harry's jacket falls open to reveal that most of his stomach has been shot away. "Who was it, Harry?" says Ira. "Nobody can palm a .45." Harry falls to the floor. He tries to say something but expires, leaving Ira with a cold one on his hands and the thought. "You were real good company, pal, the best."

Several days later, when Ira is leaving Harry's funeral, he's approached by a would-be theatrical producer who is also a part-time bartender and full-time creep, a fellow by the name of Charlie Hatter (Bill Macy), and Charlie's dolly named Margo (Lily Tomlin), a loony who wants Ira to find her cat, who's been kidnapped. Charlie tries to fan them off. He knows nuts when he sees them, but Margo persists. She shows Ira a snapshot. "Please, Mr. Wells, give this little cat a break. . . ."

Quicker than you can say Raymond Chandler or even Ross MacDonald, Ira finds himself up to his hearing aid in a series of double- and triple-crosses that involve not only the dead Harry Regan and Margo's kidnapped cat, but also a big-time Los Angeles fence, who lives in a mansion empty except for crates of stolen appliances and clothes, the fence's beautiful young wife, the beautiful young wife's lover—shot to death on his water bed—and a sadistic bodyguard, among others.

The plotting is marvelously convoluted but even if it weren't, I can't imagine not enjoying "The Late Show," which has, as its living, breathing center, the growth of an affecting relationship between old Ira, the loner, and the goofy, fad-prone Margo, whose vulgar language so shocks the courtly older man.

If Ira represents a downtown Los Angeles that no longer exists, Margo is the swinging Los Angeles that never was. Now of a certain age, she is, most of the time, at manic loose-ends. She thinks of herself as an actress who's retired—"I couldn't play the Hollywood game." She calls herself a dress designer and pushes pot to pay for her psychiatrist. She never stops talking and probably because of that, she lives alone and hates it. It's a great role and Miss Tomlin is superb.

One of Mr. Benton's gifts is being able to catch the rhythm of not only how people talk, but also of how they think they should talk, their affectations. This allows "The Late Show" to function effectively on two levels at once, as a recollection of an earlier kind of film as well as an original film complete in itself. This particular talent was also evident in the tragicomic "Bad Company," Mr. Benton's first film as a director, and a film that's been seen by too few people. As a writer, of course, he is better known for his collaborations with David Newman, including work "Bonnie and Clyde."

Credit, too, must also be given to Robert Altman, who produced "The Late Show" and whose "The Long Goodbye," in which Elliott Gould played a contemporary Philip Marlowe, was a totally different but equally effective homage to the private-eye genre. "The Late Show" deserves to be the year's first unequivocal hit.

•

"The Late Show," which has been rated PG ("Parental Guidance Suggested"), includes some vulgar language, which one never would have heard in a movie in 1950, and some bloody, if almost ritualized violence, which one would have seen in 1950, but not in full color.

1977 F 11, C4:1

Short Forms

OSKAR FISCHINGER RETROSPECTIVE, 22 examples of abstract animation dating from 1921 to 1947. Among them are: SPIRITUAL CONSTRUCTIONS; STUDIES 5, 6, 8, 11; MURATTI PRIVAT; COMPOSITION IN BLUE. AN AMERICAN MARCH, TV COMMERCIALS and MOTION PAINTING NO. 1. Total running time: 81 minutes. At the Film Forum, 15 Vandam Street, today through Sunday, and Feb. 17 through 20 at 7:30 P.M.

IN ITS RETROSPECTIVE of 26 years of work by the abstract film maker Oskar Fischinger, the Film Forum manages to demonstrate a good deal about the limitations of the form.

A great many of the 22 short pieces consist of groups of shapes moving, usually to music. Small oblongs and small boomerangs are two of the most frequent. They are so minimal that the music, some of it good and some of it 1930's German tea-house, takes over. The shapes become an accompaniment. They are like an exotic stop on an organ—glockenspiel, say—that contributes little besides trivial decoration.

•

Several of the pieces are commercials whose interest, if any, has more to do with design than with film. On the other hand, the last piece in the show—"Motion Painting No. 1"—manages, with its textured, lichenlike forms, to go beyond experiment and make an expressive statement.

Mr. Fischinger is, at least, a genial experimenter. For example, all the pieces are extremely short. He makes no pretensions, as later abstract film makers do, to enlisting time as a kind of field marshal and organizing 50-minute parades.

Besides influencing younger film makers, Mr. Fischinger's work was studied by Walt Disney's people in the preparation of "Fantasia." He was, in fact, hired to design the Bach Toccata and Fugue section, but Disney insisted on lessening the abstraction, and the arrangement did not hold.

RICHARD EDER

1977 F 11, C14:5

FELLINI'S CASANOVA, directed by Federico Fellini; screenplay by Mr. Fellini and Bernardino Zapponi; produced by Alberto Grimaldi; director of photography, Giuseppe Rotunno; editor Ruggero Mastroianni; music, Nino Rota; distributed by Universal Pictures. Running time: 165 minutes. At the Cinema 1 Theater, Third Avenue near 60th Street. This film has been rated R.

Giacomo Casanova	Donald Sutherland
Maddalena	Margareth Clementi
Anamaria	Clarissa Mary Roll
Giselda	Daniela Gatti
Madame D'Urfe	Cicely Browne
Marcolina	Clara Algranti
DuBois	Daniel Emilfork Berenstein
Henriette	Tina Aumont
Giantess	Sandra Elaine Allen
Lord Talou	John Karlson
Prince del Brando	Hans Van Den Hoek
Isabella	Olimpia Carlisi
Duke of Wurtenberg	Dudley Sutton
Faulkircher	Reggie Nalder
The Pope	Luigi Zerbinati
Doll Woman	Adele Angela Lojodice
Madame Charpillon	Carmen Scarpitta
Silvana	Silvana Fusacchia

By VINCENT CANBY

The initial sequence says it all. It is carnival time in Venice. Fireworks are raining down on the citizens, the young and the old, the beautiful and the misshapen. Suddenly, with the help of an elaborate system of weights and pulleys, the giant head of Venus begins to emerge from the Grand Canal. The crowd cheers as the master of the revels extols the goddess of love. The head rises creakily to eye level and a cable breaks. Slowly she sinks back into the dark waters. A mother screams to a child, "Cross yourself!"

Using as his text Giacomo Casanova's "The Story of My Life," Federico Fellini has created another revel of a movie—spectacular, but singularly joyless—that has the effect of celebrating the absolute end of romance and eroticism. There's nothing left but sex, and sex is a terminal disease. Love is a placebo.

•

"Fellini's Casanova," which opened yesterday at the Cinema 1, is much less about the self-proclaimed 18th-century philanderer, his life and his times, than it is the surreal, guilt-ridden confessions of a nice, middle-class Italian husband of the 20th century. This fellow, on reaching middle age shortly before the sexual revolution, is still tormented by fantasies that seem to him to be wicked and to the rest of us merely exhausting.

I don't know how else to interpret this strange, cold, obsessed film, which I find fascinating, because I find the man who made it fascinating, a talented mixture of contradictory impulses, and as depressing as an eternal hangover. Other people, less convinced of the Fellini genius, may be driven up the wall.

With "Juliet of The Spirits" in 1965, Mr. Fellini seems, in retro-

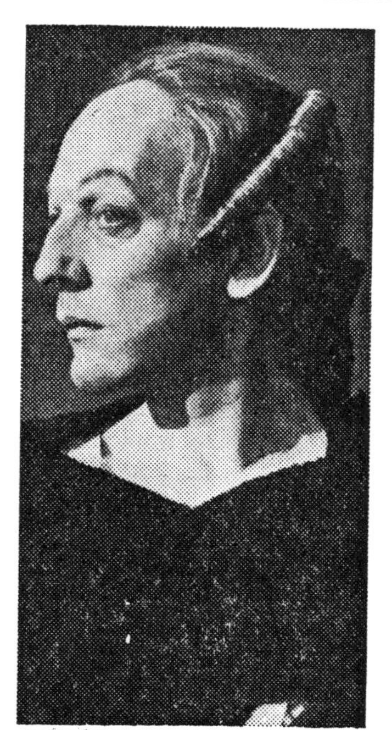

Donald Sutherland as Giacomo Casanova.
Less characterized than he is presented in a pageant.

spect, to have entered his Roxy Theater-Radio City Music Hall period by making a series of films in which he has steadfastly insisted on giving the customers more than their money's worth of movement, color, sound, light, costumes, décor, specialty acts, sideshow freaks, quick changes and dazzling, theatrical artifice.

"The Clowns" and "Roma," documentary variations on themes close to Mr. Fellini's heart, were virtually meditations upon his methods. In "Amarcord," his best film since "8½," the superabundance of style was given purposeful shape by benevolence and good feelings.

"Fellini's Casanova" recalls "Fellini's Satyricon." Though its concerns are narrower, it's as otherworldly as that nightmare vision of the pre-Christian Roman Empire. Like that film, too, "Casanova" makes no attempt to re-create an identifiable era, but, rather, to create a completely subjective impression.

•

Nothing is real. Mr. Fellini, who now works exclusively within a studio, creates everying himself. The studio is the locus of his interior world. It's not for him to go on location to shoot a tree or a sky when he can choose the sort of tree or sky he wants from the scenic designer. Never for a moment does he ask us to believe that any tree or sky ever looked this way, only to understand that this is how he feels about them.

Now, in "Casanova," Mr. Fellini has gone one step further by, in effect, constructing his leading actor. He has molded the features of Donald Sutherland, who plays Casanova, much as he were constructing a set, adding an imperial forehead and extending the nose and chin so that no matter how the actor turns, no mater how he is photographed, they define a grotesque absurd condition.

In one of the more chilly sequences of the movie, Casanova becomes infatuated with a beautiful, life-sized mechanical doll, which he takes to bed with him. The always chastely, almost prudishly photographed sexual encounter that follows has no more, or less, meaning than any of Casanova's other affairs. It's all close-ups of Casanova's sweating forehead, accompanied by panting of the sort that suggests a critical shortness of breath. In these encounters, the orgasm is a death rattle.

The closing image of the film is the aged Casanova dreaming of his youth, dancing with this mechanical doll across the frozen waters of the Grand Canal, where, below the ice, we can see the head of Venus with its empty eyes.

•

The image is daring and beautiful, but it is repeating the film's single note for one more time than is easily supportable. Like "Satyricon," "Casanova" has the form of a frieze that ends by meeting itself where it began. With the exception of a casual reference to Casanova's father, and a sequence —the best in the film—in which he runs into his aged mother in Germany, Casanova is less characterized than he is presented as if he were someone in a pageant.

"Fellini's Casanova" is a Dispassion Play that inventories Casanova's conquests, one after another, in Venice, Paris, London and the courts of Germany, as his lechery leads him to lonely, cranky old age.

There is, I'm afraid, a terrible puritanism at work here, for though the film is often witty, it is without much humor. There's one curious moment when Mr. Fellini has Casanova defend the intelligence and strength of women, and another in which the director shows us that poor Casanova is as much the faceless sex object to his mistresses as they are to him.

The production is gigantic, but the ideas and feelings are small. One longs to go home and listen to Mozart's "Don Giovanni."

1977 F 12, 12:1

THE SENTINEL, directed by Michael Winner; written and produced by Mr. Winner and Jeffrey Konvitz; director of photography, Dick Kratina; music by Gil Melle; special effects, Albert Whitlock. Released by Universal. At the Rivoli, Columbia II and other theaters. Running time: 105 minutes. This film has been rated R.

Michael Lerman .... Chris Serandon
Allison Parker .... Cristina Raines
Professor .... Martin Balsam
Halliran .... John Carradine
Robed Figure .... Jose Ferrer
Miss Logan .... Ava Gardner
Franchino .... Arthur Kennedy
Chazen .... Burgess Meredith
Gerde .... Sylvia Miles

If the movie industry is going to go on turning out works about Satanism, perhaps some of the larger film schools should consider adding a course in Theology, or at least Pastoral Protocol.

It is the kind of nagging thought that arises at a viewing of Michael Winner's "The Sentinel," which opened yesterday at the Rivoli, Columbia II and other theaters.

Nagging thoughts are not supposed to arise in horror pictures —last summer Mr. Winner predicted that this picture would be extremely horrifying — but "The Sentinel" has long stretches where there is nothing to do but notice things.

•

For example, the film's thesis is that there is a tiny unplugged passageway to Hell in Brooklyn Heights. The Roman Catholic Church periodically chooses, by lot, some unfortunate nonvolunteer to sit by the hole and make sure the devils don't get out.

I'm not saying that this is totally impossible—unlikely, of course, but not impossible. There are a lot of holes in Brooklyn Heights. But the film shows us an assemblage of what look like cardinals and canons-major meeting to choose the next nonvolunteer: in this case a New York fashion model played by Cristina Raines. We all know that such decisions are not made by the top brass but by strange old priests on pension in Cape May.

Then again, the inscription on the chink comes from Dante. It is the line about "abandon all hope ye who enter." Now it is not generally held that Dante actually visited Hell. He stayed around Florence, pretty much, and worked from second-hand reports. What is quite certain is that he never got to Brooklyn.

Are these pedantic objections, considering Mr. Winner's strenuous effort to remind us of "Rosemary's Baby"—a magnificent old apartment, a hopeful young couple, sinister neighbors and so on? The point is he has not given us much else.

There is Miss Raines as Alison Parker, looking sicker day by day. There is her crooked lover, Michael Lerman (Chris Sarandon) and just whose side he is on isn't clear until the end, and then he switches. There is a great deal of latex and makeup.

The film's plot need not be revealed much further, other than to say that it is a struggle. On one side is the Church trying to get Alison—who has rented the apartment simply because it has a nice view of New York—on the job as the sentinel. On the other side are a lot of devils, in the form of reincarnated murderers, who try to persuade her to kill herself first.

•

This is where the latex comes in. At first, the devils simply take the form of odd neighbors. As the movie goes on, they reveal their real shapes—gaping wounds, absent noses, melted features and so on. Her own father, an unpleasant man given to orgies in the upstairs bedroom, is one of the gang.

The confrontations are supposed to be terrifying but the most they offer is some mild creepiness. Miss Raines does a pretty good job as the distraught woman in a no-win situation. Mr. Sarandon and actors such as Burgess Meredith and Sylvia Miles, who are devils, drop by to collect their pay. Mr. Winner has sweetened the mess with some nudity, a little masturbation and a dash of lesbianism.

RICHARD EDER

1977 F 12, 12:1

STRANGE SHADOWS IN AN EMPTY ROOM, directed by Martin Herbert; screenplay by Vincent Mann and Frank Clark; produced by Edmondo Amati; director of photography, Anthony Ford; editor, Vincent P. Thomas; Music, Armando Trovajoli; distributed by American International Pictures. Running time: 99 minutes. At the Cinerama 2 and other theaters. This film has been rated R.

Tony Saitta .... Stuart Whitman
Sergeant Matthews .... John Saxon
The doctor .... Martin Landau
Julie .... Tisa Farrow
Louise .... Carole Laure
Margie Cohn .... Gayle Hunnicutt

"Strange Shadows in an Empty Room" starts when a pretty student at a university in Montreal is murdered. Her brother (Stuart Whitman), a detective, sets out to solve the mystery but he is always getting sidetracked by unconvincing red herrings, car chases, friends and unlikely suspects. These characters are played by John Saxon, Martin Landau, Tisa Farrow and Gayle Hunnicutt, among others.

The film was apparently photographed in Montreal and might have been designed as a tourist brochure except that the pictures, as seen at the Cinerama 2 yesterday afternoon, were often so far out of focus it could as easily have been a promotion film for Omaha.

VINCENT CANBY

1977 F 12, 13:2

THIEVES, directed by John Berry; written by Herb Gardner; produced by George Barrie; directors of photography, Arthur J. Onitz and Andrew Lazlo; edited by Craig McKay. Released by Paramount. At the Coronet Theater. Running time: 103 minutes. The film has been rated PG.

Sally Cramer .... Marlo Thomas
Martin Cramer .... Charles Grodin
Joe Kaminsky .... Irwin Corey
Man below .... Hector Elizondo
Street woman .... Mercedes McCambridge
Gordon .... John McMartin
Carlton .... Larry Scott
Mr. Day .... Bob Fosse
Mr. Night .... Norman Matlock

By RICHARD EDER

A film comedy is a windup toy that performs, when released, at its own eccentric and quirky gait. "Thieves," an expensive-looking romantic comedy, is like a windup toy whose movements are being forced by a jaded and impatient child.

It has some good notions, some good jokes and some good performers. But, with rare interludes, it is wrenched and graceless. It seems to be made for an audience whose humor and emotional receptiveness have gone deaf and astigmatic. It shouts and writes extra-large; we feel like Gulliver among giggling and sighing Brobdingnagians.

•

A dozen years ago Herb Gardner wrote "A Thousand Clowns," a play that became a movie. It was about the comic and successful effort of an eccentric—played by Jason Robards—to live in a pleasantly nonproductive manner with his nephew and a social worker—Barbara Harris—who came to reform him and stayed to join him. It was sometimes preachy and longwinded; but, in general, it was a winning and very funny defense of nuttiness in the big city.

With "Thieves," which opened yesterday at the Coronet Theater, mr. Gardner has tried to do the same thing. He even uses a ukulele, once again, to pluck out the musical theme. His kook, this time, is a woman and she is played by Marlo Thomas. The descending distance from "Clowns" to Thieves" is as the distance between Mr. Robards, who mostly surmounted the squashy bits, to Miss Thomas, who wallows in them and makes them bigger.

•

"Thieves" starts with an enormous East Side apartment house. It is nighttime and the camera scoots along the windows while the microphone picks up a collage of rich urban murmuring, largely having to do with sex and lack of purpose. We go through a window. It belongs to Martin Cramer (Charles Grodin), principal of a flossy private school, and Sally Cramer (Miss Thomas), teacher at a public, slum school.

"THIEVES"—Marlo Thomas is eavesdropped upon by Mercedes McCambridge as she phones a would-be lover in Herb Gardner's comedy.

They've been married 12 years; their fortunes are rising and their morale is sinking. He is not the fearless and funny young rebel he was when they married. She is; and to prove it she wakes him up nights and asks what his name is. Furthermore, she has just sent all their valuable furniture away to be stored in the one-room cold-water flat they first lived in.

They argue, she walks out, she comes back a week later because she has decided to have an abortion, they argue some more, she walks out again. This time she goes to the apartment of an admirer and they discuss their way into bed. Next morning she is up at dawn and off to see her septuagenarian, taxi-driving father. This father, played by Irwin Corey, is a boorish, loud-mouthed street philosopher. He comes on with the effect of 10 fingernails scraping a blackboard.

•

The husband, meanwhile, has slept with a lonely neighbor but doesn't like it. He goes back to the Lower East Side to visit the furniture, finds it's gone, has a brush with some policemen and two bums, and returns uptown. Filled with rediscovered romance, he rejoins Sally and fires off a pistol in the air to prove he is no longer stuffy, they join hands and run twinkling up the street.

The ukulele plays.

There are some good, periodic touches in the film. One of Sally's small pupils steals a set of passkeys and a hand-truck and collects typewriters and television sets from every apartment in the building to offer to her. In exchange, he proposes, she is to let him pass into the seventh grade. There is a doorman who does nothing but sleep, or seems to: In fact, he's dead.

•

The best character in the film is a mournfully choleric downstairs neighbor who is being beaten into anomie by noise, soot and urban discomfort. Hector Elizondo plays him beautifully. As Martin Cramer, Mr. Grodin is fairly characterless, but considering some of the lines he has to say, this may be a virtue.

The other day John Leonard mentioned a German author who wrote delightedly that cats have two holes in their coats coinciding neatly with their eyes. Miss Thomas has holes in her skin for eyes and mouth—those devices used by actors for expressiveness. But the holes don't coincide: they are much larger.

•

"Thieves" has been rated PG ("Parental Guidance Suggested"). The symmetrical adulteries of Sally and Martin, though not actually shown, are probably responsible.

1977 F 12, 13:1

FILM VIEW

VINCENT CANBY

The Writer as Movie Director

If someone twisted my arm and forced me to categorize in one word Robert Benton's new film, "The Late Show," I suppose I'd have to call it a parody, since it deals in the attitudes and gestures of the Sam Spade-Philip Marlowe movies of the forties and fifties, but "The Late Show" is much more than a parody. It's a contemporary private-eye melodrama that is also a bewitching, touching comedy with a life of its own, independent of our knowledge of and affection for those earlier films. In the same manner I suppose I'd have to label as satire Frank D. Gilroy's funny, off-beat Western, "From Noon Till Three," which is, I know, to diminish its appeal for many movie goers who don't like their genres fiddled with. What "From Noon Till Three" ridicules are not the manners and morals of the Old West as much as the sort of instant myth-making and overnight celebrityhood that are possible in this age of television and the mass distribution of paperback books.

Both films are risk-taking ventures. Neither conforms to patterns that producers like to follow to obtain a sure-fire hit, though "From Noon Till Three" stars Charles Bronson, a piece of box-office insurance that is immediately cancelled by Bronson's being cast as an outlaw who is not only faint of heart but a fairly nice fellow. It's no accident, that both "The Late Show" and "From Noon Till Three" are the work of directors whose principal reputations have been made as writers, though each has already directed one highly creditable film—Benton having done the largely underrated "Bad Company," from an original screenplay by himself and his "Bonnie and Clyde" partner, David Newman, and Gilroy, a Pulitzer Prize-winning playwright ("The Subject Was Roses"), having earlier directed "Desperate Characters," which he adapted from Paula Fox's novel.

Writers as their own directors are nothing new in this country, though it's not what virtually amounts to the established practice it is among the best European directors. Some of the best American directors (Preston Sturges, Billy Wilder, Woody Allen) have always written their own screenplays, either alone or in collaboration, while some equally talented and successful directors (Alfred Hitchcock, George Cukor, among others) limit their participation in the writing of a screenplay to story conferences, where, of course, they order exactly what they want as if from "21."

"The Late Show," with Art Carney and Lily Tomlin, was written and directed by Robert Benton.

While looking at "From Noon Till Three" and then at "The Late Show" it occurred to me how pleasant it was also to be able to listen to a film, not just to what was being said, but also to impulses behind the film—impulses that seem to be more common among writers than directors.

"From Noon Till Three," with Jill Ireland and Charles Bronson, is "a funny, offbeat western" written and directed by Frank D. Gilroy.

"The Late Show" is a private-eye melodrama, all right, but it's not the kind that would (or could) have interested Howard Hawks in his great "Big Sleep" period. Here is Philip Marlowe, now called Ira Wells and played by Art Carney, approaching old age with his hearing impaired, an active ulcer, a bay window and a limp, living alone in a clean but tacky Los Angeles rooming house. After a lunatic encounter with a woman named Margo (Lily Tomlin), who wants him to retrieve her kidnapped cat, Ira Wells finds himself up to his neck in classic L.A. skullduggery involving adultery, blackmail and murder. This is played straight but is given an unexpectedly humane dimension in the relationship that grows up between the crusty old detective and the lonely younger woman whose vulgar language so shocks him.

Though "The Late Show" is a cleanly conceived and executed film, with fine performances by Carney, Miss Tomlin, Bill Macy (of the "Maude" show) and Eugene Roche, its sensibility is essentially that of a writer, someone who is intrigued, moved and amused by the plight of an aged private-eye who is as out-of-date in fiction as he is in life. It's a literary conceit that happens to work beautifully on film.

This is the difference between "The Late Show" and "The Long Goodbye," directed by Robert Altman, the producer of the Benton film. In "The Long Goodbye," which remains one of the director's most original and flamboyant films, Altman set himself the task of updating the 1953 Raymond Chandler story to the over-privileged seventies, a cinematic problem since it involved finding equivalents to and substitutes for the basic ingredients in a Chandler story of another era. Time hasn't passed in "The Long Goodbye," but it hasn't congealed, either. Philip Marlowe is still a young man in the Altman film, but instead of being Humphrey Bogart, he is Elliott Gould.

Writers see things differently from directors, not more clearly nor accurately, but from a different perspective that can make certain aspects of character and life seem more important than others. Gilroy's "From Noon Till Three," like the Benton film, is also, at heart, a literary conceit, though it's one that's been given a first-rate physical production with photography by Lucien Ballard and elegant production design by Robert Clatworthy.

Here is a Western in which the only hold-up takes place in a dream sequence, and in which Bronson's casual seduction of a chaste widow-lady unleashes terrible forces not of outraged morality but of rampant hucksterism. The narrative shape of "From Noon Till Three" is as symmetrical as that of an O. Henry short story though its concerns are more complex: the widow (Jill Ireland), believing her lover of three hours to be dead, sets about to tell the world of this immortal passion that redeemed her life, through a best-selling "as-told-to" book and song. The small Western town becomes a tourist center, her mansion a museum, and she a public figure. When, several years later, the dead lover returns — shorter, uglier and much more commonplace than anyone remembers him—the result is an insupportable loss of illusion. Fatal, in fact.

"From Noon Till Three" is an extremely good-natured though chilly film, but it's not the sort of film that Charles Bronson fans expect to see when they go to a Charles Bronson picture. This, I guess, explains why it's not done well at the box office and why it was allowed to slip in and out of New York several weeks ago without causing any stir whatsoever. It deserves much better, not only because I think a lot of people would be amused by it but also because it represents an attempt to broaden the scope of popular filmmaking that, with the economic pinch, is being constantly narrowed, limited to sure-fire subjects as well as to so-called sure-fire stars (like Bronson) who often aren't.

Writers who have turned directors haven't had much luck at the box office in the last several years, though not, necessarily because their films were unworthy but often because the films attempted to do things not found in more conventionally conceived films.

I think particularly of Terrence Malick's "Badlands" and Thomas McGuane's "92 in The Shade." It wasn't any obviously unusual form of these films that threw the public (and many critics) off stride. Each looks like any other commercial film. There was no fancy tippy-toeing back and forth between reality and fantasy in either film, nor between contradictory memories, the sorts of thing that Alain Resnais is doing in his preciously conceived new film, "Providence," and which define intellectual filmmaking even to the dimmest minds. Using a conventional narrative form Malick attempted to picture a society that could produce a mass-murderer (Charlie Starkweather) but he did it without offering explanations, only suggestions, and those presented in a style so dispassionate as to seem as unfeeling and cruel as his hero. "Badlands" was unsettling (and, if you want, much more unconventional than a film like "Providence") because it required the viewer to find his own relationship to what was on the screen.

McGuane's "92 in The Shade," which he adapted from his novel, was an uproariously untidy movie, stuffed with character, incident, and unexplained eccentricities of the sort a lot of people will accept on the printed page but refuse to tolerate on the movie screen. Why this is true I'm not sure. Maybe it has to do with conditioning—untidy books are okay but untidy movies are unseemly—or with the conviction that movies simply cannot deal with ideas, even when they're disguised as emotions.

Writers like Benton and Gilroy and Malick and McGuane (especially if they have experience outside films), who want to direct movies as well, should be encouraged within all reasonable bounds. They possibly can bring something new and vital to filmmaking, which I fear, will become increasingly inbred if it is allowed to be the exclusive province of people who've grown up on films and nothing else.

1977 F 13, II:1:4

Screen: A Homicidal Maniac

By VINCENT CANBY

"The Town That Dreaded Sundown" is about a homicidal maniac who terrorized Texarkana, Ark., during the spring and summer of 1946. If, as the off-screen narrator tells us, the facts are true (only the names have been changed), then the phantom killer was actually a pair of unidentified male feet.

Charles B. Pierce, the director and producer, shows us those feet, from the trouser cuffs down, when he isn't showing us a couple of police cars screeching around corners at 25 miles an hour, or an atrocity being committed by the killer, who loved to lurk around lovers' lane.

A couple of professional actors, Ben Johnson and Andrew Prine, head the cast, but the film looks nonprofessional in every other respect. It opened yesterday at the Cinerama 2 and other theaters.

The Cast

THE TOWN THAT DREADED SUNDOWN, directed and produced by Charles B. Pierce; screenplay by Earl E. Smith; director of cinematography, Jim Roberson; editor, Tom Boutross; music, Jaime Mendoza-Nava; distributed by American International Pictures. Running time: 90 minutes. At the Cinerama 2, Broadway at 47th Street, and other theatres. This film has been rated R.

Capt. J. D. Morales .... Ben Johnson
Deputy Norman Ramsey .... Andrew Prine
Helen Reed .... Dawn Wells
Sgt. Mal Griffin .... Jimmy Clem
Patrolman Athletic Club Benson .... Charles B. Pierce
Peggy Loomis .... Cindy Butler
Dr. Kress .... Earl E. Smith
Linda Mae Jenkins .... Christine Ellsworth
Sammy Fuller .... Mike Hackworth
Pol. Chief Sullivan .... Jim Citty
Sheriff Barker .... Robert Aquino
Emma Lou .... Misty West
Buddy Turner .... Rick Hildreth
Roy Allen .... Steve Lyons
Phantom Killer .... Bud Davis
Narrator .... Vern Stiersen

1977 F 19, 15:3

FILM VIEW

VINCENT CANBY

Hollywood as Social Critic: Reducing Our Ills to Absurdity

This country, which has successfully weathered the revelations of the Pentagon Papers and Watergate, among other national surprises, is not going to be much shaken by the more or less institutionalized views of America The Ugly presented in a number of new films. However, their almost simultaneous appearance makes one wonder at what point does serious social-political concern turn into just another money-making spin-off from a healthy kind of national skepticism. Are the following movies making us think, or are they making something as unthinkable as nuclear war was seem safely remote? When does satire cease being an instrument for change and become, instead, an endorsement of the institution being satirized?

In Robert Aldrich's new suspense melodrama, "Twilight's Last Gleaming," set mostly at a remote Titan missile installation in Montana though the movie was shot in West Germany, Burt Lancaster plays a liberal-minded Air Force general who tries to force the United States Government to disclose the "real" facts behind U.S. involvement in Vietnam by threatening to blow up a large part of the Soviet Union and, perhaps, of the world.

In "The Cassandra Crossing," an Anglo-Italian coproduction photographed in Italy, Switzerland and France, Lancaster appears again, this time as a hard-headed colonel in U.S. Intelligence who tries to cover up the fact that the U.S. Government has been hiding lethal bacteria for use in germ warfare in, of all places, the World Health Organization headquarters in Geneva. To this end he is prepared to sacrifice the lives of 1,000 passengers on a train known to be carrying a peacenik who discovered the secret and who, in so doing, stands to spread a disease that could wipe out the human race.

In "Shoot," a Canadian film, a bunch of what are supposed to be ordinary, down-home, middle-class American, Sunday afternoon hunters (that is, beer-guzzling, impotent gun-nuts) engage in a suicidal battle with another group of Sunday hunters much like themselves, in what is meant (I think) to be a metaphor that defines the idiocy of stockpiled weaponry and the easy availability of guns to ordinary citizens, as well as a warning about war's intoxicating appeal to a certain kind of male mentality.

In "Fun With Dick and Jane," a comedy, two nice, middle-class Americans (an aerospace engineer played by George Segal and his wife played by Jane Fonda) turn to crime when the husband loses his job and they can't maintain their upwardly mobile progress in the land where obsolescence is built into everything, including a booming economy.

In "Network," Paddy Chayefsky's manic satire about television, a go-getting TV network obtains the sort of ratings that are usually found at the foot of the rainbow by putting a raving maniac on the air in prime-time and, when the occasion warrants, by having him assassinated on-camera.

When it misses the mark, social-political criticism has a way of boomeranging, of coming back and hitting its author. So does a faulty argument. Not long ago a U.S. Senator was carrying on about the need for this country to maintain a firm, turn-of-the-century grip on the Panama Canal and though I assume he was being sincere, he sounded less like a responsible legislator than a spoiled child who wanted his security blanket with him in the bathtub. The Senator didn't really know why the canal was important but he wanted to have it around where he could touch it. Children must sometimes be indulged but one has a right to expect that Senators make sense.

This particular fellow, by presenting a shrill, unconvincing argument, probably did more for his opposition than any amount of impassioned editorializing could have done. Loony logic is a dangerous thing. It's a pistol aimed not at the opposition but at one's own temple.

• • •

Burt Lancaster is not only a good actor when the circumstances allow him to be but he's also a committed actor who wants to do films that "say something," which is not always so good. It's not a coincidence that he's appeared in such films as "Seven Days in May," which warned us about the possibility of a military coup in Washington, or "Executive Action," based on the premise that the assassination of President Kennedy was a conspiracy of the industrial-military complex whose members were afraid that Kennedy was going to sign a test-ban treaty, lead a black revolution and pull out of Vietnam. When he can Lancaster makes liberal-line movies.

I would assume that he wanted to make "Twilight's Last Gleaming" because it gives him a chance to say, among other things, "The military always thinks it can solve everything with fire power," and because the suicide mission, which is led by the character he plays, is on behalf of "open government." That's all well and good except that the facts about the Vietnam war, as fully disclosed by "Twilight's Last Gleaming," are so much less astonishing than those we already know that the point of the film is thus weakened to make the liberals look like idiots—nicer, perhaps, but just as wooly-headed as the members of the U.S. Cabinet who are the film's real villains.

I'm sure it has no bearing on the content of "Twilight's Last Gleaming"—Robert Aldrich being one of the most independent of independent American filmmakers—but I find it curious that this film, with its completely American subject and setting, should have had to be made in West Germany. Wasn't there American money to back the production?

I also wonder whether Lancaster thought there was something important being said when he agreed to play in "The Cassandra Crossing." Though it suggests that the American military may be up to all sorts of hideous hanky-panky, re bacteria research, the movie makes its suggestions in a fashion so ludicrous as to deny their reality, and by so doing, to transform the subject of germ warfare into science-fiction, which it unfortunately isn't.

Among the more peculiar assumptions of this movie, which was directed by George Pan Cosmatos, a Greek who lives in Italy, and is being "presented" by Sir Lew Grade, an Englishman, and Carlo Ponti, an Italian, is that the American colonel played by Lancaster would have the clout to re-route the death-train all over Europe and, finally, to persuade the Polish government to accept it. Why Poland, home of the Warsaw Pact? We never are told. This involves a lot of hilariously weak exposition relating the reasons the train just can't be flagged down and its passengers tended to immediately, but then there wouldn't be a movie.

I can't see that "The Cassandra Crossing" represents some kind of anti-American conspiracy on the part of profit-motivated European movie-makers. Though the people who wrote the film's screenplay obviously aren't loaded with brains, they do know enough to realize that the audience's gullibility, which they are already stretching dangerously, might snap completely had the colonel been identified as, say a representative of Luxembourg. The American military is known to have conducted extensive research into germ warfare, but beyond that the movie is its own trip.

You know exactly what "Shoot" thinks of the poor old American middle-class in the first sequence when you see the game room of its hero, an appliance store owner played by Cliff Robertson. The walls are lined with gun racks and standing in the corner, like a year-round Christmas tree, is the American flag. In movies these days the flag is a symbol of right-wing madness. When Cliff's wife gets up in the morning she laces her first cup of coffee with booze. Instead of sleeping with his wife, Cliff likes to clean his guns. The husbands in this community like to talk about sex but they don't make love, they make their own mini-war with high-powered rifles, mortars and hand-grenades. But "Shoot" is so confused that it's only importance is as an indicator of how Vietnam has shrivelled the imaginations of moviemakers.

Much more successful are the comedies of this group, including "Network," which doesn't mean to be an accurate reflection of real life, but a fantastic projection of contemporary tastes, manners and attitudes.

• • •

"Fun With Dick and Jane," written by David Giler, Jerry Belson and Mordecai Richler, and directed by Ted Kotcheff, is not in the same class with "Network" but it displays a lot of good healthy skepticism toward the quality of contemporary American life. This is represented not only by Dick and Jane, for whom crime pays in such small installments it isn't worth the wear and tear, but also by Jane's self-righteous parents who, having made their bundle, refuse to help the younger couple, preferring, instead, to see their problems as a golden opportunity for developing self-reliance.

"Fun With Dick and Jane" is basically a series of revue sketches that dramatize—sometimes hilariously—the vulgarity and essential pointlessness of a certain kind of American, two-car, heated-swimming-pool affluence. The film often makes its points vulgarly but its main weakness is that we never for a moment believe that Dick and Jane, as performed by Segal and Miss Fonda, are as nutty as the society they're trying so hard to keep up with. This softens the seriously satiric edge of the film to the point that Dick and Jane themselves become ideal models for the rest of us to keep up with.

This is not true of "Network," which is deadly serious even at its funniest, though its huge popular success makes me wonder if it may not be having the effect of somehow sanctifying the role that TV plays in our life. Do people come out of the theater after seeing "Network," shaking their heads, vowing to spend less time watching and more time reading? I suspect not. They can't wait to get home to see who Dean Martin has "roasted" live-on-tape, to find out whether Nancy Walker has gotten herself a hit series yet, and whether whatsisname's dog has been allowed into the studio.

American movies don't set trends anymore, if, indeed, they ever did. I suspect much of the time that movies that warn of nuclear destruction, call our attention to germ warfare, criticize our social aims or have Burt Lancaster saying rude things about the military have the effect of soothing our fears. They are background music. By fictionalizing our doubts, movies may often be neutralizing them.

1977 F 20, II:1:1

SLAP SHOT, directed by George Roy Hill; screenplay by Nancy Dowd; produced by Robert J. Wunsch and Stephen Friedman; editor, Dede Allen; director of photography, Victor Kemper; music supervision by Elmer Bernstein; a Pan Arts presentation, distributed by Universal Pictures. Running time: 122 minutes. At the National Theater, Broadway at 43d Street; Beekman Theater, Second Avenue at 65th Street, and Murray Hill Theater, 34th Street at Third Avenue. This film has been rated R.

Reggie Dunlop .... Paul Newman
Ned Braden .... Michael Ontkean
Lily Braden .... Lindsay Crouse
Francine Dunlop .... Jennifer Warren
Suzanne .... Melinda Dillon
Joe McGrath .... Strother Martin
Dave "Killer" Carlson .... Jerry Houser
Denis Le Mieux .... Yvon Barrette
Steve Hansen .... Steve Carlson
Jeff Hansen .... Jeff Carlson
Jack Hansen .... Dave Hanson
Jim Carr .... Andrew Duncan
Dickie Dunn .... Emmett Walsh
Jim Ahern .... Stephen Mendillo
Johnny Upton .... Allan Nicholls
Helen Upton .... Swoosie Kurtz
Drouin .... Yvon Ponton
Wanchuk .... Brad Sullivan
Anita McCambridge .... Kathryn Walker
Tim McCracken .... Paul D'Amato
Charlebois .... Guido Tenesi
Brophy .... John Gorfton
LeBrun .... Ronald L. Docken
Charlie .... Matthew Cowles

By VINCENT CANBY

Charlestown is a middle-sized New England mill town where things are going from bad to worse. The mill is laying off 10,000 workers and the Charlestown Chiefs, the city's professional hockey team, once a source of pride, has become a third-rate club in a league of the second rank. Reggie Dunlop (Paul Newman), the team's player-coach, is getting old and feeling it. He knows it's his last season. He's about to be junked.

Things are so bad that at one point we overhear the Chief's manager, Joe McGrath (Strother Martin), trying to unload some of the team's equipment, including its massage table. The Chiefs are nice guys. Though they don't win many games, they play clean and only talk dirty.

George Roy Hill's unruly, funny new comedy, "Slap Shot," which opened at three theaters yesterday, dramatizes the age-old contest between good and evil as clean vs. dirty, and it's dirty that wins, hands (and pants) down.

"Slap Shot," which follows the fortunes of the Chiefs through their last, dizzy season, was written by Nancy Dowd, a Smith College graduate with a master's degree from the University of California School of Cinema Arts. She's a young woman who appears to know more about the content and rhythm of locker-room talk than most men.

She knows the favorite word that can be used as a noun, verb or adjective, sometimes all in one sentence. She also knows the favorite sexual image that haunts the language of these hockey players as if all living had been reduced either to committing a sexual act or to preventing one, which is more or less a reflection of what the guys are doing out there on the ice with their hockey sticks and the puck. If you don't invade the enemy territory, the enemy will invade yours.

•

I don't know enough about professional hockey to judge how accurate a picture "Slap Shot" is, but it does seem a stretch of the imagination to ask us to believe in this day and age, that neither the Chiefs' manager nor coach would have known that a dirty, violent game, accompanied by a lot of publicity hoopla, would bring in the crowds. Which is pretty much what happens to the Chiefs, first by accident, then on purpose, as the team goes onward and upward to the top of the league.

Film: History of Newsreels

By RICHARD EDER

THE NEWSREELS died on American screens in 1967, but they were in poor shape for 10 years or so before that. There was no way they could compete with television news footage, either in speed or convenience. Nor, generally speaking, in quality. Most of the time they were patchy views of a rather scatter-brained reality. Sneezing contests would alternate with politicians cutting ribbons and South Americans rioting.

But once in a while there was something unforgettable: the Hindenburg floated loftily into sight and suddenly settled on the ground like burning tinsel; a middle-aged Frenchman wept at Toulon when the fleet was scuttled. The newsreel cameras and the big screen provided an authority to these things that television equipment couldn't manage. Also there was the effect of waiting a day or two to see a disaster you had read of. World events were discrete, individual, weighty. They did not flood us.

A diffuse, somewhat unsatisfactory but reasonably interesting retrospective of newsreels in America is provided by "Yesterday's Witness," which opened yesterday at the Film Forum.

Starting with the logos of the different companies—the Warner-Pathé rooster, the globe circled by the word "Universal," the Paramount cameraman standing in profile and turning his camera to the audience—it goes on to show the newsreel's history and format.

Some of the footage is worth remembering. There is the sinking of the United States gunboat Panay by the Japanese in the 1930's. A cameraman was aboard and got the whole thing. There is the execution of a Cuban by firing-squad, again in the 30's; and a lovely scene of Bess Truman trying unsuccessfully to break a champagne bottle on a new airplane.

The film does not try to show the best footage, however. It tries for a mix of the devastating and the trivial—as any ordinary week's newsreel might have shown. The result is authentic, but sometimes tedious.

Intercut with this are interviews with the old, organ-toned commentators, and with some of the principal cameramen. Unused footage from the crash of an airplane into the Empire State Building shows the charred bodies inside the office where the plane struck. After it we are shown a touching interview with Max Markman, who was the photographer. He breaks down recalling the scene and mutters "Cut, cut," as the camera captures his tears.

There are several short items on the same program. One is a take-off on the newsreel style. Called "The Ritz Newsiola," it is funny for a few minutes, but turns fairly pointless. There is a tiny film about a rudimentary portable movie projector in a Pakistani market; and one about a mobile movie-showing team in Cuba.

1977 F 25, C18:1

Paul Newman

The film's point of view also appears to be ambiguous, for though it seems to want to be on the side of the clean, old-fashioned game, played by the rules, "Slap Shot" itself, like the Chiefs, largely triumphs by exploiting—sometimes uproariously—the brutality of the game and the protective vulgarity of the players.

Mr. Hill, a director of real sensibility, is certainly aware that people as thick-headed and slow-witted as are most of these characters aren't very interesting when seen in close-up for very long. Seen as a collective spectacle in a long-shot, though, they make a sometimes bitterly comic comment on one aspect of the industry that is professional American sports.

The performances—which have a lot to do with the right casting, particularly in the smaller roles—are impeccable. Paul Newman maintains an easy balance between star and character-actor. The leading-man authority is there, but it's given comic perspective by the intensity of the character and by its tackiness, evident even in the clothes he wears.

Michael Ontkean, a young actor I've not been aware of before, is equally good as the film's one unequivocal good guy, a Princeton graduate turned pro, which may be one of the nicest things Hollywood has said about the Ivy League in years. Jennifer Warren, who was so good in Arthur Penn's "Night Moves," plays Mr. Newman's estranged wife, a self-reliant beautician, and Lindsay Crouse is seen as Mr. Ontkean's heavy-drinking wife, a role that doesn't make too much sense as written.

There isn't space to credit all of the vivid supporting performers but, in addition to Strother Martin, you're likely to remember Jerry Houser as a goalie who thinks of himself as a mystic, and Andrew Duncan as a hilariously phony-talking radio announcer.

"Slap Shot," which has been R-rated as much for its language as for the violence on the rink, has a kind of vitality to it that overwhelms most of the questions relating to consistency of character and point of view. Much in the manner of "Network," you know that it's an original and that it's alive, whether you like it or not.

1977 F 26, 11:1

'F for Fake' Is an Illusionist's Trick With Bogus Heroes and Expert True-Life Villains

"F for Fake" was shown at the 1975 New York Film Festival. The following are excerpts from Vincent Canby's review, which appeared Oct. 28, 1975. The film opened yesterday at the Griffith Theater.

"I'm a charlatan," says Orson Welles, looking very fit, his manner that of the practiced con artist who knows that if he confesses to everything, he will be held accountable for nothing. Or is it the other way around?

This is the beginning of Mr. Welles's latest film, "F for Fake," a charming, witty mediation upon fakery, forgery swindling and art, a movie that may itself be its own Exhibit A.

Mr. Welles, the master of ceremonies, the credited director and writer as well as star of "F for Fake," welcomes us with some sleight of hand, turning a small boy's key into a coin and back again. "The key," says the charlatan, "is not symbolic of anything." The warnings keep coming, and you may be reminded of the late Old Gold slogan: "It's fun to be fooled, but more fun to know." Perhaps sometimes.

"F for Fake" is a documentary compounded of tricks, reversals, interviews with real forgers and re-creations of events that never happened. It's as much magic show as movie, a lark that is great fun even when one wishes the magician would take off his black slouch hat and his magician's cape and get back to making real movies. But did he really make this one? And is "F for Fake" not a real movie?

There are amused rumors to the effect that Mr. Welles did not actually direct a large part of "F for Fake." This part is an extended sequence set in Ibiza involving interviews with Elmyr de Hory, the well-publicized art forger, and Clifford Irving, who wrote Mr. de Hory's biography ("Fake") and later went on to make his own name by attaching it to Howard Hughes's.

The rumors are that these scenes were shot by François Reichenback, one of the first practitioners of cinéma vérité, who himself shows up throughout "F for Fake," for which he receives credit as the production coordinator. "F for Fake" is so stylish in all its parts, in its editing and particularly in a final fiction sequence that, if it is a fake, it's a marvelous one, and to hell with the signature on it.

Which is one of the things that "F for Fake" is all about. Midway through the film, after we've listened to stories that may or may not be true about Mr. de Hory's success in supplying the art world with fake Matisses, Picassos and Modigilanis, Mr. Welles reminds us that there are no signatures on the cathedral at Chartres. Chartres needs no "experts" to authenticate its grandeur, he says. "Experts" are the villains of "F for Fake"—people who must tell us whether we should swoon when looking at a particular painting or turn up our noses in disgust.

•

I have some minor reservations about "F for Fake." I don't share Mr. Welles's affection for either Mr. de Hory or Mr. Irving. Unlike the generous Mr. Welles, they are small potatoes. When Mr. Welles asks, "Doesn't it say something about our time that Cliff [Irving] could only make it through trickery?," my answer is no. It says more about Mr. Irving, who, as far as I can tell, hasn't made it at all.

1977 F 26, 10:3

FILM VIEW

VINCENT CANBY

Sometimes The Decor Is the Thing

As I write this in an apartment on Manhattan's Upper West Side, an elderly man and his wife, who live across the street on the fifth floor of what can be described as Old Lower-Income Housing, sit, one to a window, watching the activity on the sidewalk below as if it were an unending Passion Play. When the incidents become juicy, the man sometimes allows the woman to use his opera glasses. Mostly, though, he hogs them. Day and night, summer and winter. From my vantage point four floors above them I can see their television set, but they seldom turn it on, even when the pace of real life slows down to an argument over an inconveniently double-parked car. Why should they watch television when at any moment they may chance upon a mugging, a rape, a lovers' quarrel, a car being stripped or stolen? Angie Dickinson flashing her badge at a narcotics dealer isn't half as riveting as watching David, our postman, coping with someone's uncurbed, unleashed dog.

Which is one of the reasons, I suspect, that we go to the movies and, even when they're disappointing or downright bad, sit through them with a certain amount of interest.

Unlike television, which pretends to reality in stars who are just folks and human-interest dramas about Important Issues of The Day, films deal principally in illusion, sometimes, admittedly, in the illusion that what we're seeing is a mirror reflection of life, but also, and most interestingly, in the kind of illusion that can suggest emotions and ideas that are beyond the scope and interest of filmmakers-as-journalists.

These thoughts occurred to me after having sat through two new, extremely ambitious films that I'd anticipated with great hopes but that seem to me to fail in fatally important ways. Because they fail, however, they allow the eye and the mind to wander productively. The films are "Fellini's Casanova," Federico Fellini's exuberantly over-produced carnival of a movie about sex as a deadend, and Alain Resnais's "Providence," a sort of haughty, intentionally mannered comedy that seems to be about the creative processes of a second-rate artist among other things. What makes each film more interesting in retrospect than it was during the sometimes painful experience of watching it is the enthusiastic way in which both Fellini and Resnais employ artifice and artificiality in a medium in which tricky decor—the sort that calls attention to itself—is seldom seen outside science-fiction films.

• • •

"Providence," Mr. Resnais's first English-language film, was written by English playwright David Mercer (who also wrote the much wittier "Morgan: A Suitable Case for Treatment"). It stars John Gielgud as a 78-year-old novelist who boozes and dreams one night away while making notes for his new novel. These notes—fantasies—make up approximately 95 percent of the film as the self-pitying, quarrelsome old man, who appears to be barren of any vital inspiration, attempts to visualize his new novel by using members of his family as the characters. There are his elder son (Dirk Bogarde), a priggish barrister; the son's pretty wife (Ellen Burstyn); another young man (David Warner), who turns out to be the novelist's illegitimate son; and a woman (Elaine Stritch), who is both Bogarde's mistress and Gielgud's long-dead wife. This may sound compellingly complex but it's not.

The novelist has an appalling knack for cliche and for writing dialogue that sounds as if his artistic development had been arrested during a community-theater production of one of Terence Rattigan's lesser works. "Do you approve of suicide?" says one. "Certainly not," says two. "Neither do I," says one. "It reeks of spontaneity." I assume that it's one of the points of the film that this is meant to sound pretty ghastly, but to what purpose, I don't know.

I think Mercer and Resnais mean to be making some observations on family relationships but they're very small observations and it's difficult to take them seriously when the characters are so thin and their talk so wanly sardonic. However, the film's physical production, by Jacques Saulnier, is stunning in these fantasy sequences. Nothing is real nor is it meant to be. Saulnier, who was the production designer for "What's New, Pussycat?" as well as for Resnais's "Stavisky" and "Last Year at Marienbad," creates a dreamlike atmosphere that has the curious effect of making the activities taking place within them seem much more artificial than the waves on a painted backdrop.

Good production design, I know, isn't supposed to call attention to itself (though I'm not convinced that's true in a lot of films, including "Barry Lyndon," which was designed by Ken Adam). Yet in "Providence" it's about

"Fellini's Casanova" is "dazzling to look at but surprisingly pious."

the only aspect of the film that works, making possible the effectiveness of the last scene, in which the real-life models for the phantoms of Gielgud's nightmares, and their author, emerge from night to have an untroubled birthday luncheon together in the sunlit open air.

Danilo Donati is responsible for the extraordinary production design of "Fellini's Casanova," as he was for "Fellini's Satyricon." Between the two of them, Fellini and Donati have created within the studio an eye-popping landscape that is as barren and grotesque as the interior landscape that is travelled, from one female conquest to another, by their Casanova played by Donald Sutherland, whose facial features have been reordered by Fellini in much the manner that he's reordered the look of what we take to be the real world.

"Fellini's Casanova" is dazzling to look at but it's also a surprisingly pious, humorless essay on the wages of sex-without-love (lonely old age and exhaustion), the film's single lesson that is repeated for 15 minutes short of three hours. That we can tolerate this is largely due to assaults on our vision made by Donati and Fellini, from the opening carnival in Venice to the closing image of Casanova dancing with a life-sized doll across the frozen surface of the Grand Canal, observed from beneath the ice by the empty eyes in the head of a giant Venus, a carnival leftover.

• • •

The most interesting movies find a way of distilling reality to achieve whatever greater reality works for them. Wim Wenders's superlative film adaptation of Peter Handke's novel, "The Goalie's Anxiety at the Penalty Kick," looks to have been photographed entirely on actual locations, but the landscapes, interior as well as exterior, have a nightmarish clarity and emptiness about them that has nothing to do with reality. The films of Rainer Werner Fassbinder, the most talented of the young German directors, also achieve a kind of purposeful distance from reality though they too seem to have been shot mostly in actual settings. It's not necessary to stay inside the studio, but it must help, given a sizeable budget.

As television comes increasingly to dominate our consciousness there is something immensely liberating to the imagination by this kind of artifice, which is, of course, as old as films themselves. Anyone interested in the history of film design might well pick up a copy of an especially informative book on the subject that came out last year: "Caligari's Cabinet and Other Grand Illusions," by Léon Barsacq, who was the production designer for Jean Renoir's "La Marseillaise," Marcel Carnés "Les Enfants du Paradis" and many other French films. The book, revised and edited by Elliott Stein, with a foreward by René Clair, was published by Little, Brown & Co.

1977 F 27, II:17:1

THE WONDERFUL CROOK ("Pas si Mechant Que Ca—Not Really That Bad"), directed by Claude Goretta; screenplay (French with English subtiteles) by Mr. Goretta; executive producers, Yves Gasser and Yves Pevrof; director of photography, Renato Berta; editor, Joele van Effenterre; music, Arie Dzierlatka; produced by Citel Films, Artco Films, Action Films and M.J. Productions. Running time: 112 minutes. At the 68th Street Playhouse. This film has not been rated.

"The Wonderful Crook" was shown at the 1975 New York Film Festival under the title "Pas Si Mêchant Que Ca." The following are excerpts from Vincent Canby's review, which appeared Oct. 1, 1975. The film opened yesterday at the 68th Street Playhouse.

Switzerland, Swiss film makers seem to be telling us, is a perfect Swiss movement that doesn't deliver the correct time. None of the best Swiss films we've been seeing here recently—"La Salamandre," "The Middle of the World" and "The Invitation," among others—could be easily categorized as social or political in content. They share a comically reserved manner that is hardly the thing for agit-prop. Yet each in its way is as deeply concerned about the quality of life as any of Godard's more revolutionary films.

Such a film is "The Wonderful Crook" ("Pas Si Méchant Que Ca), the second feature by the extremely gifted Claude Goretta, whose first was "The Invitation."

"The Wonderful Crook" is not a comedy that will have you rolling in the aisles or tossing your hat in the air or even laughing all that much. Which may be a terrible thing to say about a comedy early in a review, but I suspect that audiences need a bit of preparation for this particular Swiss film.

It deals in small events, in details so practical that one is apt not to notice the comic attitude it wears. Its method is either carefully elliptical or understated. Indeed, even its overstatements are understated—and it is delightful.

"The Wonderful Crook" is the story of a not quite perfect son's coming of age in a perfect world. There is some irony in this, of course. He is Pierre (Gerard Depardieu), a happy-go-lucky fellow, married to a sweet, earthy girl and the father of a small child. Pierre works, though not very hard, in his father's small furniture factory, where everything is fashioned with care by hand, of wood that, his father says, breathes.

Gerard Depardieu and Marene Jobert
Even the film's overstatements are understated.

When Pierre's father is incapacitated by a stroke Pierre must take over the factory and learns to his sorrow that it's such a financial failure it's on the edge of bankruptcy. To meet the payroll Pierre takes to robbing post offices and banks.

Mr. Goretta apparently has a cheerfully open mind about bank robbing, which is one of the pleasures of the film, but not about Pierre, which is what gives the film its impact.

Pierre, as charming as he is, deceitfully implicates everyone he would protect, including both his wife, Marthe (Dominque Labourier) and the plucky young woman, Nelly (Marene Jobert), whom he meets in the course of a heist and who subsequently becomes his mistress.

Pierre has style and he displays a good deal of grace under pressure, but he's a crybaby too. With the best of intentions, he winds up failing everyone, especially Nelly, who has joined his life of mini-crime with her eyes wide open.

Mr. Goretta's direction looks deceptively simple. The characters and situations seem familiar at the start, yet little by little, scene by scene, you realize that the film is not simple at all, as when Pierre, rough-housing with his son, becomes just as excited and semi-hysterical as the child. In another scene the patrons of a corner bar watch an Italian immigrant worker dancing drunkenly with a vase of flowers, making everyone desperately uncomfortable. Obliquely we learn more than we ever thought possible.

Mr. Depardieu is very funny and complex in the pivotal role, which is not totally appealing, though the women's roles are. Philippe Leotard, the hero of "The Middle of the World," is fine in a supporting role, as is Michel Robin, the lonely bachelor of "The Invitation." A whole different subject is the superior quality of the ensemble acting in these new Swiss productions.

1977 Mr 5, 10:1

SANDSTONE, a documentary directed and produced by Jonathan Dana and Bunny Peters Dana; directors of photography, Patrick Darrin and Robert Primes; edited by Mr. Darrin with Mr. and Mrs. Dana; music produced by Dennis Dragon; released by Don Henderson Film Distribution Inc. Running time: 80 minutes. At the Cinerama and showcase theaters. This film is rated X.

By RICHARD EDER

"Sandstone" is supposed to be a documentary about new styles of sexual relationships. Instead, it comes across as a commercial for them and for the Southern California establishment — more resort than commune, it appears, where the relationsips are conducted.

As with a commercial, the faces above these unclad bodies seem to be demonstrating a product rather than using it. There is that quality of vehemence. A naked, middleage man wobbles vehemently behind a power mower over a bit of lawn. A naked woman vehemently pushes a vacuum cleaner. Some partly naked people vehemently prepare lunch. The viewer meditates upon the unsuitable, the perilous proximity of naked flesh to household appliances.

"Sandstone," which opened yesterday at the Cinerama and showcase theaters, avoids narration. It gives us our information through the words of the people being filmed, and this leaves a number of things fuzzy. From what can be gathered, it is a well-appointed place run by a dozen or so permanent members, augmented by crowds of weekenders. The economic basis of the enterprise is unclear, except that people pay to go, or strictly speaking, to belong.

Sex is the place's most specific function—it is shown with only partial explicitness—but there are other activities. Cooking, eating, drinking, self-congratulation and a lot of small talk.

With less vehemence, more clothes and about the same amount of film competence, "Sandstone" could be a home movie about a weekend in the Catskills.

1977 Mr 5, 10:2

FILM VIEW

VINCENT CANBY

Rainer Fassbinder—The Most Original Talent Since Godard

A title card at the beginning of Rainer Werner Fassbinder's 1969 film, "Katzelmacher," says sternly with no hint of apology, "It's better to make new mistakes than to repeat old ones until the mind goes numb." "Katzelmacher" was only Fassbinder's second film but this extraordinary German filmmaker, who's now just 31, was already off and running. It's as if he were perfectly aware that this talent that was bursting forth would lead him into occasional dead-ends and he didn't want to waste time in critical quibbling. So what if there are mistakes? The important thing is to move on, to explore, to develop, to push oneself to the furthest limits.

In seven years Fassbinder has made either 25 or 29 features, the exact number depending on whether or not one counts the features made exclusively for television. Taken together they make up the most exciting and original body of work by any modern director anywhere in a comparable period of time. The possible exception is the work of the early Jean-Luc Godard who, in the 1960's, was also dealing with an obsessive talent so idiosyncratic and exuberant that he was always about three pictures ahead of his critics and the public. Just at the point when we'd thought we'd cottoned on to him, Godard would be off on a new tangent that seemed destined to carry him over the edge. To many of his greatest admirers Godard did go over the edge with the series of Mao-Marxist films that appeared in the early 1970's, but anyone who saw his "Numero Deux" at the Museum of Modern Art last year is aware that the talent is as strong and firm as ever, though it's of such undisguised keenness that his films have become intolerable for the blue-collar audiences he wants to reach. Committed to an ideology that even he (the few times I've heard him speak) is hard-put to define, Godard skates in dazzling figures on an icy kind of political obscurantism.

On the basis of the Fassbinder retrospective that begins today with "Mother Kusters Goes to Heaven" at the New Yorker Theater, no such fate is immediately in store for Fassbinder who, though as politically self-aware as Godard, and as prodigiously talented, is a skeptic above all else. He's a free-lance agent, suspicious of all man-made modes, an artist who continues to work while picking his way along a narrow path, avoiding the lure of cynicism on one side and, on the other, the obvious comforts of some form of prefabricated faith, either political or mystical.

No film in the Fassbinder retrospective better illustrates this particular aspect of the filmmaker than the political comedy that opens the show. Though I'll be reviewing each of the seven new Fassbinder works included in the retrospective as it begins its commercial engagement, some advance comments are in order here.

"Mother Kusters Goes to Heaven," which Fassbinder made last year, is his variation on a 1929 Bertolt Brecht film unknown to me, "Mutter Krausens Fahrt in Glück," in which Brecht sought to capture what he called the "reality" of the Weimar Republic. In "Mother Kusters" Fassbinder seeks to capture the reality of West Germany today in a bitterly funny tale about a sweetly gullible little old lady (Brigitte Mira) whose husband one day with no warning whatsoever, goes berserk at the factory, killing the foreman and then himself. Why would poor, gentle old Kusters do such a thing?

His pregnant daughter-in-law (played by Fassbinder regular, Irm Hermann), who doesn't let the tragedy spoil a long-planned vacation in Finland, shrugs her shoulders and says, "Sometimes he looked tired but all he ever said was, 'We're not getting any younger.'" The popular press has a field day with the story. Kusters' daughter uses the publicity to further her singing career. When it turns out that on the fatal day Kusters had learned he was getting the sack, the Communists swoop down on the widow hoping to use her, which they do, then the anarchists, but none of them answers her needs.

Fassbinder's political sympathies are clearly with the left, but he remains an uncommitted outsider to the left, even as in his overtly homosexual melodrama, "Fox" (which will be included in the retrospective), Fassbinder, an acknowledged homosexual, remained outside the political politicking of gay liberation. "Fox" is no more "about" male homosexuality than his elegantly composed, breathtakingly cinematic "The Bitter Tears of Petra Von Kant" (1972) is about lesbians or "Beware The Holy Whore" (1970) is about movie-making. Those things are simply decor. The continuing theme that binds his films together has to do with the uses of power and the consequences of oppression. This is what makes his films seem uniquely post-World-War-Two German and, because of that, immediately accessible even to those of us who don't know Germany and don't even speak the language. He uses German life and experience as if it were a musical instrument.

Though this is only March, I'm willing to say that the Fassbinder retrospective is one of the major events of the film year. Beginning with the American premiere today of "Mother Kusters," the New Yorker will show in the following order, at intervals dictated by the public response to the programs: a double bill of "Fox" and "Petra Von Kant," "Chinese Roulette" (1976, American premiere), a double bill of "Ali: Fear Eats The Soul" (1974) and "The Merchant of Four Seasons" (1971), "Jail Bait" (1972, American premiere), a double bill of "Beware The Holy Whore" and "Katzelmacher" (1969, American premiere), a double bill of "The American Soldier" (1970) and "Gods of The Plague" (1969, American premiere), and "Effie Briest" (1974, American premiere). At the end of the New Yorker retrospective, the Waverly Theater will present the American premiere of "Satan's Brew," which was also made last year.

Missing (I think, unfortunately) from the retrospective are two other Fassbinder films that have been seen here at the New York Film Festival: "Recruits in Ingolstadt" (1970), Fassbinder's fascinating film version of the very Brechtian 1929 play by Marieluise Fleisser, and "Fear of Fear," which was shown at the festival last year and, in the form of a close-up study of a schizophrenic breakdown, dramatizes one possible end of capitalism, when life has become perfect and, suddenly, nothing works.

How has Fassbinder been able to keep to this extraordinary pace that is, I think, unequalled in Europe and certainly in this country? Among other things, he works with a closely knit association of actors and technicians that is as near to being a film stock company as has existed since the days of Griffith.

When you attend the retrospective you'll come to recognize a group of superlative performers who, in the course of the films, take on the properties of epic characters, as representative as hieroglyphs, though they miraculously are never quite the same from one film to the next. They include Brigitte Mira, who stars as the old chariady in "Ali," turns up in one scene in "Fox" as a lottery-ticket seller, plays the title role in "Mother Kusters," and appears throughout "Chinese Roulette" in a supporting role as a menacingly obsequious housekeeper who, it's easy to imagine, was once a guard at Buchenwald. The delicate, idealized beauty of Hanna Schygulla, who was Petra Von Kant's faithless friend in that film, turns up again and again in Fassbinder films, in "The Merchant of Four Seasons," "Katzelmacher" and, most spectacularly, in the title role in "Effie Briest," Fassbinder's cool, delicate, marvelously literary adaptation of the 19th century German novel by Theodor Fontane (and, I think, one of Fassbinder's most completely realized works). There also are Margit Carstenson, the mannequin-like beauty of "Petra Von Kant," Irm Hermann, who was Petra's quietly furious slave-secretary, Harry Baer, the fastidious, prissy, spurned lover in "Fox" who, in "Jail Bait," plays a decent enough roughneck who makes the mistake of falling in love with a 14-year-old Salome.

Manny Farber, in writing about Fassbinder a year ago in Film Comment, remarked on Fassbinder's "radical mix of snarl and decoration," which is, I think, an almost perfect way of describing the curious combination of methods that Fassbinder employs to create a new kind of reality in his films. Too much, I'm afraid, has been written about Fassbinder's affection for the films of Douglas Sirk (a lot of it by Fassbinder), but the young German's admiration for films like "Imitation of Life," "All That Heaven Allows" and "Written on The Wind" can lead to a lot of fatuous analysis, of which there's already been plenty. In the same issue of Film Comment that carried the excellent Farber piece, there was an interview with Fassbinder that contained the following exchange:

Interviewer: "Isn't the main thing you've gotten from Sirk the use of mirrors and framing devices in shots to indicate the uncontrollable fantasies of bourgeois society?"

Fassbinder: "I did it before I ever saw Sirk, but since I've seen Sirk, I do it more consciously."

That says a lot more about a certain kind of film criticism than it does about Fassbinder's films. Given the opportunity afforded by this excellent retrospective, one can note the use of devices like mirrors and immediately move on to the contemplation of more important things. **This retrospective should be a celebration, not an autopsy.**

1977 Mr 6, II:1:1

MOTHER KUSTERS GOES TO HEAVEN, directed by Rainer Werner Fassbinder; screenplay (German with English subtitles) by Mr. Fassbinder and Kurt Raab; produced by Christian Hohoff; director of photography, Michael Ballhaus; music, Peer Raben; editor, Thea Eymes; a Tango Film production, distributed by New Yorker Films. Running time: 108 minutes. At the New Yorker Theater, Broadway at 89th Street. This film has not been rated.

Mother Kusters .... Brigitte Mira
Corinna Corinne .... Ingrid Caven
Ernst .... Armin Meier
Helene .... Irm Hermann
Journalist .... Gottfried John
Mr. Thalmann .... Karlheinz Bohm
Mrs. Thalmann .... Margit Carstensen

By VINCENT CANBY

Mrs. Kusters is one of those people strangers take to be prototypical, though secretly she's far from ordinary. She simply appears to be. She's short, stocky, middle-aged, soft-spoken, naïve and inclined to be optimistic as she presents the world with a face that looks as if it had been shaped in modeling clay that fell to the floor before the features had been firmly set. People she doesn't know call her Mother Kusters and assume that she is Everywoman, which she isn't.

Mrs. Kusters is the sort of exception to the rule about the common person that was the inspiration of so much left-wing literature of the Depression about worms that turned, about little guys who fought heroically (and often futilely) back.

In the indomitable presence of Brigitte Mira, the German actress, she's also an essentially comic, idiosyncratic life-saving force that separates Rainer Werner Fassbinder's "Mrs. Kusters Goes to Heaven" from most other agit-prop drama that you've ever seen.

•

If you weren't already aware that Mr. Fassbinder, the 31-year-old German director ("Ali," "Fox and His Friends," "The Bitter Tears of Petra Von Kant," etc.), refuses to make movies that are like anyone else,'s, you have a far from solemn obligation to go to the New Yorker Theater where "Mother Kusters" opened yesterday. This fine film, which is being given its New York premiere, is the initial attraction in the first reasonably complete Fassbinder retrospective we've ever had here.

In addition to revivals of six Fassbinder films already seen in New York, the retrospective will include six Fassbinder works, dating from 1969 through 1976, that have never before been given theatrical showings locally. They are not all equally successful. They include a couple of films that look like clever doodling, but they also include one, "Effie Briest," that is

Brigitte Mira
"Idiosyncratic life-saving force."

as beautiful as anything that Mr. Fassbinder has done. Taken together, they constitute the most remarkable, original group of films made by a single director anywhere in recent years.

"Mother Kusters Goes to Heaven" is Mr. Fassbinder's contemporary variation on a 1929 German film, "Mother Krause's Journey to Happiness," directed by Piel Jutzi, which, as far as I can tell, was never released in this country. The screenplay of that film, which some sources (incorrectly, it seems) have attributed to Brecht, was set in the Berlin slums, and the title referred to Mrs. Krause's suicide after her daughter had been seduced and her son arrested for theft.

Mr. Fassbinder's pessimism is far more complex. "Mother Kusters," which Mr. Fassbinder wrote with Kurt Raab, who often acts in Fassbinder films and is sometimes their art director, is a furious morality tale that's been slightly bent. Set in contemporary West Germany, it's about Mrs. Kusters, a working-class housewife, who answers the door one evening to be told that her husband, Herman, has, that afternoon, run amok at his factory, murdered the boss's son and then committed suicide. Why would old Herman do such a thing?

Mrs. Kusters can't imagine. "He never complained," she says. "We just lived our life day by day. He was too good for this world." Her daughter-in-law (Irm Hermann), who's preoccupied with her pregnancy and a promised vacation in Finland, says, "Sometimes he looked tired, but all he ever said was, 'We're not getting any younger.'"

When it's learned that old Herman had been told he was going to be discharged, an extremely chic, elegant Communist couple (Karlheinz Bohm and Margit Carstensen) swoop down on Mrs. Kusters. They persuade her that Herman's act was revolutionary, "in a way," and proceed to use her in an election campaign.

All Mrs. Kusters wants is that her husband's name be cleared of smears that appeared in the tabloid press. She puts her faith first in the Communist Party, because she likes the friendliness of the meetings, and when the Communists don't help, she joins an anarchist whose "party" consists of himself and his girlfriend. They, too, fail the widow, which leads to an ending that some people interpret as Mr. Fassbinder in a gentle mood, though the way I read it, it's far more bleak than sentimental.

As a social critic, Mr. Fassbinder is skeptical of all prefabricated solutions. His sympathies are with the left, but he doubts everything except the will to survive. All other impulses, he seems to be saying, can be co-opted and exploited by the Establishment.

"Mother Kusters" is a witty, spare, beautifully performed political comedy that, according to an early synopsis I have, was supposed to end with Mrs. Kusters being gunned down by the police. Nothing so wild happens—which makes me wonder about the system of checks and balances that is at work within the artist. The original ending of his "Ali" also was to be a murder instead of the reconciliation that now ends the movie.

It's not, I think, that Mr. Fassbinder has gone soft but, rather, that he sees a gradual, peaceful accommodation to outrageous circumstances as the worst surrender of all.

1977 Mr 7, 33:1

MOHAMMAD, MESSENGER OF GOD, produced and directed by Moustapha Akkad; written by H.A.L. Craig; director of photography, Jack Hildyard; music by Maurice Jarre; edited by John Bloom. Running time: 3 hours. This film has been rated PG.

Hamza .... Anthony Quinn
Hind .... Irene Papas
Bu-Sofyan .... Michael Ansara
Bilal .... Johnny Sekka
Khalid .... Michael Forest
Zaid .... Damien Thomas
Ammar .... Garrick Hagon

The following review was written on the basis of a preview.

By RICHARD EDER

The three-hour-long, achingly clumsy "Mohammad, Messenger of God" does perform one backhanded service for the religion of Islam. It is, of itself, a convincing justification for the traditional Islamic hostility to pictorial representation.

The film, financed by money from Morocco, Libya and Kuwait, has one potentially important resource. It is an extraordinary story: The middle-aged caravan trader who amplified the voices he heard till they leaped across the empty desert and within 20 years conquered important portions of the Byzantine and Persian empires. By comparison, Christianity was a sluggard.

Occasionally, a spark of wonder slips through; mostly in some of the battle scenes toward the end. But it seems almost by accident. Generally speaking "Mohammad" botches its opportunities and succumbs to its problems.

•

Its main problem, of course, is its inability to show Mohammad, for fear of offending Islamic sensibilities. This behemoth of a film, in fact, treads on eggshells. In London it was shown without the word "Mohammad" in the title so as to forestall protest; and at the start there is a note saying it was approved by the "High Islamic Congress of the Shiiat in Lebanon."

The film makers have adopted a grotesque solution. Mohammad, as a character, is constantly there. People speak to him—that is, they address the camera. He goes places, he fights battles; and he is always just off-camera. When he fights we see his sword but not his hand; when he arrives at Medina at the end of the hegira from Mecca, crowds greet him but all the crowds seem to be greeting the camel. The whole awkward effect is like one of those Music Minus One records: a Tchaikovsky piano concerto with the piano missing.

But if what we don't see is awkward, what we do see is generally worse. The film begins in Mecca, whose prosperity rests on the visit of pilgrims —who also trade—to the 300 dieties housed in it. The town's rulers are upset when Mohammed begins preaching a religion of one god. Fewer gods—less business.

The growth of faith is shown in a series of vignettes. We see the town elders expressing outrage that their sons are following the new teachings; immediately we see a son converting his father and mother. Disciples sit in a room; a man arrives with a parchment containing the latest teaching; they roll their eyes and look stunned.

The unbelievers are totally villainous until they are converted, and then they assume expressions of total soulfulness. The acting is on the level of crudity of an early Cecil B. DeMille Bible epic, but the direction and pace is far more languid.

It is only in the last of the three hours that things begin to improve. Mohammed has led his followers out of Mecca to Medina, and there is war between the two cities. At least Moustapha Akkad, who is both director and producer, does his battles well. The dun desert background—the film was shot in Morocco and Libya—sets off the white costumes of the Moslems and the varicolored robes of the Arab unbelievers. There is a fine balance between the seething mass and individual savagery, with the broadswords wielded as axes.

The film ends with shots of mosques and worshipers all over the world; a montage expressing the great spread of Islam. More effective than these, and perhaps the only moment of unalloved power and beauty in the whole film, is the muezzin's call to prayer given by one of Mohammed's followers, played by Johnny Sekka. Whether the voice is Mr. Sekka's or another's dubbed in, its lilts and bitten-off silences are hair-raising: for once some part of the power and beauty of this major religion is expressed.

•

"Mohammad"—the spelling is idiosyncratic—opened yesterday at the Rivoli, Columbia II and two suburban theaters. It is rated PG "Parental Guidance Suggested"), presumably for the occasional violence of the battle scenes.

1977 Mr 10, 28:4

"ISLANDS IN THE STREAM"—George C. Scott, as a famous artist living in the Bahamas, prepares to bury his friend David Hemmings at sea in the film based on Ernest Hemingway's novel.

ISLANDS IN THE STREAM, directed by Franklin J. Schaffner; screenplay by Denne Bart Petitclerc, based on the novel by Ernest Hemingway; produced by Peter Bart and Max Palevsky; director of photography, Fred J. Koenekamp; music, Jerry Goldsmith; editor, Robert Swink, distributed by Paramount Pictures. Running time: 110 minutes. At the Coronet Theater, Third Avenue at 59th Street. This film has been rated PG.

Thomas Hudson .... George C. Scott
Eddy .... David Hemmings
Captain Ralph .... Gilbert Roland
Lil .... Susan Tyrrell
Willy .... Richard Evans
Audrey .... Claire Bloom
Joseph .... Julius Harris
Tom .... Hart Bochner
Andrew .... Brad Savage
David .... Michael-James Wixted
Helga Ziegner .... Hildy Brooks
Andrea .... Jessica Rains
Herr Ziegner .... Walter Friedel
Constable .... Charles Lampkin

By VINCENT CANBY

As played with fine, disciplined intensity by George C. Scott in "Islands in the Stream," the film adaptation of Ernest Hemingway's posthumously published novel, Thomas Hudson is a perfectly realized late-Hemingway hero; that is, he's an idealized projection of the way Hemingway wanted to see himself. Hudson is strong, wise, secure, and though he is aware of losses—those that could have been prevented and those that were inevitable—he is not thrown by them.

The time of the film, which was written by Denne Bart Petitclerc and directed by Franklin J. Schaffner, is the summer of 1940, shortly before the United States entered the war. Thomas Hudson, a successful sculptor, twice married, twice divorced, lives in comfortable isolation on the island of Bimini in the Bahamas. He has reached a carefully maintained accord with himself — which means working well, eating and drinking well, fishing well, having friends who are good company but who don't interfere with his emotional machinery.

This particular summer begins edgily with the arrival on the island of the sons he hasn't seen in four years—Tom, 19 years old; David, 14, and Andrew, 10. They descend on him as ciphers except for their associations to lives and women he has abandoned or who abandoned him. The summer, though, becomes something quite splendid.

•

The boys fish and swim and fight, and come to appreciate themselves as well as their father, whose satisfaction in them contains a kind of terrible radiance. He gets to know and love them, but now they represent a loss that is not so easily dealt with.

This is more or less the first half of "Islands in the Stream," which opened yesterday at the Coronet Theater. It's a film that begins so well, with so much genuine feeling that, as it goes on, sort of petering out, one starts wishing one could control it. Two-thirds of the way through, the wish is desperate. It is like sitting in the back seat of a car that is going gently, but unmistakably, out of control. At the end, after you've run into the tree, you aren't hurt, only very impatient.

•

Mr. Petitclerc, a journalist and novelist who apparently has had the blessing of Hemingway's widow, Mary, in adapting the novel, has been understandably free in his work, though neither he nor Mr. Schaffner has used his freedom very interestingly. The novel, which I like and which contains some of Hemingway's most moving and funniest work, is awkward screen material, but in their changes the writer and the director have simply exchanged one sort of awkwardness for another.

They haven't tightened a sprawling novel to fit the screen, they've let it sprawl in other directions, with very little grace and no feeling. "Islands in the Stream" is a movie in which a climactic death scene has less emotional impact than an earlier encounter between father and son while tinkering with an outboard motor.

Especially unrewarding is the film's concluding sequence, in which Thomas Hudson and his faithful rummy of a friend, a Petitclerc invention played by David Hemmings, attempt to run through the Cuban Coast Guard to deliver some German Jewish refugees to sanctuary in Cuba.

The concluding sequence in the book, no less melodramatic, is about Thomas Hudson's confrontation with the crew of a German U-boat. The film's invention, watered down "To Have and Have Not," seems almost opportunistic, as if the appearance of Jewish refgees would guarantee the film an emotional response lacking in the book.

It doesn't work. Somewhat better is the central sequence in the film, when Claire Bloom, looking taut and tired as Thomas Hudson's first wife, the only woman he ever really loved, turns up on the island to mull over the past. Not all of Hemingway's dialogue can actually be spoken, but this sequence contains some marvelous lines that suggest depths of feelings that the film doesn't know what to do with. The former lovers, now middle-aged, go to bed together. They bicker, drink, remember the old days when they were poor in Paris. Says the wife, "How could we all have been such good friends, and had such a lovely time, and had it turn out so badly?"

•

That sense of loss is what "Islands in the Stream" is all about, something that the film explores most successfully in the initial sequence with the boys and their father. I'm aware that film criticism should be more than an inventory of a film's parts, but "Islands in the Stream" is such a mixture of good and bad that it's impossible not to see the trees instead of the forest.

Everyone's performance is more or less defined by the material. The young actors who play the sons have very decent moments, especially Michael-James Wixted, as the troubled middle boy. Mr. Hemmings is even better than his material, but Gilbert Roland as an ancient sea captain and Susan Tyrrell as Bimini chief hooker are enough to snap the imaginations of even the most kindly disposed.

1977 Mr 10, 46:1

THE FARMER, directed by David Berlatsky; screenplay by George Fargo, Janice Colson-Dodge, Patrick Regan and John Carmody; executive producer, Peter B. Mills; produced by Gary Conway; music, Hugo Montenegro; director of photograph, Irv Goodnoff; editor, Richard Weber; a Milway production, distributed by Columbia Pictures. Running time: 98 minutes. At Loews State 2, Broadway at 45th Street, and other theaters. This film has been rated R.

Kyle Martin	Gary Conway
Betty	Angel Tompkins
Johnny O'	Michael Dante
Passini	George Memmoli
Weasel	Timothy Scott
Gumshoe	Ken Renard
Conners	John Popwell

"The Farmer," which opened yesterday at Loews State 2 and other theaters, is a viciously violent R-rated melodrama that apparently thinks it's preaching against violence while exploiting it. The film was written by four people (see above), directed ineptly by David Berlatsky and produced by Gary Conway, who also stars in it. Though the movie is R-rated and essentially unsuitable for audiences of any age, only a 6-year-old's sensibility could describe it properly:

A soldier comes home from a war (World War II) and we know he's nice because he won something (a Silver Star) but his farm is poor and the bank wants to take it away from him when a cow gets in the middle of the road one night. The cow is important because a nice gangster who is drunk runs into it and turns over (his car) though we never see the cow again.

The gangster thanks the farmer for saving his life and they become friends, including the gangster's girl (Angel Tompkins) and when the gangster is blinded by some bad gangsters he asks the farmer to get even for him to make money to save the farm.

The farmer shoots two of the gangsters, pushes one out of a window and pulls a wire around the neck of another. But the farmer hates violence and looks unhappy, except when he's with the gangester's girl and then they both take off their clothes and roll around for a long time as if their batteries were running low (in slow motion). After the farmer kills a lot of people he and the gangster's girl settle down on the farm, where she stops wearing lipstick because that isn't nice.

VINCENT CANBY

1977 Mr 10, 47:1

A scene from Alain Tanner's 1966 documentary, "A City at Chandigarh"
It's immensely satisfying to see a film that's also well worth listening to

High on India

A CITY AT CHANDIGARH, directed by Alain Tanner; written and narrated by John Berger; director of photography, Ernest Artaria; distributed by New Yorker Films. Running time: 54 minutes.
MAHATMA AND THE MAD BOY, directed and produced by Ismail Merchant; director of photography, Subrata Mitra. Featuring Sajid Khan. A Merchant Ivory production. Running time: 28 minutes.
THE DAM AT NAGARJUNSAGAR, directed by Gene Searchinger; distributed by Carousel Films. Running time: 9 minutes. At the Film Forum, 15 Vandam Street.

By VINCENT CANBY

IN 1950 the Indian Government commissioned Le Corbusier, the great Swiss-born French architect, to build from scratch a new capital city in the Punjab. For Le Corbusier, who died in 1965 at the age of 77, the commission was the unique opportunity to put into practice his theories of urban planning. Sixteen years later the new city of Chandigarh provided Alain Tanner, the Swiss film director, and particularly his collaborator, John Berger, the English critic and novelist, with material for what amounts to a meditation upon all social progess, government, the uses of tradition, and architecture.

"A City At Chandigarh," a fascinating 54-minute film directed by Mr. Tanner, with narration written and spoken by Mr. Berger, is one of the earliest collaborations of the two men who later went on to make such original, stylish, poltically informed fiction features as "La Salamandre," "The Middle of the World" and "Jonah Who Will Be 25 in the Year 2000."

•

The 1966 documentary opened yesterday at the Film Forum on a program of short films about India that also includes Ismail Merchant's lyrical, ironic "Mahatma and the Mad Boy" (28 minutes) and Gene Searchinger's comparatively conventional, nine-minute documentary, "The Dam at Nagarjunasagar," about the construction of a huge dam near Hyderabad. The program will be shown at the Film Forum tonight through Sunday at 7:30 and next week, Thursday through Sunday, at the same time.

"Mahatma and the Mad Boy" is the first film to be directed by Mr. Merchant, best known at the producer half of the Ismail Merchant-James Ivory producer-director team ("Shakespeare Wallah," "Bombay Talkie," "The Guru," etc.). Set on Bombay's Juhu beach, which takes on the aspect of a setting for a Beckett play, "Mahatma" is one day in the life of a persistently optimistic beggar boy who, with his monkey, scavenges the beach, confides his woes to a statue of Gandhi and is rebuffed by absolutely everybody.

Though the boy is a bit too sweet and garrulous to be completely winning, the photography is beautiful and menacing and the monkey most winning, with the personality of a forthright, affectionate, common-sensical alley cat who can walk on his hind legs when the need arises.

•

Anyone who has seen the Tanner-Berger features is aware that the two men have enormous, exuberant faith in words and that they don't hesitate to employ them in films where the meaning of one picture can often be heightened by the use of the spoken language. In Mr. Tanner's camera Chandigarh looks a bit like Kennedy Airport without the planes. Spread out over a broad plain, Le Corbusier's extraordinary structures look, at first, like uninhabited terminals.

Little by little, though, Mr. Berger's enthusiasm and feeling for the purpose as well as the achievements of the city transform the quite ordinary pictures we see into a kind of political manifesto. Chandigarh, says Mr. Berger, is neither a futurist city nor an imposed one. Rather it's a city that recognizes a traditional way of life while at the same time changing it.

In a time when documentary films are supposed to speak for themselves (and often don't, at least not with any coherence), it's immensely satisfying (as well as unusual) to see a film that's also well worth listening to. The narrative by Mr. Berger, a Marxist in the free-wheeling, European intellectual tradition, is not only beautifully written and spoken, it's also full of information and ideas one doesn't often get in a movie theater.

The result, though only 54 minutes long, is the best movie I've heard since "Jonah."

1977 Mr 11, C12:2

Boring Coterie

WELCOME TO L.A., written and directed by Alan Rudolph; produced by Robert Altman; director of photography, Dave Myers; music and songs by Richard Baskin; edited by William A. Sawyer and Tom Walls. Released by United Artists. At the Baronet Theater. Running time 106 minutes. This film has been rated R.

Carroll Barber	Keith Carradine
Ann Goode	Sally Kellerman
Karen Hood	Geraldine Chaplin
Ken Hood	Harvey Keitel
Nona Bruce	Luren Hutton
Susan Moore	Viveca Lindfors
Linda Murray	Sissy Spacek
Carl Barber	Denver Pyle
Jack Goode	John Considine
Eric Wood	Richard Baskin

By RICHARD EDER

WHEN KEITH CARRADINE and Geraldine Chaplin, the two almost-lovers in "Welcome to L.A.," talk by phone, each looks into a mirror. So does the movie: a very talented effort at very little, a sinewy jaw closing on a noodle, a fashion pose masquerading as a position.

"City of the One-Night Stands" is the theme song of the film, written and directed by Alan Rudolph and produced by Robert Altman, his mentor. Like "Shampoo," it is about the greed, boredom and decadence of a small, rich and talented cluster of West Coasters. But "Shampoo" said, in effect: These are some lives. "Welcome," with far less vitality and with more style than wit, says: This is life.

It doesn't make the case. It is a picture that has the smell of a coterie, of inside allusions and illusions, of private jokes or, rather—because there are few jokes—of private hangovers. The film is a very rich man in beautiful clothes telling you what a bad night he's had. You are sorry, but it was his night.

•

"Welcome" begins with Carroll Barber (Mr. Carradine), after three years of drifting in Europe, returning to Los Angeles. The return is engineered by his father, Carl (Denver Pyle) a self-made millionaire who wants to bring him into his business. The bait is the offer by a pop singer (played by Richard Baskin who, in fact, wrote the film's songs) to record one of Carroll's pieces. It is a phony offer; paid for, in fact, by Carl.

Carroll, rich, languid, untouchable, drifts through, drinking Southern Comfort out of a pint bottle, driving an expensive car with one hand, and sleeping with a succession of frantic women.

Why are they frantic? Susan Moore, an agent (Viveca Lindfors) is frantic because she is aging and life is all grappling and no grasp. Ann Goode, a real-estate woman played with a kind of defeated enthusiasm by Sally Kellerman, is frantic because her husband sleeps around. Karen Hood (Geraldine

Lauren Hutton, right, with Geraldine Chaplin in "Welcome to L.A."

A very talented effort at very little

Chaplin) is frantic because her husband, Ken, a comically ambitious assistant to Carl Barber, is totally wrapped up in himself.

The men, incidentally, are equally frantic, but have a little more breathing space. They need to score instant successes—with sex, work, lifestyle—and flee imtimacy. They love their wives, but play around on Christmas Eve.

•

We see these things in episodes, sometimes clever, usually well-acted, but excessively contrived. Harvey Keitel as a man twisted out of all shape by the need to succeed—he bounces like Silly Putty—is funny and grotesque, but never touching. Sissy Spacek has a perfectly polished role as a live-in maid who does her vacuuming topless, and entertains clients when Carroll Barber goes out. She adds a corrosive kind of humor to the movie, but no life.

The only figure that does have life—in other words, she is not defined completely at her first appearance, but goes on changing — is Karen Hood, played by Miss Chaplin. She rides around in taxis, talking to herself; cultivatesan interesting cough, and rather endearingly attributes to Benjamin Franklin, not Goya, the phrase about the sleep of reason producing monsters.

The role, as written, is more winsome than moving, but Miss Chaplin gives it a genuine wildness, and a rhythm that sounds like static and feels like electricity. In her absurdly miscalculated relationship with Mr. Carradine she is far better than anything else in the movie.

•

And Mr. Carradine is worse. Perhaps it is the director's fault more than his, but he sinks the film. We see interminable shots of him staring out windows, drooping around, driving. He is sullen and laconic, and we get dreadfully tired of him. He is the equivalent of the Poor Little Rich Girl. His deadness is supposed to be the film's judgment upon the hyperactive life of its characters. But except for Miss Chaplin, the characters are neither alive nor interesting. Mr. Rudolph is mowing down lead soldiers.

The songs are a particular torment. The music whines, the lyrics complain, and Mr. Carradine sings them with a kind of hushed writhing, like a worm dying at the bottom of a barrel.

1977 Mr 11, C18:1

THE GREAT TEXAS DYNAMITE CHASE, directed by Michael Pressman; screenplay by David Kirkpatrick and Mark Rosin; produced by David Irving; executive producers, Marshall Backlar, Marshall Whitfield and Karen Whitfield; director of photography, Jamie Anderson; editor, Millie Moore; music, Craig Safran; distributed by New World Pictures. At the Cinerama 2, Broadway near 47th Street, and other theaters. This film has been rated R.

Candy Morgan .... Claudia Jennings
Ellie Jo Turner .... Jocelyn Jones
Slim .... Johnny Crawford
Jake .... Chris Pennock
Pam Morgan .... Tara Strohmeier

and

NEW GIRL IN TOWN, directed by Gus Trikonis; written and produced by Peter J. Oppenheimer; director of photography, Irv Goodnoff; editor, Jerry Cohen; music, Kim Richmond; distributed by New World Pictures. Running time: 90 minutes. At the Cinerama 2 and other theaters. This film has been rated R.

Jamie Barker .... Monica Gayle
Jeb Hubbard .... Glenn Corbett
Kelly .... Roger Davis
Johnny Rodriguez .... Himself
C.Y. Ordell .... Jesse White
Alice .... Marcie Barkin

By VINCENT CANBY

There's a bit of real humor in the reverse sexism rampant in "The Great Texas Dynamite Chase" about two pretty, small-town Texas girls, one an escaped con and the other former, very rude bank teller, who join forces to rob banks, outwit the cops and ravish the men of their choosing. The film, directed by Michael Pressman and written by David Kirkpatrick and Mark Rosin, opened yesterday at the Cinerama 2 and other theaters on a bill with "New Girl in Town."

"The Great Texas Dynamite Chase" stars Claudia Jennings and Jocelyn Jones as the two young women who successfully manage their heists without anyone's being seriously injured until near the end. An ironic end-credit card attempts to recoup the film's earlier, lighthearted cynicism and almost succeeds.

•

Like every other low-budget, regional melodrama of this kind, the movie is virtually constructed of automobile chases in which every shot of the lead car turning a corner, hitting a bump or swerving to avoid a truck must be repeated by a shot of the pursuing car dealing with the same set of circumstances. Instead of increasing suspense, this sort of duplication cuts suspense in half. Why don't movie makers learn?

"New Girl in Town" is set largely in Nashville, where it was apparently made, and tells the sad story of a once-sweet little farm girl named Jamie Barker (Monica Gayle), who climbs to the top of the country-and-western ladder by sleeping with or being raped by the right people.

When she reaches her goal, Jamie realizes such success is just a sham. She has paid too high a price for the pot of gold at the end of the rainbow and the blue bird of happiness should have listened to the handwriting on the wall. It's that kind of film.

1977 Mr 12, 15:2

NASTY HABITS, directed by Michael Lindsay-Hogg; screenplay by Robert J. Enders, based on the Muriel Spark novel, "The Abbess of Crewe;" executive producer, George Barrie; produced by Mr. Enders; editor, Peter Tanner; music, John Cameron; director of photography, Douglas Slocombe; distributed by Brut Productions. Running time: 91 minutes. At the Cinema 2 Theater, Third Avenue near 60th Street. This film has been rated PG.

Alexandra .... Glenda Jackson
Gertrude .... Melina Mercouri
Walburga .... Geraldine Page
Winifred .... Sandy Dennis
Mildred .... Anne Jackson
Geraldine .... Anne Meara
Felicity .... Susan Penhaligon
Hildegarde .... Edith Evans
Priest .... Jerry Stiller
Maximilian .... Rip Torn
Monsignor .... Eli Wallach
Bathildis .... Suzanna Stone
Baudouin .... Peter Bromilow
Officer .... Shane Rimmer
Ambrose .... Harry Ditson
Gregory .... Chris Muncke

By VINCENT CANBY

The nuns at the Abbey of Crewe are in a swivet. The old Abbess Hildegarde has died 30 seconds prematurely—before putting her signature to a declaration of intent that Sister Alexandra should succeed her. A contested election is in the offing: Sister Alexandra, handsome, aristocratic, obsessed with power and sense of mission ("Unless I fulfill my destiny, my mother's labor pains were pointless"), versus Sister Felicity, who, while carrying on a madcap affair with a Jesuit brother, draws the support of the younger nuns with her promises to turn the convent into a "love-abbey."

The furious Alexandra instructs her two most trusted associates, Sister Walburga, the prioress, and Sister Mildred, chief of the novices, to fix upon a plan—without Alexandra's knowledge, of course.

That plan is to steel Felicity's love letters and publicize them in order to discredit her. Unfortunately, the two Jesuit seminarians who are commissioned to carry out the theft bungle it. They're caught in the act. At first it's all explained as simple high spirits. Nobody pays much attention. Alexandra wins the election by a landslide.

Then, slowly but inexorably, the word of the strange procedures at Crewe begins to leak out. Stories appear in the press. The Abbey, it's reported, is bugged. Rome becomes interested. Felicity leaps over the wall with her Jesuit lover to appear on television to promote her cause with the determination of a pop singer plugging her autobiography. What to do? Late at night, in the Abbess's elegantly cloistered quarters, Alexandra, Walburga and Mildred discuss possible scenarios.

Because most of us know the ending of the Watergate scandal, we know the ending of "Nasty Habits," the screen adaptation of Muriel Spark's 1974 satire, "The Abess of Crewe." Thus our attention must be held not by what happens, but how it's done. Approximately half of "Nasty Habits," which opened yesterday at the Cinema 2, is very funny. The other half is anywhere from awful to merely poor, which isn't good enough for a movie like this any more than it would be for a bottle of wine.

The most peculiar thing about the film, which was written by Robert J. Enders and directed by Michael Lindsay-Hogg, is that even as it utilizes great chunks of Miss Spark's marvelous dialogue (I like particularly Alexandra's talk to the nuns in which she defines the difference between "a lady" and, with a sneer, "a bourgeoise"), it also calls attention to the fragility of the novella, emphasizing the ways in which Miss Spark's comic conceit is least effective.

Take Sister Alexandra as written by Miss Spark and as played by Glenda Jackson (in her best role in years), she's a supremely interesting comic character — witty, clever, quick-minded, erudite, the sort of woman who, because she is the mistress of great traditions, can bend them. The gulf between Alexandra and the Whittier-educated President she's meant to satirize is funny in the book. On screen, it simply serves to make the satire silly.

We root for Alexandra. We cheer her brilliantly devious responses to Rome's criticism about the bugging. It's a paradox, she says airily. The Scriptures, she points out, tell us " 'to watch and pray,' which itself is a paradox since the two activities cannot effectively be practiced together, except in the paradoxical sense."

Miss Jackson as Sister Alexandra is great fun, but the film that contains her moves uneasily between high comedy and conventional low comedy about a bunch of nuns doing things that are supposed to be funny because nuns are doing them. It's as simple-minded as Leo McCarey's "Bells of St. Mary's," updated without sentiment.

The film's setting has been switched from England, the setting of the book and where most of the film was shot, to Philadelphia, perhaps to explain the presence of such American actresses as Geraldine Page and Anne Jackson, who play Haldeman and Erlichman types and who match Glenda Jackson's stylish performance line by line, gesture by gesture. I also very much liked Anne Meara as the Gerald Ford of Crewe Abbey.

Nothing, though, can explain or make palatable the casting of Melina Mercouri as the abbey's Henry Kissinger and Sandy Dennis as a John Dean sort. Miss Mercouri has the touch of a bull elephant tap-dancing on the floor above.

Miss Dennis, mugging outrageously and badly, gives the kind of performance that, 40 years ago, would have sent her to bed without her supper. It's rude, show-offy and, worse, it's incompetent. Watching her do a double-take is like watching a small tug trying to work the QE2 into her Hudson River berth in a gale. It's long and boring.

Mr. Lindsay-Hogg has allowed Miss Dennis to go for the easy laugh at the expense of undermining the legitimate performances of the other actresses, including Susan Penhaligon, who plays Sister Felicity, and of the actors like Eli Wallach, Rip Torn and Jerry Stiller, who have small roles as church fathers.

Apparently afraid that movie audiences would miss the point, the director and Mr. Enders, who was the film's producer as well as writer, have added lines not in the book ("You won't have Sister Alexandra to kick around anymore") that eventually coarsen Miss Spark's work, making it sound less witty than desperate in the manner of an extended television sketch.

1977 Mr 19, 11:1

FILM VIEW

VINCENT CANBY

Where Have B-Movies Gone?

The B-movie, or what used to be called the "supporting feature" in the days of the double-bill, did not die when the major studios cut back on their production schedules in favor of A-films, the better to compete with television. The B-movie, like a large part of the rest of America, moved to the country. One of the more interesting phenomena in recent years has been the survival of the low-budget program picture and its transformation, almost accidentally, into something that might be classified as the regional film.

There's no one regional film. There are as many different regional films as there are regions, but because the vast majority of them are produced in the south, future anthropologists studying these movies of the 1970's, could well get the idea that everything outside New York City and Los Angeles was red-neck country ruled by corrupt sheriffs and inhabited by repressed, middle-aged parents of hell-raising teen-age children who left their automobiles from time to time to sleep and eat and sometimes to make love. It may have something to do with the popularity of country-and-western music, but I also have the impression after having watched these films for some years that even when they aren't actually set in an identifiable southern locale, the characters tend to speak hillbilly-ese, less to identify place of origin than to certify sincerity.

The chances are that not many New Yorkers who follow the film scene, especially as it is represented at east side first-run theaters, are aware of these movies. They usually pass through New York quickly, like nervous travellers, often months after they've played their principal engagements in the south, southwest and middle west. They are the kind of movies that do best in drive-ins, and though I've never seen one in a drive-in, I wonder if there might not be some kind of automatic association between the movie and the drive-in setting that enhances the action on the screen. Since 90 percent of the action in these films has to do with one automobile's pursuit of another, watching this while sitting in an automobile could well set up sympathetic responses that are missing when, if you are in my position, you watch that action in the dank and dark of a Broadway movie theater at 11 a.m.

Some of these regional films have urban settings. Louisville, looking awfully sleepy and somewhat empty, has served as the locale for several melodramas made by William Girdler, the Louisvillian who wrote, directed and produced "Abby," a sort of black version of "The Exorcist." Chicago and Kansas City turn up in regional films occasionally. Seattle was the principle setting for "Scorchy," a really dopey film about dope-running, with Connie Stevens as an undercover agent.

Nashville is the setting for "New Girl in Town," a current, very homely melodrama about a farm girl who wants to get ahead as a country-and-western singer so badly she sleeps her way to the top of the charts, only to find success to be a hollow victory. Most of "Pipe Dreams," a modest little romantic melodrama in which Gladys Knight, the pop singer, made her acting debut, was filmed in Alaska and had to do with the building of the Alaskan pipeline.

• • •

Though the locales are often easily recognized, they are as often as disconnected to any plot point as the denatured studio setting for the B-films of the 1930's and '40's. I suspect that "Scorchy" was made in Seattle because somebody connected with the film, possibly a backer, lives in Seattle. "Squirm," last year's horror film about man-eating worms, was shot in Georgia, as were "Grizzly" (William Girdler's "Jaws" variation that featured a bear instead of a shark), and "The Farmer," a new R-rated revenge melodrama of extraordinary viciousness that pretends to take a stand against violence. (Georgia is one of the busier states when it comes to attracting movie people with promises of technical and financial cooperation.)

A quality that most regional melodramas share, with each other as well as with many B-pictures of old (and A-pictures, too), is a kind of mock outrage with the sort of injustices that keep their plots going (racial bigotry, political corruption, senseless killings), coupled with a desire to show everything in as explicit detail as is now cinematically possible. The original "Walking Tall," based on the life of the late Buford Pusser, the crusading Tennessee sheriff, depicted Sheriff Pusser as a man of peace who, from beginning to end, was bathed in blood, much of it other people's.

Another quality they share is a kind of romantic cynicism, which though not new, is much more frequently seen these days. "Dirty Mary Crazy Larry" (1974) is about an attractively wanton trio (two young men and a young woman) who hold up a supermarket in the southwest and then spend the rest of the film attempting to outrun the cops. It has no real ending. It just stops when the getaway car is hit by a train, incinerating the carefree youngsters. In "Macon County Line," set in (I think) Georgia, local law officers go after three nice young kids who are suspected (wrongly) of murder. Two of the young people are shot down by the cops who learn the truth, but too late. In last year's "Jackson County Jail," a young Los Angeles woman, while driving alone through the southwest, is held up by hitchhikers who make off with her car and all indentification. She is later thrown into jail by the county cops when she can't prove who she is and raped by the night guard, whom she murders in self-defense. Less than two days out of L.A., she finds herself a wanted criminal with little hope of ever proving her innocence.

The cynicism in "Jackson County Jail," by far the most interesting regional film I've yet seen, is anything but romantic, yet it deals in the same kinds of action (murder, rape, extended auto chases) that the other, lesser films are constructed of. What is the appeal of this tank-town nihilism? Do the Saturday night patrons at a rural Texas drive-in watch characters like Dirty Mary and Crazy Larry burn up at the end of a movie and think how tragic it is? Do they take it with a grain of salt? Do they simply enjoy all that running around in cars and wish their lives were as exciting? I'm not sure but films on the order of "Dirty Mary Crazy Larry" and "Macon County Line" are turning up with increasing frequency among the top money-making films every year.

Because regional films are remarkably short of real humor, a new one like "The Great Texas Dynamite Chase" is somewhat unusual. In this picture, made, I assume in Texas, two tough-talking, very pretty young women, one an escaped con and the other a bored bank teller, form a team to rob banks and have their way with various men they meet along the way. The film is stuffed with car chases, hold-ups and a crucially violent death scene, but the people who made the movie get all the humor they can out of the role-reversals by which the young women have become the aggressors and all the men their playthings. An end-credit card informs us that after their last shoot-out the two women escaped over the border, one to marry and live happily in a suburb of Mexico City, the other to become the companion to the president of the Bank of Brazil.

Few regional films conclude so cheerfully. If the heroes and heroines aren't dead, they've attained varying degrees of knowledge that almost always guarantee them a certain amount of unhappiness. The films are of greater interest as social history than as cinema. Just about everybody who lived in Sherwood Anderson's Winesburg, Ohio, was repressed. These regional films tell us that things in small-town and rural America haven't changed much in 50-some years. Life, in fact, may be more grim. But there is a difference.

If you're young and vital and know how to drive you can always jump into a car, even if you have to steal it, and spend a few merry hours roaring around on blacktop highways demonstrating an impulse for something better that, more often than not, is nothing more than that demonstration of how to turn corners fast. The two young women in "The Great Texas Dynamite Chase" don't want to go any place in particular. They simply want to keep moving.

1977 Mr 20, II:15:4

Obscure Mystery

THE DOMINO PRINCIPLE, directed and produced by Stanley Kramer; screenplay by Adam Kennedy, based on his novel; executive producer, Martin Starger; directors of photography, Fred Koenekamp and Ernest Laszlo; editor, John Burnett; music, Billy Goldenberg; presented by Sir Lew Grade for Associated General Films; distributed by Avco Embassy Pictures. Running time: 100 minutes. At the Cinema 1 Theater, 34th Street East Theater and Loews Orpheum Theater. This film has been rated R.

Roy Tucker	Gene Hackman
Ellie Tucker	Candice Bergen
Tagge	Richard Widmark
Spiventa	Mickey Rooney
Ross Pine	Edward Albert
Gen. Tom Reser	Eli Wallach
Ditchner	Ken Swofford
Gaddis	Neva Patterson
Captain Ruiz	Jay Novello
Ruby	Claire Brennan

By VINCENT CANBY

STANLEY KRAMER, the producer-director of such films as "Guess Who's Coming to Dinner," "The Secret of Santa Vittoria," "RPM" and "Oklahoma Crude," continues to be a pacesetter. As they say in Hollywood, Mr. Kramer is not content to rest on his laurel—the 1961 Irving Thalberg Memorial Award for achievement in film production. He must always push on.

"The Domino Principle," his new movie, is without doubt the definitive work to date in that growing body of screen literature devoted to instructing us in how to make a suspense film totally devoid of tension, intelligence, excitement, imagination, wit, reality and surprise. Like the prose in many how-to manuals, it is complicated without being informative, and it's also rigorously humdrum.

The film, which opened at three theaters yesterday, seems to be about a conspiracy to assassinate someone. I sound vague with good reason. So many people are involved in this murder plot—businessmen, the military, secretaries, chauffeurs, private-airline pilots, convicts and law-enforcement officers—that it seems to be less a conspiracy than the will of the majority.

At the center of the plot is a convict named Roy Tucker who's doing time in San Quentin on a murder rap. As played by Gene Hackman, Roy sweats a lot in the way of someone who drinks too much beer and he gets angry in the manner of a guy who's none too bright and knows it. While in prison, Roy is visited by a fellow named Tagge (Richard Widmark) and another named Pine (Edward Albert). They are identified as Establishment WASP's by their rep-tie haberdashery and arrogant manners. They promise to spring Roy from the slammer, deposit $200,000 to his account and give him title to a house in Spain if Roy, superb marksman that he is, does a job for them. He agrees.

Roy is allowed to escape from prison and everything starts to go according to plan, although when he is given a brief preview of the house he's been promised, it turns out to be in Costa Rica instead of Spain. The day before he's to pull off the job, the conspirators take Roy for a helicopter ride over Southern California to show him "the compound" where he'll find his victim. Roy is shocked. "I'm no good," he says, or something to that effect, "and I done some lousy things for money in my time, but I ain't going to do this."

Gene Hackman

This? What, or better yet, who is This? We never are told. It's one of Mr. Kramer's failed conceits that by his not identifying the victim of the assassination plot, we in the audience must somehow be even more horrified than if we knew. We see the man once, and I guess we're meant to imagine that he's the United States President or, at least, the Governor of California. To me, though, he suggested someone who might be the membership officer of a private country club. "The Domino Principle" doesn't expand the imagination. It makes it small.

The screenplay by Adam Kennedy, who adapted his own novel, is full of fruity truisms—"If we can't tell each other the truth, we don't have anything"—and fruity not-so-truisms—"It's like a train going down hill. You either ride it or it runs over you."

The performances are uniformly dreadful, although Mr. Widmark looks especially silly doing a late-autumn reprise of his "Kiss of Death" mannerisms, and Eli Wallach, playing a general, would seem to be certifiably insane. Candice Bergen, whose beauty and presence virtually describe contemporary chic, is cast as Mr. Hackman's lower-middle-class wife, a role she attempts more or less to represent by wearing brown hair that appears to be teased goat fur sprayed with deck varnish. Mickey Rooney, as a San Quentin convict, looks like an over-the-hill elf.

1977 Mr 24, C23:5

Film: Dilemma of Incest

Somewhere between Greek tragedy and soap opera is the sodden territory occupied by "Bittersweet Love," a movie that may best be remembered for bringing the name of Lana Turner back to screens in the neighborhoods where it opened yesterday.

Apart from serving as a reminder that Miss Turner was never one of our subtler actresses, "Bittersweet Love" is the movie that asks the question, "Can a young, married couple about to become parents recapture love and happiness after discovering they share the same sire?"

•

Yes, it seems that back in 1944 in New London, Conn., a young Navy officer (Robert Lansing) and a young woman he met at a U.S.O. dance (Miss Turner) spent a night in a motel before going their separate ways. She became pregnant, married the man who loved her (Robert Alda) and never told him he wasn't the father of their daughter (Meredith Baxter Birney).

The trouble with "Bittersweet Love" is not with the questions raised by the unlikely but innocently incestuous relationship resulting from the marriage of Miss Turner's daughter and Mr. Lansing's son: Should the pregnancy be terminated? Can the marriage continue? Should it?

It's simply that despite the earnestness of the cast, inspiration seems to have died with the posing of the problem. Right to the end, the young couple remain two Nice People who have been given a Terrible Problem. What they haven't been given is sufficient depth of character to make anyone care long or profoundly about them.

•

The PG rating seems primarily attributable to the movie's theme: incest.

LAWRENCE VAN GELDER

1977 Mr 24, C26:5

MAN ON THE ROOF, produced by Svensk Filmindustry and Svenska Institutet; directed by Bo Widerberg; screenplay by Bo Widerberg; based on the novel "The Abominable Man," by Maj Siowall and Per Wahloo; photography by Odd Geir Safther; editor, Bo Widerberg; music, Bjorn Jason Lindh. At the Plaza Theater. This film has not been rated.

Martin Beck	Carl-Gustaf Lindstedt
Einar Ronn	Hakan Serner
Lennart Kollberg	Sven Wollter
Gunvald Larsson	Thomas Hellberg
Hult	Carl Axel Heiknert
Ake Eriksson	Ingvar Hirdvall

AT about 2 o'clock on a March morning in Stockholm, a hospitalized police inspector named Stig Nyman is slashed to death in his room with a bayonet.

So begins "Man on the Roof," a bloody but keen-eyed, unsparing and absorbing, multilayered Swedish film that opened yesterday at the Plaza.

Written and directed by Bo Widerberg, who is probably best remembered here for "Elvira Madigan," "Man on the Roof" is based on "The Abominable Man," one of the novels in the highly praised Detective Martin Beck series by the late Per Wahloo and his wife, Maj Sjowall. What elevated these novels beyond the traditions of the genre was a master plan by the authors to use them as the basis for an exploration of society, and director Wilderberg remains faithful to that intent.

•

On one level, "Man on the Roof" stands as a simple mystery. Who killed Nyman and why? But to discover the answer, it is first necessary to know who Nyman was. A policeman, of course. But what is a policeman? One man's brute, it seems, is another's estimable protector of society's decent people. And finally, when the killer is revealed and begins one of those familiar killing sprees on a roof that drew spectacle-thirsty crowds and ringmasters in the form of importunate television newsmen and squads of specially trained and equipped police and their helicopters, the film becomes a study in the rationality of response.

As mysteries go, "Man on the Roof" is not a difficult puzzle. Straightforward, routine police procedures, carried out in a matter-of-fact way by sometimes weary men, yield the answer.

What invests this film with seriousness and a claim on our attention are the characters themselves. They inhabit a real world, and Widerberg sketches them, their environment and their relationships swiftly and deftly. That is true even of some of the few who appear for a matter of seconds, disappear never to be seen again and probably could be dispensed with in the name of brevity.

•

The chief roles are played remarkably: Carl-Gustaf Lindstedt as Beck, with an economy and grandeur reminiscent of Gabin as Maigret; Einer Ronn as his little chief assistant, with a vertical furrow between his brows that speaks volumes; Sven Wollter and Thomas Hellberg as the two younger detectives who mix like oil and water.

But behind it all looms Widerberg. "Man on the Roof" may suffer from a slow section in the middle, but over its length, the director displays several varieties of excellence—from the conjuration of horror by a single eye seen peering through a dark curtain; to the affectionate depiction of a city as background; to the succinct revelation of character; to the concoction of excitement, terror and suspense in the climactic stage. Not the least of his excellences is his willingness, at a time when it seems that technique is everything and coherence nil, to treat his audience to ideas as well.

LAWRENCE VAN GELDER

1977 Mr 24, C26:3

Austerity in Life

MY CHILDHOOD (55 minutes) and MY AIN FOLKS (48 minutes), directed and written by Bill Douglas, produced by the British Film Institute, and disributed by Films Inc. At the Film Forum, 15 Vandam Street.

Jamie	Stephen Archibald
Tommy	Tommy Hughie Restorick
Jamie's maternal grandmother	Jean Taylor Smith
Tommy's father	Bernard McKenna
Jamie's grandfather	Mr. Munro
Jamie's father	Paul Kermack
Jamie's paternal grandmother	Helen Gloag
German P.O.W.	Karl Fieseler

"My Childhood" (55 minutes) and "My Ain Folks" (48 minutes), which opened at the Film Forum yesterday, are, in effect, a single autobiographical feature film in which Bill Douglas, their writer and director, recalls his childhood in a small Scottish mining community after World War II. The films, photographed in black and white, have an intensely naturalistic look, but Mr. Douglas's interest is less in event than in remembered feelings of loneliness and desolation.

The principal characters are a little boy named Jamie (Stephen Archibald), the Douglas surrogate, an older boy named Tommy (Tommy Hughie Restorick), who may be either Jamie's half brother or first cousin—the film never bothers to make that clear—and the boys' grandmother, who raises them by letting them do pretty much what they please. She's neither cruel nor without love, just old and forgetful.

Stephen Archibald in "My Childhood"
The director's method is as austere as the life he evokes.

Mr. Douglas's method is as austere as the life he portrays. Jamie, who looks exhausted, with deep circles under his eyes, never cries and seldom smiles. He has already accepted the unfortunate facts of his life—his illegitimacy, his mother's mental illness and the presence of his father, a weak, not unpleasant sort of man who lives across the street with a dominating mother.

"My Childhood" and "My Ain Folks" evoke a world of such bleakness that even the sunlight looks chilly. Affection is something that is distantly remembered or found by chance, as in Jamie's friendship with a German P.O.W. The end of the war, which brings peace to everyone else, simply means that Jamie loses his only friend.

•

I can admire Mr. Douglas's discipline. He recalls all this without a bit of sentimentality. Yet after a while the unremitting gloom comes to be a reverse sentimentality, a sort of angry self-pity that is as off-putting as phony melodramatics. Like Jamie, we in the audience long to run away to some place warm, where people talk to each other and, occasionally, even laugh. The film's emotions are as bottled up as Jamie's.

"My Childhood" and "My Ain Folks" will be shown at the Film Forum tonight through Sunday at 7:30 and at the same time next week, Thursday through Sunday.

VINCENT CANBY

1977 Mr 25, C8:3

Cheery and Decent

LES ZOZOS, directed by Pascal Thomas; screenplay (French with English subtitles) by Mr. Thomas and Roland Duval; produced by Albina du Boisrouvray; director of photography, Colin Mounier; editor, Mr. Thomas; music, Vladimir Cosma; distributed by Bauer International. Running time: 105 minutes. At the Jean Renoir Cinema, Second Avenue near 10th Street. This film has not been rated.

Frederic ..... Frederic Duru
Francois ..... Edmond Railard
Paringaux ..... Jean-Marc Chollet
Venus ..... Jean-Claude Antezack
Uncle Jacques ..... Daniel Ceccaldi
Elisabeth ..... Annie Cole
Martine ..... Virginie Thevenet
Nelly ..... Caroline Cartier
Jacqueline ..... Michele Andre
French teacher ..... Serge Rousseau
Vice principal ..... Jacques Debary

A scene from Pascal Thomas's "Les Zozos" at the Jean Renoir Cinema
To criticize it is like returning a birthday greeting unopened

By VINCENT CANBY

PASCAL THOMAS, the young French director, makes the kind of films that many critics—incorrectly, I think—accuse François Truffaut of having made in his Antoine Doinel cycle. Mr. Thomas's films are definitely "pleasant," which means they are so cheerful and engaging that they come dangerously close to being sentimental. They please. They amuse. They appreciate the uses of irony.

Yet they never once surprise you with the comic perspective one gets in the Truffaut comedies. Antoine Doinel, the complete outsider, passionately aspires to join the bourgeoisie, whose manners and customs he studies with the dedication of a loony anthropologist. The bourgeoisie, seen through Antoine's admiring eyes, is simultaneously exotic and hugely comic. Mr. Thomas makes films about people who already belong, who have no idea that any other sort of existence is possible. Their view is limited.

•

Such a film is "Les Zozos," Mr. Thomas's first film, a sweet-natured comedy about several months in the lives of some teen-age boys who are neither better nor worse than they should be. Mr. Thomas knows perfectly well that they'll all grow up to be somewhat stuffy and to the right of center—knowledge he seems to accept with a sort of benign shrug.

"Les Zozos," which was included in the Museum of Modern Art's 1973 New Directors/New Films program, opened yesterday at the Jean Renoir Cinema, and follows by two years the commercial release of the directors second film, "Don't Cry With Your Mouth Full." It's so decent and well-meaning that to criticize it in any way is rather like returning a birthday greeting unopened.

"Les Zozos" is about two friends, Frederic (Frederic Duru), a would-be ladies' man, and François (Edmond Railard), a shy sort who admires Frederic's worldliness as, in the course of the film, he begins to understand Frederic's shortcomings.

•

This insight comes slowly, gently, as the two boys carry out their various romantic maneuvers, first with a couple of pretty girls who live near their boarding school, and then, most hilariously, when they make a trip to Sweden, whose girls, Frederic has been told, are notoriously easy marks. The Swedish excursion is a disaster for both boys. François is incapecitated by food poisoning and Frederic by his inability to understand the language. When a pliant young woman invites him home, he thinks she is telling him to go home.

All of the performances are attractive in the low-key way of the entire film. Annie Cole, who played the ripe young heroine in "Don't Cry With Your Mouth Full," has a small role of a girl who, for reasons that are never adequately explained, can't get a boy of her own. As was "Don't Cry," "Les Zozos" was photographed mostly in landscapes of such idealized beauty that after a while one longs to see evidence of a little pollution.

1977 Mr 25, C8:3

AIRPORT '77, directed by Jerry Jameson; screenplay by Michael Scheff and David Spector, "inspired by" the film, "Airport," based on Arthur Hailey's novel; executive producer, Jennings Lang; produced by William Frye; director of photography, Philip Lathrop; editors, J. Terry Williams and Robert Watts; music, John Cacavas; distributed by Universal Pictures. Running time: 117 minutes. At the Forum Theater, Broadway at 47th Street, and other theaters. This film has been rated PG.

Don Gallagher ..... Jack Lemmon
Karen Wallace ..... Lee Grant
Eve Clayton ..... Brenda Vaccaro

Jack Lemmon
Latest in series of reclamation projects for elderly actors.

Joe Patroni ..... George Kennedy
Philip Stevens ..... James Stewart
Nicholas St. Downs 3d ..... Joseph Cotten
Emily Livingston ..... Olivia De Havilland
Stan Buchek ..... Darren McGavin
Martin Wallace ..... Christopher Lee
Chambers ..... Robert Foxworth
Eddie ..... Robert Hooks
Banker ..... Monte Markham
Julie ..... Kathleen Quinlan
Frank Powers ..... Gil Gerard
Ralph Crawford ..... James Booth
Anne ..... Monica Lewis
Dorothy ..... Maidie Norman
Lisa ..... Pamela Bellwood
Mrs. Jane Stern ..... Arlene Golonka
Steve ..... Tom Sullivan
Dr. Williams ..... M. Emmet Walsh
Benjy ..... Anthony Battaglia

In "Airport," based on Arthur Hailey's novel, a Boeing 707 jet proved its durability by surviving the explosion of a bomb with scarcely a wobble of the wings. In the sequel, "Airport '75," a Boeing 747 jumbo jet was brought safely home to base after a collision with small private plane. Now, in the second sequel, "Airport '77," which opened at a number of theaters yesterday, a Boeing 747, converted into what is described as a "prototype executive aircraft" but looking more like a flying Beef 'n Brew, crash-lands at sea, sinks into 100 feet of water and remains almost as airtight as a diving bell and a lot safer than your own living room.

But, some wag is sure to ask, can a 747 boil an egg? Probably not. The Boeing genius has its limits, though you'd never know it from this series of popular, immensely silly films that look like reclamation projects for elderly actors.

Never, of course, does anything happen to these Boeing aircraft that could conceivably be attributed to equipment failure. The lunacy of man is responsible with such consistency that one begins to feel a quasi-religious emotion in the presence of such perfect planes. You sense the world would be a much better place if people retired and put their destinies on automatic pilot.

The tiny story of "Airport '77" concerns a rich art collector, played by James Stewart, who invites a planeload of friends, other art collectors and art critics to the opening of his Palm Beach museum. En route from Washington to Florida, thieves attempt to hijack the plane to get its cargo of paintings, but succeed only in crashing everyone into the ocean. Most of the picture is occupied with the passengers' panic, resolution and heroism as Navy divers attempt to raise the plane by huge floats.

•

The characters include the stalwart pilot (Jack Lemmon), his fiancée (Brenda Vaccaro), a frisky, pretty art patron (Olivia De Havilland) whose loyal black maid (Maidie Norman) is among the few people killed, an old (very old) flame of Miss De Havilland's (Joseph Cotten), assorted bratty children, an estranged married couple (Lee Grant and Christopher Lee) and a blind musician (Tom Sullivan), who plays cocktail piano and sings "Beauty Is in the Eye of the Beholder."

The film was directed by Jerry Jameson, most of whose experience has been in television, but "Airport '77" looks less like the work of a director and writers than like a corporate decision.

•

"Airport '77," which has been rated PG ("Parental Guidance Suggested"), contains some mildly bloody sequences involving passengers and furniture they bump into during the plane's crash-landing.

VINCENT CANBY

1977 Mr 26, 10:1

THE EAGLE HAS LANDED, directed by John Sturges; screenplay by Tom Mankiewicz; based on a novel by Jack Higgins; produced by Jack Wiener and David Niven Jr.; music, Lalo Schifrin; director of photography, Anthony Richmond; editor, Anne V. Coates; a presentation of Sir Lew Grade for Associated General Films; distributed by Columbia Pictures. Running time: 123 minutes. At Columbia Premiere theaters. This film has been rated PG.

Col. Kurt Steiner	Michael Caine
Liam Devlin	Donald Sutherland
Col. Max Radl	Robert Duvall
Molly Prior	Jenny Agutter
Heinrich Himmler	Donald Pleasence
Adm. Wilhelm Canaris	Anthony Quayle
Joanna Grey	Jean Marsh
Captain von Neustadt	Sven-Bertil Taube
Pamela Verecker	Judy Geeson
Sergeant Brandt	Siegfried Rauch
Father Verecker	John Standing
Capt. Harry Clark	Treat Williams
Colonel Pitts	Larry Hagman

By VINCENT CANBY

"The Eagle Has Landed," directed by John Sturges, is a good old-fashioned adventure movie that is so stuffed with robust incidents and characters that you can relax and enjoy it without worrying whether it actually happened or even whether it's plausible.

The time is late 1943 and the adventure concerns the efforts of some German commandos to kidnap Winston Churchill and carry him back to Berlin, in order—says the film—to allow Hitler to negotiate peace with the Allies.

•

Michael Caine plays the leader of the raiding party, a German paratroop officer whose credentials as a humanitarian are established early n the film when, en route to Germany from the Russian front, he attempts to save a Polish Jewish woman from mistreatment by Nazi soldiers. With the exception of Heinrich Himmler (Donald Pleasance), all the Germans in the movie are decent felows, the sort who risk their ives to save the world's less fortunate when they aren't kidnapping the world's leaders.

Michael Caine
First-rate performance

These Germans include Anthony Quayle as Adm. Wilhelm Canaris, who has a very funny scene early in the picture, when he describes a strategy meeting with Hitler that sounds a bit like a Darryl Zanuck story conference, and Robert Duvall, as the German officer whose job it is to make a feasibility study for the raid.

Most of the film, though, is set on the beautiful Norfolk coast of England, where the German raiders, disguised as Free Polish troops, settle down to await Churchill's arrival on a weekend rest visit. Mr. Caine's chief accomplice is a fast-talking Anglophobic Irish patriot played by Donald Sutherland with great dash and a brogue that seems to rise and fall according to a mysterious inner timetable.

•

Among other characters are a sweet English girl (Jenny Agutter) who falls in love with the Irishman, and an American Army officer (Larry Hagman) who's such a nitwit he almost wins the day for the Germans.

Tom Mankiewicz's screenplay, based on a novel by Jack Higgins, is straightforward and efficient and even intentionally funny from time to time. Mr. Sturges ("Bad Day at Black Rock," "Gunfight at the O.K. Corral" and "The Great Escape") obtains first-rate performances building the tension until the film's climactic sequence, whch, as you might suspect, concludes with a plot twist.

With so many failed suspense melodramas turning up these days, it's refreshing to see one made by people who know what they're about and, in that knowledge, have no delusions of grandeur. The film opened yesterday at Columbia Premiere theaters.

"The Eagle Has Landed," which has been rated PG ("Parental Guidance Suggested"), ends with an extended battle sequence that might frighten very small children who have never been exposed to prime-time television.

1977 Mr 26, 10:1

UNCLE VANYA, a filmed recording of the 1963 Chichester Festival theater production directed by Laurence Olivier; directed for the screen by Stuart Burge; written by Anton Chekhov and translated by Constance Garnett; a British Home Entertainment production, distributed by Arthur Cantor Productions. Running time: 120 minutes. At the Thalia Theater, 95th Street west of Broadway. This film has not been rated.

Nurse	Sybil Thorndike
Astrov	Laurence Olivier
Vanya	Michael Redgrave
Telyegin	Lewis Casson
Sonya	Joan Plowright
Ilyena	Rosemary Harris
Maman	Fay Compton
Yefim	Robert Lang
Professor	Max Adrian

The "Uncle Vanya" now in its New York premiere engagement at the Thalia Theater is a noteworthy movie curiosity. It's the filmed recording of the production staged in 1963 at the Chichester (England) Festival by Laurence Olivier with a cast that included Michel Redgrave (Vanya), Joan Plowright (Sonya), Rosemary Harris (Illyena), Max Adrian (the Professor) and Mr. Olivier (Astrov).

Photographed entirely on the Chichester stage in black and white, the production really is neither a movie nor a play, but the sort of on-the-spot report that looks best on television. Stuart Burge, who directed the production for the screen, uses the kind of medium shots and close-ups most of the time that have the effect of isolating an individual actor from his fellow players.

•

The shape of the Chichester stage probably made this necessary. Long shots, which would establish the physical and emotional relationships of the characters, are used so sparingly that it's impossible to judge accurately the effect of the ensemble acting. One gets the feeling after a while that the actors, usually seen only from the waist or chest up, are standing in high grass.

Chekhov's text, in the durable Constance Garnett translation, comes through in some marvelous moments, though, especially in the hysterical confrontation between the distraught Vanya and the Professor that ends the third act. Mr. Redgrave and Mr. Olivier are splendid. The other actors don't always fare too well before a camera taking close-up shots of performances designed to be seen from a certain fixed distance. Keeping these things in mind you should be able to enjoy this "Vanya" as one of the best readings of the play you're ever likely to hear.

VINCENT CANBY

1977 Mr 29, 36:1

Earnestly Aimless

OFF THE WALL, directed and written by Rick King; produced and edited by James Gregory; directors of photography, Chris Beaver, Jon Else and Judy Irving; an Oz Associates production, distributed by the Oz Releasing Company. Running time: 83 minutes. At the Whitney Museum of American Art, Madison Avenue at 75th Street.

John Little	Harvey Waldman
Dan	Gary Schnell
Rob	John French
Jane	Katy Roberts
Betsy	Judy Feil
Lennie Howe	Pat Crowley

By VINCENT CANBY

"OFF THE WALL," which opened a week's run yesterday at the Whitney Museum, looks very much like a movie made by film-school graduates before they had anything of interest to make a movie about.

It pretends to be the footage shot by a television crew studying—for reasons never explained—the life of a young, middle-class drifter named John Little (Harvey Waldman), a fellow who describes himself as "the last of the hippies" but who looks and behaves more like a bearded actor improvising aimlessness on film. About halfway through the movie, John holds up a bank in California and steals $5,000 as well as the television crew's camera and sound equipment, thus to continue photographing his story himself.

In its preoccupation with the movie camera and with the notion that the camera must be able to capture truth, "Off the Wall" recalls Jim McBride's classic send-up of cinéma vérité, "David Holzman's Diary," about a young man who became so obsessed with photographing his life he could no longer live it.

"Off the Wall" is neither satiric nor funny. It's as earnest and unsurprising as a term paper. As John wanders from California to New York and back again, he keeps attempting to get a fix on where his head is at.

•

When he fails, he gets mad and kicks television sets, refrigerator doors and Coke machines. Looking at a naked light bulb, he lunges at a poetic truth, wondering if he could stare at the bulb until it goes out. "It's—like—the opposite of enlightenment," he muses. "Instead of waiting for the light, you wait for the dark."

Rick King directed and wrote the film, although Mr. Waldman receives screen credit for additional dialogue.

1977 Mr 30, C17:5

It's About Blimps

BLACK SUNDAY, directed by John Frankenheimer; screenplay by Ernest Lehman, Kenneth Ross and Ivan Moffat, based on the novel by Thomas Harris; produced by Robert Evans; executive producer, Robert L. Rosen; director of photography, John A. Alonzo; music, John Williams; editor, Tom Rolf; distributed by Paramount Pictures. Running time: 143 minutes. At the Loews State 1 Theater, Broadway near 45th Street, and Loews Tower East Theater, Third Avenue near 72d Street. This film has been rated R.

Kabakov	Robert Shaw
Lander	Bruce Dern
Dahlia	Marthe Keller
Corley	Fritz Weaver
Moshevsky	Steve Keats
Fasil	Bekim Fehmiu
Muzi	Michael V. Gazzo
Pugh	William Daniels
Col. Riaf	Walter Gotell
Nageeb	Victor Campos
Joseph Robbie	Himself
Pat Summerall	Himself
Tom Brookshier	Himself
Fowler	Walter Brooke
Watchman	James Jeter
Ship Captain	Clyde Kusatsu

By VINCENT CANBY

THE DATE is Nov. 12. We know because an opening credit card informs us of this fact and during the rest of John Frankenheimer's "Black Sunday" more cards are forever telling us dates—Nov. 14, Nov. 17, etc.—as if to suggest that time is running out instead of just running on. The film, which had a single showing at Loews State 1 last night, begins regular showings at the State and Tower East today.

"Black Sunday," the screen adaptation of Thomas Harris's best-selling

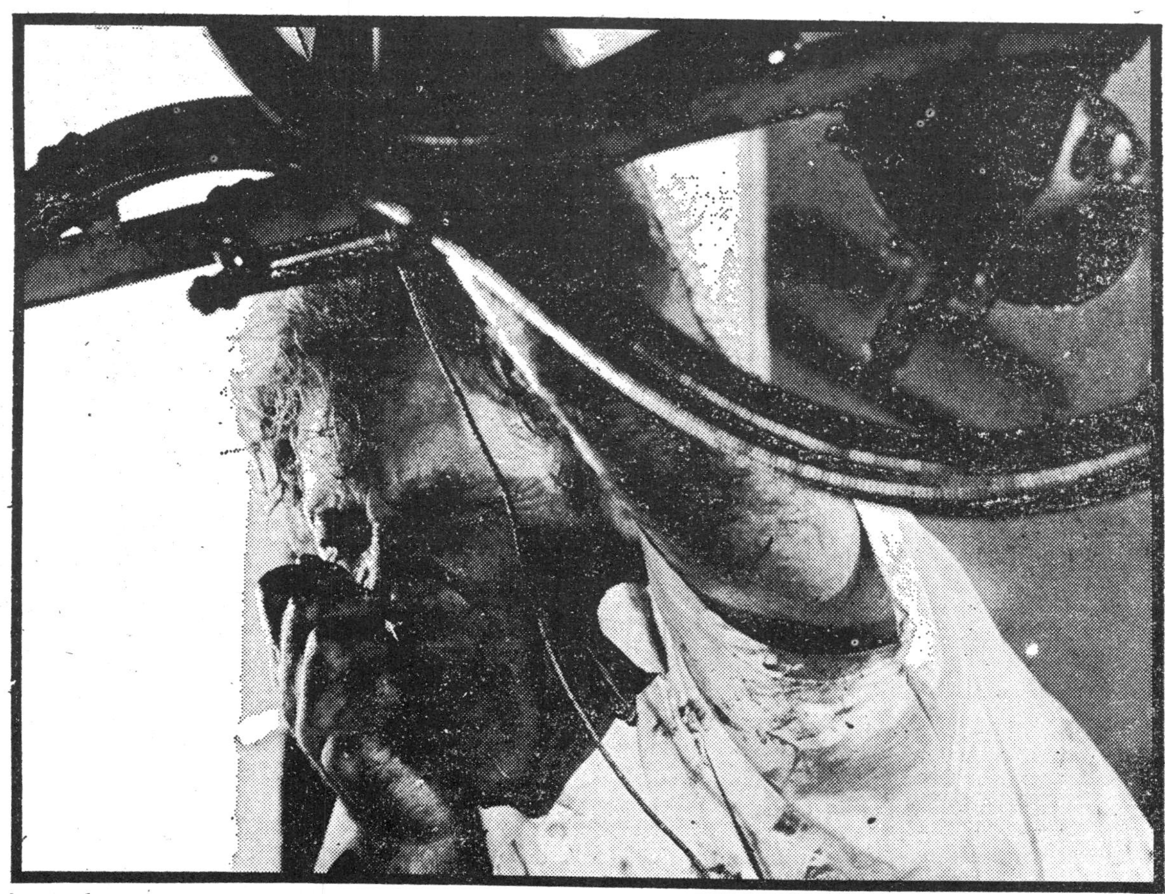

A wounded Bruce Dern stays at the controls of a hijacked blimp in "Black Sunday"
Vastly superior to other such junk movies

suspense novel, starts in Beirut where members of the Black September, the Arab terrorist group, are plotting to dramatize the Palestinian liberation cause by hitting Americans "where it hurts, where they feel most safe."

•

Their plan, as we come to learn it, is to kidnap a friendly old Goodyear blimp, load it with high explosives and dartlike shrapnel and send it put-putting over the Miami Super Bowl to assassinate the United States President and 79,999 other football fans. The question is not whether they will succeed as much as how they will fail, and at what last split-second.

Though "Black Sunday" is vastly superior to such junk movies as "Airport '77," "The Domino Principle" and "Two Minutes Warning," it belongs to that same category of film so involved with techniques and logistics that even when it generates some awe it is never once surprising.

"Black Sunday" is a Disneyland exhibit where people look real but are made out of rubber activated by transistors. It is a superior example of a kind of contemporary film making that has become much less involving and fun as its subjects have become more serious—and you can't get more serious than Presidential assassination and terrorism on the scale threatened in "Black Sunday."

Why doesn't it work for me?

I suspect it has to do with the constant awareness that the story is more important than anybody in it. The screenplay, written by Ernest Lehman, Kenneth Ross and Ivan Moffat, has the efficient manner of something hammered out—as they say in Hollywood—in a story conference. The characters don't motivate the drama in any real way. They are cut and shaped to fit it, and if the cast of "Black Sunday" were not so good, and if Mr. Frankenheimer were a less able director, the movie would be unendurably boring.

The film moves from Beirut to Los Angeles and Washington, then back to Los Angeles again and finally to Miami, cutting between the activities of the principal plotters (Bruce Dern as a psychotic Vietnam veteran and Marthe Keller as a Palestinian fanatic) and the Israeli intelligence officer (Robert Shaw) who has gotten wind of the plan during a commando raid on Black September headquarters in Beirut. We watch one side, then the other as if we were spectators at a Ping-Pong game.

•

Mr. Shaw brings to the role a mixture of tough resolve and weary skepticism that are as much his own contribution as the script's. Mr. Dern, slimmed down to skeletal proportions, is so convincing as the former prisoner of war who now flies Goodyear blimps that he effectively reminds us of Mr. Frankenheimer's best film, "The Manchurian Candidate," though "The Manchurian Candidate" was about brainwashing and politics and "Black Sunday" is about blimps (as much as anything else).

The action sequences, including the climactic attack on the Super Bowl (where we recognize a President who looks very much like Jimmy Carter) are well staged without being especially convincing. The film's best sequence has nothing to do with the action. It's the quiet recollection by Mr. Dern of his feelings when, as a prisoner of war, he received a snapshot of his wife and children and immediately realized that his wife had taken a lover.

•

Miss Keller has some difficulty portraying a Palestinian terrorist, looking, as she does, as beautiful and healthy and uncomplicated as a California surfer. She also shares a speech problem with the young Marlene Dietrich (Beirut is "Baywoot" and arranged is "awanged"), while lacking Dietrich's camp majesty.

1977 Ap 1, C10:3

Pluck and Ponies

THE LITTLEST HORSE THIEVES, directed by Charles Jarrott; screenplay by Rosemary Anne Sisson, based on a story by Burt Kennedy and Miss Sisson; produced by Ron Miller; director of photography, Paul Beeson; music, Ron Goodwin; editor, Richard Marden; a Walt Disney production, distributed by Buena Vista. Running time: 104 minutes. At Radio City Music Hall, Avenue of the Americas at 50th Street. This film has been rated G.

Lord Harrogate .... Alastair Sim
Mr. Sandman .... Peter Barkworth
Luke .... Maurice Colbourne
Violet .... Susan Tebbs
Miss Coutts .... Geraldine McEwan
Dave Sadler .... Andrew Harrison
Tommy Sadler .... Benjie Bolgar
Alice .... Chloe Franks
Mrs. Sandman .... Prunella Scales
Bert .... Joe Gladwin
Carter .... Leslie Sands

"THE LITTLEST Horse Thieves," which opened at the Radio City Music Hall yesterday as the theater's "new" Easter attraction (its "old" one, "Mr. Billion," having been a box-office flop), is a sweet-tempered, charming Walt Disney comedy about three children possessing the kind of modest pluck one associates with children's stories written at the turn of the century.

The time, indeed, is 1909 and the setting is an idyllically pretty, mostly dust-free Yorkshire. The story is about the efforts of the two young stepsons of a coal miner and the spunky daughter of the mine manager to save the lives of the pit ponies who have been rendered obsolete by new mine equipment. With the help of a volume called "The Wonder Book of Science," the children successfully restore to use the winding engine in an abandoned mine shaft, thus to steal the ponies out of

Chloe Franks and Andrew Harrison in "The Littlest Horse Thieves" at the Radio City Music Hall

the mines before they can be sent away to the glue factory.

Andrew Harrison and Benjie Bolgar play the two boys with the sort of gravity that doesn't allow for cuteness. Chloe Franks is the young heroine, a little girl who has to put up with a nanny who says things like "Mercy me, we *are* Miss Grubby Paws today, aren't we?" Most prominent among the older actors are the late Alastair Sim as the mildly eccentric old lord who owns the mine and Geraldine McEwan, who plays the bossy nanny.

•

The screenplay, written by Rosemary Anne Sisson, was directed by Charles Jarrott, whose stately earlier credits ("Anne of a Thousand Days," "Mary Queen of Scots") give no hint that he could scale down his talent to embrace this movie's genuine feelings for childhood adventure. In its own unpushy way, "The Littlest Horse Thieves" also manages to be as intelligent about miners' rights and social caste as it is about beneficial rights due to faithful, over-age pit ponies.

VINCENT CANBY

1977 Ap 1, C10:3

life is not the cure for black outlawry in our society. But, sadly enough, inhumanity has been a grim fact of jail societies ever since they were invented. And, however terrible or unjust, today's penal ills are not all racist-oriented, as implied here.

•

In filming lengthy sequences in North Dakota State Penitentiary, the director, Arthur Barron has caught the raw reality of both the jail and its actual inmates. Bernie Casey, the ill-fated, driven hero, contributes a taut, thoughtful characterization of a man educated into organizing his fellow black inmates toward a seeming, ultimate victory. Vonetta McGee is decorative as the political activist the hero comes to love in a tender, underplayed affair. And Ron O'Neal is quietly forceful as the brainy inmate who introduces him to the practical values of education.

Like the writers and the rest of the cast, however, they raise doubts by an oversimplified, approach to important issues. Their bias vitiates what could have been compelling drama.

1977 Ap 1, C10:6

Raggedy Andy
A rare and welcome addition

Importantly, the artisans hired by the producers were largely expert in handling their two-year production chore and the $4 million budget supplied by the International Telephone & Telegraph and Bobbs-Merrill, their literary subsidiary, in this, their first feature-length animated présentation.

The large team of veteran animators headed by Richard Williams, whose young daughter, Claire, appears in the film's sole live-action sequences, contributes meticulous interpretations so that Raggedy Ann, the pirate Captain and the comically lonely Camel, for example, seem to be properly mouthing and singing their delights and fears.

In most instances, their voices—supplied by such actors as George S. Irving, Joe Silver, Didi Conn and Alan Sues—provide them with fairly convincing juvenile and comic conviction. And if the music and lyrics of 17 songs by Joe Raposo ("Sesame Street," etc.) are not extraordinary, they are, like "Candy Hearts," pleasantly tuneful.

"Raggedy Ann & Andy" should charmingly fill the bill for the young fry who haven't had their kind of animated feature since Disney's "Robin Hood" in 1973.

1977 Ap 2, 10:1

Outrage Vented

BROTHERS; written and produced by Edward and Mildred Lewis; directed by Arthur Barron; edited by William Dornisch; John Morrill, director of photography; music composed and performed by Tai Mahal, a SoHo Associates Production distributed by Warner Bros. At the National, 44th Street and Seventh Avenue, and the Fine Arts, 58th Street, West of Lexington Avenue. Running time: 104 minutes. This film has been rated R.

David Thomas .... Bernie Casey
Paula Jones .... Vonetta McGee
Walter Nance .... Ron O'Neal
Lewis .... Rennie Roker
Robinson .... Stu Gilliam
Chief Guard McGee .... John Lehne
Joshua Thomas .... Owen Pace
Warden Leon .... Joseph Havener

By A. H. WEILER

ANGER IS THE STRIDENT keynote in "Brothers," the thinly disguised dramatization of some bloody, black militancy of fairly recent history in California. Hatred, like love, cries for balanced treatment, but "Brothers," which opened at the Fine Arts and National Theaters yesterday, is dedicated to venting its outrage unalloyed and largely without benefit of doubt.

Although its principals are named Thomas and Jones, viewers may see close parallels between "Brothers" and the actual cases of George Jackson, the black San Quentin prisoner who was killed a few years back; his younger brother and a judge who were slain in a shootout at a courthouse, and Angela Davis, the brilliant political, teacher-activist, who was arrested and then acquitted of charges of helping to stage a prison escape.

•

Obviously, Edward and Mildred Lewis, the husband-and-wife writing team, are convinced that their fictionalized edition of the varied documentations of these cases is the truth. Their ill-fated hero is innocent of being an accessory in an armed robbery but is railroaded into copping a plea and a short sentence. But as white guards and white inmates mistreat blacks, his sentence and rage increase up to that final, explosive revolt.

One wonders about some fuzzy but crucial points in this bleak saga. Who did kill that white guard? Who did plant those guns in white inmates' hands? "Brothers" stresses that prison

RAGGEDY ANN & ANDY, screenplay by Patricia Thackray and Max Wilk; based on the stories and characters created by Johnny Gruelle; production supervised and directed by Richard Williams; production designed by Corny Cole; edited by Harry Chang, Lee Kent, Kenneth McIlwaine and Maxwell Seligman; music by Joe Raposo; sequence director, Gerald Potterton; backgrounds by Sue Butterworth; Xerox and animation photography by Al Rezak Inc., animators include Grim Natwick, Art Babitt, Emory Hawkins, Tissa David, Gerald Potterton, Gerry Chiniquy; produced by Lester Osterman Productions; Richard Horner producer; presented by Bobbs-Merrill, the Publishing People of I.T.T. and released by 20th Century-Fox. Running time: 84 minutes. This film is rated G. At the Guild, 50th Street west of Fifth Avenue, and other local theaters.

Marcella .... Claire Williams
Voice characterizations by: Didi Conn, Mark Baker, Fred Struthman, Niki Flacks, George S. Irving, Arnold Stang, Joe Silver, Alan Sues, Marty Brill, Paul Dooley, Mason Adams, Allen Swift, Hetty Galen, Sheldon Harnick, Ardyth Kaiser, Margery Gray, Lynne Stuart.

By A. H. WEILER

"This is too good to be true," one of the animated innocents happily exclaims early in the fairy-tale capers of "Raggedy Ann & Andy" that turned up yesterday at 50 theaters in the metropolitan area. That ecstatic, if double-edged, observation is truthful. The moppets who for decades, have been cuddling up to the titular stories and those floppy dolls are likely to agree with it even if curmudgeons over the age of 12, say, probably would quibble over such superlatives.

Considering the largely rudimentary animated subjects dealt to kids on television, the technical professionalism of "Raggedy Ann" is both a rare and welcome addition to the entertainment offered pre-teens these days. At any rate, the script concocted from the ever-popular tales introduced more than 50 years ago by Johnny Gruelle for his ailing, young daughter, Marcella, needs no more justification for youngsters than a lollipop.

The adventures the scenarists have devised are, essentially, a search, starting from Marcella's toy and doll-filled playroom, for Babette, the French doll, who is kidnapped by another doll, the Captain. If the peripatetic Raggedy Ann and her brother, Andy, make it successfully through a forbidding forest, a tossing sea, a looney kingdom ruled by a wacky sovereign and the dangers of a blob called Greedy, it shouldn't hurt the youngsters more than a second lollipop.

FILM VIEW

VINCENT CANBY

Suspense Films

Near the climax of "Black Sunday," at that point in the film when all the people watching it are supposed to be sitting on the edges of their seats, I was slumped back in mine asking myself boring questions about plausibility. There on the screen in front of me was the explosives-laden Goodyear blimp, poking its way lazily through blue sky toward Miami's Super Bowl, carrying two terrorists intent on assassinating the United States President and 79,999 other football fans, but all I was worrying about was why the intelligence officers aboard the pursuing helicopter simply hadn't radioed ahead to clear the stadium. John Frankenheimer, the director, three very expensive screenwriters and some excellent actors, including Bruce Dern and Robert Shaw, were knocking themselves out to make this nightmare fantasy come true but my principal concern was with communications. I'd been disconnected.

Usually I want to know what happens next in any film as much as the next fellow. Even when I know what must happen next, I want to know what happens, as in another new suspense melodrama, "The Eagle Has Landed," which is about the attempt by some Nazi commandos to kidnap Winston Churchill during World War II. Since we all know that the Nazis never did kidnap Churchill, the suspense must lie in the manner in which they don't succeed, and though John Sturges, the director of "The Eagle Has Landed," and Tom Mankiewicz, who wrote the screenplay, do their work well, it's the sort of work that at best can earn only a B-plus. You really must be addicted to suspense melodramas to allow yourself to get caught up in finding out why something you know didn't happen ever took place.

• • •

Suspense melodramas are coming at us so thick and fast these days that I'm wondering whether a perfectly respectable movie genre will be able to survive the glut of mostly second-rate work. I'm also wondering what their producers are thinking of. "Black Sunday" and "The Eagle Has Landed" are not second-rate films. Each is actually a fairly stylish movie of its kind, but neither is about anything at all, and in this respect they are no different from truly dreadful movies like "Airport '77" and Stanley Kramer's "The Domino Principle."

Though "Airport '77" has the form of a suspense film and means to keep us interested in the fate of the passengers aboard a 747 jumbo jet that crashes into the Bermuda triangle, it's really another feature-length commercial for the Boeing airplane, which, this time, is demonstrated to be so structurally sound and watertight that it allows for the survival of its passengers for approximately 12 hours under 100 feet of water. As such it's less successful as a movie than as a hype for Boeing stock.

● ● ●

"Airport '77" is frivolous and foolish. "The Domino Principle" is ponderously mini-minded. Kramer and his writer, Adam Kennedy, have obviously thought long and hard about their movie and, after due consideration, made all the wrong decisions. Here is a film about an assassination conspiracy that never identifies the fellow to be assassinated or the conspirators, which, I suppose, is the moviemakers' way of urging us to think about assassination as an abstract concept. It doesn't work. "The Domino Principle" is utter confusion. It's not about its hero, a dour convict played by Gene Hackman, who is sprung from San Quentin to carry out the assassination, but about all the modes of transportation employed to get characters from one spot to another—bakery trucks, limousines, jet airplanes (private and commercial), Volkswagen jeeps. "The Domino Principle" is, indeed, so empty of ideas and so transparent in its intent that it becomes a kind of X-ray picture of what's wrong with much better films on the order of "Black Sunday" and "The Eagle Has Landed." They're movies exclusively concerned with physical action and mechanics. They have been conceived only in terms of event. People—characters—come second. Genuine feelings and ideas are excess baggage.

Throughout their history motion pictures have embraced the spectacle of particular events, from the first sneeze recorded by Edison through great train robberies, the births of nations and the falls of empires. Action is cinema but the greatest commercial directors (Hitchcock, Hawks, Lang, among others) have somehow succeeded in making films in which characters, feelings and even intellectual points of view were expressed by and within action. At the top of his form in films like "Rear Window," "Shadow of A Doubt" and "The Man Who Knew Too Much," Hitchcock works so skillfully that it's impossible to imagine the individual characters in any circumstances other than those we've witnessed.

The sort of suspense melodramas we're seeing today are inhabited by characters who've been cut and shaped to fit the events. They are characters born in story conferences. If we're lucky, the film is cast with actors who bring to the melodrama various idiosyncracies that are not necessarily in the screenplay.

One of the reasons that "Jaws" worked as well as it did was the casting—the quality of personal presence brought to their roles by Robert Shaw, Roy Scheider and Richard Dreyfuss. Shaw, who plays the Israeli intelligence officer in "Black Sunday," and Bruce Dern, who plays the psychotic former Vietnam P.O.W. veteran who joins forces with the Black September terrorist organization, are of immense help in persuading us to take "Black Sunday" seriously. And, I suppose, we should take it seriously in light of the fact that such acts of terrorism are certainly possible. Yet as I watched the film, I went through successive stages of withdrawal from involvement with the events on the screen until, at the end, I was asking myself, "So what?"

It's not that the film stretches the imagination too far, but not far enough. It exploits the subject of terrorism with no more thought about the roots of terrorism than "The Towering Inferno" gave to building codes.

I don't especially want to see a movie about building codes but I can imagine a film about terrorism that would be terrifying because we would be moved by the inevitability of events and by the characters involved, and not just by the physical spectacle, something that John Frankenheimer handles as well as the "Black Sunday" screenplay allows. There are some isolated moments in "Black Sunday" that are as fine as anything Frankenheimer has ever done, including a shoot-out on a crowded Miami beach and a scene in which Dern recalls his reactions when, as a P.O.W., he received a snapshot of his wife and children but noticed only the shadow of the man who had held the camera.

Yet "Black Sunday" is not about this fellow, or about the dedicated Israeli intelligence officer, or about Arab terrorism. It's about a malignant blimp.

"What happens next?" is a perfectly respectable question to ask in the course of any fiction, but in wanting to know what happens next, we also want to know why and to whom? The whys and to-whoms are getting short shrift in today's films. We aren't being asked to think, only to experience fear, which is not only one of the least exalting of emotions but also one of the easiest to communicate in films. A film like "Black Sunday" is not easy to make. A lot of money and technical skill went into its production but for all that, the only thing it does is kill time. Is it too much to expect that movies do something more?

1977 Ap 3, II:17:4

AGUIRRE, THE WRATH OF GOD, directed by Werner Herzog; screenplay (German with English subtitles) by Mr. Herzog; music, Popol Vuh; director of photography, Thomas Mauch; distributed by New Yorker Films. Running time: 90 minutes. At the D. W. Griffith Theater, 59th Street near Second Avenue. This film has not been rated.

Aguirre .... Klaus Kinski
Don Pedro de Ursua .... Ruy Guerra
Inez .... Helena Rojo
Flores .... Cecilia Rivera
Emperor .... Peter Heiling
Slave .... De Negro

By VINCENT CANBY

In 1560, not quite 20 years after the death of Francisco Pizarro, who had conquered Peru for Spain, an elaborately provisioned party of conquistadores set out from Quito to find the land of El Dorado. It was a fearful journey first to cross the Andes but even worse on the other side. Those who didn't starve, drown or die of fever in the Amazon jungles were in constant danger of being killed by Indians.

When it became apparent the entire expedition could not go on, a small task force was commissioned to continue down the Amazon for a week. In command were Pedro de Ursua and his aide, Lope de Aguirre, sometimes referred to in history books as Aguirre the Madman or Aguirre the Traitor. They never returned.

●

Exactly what happened afterward is unclear but it seems that Aguirre murdered Ursua, declared the little band's independence from Spain and crowned a man named Fernando de Guzman, the ranking nobleman among them, "Emperor of El Dorado." He eventually murdered Guzman and was himself murdered by his own men when they at last reached South America's northeast coast.

This story, one of the more bizarre and bloody footnotes to the history of hte Spanish conquests, is the basis for Werner Herzog's absolutely stunning 1972 German film, "Aguirre, the Wrath of God," which opened yesterday at the D. W. Griffith Theater. The movie was shot by Mr. Herzog ("The Mystery of Kaspar Hauser," "The Great Ecstasy of The Sculptor Steiner," "Even Dwarfs Started Small") on locations of breathtaking beauty (and, I must assume, of horrendous difficulty in South America, but it's no ordinary, run-of-the-rapids adventure.

"AGUIRRE, THE WRATH OF GOD"—Klaus Kinski plays a conquistadore in Werner Herzog's fil mwhich opens today at the D. W. Griffith.

"Aguirre, The Wrath of God" is simultaneously a historical film (to the extent that it follows events as they are known) and a meditation upon history. Aguirre is truly mad, but as played by Klaus Kinski, whose crooked walk and undiluted evil recall Laurence Olivier's Richard III, he is the essential civilized man, a fellow who, in Mr. Herzog's vision of things, must be lunatic.

There's an eerie moment in the middle of the film when the Emperor, sitting in rags under an improvised shade on the makeshift raft that is carrying the party down the Amazon, picks at his fish dinner (the other men are starving) and thinks with satisfaction that his "empire" is now six times as large as Spain's. No matter that he too may never eat again, nor that his empire is jungle swamp, the sense of power is so intoxicating that it overwhelms all other considerations.

It's as if Mr. Herzog were saying that civilization—our assumption that we have conquered nature or even come to some accommodation with it—is as ridiculous as the Emperor's pleasure.

From the film's opening sequence, when we see the conquistadores, their women (including Ursua's wife being carried in an elegant litter) and their Indian porters making their way down an Andean slope, looking like the inhabitants of an ant palace, to the concluding shots of Aguirre on his raft in the company of hundreds of tiny marmosets, Mr. Herzog views all the proceedings with fixed detachment. He remains cool. He takes no sides. He may even be slightly amused. Mainly he is a poet who constantly surprises us with unexpected juxtapositions.

•

The film is incredibly rich and lush looking. It is tactile. One can feel the colors of the jungle and see the heat. The conquistadoree endure terrible trials—whirlpools, Indian attacks, rebellion within their own ranks—yet the mood of the film is almost languid. Ursua's faithful, loving wife, played by a classic beauty named Helene Rojo, throws no tantrums when her husband is executed. She watches and waits, and when the opportunity arises, she walks off to her own death in the jungle as if going to a tea.

Contrasting with this peculiar languor is the radiant madness of Aguirre, who hypnotizes his soldiers into following his wildest instructions, who sneers at men who seek riches when power and fame are all that matter, who aspires to be nothing less than the wrath of God and who, at the end, is planning to create a new dynasty by marrying his dead daughter. He's mad but he's a survivor.

This is a splendid and haunting work.

1977 Ap 4, 43:1

Folk Documentaries Capture Intimate Scenes

By ROBERT PALMER

Two young film makers were shooting a black religious service in the home of a Centerville, Miss., faith healer late one night when the unexpected happened. In the midst of pressing, sweating bodies and overpowering gospel singing, the faith healer passed into a trance state and began speaking "unknown tongues," a rapid-fire form of utterance that comes directly from the subconscious.

"Some people carried her out of the room into another, smaller room," one of the film makers, Bill Ferris, remembers, "and we went in there, plugged a light in and fastened it to the door. It gave us just enough light to shoot. When you're making documentary films, you have to be ready for the unexpected to happen."

Mr. Ferris and Judy Peiser, his fellow film maker, were ready, and the dramatic, unforgettable footage that resulted found its way into their film "Fannie Bell Chapman: Gospel Singer," a 42-minute color documentary.

The Chapman film and two other recent works by Mr. Ferris and Miss Peiser, "Give My Poor Heart Ease: Mississippi Delta Bluesmen" and "Two Black Churches," will be shown today at th Donnell Library Center, 20 West 53d Street, and at the Museum of Modern Art. The Donnell Library showing is at 12 noon and admission is free. The Museum of Modern Art showing is at 6 P.M. and, because Tuesdays are donation days at the Modern, the patron decides how much to pay.

Striking Insights

The "unknown tongues" sequence in the "Fannie Bell Chapman" film is one of a number of unusually intimate scenes that have been captured on film by Mr. Ferris and Miss Peiser. Working out of the Center for Southern Folklore in Memphis and at Yale University, where Mr. Ferris teaches folklore, aided by the Yale Media Design Studio and foundation financing, Mr. Ferris and Miss Peiser have rapidly established a reputation as two of the more-creative film makers documenting American folklore.

Their deep penetration into the homes and communities of their subjects is practically without precedent: The "tongues" episode, a holy-dance and faith-healing service from a New Haven church, in "Two Black Churches," and the footage of a back-country juke joint and a prison-farm work gang in "Give My Poor Heart Ease" offer some of the most striking insights into black folk culture in America ever captured on film.

Bill Ferris first began recording Fannie Bell Chapman's gospel music in 1967, and he visited the Chapman family repeatedly before filming began. "I was struck by their music," he says, "and by the warmth of the family. The whole dimension of faith healing wasn't evident until we were already filming." In other scenes in the film, Mrs. Chapman builds altarlike structures out of milk cartons and makes tablecloths by typing together plastic six-pack rings, talking all the while about the visions she receives and about her healing abilities. "I cut sickness as fine as cat's hair," she explains, chopping with her hands so rapidly that they become a blur.

"Once we've started filming in a community," Miss Peiser says, "we go back and show the people rushes, and ask them what they think we should include. The folk artists are the first to see the finished films and the first to receive copies."

Mr. Ferris concedes that filming in a community effects some changes as primarily salutary. "When we film a folk artist," he says, "the community begins to see the person more as a real artist. It means that folk traditions are revitalized. I think the most important thing for the film maker to do is to develop a friendship with the people he's filming, to become sensitive to their feelings. Then when you're working with the camera, if things aren't quite right, you sense it. You also begin to be able to sense when things are going to move in an unexpected direction, and of course you have to be ready to move with that unstructured flow."

Mr. Ferris and Miss Peiser are not the sort of folk purists who try to find isolated communities that have been relatively unsullied by outside influences. "Give My Poor Heart Ease" is a particularly valuable film on the blues because it sketches a continuum, from the place of semiprofessional bluesmen in rural Mississippi to the show-business world of B. B. King, a successful blues star. In the course of the 20-minute film, a rural barber, a prisoner at the notorious Parchman Farm, and a clothing salesman on Memphis's Beale Street offer their own interpretations of what it means to sing and have the blues.

Part of a Series

"Two Black Churches" contrasts services at a Baptist church in Rose Hill, Miss., where old hymn tunes from the Rev. Isaac Watts's hymnal are sung, with the more contemporary and unrestrained services at the St. James United Free Will Baptist Church in New Haven. The minister of the urban church characterizes worship in terms of "grooving" and "doing our thing," and the music is provided by electric guitars and a choir. At the end of the New Haven service there is a "laying on of hands" sequence in which the minister uses upper spinal manipulation to make a young man get out of a wheelchair and walk. The minister's wife begins to gyrate uncontrollably in the throes of spirit possession. According to a review of this film in the Journal of American Folklore, "the scenes of spirit possession and healing . . . are outstanding, and the camera work in them is brilliant."

The films by Mr. Ferris and Miss Peiser are part of a continuing series of showings of independently made social documentaries, the What's Happening Series. All the showings are on Tuesdays, at noon at the Donnell Library and at 6 P.M. at the Museum of Modern Art. Bill Ferris feels that the showing of such films is particularly important.

"The voices of the people in these films are normally invisible to the media," he says. "You don't see or hear them on network television, rarely on public television, never in the movies or on the radio. You can look at them purely as entertainment, but they're also a means of leading into a more-sophisticated view of what it means to be a member of a folk or minority culture in America."

Fannie Bell Chapman

"The whole dimension of faith healing wasn't evident until we were already filming."

1977 Ap 5, 40:2

Poor Little Girl

AUDREY ROSE, directed by Robert Wise; screenplay by Frank De Felitta, based on his novel; produced by Joe Wizan and Mr. De Felitta; director of photography, Victor J. Kemper; music, Michael Small; editor, Carl Kress; distributed by United Artists. Running time: 113 minutes. At Loews State 2, Broadway at 45th Street; Loew's Cine, Third Avenue near 86th Street and UA Eastside Cinema, Third Avenue at 55th Street. This film has been rated PG.

Janice Templeton	Marsha Mason
Elliot Hoover	Anthony Hopkins
Bill Templeton	John Beck
Ivy Templeton	Susan Swift
Dr. Steven Lipscomb	Norman Lloyd
Scott Velie	John Hillerman
Brice Mack	Robert Walden
Judge Langley	Philip Sterling
Mary Lou Sides	Ivy Jones
Russ Rothman	Stephen Pearlman
Maharishi Gupta Pradesh	Aly Wassil
Mother Veronica	Mary Jackson

By VINCENT CANBY

"AUDREY ROSE" is supposed to be about reincarnation, but it's really about the potentially dangerous side effects when a soul passes from one body to another without a proper interval. Lightheadedness, depression, disorientation and worse—they sound like the warnings on a bottle of prescription tranquilizers.

The new film, directed by Robert

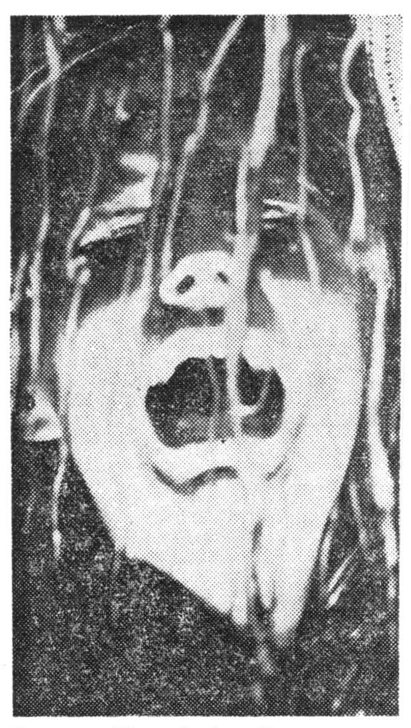

Susan Swift as Audrey Rose

Wise with a perfectly grave face, is about Ivy, who, in 1965 at the age of 5, was killed with her mother in an automobile accident in Pittsburgh and two minutes later was born again in New York and was named Audrey Rose, the daughter of upwardly mobile parents who live in the Hotel Des Artistes.

Two minutes, this film clearly understands, are not enough time for anyone, least of all poor little Ivy, to have a karma cleaned, pressed and packed and still arrive in New York from Pittsburgh on schedule. No wonder Ivy/Audrey Rose is a mess.

When the movie begins, Audrey Rose is 11 years old and pretty as a picture, but she has these dreadful nightmares about being in a fiery auto accident. They are particularly severe when her birthday rolls around. She beats her head hysterically against rain-splattered windows and burns her hands on cold radiators, behaving more or less like someone possessed.

"Audrey Rose," which opened at three theaters yesterday, is the first movie to expose ineptitude in the traffic-managing of domestic souls. It's a subject that might well be investigated by the Interstate Commerce Commission because the job has been bungled by Mr. Wise and Frank De Felitta, the man who wrote the screenplay and the best-selling novel on which it's based.

On closer examination, though, "Audrey Rose" turns out to be less about the side effects of all-too-hasty soul transfers than a demonstration of those dangers. The soul of the movie is that of "The Exorcist" instantly recycled.

Playing the Ellen Burstyn role is another fine actress who is wasted—Marsha Mason—while Anthony Hopkins, the English actor who was so splendid on the stage in "Equus," plays the role of the exorcist, and he's terrible. Actually he's not an exorcist, but the father of the long-dead Ivy. He is a scientist who has been to India to study up on souls and knows what to do to separate Ivy from Audrey Rose.

The father of the little girl in "The Exorcist" remained off screen, and Audrey Rose's father, as played by John Beck, is such a nonentity that it amounts to the same thing. It even appears that Susan Swift, who has the title role, has been photographed to resemble Linda Blair at her most bedeviled. I'd like to know the exact hour and minute this movie was born.

I suppose that's not really important, but it is depressing to see money and intelligence thrown away on material of this hustling, completely unimaginative sort. Mr. Wise does nothing to transform it. Instead he meets every cliché of the script with one of his own, and even manages to pull off a climactic courtroom scene of absolutely no suspense. That's not easy.

"Audrey Rose," which has been rated PG ("Parental Guidance Suggested"), contains an unpleasant sequence in which the troubled heroine attempts to crawl into a bonfire.

1977 Ap 7, C21:4

DEMON SEED, directed by Donald Cammell; screenplay by Robert Jaffe and Roger O. Hirson, based on the novel by Dean R. Koontz; produced by Herb Jaffe; music, Jerry Fielding; director of photography, Bill Butler; editor, Francisco Mazzola; distributed by United Artists. Running time: 95 minutes. At the Criterion Theater, Broadway at 44th Street, and other theaters. This film has been rated R.

Susan Harris	Julie Christie
Alex Harris	Fritz Weaver
Walter Gabler	Gerrit Graham
Petrosian	Berry Kroeger
Soon Yen	Lisa Lu
Cameron	Larry J. Blake
Royce	John O'Leary
Mokri	Alfred Dennis
Warner	David Roberts
Baby	Tiffany Potter
Baby	Felix Silla

By VINCENT CANBY

"Demon Seed," which opened yesterday at the Criterion and other theaters, is gadget-happy American moviemaking at its most ponderously silly.

A group of scientists in Southern California works eight years to build an artificial intelligence system that contains all the knowledge of the world and that thinks for itself. They call it "Proteus Four" and intend to use it as "the ultimate instrument of financial power," but Proteus Four has other ideas.

One day, after finding a cure for leukemia, Proteus Four falls in love. Aware that he is in something approximating mortal danger (that the scientists will pull his plug when they realize how independent he is), he desires to have a child to carry on his knowledge and his work. Among other things, he tells us in his gravelly voice that he is "interested in the uncertain future of seashores, deserts and children." Proteus Four isn't all bad but he gets his priorities mixed up.

•

"Demon Seed" is virtually a one-woman, one-computer movie. It's about Proteus Four's courtship and rape of Susan Harris, a pretty, suitably bewildered psychiatrist played by Julie Christie. All this happens after Susan and her husband, Alex (Fritz Weaver), Proteus Four's chief designer, have split and Alex has made the mistake of leaving Susan alone in their house with an open computer terminal connected to Proteus Four.

Miss Christie is too sensible an actress to be able to look frightened under the circumstances of her imprisonment. Most of the time she just looks bloody impatient, as the computer, with the help of an automated wheelchair and electric eyes that open and close doors, keeps her prisoner, makes medical tests on her and busies himself with creaing his own—are you ready?—demon seed.

Donald Cammell, a painter who was the co-director (with Nicholas Roeg) of "Performance," directed "Demon Seed" with more apparent interest in the machinery of the movie than in its sense. Some of this machinery is quite impressive, including the large metal tetrahedron that becomes the material manifestation of Proteus Four.

Yet most of these effects are more mind-depressing than mind-expanding. At best, they are unintentionally funny, as in a sequence in which the movie attempts to find video-image equivalents to a woman's feelings as she reaches the peak of pleasure with a computer. For those of us who've seen "2001," it looks as if she were landing on Jupiter.

The screenplay was written by Robert Jaffe and Roger O. Hirson with no humor and a great deal of self-consciousness of the sort that seeks to separate the writers from what they've written. "This is ridiculous," someone says desperately at one point, or, says another, "At the risk of sounding simplistic. . . ." before he goes on to sound simplistic. Miss Christie and Mr. Weaver are bearable and two actors were used to play the computer-baby. Both look like brass-dipped Mickey Rooneys.

1977 Ap 9, 11:1

The Japanese Film Festival

By JOAN MELLEN

The Japanese film returns to New York today with the Regency theater's opening of a festival of 51 movies ranging from masterpieces by Kurosawa, Ozu and Mizoguchi to potboilers featuring the superhuman exploits of a blind samurai named Zatoichi. Japanese movies nearly always involve a search for identity—what it means to be a Japanese and how the "Japanese spirit" may be recovered after a century of westernization and industrial development. Often violent, sensual

Joan Mellen, who teaches film at Temple University, is the author of "Voices From the Japanese Cinema" and "The Waves at Genji's Door: Japan Through Its Cinema."

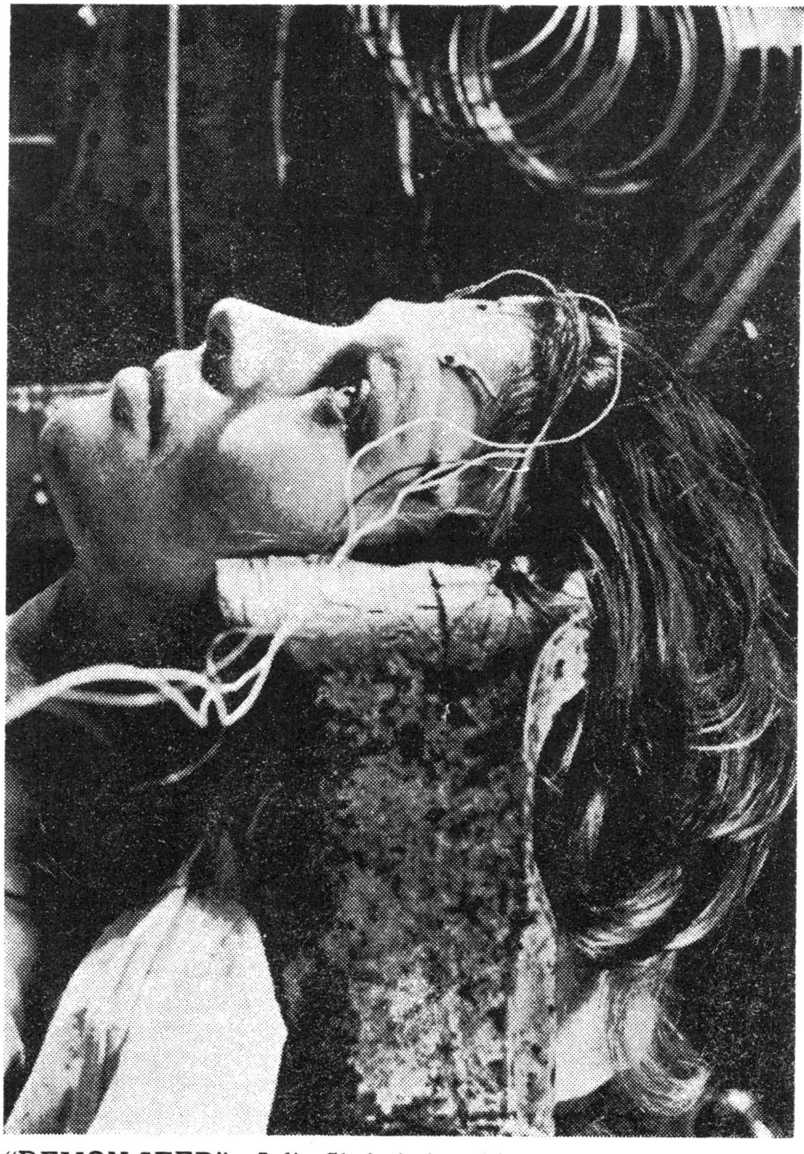

"DEMON SEED"—Julie Christie is subjected to brainwashing by an amorous computer in Donald Cammell's science-fiction film.

Toshiro Mifune stands by for action in "Yojimbo," one of 51 Japanese films to be shown at the Regency.

and intensely passionate, Japanese films are about people struggling within alien circumstances to remain true to an authentically Japanese style of life always in danger of being lost and submerged beneath the frantic pace of commercial life in contemporary Japan.

Unlike the American or European director, the Japanese filmmaker often sees himself as a prophet and savior, a cinematic D. H. Lawrence who, through his art, quests for the truth about how to live. In the 50's, in a trilogy like Inagaki's "Samurai," *bushido*— the ethical code of the samurai—is perceived as the spiritual core which expresses Japan of the present at its best. The supremely loyal retainer, forever testing his self-control and bathing in cold streams to tame unruly sexual desire, was not felt to be merely an antiquated relic of medieval times equivalent to our Sir Lancelot, Percival or King Arthur. The truths he discovered could fortify post-war Japanese as well.

•

The Japanese director, from the conservative Ozu to the daring Oshima, whose latest film is the pornographic "In the Realm of the Senses," urgently hopes to bring the Japanese back to the most vital of their traditions. The directors differ only in *which* of those past values they find most purely Japanese, whether those of the self-contained samurai world so beloved by a novelist like Mishima or values belonging to an earlier, more primitive Japan. In "The Woman in the Dunes" the hero leaves behind his urban "civilized" existence, choosing to spend the remainder of his life in an isolated rural community.

In "Tokyo Story," "The Flavor of Green Tea Over Rice" and "An Autumn Afternoon," all included in this program, Ozu finds the essence of Japanese identity in the traditional Japanese family and the delicacy of feeling it permits between its members, made possible by *enryo* or the restraint of one's personal demands for the sake of the harmony of the group. Oshima, of the next generation, focuses in "The Ceremony"—happily included in this restrospective—on the Japanese family as a threat to the freedom of the individual.

•

History comes alive in these films because it is so real, so coexistent with the present for the Japanese. The finest Japanese movies, like "Seven Samurai," take place at moments of historical transition when the whole world seems to be in upheaval, with the old dying out and the new not yet securely defined. "Seven Samurai" itself is actually about six *ronin*, or masterless samurai, retainers without a job, like medieval knights no longer attached to a castle. Those who truly live by the samurai ethic choose to aid the weak. Only in this way can they justify their continued existence in a society where they fulfill no useful productive function. In his closing scene, Kurosawa, full of nostalgia over the passing of the noble samurai, allows his hero, who has just overcome a passel of bandits, to murmur, "again we're defeated. The winners are those farmers, not us." "Seven Samurai" may be the most beautiful film elegy to the passing of a social group. The uncut 3-hour-and-28-minute version, to be shown at the Regency, is considered by many critics to be one of the finest examples of film art.

By the early 17th century, when the Tokugawa family began their rule of Japan with a peace which would last until 1867, the days of the samurai were already numbered. From the many sword-slashing films which are included in this retrospective, to the more serious period films—such as Kobayashi's "Hara Kiri"—in which important historical issues are always raised, the hero is aware that he is already obsolete. This perception suffuses the samurai film, adding a poignancy to the most outrageous exploits and providing the director with an opportunity to show the psychological wear and tear on a proud warrior confident of his social importance yet conscious that his day is done. It is in part his fury over this historical inevitability which leads to so much blood-splashing in the run-of-the-mill *chambara*, or sword film. The hero, a potent man, feels the ground giving way beneath his feet, and his impulse is sometimes to express his despair in boundless cruelty and destruction.

Apart from 1868, the date of the Meiji Restoration when feudalism was outlawed, the other significant historical moment during which so many classic Japanese films are set is immediately after World War II. The defeat of the militarists brought an end to decades of political repression and was accompanied by an outpouring of creative energy in film. Aided by the American Occupation which officially encouraged directors to make films in protest against feudal remnants in their culture —one of its edicts actually called for films about the emancipation of women —a renaissance of the Japanese film began in 1946 and continued into the 1960's. The country suffered famine and moral chaos as the Japanese sought to wed their style of life to a concern for the liberty of the individual who was to be valued for himself, apart from his function as a member of a group. The masterpiece depicting this struggle was Kurosawa's "Ikiru," with its bureaucrat-hero whose affliction with terminal stomach cancer leads him to search in his remaining months for a reason "to live," the literal translation of the film's title.

Watanabe's quest takes him to a tawdry, westernized nighttown of strippers, boozers and clip joints for the lonely, to a friendship with a very young woman co-worker, much to the chagrin of his rigid son and selfish daughter-in-law. Finally, it leads him to the first self-assertions of his life, as he defies his superiors to help a group of neighborhood women build a playground on the site of a swampy ditch.

The goal seems simple, even sentimental, yet to break through the red tape of paperwork, Kurosawa's hero must dare to do what only a postwar Japanese could. Watanabe defies the age-old Japanese decorum which decrees that an inferior never question the decisions of his superiors. When Watanabe asks the callow Deputy Mayor to "reconsider" his rejection of the playground, the very foundation upon which Japanese society has functioned for centuries begins to totter. The analagous moment in western drama would be Ibsen's Nora slamming her door in "A Doll's House." Watanabe bows, he looks uncomfortable, but he stands his ground; it seems to the Japanese audience as if history were being made on the screen, producing a most exhilarating experience, Kurosawa, like so many directors after the war, urges the Japanese to place a new, greater value on individual initiative and judgment and less unqualified faith in obedience to authority and obeisance to precedent.

Antiwar films have been few and far between in the United States, from "All Quiet on the Western Front" to "Paths of Glory" to "Dr. Strangelove" to "Mash," seeming to come but once in a decade. But the antiwar film flourished in the Japan of the 50's, fierce in its determination to see the Japanese soldier himself as a victim, abandoned on the Pacific Islands with neither food nor medical supplies, and ordered to commit suicide by superior officers when time ran out. Kon Ichikawa, in the expressionistic "Fire on the Plain," to be shown in this series, finds the Japanese soldier reduced to cannibalism. Crazed and horrified, the hero, Private Tamura, kills his less scrupulous companion who has become an expert butcher. He then walks out onto the open plain to his death. The real horror for Ichikawa is not merely the eating of human flesh, which is portrayed as an aberration of the desperate, but the atrocity of war itself.

One of the rarest viewing opportunities of this festival is Masaki Kobayashi's antiwar trilogy "The Human Condition," with its hero Kaji, so beloved by Japanese audiences that people wrote to Kobayashi begging him to allow Kaji to survive at the end of Part III. Played by Tatsuya Nakadai, familiar to Western audiences as the samurai hero of "Hara Kiri," Kaji enacts the great moral issues of the war. As labor supervisor at a Chinese prisoner of war camp, can he be both a compassionate man and a loyal Japanese? He learns that he cannot. Tortured by the secret police, he finds himself cannon fodder at the front, where officers protect themselves and raw recruits are sent out armed only with rifles against the superior tanks and artillery of the enemy. Captured by the Russians in Part III, Kaji, risking his life for a weaker friend, is dubbed a "fascist samurai." The Japanese prisoners must endure slave labor for the Russians, just as they had ordered the Chinese to serve them. His faith in such socialism as an alternative for a new Japan shattered, Kaji must die, lost spiritually as he literally freezes to death amid the ice and snow of Manchuria.

The Japanese became masters of the wide screen in the late 50's, creating grand epic landscapes appropriate to the quest of heroes like Kaji for the key to a revitalization of their culture. To depict his satire of one samurai's impossible stand against the coming commercialization of Japan, Kurosawa uses CinemaScope to the same effect in his brilliant "Yojimbo." In battle with authority and with a world he will not be able to influence, Toshiro Mifune plays a *ronin* who at times appears very small within the wide screen, addicted as he is to the mannerism of hunching his shoulders, as if to ward off a hostile universe. Yet, through the grandeur of his absurd efforts to improve a milieu so recalcitrant to humane concerns he, like Kaji, seems to our eyes even more valuable for his ultimate defeat.

The classics of Kurosawa and Kobayashi, with their moral and historical focus, predominate in this series. The three Ozu films take us closer to the individual. Men and women are invariably placed by Ozu in the bosom of the family. When its harmonies remain intact, it is here that Ozu's characters are most fully themselves. Of particular interest is a little-seen Ozu film, "The Flavor of Green Tea Over Rice," about how a restless wife comes to appreciate her seemingly dull, taciturn husand. Ozu's "An Autumn Afternoon" finds a widowed father reconciling himself to the marriage of his daughter with that quintessential emotion so savored by the Japanese, *mono no aware*, the sweet sense of the transience of all earthly things. It is also the mood at the end of his masterpiece, "Tokyo Story." The last shots, of a river on which a passing boat steams by—images of the inevitability of time and change—soothe us with their incontrovertibility and immunity to human selfishness.

But if Ozu is present, so are the angry young men of the following generation, who, like Shinoda, could make a complex film about gangland honor "Pale Flower" or, like Oshima, unfold the connections between Japanese industrialists, militarists and the patriarchal family. Oshima's "The Ceremony" must be seen, if only for its satiric sequence in which the hero's brutal grandfather insists that he go through with his marriage ceremony even though the bride has failed to show up for the wedding; the absent young woman is toasted by family members as a pure Japanese girl "free of the taint of foreign postwar influences." When postwar Japan promises to be as stifling as the past, the most accomplished young member of the family decides to kill himself and put an end to the powerful Sakurada line.

Missing only from the Regency's varied collection are those passionate Japanese films protesting the subjugation of women, from Mizoguchi's "The Life of Oharu" to Hani's "She and He" and Naruse's "When a Woman Ascends the Stairs." We do have from Mizoguchi, the greatest stylist of all Japanese directors, his lyrical biography of the famous woodblock printmaker Utamaro ("Utamaro and His Five Women"), as well as "Sancho the Bailiff," with its integration of anti-feudal protest and visual magnificence. In "Sancho the Bailiff," an epic set in the 11th century, just before the era of the samurai, an aristocratic brother and sister are kidnapped into a slave camp where they learn how rare it is for people to abide by their benevolent father's credo: "Without mercy a man is like a beast. Be sympathetic to others. Men are created equal." As with all Japanese films, past collides with present. Mizoguchi's point is aimed, of course, at his contemporary audience, encouraged to examine themselves, if gently, through the cushioning lens of the past.

Classic Japanese films like "Seven Samurai," "Ikiru," "Tokyo Story" and "Sancho the Bailiff" are seen almost as infrequently in Japan as they are in the United States. For a look at the kind of popular, lower-middle-class domestic soap opera that does make money, see "Tora-San the Intellectual," if for sociological interest alone. Nearly all Japanese films are long (at least two hours), and sometimes they seem slow. Often they are demanding, as we must always adjust to their unique cultural settings, even with films whose themes—the marriage of a daughter, the struggle for justice, the horrors of industrialization—are indeed familiar. But the Japanese film almost always justifies the effort. And—as "Rashomon," another welcome revival, indicates—the best of these films provide us with richer visual experiences than the films of any other nation. ■

1977 Ap 10, II:19:1

"3 WOMEN"—Sissy Spacek gets set to swill down a stein of beer as Shelley Duvall, her new roommate, looks on with despair.

WOMEN, directed, written and produced by Robert Altman; editor, Dennis Hill; director of photography, Chuch Rosher; music, Gerald Busby; a Lions Gate Films production, distributed by 20th Century-Fox. Running time: 125 minutes. At the Coronet Theater, Third Avenue near 59th Street. This film has been rated PG.

Millie Lammoreaux .... Shelley Duvall
Pinky Rose .... Sissy Spacek
Willie Hart .... Janice Rule
Edgar Hart .... Robert Fortier
Mrs. Rose .... Ruth Nelson
Mr. Rose .... John Cromwell
Mrs. Bunweill .... Sierra Pecheur
Dr. Maas .... Craig Richard Nelson
Doris .... Maysie Hoy
Alcira .... Belita Moreno
Polly .... Leslie Ann Hudson
Peggy .... Patricia Ann Hudson
Deidre .... Beverly Ross
Dr. Norton .... John Davey

By VINCENT CANBY

Millie Lammoreaux is a joke. Her conversation is a confusion of clichés, brand names and affectations. "I'm famous for my dinner parties," she might say, or, "This is my parking space. It's the best one," as if today's Cosmopolitan Girls were graded on their parking spaces as well as on their grooming. Millie is nothing if not perfectly groomed, though when she hops into her car to go cruising for men she never quite succeeds in pulling all of her skirt inside. A bit always hangs out the door, like a distress pennant.

Millie Lammoreaux is the central figure in Robert Altman's funny, moving new film, "3 Women," and, as played as well as largely created by Shelley Duvall, she's one of the most memorable characterizations Mr. Altman has ever given us. Miss Duvall's large, round dark eyes are windows through which a tiny creature inside looks out upon a world whose complete disinterest Millie Lammoreaux refuses to accept.

•

Mr. Altman says that "3 Women," which he wrote, directed and produced, had its origins in a dream he had in which he saw two young women in a desert setting. Ordinarily, I'm not sure that we should ever know too much about the particular inspiration for any work of fiction. Such knowledge has a way of sidetracking us from the work itself, or of prompting us to read into it things that are no longer there.

It's apropriate in this case, though, since "3 Women" is still a dream—Mr. Altman's—and, like a dream, it is most mysterious and allusive when it appears to be most precise and direct, when its images are of the recognizable world unretouched (as happens in the film from time to time) by camera filters or lab technicians.

It's been a moviemaker's convention for a long time to smear Vaseline around the edges of an image, or to blur it in some other way, to indicate a dream, even though an image of blinding clarity more accurately reflects the condensed nature of the dream experience, when, for example, without the slightest hesitation, we may accept one person as being two different people at the same time. Logic is beside the point in dreams.

Because "3 Women" is a dream, one must know what happens before one attempts to find out what it's about. What happens, briefly, is this:

Millie Lammoreaux, a physical therapist in a Palm Springs spa for old folks with fat incomes, finds herself the adored object of another young therapist who calls herself Pinky Rose (Sissy Spacek). Pinky seems to have no past of her own, not even a Social Security number. At first, it seems that Pinky might be retarded but then it's apparent she's simply a blank, possessing nothing but her worshipful appreciation of Millie.

Millie accepts Pinky's praise and affection as if she'd always been a prom queen instead of the figure of ridicule she really is, both at work and at the Purple Sage Apartments, the singles complex where she lives and that Pinky comes to share with her. Pinky doesn't notice the snubs given to Millie. She doesn't envy Millie. Because she loves Millie — idolizes her — she comes to *be* her, to take over her life being both herself and Millie.

The third woman in the composition is a reclusive painter named Willie Hart (Janice Rule), the wife of a philandering, middle-aged, ex-stunt man (Robert Fortier) and the owner, with her husband, of the seedy desert recreation area where Millie likes to hang out and look for men.

In the course of the film, in sequences that sometimes seem absolutely natural and at other times absurdist, these three women merge into one person, who is mother, daughter and granddaughter, isolated but serenely self-sufficient.

Now, I suppose, someone is bound to ask what it really is about. I'm not sure, but there are a number of possibilities. Since it is the moviemaker's dream more than that of the characters within, it seems to be a consideration of today's women. It's not a narrative in any strict sense but a contemplation of three stages of a woman's life by a man who appreciates women and may not be without a bit of guilt. It's also about youth and age and (as are all Altman films) about the quality of American life. Let it go at that and don't worry too much.

•

Having no easily discernible surface logic, "3 Women" must depend on internal logic, and this only falters when Mr. Altman loads his dream with more or less conventional dreams within, when we are given superimposed images, standard nightmare visions and images seen through water. This fanciness is unnecessary. "3 Women" is most strange and poetic when it's played straight, as when poor Millie one night comes upon an elderly couple making love, or when someone says cheerily of a character in a deep coma, "I'm sure she'll wake up when she sees you."

Logic has nothing to do with films' effeciveness, though it does with all of the performances, beginning with Miss Duvall's. In this film Miss Spacek adds a new dimension of eeriness to the waif she played so effectively in "Carrie." Also noteworthy are Miss Rule, Mr. Fortier and veteran actor-director John Cromwell and his real-life wife, Ruth Nelson, who play Pinky's possible parents.

•

"3 Women," which has been rated PG ("Parental Guidance Suggested"), contains some nudity and one scene of discreetly photographed sexual intercourse.

1977 Ap 11, 40:1

A FESTIVAL OF THE UNRECOGNIZED

By VINCENT CANBY

FILM FESTIVALS are the worst possible circumstances in which to see movies that are of somewhat less than spellbinding interest. The competition for our attention at a festival, as well as the expectations created by the nature of a festival (which, I always assume, should be a celebration), guarantees a certain number of disappointments. Truly good movies are no problem. They are as tough as they are rare. They hold up no matter what goes on around them while lesser, even quite decent movies suffer dearly. They are vulnerable. It's as if mediocrity were a contagious disease.

•

These thoughts are prompted by the sixth annual New Directors/New Films series starting today at the Museum of Modern Art. At this writing I've seen six of the 12 films that will be shown in the minifestival, sponsored by the Film Society of Lincoln Center and the museum's film department, but I haven't yet seen one that could be said to make the entire occasion worth the time, effort and funding that have gone into it.

It's unfortunate that film festivals are as locked into annual models as Detroit. Some years it might be better to pass — to admit that the festival material simply wasn't there.

Because the films in this series have no common denominator other than that each is the work of as yet unrecognized film makers, I deal with them separately in the chronological order in which they'll be screened at the museum.

•

"When Joseph Returns" (today at 6 P.M., Sunday at 8:30 P.M.) is an unsentimental Hungarian film about the edgy relationship between a middle-aged woman and her young, restless daughter-in-law when the son/husband goes to sea for six months. The film, directed and written by Zsolt Kesdi Kovacs, is beautifully acted by Lili Monori as the younger woman and Eva Ruttkai as the mother-in-law, and though the outcome is never in doubt, the manner in which the two women arrive at mutual understanding is surprisingly harrowing in its close-up details.

The girl, whose life had previously been more or less determined by equal doses of television and sex, is a slob, though an extremely pretty one, a person who never stands unsupported if there's a wall to lean against. At first she misses her husband, then resents his absence and eventually she tears loose to enjoy herself, which, of course, she doesn't. "When Joseph Returns" is the sober sort of movie that one can admire without really liking it a lot.

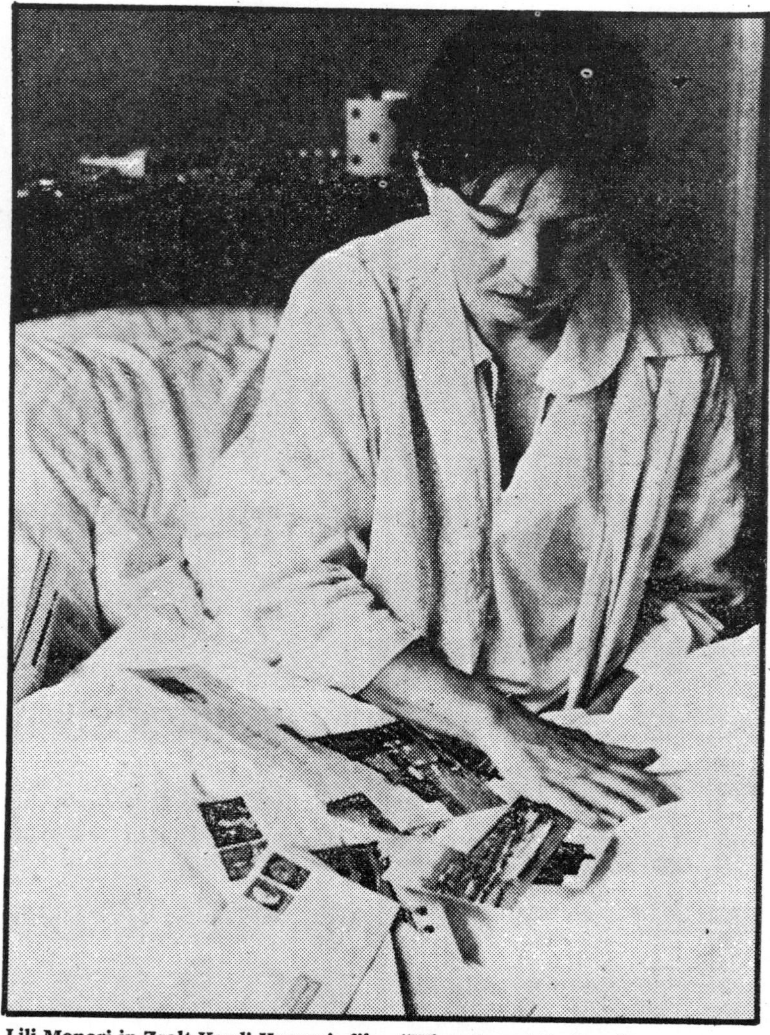

Lili Monori in Zsolt Kezdi Kovacs's film, "When Joseph Returns"
The sober sort of movie that one can admire without really liking it a lot

•

"The First Swallow" (today at 8:30 P.M., Sunday at 6 P.M.) has the determined jollity of a political operetta. The Russian (Georgian) film, directed by Nana Mchedlidze, is about the efforts of some ferociously quaint Georgian men to organize themselves into a respectable soccer team at the turn of the century, but if you think that's all it's about, you are wrong. The fellow who pulls the team together and keeps their spirits up is a dead-ringer for Uncle Joe Stalin. The acting and often epic-looking photography are terrible.

•

"11x14" (Saturday at 8:30 P.M. and Monday at 6 P.M.) is an independent American film, "conceived and executed' (say the credits) by James Benning. The objective of the film, according to Mr. Benning, is "to formulate a number of ideas using methods that are conventionally thought to be contradictory to the ideas themselves. The contradictions are used to develop a continual feeling of paradox." For paradox read impatience.

Mr. Benning's way of creating a new narrative form is to dispense with narrative completely. The film is composed of fragmentary scenes sometimes shot with a stationary camera, of landscape, viaducts, highways, fields, people getting in and out of automobiles, two women making love, a number of golfers teeing off, each in his/her turn.

Though Mr. Benning claims to have conceived and then executed his movie, I suspect it was made the other way around. "11 x 14" looks to have been assembled from available fragments, some not very well photographed, and then justified by program notes on the order of "'11 x 14' is also an attempt to create spherical time-space. The editing structure emphasizes the inherent linear quality of film. . . ."

•

"Anatomy of A Relationship" (Tuesday at 6 P.M. and next Friday at 8:30 P.M.) is a funny French film, jointly directed by Antonietta Pizzorno and Luc Moullet, in which a liberated young woman (Christine Herbert) and her cheerfully chauvinist lover (Mr. Moullet) try to reach some accord on her demands that she too receive sexual satisfaction. He calls himself "natural." She sniffs that he is only "traditional."

Mr. Moullet is especially comic as he attempts to deal with a girl who is completely normal except for saying things like "I feel I'm in touch with my body again." He vows to give up sex for bicycling, that being a relationship he can "dominate," but it's not really the same thing. As he rides around Paris he finds himself envying all nonintellectuals who, in his fantasies, never have sex hang-ups. The movie goes a bit self-conscious at the end when the actors discuss their roles with the director, but until then it's true comedy.

"Coming of Age" (Tuesday at 8:30 P.M. and next Friday at 6 P.M.) is an East German film directed by a young Iranian, Sohrab Shahid Saless, with the sort of obsessive concern for literal detail that, with repetition, is meant to become a kind of poetry. The movie never quite succeeds—one is never unaware of its composition—though it is nicely acted by 9-year-old Mike Henning, who, in the course of things, comes to realize that his mother (Eva Manhardt) is a whore.

•

"Local Color" (Wednesday at 8:30 P.M. and Saturday, April 23 at 6 P.M.) is a failed attempt to make a camp melodrama in the style of the Kuchar brothers. It's the work of Mark Rappaport, a fellow who all too often means to be facetious, as if he believed consciously heavy-handed parodies of soap opera could somehow find layers of truth behind the jokes. They don't. The purposely dense plot concerns, among others, a set of incestuous twins, an amorous barber and the barber's dissatisfied wife.

One actress—Jane Campbell—almost makes the film sit-throughable, though. Looking like a young Alice Ghostley in her "Boston Beguine" days, her mouth always turned down, she wears an expression of earnest reproach that, for reasons that I don't understand, seems very funny under the circumstances. The rest of the film, however, is more than a teeny tiny bit precious.

1977 Ap 15, C10:3

THE BEAST, directed by Walerian Borowczyk; screenplay (French with English subtitles) by Mr. Borowczyk; photography, Bernard Daillencourt and Marcel Grigon; cameraman, Noel Very; produced by Anatole Dauman; distributed by Jayson Allen. At the 59th Street East and Cinerama I Theaters. Running time: 100 minutes. This film has been rated X.

Romilda de l'Esperance .... Sirpa Lane
Lucy Broadhurst .... Lisbeth Hummerl
Virgina Broadhurst .... Elisabth Kaza
Mathurin de l'Esperance ...... Pierre Benedietti
Marquis Pierre de l'Esperance ...... Guy Treian

By GUY FLATLEY

A flabby-fleshed, perverted priest plants a soggy kiss on the lips of a passive, doleful-eyed adolescent, pops a sweet into the boy's mouth and greedily kisses him again. Later the good father will accept a bribe and agree to lie to his religious superior, to say that he has baptized a certain notorious heathen, thus paving the way for his marriage to a wealthy young woman. It could be a scene from Luis Buñuel at his most scathingly sacrilegious, but the passion and wit are missing, the vigor and the venom.

•

Sunlight floods the branches of a forest as a tense maiden with silvery tresses picks her way gingerly along a leaf-strewn path. It could be a scene from Bo Widerberg in prettily pastoral mood, but the pulsating music on the soundtrack is Scarlatti, not Mozart, and the presumably pure wanderer is soon to shed her powdered wig and fragile frock and tumble into an illicit, bittersweet liaison with a lover far more forceful, and furry, than any man ever to stir the dreams of Elvira Madigan, or even Jessica Lange in "King Kong."

The syrupy, hypocritical prelate and the lascivious lass with the deceptively delicate air represent flip sides of a tarnished coin in "The Beast," a sleazy blend of fairy tale, Freudian foolishness and Eighth Avenue peep show. Written and directed by Walerian Borowczyk—a Polish émigré to Paris who has been praised for such bizarrely erotic works as "Immoral Tales" and "Story of Sin"—this unsavory descent into black comedy focuses on the scheme of a decadent marquis to marry off his only son —an imbecilic oat who is obesessed with the mating habits of horses —to a stunning, sexually repressed heiress, a blond nitwit given to elaborate masturbatory fantasies, one of which centers on a rumored relationship between an ancestor of her prospective husband and a rapacious creature of the forest.

There are occasional flashes of humor in "The Beast." For the most part, however, Mr. Borowczyk's handling of his actors and his themes is sledgehammer-heavy, painfully in keeping with his evident contempt for humanity. If there is a message in "The Beast," it is to be found in the leeringly prolonged scenes of copulation and oral sex between the wanton woman and the panting animal. And that message is unfit for man or beast.

1977 Ap 16, 14:4

JABBERWOCKY, directed by Terry Gilliam; screenplay by Charles Alverson and Mr. Gilliam; produced by Sandy Lieberson; director of photography, Terry Bedford; editor, Michael Bradsell; music, De Wolfe; an Umbrella Entertainment production, distributed by Cinema 5. Running time: 104 minutes. At the Cinema 1 Theater, Third Avenue near 60th Street. This film has not been rated.

Dennis Cooper	Michael Palin
King Bruno	Max Wall
Princess	Deborah Fallender
Chamberlain	John Le Mesúrier
Griselda Fishfinger	Annette Badland
Mr. Fishfinger	Warren Mitchell
Mrs. Fishfinger	Brenda Cowling
Squire	Harry H. Corbett
Other squire	Rodney Bewes
Landlord	Bernard Bresslaw
Betsy	Alexandra Dane
Bishop	Derek Francis
First merchant	Peter Cellier
Second merchant	Frank Williams
Third merchant	Anthony Carrick
Mr. Cooper Senior	Paul Curran
Poacher	Terry Jones

By VINCENT CANBY

The time is the mythic long-ago, a period after the eclipse of Camelot, but not yet the time of recorded history. The place is the kingdom of Bruno The Questionable, who is not a bad tyrant under the circumstances. Bruno's realm is being ravaged by a monster so terrible that the sight of it once turned an old peasant's teeth snow-white over night.

Who will slay the monster to restore law and disorder, thus to win half of the Princess's hand and all of the kingdom (or perhaps it's the other way around)? From the opening sequence of "Jabberwocky," there's no doubt but that it must be Dennis-the-cooper's-son. Dennis (Michael Palin), disowned by his father in an embarrassing deathbed speech (his father was out of sorts), is the quintessential naif. Being profoundly and cheerfully stupid, slavishly faithful to the obese Griselda, polite in all situations, and ever optimistic, Dennis is fate's triumphant plaything.

He is also the hero of "Jabberwocky," the most marvelously demented British comedy to come along since "Monty Python and The Holy Grail," to which "Jabberwocky" is a sort of stepson. The film, which opened yesterday at the Cinema 1, was directed by Terry Gilliam, who co-directed "The Holy Grail" and is, like Mr. Palin, a member of the group that calls itself Monty Python's Flying Circus.

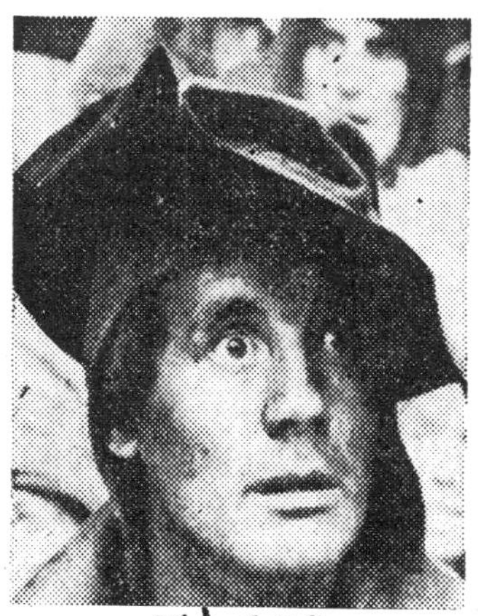

Michael Palin
The quintessential naif

Taking as their inspiration some lines from Lewis Carroll's "Through The Looking-Glass," ("Beware the Jabberwock (my son!/The jaws that bite, the claws that catch. . . ."), Mr. Gilliam and Charles Alverson, with whom he collaborated on the screenplay, have written a wickedly literate spoof of everything from "Jaws" through "Ivanhoe" to "The Faerie Queen."

It's a monster film with heart, a movie romance with bite, a costume picture without zippers, and a comedy with more blood and gore than Sam Peckinpah would dare use to dramatize the decline and fall of the entire West.

The world through which Dennis stumbles ever upward is an unending landscape of misery, torture, filth, slop buckets, sudden death, and all-round decay—"Jabberwocky's" comment on movie makers' comparatively recent obsession with showing us the past as it supposedly really was.

Mr. Palin's Dennis is a fully realized comic character as much because he seems a mite old to be so innocent as because of his sturdy faith in his own small goals. All Dennis wants to do is to make his way enough to be able to claim the hand of the grouchy, overfed Griselda, but fortune keeps smiling on him. By chance he finds himself squire to the knight chosen to slay the monster, and eventually the sole survivor of the battle with a creature that looks like something out of a medieval Sesame Street.

The movie's gags are nonstop, both verbal and visual, with lots of cross-references. "At last," proclaim the movie's ads, "a movie for the squeamish!" though some audiences may find the blood and scatology difficult to take. If there's anything unpleasant to be walked under or stepped into, Dennis will find it.

Supporting Mr. Palin are a number of excellent character actors, many of whom are unknown to me. They include Max Wall as King Bruno, Warren Mitchell as Dennis's would-be father-in-law, and Harry H. Corbett as a squire who's fallen upon bad times. The performances are fine, but even more remarkable for a comedy of this sort are Roy Smith's stylish production design and the camera work of Terry Bedford.

"Jabberwocky" is very funny, yet it looks like an epic.

1977 Ap 16, 14:4

FILM VIEW

VINCENT CANBY

'3 Women' Lights Up A Dark Movie Season

So far it has not been a good year. To be a bit more blunt about it, these last three and a half months have been about as bleak a period for commercial films as any recent time I can remember. We've been over-loaded with suspense melodramas to the point where our fuses are giving out. It's next to impossible to tell the difference between those that are well-made ("Black Sunday," "The Eagle Has Landed") from those that are especially mindless ("The Domino Principle," "The Cassandra Crossing,") and one that is both well-made and mindless ("Twilight's Last Gleaming"). And does anyone really care? I suspect not since the movies aren't about anything at all.

These are films for short-term escape, movies to browse through in life's waiting room, works that occupy time without leaving the slightest traces behind. Biodegradable entertainment. It's as if movie-makers had taken a lesson from soap manufacturers who know we no longer wash our hands because our hands are dirty but because the soap is there. Want not but waste not.

The feverish competition among moviemakers to come up with mass-audience films has never before resulted in a glut of movies of such consistent banality and lack of adventurousness as those we've been seeing this year. Or so it seems. Particularly when in one week, virtually side by side, we are given things like "Audrey Rose" and "The Demon Seed."

"Audrey Rose," directed by Robert Wise, who once made a good scary movie called "The Haunting" (based on a Shirley Jackson story), purports to be about reincarnation but it's really only an anemic reincarnation of "The Exorcist" without the presence of the devil. Audrey Rose, its 11-year-old heroine, is possessed not by Old Scratch but by the soul of a Pittsburgh girl named Ivy who was killed in an automobile crash at age five and was born again two minutes later in New York as Audrey Rose. The movie pretends that a belief in reincarnation facilitates the acceptance of life but it demonstrates that reincarnation can be a fate worse than death when God's timetable is just a few minutes off.

• • •

"The Demon Seed" is an even more absurd rip-off, being an attempt to breed "Rosemary's Baby" with any number of sci-fi fictions about the computer that outgrows the men who made it. In this case the computer, who's named Proteus Four, falls in love with a psychiatrist named Susan (Julie Christie) by whom he's determined to have a baby to carry on his knowledge and his work. Miss Christie spends most of the movie as a prisoner in her own house, running around hysterically batting at locked doors and fighting off (unsuccessfully) Proteus Four's advances that, 28 days later, produce something that looks like a fat brass candlestick with a voice like Andy Devine's.

In the context of all of this junk, the multiple activities of Robert Altman this spring give him the aspect of a one-man wave, which, if not exactly new, is certainly refreshing, reviving, as his films do, one's faith in the odd possibilities of movies made for the commercial market. Altman is currently represented as the producer both of Robert Benton's charming "The Late Show," featuring the superb performances of Art Carney and Lily Tomlin, and of Alan Rudolph's somewhat less than charming though not uninteresting "Welcome to L.A.," a languid, fashionably disenchanted view of life and love in Los Angeles seen as a sort of Sunset Strip "La Ronde."

On his own—as producer, writer and director—Altman has just presented us with "3 Women," a most singular, dreamy kind of movie that has as its center of gravity a comic performance by Shelley Duvall that is as funny and moving as anything you're likely to see the rest of this year.

Before saying more about Miss Duvall I suppose I have to describe "3 Women," and that's something of a chore because I don't know how to describe it without making it sound impossible to sit through. "3 Women" has the form and illogic of a vivid dream (Altman's). As with a dream, one remembers haunting details though the precise nature of what it's about means to be mysterious, which I'm prepared to accept in my own dreams but not always in those of others.

The narrative concerns Millie Lammoreaux (Miss Duvall), who works as a physical therapist in a Palms Springs spa for old people, as well as a strange, worshipful younger woman named Pinky Rose (Sissy Spacek) who, in the course of the dream, comes to assume Millie's personality, and an older woman, a reclusive painter named Willie Hart (Janice Rule), who, until the end, remains a dimly seen specter in the lives of the others. That is more or less the story line.

The locale is the outskirts of Palm Springs, on the edge of the desert, the setting of the singles complex called the Purple Sage Apartments, where Millie lives, and a run-down recreation area called Dodge City, featuring an empty swimming pool, a long-unused miniature golf course, a track for motorcyclists and, most important, a bar where Millie can pick up men.

• • •

As much as anything else, "3 Women" is about the metamorphosis of the three women into a longed-for family relationship (mother, daughter and grand-daughter) that effectively seals off the world that has treated each so ferociously. To say that is to insist on reading the film from beginning to end as if it were something like "Audrey Rose" or "The Demon Seed," which it isn't. Rather it's a succession of arresting sequences, some of which make more sense than others.

There is little Pinky Rose's curious courtship of Millie, which begins as a girlish crush and turns into the embrace of a boa constrictor as Miss Spacek assumes first the other woman's social security number, her diary and then the society of friends that Miss Duvall's Millie was never successful with.

Among the film's several concerns is identity as a virtually tangible asset. At one point Pinky says of a pair of identical twins who work with her and Millie at the Desert Springs Rehabilitation Center, "I wonder if they're always the same." Says Millie, whose mind is determinedly literal, "What do you mean?" "Maybe," says Pinky, "one day Peggy becomes Polly and Polly Peggy. Nobody would know."

Miss Spacek is both innocent and eerie as Pinky, a sort of metachild. She is not quite of this world. Miss Duvall's Millie, though, is totally of this world, a desperately unhappy creature hanging onto life by her fingernails and making do with whatever wisdom she can pick up from Cosmopolitan, McCalls, Women's Day and House Beautiful. "Clean is sexy," Millie reminds herself with a note on the bulletin board in her kitchen, though no matter how clean and well-groomed she is, she comes on so strong with all of the other singles at the Purple Sage Apartments she's become a figure of ridicule.

If there were one image that summed up the feeling of "3 Women" for me it would be the sight of Miss Duvall, reed-slim, her large dark eyes open but somehow protected against visible insults, moving past the young people lounging beside the Purple Sage Apartments swimming pool, graciously declining a dinner invitation that's never been given.

There was something of Millie in Miss Duvall's portrayal of L.A. Joan, the pushy country-and-western groupie in "Nashville," but where L.A. Joan's gall was a sympton of her toughness and her total self-interest, Millie's gall is simply her determination to survive. She's a brutally funny, infinitely touching contemporary character and she transforms "3 Women" into a film of immediate emotional impact, while "3 Women," in turn, lights up an otherwise dreary movie season of recycled formula films.

1977 Ap 17, II:13:1

Oft-Told Tale

WIZARDS; writien, produced and directed by Ralph Bakshi; edited by Donald W. Ernst; animation cameraman Ted C. Bemiller; music by Andrew Belling; sequence animation by Irwin Spence; layout by John Sparey; with the voices of Bob Holt (Avatar), Steve Gravers (Blackwolf), Jessie Wells (Elinore), Richard Romanus (Weehawk), David Proval (Peace), James Connell (President); released by 20th Century-Fox. At the Trans-Lux East, Third Avenue and 57th Street and other theaters. Running time: 82 minutes. This flim has been rated PG.

By A. H. WEILER

IF RALPH BAKSHI'S "Fritz the Cat" and "Heavy Traffic" were as explicit as, say, sex and their X ratings, his "Wizards," which arrived in local theaters yesterday avoids that stigma. It offers ample proof once again that Mr. Bakshi has no connection with the sunlit Disney school of animated fantasy. But in concentrating on the distant future and a war between the surviving forces of good and evil in a ravaged world, "Wizards" evolves, at best, as only a mildly interesting mixture of clashing polemics and shoot-'em-up melodrama.

Of course, he has fashioned a fable, but one that is as contemporary as Hitler. His "Wizards" are brothers in the persons of Avatar, the leader of the good guys, and Blackwolf, chieftain of the opposing, mutant bad guys, whose techniques of intimidation and attack are literally borrowed from Nazi Germany.

Mr. Bakshi's allegory is fairly obvious from the outset, but he and his animators are convincingly professional. They have devised a mélange of animation and live footage that gives their feature mystical, slightly scary and, occasionally, comic tones.

A couple of frightened elves praying in a Yiddish-Hebrew gibberish is neither relevant nor funny. But Avatar is a bumbling, aged magician, who —shades of Disney!—looks a bit like a bearded Grumpy and speaks like Archie Bunker. The film's nubile queen, Elinore, is wispily clad and curvaceous enough to make Snow White blush. And a cadaverous Blackwolf, Avatar's tough, little general, Weehawk, as well as a slew of elves, fairies and a zoo of far-out fauna, are colorful creations.

"Animation can be used to tell all kinds of stories," Mr. Bakshi said after the arrival of the iconoclastically sexy and hip "Fritz the Cat" and "Heavy Traffic." And, that observation also applied to his ensuing, controversial "Coonskin." With "Wizards" he has ably illustrated his ability to tell another kind of story, but one that merely restates the already all too obvious, dire results of nuclear war and man's inhumanity to man.

•

This film has been rated PG ("Parental Guidance Suggested") probably because of its violent war scenes.

1977 Ap 21, C22:5

Somber Comedy

ANNIE HALL, directed by Woody Allen; screnplay by Mr. Allen and Marshall Brickman; produced by Charles H. Joffe, executive producer, Robert Greenhut; director of photography, Gordon Willis; editor, Ralph Rosenblum; distributed by Untied Artists. Running time: 94 minutes. At the Baronet Theater, Third Avenue near 59th Street; Little Carnegie Theater, 57th Street east of Seventh Avenue, and 34th Street East Theater, 34th Street near Second Avenue. This film has been rated PG.

Alvy Singer	Woody Allen
Annie Hall	Diane Keaton
Rob	Tony Roberts
Allison	Carol Kane
Tony Lacey	Paul Simon
Mom Hall	Colleen Dewhurst
Pam	Shelley Duvall
Robin	Janet Margolin
Duane Hall	Christopher Walken
Dad Hall	Donald Symington
Grammy Hall	Helen Ludlam
Alvy's Dad	Mordecai Lawner
Alvy's Mom	Joan Newman
Alvy, age 9	Jonathan Munk
Alvy's Aunt	Ruth Volner
Alvy's Uncle	Martin Rosenblatt
Joey Nichols	Hy Ansel
Aunt Tessie	Rashel Novikoff
Man in theater line	Russell Horton
Marshall McLuhan	Himself
Dorrie	Christine Jones
Miss Reed	Mary Boylan
Janet	Wendy Gerard
Coke Fiend	John Doumanian

By VINCENT CANBY

ALVY SINGER (Woody Allen) stands in front of an orangey sort of backdrop and tells us, the movie audience, the joke about two women at a Catskill resort. "The food," says the first woman, "is terrible." "Yes," the second woman agrees, "and the portions are so small."

This, says Alvy Singer, is just about the way he feels about life. It's not great—in fact, it's pretty evenly divided between the horrible and the miserable—but as long as it's there, he wants more.

In this fashion, Woody Allen introduces us to the particular concerns of his fine new film, "Annie Hall," a comedy about urban love and incompatibility that finally establishes Woody as one of our most audacious film makers, as well as the only American film maker who is able to work seriously in the comic mode without being the least bit ponderous.

Because Mr. Allen has his roots as a writer of one-liners and was bred in television and nightclubs, standing up, it's taken us quite a while to recognize just how prodigiously talented he is, and how different he has always been from those colleagues who also make their livings as he once did, racing from Las Vegas to the Coast to Tahoe to San Juan, then back to Las Vegas. Among other things, he's the first major American film maker ever to come out of a saloon.

For all of Mr. Allen's growth as a writer, director and actor, "Annie Hall" is not terribly far removed from "Take the Money and Run," his first work as a triple-threat man, which is not to put down the new movie but to upgrade the earlier one. "Take the Money and Run" was a visualized nightclub monologue, as freely associated as an analysand's introspections on the couch.

This also is more or less the form of "Annie Hall," Alvy Singer's free-wheeling, self-deprecating, funny and sorrowful search for the truth about his on-again, off-again affair with a beautiful young woman who is as emotionally bent as he is. The form of the two films is similar, but where the first was essentially a cartoon, "Annie Hall" has the humane sensibility of comedy.

•

It is, essentially, Woody's "Scenes From a Marriage," though there is no marriage, only an intense affair to which Alvy Singer never commits himself enough to allow Annie Hall (Diane Keaton) to give up her apartment and move in with him. Just why, we aren't told, though we can make guesses on the basis of the information furnished.

Alvy, who grew up as a poor Jewish boy in Brooklyn in a house under a Coney Island rollercoaster, is chronically suspicious and depressed. It may have started when he was 9 and first read about the expanding universe. What kind faith can you have if you know that in a couple of billion years everything's going to fly apart? With the firm conviction that the scheme is rotten, Alvy becomes a hugely successful television comedian somewhat on the scale of—you can guess Woody Allen.

Annie Hall is no less ambitious and mixed up, but for other reasons that, we must assume, have to do with the kind of WASPy, Middle Western household where Mom and Dad tend guilts as if they were prize delphiniums.

As Annie Hall, Miss Keaton emerges as Woody Allen's Liv Ullmann. His camera finds beauty and emotional resources that somehow escape the notice of other directors. Her Annie Hall is a marvelous nut, a talented singer (which Woody demonstrates in a nightclub sequence that has the effect of a love scene), generous, shy, insecure and so uncertain about sex that she needs a stick of marijuana before going to bed.

Alvy, on the other hand, embraces sex as if it were something that wouldn't keep, even when it means going to bed with a dopey reporter from Rolling Stone (Shelley Duvall in a tiny role). The most Alvy can do to meet Annie's fears is to buy a red light-bulb for the bedroom lamp. He thinks it's sexy.

•

"Annie Hall" moves back and forth in time according to Alvy's recollections, from his meeting with Annie on a tennis court, to scenes of his childhood, to a disastrous visit with her family in Chippewa Falls, to trips to Hollywood and scenes of reconciliations and partings in New York. Throughout there are explosively comic set-pieces having to do with analysis, Hollywood, politics, you-name-it, but the mood, ultimately, is somber, thoughtful, reflective.

One of Mr. Allen's talents as a director is his casting, and "Annie Hall" contains more fine supporting performances than any other American film this year, with the possible exception of "The Late Show" and "Three Women." Most prominent are Paul Simon as a recording industry promoter, Carol Kane as Alvy's politically committed first wife, Tony Roberts as Alvy's actor-friend, Colleen Dewhurst as Annie Hall's mother, and Christopher Walken as Annie's quietly suicidal brother. That's to name only a few.

There will be discussion about what points in the film coincide with the lives of its two stars, but this, I think, is to detract from and trivialize the achievement of the film, which, at last, puts Woody in the league with the best directors we have.

•

"Annie Hall," which has been rated PG ("Parental Guidance Suggested"), contains some mildly explicit sex scenes, which, since sex is one of the things it's all about, could have been avoided only if it were a different film.

1977 Ap 21, C22:5

Camp Lyricism

CHINESE ROULETTE, directed by Rainer Werner Fassbinder; screenplay (German with English subtitles) by Mr. Fassbinder; director of photography, Michael Ballhaus; editor, Ila Von Hasperg; music, Peer Rabin; a Films du Losange-Albatross-Multicine production, distributed by New Yorker Films. Running time: 96 minutes. At the New Yorker Theater, Broadway at 89th Street. This film has not been rated.

Ariane .... Margit Carstensen
Kolbe .... Ulli Lommel
Irene .... Anna Karina
Gerhard .... Alexander Allerson
Angela .... Andrea Schober
Traunitz .... Macha Meril
Kast .... Brigitte Mira
Gabriel .... V. Spengler

By VINCENT CANBY

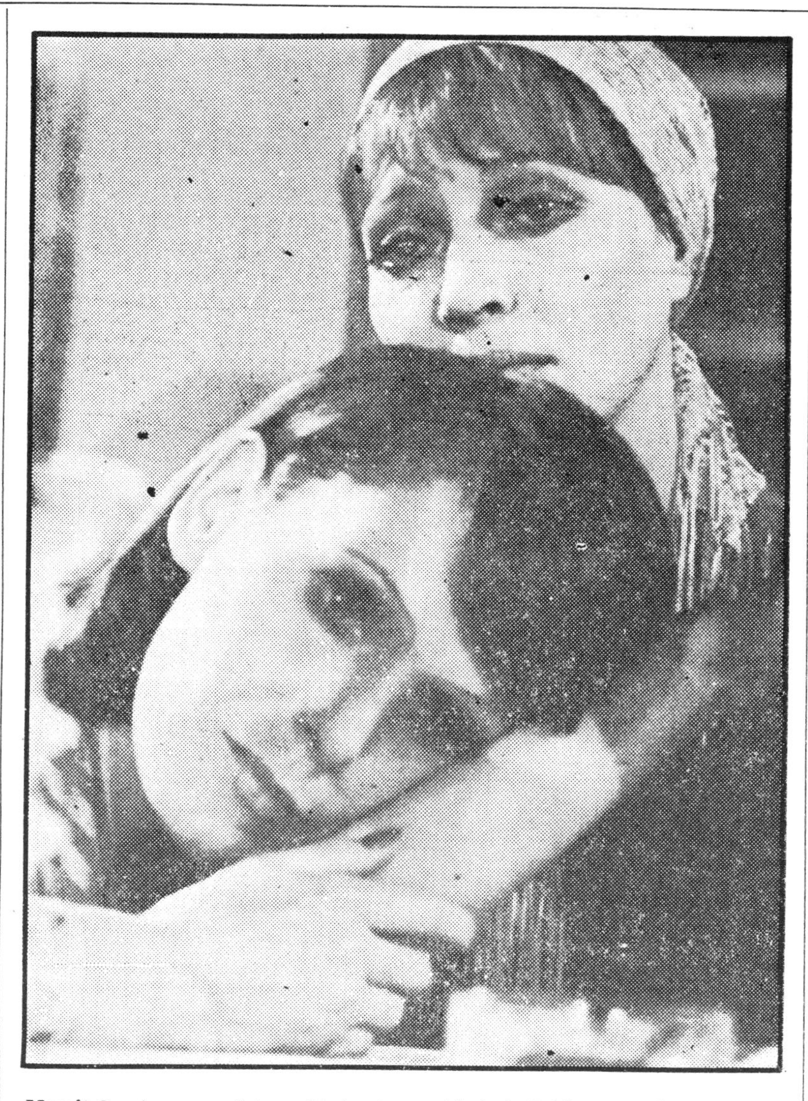

Margit Carstensen and Anna Karina in Fassbinder's "Chinese Roulette"
Though the mood is cool and distant, the film is hypnotic

RAINER WERNER FASSBINDER'S "Chinese Roulette," which opened yesterday at the New Yorker Theater as part of the current Fassbinder festival, is a mysterious comedy of such deliberate elegance that it constitutes a kind of introduction to the later, so-called Sirkian (after Douglas Sirk) period of this extraordinary young German director—as he himself might write it after submitting to his fifth or sixth solemn interview in one day.

The film is still very much about one of the principal Fassbinder concerns—power—here demonstrated in the hold exercised by a tyrannical teen-age girl, whose legs are paralyzed, over her self-absorbed but essentially innocent parents. The concern with power is there all right, but even more apparent, intentionally so, is the film's style, which is camp lyricism of such density it becomes a lethal weapon.

One could die of acute dizziness watching the Fassbinder camera as it circles around a drawing room, capturing images partially distorted by glass or seeing someone reflected not just once but two or three times in mirrors. The characters are full of ferocious emotions that are revealed only within long, pensive glances or small insults. Hands touch briefly. A wife compliments her husband's mistress on her beauty. Later she gently kisses the younger woman's neck. She might well be taking a bite out of it.

The setting is a castle that is the weekend retreat of Gerhard (Alexander Allerson) and his wife, Ariane (Margit Carstensen), a wealthy Munich couple who seem to be ideally happy when we first meet them with their pretty, partially disadvantaged daughter.

On this particular weekend Alexander, having told Ariane he was going to Oslo on business, accompanies Irene (Anna Karina), his French mistress, to the castle, only to find that Ariane is already there with her lover. Being, they think, sophisticated, the four decide to stay on as each couple had originally planned, but before they can finish their first, edgy dinner together they are joined by the daughter, Angela, and the daughter's mute companion.

The cast of characters does not end there, though. It also includes the castle housekeeper, Kast, played by Brigitte Mira at a far remove from her title role in "Mrs. Kusters Goes to Heaven." Kast wears brilliant red lipstick, bouffant hair and eyelashes so long and sharp they look as if they could scratch the finish of a Mercedes-Benz. Instead, she simply bosses around her androgynous son (V. Spengler) and laughs with delight when the crippled child falls off her crutches.

The weekend is one of circling camera movements and emotions, as if no one wanted to be caught in a sitting position (metaphorically speaking, of course), and it's climaxed when Angela persuades her parents and their guests to play an after-dinner truth game called Chinese roulette. The results are seemingly fatal. I emphasize seemingly since the film is full of unexplained actions, references, connections. It's also full of jokes, some less dour than others, such as the blind man who comes to beg alms at the castle and drives off in his own car that has an obscene license plate.

•

Ordinarily I'm not particularly taken with this kind of film making. Yet "Chinese Roulette" is fascinating even when it's frustrating, but then, I suppose, it's not really frustrating. Though the mood is cool and distant, the film is hypnotic. One can't break away from it. It's not a movie that attempts to imitate life but to create another reality through artifice, which becomes an end itself. One tends not to notice feelings and ideas, but only the dazzling technique.

This, of course, is the Fassbinder way of italicizing his ideas and feelings, but it's also something that one should be prepared for when one goes into the theater. Otherwise it might be rather a shock.

The performances, as in the brilliant "Bitter Tears of Petra Von Kant," have as much to do with the physical look of the actors and with choreographed gestures as with any conventional communication of emotions. Thus Miss Carstensen, with her ideally planed mannequin's face, which is more a representation than reality, is the perfect Fassbinder actress, but Miss Karina's beauty—magnificent eyes set in a virtually impassive face—works almost as well, as do the furious little-girl features of Andrea Schober, who plays Angela.

Taking one step at a time, Mr. Fassbinder is exploring new methods of cinema narrative that are more original and daring than anything I've yet to see by film makers who call themselves avant-garde. One must not be too ponderous about him, though. Where Douglas Sirk expressed himself through glass, the medium, in this film seems most often to be Lucite, and that's another joke.

1977 Ap 22, C10:3

Men of Notes

A GOOD DISSONANCE LIKE A MAN; directed and produced by Theodore W. Timreck; based on the composer Charles Ives's memos and reminiscences and taped interviews with relatives and friends; director of photography, Peter Stein. Running time: 60 minutes.

Charles E. Ives .... John Bottoms
George E. Ives .... Richard Ramos
Harmony Ives .... Sandra Kingsbury
George W. Chadwick .... Louis Zorich
Franz Milke .... Louis Turenne
Young Charles .... Joshua Hamilton
Horatio Parker .... Bob McIlwain

and

THE DREAMER THAT REMAINS: A PORTRAIT OF HARRY PARTCH; directed by Stephen Pouliot; produced by Betty Freeman and released by Macmillan Films. Running time: 27 minutes.

Both films at the Film Forum, 15 Van Dam Street, tonight through Sunday. These films have not been rated.

By A. H. WEILER

THANKS TO the new program at the Film Forum, the decidedly unusual characters of two gifted, proud, unreconstructed musical loners, Charles Ives and Harry Partch, are brought into colorful focus in screen treatments that, however partial, do them and their innovative work a deserved service.

As the more ambitious subject, the feature-length "A Good Dissonance Like a Man" is a dramatization that, through meticulous use of authentic sources and places, leaves the satisfying impression of fact-filled, documentary truth. Charles Ives, in this case, is not a misty legend. He is the boy immersed in music by his father, a musician and experimenter whose diversions from musical norms rubbed off in historic style on the son.

•

If Ives is now regarded as one of America's greatest composers, recognition of his avant-garde tonal works, the film makes clear, came late in his career. The film traces major influences on the composer's life—the inspiration of the New England countryside, his heritage, college days at Yale, his happy, if illness-plagued, family life, the insurance business that made him well-to-do and free to compose in his own time and own way and, above all, his rebellion against musical regimentation—to evoke a three-dimensional, all-too-human artist.

The characterizations of the principals are realistic and convincing, as are the taped, narrated reminiscences of relatives and friends. And, they are colorfully abetted by scenes shot at family homes and at Yale. One may yearn for more of the Ives music (and its identification) than we get here, but it is obvious that Theodore W. Timreck, the producer-director, and his associates have given us, not dissonance, but a lucid and vivid portrait of an extraordinary man.

•

The 27-minute study of Partch, filmed in California in 1973, a year before his death, is largely an interview but he, too, emerges as a man decidedly apart from the crowd. White-bearded, thin and casually dressed, he projects his musical and social views simply and directly—recollections of the hobo's life in the West, his youth, the Depression.

The weird instruments he invented and built—a 72-string, lyrelike cithara, glass bells cut from bottles, and the like—were designed to fit his individualistic compositions, music often inspired by the times and the places in which he lived. Although the film is merely an excerpt from the annals of a full and fulfilled life, it makes its "dreamer" strikingly real.

1977 Ap 22, C11:1

New Directors

By VINCENT CANBY

For those who may want to see some of the entries in the second half of the New Directors/New Films series currently at the Museum of Modern Art, the following comments are presented in the chronological order in which the films will be shown. The series, sponsored by the Film Society of Lincoln Center and the Museum's department of film, ends Wednesday.

"Well-Spring of My World," tonight at 8:30, is a sad, gently rueful Danish documentary in which its director, Christian Braad Thomsen, returns to the tiny town where he grew up to interview old friends and reflect on the once rich, fertile countryside that's being gobbled up by housing projects and superhighways. Most of Mr. Thomsen's subjects seem slightly inhibited by the camera, but the stories they tell are occasionally very moving and surprisingly poignant.

•

"Rubber Gun" and "The Preparatory,"Sunday, 6 P.M., and Tuesday, 8:30 P.M., is one of the better programs to be offered in this series. "Rubber Gun" is a 90-minute Canadian feature directed by Allan Moyle and written by him and Stephen Lack, both of whom are also actors in the film, which appears to be as much improvised as conventionally planned and directed.

The film, a tombstone marking the end of the drug culture, concerns the coming apart of a group of young Canadian druggies and pushers pursued by time and the cops. It's one of those movies in which you're never sure who's giving a performance and who's simply allowing the camera to record him. There is a difference. "Rubber Gun" will be released here commercially later this year, at which time it will be reviewed.

"The Preparatory," written and directed by Terence Cahalan, an American, is an effective, clear-eyed, unsentimental remembrance of life in a Catholic preparatory school. The film, Mr. Cahalan's master's project, shows talent and discipline. Running time: 25 minutes.

•

"Brandos Costumes," also known as "Mild Manners" and "Gentle Customs," Sunday, 8:30 P.M., and Tuesday, 6 P.M., is the first feature of a Portuguese director named Alberto Seixas Santos and is by

Stephen Lack in "Rubber Gun"
In one of the better programs

far the most ambitious and interesting feature in the current program.

The film intercuts between old newsreel footage and highly theatrical, sometimes melodramatic, tableaux to draw parallels between the late Portuguese dictator Dr. António de Oliveira Salazar and a typical, upper middle-class family man who is a free-thinking liberal outside his house and a tyrant at home. Not all of the associations are clear to someone not familiar with recent Portuguese history, but the film's bold style, which copies no contemporary director I can think of, and its wit and passion are worth attention.

•

"Devices and Desires" and "Elizbeth Swados — the Girl With the Incredible Feeling," Monday, 8:30 P.M., and Wednesday, 6 P.M. are a mixed bag.

Giles Foster's "Devices and Desires" (55 minutes) is a fond picture of an eccentric, early 19th-century English clergyman named John Skinner. In Mr. Foster's film he is brought up to date, named Granville Moulton and played with fine, understated madness by Frederick Treves. Mr. Moulton is convinced that he has discovered the ruins of the Roman capital of Britain and digs at his site instead of attending to his parishioners.

We never know the reasons behind the old man's obsession which eventually alienates even those who would like to help him, but we can appreciate its hold on him, as well as his impatience with the dull world around him. "Weddings, christenings and funerals," says the testy message on Mr. Moulton's telephone-recording mechine, "state your business.'

"Elizabeth Swados" is something else. It, too, is a fond picture of its subject, the gifted young woman who sings, plays and composes for the contemporary theater, but it's hardly more than a grab bag of impressions by the director, Linda Feferman.

The 37-minute film uses a lot of footage shot by other people, including home movies shot by Miss Swados' loving parents. There is also a quite nice cartoon based on a children's book written by Miss Swados, about a girl who had an incredible feeling, pictured as an amorphous mass that looks like a bag of laundry, which disappeared when it was explained. Something of the same sort happens when you try to explain Miss Swados.

•

"L'Affiche Rouge," Monday, 6 P.M., and Wednesday, 8:30 P.M., is one of those movies that sound much more interesting to hear about than they ever are to watch. It's about a group of Parisian actors who plan to make a movie about the Manounchian Band, a group of left-wing resistance fighters, mostly young and mostly foreign, who were executed by the Nazis in the last months of the German occupation.

As the actors gather at the studio for a picnic, they try on costumes, dance, act out brief scenes from the film they want to make, discuss the meanings of their roles and generally try to persuade us of the importance of the project.

The film, in French, was directed by Frank Cassenti. It strains very hard to look improvised and politically committed, but it only seems phony, arch and self-important. The cast includes Pierre Clementi, who has probably made more appearances in failed avant-garde films than any other actor of his generation.

1977 Ap 23, 10:1

FILM VIEW

VINCENT CANBY

Woody Allen Is the American Bergman

The day after I saw Woody Allen's new film, "Annie Hall," the man with the tape recorder started haunting me, turning up on the next stool at Chock Full o'Nuts, staring dumbly at me from across the aisle on the No. 104 bus when I was trying to read about Zaire, standing in line behind me at the bank with no check or withdrawal slip in his hand, only the damned tape recorder. I made a mental note: if art is life recorded, as now seems to be the fashion, the triumph of our age is the instant replay. The time spent on the creative process has been brought to the irreducible minimum. Eradicated. The man's expression was always the same, a mixture of disbelief and reproach. Because movie buffs are like drunks—at any minute they can turn mean—I finally submitted to the interview, as much to put my own thoughts in order as to get rid of him. He didn't waste words making his point.

Q.: "You aren't serious?"

A.: "I think I am . . ."

Q.: "You say you 'think.' . . . Aren't you sure?"

A.: "Yes . . ."

Q.: "You believe that Woody Allen is America's Ingmar Bergman?"

A.: "Exactly . . . or as close as we have at the moment, or are likely to have."

Q.: "You are telling me that a stand-up comic, a fellow who began as a freelance gag-writer for Sid Caesar and then went on to perform one-liners in nightclubs and on television, is some kind of reflection of America's collective subconscious?"

A.: "I'm not sure I know exactly what the collective subsconsious is. Or whether that has anything to do with Bergman. What I mean is that I think it's about time that we recognized Woody Allen as one of our most original, most personal, most passionate, most introspective filmmakers. And I think that the background you've just cited, with what sounded like a small, inhibited sneer, is one of the reasons that he may speak for our time and place in a way that would be forever beyond the reach of people we treat much more seriously. You know, Robert Altman, Francis Ford Coppola, Martin Scorsese . . ."

Q: ". . . 'most introspective'?"

A.: "The way American life is set up, we aren't meant to have much time for introspection. And it's apparent from all of Woody's films, from 'Take the Money and Run' through 'Sleeper,' 'Love and Death' and now 'Annie Hall,' that Woody is as introspective as any American can be and attend Knicks games, play a clarinet, go to movie revivals, write essays, stories and film scripts, see friends, watch television, have a relationship and still be in analysis. It's not easy. You've got to be ready to introspect at any free moment, as when you're at the analyst's, on the couch, and the super interrupts to install a new light switch."

Q.: "You're sending me up?"

A.: "Not at all. Woody is the poet of America's emotionally disenfranchised, urban, upwardly mobile males who seek fame, fortune and girls they can relate to. Like all artists, he's a bit schizoid. He's a participant in the American Dream but never for a moment isn't he standing a little to one side, watching himself. I suspect he's a note-taker."

Q.: "Well *I* suspect that the principal reasons you're associating Woody Allen to Ingmar Bergman at this point are because he's on the record as being a Bergman admirer and because 'Annie Hall' has all the aspects of a film-ah-clay, if you know what I mean. It's about a Jewish boy from Brooklyn who becomes a successful comedian— Woody—who falls in love with a beautiful, talented, WASPy actress-singer played by Diane Keaton, the beautiful, talented, WASPy actress-singer with whom Woody has a relationship in real life."

A.: "It's not just that. It also has to do with the concerns of the film, and their quality. I haven't seen an American film in years that was as seriously interested in the relations between men and women as 'Annie Hall.' Or, for that matter, a film that was as seriously interested and as funny and perceptive . . ."

Q.: ". . . and Diane Keaton is Woody's Liv Ullmann?"

A.: "I think so. As Bergman has a way of transforming Liv Ullmann into one of the world's great beauties, so does Woody have a way of permitting us to share his appreciation of Keaton's beauty, talent, intelligence and wit, as well as her idiosyncracies. There's a scene in 'Annie Hall'—the one in the nightclub in which Woody allows Diane Keaton to sing 'It Seems Like Old Times' from start to finish, without a cut—that is comparable to the great monologues that Bergman has given Ullmann, and, to go further back, comparable to Chaplin's treatment of Paulette Goddard in 'Modern Times' and 'The Great Dictator.' "

Q.: "Woody Allen is an auteur?"

A.: "As much as is any man making American movies today. More so, since he not only writes and directs his films, he also acts in them."

Q.: "He's a Chaplin?"

A.: "No, he's an Allen. . . ."

Q.: ". . . but all those Catskill jokes. He's so . . . verbal, and they are, after all, only jokes."

A.: "They are brilliantly used. And if you think his films are too verbal, you aren't looking at them. They have a disciplined simplicity that is in the style of a Bergman or a Buñuel. No irrelevant camera movements. Everything is in the service of the screenplay. Nothing interferes, which is why 'Annie Hall' is so effective—both hilarious and moving."

Q.: "I can't help feeling he's frivolous. I don't buy all his name-dropping—Kant, Kierkegaard, Nietzsche, Dostoyevsky, death, God. It's a kind of flag-waving—of status-symbol-waving."

A.: "I think it is and it's meant to be, but I also believe it. Woody is a seeker. There is in him still the small child who goes into the library and wants desperately somehow to absorb all those volumes, as if once he had plowed through them, he would have found the answer to life. Woody is no Edgar Cayce. He can't put a volume under his pillow when he goes to bed and wake up in the morning with the contents having seeped up into his brain. He's a reader. He also is a cross-indexer, which is the source of some of his funniest routines."

Q.: "But he's always the same."

A.: "I disagree. One of the most interesting things about 'Annie Hall' is the emergence of the public Woody Allen character as a hero. His persona has travelled a long way from 'Take The Money and Run' to 'Annie Hall,' from the nebbish who wouldn't have dared to entertain a real feeling to the tortured (if comically) mover and doer who is the hero of 'Annie Hall.' The rake's progress has been audacious."

Q.: "Can you imagine Woody Allen ever making a movie like 'Wild Strawberries' or 'Face to Face'?"

A.: "Can you imagine Ingmar Bergman ever making a movie like 'Bananas' or 'Sleeper'? That's not the point. Because Woody works with the materials of the pop comedians, it may be difficult for us to see just how original and adventurous a film like 'Annie Hall' really is. It's time to pay attention."

1977 Ap 24, II:19:1

"JACOB THE LIAR"—Erwin Geschonneck and Vlastimil Brodsky play Jewish laborers in Nazi-occupied Poland.

By A. H. WEILER

JACOB THE LIAR, screenplay by Jurek Becker based on his novel of the same title; directed by Frank Beyer; a DEFA Film-Fernsehen co-production, East Germany; photography by Gunter Marczinkowsky; edited by Rita Hiller; presented by Macmillan Films Inc. At the Plaza Theater, 58th Street east of Madison Avenue. Running time: 95 minutes. This film has not been rated.

Jacob Heym .... Vlastimil Brodsky
Kowalski .... Erwin Geschonneck
Lena .... Manuela Simon
Misha .... Henry Hubchen
Rosa .... Blanche Kommerell
Herr Frankfurter .... Dezso Garas
Frau Frankfurter .... Suzana Gordon
Prof. Kirchbaum .... Friedrich Richter

World War II film records of the attenuated terrors of Polish ghetto life are all too familiar now, but "Jacob the Liar" tempers the terrible truth in serio-comic style. Of course, laughter is not precisely what Frank Beyer, the director, and Jurek Becker, who adapted his own novel to the screen, had in mind, but they make Jacob's falsehoods the courageous and often lightly funny stuff that bound a doomed people together momentarily in hope.

•

As an East German production and one of the five candidates for this year's foreign-language Academy Award, "Jacob the Liar," which opened at the Plaza yesterday, is surprisingly devoid of anything resembling Communist propaganda. And, in focusing on Jewish ghetto inmates, the director and his scenarist pointedly stress the togetherness of these inmates as against the callousness of survival in, say, the concentration camp of Lina Wertmuller's "Seven Beauties."

Their Jacob Heym, once a cafe owner, is now simply one of the town's downtrodden, unkempt laborers under Nazi occupation forces who, by chance, overhears a radio communiqué in local Gestapo headquarters about Russian victories in the vicinity. And our woebegone hero then passes the happy news to other Jews, stating with underplayed pride that he heard it on his own clandestine radio. Naturally, his neighbors, clinging to this newly found promise of deliverance, demand more news daily and our increasingly reluctant Jacob is forced to invent it.

As a series of vignettes, "Jacob the Liar" illustrates recollections of a happier past and the glimmer of cheer as well as the fear of reprisals felt by the ghetto's inmates. Henry Hubchan and Blanche Kommerell, a pretty brunette, grasp desperately for moments of love in a crowded, decrepit room. Dezso Garas and Suzana Gordon, as Miss Kommerell's actor-parents, cower in anticipation of a concentration camp destiny, and, Erwin Geschonneck, gives a sensitive performance as a former barber and close friend of Jacob, who resorts to the grimmest solution when hope is lost.

•

Vlastimil Brodsky, a noted Czech actor, is forceful, funny and poignant as the ever helpful, if married, Jacob, whose sad, sagging face mirrors the tragedy of the ghetto's plight. He is nobly abetted by Manuela Simon, an endearing natural, pretty little moppet, playing his inquisitive niece, whom he entertains in one charming scene by imitating Winston Churchill's sonorous voice as it seemingly emerges from his alleged radio.

Although English subtitles make the action clear, a viewer may be disturbed by some abrupt transitions and by Poles speaking German. But if there is little doubt as to the drama's inevitable, tragic denouement, "Jacob the Liar" is, in effect, a heartwarming saga and one that illustrates Mark Twain's observation that "courage is resistance to fear, mastery of fear, and not the absence of fear."

1977 Ap 25, 39:1

Kind Bumbler

TORO-SAN, THE INTELLECTUAL (OTOKO WA TSURAI TORAJIRO KATSUSHIKA RISSHI HEN), screenplay, original story and direction by Yoji Yamada; edited by Iwao Ishii; director of photography, Tetsuo Takaba; produced by Kiyoshi Shimazu; distributed by Shochiku Films of America Inc. At the Regency Theater, Broadway and 67th Street. Running time: 97 minutes. This film has not been rated.

Kuruma Torajiro ... Kiyoshi Atsumi
Sakura ... Chieko Baisho
Reiko Kakei ... Fumie Kashiyama
Junko Mogami ... Junko Sakurada
Ryuzo Kuruma ... Masami Shimojo
Tsune Kuruma ... Chieko Misaki
Hiroshi Mogami ... Gin Maeda
Mitsuo Mogami ... Hayato Nakamura
Prof. Tadokoro ... Keiju Kobayashi
Policeman ... Masakane Yonekura
Priest ... Hideji Otaki
Genko ... Gajiro Sato

By A. H. WEILER

"TORO-SAN, the Intellectual," a new feature which today opens a two-day stand in the Japanese film revival series at the Regency Theater, is proof that East and West can meet on some cultural levels. In the case of this "Toro-San," the Orient's customs may still be somewhat exotic but the succession of joys, sorrows and misconceptions are as Western as any soap opera.

This is not meant to denigrate the sudsy but obviously profitable techniques of those enduring television sagas. Like them, this latest Toro-San adventure, reportedly the 17th filmed in the last eight years starring the title character, ranks among the most popular film series with Japanese moviegoers. But the work of Yoji Yamada, who wrote and directed many of them, is—except for a retrospective showing of 11 Toro-San features he presented at the Japan Society here last January—fairly unfamiliar in local houses.

His current "Toro-San" is the same simple, unlettered, kindly, bumbling wanderer who manages to get himself into and out of scrapes while scattering good deeds along the way. This time, he returns home to the candy shop run by his uncle, aunt, sister and brother-in-law only to find himself accused of being the father of the pretty 17-year-old girl waiting for him.

Toro is guiltless, of course; he was only the self-effacing benefactor of the girl and her late mother, whom he befriended when she was deserted by her husband. Those misunderstandings do pile up, however.

On a visit to the mother's grave, a priest instructs the naïve Toro to "know yourself, it's never too late to learn." And, before you can say sayonara, he's smitten by a demure, attractive archeology student — a roomer with his family—and he's off and running.

Naturally, the results are bittersweet but unrewarding for all. There's a middle-aged, girl-shy archeology professor who thinks he's been spurned by his pupil, who happens to be Toro's teacher. Toro is equally confused by her purely platonic intentions and, obviously, the lady is left unrequited.

•

His script may be convoluted and his direction uneven, but Mr. Yamada is decidedly professional in shaping a colorful and briskly moving story. No amount of English subtitles fully clarifies his opening sequence—presumably a fantasy shoot-'em-up showdown in an old western saloon—that is a larger-than-life lampoon only vaguely related to subsequent events. But there's little doubt that Mr. Yamada and his cast project contemporary Japanese family life and ties realistically and affectionately.

As Toro, Kiyoshi Atsumi is an endearing buffoon whose love for his clan and others is unmistakably honest while he endures their jibes about his oafishness, his "square face" and the unnecessary glasses he takes to wearing during his brief schooling.

The town, its streets and shops, the wooded hills, and a pick-up baseball game, add to the color of the comedy-drama. If, like soap operas everywhere, this "Toro-San" seems to be much ado about nothing that is momentous, it generally manages to be genuinely warm and charming.

1977 Ap 27, C19:1

A Crawler

IT'S ALIVE, directed, written and produced by Larry Cohen; director of photography, Fenton Hamilton; editor, Peter Honess; executive producer, Peter Sabiston; music, Bernard Herrmann; distributed by Warner Brothers. Running time: 91 minutes. At neighborhood theaters. This film has been rated PG.

Frank ... John Ryan
Lenore ... Sharon Farrell
Professor ... Andrew Duggan
Clayton ... Guy Stockwell
Lieut. Perkins ... James Dixon
Captain ... Michael Ansara
Executive ... Robert Emhardt
Charlie ... William Wellman, Jr.
Doctor ... Shamus Locks
Nurse ... Mary Nancy Burnett

Larry Cohen's "It's Alive," which opened at neighborhood theaters yesterday, is a horror film about a newborn baby who loses no time in making a mess of things. He murders everyone in the delivery room except his mom. Thereafter he lays waste a large part of Los Angeles, getting around town so rapidly you suspect he must have his own Porsche, though when we see him he's always crawling.

Mr. Cohen is not unintelligent, but the few interesting ideas in his horror films, including the recent "Demon," are drenched in supreme silliness by way of the dialogue and special effects. The performances in this film are especially unpleasant, and the music score by the late Bernard Herrmann sounds as if it might have been composed to accompany World War II.

"It's Alive," which has been rated PG ("Parental Guidance Suggested"), contains a scene of childbirth that's grizzly enough to put anyone off both motherhood and fatherhood.

VINCENT CANBY

1977 Ap 28, C22:5

Pages of an Album

SHINING STAR, produced and directed by Sig Shore; original story and screenplay by Robert Lipsyte; director of photography, Alan Metzger; editor, Bruce Witkin; original score composed and performed by Earth, Wind and Fire. At neighborhood theaters. Runing time: 100 minutes. This film is rated PG.

Coleman Buckmaster ... Harvey Keitel
Carlton Jones ... Ed Nelson
Velour Page ... Cynthia Bostick
Franklyn Page ... Bert Parks
Gary Page ... Jimmy Boyd
Mike Lemongello ... Michael Dante
Early ... Maurice White
The Group ... Earth, Wind and Fire

WHEN IT STAYS with its pop-music sounds and its recording-studio settings, "Shining Star," which opened yesterday at neighborhood theaters, possesses the instructive quality of a competent documentary on an interest-element of show business.

The trouble is that "Shining Star" isn't a documentary at all. As fiction, it is an occasionally choppy looking movie with aspirations toward exposing the seamy side of the recording industry—the marketing of no-talent performers by cynical executives of companies controlled by the underworld. Unfortunately, its people are unconvincing—stereotypical characters depthlessly performed.

It is a handicap that cannot be overcome, even by the musical contributions of Earth, Wind and Fire, appearing as a relatively unknown act shunted aside in favor of a wretched family group, the Pages. "Shining Star" is, after all, a movie, not a recording.

Harvey Keitel

As a moral tract, it offers indignation but cannot kindle outrage, which leaves it long on soul but short on art.

Although not shown previously in this area, "Shining Star" has played elsewhere under the title "That's the Way of the World."

•

Scenes of drug use (heroin and cocaine) as well as some standard street language and one lyrical, unrevealing scene in bed are probably responsible for the PG ("Parental Guidance Suggested") rating.

LAWRENCE VAN GELDER

1977 Ap 28, C22:5

Cause and Effect

BETWEEN THE LINES, directed by Joan Micklin Silver; screenplay by Fred Barron, based on a story by Mr. Barron and David M. Halpern Jr.; produced by Raphael D. Silver; music, Southside Johnny and the Asbury Jukes; additional music by Michael Kamen; director of photography, Kenneth Van Sickle; editor, John Carter, distributed by Midwest Film Productions. Running time: 101 minutes. At the Sutton Theater, 57th Street east of Third Avenue. This film has been rated R.

Harry ... John Heard
Abbie ... Lindsay Crouse
Max ... Jeff Goldblum
Lynn ... Jill Eikenberry
David ... Bruno Kirby
Laura ... Gwen Welles
Michael ... Stephen Collins
Stanley ... Lewis J. Stadlen
Hawker ... Michael J. Pollard
Roy Walsh ... Lane Smith
Danielle ... Marilu Henner
Sarah ... Susan Haskins
Herbert Fisk ... Ray Barry
Doug Henkel ... Douglas Kenney
Frank ... Jon Korkes
Ahmed ... Joe Morton
Wheeler ... Richard Cox
Jason ... Gary Springer
Paul ... Charles Levin
Austin ... Guy Boyd

By VINCENT CANBY

ETWEEN THE LINES," the second feature by Joan Micklin Silver ("Hester Street"), is an appealing, low-key, counter-culture newspaper comedy, meaning that it doesn't have a great deal of conventional newspaper narrative, though toward the end someone does tell "the kid," a would-be reporter who has just come up with his first scoop, "You're going to nail those punks with that story!"

The newspaper in question is The Back Bay Mainline, a Boston weekly that suggests both The Boston Phoenix and The Real Paper, which is not terribly surprising because the film was written by Fred Barron, who once worked on each.

•

Like so many once-underground papers today, The Mainline and the members of its staff are going through an identity crisis. Founded in the late 1960's, when there were easily recognized battles to be fought, the formerly hard-swinging, radical, antiwar paper has grown fat. It's running out of causes. The Mainline is so profitable, in fact, that a newspaper tycoon is negotiating to buy it.

Harry (John Heard), The Mainline's chief investigative reporter, a fellow who once won a national journalism award for a series exposing nursing home scandals, is suffering from career-bends. He tells Abbie (Lindsay Crouse), a pretty, still-ambitious photographer who is his occasional girlfriend, "It isn't exciting anymore." No matter how many exposés one writes, nothing ever changes.

Michael (Stephen Collins), who made his reputation reporting on the activities of flower children, hippies, yippies and druggies, is planning a book on the counterculture years. Even before he has received his advance, he has started to talk in the vocabulary of the literary hustlers who never put finger to typewriter before knowing the probably financial disposition of all of the subsidiary rights. You know he's going to be the perfect talk-show guest.

•

Laura (Gwen Welles), who lives with Michael and says every other day that she's leaving him, is also a reporter but one with no great drive. When Michael decides to move to New York, Laura at first refuses to tag along. She has her own career, her own friends, she says, but then she changes her mind. It's probably her first major compromise. Max (Jeff Goldblum), the paper's rock critic and resident comic, talks big but he, too, compromises at the first sign of a crunch.

"Between the Lines" is, technically, I suppose, a newspaper film, but what distinguishes it is the gently perceptive way it captures the emotional confusions of its characters. They are young, talented, ambitious people who once had the great good fortune to be enthusiastically committed and to have had professional lives that were the same as their private lives. Just how lucky they were they begin to realize only now that the time has passed. The 1960's have become their roaring 20's.

"Between the Lines" is about growing up after you've already grown up. Harry, the investigative reporter, experiences his first intimations of obsolescence at 30. He's suddenly baffled by the fact that Abbie continues to enjoy her job—it's as if he'd never really known her. They quarrel, break up and come back together, but each knows that it will never be the same again.

Somewhere in "Life on the Mississippi" Mark Twain remembers coming into Hannibal for the first time after he received his pilot's license. The river was no longer beautiful to him. Unusual ripples on the surface had become warnings of new shoals. A brilliant red sunset was simply a weather forecast.

"BETWEEN THE LINES"—Lindsay Crouse, Gwen Welles and Jill Eikenberry, staff members of a crusading independent newspaper, clown around in their off hours.

He'd lost something very precious and he had to move on.

So do Mrs. Silver's characters and "Between the Lines" is at its best when it ambles in and out of their lives, overhearing lovers' quarrels, professional conflicts, office politics. It's not so convincing when it tries to work along conventional plot lines that have to do with the selling of the paper and with some underworld activities. Then it's awkward and amateurish.

Not so the performances, which are uniformly first-rate, the kind of ensemble work in which no actor is more or less important than another. That includes Jeff Goldblum, who has received a good deal of publicity as the nutty rock critic. His is a more colorful role, but Mr. Heard, Mr. Collins, Miss Crouse and Miss Welles are quite special, too.

Among other things, "Between the Lines" is one of the few films I've seen dealing with the counterculture years that doesn't rip it off or send it up. Time, says Mrs. Silver, catches up, even with the young.

1977 Ap 28, C22:5

Cogent and Moving

ALICE IN THE CITIES (Alice in den Stadten), directed by Wim Wenders; screenplay (German with English subtitles) by Mr. Wenders and Velia von Fustenberg; photography, Robby Muller and Martin Schafer; editor Pater Przygodd; music, Can; executive producer, Peter Genee; production companies, Producktion/Filverlag der Auloren. Running time: 110 minutes. At the Jean Renoir Cinema, 2d Avenue between 10th and 11th Streets.

Philip	Rudiger Vogeler
Alice	Yella Rottlander
Lisa	Elizabeth Kreuzer

"Alice in the Cities" ["Alice in den Stadten") was shown at the 1974 New York Film Festival. The following are excerpts from Lawrence Van Gelder's review, which appeared Oct. 9, 1974. The film opened yesterday for one week at the Jean Renoir Cinema.

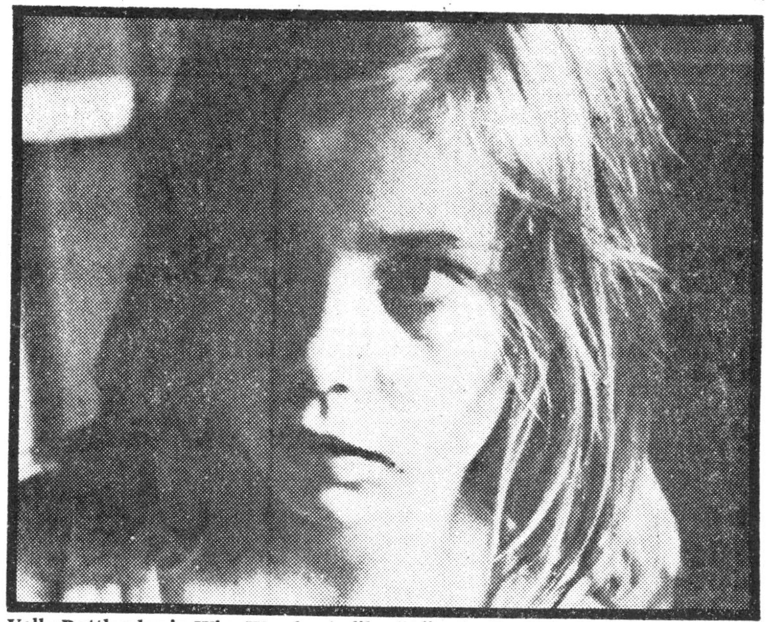

Yella Rottlander in Wim Wenders's film "Alice in the Cities"
Tightly controlled, intelligent and ultimately touching

IF YOU ARE searching for a fine, tightly controlled, intelligent and ultimately touching film, "Alice in the Cities" ("Alice in den Stadten"). It is a West German film directed and, in part, written by Wim Wenders, a young German who received praise here two years ago when his second feature, "The Anxiety of the Goalie at the Penalty Kick," was shown at the Museum of Modern Art in the New Directors/New Film series.

•

Ostensibly, "Alice in the Cities," filmed in black and white, tells what happens when a footloose 31-year-old German journalist suddenly finds himself saddled with a well-traveled 9-year-old girl on a journey from the United States back to Europe.

To suggest that this is a foreign version of "Paper Moon" is like fostering the belief that Otto Soglow's Little King is creative kin to Shakespeare's Hamlet because both, after all, share a preoccupation with royalty.

"Alice in the Cities" is a film with a great deal to say about Europe and America, about the exhaustion of dreams and the homogenization of nations, about roots and the awareness of time, about sterility and creativity, about vicarious and real adventure and eventually, about the possibilities of the future.

At the outset, Phillip, the journalist, played with a seemingly effortless skill by Rudiger Vogeler, is an emotionally and creatively exhausted man caught up in and overwhelmed by a standardized ugly America.

He misses the deadline for a story about America and decides to return home, only to discover that an airline strike has grounded all flights to Germany. At the airport, he meets Lisa, who has decided to abandon her husband and return to Germany, and her daughter, Alice. Lisa abandons Alice with Phillip and tells him she will meet them in a couple of days in Amsterdam, but she fails to turn up. After a time, Phillip and Alice go looking for her grandmother.

Arrival in Europe unfolds the lovely symmetry of this film—beginning with the change of time. There is, too, the contrast of music from the radio, the slackening of photography and the increase in writing, a seemingly idle bedtime story that sounds a note first struck in New York and is not very idle at all; the abandonment of old homes, and the contrast between the German women who refuse to sleep with Phillip in New York and the one who will in Germany.

"Alice in the Cities" is not sentimental about its people. Better than that, it is concerned about what is to become of all of us.

1977 Ap 29, C6:1

Close Quarters

THE WILD DUCK, directed by Hans W. Geissendorfer; screenplay (German with English subtitles) by Mr. Geissendorfer, based on the play by Henrik Ibsen; produced by Bernd Eichinger; director of photography, Harry Nap; editor, Gunther Witte; music, Nils Janette Walen; a Solaris Film production in cooperation with Sasha Film/Wein and the West German Broadcasting Company, distributed by New Yorker Films. Running time: 100 minutes. At the 68th Street Playhouse, Third Avenue at 68th Street. This film has not been rated.

Gina	Jean Seberg
Hialmar	Peter Kern
Gregers	Bruno Ganz
Hedwig	Anne Bennent
Old Ekdal	Martin Florchinger
Relling	Heinz Bennent
Consul	Heinz Moog
Mrs. Sorby	Sonia Sutter
Molvik	Robert Werner
Petersen	Guido Wieland

By VINCENT CANBY

THE DENSITY of the pain in any Ibsen play has to do not only with the accumulation in time of tragic, misbegotten deeds but also with the playing area of the stage. As his characters are locked into their lives, they are caged in theater sets.

Double doors at the rear may lead to an inner room, and stairs at stage left suggest the existence of another floor. Yet there is no true escape from the small, realistically furnished, 19th-century interior landscape that, as often as not in Ibsen, is a living room. In English, if not in Norwegian, that's a joke. By the time we reach the fifth Ibsen act the feeling of confinement has become so intense that violence is inevitable.

This is one of the reasons why Ibsen's plays don't easily translate from stage to films, which are as big as all outdoors. It is also one of the achievements of Hans W. Geissendorfer's German-language adaptation of "The Wild Duck" that this physical evocation of emotional pressure is not lost in his very moving film.

•

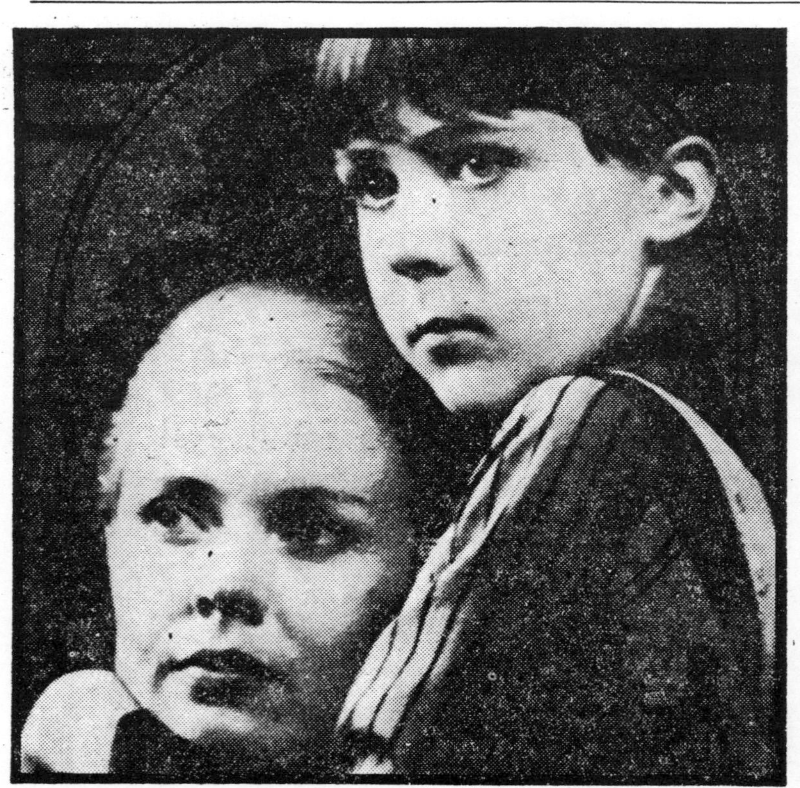

Bruno Ganz and Jean Seberg in Hans W. Geissendorfer's "The Wild Duck"
A very moving film that closely adheres to the true Ibsen spirit

"The Wild Duck," which opened yesterday at the 68th Street Playhouse, has no spectacular performance to equal Glenda Jackson's in the film version of "Hedda Gabler" last year, but its spirit seems truer to Ibsen, even with necessarily foreshortened English subtitles translating the German dialogue.

Mr. Geissendorfer, the young German director who created considerable interest here five years ago with an elegant vampire film called "Jonathan," has cut the text a bit and shifted some of it around. The point of his treatment, though, is not to modernize the original in any way but to make us respond to and understand the conventions of one of Ibsen's best-made plays.

In no other work by the Norwegian playwright, whom Shaw ranked (along with himself, of course) ahead of Shakespeare, has so much rotten business been going on for so long before the beginning of Act One, which must tempt the film director to find all sorts of cinematic equivalents for the exposition spoken on stage. Mr. Geissendorfer resists all this and sticks to the fury at hand, an ironic self-appraisal by a playwright who had once championed idealism so forcefully.

The time is 1884 and the setting is a small Norwegian city where Hjalmar (Peter Kern), a good-natured, self-deluding, former member of the bourgeoisie, lives happily with his wife, Gina (Jean Seberg), his daughter, Hedwig (Anne Bennent), and his disgraced old father.

Into this placid family circle comes Hjalmar's old schoolmate, Gregers (Bruno Ganz), whose mission is to make people see the lies they live in order to attain the enlightenment of truth. In so doing he destroys the family and, it seems likely, himself.

Mr. Geissendorfer opens up the play but not in such a way that he lets the life out of it. The camera moves freely around Hjalmar's tidily run-down flat, from the studio where Gina runs his photography business to the adjacent attic where the senile grandfather stalks game (penned-in rabbits) and where Hedwig keeps her wild duck.

There are brief glimpses of the outside world—a barroom, the courtyard of the apartment building—but none of these has the effect of diminishing the drama of financial fraud and concealed parenthood that's being revealed in breathtaking order upstairs.

•

With the exception of Miss Seberg, who is too chicly beautiful to be believable as the sort of waddling, once-ripe housemaid she's supposed to be, the casting is nearly perfect.

Anne Bennent is a lovely Hedwig with her open, solemn face and her way of walking with her hands drawn to her sides, as if she were always afraid of breaking something. Peter Kern, who has appeared here in Fassbinder films and looks a bit like Gene Wilder, is less comic than one expects as the foolish Hjalmar, but he has a kind of witty self-importance that makes the character more easily tolerable. The star, though, is Bruno Ganz, fanatically self-assured as the terrifying idealist who, you know, is himself teetering on the edge of suicide.

The color photography is uncommonly good—not so dramatically underlighted that one feels the need of wiping one's glasses, but soft and a little smoky, as if one should open the windows of the flat. They would do just that except that it's midwinter and the choice is either to have clean air and freeze or to put up with leaky flues and cooking odors to stay warm. The cold finally does invade their lives, but it is bitter truth, which in this film can be physically felt.

1977 Ap 29, C12:1

Hollywood's Secret Star: The Special-Effects Man

By CAROLYN SEE

LOS ANGELES

Once upon a time, when a moviegoer walked out of a theater his head was full of images of striking personalities who had made a powerful impact on his emotions. These bigger-than-life individuals had names like Bogart and Gable, Crawford and Davis, and they were acknowledged to be stars. Today, Hollywood is entering a new era, one in which the biggest stars of all seem to be those spectacularly impersonal attractions known as Special Effects, and the images that cling to a moviegoer's mind are apt to be those of burning skyscrapers, crumbling cities, grumpy sharks, enormous bees and giant locusts.

The success of films like "Earthquake," "Jaws," "The Towering Inferno" and "King Kong" has led to a remarkable proliferation of grotesque adventures. In the coming months, we can look forward to "Exorcist II: The Heretic," "Orca" (about a killer whale), "Swarm" (about killer bees), "Empire of the Ants" (about killer ants), "Survival Run" (about nuclear devastation), "The Island of Dr. Moreau" (about a scientist who turns men into beasts and beasts into men), "Jaws II" and a couple of ambitious entries in the field of science-fiction—George Lucas's "Star Wars" and Steven Spielberg's "Close Encounters of the Third Kind," which is said to feature an invasion by little green men from Mars.

It may be that special effects are simply this year's fad, yet it could be that the achievements in this area are at the heart of what moviemaking really is, and that their unique quality cannot be duplicated in any other art. As Vincent Canby says elsewhere in this section, special effects are an essential aspect of "the emotionally liberating effects of movies."

His message is seconded by that master of the medium, Marshall McLuhan. "Of course! Of course!" he shouts out from his Toronto home. "It's not very mysterious—all these disaster movies with giant insects and green men reflect the way ordinary people feel about the new, non-human environment. Every time we get on the phone, every time we listen to the radio, we become humans without bodies, and without our bodies, we become free to roam in our fantasy worlds, and to dredge up every horror we find there. It's not necessarily bad, you know. Horror movies give us a real lift. If we can respond to the sound of angry bees or pigs being slaughtered, we're still alive, and that's terrific!"

From Hollywood, one hears different explanations for the moviemakers' passion for mechanically inflated beasts and trick-photography holocausts. Frank Van De Vere, the veteran special effects expert who recently won an Oscar for "King Kong," has his own theories about the subject. "When television came in, we went through a whole series of life-can-be-miserable movies," he says. "Established producers would spend $6 million on a movie about something real sad and the movie would go right down the tubes. Pretty soon, you got the inexperienced kids making things like 'Woodstock.' They were nice kids, with longhair and bare feet, and they were real creative. They used diffusion and shot into the sun—things their grandfathers had given up doing 50 years ago because they didn't work. Finally, people got tired of all that misery and experimentation, so now we're in a new era here."

Van De Vere, a quiet, silver-haired man, has devoted a great portion of his life to the art of good-natured deception. In "King Kong," for example, the world the audience sees does not really exist. The enormous wall which keeps Kong on his side of the South Pacific island exists somewhere in miniature, and scraps of it are lodged on life-size sets. But the main wall is the intricately detailed matte painting on glass by Lou Lichtenfield, a work now to be found on the wall of Van De Vere's office. The tiny painting, mounted on glass, appears to float in the air, with nothing above it, and nothing but clear glass below. But when the audience sees the film, it sees the sky above illuminated with fireworks while the natives scurry about below. All of this is combined in three or four sets of film by the complex art of "blue screen."

"Say you want to blow up a ship for a movie you're making," says Van De Vere, "but it costs too much to blow up a ship. So you send somebody out to take a shot of the ocean. Then you find a stock shot of a ship blowing up. Then suppose you want a moon up in the sky. We can put all that together for you so that when we're through with it, you've got a ship blowing up on an ocean with a moon in the sky."

"Just think about Kong for a minute," he says. "Dino de Laurentiis would like to have you think that the 42-foot gorilla was in every shot. Actually, he was only in about 25 feet of film. The rest of the time, it was a guy named Rick in a gorilla suit. What we really worked with was that 19-foot arm with the hand on it. Those shots were blue-screen shots. Remember when Kong wakes up that first morning with Dwan and she tries to run away and he plays cat-and-mouse with her? Well, first Rick plays it, in his gorilla suit, with his own arm behind him. Then, another time, another day maybe, we've got the arm out there, and the girl. We work out the whole scene with her and the arm. Then we put it all together, the island, the moon. . . ."

•

Later that day, in his cluttered studio, Van De Vere observes white-gloved workers bending intently over strips of film. "Here's one of the bees in 'Swarm,'" he says. "With the blue screen we can put in the picnickers later on. The whole aim of this art, of course, is not to let people figure out what we're doing. If you're conscious of the special effect you're watching, then it isn't a very good special effect."

Carolyn See is a freelance writer based in Los Angeles

Van De Vere then checks out some footage from "Exorcist II" in which a giant locust attacks a tribe of terrified Africans. "These are some of the hardest shots that have ever been done with the blue-screen process, because of those wings. They're transparent—you can actually see through them."

Surprisingly, there are really only three basic techniques used for creating special effects. First, the miniature, which looks terrific in repose but even better when it blows up or burns down or is swept away in a flood. Second, the mechanical effect, which includes fog and fire, as well as those astonishingly realistic bullet holes (tiny pockets of explosives taped to asbestos plates, attached to wires that run down the pantsleg of a stuntman and across the room to where a special-effects man pushes buttons for the prescribed dosage of death and destruction). And, finally, there is the blue-screen process itself, which composes all these effects— together with the blonde model and the bogus gorilla—into the final, technologically sophisticated nightmare.

Despite, or perhaps because of, the explainability of most of these special effects, great care is customarily taken to keep them secret. It doesn't take a giant mind to figure out that Irwin Allen must be using "macrophotography"—the art of photographing small things to look large—for "Swarm," his upcoming epic about villainous bees, just as Jacques Cousteau has photographically blown up tiny crayfish to the size of blimps for his television series.

If a particularly strict hush falls over the filming of all outer space moves. A spokesman—or *non*-spokesman—for "Close Encounters of the Third Kind" reacts with such horror when asked to discuss the film's special effects that it's as if he'd been asked to divulge germ-warfare secrets to a Soviet agent. A technician on the set will say only that plenty of night photography has been used, and bolts of black velvet to simulate galactic gloom.

•

The special-effects star of "Orca" is an enormous, hydraulically-powered whale that a team of Italian technicians operate by remote control—one man for eyes, one man for jaws, etc. Dino De Laurentis promises that his whopper of a whale will be more lifelike than his 42-foot King, who was distressingly arthritic in his movements.

Sometimes the impulse to boast outweighs the instinct for secrecy. In Peter Benchley's "The Deep," a genuine sunken ship, the British vessel H.M.S. Roan, was chosen as the prime location. Robert Shaw, Nick Nolte and Jacqueline Bisset, along with director Peter Yates and his cameraman, were all taught to dive 15 fathoms below the surface for establishing shots. Later, they did their diving and emoting in Bermuda, in the world's largest underwater set, a disc-shaped excavation measuring 30 feet deep and 120 feet across and containing 1 million gallons of water, as well as a perfect "miniature" reproduction of the Roan.

Working with special effects requires enormous partience, according to Elliot Shick, who is fresh from months on location with H.G. Wells's "The Island of Dr. Moreau." "The main special effect we had was the burning down of Dr. Moreau's compound and all the animals," he recalls. "And I want to say right now that we didn't injure one animal during the filming."

A multitude of monsters and other mechanical marvels will reign supreme in such forthcoming films as "Orca," "Close Encounters of the Third Kind," "Rollercoaster" and "Star Wars."

By the end of the burning—which took almost three weeks—stuntmen and crew were exhausted. Inside the compound, flame pots, which are similar to the pipes in a gas fireplace, were used after being being doctored with various powders to produce spectacular colors. The interiors of the building were set fire to again and again. Stuntmen, wearing asbestos suits dabbed with rubber cement, were sent running through flames that appeared to be burning animals to death but actually were pointed in the direction of the cameras rather than at the animals. In one scene, a "numanimal" (one of Dr. Moreau's dastardly experiments) wrestles a leopard; then both of them crash through a pane of artificial "candy" glass to a fiery death.

For many, the king of mechanical miracles is Glen Robinson, the man who destroyed the city of Los Angeles in "Earthquake," blew up the "Hindenberg," all the 30-year-olds to a flaming death in "Logan's Run," conjured up the mysterious fog bank in "King Kong," and built the hydraulically-powered 42-foot Kong himself.

For "Earthquake" Robinson built a 25-foot "miniature" dam, with five separate systems to destroy it. The flood waters came out of a giant Robinson-made flume, with enough calculated force to break the dam. In case that didn't work, a network of miniature primacord would blow it up. In case that didn't work, a giant cable with a pair of tongs would rip it apart. In case that didn't work, Robinson constructed a hydraulic ram to punch it out. In case that didn't work, a final cable system with a winch would pull it to bits. None of the extra four systems were necessary; the pure force of water broke the dam, as Robinson has known it would. God makes mistakes, Robinson never.

"He can build you a little cloud and it'll stay right there while you film it," says a co-worker. "He can set you on fire and put you right out again. He can blow you up and it won't hurt. You know something funny? M-G-M canned him a little while ago because he was too old. Then they had to keep hiring him back because he was the only one who knew what he was doing. Now he works all the time." ■

1977 My 1, II:1:5

FILM VIEW

VINCENT CANBY

Picturing Fantasy Is Central To Cinema

Encouraging news: the word from Hollywood this week is that the special effects people have never been busier whomping up the kind of fantasies that have been an essential part of cinema ever since man's first successful space trip in Georges Melies's "Voyage to The Moon" (1902). I wasn't around then but I was around at the age of four or five, in the early thirties, to see a film called "Hell Below." It was a submarine melodrama much like others of that era but it was apparently so effective that when poor, croaker-voiced Sterling Holloway was caught in a flooded compartment, which had been locked against his escape in order to save the rest of the ship, I had some trouble sorting out reality from movie illusion.

Me (to parent): "Was he drowned?" Parent (trying to watch the movie): "Yes." Me: "You mean he was really killed?" Parent: "Of course not. He's alive but he's supposed to be dead." Me: "He's pretending? He's not really drowned?" Parent: "He's not pretending." Me: "Then he is dead." Parent (with impatience): "No. He's perfectly all right." Me: "Then why are all of the other sailors crying?" Parent: "Because they think he's dead." " Me: "But he isn't?" Parent: "Yes, he is, in the movie." Me: "But not really?" Parent: "No." Me: "But if he isn't drowned really . . . ?"

And so on. I've no idea how long that discussion rambled on before I had a mitten stuffed into my mouth or before I grasped my first awareness of one of the things that makes movies so special. No matter how extraordinary and unusual they may seem, the events we see on the screen have reality even when we know they couldn't possibly be real. I suspect that one of the emotionally liberating effects of movies is this sort of bifocal response to them. In childhood, we can enjoy watching the spectacle of Vesuvius erupting and of lions tearing apart Christians secure in the knowledge that it's not really happening. Later on, I think, we enjoy a sight as remarkable as the destruction of Los Angeles in an earthquake because of the mock-terror of the event itself and because of the uncanny success of the special effects people who, through a variety of processes, make us believe that if and when it ever happens, it will probably look very much this way.

But then I may not be the toughest critic of what the special effects people do. To someone who still doesn't understand why his radio works, all cinema is a special effect, a grand illusion, at its best, sheer poetry and magic. Think of the first breath-taking sight of the relay station slowly revolving in the space of Stanley Kubrick's "2001," or the dazzling descent through the moons of Jupiter in the same film. Remember the peculiar beauty of the dust storm sweeping through Texas in "Bound for Glory," the hurricane in "Hurricane" and the sight of the Hindenberg sailing majestically over lower Manhattan in "The Hindenberg." A movie doesn't have to be especially good to be able to enchant us with such moments, though the special effects have to be of consistent quality. A little bit of tackiness can destroy everything. I recall seeing the 1951 "Quo Vadis" at the old Astor Theater the day after its premiere. Sitting in front of me in the packed house was a small boy, only slightly older than I had been when I first wrestled with the matter of illusion and reality in "Hell Below." The boy had been following the film with the devoted attention of the true cinema believer, squirming with delight as he watched Christians being eaten, gladiators having at each other, Rome going up flames, all of which was followed by one quick sequence, necessary to keep the plot moving, in which Deborah Kerr, looking prettily smudged, met Finlay Currie as Simon Peter on a road outside Rome.

The two actors had been photographed against a miniaturized view of Rome's smoldering ruins, projected onto a screen behind them in such a way that both actors were outlined with head-to-foot blue halos. The little boy, who had been struck pleasurably dumb by the magic of all the earlier spectacle scenes, snapped to attention. "Fake!" he shouted, thereby vitrually ending the movie for everyone else in the house.

• • •

Tacky special effects can sometimes exert their own kind of charm, as they do in the old Flash Gordon serials, but special effects aren't special when they are tacky. They are a breach of trust. For all the pains and trouble he took over his films, Cecil B. DeMille often asked us to accept patently phony stuff as the real thing. When Victor Mature pulled down the temple in "Samson and Delilah," I swear I saw some of the rocks bounce as if it the temple has been made of rubber. The parting of the Red Sea in "The Ten Commandments" still looks to me as if three pieces of film had been spliced together. The splicing was very neatly done but it hasn't much to do with the way I might have imagined the original event.

The effectiveness of special effects has as much to do with their use, with how they are placed within a film, as with the genius of the men who design them. This is something that the Japanese have never understood, or perhaps have never cared to understand. In Japanese spectacle films, more is more and that's all there is to it. In a film about the destruction of Tokyo, one of the favorite targets of Japanese special effects people (are they trying to tell the Emperor something?), they might open with a tidal wave to be followed with a new disaster every nine minutes. It's too much, too soon. One first gets bored, and then one starts to notice all the little failures of illusion—cars out of scale with buildings, buildings out of scale with monsters.

• • •

It was a wise decision on the part of the people responsible for "Jaws" to withhold any close-up shots of their man-made shark until the climax of the film, by which time the audience had been worked up to such a pitch of apprehension and excitement that it probably would have accepted as terrifying stock footage of an out-of-sorts guppy, magnified, of course.

Effective special effects can be mind-expanding (the shots of Fritz Lang's futurist city in "Metropolis"), lyrical (the balloon sequences in "Around The World in 80 Days"), terrifying (the progress of the fire in "The Towering Inferno") or simply funny (the disintegration of the United Nations Building in "The Pink Panther Strikes Again"). Sometimes, as in too many science-fiction movies the special effects people run away with the film.

What do you remember of "Logan's Run"? Aside from the beautifully photographed "carousel sequence, in which old people of 30 were ritually reborn (executed), all I remember are the ray guns, TV screens the size of "Guernica," giant shopping centers and a lot of people walking around on shiny floors that never showed scuff marks.

• • •

Although I have great affection for the most outrageous of movie tricks—King Kong scaling either Empire State Building or the World Trade Center, the Invisible Man puttng on a trench coat, hat and dark glasses, Dorothy being swept away to Oz by a Kansas tornado, Fred Astaire dancing on a ceiling—there are some special effects I never buy. These include the kind of mythical monsters created by Ray Harryhausen in a film like "The Seventh Voyage of Sinbad" and by the Japanese in their various Godzilla pictures. I can marvel at the cleverness of the special effects people but what they've fabricated bears no relation to my fantasies. I also have trouble accepting the virtual indestructability of the Boeing airplanes in the "Airport" movies. You'd think they were made out of reinforced concrete. Rabbits photographed to look as if they were 10-foot-tall mutants that weigh a ton simply are not frightening. They are Easter bunnies and about as scary as giraffes.

The term "special effects" takes in a lot of territory, and many are as benign as Mary Poppins taking flight or the split screens that Woody Allen uses so comically in "Annie Hall." I suppose we remember the spectacle of various disasters most vividly because they are the sort of things we're not likely to see, or, if we do, to see and live to tell about. But whether the special effect is the destruction of Rome, the capsizing of the Poseidon or the levitation of a Volkswagon, we delight in witnessing something that can't be done anywhere or, certainly, not done as well. Our imaginations can be tickled even when aesthetics are forgotten. This is the way it was, says the special effects man, or, this is the way it might be.

1977 My 1, II:15:1

ANDY WARHOL'S BAD, directed by Jed Johnson; screenplay by Pat Hackett and George Abagnalo; produced by Jeff Tornberg; music, Mike Bloomfield; director of photography, Allan Metzger; editor, David McKenna; an Andy Warhol/Jeff Tornberg production, distributed by New World Films. At the Cinerama 2, Broadway near 47th Street, and other theaters. This film has been rated X.

Mrs. Aiken	Carroll Baker
LT	Perry King
Mary Aiken	Susan Tyrrell
PG	Stefania Cassini
RC	Cyrinda Foxe
Grandmother	Mary Boylan
Detective Hughes	Charles McGregor
Ingrid Joyner	Tere Tereba
Estelle	Brigid Polk
Young Mother	Susan Blond
Mr. Aiken	Gordon Oasheim
Marsha	Maria Smith
Glenda	Geraldine Smith
O'Reilly	Lawrence Tierney
Russell Joyner	Joe Lamba
Joe Leachman	John Starke
Mrs. Leachman	Renee Paris

By VINCENT CANBY

IF ANDY WARHOL and the gang down at the Factory are trendsetters, heaven help the human race. Sex, even in its kinkier manifestations, is out. Gone, if not totally forgotten. It's so passé in "Andy Warhol's Bad," the newest film to be put out under the Warhol franchise, that we may now have to consider "Blue Movie" and "Trash" as the supreme examples of the Warhol romantic period.

"Bad," which opened yesterday at the Cinerama 2 and other theaters, was directed by Jed Johnson and written by Pat Hackett and George Abagnalo, two young but longtime Factory members, without the apparent help of Paul Morrissey, the achitect of the Warhol "Dracula" and "Frankenstein" films.

•

"Bad" is not only the most stylistically conventional Warhol comedy to date, it is also the most forthrightly satirical, being a picture of an America that looks like middle-class Queens, coast to coast, in which the men are either impotent or disinterested and the women concerned solely with the acquisition of clothes, getting revenge of one sort or another, and seeing that the house is neat and tidy. Having triumphed over their sexual obsessions, the Warhol characters have become lobotomized members of the consumer society.

Keeping things moving in this society is Mrs. Aiken, a Queens beautician whose specialty is hair-removal, a character marvelously well-played by Carroll Baker as if she were a nastily efficient Schrafft's hostess.

•

Mrs. Aiken, a handsome blonde whose figure has the look of something encased in a steel corset, is the archetypal American mom who has had to take things in hand when dad proved wanting. In addition to the electrolysis treatments—"650 hairs an hour"—she gives in her dining room-office, Mrs. Aiken presides over a sort of mini-Murder Inc. Thirty years ago she might have run a lending library from her house. Today she provides, on contract, assassins who are mostly bored young women who like the easy hours.

"Bad" is not to be interpreted as a Major Statement on our time. It is, indeed, as much an artifact of our time as a comment upon it. It's a dead-panned, Grand Guignol comedy about several days in the life of Mrs. Aiken as she goes about keeping her house in order, removing unwanted hair, putting up with her dimwitted daughter-in-law (Susan Tyrrell), who has been abandoned by Mrs. Aiken's son, tending to her senile mother, and grimly sending her husband off to spend a day at the nearest Off Track Betting parlor.

A lot of the film is taken up with watching Mrs. Aiken's operatives at work, and it's these squences that have landed the film its X rating, which should be an alarm to anyone who objects to blood and gore even when they are so patently fake.

One sequence in particular, in which a baby, a chronic screamer, is tossed out the window by its mother, isn't easy to take even when you can clearly see it's a doll. Some other set-pieces include the the amputation of a finger and the murder of a dog, the latter carried out for a customer who demands, "You've got to do it viciously —not ouchless."

•

"Bad" comes close to the sort of thing that Joe Orton, the late English playwright, was doing in plays like "Entertaining Mr. Sloane" and "Loot." It means to be outrageous. It also presents the audience with a dilemma. If we become outraged and walk out, as one might in the baby-murder scene, it laughs at us: This is, after all, only a film, so why don't we become outraged at the various real horrors in the world around us? If we don't become outraged, says the film, we may not be too different from the robots in the movie.

In addition to Miss Tyrrell, the supporting cast includes Perry King as Mrs. Aiken's only male operative, a fellow who explains his impotence by saying, "I got a disability. I committed suicide last year," and Brigid Polk, a Warhol veteran ("Chelsea Girls"), as the dog-hater. They all are very peculiar and very good.

"Bad" is not a movie to recommend to anyone without a warning, but the film is more aware of what it's up to than any Warhol film I've seen to date.

1977 My 5, C22:5

Fury Left and Right

REBELLION IN PATAGONIA, directed by Hector Olivera; screenplay (Spanish with English subtitles) by Osvaldo Bayer, Fernando Ayala and Mr. Olivera, based on the novel by Mr. Bayer; produced by Mr. Ayala; director of photography, Victor Hugo Caula; music, Oscar Cardozo Ocampo; editor, Oscar Montauti; produced by Aries Cinematografica Argentina, and distributed by Transcontinental Film Center. Running time: 109 minutes. At the Thalia Theater, Broadway at 95th Street, and Jean Renoir Cinema, Second Avenue at 10th Street. This film has not been rated.

Antonio Soto .... Luis Brandoni
Jose Font .... Federico Luppi
Schultz .... Pepe Soriano
Commander Zavala .... Hector Alterio
Outerello .... Osvaldo Terranova

By VINCENT CANBY

THE HISTORY of Hector Olivera's 1974 Argentine film, "Rebellion in Patagonia," is almost as full of reversals in fortune, followed by success, followed by other setbacks, as the tumultuous social history it documents.

The film, which opened yesterday at the Thalia and Jean Renoir Cinema on a double-bill with "Union Maids," is about the series of bloody strikes that marked the first attempts to organize by urban and rural workers in the southernmost province of Argentina in the early 1920's.

Those attempts succeeded, failed, succeeded, and ultimately were decisively destroyed by the government. The Argentine Army imposed a sort of order-by-execution that has since become a way of life for the huge, potentially rich, underpopulated country that stretches from the subtropics almost to the Antarctic.

"Rebellion in Patagonia" takes a long view of history but when it was ready for release in 1974, at the time the presidency of Juan Perón was turning more and more to the right, the military men thought it advisable that the film be shelved. When, after a lot of controversy, the movie finally was released in Buenos Aires, it became a hit and then went on to be honored at film festivals in Berlin and Taormina.

Since then, several of its principal actors, their lives threatened by the Argentine Anti-Communist Alliance, a very busy, aggressive, right-wing vigilante group, have taken up residence abroad. The furies that motivated the action in the film—the historic schisms between the Argentine right and left—live on.

To use the terms right and left implies that the disagreements that separated Argentinians after World War I were politically more sophisticated than they really were.

It was the haves versus the have-nots, the wealthy landowners allied with city interests against the rural and urban workers. Though each group had many members who were not Argentinians, each liked to warn against the influences of "foreigners" in the ranks of their enemies. In a land populated by immigrants, there's nothing lower than the late arrival.

"Rebellion in Patagonia" covers a great deal of ground in the sweeping style of the muralist, opening with the assassination of an Army colonel in Buenos Aires in 1923 and then going back several years to describe the events leading up to that assassination.

Most of the action takes place on the broad plains of Patagonia, one of the most beautiful, most spooky landscapes on earth. It was there that a coalition of Communists and anarchists had successfully organized the workers on the sheep farms. When the landowners later refuse to honor their agreements, new strikes break out and the Army chief, once sympathetic to populist cause, sets out to break the movement in a campaign that's estimated to have taken the lives of 3,000 workers.

The film is a collection of vignettes, richly detailed with the sort of character and incident that recall nostalgically but without sentimentality the sense of high purpose of early trade-unionism. The movie has a great fondness for these seminal labor fighters, including a young Spanish activist (Luis Brandoni) who is also a realist, and a fine old German idealist (Pepe Soriano) who puts his life on the line for his beliefs.

It's not all black versus white, though. Mr. Olivera defines divisions within the ranks of both sides, sometimes tragically and often wittily, as in an early trade-union meeting when the success of a strike is celebrated by the Communists with a rousing anthem while their nonpoliticized Chilean compatriots look on aghast. They haven't yet been taught that politics can be expressed in song.

1977 My 6, C10:3

The Argentine army is called in to crush a strike in the film "Rebellion in Patagonia"

Trauma of Imprisonment

LES ORDRES (The Orders), directed by Michel Brault; screenplay (French with English subtitles) by Mr. Brault; directors of photography, Mr. Brault and Francois Protat; distributed by New Yorker Films. Running time: 107 minutes. At the Film Forum, 15 Vandam Street.

Marie Boudreau .... Helene Loiselle
Clermont Boudreau .... Jean Lapointe
Dr. Beauchemin .... Guy Provost
Richard Lavoie .... Claude Gauthier
Claudette Dusseault .... Louise Forestier

"Les Orders," written and directed by Michel Brault, is an angry, beautifully acted French-Canadian film based —like those of Costa-Gavras—on an actual event. The time is October 1970, shortly after the kidnapping of a British diplomat and a provincial cabinet minister by an urban guerrilla group calling itself the Quebec Liberation Front. The Canadian Government subsequently suspended civil liberties in Quebec arrested 450 people, few of whom apparently had anything to do with the kidnapping, and held them without charge, some for as long as several months.

'Les Ordres" is not about French-Canadian liberation, though it clearly finds the English to be villains. Rather it's about the terrifying speed with which democratic processes can be liquidated and even more about the psychological effects of imprisonment.

The film follows the case histories of five persons who had peripheral associations to politics — a union representative and his wife, a physician, an unemployed laborer and a social worker. Although only one man is tortured, by being made to endure what turns out to be a mock-execution, each of the victims is effectively traumatized through humiliation, fear and loss of identity.

These scenes are harowing to watch, but one suspects that the director has loaded his dice. Would such treatment be condoned if the victim was known to be guilty? That question isn't answered, but because the characters in "Les Ordres" are presented as innocent, one wonders, whether the film's humanitarianism has its limits.

Mr. Brault, who was the cameraman for Claude Jutra's "Mon Oncle Antoine" and "Kamouraska," is immensely good with his actors, none of whom is known to me, but he hasn't been able to resist some of the less interesting stylistic affectations of the day.

These include the arbitrary switching back and forth between color and black and white, overlapping sound and terribly tedious, phony interludes in which the narrative is interrupted to have the actors talk about their roles. Ingmar Bergman got away with this once ("The Passion of Anna") and once turns out to have been enough.

"Les Ordres," which opened at the Film Forum yesterday, will be seen there through Sunday at 7:30 P.M. and repeated at the same hour next Thursday through Sunday. VINCENT CANBY

1977 My 6, C10:5

BLACK AND WHITE IN COLOR, directed by Jean-Jacques Annaud; screenplay (French with English subtitles) by Mr. Annaud and Georges Conchon; produced by Arthur Cohn, Jacques Perrin and Giorgio Silvagni; director of photography, Claude Agostini; music, Pierre Bachelet; editor, Francoise Bonnot; an Arthur Cohn production, distributed by Allied Artists. Running time: 91 minutes. At the Paris theater, 58th Street west of Fifth Avenue. This film has been rated PG.

Sergeant Bosselet .... Jean Carmet
Paul Rechampot .... Jacques Dutilho
Marinette .... Catherine Rouvel
Hubert Fresnoy .... Jacques Spiesser
Maryvonne .... Dora Doll
Caprice .... Maurice Barrier
Jacques Rechampot .... Claude Legros
Pere Simon .... Jacques Monnet
Pere Jean De La Croix .... Peter Berling
Barthelemy .... Marius Beugre Boignan

"BLACK AND WHITE IN COLOR"—Jacques Monnet, a French priest, is carried to the front to watch a World War I skirmish between Africans conscripted by French and German colonialists.

Lamartine .... Baye Macoumba Diop
Fidele .... Aboubaker Toure
Kraft .... Dieter Schidor
Major Anglais .... Marc Zuber
Haussmann .... Klaus Huebl
Oscar .... Mamadou Coulibaly
Assomption .... Memel Atchori

By VINCENT CANBY

The setting is the dry, hot savannah of West Africa in late 1914. The inhabitants of a small French trading post in the interior live in easy alliance with the members of a tiny German garrison a few miles away. They don't fraternize exactly, but they get along in their separate spheres of boredom.

The German sergeant spends his days seeing that his handful of black troops maintains military routine. The French sergeant, though, lazes about, drinks wine with the French shopkeepers and their wives and gossips about the peculiar geologist who shares their existence, but never seems to be a part of it. The young Frenchman is different from them, meaning he's educated.

This somnolent peace is destroyed with the arrival of an old Paris newspaper with the word of the outbreak of war. "Who with?" asks one Frenchman. "Germany." "That's strange," says the first. "I would have thought it would be with England." The small crew of boozing, foolish French patriots, with the spiritual support of their two resident priests, decides to march on the German fort for the greater glory of France.

Their war begins cheerfully with a picnic lunch attended by the ladies, who have come along to watch the tricolor raised over the German fort. Instead, they see their troops (about two dozen hastily impressed, disinterested blacks who carry their guns on their heads) vanquished by a single machine gun.

This is the beginnig of "Black and White in Color" and it is not terribly promising. There's hardly a cliché overlooked by Jean-Jacques Annaud, the director, as he sets his scene for yet another film on the senselessness of war. The Germans are bears for discipline. The French are hysterical, convivial. The priests are fat-bellied and venal and the blacks infinitely patient with the idiosyncracies of the civilized.

But stick with "Black and White in Color" a little longer. What starts as a broad, obvious, rather pious comedy peopled by musical-comedy types turns into something much more complex as it goes along. It's less about the senselessness of war (a movie that is pro-war on principle might be more easy to become excited about) than it is about the way extraordinary times and circumstances can create leaders.

The central figure of the film is Hubert, the French geologist (Jacques Spiesser), the soft-spoken, self-assured, almost pretty young man who, after unsuccessfully trying to stop the original attack against the German fort, becomes the acknowledged commander of the desperate Frenchmen. The way Hubert takes charge is comic and mysterious. He is decisive, blunt, polite, cruel, high-handed and distant. Like De Gaulle, he always behaves properly, but he doesn't tolerate fools.

As the young man finds his character, so does the movie. In an excellent scene in the midst of the crisis, after Hubert has bulldozed his compatriots into some form of order, the young man makes his first official appearance (at a review of the French "troops") with his stunning-looking, ever-mute but extremely haughty black mistress on his arm. There's nothing for these cowed, petit-bourgeois French shopkeepers to do but bow and curtsy to the consort.

Jacques Spiesser
Like DeGaulle he behaves properly, but doesn't tolerate fools.

The performances also improve immensely as the film moves on. At the beginning, Jean Carmet and Jacques Dufilho as, respectively, the lazy sergeant and the hysterical shopkeeper (a sort of spin-off of the characters played by Louis De Funes), are numbingly predictable, but later, as supporting characters, they become very funny. Mr. Spiesser is fine as the assertive young leader. It's a performance that reveals itself so quietly that it's not until the film is almost over that one understands what's happening—and because I'm not allowed to reveal the ending, I can only say that the final sequence of the film makes everything that's gone before worth attending to.

"Black and White in Color," which opened yesterday at the Paris Theater, was awarded the Oscar as the best foreign-language film this year as the entry from the Ivory Coast, where the movie was shot. There's been some flak about this because the film's executive producer is Swiss and its director, writers and most of the cast are French. In winning the Oscar, it had to beat both "Seven Beauties" and "Cousin, Cousine," which says less about the quality of the winner than the peculiar rules by which the members of the Academy of Motion Picture Arts and Sciences vote in this category.

●

"Black and White in Color," which has been rated PG ("Parental Guidance Suggested"), includes some minor nudity and a few vulgar expressions that, in subtitles, look like the sort of graffiti one might see scribbled in much larger print on any New York bus or subway car.

1977 My 9, 27:1

All Are Engulfed

TOKKAN (BATTLE CRY). Screenplay written, and directed by Kihachi Okamoto; director of photography, Daisuke Kimura; a Kihacni Production released by ATG Productions of Tokyo. At the Regency, Broadway and 67th Street. Running time 95 minutes. This film has not been rated.

Senta .... Toshitaaka Ito
Manjiro .... Yusuke Okada
Judayu Hoseya .... Etsushi Takahashi
O-Ito .... Hiroko Isayama
Teru .... Emiko Senba

By A. H. WEILER

KIHACHI OKAMOTO, one of Japan's industrious director-writers, illustrates once again in "Tokkan," the new offering in the Regency Theater's Nipponese film series, that wars are hellish and fruitless for the men who fight and die in them. If that horribly truthful idea is not precisely new to Japanese movie-makers, Mr. Okamoto's perceptive concentration on the personalities of those caught up in conflict and his sense of humor make "Tokkan" an interesting, sometimes exciting appreciation of the unchanging nature of men in war, even though it is set in a century-old fuzzy past.

For the record, Mr. Okamoto has been dealing with Japanese history in such sword-swinging adventures as "Samurai Assassin," "Sword of Doom" and "Red Lion," all of which starred Toshiro Mifune, as well as the World War II dramas "The Emperor and the General" and "The Battle of Okinawa."

●

In "Tokkan" he is cleaving to the 1868 period of "Red Lion" and the clashes between the dying Tokugawa Shogunate and the emerging Meiji powers.

Of course, the historical aspects of "Tokkan," which probably will be foggy to most local viewers, are indicated by

English subtitles. But despite the time, place and exotic circumstance, most of the principals are simple citizens who don't appear to be making history so much as they are naïvely engulfed by it.

With the aid of an ancient narrator, "Tokkan" evolves largely as the tale of Senta, a wide-eyed peasant farm youth whose urge to become involved in the excitement of the clan wars in his bailiwick is almost as desperate as his need for sex. It's also the story of Manjiro, who isn't as cloddish, but is out for as much loot as possible, while not overlooking the girls during this civil strife.

Naturally, Mr. Okamoto's fiction bristles with action. His leading characters —including Judayu Hoseya, as Senta's tough military leader, and Emiko Senba, as the prostitute that Senta comes to love, among many others—are caught up in a succession of skirmishes. The fact that these are highly stylized, as is the broad acting, the grimaces and the studied posturing, does not detract from the explicitly gory consequences of battle and the indifference of the entrenched feudal lords to war's effects.

•

Toskitaaka Ito and Yusuke Okada, as Senta and Manjiro, respectively, are vigorously athletic in the martial and sexual bouts that are reeled off with regularity between moments of self-appraisal. If the plot and subplots seem convoluted, they stand out as the simple, occasionally funny characters who project the confusion and waste of war as well as the climactic observation that "you fight from morning till night, but nobody makes a gain."

"Tokkan" is being shown today through Saturday, together with the 1973 adventure "Zatoichi Meets His Equal."

1977 My 11, C16:5

Invasion of Privacy

THE HOUSE BY THE LAKE. Written and directed by William Fruet; produced by Ivan Reitman; executive producers, Andre Link and John Dunning; edited by Jean LaFleur and Debbie Karjala; cinematography by Robert Saad; released by American International Pictures. At local theaters. Running time 89 minutes. This film has been rated R.

Diane	Brenda Vaccaro
Lep	Don Stroud
Harry Blatt	Chuck Shamata
Runt	Richard Ayres
Frankie	Kyle Edwards
Stanley	Don Gransbery
Spragg	Ed McNamara
Ralph	Michael Kirby

By A. H. WEILER

THERE'S A GOOD DEAL less than meets the eye in "The House by the Lake," which opened at local theaters yesterday. Despite the fact that this Canadian-made shocker leaves a trail of rape, burning, drowning and seven corpses, the bloodletting is as mindless as the wanton wrecking of the handsomely appointed, titular Tudor mansion set amid "10 miles of privacy" in beautifully rustic Ontario where all the carnage was filmed.

William Fruet, the director-writer, may not be long on logic, but he appears to be as devoted to fast cars as he is to explicitly earthy dialogue and violence. It's obvious from the start, when Chuck Shamata, the young, successful, swinging dentist dreaming lustful dreams of conquest at his "house," allows Brenda Vaccaro, his date, to drive his Corvette in a race with four menacing, drunken hoodlums led by Don Stroud. Of course, she forces them into a ditch and, naturally, the vengeful gang tracks the pair to the secluded mansion with the resulting goings-on.

There may be a touch of validity to the frustrating helplessness of the couple faced by all of this murderous idiocy. But Don Stroud, no stranger to villainy, is, in this case, simply a largely unmotivated, unrestrained killer who is no better than the equally ill-fated Richard Ayres, Kyle Edwards and Don Gransbery, as his unkempt, moronic mates.

Mr. Shamata has a fatuous moment or two as the bragging sybarite dentist, but Miss Vaccaro, who ducks his advances easily, is defeated by an unbelievable role that requires her to be an expert driver and mechanic, traumatized rape victim and avenger. It should have been obvious to her, as it is to this observer, that "The House by the Lake" is hardly a place to visit, despite its lovely surroundings.

1977 My 12, C22:3

Sifting Sand

CROSS OF IRON, directed by Sam Peckinpah; screenplay by Julius J. Epstein, Walter Kelley and James Hamilton; produced by Wolf C. Hartwig and Alex Winitsky; executive producer, Arlene Sellers; music, Ernest Gold; editors, Tony Lawson, Herbert Taschner and Murray Jordan; director of photography, John Coquillon; distributed by Avco Embassy Pictures. Running time: 120 minutes. At Loews State 2, Broadway at 45th Street; Orpheum, 86th Street near Third Avenue, and other theaters. This film has been rated R.

Sergeant Steiner	James Coburn
Captain Stransky	Maximilian Schell
Colonel Brandt	James Mason
Captain Kiesel	David Warner
Kruger	Klaus Lowitsch
Zoll	Arthur Brauss

By VINCENT CANBY

WATCHING Sam Peckinpah's "Cross of Iron," you realize it's still possible to take this erratic director —"The Wild Bunch," "The Ballad of Cable Hogue" and "The Killer Elite"— seriously but it's no longer very rewarding. It's like sifting Coney Island sand for pennies. You work all day to come up with a backache.

"Cross of Iron" is Mr. Peckinpah's least interesting, least personal film in years, a hysterically elaborate, made-in-Yugoslavia war spectacle, the work of international financiers and a multinational cast, most of whom are supposed to be Germans although they sound like delegates to an international PEN convention.

The film, which opened at Loews State 2, the Orpheum and other theaters yesterday, is about a small detachment of German troops on the collapsing Russian front in 1943. There's the gracious German colonel, played by James Mason, who is English; the stiff-backed Prussian captain, played by Maximilian Schell, who is Swiss; the rugged German corporal, played by James Coburn, who is from Nebraska, and the German enlisted men who are played by real Germans.

Although throughout the film the artillery barrages are nonstop, the rations are meager, and disease is everywhere, the worst thing these soldiers endure is a speech contagion. Whenever Mr. Schell or the German actors have a scene with the English or American actors, the accents of the English and Americans go suddenly Teutonic as if in the siege of belligerent consonants.

There's not a decent performance in the entire film, something for which the director must be held accountable, along with the people who provided the screenplay. This is nothing much more than a frame for the special effects and a slight story about the antagonism between the brave, disillusioned corporal (a Good German) and the aristocratic Prussian (the Bad German). It may be of historical interest to note that there's only one Nazi in the movie and although he's not nice, it's the Prussian who's the villain.

Mr. Peckinpah's continuing concern for the corruptibility of children is something, given the once-over-lightly treatment behind the opening credits, which detail the rise and fall of the Nazi war machine, while the rest of the movie is virtually a parody of his machismo themes. "A man is generally what he feels himself to be," says Mr. Coburn at one point, but these characters don't have a convincing feeling among them.

I can't believe that the director ever had his heart in this project, which, from the beginning, looks to have been prepared for the benefit of the people who set off explosives. However, the battle footage is so peculiarly cut into the narrative that you often don't know who is doing what to whom. The visual effect, especially when bodies, buildings and vehicles are blown up in slow motion, becomes as Abstractly Expressionistic as a Jackson Pollock. The blood is thicker than water. It's paint.

1977 My 12, C22:4

"CROSS OF IRON"—Maximilian Schell and James Coburn, grimly determined German soldiers, open fire on the advancing Russians.

Poignant Middle Age

COUSIN ANGELICA (La Prima Angelica), directed by Carlos Saura; screenplay (Spanish with English subtitles) by Rafael Azcona and Mr. Saura; produced by Elias Querejeta; music, Luis de Pablo; distributed by New Yorker Films. Running time: 106 minutes. At the D. W. Griffith Theater, 59th Street near Second Avenue. This film has not been rated.

Luis	Jose Luis Lopez Vazquez
Angelica (adult)	Lina Canalejas
Angelica (child)	Maria Clara Fernandez
Anselmo	Fernando Delgado
Aunt Pilar (old)	Josefina Diaz
Aunt Pilar (middle-age)	Lola Cardona
The nun	Julieta Serrano
Mother of Luis	Encarna Paso
Father of Luis	Pedro Sempson

By VINCENT CANBY

LUIS (José Luis Lopez Vazquez) is an unmarried, middle-aged, Barcelona businessman. He's soft-spoken and has the manner

"COUSIN ANGELICA"—Jose Luis Lopez Vasquez, a middle-aged bachelor, fantasizes about Maria Clara Fernandez, his childhood sweetheart during the Spanish Civil War.

of someone who keeps to the background. Perhaps he's self-conscious about his lack of hair and about the oval face that recalls the faces of clowns who are meant to seem most comic when they are most sad, though Luis is not a comic character. He's self-contained and intelligent, the sort of man, you feel, who has made a satisfactory adjustment to life by scaling down his dreams to fit an overnight bag.

At the beginning of Carlos Saura's fine, sorrowful and poignant Spanish film, "Cousin Angélica," Luis is taking the bones of his long-dead mother from Barcelona to her family's crypt in southern Spain, where Luis grew up with his Falangist relatives while his father was fighting for the Republican cause.

"Cousin Angélica," which opened yesterday at the D.W. Griffith Theater, is a voyage into the past quite unlike any other I've ever seen in a movie, both because Spain's recent history is so particular and because of Mr. Saura's way of always dealing with memory so that it becomes an extension of the immediate present.

"Cousin Angélica" is not simply about Luis's childhood before and during the civil war. It's about Luis's recollections of his childhood as he renews contacts with his family, especially with his cousin Angélica, the sweet, pigtailed little girl he once loved and who has grown into a handsome, rather ordinary woman whose disappointments frighten him.

Mr. Saura doesn't use conventional flashbacks, which are as isolated from time and feeling as postcard pictures are removed from a tourist's actual experiences. When Luis recalls scenes from his childhood, he walks into them as the middle-aged man he is, a theatrical device that works in films much more effectively than I might have imagined.

En route once again to his relatives, the tearful Luis is comforted by his mother and father. There is nothing exceptional about this scene except that when we see the middle-age, cardigan-wearing Luis being soothed by parents younger than he is we are suddenly presented not only with a memory of the past but with everything that's accrued in the intervening years—with fear, anger and humiliation, but, also with the sense of loss that has haunted his maturity.

The older Luis sits in his schoolroom listening to a priest tell a horror story about a little classmate, killed in an air raid, who may or may not be eternally damned depending on whether or not the boy had "given in to temptation" the morning he was killed. No wonder Luis never married.

The recollected scenes of tentative courtship between Luis and the young Angélica, played by a beautiful, dark-haired actress named María Clara Fernandez are both intensely moving and slightly perverse, being simultaneously a remembrance of not-quite-forgotten intimacies and a description of where Luis is now, a contemporary Spaniard whose scars remain raw, if unseen. He's a Humbert Humbert with no will to act, without even a fantasy life.

José Luis Lopez Vazquez is super as Luis, apparently cheerful, self-contained and settled, though forever disconnected from the kind of family life he remembers with such mixed feelings.

Spain, though, is the real subject of the film, and at the time it was released there — 1974 — "Cousin Angélica" caused quite a stir with its references to the war, Spanish Catholicism and the possible nobility of at least some members of the Republican cause. Even if it's difficult for someone not familiar with the subtleties of Spanish life to get all of these references, the movie is extraordinarily compelling, an invitation into a world until recently closed, but whose vitality has remained undiminished.

1977 My 13, C5:3

Science-Fiction Horror Story Backfires All the Way

THE CAR, directed by Elliot Silverstein; screenplay by Dennis Shryack and Michael Butler and Lane Slate. based on a story by Mr. Shryack and Mr. Butler; produced by Marvin Birdt and Mr. Silverstein; director of photography, Gerald Hirschfeld; editor, Michael McCroskey; music, Leonard Rosenman; distributed by Universal Pictures. Running time: 98 minutes. At the National Theater, Broadway at 43d Street, 86th Street East Theater, near Third Avenue, and Murray Hill Theater, 34th Street near Third Avenue. This film has been rated PG.

Wade Parent..............James Brolin
Luke..............Ronny Cox
Lauren..............Kathleen Lloyd
Everett..............John Marley
Amos..............R. G. Armstrong
John Morris..............John Rubinstein
Margie..............Elizabeth Thompson
Ray Mott..............Roy Jenson
Lynn Marie..............Kim Richards
Debbie..............Kyle Richards
Miss McDonald..............Kate Murtagh
Metcalf..............Robert Phillips
Bertha..............Doris Dowling
Chas..............Henry O'Brien

By VINCENT CANBY

"The Car," which opened at three theaters yesterday, has all the ingredients of a parody, although someone has made the mistake of doing it straight. It's a cross between a science-fiction and a horror film about an angry, driverless automobile that terrorizes a small Utah town for several days, squashing one hitchhiker, two bicyclists, one sheriff, one school teacher and assorted policemen.

The people who made the film (see box, if you really care) clearly didn't have enough interest in the project to provide it with any kind of mythological substructure. This car is simply mean—perhaps its spark plugs hurt. I think we are supposed to believe the car is demonically possessed because it won't go into cemeteries, but I know people who won't go into cemeteries and have never suspected they were more than superstitious or lazy. The performances are terrible—thin and overwrought in the manner of actors trying to improvise without an idea in their heads.

•

"The Car," which has been rated PG ("Parental Guidance Suggested"], is such an inept movie that even its vulgar language is unbelievable—it sounds worse than it really is. The actual gore is minimal.

1977 My 14, 14:2

JAIL BAIT (Wildwechsel), directed by Rainer Werner Fassbinder; screenplay (German with English dialogue) by Mr. Fassbinder, based on a novel by Franz Xaver Kroetz; director of photography, Dietrich Lohmann; music, Ludwig van Beethoven; distributed by New Yorker Films. Running time: 99 minutes. At the New Yorker Theater, Broadway at 89th Street. This film has not been rated.

Hanni..............Eva Mattes
Franz..............Harry Baer
Hanni's father..............Jorg von Liebenfels
Hanni's mother..............Ruth Drexel
Doctor..............Hanna Schygulla
Franz's friend..............El Hedi Ben Salem
Factory manager..............Kurt Raab
Prison matron..............Irm Hermann

By VINCENT CANBY

"Jail Bait" is the intentionally slangy English rendering of the original German title of Rainer Werner Fassbinder's 1972 German film, "Wildwechsel" (literally, "Wild Game"), a melodrama that mixes the tacky with the sublime in much the same way that its soundtrack switches back and forth between early 1960's-sounding pop records, full of loudly proclaimed laments for that week's lost love, and the music of Beethoven.

"Jail Bait," which opened yesterday at the New Yorker as part of the theater's continuing Fassbinder festival, is Mr. Fassbinder's "La Peau Douce," a close-up examination of the sort of event that might make a two- or three-paragraph item in the local newspaper.

•

In "La Peau Douce," François Truffaut found evidence of poetic misalliance in a banal murder story. Mr. Fassbinder finds fury in the shape of a mindless Erinyes who destroys because she's peeved. "Jail Bait" touches on a number of other things, but misogyny is the dominant theme. Beware, it says. The danger presented by women is not symbolic—it's real, lethal and wanton and, in this case, it's named Hanni.

Hanni (Eva Mattes) is an astonishingly well-developed 14-year-old, as full-breasted and round-hipped as a Rubens model with a fondness for ice cream and Cokes. She wears her hair in braids, frolics unselfconsciously with her truck-driver father and would appear to be the perfect child in a household where no room is without its crucifix or picture of Jesus, Mary or one of the saints.

One day after school Hanni allows herself to be picked up by Franz (Harry Baer), the sort of 19-year-old who has been told too often that he looks like James

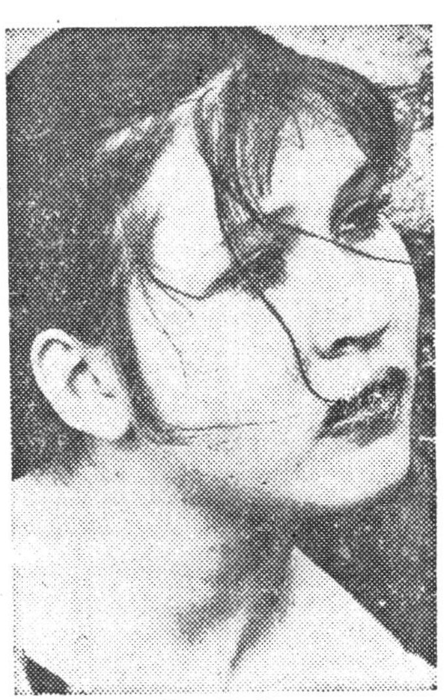

Eva Mattes
Staggering self-assurance

Dean. Harry wears his well pomaded hair in an artfully teased pompadour, favors studded jeans and drives a motorcycle. That afternoon in a haybarn, Franz deflowers Hanni with a good deal less fuss than he'd anticipated. When he mentions this, she shrugs and points out that if it hadn't been him, it would have had to be someone else. "Why are you getting dressed?" he says. "Why not?" is the reply. "There's nothing else to do."

•

"Jail Bait" is "The Blue Angel" without the hysterics of Jannings and the mystery of Dietrich. It's a tragedy for the soft-drink, fast-food, drive-in generation—cryptic and almost as cold as Hanni, who, having once been responsible for Franz's being sent to jail (for impairing the morals of a minor), immediately takes up with him again on his release.

Franz, of course, is no great brain, though he swaggers as he thinks a man should. As written, and as played (gently) by Mr. Baer, he's no match for the rapacious Hanni. When she suggests that their only recourse is to murder her father, he finally agrees. He tells himself—perhaps vaguely remembering a movie he's seen—that "it's men's work."

From this outline you might think that "Jail Bait" is less political than such other Fassbinder films as "Mother Kusters Goes to Heaven," "Fox," "The Bitter Tears of Petra Von Kant" and "Ali," but its quite as concerned as those films with the uses of power and the quality of life in bisected, postwar Germany.

It's also obsessed with a particularly adolescent fantasy about the difference between men and women. At one point Hanni, a role played by Miss Mattes with staggering self-assurance, kids Franz about the possibility of her father's catching them and castrating the younger man. "Then," she says, "you'd be just like me."

•

When Hanni's father first learns of his daughter's seduction, he cries out for the death penalty, which, Hanni's mother notes, has been abolished since the fall of the Nazis. "That," says the father, "was a regime. Now all we have is a government." He's the kind of fellow who says he doesn't believe in murdering Jews but adds, "Better to gas 100,000 Jews than to have a pig like that messing around with my daughter."

"Jail Bait," though it is beautifully and, intelligently controlled, is not an easy film to like. It certainly doesn't lift the spirits in any conventional way. It does contain moments of real pathos—unusual in a Fassbinder film — in those scenes involving Hanni's mother, a role acted with desperate sadness by Ruth Drexel. However, the film's fascination lies not in any particular character or event but in the meanness of the total drama that Mr. Fassbinder sets before us. It's as blunt and simply drawn as a cartoon. The times, he says, deserve no more.

1977 My 16, 24:1

LOOKING UP; screenplay by Jonathan Platnick; producd and directed by Linda Yellen; co-produced by Karen Rosenberg; edited by John Carter; photography by Arpad Makay and Lloyd Friedas; music by Brad Fiedel; a First American Films release; distributed by the Levitt-Pickman Film Corporation. At the Fine Arts Theater, 58th Street, west of Lexington Avenue. Running time: 94 minutes. This film has been rated PG.

Rose Lander .... Marilyn Chris
Manny Lander .... Dick Shawn
Becky .... Jacqueline Brookes
Libby Levine .... Doris Belack
Sy Levine .... Harry Goz
Grandma .... Naomi Riseman
Grandpa .... Will Hussing
Myra .... Neva Small
Stan .... George Reinholdt
Ann Reeny .... Gillien Goll
Francine Levine .... Ellen Sherman
Barbara Lander .... Susan McKinley
Irma .... Estelle Harris
Gene .... Izzy Singer

By A. H. WEILER

As the first feature-film producing effort of Linda Yellen and Karen Rosenberg, "Looking Up" bears a stamp of maturity not normally associated with a pair of 27-year-olds. Their dramatization of the relationships of members of a middle-class New York Jewish family leaves the nagging impression of a dizzying succession of people caught up in a variety of troubles. But, despite its disturbing realties, "Looking Up," which had its premiere yesterday at the Fine Arts Theater, projects its sincerity with heartfelt emotion and a seemingly autobiographical remembrance of things present and past.

In essence, Jonathan Platnick's script focuses on three generations of the family, particularly on Rose Lander, her two sisters, their husbands, children and their grandparents. More directly, it concentrates on their anxiety-ridden, largely unsuccessful drives for the better (i.e. richer) life in such authentic surroundings as, say, Washington Heights or Forest Hills.

•

Practically all of the clan is involved in a frantic dash for the golden end of the rainbow while planning a diamond anniversary party for the grandparents. Rose is desperately striving for the fast-food franchise that will free her husband, Manny, from his failing seltzer business as she worries about her daughters and grandchildren, copes with grandma's geriatric fantasies, constantly shops and works part time in an envious cousin's luncheonette.

Her sister, Libby, is also defeated as her plans for her daughter's marriage to a rich suitor are shattered when her husband is indicted in a real estate flim-flam. It also happens that Rose's married daughter has turned into a pill-popping psychiatric case. And Rose also discovers that her husband had sired Libby's child.

•

"Looking Up," however, does live up to its title when the sisters join to face the future bravely as they gather at that party in one of those pseudo-elegant palaces where you can get a swan sculptured out of chicken liver with the hors d'oeuvres. "We'll do the best we can," says Becky the spinster sister, if we can just hold on."

Despite the plot's soap-opera overtones, Miss Yellen, who directed with an eye for visual movement and character delineation, and the large cast—mostly drawn from local stage and television ranks—manage to avoid many of the sudsy banalities of the genre.

Some of the roles are too broadly played, but quite a few of the principals score with natural portrayals. Marilyn Chris is a truly impressive and poignant figure as the undaunted Rose, either as a canny supermarket shopper or as the tigerish leader of her brood. Jacqueline Brookes is properly self-reliant as the realist Becky; Naomi Riseman is fine as the bumbling grandma, as are a serious Dick Shawn as Rose's inadequate, if devoted, husband and Doris Belack and Neva Small, as the beleaguered Libby and her problematic daughter.

Many of the parts of "Looking Up" are greater than the whole, but its sobering, specialized drama rings as true as its real street scenes.

•

"Looking Up" received a PG ("Parental Guidance Suggested") rating probably because of some explicit dialogue and a near-nude scene, neither of which should be especially traumatic for young viewers.

1977 My 16, 24:1

Period Rite

ALTHOUGH the Whitney Museum's presentation of the 1939 Yiddish film. "Mirele Efros," is billed as the first of a two-part series devoted to the Yiddish cinema in America, the film has much closer connections to theater than movies. The screenplay, an adaptation of the turn-of-the-century Jacob Gordin play, fondly and solemnly preserves all of the gestures associated with the kind of performance that was as much ritual as theater.

The story, about a rich, wise, hard-working mother's ill-treatment at the hands of her venal daughter-in-law, is shot entirely within three-sided interior sets. The camera moves around within them gingerly, as if it didn't want to bump into the bric-a-brac.

The film was directed by Josef Berne and stars Berta Gersten in the title role. It was originally reviewed in The New York Times Oct. 21, 1939, the day after it opened at the Cameo Theater, and can now be seen at the Whitney through Sunday. VINCENT CANBY

1977 My 18, C21:1

The Good Guy

BREAKER! BREAKER!; screenplay by Terry Chambers; produced, directed and music by Don Hulettte; cinematography by Mario DiLeo; edited by Steven Zaillian; executive producers Samuel Schulman and Bernard Tabakin; a Paragon Films Production released by American International Pictures. At local theaters. Running time: 86 minutes. This film has been rated PG.

J. D. Dawes .... Chuck Norris
Judge Trimmings .... George Murdock
Arlene Trimmings .... Terry O'Connor
Sgt. Strode .... Don Gentry
Arney .... John DiFusco
Deputy Boles .... Ron Cedillos
Billy Dawes .... Michael Augenstein
Wilfred .... Dan Vandegrift
Drake .... Douglas Stevenson

By A. H. WEILER

TRUCKING, citizen's band radio and movies may help swell the gross national product, but they don't do a thing for "Breaker! Breaker!" a shoddy amalgam of those elements that crashed into local theaters yesterday. Terry Chambers's rudimentary script about an indomitably good guy of a trucker who takes on a whole corrupt town to rescue his kidnapped younger brother, is matched by Don Hulette's wooden direction of a sophomoric cast.

Chuck Norris, a program note states, is the undefeated American karate champ and he is also blond, square-jawed and about as emotional as a statue as the Zen master and martial-arts maven, who kicks or beats up practically all the sleazy citizens of Texas City, Calif. George Murdock is just as believable as the town's drunken, Shakespeare-spouting judge and boss.

Chances are most moviegoers over the age of 12, say, might have the urge to shout "Breaker! Breaker!" long before fellow truckers come to the aid of our jailed hero via that C.B. radio call for help.

•

The film is rated PG (Parental Guidance Suggested)" probably because of some explicit dialogue and some violence, neither of which is as startling as these juvenile proceedings.

1977 My 19, C20:1

Growing Pains

CRIA! (Breed), directed by Carlos Saura, screenplay (Spanish with English subtitles) by Mr. Saura; produced by Elias Querejeta; editor, Pablo G. Del Amo; director of photography, Teodoro Escamilla; distributed by Jason Allyn. Running time: 115 minutes. At the Plaza Theater, 58th Street, east of Madison Avenue. This film has been rated PG.

Ana (adult, mother) .... Geraldine Chaplin
Ana (child) .... Ana Torrent
Irene .... Conchita Perez
Maite .... Maite Sanchez Alexandros
Paulina .... Monica Randall

By VINCENT CANBY

CHILDHOOD CAN BE a most terrifying time. One must constantly observe the proscriptions of a primitive system of cause and effect that can be questioned only by the reckless or the ignorant. Squash a spider and it will rain. Step on a crack, break your mother's back. Sleep in the light of a new moon and you may never wake up. There is power in the knowledge of these things, as well as awful responsibility. One must be vigilant. One has to be alert for signs.

Such a child is Ana (Ana Torrent), the 9-year-old heroine of Carlos Saura's beautifully acted, haunting Spanish movie, "Cria!" about a childhood so packed with trauma that one can scarcely believe that this acutely sensitive child will ever grow up to be the apparently composed, articulate woman that Geraldine Chaplin plays.

In his 1973 film, "Cousin Angelica," which opened here last week, Mr. Saura looked back on a Civil War childhood from the position of a middle-aged man forever stuck on the dead-center of his memories. "Cria!" is more ambitious but, without the focal point of a strongly defined present, it lacks the cumulative impact of the earlier movie.

Its dreamlike reality is fragile. As it cuts among three time periods—Ana at 9, Ana a few years earlier at the time of the death of her mother (also played by Miss Chaplin), and snippets of the grown-up Ana—one begins to wonder whether the movie is much more than an outline for another movie. One wants more than mood and memory, though that may be asking for more than Mr. Saura ever intended.

He's quoted as having said he conceived "Cria!" after seeing Miss Torrent in Victor Erice's "The Spirit of the Beehive," which is easily understood. This extraordinary little girl, with large dark eyes and the grave manner of someone who has been given the secrets of the universe, is childhood not as it ever was, but as adults remember it.

The childhood that Mr. Saura imposes on Ana is enough to have crushed even someone who's gone through a successful Freudian analysis, much less someone of Ana's age and temperament. She watches her mother die—painfully—of cancer and blames her philandering father. Using a substance that her mother has told her is poison (but actually may be no more than bicarbonate of soda), Ana doses her father's glass of milk and shoulders the responsibility of his death while he's in the act of making love to his best friend's wife.

It's one thing, I suspect, for a child like Ana to fantasize about murder and even to accept responsibility for a murder obtained through charms or prayers, but it's quite another kind of drama when you have a little girl running around and believing that she's knocking off people with poison. Mr. Saura stacks the cards against Ana. Unlike her two sisters, she has an uncanny knack for walking into rooms at the wrong time. She's more than vigilant. She's emotionally accident-prone.

Though "Cria!" seesm arbitrarily and artificially structured, individual sequences are remarkably fine—Ana's attempts to make contact with her mute, paralyzed grandmother, her longing memories of her mother's combing her hair, her matter-of-fact questioning of the maid about what a woman's breasts look like, and a scene in which Ana and her two sisters become giddy and dance rock to a rock recording.

Geraldine Chaplin and Ana Torrent in "Cria"

"Cria!" is a movie of marvelous moments and two superb performances, by Miss Torrent and by Miss Chaplin, who has never before in a film that I've seen so thoroughly realized herself as an actress. She's awfully good in the otherwise messy "Welcome to L.A.," but she's excellent in "Cria!"

•

"Cria!" which has been rated PG ("Parental Guidance Suggested"), contains a sequence in which Ana comes upon Freud's primal scene (most delicately suggested), something that may well terrify more adults than children who see the movie.

1977 My 19, C20:4

THE SAGA OF ANATAHAN, directed, written and photographed by Josef von Sternberg; adapted from a book by Maruyama; produced by Takimura; distributed by Twyman Films. Running time: 95 minutes. At the Thalia Theater, Broadway at 95th Street. This film has been rated PG.

Queen Bee .... Akemi Negishi
Husband .... Suganuma
Drones .... Sawamura, Nakayama, Fujikawa, Kondo, Miyashita
Skippers, ... Tsuruemon, Kikuji
At the Shamisen .... Kokuizo
Homesick Ones .... Tamura, Kitagawa, Suzuki
Patriot .... Amikura
Narrator .... Josef von Sternberg

THE "RECONSTRUCTED" version of Josef von Sternberg's "The Saga of Anatahan," which opened yesterday at the Thalia Theater, is virtually a one-film retrospective of that great, idiosyncratic, often off-putting director's work. The film, in a fine new print, has been put together from footage that was originally released here in 1954—and reviewed in The New York Times on May 18, 1954, as "Ana-Ta-Han"—with supplemental nude footage that von Sternberg cut into the first version in 1958.

The amount of care and money that have gone into this reconstruction is testimony to the success of the keepers of the von Sternberg legacy. When he died in 1969, the reputation of the director appeared to be based entirely on the seven films he had made with Marlene Dietrich, beginning with "The Blue Angel." Mostly forgotten were "Underworld" (1927) and "The Docks of New York" (1928), and seldom ever mentioned was "Anatahan," which was his last production, though "Jet Pilot," begun in 1949, was not released until 1957.

•

"Anatahan" is not a film to use as an introduction to the von Sternberg work. One can snicker at the pomposities of its voice-over narration, written and spoken by the director, which recalls the conventions of silent movies, but even this narration, as much as visual style, constitutes a kind of coda to the von Sternberg career.

The film, which the director made in Japan with an entirely Japanese cast and crew, must have been supremely satisfying to the director's ego, even if he was obviously somewhat short of studio space. Von Sternberg wrote, directed and photographed the film and speaks the only dialogue that can be understood.

The story is about a group of Japanese sailors and one woman who are marooned on a Pacific island for something like five years after World War II.

How this little society, dominated by one female, goes to pieces is depicted in what amounts to a series of virtually actionless tableaux. The melodrama is as passionless as a parable. Instead of being erotic, the film is obsessed by the idea of eroticism.

•

It's not easy to accept Akemi Negishi as a femme fatale. She is sweetly pretty and rather chubby-kneed, and when she does a seductive, hip-swinging dance that is meant to drive the men out of their minds with desire, she looks more like a preteen practicing an awkward hula. We do see, however, von Sternberg's obsession with a concept of sexual desire as a destructive force.

The obsession is reflected in the romantically highlighted black-and-white photography, as well as in the tightness of the space in which he had to work. Except for stock footage of the sea, there's hardly a long shot in the film. The marooned sailors and their queen bee are locked as much into the medium-shot frame as they are on their island. There are some sequences that are bound to prompt giggles from newcomers to von Sternberg, but there are others that immediately evoke some of the best work ever done by this great motion-picture stylist.

The effect of the film is simultaneously sad, beautiful and a bit outrageous. Only von Sternberg would think to insert an opening-credit card informing us that the film had been produced entirely in "a studio constructed for this purpose in Kyoto, the ancient capital of Japan." He was a fellow who needed the proper vibrations.

•

"The Saga of Anatahan," which has been rated PG ("Parental Guidance Suggested"), contains some discreet female nudity photographed with the sort of impersonal prettiness one used to see on pinup calendars.

VINCENT CANBY

1977 My 19, C22:4

SMOKEY AND THE BANDIT, a Rastar Production; produced by Mort Engelberg; directed by Hal Needham; a screenplay by James Lee Barrett, Charles Shyer and Alan Mandel; director of photography, Bobby Byrne; music by Bill Justis and Jerry Reed. At the Radio City Music Hall. Running time: 97 minutes. This film is rated PG.

Bandit .... Burt Reynolds
Carrie .... Sally Field
Cledus .... Jerry Reed
Sheriff B. T. Justice .... Jackie Gleason
Junior .... Mike Henry
Little Enos .... Paul Williams
Big Enos .... Pat McCormick

WHENEVER the weather starts to turn warm and Americans begin to take to the roads and drive-ins again, the Hollywood assembly line disgorges another series of movies that employ cars as stars.

In the case of the latest example, "Smokey and the Bandit," which opened yesterday at the Radio City Music Hall, the advertising and publicity would have it that the principal performers are Burt Reynolds, Sally Field, Jackie Gleason and Jerry Reed.

But that is misleading. This is a movie for audiences capable of slavering over a Pontiac Trans Am, 18-wheel tractor-trailer rigs, dismembered police cruisers and motorcycles. It is also for moviegoers likely to use one hand to pound arm rests with sheer zest of a race against time involving 400 cases of Coors beer and the other hand to smite thighs with glee at what happens when a couple of good old boys and a passel of pursuing redneck sheriffs and state troopers match alleged wits.

•

And just in the event that there is somebody out there incapable of recognizing the difference between a 6.6 liter Trans Am and a Hudson Terraplane or a new Peterbilt rig and a decrepit Reo truck, there is sufficient use of C.B. radios to let everyone know that while "Smokey and the Bandit" may not be a very original motormayhem movie, it is at least a new one.

Mr. Reynolds, playing Bandit, a driver of legendary skill, takes on an $80,000 bet that requires him to race 1,800 miles from Georgia to Texas and back in a span of 28 hours, returning with the aforementioned beer. Bandit commandeers his friend Cledus (Jerry Reed) to drive his rig while he takes the wheel of the Trans Am to act as the blocker, or diversionary force, when Smokey—the law—turns up.

•

All proceeds smoothly until the homebound trip, when Bandit picks up a runaway bride-to-be (Sally Field), touching off interstate pursuit by her prospective father-in-law, an outraged Texas sheriff named Buford T. Justice (Jackie Gleason), who is accompanied by the bridegroom-to-be, his hulking nincompoop of a son (Mike Henry).

With Mr. Reynolds playing it cool and Mr. Gleason doing his burns and investing the film with a certain raunchy humor, the rest is up to the vehicles. And they don't do anything that hasn't been seen before.

•

Th movie carries a PG ("Parental Guidance Suggested") rating. Despite its regional settings and characters, "Smokey and the Bandit" abounds with scatology, profanity and obscenity neither uncommon to the streets of New York nor unknown to most of its inhabitants from the age of 2 onward, or unspoken by most of them at one time or another.

LAWRENCE VAN GELDER

1977 My 20, C8:5

Boys Will Be Victims

TENDERNESS OF THE WOLVES, directed by Ulli Lommel; screenplay (German with English subtitles) by Kurt Raab; produced by Rainer Werner Fassbinder; director of photography, Jurgen Jorges; music, Peer Raben; editors, Thea Evans and Franz Walsch; a Tango Film production, distributed by Monument Film Corp. Running time: 95 minutes. At the Jean Renoir Cinema, Second Avenue at 10th Street. This film has not been rated.

Haarmann .... Kurt Raab
Granz .... Jeff Roden
Frau Linder .... Margit Carstensen
Cafe Owner .... Brigitte Mira
Dora .... Ingrid Caven
Frau Bucher .... Hannelore Riefenbrunner
Frau Am Schluss .... Tanara Schanzara
1st Commissar .... Wolfgang Schenk
2d Commissar .... Rainer Hauer
Wittkowski .... R. W. Fassbiner
Einarmiger .... Heinrich Giskes

By VINCENT CANBY

TENDERNESS of the Wolves," which opened yesterday at the Jean Renoir Cinema, follows "Jail Bait" as the second movie this week to come out of the Rainer Werner Fassbinder film factory, where, it seems, they make movies in their lunch breaks while making movies.

"Tenderness of the Wolves" was produced in 1973 by Mr. Fassbinder and directed by Ulli Lommel, the actor who

Kurt Raab and his victim in "Tenderness of the Wolves"
The fun is a particularly chilly sort

was most recently seen as the wife's lover in "Chinese Roulette" and will be seen again soon in another Fassbinder film, "Effie Briest," when it opens as part of the Fassbinder festival at the New Yorker Theater. This sudden surfacing within a short time of so many films directed by Mr. Fassbinder, or associated with him, carries with it both rewards and punishments.

The situation would be intolerable were the young German director and his colleagues less talented, but it's difficult in any case. Just because one admires them, one tends to expect each new film to be something of a revelation, and when it isn't, one is inclined to draw back a bit, to re-examine earlier reactions, to find fault.

People with such gifts aren't allowed to have fun, which is pretty much what "Tenderness of the Wolves" seems to be doing, though if you are familiar with the Fassbinder mode, the fun is of a particularly chilly sort.

"Tenderness of the Wolves," written by Kurt Raab, who also plays the leading role, is the gospel according to Mr. Fassbinder about Peter Kurten, the Düsseldorf mass murderer whose crimes inspired Fritz Lang's 1931 classic, "M."

Kurten, here named Haarmann and played by Mr. Raab, lives in an unidentified German city in the late 1940's. A sneak thief, forger and occasional fence, Haarmann has as his principal source of income dealings in black-market meat, which may or may not be leftovers from his victims, mostly destitute young men whom he takes home to fondle and then to drink. Haarmann, you see, is a vampire.

•

Mr. Lommel regards the activities of Haarmann as he moves about the city—picking up his victims, acting as a police informer, attending convivial dinners at the neighborhood pub (with the main course usually supplied by him)—with a deadly cool that, in the Fassbinder troupe, passes for humor.

Haarmann's neighbors treat him as a harmless eccentric with a taste for boys. True, he's something of a sight-gag, with his totally bald head, odd clothes and manic expression, but as any one of the local hookers or pimps or black marketeers would say, nobody's perfect. Only one person, an irritable, nosey woman (Margit Carstensen), who lives just downstairs, has the courage of her suspicions when she starts counting the number of young men who go upstairs and the number of brown paper parcels that come down.

•

"Tenderness of the Wolves" may be about the least erotic vampire movie ever made, which is, I suspect, the intention of Mr. Lommel and his associates. The movie deals in sleaziness—physical and emotional—of such intensity that second-rateness becomes virtually the subject of the film as well as its style. This is not to say the film is sloppy.

It is beautifully and enthusiastically performed and it doesn't contain a single superfluous or redundant camera movement. Like Mr. Fassbinder's own early films, "Tenderness of the Wolves" is cryptic, tough-talking and swaggering in the manner of someone who means to shock his elders. Like the early Warhol work, "Tenderness of the Wolves" seems to be sending up everyone and everything, but, unlike the Warhol movies, it takes filmmaking—the possibilities of the discipline—with complete seriousness, which becomes the redeeming factor in Fassbinder films, even when the subjects are off-putting.

In addition to Mr. Raab, an exceedingly witty actor, and Miss Carstensen, the Fassbinder regulars who appear in the film include Brigitte Mira as the tough, cheery proprietor of the local pub, Ingrid Caven as a hard-luck hooker and Mr. Fassbinder as a small-time crook. Wearing a loud pin-stripe suit and seeming to be 100 pounds heavier than usual, Mr. Fassbinder scowls through his scenes as if he thought of himself as a young Orson Welles. He may well be—gifted, arrogant and indefatigable.

1977 My 20, C21:1

THE CITY (1939); photographed and directed by Willard Van Dyke and Ralph Steiner; screenplay by Henwar Rodakiewicz from an outline by Pare Lorentz; commentary written by Lewis Mumford and narrated by Morris Carnovsky; edited by Theodore Lawrence; music by Aaron Copland; produced by American Documentary Films. Running time 43 minutes.

THE RIVER (1937); written and directed by Pare Lorentz; photographed by Willard Van Dyke, Floyd Crosby and Stacy Woodard; narrated by Thomas Chalmers; produced by the Farm Security Administration; edited by Leo Zochling and Lloyd Nosier; music by Virgil Thomson. Running time: 30 minutes.

PIE IN THE SKY (1934); made by Elia Kazan, Ralph Steiner, Irving Lerner and Leo Hurwitz with Mr. Kazan, Russell Collins and members of the Group Theater. Running time: 16 minutes, silent.

At the Film Forum, 15 VanDam Street, tonight through Sunday night, and Thursday through Sunday nights.

By A. H. WEILER

The passage of time inevitably has relegated "The River" and "The City" to the comparative anonymity of archives or to all too infrequent exposure on college, museum and public television circuits. But the Film Forum's current assemblage of these noted documentaries, coupled with the even rarer short, "Pie in the Sky," is vivid proof that their highly spirited style is still forcefully unusual and effective even if the subject matter has become slightly quaint with age.

It's not too chauvinistic to note that Pare Lorentz, a reformed movie critic (The New York American, Judge, etc.), became the moviemaker of the 1930's whose outstanding social awareness is still fairly germane in both "The River" and "The City." With the considerable aid of Willard Van Dyke and Stacy Woodard, the photographers, and Virgil Thomson, the composer, "The River"—the Mississippi, of course—continues to flow with imagery and power.

•

The poetry of the script narrated by Thomas Chalmers captures the cadence of that awesome and often destructive waterway, as well as its running history, in such purposely repetitive lyric lines as "from as far West as Idaho—from as far East as Pennsylvania—the mighty river flows down to the Gulf." And, Mr. Thomson's score, which is properly reminiscent of American ballads and folksongs, is as complementary to those lines as the pictorially pointed scenes of floods and man's misuse of the land that helped generate them.

Pare Lorentz cannot be faulted for touting the monumental work done by the government in partly harnessing Ol' Man River for life saving, enriching ends, since, after all, his producer was the Farm Security Administration. But even at this late date and changes in our biggest waterway and administrations, "The River" is a testament to fine reporting and film making.

This is, perhaps, a mite truer, especially for New Yorkers, as far as "The City" is concerned. Willard Van Dyke and Ralph Steiner, who shot and directed this analysis of towns and cities past and present from Mr. Lorentz's outline and Lewis Mumford's script, made it a still captivating study of the dehumanizing effects of so-called progress.

Despite the 38 years since "The City" was shown at the World's Fair here, Mr. Mumford's words, as spoken by Morris Carnovsky and abetted by Aaron Copland's colorful music, ring with passionate truth in comparing the past's peacefully bucolic towns with busy but demeaning metropolises. New York comes in for a cynical, sometimes comical dissection in the plea for planned industrial-living communities, which, of course, are constantly being implemented these days.

History is beautifully served by Our Town's 1938 traffic jams, subway and elevated straphangers, slum dwellers, street accidents, lunches on the run or a deserted Wall Street on a Sunday and, pointedly, would-be escapees from the torrid sidewalks trapped in endless lines of cars en route to the country. "The City" remains an admirable reminder of some of our society's misplaced values, as well as some remedies for some of those ills.

Call "Pie in the Sky" an intriguing curiosity. The 16-minute silent comedy, a decidedly unusual filming technique in 1934, illustrates disdain for handouts and welfare and reflects on th Depression in a series of miming japes by a youthful Elia Kazan and other members of the leftist Group Theater. While it evolves as a somewhat jerry-built, fragmentary acting exercise now, which doesn't fit the Film Forum's "Classics From the 1930's" title, it cleaves to the period and mood of the classics in the program.

1977 My 20, C24:3

THE GREATEST, directed by Tom Gries; screenplay by Ring Lardner Jr., based on the book by Muhammad Ali, Herbert Muhammad and Richard Durham; produced by John Marshall; director of photography, Harry Stradling Jr.; editor, Byron (Buzz) Brandt; music, Michael Masser; a Columbia/EMI presentation, distributed by Columbia Pictures Running time: 114 minutes. At the Criterion Theater, Broadway at 44th Street, and other theaters. This film has been rated PG.

Muhammad Ali .... Himself
Angelo Dundee .... Ernest Borgnine
Dr. Ferdie Pacheco .... John Marley
Bill McDonald .... Robert Duvall
Cruikshank .... David Huddleston
Hollis .... Ben Johnson
Malcolm X .... James Earl Jones
Velvet Green .... Dina Merrill
Sonny Liston .... Roger E. Mosley
Draft lawyer .... Paul Winfield
Herbert Muhammad .... Lloyd Haynes
Payton Jory .... Malachi Throne
Mrs. Fairlie .... Lucille Benson
John the gardener .... Theodore R. Wilson
Belinda Ali .... Annazette Chase
Ruby Sanderson .... Mira Waters
Cassius Clay, age 18 ... Philip (Chip) McAllister
Cassius Clay Sr. .... Arthur Adams
Odessa Clay .... Dorothy Meyer

By VINCENT CANBY

"The Greatest," the screen biography of Muhammad Ali, a.k.a. Cassius Clay, is a charming curio of a sort Hollywood doesn't seem to make much any more. It's a movie about a real-life personality who plays himself in reconstructions of those events that brought him to success's pinnacle, which, in turn, prompted movie producers to want to make this movie about him.

As serious fictcion, it's product merchandising such as T-shirts, bumper stickers and personality posters. Yet once you get beyond the embarrassingly simple-minded introductory sequences, "The Greatest" is winning entertainment. I suspect this is because Muhammad Ali, unlike Audie Murphy ("Beyond Glory") and Douglas (Wrong Way) Corrigan ("The Flying Irishman"), to name two others who replayed their lives in film, has spent the last 15 or 20 years shaping a public personality big enough to fill a movie screen.

•

"The Greatest," which opened yesterday at the Criterion and other theaters, glosses over a lot of rocky material and smoothes the rough edges of one of the most fascinating careers in boxing history, but this, too, is the way of such movies. One of the pleasures of "The Greatest" is in not getting bogged down in details not easily explained by a piety.

The film, written by Ring Lardner Jr. and directed by Tom Gries (who died shortly after the completion of producton), is old-fashioned, upbeat movie-making with a marvelous personality at its center. You might call Muhammad Ali a natural actor, but that would be to deny his wit, sensibility, drive, ability, enthusiasm, poise and common sense, all of which are the conscious achievements of an ambitious man who has known exactly what he has wanted for a long time.

Part of the fun of watching "The Greatest" is in being in on another Ali victory, and in being aware that he himself has such a clear perspective of what he has been up to in defining his career as much through public relations as determination, belief and talent.

•

The film itself is an extension of that public-relations sense. It opens with the young Cassius Clay—nicely played by Phillip (Chip) McAllister — returning home to Louisville from Rome with an Olympic medal to face obligatory discrimination, thus to acquire the

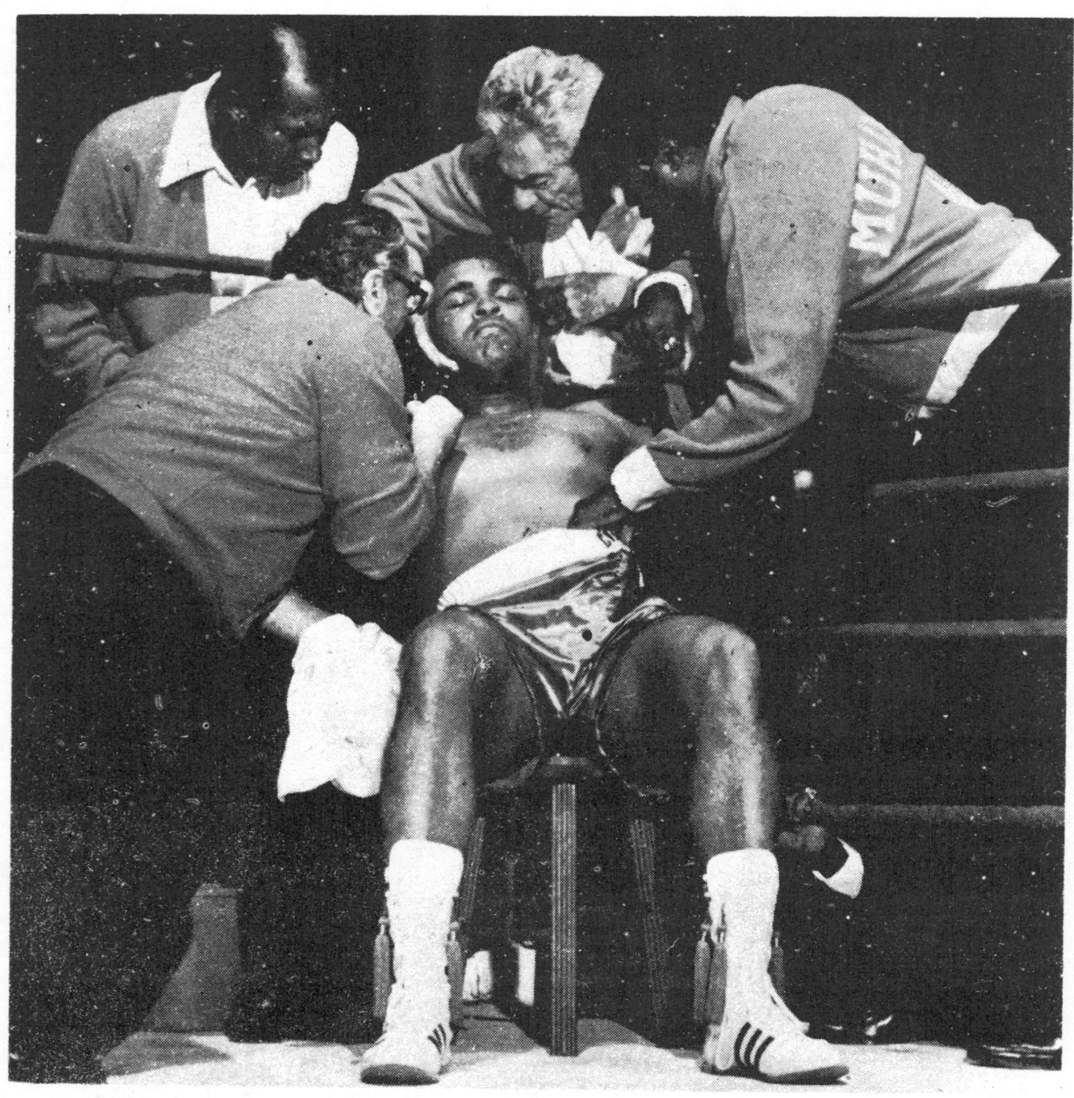

"THE GREATEST"—Muhammad Ali is briefly subdued by a blow to the jaw delivered by George Foreman.

inspiration to go on to his success as a professional fighter.

At the point he turns pro, Muhammad Ali takes over his own role in what amounts to a resume of the published facts of his life—his friendship with Malcolm X and conversion to the Muslim religion, his successes in the ring and then ostracism after he refused induction into the Army, followed by his victory before the Supreme Court and his victory over George Foreman in the title fight in Zaire.

The fight sequences (actual footage) are cannily placed within the film to build to the climatic bout with Foreman. The facts of the champ's private life are treated much in the manner of a "Dick and Jane" story, but so ingenuously that it's difficult to complain about the disappearancce of Malcolm X (James Earl Jones) without comment halfway through the movie, or about the apparent elimination of one entire first marriage.

I say apparent because I don't know that much about the champ's love life. I wouldn't have realized that Annazette Chase, who plays the Muslim girl he marries in the film, was not his first wife without having read the program notes in which her role is described as that of "Ali's controversial second wife, Belinda." Why she is controversial is not explained by the film. Could it be because she has since been replaced?

The huge supporting cast includes a lot of fine actors doing little more than bits, though Robert Duvall stands out as one of Ali's earlier backers and Roger E. Mosley is very funny as Sonny Liston in the film's most uproarious sequence—when Ali sets out to insult the humorless Liston into a title bout. Ernest Borgnine and John Marley are staunch as, respectively, the champ's trainer, Angelo Dundee, and his doctor, Ferdie Pacheco.

"The Greatest," though, is entirely Muhammad Ali's. His presence dominates the screen and turns a rather ordinary, one-in-a-million success story into a first-rate piece of popular Americana.

1977 My 21, 11:1

Muhammad Ali and Mira Waters

FILM VIEW

VINCENT CANBY

The New Disorienting Movie

At the start of the next century it may well be possible to look back on these years of the 1970's and identify this very particular period—if not as the turning point from the Old Movie to the New, then as the time when New Movies began to supplement Old in such number that it wasn't always easy to tell them apart. The situation is disorienting. To experience some current movies is to go scuba-diving in murky water. Which way is up?

This, I think, has as much to do with the various degrees of turn-off we all feel in relation to certain films as with whether or not the films are really any good. Robert Altman's "3 Women" is very much a New Movie, but its dreamlike form makes that self-evident. We don't expect to be told everything. We—especially if we have admired Altman's work in the past—are prepared to make all sorts of adjustments when looking at one of his films, which we aren't when, say, we watch a rather absurd little horror film like Larry Cohen's "It's Alive" (about a murderous newborn child), which is also a New Movie.

It says something about the movies' traditional role as a mass entertainment medium (which, of course, is no longer true) that so many people who have peacefully and sometimes enthusiastically accepted experiments in drama, fiction and painting, refuse to allow filmmakers to seek new forms of expression. That could be because the new movie forms of expression don't look so flamboyantly new. If they did, there would be a lot less trouble. Nobody is running old socks through the projector and calling it art. New Movies look like Old Movies but they aren't providing the same kind of release.

There is also a lot of reverse snobbism involved in the way New Movies are watched by people who would rather die than say anything nice about Andrew Wyeth. Movies aren't supposed to be different from what they were when we were kids. This is the sort of person who goes to see "Rocky" and loves it just because it *is* schlocky. The other-half goes to see it and loves it because it is a slice of romanticized real-life.

These thoughts are partially inspired by "Andy Warhol's Bad," the latest film to come out of the Warhol Factory and certainly a New Movie though not exactly a supreme example. Like all Warhol films, especially "Trash" and "The Chelsea Girls," "Bad" means to bewilder the audience by presenting, without moral comment and with a certain amount of glee, a picture of an absolutely rotten society. In this case the absolutely rotten society is the household of a well-upholstered, bleached-blonde Queens housewife, a Mrs. Aiken (Carroll Baker) who, in addition to removing unwanted hair (650 hairs an hour) from customers who come to her dining room-clinic, also runs a local Murder, Inc.

Mrs. Aiken is less malicious than supremely acquisitive. Because her husband is ineffectual, she does what she has to do to make ends meet as a member of the great consumer society. She acts as the booking agent for a string of operatives—mostly ill-tempered young women — who are prepared to carry out such contracts as the murder of unpleasant babies and autistic children and the maiming of other beings (including a dog) and who, simply out of boredom, may spend an off evening burning down a movie theater.

"Bad" is a New Movie but it is a less pure New Movie than the earlier Warhols in that it contains a hint of sentimentality and there is little doubt what we are meant to feel about what is happening on the screen, even when it's not easy to watch the gory details. "Bad" is a conscious send-up of America-The—Absurd, a satire, but its own fondness for bad taste forces the audience to come to some adjustment to it, to find a way to accommodate its piled-on vulgarities. It is this insistence that we come to it, rather than the other way around, that is one of the distinguishing features of the New Movie, which is more truly avant-garde than any 80 hours of films that experiment with abstract images, superimposition of images, associative images and single-frame editing.

The difficulty with the New Movie is that we still tend to bring to every film the same set of expectations and demands we carried with us when we went to see "Gone With the Wind," "North By Northwest," "Grand Illusion" and "Potemkin." That would seem a perfectly reasonable thing to do, since we're still sitting in the same old theater seats, looking at the same old theater screen from the same old point of view. Yet we aren't always walking out of the theater with the same old feelings. Something most unsettling is taking place.

In such Rainer Werner Fassbinder films as "Mother Kusters Goes to Heaven," "Chinese Roulette" and "The Bitter Tears of Petra von Kant," there is often a complete lack of psychological background. Fassbinder couldn't care less about how his characters get to be the way they are—I suspect he'd say that to attempt to explain would be to oversimplify and thus to mislead, which is not the purpose of his films. All that we can know about a Fassbinder character is revealed on the screen in the course of the contemporary action but because the contemporary action is not always clear, we have to step in and make our own assumptions. We can, and there's nothing wrong in that but it may be a waste of time. In Fassbinder's films people, place, time and event are so thoroughly fused that we simply cannot isolate and analyze characters in any conventional way, any more than we can criticize a piece of non-representational sculpture in terms of whether or not it physically resembles its model. Freud is not dead for the New Moviemaker, but someone like Fassbinder sees a totality that involves a great deal more than character explanation.

• • •

Strictly speaking, the New Movies aren't new. Luis Bunuel has been making them since 1928. Sometimes, as in "Un Chien Andalou" and "The Discreet Charm of the Bourgeoisie," they have been surreal, but quite as frequently they've been as straightforward as "Tristana." Bunuel's films have the fantastic clarity of a landscape lit by a bolt of lightning. We see more detail than we can immediately understand—and more than he cares to waste his time and ours by explaining. There's seldom any music on the soundtrack of a Bunuel film to tell us whether we should laugh, cry, be furious or shocked. The delight in a Bunuel film is that we may feel all those emotions in a succession of splitseconds. Movies like that don't quickly pass from the mind.

Another difficulty with the New Movie is that it doesn't present us with any obvious point of identification. Sometimes there's no one with whom we can sympathize, which, as a rule of thumb, is not great box office, though Stanley Kubrick has brought off such successful New Movies as "2001" and "A Clockwork Orange." The success of these films, I suspect, lies in their "spectacle"—the mind-boggling visions of space in "2001" and the wittily grotesque projection of the-way-we-are-now into the future of "Clockwork."

Without their spectacle the Kubrick films would probably be intolerable for many people. Audiences accustomed to Old Movies equate the dispassion of "A Clockwork Orange" with

Altman's dreamlike "3 Women"

Fassbinder's enigmatic "Tears"

Warhol's amoral "Bad"

a conviction that Kubrick himself takes no moral stand on the events depicted. He does, of course, but he doesn't announce it. He refuses to make things easy for us. He doesn't footnote his movies with reassuring messages. Instead, he insults our sense of order by showing a system of rewards and punishments that is totally confused. There is no Clark Gable or even a Steve McQueen to act as our surrogate in "A Clockwork Orange"—no one we immediately recognize and whose popular identity establishes our relation to the film. We watch the New Movie at a distance, on our own. It's no coincidence, I think, that there has been an increasing number of New Movies since the decline of the old star system. New Movies deal in the unfamiliar.

Many horror films are New Movies, including the dreadful "The Omen," if only because they require audiences to swallow nonsense that they'd reject in the light of day. But people who go to horror films are prepared to make adjustments—to stand comfortably ouside the film—as the price of thrills. Horror movies are spectacles, too.

Fellini's "Casanova" is a New Movie and "Amarcord," which is awash in sentiment of the most appealing kind, is Old. There's no doubt about how one is supposed to feel about the characters of Fellini's recollected youth, but "Casanova" is as cold as ice. Temperature is not necessarily a surefire way of determining the difference between New and Old Movies, but it is an indicator. The New Movie tends to be cool, distant, without reproach. It says, "This is the way it looks. How do you feel about it?" and then it leaves you on your own. It is suspicious of answers. Bergman's films are Old in the best sense, and they are Old even when they are ambiguous. They are full of unmistakable emotions—love, sorrow, longing, dread, confusion.

• • •

Wim Wenders's screen adaptation of Peter Handke's "The Goalie's Anxiety at the Penalty Kick" is a quintessential New Movie, being a vivid film equivalent of the kind of New Novel written by Handke in Germany and Alain Robbe-Grillet and Marguerite Duras in France. Both Robbe-Grillet and Duras have made their own New Movies but they've been unendurably boring. Duras ("Nathalie Granger" and "India Song") refuses to give us enough information of any kind to excite our interest, while Robbe-Grillet ("L'Immortelle") displays a fondness for fashion-magazine photography and pretty images that have the effect of denying any emotions whatsoever. While his writing is clean, his movies are full of purple prose.

"The Goalie's Anxiety at the Penalty Kick" is a stunningly straightforward story of a man cutting himself loose from his society, going over the edge into lunacy the way the rest of us take off on a summer vacation. Methodically. Wenders uses no tricks. We recognize the world in which his hero travels. It is so ordinary that for about the first third of the movie we wonder what is up, at which point we begin to notice that although we recognize the world of the goalie, it's not all that ordinary. Everything is a bit too precise. We are aware of noises we wouldn't usually hear. At times the landscape seems uninhabited, then suddenly full of menacing strangers. There are portents of disaster everywhere, sometimes in the hysterical way children play when they're excited.

• • •

The manner in which Wenders draws us into the goalie's mind (without one subjective camera movement) is so remarkable that the film rivets us, though to this day I'm not sure why or what it all means. It's too easy to call it a study in alienation. The film and the responses it prompts are more mysterious than that. The New Movie need not be gloomy. I think an argument can be made to the effect that all of Woody Allen's comedies from "Take the Money and Run" through "Love and Death" are New Movies, while his new movie, the marvelously affecting "Annie Hall," is Old. A lot of people who had trouble finding a handle for the "early" Woody—the out-and-out rat—are discovering him for the first time in "Annie Hall," which is the first time he's presented himself as a character of intelligence and feeling.

New Movies are neither better nor worse than Old. They are different. They ask us to look at the screen with skepticism instead of expecting to be lulled into euphoria or having our prejudices (good and bad) reaffirmed. Sometimes New Movies aren't worth the effort. Sometimes, though, as in films like "Mother Kusters" or Terrence Malick's "Badlands" or Woody Allen's "Bananas," the experience is to remind us that movies have only scratched the surface of their possibilities. ■

1977 My 22, II:1:1

Film: Journey to the Altar

NOTHING IN THE WAY of heightened perception, late-flowering appreciation or guilt-laden hindsight has come along in the last 37 years to give rise to revisionist theories about Edgar G. Ulmer's "Americaner Shadchen" ("American Matchmaker"), the Yiddish film that opened yesterday for a run through Sunday at the Whitney Museum of American Art.

•

Then, as now, this is an innocent comedy about a man who is successful in business but unlucky in love. After eight broken engagements, he sets himself up as modern matchmaker with a suite of offices on the Grand Concourse. And when the girl he loves (and who loves him) is left at the altar by the bridegroom he has found for her, he winds up married. Now, as then, it must be said that this movie, which was reviewed in The New York Times on May 7, 1940, takes too long to reach the romantic heart of its plot.

For Edgar G. Ulmer, the Vienna-born film maker who producer and directed it, "Americaner Shadchen" was one of four Yiddish films in an extensive career that included work in Hollywood. But unlike such movies as "Bluebeard," "Strange Illusion," "Detour" and "The Cavern," it is not among the explorations of nightmarish worlds that have earned him a certain following.

With Leo Fuchs as the matchmaker and Judith Abarbanel as his love, "Americaner Shadchen" is an entertainment so simple and obvious that even non-Yiddish-speaking audiences are unlikely to find their understanding of the action impaired by the occasional difficulty of reading white subtitles on a white background.

LAWRENCE VAN GELDER

1977 My 25, C22:5

WE ALL LOVED EACH OTHER SO MUCH, directeed by Ettore Scola; screenplay (Italian with English subtitles) by Age, Scarpelli and Mr. Scola; director of photography, Claudio Cirillo; music, Armando Travaiola; editor, Raimondo Crociani; produced by Pio Angeletti and Adriano De Micheli; distributed by Cinema 5. Running time: 124 minutes. At the Beekman Theater, Second Avenue at 65th Street. This film has not been rated.

Giovanni .... Vittorio Gassman
Antonio .... Nino Manfredi
Luciana .... Stefania Sandrelli
Nico .... Stefano Satta Flores
Elide .... Giovanna Ralli
Catenacci .... Aldo Fabrizi
Landlady .... Isa Barzizza
Nico's wife .... Marcella Micheiangeli

By VINCENT CANBY

"We All Loved Each Other So Much" is the forgettably awkward title of Ettore Scola's wise, reflective Italian comedy that examines 30 years of recent Italian social history in terms of the friendship of three men and the one woman each man has loved at one time or another. It's the sort of thing for which European filmmakers, especially Italian, have a special feeling, while Americans have none whatsoever, if only because American producers are made uneasy by movies that are about friendship and that attempt to cover so much time.

"We All Loved Each Other So Much," which opened yesterday at the Beekman, is full of fondness, rue, outraged and high spirits. It is also—surprising for an Italian film—packed with the kind of movie references that French filmmakers like, and it is dedicated to the late Vittorio DeSica, whose "Bicycle Thief" plays a prominent part in the picture.

The three men, who have become friends as leftist partisans near the end of the Nazi occupation of Italy, are Giovanni, a lawyer (Vittorio Gassman), Antonio (Nino Manfredi), who begins his postwar career as a hospital orderly (and remains one for the rest of his life, and Nico (Stefano Satta Flores), a politically committed movie nut who doesn't hesitate to abandon his wife and child to go off to Rome after a disagreement over the merits of "The Bicycle Thief."

The woman who moves in and out of their lives is Luciana (Stefania Sandrelli), an aspiring actress, the high point of whose career (and one of the high points of the film) comes when she is cast as an extra in "La Dolce Vita." The scene that Mr. Scola recreates is the preparation for Anita Ekberg's walk through the Trevi fountain, complete with Marcello Mastroianni actually sitting on the sidelines as Federico Fellini directs (and receives a tribute from a polictman who says, "I've always admired your films, Mr. Rossellini").

The film's principal storyline has to do with the decline and fall of the lawyer, Giovanni, into successful opportunism, a role that Mr. Gassman has played before, but which he does with immense gallantry and humor as he goes from youth to middle-age. Also extremely good are Aldo Fabrizi, as the crooked industrialist who becomes Giovanni's father-in-law, and Giovanna Ralli as the fat, bird-brained rich girl whom Giovanni marries and transforms into a chic, bored woman who comes to identify herself—fatally—with the women in Antonioni movies.

Mr. Scola, who has been represented here both as a writer ("Il Sorpasso") and director ("Made in Italy," "The Pizza Triangle," among others), employs a comic style that is effective for being loose, allowing him to introduce real people as themselves, to parody "Strange Interlude's" spoken interior thoughts, to go from slapstick to satire and then to drama of genuine feelings.

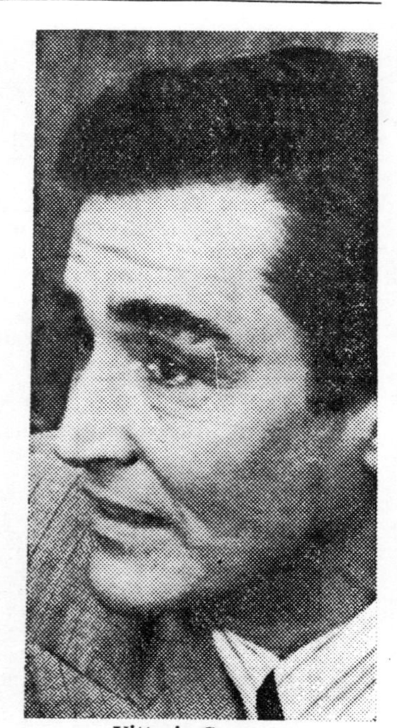

Vittorio Gassman
Plays role of the lawyer with immense gallantry and humor.

At its best, the film combines a number of different emotions at once, as when the film-obsessed Nico attempts to teach Luciana the fundamentals of Sergei Eisenstein's theory of montage on Rome's Spanish Steps, all the while seducing her.

Though the film is very funny at moments, the dominant mood is a sense of loss, but even here the film makes its point in a backhanded way. "We wanted to change the world, but the world changed us," says Antonio, the aging hospital orderly. Yet Mr. Scola recognizes this as the windy cliché of someone given to self-dramatization. After 30 years the three friends are more worn, more tired, more experienced than they were as young men, but neither the world nor time has changed them in any essential ways. That's the bitter truth.

1977 My 24, 31:1

Comic-Book Sci-Fi

STAR WARS, directed and written by George Lucas; produced by Gary Kurtz; production designer, John Barry; director of photography, Gilbert Taylor; music, John Williams; editors, Paul Hirsch, Marcia Lucas and Richard Chew; a Lucasfilm Ltd. production, distributed by 20th Century-Fox. Running time: 123 minutes. At the Astor Plaza, 44th Street west of Broadway, Orpheum Theater, 86th Street near Third Avenue, and other theaters. This film has been rated PG.

Luke Skywalker .... Mark Hamill
Han Solo .... Harrison Ford
Princess Leia Organa .... Carrie Fisher
Grand Moff Tarkin .... Peter Cushing
Ben (Obi-Wan) Kenobi .... Alec Guinness
See Threepio .... Anthony Daniels
Artoo-Deetoo .... Kenny Baker
Chewbacca .... Peter Mayhew
Lord Darth Vader .... David Prowse
Uncle Owen Lars .... Phil Brown
Aunt Beru Lars .... Shelagh Fraser
Chief Jawa .... Jack Purvis
General Dodonna .... Alex McCrindle
General Willard .... Eddie Byrne
General Taggi .... Don Henderson
General Motti .... Richard Le Parmentier

"STAR WARS"—A villainous soldier on the planet of Tatooine fires upon a fleeing princess.

By VINCENT CANBY

STAR WARS," George Lucas's first film since his terrifically successful "American Graffiti," is the movie that the teen-agers in "American Grafiti" would have broken their necks to see. It's also the movie that's going to entertain a lot of contemporary folk who have a soft spot for the virtually ritualized manners of comic-book adventure.

"Star Wars," which opened yesterday at the Astor Plaza, Orpheum and other theaters, is the most elaborate, most expensive, most beautiful movie serial ever made. It's both an apotheosis of "Flash Gordon" serials and a witty critique that makes associations with a variety of literature that is nothing if not eclectic: "Quo Vadis?", "Buck Rogers," "Ivanhoe," "Superman," "The Wizard of Oz," "The Gospel According to St. Matthew," the legend of King Arthur and the knights of the Round Table.

All of these works, of course, had earlier left their marks on the kind of science-fiction comic strips that Mr. Lucas, the writer as well as director of "Star Wars," here remembers with affection of such cheerfulness that he avoids facetiousness. The way definitely not to approach "Star Wars," though, is to expect a film of cosmic implications or to footnote it with so many references that one anticipates it as if it were a literary duty. It's fun and funny.

The time, according to the opening credit card, is "a long time ago" and the setting "a galaxy far far away," which gives Mr. Lucas and his associates total freedom to come up with their own landscapes, housing, vehicles, weapons, religion, politics — all of which are variations on the familiar.

•

When the film opens, dark times have fallen upon the galactal empire once ruled, we are given to believe, from a kind of space-age Camelot. Against these evil tyrants there is, in progress, a rebellion led by a certain Princess Leia Organa, a pretty round-faced young woman of old-fashioned pluck who, before you can catch your breath, has been captured by the guardians of the empire. Their object is to retrieve some secret plans that can be the empire's undoing.

That's about all the plot that anyone of voting age should be required to keep track of. The story of "Star Wars" could be written on the head of a pin and still leave room for the Bible. It is, rather, a breathless succession of escapes, pursuits, dangerous missions, unexpected encounters, with each one ending in some kind of defeat until the final one.

These adventures involve, among others, an ever-optimistic young man named Luke Skywalker (Mark Hamill), who is innocent without being naïve; Han Solo (Harrison Ford), a free-booting freelance, space-ship captain who goes where he can make the most money, and an old mystic named Ben Kenobi (Alec Guinness), one of the last of the Old Guard, a fellow in possession of what's called "the force," a mixture of what appears to be ESP and early Christian faith.

•

Accompanying these three as they set out to liberate the princess and restore justice to the empire are a pair of Laurel-and-Hardyish robots. The thin one, who looks like a sort of brass woodman, talks in the polished phrases of a valet ("I'm adroit but I'm not very knowledgeable"), while the squat one, shaped like a portable washing machine, who is the one with the knowledge, simply squeaks and blinks his lights. They are the year's best new comedy team.

In opposition to these good guys are the imperial forces led by someone called the Grand Moff Tarkin (Peter Cushing) and his executive assistant, Lord Darth Vader (David Prowse), a former student of Ben Kenobi who elected to leave heaven sometime before to join the evil ones.

The true stars of "Star Wars" are John Barry, who was responsible for the production design, and the people who were responsible for the incredible special effects—space ships, explosions of stars, space battles, hand-to-hand combat with what appear to be lethal neon swords. I have a particular fondness for the look of the interior of a gigantic satellite called the Death Star, a place full of the kind of waste space one finds today only in old Fifth Avenue mansions and public libraries.

There's also a very funny sequence in a low-life bar on a remote planet, a frontierlike establishment where they serve customers who look like turtles, apes, pythons and various amalgams of same, but draw the line at robots. Says the bartender piously: "We don't serve *their* kind here."

It's difficult to judge the performances in a film like this. I suspect that much of the time the actors had to perform with special effects that were later added in the laboratory. Yet everyone treats his material with the proper combination of solemnity and good humor that avoids condescension. One of Mr. Lucas's particular achievements is the manner in which he is able to recall the tackiness of the old comic strips and serials he loves without making a movie that is, itself, tacky. "Star Wars" is good enough to convince the most skeptical 8-year-old sci-fi buff, who is the toughest critic.

•

"Star Wars," which has been rated PG "Parental Guidance Suggested"), contains a lot of explosive action and not a bit of truly disturbing violence.

1977 My 26, C18:1

DAY OF THE ANIMALS, produced by Edward L. Montoro; directed by William Girdler; screenplay by William and Eleanor Norton; music by Lalo Schifrin; animal and stunt coordinator, Monty Cox; special effects by Gene Griggs. Running time, 97 minutes. At Loews State II, UA East Side and RKO 86th Street Twin I theaters. This film has been rated PG.

Steve Buckner	Christopher George
Paul Jensen	Leslie Nielsen
Terry Marsh	Lynda Day George
Taylor MacGregor	Richard Jaeckel
Daniel Santee	Michael Ansara
Shirley Goodwyn	Ruth Roman

LAWRENCE VAN GELDER

DAY OF THE ANIMALS," which opened yesterday at Loews State II, the UA East Side and RKO 86th Street Twin I theaters, is "The Birds" recycled by an equal-opportunity employer with an eye more on shock than suspense.

So when the participants in a trek of fools into the Western high country come under attack, they have more than talons and beaks to fear. Wolves, mountain lions, bears and packs of dogs are stalking and savaging them, as well as the birds; and in more civilized areas, rats run amok and poisonous snakes slither in sinuous multitudes in abandoned cars and trucks.

•

Why all this unseemly behavior? Well, "Day of the Animals" is a movie speculating about what could happen if the ozone layer protecting the earth were diminished because of mankind's use of aerosol sprays. And it decides that this would give rise to a mutant virus that would turn animals into mankillers.

Naturally, we are told, this phenomenon would manifest itself initially in the high country, where Steve Buckner (Christopher George) and Daniel Santee (Michael Ansara) are leading a no-weapons, no-food wilderness tour. Among the participants are a megalomaniacal advertising executive, a television newswoman, a science professor, a divorced mother and her son, a football player dying of cancer and a couple trying to patch up their marriage.

"Day of the Animals" offers pretty scenery, and some repulsive animal attacks. Despite its putative concern for the environment, it is calculated more to incite terror than to inspire restraint.

This film has been rated PG ("Parental Guidance Suggested"). Animal and human savagery, the latter in the form of an attempted rape, are apparently the reasons.

1977 My 26, C22:3

Kinuyo Tanaka and Shin Saburi in Yasujiro Ozu's "Equinox Flower"
Ozu, uncharacteristically buoyant

A Resourceful Father

EQUINOX FLOWER (Higanbana), directed by Yasujiro Ozu; screenplay (Japanese with English subtitles) by Mr. Ozu and Kogo Noda, based on the novel by Ton Satomi; director of photography, Yushun Atsuta; music, Takayori Saito; editor, Yoshiyasu Hamamura; distributed by New Yorker Films. Running time: 118 minutes. At the Cinema Studio Theater, Broadway at 66th Street. This film has not been rated.

Wataru Hirayama....................Shin Saburi
Kiyoko Hirayama....................Kinuyo Tanaka
Setsuko Hirayama....................Ineko Arima
Hisako Hirayama....................Miyuki Kuwano
Masahiko Taniguchi....................Keiji Sada
Hajime Sasaki....................Chieko Naniwa
Yukiko Sasaki....................Fujiko Yamamoto
Toshihiko Kawai....................Nobuo Nakamura
Shukichi Mikami.................... Chishu Ryu
Fumiko Mikami.................... Yoshiko Kuga
Shotaro Kondo....................Teiji Takahashi
Ichiro Naganuma....................Fumio Watanabe

By VINCENT CANBY

WATARU HIRAYAMA (Shin Saburi), the hero of the late Yasujiro Ozu's 1958 film, "Equinox Flower," is a successful Tokyo businessman, contentedly married to an old-fashioned wife who never argues and who picks up after him, the father of two pretty daughters, one of whom is reaching the marriageable age.

When we first meet him at the wedding dinner for the daughter of one of his old friends, Hirayama delivers an amused, affectionate toast to the bridal couple, noting that theirs is a love match, not a "prosaic, unromantic" arranged marriage, as his own had been. When the guests laugh, even his wife giggles.

To the world at large Hirayama seems as flexible and resourceful as the nation that turned the military defeat of World War II into economic victory. At home, though, he's still a rigid 19th-century tyrant.

•

"Equinox Flower," which opened yesterday at the Cinema Studio, is about Hirayama's desperate attempts to thwart his liberated daughter, Setsuko (Ineko Arima), from making just the sort of love match that he has encouraged when the daughter was not his own. Hirayama at first refuses to allow any marriage at all. He resorts to comically transparent stratagems to find out the worst about the young man, who is revealed to be without blemish.

When Hirayama's wife (Kinuyo Tanaka) points out—very delicately—that her husband is not being consistent, he explodes that this has to do with parental love and, besides, inconsistencies are the way of the world. It's a witty scene and a very moving one.

"Equinox Flower"—a particularly inscrutable title even for this great Japanese director—is one of Ozu's least dark comedies, which is not to say that it's carefree, but, rather, that it's gentle and amused in the way that it acknowledges time's passage, the changing of values and the adjustments that must be made between generations.

•

Hirayama is as charming a character as Ozu has ever given us—intelligent, thoughtful, sensitive, impatient with pretense, practical, a good friend and a dutiful parent, and, when it comes to his own children, a total hypocrite. His defense of traditional values, which Ozu again and again saw in terms of the relations between fathers and daughters ("Late Spring," "Autumn Afternoon," "End of Summer"), is doomed from the start, yet there is in "Equinox Flower" less a sense of defeat than in any of the other films.

"Equinox Flower" is uncharacteristically buoyant, as in a crucial sequence when his daughter Setsuko's best friend tricks the father into giving his consent to Setsuko's marriage. The trick is farcical, though its implications are genuinely dramatic, creating the mixture of contradictory emotions that make Ozu's meticulously observed family dramas unique in film literature.

•

The performers are flawless, including Chishu Ryu, the leading player in a number of other Ozu works who here plays a supporting role, that of Hirayama's best friend, a gentle man completely baffled when his own daughter moves out of her home to live with her lover. But even this father and daughter are reconciled by the end. Neither understands the other, yet there is acceptance, which is Ozu's way.

One word about the print being shown at the Cinema Studio: "Equinox Flower" was Ozu's first color film, which makes the drearily purplish cast of this print so disappointing. Ozu used color with the same discipline that he devoted to all other aspects of filmmaking, though it's impossible to tell here.

1977 My 27, C10:3

Fabulous Sword

TANGE-SAZEN, directed and adapted by Seiichiro Uchikawa from the novel by Fubo Hayashi; photography by Yoshikawa Ototu; a Shochiku Production distributed by Shochiku Films of America Inc. At the Regency Theater, Broadway and 6/th Street. Running time: 95 minutes. This film has not been rated.

Tange-Sazen / Genzaburo Yagyu....................Tetsuro Tamba
Gennoio Yagyu....................Keisuke Sonoi
Hagino....................Haruko Wanibuchi
Ofuji....................Michiko Saga

By A. H. WEILER

IF MEMORY and records serve, the work of Seijiro Uchikawa, the director-writer, had not surfaced here before the arrival yesterday of "Tange-Sazen," the latest offering in the Regency Theater's Japanese film series. More than anything else, it indicates that the prolific Nipponese movie industry is not suffering from any dearth of directors or Samurai sagas.

As may be surmised, stylization is the keynote of the period, the performances and the settings of this sword-swinging mystery-adventure. Mr. Uchikawa's direction, as well as his script, conforms to the exotic standards demanded by these legendary fictions. The fact is that once again the plot is multifaceted enough to make a Westerner blink, although English subtitles point the way through some of its labyrinths.

•

Tange-Sazen is not your Japanese garden variety hero. A one-armed, one-eyed swordsman, he is scorge of all bad guys and hero to his fellow slum dwellers. The time is 1730 and it appears that the Yagyu clan has been ordered to repair a certain shrine, which will take all kinds of money. It's a problem that can be solved only by a fabulous sword that is the key to a vast, buried treasure.

But the twists are dizzying. That coveted blade not only draws Tange-Sazen but also the clan chief's son, his fiancée, his younger brother and a clutch of assorted villains into the chase for the fortune. And it isn't ungallant to hint that Tange-Sazen also turns out to be one of clan lord's twin sons who was abandoned as an infant.

Amid these gnarled proceedings, however, are moments of pastoral beauty captured in lovely pinks and browns as well as some colorfully broad performances, particularly by the gruff, grimacing, athletic Tetsuro Tamba in the dual roles of the indomitable Tange-Sazen and the lord's older son, and Keisuke Sonoi, as the pretty, high-born fiancee, who is smitten both by love and tragedy. In guiding this often foggy fable, which was produced in 1963, Mr. Uchikawa has concentrated on some unlikely action, which, like Tange-Sazen, is likely to hold a viewer's attention.

"Tange-Sazen" is being shown today and tomorrow with "Three Ronin," another Samurai adventure.

1977 My 27, C15:1

FILM VIEW

VINCENT CANBY

Thoughts About the Fear of Kids In Current American Movies

America's domination by its youth culture will not have properly peaked until we have as the nation's number-one television entertainer a stand-up comic no older than 8. At that point everything will have come together—our fear of the young, our desire to appear hip, our inclination to give children more material rewards than they could possibly think of on their own, and our worst nightmare, the expectation that one day we'll wake up to find ourselves rendered obsolete by toddlers, who then may well decide at what hour *we* should be put to sleep.

This is the only way I can explain the extraordinary fear and loathing of children, including babies, being expressed in current American movies. These films seem as determined to alert us to the potential dangers of totdom as the Warner Brothers films of the late 30's and early 40's were devoted to exposing the Nazis. Look closely at your kid, says "Demon Seed," because its father may have been a computer. "There's only one thing wrong with the Davis baby," says the ad for another film. "It's alive!" (which is also the title of the movie).

This peculiar American obsession with children-as-monsters is made even more apparent by the availability here of a number of European films that persist in treating children seriously and childhood as a normal part of the maturation process, not as a sentence to Hell.

In the space of one week there opened in New York "Cousin Angelica" and "Cria!", two unusually sensitive and sensible films about childhood, both directed by the Spanish filmmaker, Carlos Saura, and one ("Cria!") starring Ana Torrent, the tiny, dark-eyed 9-year-old whose responsive face made last year's "The Spirit of the Beehive" so memorable.

They regard children unsentimentally in European films, and with admiration and affection, as in Truffaut's "Small Change." Here we've reached the stage where it's a laugh to watch a short-tempered mom, fed up with non-stop squalling,

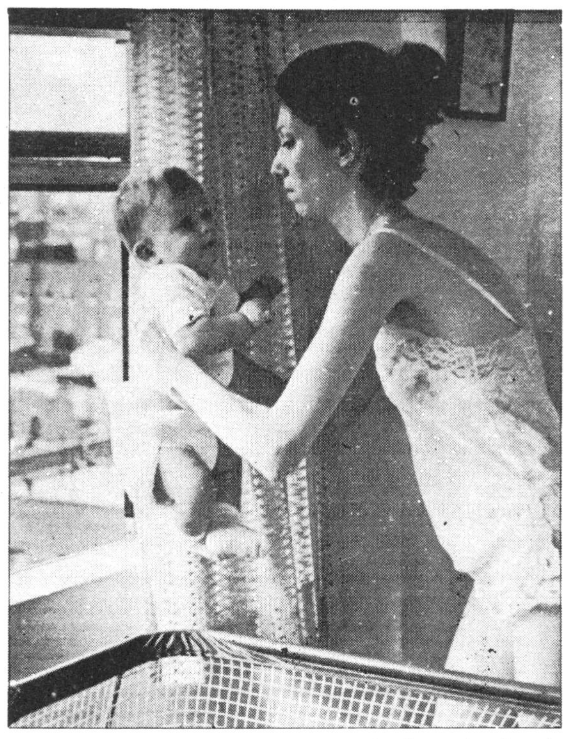

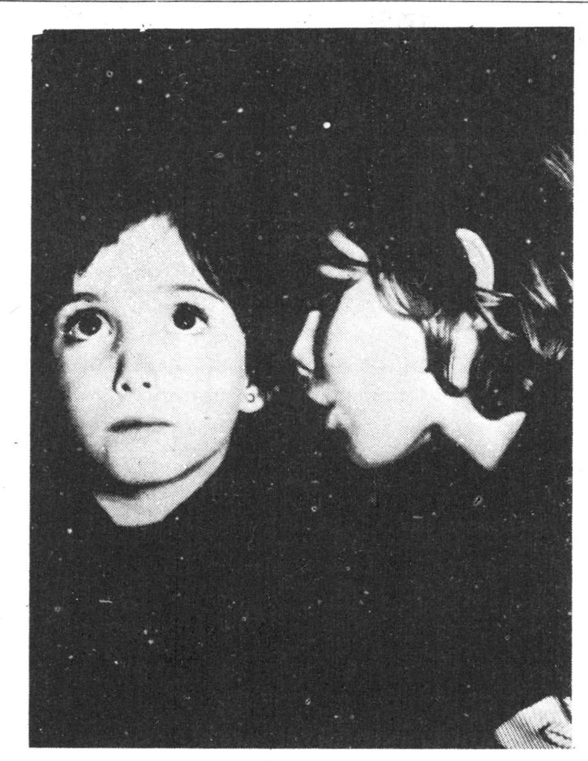

In Warhol's "Bad," kids as victims; in Spain's "Beehive," kids as kids

:oss her baby out the window of her high-rise. ("Andy Warhol's Bad").

About the only normal—or normally neurotic—children :o be seen in a recent American film are the three boys in Franklin Schaffner's screen version of Hemingway's "Islands in the Stream," and the film isn't really about the boys. It's about their Hemingway-like dad and what *he* feels about *them*. More in the fashion of the day is "Audrey Rose," the Robert Wise-Frank De Felitta spin-off from "The Exorcist" about an 11-year-old New York girl named Audrey Rose, who was killed two minutes before Ivy was born.

• • •

The movie is supposed to be about reincarnation (and its pitfalls) but it's essentially an exercise in the good old pastime of Kick the Kid (Before He Kicks You). The little girl in "Audrey Rose" is a tortured nonentity, a spectacle to be observed much as we might watch Old Faithful in Yellowstone National Park. We don't feel any special sympathy for the child, and I don't think we are meant to, only a terrific relief that she's theirs, not ours.

The little boy in "The Omen," we are given to believe, is the natural son of the Prince of Darkness, come to earth to claim his legacy. "It's Alive" is about a murderous new-born infant who, after dispatching the doctors and nurses in the delivery room, crawls around Los Angeles at will, killing milkmen, senior citizens and other innocent adults. Near the end of "Demon Seed" we witness the birth of the child that's been "given" to Julie Christie by an amorous, ambitious "artifical intelligence system" that wishes to rule the earth. The baby, which we see briefly, is a superbeing who looks like a brass-dipped Mickey Rooney.

Ray Bradbury has wittily exploited adult fears of and guilts about children in a number of short stories, but the movies we're getting today have less to do with wit than with paranoia. That paranoia, though, in being a delusion, is not too different from the unreal way in which American movies have always depicted children, particularly as represented by such child stars as Mary Pickford, Shirley Temple, Jackie Cooper, Margaret O'Brien and Hayley Mills. These idealized representations of children—wise beyond their years, stanch, loyal, self-sufficient—have little need of the state of grace that Truffaut says, in "Small Change," envelops childhood. They are plaster saints, and quite as kid-freaky as the malignant monsters American movies are now presenting to us.

It's no wonder that the best child actor to appear in American movies lately, Jodie Foster, has made her mark playing essentially adult roles (the teen-age prostitute in "Taxi Driver," the speakeasy singer in "Bugsy Malone" and the daughter in the daughter-mother role-switching Disney comedy, "Freaky Friday"). Actresses complain about the dearth of good roles for women, but there are none at all for children as children.

• • •

That European filmmakers are able to explore childhood so successfully while Americans deal largely in distortions has, I suspect, more to do with the difference between the way films are made here and abroad than with any innate difference in sensibility. The best European films, which are the ones we see here, are the product of a cottage industry, of director-writers who pursue their personal visions away from the kind of pressures that have historically shaped American films since they became a global business. Though American movies are not exactly mass-produced, children in American movies tend to be as doll-like as toys produced for sale both at home and abroad. Would anyone want to buy a Barbie Doll with a crooked nose or thin hair? Perhaps a few eccentric little girls, but most want dolls that look exactly like the dolls their friends have.

European filmmakers recognize that movies that contain child actors needn't be designed for children. This is something that has perpetually confused Hollywood filmmakers and, I think, has been responsible for the odd distortions we've come to accept by saying with a shrug, "That's Hollywood." In American movies children tend to be miniature adults, and thus without any real stature or individuality. Not so in a film like Saura's haunted "Cria!", which is about the desperate attempts of a 9-year-old child to make some sense out of the chaos she sees in the adult world around her. It's not a film for children (though I don't believe it would disturb a child). It's a film for adults who haven't forgotten that they too were once at a terrible disadvantage for being small and, in the ways of the world, ignorant.

Saura, Truffaut, Hans Geissendorfer (director of the excellent German adaptation of "The Wild Duck"), Pascal Thomas (director of "Les Zozos") recognize that children are different from you and me by taking them on their own terms. The reaction of American moviemakers is to turn kids into either saints or beasts, a process that not only facilitates the product merchandizing but also relieves us of any responsibility towards them. ■

1977 My 29, II:11:1

Living Lessons

THE NEW SCHOOL, a documentary feature directed by Jorge Fraga; in Spanish with English subtitles and English narration; produced by the Cuban Film Institute (ICAIC); distributed by Tricontinental Films. Running time: 90 minutes. At the Film Forum, 15 Vandam Street.

A junior high school student in the Cuban documentary "The New School"

By VINCENT CANBY

THE NEW School," which opened yesterday at the Film Forum, is a 90-minute documentary about Cuba's intensive program to build and staff dozens of new junior high schools throughout the country. The subject sounds deadly dull, and in truth, there are a number of predictable aspects to the movie, produced by the Cuban Film Institute and directed by José Fraga.

The faces of the students, teachers and parents run the gamut from earnestly sincere to just plain happy, but then one would not expect a documentary of this sort to record failure, skepticism or hopelessness. Untroubled cheerfulness is the accepted expression of revolutionary propaganda. Optimism is its mode.

As soon as one sees beyond the manners of the genre, "The New School" becomes a fascinating report on what appears to be an extraordinary project involving educational concepts as well as physical construction. The film concentrates on five new junior high schools, in Cuba and on the Isle of Pines, which are part of the program designed to make junior high school education available to every child in the country.

Though the oblong, three-story school buildings are about as architecturally interesting as airport hotels, the students and their teachers are clearly experiencing adventures that are anything but prefabricated.

To help pay for the buildings and maintain the schools, each is set within an area of farm land that the students work as part of their daily routine. Because of the shortage of teachers, older students are drafted to instruct younger students while continuing with their own education, a system that further extends the sense of student participation in the shaping of their own lives.

Revolutionary fervor of the sort pictured here is most appealing as we see students conduct auto-critique sessions, taking one boy down a notch for not having the right attitude, another for cheating, and questioning one girl who pops phosphorus pills before exams to "improve" her memory. It may look a bit naïve to those of us in the land of overdevelopment, where a belief in the possibilities of the future must be thought delusory at the very least; otherwise, utterly mad. I hope not.

Premier Castro shows up in several sequences in his role as "Papa Fidel," playing basketball, baseball and Ping-Pong with the students and, at one point, emceeing a fashion show at which students and teachers vote on what will be the school uniforms.

It's terribly, terribly jolly, but even here the film cleverly manages to turn a stereotyped conception to its own advantage. As we watch Premier Castro kid around with the students, one's first thought is to wonder who's running the government that day and then to think, well, Cuba is not all that big and so it may be perfectly possible that the father of the Cuban revolution can act out his partriarchal role in daily life.

"The New School" is not cinematic art but it is shrewd and effective. It may be seen at the Film Forum today through Sunday at 7:45 P.M. and next Thursday through Sunday at the same time.

1977 Je 3, C11:1

Psychedelia

THE GRATEFUL DEAD, distributed by Monarch Noteworthy; produced by Eddie Washington; editorial direction by Jerry Garcia; location direction by Leon Gast; executive production by Ron Rakow; edited by Susan Crutcher; animation by Gary Gutierrez; sound mixed by Dan Healy; at The Ziegfeld Theater. Running time 131 minutes. This documentary has not been rated.

ABOUT 40 MINUTES into "The Grateful Dead," a documentary that opened yesterday at the Ziegfeld Theater, two fans of that comparatively long-lived rock group are recorded by the camera in the midst of a debate.

In the corridor of an auditorium where The Grateful Dead are playing to a gathering of their ecstatic faithful, one debater argues that the documentary-in-the making is more than a record album on film. In a few years, he asserts, his opponent will gladly pay $4 or $5 to see the movie.

The other argues vehemently that the film is nothing, that the fans of the group, which had its beginnings in Haight-Ashbury a decade ago and retains a devoted cult following, are being exploited by the moviemakers.

•

Because both parties to the debate are clearly fans of the group, whose early acid-rock style also made it a favorite among the Hells Angels, the music is not an issue. But now that the movie is here, the opportunity for judgment is at hand.

"The Grateful Dead" is little more than a record album on film—more than two hours of it, not including an intermission. And while the advertising promises insight, the film settles for superficiality. A few minutes are devoted to showing the group offstage; a few minutes reflect a willingness to let them reveal themselves as best they can, but not an effort to probe.

What remains, despite some nostalgic stills from San Francisco in the youthful efflorescence of a decade ago and an animated sequence that looks like a psychedelic version of "Star Wars," are images devoid of illumination.

Angled closeups fill the screen. Again and again, the cameras zoom in close on The Dead. Lips sing into microphones; fingers scuttle along the necks of guitars; sweat runs down the drummer's face; fans dance in the aisles; they cheer; they writhe against the stage.

Aural excitement is pitted against visual monotony. Monotony wins.

LAWRENCE VAN GELDER

1977 Je 3, C11:5

KATZELMACHER, directed by Rainer Werner Fassbinder; screenplay (German with English subtitles) by Mr. Fassbinder; director of photography, Dietrich Lohmann; editor, Franz Walsch; music, Peer Raben (after Franz Schubert); an Antiteater production, distributed by New Yorker Films. Running time: 88 minutes. At the New Yorker Theater, Broadway near 89th Street. This film has not been rated.

Marie	Hanna Schygulla
Erich	Hans Hischmueller
Helga	Lilith Ungerer
Paul	Rudolf Waldemar Brem
Rosy	Elga Sorbas
Franz	Harry Baer
Elisabeth	Irm Herman
Peter	Peter Moland
Gunda	Doris Mattes
Jorgos	Rainer Werner Fassbinder

By VINCENT CANBY

Erich, who's becoming pudgy, wears a perpetual frown as if it were a fashion accessory. Marie, his pretty, romance-minded friend, clings to his arm as proudly as if Erich were an Olympics champion and not a petty hood.

Paul, who's also getting fat, is proud of his hair, which he carefully combs whenever a lock might be out of place. Helga, who loves Paul, chatters too much and every now and then needs to be slapped into silence. Gunda has no guy but she hangs out with the others, hoping, probably, to pick up a castoff.

Lower middle-class layabouts, they sit on—or lean against—the railing outside a Munich apartment house in various positions of boredom. They bicker. They brood. Mostly they just stare into space, lined up all in a row like the crows in Hitchcock's "The Birds."

•

As they walk into or out of the frame, the camera rather ostentatiously refuses to follow them. Instead, it continues to stare straight ahead at the railing, as if mocking the world-weary attitudes it's been recording so patiently.

Occasionally the scene shifts to the corner pub where Erich and Marie and Helga and Paul, sometimes with Gunda and Franz and Rosy, play cards. Sometimes they pair off to make love quickly and perfunctorily in barren rooms, only to return to the railing.

Nothing much changes. Nothing changes, that is, until Elisabeth, who lives across the way, rents a room to a Greek worker named Jorgos. The rumors begin to fly. Jorgos is said to be a sexual wonder. Gunda reports a chance meeting in the park with Jorgos as an attempt at rape. The other young men feel threatened. Something has to be done.

•

This is more or less the form of "Katzelmacher," Rainer Werner Fassbinder's second feature film, made in 1969 before he went on to become virtually a one-man German New Wave. "Katzelmacher"—a slang term for troublemaker—opened yesterday at the New Yorker as part of the theater's continuing Fassbinder festival. It is, with "Effie Briest," one of the two remaining Fassbinder festival films not to be missed.

I've described the style of the film in some detail because it is so hypnotic and eventually so comic. Mr. Fassbinder, even in those early days when the influence of Godard was still apparent, was a complete original, one of the few directors who could make a deadpan film about lethargy, greed and small-mindedness that is simultaneously funny and tough, sympathetic and caustic.

His characters, with the possible exception of Jorgos (played by Mr. Fassbinder), who never says much, are either slobs or dimwitted, and though they are totally self-absorbed and given to parroting clichés, they are sometimes capable of the unexpected gesture, as when Marie decides to leave Erich for Jorgos. Paul frets when Helga becomes pregnant; he considers murdering her, or, at the least, of aborting the child. When she loses it anyway, he decides to marry her.

•

The static camera, the exaggerated mannerisms of the actors, the jump-cuts, the repeated themes and variations of scenes, all recall Godard, but the major influence on the film appears to be Mr. Fassbinder's early work in the theater.

The screenplay, in fact, is an adaptation of a Fassbinder play, but having seen the film twice I find it difficult to imagine it as anything except an extraordinarily stylish film. It's quite unlike anything else I've seen, with the exception of another early Fassbinder film, "Recruits at Ingolstadt," which was also adapted from a theater piece.

Unlike some of the later Fassbinder works, there's little ambiguity about what the director is up to here. "Katzelmacher" is scathing about the postwar German economic boom that has, of course, been so kind to the film maker himself. More importantly the flim is an early glimpse of his dazzling talent and the talents of the stock company of performers and technicians who, with him, have created a body of film work unique in any country in recent years.

1977 Je 4, 11:1

OSSESSIONE (Obsession), directed by Luchino Visconti; screenplay (Italian with English subtitles) by Mario Alicata, Antonio Pietrangeli, Gianni Puccini, Giuseppe de Santis and Mr. Visconti; directors of photography, Aldo Tonti and Domenico Scala; editor, Mario Serandrei, executive producer, Liberto Solaroli; a production of ICI (Rome). Running time: 135 minutes. This film has not been rated. At the D. W. Griffith Theater, 59th Street and Second Avenue.

Giovanna	Clara Calamai
Gino	Massimo Girotti
The husband	Juan de Landa
The "Spaniard"	Elia Marcuzzo
Anita	Dhia Cristani
Lorry driver	Vittorio Duse

"Ossessione" ["Obsession") was shown at the 1976 New York Film Festival. The following are excerpts from Vincent Canby's review, which appeared Oct. 2, 1976. The film opened yesterday at the D. W. Griffith Theater.

Although there are almost as many definitions of Italian neo-Realism as there are Italian neo-Realist films, Luchino Visconti's first feature, "Ossessione," made in 1942, is generally accepted as having begun the movement whose name was later applied to the work of Antonioni, Rossellini, De Sica and others.

•

The film is being shown here commercially for the first time. Earlier showings in the United States had been prohibited because Mr. Visconti had, without permission, helped himself to James M. Cain's novel, "The Postman Always Rings Twice," the rights to which were owned by M-G-M, the studio that later filmed it in 1946 with John Garfield and Lana Turner under Tay Garnett's direction.

Comparing the Visconti "Ossessione" with the Garnett "Postman" is to stand a production of "Traviata" next to a McDonald's television commercial, which is not meant to underrate the American film, which is as effectively steamy, tough and terse as the Hollywood law allowed in those days.

Mr. Visconti follows with remarkable fidelity the Cain story about the handsome young drifter and the youngish wife who, driven by their sexual passion and greed, murder the woman's old husband to get his money and his business, a combination hamburger stand and filling station.

"Ossessione" today looks to be an extraordinarily majestic, elegant and romantic movie to have started anything labeled neo-Realism. There is even something grand about that bleakness of the Italian landscapes, to say nothing of the mood. When the illicit lovers, Gino (Massimo Girotti) and Giovanna (Clara Calamai), are exchanging lustful glances at the dinner table, the soundtrack rumbles with the sounds of distant thunder and frantic cries of caged farm animals. Under these circumstances, one is disappointed that the characters don't sing.

"Ossessione," which also began the late Mr. Visconti's remarkable film career, may be slow going to the uninitiated, but its historical importance is not to be denied.

1977 Je 4, 12:1

FRATERNITY ROW, directed by Thomas J. Tobin; written and produced by Charles Gary Allison; director of photography, Peter Gibbons; editor, Eugene A. Fournier; music, Don McLean; distributed by Paramount Pictures. Running time: 104 minutes. At neighborhood theaters. This film has been rated PG.

Rodger	Peter Fox
Zac	Gregory Harrison
Chunk	Scott Newman
Jennifer	Nancy Morgan
Betty Ann	Wendy Phillips
Brother Abernathy	Robert Emhardt
Narrator	Cliff Robertson

Not since "Lifeguard" has any American movie confronted secondary problems as steadfastly as "Fraternity Row," a film about one idealistic student's attempt to change the fraternity system at what is described as a small, elitist eastern college in 1954.

"Fraternity Row," which opened at neighborhood theaters yesterday, is itself a sort of campus product, having been written and produced by Charles Gary Allison to get material for his Ph.D. in philosophy and communications at the University of Southern California. Considering the lack of experience of both Mr. Allison and Thomas J. Tobin, the director, the film is something of a technical achievement.

It really looks and sounds like a 50's movie. The color is just garish enough and the actors all a bit too pretty—like studio contract players in the 50's—and it repeats its few ideas so many times that even the most dimwitted third-grader can get the point.

•

"Fraternity Row" comes out firmly against bigotry, hypocrisy and hazing in its story about a fraternity pledge named Zac (Gregory Harrison) who attempts to change the system from within, though his girlfriend, Jennifer (Nancy Morgan), remains properly skeptical. The movie also comes out firmly against the tactics of the late Senator Joseph R. McCarthy when his charges were made against non-Communists. At the same time it displays great affection for the dopier rituals of the day, including solemn ceremonies in which a young man would publicly give his fraternity pin to the young woman of his choice ("With this pin I pledge thee my heart. . . .").

The actors are all very attractive under the circumstances, which at best, are facetious and, at worst, embarrassing. They include Mr. Harrison, Peter Fox (as an upper classman), Miss Morgan, and, most effective of all, Scott Newman (Paul's son) as the fraternity's cheerful sadist. In another time these roles would have been played by Robert Wagner, Terry Moore and Jeffrey Hunter, and they wouldn't have been half as good.

VINCENT CANBY

1977 Je 4, 12:1

FILM VIEW

VINCENT CANBY

Not Since 'Flash Gordon Conquers The Universe'...

It may well be true, as some of my colleagues apparently fear, that the immense success of "Annie," the Broadway musical incarnation of Harold Gray's "Little Orphan Annie," and George Lucas's "Star Wars," a gigantic comic-strip of a sci-fi movie, are the seminal works of a new age of Non-Think, an anti-intellectual reaction to plays and films that go out of their way to insult, shock, provoke and disturb, that question everything including the system that allows the artist to express his outrage. One can easily make a case for this argument.

Among other things, "Annie" virtually reduces the first term of Franklin Delano Roosevelt to one cabinet meeting at which Annie gives FDR the inspiration for his New Deal. The show doesn't seem to have a thought in its head, being composed of a series of sure-fire stimuli that call forth the sort of preconditioned responses that everyone who is not a card-carrying ogre has to orphans, stray dogs, mean overseers, kindly benefactors and tap-dancing toddlers.

At the same time "Star Wars" is the first science-fiction film since "Flash Gordon Conquers the Universe," a 12-episode 1940 serial, that makes absolutely no meaningful comment on such contemporary concerns as nuclear war, overpopulation, environmental pollution, depersonalization and sex. Reduced to their lowest common cliche, "Annie" and "Star Wars" are escapist entertainment. Each is guaranteed not to disturb the tired businessman who wears his fatigue like a battle ribbon.

This is, I think, quite true, but to leave it at that is to miss the point of what is too glibly described as escapist entertainment, as if everybody's escapist entertainment were the same thing and as if there weren't effective escapist entertainment and escapist entertainment to which one can be allergic, like penicillin. "The Sound of Music," which soothed the ragged nerves of almost everybody else, brought me out in spots. It depressed me as much as if I'd been listening to Dr. Martin Abend talking about Red China.

There's no need for me to analyze "Annie," which has already been gone over at some length in these pages. It was agreeable and my only reservations had to do with not seeing enough of Sandy and with length. Two hours and 45 minutes, with one intermission, is too long for something that's supposed to be escapist. After that long a sit, you begin wishing to escape from the escape.

"Star Wars" is also too long—which is the sort of criticism that I don't usually believe critics should indulge in. An artist's choice of scope, dimension and size should be as beyond criticism as his choice of subject. You accept these things and go on from there, in everything, that is, except escapist entertainment. There comes a point when enough is enough. That, of course, has to do with me, with my age and with my tolerance for comic strips. On the other hand, I know one 10-year-old who could have sat through another six hours of "Star Wars" without visible fidget.

"Star Wars" pretty much defines what most people mean when they speak of escapist entertainment. It isn't about anything at all in any serious way, though it is so beautifully and cheerfully done, and it is so full of references to the literature of one's childhood, that the escapism is of a particularly invigorating sort. The movie's cinematic and literary richness are such that it cannot honorably be associated with other film and theater works that, by their blandness of subject and safe, unimaginative treatment, describe themselves as artifacts of the Age of Non-Think.

• • •

I refer to most movies about the glories of the wilderness, about the foolishness of war, about unidentified political conspiracies and about the emptiness of success achieved at the price of love. I refer to almost all Broadway musicals (though I like watching their scenery being moved about) and to virtually all of television's situation comedies and regularly scheduled news programs.

If, as I believe, the works of the Age of Non-Think can be identified as much by their lack of style as by their lack of substance, then "Star Wars" escapes such classification by a mile. "Annie" I'm not so sure about.

In "Star Wars" Lucas has created a jumbo-sized fantasy that pays homage first to those movie serials of our youth—including the "Flash Gordons," "Buck Rogerses" and "Captain Marvels"— that, in spite of their tackiness, liberated the imagination of millions of children around the world. Lucas glorifies the memory of those serials, more than the serials themselves. He isn't saying that "Star Wars" is the way these quickie productions actually were, but it's the way we thought of them as we watched them, when the heart was in the mouth, when one's reason (even of the youngest patron) was put on hold, and when one allowed one's emotions to be grabbed, secure in the knowledge that everything would eventually come out all right.

"Star Wars" pays homage to the old movie serials but it has roots that extend into comic strips ("Flash Gordon," "Terry and the Pirates"), into boys' books on the order of the Hardy Boys series, into classics like "The Wizard of Oz" and "A Connecticut Yankee in King Arthur's Court," into the legends of King Arthur and his Knights of the Round Table, into any number of simple-minded war movies, "Quo Vadis?" as well as into various gospels in the New Testament.

Set "a long time ago in a galaxy far far away," the Lucas screenplay is about the efforts of a couple of knights errant, a fresh-faced young man named Luke Skywalker (Mark Hamill) and the captain of a space-freighter, Han Solo (Harrison Ford), the sort of fellow who has been in every dive from one end of the galaxy to the other, to save the galactal empire from the evil forces now in control. Their principal mission is to rescue the virtuous Princess Leia Organa (Carrie Fisher), who has in her possession SOME VERY IMPORTANT SECRET PLANS. (The story really is nonsense, but don't worry about that.)

Helping the two space-knights are an old wise man, Ben (Obi-Wan) Kenobi, played by an amusingly dignified Alec Guinness, and a pair of marvelously funny robots, a tall, thin, Tin woodman-type made out of brass, a fellow who says such things as, "Sir, if you don't need me, I think I'll shut down for a while," and a short, squat, tubby one, who looks like a portable washing machine and communicates in sqeaks and blinking of lights. They are an enchanting comedy team, often in disagreement with each other, given to spats, but when the chips are down, they are steadfast squires.

Lucas populates his galaxy with all sorts of curious beings, including nasty, pint-sized Sand People, hybrid animals that must be seen to be appreciated, talking griffons, a wino who looks like the Creature from the Black Lagoon, and one Wookie, Han Solo's first mate, a fellow who is supposed to be a hairy anthrapoid but who looks more like Lucas's version of the Cowardly Lion.

Not since "The Wizard of Oz," I think, has a moviemaker so successfully created such a series of original monsters, some less nice than others. One of the film's two main villains is played by Peter Cushing of Hammer Films renown, and I'm sure that it's no accident that he looks like a classy edition of Charles Middleton, the man who played the unspeakably treacherous Emperor Ming in the Flash Gordon serials.

• • •

"Star Wars" has been rated PG ("parental guidance suggested") though I can't figure out why. The movie is full of extraordinary action (space-ship battles, duels with swords that look as if they were fluorescent, ray-gun attacks, and such) but the action is anything but violent. No one is harmed in any believable or frightening way. This is not the sort of film that will send a child screaming for shelter under his seat. He may be pleasantly scared but he won't dare look away for fear of missing some further pleasure.

The chances are that parents will share that pleasure most of the time. It does go on a bit long, but those of us over 8 will appreciate the film's remarkable techniques, including the miniatures, and camera tricks, as well as the wit that never becomes facetious. This is not a film of the Non-Think Age. Actually, I may have to see it again. A friend of mine had to point out something I missed the first time—that the last scene is a direct quote from Leni Riefenstahl's "Triumph of the Will." Is Lucas, in that last scene, making some comment on the totalitarianism inherent in so many fairy tales and visions of extraterrestrial life? I suppose so. I also suppose he was having a terrific time thinking it all up, anticipating just such comments. ■

1977 Je 5, II:15:1

Von Kluck's Day

THE MARCH ON PARIS 1914—OF GENERALOBERST ALEXANDER VON KLUCK—AND HIS MEMORY OF JESSIE HOLLADAY, directed by Walter Gutman; directors of photography, Mr. Gutman and Mike Kuchar; music, Jessie Holladay Duane; a Walter Gutman production. Running time: 70 minutes. At the Whitney Museum of American Art, Madison Avenue at 75th Street.

Young general ..... Wulf Gunther Brandes
Jessie Holladay ..... Jessie Holladay Duane
Old general ..... Barrows Mussey
Narrators ..... Wulf Gunther Brandes, Walter Gutman

By VINCENT CANBY

THE MARCH ON PARIS 1914—of Generaloberst Alexander von Kluck—and His Memory of Jessie Holladay," which opened yesterday at the Whitney Museum of American Art, is the wittiest, most appealing film yet made by Walter Gutman, the stock-market analyst, art critic and patron, painter, philosopher and lover of beauty who, at 74, is one of the more exuberant of independent American filmmakers.

In his program notes for the film, Mr. Gutman would have us believe that the making of the movie was really just an excuse to take a trip to France last summer in the company of Jessie Holladay Duane, whom he describes as "a beautiful young woman who, curse the fates, is a half century younger than me (sic). . . ." Don't you believe it. The film is much more complicated than that.

•

It's a meditation on love—idealized sexual love, love of war and Mr. Gutman's own love of the beautiful women he appreciates with the intensity of an obsessed collector. The form of the film is free, almost haphazard, though sophisticated in its intent.

The inspiration is a book written by Alexander von Kluck (whose name prompts some Gutman jokes), the German general who led the advance on Paris in 1914 and who was turned back at the outskirts of Paris by, among other things, the "taxicab army."

It is Mr. Gutman's fantasy that von Kluck, some years before 1914, met and had an idyllic affair with a young American woman (Miss Duane) as he was reconnoitering the northeastern French countryside disguised as a painter. The film cuts back and forth between scenes of this affair, chastely mimed and set with no embarrassment at all in contemporary landscapes and scenes detailing von Kluck's drive on Paris, complete with military maps and lengthy quotations from von Kluck's memoirs.

Did von Kluck fail because he was bemused by memories of his lost love as he drove his armies through France toward Paris? Probably not. I don't think that's the sort of thing that would appeal to Mr. Gutman's sense of history, though at one point he suggests that the American Civil War could have been over in two years if the Union's Gen. Winfield Scott Hancock had not made the unfortunate decision to go on the wagon. Hancock without booze, says Mr. Gutman, lacked the necessary boldness. Von Kluck was not a great general, drunk or sober.

In "The March on Paris" Mr. Gutman is not especially concerned with causes and effects. Mostly he is recalling for us his feelings about the war he remembers as a little boy, a war, he says, almost crossly, that few people know anything about any more. He evokes those feelings in still photographs, newsreel footage and drawings, and especially in the recurring images of Miss Duane, whose dark-haired beauty, by seeming so fresh, immediately suggests something so impermanent that it must already have disappeared in the time it took to process the film.

•

Miss Duane is a far cry from earlier Gutman heroines—the aggressive circus performers and "strong" women he so lovingly presented in films such as "The Grape-Picker's Daughter" and "Unstrap Me." When he photographs her walking through a wheat field, chest-high, we see her as the director does—desirable, ripe, but also a bit self-conscious, squinting into the sun, quite puzzled about the project she has somehow become a part of.

"The March on Paris 1914" is most personal, original and charming, the best film by far in the Whitney's current season.

1977 Je 8, C14:5

Gems and Jets

THE OTHER SIDE OF MIDNIGHT. Directed by Charles Jarrott; screenplay by Herman Raucher and Daniel Taradash, based on the novel by Sidney Sheldon; produced by Frank Yablans; executive producer, Howard W. Koch Jr.; music, Michel Legrand; editors, Donn Cambern and Harold F. Kress; director of photography, Fred J. Koenekamp; distributed by 20th Century-Fox. Running time: 163 minutes. At the Coronet Theater, Third Avenue near 59th Street, and National Theater, Broadway at 43d Street. This film has been rated R.

Noelle Page ..... Marie-France Pisier
Larry Douglas ..... John Beck
Catherine Douglas ..... Susan Sarandon
Constantin Demeris ..... Raf Vallone
Bill Fraser ..... Clu Gulager
Armand Gautier ..... Christian Marquand
Barbet ..... Michael Lerner
Lanchon ..... Sorrell Booke
Paul Metaxas ..... Antony Ponzini
Demonides ..... Louis Zorich
Chotas ..... Charles Cioffi
Sister Theresa ..... Dimitra Arliss
Warden ..... Jan Arvan
Madame Rose ..... Josette Banzet
Doc Peterson ..... John Chappell
Female guard ..... Eunice Christopher
Jacques Page ..... Roger Etienne

By VINCENT CANBY

SIDNEY SHELDON'S "The Other Side of Midnight" is one of those best-selling novels that all too soon has become not a major motion picture, but a lengthy, expensive one.

Written in eau de cologne by Herman Raucher and Daniel Taradash and directed by Charles Jarrott, who seems to have been paid by the yard, the movie takes almost three hours to tell us how miserable it is to be rich, famous and powerful, to be showered with jewels, to have a private airplane to go with your private Greek island, and to sleep in gigantic beds mounted on raised platforms that are, of course, sacrificial altars in fiction of this sort.

•

"The Other Side of Midnight" is about sweet, innocent Noelle Page (Marie-France Pisier) who, when still in her teens, is apprenticed by her father to the lecherous middle-aged owner of a dress shop in her native Marseilles. The time is 1939. War clouds are—how does one say?—gathering. When Noelle realizes that she's been sold into concubinage, she runs away to Paris, where the war is suddenly on, the clouds having apparently broken while she was taking the train north.

In Paris, after being fleeced by a cab driver, the penniless Noelle is befriended by handsome debonnaire Larry Douglas (John Beck), an American serving with the Royal Canadian Air Force. Larry is charming, but he is also a rat. After a short affair of idyllic intensity and a great deal of conventional sight-seeing, Larry leaves Noelle without a forwarding address, though he has promised to return in three weeks to marry her. In six weeks she gets the word: she's—how does one say?—with child.

Though "The Other Side of Midnight" contains lots of other characters and moves earnestly from Paris to Washington to Hollywood to Greece and back to Paris again (and again), it's mostly about Noelle's elaborate plans for revenge on Larry. It grows into an obsession as she becomes, with no great effort, first a successful fashion model, then the most famous movie star in France and, finally, the mistress of Constantin Demeris (Raf Vallone), a Greek shipping tycoon who also happens to be the richest man in the world.

"The Other Side of Midnight," which opened at two theaters yesterday, is movie fiction of the sort that sometimes becomes immensely popular because it satisfies both the people who want to believe it and those who feel superior to it and like to giggle helplessly at clichés of an elephantine scale and solemnity that one doesn't often see anymore.

•

I feel somewhat less charitable, almost as if I wanted to defend the rich and famous and powerful who are ripped off in fiction that doesn't do justice to their idiosyncracies. This particular film also has the effect of making everyone connected with it look ridiculous, including Miss Pisier ("Cousin, Cousine," "French Provincial"), Mr. Vallone, Mr. Beck, and especially Susan Sarandon, who might well be a very good actress but who here plays Mr. Beck's victimized wife as if she'd been told to liven up a dull party. It's a terrifically busy performance.

Over each scene Michel Legrand's music hangs like a comic-strip balloon, spelling out what people are feeling in much the same manner that announcers on television commercials repeat the words we see written on the screen.

1977 Je 9, C16:1

Bump in the Night

JOURNEY INTO THE BEYOND, created and directed by Rolf Olsen; photography, X. Franz Lererle; narration written by Paul Ross; film editors, Alfred Srp and Ric Eisman; music, Don Great; produced by Rudolf Kalmowicz; released by Burbank International Pictures. At the Rivoli, Broadway and 49th Street, and other theaters. Running time: 95 minutes. This film is rated R.

WITH: John Carradine as narrator.

By A. H. WEILER

THERE'S NO DOUBT that the supernatural is a natural for the movies. And the current stop of "Journey Into the Beyond" at local theaters yesterday is another illustration of the commercial value of filmed things that go bump in the night. As a collage of color and black-and-white footage, from the laying on of hands to levitation, this exotic "Journey" should keep viewers awake and, perhaps, occasionally startled, if not convinced that seeing is believing.

One may wonder how the camera happened to be where it is at just the right time, but a viewer might also be puzzled how photographers managed to be on hand in that remote village in Benin when the local necromancer, Nana Owaku, rose from the ground without visible means of support. Or, for that matter, when "the great Issah," an African witch doctor, performs the dual feats of bloody eye cataract surgery and rainmaking.

Although the squeamish, who are warned in advance, may not take to the "psychic" abdominal surgery, performed, it seems, without anesthesia or antiseptics, both in the Philippines and in Brazil, they are treated to a variety of less traumatic events. Included among these are the "psychic" healing done by a couple of Italian practitioners as well as religious occurrences such as statues and madonnas and humans with unexplained stigmata or tears.

"Is there life after death?" the film's ads teasingly inquire. The commentary in this "Journey" is short on explanations and as full of disclaimers as the raisins of a fruit cake. With the decidedly abnormal life depicted here, inquiry into death doesn't appear to be absolutely necessary.

1977 Je 9, C19:1

GODS OF THE PLAGUE (Gotter der Pest), directed by Rainer Werner Fassbinder; screenplay (German with English subtitles) by Mr. Fassbinder; directors of photography, Dietrich Lohmann and Herbert Paetzold; editor, Franz Walsch (Mr. Fassbinder); music, Peer Raben; produced by Antitheatre; distributed by New Yorker Films. Running time: 90 minutes. At the New Yorker Theater, Broadway near 89th Street. This film has not been rated.

Franz Walsch ..... Harry Baer
Joanna ..... Hanna Schygulla
Margarethe ..... Margarethe von Trotta
Guenther ..... Guenther Kaufmann
Carla ..... Carla Aulaulu
Magdalena Fuller ..... Ingrid Caven
Policeman ..... Jan George
Marian ..... Marian Seidowski
Commissioner ..... Yaak Karsunke
Joe ..... Micha Cochina
Supermarket manager ..... Hannes Gromball
Mother ..... Lilo Pempeit
Porn purchaser ..... R. W. Fassbinder

By VINCENT CANBY

"Gods of the Plague" (Gotter der Pest), this week's new Rainer Werner Fassbinder film, was made in 1969, the year he also made his second film, "Katzelmacher," which is still one of his best, as well as his first, "Love Is Colder Than Death," which has not yet been released in this country. "Gods of the Plague" opened yesterday at the New Yorker Theater on a double bill with "The American Soldier," a 1970 Fassbinder film that had its premiere here in January 1976.

I mention this chronology because the New Yorker Theater's Fassbinder festival is presenting so many of the director's films in such short order that keeping them straight can be as difficult as sorting out which plots go with which titles of Frank L. Baum's Oz books.

•

Although "Gods of the Plague" is described as a sequel to "Love Is Colder Than Death," which I haven't seen, it makes an appropriate companion piece to "The American Soldier," a comically dead-panned contemplation of American gangster films of the 30's and 40's. Where "The American Soldier" comes close to parody, though, "Gods of the Plague" is absolutely straight, which is not to say that it's realistic or that its narrative is important for itself.

"Gods of the Plague" is a distillation. It's as if Mr. Fassbinder and his actors had taken a half-dozen Bogart films, mixed in an equal number of Cagneys and Robinsons, added a few Rafts and maybe one or two Monogram melodramas for flavor, boiled them until the stock was almost entirely reduced, and then used the residue to make this film in which gestures and attitudes, characters and events, have the formality of an art that's been dead for 200 years.

•

"Gods of the Plague" is the quintessential American gangster film if the quintessential American gangster film had been adapted and updated to accommodate a bunch of small-time Munich hoods for whom the holdup of a rather ordinary suburban supermarket is "the big job." If "The American Soldier" is about movies, "Gods of the Plague" is one of the movies it's about.

Its hero is Franz (Harry Baer), a taciturn ex-con whose release from prison opens the film. When he goes to a restaurant with his girlfriend for his first taste of freedom, he orders Spam and eggs. He likes Spam and eggs, he says. Joanna (Hanna Schygulla) asks what it was like in prison. "No worse than on the outside," says Franz. His joylessness is profound, and it's consistent with his vision of a world in which everyone is an inmate.

The plot of "Gods of the Plague" is not quite as complex as that of "The Big Sleep," but it helps to have some program notes, because Mr. Fassbinder, aping Franz's taciturnity, doesn't waste time on explanations. Franz drifts from woman to woman, becomes implicated (wrongly) in his brother's murder, resumes a relationship with a black hood nicknamed Gorilla (Guenther Kaufmann), who actually murdered his brother, and agrees to participate in the supermarket heist to finance an escape to a paradise that may or may not be Greece.

•

It's a world of perpetual gray, of chance meetings, faithlessness, revenge, informers and crooked cops. People talk but they don't communicate. Someone says something and there's a 10-second delay before there's any response, as if the person spoken to felt that if he waited long enough there'd be no reason to answer. Everyone is mannered, even Franz's loony mom, who is not unlike the mom in "The American Soldier." Occasionally it recalls Jean-Luc Godard's "Breathless," but where Mr. Godard's characters have dreams, Mr. Fassbinder's have been sentenced to life imprisonment and know it.

"Gods of the Plague" is the work of a very young man who has just discovered the secret pleasures of angst. It's full of the movie associations that once so amused Godard, Truffaut and Chabrol, and it's impeccably performed by members of the Fassbinder stock company.

1977 Je 11, 11:1

ROLLERCOASTER, directed by James Goldstone; screenplay by Richard Levinson and William Link, based on a story by Sanford Sheldon, Mr. Levinson and Mr. Link, suggested by a story by Tommy Cook; produced by Jennings Lang; director of photography, David M. Walsh; editors, Edward A. Biery and Richard Sprague; music, Lalo Schifrin; distributed by Universal Pictures. Running time: 119 minutes. At the Forum Theater, Broadway at 47th Streete; 86th Street East Theater, near Third Avenue; Murray Hill Theater, 34th Street near Third Avenue, and other theaters. This film has been rated PG.

Harry Calder.......George Segal
Hoyt.......Richard Widmark
Young man.......Timothy Bottoms
Simon Davenport.......Henry Fonda
Keefer.......Harry Guardino
Fran.......Susan Strasberg
Tracy Calder.......Helen Hunt
Helen.......Dorothy Tristan
Benny.......Harry Davis
Lyons.......Stephen Pearlman
Wayne Moore.......Gerald Rowe
Christie.......Wayne Tippit
Demerest.......Michael Bell
Rock concert M.C.......Charlie Tuna
Quinlan.......William Prince

"Rollercoaster," which opened at theaters all over town yesterday, is effective pop entertainment that, like an amusement-park ride, deals in the sensation of suspense for the foolish fun of it. It is not, as you might suspect, one of those not-quite-all-star, group-jeopardy movies ("Earthquake," "The Towering Inferno") in which disaster strikes in the first reel and continues to pick off actors for the next two hours or so.

"Rollercoaster" is a suspense melodrama of the sort that Alfred Hitchcock does best and most wittily (and sometimes most cruelly), and one wonders what he might have made from the material that James Goldstone, the director, treats benignly, as if he didn't want to rattle the teeth of the very young or those of the somewhat older crowd who wear detachable replacements. The Sensurround sound effects, though noisy, are more amusing than scary.

•

The screenplay has the air of something assembled through the good old Hollywood process of, first, treatment, then screenplay, followed by suggestions, counter-suggestions, compromises and rewrites. In whatever manner it was written, it accomplishes what it sets out to do. With a minimum of wasted energy it dramatizes the attempts of various safety officials and law officers to apprehend an extortionist who has been sabotaging rollercoasters from coast to coast.

There's no mystery to the audience about the identity of the fellow, played by Timothy Bottoms, a cool young man who carries on a cat-and-mouse game with his principal adversary, a Los Angeles safety inspector played by George Segal.

"Rollercoaster" opens with one quite spectacular rollercoaster crash, but after that it's mainly concerned with tracking the killer from Los Angeles to

George Segal

Pittsburgh to Chicago, to Richmond and then, for the grand finale, back to Los Angeles for a rollercoaster ride that features a 360-degree loop.

•

Considering the material, Mr. Goldstone rather resolutely refuses to allow the rides themselves to dominate the film. As if to emphasize that this is a man-hunt movie instead of a series of cinematic simulations of roller-coaster rides (like the one featured in "This Is Cinerama," which made a number of non-fans queasy), he continually cuts between his subjective camera, mounted on a speeding roller-coaster and the point of view of people on the ground (including us, who always expect the worst).

It is just one of the various intelligent options he has exercised to make a movie of such good sport, and one that makes few unreasonable demands on our credulity. The actors, including Richard Widmark as a gritty Federal agent and Henry Fonda as a safety executive, take their roles with the sort of graceful gravity that never betrays the nature of the film.

•

"Rollercoaster," which has been rated PG ("Parental Guidance Suggested"), treats its mayhem so discreetly that, indeed, one has to look fast on a couple of occasions to know exactly what dreadful event has taken place. The fun is not in the violence, which is almost nonexistent, but in its possibility.

VINCENT CANBY

1977 Je 11, 12:1

FILM VIEW

VINCENT CANBY

Andy Hardy Updated to The Sexy 70's

Bobby, proclaim the ads for "The Van," "couldn't make it . . . till he went fun-truckin'!" No matter how you judge movies, "The Van" must rate as a foolish, technically poor, outrageously sexist, cheapie exploitation-movie. It's entertainment designed primarily for sale at Hollywood's take-out counter—the drive-in theater. Brought to us by the producers of "The Pom Pom Girls," another movie you've never heard of but which earned an estimated $4,300,000 last year, "The Van" is an exuberantly crass, R-rated, California comedy about a young man named Bobby, played by actor Stuart Getz who looks a little bit like a real-life Raggedy Andy. Bobby works in a car-wash and has as his dream the ownership of a van, a sort of super-panel truck whose interior is outfitted with a bar, a mirrored ceiling and a waterbed. Bobby, you see, is shy and is convinced that the only way he'll ever be able to get a girl of his own is to be able to dazzle her with his vehicle. There once was a time when a young man's vehicle was a bicycle with (if he were a fellow of style) balloon tires and a battery-operated headlight. Next came reconditioned jallopies, followed by motorcycles, followed by souped-up Thunderbirds, Corvettes and other conventional automobiles.

Now, says "The Van," we are in the era of the van—which was news to me but, as has gone California, so eventually go all the rest of us. I don't argue. I just look. When a movie like "The Van" comes along, attention must be paid. It's a report from our western front. It's mid-June, 1977—do you know where your children are?

According to "The Van," they are out fun-truckin', which is not to suggest that the film makes any statement about our youth/highway culture. Rather, it's a part of it. It's also one of the reasons why, every now and then, it pays to pay attention to junk movies. To hell with movies as art or personal statements. A junk movie like "The Van" can tell us as much about the state of our minds as a piece of pizza tells us about our palate.

In the past, most junk movies dealing with our youth / highway culture have catered to a sentimental kind of paranoia. In "Dirty Mary Crazy Larry" the kids wind up burned to cinders after their vehicle is intercepted by a speeding freight train. The implication is that they'd be alive today if the cops hadn't been pursuing them. In the final frame of "Aloha Bobby and Rose," Bobby is gunned down by the police while Rose looks on. However, in the final frame of "The Van," Bobby, whose van has been temporarily put out of commission in a drag race, drives off into the sunset with Tina in Tina's car. Tina loves Bobby truly but wishes he'd get rid of his van. "I can't," says Bobby as the music comes up. "It's like . . . well . . . it's my ballroom."

The double-entendres fly through the air of "The Van" with all of the grace of bags of cement, and though the film is ostentatiously vulgar, it's not pornographic nor even dirty. It's essentially innocent—Andy Hardy updated to the sexually revolutionized seventies.

The America that we see pictured in "The Van" has been effectively reduced to a strip of highway that seems to run between Los Angeles and Santa Monica. Its wonders are filling stations, automobile salesrooms, Pepe's Pizza Parlor, car washes, side roads for drag-racing, at the end of which is the Pacific Ocean and a beach where one can park one's van and make out. So much of the action takes place either in or adjacent to vehicles that it comes as a real shock when, in one brief sequence, we see Bobby at his parents' handsome, white clapboard, upper-middle-class suburban home. You might have assumed Bobby had been bred in a glove compartment.

Money appears to be no desperate problem for Bobby. He has apparently saved enough from his job at the car wash to put a down payment on his van, a canary-yellow job called "Straight Arrow," and which might cost a total of anywhere between $4,000 and $9,000. At one point, he's short $200 for an upcoming payment but that's due to special plot circumstances and has nothing to do with the general affluence of everyone in the film.

This, says "The Van," whether it knows it or not (and I suspect it does), is not necessarily how things are but how they might be in the perfect world desired by the audiences for whom the movie was made. There's no smog in this Los Angeles. No air pollution, though you wonder why, since there's at least one vehicle for every member of the cast. More important, there's no awareness of any fuel shortage. At the rate that Bobby and his friends consume gasoline, the world's total known petroleum deposits would be depleted by mid-1978.

Times have changed, but not all that much. Andy Hardy's life in Carvel was pretty much a vehicle-oriented existence. The only difference is that where Andy and Polly used to make a big deal out of stealing kisses in Andy's convertible, Bobby and Tina (and Sally and a number of other girls) go, as Andy would have said, all the way (time and time again) as Bobby seeks his manhood on the waterbed in his van. Innocence, which once described physical inexperience in movies, has now become a state of mind, which is not a bad thing at all, though the grasp of an abstract concept would clearly be beyond anybody in "The Van" and, by extension, of anyone in the California youth / highway culture.

One of the refreshing things about a junk movie like "The Van" is the way in which it allows us to make up our own minds about what we're seeing. Though it means to celebrate a sort of never-ending life on wheels, it does it with such unreserved artlessness that it can be read two ways at once. Bobby, Tina and their friends drink beer almost non-stop, but they never get drunk and never appear to gain an ounce. Their favorite foods are pizza and hamburgers, but their teeth are so perfect they look capped. They guzzle wine while racing around highways but the only drivers who have accidents are the cops who race after them. The whole point of a young man's existence is to make out, and the whole point of a young woman's existence is to make possible the making out of the young men. Life is informal—and it is perfectly ordered. It's why people move to California.

I hesitate to recommend "The Van," but as someone who sits in New York reading California trends as if he were a China-watcher based in Hong Kong, I found it fascinating and a little scary—a report from the future, provided that the OPEC countries don't get frisky. ■

1977 Je 12, II:15:1

'Tora-San' From Japan Is Playing at the Regency

Tora-San, the peripatetic catalytic figure at the core of one of Japan's most popular film series, is back again. In "Tora-San, Love Under One Umbrella," which opened a two-day run yesterday at the Regency Theater, the gentle, ponderous wanderer, portrayed by Kiyoshi Ataumi, finds himself playing nursemaid to a runaway businessman suffering a midlife crisis, and being compelled to entertain the idea of marriage to an old friend—Lily, a divorced cabaret singer.

This "Tora-San" is the 15th of the 19 films so far made in the series built around this character and the members of his family who wait for him and worry about him in their little sweet shop in Tokyo.

"Tora-San, Love Under One Umbrella," is filled not with the conflicts and agonies of great drama, but with the ingredients of ordinary life—moments of pleasure and disappointment that evoke from the participants anger, laughter, remorse, compassion, understanding and forgiveness.

Like its principal character, "Tora-San" is an unassuming movie, much like an episode in a television serial, and valuable in its modest way for what it reveals about manners, morals and mores in contemporary Japan.

LAWRENCE VAN GELDER

1977 Je 13, 36:3

Stars at War

A BRIDGE TOO FAR, produced by Joseph E. Levine and Richard P. Levine; directed by Richard Attenborough; screenplay by William Goldman, based on the book by Cornelius Ryan; music, John Addison; director of photography, Geoffrey Unsworth; editor, Anthony Gibbs; distributed by United Artists. Running time: 176 minutes. At the Rivoli Theater, Broadway at 49th Street. This film has been rated PG.

Lieut. Gen. Frederick (Boy) Browning .. Dirk Bogarde
Staff Sgt. Eddie Dohun .... James Caan
Lieut. Col. (Joe) Vandeleur .... Michael Caine
Maj. Gen. Robert Urquhart .... Sean Connery
Lieut. Gen. Brian Horrocks .... Edward Fox
Col. Bobby Stout .... Elliott Gould
Maj. Gen. Stanislaw Sosabowski ...... Gene Hackman
Lieut. Col. John Frost .... Anthony Hopkins
General Ludwig .... Hardy Kruger
Dr. Spaander ....Laurence Olivier
Brig. Gen. James M. Gavin .... Ryan O'Neal
Maj. Julian Cook .... Robert Redford
Lieut. Gen. Wilhelm Bittrich ...... Maximilian Schell
Kate ter Horst .... Liv Ullmann
Tough colonel .... Arthur Hill
Field Marshal Gerd von Rundstedt ... Wolfgang Preiss
Underground leader .... Seim Vroom
Kid with glasses .... Eric Van't Wout
Old Dutch lady .... Mary Smithuysen
Wife..............................Marlies Van Alonaer
Captain Glass .... Nicholas Campbell
Major Carlyle .... Christopher Good
Lieutenant Cornish ....Keith Drinkel
Captain Harry .... Peter Faber

By VINCENT CANBY

JOSEPH E. LEVINE's "A Bridge Too Far," the film version of Cornelius Ryan's best-selling book about the disastrous Allied push into the Netherlands in September 1944, proves that there's life in the Old War yet. The movie is massive, shapeless, often unexpectedly moving, confusing, sad, vivid and very, very long.

Directed by Richard Attenborough and acted by a cast of thousands, including some very expensive stars, "A Bridge Too Far" is certainly equal to Darryl F. Zanuck's "The Longest Day," the film version of the Ryan book about the 1944 Allied invasion of Normandy. In saying that, however, I should admit that this sort of film seems to me to have less to do with the art of movie-making than with the logistics of transportation, housing, food, actors' schedules, demolition, military cooperation and morale. One watches it not so much in admiration as in awe.

Frank Connor

Allied paratroopers attacking in a scene from the motion picture

"A BRIDGE TOO FAR"—Robert Redford, right, leads his men into bloody battle in Richard Attenborough's film.

Unlike "The Longest Day," which recalled one of the Allies' most stunning victories, "A Bridge Too Far" recalls one of their most tragic and costly defeats, when, in an attempt to conclude the war before the end of 1944, the English and Americans dropped 35,000 troops behind the enemy lines in the Netherlands to secure five bridges over the Rhine into Germany.

The plan was the brainchild of British Field Marshall Bernard L. Montgomery, usually a cautious man, and it would have worked if intelligence reports had been heeded, if the weather had been perfect, if one German army had been surrounded and, if luck had been with the attackers.

Instead, just about everything that could go wrong did go wrong. At the end of the operation, which was supposed to last four or five days but went to nine, the Allied casualties—killed, wounded and missing—were more than 17,000, compared to an estimated 10,000 to 12,000 in the Normandy landings.

If one doesn't quite grasp the import of this in the film it's because, after a couple of hours, scenes of tanks, buildings and bridges being blown up, of shells exploding, of soldiers being mutilated and of other carnage are all pretty much alike, no matter who ultimately wins the day. Missing is some point of view more particular (and more historical) than the idea that war is hell.

What Mr. Levine, Mr. Attenborough and William Goldman, who wrote the screenplay, have successfully brought off, though, is, in the initial sequences, the orderly exposition of what Operation Market Garden was all about, and, in the following sequences, an effective illustration of some of the things that went so wrong. The film is technically a wonder. The shots of the paratroop drops are breathtaking and, if one knows anything about the problems of such filmmaking, the very fact that all the color shots match so well is a major accomplishment.

"A Bridge Too Far," which opened yesterday at the Rivoli, also seems to me to demonstrate the wisdom of a policy that, until now, I've been inclined to scoff at, that is, the decision to cast star actors in so-called cameo roles. These dozen or so stars are as much the means of such a film—as necessary to narrative coherence—as the screenplay. Not many moviegoers, I suspect, would be able to keep track of the cascading incidents without the aid of the immediately identifiable actors who enact them. Their familiar faces are visual program notes.

In addition, some of these actors are very good. Anthony Hopkins is fine as the British officer assigned to capture the bridge at Arnhem and whose troops, without any support whatsoever, hold one end of the bridge for nine days before being overtaken. James Caan stars in a furiously effective episode about a sergeant who forces a doctor, at gunpoint, to operate on his wounded captain. Laurence Olivier and Liv Ullmann give recognizable emotions to Dutch civilians caught in the crossfire, and Edward Fox is quietly but brilliantly funny as a gung-ho British officer.

Some of these stars have more to do than others. Elliott Gould is on and off like a station break. Gene Hackman scowls a good deal as the commander of the Polish paratroopers and Gen. James M. Gavin, played by Ryan O'Neal, appears to be growing mysteriously young, having been played by Robert Ryan in "The Longest Day."

Not all of the episodes are star-studded. There's an eerie moment early in the film when paratroopers come upon the newly liberated inmates of a mental hospital, wandering through a forest like smiling, catatonic ghosts. At Arnhem, in the midst of a German attack, a little old woman, whose house has been taken over by the British forces, frets about the disorder and unseemly noise.

If "A Bridge Too Far" finally leaves one exhausted instead of exhilarated, this has to do not only with length, but also with the nature of a particular operation that failed. The scale of the failure is impressive, but it doesn't ennoble.

"A Bridge Too Far," which has been rated PG ("Parental Guidance Suggested") includes some graphic battlefield footage that, under the circumstances, could not easily have been avoided.

1977 Je 16, C20:5

Flouting Convention

EFFI BRIEST, directed by Rainer Werner Fassbinder; screenplay (German with English subtitles) by Mr. Fassbinder, based on the novel by Theodor Fontane; directors of photography, Jurgen Jurges and Dietrich Lohmann; editor, Thea Eymes; music Camile Saint-Saens; produced by Tango Films; distributed by New Yorker Films. Running time: 140 minutes. At the New Yorker Theater, Broadway at 89th Street. This film has not been rated.

Effi Briest .... Hanna Schygulla
Baron von Instetten .... Wolfgang Schenck
Major Crampas .... Ulli Lommel
Frau Briest .... Lilo Pempeit
Herr Briest .... Herbert Steinmetz
Gieshubler .... Hark Bohm
Roswitha .... Ursula Stratz
Johanna .... Irm Hermann
Wullersdorf .... Karl-Heinz Bohm

By VINCENT CANBY

THE SETTING is a handsome old country house outside Berlin in the 1890's, the home of a well-to-do upper-middle-class businessman, his wife and their 17-year-old daughter, Effi Briest. Effi, as played by the enchanting Hanna Schygulla, is all sun-lit curls and radiant beauty, a combination of naïveté, native intelligence, forthrightness and willful self-interest.

When the somewhat older Baron von Instetten (Wolfgang Schenck), whom Effi doesn't know, asks for her hand, Effi is as happy as her ambitious mother. Several days before the wedding, though, she is apprehensive. She and her mother are taking the air, walking across a field of untended grass, when Effi stops short. "The baron," she says, "is a man of firm principles." Her mother agrees, pleased that a 17-year-old might grasp such a point. Effi, desolate for the briefest of moments, adds, "I have none at all."

•

Rainer Werner Fassbinder appends to "Effi Briest," his film adaptation of Theodor Fontane's 1894 German novel, the subtitle: "Or many who have an idea of their possibilities and needs nevertheless accept the prevailing order in the way they act, and thereby strengthen and confirm it absolutely." Mr. Fassbinder is being both funny and severe in the manner of the Fontane novel, which describes the decline and fall of Effi Briest after she has flouted convention not out of passion but boredom and whim.

Nothing seen earlier in the New Yorker Theater's current Fassbinder festival, where "Effi Briest" opened yesterday, quite prepares one for the special pleasures of this beautiful, ironic, intentionally literary-sounding film. It's an achievement of several kinds. In the way it uses language (narration as well as dialogue) it reminds me of both Robert Bresson's "Diary of a Country Priest" and Francois Truffaut's "The Wild Child." It's visually beguiling—its cameramen having found shades of gray between black and white I'm not sure I've seen before—and it is performed by the Fassbinder stock company with the precision and style one seldom finds outside the legitimate theater.

•

Mr. Fassbinder made "Effi Briest" three years ago, and though I've no way of knowing for sure, I suspect one of the reasons he wanted to do it would be to show his critics that he was quite capable of putting his formidable talent to the service of someone else's work. His success is such that I think "Effi Briest" might well have pleased André Bazin, the late French critic who dared suggest that, in a film adaptation of a literary work, one picture was not necessarily worth 1,000 words.

Mr. Fassbinder has certainly not been stingy with Fontane's words. They

Ulli Lommel and Hanna Schygulla in Fassbinder's "Effi Briest"
A beautiful, ironic, intentionally literary-sounding film

are spoken as dialogue, as the texts of letters, as chapter headings and as narration, which are the words of the author who, though all-seeing, is not as much a moralist as an observer. Fontane's attitude toward the events observed matches the cool—the dispassion—that has been method of such dissimilar Fassbinder films as "Katzelmacher," "Mother Kusters Goes to Heaven," "Chinese Roulette" and "The Bitter Tears of Petra Von Kant."

•

Unlike Anna Karenina's and Emma Bovary's, Effi's problem is not that she loved—which she didn't—but that she carried on a harmless flirtation that, eventually, made her feel as guilty as her husband suspected her of being. The society of "Effi Briest" is as closed and airless as ancient Egypt's. In the tiny bourgeois community where she settles with the baron, the virtually uneducated Effi is regarded as (1) an atheist, (2) a deist or (3) "a superficial Berliner."

In loneliness she responds to the courtship of a handsome young officer, Major Crampas (Uli Lommel), who is a bit of a rake, unhappily married, and fully aware of the baron's various ways of intimidating Effi into fidelity. The major also writes Effi letters that the foolish Effi preserves. Some years after the baron and Effi have moved to Berlin, the baron finds the letters and, to uphold his "duty to the community," challenges the major to a duel. The end is tragic, not because people die but because Effi ultimately believes guilt to be her duty.

•

The film is composed of short scenes, some almost subliminal, often separated by fades to a white that suggest the empty space on a page at the end of a chapter. Each member of the cast is superb, though Miss Schygulla is stunning in a role that bears little resemblance to her work in "Katzelmacher" and "Petra Von Kant."

As the film understates its ideas, though at some length, the characters overstate their feelings in such a way that seems to prevent them from seeing the truth. It's in keeping that Effi, at wit's end toward the conclusion of the film, should say tearfully, "Too much is too much." She means "enough is enough," but she can't recognize the fact, thus to do something about it. It's the peculiar fate of the naïve Effi, in the words of the film's subtitle, to "strengthen and confirm the ruling order absolutely."

1977 Je 17, C5:1

Last of a Breed

WE'RE NOT THE JET SET, a documentary feature directed by Robert Duvall; produced by Barbara Duvall; editor, Stephen Mack; cameraman, Tony Donovan, Tony Foresta and Joseph Friedman. Running time: 86 minutes. At the Film Forum, 15 Vandam Street.
WITH: B. A. and Eunice Peterson and members of their family.

B. A. PETERSON, an exceedingly self-assured, tough and robust Nebraska farmer; his wife, Eunice, a small, proud woman always ready to tell B. A. he's absolutely right; their six sons, two daughters and assorted grandchildren and in-laws are the subject of "We're Not the Jet Set," a funny and slightly scary documentary feature made by Robert Duvall, heretofore known

Robert Duvall
One of our finest actors turns film maker with this effective chronicle

mainly as one of our finest actors ("Network," "The Seven-Per-Cent Solution," etc.).

The film, which opened at the Film Forum yesterday and will be seen there this weekend and next, will open a regular theatrical engagement at the New Yorker Theater next month.

•

"We're Not the Jet Set" appears to regard the Petersons, especially B. A., with a mixture of awe and admiration that is ultimately ambiguous. They don't make families like that anymore, or, if they do, they don't survive very long without the commanding presence of a patriarch like B. A., who, as Mr. Duvall's camera catches him, may be the last of a breed. B. A. is the macho father-figure, the individualist who is a hero on the frontier and an overbearing, bigoted tyrant in any civilized context.

The Peterson family is totally dominated by B. A. and his sons. The women don't count except when they are expressing approval or when, as we see in one scene, a daughter is needed to remove blackheads from her father's chin.

Mr. Duvall's method is to let the Petersons speak for themselves to create a group portrait that, as the details accumulate, becomes increasingly critical, if not harsh. B. A. encourages his sons to be tough, to take chances, to compete with each other and outsiders. Commenting on one son's apparently severe rodeo accident, B. A. says simply, "I'd rather have them killed or hurt in the arena or on the farm than in Vietnam or on the highway." Those are the choices as he sees them.

•

Without appearing to comment himself, Mr. Duvall shows us the daily life on the huge Peterson farm, which is still a fairly rugged existence, crosscutting with scenes at the rodeos, where the Petersons sons excel, and with other scenes of unexpected candor. One of the older boys suddenly admits that in spite of the apparent good feelings, he wouldn't hang around home for a minute if his father weren't alive. And, says the son, his father has a bad heart, "though he won't never admit it."

Another son remembers, without rancor, a family fight in which B. A. broke the son's thumb and three fingers to make a point. In an earlier sequence we have watched B. A. bathing his small grandson with a nanny's care. Hidden in this family are unacknowledged deposits of tenderness and fury, the awareness of which, as much as anything else, makes "We're Not the Jet Set" so interesting as an American chronicle and so effective as the work of a new film maker.

VINCENT CANBY

1977 Je 17, C10:5

Japan Galahad

THE LAST SAMURAI (Okami Yo Rakujitsu O Kire); screenplay by Takeo Kunihiro; based on an original story by Shotaro Ikenami; directed by Kenji Misumi; photography by Masao Kosugi; a Shochiku Production; distributed by Shochiku Films of America Inc. At the Regency Theater, Broadway and 67th Street. Running time: 160 minutes. This film has not been rated.
Toranosuke Sugi .... Hideki Takahashi
Hanjiro Hito Kiro .... Ken Ogata
Ikemototo Shigehei .... Takahiro Shimura
Iba Hachiro .... Masaomi Kondo
Okita Soshi .... Teruhiko Saigo
Reiko .... Keiko Matsuzaka
The Nun .... Kiwako Taiji

By A. H. WEILER

SAMURAI SWORDSMEN are, of course, as indestructible and legendary to Nipponese moviegoers as cowboys are to Occidental film fans. And, naturally, they both fill obvious needs. But in "The Last Samurai," the latest entry in the Regency Theater's Japanese movie series, the truly dramatic sadness of the end of an epic age is overshadowed by the familiar, complex, stylized adventure that is often confusing and a strain on Western credulity.

Kenji Misumi, the director, and his writers, however, are not exclusively concerned with mere melodrama. Their sweeping, two-part, two-hour-and-40-minute composite of war and personal drama shot in arresting colors is based, in essence, on the divisive, politically explosive upheavals of 19th-century Japan.

•

The civil wars between the Tokugawa Shogunate and the Meiji Restoration forces are, anachronistically, not new to Japanese movies, but are still a mite too specialized for most Western viewers. And "The Last Samurai" isn't especially clear on this issue. But Toranosuke Sugi, the titular hero on whom this saga focuses from 1868 through 1877, is literally a towering figure whose Galahad-like qualities are as obvious as his postured sword-swinging.

The labyrinthine script has him following the Shogunate against the wishes of his revered instructor and foster father, who is slain in one of the film's many gory hand-to-hand battles. And it is his incessant drive that dominates a good deal of the action.

If the introduction of modern, more proficient slaughter with rifles and cannon, as against Samurai swordplay, is somewhat theatrically staged, the director must also be credited with injecting more than a hint of Western sentimentality and compassion that perhaps clashes with the style of classic Japanese period drama.

•

The romance between Toranosuke, played in vigorous and expressive fashion by the tall handsome Hideke Takahashi, and an extremely decorative Keiko Matsuzaka, as his demure, loving, ill-fated wife, is believably tender to any eyes. And Ken Ogata, as Toranosuke's friend and the unwitting killer, who, despite his military success, forsakes the martial arts for farming, is a convincingly tough, if happy-go-lucky, peasant-Samurai.

When Toranosuke abandons his sword for the peaceful life after a bloodless, climactic bout with his pal, it is a wistfully touching gesture. But "The Last Samurai" remains devoted a good deal more to swordplay than to peace, sentiment or history.

1977 Je 17, C10:5

C'est la Vie

TOUCHED IN THE HEAD, produced and directed by Jacques Doillon; screenplay by Mr. Doillon and Phillippe Defrance; photography by Yves Lafaye; edited by Noelle Boisson; released by Bauer International. At the Jean Renoir Theater, 100 Seventh Avenue South. Running time: 104 minutes. This film has not been rated.
Liv .... Ann Zacharias
Chris .... Christophe Soto
Leon .... Olivier Bousquet
Rosette .... Roselyne Villaume
Boss .... Martin Thevieres
Union Officcial .... Pierre Fabien
Replacement .... Gabriel Bernard

"TOUCHED IN THE HEAD," the French comedy-drama that arrived at the Jean Renoir yesterday, leaves a disturbing feeling of youth being wasted on the young. As a bittersweet, somewhat comic diary of a small slice of the lives of four Parisian adolescents, it is despite its obvious good intentions, a roughly drawn portrait whose parts are a good deal more memorable than the whole.

Perhaps the muddy black-and-white print, an often muddled sound track and shimmering, sometimes illegible English subtitles can be held partly accountable for the unevenness of this 1974 first feature by Jacques Doillon. It is clear, however, that he is a compassionate observer and critical of the social forces involving the young baker's assistant, his provincial girlfriend, his auto-mechanic pal and the uninhibited Swedish girl who brings temporary emotional upheavals and liberation into their orbit.

Since it focuses largely on the room in which the baker's assistant has locked himself as a protest against the boss who has dismissed him, "Touched in the Head" has a constricted, shabby look. But since the others join him in what is essentially a lark, they become a ménage à quatre that is decidedly unusual, if not strikingly dramatic.

They are, with the exception of Ann Zacharias, as the pretty Swedish catalyst, a basically aimless, callow group still bound by their lower-class social mores, despite this extraordinary fling.

As the baker, Christophe Soto is mostly glum but still tender with the shy Roselyne Villaume, whom he seems to love but who, naturally, is confused and hurt when he also makes it with the liberated Miss Zacharias. And Olivier Bousquet is just as frustrated as the apparently unrequited member of the triangle. Miss Zacharias, on the other hand, contributes a charmingly natural performance as the understanding siren, who gives them a momentary glimpse of a more exciting existence.

They may be temporarily "Touched in the Head" but their sincere, occasionally humorous story remains as fragmentary and inconclusive as their freewheeling, somewhat juvenile capers.

A. H. WEILER

1977 Je 17, C10:5

THE DEEP, directed by Peter Yates; screenplay by Peter Benchley and Tracy Keenan Wynn, based on a novel by Mr. Benchley; produced by Peter Guber; director of photography, Christopher Challis; music, John Barry; second-unit directors and underwater photographers, Al Giddings and Stan Waterman; editor, Robert Wolfe; distributed by Columbia Pictures. Running time: 123 minutes. At Loews State 2, Broadway at 45th Street, and other theaters. This film has been rated PG.

Jacqueline Bisset in one of the underwater sequences from "The Deep"

One of cinema's natural splendors . . . despite this film

Romert Treece .... Robert Shaw
Gail Berke .... Jacqueline Bisset
David Sanders .... Nick Nolte
Cloche .... Lou Gossett
Adam Coffin .... Eli Wallach
Kevin .... Robert Tessier
Slake .... Dick Anthony Williams
Ronald .... Earl Maynard
Wiley .... Bob Minor

By VINCENT CANBY

The opening yesterday of "The Deep" at Loew's State 2 and other theaters, as well as of "Exorcist II: The Heretic" (see separate review), mark the arrival of the silly season that more or less coincides with hot weather, out-of-control air-conditioning and asphalt pavements as luxuriously soft as deep-pile carpets.

"The Deep," which is even sillier than the Peter Benchley novel, recalls—though not to its own advantage—the sort of adventures Frank and Joe Hardy used to have on their summer vacations.

Jacqueline Bisset, one of Cinema's natural splendors whether she's wearing a white evening dress composed by a poet or a soaping-wet T-shirt, plays the Joe Hardy role. Nick Noltt, a blue-eyed blond fellow who appears to have been cloned (clufsily) from Robert Redford's press clippings, plays Frank Hardy.

●

While scuba diving off Bermuda, Jackie and Nick come upon the remains of a sunken vessel that turns out actually to be two. One is a World War II ammunition ship, with a $2 million cargo of morphine intact, and the other an 18th-century French merchantman that was apparently hauling something that someone has to call—at least once in a review such as this—a king's ransom in precious jewels.

Also figuring in the adventure is a gruff but honorable scuba diver, a role played by Robert Shaw with so much colorful crustiness that if he were a boat, and if crustiness were barnacles, he'd immediately sink. Lou Gossett plays the leader of the bad guys, all of whom are black, which may or may not have sociological significance. I doubt it. As a local beach rat, Eli Wallach looks as if he had been gotten up for a hard-time party.

The story, as well as Peter Yates's direction of it, is juvenile without being in any attractive way innocent, but the underwater sequences are nice enough, alternately beautiful and chilling. The shore-based melodrama is as badly staged as any I've seen since Don Schain's "The Abductors" (1972), which is to remember incompetence of stunning degree.

●

"TheDeep," which has been rated PG ("Parental Guidance Suggested"), contains a lot of gratuitously unpleasant moments, including a scene in which Miss Bisset is massaged with chicken blood (against her will), a life-and-death fight on an outside elevator that I still can't figure out and another fight in which one man breaks the neck of his opponent, accompanied by an exceedingly noisy "click" as the bone is snapped.

1977 Je 18, 10:1

EXORCIST II: THE HERETIC, directed by John Boorman; screenplay by William Goodhart; produced by Mr. Boorman and Richard Lederer; director of photography, William A. Fraker; editor, Tom Priestley; music, Ennio Morricone; distributed by Warner Brothers. Running time: 117 minutes. At the Criterion Theater, Broadway at 44th Street, and other theaters. This film has been rated R.

Regan .... Linda Blair
Father Lamont .... Richard Burton
Dr. Gene Tuskin .... Louise Fletcher
Father Merrin .... Max von Sydow
Sharon .... Kitty Winn
The Cardinal .... Paul Henreid
Kokumo .... James Earl Jones
Edwards .... Ned Beatty
Liz .... Belinha Beatty
Spanish girl .... Rose Portillo
Mrs. Phalor .... Barbara Cason

Linda Blair may be the least fleet-footed actress Hollywood has produced since the incomparable Joan Crawford attempted to keep up with Fred Astaire in "Dancing Lady." Seen tap-dancing, as she is on two occasions in "Exorcist II: The Heretic," the chubby-kneed Miss Blair appears to be stomping on live cigar stubs. The rest of the movie is even heavier and more lugubrious.

Given the huge box-office success of the William Peter Blatty-William Friedkin production of "The Exorcist," there had to be a sequel, but did it have to be this desperate concoction, the main thrust of which is that original exorcism wasn't all it was cracked up to be? It's one thing to carry a story further along, but it's another to deny the original, no matter what you thought of it.

●

I thought it was something even less than good, but this new film, which opened yesterday at the Criterion and other theaters, is of such spectacular fatuousness that it makes the first seem virtually an axiom of screen art. It was written by William Goodhart (with no reference that I could see to Mr. Blatty's original conception, which may be his wish), and directed by John Boorman, a man who makes films ("Leo The Last," "Deliverance") just fuzzy enough to seem complex, thus to invite closer scrutiny.

"Exorcist II" is a fancified exercise in what might be called "simultaneity," which simply means it contains lots of cross-cutting between scenes of simultaneous action, in this case involving characters who are supposed to be in telepathic communication. It all looks very busy, though not much happens.

Mr. Goodhart's screenplay picks up the exorcised Regan (Miss Blair) four years after the startling events in Georgetown. Father Lamont (Richard Burton), a failed exorcist himself, is commissioned by an old friend, a Cardinal (Paul Henreid), to investigate the original exorcism conducted by the late Father Merrin (Max von Sydow), whom we see in flashbacks alive and, all things considered, fairly well.

●

When Father Lamont cooperates with Regan's psychiatrist (Louise Fletcher) in some experimental work involving "synchronized hypnosis" (when the therapist joins the patient in the latter's trance), all hell breaks loose again, though the being that Father Lamont sees still in possession of Regan is no longer identified as the devil. He's now called "Bazoozoo, king of all the evil spirits of the air." Even the mythology of the movie is second-rate, less mysterious than opportunistic, as if designed to offend the fewest possible people.

"Exorcist II" begins by looking foolish and slowly becomes a straightfaced film of the absurd. The fight for possession of Regan's soul entails several trips to Africa, two to Rome, and finally a climactic one to the same Georgetown house that figured in the first film.

Linda Blair

No tap dancer,

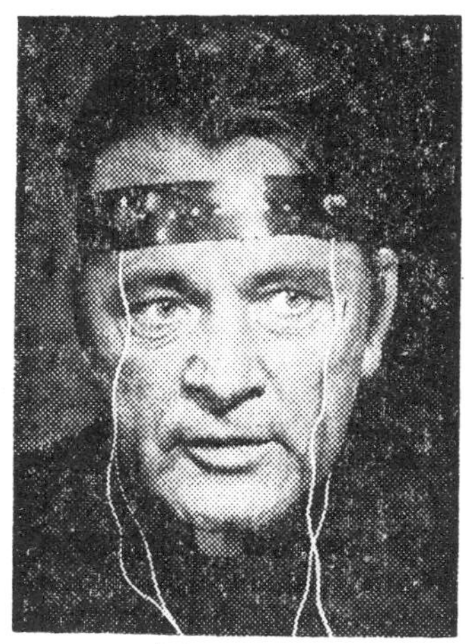

Richard Burton

Plays a failed exorcist

Mr. Boorman's strength, however, is not in his narrative or in his handling of actors, all of whom (especially Miss Blair and Miss Fletcher) look extremely ill at ease. It's in his sets and dècor. I especially liked the psychiatric clinic in a large New York hospital, which looks like the Charles Jourdan Fifth Avenue shoe store without the shoes, and the mirrored terrace of Regan's New York penthouse that contains a pigeon cote that seems to be a homage to Louise Nevelson. Everything else, including two immolations, is cold mashed potatoes..

VINCENT CANBY

1977 Je 18, 10:1

HOMAGE TO CHAGALL—THE COLOURS OF LOVE; written, produced and directed by Harry Rasky narrated by James Mason and Joseph Wiseman; photography by Kenneth W. Grigg; edited by Arla Saare; music by Louis Applebaum; lighting by Erik Kristensen; animation camera by Robert Mistysyn. At the Little Carnegie, 57th Street, east of Seventh Avenue. Running time: 90 minutes. This film has not been rated.

By A. H. WEILER

As the world's most renowned living artist, Marc Chagall, who will be 90 on July 7, is proof that Hippocrates wasn't precise in observing that "life is short and art is long." And Harry Rasky, the Canadian writer-producer-director of

Madame and Marc Chagall
Engagingly wise, natural and unassuming

"Homage to Chagall—The Colours of Love," which had its premiere yesterday at the Little Carnegie, is lovingly true to his title in projecting a fairly justifiable admiration of the now legendary man and his immense artistic output.

If he ignores critical apathy toward some of Chagall's later work, his unabashed "Homage" is, perhaps, more of a tribute to the range and detail captured by the color camera eye, and often poetic dialogue, than it is to extensive analysis or all-inclusive biography.

But as a dedicated professional known for such documentaries as "Tennessee Williams' South" and "The Wit and World of G. Bernard Shaw," Mr. Rasky, with the aid of appreciative narration by James Mason and Joseph Wiseman, portrays Chagall as an all-too-human figure, as memorably lively and colorful as some of his noted spirited, if mystical, paintings.

Tracing Chagall's life through his art from Czarist Vitebsk, where he was born, to his present, flower-filled sanctuary in Provence's sunlit St. Paul de Vence, makes for a color-drenched odyssey that obviously includes a good deal more than the "Fiddler on the Roof" or the Metropolitan Opera's immense "Sources" and "Triumph of Music" murals that most easily come to mind.

The succession of dream-world-like paintings teeming with Vitebsk Jewish elders, roosters, donkeys and levitated lovers featuring Bella Rosenfeld, his late first wife, who often served as his model, are minutely inspected and annotated. But this happy, post-1910 Parisian period is balanced by the likes of the fairly moody "L'Exode," which reflects his shock and sorrow for Jewish persecution in his figure of Christ on the cross dominating masses of Jews.

There are, of course, a variety of paintings, murals and mosaics on religious and other themes stretching from the United Nations Building stained glass windows to the museums in Jerusalem and Nice and Chagall's own garden in St. Paul. But these, and notably the close-up views of his paintings on the ceiling of the Paris Opéra, are a credit to photographic expertise.

•

More important, from a moviegoers' view, is the fact that the white-haired but robust Chagall is engagingly wise, natural and unassuming in seemingly unrehearsed, carefully considered answers translated from the French by his wife, Vava, the former Valentine Brodsky whom he married in 1952. They are, it is also more obvious on film than in words, both a serenely contented couple and in love.

The recently closed exhibition of some of Chagall's finest paintings at the Pierre Matisse Gallery here deserved the praise it received. And, although this "Homage," which was televised in Canada on March 30, may be specialized biography stemming from Chagall's autobiography, the Bible and other sources, it is an affectionate and visually beautiful celebration of both the man and his art painted with what André Malraux termed "the colours of love."

1977 Je 20, 33:1

Bumbling Infidelity

PARDON MON AFFAIRE (Un Elephant Ca Trompe Enormement); Produced by Alain Poire and Yves Robert; directed by Yves Robert; screenplay by Jean-Loup Dabadie and Yves Robert; music by Vladimir Cosma; a Gaumont International-La Gueville Co-production; a First Artists release. At the Baronet Theater. Running time: 105 minutes. This film has been rated PG.

Etienne	Jean Rochefort
Daniel	Claude Brasseur
Simon	Guy Bedos
Bouly	Victor Lanoux
Marthe	Daniele Delorme
Charlotte	Anny Duperey
Mme. Esperanza	Martine Sarcey

IF HALF A DOZEN LAUGHS—some of them solid—spaced over nearly two hours were enough to qualify a film as outstanding comedy, "Pardon Mon Affaire" would merit designation as a hit. But as it stands, something on the order of half a dozen consecutive days of 90-degree temperatures and matching humidity plus a resolution of the Concorde dispute sufficient to touch off a wave of uncritical Francophilia will be necessary to blind audiences to the schizophrenic lopsidedness of this French movie, which opened yesterday at the Baronet.

The work of Yves Robert, who directed "The Tall Blond Man with One Black Shoe," "Pardon Mon Affaire" is basically a standard-issue French infidelity comedy — built around Jean Rochefort as Etienne, the bumbling middle-aged civil servant who takes one look at a model named Charlotte (Anny Ruperey) and decides the time has come to cheat on his wife, Marthe (Daniele Delorme).

•

Having no previous experience at infidelity, Etienne manages to make an inadvertent assignation with his receptionist; to make an idiot of himself on horseback after he discovers the model likes to ride; to find himself in Brussels while the model is waiting for him in London; to lure her to what he believes is a vacant apartment only to discover that he has brought her to his own birthday party; and to wind up on television when he takes refuge from the model's husband on a Paris window ledge.

Jean Rochefort

It's thin stuff, but it has its amusing moments, including the pursuit of Etienne's wife by a student whose ardor is matched only by his utter humorlessness.

What makes "Pardon Mon Affaire" a lopsided film is its concern with Etienne's friends—Bouly, who cheats regularly on his wife and is devastated when she leaves him; Simon, the doctor who is henpecked by his mother, and Daniel, who turns out to be a homosexual.

When they are simply adjuncts to the story of Etienne, they serve a useful purpose. But "Pardon Mon Affaire" seems to be trying to say something about the lives of these three other men and beyond that, about the friendship of all four. Unfortunately, it either lacks the time or the insight. Whatever the reason, the result is an unbalanced film, torn between the silly and the serious, doing total justice to neither.

•

This film is rated PG (Parental Guidance Suggested"). There is nothing terribly erotic about it, but there are some caresses and scenes in bed.

LAWRENCE VAN GELDER

1977 Je 22, C22:1

Warrior's Code

MATATABI ("The Wanderers"); directed by Kon Ichikawa; screenplay by Mr. Ichikawa and Shuntaro Tanigawa; cinematography by Setsu Kobayashi; edited by Saburohyoe Hirano; produced by Kon Productions and A.T.G. and released by A.T.G. At the Regency Theater, Broadway and 67th Street. Running time: 100 minutes. This film has not been rated.

Mokutaro	Kenichi Ogihara
Genta	Ichiro Ogura
Shinta	Isao Bito
Okyo	Reiko Inoue
The Boss	Tadao Ninomiya

KON ICHIKAWA, one of Japan's top-flight and veteran directors known here principally for such contemporary subjects as the World War II "Fires on the Plain" and "Tokyo Olympiad," is artistic but unclear in his period drama, "Matatabi," which arrived yesterday as the final offering in the Regency Theater's Japanese film series. His saga of wandering gangs of the 1840's may shed light on a little-known facet of Nipponese history, but his script is as circuitous as his peripatetic principals.

The existence, actions and, above all, strange ethical codes of these so-called "toseinin," or errant, peasant swordsmen for hire, are made fairly clear with the aid of an off-screen narrator and English subtitles. And it is also evident that they are dependent on the local, petty "bosses" they protect, and on their laws, by which they live.

•

The three young, unkempt peasant swordsmen in "Matatabi" adhere to the ritualistic demands of their code as they earn their keep by beating a rival gang of gamblers. But the going thereafter is as complicated as a maze.

Moreover, these complications smack of contrivance as Genta, one of the "toseinin," discovers that his father, who deserted the family for more exciting, profitable fields, is now planning to undermine Genta's gambler-boss. This leads not only to patricide, according to the code, but also to ostracism from the local gang. And, on and on, to the final decimation of the once cohesive trio into one aimless wanderer.

The director makes an interesting point of stressing the power of a code that could bind such lower-class young men in loyalty to the death for a mere pittance of patronage. And, as in previous films, he has captured eye-catching scenes of picturesque beauty, as well as the prescribed, fairly constant vignettes of often gory action.

He has also elicited tender sequences between Ichiro Ogura, as the driven Genta, and Reiko Inoue, as the young farm woman who leaves her husband for him. If Isao Bito and Kenichi Ogihara also display nuances of genuine emotion as members of his brotherhood, they are, in the main, wanderers through a complex series of foggy, seemingly unfinished adventures.

A. H. WEILER

1977 Je 23, C19:1

Nostalgic Doings

NEW YORK, NEW YORK, directed by Martin Scorsese; screenplay by Earl Mac Rauch and Marik Martin, based on a story by Mr. Mac Rauch; produced by Irwin Winkler and Robert Chartoff; director of photography, Laszlo Kovacs; original songs by John Kander and Fred Ebb; supervising film editors, Irving Lerner and Marcia Lucas; editors, Tom Rolf and B. Lovitt; distributed by United Artists. Running time: 153 minutes. At the Ziegfeld Theater, 54th Street near the Avenue of the Americas. This film has been rated PG.

Francine Evans	Liza Minnelli
Jimmy Doyle	Robert De Niro
Tony Harwell	Lionel Stander
Paul Wilson	Barry Primus
Bernice	Mary Kay Place
Frankie Harte	Georgie Auld
Nickie	George Memmoli
Palm Club owner	Dick Miller
Horace Morris	Murray Moston
Artie Kirks	Lenny Gaines
Cecil Powell	Clarence Clemons
Ellen Flannery	Kathi McGinnis
Desk clerk	Norman Palmer
Eddie Di Muzio	Frank Sivera
Jimmy Doyle Jr.	Adam David Winkler
Desk clerk	Dimitri Legothetis
Harlem Club singer	Diahnne Abbott

By VINCENT CANBY

ROBERT DE NIRO is an actor of too much furious intelligence and humor to be contained very long by the ritualized conceits of "New York, New York," Martin Scorsese's elaborate, ponderous salute to Hollywood movies of the 1940's and early 50's in the form of a backstage musical of the period.

Seeing Mr. De Niro as Jimmy Doyle, a talented, selfish, womanizing saxophonist, a variation on the sort of role

Robert De Niro as the musician and Liza Minnelli as the band singer

Sygma

that Tyrone Power played more than once, is to watch a man running to catch a train, only to pass right by it. The movie can't keep up with him.

Nor, eventually, does it well serve Liza Minnelli as Francine Evans, the Helen Forrest-Kitty Kallenlike singer whose career, for a brief period of time, coincides with Jimmy Doyle's in the last years of the big-band era. Miss Minnelli doesn't outrun the film. With her apparently whole-hearted cooperation, the film uses her, especially toward the end when she's placed front-and-center to perform a series of evocations of her mother, Judy Garland, that are effectively eerie without being in the least bit moving.

•

"New York, New York," which opened yesterday at the Ziegfeld, means to recall the lost sights and sounds of post-World War II movies with affection and wit. Indeed, the good will is immense in the early scenes that establish the characters of the saxophonist and the singer, who meet as cute as Tyrone Power and Alice Faye ever did, and who become a "boy-girl" act after she, a nonlooker, saves his first audition by singing with him.

The big-band sounds are right, as are the sets and costumes and especially the movie conventions. "New York, New York" knowingly embraces a narrative line as formal and strict in its way as the shape of a sonnet. Even the sets are meant to look like back-lot sets, not the real world. When Jimmy and Francine walk down a New York street, it's that New York street so many of us grew up with, the one that abruptly terminates in a row of brownstones because, after all, there was only so much studio space.

Yet, after one has appreciated the scholarship for about an hour or so, admiring Mr. De Niro's manic intensity and Miss Minnelli's way of desperately throwing out comic lines as if they were failed lassoes—things that are often funny in themselves—one begins to wonder what Mr. Scorsese and his writers, Earl Mac Rauch and Marik Martin, are up to.

•

"New York, New York" is not a parody," but the original genre is really not interesting enough to have had all of this attention to detail spent on it. It's not that the movie runs out of steam long before it has gone on for two hours and 33 minutes, but that we have figured it out and become increasingly dumbfounded. Why should a man of Mr. Scorsese's talent ("Mean Streets," "Alice Doesn't Live Here Anymore," "Taxi Driver") be giving us what amounts to no more than a film buff's essay on a pop-film form that was never, at any point in film history, of the first freshness?

Even more disturbing is the movie's lack of feeling for the genuine feelings that those old movies were meant to inspire.

Toward the end of the film, when Miss Minnelli is being photographed in such a way as to recall Miss Garland (in "The Man Who Got Away" number from "A Star Is Born"), or being dressed in the black tights and mandarin jacket that her mother favored late in her career, it seems that nothing is sacred. That suspicion is confirmed by the film's title song, a new number written by John Kander and Fred Ebb that is not to be confused with the classic from "On the Town," written by Leonard Bernstein with Betty Comden and Adolph Green.

The three other new Kander and Ebb songs are not objectionable, and the dozen or so old songs are fine, including those sung by Miss Minnelli and one, "Honeysuckle Rose," sung by Diahnne Abbott (Mrs. De Niro), in what appears to be a recollection of Billie Holiday. Mary Kay Place, one of the great attractions of "Mary Hartman, Mary Hartman," has some good moments as another band singer, and Lionel Stander and Lenny Gaines are among the more prominent supporting players.

"New York, New York" is not a disaster of the order of Peter Bogdanovich's "At Long Last Love." Mr. De Niro and Miss Minnelli have talent in excess. Yet "New York, New York" is a somehow more painful movie, being nervy and smug. "At Long Last Love" was appealing in the way of someone who gallantly refuses to acknowledge having two left feet.

•

"New York, New York," which has been rated PG ("Parental Guidance suggested"), contains some mildly vulgar language, but is otherwise not much more explicit than films of the period that it recalls.

1977 Je 23, C19:1

A Dog's Life

FOR THE LOVE OF BENJI, directed and written by Joe Camp; original story by Ben Vaughn and Mr. Camp; produced by Mr. Vaughn; executive producer, Mr. Camp; music, Euel Box, director of photography, Don Reddy; editor, Leon Seith; distributed by Mulberry Square Productions. Running time: 85 minutes. At the Guild Theater, 50th Street west of Fifth Avenue, and other theaters. This film has been rated G.

Mary	Patsy Garrett
Cindy	Cynthia Smith
Paul	Allen Fiuzat
Chandler Dietrich	Ed Nelson
Stelios	Art Vasil
Ronald	Peter Bowles
Elizabeth	Bridget Armstrong
Baggage room man	Mihalis Lambrinos

"BENJI II" or, as it is officially titled, "For the Love of Benji," takes the small, quizzical mutt-hero of Joe Camp's very popular "Benji" and sends him to Athens, where he becomes the pawn in a spy caper. Though Olympic Airlines gets a big fat plug from the film, you may want to switch your reservations to Trans World Airlines after watching "For the Love of Benji."

Poor Benji, en route from Olympic's check-in counter at Kennedy to the baggage compartment, is dognapped, drugged and has his paw printed with a code message. At another point, when Benji and his human companions are changing planes in Athens for Crete, the Olympic baggage handlers forget to trans-ship his carrying case so that he is left behind. This is the sort of thing I thought happened only when one attempted to island-hop through the Caribbean.

"For the Love of Benji" has a sort of plot that involves a formula for transforming one barrel of oil into 10 (could the secret ingredient be water?). Mostly the movie is about Benji's adventures in Athens, finding friends being chased by villains, being caught, escaping and being chased again. As dog stars go, Benji can cock his head with the best of them. He also runs with fierce sincerity. The human actors have the vacant look of models you see in mail-order catalogues.

The film opened yesterday at theaters all over town, including the Guild where, at 11 A.M., the members of the very young audience appeared to be eating their way through the movie—sandwiches, popcorn, lollipops, cake, soft drinks and paper napkins, which were sometimes chewed in anxiety. The card announcing the film's G rating was roundly booed by the youngsters though at almost every sight of the dog they screamed with mouth-filled delight.

VINCENT CANBY

Benji, the star of the film

1977 Je 23, C22:1

Stately Spectacle

PHARAOH; directed by Jerzy Kawalerowicz; screenplay by Mr. Kawalerowicz and Tadeusz Konwicki; based on the novel by Boleslav Prus; photography by Jerzy Woicik; edited by Wieslawa Otocka; music by Adam Walacinski; sets by F. Trzaskowski, A. Weiman and R. Korczak; English dialogue by Robert Cushman and John Henderson; dubbing by Les Films Jacques Willemetz, Paris; produced by KADR Film Unit-Film Polski; distributed by Horizon Films. Running time: 140 minutes. At the Thalia Theater, 95th Street, west of Broadway. This film has not been rated.

Rameses XIII	George Zelnik
Sarah	Christine Mikolayevska
Kama	Barbara Bryl
Herhor	Piotr Paulovski
Penther	Leszek Herdegen
Tutmosis	Jerzy Buczacki
Mephres	Stanislav Milski
Hebron	Eva Kryzyevska

By A. H. WEILER

"PHARAOH," Jerzy Kawalerowicz's Polish-made dramatization of an ancient struggle for power, which opened yesterday at the Thalia more than a dozen years after it was completed, is as much of an enigma as the Sphinx's smile, for its important issues remain simple, obvious and unresolved. The picture is a stately spectacle of evil men triumphing over good intentions with a Cecil B. DeMille-like cast of thousands in panoramic battles or demonstrations.

Like such veterans as Andrezj Wajda and Aleksandr Ford, the 65-year-old Mr. Kawalerowicz, remembered for his 1962 mystical 17th-century drama "Joan of the Angels?" again illustrates his fascination with history in "Pharaoh," which he helped adapt from a 19th-century Polish novel. In the film, he focuses on a young, handsome, socially conscious sovereign of an Egypt threatened by its neighbors and dominated by its covetous priests.

•

Rameses' entanglements with his machinating priests, who refuse to relinquish their grip on the people or their secreted treasure, evolves as a series of largely orotund declamations that smack more of debate than drama. If further explanations seem needed for the film's abrupt passages, perhaps they can be attributed to the cutting of a lengthy work.

Mr. Kawalerowicz's cameras, moving through authentic, picturesque locales in Luxor, Cairo and Bokhara in Uzbekistan, have captured the vivid colors of Egypt's mammoth temples, pyramids and statuary and the dun desert wastes on which those thousands of extras, lined up in military array, clash to the sounds of roaring voices, horns and drums.

Despite the slowly measured pace of his early sequences, the director has elicited grimly sincere but occasionally emotional performances from some of his principals. George Zelnik, as the beleaguered heir to the throne and as the ill-fated Pharaoh, is confused, driven and torn by his desire for supremacy, by an inherent solicitude for his subjects and by the destructive cabals of his priests and foreign powers.

•

Piotr Paulovski is moodily forbidding as the austere, conniving high priest Herhor, who is aided by, among others of his order, the oily, manipulative Stanislav Milski. And, Christine Mikolayevska, as the tragic Hebrew concubine and mother loved by Pharaoh, and Barbara Bryl, as the Assyrian priestess, who seduces him, are not only obviously decorative in near-nude portrayals but also fairly convincing in their involvements with him.

Their "Pharaoh," dubbed into English of varying accents is an impressive sweeping, if fairly familiar, picturization of a historical past, even if its humans and their conflicting causes are not fully realized.

1977 Je 23, C22:1

Hitler Legacy

HIGH STREET (Rue Haute); directed by Andre Ernotte; screenplay by Andre Ernotte and Elliot Tiber; music by Mort Schuman; director of photography, Walter van den Ende; executive producers; Pierre Drouot and Alain Guilleaume; a co-production of Cine Vog Films, Brussels and Filmel, Paris. At the Quad Cinema 3, 13th Street between 5th Avenue and the Avenue of the Americas. Running time: 90 minutes. This film has not been rated.

Mimi .... Annie Cordy
David Rheinhardt .... Mort Shuman
The Man .... Bert Struys
Young Mimi .... Ester Christiniat
The Boy .... Olivier Krickler
David Blum .... Claude Batelle

By LAWRENCE VAN GELDER

A CHILLING AND VOLATILE depiction of agony, profound rage, grief and madness—the hideous legacy of Nazi inhumanity in Brussels during World War II—seizes the eye and wrenches the heart in "High Street," a Beligian-French film that opened yesterday at Quad Cinema 3.

A tour de force by the French actress Annie Cordy constitutes the visual and emotional centerpiece of this prize-winning film based on case histories of people who carry through life the ineradicable psychic wounds inflicted as an almost careless byproduct of the captivity and murder of six million Jews.

•

Miss Cordy portrays Mimi, a deranged woman who attends more than operates a fish stand, who lives in a cruel yet understanding symbiotic relationship with a mysterious silent man, and who rails at her neighbors, the clergy and the tourist buses that stop near her pauper's flat in a lower-class section of Brussels called the Marolles.

She is an embarrassment to the clergy, a scold to the churchgoers, an unexceptional case to medicine, an object of derision and abuse to some of her neighbors and a disquieting lunatic to the passengers aboard the tourist buses whose arrival ignites some of her most unsettling outbursts.

•

Annie Cordy in "High Street"

To David Rheinhardt, an expatriate American artist who lives in an adjacent quarter of the city, this traumatized woman who calls his name is, at first, an inescapable aberration in the local landscape, then an irresistible riddle who propels his art from the abstract to the real as he seeks to fathom it.

•

And finally, as he moves beyond art to an involvement in her life through pity and protection, he gains a measure of her trust. But there is no eradicating the wounds inflicted one night in 1943, when Gestapo agents and German troops seized David Blum, her Jewish husband, and left her with a dead child amid indifferent neighbors.

•

In the climactic image of this haunting film, David Rheinhardt is seen venting his agony and rage against the windows of one of the tourist buses. They are not, of course, what the insane Mimi has perceived them to be—vehicles that will someday bring David Blum home. He will never come home. They are metaphors of indifference—of life perceived at a remove, in passing, by creatures whose anatomy qualifies them as people, but whose failure to rise up, to speak out in the face of vile outrage excludes them from the ranks of humanity.

•

For all its power, "High Street" is not a movie without faults. Not all the performances are up to the standards set by Miss Cordy and Bert Struys, the mysterious man who cares for her. Secondary roles are sometimes amateurishly rendered. And in its will not merely to reach out to the emotions, but to seize them with barbed talons, the narrative is warped. The cause of Mimi's trauma—hinted at to the audience in brief, rapid flashbacks cut into her bouts of madness—is withheld from David Rheinhardt long beyond the time when reason tells us he would have learned the entire story.

Nevertheless, "High Street" is an extraordinary movie, as shrill and emotional, perhaps, as its central character, and for the same good reason. It has something to say worth saying for as long as there is any danger that mankind may forget the awful sins of the past.

1977 Je 23, C22:1

A Disaster

CONVERSATION PIECE, (Gruppo di Famiglia in un Interno), directed by Luchino Visconti; screenplay by Suso Cecchi D'Amico, Enrico Medioli and Mr. Visconti, based on an idea by Mr. Medioli; executive producer, Giovanni Bertolucci; director of photography, Pasqualino de Santis; editor, Ruggero Mastroianni; music, Franco Mannino; produced by Rusconi Film (Rome) and Gaumong International Sarl (Paris). Running time: 122 minutes. At the D. W. Griffith Theater, 59th Street and Second Avenue. This film has not been rated.

Professor .... Burt Lancaster
Bianca Brumonti .... Silvana Mangano
Konrad .... Helmut Berger
Lietta .... Claudia Marsani
Stefano .... Stefano Patrizi
Erminia .... Elvira Cortese
Mother .... Dominique Sanda
Wife .... Claudia Cardinale

By VINCENT CANBY

THE VERSION of Luchino Visconti's "Conversation Piece" that opened yesterday at the D. W. Griffith Theater is virtually the same film I saw and reviewed when it was shown at the 1975 New York Film Festival. There is one difference. The festival film was in English, while the Griffith version is in Italian with English subtitles.

One might be tempted to believe that the Italian language version is the original though, as it so often the case with Italian films with international casts, there really is no original version. At least some of the actors in each version—Italian, French or English—are dubbed by other actors for the postsynchronized soundtrack.

It is important to point this out because a number of observers tended to blame the mostly unfavorable critical reception to the film in 1975 on the fact that the festival showed it in English. Having just seen the Italian version, I stand by my original review, though the Italian dialogue, translated by subtitles, does have the effect of slightly distancing some of the screenplay's banalities. It is thus easier to see the film as an old man's musings, which are sad because they are so impotent, and because the film that contains them is so vulnerable.

The following are excerpts from my original review, which appeared Sept. 27, 1975.

"Conversation Piece" is a disaster, the kind that prompts giggles from victims in the audience who, willingly, sit through it all feeling as if they were drowning in three inches of water.

The film continues to explore concerns that occupied Mr. Visconti in both "The Leopard" and in his later, much less successful screen adaptation of "Death in Venice." The barbarians, the forces that represent social and political change and that acknowledge their physical passions, are attacking a citadel of the intellect, a place where reason has reigned at the cost of any possibility of love or commitment. It's one of Mr. Visconti's more dubious propositions that a person of taste and intelligence must always sleep alone in sterile splendor.

In "Conversation Piece" the citadel is the handsome old Roman palazzo owned by the Professor (Burt Lancaster), an aging, American-born, Roman-bred art historian who devotes his life to his books, his paintings by Old Masters, and his stereo recordings of Mozart. His life is turned upside down when his house is invaded by the real world as represented by a rich, pushy, overdressed marquesa, played by Silvana Mangano, the wife of a Fascist industrialist, her teen-age daughter (Claudia Marsani), her young German lover (Helmut Berger) and her daughter's lover (Stefano Patrizi).

The members of this rampaging horde of four are supposedly so vital and so fascinating that they are able to persuade the Professor to lease to them his upstairs apartment for a year, though to anyone watching the movie they seem less interesting than a group of ordinary, run-of-the-play dress extras. Part of it has to do with what they say and the way we hear it.

The screenplay is by Mr. Visconti and his longtime associates, Suso Cecchi D'Amico and Enrico Medioli and is said to be based on "an idea" by Mr. Medioli, which may well have once been a one-set play, the kind that has carefully timed entrances and exits and makes frequent use of the telephone to pass on information to us, if not people offscreen.

"Conversation Piece" is a movie made up of one part chitchat ("May I use your telephone?), one part unwanted confessions ("I threw myself into the student movement—deeper than most") and one part lumpy aphorisms ("The way of progress is destruction").

As in bad plays, everyone always means exactly what he says and never has to think a second before saying it. There is no feeling for the complexity of the mental processes, for the mysterious ways in which the mind works. This, of course, wouldn't be bad if these people had the wit and insight of George Bernard Shaw characters, but they don't.

•

As the invaders ultimately destroy the old professor, they also are the undoing of the German gigolo who, we are asked to believe, was once politically committed until ravaged by the bourgeoisie. Possibly some other actor could have handled this part, but Mr. Berger (who played the title role in Mr. Visconti's "Ludwig") is such a lightweight he can function no more than as an ideogram for decadence.

Miss Mangano is grotesque in a grotesque role, while Miss Marsani, as her daughter, acts as if she'd seen too many "Gidget" movies.

Mr. Lancaster, fine old professional that he is, is awful, adopting that humble, "Birdman of Alcatraz" manner he uses when employed in what he apparently thinks is serious movie-making. "Conversation Piece" is the kind of fatuous film that the professionally pragmatic Burt Lancaster, the action movie hero, would snort at and leave in the middle of.

1977 Je 24, C10:5

SORCERER, directed and produced by William Friedkin; screenplay by Walon Green, based on the novel "The Wages of Fear" by Georges Arnaud; editor and associate producer, Bud Smith; directors of photography, John M. Stephens and Dick Bush; music, Tangerine Dream; distributed by Paramount Pictures and Universal Pictures. Running time: 122 minutes. At Loew's State 1, Broadway at 45th Street, and Loew's Cine Theater, Third Avenue near 86th Street. This film has been rated PG.

Scanlon/"Dominguez" .... Roy Scheider
Victor Manzon/"Serrano" .... Bruno Cremer
Nilo .... Francisco Rabal
Kassem/"Martinez" .... Amidou
Corlette .... Ramon Bieri
Lartigue .... Pater Capell
"Marquez" .... Karl John
"Carlos" .... Frederick Ledebur
Bobby Del Rios .... Chico Martinez
Spider .... Joe Spinell
Agrippa .... Rosario Almontes
Billy White .... Richard Holley
Blanche .... Anne Marie Descott
Pascal .... Jean-Luc Bideau
Lefevre .... Jacques Francois
Guillot .... Andre Falcon
Donnelly .... Gerard E. Murphy
Boyle .... Desmond Crofton
Murray .... Henry Diamond
Ben .... Ray Dittrich
Marty .... Frank Gio
Vinnie .... Randy Jurgensen
Carlo Ricci .... Gus Allegretti

By VINCENT CANBY

The memory of Henri-Georges Clouzot's suspense melodrama, "The Wages of Fear," is not so vivid in my mind that it seems to be any sort of sacrilege that William Friedkin should make a new film based on the same Georges Arnaud novel that had been adapted by Clouzot. About all that I remember of the earlier movie was the performance by a very young Yves Montand, the steamy Latin American locale and the hair-raising climactic sequences: Mr. Montand and three other desperate characters attempting to drive two truckloads of nitroglycerine across 200 miles of mountain and jungle obstacles to fight an oil-well fire.

I'm not at all sure that the film is a classic, but it is remembered fondly, even though the version we saw in this country was drastically pruned, reportedly to remove a lot of anti-American propaganda about the ruthlessness of an American oil company. Apparently moviegoers in 1955 were not thought to be ready for a French film that questioned a sacred American trust.

•

Now that I've seen "Sorcerer," the meaningless title that has been attached to the Friedkin film (perhaps because his last film was the terrifically successful "The Exorcist"), I'm no longer certain that what was cut from the Clouzot film was anti-Americanism. Maybe it was just a great deal of introductory exposition of the sort that keeps "Sorcerer" from getting under way until it's almost an hour long—which may be nothing in the life of an infant, but is middle-age for a movie.

Like "The Wages of Fear," Mr. Friedkin's film is essentially about four men, each at the end of his tether, who find themselves broke—and both emotionally and socially outcast—in the squalid outback of an unnamed Latin American country where they slave for the oil company.

They are Scanlon (Roy Scheider), a small-time American hood who has fled a gangland execution; Victor Manzon (Bruno Cremer), a rich French investment banker charged with fraud; Nilo (Francisco Rabal), a Mexican assassin, and Kassem (Amidou), a Arab terrorist.

To give these characters contemporary relevance Mr. Friedkin and Walon Green, who wrote the screenplay, have gone to a lot of trouble and expense that are not only unnecessary but diminish the impact of the sometimes stunning melodrama that unfolds in the Latin American petroleum republic.

Four virtually separate short movies, filmed in Mexico, Paris, Jerusalem and this country, introduce the characters in a way that is meant to establish their predicaments as unique but, instead, has the effect of turning each into a sterotype out of any number of other films, including "Black Sunday" and Mr. Friedkin's own "The French Connection." For moviegoers who are convinced that more is more, "Sorcerer" is a big, fat, satisfyingly shapeless spectacle. For the rest of us it's a walnut of a movie—a good little melodrama surrounded by thick pulp.

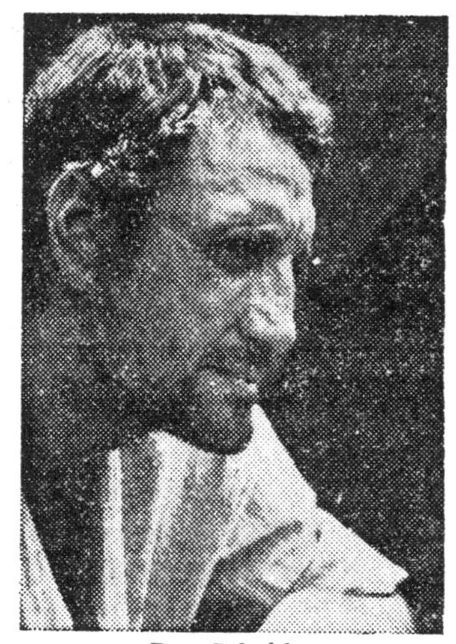

Roy Scheider
Provides the film's dominant note of reckless desperation.

Once the focus is shifted to Latin America, to one of the most convincingly seedy locations I've seen recently, and just as soon as the four men take off in their two nitro-laden trucks, the movie comes to life. It is apparent that everything we need know about them is revealed in the action, in the course of their cross-country journey, meticulously photographed in heat, rain and sunlight, in swamps, jungles and mountains.

•

Each of the four leading actors gives a tough, unsentimental performance of the sort demanded by an action movie when characters are a function of plot and not its point. In the way he moves and looks, Mr. Scheider is the film's dominant note of reckless desperation; Mr. Cremer is the civilized man who gives up his manners as if he were digging into capital.

Considering how politically bold the Clouzot film was thought to be, "Sorcerer," which opened yesterday at Loew's State I and Cine Theaters, seems pretty tame. We see the poverty of Latin America and the ruthlessness of the oil company, but they are of less political than atmospheric importance. The most political moment in the film—a fine, strange scene—occurs when the drivers come upon a young Indian man who runs ahead of the nitro truck, laughing at the foreigners and making rude gestures.

•

"Sorcerer," which has been rated PG ("Parental Guidance Suggested"), contains rather more bloody violence than one is likely to see in other PG movies these days.

1977 Je 25, 11:1

FILM VIEW

VINCENT CANBY

'Tis the Season to Be Silly

The man with the tape recorder came by the office in the middle of an afternoon so hot and muggy that the telephone couldn't ring. It gurgled. I had no will to make an exit. As it usually is, giving-in was the easiest way. The man wasted little time with preliminaries, which are never transcribed anyway, and got straight to the point.

Q: In a recent review you announced the arrival of "the silly season." Is this information that's been given only to you? Is it privileged?

A: Hardly. . .

Q: When does it start?

A: Some people use a church calendar to compute the actual date. . . . It has something to do with so many days after Whitsunday, depending on the first full moon. This year the silly season officially began June 8.

Q: That was how long after the first full moon?

A: I've no idea. It was the day that Paramount opened "A Frank Yablans Presentation," that is, "A Martin Ransohoff-Frank Yablans Production," that's to say, "The Other Side of Midnight," which was "Produced by Frank Yablans." I'm quoting the billing in the ads.

Q: Frank Yablans . . . Haven't I heard that name before?

A: Probably. Last year he produced "Silver Streak" with Gene Wilder, Jill Clayburgh and Richard Pryor. It was terrible.

Q: But it made a lot of money. Could it be that Frank Yablans knows what most of the American people want?

A: If he does, the rest of us should investigate Bulgarian citizenship.

Q: You didn't like "The Other Side of Midnight"? Don't you respond to romances of passion and power?

A: I do, but only in the privacy of my bedroom. However, "The Other Side of Midnight" is not pornographic. It's simply boring. There's no constitutional way to prevent adults, as well as children accompanied by a parent or an adult guardian, from seeing such a film.

Q: Would you label it "dangerous"?

A: If by "dangerous" you mean a movie that's like an unmarked curve, yes. To watch it is to find oneself suddenly sinking up to the armpits in a sea of lime Jello. It's an extremely sticky way to go.

Q: Please explain.

A: Well, it's about this pretty French girl in Marseilles in 1939 whose father sells her to a lecherous old man who runs away to Paris and who becomes a famous model after having been loved, made pregnant and then abandoned by an American flier in the Royal Canadian Air Force, and then becomes a famous film star. . . .

Q: The lecherous old man?

A: No, the girl.

Q: What about the baby?

A: She gets rid of it with a coat hanger, but she stays mad at the American for years. All the while she's becoming rich and famous and powerful and the mistress of a Greek shipping tycoon, she remains furious with the flier, who has gone home and married somebody else.

Q: She hates him?

A: You haven't been listening. She loves him, and she gets him back after the war by hiring him as her private airplane pilot, but she doesn't reckon on the fury of the Greek shipping tycoon who likes to play God. . . .

Q: I like that phrase . . .

A: . . . I thought you would.

Q: It seems to have a lot of plot . . .

A: And I haven't told you half of it.

Q: But aren't the actors any good?

A: Marie-France Pisier, who was so fine in "Cousin, Cousine," walks through the movie as if she'd been lobotomized. Maybe she's just tired. All the beds in the movie are set on raised platforms, so she has to walk up a small flight of stairs to get into bed even when she sleeps in her own room, which isn't often.

Q: Is she sexy?

A: Catherine Deneuve selling Chanel No. 5 in a 60-second spot is sexier.

Q: But what about all the romantic locations? Paris? Greece? Hollywood? Washington? And the fancy palaces with marble floors so you can smash champagne glasses on them?

A: Women who insist on smashing champagne glasses make me nervous. I like to walk around in bare feet.

Q: I think I want to see "The Other Side of Midnight." Are there any other silly movies you want to warn me about?

A: You should certainly try to avoid "Exorcist II: The Heretic," the sequel of a film whose title has slipped my mind for the moment.

Q: Is there nothing good about it?

A: Yes. It's so silly it makes an "Exorcist III" extremely unlikely.

Q: What's this one about?

A: I thought you'd never ask. Well, it takes place four years after the little girl in "The Exorcist" played by Linda Blair—in both films—was exorcised by the exorcist played by Max von Sydow. It now seems that von Sydow, or Father Merrin as he was called, was a bit sloppy—if it had been an appendectomy, Linda's mom would have grounds for a malpractice suit. Another priest, played by Richard Burton, and a psychiatrist, played by Louise Fletcher, discover that in doing the original job Father Merrin sewed up the wound without getting out all of the infection. So to speak. But this time it's not the devil who's after Miss Blair's soul, but a demon only identified as "Bazoozoo, king of the evil spirits of the air . . ."

Q: I love it already.

A: John Boorman, who directed the film, and William Goodhart, who wrote it, play down the possession stuff, which, in the original, was at least photogenic. Instead they favor a lot of hocus-pocus about "synchronized hypnosis," in which two people are able to share a trance much as they might a comic book.

Q: How is sweet little Linda Blair?

A: Putting on weight.

Q: Louise Fletcher?

A: Decidedly nervous. But Burton is so calm he seems almost somnambulant. The sets are outrageous to the point of being intentionally, comically pseudo-expressionistic.

Q: Tell me just one thing . . .

A: Yes.

Q: Does anybody get the chance to say, "We are . . . here . . . in the presence of evil"?

A: Yes, Burton, but he pronounces it as if it were an entree—"eee-veal."

Q: Wild horses couldn't keep me away. What other silly movies shouldn't I see?

A: "The Deep" must go onto your list.

Q: Isn't that the sequel to "Jaws"?

A: The picture in the ad is the sequel to the picture in the "Jaws" ad. The movie isn't. It's based on the how-I-spent-my-summer-vacation novel by Peter Benchley, about a young couple—Jacqueline Bisset and Nick Nolte—who have a series of adventures on their all-expenses-paid (including airfare, two-to-a-room) vacation in Bermuda after finding a sunken treasure ship just offshore.

Q: You like to scuba-dive. Didn't you find all the underwater footage interesting?

A: It's pretty good, but it looks so clean and well-lit that it reminded me less of scuba-diving than of a ride in a glass-bottomed boat. Then, too, the story is essentially just haunted-house stuff—only underwater.

Q: Sounds fine for kids, like "Star Wars."

A: It's fine for kids if the kids are into voodoo, and if they can get their kicks watching Jackie Bisset being smeared with chicken blood. Or if they enjoy seeing a cat that's been nailed to a wall. Or if they like to hear the "click" when somenone's neck is broken. If your kids are kinky, this is the picture for them.

Q: It doesn't sound as violent as "Jaws."

A: I suppose it isn't, but the violence in a witless movie, one that's not very well made or thought-out, is ten times more repulsive and disturbing than the violence in a well-made movie.

Q: Aren't there any decent performances?

A: None, though Miss Bisset is well worth watching, especially in a white T-shirt that sea water has made attractively transparent. Robert Shaw, who plays a crusty scuba-diver who befriends the young couple, carries calculated lovability to a high (or low) that only Spencer Tracy ever got away with.

Q: What's the scenery like?

A: Intensely blue in various shades from turquoise to royal . . . Does that convince you?

Q: It certainly does. I'll go see it tonight. Thank you for the time.

A: Thank you. It's always satisfying to realize that one has reached his public. ■

1977 Je 26, II:1:4

It's No Picnic

EMPIRE OF THE ANTS; produced, directed and story by Bert I. Gordon; screenplay by Jack Turley; based on a story by H. G. Wells; photography directed by Reg Morris; edited by Michael Luciano; special effects by Roy Downey; a Cinema 77 Film released by American International Pictures. At local theaters. Running time: 91 minutes. This film has been rated PG.

Marilyn Fryser .... Joan Collins
Dan Stokely .... Robert Lansing
Charlie Pearson .... Edward Power
Joe Morrison .... John David Carson
Margaret Ellis .... Jacqueline Scott
Sheriff Art Kincade .... Albert Salmi
Coreen Bradford .... Pamela Shoop
Larry Graham .... Robert Pine
Christine Graham .... Brooke Palance
Harry Thompson .... Harry Holcombe
Velma .... Irene Tedrow

By A. H. WEILER

BERT I. GORDON seems to be fascinated by the Animal Kingdom. Last year he conjured up a menagerie of mammoth voracious rats, chickens and bees for "Food of the Gods," a film inspired by an H. G. Wells story. Now Mr. Gordon has come up with a man-hungry colony of giant insects in "Empire of the Ants," also derived from a work by H. G. Wells. The movie swarmed into local theaters yesterday; unfortunately, the insects and the people in this mélange of ersatz science-fiction and dull adventure deserve one another.

There are some "15,000 different species of ants," an off-screen narrator tells us, whose industry and intelligence are astounding. But these king-sized insects don't appear to get much competition, intellectual or otherwise, from the covey of humans who figure in this picture. The humans are a group of prospeceive buyers conned to undeveloped acres apparently in the vicinity of the Everglades, where some of the film was shot.

•

In any case, salesmanship soon gives way to special effects as the ants, keening and racketing like helicopters, start stalking and decimating the group as the humans try to escape via a river and the swampy, jungle-like terrain. If credulity isn't strained at this point, it certainly is when the humans finally make it to a village and sugar refinery controlled by, you guessed it, sugar-loving ants.

As a laconic charter boat skipper, Robert Lansing seems to be more level-headed than the rest as he leads this largely ill-fated party out of a frightening mess. But the human's fright is seen as play acting, and the account of their progress over a gory trail is slow and repetitive. And, aside from some multifaceted ant's-eye views of humans, the special effects are artificial and unexciting.

This "Empire of the Ants," as Albert Salmi, in the small role of the village sheriff, puts it, is "hard to believe."

•

This film is rated PG ("Parental Guidance Suggested") probably for its occasional bloody scenes and its ant attacks, but these simulated terrors are not likely to shock viewers past the age of, say, 10.

1977 Je 30, C18:3

A la Actors Studio

THE THREE SISTERS, screen direction by Paul Bogart, based on the theater production of the Chekhov work staged by Lee Strasberg; executive producer, Cheryl Crawford; produced by Ely Landau; English version by Randall Jarrel; recorded on videotape, transferred to film. An Actors Studio Theater production, distributed by NTA. Running time: 166 minutes. At the Thalia Theater, 95th Street west of Broadway.

Andrei .... Gerald Hiken
Nataiya .... Shelley Winters
Olga .... Geraldine Page
Masha .... Kim Stanley
Irina .... Sandy Dennis
Kulygin .... Albert Paulsen
Vershinin .... Kevin McCarthy
Baron Tuzenbach .... James Olson
Solyony .... Robert Loggia
Chebutykin .... Luther Adler
Fedotik .... John Harkins
Roday .... David Paulsen
Ferapont .... Salem Ludwig
Anfisa .... Tamara Daykarhanova

By VINCENT CANBY

THE THALIA THEATER, under its new management, has been maintaining one of the most original, unusual and, sometimes, odd programming policies of any theater in New York. In recent months they've allowed us to see a filmed recording of Laurence Olivier's extraordinary Chichester Festival production of "Uncle Vanya," Josef von Sternberg's last film, "Anatahan," and the huge Polish epic called "Pharaoh."

When you drop into the Thalia, the chances are you'll find something out-of-the-ordinary, a film that isn't likely to turn up in any cricuit house. It might not be great or even good, but it will be rare.

•

Such is the Thalia's newest program, which opened yesterday. It's the 1965 videotape version, transferred to film, of the Actors Studio Theater production of Chekhov's "The Three Sisters" as it was staged by Lee Strasberg. The production was originally done in 1964 in New York, where it received more or less mixed notices, and later went to London, where theater people behaved as if we'd sent them a red-white-and-blue stinkbomb.

As it looks now, we had.

Yet it's a fascinating footnote to the history of the New York theater and, especially, of the Actors Studio. This production is virtually bulging with the self-assurance of an organization that thought it could do anything if everyone just sweated and fretted long enough. Never have I seen a "Three Sisters" half as long, for four actresses —who play the three sisters and their sister-in-law—who seem less likely to become victims of anything except a natural disaster on the order of a major —magnitude nine on the Richter scale —earthquake.

The cast includes some fine performers, as well as some not-so-fine, but what wrecks the production is the aggressive tone, for which, I assume, Mr. Strasberg was responsible. Everything is too literal, too calculated, too coarse, too busy—even the pauses rattle the screen. The accents don't match, some are out of Topeka, Kan., some out of Broadway and some out of the Yiddish theater. It's less a production than a convention of actors on fire for what they think is a good cause.

•

Two performers who come close to achieving some kind of unity of style and feeling are Kim Stanley as Masha, the middle sister, and Kevin McCarthy as Vershinin, the unhappily married army officer who, briefly, lights up the lives of the sisters in the dreary Russian provincial city where they are forever marooned.

Geraldine Page, one of the best actresses we have, seems misdirected as the oldest sister, Olga. Sandy Dennis as Irina, the youngest, acts as if she were afraid her upper teeth were going to pop out. The recurring gesture of a hand reaching up to the mouth evokes not emotional desperation but severe orthodontic panic.

Shelley Winters, as the arriviste sister-in-law, Natalya, who methodically dispossesses the sisters, is out of control from start to finish. She's as pushy as a waitress in a hamburger joint who wants to get the customers out by closing time. James Olson has some decently theatrical moments as Baron Tuzenbach, Irina's suitor. No one else need by mentioned by name.

Geraldine Page

The film quality is not at all bad considering the videotape origins, but Paul Bogart, who directed the taping, favors too many close-ups that have the effect of isolating actors when they are, in fact, part of an ensemble. It is, however, a fitting metaphor for a production in which each actor seems so occupied with his own performance that he's incapable of communicating with someone no more than a foot or two away.

1977 Je 30, C19:1

MACARTHUR, directed by Joseph Sargent; screenplay by Hal Barwood and Matthew Robbins; produced by Frank McCarthy; director of photography, Mario Tosi; music, Jerry Goldsmith; editor, George Jay Nicholson; a Richard D. Zanuck-David Brown production, distributed by Universal Pictures. Running time: 122 minutes. At Radio City Music Hall, Avenue of the Americas at 50th Street. This film has been rated PG.

General MacArthur .... Gregory Peck
General Sutherland .... Ivan Bonar
General Marshall .... Ward Costello
Colonel Huff .... Nicholas Coster
Mrs. MacArthur .... Marj Dusay
President Truman .... Ed Flanders
Secretary .... Art Fleming
Admiral King .... Russell D. Johnson
General Wainwright .... Sandy Kenyon
Representative Martin .... Robert Mandan
Colonel Diller .... Allan Miller
President Roosevelt .... Dan O'Herlihy
Colonel Whitney .... Dick O'Neill
Admiral Nimitz .... Addison Powell
General Sampson .... Tom Rosqui
General Eichelberger .... G. D. Spradlin
Admiral Halsey .... Kenneth Tobey
General Walker .... Garry Walberg
General Marquat .... Lane Allen
Castro .... Jesse Dizon
Emperor Hirohito .... John Fujioka
General Blamey .... Gerald S. Peters
Ah Cheu .... Beulah Quo
General Derevyanko .... Alex Rodine
Lieutenant Bulkeley .... William Wellman Jr.

By VINCENT CANBY

IT SAYS something about the traditional populism of Hollywood that all of us are inclined to feel a bit uneasy with movies that treat generals as seriously and/or as sentimentally as movies have always treated enlisted men.

It seems almost un-American, as if we were being accused of some secret royalist tendencies. Yet I don't think one has to be an elitist to find characters like Gen. George S. Patton Jr. and Gen. Douglas MacArthur quite as fascinating as Sergeant York and Willie and Joe. Generals are people, too, even if they tend to take a fairly cosmic view of themselves and the world around them.

"MacArthur," which opened yesterday at the Radio City Music Hall, consolidates the beachhead on top-brass movies established by "Patton," which was also the work of Zanuck-Brown Productions and was produced by Frank McCarthy, himself a former World War II general.

Its subject is not as colorful as Patton (colorful may or may not be a euphemism for nutty and brilliant), but MacArthur comes in a close second. More important, he played a unique role in modern American history, being the chief architect of United States strategy in the southwest Pacific in World War II, as well as the American mikado who ruled Japan and set its postwar policies in the years immediately after that country's defeat.

•

The movie, written by Hal Barwood and Matthew Robbins and directed by Joseph Sargent, covers too much ground too quickly (and thus superficially). It is extremely effective in delineating the extraordinary contradictions in the man—his military brilliance, his sentimentality, his arrogance, his vanity, his compassion and, ultimately, his aristocratic, 19th-century way of looking at things in a 20th-century democratic republic.

"A dangerous concept!" MacArthur roared when President Truman recalled

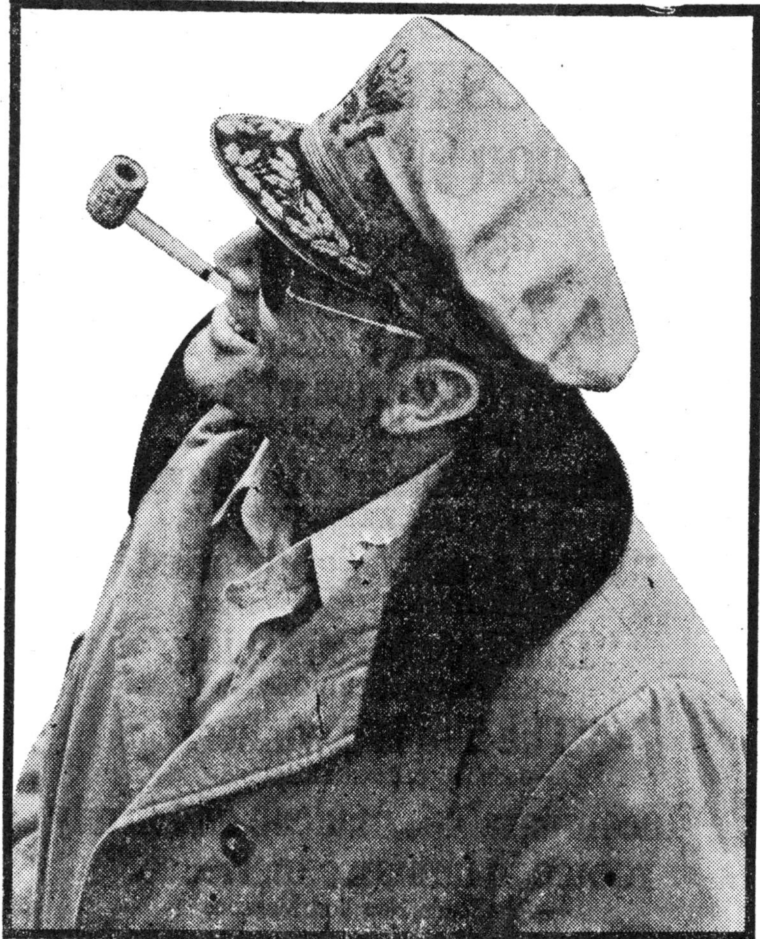

Morgan Renard/Sygma

Gregory Peck in Joseph Sergent's film "MacArthur"
Peck's wit gives an edge to the performance and humanity to a character

him from Korea after the general had disobeyed specific orders. MacArthur thought it nothing less than idiocy that a general owed his loyalty to an elected official who held office temporarily rather than to the Constitution (as he might interpret it) and the people.

In the title role, Gregory Peck is remarkably good. He not only looks and sounds like the general, he also makes the character disgracefully appealing, even when he is being his most outrageous. Though he's a well-known libertarian, Mr. Peck has a kind of lofty manner—even when he's being humble—that well suits MacArthur. In addition, the actor displays a wit that gives an edge to the performance and humanity to a character who it might well have been impossible to be around.

The film, a series of flashbacks set in the frame of MacArthur's 1962 farewell address to the students at West Point, is further reinforced by the fact that, next to Winston Churchill, no man of his generation could so successfully recall the glories of 19th-century oratory. His speeches, including the "Old Soldiers Never Die" address to Congress, are so cannily handled by the film and Mr. Peck that one is constantly finding oneself at equal distances between the sneer and the tear.

In terms of actual chronology, the movie covers MacArthur's career from his departure from Corregidor in 1942, just before the fall of the Philippines, through his stay in Australia and his return to the Philippines via New Guinea, through his term as supreme commander in Japan and his ultimate falling-out with President Truman over policies in the Korean War.

So many events have to be eliminated or ellipsized that one would have a tough time realizing from the film that, among other things, the Philippines consist of more than a single island and that the Pacific war involved a number of other campaigns every bit as brilliant as MacArthur's.

The supporting characters are little more than mouthpieces, though the actors who play President Roosevelt (Dan O'Herlihy) and President Truman (Ed Flanders) come across as extended caricatures. Mr. Peck's is the only true character. Even this seems fitting, as MacArthur was not a fellow who took kindly to independence in his subordinates, though he himself was as insubordinate as his will dictated.

"MacArthur" contains very little in the way of conventional battle spectacle, yet those battle scenes it has are effectively done—and always in a scale that allows MacArthur to dominate them as he does the film. Though the movie gets a number of laughs at the expense of the general's vanity and rightist political sympathies and aspirations, the final tone is one of respect and awe. This, I suspect, is something that will be difficult for people who like easy judgments to accept. One of the reasons "MacArthur" is so disturbing is because, at unexpected moments, it's so moving.

•

"MacArthur," which has been rated PG (Parental Guidance Suggested) contains war footage that is, necessarily, violent and bloody.

1977 Jl 1, C8:1

Stern and Sober

THE OTHER FRANCISCO, directed by Sergio Giral; screenplay (English subtitles) by Mr. Giral, based on the novel "Francisco," by Anselmo Romero; director of photography, Livio Delgado; editor, Nelson Rodriguez; music, Leo Brouwer; produced by the Instituto Cubano del Arte e Industria Cinematograficos (the Cuban Film Istitute); distributed by Tricontinental Film Center. Running time: 100 minutes. At the Jean Renoir Cinema, 100 Seventh Avenue. This film has not been rated.

Francisco .... Miguel Benavides
Dorotea .... Alina Sanchez
Ricardo .... Ramon Veloz
Richardo's mother .... Margarita Balboa
Overseer .... Adolfo Llaurado

"THE Other Francisco" the 1975 Cuban film that opened yesterday at the Jean Renoir Cinema, is an unusually fresh example of the sort of didactic movie making that often leaves a lot to be desired. Directed by Sergio Giral, "The Other Francisco" is both an adaptation of Anselmo Suarez Romero's "Francisco," a Cuban anti-slavery novel written before "Uncle Tom's Cabin," as well as a critique of the novel and of the methods and motives of 19th-century Cuban liberals and abolitionists.

Mr. Giral cross-cuts between scenes from the novel—a sentimental story about a young slave who kills himself when his beloved is taken into the master's bed—and scenes that attempt to show what slavery was really like. There also are interludes in which the novelist discusses the writing of his book, which, he admits, attributes romantic motives to characters who were incapable of romantic notions.

•

Photographed in black-and-white that has the quality of newsreel battle footage, the film both appreciates the novel's abolitionist sentiments and analyzes the distortions. Slaves, the movie says, were hardly as docile and passive as the novelist pictured. They might commit suicide to escape the system but never because of broken hearts. Women slaves were treated as badly as the men. Although Cuban liberals were against slavery, they were apprehensive about full independence from Spain, fearing a black-majority rule.

"The Other Francisco," which begins the Renoir Cinema's retrospective of Cuban films (including the superb "Memories of Underdevelopment"), is a stern, sober, opinionated work. It's also another demonstration of the great vitality of the contemporary Cuban film industry.

VINCENT CANBY

1977 Jl 1, C8:1

FILM VIEW

VINCENT CANBY

WORLD WAR II WON'T FADE AWAY — NOT IN THE MOVIES, THAT IS

Am I getting old? Unreasonable? Irritable? Maybe even eccentric? Obviously I don't think so but I do have doubts. The thing is, I don't want to see any more World War II movies for at least a month. Make that six weeks and classify it as R & R. This season I've slogged through the Allied defeat at Arnhem in Joseph E. Levine's "A Bridge Too Far." In "MacArthur" I was holed up with the General on Corregidor for weeks before finally being forced (against my will) to abandon "the Rock" to go into testy exile in Australia. I then fought my way up through New Guinea and the Philippines to Japan where I decreed the formation of a labor movement and gave Japanese women the right to vote. Just when I was getting bored by being so uplifting, I received a reprieve. That is, the Korean War or, as Mac himself calls it in the movie, "One last gift to an old soldier."

As if that weren't enough, in John Sturges's "The Eagle Has Landed" I was dragooned into joining a group of incredibly gallant German commandos in their attempt to kidnap Winston Churchill. We failed but at what price! After that there was what seemed an interminable stretch with a small detachment of German troops on the collapsing Russian front in Sam Peckinpah's "Cross of Iron." Anyway, the guys said they were German but the colonel (James Mason) had an English accent, the captain (Max Schell) a Swiss-German accent, the corporal (James Coburn) was strictly from Nebraska, while all of the other enlisted men sounded like variations on Baron Munchausen.

This tour was the worst. It wasn't simply that when the guys were hit by mortars they suddenly spurted blood in slow motion—like fountains of thick cherry syrup. We're more or less used to that with Peckinpah. More intolerable was all of that manic horsing around in the enlisted men's quarters—everyone acting all over the place and throwing their machismos back and forth like thug-Boy Scouts in a perpetual pillow fight.

For years after World War II about the only movies we saw from the Soviet Union and Eastern Europe were movies about the war. Movies about how the Poles stood up to the Nazi invaders, about Tito's partisans, about the extraordinary resilience of the little people who were the children of Mother Russia. Some of the films were extremely good—Wajda's "Kanal" and "Ashes and Diamonds," Menzel's "Closely Watched Trains," Chukhrai's "Ballad of a Soldier." Yet, after a while, one began to wonder why there was all of this looking-back in the Soviet bloc. Granted that the war had had devastating social, economic and psychological effects on those countries, but weren't there other, more contemporary subjects that interested them? As we learned during the brief Czech "spring," there were plenty of other subjects, but the only safe subject was the war. It was the subject about which everyone could agree.

Something of this same sort holds true here. It's not that our World War II films have to be especially safe in a political sense but, rather, that they are sound economics. World War II movies are action movies and an action movie—all other things being equal—comes as close as any movie can to being a safe investment in a business where there are no such things. Then, too, World War II was the last of the "good" wars. Not only were the issues clear-cut and the sides chosen early, but we won. There were no nagging doubts about whether or not we should have been in it. There was no other way.

This knowledge, as much as anything else, explains why our war movies are always set in World War II. If it were simply a matter of picking a war to make a movie about, we would have had many more about Korea and, certainly, about Vietnam. World War I is now too far in the past to be of great interest to most audiences, which leaves World War II to be exploited as freely as anything else in the public domain.

What amazes me about our war movies is how little they've changed over the years and, by not changing in any important way, how they have become testimonials not to heroism, endurance and faith but to the melodrama and excitement of war. Peckinpah has said somewhere that "Cross of Iron" is anti-war because it shows all the nasty things that happen to men in war, which is nonsense. It trafficks in the spectacle of battle for a viewer who is safe in his theater seat and knows that war has a beginning, a middle and an end, like any movie. If someone could make a film that accurately reproduced the pain, panic, ugliness, confusion and desperation of a battle, as well as the wary acceptance of death too soon, no one, I'm sure, would be able sit through it. So much for war movies that are supposed to be anti-war.

The truly anti-war movies must be unpleasant, rude and depressing, which were qualities that were caught in Stanley Kubrick's "Paths of Glory" and in isolated sequences in Lina Wertmuller's "Seven Beauties." There are very few others.

Sturges's "The Eagle Has Landed" belongs to the war-as-adventure subcategory and, as such, is quite decent entertainment, though I have a friend who strenuously objects to the fact that the film's heroes are German. This is one of the minor variations on the war theme that has developed in recent years, and one that takes into consideration three factors: (1) there were some "good" Germans; (2) you can't stay mad forever; and (3) the German market is very important to the financial success of any commercial American movie.

"MacArthur," produced by Richard Zanuck and David Brown, the men responsible for "Patton" (along with director Franklin J. Schaffner), is their attempt to hit the jackpot again with another supposedly candid portrait of a military hero who is shown to be vain, brilliant, compassionate, egocentric, ambitious and petty, a man who hated war but who only was fully realized when fighting one. The movie, directed by Joseph Sargent, attempts to cover too much ground too quickly and it lacks a central character as peculiarly compelling as Patton and an actor as spellbinding as George C. Scott. But it has its moments. Though it's difficult to transform MacArthur into an appealingly colorful character, Gregory Peck does well. He both looks and sounds right, perhaps because Peck's stately bearing in some way coincides with MacArthur's regal view of himself.

"MacArthur" is a war film with so little battle footage that one comes away with the impression that the Pacific campaign was fought and won entirely in conference rooms. It may well be that that's where generals must do most of their fighting. Yet "MacArthur" never dramatizes convincingly the genius of his campaigns. Most of the battles are reported as events that happen off-screen, thereby diminishing somewhat the extraordinary efforts and sacrifices of the armies and navies that made it possible for MacArthur to realize his plans. It's a sort of "closet" war movie.

"A Bridge Too Far," directed by Richard Attenborough, is another thing entirely, a massive recreation of a disastrous Allied operation that lasted nine days and that, as detailed in Cornelius Ryan's best-selling book, failed as the result of a singular series of wrong-headed decisions, bad judgment and bad luck.

The film is in the tradition of "The Longest Day" and is, if that's your idea of movie art, very impressive. The battle scenes are as spectacular as any you've ever seen and may ever see again. There are dozens of star-actors playing real-life characters in dozens of separate but interlocking incidents. Following its various narrative lines is like watching an ant-palace as big as the Ritz. One never quite knows where to look, or who is doing what to whom. In dramatizing the confusion inherent in such a gigantic operation the movie lets some of that confusion spill into the audience. Yet as an example of big-budget, literal-minded moviemaking, "A Bridge Too Far" is probably as good as one can get.

But, exactly, what does one get? A distaste for war? A sense of the futility of such battles? A renewed dedication to fight for a just peace for everyone? Not at all. Though this battle was lost, the war was eventually won, which effectively undermines any point the film might be making about the horrors of war. Perhaps British Field Marshal Montgomery, who masterminded the operation and who insisted it was a success even when it failed, was right. Perhaps it did contribute to the war's end.

"A Bridge Too Far" may want to tell us that war is awful, but instead it shows us a comparatively tidy spectacle in which the amount of blood and guts is held to the minimum that will allow the movie its PG rating. An R-rated war would be bad business.

Our world changes but our World War II movies don't. For the time being, I've had enough. I've put in my time. I've got my points. I want out. ■

1977 Jl 3, II:1:4

Comic-Book Fare

THE PEOPLE THAT TIME FORGOT; screenplay by Patrick Tilley based on "The People that Time Forgot" by Edgar Rice Burroughs; directed by Kevin Connor; produced by John Dark; executive producer, Samuel Z. Arkoff; edited by John Ireland and Barry Peters; special effects supervised by Ian Wingrove; a Max J. Rosenberg Production presented by American International Pictures. At the Cinerama 1, Broadway and 47th Street, and local theaters. Running time: 90 minutes. This film has been rated PG.

Ben McBride	Patrick Wayne
Bowen Tyler	Doug McClure
Ajor	Dana Gillespie
Charly	Sarah Douglas
Norfolk	Thorley Walters
Hogan	Shane Rimmer

By A. H. WEILER

HAT WE NEED is a winch," says one of the passengers of a World War I biplane that has crashed on a mysterious volcanic island during a search for a lost American explorer in "The People That Time Forgot." What is really needed, it soon becomes obvious in the film that landed at local theaters yesterday, is a creative script, imaginative direction and acting and some levity to lift this vehicle out of its comic book trappings.

•

The producers, who previously delved into another Edgar Rice Burroughs fiction to give us "The Land That Time Forgot," apparently were happy with the pattern that they had set the first time around. Their "People That Time Forgot" again are cavemen, who, defying evolution and Darwin, are struggling for lebensraum with dinosaurs, pterodactyls and the like. But despite that awesome competition, it's clear that they will also resent these strange newcomers.

•

Included among the intruders are Patrick Wayne, as a boyishly resolute World War I aviator, and Doug McClure, his buddy and the sought-after explorer held captive by the natives. Associated in this trip that doesn't seem quite necessary are Sarah Douglas, as a pretty, but somewhat wooden, British newspaper photographer; Shane Rimmer, as a rough-hewn airplane mechanic-gunner, and Thorley Walters, as a proper English scientist.

However, they're no match physically for the largely undraped Dana Gillespie, as a gorgeous Cave Girl, who leads them to the eventually ill-fated exploder from whom, by the long arm of coincidence, she has learned some rudimentary English. Her limited dialogue is a mite less artificial than the fabricated prehistoric fauna, volcanic eruptions and other simulated dangers the group encounters en route to freedom. All things considered, these "People That Time Forgot" are fairly easy to forget.

•

This film has been rated PG ("Parental Guidance Suggested") which probably fits the bill for preteen-agers, although its beasts, battles and volcanic action are perhaps a good deal less scary than was intended.

1977 Jl 7, C18:1

Year of the Orphan

THE RESCUERS, directed by Wolfgang Reitherman, John Lounsbery and Art Stevens; produced by Mr. Reitherman; executive producer, Ron Miller; story by Larry Clemmons, Ken Anderson, Vance Gerry, David Michener, Burny Mattinson, Frank Thomas, Fred Lucky, Ted Berman, Dick Sebast; suggested by "The Rescuers" and "Miss Bianca," by Margery Sharp; directing animators, Ollie Johnson, Frank Thomas, Milt Kahl and Don Bluth; music, Artie Butler; editors, James Melton and Jim Koford; a Walt Disney Productions presentation, distributed by Buena Visa. Running time: 76 minutes. At the Cinerama Two, Broadway at 47th Street, and other theaters. This film has been rated G.

With the voices of Bob Newhart (Bernard), Eva Gabor (Miss Bianca), Geraldine Page (Madame Medusa), Joe Flynn, Jeanette Nolan, Pat Buttram, Jim Jordan, John McIntire, Michelle Stacy, Bernard Fox, Larry Clemmons, James Macdonald, George Lindsey, Bill McMilan, Dub Taylor and John Fiedler.

By VINCENT CANBY

WITH "ANNIE" already established as one of the bigger hits on the Broadway stage, the arrival of "The Rescuers"—the first animated feature from the Walt Disney organization since 1973—could make this the year of the transcendent orphan. Like Little Orphan Annie, Penny, the small heroine of "The Rescuers," is parentless and subject to all sorts of evil designs by people, who fortunately, are so incompetent that they are virtually self-destruct mechanisms.

"The Rescuers," which opened yesterday at the Cinerama Two and other theaters, is efficiently short, charming, mildly scary in unimportant ways, and occasionally very funny. It's a perfect show for the very, very young who take their cartoons seriously.

•

The screenplay, based on two stories by Margery Sharp, is principally about the efforts of two do-gooding New York mice, Bernard and Miss Bianca, members of something called the Rescue Aid Society, to rescue Penny after she's been kidnapped by a certain Madame Medusa. The last, who runs Madame Medusa's Pawn Shop Boutique, has stolen the child and whisked her off to Louisiana because Penny is the only person small enough to crawl into a pirate's cave there and retrieve a diamond as big as a baseball.

I doubt that even small children will pay too much attention to the story, which, as it should be, is simply the excuse for a series of marvelously improbable adventures. There is, for example, the hectic journey that Bernard, whose voice and something of his personality are supplied by Bob Newhart, and Miss Bianca (voice by Eva Gabor) take to Louisiana via Albatross Air Charter Service. The "equipment," as it's called in timetables, is a very tired albatross named Orville who hasn't yet mastered takeoffs or landings.

In the Devil's Bayou in Louisiana there are split-second escapes from Madame Medusa, a fine, flame-haired Gorgon for whom Geraldine Page supplies the voice and comic presence, and encounters with various swamp types, including a dragonfly named Evinrude who runs a local boat service.

•

With periodic timeouts for obligatory songs of an especially forgettable nature, "The Rescuers" moves quickly and without fuss from one episode to the next, never creating a sense of any real dread or fear. The animation is pretty in a conventional fashion that may be as fascinating to children as the bold innovations of someone like Ralph Bakshi are to the rest of us.

"The Rescuers" doesn't belong in the same category as the great Disney cartoon features ("Snow White and The Seven Dwarfs," "Bambi," "Fantasia") but it's a reminder of a kind of slickly cheerful, animated entertainment that has become all but extinct.

1977 Jl 7, C18:1

Bernard and Bianca are do-gooding mice in Disney's cartoon film "The Rescuers." Bob Newhart and Eva Gabor supply their voices.

Marxist History

VIVA LA REPUBLICA! a documentary feature directed by Pastor Vega; screenplay (in Spanish with English subtitles and in English) by Mr. Vega. Victor Casaus, Julio Garcia Espinosa, Jesus Diaz and Mirita Lores; editor, Miss Lores; produced by the Cuban Film Institute; distributed by Transcontinental Films. Running time: 91 minutes. At the Jean Renoir Cinema, 100 Seventh Avenue. This film has not been rated.

"VIVA LA REPUBLICA!" which opened at the Jean Renoir Cinema yesterday, is an effective, hard-hitting Marxist history of Cuba from the Spanish-American War, by which the United States came to dominate Cuban affairs, until the successful 1959 revolution led by Fidel Castro. The film is composed of newsreel footage supplemented by political cartoons, footage from fiction films and from television films and commercials.

•

Though the method is sophisticated, the purpose is simple—to recall the years of United States economic, social and political domination of the island republic, as well as the almost impossible odds that faced all nationalist movements.

"Viva La República!" which was directed for the Cuban Film Institute by Pastor Vega, is moving and thought-provoking, not only for what it says about Cuba, but also for its indictment of what was fairly standard United States policy throughout Latin America for so many years. Everything could be expropriated, including history. Says the film's narrator of the 1895 Cuban revolution that was later joined by the United States to make the Spanish-American War, "The name of the war didn't even mention Cuba."

VINCENT CANBY

1977 Jl 7, C18:5

FILM VIEW

VINCENT CANBY

Let's Call It 'The Accountant's Theory' of Filmmaking

Second thoughts on two first-run movies: For more than a decade now we've accepted the auteur theory to the effect that there are dominant themes in a filmmaker's work, our awareness of which distinguishes the director's output and enriches our appreciation so that even when a film is not great, we may find it rewarding. To this theory, which can be applied only to a limited number of directors with coherent results, I'd like to suggest another way of regarding a filmmaker's work—something of more general application. In France they would call it the *Politique des Comptables*. Here: the accountant theory. Put another way, it's "you're as good as your last picture, Sam," meaning that the amount of freedom and clout that a director has at any moment depends pretty much on the grosses of his most recent film. This helps to explain (and if theories don't help to explain something, what good are they?) why directors of very profitable films so often follow up with films that are in some fashion self-indulgent and out-of-control.

The case in point this week is Martin Scorsese and his new movie, "New York, New York," a fond, extravagant, shapeless salute to the big-band musicals of the 1940's. It takes the form of a period boy-girl backstage romance about a singer (Liza Minnelli) and tenor-sax player (Robert De Niro) who meet on V-J Day, more or less fall in love, marry, have a kid, and then are swept apart by their ambitions and their careers when the big-band era collapses in the early 50's.

The first third of "New York, New York" is terrifically promising, beginning with the initial encounter of the boy and the girl in the chaos of a victory celebration in one of those huge Hollywood versions of a New York nightclub. Miss Minnelli, in her USO uniform, her hair rolled up, Ann Sheridan-style, around her overseas cap, sits alone at a table and trades put-downs with De Niro, who is dressed in civvies, including an oversized Hawaiian sport shirt, when he tries to pick her up. His pushiness and her nasty retorts are in the best tradition of what so long passed for comedy in Hollywood films when the boy and the girl were required to "meet cute." The language of love was largely a language of insult. Miss Minnelli is very funny and on-the-mark and De Niro is self-assured and aggressive—so much so that he eventually busts out the other side of a movie that is an imitation of what originally was papier-maché. Which leaves "New York, New York" as a sort of a dream of a dream.

Watching the movie was, for me, a process of galloping disenchantment, though not because the movie goes to pieces in any spectacular manner. After first appreciating Scorsese's appreciation of the form—the movie manners, the costumes, the elaborately recreated artificiality of the sets, the big-band sounds, Miss Minnelli's singing of a bunch of golden oldies and some tinny newies (by Kander and Ebb)—I began to wonder if this was all there was to be. The answer: yes. But there simply isn't enough to justify a running time that seems longer than "Gone With The Wind's" and a budget that's probably bigger.

Scorsese is one of our new generation of directors who comes out of a film school (New York University). He grew up with Hollywood movies, knows them inside out and, what's more important, has his own particular talent (as he's shown in "Mean Streets," "Alice Doesn't Live Here Anymore" and "Taxi Driver"), which has assimilated the films of the past but is separate from them.

His contribution to what was always a second-rate Hollywood genre (which would include films like "Alexander's Ragtime Band," "Rose of Washington Square," "Orchestra Wives") is to make something that's 10 times as big, half as fast, and almost totally devoid of emotion. The latter, I suppose, can be taken as Scorsese's "comment" on such films but that, I think, is stretching a point in the director's favor.

"New York, New York" is so full of movie lore and references that it boggles the non-pro mind. What it totally lacks is pace—it's the sort of movie that would drive Darryl F. Zanuck through five cigars without knowing he'd lit the first— as well as any sense of fun. What some of my colleagues find bold and fascinating—its coldness—seems to me to be nothing more or less than an inability to come to grips with the sentimental nature that gave shape to the original. "New York, New York" doesn't fall apart. It just slips into a series of so-so musical numbers, between which we are given to understand that both the singer and the sax player are achieving success separately.

Much has been written about the film's original four-hour (or was it four-and-one-half-hour?) rough cut, the paring down of which necessarily meant dropping a lot of essential material. I don't doubt that, but I wonder why someone would conceive of a film like this in a four-hour form. Can you imagine sitting through a three-hour Gene Autry western? I can't.

What happened? Because I have no privileged information I feel perfectly free to apply the *Politique des Comptables*. "Mean Streets" was no big deal at the box office—actually it was a prestigious flop—but "Alice Doesn't Live Here Anymore" was a surprise hit. This was followed by "Taxi Driver," which was not only successful financially but was "controversial" enough to give Scorsese a reputation as a man who could make films that were profitable and would be taken seriously by the critics. It seems as if it became "sign Marty" time in Hollywood and to sign Marty, one gave Marty what Marty wanted, which, I assume, was freedom to work in his own way and to spend as much money as he needed. Even if "New York, New York" becomes a hit in spite of itself, I hope Scorsese will go back to working on a smaller scale, with subjects that have lives of their own.

The *Politique des Comptables* is the only possible way one can justify the expense, the complicated logistics and even the title of William Friedkin's "Scorcerer." This is a $21,000,-000 to $23,000,000 suspense-adventure film based on Georges Arnaud's French novel "The Wages of Fear," which was earlier made into a movie by the late Henri-Georges Clouzot, to whom Friedkin, rather patronizingly, dedicates his film. "Scorcerer" looks like a movie in desperate need of a strong —maybe even a stingy—producer, but Friedkin was his own producer and what the director wanted the producer saw he got.

Friedkin, you may remember, was the director of "The Exorcist," which has so far earned more than $82,000,000 in the domestic market alone, according to a January accounting. Profits like that don't grow on trees, so when Friedkin turned his attention to a follow-up project he was able to call the shots in a way that, ultimately, may be to his disadvantage.

Inside this two-hour-plus film that was photographed n location in France, Israel, Mexico and New Jersey there is a good, tight one-hour movie, shot in the Dominican Republic, about four bums, outcasts from their own countries, who agree to drive two truckloads of nitroglycerine through virtually impassable Latin American terrain to fight an oil-well fire. Instead of being as simple and straightforward as that, though, Friedkin had seen fit to spend almost an hour of screen time showing us how each of the four men wound up in such desperate circumstances in the jungles.

Friedkin is a good director ("The Birthday Party," "The Night They Raided Minsky's") but he's not the god that the grosses of "The Exorcist" would indicate to financial types. To make a good suspense-adventure film one doesn't stretch the material. One compresses it so that it becomes a dangerously explosive element. Somebody must have been aware of this but Friedkin, riding the crest of "The Exorcist" wave, was out of reach.

The movie has some extremely good performances, by Roy Scheider and Bruno Cremer among others, but it should have been much, much tighter, less cinematically grand. It should also have had almost any title but "Scorcerer," which is justified by being the name written on the side of a truck within the movie, but which we know was attached to the movie to associate it with Friedkin's last film.

By some fluke coincidence, "Scorcerer" was released in New York a week after the release of "Exorcist II: The Heretic," and I've heard more than a dozen people (including myself) use the title of the Friedkin film when talking about the "Exorcist" sequel. Nobody wins in that sort of confusion.

Note to Liza Minnelli fans: In my daily review of "New York, New York,"I referred to Miss Minnelli in a specific scene as "an onlooker," but through a typographical error it came out as "a nonlooker." I'm neither a cad nor unappreciative of Miss Minnelli's appeal. ■

1977 Jl 10, II:11:1

El Dorado-Bound

STROSZEK, directed by Werner Herzog; screenplay, in German with English subtitles and in English, by Mr. Herzog; director of photography, Thomas Mauch; editor, Beate Mainka-Jellinghaus; music, Chet Atkins and Sonny Terry; a Werner Herzog Filmproduction/Skellig Edition, distributed by New Yorker Films. Running time: 108 minutes. At the Cinema Studio, Broadway at 66th Street. This film has not been rated.

Stroszek .... Bruno S.
Eva .... Eva Mattes
Scheitz .... Clemens Scheitz
Pimp .... Wilhelm von Hamburg
Pimp .... Burkhard Driest
Pimp .... Pitt Bedewitz
Mechanic .... Clayton Szlapinski
Mechanic .... Ely Rodriguez
Prison Governor .... Alfred Edel
Bank Employee .... Scott McKain
Auctioneer .... Ralph Wade

By VINCENT CANBY

WERNER HERZOG, the young German director of "The Mystery of Kasper Hauser," "The Great Ecstasy of the Sculptor Steiner" and "Aguirre, the Wrath of God," doesn't make movies that are easy to describe, "Kasper Hauser," Mr. Herzog's variation on the "wild child" story, is a beautiful, ghostly movie, a parable almost too refined for mortal comprehension.

In his short film about Walter Steiner, Mr. Herzog demonstrates the ecstasy of the champion ski-jumper in sports footage so breathtakingly, we see doom in every triumph.

"Aguirre," about the mad, power-obsessed Spanish conquistador, is a meditation upon human futility photographed in Peru and Brazil in some of the world's most spectacular scenery. Among other things, Mr. Herzog visually dazzles us while he's pulling the rug from under our feet.

•

In a Herzog film we have to keep checking what we are hearing against what we're seeing. They are seldom the same things, but forcing us to reconcile contradictions is one of the ways in which he works.

"Stroszek," which opened yesterday at the Cinema Studio, is described by Mr. Herzog as a ballad, which is probably as good a way as any to categorize it initially. It's a "road" picture. In some distant way it reminds me of "Easy Rider," but it's an "Easy Rider" without sentimentality or political paranoia. It's terrifically, spontaneously funny and, just as spontaneously, full of unexpected pathos.

"Stroszek" is the tale of three mismatched friends—each a loser—who set out from Berlin to find El Dorado in northern Wisconsin, in winter, with very little money and hardly any knowledge of English. It would be difficult to imagine three people less fit for such a journey.

Scheitz (Clemens Scheitz) is in his 70's, small, frail, modest, a fellow who seems always to be suffering from a chill. Eva (Eva Mattes) is a buxom but none-to-bright Berlin streetwalker, the sort that pimps can beat up and double-cross endlessly without seriously damaging her dogged dependence on them.

Most importantly there is Stroszek, played by Bruno S., the Berlin street musician who played the title role in "Kasper Hauser." Stroszek, 40-ish, is a worldly innocent who, when we first meet him, seems to be simple-minded. He is being released from prison by a not-unsympathetic warden who warns him to stay out of bars and to try to remember to shave and keep his fly zipped. It's not that Stroszek has tendencies. He simply doesn't pay attention to minor details. Something is missing from Stroszek, but what it is is not intelligence.

•

As an actor, Bruno S. is a found object. Much of the tension of the early scenes of "Stroszek" is created by our attempting to fit Bruno S. into some normal scheme of things. Is he acting? Is he following Mr. Herzog's directions like a trained dog? Is he improvising, sometimes with immense wit? I suspect it must be a combination of all three.

In whatever way the performance is created, it's an extraordinarily compelling one, and one that is virtually a physical manifestation of what the film is about. The Stroszek we get to know is a compassionate, patient, common-sensical man incapable of rage or physical assertiveness. This small, curious personality is imprisoned within a large, stocky, man-sized body that seems too big for him, a vehicle that can maneuver with only the utmost effort and concentration. When he glances around him, he looks like a child peering apprehensively out of the pilot's seat of a 747.

The adventures of these three contemporary pilgrims as they attempt to settle into what they believe to be the American way of life are both bleak and uproariously funny. Eva, who works as a waitress—for a while—and Stroszek, who gets a job as a mechanic, buy a huge mobile home of an indescribably fancy awfulness. Scheitz, who appears to shrink even smaller in the Wisconsin cold, becomes politely disoriented and decides he has discovered the means to measure "animal magnetism" by using a conventional ammeter.

Constantly working against Mr. Herzog's very cool view of the human condition is not only the humor—"Stroszek" contains one of the shortest, funniest holdups I've ever seen in a movie—but also the physical beauty of the landscapes, the cityscapes and the squalid interiors. This visual lyricism, which at first seems at odds with the subject, eventually becomes a further celebration of Stroszek's survival.

•

That the pilgrims must eventually be disappointed is a foregone conclusion, but the way it happens is anything but predictable. Among the dozens of images in the film I'll remember for a very long time is one near the end of a chicken that can't stop dancing and another of a premature baby, hardly bigger than a man's hand, whose capacity to hang on is nothing less than ferocious. It's this mixture of feelings and attitudes that gives the Herzog works their haunting lives.

1977 Jl 13, C14:1

Elliptical Marxism

THE MAN FROM MAISINICU; written and directed by Manuel Perez; produced by the Instituto Cubano del Arte e Industria Cinematographicos (ICAIC-the Cuban Film Institute); director of photography, Jorge Herrera; edited by Gloria Arguelles; released by Tricontinental Film Center. At the Jean Renoir Theater, 100 Seventh Avenue. Running time: 124 minutes. This film has not been rated.
With Sergio Corrieri as Alberto Delgado Delgado and featuring Reinaldo Miravalles, Raul Pomares and Adolfo Llaurado.

By A. H. WEILER

AS A POLITICAL DRAMATIST, Manuel Perez, the writer-director of "The Man From Maisinicu," the Cuban feature that opened at the Jean Renoir Theater yesterday, is forthright in his dedication to Fidel Castro's Marxism, but confusingly elliptical in dramatizing it. The aims and politics of the man from Maisinicu may be properly shrouded in mystery, but the tortuous flashbacks and flash-forwards on the violent road he travels tend to obscure rather than spotlight the film's heroes and villains and their goals.

•

The 37-year-old documentary-film maker, who made "The Man From Maisinicu" four years ago as his first dramatic effort, generates suspense and realism at the outset as the badly beaten body of his man is discovered in the brush near the state farm he managed in the wooded hill country of Maisinicu. Is he a Castro loyalist or the under-cover counterrevolutionary he seems to be?

With the aid of English subtitles and off-screen narration, he is revealed as a former soldier who, angered by bureaucratic mistreatment, apparently has switched his allegiance to counter-revolutionary forces. An intrepid type, he is exposed to the questions and gun-fire of Castro's militia and the mounting suspicions of the rebels he is harboring and apparently aiding to escape to safety in Miami.

References to CIA machinations in behalf of these anti-Castro "bandits," are made, of course. But the off-screen citing of names, dates and places, which probably were intended to heighten the adventure's cinéma vérité look, often are a mite more perplexing than necessary to a viewer unfamiliar with the intricacies of Cuban geography and revolutionary history.

As "The Man From Maisinicu," Sergio Corrieri provides a fully realized portrait of a natural, rugged, heroic citizen who appreciated and was ready to accept the awesome wages of patriotism. But Mr. Perez's unbilled supporting cast, though fiercely determined in numerous confrontations and clashes, is made up largely of rough-hewn, undefined characters.

The director-writer, a program note states, purposely used a circuitous approach not only to create suspense but also to underscore the "heroism of revolutionaries." He has partly succeeded. His truly heroic "Man From Maisinicu" may be enveloped in authentic mystery and tensions, but they are slackened in a maze of bewildering flashbacks. And his drama's politics are, like the film on which it was shot, simply black and white.

1977 Jl 13, C14:5

THE ISLAND OF DR. MOREAU, directed by Don Taylor; screenplay by John Herman Shaner and Al Mamrus, based on a novel by H.G. Wells; executive producers, Samuel Z. Arkoff and Sandy Howard; produced by John Temple-Smith and Skip Steloff; director of photography, Gerry Fisher; music, Laurence Rosenthal; editor, Marion Rothman; distributed by American International Pictures; Running time: 104 minutes; At the Cinema 1 Theatre, Broadway at 47th Street, and other theaters. This film has been rated PG.

Dr. Moreau	Burt Lancaster
Braddock	Michael York
Montgomery	Nigel Davenport
Maria	Barbara Carrera
Saver of the Law	Richard Basehart
M'Ling	Nick Cravet
Boarman	The Great John "L"
Bullman	Bob Ozman
Hyenman	Fumio Demura
Lionman	Gary
Tigerman	John Gillespie

Beauty and the Beasts: Barbara Carrera, surrounded by a bevy of "humanimals," who act with her in "The Island of Dr. Moreau."

by VINCENT CANBY

WHAT SOMEONE should always refer to at some point as "the sacred mystery of life" is being interfered with in high old style in Don Taylor's creepy new film adaptation of H. G. Well's novel, "The Island of Dr. Moreau." The horror movie, which belongs to the man-made-monster sub-category, opened yesterday at the Cinema and other theaters.

The film sticks to its turn-of-the-century period and is beautifully set on a tropical Pacific isle (actually St. Croix without golfers), where Dr. Moreau (actually Burt Lancastar with a beard) conducts the insidious experiments that earlier got him tossed out of every medical society from Boston to Port Said. The doctor, like Baron Frankenstein, is positively obsessed with the sacred mystery of life, which he wants to control through chromosomes.

To this end, he has set up his laboratory on a remote island where, with the companionship of a beautiful, now chaste, ex-Panamanian whore named Maria (Barbara Carrera) and a hired-gun named Montgomery (Nigel Davenport), he injects what appears to be pure mountain spring water into horse, tigers, hyenas, wolves and such.

After 11 years of hard work Dr. Moreau has a whole island full of near-misses that the film calls "humanimals," a term that has been trade-marked with an eye, I suppose, to the toy and T-shirt markets. The humanimals are slow-witted, manlike beasts who walk around on their behind legs, menace strangers, but with Dr. Moreau, behave with the sort of tense over-politeness one would expect at a Friday night social designed to allow inmates to meet and get to know their prison guards.

Dr. Moreau might still be carrying on his work, populating the world with his mistakes, if there hadn't arrived at the island a shipwrecked sailor named Braddock (Michael York), who had scruples about the sacred mystery of life but none when it came to grabbing Maria, who still remembered a trick or two.

This is more or less the plot of "The Island of Dr. Moreau," which, according to my research, was also the general outline of the 1933 screen adaptation that starred Charles Laughton and was called "Island of Lost Souls." Having neither read the novel nor seen the earlier film directed by Eric Kenton, I feel no sense of loss in the mostly clever foolishness that Mr. Taylor has directed.

Mr. Lancaster is a very benign madman, courtly, gentle-mannered, a perfect host to the uninvited guest until Mr. York goes poking around and stirring up trouble with the homemade help. Then, but only then, does the doctor decide he must take "steps." That is, he is forced to begin some new experiments with the younger man.

"The Island of Dr. Moreau is a Saturday night movie that needn't be ashamed to come out the rest of the week. The screenplay by John Herman Shaner and Al Mamrus, sounds as if it would have been fun to write. Though it's never facetious, it enjoys such extravagances as the doctor's saying, "if they (the humanimals) spill just one drop of blood, it will drown us all."

The performers display a kind of disciplined intelligence that keeps them from bursting through the style of the film into comic limbo. These include Mr. Davenport as the foreman who, to relax, listens to an amazingly high-quality recording of "The Magic Flute" and Richard Basehart as the most intelligent, most peace-loving of the humanimals, a fellow who winds up like Neville Chamberlain—totally discredited.

Most of the work, though, is done by John Chamber, Sam Striepeke and Tom Burman, who designed the make-up and by Mr. Lancaster, and Mr. York, who are steadfast. Miss Carrera is so beautiful she's a sacred mystery of life all by herself.

1977 Jl 14, 12:1

I NEVER PROMISED YOU A ROSE GARDEN, directed by Anthony Page; screenplay by Gavin Lambert and Lewis John Carlino, based on the novel by Joanne Greenberg; executive producers, Roger Corman and Edgar J. Sherick; produced by Terence F. Deane, Daniel H. Blatt and Michael Hausman; director of photography, Bruce Logan; editor, Garth Craven; music, Paul Chihara; an Imorch production, distributed by New World Pictures. Running time: 96 minutes. At the Cinema II Theater, Third Avenue near 60th Street. This film has been rated R.

Dr. Fried	Bibi Andersson
Deborah Blake	Kathleen Quinlan
Miss Coral	Sylvia Sidney
Mr. Blake	Ben Piazza
Mrs. Blake	Lorraine Gary
Carla	Darlene Craviotto
Hobbs	Reni Santoni
Lee	Susan Tyrrell
Helene	Signe Hasso
McPherson	Norman Alden
Secret Wife of Henry VIII	Martine Bartlett
Anterrabae	Robert Viharo
Lactamaeon	Jeff Conaway
Dr. Haile	Dick Herd
Mrs. Forbes	Sarah Cunningham
The Spy	June C. Ellis
Sylvia	Diane Varsi
Kathryn	Patricia Singer
Eugenia	Mary Carver
Idat	Barbara Steele

By VINCENT CANBY

TO ESCAPE—actually, to renaer neutral—the terrors, real and imagined, of this world, Deborah Blake, a pretty, middle-class teen-ager, has created another much more exotic and much more terrifying world that exists just beyond reality. Though she is its ruler, she's also its slave, subject always to the laws and rituals she herself has designed to keep herself in line. At the age of 16, Deborah Blake is a certified schizophrenic.

Among the achievements of Anthony Page's screen adaptation of Joanne Greenberg's novel, "I Never Promised You A Rose Garden," is our immediate acceptance of Deborah's fantasy world, a desert landscape inhabited by half-naked pagans whose origins could be comic books perused at some preliterate age. Deborah's demons are both ferocious and absurd and never for a moment do we doubt their existence.

Unlike "One Flew Over the Cuckoo's Nest," "I Never Promised You A Rose Garden" makes no pitch on behalf of the proposition that the mentaly ill may be more sane and happy than the straights walking around loose outside. Mental illness, it knows, is sad and depressing, full of such breathtaking, manifold possibilities for failure and harm that one always has to be alert. It's exhausting, physically and phychically.

"I Never Promised You A Rose Gar-

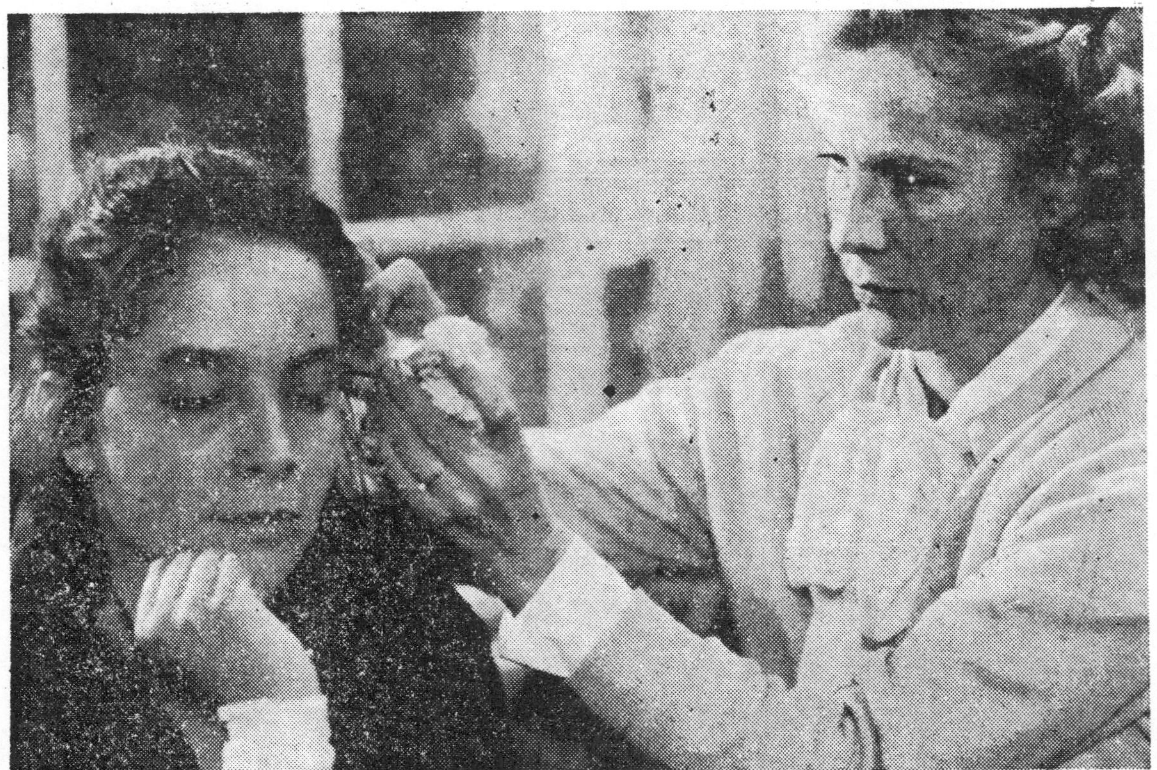

The New York Times/Jack Manning

Kathleen Quinlan as a mentally ill girl, Bibi Andresson as her psychiatrist in "I Never Promised You a Rose Garden"
Miss Quinlan projects "a sense of panic barely contained, of intelligence and feeling struggling to break free"

den," which opened yesterday at the Cinema II, is the carefully realized story of Deborah's treatment at a hospital that is probably better than most but still frightening enough, it would seem to us, to drive even someone who's well-balanced over the edge.

There's the male nurse who, to assert his own tenuous superiority over the patients, beats them up at will and, when he's feeling at ease, simply teases them. There are fatuous doctors and patronizing nurses. Mostly though, there are the other patients who insist on imposing their own worldly, surreal views on everyone around them, who slide in and out of temper tantrums, feuds and passionate friendships, who effectively befuddle even the simplest logic. To move among them without a collision is to sail without benefit of a centerboard or rudder.

How Deborah, with the help of one remarkable doctor, is eventually able to recognize her own pain and thus come to some kind of terms with her demons is the moving substance of this film that leaves one almost as exhausted as its heroine.

Mental illness is always a tricky thing to dramatize, not because it's especially difficult but because it's such an acute form of distress that it exists outside all conventional experience. Mr. Page and his screenwriters, Gavin Lambert and Lewis John Carlino, never quite succeed in convincing me that Deborah's triumph has much to do with the world at I know It. Most of us can identify in some fashion with astronauts, pearl divers, pirates and presidents, but madness is difficult to comprehend—maybe we are afraid of comprehending it. Whatever the reason, "I Never Promised You A Rose Garden' is something I can say I admired much more than I really liked.

The tone of the film is straightforward, terse, even as it shares with us Deborah's melodramatic visions of secret ceremonies and sacrifices, which suggest she's seen more than one movie on the order of "King Kong." Unless you're someone who finds psychotic behavior intrinsically funny, however, you're likely to be ground-down by the ward sequences in which aimlessness and violence are so effectively portrayed you may wish for a weekend pass before the movie's end.

Kathleen Quinlan, who had small parts in "American Graffiti" and the California problem-picture, "Lifeguard," gives a remarkably fine, contained performance as Deborah. There are no mannerisms, no tricks, only a sense of panic barely contained, of intelligence and feeling struggling to break free. Bibi Andersson is almost equally good as the psychiatrist, nobly free of platitudes and mock-doctor self-importance.

Among the inmates you'll recognize Signe Hasso, Susan Tyrrell, Diane Varsi (looking very plump) and Sylvia Sidney. They're all colorful and slightly too-much, as I suppose they should be, though Miss Sidney is achingly pathetic as an old lady who, for a brief time, becomes a legend in the ward after she wins her release.

1977 Jl 15, C10:1

THE LAST REMAKE OF BEAU GESTE, directed by Marty Feldman; screenplay by Mr. Feldman and Chris Allen, based on a story by Mr. Feldman and Sam Bobrick; executive producers, Howard West and George Shapiro; produced by William S. Gilmore; director of photography, Gerry Fisher; editors, Jim Clark and Arthur Schmidt; music, John Morris; distributed by Universal Pictures. Running time: 83 minutes. At the Sutton Theater, 57th Street east of Third Avenue. This film has been rated PG.

Flavia Geste .... Ann-Margret
Digby Geste .... Marty Feldman
Beau Geste .... Michael York
Markov .... Peter Ustinov
Sheikh .... James Earl Jones
Sir Hector .... Trevor Howard
General Pecheur .... Henry Gibson
Governor .... Terry-Thomas
Boldini .... Roy Kinnear
Crumble .... Spike Milligan
Camel Salesman .... Avery Schreiber
Judge .... Hugh Griffith
Miss Wormwood .... Irene Handl
Captain Merdmanger .... Henry Polic II
Blindman .... Ted Massidy
Father Shapiro .... Burt Kwouk
Dostoyevsky .... Val Pringle
Lady in Courtroom .... Gwen Nelson
Young Beau (6) .... Philip Bollard
Young Beau (12) .... Nicholas Bridge
Young Digby (12) .... Michael McConkey
Young Isabel .... Bekki Bridge
Dr. Crippen .... Roland MacLeod
Valentino .... Martin Snaric
Henshaw .... Stephen Lewis
Arab Horseman .... Ed McMahon

By VINCENT CANBY

Marty Feldman, the wild-eyed, cheerfully low-minded English comedian who was indispensable to Mel Brooks's "Young Frankenstein" ("Call me Eye-gore") and Gene Wilder's 'Sherlock Holmes' Smarter Brother," has now spun himself off, so to speak, as the star, director and co-author of his own frontal assault on cinema tradition and sensibility.

"The Last Remake of Beau Geste," which opened yesterday at the Sutton Theater, sends up just about everything, including a lot of things you may think you'd forgotten—such as the original Percival Christophere Wren novel, William A. Wellman's 1939 film version with Gary Cooper and all Foreign Legion movies. It also takes an extended dim view of gallantry, heroism, true love and honor while dealing in old husband-young wife jokes, jokes about female breasts, as well as a whole range of similar jokes that are funny primarily because they are in absolutely terrible taste.

It is Mr. Feldman's marvelous conceit to cast himself and Michael York as identical twins, the adopted sons of aging Sir Hector Geste (Trevor Howard), who was so angry after his wife died in childbirth, leaving him with an infant daughter, that he took into his home (Geste Manor) a pair of ragamuffins from the Wormwood and Gaul Orphanage. Sir Hector raises Beau (Mr. York) to be a leader of men and poor little Digby (Mr. Feldman) to follow as well as to love his adopted sister, "the fair Isabel" (Sinead Cusack), from afar.

The arrangement seems to work quite well until the very decrepit Sir Hector returns from a war in the Sudan with a new wife, Flavia, (Ann-Margaret). One night with Flavia and Sir Hector spends the rest of the movie in bed "alive," as the doctor says periodically, "and dying." After the famous Geste "Blue Water diamond" has been stolen, and the scheming Flavia has asserted her will to take control of the family, Beau and Digby, by separate routes, take off to join the French Foreign Legion.

I think I may be telling you somewhat more of the plot than is necessary in an effort to keep from myself describing the film's gags, which are really what it's all about. I am trying not to tell you about Digby's brilliant break from jail with the wholehearted cooperation of the prison guards, and about his later meeting, in a desert mi-

"THE LAST REMAKE OF BEAU GESTE"—Foreign Legionnaire Marty Feldman blows up a storm, and the desert will never be the same.

rage, with Gary Cooper in a secene from the Wellman film. Like many of the gags in the film, this latter involves some brilliantly clever crosscutting and results in a rather new image for Cooper.

The movie's momentum, like that of 'Blazing Saddles," is dependent not at all on any narrative devices and entirely on the individual gags and the performances. Mr. Feldman has surrounded himself with some of the funniest people in the business. They include Mr. Howard; Spike Milligan as Sir Hector's ancient manservant, a fellow who sways like a pendulum when he walks; Peter Ustinov as the sadistic Foreign Legion sergeant, who calls his men "my little fledermouses," and rides a horse that has a pegleg like his own; James Earl Jones as a very Anglicized Arab chieftain, as well as Ann-Margaret and Mr. York, who must play things fairly straight.

I'm not sure that Mr. Feldman, as a film's principal comedian, is as much fun as he is when he's part of an antic combination, as he was in both "Young Frankenstein" and "Sherlock Holmes' Smarter Brother." It's the nature of his comic personality that he is funniest when he is a member of a gang, adding a surreal visual touch as well as a presence that's slightly menacing because it's so unpredictable. As the star—as well as the director—there are moments when the desparation is apparent.

Yet there are so few comedies of this rakish sort that one can't afford to be too particular. Also, one should not overanalyze it or overreport its comic highlights. Its laughs come as much from the shock of discovery as from what's being said or done.

"The Last Remake of Beau Geste," which has been rated PG ("Parental Guidance Suggested"), contains a lot of explicit sexual and anatomical references that, if they don't go over the heads of youngsters, will probably strike them as the highest form of wit, mostly because they are consistently, often hilariously irreverent.

1977 Jl 16, 12:1

ORCA, produced by Luciano Vincenzoni; directed by Michael Anderson; original story and screenplay by Mr. Vincenzoni and Sergio Donati; director of photography, Ted Moore; music by Ennio Morricone; second unit and underwater director, Folco Quilici; a Dino De Laurentiis presentation; a Paramount release. At the Criterion and other theaters. Running time: 92 minutes. This film has been rated PG.

Nolan .... Richard Harris
Rachel Bedford .... Charlotte Rampling
Umilak .... Will Sampson
Annie .... Bo Derek
Novak .... Keenan Wynn
Ken .... Robert Carradine
Paul .... Peter Hooten
Swain .... Scott Walker

If it were medically possible to overdose on claptrap, "Orca," which opened yesterday at the Criterion and other theaters, would be compelled to carry a warning from the Surgeon General.

Awash in pseudo-science, blarney, Indian munbo-jumbo, anthropomorphism, plain old-fashioned superstition, bug-eyed fear and the ill-concealed yearning of its screenwriters to humble "Jaws," this film about whales and men flounders after about 15 minutes.

•

By that time, "Orca" has informed its audience that the killer whales, which are its chief grace, may possess an intelligence superior to man's. Nothing said by the humans for the rest of the movie does anything to raise doubts about that.

Speaking in simple idiocies, the characters in "Orca" (Latin for whale)—chief among them Richard Harris as a fisherman, Charlotte Rampling as a cetologist, Will Sampson as a font of Indian lore, and Keenan Wynn, Bo Derek and Peter Hooten as various forms of whale fodder — proceed on a doomed course.

It begins when Mr. Harris, hoping to pay off the mortgage on his boat by capturing a killer whale, manages instead to mortally maim a pregnant female of the species. Such whales, the audience has been informed, are monogamous. The bereaved male then proceeds to stalk Mr. Harris and to challenge him to a duel.

Before the finale amid the ice floes off Labrador, several people have been killed, one has lost a leg, a few boats have been sunk, a house has been destroyed and a fuel dump has gone up in flames.

The finale is chiefly notable for diverting the audience's attention from the action by raising the possibility that Miss Rampling concealed a couturier and a makeup expert aboard Mr. Harris's boat en route to the showdown.

The outset of "Orca" is marked by some lyrical and touching scenes involving killer whales. But thereafter this movie offers nothing but total immersion in the ridiculous.

•

"Orca's" PG rating ("Parental Guidance Suggested") is probably attributable to a goriness that revolts even its characters, and not to the single rapid scene of the attractive, carefully draped Bo Derek in bed with Peter Hooten nor to some mild expletives.

LAWRENCE VAN GELDER

1977 Jl 16, 12:2

OUTLAW BLUES; directed by Richard T. Heffron; written by B. W. L. Norton; produced by Steve Tisch; executive producers, Fred Weintraub and Paul Heller; director of photography, Jules Brenner; edited by Danford B. Greene and Scott Conrad; music by Charles Bernstein; presented by Warner Bros. At neighborhood theaters. Running time: 101 minutes. This film has been rated PG.

Bobby Ogden .... Peter Fonda
Tina Waters .... Susan St. James
Buzz Cavanaugh .... John Crawford
Garland Dupree .... James Callahan
Hatch .... Michael Lerner
Elroy .... Steve Fromholz
Associate Warden .... Richard Lockmiller
Billy Bob .... Matt Clark
Cathy Moss .... Jan Rita Cobler
Leon Warback .... Gene Rader

By A. H. Weiler

Like many junk foods, "Outlaw Blues," which went on sale at neighborhood theaters yesterday, is pleasantly palatable if not especially nutritious. Despite its aura of contrivance, Peter Fonda and the rest of an energetic cast help transform these "Blues" into a fairly lighthearted adventure set against the background of the country-and-western music scene.

Of course, they make the most of a musical genre that has millions of devoted fans. Mr. Fonda makes his movie debut as a vocalist and guitarist, singing the title tune by John Oates, as well as other plaintive rural ditties by such country stalwarts as Lee Clayton and Harlan Sanders. But, to the credit of B. W. L. Norton's script, the film also strongly indicates the vicious

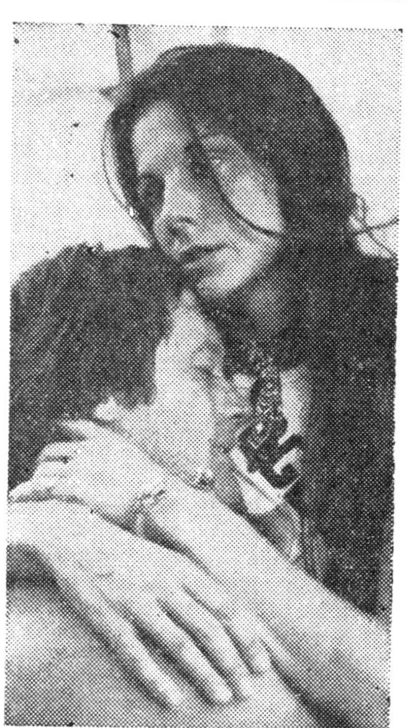

Peter Fonda and Susan St. James
Amiable, if lightweight, diversion

competition and sleaziness that could lurk behind the glamorous facades of some of the medium's recording giants.

Essentially, "Outlaw Blues" is a Mack Sennett-like chase with Mr. Fonda, as an ex-convict, in pursuit of James Callahan, playing the ruthless country star who has stolen Mr. Fonda's titular ballad. If our hero is a naïve tyro at first, he is soon shown the light by Susan St. James, as a decorative tough cookie wise in the ways of this division of show business. As might be expected, sex and love get into the act.

Richard T. Heffron, the director who has focused largely on documentaries, for example "Fillmore," has kept his cast in fairly constant motion in such authentic locales as Huntsville (Ala.) Prison, San Antonio and Austin, Tex., where the chase is centered. As noted, Miss St. James knows a good thing when she sees one, and, using a fracas in which the thieving star is accidentally shot, she proceeds to make a sought-after luminary out of her ex-con lover.

•

If speeding cars and a speedboat are not particularly original action devices, they are colorful and occasionally funny as our fleeing principals and the police, headed by Buzz Cavanaugh (John Crawford), make their roaring, breakneck rounds through the city and its river.

Come to think of it, the athletic cast is broadly oafish or devious in proper tongue-in-cheek style; Peter Fonda manages to be gently appealing and has a pleasant tenor voice, while Miss St. James is convincing as an expert conniver as well as being flip and pretty. "I've got the last laugh on you," Mr. Fonda's "Outlaw" sings, which isn't quite true considering his slight saga. But he and his company make it an amiable, lilting, if lightweight, diversion.

•

Although the young fry are certainly accustomed to the type of violent speeding scen in "Outlaw Blues," some raunchy dialogue probably earned it its PG ("Parental Guidance Suggested") rating.

1977 Jl 16, 14:1

Tatsuya Fuji in scene from "In the Realm of the Senses."
In the last few minutes, a trying film became intolerable.

IN THE REALM OF THE SENSES (L'EMPIRE DES SENS), directed by Nagisa Oshima; screenplay (Japanese with English subtitles) by Nagisa Oshima; photography, Kenichi Okamoto and Hideo Ito; editor, Keiichi Uraoka; music, Minoru Miki and traditional Japanese songs; produced by Anatole Dauman; production companies Arges Films (Parix/Oshima Productions), Tokyo. Running time: 115 minutes. This film has not been rated. At the Plaza Theater, 58th Street east of Madison Avenue.

"In the Realm of the Senses" ("L'Empire Des Sens") was shown at the 1976 New York Film Festival. The following is adapted from Richard Eder's review, which appeared Oct. 2, 1976. The film opened yesterday at the Plaza Theater.

It's impossible to see a painting if your nose is squashed right up against the canvas. Even with the contemporary pleasure in turned-up volume, there is a point at which music is so loud it can't be heard. Excessive visual shock will turn an audience's attention from any other quality a movie may possess and center it exclusively on its own pain.

Nagisa Oshima's film about sexual obsession, "In the Realm of the Senses," was not, in fact, doing very well when, in the last couple of minutes, he turned the volume up. It had become tedious and repetitious; its limited strengths had long since been exhausted from overuse. And in those last couple of minutes a trying film became an intolerable one.

•

I am using the word "intolerable" as a critic and not to justify the United States Customs ban on the film last fall. "Senses" does not show anything that has not been available in hard-core porn houses around Manhattan. Except an undeniable — though I think poorly used — artistic imagination.

"Senses" which, with the Customs ban reversed, has opened at the Plaza Theater, is about the literally consuming passion of a man and a woman. He is married to the owner of a geisha house: she is a newly arrived geisha.

The film consists of virtually nothing but their love-making. He is a man of infinite capacity and she is a woman of infinite desire—her doctor's term is "hypersensitive," she delicately explains—

and so the sex is incessant. It takes place furtively at first, then more and more openly, alone and in company.

The sex scenes, totally explicit, are much more than gymnastics. Both actors are good. Eiko Matsuda is appealing and even touching in her insatiability; Tatsuya Fuji has a haunting gentleness and passivity as he comes to recognize his destiny: to be literally loved to death.

The sex is never divorced from emotion, and this, for such a graphic presentation, is a novelty. Mr. Oshima is an artist. The movie, though, is not a work of art; at most, it is an artistic blunder.

•

Any life outside that of the couple is shadowy. The sex becomes an abstraction; so do the two lovers. Their lovemaking becomes more and more knotted, more and more obsessed with death.

For the viewer, there is little to do but wait the obsession out. It is a mathematical development. It is quite clear that she will kill him, and she does.

What is not, perhaps, foreseeable is the particularly repulsive form that the killing takes. After strangling her lover, the woman cuts off his sexual organs and displays them, prolongedly and bloodily.

There is some logical justification for the act—a final barbaric rite in a deadly sexual ritual. But there's no real emotional justification for it. The movie was dying anyway; now, after pretty well stupefying, it wounds.

1977 Jl 18, 34:1

LA GRANDE BOURGEOISE, directed by Mauro Bolognini; produced by Lira Films-Filmarpa/Rome; director of photography, Ennio Guarnieri; music by Ennio Morricone; distributed by Atlantic Releasing Corp.; at the Paramount and Beekman theaters. Running time: 115 minutes. This film has not been rated.

Linda Murri .... Catherine Deneuve
Tullio Murri .... Giancarlo Giannini
Augusto Murri .... Fernando Rey
Rose Bonetti .... Tina Aumont
Francesco Bonmartini .... Paolo Bonicelli
Pio Naldi .... Corrado Pani
Carlo Secchi .... Ettore Manni
Augusto Stanzani .... Marcel Bozzutti

By LAWRENCE VAN GELDER

Style wars with substances in "La Grande Bourgeoise," the Italian movie with a French title that opened yesterday at the Beekman and Paramount theaters. And style wins.

Not only does substance lose; so does the audience, for in the hands of a director less enamored of surfaces and more insistent on revelation than Mauro Bolognini, "La Grande Bourgeoise" might have been an uncommonly fascinating film.

Based on the Murri affair, a turn-of-the-century Italian murder case, "La Grande Bourgeoise" raises all sorts of worthy issues: It pits socialism against monarchy; Christianity against atheism; intellectualism against narrow-mindedness, class against class.

•

It sets conventional moralists against perceived libertines; conservatives against liberals.

It traffics in the hostility of civil servants toward those they view as their betters, in the consequences of deceit, in conspiracy theories, in guilt and innocence, and the sort of punishments meted out when scandal shocks a community.

The film roots about in the perversion of journalism and politics. Its action pivots on a hellish marriage and touches upon questions about the role of women, the limits of tolerance in the face of tyranny and the justifications for divorce and murder. It has licit hate and illicit love; it has the love of brother for sister and of parent for child; the awful defeat of parental expectations; the spectacle of wasted lives.

And to all of those can be added a bit of mystery; some dogged detective work and a courtroom scene.

•

Out of the stuff of greatness, Mr. Bolognini has brought glitter. "La Grande Bourgeoise" is a movie so busy beguiling the eye with Mr. Bolognini's overwrought visual style and underscoring its action with the aural dayglo of Ennio Morricone's music that it forgets to nourish the mind or the heart.

Little wonder, then, that the big names marshaled for this film seem, like everything else in it—from clothes to landscapes to cities to interiors—to be nothing more than the surfaces against which Mr. Bolognini preens his style.

Actually, Catherine Deneuve, Giancarlo Giannini and Fernando Rey are meant to portray three members of a distinguished and highly intellectual Bologna family by the name of Murri. Miss Deneuve as Linda, to descend into description worthy of "La Grande Bourgeoise"—is locked in a hateful marriage to a cruel and reactionary boor. Mr. Giannini, as Linda's devoted brother Tullio, a brilliant lawyer and leading Socialist, plots to end her misery by murdering Francesco. And Fernando Rey, as Augusto Murri, is one of the country's great doctors and an influential, free-thinking scholar crushed by his acceptance of responsibility for his children's actions.

•

But Mr. Bolognini leaves them little scope for depth. Miss Deneuve, whose supposed frail health raises the possibility that her husband's cruelty may result in her death, appears to be afflicted with nothing more than eye strain. She puts drops in her eyes and sometimes wears granny glasses. Mr. Giannini seems to do most of his acting between the tops of his cheekbones and the base of his forehead. Furrow between eyes equals concern. Big eyes: suffering.

When mouths open, out comes sententiousness. A partial list includes: No one knows everything. Misery can't last forever. And—a man who kills another man commits a reprehensible act.

What Mr. Bolognini really likes is playing with light. It glares off faces, hands, foreheads, noses. Aureoles everywhere. Swans' necks, starched collars, glass globes, wood paneling. Bologna and Venice look lovely. People and places are seen through filters, steam, curtains and haze.

What we have here, ladies and gentlemen is "The Other Side of Midnight," Italian style. "La Grande Bourgeoise" is a movie peddling luster in the guise of illumination.

1977 Jl 19, 29:1

STRONGMAN FERDINAND, written and directed by Alexander Kluge; produced by Kairos-Film/Reitz-film; photographed by Thomas Mauch; edited by Heidi Genee; in German with English subtitles; Running time: 98 minutes. This film has not been rated. At the Jean Renoir Cinema, 100 Seventh Avenue.

Ferdinand Rieche .... Heinz Schubert
Gertie Kahlmann .... Verena Rudolph
Kniebeling .... Joachim Hackethal
Ganter .... Heinz Schimmelpfenning
Wilutzki .... Gert Guenther Hoffmann

Heinz Schubert as "Strongman Ferdinand"
Something like Hitler played by Chaplin

"Strongman Ferdinand" was shown at the 1976 New York Film Festival. The following review by Richard Eder appeared last Oct. 9. The film opened yesterday at the Jean Renoir Cinema.

THE MORNING IS SOUR and dark. Ferdinand Rieche, a security policeman demoted for overzealousness, is having breakfast. With a mournful countenance, a prominent nose and a face that resembles both mousetrap and mouse, he devours raisin cake. The radio announces a tropical storm approaching Wiesbaden.

Ferdinand grabs his atlas, locates Wiesbaden, assesses its distance from the East German frontier, road routes, rivers. He chews and ponders: who can be behind this storm?

•

This is part of the prologue of Alexander Kluge's "Strongman Ferdinand" a satire on West German society that opened yesterday at the Jean Renoir Theater. It is obsessively narrow in its focus and drawn out too far, but in its better moments—and there a lot of them—it is original, apt and very, very funny.

Nothing is so troublesome to a society as a man who follows its principles literally. To Kluge, West Germany is a society that maintains a fat complacency by making an idol of order and resistance to change.

Rieche is the dangerous total believer. He pursues order to the point where it becomes outlawry, mad yet oddly logical. Security is his profession and his obsession. When a superior at the factory where he has become chief of security—after leaving the police force—questions the usefulness of his elaborate measures, he retorts:

"With security, it's not a question of usefulness. It is a question of the whole purpose of life."

•

"Strongman Ferdinand" is the tragicomic story of what happens when Rieche—50, in poor health, his career broken by his tendency to harangue his police superiors on the need to arrest people *before* they break the law—gets a last chance.

The factory security post becomes vacant. The previous chief was discharged for placing snipers to shoot workers who break plant discipline. The press had got on to the story, and so the bosses—bland, hypocritical men—hire Rieche. They order him to do "enough, but not too much" but they have hired a one-man disaster.

Within 48 hours, Rieche has knocked down his office walls with a sledgehammer to make it bigger, turned it into an advanced communications post, begun drilling the middle-aged factory guards as an élite commando force, and put in so many locks that the washroom attendant is locked in.

Obstacles are put in the way of this small figure with the enormous head who storms around in a green trenchcoat, upsetting everything. He has to take a medical exam: his solution is to force a young woman employee caught pilfering to give him her urine sample. "Very young urine," the doctor congratulates him. "In fact, if you were a woman, I'd say you were three months pregnant."

More seriously, the factory bosses keep cracking down on him for excess; as when he and his guards raid another factory for a training exercise, or when he insists on body-searching a group of visiting American industrialists. It becomes a mounting war between Rieche and management and eventually, as the battles become more and more comically outrageous, between Rieche and a society that can't understand his efforts to defend it.

The movie is done in short, clipped sequences—there are too many of them, though—each like a brief stanza in the ballad of Rieche. The dry, deadpan style of this social fantasy is counterpointed beautifully by a camera that becomes lyrical: focusing on a full moon wrinkled by chimney smoke, or showing the security guards drilling on the beach at dawn and lit up in profile like a line of long-legged wading birds.

The harshness is redeemed even more by the character of Ferdinand himself, memorably played by Heinz Schubert. He is fond of cake and his blond taxi-driving girlfriend, Gertie. They celebrate birthdays at a midnight feast in cheap restaurants, and go on a winter trailer trip to practice for Christmas.

"Christmas needs training or it won't work," Rieche says. He is something like Chaplin; something like Hitler played by Chaplin. The combination is unforgettable.

1977 Jl 22, C9:1

THE FIRST NUDIE MUSICAL, directed by Mark Haggard and Bruce Kimmel; screenplay by Mr. Kimmel; director of photography, Douglas H. Knapp; music by Mr. Kimmel; film editor, Allen Peluso; produced by Jack Reeves; an Albert Schwartz and Imre J. Rosenthal presentation; released by Northal Film Distributors, Ltd. Running time: 95 minutes. This film is classified R. At the 68th Street Playhouse, at Third Avenue.

Harry .... Stephen Nathan
Rosie .... Cindy Williams
John .... Bruce Kimmel
Susie .... Leslie Ackerman
George .... Alan Abelew
Juanita .... Diana Canova
Mary La Ru .... Alexandra Morgan

By JANET MASLIN

At the conclusion of "The First Nudie Musical," Stephen Nathan and Cindy Williams, a clean-scrubbed couple with matching pug noses, decide to get married, he proposing shyly and she all aglow. This show of naïveté, however touching, comes as something of a surprise, since the pair have just shuffled their way through a musical number about oral sex.

Mr. Nathan is playing the son of the head of a failing movie studio, and it seems his only means of salvaging the family business involves producing, and even performing in, the world's first pornographic musical (hence the title). Surely there must have been a better way.

Since sex, at least under optimum conditions, is no laughing matter, and since comedy isn't often erotic, Mr. Nathan's brainstorm turns out to be a losing proposition—even though, according to Bruce Kimmel's screenplay, the movie-within-a-movie knocks 'em dead and saves the day.

Mr. Kimmel is something of a quadruple threat, since he has also composed a tuneless score

Cindy Williams in scene from "The First Nudie Musical."

(sample lyric: "Gotta sing, gotta dance/While I'm taking off my pants"), co-directed with Mark Haggard (on a $200,000 budget during two weeks' time, though the finished product looks considerably more fly-by-night than the figures would indicate), and cast himself in the third lead, as a fledgling director whose bashfulness borders on idiocy.

At the other end of the acting spectrum is Miss Williams. Her performance, despite some gamy dialogue, isn't much of a departure from her television work, but her pure sit-com mugging makes her the most mercifully subdued player in the bunch.

1977 Jl 25, 29:1

Barbara Bach and Roger Moore in "The Spy Who Loved Me"

THE SPY WHO LOVED ME, directed by Lewis Gilbert; screenplay by Christopher Wood and Richard Maibaum; director of photography, Claude Renoir; film editor, John Glen; music by Marvin Hamlisch; produced by Albert R. Broccoli; released by United Artists. At Loews State I, Cine, Columbia I and other theaters. Running time: 125 minutes. This film is rated PG.

James Bond .... Roger Moore
Maj. Anya Amasova .... Barbara Bach
Stromberg .... Curt Jurgens
Jaws .... Richard Kiel
Naomi .... Caroline Munro
General Gogll .... Walter Gotell
Minister of Defense .... Geoffrey Keen
"M" .... Bernard Lee
Captain Benson .... George Baker

By JANET MASLIN

DURING THE COURSE OF "The Spy Who Loved Me," James Bond vanquishes an amphibious building that looks like a giant spider, a 7 foot 2 inch villain with metal fangs, hundreds of hapless extras and one very beautiful broad, but he hardly ever comes to grips with his most insidious adversary, the James Bond formula.

The same conventions that have provided 10 Bond movies with their patent pizazz also serve as a straitjacket, and these days a Bond film is interesting only insofar as it quietly subverts the series' old tricks. Happily, "The Spy Who Loved Me" has its share of self-mockery—not enough for a full-scale send-up, but enough to give shopworn old 007 a shot in the arm.

•

The motivating sentiment behind the Bond movies has always been envy: The viewer, poor slob, is expected to covet Bond's women, admire his elaborate playthings and marvel at his ability to chase through the desert in evening clothes without getting dusty. Fifteen years ago, at the time of "Dr. No," this sort of thing was a great deal more effective than it is today, because the notion was new and the gadgets could be genuinely dazzling. But by now Bond fans have seen so many fast cars and floozies come and go that they may be almost as jaded as James himself.

Almost, but not quite: Roger Moore is so enjoyably unflappable that you sometimes have to look closely to make sure he's still breathing. Presented with a fabulous new white Lotus, he drives off impatiently without even examining the car's special accessories (as it turns out, the Lotus can swim). Seduced by a conniving cutie, he looks desperately bored.

Mr. Moore has the anonymous aplomb of a male model—appropriate, because the film is littered with trade-mark-bearing merchandise — and he seems incapable of bringing much individualized zest to the role. But his exaggerated composure amounts to a kind of backhanded liveliness. Though Mr. Moore doesn't compromise the character, he makes it amusingly clear that hedonism isn't all it's cracked up to be.

The plot this time, which bears no resemblance to that of Ian Fleming's novel, features Curt Jurgens as a shipping magnate determined to destroy the world and Barbara Bach as a Russian agent who grudgingly joins forces with Bond to pole-ax this scheme. Miss Bach is spectacular but a little dim, even by Bond standards; certainly she makes no sense as a master spy who is almost (but not quite) as ingenious as 007 himself.

In all fairness, Miss Bach's is an impossible role: Beauty and brains needn't be incompatible, but maintaining the requisite level of pulchritude of a Bond heroine is such a full-time job that it precludes any other work more strenuous than, say, watching Bond sip his very dry martini (shaken, not stirred).

•

The film moves along at a serviceable clip, but it seems half an hour too long, thanks to the obligatory shoot-'em-up conclusion, filmed on the largest soundstage in the world, but nevertheless the dullest sequence here. Bond's final blowout, however lavishly produced, has long since gotten to be old hat, and besides, it's the attention to smaller details that has helped the series maintain its high gloss.

The theme song, sung by Carly Simon, ranks with Paul McCartney's theme from "Live and Let Die" as one of the most delightful surprises the series has had to offer—even if it *is* accompanied by footage of a naked woman, in silhouette, doing silly calisthenics on the barrel of an enormous gun.

•

"The Spy Who Loved Me" has a PG ("Parental Guidance Suggested") rating even though Bond indulges in his favorite means of exercise a little more listlessly than usual. A number of extras are gunned down almost bloodlessly, and arch-villain Curt Jurgens feeds his secretary to a shark.

1977 Jl 28, C17:1

VIVA KNIEVEL!, directed by Gordon Douglas; screenplay by Antonio Santillan and Norman Katrov; story by Mr. Santillan; director of photography, Fred Jackman; music, Charles Bernstein; film editor, Harold Kress; produced by Stan Hough; distributed by Warner Bros. At neighborhood theaters. Running time: 106 minutes. This film is rated PG.

Evel Knievel .... Himself
Will Atkins .... Gene Kelly
Kate Morgan .... Lauren Hutton
Ben Andrews .... Red Buttons
Stanley Millard .... Leslie Nielsen
Frank Gifford .... Himself
Sister Charity .... Sheila Allen
Barton .... Cameron Mitchell
Tommy Atkins .... Eric Olson

THE FIRST WE SEE of Evel Knievel he is visiting an orphanage, handing out toys to children and fudge to the nuns. Then he stops by a stadium to sign some autographs and chat with his fans. Later, he returns to the stadium to make a little speech about why America's youth shouldn't get mixed up with drugs and, almost incidentally, to jump his motorcycle over a cage full of lions and tigers.

The peculiar passions that have led Mr. Knievel into his much-renowned line of work have no place in a movie hell-bent on depicting him as a wonderful guy. As far as "Viva Knievel!" is concerned, he might just as well be the world's most glamorous plumber.

Mr. Knievel—"a king of the road with a helmet for a crown," according to the title song—plays himself, more or less, in a story about crooks who plan to sabotage a motorcycle jump he will perform in Mexico and then smuggle a load of cocaine back into the United States by hiding it in his coffin. Along the way he encounters Lauren Hutton, playing a photographer who doesn't like him.

Eventually, Miss Hutton changes her tune. "Don't let it end," implores Mr. Knievel, in his characteristically expressionless tone. "I have to," Miss Hutton replies, in hers. "I'm flying out to cover that new revolution in South America." "Big deal!" Mr. Knievel snaps. "There's *always* a revolution in South America!"

Mr. Knievel and Miss Hutton are both ringers, and they should never have been forced to converse without benefit of supporting players. "Viva Knievel!"'s one noteworthy performance comes from Gene Kelly, unexpectedly touching in the role of a rummy, embittered old has-been who, through the benevolence of Mr. Knievel, gets a new lease on life. Mr. Knievel is a sedentary-looking fellow who wears diamond jewelry and white loafers even during his action sequences; Mr. Kelly is as spry as ever and puts him to shame.

JANET MASLIN

1977 Jl 28, C17:3

Is 'Senses' In the Realm Of Pornography?

By JOAN MELLEN

To Western audiences, "In the Realm of the Senses," which is graphically explicit in its depiction of an obsessive sexual affair, may seem both tediously repetitive and ultimately pornographic. True, record-breaking crowds have descended upon the Plaza theater, where the film—seized by United States Customs last fall before it could be shown at the New York Film Festival—has at last opened; yet, many people have undoubtedly been surprised and confused by what they have found.

For at the heart of Nagisa Oshima's film lie impulses quite foreign both to the Western approach to sexuality and to pornography. Oshima—known in Japan as a political filmmaker whose highly abstract work attacks social injustice and appears primarily in art houses—is here evoking an uninhibited, joyous sensuality which is said to have flourished in 10th-century Japan as an intrinsic part of an aristocratic culture in which people dedicated themselves to the appreciation of lovemaking, free of inhibition or anxiety; it was a mood reinvoked for the last time in the flurry of pleasure-seeking just prior to the opening of Japan to the West.

Out of the tradition of Prince Genji himself, hero of Lady Murasaki's celebrated novel, "The Tale of Genji," come Oshima's Sada and Kichizo, survivors of a world of sexual refinement long since lost by the 1930's—the period in which "In the Realm of the Senses" is set. Sada and Kichizo pursue the pleasure that was possible in that ancient and more beautiful Japan, heroically unwilling to allow themselves to be repressed by the culture of their own time, one in which Japan has already invaded Manchuria. Oshima suggests that sex in this old Japan was pure, divorced from psychopathology and Oedipal burdens, transcending social class. The body was as important as the spirit. He defies the premise at the heart of "Last Tango in Paris" (to which "In the Realm of the Senses" has been mistakenly compared) that we bring all that we are and have been to the act of love. In Oshima's vision, equality is at the heart of Japanese sensuality.

•

Sada begins as a maid in the brothel run by Kichizo and his wife; she calls him Master. Later she becomes the dominant partner and uses words in the Japanese language which came to be used only by men and were to be shunned by polite, well-bred women. Social position is of no relevance to the relationship between lovers.

Kichizo first approaches Sada holding a sprig of cherry blossoms, Oshima's signal that we are exploring a last flowering of authentic Japanese culture in which sensuality was sufficient unto itself, sex neither mystical nor dirty. The Japanese, says Oshima, were once capable of love without shame. As opposed to the natural Japan of the past, the modern world in which Sada and Kichizo are called "perverts" because they never cease making love is ruled by militarists; the year is 1936, that of the famous aborted Officers' Coup which finally strengthened the army's stranglehold over the country. This fascism of the 30's Oshima depicts in terms of a denial of the senses. As a troop of soldiers parade, impassive women mechanically wave Japanese flags on one side of the street. On the other, immune to nationalistic fervor, passes Kichizo, self-absorbed, fulfilled and the only one among all these people who is capable of the uninhibited physical life which, for Oshima, represents Japanese culture at its best.

In its uniquely Japanese approach to love, "In the Realm of the Senses" utterly transcends Western pornography, even though we are witnesses to the sexual act. The idyll of Sada and Kichizo, devoid of brutality, offers delight for both the man and the woman. Unlike pornography, and following the tradition of erotic art by Japanese woodblock printmakers like Utamaro and Hokusai, the love scenes focus on the sexual ecstasy of the *woman*, the pleasure in which she is an active participant rather than a victim. The male feels no need to exhibit excesses of masculinity in violence. The eroticism is based not on the woman's being humiliated or overwhelmed, but upon mutual abandon.

The Japanese ideal is for the male to be passive, the receiver of pleasure; his pride comes not from dominance but in the degree to which the woman responds. Sada pleases Kichizo by her enthusiasm and we learn that she was so successful as a prostitute because she was happy and enjoyed sex so much—another particularly Japanese point of view. With reverence, Oshima invokes the Sada who in real life became a national figure precisely because she recreated that old Japan in which nothing about the body was felt to be disgusting and in which man and woman could alternately be givers and receivers of pleasure. In defiance of any pornographic impulse, the camera focuses on their faces or on their full figures, refusing to allow the viewer to play the role of salacious voyeur. Vicarious pleasure would indeed be perverse; such satisfaction can be ours only if we become as uninhibited as are Sada and Kichizo themselves. People continually happen in upon the lovers, but such intrusions are treated with humor, not prurience, just as the lovemaking is presented beyond the claims of puritanical morality.

•

The insatiable lovers of "In the Realm of the Senses"—"an uninhibited, joyous sensuality"

'In its uniquely Japanese approach to love, the film transcends pornography, even though we are witnesses to the sexual act.'

The ending, in which Sada strangles and then dismembers Kichizo, is disturbing, but no evocation of de Sade is intended, Sada's name notwithstanding. Oshima imitates the rupture of conventional vision practiced by Bunuel, who, in the opening shot of "Un Chien Andalou," slit open an eyeball with a razor. But Kichizo's death is freely chosen as a gift to his lover, that she may "be happy strangling me." Dying, he sees everything "in red," reminded of his birth in this vision where death is as natural a phenomenon as sex. As in Western thought (c.f. de Rougemont), love and death are finally facets of the same experience. Violence has been only one element of a love affair which has also included playfulness, patient good will and joy, and Sada emasculates Kichizo with a carving knife not out of anger or hatred, but to unite herself with a lover now immune to suffering.

•

Oshima's sympathies are with this Sada who wandered around Toyko "carrying what she had cut off. . .resplendent with happiness." He has consistently shot her dressed in a red kimono, a last flame of vitality against a black background, courageously sustaining the by-now anachronistic capacity to feel purely. Sada and Kichizo are liberated, holy and sanctified, from a Japan which can no longer understand them, free from a tradition which associates sex with shame. In Sada, the sensuality of the old Japan lives on, as the real-life Sada devoted herself to further pursuits of pleasure after her four-year jail sentence expired.

Like the Japanese audience for whom Oshima has made his film, so remote are we from undiluted sensuality that much of "In the Realm of the Senses" becomes almost intolerable to watch. But, at its best it presents a striking picture of that bygone era of Japanese culture in which pornography was inconceivable and sensuality flourished, immune to any sense of sin or shame or guilt. ■

Joan Mellen is the author of "Big Bad Wolves: Masculinity in American Films," to be published in January.

1977 Jl 31, II:1:1

FILM VIEW

NORA SAYRE

Films From the Past That Still Have the Power to Panic

Those who relish being frightened by movies may be disappointed on re-examining their favorites: it's difficult to dissolve with dread a second time, and the test is probably unfair. Meanwhile, I'm told that almost nothing achieves the results of a particular training film for fledgling fathers, where the details of childbirth have prompted some punctual faintings in mid-reel.

In search of fear, your standards can soar to nearly impossible heights. You may reflect on key moments in Hitchcock: the finger missing above the knuckle in "The Thirty-Nine Steps," or the temporary blinding of a killer by flashbulbs in "Rear Window," or the desperate tennis game in "Strangers on a Train," where Farley Granger needed to win the match in three sets in order to prevent the murderer from planting a clue that would incriminate him—it was no mere question of winning, but of winning quickly enough. And seeing "Psycho" again is rather like visiting a historical monument or a national shrine; when anyone approaches the legendary staircase where Martin Balsam was stabbed—falling backward downstairs, his slashed face contorted with horror at what he'd seen—you're awed to think that this is where it happened, as though you were surveying one of the battlefields of the Civil War.

Yet "Psycho" still seems to lead when moviegoers are asked what film alarmed them most. "Diabolique" and "Repulsion" run as brisk seconds, while some mention "The Uninvited" (ranked as one of the few persuasive ghost stories, made in 1944), and Claude Chabrol's "Le Boucher," where blood dripping onto a sandwich is respectfully recalled.

Nora Sayre is the author of "Sixties Going on Seventies. She is currently working on a book about the 1950's.

Touring the terrain of the last three decades, I found sites that were certainly unnerving, granted that most of us are more fear-proof now than in the past. Although old movies are encumbered with quavery or pulsating music that diminishes the excitement for contemporary audiences, many are crammed with ingredients that enrich fear. In a truly suspenseful picture, even a sentence like "You should get some rest" can sound ominous, as can "You stay here. I'll get the car."

Much of the British "Dead of Night" (1946; sequences directed by Alberto Cavalcanti, Basil Dearden, Charles Crichton and Robert Hamer) is still delectable. The movie plays with precognition, as in the dream of the hearse driver who asserts, "Just room for one more inside, sir!," or within the coziness of the old farmhouse in Kent, where the bewildered Mervyn Johns admits that he has already dreamt about the strangers who offer him tea with milk and sugar. The film honors the tradition that a rational world can be infected by one demented person, who turns ordinary lives inside out. As is common in such movies, some are unable to convince others of the wonders or the terrors that they've seen, and their frustration intensifies the spectator's anticipation of the shocks to come.

Like many of the films of the late 1940's, "Dead of Night" seethes with psychology. A man who feels that his sanity is collapsing is told, "It's no good bottling things up, you know." Seeing a sinister, unknown room reflected in a newly-acquired mirror, he fears that the problem isn't in the furnishings, but in his mind. As his perceptions compel him to assume the personality of another, you realize how often this standby has been revived, in movies ranging from "Persona" to "3 Women." From there, it's only one step to possession, demonic or not.

Bettmann Archives

A ventriloquist is frightened by his dummy in "Dead of Night"; a wife drugs her husband in "Diabolique."

Michael Redgrave's marvelous performance in "Dead of Night" as the crazed ventriloquist who's dominated by his dummy stresses how very dangerous a rejected person can be. Frantically jealous if anyone handles the little object, he's certain that it will leave him for another partner, and the conviction hurls him into homicidal rage. Real or imagined rejection quite often ignites movie murderers: in "Strangers on a Train," Robert Walker behaved like a spurned suitor as Farley Granger grew wary of him, and few can forget how Anthony Perkins felt about his mother's lover in "Psycho."

Dreams are cleverly employed in "Dead of Night," and you can't accuse the filmmakers of trickery—as you may when a movie depends on dreaming to package a plot. Three years ago, the late Nunnally Johnson told me about his anxieties concerning "The Woman in the Window," which he wrote and Fritz Lang directed in 1944. Toward the end, Edward G. Robinson took poison. Dying slowly in a chair in an empty house, Robinson couldn't answer a ringing phone that might have meant rescue; his eyes closed. There was a close-up of his face. Then a hand shook his shoulder, the camera pulled back without a cut, and he was seen awakening at his club. The movie had a sneak preview at Pomona, where Johnson was appalled by the reaction. "When that camera pulled back, the audience let out a sound I'd never heard before—it was a wild animal sound. I didn't know if they were outraged because they'd been fooled"—or if they'd hated the entire picture. "I thought: are they going to throw things at the screen, are they so mad, do they feel cheated?" However, the movie had a succulent success.

● ● ●

The psychology of the 1940's is also conspicuous throughout Robert Siodmak's "Spiral Staircase" (1946), in which Dorothy McGuire, as a mute, is tracked by a killer who hates defects—he has already strangled a cripple, a scarred woman, and one who was retarded. His determination to rid the land of imperfections is unsettling, and the handicapped targets are particularly defenseless. (It turns out that he too was a rejectee.) Since the heroine lost her voice during a childhood trauma, it's implied that a shock will be therapeutic; even though she's "adjusted to her condition," a jolt might heal her completely. As the murderer closes in, it's apparent that he could cure almost anyone's siege of hiccups.

Miss McGuire maintains a modest dignity; although her part was a forerunner of the Audrey Hepburn roles of the 1950's, she avoids winsomeness. With its ultra-upholstered mansion rippling with chandeliers and fraught with mirrors, "Staircase" is a lavishly romantic movie, and it's too thundery and candle-ridden: the cobwebs stir too easily in any breeze. But the pace is swift, and there are many rewarding passages, as when the camera enters a closet to reveal that the killer is hiding behind a rack of clothes (we see one glaring eyeball), or when the apprehensive mute drags a stick across a fence railing to make a noise that will give her courage. Repeatedly, we're disconcerted to hear the voice of someone we didn't know was in the room—then the camera retreats to include him in the shot, and it's as though a disembodied figure had suddenly materialized.

The film is full of people who watch each other intently, hence suspicion spreads like a vast stain. In fact, "Staircase" is constructed to make you distrust almost every man who appears on the screen. Whenever there's a knock at the front door, you expect Laird Cregar or Peter Lorre, not that they're listed in the credits. Ethel Barrymore, bedridden and bad tempered as usual, contributes sombre allusions throughout.

Hitchcock was once interested in obtaining the rights to the novel on which "Diabolique" was based; it was written by the same team whose book inspired his "Vertigo." But it's hard to imagine the material in Hitchcock's hands, instead of Henri-Georges Clouzot's, whose "The Wages of Fear" (1953) is much akin to "Diabolique" (1954). In both movies, Clouzot establishes acutely dislikable characters whom he treats with contempt; then he tortures them to such an extent that you're forced to agonize over people you can't stomach. In the past, I resented that experience: I was angry as well as offended. But there's no question of Clouzot's abundant talent for manipulation.

At the boys' school in "Diabolique," the headmaster's mistress (Simone Signoret) and his wife (Vera Clouzot) plan his murder. The husband (Paul Meurisse), a suave sadist who slaps both women around and tyrannizes his staff and students, is clearly capable of intricate and lurid cruelties, so we can't feel for the potential victim. The Signoret of the mid-fifties is muscular yet lush: there's a brutal authority in all of her gestures and movements, whether she's disciplining small boys or giving someone an injection or smoking impatiently. Deft at deceit—she's splendid when she performs a role within a role—she conveys a merciless hostility toward everyone. Vera Clouzot is probably the most replellent of the three: a pathetic invalid who's also a spiteful hypocrite. Dishonest with herself, she's as flaccid as a crab that's lost its carapace. The director forbids us to even pity her, and her illness is rather sickening in itself.

The main characters endow the whole picture with a bitter moral stink. A pool festering with the scum of floating algae sets the tone. Due to the headmaster's obscene stinginess, the school food is polluted, and you're made to feel that the unhappy children are unpleasant. As in "The Wages of Fear," we're driven to expect extreme physical suffering—although it may not actually occur. In the grimmest scenes, there's an intelligent use of silence, flavored by an occasional creak—no obtrusive music here. And I savor the appearance of a classic figure: the benign detective who is so threatening to others, played with rumpled zest by Charles Vanel. The audience is on marshy ground at the movie's midpoint: we're slugged with suggestions of the supernatural, but don't know whether to accept them. The build-up is slow and the film does lag at times, but the famous bathtub sequences could still electrify a first-time viewer.

Although Roman Polanski's "Repulsion" (1965) is tremendously dated, the first half is worthy of inspection. Polanski once said that he would like to make a movie that contained only one character; solitude has always engrossed him. Here, the deepening isolation of a young woman who's sliding into insanity explores the theme that Polanski would later garble in "The Tenant." Catherine Deneuve, the manicurist who bites her nails, has two parallel aversions: food and sex. Dressed and coiffed to attract the men she flees, she feels violated by the mere presence of a male. (Deneuve was fleshier, more tangible then—she hadn't yet borrowed the lofty perfections of Grace Kelly.) When she cautiously brushes a speck of grit from her face, it's plain that she can't bear to be touched—not even by her own hands. As her mind crumbles while she's alone in an empty apartment, we share her hallucinations, such as a sudden, terrifying glimpse of an imaginary man reflected in a swinging mirror. Nothing around her is stable: the walls crack noisily when she touches or looks at them, as though she were in an air raid. But she's only being bombarded by her own emotions.

The film moves from quiet agitation to outright fury. When Miss Deneuve slays two men, the style of stabbing is drawn from "Psycho"; a tribute to the plumbing in "Diabolique" follows. Halfway through, the performances and the images deteriorate. Miss Deneuve lapses into a witless stare and then becomes a cut-rate Ophelia, equippped with a mad little smile. She has some trite rape fantasies, but one doubts the aggressiveness of the real men who pursue her, especially a barking landlord who's instantly converted into a jolly lecher. As scores of hands burst through the walls to clutch at her, Polanski rings up a debt to Cocteau, and the movie lunges into the pretentious. (Wild improbability doesn't diminish a frightening film, but artificiality is fatal.) Moreover, you grow restless because you never learn what ails this deranged creature, although Polanski seems to nurture the notion that all a woman needs is one good rape.

Early on, there is a sense of genuine disintegration. But later, the film's murky affectations sabotage the spectator's respect. The camera returns lovingly to some sprouting potatoes and a rotting rabbit: a meal that was never prepared. Some might deduce that the heroine would not have gone berserk if she had cooked them, and that the moral of the movie is to stay in the kitchen and have a good dinner. ■

1977 Jl 31, II:11:1

OUTRAGEOUS!, written and directed by Richard Benner, based on a story from "Butterfly Ward" by Margaret Gibson; director of photography, James B. Kelly; editor, George Appleby; music by Paul Hoffert; produced by William Marshall and Hendrick J. Van Der Kolk; a Herbert R. Steinman and Billy Baxter Presentation. At the Cinema I Theater, Third Avenue and 60th Street. Running time; 96 minutes. This film is rated R.

Robin Turner .... Craig Russell
Liza Connors .... Hollis McLaren
Perry .... Richert Easley
Martin .... Allan Moyle
Bob .... David McIlwraith
Jason .... Jerry Salzberg
Anne .... Andree Pelletier
Jo .... Helen Shaver

By JANET MASLIN

"Outrageous!" tells two stories, only vaguely connected, one about a schizophrenic girl and the other about a homosexual hairdresser. Liza, the girl, has recently escaped from a mental hospital and moved into Robin's apartment, where she chatters hysterically about how, because she is the one who was born dead, the bone-crushers are going to come and grind her bones to powder.

Robin isn't much more lucid himself. One evening, after a hard day at the salon, he complains that "these women here, they live life like it's a can of Coke and they're afraid to drink it too fast or it'll all be gone. Life *isn't* a can of Coke."

●

"Outrageous!" is entirely sympathetic to these characters, trying to show how the rest of the world misunderstands them and why their wackiness makes them wonderful. Unfortunately, the movie winds up exploiting them in an insidious and very unpleasant way. Robin and Liza seem to define themselves through their ability to shock or at least unsettle those around them. The camera, in attempting to play along with this, merely ogles them, accentuating their freakishness without offering much insight into why, for each of them, flamboyance is so desperately important.

It could be argued that "Outrageous!," a low-budget Canadian production set mostly in Toronto, presents a no-holds-barred look at a certain stratum of homosexual culture and is thus noteworthy for its verisimilitude. But a film in which nobody ever seems to stop screaming unwittingly enforces stereotypes as dangerous as those favored by Anita Bryant.

Craig Russell and Hollis McLaren are more than convincing as Robin and Liza, but they're a little hard to watch; Miss McLaren, in particular, is either a brilliantly skittish performer or an authentic nervous wreck. Much of the film is devoted to showcasing Mr. Russell's talents as a female impersonator, because he eventually hangs up his blow dryer ("I'm *sick* of doing everyone else's head!") to seek his fortune in Manhattan's homosexual nightclubs.

1977 Ag 1, 20:1

Mechanical Mind

HERBIE GOES TO MONTE CARLO, directed by Vincent McEveety; produced by Ron Miller; director of photography, Leonard J. South; written by Arthur Alsberg and Don Nelson; music by Frank De Vol; distributed by Buena Vista Distribution Co., Inc.; presented by Walt Disney Productions; at neighborhood theaters. Running time: 105 minutes. This film has been rated G.

Jim Douglas .... Dean Jones
Wheely Applegate .... Don Knotts
Diane Darcy .... Julie Sommars
Inspector Bouchet .... Jacques Marin
Quincey .... Rory Kinnear
Max .... Bernard Fox
Bruno Von Stickle .... Eric Braeden
Detective Fontenoy .... Xavier Saint Macary

HERBIE, the 1963 Volkswagen Beetle with a mind—and heart—of his own and the power to cloud juvenile minds, is back again.

This time, the little car that became a box-office star in "The Love Bug" in 1969 and demonstrated continuing popularity in "Herbie Rides Again" (1974) is off to the races in Europe. The latest vehicle for the vehicle is "Herbie Goes to Monte Carlo," which opened yesterday at neighborhood theaters.

Herbie, already the under-Beetle in a race from Paris to Monaco against more dazzling looking cars and more dashing crews than folksy Dean Jones and pop-eyed Don Knotts, faces a couple of additional complications: a $6 million diamond dropped in his gas tank by jewel thieves led by a crooked police inspector; and falling in love with a powder blue Lancia that is one of his rivals in the race.

•

Does Herbie win? Does Herbie help foil the jewel thieves? Does true love triumph?

Countless people will probably pay to find out the answers despite special effects in which the actors appear repeatedly in black outline and occasionally distorted perspective; and an assortment of tricks (rearing up on hind wheels, blushing and blinking his lights) that possesses a somewhat limited power to captivate.

Reluctant adults marched off to "Herbie" by tiny press gangs may take what consolation they can from the scenery, featuring France and Monaco.

LAWRENCE VAN GELDER

1977 Ag 4, C14:1

Driving Ambition

GREASED LIGHTNING, directed by Michael Schultz; written by Kenneth Vose and Lawrence DuKore, Melvin Van Peebles and Leon Capetanos; director of photography, George Bouillet; edited by Bob Wyman, Christopher Holmes and Randy Roberts; music by Fred Karlin; produced by Hannah Weinstein; released by Warner Bros.; a Third World Cinema Productions Film. At the New Amsterdam, Victoria and other theaters. Running time: 96 minutes. This film is classified PG.

Wendell Scott	Richard Pryor
Hutch	Beau Bridges
Mary	Pam Grier
Peewee	Cleavon Little
Sherriff Cotton	Vincent Gardenia
Woodrow	Richie Havens
Russell	Julian Bond

RICHARD PRYOR isn't very funny in "Greased Lightning," and if you don't think that sounds like an accomplishment, well, think again. Mr. Pryor has a gift for being almost effortlessly amusing, so much so that movie audiences often burst out laughing at the mere sight of him. The first few minutes of "Greased Lightning" are a little dicey for that reason, until it becomes clear that Mr. Pryor is out to give a coolly sustained dramatic performance, even a rather subtle one. After that, it's smooth sailing all the way.

•

"Greased Lightning" is a winning biography of Wendell Scott, the first black stock-car racing champion. Mr. Scott started out driving a taxi after World War II, learned his craft by briefly running moonshine in the backwoods of Virginia. By the mid-1960's he was a veteran driver who had won his battles with those white racetrack owners and law officers who once hoped to cramp his style.

The film notes this passage of time inexpensively, mostly through ever-changing car models and different amounts of talcum powder in Mr. Pryor's hair. But it lavishes a great deal of energy upon tracing Mr. Scott's evolution from a secretive figure, both frightened and exhilarated by his own ambitions, to a hero a little saddened by the fact that his triumphs are mostly behind him. Mr. Pryor is especially successful in presenting Mr. Scott as a man who guards his energy and intelligence carefully, betraying very little to his enemies and saving a great deal for the moments that matter.

•

Michael Schultz, the erratic and innovative black director responsible for both the verisimilitude of "Cooley High" and the jive of "Car Wash" is this time at his most quietly telling, as he incorporates a warm sense of Mr. Scott's family ties into a broader,

Richard Pryor.

slightly harsher portrait of the era in which he came to maturity. The film perceives a symbiotic relationship between black and white cultures of the day, and it presents racism almost matter-of-factly, as a by-product of cross-cultural confusion.

In one scene, Mr. Scott became so furious that he calls a white man a "nigger." Beau Bridges, as a white driver who taunts Mr. Scott at their first meeting, is shown to be an all-around sorehead who uses racism as a convenient outlet for his otherwise-undirected rage. He and Mr. Scott soon become fast friends, the early trouble between them apparently forgotten. In one of the film's most crowd-pleasing episodes, they use a steak dinner and a Confederate flag to hold at bay a restaurant full of white patrons, who clearly find Mr. Bridges' character the more dangerous and unsavory of the two.

•

Mr. Bridges has been giving all the right performances in all the wrong movies lately, but this time he comes into his own; his performance here, which recalls his brother Jeff's in another movie about a racing driver, "The Last American Hero," has a crackling vitality, especially when he banters with Mr. Pryor. Mr. Schultz has taken chances in his casting, with performers ranging from Julian Bond to Richie Havens, but everyone does

Cleavon Little is especially effective as Mr. Scott's friend and confidant. Pam Grier, as Mr. Scott's preternaturally patient wife, manages at times to make herself seem almost inconspicuous, which constitutes a triumph of willpower over natural assets even more impressive than that of her co-star.

•

"Greased Lightning" is rated PG ("Parental Guidance Suggested"), partly because of the words that are tossed around when tempers flare, and partly because of the sweet, low-key sexual chemistry that seems to exist between Mr. Pryor and Miss Grier.

JANET MASLIN

1977 Ag 4, C14:1

Shell Game

RACE FOR YOUR LIFE, CHARLIE BROWN, directed by Bill Melendez; written and created by Charles M. Schulz; animation by Don Lusk, Bob Matz, Hank Smith, Rod Scribner, Ken O'Brien, Al Pabian, Joe Roman, Jeff Hall, Sam Jaimes, Bob Bachman, George Singer, Bill Littlejohn, Bob Carlson, Patricia Joy, Terry Lennon and Larry Leichliter; music by Ed Bogas; editing, Chuck McCann and Roger Donley; released by Paramount Pictures. At the Olympia and other theaters. Running time: 75 minutes. This film is classified G.

"RACE FOR YOUR LIFE, Charlie Brown" packs the "Peanuts" gang off to a summer camp that doesn't require counselors, because the kids come equipped with adults-sized neuroses of their own. Sally moons over Linus, Peppermint Patty rigs all the bunk elections and Charlie Brown worries about whether he has leadership qualities, especially after one of the local bullies declares that "that round-headed kid is a *joke*." Snoopy, ever the scene-stealer, races across the desert on a souped-up cycle, "Easy Rider"-style. In short, everyone is up to his or her perennially adorable old tricks.

This is the third of the Charlie Brown features (there have also been 16 television specials, and a 17th is in progress), but the animated "Peanuts," as directed by Bill Melendez, isn't that much of a departure from Charles M. Schulz's 25-year-old comic strip. The film runs an hour and quarter and has a rambling plot about a regatta, but it seems less like a continuous story than a series of droll blackout sketches, many of them ending with the obligatory "Good Grief!"

The animation is as purposefully spare as the format, often seeming even more two-dimensional than Mr. Schulz's newspaper drawings. The net effect is that of having read the comic strip for an unusually long spell, which can amount to either a delightful experience or a pleasant but slightly wearing one, depending upon the intensity of one's fascination with the basic "Peanuts" mystique.

JANET MASLIN

1977 Ag 4, C14:1

A 'Jaws' With Flaws

TENTACLES, directed by Oliver Hellman; executive producer, Ovidio Assonities; produced by Enzo Doria; written by Jerome Max, Tito Carpi and Steve Carabatsos; director of photography, Roberto D'Ettore Piazzoli; music by S. W. Cipriani; director of marine and underwater sequences, Nestore Ungaro. An American International Release; at negihborhood theaters. Running time 90 minutes. This movie has been rated PG.

Ned Turner	John Huston
Tillie Turner	Shelley Winters
Will Gleason	Bo Hopkins
Mr. Whitehead	Henry Fonda
John Corey	Cesare Danova
Mike	Alan Boyd
Captain Robards	Claude Akins

By LAWRENCE VAN GELDER

BACK IN THE days before Bruce the shark and Orca the killer whale, people who were foolhardy enough to venture near salt water in adventure movies—especially those set in the South Seas—were likely to find themselves in the toils of a giant octopus.

Well, it's back to those thrilling days of yesteryear in "Tentacles," the all-too-familiar giant octopus movie that opened yesterday at neighborhood theaters.

This one isn't set in the South Seas. Influenced by "Jaws," and up-to-date in its use of this summer's fad mammal, the killer whale, "Tentacles" is set on the California coast, where underwater radio waves of illegal frequency, authorized by a corrupt executive of a construction company, rile a giant octopus.

Among the dozen or so victims are a baby, a boatyard worker, a very fat man and the wife of the oceanographer who ultimately solves the mystery of the deaths and settles the monster's hash with the aid of a pair of killer whales.

John Huston plays the nosey reporter; Claude Akins is the local lawman who wants to keep the lid on the strange doings. Henry Fonda turns up as the industrialist initially unaware of the use of the illegal radio frequencies by his aide, Cesare Danova. Shelley Winters plays the blowsy sister of the reporter and the mother of a young boy imperiled by the monster during a children's sailboat race; and, in a generally unelectrifying cast, Bo Hopkins takes honors for torpidity with his depiction of the oceanographer.

People who are immune to atrocious acting in minor roles; to occasionally poor dubbing; to a totally unoriginal story; to the sort of sloppiness that allows at least one reference to the octopus as a squid; and to a climactic sequence that looks like feeding time at the aquarium when it is at all intelligible, will cull the exceedingly minor rewards of "Tentacles" from some realistic underwater photography, a nicely manipulative opening sequence in which the baby vanishes; and the bobbing corpse gimmick that was more shocking than anything else in "Jaws."

•

The PG (Parental Guidance Suggested) rating of "Tentacles" is probably attributed to its one scary sequence, involving a corpse, and to the high death toll.

1977 Ag 4, C14:5

Root of All Good

THE GREAT MADCAP (EL GRAN CALAVERA), directed by Luis Bunuel; screenplay (Spanish with English subtitles) by Raquel Rojas and Luis Alcoriza, from a comedy by Adolfo Torrado; photography, Ezequiel Carrascu; music, Manuel Esperon; editing by Carlos Savage; produced by Ultramar Films S.A. (Oscar Dancigers). At the Jean Renoir Cinema, 100 Seventh Avenue. Running time: 90 minutes. This film has not been rated.
WITH: Fernando Soler, Andres Soler, Luis Alcoriza, Rosario Granados, Maruja Grifell, Antonio Bravo, Ruben Rojo, Gustavo Rojo and Francisco Jambrina.

By JANET MASLIN

"THE GREAT MADCAP" is an atypically sunny, relatively slight Luis Buñuel film, made in Mexico in 1949 but only now enjoying its first New York theatrical run at the Jean Renoir Cinema, which will be the local host of premieres of three more Buñuel films in weeks to come.

The title refers to a Mexican millionaire who begins drowning his sorrow after his wife's death and, as the film opens, has just spent a night in the cooler, cheek by jowl with a bunch of friendly bums. He fits in quite nicely, which is convenient, because the millionaire's good-for-nothing family is hatching a plot that will leave him in rags for real.

It seems that the family—a socialite daughter, playboy son, snooty brother and hypochondriac sister-in-law—has decided that the only way to keep everybody's favorite moneybags sober is to convince him that he has already squandered his fortune. The relatives forsake their hacienda to rent a shabby apartment and don very neat work clothes, in an effort to convince him that times are rough. Their ruse doesn't work—and why should it? They still sneak cream puffs when the old man isn't looking.

•

Rosario Granados and Ruben Rojo in "The Great Madcap"
In a Bunuel film, a happy ending?

But the millionaire comes up with a scheme of his own, and it's a wonderful success: He convinces the others that they really *are* poor and, as if by magic, these freeloaders learn to support themselves. Pretty soon everyone is back home in the mansion, where the snooty brother mends gilt furniture and the sister-in-law bakes bread. The lazy son decides to go back to college, and the daughter breaks off with a gigolo to marry a diligent poor boy she met in the slums. Through it all, the millionaire beams wisely. Everybody lives more than happily ever after.

This story, based on a comedy by Adolfo Torrado, would have amounted only to the airiest of fluff had not Buñuel taken merry advantage of the plot's several layers of deceit. The film, which has an exaggerated visual elegance to match its characters' fine manners, contains several delightful episodes in which the family's cordiality, never worth much in the first place, is worn even thinner than usual by everyone's complete uncertainty about just what everyone else is up to. But, Buñuel being Buñuel, politesse easily prevails at the expense of reason.

1977 Ag 5, C7:1

MARCH OR DIE, directed by Dick Richards; screenplay by David Zelag Goodman; story by Mr. Goodman and Mr. Richards; cinematographer, John Alcott; music by Maurice Jarre; film editor, O. Nicholas Brown; produced by Mr. Richards and Jerry Bruckheimer. At Loews State 2, Tower East, 34th Street East and neighborhood theaters. Running time: 106 minutes. This film is classified PG.

Major William Sherman Foster....Gene Hackman
Marco Segrain....Terence Hill
Francois Marneau....Max Von Sydow
Simone Picard....Catherine Deneuve
El Krim....Ian Holm
Sgt. Triand....Rufus
Ivan....Jack O'Halloran
Lt. Fontaine....Marcel Bozzuffi

By JANET MASLIN

Because he has almost nothing to say, and especially because he always seems to be winking at the camera, spaghetti-western star Terence Hill is the only truly lively figure in "March Or Die." No one else in the film's peculiarly listless all-star cast has much to say either—but none of these others has the good grace to keep still.

Gene Hackman and Catherine Deneuver in "March or Die."
Part of a peculiarly listless all-star cast.

Take Gene Hackman, for instance, as a Foreign Legion major who has clearly been out in the hot sun too long; Mr. Hackman is forever muttering about "the trenches," and the horrors he has seen while fighting in them. Catherine Deneuve, as a gorgeous (though slightly less gorgeous than usual) widow, likes to rattle on about amour and archeology, the latter also being a pet subject of Max Von Sydow's (he plays a scientist out on a dig). "March Or Die" is an extraordinarily wooden movie that, while ostensibly being about the futility of battle, actually has more to do with the futility of making movies about that futility.

Dick Richards, who also directed "Farewell, My Lovely," has a good eye for eccentric faces and backgrounds; he comes up with a few memorable human tableaux here, as when a bunch of legionnaires stand quietly in a sepia-toned glow, listening to a pianist play "Plaisir D'Amour." Unfortunately, Mr. Richards's talents are ill-suited to his material here, and the static quality of the film's better movements only calls attention to the inadequacy of its action sequences.

The story is complicated, comprising a dewy-eyed love affair between Miss Deneuve and Mr. Hill, an apparent one-nighter between Miss Deneuve and Mr. Hackman, a variety of lost souls who have come to the desert to forget their grubby pasts, a Legion assignment to protect Mr. Von Sydow as he excavates a priceless tomb, and the Arabs' indignation at these intruders and their grave-robbing. Although a few of these subplots may have a romantic ring to them, the movie's general tone is as hard-boiled as its title.

Blood is shed messily and often, and many vignettes are designed to illustrate what a he-man a true legionnaire must be. One particular episode, which culminates in a weakling legionnaire's suicide after the others find out he has been impotent with a whore, is aimed strictly at the sort of filmgoer who eats carpet tacks for breakfast.

•

"March Or Die" is rated PG ("Parental Guidance Suggested"), and for good reason; it contains some extremely gruesome scenes of mutilation that may well bother small children.

1977 Ag 6, 9:1

FILM VIEW

NORA SAYRE

Did Cooper and Stewart Have to Be So Stupid?

Dogs don't hesitate: they fold up at their feet. And although they respond easily to "the wonders of nature," they're apt to be caught in the rain: innocence is established by a drenched coat and a sopping hat. Quick grins or brief guffaws convey integrity. Colliding with furniture and lamps, they fumble with their fedoras, and frequently get lost: there's a tendency to take the wrong bus, also to eat cookies out of a paper bag, or to order milk in a saloon. Brass bands that blare in their honor make them flinch, and they recoil from admirers who rush to clasp their paws. Unhappy in tuxedos, enlivened by harmonicas, worshipful toward women—one of them was once seen kissing a wilting corsage before he pressed it between the pages of a book—prone to hurl sudden punches at impious persons, they rub their cheeks slowly when bewildered, and close their eyes before making a big decision. Quite often, reading seems difficult for them. But the backs of their necks tingle when they hear the national anthem, and their lips constantly part with awe—or their jaws drop with pleasure or shock. They seem likely to pant when eager, and perhaps it's the perpetual dogginess of these men that captivates their canine counterparts.

The male naif, as embodied by Gary Cooper and James Stewart some three to four decades ago, is a startling and even rather disturbing phenomenon when inspected in the 1970's—not merely because we're accustomed to anti-heroes. Granted that goodness used to be popular, and that the rustic who triumphs over the treacheries of the city is an American favorite, the fact that Cooper and Stewart persisted as stars throughout the sophistications of the 1930's and 40's seems quite amazing today. Probity and purity can be appreciated; these are men you can't bribe. But must they be stupid? Again and again, their roles proclaimed stupidity as a virtue: With radiant pride, they uttered such lines as "I'm just a simple guy still wet behind the ears," or "I'm just a mug and I know it." Since many historians have been re-evaluating womens' parts in old movies, it seems time to do the same for a couple of the men—and Cooper and Stewart were hardly flattering to their sex.

You might argue that stupidity was associated with strength, due to the frontier tradition. But often, these two weren't loners or frontiersmen—in Frank Capra's films, for example, Cooper and Stewart were terribly dependent on being coached and propped up by women like Jean Arthur, whose brainpower outran the simpletons'. In "Meet John

Nora Sayre is the author of "Sixties Going on Seventies." She is currently working on a book about the 1950's.

Bettmann Archives

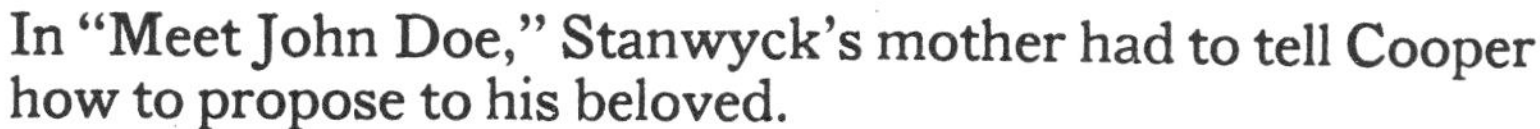

In "Meet John Doe," Stanwyck's mother had to tell Cooper how to propose to his beloved.

Sex was foreign territory to Stewart in "Mr. Smith Goes to Washington."

Doe," Cooper is Barbara Stanwyck's creation: not only does she comb his hair while moulding his character, but her mother has to tell him how to propose to his beloved. (Actually, he wants the mother to do it for him.) In many of his movies, Cooper's mind works so sluggishly that he seems mentally deficient: the thoughts rise as slowly as bubbles in a gassy swamp. Early in Sam Wood's "The Pride of the Yankees" (1942), when approached by the renowned team, he asks warily, "You mean—the New . . . York . . . Yankees?" as though he fears that he might be drafted to fight the Civil War.

In "Mr. Smith Goes to Washington," Claude Rains as a perfidious Senator sternly warns Stewart: "This is a man's world . . . You'll only get hurt." The naif is a small boy without Tom Sawyer's or Huck Finn's ability to outsmart his seniors. Rains repeats: "It's a man's world." In that realm, the vast child is also told, "You gotta face facts," which means "playing ball" in unsavory situations.

Invariably, the child-man was supposed to make women feel maternal: to want to draw the covers up to his chin and tuck him in. And certainly, after years of watching macho actors, one finds the gentleness of the early Stewart or Cooper appealing. But, eventually, what's troubling about their personae becomes clear; as children and fools they're not equals—therefore not attractive to a contemporary woman. Dumbness was meant to be lovable, but now retardation seems no more alluring than the image of the backward blonde.

The naifs were also assumed to be admirable because they would not—or could not—express emotions. Masculinity in movies used to mean being unmoved. Stewart spent much of his career chewing on an imaginary cud, and Cooper seemed to be zippered into some girdle of the emotions, which was appropriate for Fred Zinnemann's "High Noon" (1952), but not the best foundation for melodrama or romantic comedy. It's almost inconceivable that filmmakers would put such creatures on the screen today, and these roles began to change after the 40's. Although Anthony Perkins in the 50's and Dustin Hoffman in the 60's did play updated naifs, both were allowed to be intelligent as well as vulnerable. But you can't picture either Al Pacino or Robert De Niro being astounded when a woman has the boldness to telephone him, or gasping "Holy mackeral!," or encouraging his mother to sit on his lap—then giving her his fraternity pledge pin and adding, "You'll have to go steady with me."

Sex was foreign territory for Cooper and Stewart; as they trudge through some of the most tepid courtships in film history, you may wonder which was the least erotic actor. But my choice would be Cooper. When he played Lou Gehrig, he had a line that was quintessential for both actors: "What does it mean when a girl says that you remind her of a Newfoundland puppy?" In "Meet John Doe," he gazes at a sandwich with more longing than he ever bestowed on a woman, though he does focus guiltily on a small nude statuette. Elsewhere, paired with Marlene Dietrich, he was a totally dry blanket; few could say "We're alone" with so little zest. And when he had to exclaim, "I'm insane about you," he sounded as though he was ordering some golf clubs. During King Vidor's "The Fountainhead" (1949), where he was meant to be lustful as well as worldly, he grew more passive as Patricia Neal became more passionate, and he could only raise an eyebrow when she bared her teeth. Straining for sexuality, he managed to look kindly and benign. Even as an Ayn Rand hero, an architectural genius who electrified the public by his daring, he kept the habit of peering at his shoes, or tugging at his lapels to convey individuality.

• • •

"There's something swell about the spirit of Christmas": the lines that were constructed for the naifs must sometimes have convulsed the script writers; even when a comedy was built around Cooper or Stewart as a straight man, it must have been amusing to make the handsome stumblewits assert that "Things sure do happen fast around here, don't they?" or "Gee whiz, I'm all mixed up." Jokes were not their domain; instead, the audience laughed at what happened to them or in spite of them. Still, Cooper is at his most comic in "The Fountainhead," where he has to torture his tongue around sentences like "A building has integrity, just like a man—and just as seldom," or "There is no such thing as a collective brain."

Blinking was crucial to the style of both actors. However, when one reflects on Cooper, one's respect for Stewart expands: despite his limitations, he was far more skilled as an actor. Predictably, directors like Capra and Hitchcock brought out his best. While he was hopelessly dreary in pictures like Sam Wood's "The Stratton Story" (1949), he flourished in Capra's "It's a Wonderful Life" (1946), where he was permitted some canniness, and in George Marshall's "Destry Rides Again" (1939), where he was meant to seem clever because he pretended to be stupid. But Cooper was leaden even in an enchanting comedy like Frank Borzage's "Desire" (1936), and it's a tribute to all concerned that he didn't ruin the movie.

Stewart was gifted at listening to others: whether he was suspicious or admiring of them, his wordless stare was superior to Cooper's. In many of the latter's movies, the camera had to leave his face during the key speeches of his co-stars; sometimes we see only the back of his head when he declares his ardor on his loneliness. When acutely upset, he carefully clenches a fist; profoundly angered, he tightens his jaw slightly—he simply couldn't do more. It seems mystifying that such a phlegmatic person could have become a star—until you remember his extraordinary early beauty in Josef von Sternberg's "Morocco" (1930). The face explains his fledgling success, though not his staying power.

• • •

Let's be enduringly grateful that Cooper wasn't cast instead of Stewart in Capra's "Mr. Smith Goes to Washington" (1939). The movie seems nearly flawless today, and the pacing is delicious: The best comedies of the 1930's make many contemporary films appear to have been designed for languid responses. Then, movies made for the mass market assumed that the audience was quickwitted. The plight of the naive young Senator who was selected to be a stooge, but who defies the forces of corruption, can be seen as a rather subtle indictment of the political system. Innocence does triumph, but such a brainless man could never have been effective if the cynical establishment hadn't hired him to begin with. The character succeeds not because he's nimble but because the powers pitched against him are rotting—hence vulnerable in themselves.

Meanwhile, it's a bit surprising to learn from Capra's memoirs that he didn't foresee the indignant Washington reaction to "Mr. Smith." Some politicians were outraged that a movie dared to depict graft in the Senate, just as many local reporters were furious when a newsman was portrayed as a keen drinker. After much booing, a third of the first night's audience of celebrities walked out. Although Capra's fervent patriotism floods through the entire movie, several Senators denounced it, some Hollywood executives feared that—in

> 'The male naif is a startling and disturbing phenomenon when inspected in the 1970's—even in an era of anti-heroes.'

retaliation—Congress would pass a bill that would curtail distribution throughout the industry, and other studios put pressure on Columbia to withdraw the film from circulation. Joseph Kennedy, then ambassador to London, cabled Harry Cohn, chief of Columbia, to urge that the movie not be shown abroad; Capra recalled that Kennedy felt that "it would be a blow to the morale of our allies . . . [and] it might be construed as propaganda favoring the Axis powers." In retrospect, the uproar seems ridiculous. But, at the same time, veterans of the 60's and Watergate will catch the implication that the American system may be destroying itself; actually, we may be even more sensitive to that theme than the audiences of 1939.

Also, we're struck by the vigor of the social criticism in Sidney Buchman's script, which isn't dampened by the sentiment that irrigated Capra's other movies. (Currently, we're quite indulgent of the sentimentality of the films of the 30's and 40's: we accept it as an historical style.) "Meet John Doe" (1941), which completed Capra's political trilogy of "Mr. Deeds Goes to Town" (1936) and "Mr. Smith," is a lesser movie, but it's fascinating as a companion piece. Just as "Mr. Smith" seems rather radical in 1977, "John Doe" appears more conservative than was probably intended.

Encircled by poverty, Gary Cooper becomes the accidental leader of a totally apolitical movement, which is projected as preferable to politics per se—though the citizens do march on Washington to demand "clean government." All politics are suspect: "It's because of all those slimy politicians that we have all this unemployment!" Cooper represents the "typical American," identified as "the world's greatest stooge and the world's greatest strength." The essence of his movement is being kind to your neighbors "and asking for nothing in return." Tycoons collaborate to exploit "the little people": when the wicked gather, their snowy shirt bosoms gleam beneath chandeliers and among candelabra, and you realize that it's almost fatal to trust anyone who has a bank account.

In 1941, Capra's targets were American right-wing groups which he felt were helpful to Hitler. He wrote that "little 'fuhrers' were springing up in America, to proclaim that freedom was weak, sterile, passé. The 'new wave' was Blood Power! Destroy the weak, the Jews, the blacks, destroy Christianity . . ." But when Cooper's troops mass together in "John Doe," a spectator of the 70's can't help but remember how the concept of the Silent Majority was employed in the Nixon years. Also, in this movie, the "peoples' " conventions combine the atmosphere of a George Wallace rally of the late 60's with that of a John Birch Society conference. (I speak from experience, having attended both.) And the movie's contradictions become more intricate: When a villain says, "What the American people need is an iron hand," the director was of course protesting fascism; however, the plea for populism suggests an endorsement of the mob—which, after a surge of brutality, turns out to be warmhearted after all.

Naturally, Cooper survives; again, the male naif abides through chance rather than dexterity. For all his incompetence, the character was thought pivotal to movies aimed at audiences that were expected to be suspicious of the educated or the sophisticated. And at present, the jubilant endings of a number of Capra's other films can momentarily dilute our skepticism— because we view them as fantasy, and because the witless movie hero is now almost extinct. Hence he's no longer a threat—to Wall Street or Washington, or to anyone's self image. ■

1977 Ag 7, II:11:1

SANDAKAN 8, directed by Kei Kumai; screenplay (Japanese with English subtitles) by Mr. Kumai and Sakae Hirozawa; original story by Tomoko Yamazaki; camera, Mitsuji Kaneo; presented by Peppercorn-Wormser Inc. At the Fine Arts Theater, 58th Street between Park and Lexington Avenues. Running time: 120 minutes. This film has not been rated.

Old Woman .... Kinuyo Tanaka
Young Woman .... Yoko Takashi
Young Writer .... Komaki Kurihara

By JANET MASLIN

"Sandakan 8" is a Japanese film about prostitution, narrated from what is supposed to be a feminist point of view. However feminism, in this case, only means interjecting a particularly noxious form of man-hating where the pornographic touches ordinarily might be.

•

The film doesn't dwell on sex unnecessarily, but it's plenty lurid just the same, in a disturbingly neo-Victorian way. This kind of treatment can't pass for enlightened, not by any stretch of the imagination. It's just plain reactionary.

The story is told by a saccharine middle-class woman, a feminist historian of sorts, who encounters Osaki, a former karayuki-san, a term for girls who were sold into prostitution early in the century and then shipped out to colonies all over the Pacific. Osaki, now impoverished and nearly 70, invites the historian to her hovel, where the younger woman begins behaving like Little Miss Muffet, cringing prettily at the worms in the bath water.

The historian just barely manages to stifle her revulsion until the old lady decides to tell her story, which turns out not to have been worth waiting for. Sample pearl: "Don't fall in love, no matter what. When you're in love, you're blind."

Osaki's tale, told in flashback, repeatedly illustrates what loathsome brutes men are, and the historian, in a series of senseless cuts to the present, keeps on nodding sympathetically. Along the way, there is also some mention of Japanese imperialism, and of the homeland's hypocrisy in shunning the karayuki-san when they tried to return from the colonies. But most of the film, which is artlessly shot and acted in an exaggerated, melodramatic style, concentrates on proving that there really is a fate worse than death.

Yoko Takashi in "Sandakan 8"
She has some impressive moments

•

Yoko Takahashi and Kinuyo Tanaka, two lovely actresses who play Osaki as a young girl and an old woman, have some impressive moments, on those few occasions when Kei Kumai's direction allows for any subtlety. As the historian, Komaki Kurihara wears an impenetrably pasty smile and does more harm than good. Osaki's story might have retained some of its integrity had it not been set in flashback; this way, too many present-day ironies are allowed to interrupt it, trivialize it and blunt its power.

1977 Ag 8, 18:1

Call in the Family

SATAN'S BREW, directed by Rainer Werner Fassbinder; script (German with English subtitles) by Mr. Fassbinder; photography, Michael Ballhaus; editors, Thea Eymez and Gabi Eichel; music, Peer Raben; presented by New Yorker Films. At the Waverly Theater, Avenue of the Americas at West Third Street. Running time: 110 minutes. This film has not been rated.

Walter Kranz .... Kurt Raab
Andree .... Margit Carstensen
Luise Kranz .... Helen Vita
Lisa .... Ingrid Caven
Rolf .... Marquard Bohm
Lauf .... Ulli Lommel
Ernst .... Volker Spengler

By JANET MASLIN

IF YOU HAVE any doubt that there's such a thing as being too prolific, by all means go see Rainer Werner Fassbinder's "Satan's Brew." Mr. Fassbinder attempting physical, almost slapstick comedy, is Mr. Fassbinder at his least funny or enlightening; and the film, a kind of "Father Knows Best" on acid, showcases most of the director's worst qualities without leaving room for his best. Made in Germany early last year, this is an ice-cold work, and a stubborn and difficult one. The meager rewards it delivers are no

Volker Spengler in a scene from the film "Satan's Brew"

match for the enormous energy it demands.

Beginning and ending with a quotation from the French avant-gardist Antonin Artaud, to the effect that thinking from a non-human point of view is a way of maintaining contact with the gods, "Satan's Brew" operates as something of a sicko sit-com, with a set of domestic characters nonchalantly acting out their most bestial impulses.

•

Walter Kranz (Kurt Raab) is a beleaguered poet with a hefty wife who complains loudly about their nonexistent sex life and a brother whose hobbies are exposing himself and collecting dead flies.

The menagerie also includes a duplicitous whore and a bug-eyed, warty mistress (played through heavy makeup by the usually stunning Margit Carstensen). Kranz himself is hard at work pretending he is Stefan George, a German poet favored by the Nazis, and writing a new opus, to be entitled "No Ceremony For The Führer's Dead Dog."

Mr. Fassbinder can be both ironic and provocative when, as in "Mother Kusters Goes To Heaven," his only successful comedy, he gently contrasts people's manners with their desires. But in "Satan's Brew" his blunt directorial style merely exaggerates the coarseness of his characters, and his humor turns stolid and didactic. There are, for instance, a great many ponderous lessons here about the relationship between sex and money: a woman in kinky purple underwear goes into ecstasies while writing a check (at this point, her lover serenely shoots her), and the brother who collects flies tries to use them as both erotic offerings and as currency.

Mr. Fassbinder also pokes fun at a wide range of perversions: one character, a masochist, has scrambled egg spat onto her face and happily lets it dry there. Also, there are repeated digs at the German national temperament, including several references to anti-Semitism and someone's scornful appraisal of death as "the fate of the weak." It's hard to be sure where Mr. Fassbinder stands on these or any other issues, because the film's plot is unintelligible and its directorial vantage point is somewhere off in the ozone.

•

For all its brutishness, though, "Satan's Brew" is finally not vulgar enough. The film's premise calls for both precision and abandon and, while an exaggerated, reference-laden meticulousness is Mr. Fassbinder's specialty, he seems incapable of doing anything very freely. His characters follow their animal instincts, but they do so in such a careful way they might as well be trained seals. None of them flouts convention with the kind of spontaneity or enthusiasm that might have lent real wit to the film's bloodless, brittle scheme.

1977 Ag 10, C18:1

Horse Feathers

THE KENTUCKY FRIED MOVIE, directed by John Landis; produced by Robert K. Weiss; executive producer, Kim Jorgensen; written by David Zucker, Jim Abrahams, Jerry Zucker (the Kentucky Fried Theater); director of photography, Stephen M. Katz; music coordinator, Igo Kantor; a Ned Topham presentation for United Film Distribution Co. At the Eastside Cinema. Running time: 86 minutes. This film has been rated R.

Cleopatra	Marilyn Joi
Schwartz	Saul Kahan
Housewife	Marcy Goldman
Paul Burmaster	Joe Medalis
Claude LaMont	Barry Dennem
Boy	Rick Gates
Girl	Tara Strohmeir
Newscaster	Neil Thompson
Architect	George Lazenby
Henry Gibson	Himself
Bill Bixby	Himself
Clumsy Waiter	Donald Sutherland
Loo	Evan Kim
Pennington	Derek Murcott
Dr. Klahn	Master Bong Soo Han

By LAWRENCE VAN GELDER

ANYONE interested in the condition of humor and wit in the United States stands likely to come away depressed from "The Kentucky Fried Movie," which opened yesterday at the Eastside Cinema. The first film of the Kentucky Fried Theater, a comedy group that traces its origins to the University of Wisconsin six years ago, "The Kentucky Fried Movie" is in the tradition of "The Groove Tube" and "Tunnelvision." The range of its satire and comedy, as displayed in 22 segments running from a minute or two up to 30 minutes, is fairly narrow.

Television is both an inspiration and a preoccupation, with commercials, news shows, early morning talk-news shows, talk shows and 50's-style courtroom dramas all serving as targets.

Movies come next. "Cleopatra Schwartz," dealing with the love of a black superwoman and a Hasidic rabbi, is this movie's comment on black exploitation films.

Disaster movies, soft-core pornographic movies and martial-arts films are also the focus of a mordancy that gives the impression—particularly in the 30-minute martial-arts segment—of being undercut by the maker's affection for the original genre. Sex records and charity appeals are also inspirations for efforts at humor in this 86-minute film, which seems at least twice as long.

Reportedly made on a budget of about $1 million, "The Kentucky Fried Movie" is a good-looking production well performed by a large cast that includes Donald Sutherland, Henry Gibson and George Lazenby in brief appearances.

Television is at once this movie's nourishment and onus. The caliber of television wit and humor has never been uniformly high, and comedy derived from it is likely to have difficulty surmounting such humble origins. It is little wonder, then, that "The Kentucky Fried Movie," being freed from the restraints of television, though not from its inherent defects, occasionally descends into juvenile tastelessness (a dignified woman using four-letter words; a board game built around the assassination of President Kennedy; a charity appeal involving a child's corpse).

Other episodes, such as the one involving a television newscaster suddenly aware that he can see into the room of a lovemaking couple, last so long that the joke is dissipated by boredom; and in this case crosses the line from humor to an exercise in prurience.

Lots of people will probably like "The Kentucky Fried Movie," just as they like Kentucky Fried Chicken and McDonald's hamburgers. But popularity is still no reason for deifying mediocrity.

1977 Ag 11, C14:5

Muted Shrieks

THE LITTLE GIRL WHO LIVES DOWN THE LANE, directed by Nicolas Gessner; screenplay by Laird Koenig, based on his own novel; director of photography, Rene Verzier; editor, Yves Langlois; music by Christian Gaubert; produced by Zev Braun; a Samuel Z. Arkoff presentation; released by American International Pictures. At showcase theaters. Running time: 94 minutes. This film is rated PG.

Rynn	Jodie Foster
Frankk Hallet	Martin Sheen
Mrs. Hallet	Alexis Smith
Miglioriti	Mort Shuman
Mario	Scott Jacoby
Town Hall Clerk	Dorothy Davis
Bank Manager	Clesson Goodhue

By JANET MASLIN

EVEN THOUGH she's cast as a murderess, Jodie Foster comes her closest yet to playing a normal kid in "The Little Girl Who Lives Down The Lane," a mild-mannered horror movie for people who don't much enjoy being scared. Miss Foster's foul deeds, which prove to be not so foul after all, are committed either accidentally or off-camera. The rest of the time, Miss Foster loafs around in blue jeans, plays with her hamster, and falls so desperately in love that, when things go wrong, she can barely touch her dinner, which consists of a burger and a shake.

The story, set in the obligatory New England hamlet, involves Martin Sheen as a vicious child-moester who sees in Miss Foster the things that movie audiences have been seeing in her for the last few years, and Alexis Smith, as Mr. Shen's wicked mother. Miss Smith plays the town real estate agent and, because she wears a Valentino wardrobe and drives a Bentley, it must be quite a town.

In any case, Miss Smith has rented a house to Miss Foster and her father, a Very Famous Poet who hasn't been heard from since. Every time Miss Smith drops by to make trouble, Miss Foster announces that her father is out of town or says he is working in his study and can't be disturbed. Hah!

Though Mr. Sheen does a chillingly effective turn as the psycho, and Miss Smith an unduly nasty one as his mother, the film's real source of energy is Miss Foster's bout of puppy love with Scott Jacoby, who brings freshness and ingenuity to a humdrum role. The affair blossoms, and then some: the pair begins sleeping together, and Miss Foster is called to murmur sweet nothings like "I never knew how much I needed you."

Fortunately, there's more to it than that: they also share an easy camaraderie and a number of genial, even heart-warming moments. Nicolas Gessner's direction has a correspondingly comfortable feel, but this type of story

Jodie Foster and Scott Jacoby as adolescent lovers

is as old as the hills—no, older—and Mr. Gessner doesn't do much to make it plausible.

Filmgoers with short attention spans may find themselves wondering not where Miss Foster has been stashing all the adults in her life but, rather, why she is wearing a stiff and obvious-looking wig.

•

"The Little Girl Who Lives Down The Lane" is rated PG ("Parental Guidance Suggested"), because of a few bloody closeups of a corpse and because of the terrible things Mr. Sheen does to a stuffed facsimile of Miss Foster's hamster.

1977 Ag 11, C16:5

Old Rainmaker

CHAC, directed, written and produced by Rolando Klein; in Tzeltal and Mayan dialects with English subtitles; director of photography, Alex Phillips Jr.; editor, Harry Keramidas; music, Victor Fozado and Elizabeth Waldo; a Cientifilm Aurora production. Running time: 95 minutes. This film has not been rated. At the New Yorker Theater, Broadway near 88th Street.

Diviner.......Pablo Canche Balam
Cacique.......Alonso Mendez Ton
Mute boy.......Sebastian Santis
Father.......Pedro Tiez

"Chac" was shown at the 1975 New Directors-New Films series at the Museum of Modern Art. The following review by Vincent Canby appeared April 5, 1975. The film opened yesterday at the New Yorker Theater.

"Chac," is officially identified as a Panamanian film though it was made in Mexico by a young Chilean-born film director, Rolando Klein, who studied cinema at the University of California at Los Angeles. The film itself is equally eclectic, a sort of Museum of Natural History movie about Mayan culture, put together with all sorts of slick, elaborate, sophisticated film techniques.

The camerawork is as glossy as a layout in the National Geographic and the movie, though sincerely intended, is just a bit patronizing toward the Mayan descendants it means to appreciate.

•

Though the movie's glossy, picturesque look has the effect of denying the depth of the director's interest in the primitive culture he is studying, Mr. Klein does show real ability in obtaining simple, direct, unselfconscious performances from his Indian actors. They all perform with that kind of natural absorption that often elludes amateurs, including those women secretly photographed in supermarkets touting their favorite brand of detergent.

"Chac" has a story of sorts. It's about the members of a contemporary Mayan tribe who, when their own shaman fails to produce rain, seek the help of a possibly evil hermit called the Diviner. Mr. Klein incorporates many Mayan legends into the movie and gives us what ultimately has the effect of a fairly posh, all-expenses paid weekend in the primitive Yucatan.

1977 Ag 12, C4:5

Pedro Tiez, a Tzeltal Indian from Mexico, in the film "Chac"
Simple and direct performances obtained from the Indian actors

DAUGHTER OF DECEIT (LA HIJA DEL ENGANO), directed by Luis Bunuel; screenplay (Spanish with English subtitles) by Raquel Rojas and Luis Alcoriza; photography, Jose Ortiz Ramos; music, Manuel Esperon; produced by Oscar Dancig's, Ultramar Films S.A. Running time: 80 minutes. This film has not been rated. At the Jean Renoir Cinema, 100 Seventh Avenue South, near Sheridan Square.

Don Quintin.......Fernando Soler
Marta.......Alicia Caro
Paco.......Ruben Rojo
Jonron.......Nacho Contra
Angel.......Fernando Soto
Jovita.......Lily Aclemar

By JANET MASLIN

THERE aren't many surprises in the scenario for "Daughter of Deceit," a melodrama Luis Buñuel directed in Mexico in 1951. A happy-go-lucky man discovers that his wife is unfaithful and, when the wife spitefully announces that the couple's daughter isn't really his, he throws his wife out and then abandons the baby. Years later, when the wife makes a deathbed confession that the girl was legitimate after all, the father sets out to find her.

Alicia Caro, left, in Luis Bunuel's 1951 film, "Daughter of Deceit," at the Jean Renoir Cinema

He has by then become bitter and nasty, the owner of a nightclub called the Inferno, and when he inadvertently happens across the girl without recognizing her as his daughter, he treats her terribly. But the girl is an angel in human form, just about, and when the mix-up is discovered she forgives him, making him happy-go-lucky once more.

•

"Daughter of Deceit" was the second version of this rather slight story on which Mr. Buñuel worked—he also was executive producer of a 1935 version—and perhaps part of what attracted him to the tale was its relentless equation of love with treachery. The film begins and ends with glimpses of the father as a jolly soul, but it spends most of the time measuring love in terms of its power to destroy. The wife's infidelity turns her husband into a veritable fiend, and when the man unwittingly torments his daughter, the real drama has less to do with mistaken identity than with the question of whether she, too, will be transformed.

The story is inconsequential enough to demand a happy ending, and so Mr. Buñuel never seriously addresses himself to the notion of love's darker side. He does establish the point obliquely, though. When the daughter meets the handsome young man she will marry, for instance, their flirtation begins on a country lane, just after he has accidentally hit her with his car.

•

Fernando Soler, the actor who starred in many of Mr. Buñuel's Mexican films, is all wrong for the part of the father, but marvelous just the same; Mr. Soler's air of courtliness and good humor always shines through, even in what are supposed to be the film's blackest moments. Alicia Caro, as the daughter, is remarkable chiefly for her cool, elegant, almost formidable beauty, the kind for which the director has always had such an extraordinarily keen eye.

1977 Ag 12, C11:1

SUSPIRIA, written and directed by Dario Argento; photography, Luciano Tovoli; produced by Claudio Argento for Seda Spettacoli; music by The Goblins, with the collaboration of Dario Argento. At the Criterion Theater, Broadway and 45th Street. Running time: 92 minutes. This film is rated R.

Susy.......Jessica Harper
Sara.......Stefania Casini
Madame Blank.......Joan Bennett
Miss Tanner.......Alida Valli
Daniel.......Flavio Bucci

By JANET MASLIN

Right from the start, it's clear that the Italian-made, English-language "Suspiria" is a specialty item: The opening credits show the title of the movie carved out of pulsating glands. Writer-director Dario Argento has an unusually horrific slant on life, to say the very least, and his film's most powerful moments have a way of making one think about open-heart surgery. But "Suspiria," which opened yesterday at the Criterion Theater, does have its slender charms, though they will most assuredly be lost on viewers who are squeamish.

The plot, as transparent as the pane of glass that slices up the movie's first victim, is intentionally ridiculous, and Mr. Argento's direction has the mocking, stylized simplicity of a comic strip. A strange, pouty girl named Susy Banyon (Jessica Harper) arrives at a German ballet academy, and within minutes a monster is whittling away at her classmates. Nobody will level with Susy about what's going on and, in general, the students' compassion for one another leaves a lot to be desired. "Poor David," remarks one, "torn to pieces. Incredible!"

The headmistress, played primly by Joan Bennett, is no help either.

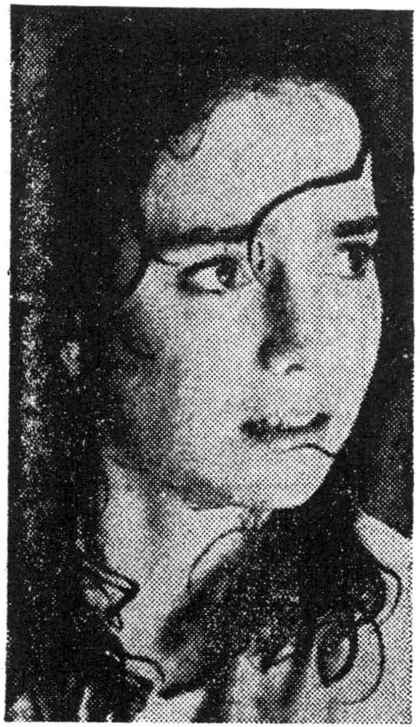

Jessica Harper in "Suspiria"

Though she puts up a great show of gentility in public, she secretly shrieks things like "She must die, die, die!"

The film's ostensible highlights include a bat on the rampage, a plague of white worms, "Tubular Bells"-type music by a group called The Goblins, and a great many graphic tips on how to carve one's fellows into rib roast.

However, Mr. Argento's methods make potentially stomach-turning material more interesting than it ought to be. Shooting on bold, very fake-looking sets, he uses bright primary colors and stark lines to create a campy, surreal atmosphere, and his distorted camera angles and crazy lighting turn out to be much more memorable than the carnage.

"Suspiria" is really quite funny, during those isolated interludes when nobody is bleeding.

1977 Ag 13, 11:1

Kids Will Like Third 'Sinbad'

By LAWRENCE VAN GELDER

Question: What has the foot of a seagull, the power of an evil sorcerer and the accent of a Gabor sister?

Answer: Zenobia, the sinister and ambitious royal stepmother in "Sinbad and the Eye of the Tiger," No. 3 in the latest generation of Sinbad movies, which opened yesterday at neighborhood theaters.

Determined to look upon the throne of ancient Charok and be able to point out her son, the Caliph, Zenobia reduces Prince Kassim, the rightful heir, to the status of baboon, albeit one who retains —at least for a time—the ability to play chess.

Things look bad in Charok until Sinbad (Patrick Wayne), seeking the hand of Kassim's sister, Farrah (Jane Seymour), returns from a voyage and determines to set things right.

Along the way, he and his allies cross paths with some of the creations of animation expert Ray Harryhausen that have given this series something of a cult following—fleshless assassins with the heads and eyes of insects; a metal bullheaded giant called Minaton; one bee that acts like a B-l; an enormous troglodyte and, in the climactic battle, a saber-toothed tiger inhabited by the spirit of the villainous Zenobia, played by Margaret Whiting.

Well, at least by becoming a tiger she has managed to rid herself of the fowl foot acquired during a potion shortage incurred while doing a turn as a tern to spy on Sinbad and his companions aboard their ship.

Under the direction of Sam Wanamaker, this latest Sinbad adventure maintains the innocent and atavistic juvenile charm of the others in the series.

In the midst of rather rudimentary acting by some of the humans, there are the admirable Harryhausen monsters; a reasonable amount of action; exotic locales, Spain, Jordan and Malta among them; Jane Seymour and Taryn Power (daughter of Tyrone Power and Linda Christian) to look good while looking frightened; and a happy ending (at least for the survivors).

No child could ask for much more.

The Cast

SINBAD AND THE EYE OF THE TIGER, directed by Sam Wanamaker; produced by Charles H. Schneer and Ray Harryhausen; story by Beverley Cross and Ray Harryhausen; screenplay by Beverley Cross; creator of special visual effects, Ray Harryhausen; director of photography, Ted Moore; music by Roy Budd; distributed by Columbia Pictures. At neighborhood theaters. Running time 113 minutes. This film has been rated G.

Sinbad	Patrick Wayne
Dione	Taryn Power
Zenobia	Margaret Whiting
Farah	Jane Seymour
Melanthius	Patrick Troughton
Rafi	Kurt Christian
Hassan	Nadim Sawaiha
Kassim	Damion Thomas
Balsora	Bruno Barnabe
Zabid	Bernard Kay
Maroof	Salami Coker
Aboo-Seer	David Sterne

1977 Ag 13, 11:2

FILM VIEW

FRANK RICH

Even Misfits Can Live Happily Ever After

Most of the movie genres spawned by the counter-culture of the 1960's have vanished along with their era. You don't see too many mod-rock comedies (à la "A Hard Day's Night") any more—or alienated "road" pictures ("Easy Rider," "Five Easy Pieces") or campus rebellion frolics ("Getting Straight"); such films now belong to nostalgia fanatics and revisionist cultural historians. Yet there is one small but durable breed of 60's movie that still exerts so strong a pull on audiences that it has survived the 70's unabated. This is the genre that's typified by such works as "Morgan!," "King of Hearts," "Trash," "Marat/Sade," "Going Places" and "The Rocky Horror Picture Show"—films that preach it is better to be crazy (or at least benignly bonkers) than sane in a dehumanized modern world.

These movies, whose philosophical roots can be traced to such 60's icons as R.D. Laing and Timothy Leary, are harmless in small doses, and, at their best, they can be hugely satisfying escapist entertainment. "One Flew Over the Cuckoo's Nest," the box-office champion of the lot, has so much visceral energy and compelling acting that you can't even pause to consider how simplistically Ken Kesey has drawn his do-or-die struggle between "crazy" hero McMurphy and "sane" villain Nurse Ratched. The Peter Shaffer play "Equus," which will be seen in a film version this fall, similarly transforms a stacked, adversary shrink-patient relationship into potent middle-brow melodrama.

• • •

Still, there's something disturbing about all of these works, however gripping they may be: at heart, they're all adolescent fantasies—designed to appeal to young people who fear they may be squelched by an adult world that doesn't tolerate non-conformist behavior. In real life, human beings have far more choices than these films, with their martyred heroes and repressive authority figures, let on. You can, after all, be certifiably sane without being as emotionally sterile as Nurse Ratched or "Equus's" Dr. Dysart or the upper-class British swells of "Morgan!"; conversely, you can be a freaky, free-spirit without having to take up residence in an insane asylum (like McMurphy and Morgan). Thanks in no small part to the social upheavals of the 60's, most forms of non-criminal eccentric behavior are now tolerated by society at large; the crazy-vs.-sane movies, which are possessed by the melodramatic us-vs.-them mentality of the contentious 60's, don't acknowledge the loosening up of mores that has occured over the past decade.

It's in this context that a new, small Canadian film with the off-putting title of "Outrageous!" is such a welcome surprise. This movie, which quietly took up residence at the Cinema II two weeks ago, incontestably belongs to the crazy-vs.-sane genre—and yet it plays new and mature variations on the theme. Unlike its peers, it is happily aware of the full range of possibilities that exist in life.

This isn't to say that the movie is wholly successful. Richard Benner, a Canadian TV director who makes his feature film debut with "Outrageous!," has some trouble juggling his various narratives, as well as a tendency to wear his heart on his sleeve. Fortunately, he also has a frisky, scatological sense of humor, loads of energy, and an ability to bring wacky characters to life—talents that overwhelm his movie's flaws. At its considerable best, "Outrageous!" has the rambunctious comic force we associate with Brian De Palma's early films, "Greetings" and "Hi, Mom" and, better still, it has a sensible, attractive view of humanity that is purely its own.

The movie's plot, adapted from a short story by Margaret Gibson, has to do with the relationship between two self-described "crazies"—Robin (Craig Russell), a pudgy homosexual hairdresser, and Liza (Hollis McLaren), a schizophrenic

Frank Rich is now writing a book about the early days of television.

young woman who has recently fled from a mental hospital. Robin and Liza are best friends who share a dreary Toronto flat, and they are miserable. They don't fit into the normal world that surrounds them, and they dream of escaping to some place where they can live lives of "dazzle"—where they can flourish on their own, admittedly mad terms.

At times "Outrageous!" is all too willing to embrace the cliches of its genre. The film's basic dramatic situation is of a piece with most of the other crazy-vs.-sane movies, and the script sometimes panders to the latent flower children in the audience: at one point, in a burst of crazies' chauvinism, Robin announces that he "never knew anyone who was worth knowing who wasn't a positive fruitcake"; at another, Robin all too rhetorically asks, "Why does everybody always want to lock each other up? Who's insane anyhow?" Meanwhile, the disco songs on the soundtrack constantly remind us that "It isn't easy in this crazy world" and that "You've got to be what you got to be."

• • •

But for all these invocations of counter-culture cant, "Outrageous!" never sinks to the level one fears it might. Benner, uniquely for a practitioner of this genre, simply refuses to supply his film with the traditional sane villains: there are no Nurse Ratcheds or Dysarts who come along to oppress the hero and heroine and force them to conform to accepted modes of behavior. While Liza continues to see her psychiatrist, she's never dragged back to the dread asylum; she's given a chance to prove she can function on her own. Nor is Robin, as one might expect, portrayed as a victim of the heterosexual world from which he is excluded; the only people who treat him cruelly in the film are homosexuals.

By refusing to turn his crazies into martyrs, Benner gradually pushes "Outrageous!" in its unexpected direction. Unlike their counterparts in similar films, Robin and Liza are not defeated by the sane world; Benner gives them the freedom to take charge of their lives and seize the "dazzle" they want. And that's precisely what they do. Robin buys some wigs and costumes, screws up his courage, and starts to assemble a female-impersonation nightclub act—an act that eventually takes him out of Toronto and that brings him acceptance from both gay and straight audiences. (Mr. Russell, who plays Robin with great feeling, is himself a professional

In "Outrageous!" Craig Russell, a wacky female impersonator, faces a bright future—unlike the majority of comtemporary movie "crazies," such as the lobotomized Jack Nicholson, below, in "One Flew Over the Cuckoo's Nest."

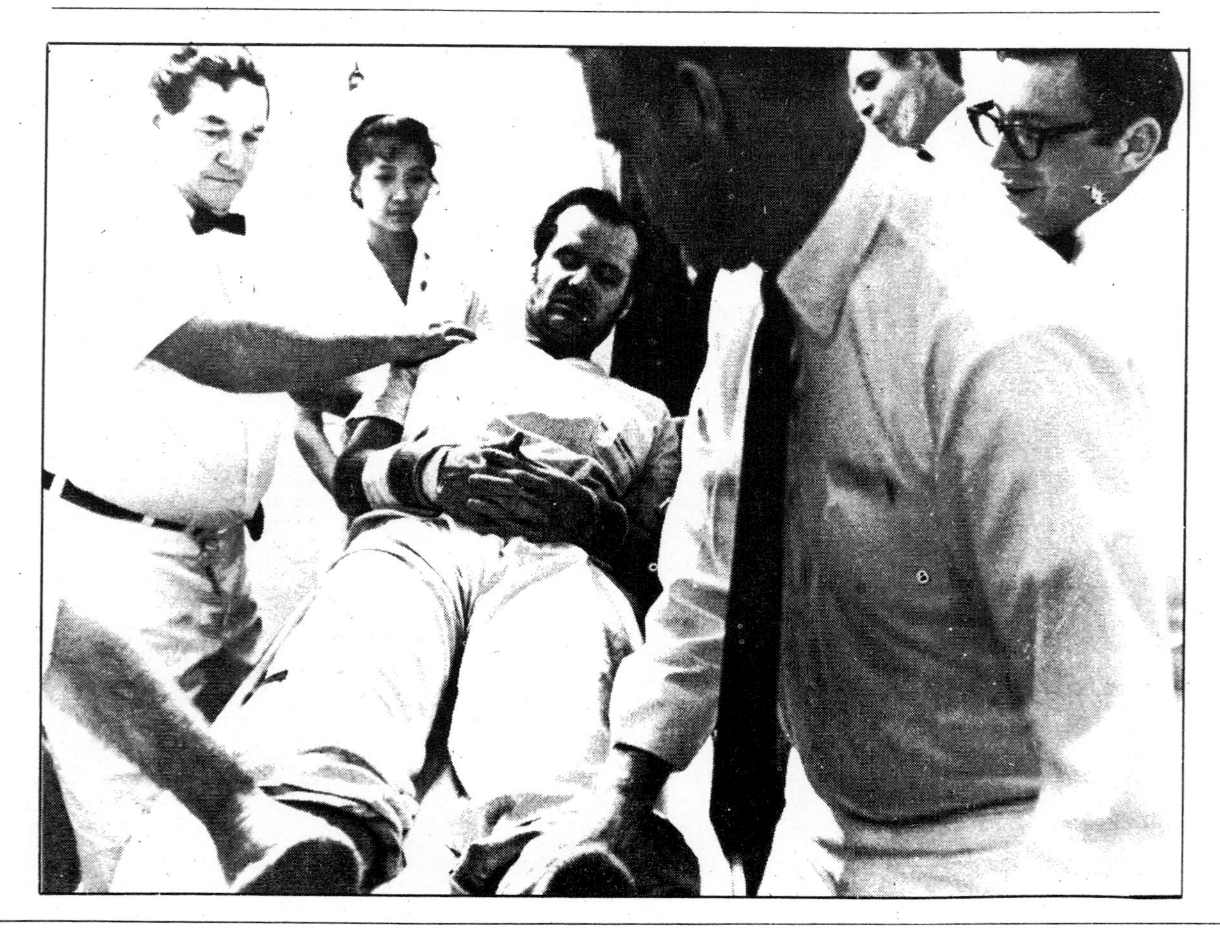

female impersonator, and his act is one of the comic high-points of the film.) For her part, Liza draws sustenance from Robin's love for her; she learns how to stop feeling sorry for herself and starts channeling her energy into "writing stories for all the crazies all over the world."

This happy resolution of Robin's and Liza's malaise may be a little too pat to be entirely convincing—but it's still more credible than the tragic fates that invariably befall the protagonists of similar movies. It's moving, for once, to see a film about crazies that doesn't end with the characters either being lobotomized, locked up in padded cells, transformed into "normal" zombies or killed. And it's more in tune with the times, too—because, in the 70's it's more possible than it once was to preserve your own special insanity without dropping out of the world. As Robin explains to Liza near the movie's end, "You'll never be normal, but you're special and you can have a hell of a good time . . . You have a healthy case of craziness—just make it work for you."

Coming from a movie that is infatuated with crazy people, that's uncommonly sane advice. ■

1977 Ag 14, II:11:1

THE SENSUAL MAN, written and directed by Marco Vicario; based on a novel by Vitaliano Brancati; film editor, Bompiani; music by Armando Trovaioli. In Italian with English titles. At the Little Carnegie Theater, 57th Street east of Seventh Avenue. Running time: 108 minutes. This film is rated R.

Paolo .... Giancarlo Giannini
Lilia .... Rossana Podesta
Il Nonno .... Lionel Stander
Edmondo .... Gastone Moschin
Marietta .... Marianne Comtell

By JANET MASLIN

The hero of "The Sensual Man" is crazy about women, and women are crazy about him, too. Right from the moment when Paolo (Giancarlo Giannini), then the barely adolescent scion of a Sicilian noble family, begins fooling around with the maid, his life becomes a hectic one. There are a tempestuous blonde, a rich Roman brunette with a lot of modern furniture, and a stern lady Communust who, rather inexplicably, wears black lace garters.

•

There are the fresh-faced girl at the chemist's and the countess with the yelowish teeth. There is the pretty nurse at whom Paolo, always at the ready, makes a pass, even though the nurse is busy ministering to his dying father. There is even, very nearly, Paolo's unusually nubile Mama.

The only problem is that "The Sensual Man" isn't a comedy, at least not intentionally. Instead, this is meant to be the long, sad story of Paolo's congenital inability to control his carnal passions (by way of an explanation, it seems it'sh ereditary; his uncle and grandfather were ladykillers, too). The tale culminates in Paolo's failure to stay married to the only woman he truly loves, a sweet young thing 20 years his junior, a creature so untainted that the very notion of sex makes her burst out crying.

There isn't much of a lesson to be learned from "The Sensual Man," and there isn't much to watch here, either. Marco Vicario's direction is stultifyingly banal; he favors dark rooms overdecorated with antique furniture, romantic strolls through the autumn leaves and swelling strings each time the billing and cooing begin.

•

Giancarlo Giannini

Looks older than the actress who plays his mother.

Giancarlo Giannini has played characters like Paolo too often to attack the role with much energy, even though he is this time confronted with an unusual difficulty. Even in 1974, when "The Sensual Man" was made in Italy, Mr. Giannini looked substantially older than the rapscalllion of 25 he is supposed, at least during the middle of the film, to be. As if that weren't bad enough, he also looks older than the actress who plays his mother.

1977 Ag 15, 34:1

RUBY, directed by Curtis Harrington; produced by George Edwards; executive producer Steve Krantz; written by George Edwards and Barry Schneider. An Aquarius Films release. At RKO Cinerama II, RKO 86th Street Twin and neighborhood theaters. Running time: 85 minutes. This movie has been rated R.

Ruby..Piper Laurie
Ruby's daughter........................Janit Baldwin
Vince Kemper.........................Stuart Whitman
Dr. Keller...................................Roger Davis
Nicky...Sal Vecchio

PIPER LAURIE and Stuart Whitman, a couple of actors who have known better days, turned up yesterday in theaters in and around New York City in "Ruby," a movie whose elements have also seen better days.

More than inciting shock and horror, this is the sort of movie that inspires genealogy. Floating around in it are large chunks of "The Exorcist"; costumes out of all those 30's and 40's movies in which gangsters affected dinner jackets and gleaming white starched shirtfronts; a soupçon of something called "J.D.'s Revenge," a summer entertainment of recent if not remarkable vintage; and a pair of eyeballs afloat in liquid—the sort of preserves usually put up by the Hammer Films folks in England.

•

What seems to be going on around the swamp-country drive-in movie theater operated by Miss Laurie and Mr. Whitman is a lot of supernatural carnage. It seems that Nicky (Sal Vecchio), the once and future lover of Ruby (Miss Laurie), a one-time chanteuse, starlet and gang moll, has risen from his watery grave to wreak some vengeance. on the underworld colleagues he holds responsible for his demise.

From time to time, he manifests his presence through Jannit Baldwin, who plays his and Ruby's silent, protuberant-eyed daughter. To provide the straight-faced mumbo-jumbo intended to lend a scientific veneer to the proceedings, Roger Davis is called in to portray Dr. Keller, a parapsychologist.

The makers of "Ruby" apparently believe that lots of gore, hints of incest and necrophilia, skeletal embraces and those preserved eyeballs are the stuff of which adequate horror films are made. Even within its own modest league, this movie is a dull concoction.

LAWRENCE VAN GELDER

1977 Ag 18, C17:5

More Than Cartoons

FANTASTIC ANIMATION FESTIVAL, Christopher Pa-[illegible], concept director; Dean A. Berko, executive director.
FRENCH WINDOWS, by Ian Emes; music by Pink Floyd.
ICARUS, by Mihai Badica.
A SHORT HISTORY OF THE WHEEL, by Loren Bowie.
COSMIC CARTOON, by Steven Lisberger and Eric Ladd.
THE LAST CARTOON MAN, by Jeffrey Hale and Derek Lamb.
CAT'S CRADLE, by Paul Driessen.
MOONSHADOW, by Cat Stevens; music by Mr. Stevens; narration by Spike Milligan.
NIGHTBIRD, by Bernard Palacios.
ROOM AND BOARD by Randy Cartwright.
BAMBI MEETS GODZILLA, by Marv Newland.
MOUNTAIN MUSIC by Will Vinton.
LIGHT, by Jordan Belson.
SUPERMAN VS. THE MECHANICAL MONSTERS, by Max Fleisher.
AWARD-WINNING ANIMATED COMMERCIALS. MIRROR PEOPLE, by Kathy Rose.
KICK ME, by Robert Swarthe.
CLOSED MONDAYS, by Will Vinton and Bob Gardner.
At neighborhood theaters. Running time: 107 minutes. This film has been rated PG.

By LAWRENCE VAN GELDER

EVERY YEAR at Academy Award time, someone stands up and hands out a prize for animation. Chances are that only a minuscule portion of the audience has seen the film in question, and those who wonder about it at all are likely to assume it to be a particularly fine example of the sort of cartoon that used to be a regular part of Saturday afternoons at the movies.

A worthwhile chance to correct that impression is now at hand in the form of a collection of 18 extraordinary animated short films grouped together under the title "Fantastic Animation Festival."

•

The show, which opened yesterday at neighborhood theaters, is a long one—an hour and 47 minutes—but a good one. The worst than can be said of it is that it may be too much of a good thing, a feast of excellence that probably would be more savory could

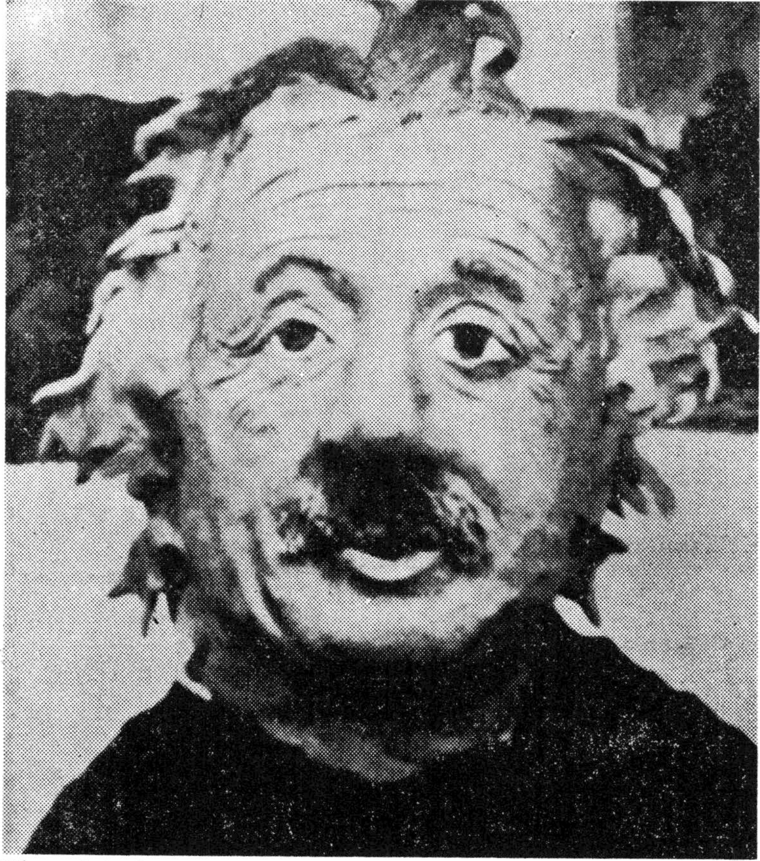

Einstein's face as sculpture in "Closed Mondays," one of the shorts in "Fantastic Animation Festival."

it be partaken of a little at a time rather than all at once.

That cavil recorded, it should be said immediately that here at once is an opportunity to examine the state of a sophisticated art that gives to the imagination wings denied to conventional film makers. Animation offers not only a medium for telling stories, for making points about human nature and society, for speaking in metaphor and wit; it offers freedom from the bonds of literal photographic image. In animation anything is possible—journeys far into space or deep into the mind; instantaneous transformations of the mundane—and "Fantastic Animation Festival" displays much of the range of these possibilities.

•

Not all of these shorts are likely to appeal equally to everyone, but everyone is likely to find something to admire, from the drama and nostalgia of the 1941 "Superman vs. the Mechanical Monsters" to the succinct wit of "Bambi Meets Godzilla" to the commentaries and humor of "Icarus," "Mountain Music," "The Last Cartoon Man," "Room and Board" and "Closed Mondays," an Academy Award-winner, to the sophisticated technique and evocations of "French Windows," "Light" and the eerie and enigmatic "Nightbird."

•

The PG ("Parental Guidance Suggested") rating is probably attributable to a couple of swift depictions of the nude female body, bare female breasts and the use of the words "crap" and "hell."

1977 Ag 18, C20:1

It's on Track

THE ILLUSION TRAVELS BY STREETCAR, directed by Luis Bunuel; screenplay by Maurice de la Serna, Jose Revueltas and Juan de la Cabada; photography by Raul Martinez Solares; music by Luis Hernandez Breton; with Lilia Prado, Carlos Navarro, Domingo Soler, Agustin Isunza. In Spanish with English subtitles; made in Mexico in 1954. At the Jean Renoir Cinema, 100 Seventh Avenue South. Running time: 84 minutes.

By JANET MASLIN

"THE ILLUSION Travels by Streetcar," the third Mexican Luis Buñuel film of the early 50's to have its American premiere at the Jean Renoir Cinema, is simultaneously the most characteristic and the most uneven of the lot. Satirical, at times almost allegorical, and full of surreal touches, it is also at times ponderous and rambling. It begins, for instance, with a somber and preachy voice-over, to the effect that life is full of small but meaningful stories and that what follows will be one of them.

From there, it details the adventures of a pair of transit workers who have lovingly repaired a ramshackle old trolley, only to learn that the streetcar company has decided the car is obsolete. The two get drunk that night and steal the trolley, piloting it around Mexico City until they can safely return it the following evening.

•

They have no set course in mind, but the car is commandeered over and over again by peculiar bands of people. An impatient schoolteacher loads her children onto the car, and soon anarchy reigns; a group of wealthy businessmen climb on board and are shocked and irritated by the crew's refusal to collect fares. In another, shabbier part of town, peasant women decide that anyone who won't take money is probably a thief.

On board the trolley, the mood is deadpan and decidedly strange. A butcher climbs on and calmly sets up shop, carving meat and hanging up carcasses. Two women carrying a plaster saint wander along in the middle of the night, on their way to church to have the saint blessed; it seems this nocturnal urge strikes them regularly, the way the craving for chip dip affects others.

This behavior is never made to seem grotesque; in fact, it hardly seems out of the ordinary. At its best, the film inhabits a cool, only slightly distorted fantasy world that has its own eccentric rules of decorum.

The film achieves this tone effortlessly much of the time, but occasionally it strains, as when a neighborhood party includes a little morality play that casts the trainmen as God and the Devil. Occasionally it meanders, too, and the trolley conceit begins to wear thin.

But its best moments combine inspired whimsy with tight control, and make it eminently recommendable to anyone even remotely interested in Buñuel's oeuvre and its evolution.

1977 Ag 19, C9:3

Lilia Prado and Fernando Soto in Buñuel's "The Illusion Travels by Streetcar"
Recommendable to anyone interested in Buñuel's oeuvre and its evolution

THE BAD NEWS BEARS IN BREAKING TRAINING, directed by Michael Pressman; screenplay by Paul Brickman, based on characters created by Bill Lancaster; produced by Leonard Goldberg; director of photography, Fred J. Koenkamp; music, Craig Safan; editor, Jack Wheeler; distributed by Paramount Pictures. Running time: 100 minutes. At the Forum Theater, Broadway at 47th Street, and other theaters. This film has been rated PG.

Mike Leak........William Devane
Sy Orlansky........Clifton James
Kelly Leak........Jackie Earle Haley
Carmen Ronzonni........Jimmy Baio
Tanner Boyle........Chris Barnes
Ahmad Abdul Rahim........Erin Blunt
Jose Agilar........James O. Escobedo
Miguel Agilar........George Gonzales
Ogilvie........Alfred Lutter
Jimmie Feldman........Brett Marx
Rudi Stein........David Pollock
Timmy Lupus........Quinn Smith
Toby Whitewood........David Stambaugh
Michael Engelberg........Jeffrey Louis Starr
Councilman Whitewood........Richard McKenzie
Officer Mackie........Lane Smith
Lester Eastland........Fred Stuthman
Mr. Manning........Dolph Sweet
Morrie Slaytor........Pat Corley

By VINCENT CANBY

Even without Walter Matthau and Tatum O'Neal, who were the stars of "The Bad News Bears," there is apparently no stopping, or even slowing down, that team of pint-sized California baseball players in their spin-off movie, titled, for no particular reason except that it has a nice ring to it, "The Bad News Bears in Breaking Training."

The film, which opened at the Forum and other theaters yesterday, is as American as Budweiser beer, Coca-Cola, Hilton Hotels and the Houston Astrodome, all of which receive such prominent plugs it seems as if the film's subsidiary purpose is to keep capitalism afloat. In this respect the film may simply be pursuing accuracy. We live in a time when it's impossible to carry on a lengthy conversation without mentioning a noun that isn't also a trademarked name.

•

"The Bad News Bears in Breaking Training" is manufactured comedy of a slick order, depending almost entirely for its effects on the sight and sound of a bunch of kids behaving as if they were small adults. It's a formula that worked for Our Gang Comedy for many years, and works again here with a bright screenplay by Paul Brickman, based on Bill Lancaster's original characters, and direction of intelligent lightness by Michael Presman. He's the young man (now 26) who made a funny movie, "The Great Texas Dynamite Chase," out of a standard road picture earlier this year.

What plot there is concerns the efforts of the Bears, whose ages run from 9 to 13 (though one or two look older), to get from California to Houston to play in the Astrodome, the winning team then to go on to play the Japanese champions. A critic is not allowed to tell you who wins the Houston game, but it's general knowledge that the next Bears film will be called something on the order of "The Bad News Bears in Tokyo."

The story of a film such as this isn't anywhere near as important as the number of variations that the moviemakers can successfully work on a severely limited number of jokes. Mr. Pressman and Mr. Brickman do well, considering that there are only so many ways that a baseball team can be made to look like losers in order to make a succesful comeback in the final sequence.

Jackie Earle Haley
Actor of real potential

They are helped by some excellent actors, including Jackie Earle Haley who, just a couple of years ago, was the brat Donald Sutherland stomped to death in "The Day of the Locust" and who now looks almost 18, but is an actor of real potential. William Devane is absolutely straight as young Haley's long-lost father, the man who coaches the young pirates to victory.

Some of the other Bears who are very funny are Chris Barnes, who appears to be smaller than Tom Thumb and who, like so many kids who are disadvantaged in height, is ready to fight at the merest slight; Erin Blunt, as the teams' black kid, and Jaime O. Escobedo and George Gonzales as the team's two Mexican-Americans.

•

"The Bad News Bears in Breaking Training," which has been rated PG ("Parental Guidance Suggested"), seeks (and finds) a number of laughs by having its young actors use vulgar four-letter words with the pounding enthusiasm of children who've just learned to speak pig-Latin.

1977 Ag 20, 13:1

Roger Moore, as the dapper, indestructible 007, deftly dispatches a villain and defends Soviet agent Barbara Bach in "The Spy Who Loved Me."

FILM VIEW

FRANK RICH

Why James Bond Is Still A Crowd Pleaser

In a culture that disposes of its pop heroes even faster than it manufactures them, James Bond is a genuine survivor. Here it is 15 years since Ian Fleming's fictional British Secret Service agent first bounded on to a movie screen—in "Dr. No"—and he's still going strong. Maybe even stronger than ever. "The Spy Who Loved Me," the latest Bond thriller, is not only one of the best in the series (which has yielded 10 movies thus far), but it is also as much of a crowd pleaser as the early Bond hits were. Indeed, the throngs of moviegoers who are turning out for "The Spy Who Loved Me" laugh and cheer almost as vociferously as the gaga audiences at "Star Wars."

The continued appeal of the Bond movies is a real phenomenon—particarly when you consider what a dated cultural artifact James Bond is. More than any other pop character, Agent 007 emblemized the romantic values of the now distant Camelot era: Bond was a cool, handsome, intellectual bon vivant who did battle against evil international forces, and in our consciousness he was nothing if not a Hollywood stand-in for John Kennedy. (Kennedy himself was a self-confessed admirer of Ian Fleming's novels.) Bond's lifestyle—his fondness for shapely women, designer clothes and mechanical gimcracks—came right out of the pages of Playboy magazine, and not since the early 60's has Playboy correctly expressed the fantasy lives of mainstream American men.

Frank Rich is now writing a book about the early days of television.

After Kennedy's death, one would have expected Bond to fade, too—but nothing fazes him. He has survived everything: The Cold War, which gave rise to the super-agent genre, has come and gone; Bond's screen imitators (Dean Martin's Matt Helm, James Coburn's Flint, Michael Caine's Harry Palmer) have come and gone; Ian Fleming has come and gone (he died in 1964). Sean Connery, who created Bond on screen and once seemed irreplaceable in the role, eventually abandoned Bond, only to be succeeded by George Lazenby and Roger Moore, the current 007. England, still vaguely a symbol of might and sophistication in the early 60's, has fallen into disrepair—but Bond continues to behave as if his home country had an empire and sound currency. You just can't keep a good guy down.

Still, it's not impossible to understand why Bond has endured; you need only look at "The Spy Who Loved Me." The new film, which carries only the title of an Ian Fleming novel (screenwriters Christopher Wood and Richard Maibaum have constructed a plot of their own), is, like its hero, a throwback to a vanished past—a happy Hollywood past. This movie takes us back to the time when craftsmanship and good humor were standard fixtures in light film entertainments; it's a movie that actually fulfills the conventional expectations that an audience brings to it. Certainly the same cannot be said of such similarly escapist current pictures as "The Deep," "Sorcerer," "A Bridge Too Far" and "March or Die"

—films that have trouble telling their stories coherently and are often cruel-spirited to boot.

There is nothing cruel about "The Spy Who Loved Me"—even though it does contain the requisite number of killings and its hero's obligatory double-entendre wisecracks. The violence, which is always accompanied on the soundtrack by comic book-style "pows!" and "bangs!," is too theatrical to threaten even the unduly squeamish, and by the standards of current movies and television shows, it's not terribly graphic. Bond's sexist one-liners are benign, too, these days: Roger Moore so italicizes those corny gags that they take on a reassuringly ritualistic quality—like classic old vaudeville routines. You can laugh without feeling much guilt.

Besides, the Bond movies are not entirely unaware of the women's movement. In the new film, Bond has a female partner in derring-do—a Ninotchka-like Russian agent, no less, called Agent Triple X (Barbara Bach). Agent Triple X joins 007 to vanquish a megalomaniacal industrialist (Curt Jurgens) who wants to destroy both the U.S. and the U.S.S.R., and she is every bit as skillful an international detective as the hero. (She's also as attractive.) To the screenwriters' credit, however, they are not showy about their acknowledgement of women's liberation and detente: They handle their revisionist updatings of the Bond formula gingerly and thus avoid the campy, self-mocking tone that was so fatal to last winter's remake of "King Kong."

• • •

Rather than make fun of their material, the creators of "The Spy Who Loved Me" go about their business with straight faces, plying the audience with the same devices that have always worked for the Bond films: We get the usual series of absurdly narrow escapes for the hero, the gorgeous settings (Sardinia and Egypt, lushly photographed by Claude Renoir), the inventive gadgetry (a sports car that converts itself into a submarine), and a linear good guys-vs.-bad guys narrative. The villains—crucial to Bond films, as they are to all comic-book fictions—are as spicy as ever. Jurgens's mad industrialist has a water fetish that matches Goldfinger's for gold: He dreams of establishing an underwater utopia after he's destroyed "civilization as we now know it," and he is forever dining on gargantuan lobsters and oysters in his lavish aquarium home. The industrialist's primary henchman is a seven foot, two inch Frankenstein look-alike known as "Jaws"; Richard Kiel, the unappetizing actor who plays the part, has been outfitted with steel teeth, and when he gives his victims (among them an honest-to-God shark) their lethal hickeys, we recall the wicked merriment that hard-kicking villainess Lotte Lenya brought to "From Russia With Love" way back in 1963.

The ingredients that go into the Bond movies are not, of course, the stuff of film art; they are the standard paraphernalia of old-time double-feature movies. But however mindless "The Spy Who Loved Me" is, there's still exhilaration to be had in watching the filmmakers execute their formula in so professional a manner. This movie cost a lot of money, and, for once, you really see the money on screen—in everything from the elegant, animated opening credits sequence (by Maurice Binder) to the mammoth soundstage sets that Ken Adam ("Barry Lyndon") has designed for the film's holocaustal climax. Though Lewis Gilbert, the movie's director, is no one's idea of a creative whirlwind, he has a sense of pace and a desire to dazzle. He doesn't waste time on padded exposition—the bane of many of this summer's clinkers—and he doesn't bother with too much talk. Unfortunately, he doesn't seem to bother too much with the actors, either—Moore and Miss Bach are better seen than heard—but then again, who goes to action movies for their acting?

• • •

What we really want from big-budget summer films like "The Spy Who Loved Me" are the simple things: a little romance, some visceral thrills, a hell of a ride. These are the goods that the Bond pictures fairly consistently deliver, and if the 007 movies are not as inspired as such blockbuster entertainments as "Star Wars" or "Jaws," they're more dependable than all the rest. Maybe we no longer need James Bond to defend the honor of the free world, but how lucky we are that he's survived to defend the increasingly endangered traditions of the well-made commercial film. ■

1977 Ag 21, II:11:1

Robby Benson and Annette O'Toole in "One on One."

Cagey and Clever

ONE ON ONE, directed by Lamont Johnson; screenplay by Robby Benson and Jerry Segal; produced by Martin Horstein; director of photography, Donald M. Morgan; editor, Robbe Roberts; music by Charles Fox and lyrics by Paul Williams; distributed by Warner Brothers. Running time: 98 minutes. At the Loews State 2 Theater, Broadway at 45th Street, and other theaters. This film has been rated PG.

Henry Steele....................Robby Benson
Janet Hays....................Annette O'Toole
Coach Smith....................G. D. Spradlin
B. J. Rudolph....................Gail Strickland
The hitchhiker....................Melanie Griffith
Malcolm....................James G. Richardson
Gonzales....................Hector Morales
Tom....................Cory Faucher

By VINCENT CANBY

HENRY STEELE (Robby Benson) is a high school basketball star who seems no more or less bright than his contemporaries but he is extremely ambitious. When, in the middle of his senior year, he is approached by university basketball scouts, Henry holds out for the best deal, which includes not only a four-year scholarship, private tutoring and various jobs to put money in his pocket, but also an automobile of his choice.

That autumn, en route to the big West Coast university that has won Henry, the car of his choice starts to steam ominously. The car looks great but it's a lemon.

This is pretty much the opinion that "One on One," directed by Lamont Johnson ("The Last American Hero") and written by Mr. Benson and his father, Jerry Segal, has of the high-pressure, big-business world of supposedly amateur university athletics.

This is not the reason that "One on One" seems so decent and entertaining. The most money-grubbing movies often are insufferably high-minded about other people's ambition and money-grubbing. "One on One" never makes any of its points lightly but never is it smug, as if it had a franchise on truth, nor is it condescending to its characters.

The Benson-Segal screenplay has an appreciation both for the formula of films of action (in this case, on the basketball court) and for chararters of unexpected backbone. In Mr. Johnson, "One on One" also has a director whose best films have been concerned with competition as a dangerously important expression of American life.

According to "One on One," which opened at Loews State 2 and other theaters yesterday, a certain amount of competition is a healthy thing—in politics as well as the fast-food business—but the need to win at all costs is a perversion of a system that otherwise is never seriously questioned.

"One on One" is mostly about the modified awakening of Henry Steele. At first, Henry is nonplussed by the professional thoroughness of the university's athletic program but later he becomes its victim when he doesn't measure up. After he refuses to renounce voluntarily his scholarship, he elects to fight the system to become the basketball star they said he never would.

In movies of mystery and suspense, predictability is fatal. In something like "One on One," predictability has the effect of enriching our interest as we wait to see not what will happen but how it's brought about. A lot of the success of the "how" in "One on One" has to do with the performance by writer-actor Benson, whose clean-cut naïveté masks a surprising moral strength, which, even if it's not very common, is something we'd all like to believe in.

Until her role becomes squeaky clean, Annette O'Toole is most winning as the beautiful, sharp-tongued young woman who is assigned to tutor the basketball star and stays on to fall in love with him. Gail Strickland is very funny as a coach's secretary, who likes to ravish her boss's players, and G.D. Spradlin is fine as her boss, a tough man who stands by the system, right or wrong.

"One on One" is the sort of pop movie that has too much music on the soundtrack and too much bright color in the photography, which, I suppose, is part of its style. Yet it also has some very good sequences that are not at all expected, including the smashing basketball game that concludes the film.

•

"One on One," which has been rated PG ("Parental Guidance Suggested"), contains some mildly vulgar language that you are as likely to hear outside a locker room as in one.

1977 Ag 25, C17:1

Drama in Aspic

DEATH IN THE GARDEN (La Mort en Ce Jardin), directed by Luis Bunuel; screenplay (French with English subtitles) by Mr. Bunuel, Luis Alcoriza, Raymond Queneau, based on a story by Jose-Andre **Lacour; produced by David Mage and Oscar Dancigers; director of photography, Jorge Stahl Jr.; music, Paul Misraki; editor, Marguerite Renoir; a co-production of Producciones Teperac (Mexico) and Dismage (Paris). Running time: 97 minutes. At the Renoir Cinema, 100 Seventh Avenue South. This film has not been rated.**

Djin .... Simone Signoret
Chark .... Georges Marchal
Father Lisardi.............................. Michel Picolli
Maria .... Michele Girardon
Castin .... Charles Vanel
Chenko .... Tito Junco
Alberto .... Luis Aceves Castaneda
Captain Ferrero .... Jorge Martinez de Hoyos
Alvaro .... Raul Ramirez
Lieutenant .... Alberto Pedret

By VINCENT CANBY

TO CONCLUDE its minifestival of heretofore unreleased films by the great Luis Buñuel, the Renoir Cinema yesterday opened "Death in the Garden" ("La Mort en Ce Jardin"), a comparatively big-budget, color, Mexican-French co-production made in 1956.

Like "Fever Mounts at El Pao," a 1959 Mexican-French co-production that Buñuel himself would like to forget, "Death in the Garden" is full of marvelous, uniquely Buñuelian moments set in a melodramatic custard. It's not a film by which to be introduced to Buñuel, but if you know and appreciate his work as I do, it's one of the few movies around that should not be missed.

"Death in the Garden," set in the backwaters and the jungles of an unidentified South American dictatorship, is a large-scale narrative that takes on state, church, the military, society and the individual in such a way that you feel the director must have intended this primeval locale to be a kind of psychological mirror-image of the Franco Spain from which he exiled himself.

Though the film's intellectual substructure is fascinating, the screenplay (by Buñuel, Luis Alcoriza and Raymond Queneau) is so packed with incident that it's all that one can do to keep up with the plot, which is at war with reflection.

Its principal characters are a beautiful hard-hearted whore (played by a very young Simone Signoret), a handsome, amoral young drifter (Georges Marchal), a well-meaning but ineffectual priest (Michel Piccoli, with all of his hair), an aging diamond miner (Charles Vanel) who dreams of opening a restaurant in Marseilles, and his pretty, mute daughter (Michele Girardon).

•

Through one ruse and another, including a bloody but ineffectual rebellion, Buñuel and his collaborators put the characters into the position of having to flee for their lives upstream and into the jungles. Nobody in the small party of fugitives either lives or dies by accident. Their fates are decided by a scheme that invites interpretation more than surprise.

It's not the story, the performances or even the ideas (much more wittily and succinctly put in both earlier and **later Buñuel films), but the sudden moments in which a Buñuel image or gesture comes shining through a haze of melodramatic conventions.**

There's an extraordinary moment when the body of a headless python, killed by the fugitives for their supper, suddenly seems to come alive again as it is attacked by an army of ants. That one image could be one entire movie. In another scene, Mr. Piccoli, the priest, recalls for no easily apparent reason a story about a fellow seminarian who once had a compulsion to eat poached eggs. In moments like this, one glimpses Buñuel's appreciation for the act of disorder.

At the time Buñuel made "Death in the Garden" he had already produced such masterpieces as "Los Olvidados," "El" and "The Criminal Life of Archibaldo de La Cruz," and he was within four years of beginning his golden age that includes "Viridiana," "Simon of the Desert," "Belle de Jour," "Tristana" and "The Discreet Charm of the Bourgeoisie."

"Death in the Garden" is a kind of halfway house for the film genius, made when he had yet to receive the acclaim that would give him full control of his movies, but after he had been taken seriously enough by the money men to be entrusted with an expensive movie with big stars.

"Death in the Garden" is a perfectly honorable compromise, but you won't see in it the simplicity and the clarity of technique and spirit that are so breathtaking in his best movies.

A word about the film as it's being shown at the Renoir: It's a 16-mm print in which the color is not first-rate and many of the white subtitles, especially at the beginning, are virtually invisible.

1977 Ag 26, C6:5

Stories Galore

YOU LIGHT UP MY LIFE, produced, directed and written by Joseph Brooks; director of photography, Eric Saarinen; editor, Lynzee Klingman; music by Mr. Brooks; released by Columbia Pictures. At showcase theaters. Running time: 90 minutes. This film is rated PG.

Laurie Robinson .... Didi Conn
Si Robinson .... Joe Silver
Cris Nolan .... Michael Zaslow
Ken Rothenberg .... Stephan Nathan
Annie Gerrard .... Melanie Mayron
Conductor .... Jerry Keller
Carla Wright .... Lisa Reeves
Charley Nelson .... John Gowans

By JANET MASLIN

"YOU'RE VERY PRETTY," says the dazzlingly handsome man to the sweet young girl he has just brought home with him. "No I'm not," she replies shyly. "Yes you are," says he. "You don't have to say that," she counters. "I wouldn't say it if I didn't mean it," he wispers. Then they kiss, the strings swell and the camera very discreetly averts its eye.

Amazingly enough, "You Light Up My Life" gets away with this kind of bushwah, and usually gets away with it in style. Joseph Brooks, who wrote, produced and directed the film, and also arranged, composed and conducted its score, has taken a number of conventional, even cloying elements and scrambled them just enough to make things fresh and interesting, in a horrifyingly contemporary way. At its best, Mr. Brooks's film captures both the longing for and the infeasibility of romance in the world of showbiz, a world so glossy that surface and substance are virtually interchangeable.

•

"You Light Up My Life" attempts to tell several stories at once, perhaps too many of them. Laurie, the girl (played very movingly by Didi Conn), is engaged to a stuffy, self-absorbed tennis instructor (Stephen Nathan) with whom she already seems to have a bad marriage, and part of the film is about the garish wedding they have planned. The bride and bridegroom will be hauled down the aisle inside a giant clam.

Laurie's father (Joe Silver) is a borscht-belt comedian who has trained his daughter to follow in his footsteps, but during the course of the film she discovers she would be better off as a musician. the audience discovers this too, during an exceptionally touching sequence in which Laurie, having been summoned to audition for a movie that — coincidence of coincidences — is being directed by the same dazzling Lothario with whom she has had an affair, (Michael Zaslow), and she performs the title song. The number is an instant hit, and so is Laurie's unexpectedly full, throaty voice, which does not happen to be Miss Conn's own.

•

Mr. Brooks's previous experience has been in composing orchestral-sounding commercials. (The "You've got a lot to live, and Pepsi's got a lot to give" was perhaps his best known). His songs have this same anthemlike sound. His experience with commercials has helped him to create, in the film's best moments, smart and talented people who have become so hopelessly adept at packaging themselves that they've lost track of what they're selling.

Mr. Brooks isn't always this delicate; in fact, when he takes on the advertising business directly by parodying the ways in which commercials are made, he gets downright mean. But his film, though often too tangled and ambitious for its own good, benefits enormously from the uncommon innocence and vulnerability of Miss Conn's manner, the delightful eccentricity of her timing and the air of invincible hopefulness she brings to even the most hearbreaking of situations.

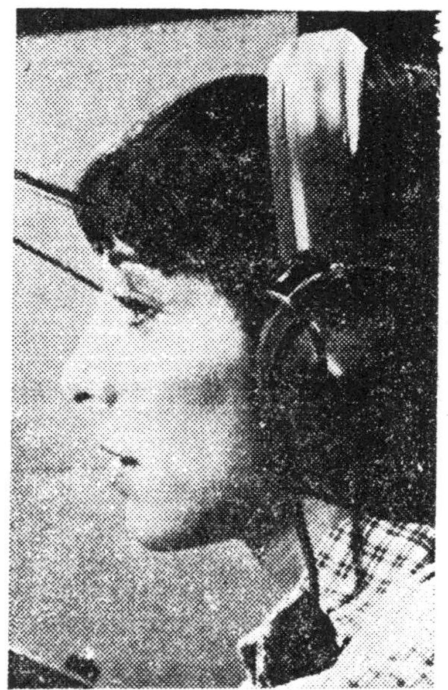

Didi Conn

•

"You Light Up My Life" is rated PG ("Parental Guidance Suggested"), perhaps because, though in only one instance, the character played by Miss Conn goes pretty far on a first date. But the rating is misleading; she really isn't that type of girl.

1977 S 1, B11:4

Flashback Drama

FINAL CHAPTER—WALKING TALL, directed by Jack Starrett, screenplay by Howard B. Kreitsek and Samuel A. Peeples; produced by Charles A. Pratt; music, Walter Scharf; editor, Houseley Stevenson; director of photography, (Robert B. Houseley; a BCP production, distributed by American International Pictures. Running time: 112 minutes. At the Cinerama One Theater, Broadway at 47th Street, and other theaters. This film has been rated R.

Buford Pusser .... Bo Svenson
Luan .... Margaret Blye
Carl Pusser .... Forrest Tucker
The Boss .... Morgan Woodward
Joan .... Libby Boone
Mike .... Leif Garrett
Grade Coker .... Bruce Glover
Martin French.............................. Taylor Lacher
Dwana .... Dawn Lyn
Lloyd Tatum .... Sandy McPeak
Johnny .... Robert Phillips
John Witter .... Logan Ramsey
O.Q. Teal .... Clay Tanner
Grandma .... Lurene Tuttle
Robbie .... David Adams
Aaron .... Vance Davis
Bulo .... H.B. Haggerty
Mel Bascomb .... John Malloy

By VINCENT CANBY

"FINAL CHAPTER—Walking Tall" is the third film about Buford Pusser, the late Tennessee sheriff whose fight against moonshiners, backwoods pimps and bleeding-heart liberals provided the material for "Walking Tall" (1974) and "Part Two, Walking Tall" (1975).

The new film, which opened yesterday at the Cinerama One and other

Bo Svenson

theaters, is full of the desperation of the moviemakers who are perfectly aware that they've already used up all of the cinematic facts of Pusser's life but are unwilling to let a good thing go without getting the last bleeding buck out of it.

This they do by having Buford (Bo Svenson) remembering (in flashback) how his wife was murdered in an ambush set for him (material covered in the first film) and by having him speak long, tear-stained monologues to his wife's tombstone to bring us up to date on what's gone before.

"Final Chapter," which was directed by Jack Starrett and written by Howard B. Kreitsek and Samuel A. Peeples, is a thin, tired movie even when the screen is awash in blood.

•

It's the conceit of this movie that Buford didn't die in a simple accident of the fancy automobile he'd bought with money received from Hollywood for rights to his life, but that the car was sabotaged by underworld figures. The movie covers rather prissily Buford's great good fortune in selling his story to the movies. It's not the sort of thing that happens to most people and it makes this man-of-the-people suddenly too special to fit in with the image created in the first picture. Maybe that's why we are never told how much money he did make, though the writers don't hesitate to speculate (lamely, I think) about the circumstances surrounding his death in 1974.

The writing, direction and acting are dreadful. The only reasons to acknowledge such a film at this length are that the first two movies were so popular, and also one might now hope that this is the absolute end of the merchandising of Buford Pusser.

1977 S 1, B11:4

FILM VIEW

VINCENT CANBY

How to Cope With Creeping 'Rockyism'

There's only one thing worse than pessimism out-of-control—it's optimism rampant. Although the pessimist may wear himself out worrying about dreary possibilities that never come to pass, he has no place to go but up. The optimist starts the day with a song, whistles a happy tune and wrestles with one disappointment after another.

If the current Hollywood trend toward what my colleague Janet Maslin has identified as "creeping Rockyism"—the rash of "cheery and uplifting" movies set in a "profoundly nice world"—bothers you as much as it does me, I've discovered a way to cope, a means of looking into the sunshine of so many recent movies to find the comforting gloom beyond.

It's not easy. One has to work, to grasp at straws, to make mountains out of molehills, to read handwriting on the wall written in invisible ink.

Take, for example, a movie as innocent of cosmic meaning as "For the Love of Benji," Joe Camp's sequel to his enormously successful "Benji." In "For the Love of Benji," the mutt-hero spends most of his time running wildly around Athens and the Acropolis being pursued by spies, policemen, other dogs, and always missing, until the last reel, the little girl and boy who are his owners. At the fadeout Benji is frolicking happily on the beach with the children while the elders describe the means by which Benji foiled a plot to deprive the world of surplus oil (at least, I *think* that's what the spy-thing was all about).

• • •

That ending, however, only seems to be happy. Actually it contains within it the seeds of the starkest kind of dog-tragedy. What Joe Camp doesn't show us, but which he hasn't been able to hide from my field of vision, is that Benji's adventures in Athens have infected him with an obsession for learning. Two weeks after he gets back to the States, Benji runs away to Miami to catch a special Caribbean cruise that features lectures and seminars by such luminaries as Erich Segal ("Hollywood and the Classics Scholar"), Dwight Macdonald ("The Old Left: Its Failures and Achievements") and others.

The first afternoon out, scampering down the deck from the Segal seminar to attend the Macdonald lecture, Benji goes around a corner too fast and—overboard! That's the end of Benji.

• • •

Do you really believe that the concluding sequence of George Lucas's "Star Wars" means that the forces of darkness have been vanquished? It's not an accident that Lucas shot the scene in such a way as to recall Leni Riefenstahl's "Triumph of the Will." You may have a lump in your throat along with Luke Skywalker and Han Solo as they are honored by Princess Leia Organa, but beware.

"The Other Side of Midnight" is a movie "people will be roaring about for years to come."

The sweet-looking, round-faced little princess is a Gorgon in Snow White drag. Two hours after the ceremonies she signs a sweeping order that restricts the civil rights of all robots as well as of those citizens who wear ape-suits, rat-suits or any other gear that sets them apart from the fair race of which she is the purest example.

If that doesn't make your heart leap down, consider the true story of what happens to Gail Berke and David Sanders, the young lovers, and Treece, the crusty salt, after their triumphal fadeout from "The Deep."

We've been led to believe that Berke and Sanders, while bringing up all that buried treasure, have discovered a deep new relationship and will probably decide to get married (in the book they are already married) when they get back to New York.

What Peter Benchley, the writer, and Peter Yates, the director, have not made clear is that in the movie, Berke (Jacqueline Bisset) is already happily married to an extremely rich stockbroker, has three small children, and is not about to give up a New York townhouse (year-round), Hyannisport (summer), Palm Beach (winter) and a Greek island (inbetween) to settle down with a fellow who's nice enough looking but probably has trouble reading a comic strip. She's been using him with her sophisticated husband's tolerant approval. The young man, disappointed and spurned, becomes a Bermuda gigolo, moves on to Acapulco and, when his physique turns to flab, becomes a bartender at the Hilton. Treece, who for years has been withholding the best treasures he's been finding off Bermuda, goes to Switzerland, opens a numbered bank account and starts speculating in currencies.

• • •

Nice people, eh? A great world we live in? Let me go on:

Were you moved—the way I was at first—when the little boy played by Chris Barnes in "The Bad News Bears in Breaking Training" has a tantrum in the middle of the Houston Astrodome and thus is instrumental in the Bears' being able to continue their game and to win it? A lot of good heart there—you may have said to yourself—good old American pluck.

What you failed to notice, though, is that the screenplay wasn't kidding when it indicated that the van in which the Bears drove from Los Angeles to Houston was stolen. After the picture ends and the championship Bears are returning to California, a hard-nosed cop attempts to arrest them as the van crosses the state line. The Bears panic. The driver of the van, Kelly Leak, played by Jackie Earle Haley, becomes rattled and accidentally runs over the cop, killing him, forcing the Bears to become fugitives from justice.

The kids want to go straight but the system won't allow it. In their extreme need for candy bars and soft drinks, they hold up a service station, in the course of which the owner is mashed with a Coke bottle and three Bears are wounded, one fatally, with a shotgun. Their end is no less tragic for being predictable: a shoot-out in which the state cops gun down all of the kids, the last to expire being little Chris Barnes who, as the lights go off in his head, hears—faintly, in the far distance—the sounds of remembered Astrodome applause.

• • •

Take another look at "One on One," which is a very appealing movie on its surface and has been hailed by one critic as "this year's 'Rocky.' " "One on One" is the decently uplifting tale of a high school basketball star named Henry Steele (Robby Benson) who becomes disenchanted with the high pressure and slick professionalism of university sports programs. The movie would like us to think that the story of Henry Steele simply ends after he has withstood all sorts of hazing to remain on the college basketball team to win the crucial game.

All that is true as far as it goes, but there is more to the story: Henry's resentment toward the university is so furious that he is fair game when the Mafia's bland, WASPy-looking campus respresentative contacts him about shaving points. Henry agrees, holding out for the best price possible, and goes undetected until his senior year.

He might have graduated in routine fashion to become a successful basketball coach had not his long-time girlfriend, Janet (Annette O'Toole), blown the whistle. After standing by him for four years, Janet gets mad when Henry attempts to dump her in favor of a pretty but dumb freshman, the daughter of a successful Hollywood film director. Henry is tried, convicted, sent to the slammer for a year where he is knifed to death in the chow line in a case of mistaken identity.

Does that make you feel better? More in touch with reality?

The shocker, though, is the true story of "Rocky," who, Sylvester Stallone has attempted to convince us, is simply a nice guy with guts, a fellow who wanted to go, as he says, "the distance."

In the movie we all saw, Rocky does go the distance in the ring. The secret the movie hints at, but never discloses, is that Rocky has been going the distance in other ways that might be described as "anti-social." Remember Rocky's concern for the young girl who smoked? Well, what the movie covered up was Rocky's weakness for nymphets.

Rocky is to be both pitied and censured, but he couldn't have picked a more inopportune time to be caught by the Morals Squad than one week before the mayoral election in which he was running at the head of a reform ticket. What will Stallone be able to do with Rocky next? The guy's over-age as a fighter and washed up in politics. Maybe "Rocky Hits Skid Row."

The "profoundly nice" worlds of these movies are open to interpretation, but you must work at them. ■

1977 S 4, II:9:1

Prettily Romantic

A WOMAN'S DECISION, directed by Krzysztof Zanussi; screenplay (Polish with English subtitles) by Mr. Zanussi; director of photography, Slawomir Idziak; music, Wojciech Kilar; produced by Film Polski; distributed by Tinc Productions. Running time: 99 minutes. At the Cinema 3 Theater, 59th Street west of Fifth Avenue. This film has not been rated.

Marta .... Maya Komorowska
Marta's husband .... Piotr Franczewski
Jacek .... Marek Piwowski

By VINCENT CANBY

KRZYSZTOF ZANUSSI, the Polish director who has been represented here by "Family Life" (1971) and "Illumination" (1973), is a serious filmmaker whose method keeps getting in the way of his concerns. His newest film, "A Woman's Decision," which opened yesterday at Cinema 3, is a sensitively acted, sometimes-moving story about the emotional indecisions of the woman who has everything.

It may not be an accident that the English translation of the film's Polish title dimly evokes some old Joan Crawford chestnut about a beautiful shopgirl torn between Herbert Marshall (money, glamour) and Franchot Tone (love, marriage).

The alternatives faced by Mr. Zanussi's heroine, Marta (Maya Komorowska), a supposedly happily married woman and mother who is successful in her career (as an accountant) are a good deal more honest and complex than any that ever faced Joan Crawford, but the method is so prettily romantic it denies much of the emotional urgency.

The photography, whenever possible, is dappled with Claude Lelouch-like reflections and the soundtrack is full of the kind of music to read a Mantovani record album's liner notes by.

This is too bad since behind this fanciness there are characters of recognizable feelings and rare decency. Mostly there is Marta who, as played by Miss Komorowska, is a woman of intelligence who can cope with everyone else's problems but is—as she sees it—thwarted by a husband (Piotr Franczewski) absorbed by his own career and unable (or unwilling) to talk about their own difficulties.

Their difficulties aren't unique. He's somewhat skeptical of her enthusiasms, proud of his position as head of the house, inclined to deal with problems by behaving as if they didn't exist. Marta, though, is a doer and a talker. When she finds herself having an affair with a man as footloose as it's possible to be in a socialist state, Marta must make her decision whether to make her break for freedom with the bohemian lover or stay with her husband.

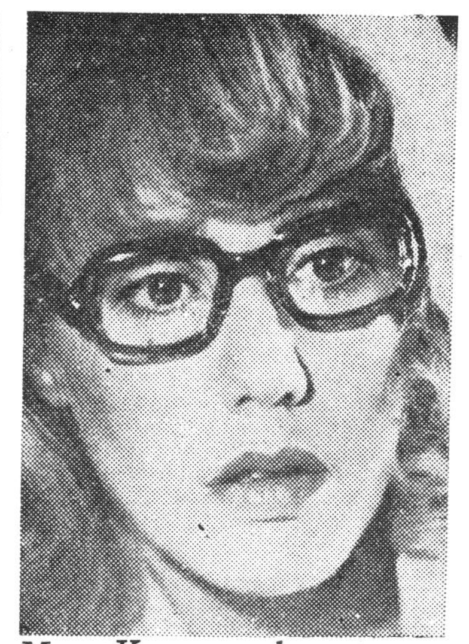

Maya Komorowska

It isn't her decision that gives the film its poignancy but the subsidiary moments by which Marta's character is defined. These include her confrontation, as the office's union representative, with the office's boss, her washroom dialogues with her tough-minded best-friend who calls Marta's do-gooding "self-indulgent," and an extremely moving sequence in which Marta calls on her terminally ill mother-in-law who, though not all that fond of Marta, warns her not to act with her husband as she thinks she should but, honestly, as she feels.

Such sequences are so strong and good, as are the performances by Miss Komorowska, Mr. Franczewski and Marek Piwowski, who plays her lover, that the movie doesn't need the lush production techniques, which, like make-up on a naturally beautiful woman, obscure the film's natural resources.

1977 S 8, B15:4

THE RIVER AND DEATH (El Rio y la Muerte), directed by Luis Bunuel; screenplay (Spanish with English subtitles) by Bunuel and Luis Alcoriza from the novel "Muro Blanco Sobre Roca Negra" by Miguel Alvarez Acosta; director of photography, Raul Martinez Solares; music, Raul Lavista; editor, Jorge Bustos; produced by Clasa Films Mundiales; distributed by Bauer International. Running time: 90 minutes. At the Renoir Cinema, 100 Seventh Avenue South. This film has not been rated.

Mercedes .... Columba Dominguez
Felipe Anguiano .... Miguel Torruco
Gerardo Anguiano .... Joaquin Cordero
Romulo Menchaca .... Jaime Fernandez

Polo....................................Victor Alcocer
Elsa....................................Silvia Derbez
Crescencio............................Humberto Almazan
Chinelas..............................Alfredo Varela·Jr.

By VINCENT CANBY

IN HIS MANY YEARS of filmmaking for the commercial Mexican market, which he embraced without condescension, Luis Buñuel turned out just about every kind of movie there is, with the possible exception of the animated cartoon. He adapted classic novels—"Wuthering Heights" and "The Adventures of Robinson Crusoe." He made screwball comedies ("The Great Madcap"), films of social consciousness ("Los Olvidados"), so-called "women's pictures" ("La Hija del Engaño") and "The River and Death," something that might qualify as Buñuel's Mexican western, though like so many of his commercial films, it twists a genre to suit his view of things.

"The River and Death" (1954), which opened yesterday at the Renoir Cinema as part of the theater's Buñuel retrospective, takes such a solemn, deadpan attitude toward its high melodrama that it virtually becomes an absurdist western, though not, I suspect, the kind that would have offended the audiences for which it was intended.

The New York Times/Jack Manning

Luis Buñuel

The film is the story of several generations of a bloody feud within a Mexican family in a small rural town where men are nothing if not macho, and women—in the "Funny Girl" lyrics of Bob Merrill—"are smaller so that men can be bigger than." Honor is as sensitive to slight as a wagonload of nitroglycerine—the merest jostle and half the town explodes.

Buñuel has been quoted as saying the film is about "death, Mexican-style." This is death so common that it becomes an acceptable part of life, not because of any great faith in a hereafter, though the town is deeply Catholic, but because it's a logical extension of the manners of the living.

The screenplay by Buñuel and Luis Alcoriza is as convoluted as an opera libretto, and understanding the relationships between characters is sometimes as difficult as figuring out the plot of an ongoing television serial after watching a single episode.

The original audiences for "The River and Death" followed these narrative details with care, I'm sure, but what interests us today is Buñuel's position in relation to them. He remains distant, as if appalled, but clear-eyed because he understands the idiocy and hypocrisy of the system. Leading characters are gunned down and carted out of the picture with little more emphasis given these sequences than those devoted to supporting characters we hardly recognize.

•

One of the film's more fascinating, Buñuelean touches is the almost casual, off-screen transformation of its leading lady who, as a young fiancée, had sought to escape life in the bullet-riddled town, into as vengeful a creature as any of its other citizens. The transformation is presented without comment, as a matter of inevitable fact.

The performances by members of the Mexican cast are as extravagant and ritualized as the furious events by which the film is moved in and out of flashbacks toward a present that is, by Buñuelean standards, comparatively full of hope. "The River and Death" is not one of Buñuel's masterpieces, but "Rehearsal for a Crime" (Ensayo de un Crimen), also known here as "The Criminal Life of Archibaldo de La Cruz," which opens at the Renoir next week, is.

1977 S 9, C9:5

Who Will Stand Up?

BY THE BLOOD OF OTHERS (Par Le Sang Des Autres), directed by Marc Simenon; produced by Mr. Simenon and Mylene Demongeot; screenplay (French with English subtitles) by Jean Max; director of photography, Rene Verzier; music, Francis Lai; editor, Etienette Muse; produced by Kangourou Films-Les Films La Boetie (Paris), Merona Produzione (Rome) and Cinevideo Inc. (Montreal); distributed by Joseph Green Pictures. Running time: 95 minutes. At the RKO 86th Street Twin 2, 86th Street near Lexington Avenue, and other theaters. This film has not been rated.

Maryse.............................Marieangela Melato
The Man.............................Yves Beneyton
Genevieve.............................Denise Feliatrault
Caroline.............................Nathalie Guerin
The Mayor.............................Bernard Blier
The Priest.............................Charles Vanel
Police Chief.............................Georges Geret
Juliette.............................Mylene Demongeot
The Prefect.............................Claude Pieplu
Dr. Senequier.............................Francis Blanche
Francesco.............................Robert Castel
Scarpelli.............................Riccardo Cucciolla
Amelie.............................Monita Derrieux
Francis.............................Jacques Godin
Georges.............................Daniel Pilon

By VINCENT CANBY

"BY THE BLOOD OF OTHERS" (Par le Sang des Autres) is a 1973 French film that examines the moral questions that must be faced by anyone dealing with hostage-taking—the most agonizing of terrorist tactics because innocents are the victims—against which there seems to be no defense whatsoever.

The film, which opened yesterday at the RKO 86th Street Twin 2 and other theaters, was directed by Marc Simenon (son of Georges) and produced by him and Mylene Demongeot, who plays a small but vivid role in the picture.

The movie, set in rural France, begins with a furious, almost unbearably cruel sequence in which a young mental patient rapes and beats a woman and then takes her and her daughter hostage, demanding as their ransom the company of the most beautiful girl in the nearby village. The mayor is alerted, then the prefect, the chief of police, the doctor and the priest. How to deal with the situation? Storm the house? Find a suitably pliant prostitute? Nothing?

•

When "By the Blood of Others" starts asking questions, the film slowly expires into a series of preconceived attitudes that ultimately have the piety—and something of the dramatic impact—of a public-service clean-air commercial. Is there anyone here who'll stand up for hypocrisy? No? Then for whom is this movie intended?

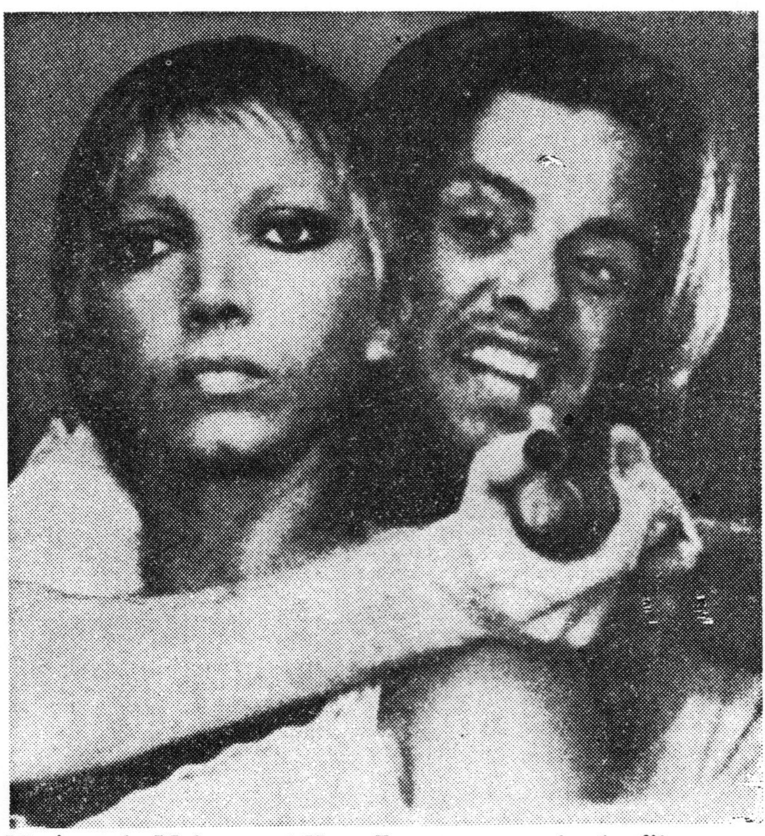

Mariangela Melato and Yves Beneyton star in the film

Given what becomes the numbing predictability of Jean Max's screenplay, Mr. Simenon obtains some decent performances, though they are all pretty much defined by how they are required to behave, not by character but by the point of the movie, which, simply put, is that anyone will compromise when his own interests are at stake.

The exception to the rule in "By the Blood of Others" is the Mayor's daughter, a spunky, beautifully tanned young woman played by Mariangela Melato—long before she met Lina Wertmüller—whose bravery and love are quite spectacular and not in the least convincing.

The supporting cast includes Yves Beneyton as the mental patient, a young man who looks as if he could be still another son of John Carradine; Bernard Blier as the Mayor; Charles Vanel as the old priest who drinks to forget how terrible his flock is, and Claude Pieplu as the despicably vain prefect. Miss Demongeot's role as the hooker who is brought to the scene is not especially surprising, but it is lively, and when she is removed from the scene the movie goes extremely glum.

1977 S 15, C20:5

Hodgepodge Salad

ALLEGRO NON TROPO, an animated film directed by Bruno Bozzetto; screenplay (Italian with English subtitles) by Mr. Bozzetto, Guido Manuli and Maurizio Nichetti; animators: Mr. Bozzetto, Giuseppe Lagana, Walter Cavazzuti, Giovanni Ferrari, Giancarlo Cereda,, Giorgio Valentini, Guido Manuli, Paolo Abicocco and Giorgio Foriani; editing, Giancarlo Rossi; music by Debussy, Dvorak, Ravel, Sibelius, Vivaldi and Stravinsky; distributed by Specialty Films, Inc. At the Little Carnegie Theater, 57th Street east of Seventh Avenue. With: Maurizio Nichetti, Nestor Garay, Maurizio Micheli and Maria Luisa Giovannini.

ONE of the most delightful things about Walt Disney's "Fantasia" is its innocence, and one of the least delightful things about Bruno Bozzetto's "Allegro Non Troppo," an ungainly takeoff on "Fantasia," is its absolute lack of same. The film opened yesterday at the Little Carnegie Theater.

Mr. Bozzetto, who has devised animated seqences to accompany classical music and interspersed a few live, black-and-white (green-and-white, actually) episodes involving an orchestra, seems dangerously conscious of the work of other animators.

That is not to suggest that he is uninventive—far from it. If anything, Mr. Bozzetto is *too* original, so feverishly determined to outdo everyone from Disney to Bakshi that he seems less suited to directing than to tossing salad. His movie is full of clashing colors and incongruous styles, with characters inspired by anything from Keane paintings to herbal shampoo commercials. The best that can be said for such a mélange is that it is genuinely exhausting.

JANET MASLIN

1977 S 16, C9:1

THE CRIMINAL LIFE OF ARCHIBALDO DE LA CRUZ, also called "Rehearsal for a Crime" (Ensayo de un Crimen), directed by Luis Bunuel; screenplay (Spanish with English subtitles) by Mr. Bunuel and Eduardo Ugarte Pages, from a story by Rodolfo Usigli; produced by Alfonso Patino Gomez; director of photography, Agustin Jimenez; music, Jorge Perez Herrera; editor Jorge Bustos; a production of Alianza Cinematografica, S.A. Running time: 91 minutes. At the Renoir Cinema, 100 Seventh Avenue South. This film has not been rated.

Archibaldo de la Cruz .... Ernesto Alonso
Lavinia .... Miroslava Stern
Patricia .... Rita Macedo
Carlota Cervantes .... Ariadna Weler
Alejandro Rivas .... Rodolfo Landa
Senora Cervantes .... Andres Palma
Chief of Police .... Carlos Riquelme
Willy Corduran .... Jose Maria Linares Rivas
Governess .... Leonor Llansas
Mother .... Eva Calvo

Ernesto Alonso, Miroslava Stern in "The Criminal Life of Archibaldo de la Cruz"
Buñuel in peak form and total command

By VINCENT CANBY

LUIS BUNUEL'S "The Criminal Life of Archibaldo de la Cruz," also sometimes called "Rehearsal for a Crime" ("Ensayo de un Crimen"), was made in Mexico in 1955 and has been seen here at screenings at the late, lamented Cinema 16 and at the Museum of Modern Art. But only yesterday did it have its commercial premiere at the Renoir Cinema, where it is that theater's evening program. Though it's 22 years late in arriving, "The Criminal Life of Archibaldo de la Cruz" is the only new movie in town about which I can say that it mustn't be missed.

Buñuel made some-not-so-good films after "Archibaldo" and before the classic "Viridiana" (1961), but "Archibaldo" is the film that really begins his extraordinarily productive late period in which he has given us such masterpieces as "Tristana" and "The Discreet Charm of the Bourgeosie," with the possibility of another coming up, "That Obscure Object of Desire," his newest work, which will be seen at the forthcoming New York Film Festival.

One might be tempted to call "Archibaldo vintage Buñuel except that that would imply the film recalls a talent since lost, worn thin, run out. "Archibaldo" is Buñuel in the peak form with which he has continued to dazzle us in recent years. It doesn't have the superb European actors who have given "Tristana," "Discreet Charm" and "Phantom of Liberty" their box-office chic, but it has the wit, the simplicity of style, the directness and, above all, the total command that make his later films seem virtually perfect realizations of the director's particular visions.

•

"Archibaldo," written by Buñuel and Eduardo Ugarte Pages, is the breezy, irreverent tale of a would-be archfiend, Archibaldo de la Cruz, well-born, rich, handsome, sensitive, who is just the tiniest bit hung up as the result of a childhood trauma.

When he was 5 and the impossibly spoiled only child of wealthy bourgeois parents, he was caught one day by his governess as he was dressed in his mother's corsets. The governess scolds him, mildly, but Archibaldo is not the sort of child to take correction lightly. A few minutes later, using a music box he's been told has magical powers, he wishes the governess dead. No sooner wished than accomplished. The young woman is immediately killed by a stray bullet from a revolution raging outside.

The sight of the boring, but very pretty, governess lying dead on the carpet, her skirts in a tangle around her upper thighs, makes a lasting impression on the boy, who thereafter goes through life confusing love, death and sexuality. Through a series of outrageous coincidences, the objects of Archibaldo's sexual desires and sadistic impulses are dispatched by circumstances over which he has no control but for which he feels increasingly guilty.

As played by Ernesto Alonso, an actor who has the charm and the wit that Fernando Rey has displayed in similar roles in more recent Buñuel films, Archibaldo is a very polite, considerate and wise nut, aware of almost everything except that he is the inevitable (in Buñuel's view) product of religious and sexual repression.

•

Archibaldo is innocent of the crimes he tries to confess to the chief of police but though this film is high comedy, his innocence is not much different from that of the delinquents of Buñuel's "Los Olvidados"—the slum kids who commit unspeakable atrocities but feel no guilt whatsoever. Archibaldo and the slum children inhabit very different kinds of films though the social orders are equally bankrupt in both.

In "Archibaldo," Buñuel's mood is light-hearted, benign and extremely funny. Archibaldo's salvation eventually is brought about by an act that might be described as a surrogate murder of the beautiful young woman he loves, and whose waxen effigy he happily burns up in his pottery oven.

Miroslava Stern, who was billed simply as Miroslava in American films ("The Brave Bulls"), is cool and self-possessed as the beautiful model and tour-guide who finally is responsible for bringing Archibaldo out of his fantasy world. Unbilled is the excellent child actor who plays the young Archibaldo. Eva Calvo is the brat's mother, the sort of woman who, when she's told she can't go to the theater because of the revolution, stamps her pretty little foot and whines, "It *would* have to be today."

1977 S 16, C9:5

Distorted Lenses

SAN FRANCISCO GOOD TIMES, directed, edited and produced by Allan Francovich and Eugene Rosow. At the Jean Renoir Cinema, 100 Seventh Avenue South. Running time: 90 minutes. This film has no rating.
With: The Good Times Commune and Timothy Leary, Bill Graham, Peter Townshend, the Magic Floating Lotus Opera Company and the Berkeley Astrology Guild.

By JANET MASLIN

"SAN FRANCISCO GOOD TIMES" is an hour-long black-and-white documentary about the underground newspaper Good Times, which was published between 1968 and 1972 by a staff that lived communally for part of that period. The newspaper and its concerns also provide the directors, Allan Frankovich and Eugene Rosow, with an opportunity to sketch a rambling, unfocused, very affectionate portrait of San Francisco hippiedom in general. The film has opened at the Jean Renoir Cinema.

So there are outdoor rock festivals, chatty astrologers and organic gardeners showing off their seeds. There are brief interviews with Peter Townshend of the Who and the rock promoter Bill Graham, and background music by the Jefferson Airplane. There is a session with Timothy Leary, who speaks knowingly of "the politics of pleasure." There is a rally in support of Huey Newton. There are also, without much explanation, the demonstrations and violence in People's Park.

The film makers approach their subject wistfully but without much insight, perhaps because their footage was assembled at exactly the wrong time. In 1973, when "San Francisco Good Times" was completed, the euphoria was over, but the evaluation process had not yet begun.

Mr. Frankovich and Mr. Rosow seem so intent on capturing the happiest memories of a lost time that they wind up depicting the era as one of pure physical ecstasy and also, to some extent, of irresponsibility. When viewed strictly in terms of be-ins and incoherent raps and LSD, hippies can be made to seem sweet in their naïveté, but, finally, too ineffectual to have made any difference. That's neither accurate nor fair.

"San Francisco Good Times" is less likely to make one mourn the passing of a movement than to speculate, without any help from the film makers, about its follow-through.

1977 S 16, C13:2

FILM VIEW

VINCENT CANBY

Actresses Stage A Comeback

Actresses may have a different opinion, since they read the available scripts long before we see them as finished films, but, based on the evidence of the year to date, 1977 is turning into a big year for women. For the first time in a number of seasons, there will be some real competition at the end of the year for awards for best performances by leading actresses as well as by actresses in supporting roles.

I haven't even seen Jane Fonda and Vanessa Redgrave in "Julia," or Shirley MacLaine and Anne Bancroft in "The Turning Point," or Diane Keaton in "Looking for Mr. Goodbar," yet I'd have trouble having to decide at this minute among those performances I have seen.

• • •

I think especially of Lily Tomlin as the slightly pulled-apart, pot-smoking, would-be actress and designer whose cat, by being cat-napped, more or less is the reason Robert Benton's "The Late Show" initially gets going. As anyone knows who saw her extraordinary one-woman show on Broadway earlier in the year, Miss Tomlin can create a dozen different characters in the time it might take another actress to say "yes," but her performance in "The Late Show" is the scrupulously disciplined portrait of a four-star nut. It's wild, unpredictable, funny and terrifically touching.

• • •

But I don't know if I'd want to vote for her over Shelley Duvall's equally touching and equally surprising performance as Millie, the ethereal eccentric with the hide of an elephant in Robert Altman's "3 Women." This is Miss Duvall's most remarkable performance so far in one of the most unusual careers in contemporary films. For that matter, though, I'm not sure I'd want to vote for Miss Duvall over her "3 Women" co-star, Sissy Spacek, who, in the Altman film, plays Pinky Rose, the waif who systematically takes over the identity, habits and life of Miss Duvall's Millie.

Miss Spacek is also one of the reasons to sit through Alan Rudolph's "Welcome to L.A.," in which she plays the sort of nature child who likes to vacuum-clean topless, though the most impressive performance in that film is given by Geraldine Chaplin as a desperately lonely middle-class wife who lives a full fantasy life.

Miss Chaplin's role in "Welcome to L.A." would, I suppose, be classified as "supporting" (as are all of the performances), thus she need not compete with herself in the same category for her sweet/strong leading performance in a dual role in Carlos Saura's "Cria," a fine Spanish film about the efforts of a small girl, played by the incredible Ana Torrent, to give some order to the adult world in which the child lives. Miss Chaplin would not be competing with herself, but she would be competing with Miss Torrent, and that competition is formidable.

• • •

Not having yet seen "Looking for Mr. Goodbar," I don't know whether Diane Keaton is going to find that her performance in that film will be competing for awards with her exuberant performance we already have seen as Woody Allen's tenderly neurotic love in "Annie Hall." The scope and wit of Miss Keaton's performance in this film, as well as her performance in Israel Horovitz's very funny Off Broadway play, "The Primary English Class," reminds me of all that talk we've been hearing in recent years about writers not writing good parts for women.

This may be true (and there are, I suspect, economic reasons for it, since there's been such a heavy emphasis on action films that are male-dominated), but that may be only part of the story. When actresses (or actors, for that matter) of unusual talent come to the surface, they have a way of inspiring directors and writers to do the sort of work they might not have attempted without the availability of particular performers.

I doubt that Woody Allen would have ever conceived of a movie like "Annie Hall" if there hadn't been Diane Keaton to play the title role. Saura has gone on record to say that he got

Geraldine Chaplin, an impressive performer, receives formidable competition from the young Ana Torrent in "Cria."

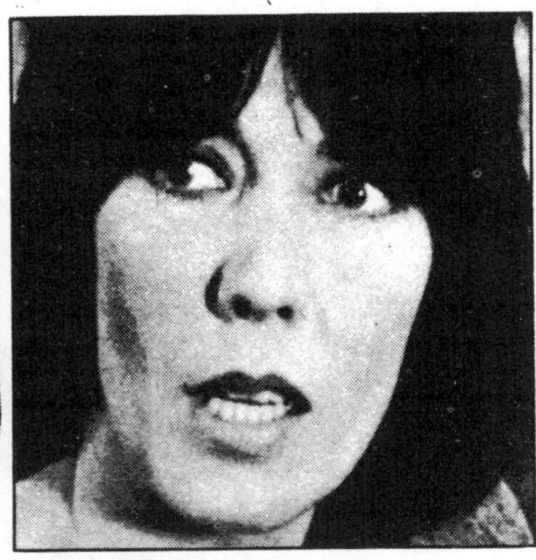

Lily Tomlin is "wild, unpredictable, funny and terrifically touching" as a four-star nut in "The Late Show."

Diane Keaton gives an "exuberant performance as Woody Allen's tenderly neurotic love" in "Annie Hall."

Kathleen Quinlan gives a major performance as the schizophrenic in "I Never Promised You a Rose Garden."

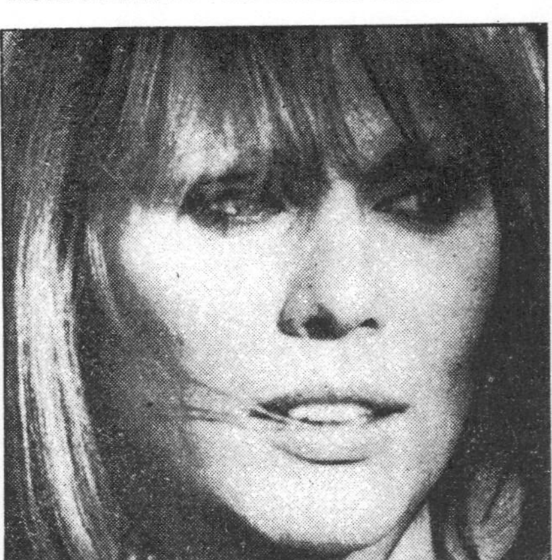

Marthe Keller, a Swiss actress with real potential, may finally make her mark in "Bobby Deerfield" and "Fedora."

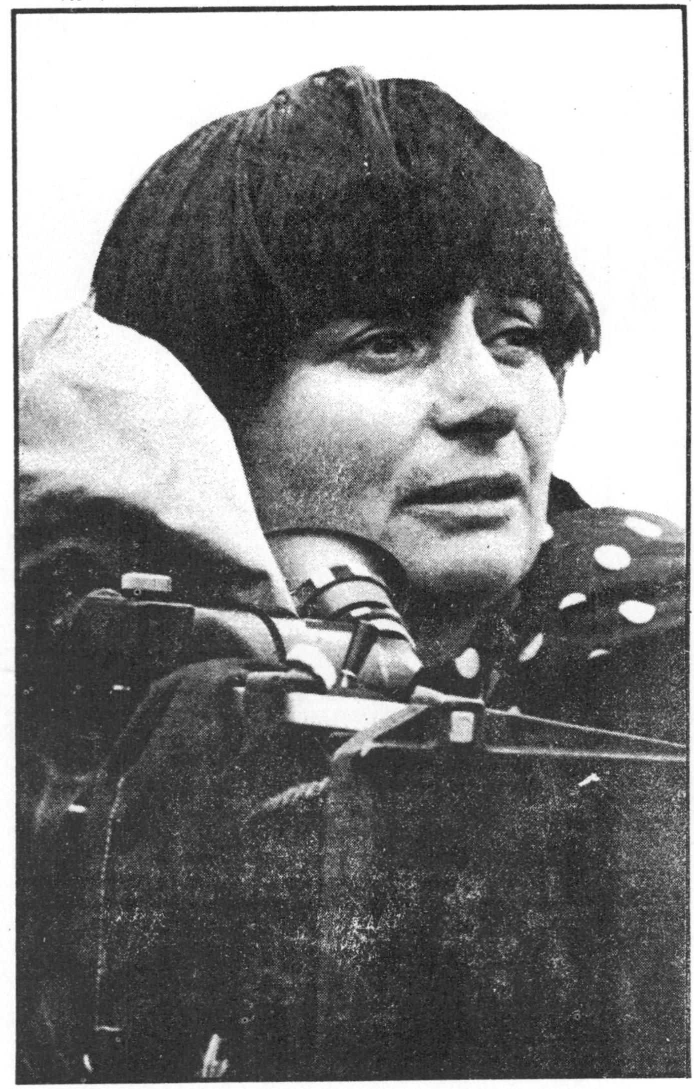

Agnes Varda, director of "One Sings, the Other Doesn't": "I'm a woman of tomorrow, but . . . "

Therese Liotard and Valerie Mairesse, who star as long-time friends in Miss Varda's film.

Jacqueline Bisset, wasted in "The Deep," will perhaps one day get "a role that matches her talent as well as her beauty."

Marie-France Pisier, despite the disaster of "The Other Side of Midnight," is clearly someone who knows how to act.

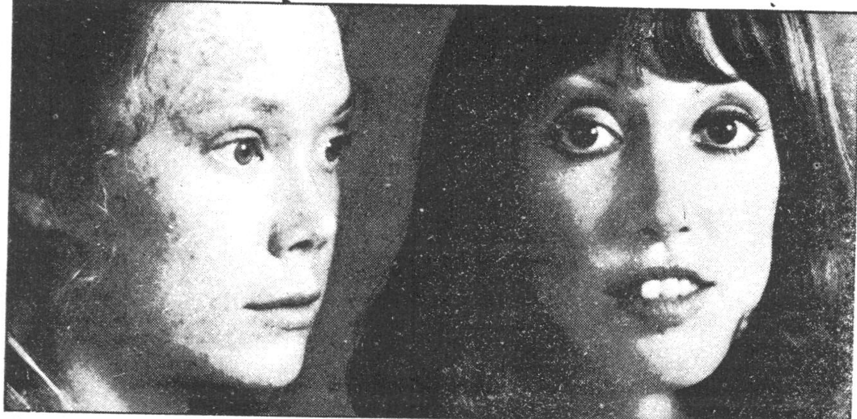

Shelley Duvall, right, is touching in "3 Women," but "I'm not sure I'd want to vote for Miss Duvall over her co-star, Sissy Spacek, who is also one of the reasons to sit through 'Welcome to L.A.' "

the idea for "Cria" after having seen Miss Torrent's performance in Victor Erice's earlier Spanish film, "The Spirit of the Bee-hive." Without a child of Miss Torrent's phenomenally expressive face and reined-in personality, "Cria" would have been an impossibility.

This availability of performers need not work exclusively on such a personal basis, though. When writers and directors are aware that there's a pool of unusual talent at hand, they are more likely to chance offbeat works than when they assume that no matter how grand the projected film, it will inevitably be ground down to fit mediocre talents.

• • •

Another major performance by an actress this year is that of Kathleen Quinlan as the schizophrenic teen-ager in "I Never Promised You a Rose Garden"—the sort of performance that is as notable for the excesses it avoids as for the honesty and simplicity of what is achieved.

One of the most enchanting performances of the year to date is Hanna Schygulla's in the title role of Rainer Werner Fassbinder's "Effi Briest," an adaptation of the novel by Theodore Fontane. My own appreciation of Miss Schygulla's delicate performance as Effi is enhanced by having seen her in all sorts of different kinds of roles in other Fassbinder films, which, unfortunately, haven't been widely distributed outside New York. Yet I doubt that anyone seeing her for the first time in "Effi Briest" will be unaffected by an actress who could be, I think, an international star.

• • •

So far I've restricted this inventory only to actresses who scored particular successes in good roles, but some other women have been doing quite well in movies of less than cosmic interest, to such an extent that it seems probable that when the right material comes along, they'll be ready.

Though "The Other Side of Midnight" is a joke by any standard except the box-office one, Marie-France Pisier is clearly someone who knows how to act ("Cousin Cousine," "French Provincial"). One of these days the splendid-looking Jacqueline Bisset ("The Deep") is going to get a role that matches her talent as well as her beauty. We've already seen glimpses of it in François Truffaut's "Day for Night" and in some of her early, low-budget Hollywood films.

Marthe Keller, the Swiss actress, seems to have real potential but somehow the roles—large ones—she's had in such American films as "Black Sunday" (as the Arab terrorist) and "Marathon Man" (the agent/girlfriend) reduce what could be a highly individualistic talent to the proportions of those of a starlet. Perhaps she'll make her mark in Sydney Pollack's forthcoming "Bobby Deerfield" and Billy Wilder's "Fedora."

I also wouldn't mind at all if someone decided to take Barbara Carrera seriously as a film personality. Miss Carrera ("The Island of Dr. Moreau," "Embryo") has the kind of looks and screen personality that an old tycoon on the order of Louis B. Mayer would have transformed into an old-fashioned motion-picture star, having taught her motion-picture behavior along the way as was done in the days of Ava Gardner and Lana Turner.

That there apparently are more decent roles for women now must have something to do with this availability of a full range of major actresses, but which comes first, the actress or the role, can only be impolitely associated to the question about the chicken and the egg. ■

1977 S 18, II:17:1

Barbara Carrera is the kind of screen personality who could become another Lana Turner or Ava Gardner.

LET JOY REIGN SUPREME (Que La Fete Commence), directed by Bertrand Tavernier; screenplay (French **with English subtitles) by Jean** Aurenche and Mr. Tavernier; produced by Michelle de Broca; director of photography, Pierre William Glenn; editor, Armand Psenny; music, Philippe d'Orleans, Regent of France; distributed by Specialty Films. Running time: 120 minutes. At the 68th Street Playhouse, Third Avenue at 68th Street. **This film has** not been rated.

Philippe d'Orleans................Philippe Noiret
Abbe Dubois........................Jean Rochefort
Marquis de Pontcallec.......Jean Pierre Marielle
Mme. de Bourbon..................Marina Vlady
Villeroi..............................Alfred Adam
Duc de Bourbon..................Gerard Desarthe
Emilie...............................Christine Pascal
Caussimon..........................Gilles Guillot

By VINCENT CANBY

"Let Joy Reign Supreme" "(Que La Fête Commence"), the second film by Bertrand Tavernier, the young French critic and film scholar who turned director with the excellent "The Clockmaker," reminds us of the special pleasures of what Hollywood used to call the "historical picture," when the historical picture was done well and wasn't just a lot of waxy-looking actors walking around in oddly cut trousers or writing with feathers instead of pens.

The title is purposely ironic. "Let Joy Reign Supreme" is a witty provocative, visually dazzling re-creation of French political and social life during the crucial last years of Philippe d'Orléans, regent for the young Louis XV, who was 5 years old at the death of his great-grandfather, Louis XIV.

•

When the old Sun King died in 1715, France had been at the peak of its power and glory. Before the end of the century, though, it would be swept by the greatest, bloodiest revolution the world had yet seen. It is the idea of Mr. Tavernier and Jean Aurenche, the veteran French filmwriter who collaborated with the director on the screenplay, that some of the factors that made the revolution inevitable were more or less locked into place by events that took place during Philippe's regency.

For the benefit of those of us who may not be quite as up on French history as they are, the writers have provided us with a brief introduction that sets the scene and the time (1720-23) for the film that follows. Some references in the movie remain obscure, but mostly it is a tumultuously vivid evocation of people, place and period, with particular emphasis on three men.

The first is Philippe, the regent, superbly played by Philippe Noiret, an intelligent, civilized, sophisticated man who says, when he remembers that his daughter is an abbess, "I don't get along with my son-in-law." Philippe is not an unenlightened ruler but he is limited by his fondness for epic debauchery and by his noble birth. He really cannot think of the lower orders except as abstract beings.

The second is Philippe's principal foreign minster, the Abbé Dubois, a cynical, ambitious, sardonic man, the son of a peasant, a churchman who has absolutely no knack for saying Mass and who schemes to be made an archbishop because the power of archbishops comes from God and need not depend on the passing fancies of any temporal rulers. It's a **marvelous role** that Jean Rochefort plays with great style, especially in the Abbé's scenes with Philippe, the lifetime friend he faithfully attends but who can say, when the chips are down, "I hope you die a painful death."

The third key figure is a Breton nationalist, the short-tempered, rugged but doomed-to-fail Marquis de Pontcallec (Jean Pierre Marielle), who has grand dreams of seceding from France to establish the Republic of Brittany. Pontcallec writes insulting letters to Philippe, negotiates for aid from the Spanish King but, when the time for rebellion arrives, find himself alone on the field.

•

"Que La Fête Commence" ("Let the Party Begin"), the film's original French title, could be the cry that begins one of Philippe's exhausting, all-night orgies, as well as one that heralds the beginning of the end of the French monarchy.

As much as he delights in the interplay of power and personalities, Mr. Tavernier delights in re-creating the look and sound (soundtrack music is by Philippe himself) of the period. "Let Joy Reign Supreme" is one of the handsomest, most densely detailed color films I've seen since "Barry Lyndon."

•

The movie, which opened yesterday at the 68th Street Playhouse, is so rich in references—to everything from the boom in New World real estate and reforms in French banking procedures to the toilet habits of the aristocracy—that it might send you to the library for more information. The panorama that Mr. Tavernier sets before us is alive. It's also seen through the bifocal lens of a moviemaker who, though fascinated by the closeup incident, never loses the long view. A fine film.

Philippe Noiret and Marina Vlady in "Let Joy Reign Supreme"
A tumultuously vivid evocation of people, place and period

1977 S 19, 45:1

DIRTY DUCK, directed, written, animated and designed by Charles Swenson; produced by Jerry Good; songs written, arranged, produced and conducted by Mark Volman and Howard Kaylan (Flo & Eddie). A Murakami Wolfe production. A New World Pictures release. At the D. W. Griffith and Quad 4 Theaters. Running time: 75 minutes. This film has been rated X.

VOICES: Mark Volman, Robery Ridgeley, Walker Edmiston, Cynthia Adler, Janet Lee, Lurene Tuttle, Jerry Good and Howard Kaylan.

FIRST, A WARNING: "Dirty Duck," which opened yesterday at the D. W. Griffith and Quad 4 theaters, is an X-rated film. And, what's more, an X-rated animated film. So people of tender sensibilities who are offended without exception by street language and repelled by the depiction and use of genitalia will not find it to their liking.

But thos who approach it with an open mind are likely to find it a rather zany, lively, uninhibited sexual odyssey that manages to mix a bit of Walter Mitty and a touch of Woody Allen with some of the innocence of Walt Disney, the urban smarts of Ralph Bakshi, the mysticism and psychedelic eclecticism of "Yellow Submarine" and the unabashed libidinous relish of the cartoonist Robert Crumb.

•

To that is added a sprinkling of Jules Feiffer's angst, an attractive rock-music score and evocations of actors like Humphrey Bogart, whose voice emerges from an immense tank that conjures up memories of "Sahara"; John Wayne, as a white-uniformed highway patrolman with a saurian neck, ultrapatriotic, ultraconservative mouthings and a body that also serves as his drag-racer patrol car; Alfonso Bedoya, as God Hat, the bandit leader in "Treasure of Sierra Madre," and Billie Burke, as Glinda, the Good Witch in "The Wizard of Oz."

"Dirty Duck" is the story of Willard Eisenbaum, a shy, lonely, inept, sexually frustrated employee of an insurance company, thrown by fate into the company of a large, sailor-suited duck that is convinced that some good sex will straighten Willard out. Off they go, on a journey that brings them eventually into each other's affections.

•

Though the film is studded with a wide variety of sexual practices and though some of its fast-talking characters and faster lyrics make satirical sport of sexual and ethnic stereotypes and of late-night television's used-car pitchmen, "Dirty Duck" manages to avoid the common trap of leering sophomorism.

For all its lustfulness, "Dirty Duck" is concerned with the condition of loneliness. And in it, Charles Swenson—who wrote, animated and designed the movie, with songs by the Flo & Eddie comedy team of Mark Volman and Howard Kaylan—has told a familiar story in an unconventional way. Beneath the zanines's and constant sexuality lie understanding and affection. Behind all the updated surface beats an old-fashioned mushy heart.

1977 S 22, C14:5

Chauvinist Game

ONE SINGS, THE OTHER DOESN'T, directed by Agnes Varda; screenplay (French with English subtitles, and English narration) by Miss Varda; directors of photography, Charlie Van Damme, Nurith Aviv and Elisabeth Prouvost; music and songs by Francois Wertheimer and Orchid, with lyrics by Miss Varda; editors, Joelle Van Effenterre, Francoise Thevenot and Elisabeth Pistorio; a coproduction of Cine-Tamaris, Societe Francaise de Production, Institut National de l'Audiovisuel and Contretemps (Paris), Paraidise Film (Brussels) and Population Film (Curacao); distributed by Cinema 5. Running time: 105 minutes. At the New York Film Festival, Lincoln Center. This film has not been rated.

Pauline, called Apple ....Valerie Mairesse
Suzanne ....Therese Liotard
Darius ....Ali Rafti
Jerome ....Robert Dadies
Apple's father ....Francis Lemaire
Dr. Pierre Aubanel ....Jean-Pierre Pellegrin

By VINCENT CANBY

THE 15TH NEW YORK Film Festival gets very fashionably under way tonight at Avery Fisher Hall with a woman's picture—a movie by, for and about women. These are women who haven't exactly done away with men but they have successfully established an emotional strength that—unintentionally, I think—makes the men around them look superfluous for everything except for the reproduction of the species and singing in the kind of harmony that requires a soprano, an alto, a tenor and a bass.

The film is "One Sings, the Other Doesn't," written and directed by Agnès Varda, who, over the years, has made so many interesting, original, surprising films ("Le Bonheur," "Lion's Love," "Daguerreotypes," among others) that critics no longer feel compelled to make a big sexist deal out of the presence of a woman in a field dominated by men.

In a peculiar way, now, "One Sings, the Other Doesn't" wipes all that away. It's as if Miss Varda had become fed up with the old integration bit and had switched to a new separate-but-equal line and, instead of demonstrating a woman's right to be taken seriously as a film artist or even as a person, had begun her own propaganda campaign.

"One Sings, the Other Doesn't" has some good sequences in it, is beautifully acted by two actresses who are new to me, is handsomely composed but, at key moments, it's as phony—as relentlessly schematic and upbeat—as Soviet neo-realist art. It's of less interest as a movie than as a statement of position.

•

The film, which opens its commercial engagement tomorrow at the Plaza Theater, is about two women and their friendship over approximately 15 years when each in her own fashion achieves some kind of liberation from the chains that bind one exclusively to kitchen, kids and kaffeeklatsch.

Suzanne (Thérèse Liotard), the more conventional of the two, and also the more interesting, is a pretty brunette who lives with an unsuccessful photographer named Jerôme (Robert Dadiès) who gives her babies and love, but whose wife refuses to divorce him. Jerôme appreciates women but he cannot cope. His studio is filled with pictures of women of all ages, shapes and dispositions. "I'm after women in their naked truth," he says at one point, but though he loves and admires them, he's incapable of doing much more than making them pregnant. Jerôme commits suicide.

Pauline (Valérie Mairesse), nicknamed Apple, several years younger than Suzanne, sees Suzanne's impossible position and resolves not to be similarly caught. She becomes a successful street-singer and women's rights worker and suddenly, to her surprise, falls

Therese Liotard and Valerie Mairesse in "One Sings, the Other Doesn't"
A movie by, for and about women

in love with a young Iranian student. Darius (Ali Raffi), her lover, appears to share her "radical" views, that is, until they go home to Iran where he's as much of a chauvinist as the next fellow.

Suzanne, abandoned by Jerome through his suicide, takes her children to the farm of her disapproving parents in the south of France. During the day she tends the stock. At night she teaches herself to type and, in the kind of transition that is typical of this film, she suddenly becomes a successful family-planning counselor whose own children are models of adjustment.

Pauline/Apple, who has given up her singing career to follow her husband home to the picture-postcard scenery of Iran, has a child and feels she must get on with her own life. She and Darius reach an agreement: he can keep the first baby if he makes her pregnant again so that she can have one of her own, which is how they work out *their* problems.

•

Throughout all these adventures, Suzanne and Apple keep up a correspondence whose principal theme is how each misses the other, feels a deep womanly kinship to the other, and longs for a reunion so that they can talk about women and women's problems.

Somehow, I never particularly believe in this friendship, nor do I believe in the sunny resolution to the various problems.

It all has the air of whistling in the dark, or maybe of positive thinking. When Apple and her all-woman combo sing in public squares, the repeated refrain is "I'm a woman—I'm me!" The self-absorption is intense. It's also abstract. If we were more aware of the toll taken of the two women in their struggles, the film would carry more emotional impact. As it is, it has a sort of high-toned perfunctoriness to it.

The two leading actresses are appealing in ways the material is not, and Miss Varda obtains some attractive performances from the children in her cast.

I admit that my tepid reaction to "One Sings, the Other Doesn't" is biased. I'm no more or less interested in "women's" pictures than in "men's" pictures. I am interested in good movies, which transcend sex.

1977 S 23, C10:3

THE AMERICAN FRIEND, directed by Wim Wenders; screenplay (English, German and French with English subtitles) by Mr. Wenders, based on the novel "Ripley's Game" by Patricia Highsmith; director of photography, Robby Muller; editor, Peter Przygodda; music, Jurgen Knieper; distributed by New Yorker Films. Running time: 127 minutes. At the New York Film Festival, Lincoln Center.

Jonathan Zimmermann	Bruno Ganz
Tom Ripley	Dennis Hopper
Marianne Zimmermann	Lisa Kreuzer
Raoul Minot	Gerard Blain
Derwatt	Nicholas Ray
The American	Samuel Fuller
Marcangelo	Peter Lilienthal
Ingraham	Daniel Schmid
Man in Paris	Sandy Whitelaw
Man in restaurant	Jean Eustache
Rodolphe	Lou Castel
Daniel	Andreas Dedecke

By VINCENT CANBY

It's one of the peculiarities of contemporary film making that three of the most interesting American underworld movies of recent years have been made in West Germany by young German directors—two by Rainer Werner Fassbinder ("Gods of the Plague" and "The American Soldier") and now one by Wim Wenders, "The American Friend," which will be shown at the 15th New York Film Festival at Lincoln Center tonight at 9 and tomorrow at 3 P.M. The film will begin its regular commercial engagement Monday at the Cinema Studio.

Strictly speaking, all three are more important as comments on the genre than as demonstrations of it, though the tone of tragic-cool, which is essentially comic in Mr. Fassbinder's brilliantly slapdash films, is made so profound and desolate in "The American Friends" that the film can stand by itself.

•

Mr. Wenders describes "The American Friend" as "an entertainment film," by which, I assume, he means that unlike, say, his fine, icy adaptation of Peter Handke's "The Goalie's Anxiety at the Penalty Kick," it's for mass audiences who demand narratives with more or less conventional beginnings, middles and ends. This is not quite true.

"The American Friend," adapted from Patricia Highsmith's novel "Ripley's Game," has those basic ingredients, plus a good deal of suspense, but it's almost as shy of easy explanation as "The Goalie's Anxiety at the Penalty Kick." Like that film, too, "The American Friend" is obsessed with the idea of personal identity, which was slowly slipping away from the goalie during that earlier film, but which is the revelation in the new work.

"The American Friend" is about a young Hamburg picture-framer named Jonathan Zimmermann (Bruno Ganz), who is happily married and has a young son and who is perfectly ordinary except that he is suffering from a rare blood disease. He knows the disease will eventually be fatal, though doctors can't tell him whether he will live two days, a month or five years. The uncertainty gives him a kind of peace, a saintly sanity. He would call himself a moral man.

This peace and sanity is upset when Jonathan is approached by an insistent Frenchman who, promising to pay him handsomely and to help him obtain special medical treatment, asks him to come to Paris to assassinate a Mafia figure. Jonathan needs the money but the idea of killing seems inconceivable to him. Watching these negotiations, and advising the Frenchman while also establishing a friendship with Jonathan, is a mysterious American, Tom Ripley (Dennis Hopper), a fellow who wears a cowboy hat, looks ravaged by time though he's certainly not old, and who appears to be part of some sort of art-forging ring.

Little by little Jonathan Zimmermann finds himself being caught up in a series of outrageous circumstances that apparently have no connection to his earlier life. It's as if the promise of a huge sum of money, which would relieve his widow of financial worries, as well as the specialized medical treatment, derail the personality he thought he had. He kills once without remorse, and then finds he must accept a second assignment.

These are the bare bones of the story, which has almost nothing to do with the why of things and very little to do with the how. Instead it consists entirely of behavior observed from a privileged position, as was "The Goalie's Anxiety at the Penalty Kick." We see Jonathan not as he is transformed into someone other, but as he strips down to his essential being. At least, that's how I read it.

Though it's fun, it's not always simple. Mr. Wenders has so spaced out sequences—consciously eliminating explanations—that he's left it up to us to read the film as we will from causes and effects.

One of the effects that most interests him is the friendship that grows up between Jonathan and the peculiar Tom Ripley, who moves through the film as he does from one continent to another, with supernatural ease. Ripley, which is the first decent role that Mr. Hopper has had in years, is the devil who buys Jonathan's soul, only to find that, eventually, their roles are, if not reversed, then rearranged. For a brief moment in between they are friends.

"The American Friend," much superior to both Mr. Wenders's "Alice in the Cities" and "Kings of the Road," is enigmatic if one insists on simple logic, which is not something that is terribly rare in movies, even bad ones. It is fascinating if you take it on its own terms. It is an extremely beautiful film, sometimes intentionally extrav-

Bruno Ganz, left, and Dennis Hopper in "The American Friend."

An enigmatic, fascinating and extremely beautiful film.

agant in visual detail, and acted with effectively insidious self-assurance by Mr. Hopper and with an appropriate sort of square intensity by Mr. Ganz, who was so good earlier this year in the German film version of "The Wild Duck."

One reservation: Mr. Wenders's decision to cast the veteran Hollywood directors Nicholas Ray and Sam Fuller as two of the villains of the piece simply disturbs the flow of the film, if you recognize them, as I do. However, since I didn't recognize either Jean Eustache or Gerard Blain, the French directors, who also appear in the film, I suppose this won't seem especially important to most moviegoers.

1977 S 24, 15:1

TENT OF MIRACLES (TENDA DOS MILAGRES), directed by Nelson Pereira dos Santos; screenplay (with English subtitles) by Mr. Pereira dos Santos and Jorge Amado, from the novel by Jorge Amado; photography, Helio Silva; editor, Raimundo Higino and Severino Dada; music, Gilberto Gil and Jards Macale; executive producer, Ney Sant'Anna; production manager, Albertino N. da Fonseca. At the New York Film Festival at Alice Tully Hall, Broadway at 65th Street. Running time: 132 minutes.

Fausto Pena .... Hugo Carvana
Ana Mercedes .... Sonia Dias
Prof. Edelweis .... Anecy Rocha
Dr. Zezinho .... Wilson Jorge Mello
Gastao Simas .... Geraldo Freire
James D. Livingston .... Laurence R. Wilson
Dada .... Severino Dada
Pedro Archanjo .... Jards Macale
Pedro Anchanjo .... Juarez Paraiso

"Tent of Miracles" is to be commended on a couple of scores: It condemns racism and it was made in Brazil, a country whose films don't receive much representation in this country. It's also the story of a very saintly man, and certainly such stories are rare these days. That said, "Tent of Miracles" is also too messy and jumbled to have many other selling points.

The subject of the film is Pedro Archanjo, a black Bahian sociologist who is also supposed to have been a brilliant philosopher, his principal theory being that miscegenation is necessary and healthy for Brazilian society. Unfortunately, his story is told and discussed by a bunch of hip young film makers, supposedly at work on a biographical movie, who aren't properly equipped to explain his genius. Their story, which takes up almost as much time as the movie-within-a-movie about Archanjo, is uninteresting and at times almost unintelligible.

•

Archanjo turns out to have been a man who enthusiastically practiced what he preached. In the film's best sequences, he appears as a young man, involved with women of all shades and persuasions and merrily outraging the supposedly white upper classes. One of Archanjo's theories is that everyone in Bahia is of mixed blood anyway, and one of his supposedly most daring acts is to publish a booklet naming black ancestors of all the fanciest white families.

Nelson Pereira dos Santos is a well-established Brazilian director, but the film is surprisingly clumsy, almost amateurish at times: for instance, it is at first difficult to tell whether the footage of Archanjo's story is meant to be a series of flashbacks or excerpts from the film being made. A white American scientist, who yells things such as "May I have my money?" at the top of his lungs, is supposed to be a Nobel Laureate but looks more like a freshman quarterback. Sonia Dias is a great beauty, but her ubiquitousness in the film goes entirely unexplained.

JANET MASLIN

1977 S 24, 15:1

L'ENFANT DE PARIS, directed by Leonce Perret; screenplay (French with English subtitles) by Mr. Perret, from the play "Les Deux Orphelines" by d'Ennery; photography, Specht; production company, Film Gaumont. At the New York Film Festival, Alice Tully Hall, Broadway and 65th Street. Running time: 104 minutes. This film has not been rated.

The little girl .... Suzanne LeBret
The boy .... Maurice Lagrenee
The kidnapper .... Louis Leubas

By JANET MASLIN

"L'Enfant de Paris" is an exceptionally well-photographed 1913 silent film that has been included in the New York Film Festival partly because it was a personal favorite of the late Henri Langlois, founder of the Cinemathèque Française. Directed by Leonce Perret, who made or appeared in an estimated 600 films (21 of them in America) before he died in 1935, the movie tells the story of an almost inhumanly sweet little girl who is kidnapped by scoundrels.

The story is unexceptional, and so is Perret's general approach. But his technical sophistication is quite impressive, particularly during a long sequence in which the kidnapper has the good taste to cart his captive off to Nice. "L'Enfant de Paris" is well worth seeing on the strength of its location footage alone.

•

As the film begins, the little girl is rich and happy, safe in the bosom of her loving family. Half an hour later her father, a soldier, has disappeared in battle, and her mother has died of grief. The sweet little girl is sent to an orphanage, where the other girls laugh at her and the teachers take her favorite doll away.

When she escapes from the orphanage and faints as a result of her exertions, a crook comes along to steal her gold locket, which of course contains pictures of her poor, lost parents. As an afterthought, he steals her, too.

The little girl, who is carried through the film like a human suitcase, winds up in the predictable den of iniquity, living with a drunken shoemaker and his hunchbacked assistant. The assistant falls in love with the little girl, rather unwholesomely, and eventually returns her to her father, who is, of course, not dead after all. In movies as treacly as this one, fathers who disappear in battle seldom are.

•

The little girl, Suzanne LeBret, has a strangely middle-aged face and an acting range that allows for little more than her extending her arms joyfully or staring tragically at the floor. The crook, played by Louis Leubas, is more interesting, because he oozes crookedness from every pore, as do his very amusing henchmen. "L'Enfant de Paris" has no dialogue subtitles, only a few printed telegrams and newspaper articles, and would seemingly lend itself to overacting of the most painful kind. Fortunately, many of the performances are as unexpectedly forthright as the stunning pre-World War I landscapes.

1977 S 24, 15:1

MEN OF BRONZE, a documentary feature directed by William Miles; produced by Mr. Miles and Paul Killiam; director of photography, Richard W. Adams; editor, Mr. Adams; a Killiam Shows Inc. production. Running time: 59 minutes.

Also, **CHILDREN OF LABOR,** a documentary feature directed by Noel Buckner, Mary Dore, Richard Broadman and Al Gedicks; screenplay by Mr. Buckner, Miss Dore and Mr. Broadman; directors of photography, Mr. Buckner, Miss Dore and Mr. Broadman; editors, Mr Buckner, Miss Dore and Mr. Broadman; a C. D. Film Workshop/C.A.L.A. production. Running time 53 minutes. Both films at the New York Film Festival at Lincoln Center.

History recollected by the people who made it and the inevitable erosion of ideals by time are the themes shared by a pair of American documentaries, "Men of Bronze" and "Children of Labor," which will be shown at the 15th New York Film Festival at Alice Tully Hall tonight at 6 and Monday at 9:30 P.M.

Of the two, "Men of Bronze," which is about the exploits of the largely black 369th U.S. Infantry Regiment in World War I, is the most moving and finished, if only because the film makers have somehow scaled their subject to the dimensions of film. "Children of Labor" examines the social and political history of Finnish immigrants to this country beginning at the turn-of-the-century, with emphasis on the radical Finnish-American tradition. The film is effective as far as it goes but the subject appears to be too big and complex to fit neatly into a 53-minute movie.

William Miles, who directed "Men of Bronze," and Paul Killiam who produced the film with Mr. Miles, have constructed their film out of old newsreel footage and stills and, most importantly, from interviews with three excellent subjects.

The first is the patrician Hamilton Fish Sr., who was a captain with the 369th and who seems to represent the best of an American aristocratic tradition long gone. Another is Melville T. Miller, is still wonderfully garrulous, witty Brooklyn man who enlisted in the 369th when it was still a part of the New York National Guard—it didn't receive its Federal designation until it was attached to the French Army in 1918.

Mr. Miller, now in his mid-seventies, appears to remember everything clearly but with the particular detachment of time that can make even the most hair-raising memories funny.

The most interesting interview, even though he says less than the other two, is the comparatively taciturn Frederick H. Williams, a grizzled old black man whose memories are not entirely sweet, and whose silences and pauses suggest that, in his case, time may not have healed all wounds.

"Men of Bronze" is a fine tribute to the history of the 369th, whose spectacular battle records proved that black soldiers were fit for considerably more than stevedore duty. This is a lesson that apparently wasn't even understood by World War Two, when the United States Navy would pressure black enlistees to take mess duty—though, of course, there was no doubt in anyone's mind by the time Vietnam came along.

"Children of Labor" is no less sincere but the subject is too vast to be covered by a short film except in a sort of textbook style that touches names, dates and places so rapidly that at the end you suspect you might be subjected to a spot quiz.

VINCENT CANBY

1977 S 24, 15:1

Movie Falters After Getting Off to Fairly Good Start

FEMMES FATALES, directed by Bertrand Blier; produced by Bernard Artigues; written by Mr. Blier and Philippe Dumarcay; cinematography by Claude Renoir; music by George Delerue. Distributed by New Line Cinema. At the Columbia II and Quad 3 theaters. In French with English subtitles. Running time: 81 minutes. This movie has not been rated.

Paul Dufour .... Jean-Pierre Marielle
Albert .... Jean Rochefort
Le Cure .... Bernard Blier
Suzanne .... Brigitte Fossey
L'Ancien Combattant .... Claude Piepiue
Le P.D.G. .... Michel Peyrelon
Le Chanoine .... Pierre Bertin
Genevieve .... Micheline Kahn
Cliente Cossue .... Claudine Beccarie

By LAWRENCE VAN GELDER

For a while, "Femmes Fatales," the French film that opened yesterday at the Columbia II and Quad 3 theaters, gives indication of accomplishing the considerable feat of being a successful comedy about misogyny.

But about halfway along it stops deriving its strength from the portrayals of Jean-Pierre Marielle as a jaded gynecologist and Jean Rochefort as an irresistible pimp who is his companion in flight from women. Instead, it shifts abruptly in mood and focus from their new lives in a tiny village where they loaf, cook, eat, drink, befriend the local clergy and counsel a young boy against the consequences of sex.

In a jarring transition from reality into fantasy, "Femmes Fatales" transforms its two principals into leaders of a horde of like-minded refugees. Pursued by a uniformed army of lubricious women, the pair are taken prisoner and turned into scientifically monitored studs before they are turned out—broken, terrified and prematurely aged—to a bleak life-on-the-run that brings them to an ironic and unexpected final destination.

The effect of the transition is very much as though Bertrand Blier, who also directed "Going Places," had lost his footing on the most slippery high wire he could find. Certainly these are not the times when the making of a movie that makes women and their sexuality the objects of scorn and revulsion can be deemed anything less than an exercise in risk and an invitation to condign condemnation.

But thanks to the credibility of Mr. Marielle as the gynecologist, Paul, and to Mr. Rochefort as the pimp, Albert, director Blier manages to teeter about halfway toward success on his own terms before turning cosmic and plunging into artistic failure.

"Femmes Fatales," sexually graphic, foul-mouthed, intermittently funny, initially deft and ultimately clumsy, is neither witty enough nor strong enough to override the current of social history. Narrow and likely to offend many, it stands like a bigot at a conference on brotherhood, capable of generating laughter, yes, but chiefly remarkable for insensitivity to time and place.

1977 S 24, 17:1

'Padre Padrone' Very Moving

By JANET MASLIN

Paolo and Vittorio Taviani, the two brothers who wrote and directed "Padre Padrone," say they first got the idea for their film from a newspaper clipping—about a shepherd who had lived in almost complete isolation in the hills of Sardinia until he turned 20, then went on to become a professor of linguistics and write a book about his experience.

When the brothers learned more about the man's story, they began to perceive him not as an unsocialized innocent, à la Truffaut's "The Wild Child" or Herzog's "The Mystery of Kaspar Hauser," but rather as a more conventional figure whose character was shaped through his battle with a single huge impediment. The obstacle in "Padre Padrone" is not the shepherd's estrangement, or even his monumental loneliness, but rather his terrifying and tyrannical father.

The film's beginning, and its most stirring segment, presents a 6-year-old boy being taken out of school and sent off to tend a flock on a desolate, ruggedly beautiful mountainside. His father, who beats young Gavino with objects as stridently symbolic as a stick and a dead snake, inducts the boy into his new way of life in the cruelest manner possible.

There are isolated instances of the father's tenderness, when he shares his perceptions of nature with his son and when he realizes, after the boy bursts into tears and then faints from fright and exhaustion, that the torture has gone far enough. But most of the father's behavior borders on sadism,

Saverio Marconi

despite the economic necessity in which it is rooted. So the father remains as inconsistent and irrational to the viewer as he might seem to a small child.

•

Years later, when Gavino begins bridling under his father's authority and angling for a chance to escape, his battle is fought along more familiar lines and his father seems a less formidable adversary. Gavino enlists in the army and travel to the Italian mainland, where he begins to educate himself and delight in the precise meaning of words. The title, which means "My Father, My Master," also refers to Gavino's sheer exultation in the nuances of his new vocabulary.

By the time Gavino returns to Sardinia, his father has begun to seem smaller, pettier, a bit more pathetic in his stubbornness. Gavino finally wins his freedom, but at a terrible cost: He is forced to witness the spectacle of his father's defeat and humiliation.

•

"Padre Padrone" is stirringly affirmative. It's also a bit simple: The patriarchal behavior of Gavino's father is so readily accepted as an unfathomable given constant that the film never offers much insight into the man or the culture that fostered him. Intriguingly aberrant behavior is chalked up to tradition, and thus robbed of some of its ferocity. But the film is vivid and very moving, coarse but seldom blunt, and filled with raw landscapes that underscore the naturalness and inevitability of the father-son rituals it depicts.

The Taviani brothers have made other films, but this is the first of their efforts to receive wide international exposure and acclaim. "Padre Padrone," which was the grand prize winner at Cannes this year, should serve less as a debut than as an introduction.

1977 S 25, 56:1

A SPECIAL DAY, directed by Ettore Scola; story and screenplay (Italian with English subtitles) by Ruggero Maccari and Mr. Scola, in collaboration with Maurizio Costanzo; produced by Carlo Ponti; music, Armando Trovaioli; director of photography, Pasqualino De Santis; editor, Raimondo Crociani; a coproduction of Canafox Films (Montreal) and Comp. Cin. Champion S.P.A. (Rome), distributed by Cinema 5. Running time: 110 minutes. At the Beekman Theater, Second Avenue at 65th Street. This film has not been rated.

Antonietta	Sophia Loren
Gabriele	Marcello Mastroianni
Emanuele	John Vernon
Caretaker	Francoise Berd
Figlia Del Cavaliere	Nicole Magny
Romana	Patrizia Basso
Arnaldo	Tiziano De Persio
Fabio	Maurizio Di Paolantonio
Littorio	Antonio Garibaldi
Umberto	Vittorio Guerrieri
Maria Luisa	Alessandra Mussolini

By VINCENT CANBY

Antonietta and Gabriele make an extremely unlikely couple. She's an overworked, barely literate housewife, the mother of six, a woman with a drawn face and the haggard expression of someone who's long since given up on what she looks like, but she accepts her lot, which includes a talking mynah bird that can't even get her name right. She is, however, an enthusiastic supporter of Mussolini, who is, for Antonietta, both a savior and a sex symbol. She keeps a scrapbook on his life.

Gabriele is a fastidious bachelor, intelligent, sensitive and sardonic, and he's at the end of his rope. He's been cashiered from his job as an announcer on the government-sponsored radio station because he's suspected of being degenerate, that is, homosexual, which he is. In Italy in 1938, homosexuals were rounded up and packed off to Sardinia, where they couldn't contaminate the Fascist culture.

In Ettore Scola's funny, humane "A Special Day"—an acting tour de force for Sophia Loren and Marcello Mastroianni—Antonietta and Gabriele are never really a couple, but their brief encounter lights up the screen with the kind of radiance you get only from great movie actors who also are great stars.

"A Special Day," which opened yesterday at the Beekman Theater, takes place on the day of Hitler's 1938 state visit to Rome, where he was given a gigantic, hysterically enthusiastic reception by Mussolini, the King, the diplomatic corps, leading Italian industrialists (whose names are still familiar) and 90 percent of the city's population and a military parade that lasted almost as long as Mussolini's campaign in Ethiopia.

After packing off her six children and her husband (all properly uniformed) to attend the rally, Antonietta sets about to clean up the debris within the cramped apartment when Rosamunda, the mynah bird, escapes and flies to the other side of the courtyard of the now-empty apartment block. This is the device that brings Antonietta and Gabriele together for almost two hours of comic and touching confidences, arguments and self-searching that lead, eventually, to a love scene that is simultaneously ecstatic and forlorn. It's something, I suspect, that only Miss Loren and Mr. Mastroianni could bring off so triumphantly.

"A Very Special Day" is pure theatrical contrivance, and this is part of the pleasure as we watch two extraordinary performers test themselves, take risks, find unexpected pockets of humor and pathos in characters that one doesn't easily associate with the public personality.

Miss Loren is magnificent in the best role she's had since "Two Women," for which she won an Academy Award. Of the two stars, she has a slightly easier time of it in that in the film's earlier scenes the character is presented to us in context, within the bosom of her uproarious family and in relation to her self-important, macho, peanut-brained husband, played by John Vernon.

Mr. Mastroianni has a somewhat more difficult time of it if only because we seem him isolated from any social-psychological landscape that might define the man he is. We have to take him at his word, but because we bring to any Mastroianni performance the memories of so many earlier ones, it's initially difficult to accept Gabriele as the distraught, suicidal homosexual he

Sophia Loren
Magnificent

is supposed to be.

Once the two characters have been brought together, though, and the revelations revealed, the movie takes off in the sort of breathtaking display of teamwork I associate with Hepburn and Tracy, Lunt and Fontanne and, of course, Loren and Mastroianni in "Yesterday, Today and Tomorrow" and "Marriage, Italian-Style."

They don't do it all by themselves. Mr. Scola, who was responsible for "We All Loved Each Other So Much" earlier this year, has provided them with good, sometimes quite extravagant material to work with. The screenplay, which he wrote with Ruggero Maccari and, say the credits, "in collaboration with Maurizio Costanzo," is full of wit and feeling even when we're aware of facile ironies.

But for all the facility, which certainly isn't bad in itself, "A Special Day" has a solid foundation in honesty. This is no middle-aged "Tea and Sympathy." The encounter doesn't turn Gabriele into a straight or Antonietta into an anti-Fascist bomb-thrower. It enriches their lives, which, on a somewhat smaller scale, is what this film does.

1977 S 26, 41:1

Animation In Sharper Focus

By A. H. WEILER

In adding an animation festival to its offerings for the first time, the New York Film Festival is not so much breaking new ground as it is bringing a fuzzy scene into sharp focus. The move is logical. After all, a variety of short subjects were scattered through previous festivals. And the Film Society of Lincoln Center, sponsors of the showings, also have had gratifying, experiences with programs of shorts in our public parks in the last few years.

However, most moviegoers are rarely exposed to such fare, even if select sources such as the Whitney Museum, the Museum of Modern Art, the Film Forum and the current Fantastic Animation Festival occasionally illustrate the idea that animation did not die with Winsor McCay's "Little Nemo" of 1911 or Disney's Donald Duck, but is alive and well and busily living here and abroad. This festival more than amply backs up that idea.

The collection, aimed largely at adults, includes more than 70 films, running from 40 seconds to 14 minutes each, predominantly made by Americans, with others from Canada, Japan, France, Poland, Czechoslovakia, Yugoslavia, England, Belgium and Germany. This bulging compilation, separated into five, approximately 90-minute programs, is being shown, beginning today and running through Friday, starting at 3:15 P.M., in Lincoln Center's Alice Tully Hall.

As might be expected, this king-sized package is qualitatively uneven, although the creative drives of most of the film makers are obvious from samplings of their output.

Of course, animation has traveled diverse roads since the heyday of McCay, Disney and Max Fleischer. If McCay is absent, Disney, Fleischer and Tex Avery, respectively, are represented by funny, typical period pieces in "Der Fuehrer's Face" (1943), "Poor Cinderella" (1934) and "Miss Glory" (1936).

Equally indicative of the imaginative efforts of contemporary American and foreign artists are "Fantabiblical," an 11-minute Italian-made comic commentary on the Old and New Testaments by Bruno Bozzeto, whose feature cartoon, "Allegro Non Tropo," has recently opened here; "The Killing of an Egg," a three-minute Dutch antic about an extremely lively egg by Paul Driessen, and "Manga," an amusing, seven-minute Japanese lampoon of the hunter and the hunted by Yoji Kuri.

Some entries, such as the one-minute "Teatime" by Mary Szilagyi, are merely fragmentary exercises, but, among other American offerings, Sally Cruikshank's four-minute "Chow Fun" is as cheerful as its rinky-dink music, and George Griffin's clever four-minute "The Club" is a sexually satiric thrust at the rich man's club life.

The comparatively recent, successful marriage of science and artistry is strikingly evident in Jordan Belson's nine-minute "Music of the Spheres." This latest creation of an experienced experimental moviemaker—a combination of computer, optical and electronic music techniques—emerges as beautiful eye-and ear-catching abstractions whirling in outer space.

In similarly inventive style, "Le Pasagiste" ("Mindscapes"), an eight-minute Canadian film by Jacques Drouin, evokes moody dream visions through the use of a "pin screen" technique developed in the 1930's by Alexander Alexeiff in which animation evolves from shadows of pins on a board. "The Nose," a 12-minute French entry by Alexeiff and Claire Parker, also is on view.

•

Kathleen McLaughlin's five-minute "Opening and Closing" is an effectively absurd focus on washing-machine doors. It is hardly as ambitious or forceful as "Rapid Eye Movements," a 13-minute mélange of various techniques and hip dialogue by Jeff Carpenter that strongly projects the humor and sadness of current swingers.

There are a number of shorts such as Oskar Fischinger's abstract "Composition In Blue," Lillian Schwartz's computerized "Googleplex" and Frank Mouris's Kaleidoscopic "Coney" that are gems known to animation aficionados in New York. These, as well as a vast majority of the others, bear the stamps of dedication and a striving for originality.

A random list should include the lovely, previously shown Canadian "Notes on a Triangle," by René Jadoin; Walt Disney's "Band Concert," Al Jarnow's repetitive but fascinating montage of a seemingly endless trip on a geometric highway, and Jane Aaron's animated figures superimposed on scenic live action in "In Plain Sight."

The work of Americans may dominate the festival, but "Phoenix," a 10-minute Yugoslav cartoon by Petar Gligarovski, seems to be a tribute to an unusual freedom accorded an artist from a Communist nation. His views of the progress of civilization, its explosive destruction by the shrieking horrors of modern warfare and a phoenix-like ensuing peace, is an amalgam of germane propaganda and colorful art.

Perhaps this import and the more than 70 other films may be too much of a specialized thing. No matter. This innovative festival is both a constructive service for the artists involved and for discriminating moviegoers, and is proof that the film-animation genre has come a long way since "Little Nemo."

1977 S 26, 41:4

Mexican Movie, Admirable in Some Respects, Is Curiosity

By LAWRENCE VAN GELDER

It's not every day that the opportunity arrives to see Patricia Hearst (a.k.a. Kane), Hernando Cortez, Juliet, Adam, Jesus Christ and a team of football players cavorting under one roof to the music of Anton Dvorak, Edvard Grieg, Antonio Vivaldi, Richard Wagner and Giaccomo Puccini, among others.

And perhaps that's reason enough to run off to the 15th New York Film Festival tonight at 6:15 P.M. or next Sunday at 3 P.M. to see the Mexican Movie "Pafnucio Santo," which may be the most eclectic extravaganza to play Lincoln Center since "The Night of the Scarecrow" by the Brazilian director Sérgio Ricardo made the festival lineup in 1974.

But audiences in search of films of less reach and greater grasp are best advised that "Pafnucio Santo" is—while admirable in some respects—chiefly a curiosity.

•

The work of Rafael Corkidi, perhaps best known as the cameraman on the Alejandro Godorowsky films "El Topo" and "Holy Mountain," this movie mixes religion, politics, Mexican history and opera.

The Cast

PAFNUCIO SANTO, directed, written and photographed by Rafael Corkidi; produced by Conacine, S.A.; executive producer, Rafael Corkidi. At the 15th New York Film Festival. Running time: 98 minutes.
Pafnucio .... Pablo Corkidi
Frida Kahlo, Sor Juana Inez de la Cruz; Cortez's captain .... Maria de la Luz Zendejas
Messenger, Cortez, Judge, Romeo, Ranger, Revolutionary .... Jorge Humberto Robles
Demon dancer, China Povlana, Zapata .... Gina Morett
Eva, Carlotta, Patty Kane, Juliet ...... Susana Kamini
Malinche .... Piya
Adam, Jesus Christ, Revolutionary .... Don Juan Barron
Soldier of Cortez .... Jose Luis Urquieta
Newspaper Boy .... Sebastian

At its simplest, it deals with the search for a woman to bear a new Messiah, undertaken by a small, football-helmented boy, Pafnucio, at the behest of a sinister-looking, black-caped heavenly emissary who has borne witness—we see—to the flight from Paradise, cross burnings by the Ku Klux Klan, the march of Jewish children into Nazi death camps and the crucifixion of Jesus.

The search undertaken by Pafnucio carries him back and forth in Mexican history from Cortez to modern revolutionaries, with Patricia Hearst thrown in as Patricia Kane, obviously a descendant of the cinema Citizen of the same name. Everybody sings, and in the case of classic compositions, the original lyrics are retained, although the subtitles on the screen have the characters saying such things as "Don't you see the Empire is crumbling?" or "Your God killed our gods—our temples, our art all lie in ruins.'

•

"Pafnucio Santo" is at its best visually. Mr. Corkidi has a keen eye for the visually striking: figures set against desolate landscapes, football players in full uniform drilling in the ruins of a cathedral, banner-waving peasant armies. But his ambitious movie is a bit like a homemade backyard shrine, admirable for what it says about the builder's capacity for compassion, regrettable in its confusion of prettiness for high art.

1977 S 27, 34:3

Film Festival: 'The Truck' Talks And Talks but It Says Very Little

By JANET MASLIN

In "The Truck," the director and novelist Marguerite Duras plays a woman whose lips curl into a joyless, knowing half-smile every time she makes mention of despair. Her film should appeal most strongly to those viewers who are similarly attuned to the romantic possibilities of gloom. However, even those who have little patience for Miss Duras's preciousness may find her work as haunting and determinedly self-possessed as it is quietly infuriating.

•

"The Truck," which will be screened this evening at 9:30 and tomorrow evening at 6:15 in the New York Film Festival at Alice Tully Hall, involves two players and a blue diesel rig. The actors—tiny, stiff-backed Miss Duras and geefy, hulking Gérard Depardieu—sit fixedly at a table, reading aloud and discussing a film script she has written. The truck, seen intermittently, rolls inexorably along highways and byways. There is no other action.

Jerry Bauer

Marguerite Duras

Her work is as haunting as it is quietly infuriating.

The script is about a woman possessed of "the noblesse of banality," to use Miss Duras's phrase. The woman is given a lift by a young truck driver. "He's exercising his profession," Miss Duras explains, "and she, she's transported by him."

In the truck, as the script has it, the woman sings and talks a great deal. Mr. Depardieu's character asks her, "But what are you talking about?" "She says, 'I'm talking,". is Miss Dura's reply.

•

"The Truck" is full of exasperatingly banal interchanges, which are in no way improved or illuminated by Miss Duras's admission of her character's banality. It is also rather coyly self-pitying, because Miss Duras and her character seem to overlap, and the character is at times made to seem pathetic.

But the scenes of the truck take on an eerie grandeur after a while, and Miss Duras's disdain for her audience's expectations becomes perversely transfixing. It's a pity that her script is not as stern and unrelenting as the film's visual style.

On the same bill, and on quite a different note, is "Grandpa," a 29-minute short by Stephen Forman and Paul Desaulniers, an affectionate and admiring portrait of Mr. Forman's feisty grandfather. The talkative grandfather says more in this film's first five minutes than Mr. Depardieu says during the entirety of "The Truck."

1977 S 27, 34:3

Victims' Victim

SHORT EYES, directed by Robert M. Young; screenplay by Miguel Pinero, based on his stage play; produced by Lewis Harris; music scored and composed by Curtis Mayfield; executive producer, Marvin Stuart; editor, Edward Beyer; director of photography, Peter Sova; distributed by the Film League Inc. Running time: 104 minutes. At the New York Film Festival at Lincoln Center. This film has been rated R.
Clark Davis .... Bruce Davison
Juan .... Jose Perez
Ice .... Nathan George
El Raheem .... Don Blakely
Paco .... Shawn Elliott
Cupcakes .... Tito Goya
Longshoe .... Joseph Carberry
Omar .... Kenny Steward
Mr. Nett .... Bob Maroff
Mr. Brown .... Keith Davis
Go Go .... Miguel Pinero
Cha Cha .... Willie Hernandez
Tony .... Tony Di Benedetto
Mr. Allard .... Bob O'Connell
Mr. Morrison .... Mark Margolis
Gomez .... Richard Matamoros
Pappy .... Curtis Mayfield
Johnny .... Freddie Fender

By VINCENT CANBY

"SHORT EYES," Miguel Piñero's screen adaptation of his stage play, is so tightly and effectively constructed within its small enclosed landscape that not until it's over does one realize that this prison melodrama reaches well beyond the walls of the Manhattan Men's House of Detention, where it's set.

"Short Eyes" has the natural eloquence and wisdom that one is supposed to find in street people—but seldom does. Without seeming to try, without straining, the movie is less a story of prison life than it is the story of a segment of modern American urban society that's on the bottom but refuses to recognize the fact, if only because there are shadowy figures even further down the scale of values.

•

The film will be shown at the New York Film Festival at Alice Tully Hall tonight at 9:30 and repeated there tomorrow evening at 6:15. It will begin its regular commercial engagements Friday at the Sutton and Paramount Theaters.

"Short Eyes" has had a long and fascinating history, having begun life as a workshop production staged by Marvin Felix Camillo and the Family, the resident company at the Theater of Riverside Church, where Mr. Piñero was a playwright in residence. It was subsequently picked up by Joseph Papp's New York Shakespeare Festival, and presented at the Anspacher/Public Theater, from which it was moved to the Vivian Beaumont Theater in May 1974. Along the way it won two Obies and the New York Drama Critics' Award as the best play of 1973-74.

Its theatrical origins are quite apparent in this furious but controlled screen version directed by Robert M. Young, who made a number of award-winning television documentaries in the 60's. He also collaborated, with Michael Roemer, on the fine feature film, "Nothing but a Man," shown at the Film Festival in 1964.

•

In this case, though, the theatrical origins contribute to the claustrophobic atmosphere that is essential to the point of "Short Eyes," which is about a kind of overcrowding that is the physical equivalent to emotional desperation. There's no way out. As lines of dialogue overlap in that supercharged way of a theatrical production, so do Mr. Piñero's characters fight for space in the single cellblock where all the action takes place.

The blacks have staked out one section, the Puerto Ricans another and the white minority still another. The one person who has no territory is the new man, a nice-looking, mild-mannered, WASPy fellow named Clark Davis (Bruce Davison), who, once the

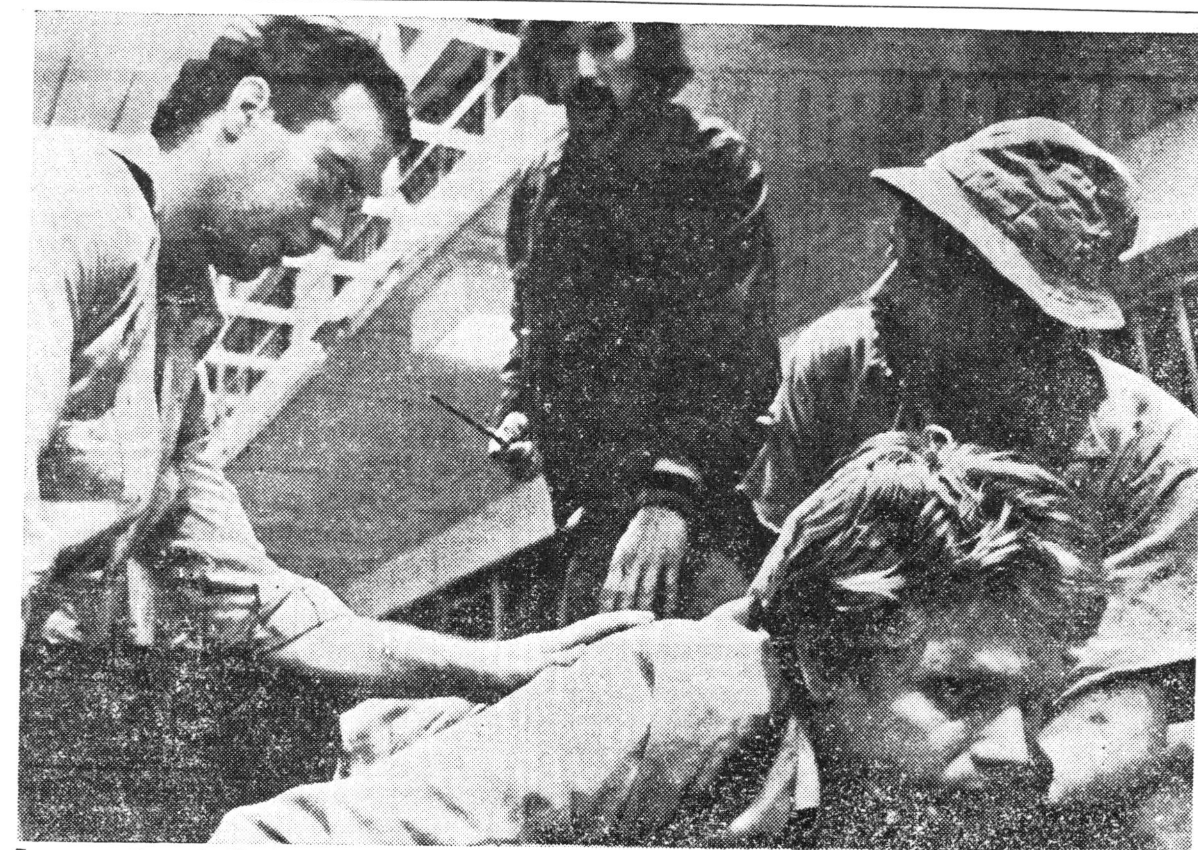

Inmates Joseph Carberry, Shawn Elliott and Kenny Steward victimize a new prisoner, Bruce Davison, in "Short Eyes," at the New York Film Festival tonight and tomorrow.

word gets out that he is a "short-eyes" —prison jargon for child molester—is subjected to the systematized torture that gives shape to the story.

Although there are only four members of the stage production in the film, the acting has the balance and the ferocity to be found in a group of actors who have been playing with—and against—one another for years. This is ensemble playing of the first rank.

•

Among those you'll remember are Jose Perez as the father-confessor figure among Puerto Rican prisoners, a man who tries unsuccessfuly to maintain some order in the ranks; Don Blakely as an angry black nationalist who, when the chips are down, is unable to commit a race murder; Shawn Elliott as a Puerto Rican prisoner whose viciousness has both grace and charm to it; Tito Goya as the "kid" who is the object of apparently unwanted attentions, and Joseph Carberry as the leader of the white prisoners, who initially befriends "Short Eyes" and then becomes his most relentless judge.

Curtis Mayfield, the singer and composer, makes a brief, very effective appearance as an older prisoner who wears "granny" glasses and believes there should be some decency even among people fighting to hang on to the bottom rung of the ladder. If Mr. Davison stands out—which he does—it's not only because of his position within the film as the victim of the victims, but also because he gives a performance so intimate it's almost painful to watch.

There is something of this quality about the entire film. "Short Eyes" is tough and depressing but it's also remarkably effective film making, which relieves the gloom at bit.

1977 S 28, C17:1

Dropout Destroyed

THE DEVIL PROBABLY (Le Diable Probablement), directed by Robert Bresson; screenplay (French with English subtitles) by Mr. Bresson; executive producer, Stephane Tcholgadjieff; director of photography, Qasqualino de Santis; editor, Germaine Lamy; music, Philippe Sarde; a production of Sunchild/Gaumont Films. Running time: 95 minutes. At the New York Film Festival, Lincoln Center.

Charles	Antoine Monnier
Alberte	Tina Irissari
Michel	Henri de Maublanc
Edwige	Laetitia Carcano
Psychoanalyst	Regis Hanrion
Valentin	Nicolas Deguy
Bookseller	Geoffrey Gaussen
Commissioner	Rogert Honorat

By VINCENT CANBY

"THE DEVIL PROBABLY" ("Le Diable Probablement") is the 12th feature film by Robert Bresson, the rigorously original French film maker who was 70 years old last Sunday. This fact should be mentioned immediately because this latest Bresson is very much the work of a man taking stock, which is not to say that it's by any means sentimental or gently autumnal.

Time hasn't softened the Bresson esthetic. The world he perceives still looks unlike that of any other director. Objects, people, places—everything is seen with a clarity so fine that his images achieve something beyond realism, as if clarity so intense could distort truth, at least as we have come to accept it.

•

The film will be shown at Alice Tully Hall tonight at 9:30 and tomorrow evening at 6:15.

"The Devil Probably" has the air of something out of the 1960's in that it recalls a time when dropping out was so fashionable it was virtually epidemic among the young of the bourgeoisie. But Bresson is not a film maker of fashion. Fashions rise and fall around him like tides around a continent.

This film, Bresson's first to be based entirely on his own screenplay, is about a young man who, realizing that he cannot support the world as he finds it, nor hope to change it through revolution or religion, nor even to adapt to it through psychoanalysis, chooses the way of the ultimate dropout—suicide. In telling you this, I'm not giving away a plot point because Bresson, as is his custom, refuses to allow us to watch his movies in anticipation of what's going to happen next.

•

He reports this suicide in newspaper headlines in the opening sequence, then proceeds backwards from there as he coolly presents us with the picture of an age that, like his hero, Charles (Antoine Monnier), whose androgynous beauty is a directorial position, is systematically destroying itself, though in preposterous arrogance and innocence. Charles's choice is an intellectual statement.

So, too, are all Bresson films, which may explain why they are so difficult on a first viewing and become, with repeated showings, increasingly rich and rewarding. One of the difficulties, as others have noted, is that Bresson films simply do not operate on the same senses that most other films do. There's no easy identification through primary emotions. His actors don't act. They exist to be moved around and so lighted and photographed to fit the director's line, which is simultaneously instinctive and stern, like a poet's.

•

Two recent Bresson films that have given me more and more pleasure over the years are "Lancelot of the Lake" (1974) and "La Femme Douce" (1969), both of which I found almost impossible when I first saw them. I didn't find "The Devil Probably" at all impossible, which makes me wonder whether I'm tuning into Bresson or if "The Devil Probably" doesn't really measure up.

The new film looks and sounds like a Bresson work, but it's not especially difficult. Furthermore, though no one comes close to smiling within the film, there are times when it's almost funny. At one point Charles and a friend, riding on a bus, argue about the responsibility for the world's dreadful state, involving suddenly the other passengers and finally the bus driver who, when he turns around to speak, rams into something. Only Bresson would have the nerve to keep his camera on the feet of the passengers instead of showing us what then happens in the street.

The pollution of the contemporary world—intellectual as well as physical—is the apparent subject of the film, but a contemplation of idealized beauty is the method, which is why the looks of the actors are so important. It's no accident that the actor who plays Charles looks startlingly like Tina Irissari, the girl Charles sometimes lives with, or that they both look like Dominique Sanda, who had never acted before she made "La Femme Douce."

No other director I can think of has come as close as Bresson to molding his players into what are, in effect, variations on a continuing personality, much the way a painter might.

What sets apart "The Devil Probably," though, are social concerns that are sometimes expressed with irony and wit. "Isn't there a limit to doing nothing?" asks Charles's friend Michel. "Yes," says Charles, "but after that there's extraordinary pleasure."

When Charles and his friends go on a picnic, ordinarily blasé Parisians exclaim when they see an old man catch what one of them describes with wonder as "a live fish!" In the world that Bresson shows us in "The Devil Probably," the catching of a live fish has become not only very rare, but also a crime.

1977 S 29, C19:4

Demolition Derby

GRAND THEFT AUTO, directed by Ron Howard; produced by Jon Davison; executive producer, Roger Corman; written by Rance and Ron Howard; director of photography, Gary Graver; stunt coordinator, Victor Rivers. A New World Pictures release. At the Harris 42d Street, Loews 83d Street and RKO 86th Street theaters. Running time: 85 minutes. This movie has been rated PG.

Sam Freeman	Ron Howard
Paula Powers	Nancy Morgan
Vivian Hedgeworth	Marion Ross
Sparky	Pete Isacksen
Bigby Powers	Barry Cahill
Preacher	Hoke Howell
Jack Klepper	Lew Brown
Priscilla Powers	Elizabeth Rogers
Slinker	Rance Howard
Curly Q. Brown	Don Steele
Collins Hedgeworth	Paul Linke

UBIQUITOUS and versatile, Ron Howard turned up yesterday at the Harris 42d Street, Loews 83d Street and RKO 86th Street theaters as star, director and screenwriter, with his father, Rance, of the latest automotive chase and crash movie, "Grand Theft Auto."

Puns aside, Mr. Howard need take a back seat to no one when it comes to competence in the genre. His debut as a director of feature films may not mark him as an innovator, but neither does it suffer from comparison to its many predecessors, including "Eat My Dust," which Mr. Howard starred in last year.

"Grand Theft Auto" may have the usual idiots for characters and it may tax credibility well beyond the fracture point, but it isn't dull, and its vehicles are better looking than the ones in "Eat My Dust" and "Smokey and the Bandit."

Nobody who has ever wanted to see a Rolls-Royce in a demolition derby is going to walk away from this movie disappointed.

As for the chase itself, it involves Mr. Howard and Nancy Morgan as the runaway lovers, bound for marriage in Las Vegas against the wishes of her wealthy and politically ambitious father and against the intentions of the wealthy incompetent she was supposed to marry.

Just about everybody, from parents to bounty hunters to preachers, to private detectives to mobsters to chicken farmers to a disk jockey and oh, yes, even the police, winds up in the chase, using everything from a camper, a commandeered bus and a Volkswagen Beetle to assorted sedans and helicopters.

•

The PG rating is doubtless attributable to a bit of the language—nothing out of the ordinary, really—and to the fact that the young lovers make it clear that they have a strong sexual attraction for each other.

LAWRENCE VAN GELDER

1977 S 29, C19:5

Back to the Track

BOBBY DEERFIELD, directed by Sydney Pollack; screenplay by Alvin Sargent, based on the novel, "Heaven Has No Favorities," by Erich Maria Remarque; produced by Mr. Pollack; executive producer, John Foreman; director of photography, Henri Decae; music, Dave Grusin; editor, Fredric Steinkamp; distributed by Columbia Pictures. Running time: 124 minutes. At the Baronet and Coronet Theaters, Third Avenue near 59th Street. This film has been rated PG.

Bobby	Al Pacino
Lillian	Marthe Keller
Lydia	Anny Duperey
The Brother	Walter McGinn
Uncle Luigi	Romolo Valli
Karl Holtzmann	Stephan Meldegg
Delvecchio	Jaime Sanchez
The magician	Norm Nielson
Tourists	Dorothy James Mickey Knox
Priest	Guido Alberti
Catherine Modave	Monique Lejeune
Bertrand Modave	Steve Gadler

By VINCENT CANBY

WHAT CAN YOU SAY about a guy who, when he's in bed with a new girl for the first time, and strokes her sleeping head, and finds that a large hank of her hair comes out in his hand, simply shrugs and replaces the hair, patting it back in place as if it were self-sticking?

Very little, I'm afraid. You might think that the next morning the fellow, using some discretion, would ask the young woman how she's feeling, or maybe whether or not she's been in chemotherapy or if she's recently come into contact with a lead-based paint. Is her ceiling flaking?

Not Bobby Deerfield, the title character in this big, expensive, ultimately ridiculous movie that appears to have been constructed to be a "Love Story" on wheels.

•

"Bobby Deerfield" may turn out to be the year's most cynical movie made by people who know better, including Sydney Pollack, the director, and Alvin Sargent, who wrote the screenplay. It stars Al Pacino as a self-centered, remarkably uninteresting (and uninterested) international race-car driver and Marthe Keller as his doomed, soon-to-be-bald beloved, a girl whose manic behavior is supposed to indicate a love of life but suggests rather more strongly that she's in desperate need of a Valium.

The film, which opened yesterday at the Baronet and Coronet Theaters, starts with a good deal of promise, that is, with a mystery: In a race in France one of Bobby's colleagues is killed when his car, a duplicate of the one Bobby is driving, cracks up for no apparent reason. Bobby, a boy from Newark who's hit the big time (French mistress, apartment in Paris, product-endorsements), sets out to find out what's wrong with the car. His hunt takes him to a fancy Swiss clinic where he interviews a man who has survived the crash. He also, unfortunately, meets Miss Keller, also a patient and someone clearly to be avoided even if you don't mind loose hair.

•

The would-be tragedy of their love story, which is supposed to resurrect Bobby's humanity, is neutralized by just about everything the film's makers think they have going for them, including the scenery (the Swiss Alps, Bellagio, Florence, Paris) to which the lovers gravitate as if they were travel agents. It's so relentlessly picturesque you may come out of the theater and walk directly to 42d Street to become reoriented.

There's also something off-putting about the lovers Mr. Pacino and Miss Keller play, sometimes coyly and sometimes with such intensity you can't believe they're in a movie of such essential fatuousness. They rattle around the script, saying its lines as if they were touching bases, but they succeed in creating not a single moment of genuine pathos.

It says something about the sort of film "Bobby Deerfield" is that the audience is inclined to applaud at the sight of hot-air balloons. It also says something about me, I suppose, that this is the first film about automobile racing I've ever seen when I wished the movie would get back to the track. I'd put up with just about anything to avoid watching Mr. Pacino doing an imitation of Mae West and hearing Miss Keller, who is supposed to be Italian describe things as "bowing" when she means boring and blab on endlessly about death.

"Bobby Deerfield," which has been rated PG ("Parental Guidance Suggested"), contains some vulgar language and partial nudity that will be seen by those members of the audience who are not taking a snooze.

1977 S 30, C8:1

Marthe Keller and Al Pacino in Sydney Pollack's "Bobby Deerfield"

Double Identity

HANDLE WITH CARE, directed by Jonathan Demme; screenplay, Paul Brickman; director of photography, Jordan Cronenweth; edited by John F. Link 2d, music, Bill Conti; executive producer, Shep Fields; released by Paramount Pictures. At the New York Film Festival, Alice Tully Hall. Running Time: 96 minutes.

Spider	Paul le Mat
Pam	Candy Clark
Dean	Bruce McGill
Papa Thermodyne	Hobert S. Blossom
Chrome Angel	Charles Napier
Dallas Angel	Ann Wedgeworth
Portland Angel	Marcia Rodd
Hot Coffee	Alix Elias
Smilin' Jack	Richard Bright
The Priest	Ed Begley, Jr.

By JANET MASLIN

MOST OF THE PRINCIPALS in Jonathan Demme's "Handle With Care" have citizens' band radios, and these people careen into one another's lives just as easily as they interrupt one another's broadcasts. The visual editing of the film is very much like its sound editing, so scenes become short and fragmented, like loosely overheard snatches of conversation. The radio conceit also provides the film with a unifying notion, because each character has a real name and a C.B. "handle," with separate identities for each. One of the characters even spells this out, though the point is hard to miss: "Everybody in this town is somebody they're not supposed to be."

•

"Handle With Care," which was originally released in other cities under the title "Citizen's Band," is so clever that its seams show. Mr. Demme's tidiest parallels and most purposeful compositions are such attention-getters that the film has a hard time turning serious for its finale, in which characters who couldn't communicate directly come to understand one another at long last.

The film will be shown tonight at 9:30 in Alice Tully Hall at Lincoln Center as part of the New York Film Festival and again tomorrow at 3 P.M.

Even though the film's energy and its intelligence are at war with each other all the way through, their incompatibility is eminently engrossing. The structure is thoughtful, and some of the imagery is so calculated it seems chilly; on the other hand, the film's surface is flippant and funny, full of talented performers in whimsical, open-ended roles. It's easy to see why "Handle With Care" was too scrambled to succeed during its first go-round. It's even easier to see that the film deserves a second chance.

The characters include a bigamous trucker (Charles Napier) and his two wives (Marcia Rodd and Ann Wedgworth), who first meet on a bus in one of the funniest sequences here; after comparing family photos and then weeping their eyes out, the wives begin to wonder if they aren't related. Another triangle includes two competitive brothers (Paul Le Mat and Bruce McGill) and their mutual sweetheart (Candy Clark), who is forced, by an otherwise-graceful screenplay, to tell one of them "I'm a woman; not a trophy."

There is also a squealy, roly-poly hooker who operates out of a mobile home, and who laments "Now with that gol-darned 55-mile limit, nobody's got time for nothin.'" There is the brothers' drunken old dad, who is forever threatening to eat the family dog. And there are a wide variety of crackpots on the airwaves, who become Mr. Le Mat's prey after he decides to do his civic duty by eliminating all improperly used C.B.'s with a baseball bat.

The plot may operate on the premise that wackiness is its own reward, but Mr. Demme's direction is decidedly, almost jarringly, on the serious side. When Mr. Le Mat and Miss Clark, whose affair has been on and off the rocks, finally get back together, Mr. Demme manages to make a high school setting look like a chapel, shooting up at the couple and letting a light bulb shower them with beatific rays. The composition has a life of its own, almost more life than it needs, and it has very little bearing on the characters as we've come to know them. But it's a stunning composition just the same.

1977 S 30, C10:3

HEART OF GLASS, directed by Werner Herzog; screenplay (German with English subtitles) by Herbert Achternbusch and Mr. Herzog; photography, Jorg Schmidt-Reitwein; editor, Beate Mainka-Jellinghaus; music, Popol Vuh and Studio der fruhen Music; Production Company, Werner Herzog Filmproduktion; a New Yorker Films Release. Running time: 93 minutes.

Also: LA SOUFRIERE, directed by Werner Herzog. At the New York Film Festival at Alice Tully Hall, Broadway at 65th Street. Neither film has been rated.

Hias, the visionary shepherd	Josef Bierbichler
Glass factory owner,	Stefan Auttler
Adalbert, the servant	Clemens Scheitz
Wudy	Volker Prechtel
Ludmilla	Sonia Skiba
Pauline, the madwoman	Brunhilde Klockner
Sam	Wolf Albrecht

By JANET MASLIN

"La Sourfrière" is only 30 minutes long, but it is one of Werner Herzog's most exquisite efforts, a perfect distillation of his talents. Made in 1976, the film is a serene, strangely clear-headed documentary about the end of the world.

"La Sourfrière" is the name of a volcano on Guadeloupe that threatened to erupt about a year ago; Mr. Herzog learned of the near-catastrophe only by chance, spotting a newspaper item about a native man who refused to leave the area after everyone else had been evacuated.

Thirty-six hours later, Mr. Herzog and two cameramen had arrived in the town of Basse-Terre, at the foot of a mountain that had begun to spew forth white clouds of sulfurous steam.

Mr. Herzog's narration deliberately skirts the question of whether he and his crew were afraid, but the implication is that they have passed beyond fear into a state of purely objective curiosity. When one of the cameramen lost his glasses, said Mr. Herzog, "we decided to pick them up the next day, if the mountain still existed by then."

•

The town is deserted, "just a few doors banging in the wind and water dripping." The sea is full of drowned snakes, which have been driven out of the mountains where they normally dwell. A shot of a civic monument becomes wonderfully ironic, because the town is now a monument in its own right. The police station, like everything else, is silent and deserted: "It was great not to have the law hanging around." Even the scientists have fled. Mr. Herzog had every reason to expect, as he says, that these pictures of the town were the last ones that would ever be taken.

The crew finds the peasant man, who is lying on the ground, waiting peacefully; turning his palms upward, he shows them the position in which he plans to die. He talks confidently about God's will, and explains that he has no fear. At Mr. Herzog's prompting, he sings a love song.

•

The film includes an extraordinary anecdote about a city on the neighboring island of Martinique that was destroyed in a volcanic eruption in 1902. There was no lava, only a burst of flame—"the whole thing can only have taken seconds," Mr. Herzog explains, showing a photograph of vultures circling the next day. There was only one survivor in a population of 32,000, and he was the town's most evil man, a convict who had been put in solitary confinement underground. He eventually became a sideshow attraction in an American circus.

La Soufrière never erupted even though the warning signs were definite enough almost to guarantee that it would. Mr. Herzog is doubtless glad to have survived, but the film reflects only his disappointment. "It all ended up a dead loss and a laughing stock," he said, almost angrily.

"La Sourfrière," one of the foremost attractions of the New York Film Festival (it will be shown tonight at 6 o'clock and Monday evening at 9:30), is on a bill with "Heart of Glass," a feature by Mr. Herzog that is far less successful. Mr. Herzog hypnotized his entire cast to film a parable about a medieval town that has thrived by producing ruby-colored glass, until the only man who knows the formula dies. After that, the town goes mad trying to recapture its lost glory.

•

In its own way, "Heart of Glass" is as much about the end of the world as is "La Soufrière," but the longer film is much less accessible, and often obscure. The actors' trance is contagious, and the film has some genuinely mesmerizing moments, as when the town seer, whose words have made little sense, suddenly begins to predict an alarmingly familiar future in which "no man will like another man." Mr. Herzog seems not to be working with real actors, but rather with apparitions.

At times, the script reads like a collection of nonsequiturs. Do you want our people to eat oatmeal bread again, that gives them headaches?" asks one character. "Rats will bite your earlobes," someone swears. Even the film's meticulousness—every trace of red anywhere, even on a goose's head, is clearly planned—is not entirely decipherable.

The elusiveness of "Heart of Glass" makes it something of a disappointment. But it is too mysteriously lovely to be regarded as a failure.

1977 O 1, 10:1

THE MAN WHO LOVED WOMEN (L'Homme Qui) Aimait Les Femmes), directed by Francois Truffaut; screenplay (French with English subtitles) by Mr. Truffaut, Michel Fermaud and Suzanne Schiffman; music, Maurice Jaubert; director of photography, Nestor Almendros; editor, Martine Barraque-Curie; a production of Les Films du Carrosse and Les Productions Artistes Associes, distributed by Cinema 5. Running time: 119 minutes. At the New York Film Festival at Lincoln Center. This film has not been rated.

Bertrand Morane .... Charles Denner
Geneviéve Bigey .... Brigitte Fossey
Delphine Grezel .... Nelly Borgeaud
Vera .... Leslie Caron
Helene .... Genevieve Fontanel
Martine Desdoits .... Nathalie Baye
Bernadette .... Sabine Glaser
Fabienne .... Valerie Bonnier
Denise .... Martine Chassaing
Nicole .... Roselyne Puyo
Uta .... Anna Perrier
Madame Duteil .... Monique Dury
Liliane .... Nella Barbier
Aurore .... Anonymous
Juliette .... Frederique Jamet
Christine Morane .... M. J. Montfajon
Doctor .... Jean Daste
Monsieur Betany .... Roger Leenhardt
Lecturer .... Henri Agel
Lecturer .... Jean Servat
Bertrand (as a child) .... Michel Marti

Bertrand Morane (Charles Denner) is a bachelor in his early 40's. He lives in Monpellier in southern France, where he makes a decent if not great living in a testing laboratory. Bertrand is polite, intelligent and sensitive, but mostly he is obsessed by women. Pretty ones, beautiful ones, plain ones, old ones, young ones. There are also one he never sees (the voice of the telephone operator who awakens him in the morning) and one he hasn't seen for many years—his mother.

When Bertrand dies, which is the way Francois Truffaut begins his lighthearted, wise new comedy, "The Man Who Loved Women," the mourners who push through the winter chill to the cemetery are, without exception, women. Though Bertrand was obsessed by women and though he might have felt guilty about using them at times, it is not an untypical Truffaut reversal that Bertrand was as much used by them, not meanly but, after all, a man who loves women with such persistence (which is not to be confused with fidelity) is rare these days, worthy of having attention paid.

"The Man Who Loved Women" will be shown at Alice Tully Hall at Lincoln Center tonight at 9 and Monday evening at 6:15. It will go into regular theatrical release here later this month.

In this new film, Mr. Truffaut's 16th feature since "The 400 Blows" in 1959, the director is working in a vein usually thought to be frivolous to examine the serious, primary game that men and women play, an ancient pastime whose rules are changing, as one of his characters notes. I suppose there's always been a little of the late Ernest Lubitsch in all Truffaut comedies, though I wouldn't want to have to prove it, but there is more than I've ever seen before in "The Man Who Loved Women."

•

It's full of the double-edged wit of the self-aware. Although it's a comedy about the sexes, it's less sexist, essentially, than Agnes Varda's liberation ode," "One Sings, the Other Doesn't." I don't mean to impose a heavier burden on "The Man Who Loved Women" than it can carry, but the Truffaut comedy, in the way it appreciates women in their infinite variety and understands what they're up against, is infinitely more liberated than most liberated films, which reduce women to abstract concepts.

Enough of that sort of talk, though.

The movie is a supremely humane, sophisticated comedy that is as much fun to watch for the variations Mr. Truffaut works on classic man-woman routines as for the routines themselves. The narrative line is so gossamer-thin it barely sustains the sentence that describes it: Bertrand, in his memoirs completed shortly before he's killed in an accident, remembers all the women he's loved, and a number he hasn't, trying in this fashion to understand why he has never been able to settle down.

There are, among others, Nicole, the theater usher who first caught his attention by the seductive noise of one silk-stockinged leg crossing the other; Helene, a woman of his age who turns him down because she's only attracted to young men; Liliane, the head-strong waitress with whom he never slept and who, he says, is his "evidence that a man and a woman can be just friends."

Most hilariously there is Delphine (Nelly Borgeaud), a married woman whose deepest passions are unlocked by the unsuspecting Bertrand and who has a way of maneuvering him into situations in which they are threatened with public exposure. "Oh," says the overheated Delphine, tearing off her clothes in the car, "the things you make me do!"

There is also — in the film's most marvelous, most surprising sequence — an encounter with Vera, beautifully played by Leslie Caron, a woman with whom he had an extended affair some years before. It's a scene that lasts no more than four or five minutes, but it's so remarkably well played and written that an entire love affair, from the beginning to the middle and the end, is movingly evoked through what is really just exposition.

The film's style is so economical it seems almost terse. The flashback to Bertrand's childhood, in which the boy was made the go-between for his mother in her affairs, suggests the young Antoine of "The 400 Blows," while Bertrand's funny, sweet encounter with a little girl he finds crying on a stairway recalls the Antoine of "Love at Twenty." Bertrand asks the little girl why she's crying and finally gets her to concede that there is a certain amount of pleasure in being so unhappy, which makes her brighten immediately.

Brigitte Fossey plays Bertrand's literary editor, the one person, you feel, who might have straightened him out if she had taken him as seriously as he had begun to take her. Perhaps not. The film is open-ended on this.

Charles Denner is very, very funny as Bertrand, a fellow who has the same single-minded purpose as the rat-exterminiator he played in "Such a Gorgeous Kid Like Me," as well as the delicacy of touch of Antoine Doinel on his best behavior.

It's not the Truffaut way to make movies that contain flat statements. Like almost every film he's ever done, "The Man Who Loved Women" considers some of the aspects and manifestations of love and then shakes its head —in a mixture of wonder, delight and sadness.

VINCENT CANBY

1977 O 1, 10:1

SALO, 120 DAYS OF SODOM, directed by Pier Paolo Pasolini; screenplay (Italian with English subtitles) by Mr. Pasolini and Sergio Citti, based on the novel "120 Days of Sodam," by the Marquis de Sade; executive producer, Alberto Grimaldi; director of photography, Tonino Delli Colli; editor, Nino Baragli; music, Ennio Morricone; a co-production of PEA (Rome) and Les Producions Artistes Associes (Paris), distributed by Zebra Releasing Corporation. Running time: 117 minutes. At the New York Film Festival at Lincoln Center. This film has not been rated.

Duke .... Paolo Bonacelli
Bishop .... Giorgio Cataldi
Magistrate .... Umberto P. Quinavalle
President .... Aldo Valletti
Signora Castelli .... Caterina Boratto
Signora Maggi .... Elsa De Giorg.
Signora Vaccari .... Helene Surgere
Virtuosa .... Sonia Saviange

By VINCENT CANBY

Had Pier Paolo Pasolini not died the way he did on Nov. 1, 1975, murdered (the Rome court found) by a 17-year-old boy who repeatedly ran Mr. Pasolini's silver Alfa Romeo over the body in a scrubby vacant lot, I'm not at all sure we'd take the film that became his last work as solemnly as we must.

The young murderer's defense was that he'd become enraged after Mr. Pasolini, who had picked him up several hours earlier near Rome's Termini Station, made homosexual advances. The boy was convicted and sentenced to prison for nine years, seven months and 10 days. Mr. Pasolini, said Michelangelo Antonioni, "was the victim of his own characters."

If Mr. Pasolini really was the victim of his own characters, then his most significant film must be his last, "Salo, 120 Days of Sodom." Mr. Pasolini's transposition of the Marquis de Sade's 18th-century novel to Italy (1944), and the puppet government set up at Salo in northern Italy when Mussolini was briefly free after his rescue by the Nazis from Italian partisans.

Mr. Pasolini, a poet and novelist as well as a film maker, an ardent Marxist who early on had been thrown out of the Communist Party for his homosexuality, made controversial films throughout his career, but none to equal "Salo," which was completed shortly before his death.

•

De Sade's novel has the small distinction of being the only novel I couldn't bring myself to finish reading. Indeed, de Sade himself hardly finished writing it—the last half being no more than a plan for the humiliations and tortures he wished to describe in greater detail when he had the time, which he never had.

De Sade saw his work, about the epic 120-day debauch of four pillars of French society, as a revolutionary act, designed to bring down the old order so that a new one might be established. As he described the debauch, though, he also indulged his own fantasies that passed through more or less commonplace sexual perversions to coprophilia, necrophilia and explicit torture of the young women and young men who had been kidnapped to share the hosts' pleasures.

Mr. Pasolini has made a very significant change in updating this work, however. The four hosts—the duke, the president, the magistrate and the bishop—are now Fascists, expressing their ultimate desires as the world is crumbling around them in the last days of the fascist regime. They are no longer rebelling against God. They are demonstrating the evil of the human spirit, which is something else entirely, though I can't help but feel that de Sade and Mr. Pasolini share a peculiar delight in speculating about the specific details of this evil.

The New York Times

Pier Palo Pasolini
His most significant film

For all of Mr. Pasolini's desire to make "Salo" an abstract statement, one cannot look at images of people being scalped, whipped, gouged, slashed, covered with excrement and sometimes eating it and react abstractedly unless one shares the director's obsessions.

•

Far from being the "agonized scream of total despair" the New York Film Festival calls the film, it is a demonstration of nearly absolute impotency, if there is such a thing. Ideas get lost in a spectacle of such immediate reality and cruelty.

"Salo" will be shown at Alice Tully Hall at Lincoln Center today at 1 P.M. and repeated there tomorrow evening at 6. It opens its regular commercial engagement Monday at the Festival Theater.

"Salo" is, I think, a perfect example of the kind of material that, theoretically, anyway, can be acceptable on paper but becomes so repugnant when visualized on the screen that it further dehumanizes the human spirit, which is supposed to be the artist's concern. When one reads, one exercises all kinds of intellectual processes that are absent when one looks at pictures. An image frequently says less than a thousand words. It's of especially limited use when dealing with the kind of ideas that Mr. Pasolini was playing with here.

•

The new film has no conventional story, being an allegory composed of tableaux in which we see the four hosts making their compact, their victims being rounded up and inspected, and finally the revels themselves. These begin with some simulated sex and move on to the series of parties in which the hosts carry coprophilia as far as it can go, and then begin their elaborate tortures. In between, a lot of high-toned talk about how the domination of one person by another is a metaphor for the capitalist's treatment of the working man, and how murder is the logical extension of such power.

The words are not nonsensical, but they are feeble in conjunction with the ferocity and explicitness of the images. The film is not without style in its settings—lots of Mussolini-era décor—or in several of its performances, including that of Caterina Boratto, who plays one of the madams who attempt to arouse the four hosts by telling them lewd stories with a piano accompaniment. Yet it all finally seems thin and superficial.

Throughout his career as a film maker, Mr. Pasolini was very good at intellectualizing, after the fact, what he was doing on the screen. His best films—"The Gospel According to St. Matthew" and "Accatone"—can stand alone. His later films, even the rambunctious "fable films" ("Decameron" and "A Thousand and One Nights") require a certain amount of rationalizing to be acceptable.

As Mr. Pasolini's vision of the world became increasingly bleak, his films became more arid. "Salo" is the bitter, empty end.

1977 O 1, 11:1

ROSELAND, directed by James Ivory; screenplay by Ruth Prawer Jhabvala; produced by Ismail Merchant; director of photography, Ernest Vincze; music, Michael Gibson; editor, Humphrey Gibson; executive producers, Michael T. Murphy and Ottomar Rudolf; a Merchant-Ivory production, distributed by Cinema Shares International. Running time: 103 minutes. At the New York Film Festival at Lincoln Center.

May	Teresa Wright
Stan	Lou Jacobi
Master of Ceremonies	Don De Natale
Marilyn	Geraldine Chaplin
Cleo	Helen Gallagher
Pauline	Joan Copeland
Russel	Christopher Walken
George	Conrad Janis
Rosa	Lilia Skala
Arthur	David Thomas
Ruby	Louise Kirtland
The Hustle Couple	Annette Rivera Floyd Chisholm
Bartender	Edward Kogan

By VINCENT CANBY

It is the basic proposition of "Roseland," the funny, moving, imaginative new movie directed by James Ivory, written by Ruth Prawer Jhablava and produced by Ismail Merchant, that the world is a dance hall in which everyone, even the comparatively young and the quite old, have been arrested in middle age. It's as if they'd been put under a spell by the music of the old-time swing band, whose anonymous players, their faces as expresionless as death-masks, pump and blow and beat away night-after-night-after-night, plus two afternoons a week.

"Roseland" is a stunt that comes off —three interlocking stories, set almost entirely within New York's famous Roseland Ballroom, about essentially lonely people who live their lives (and sometimes end them) to nonstop Waltzes, fox-trots and occasional hustles. Considering that most of the earlier efforts of the Ivory-Jhablava-Merchant team ("Shakespere Wallah," "The Guru" and "Bombay Talkie," among others) have been set in India, the success of "Roseland" is all the more dramatic.

The film will be shown at Alice Tully Hall at Lincoln Center tonight at 9 o'clock and Tuesday evening at 6:15. It will open its regular commercial engagement at the Columbia 1 Theater Oct. 16.

Most remarkable to me is Mrs. Jhablava's ear for New York speech, such as the genteel mannerisms affected by someone like May (Teresa Wright) a middle-aged widow who bores everyone with stories about her late husband, Ed. ("He wouldn't wear anything with a spot on it . . . he always had to be spotless.")

But Mrs. Jhablava is equally good with the dialogue of the elderly, heavily made-up former cook, Rosa (Lilia Skala), who wants only to win "the Champagne Hour" dance contest, and the desperate, self-deprecating lines of Pauline (Joan Copeland), a rich, uncertain woman who fusses over her gigolo and says, after making the smallest, most timid demand of him, "Oh, darling Russel, I'm spoiling your whole day!"

•

The ear is accurate, but the effect of the film is less real than surreal, less slice-of-life than so romantic that Mr. Ivory makes us accept, in the concluding episode, an explosion of outrageously overblown sentiment.

The film's enclosed setting—the dance hall, its bar, lobby and rest rooms—as well as the dominating vulgarity of its décor and the music contribute to an eerie, confined "Outward Bound" atmosphere that's maintained even when Mr. Ivory allows the camera to go outside on a couple of occasions.

The performers have a ball with the kind of roles that allow them to get on and off the screen fast, thus to leave vivid impressions. Among the best are Miss Wright, Miss Copeland and Miss Skala, who more or less star in their own vignettes. There are also Helen Gallagher, the Roseland dance teacher whose commentary provides continuity; Lou Jacobi, as Miss Wright's nononsense suitor; Christopher Walken (in his best screen role to date) as Miss Colepland's gigolo; Geraldine Chaplin, as a divorcee who spends some time briefly at the dance hall before fleeing with her sanity, and David Thomas, who is especially fine as Miss Skala's aging suitor, an old man who simply can't remember to smile while counting out the dancesteps.

Don De Natale, Roseland's real-life master-of-ceremonies, a young man with a patent-leather look and the kind of patter that Pal Joey would have admired, hovers over the show, so persistently cheerful that, finally, he becomes macabre, which is, I suspect, exactly what Mr. Ivory intended.

1977 O 2, 66:1

Lilia Skala and David Thomas in "Roseland"

OMAR GATLATO; directed by Merzak Allouache; screenplay (French and Arabic with English subtitles) by Merbak Allouache; photography, Small Lakhdar Hamina; editor, Moufida Tlatli; music, Ahmed Malek. Production company: Office National pourle commerce et l'industrie cinematographiques. At the New York Film Festival, Alice Tully Hall, 65th Street and Broadway. Running time: 94 minutes. This film has not been rated.

Omar Gatlato	Boualem Benani
Selma	Farida Guenaneche
Moh	Aziz Degga
The Singer	Abdelkader Chaou

By JANET MASLIN

"Omar Gatlato," an intriguing Algerian film at the New York Film Festival, is billed as a "human comedy," and, indeed, its opening recalls "Annie Hall," even if the jokes don't entirely translate. A small, vaguely comical-looking man in his late 20's begins speaking directly to the camera, explaining the routine of his daily life and introducing his friends. Every day, he tells us, he must grudgingly stop and talk with the neigborhood butcher "so he won't slip me any ewe meat."

This Omar (Boualem Benani) is a cheerful fellow, even though nothing in his life particularly justifies his optimism. He works at a dull office job, swims at a crowded public beach near an industrial plant and lives in a shabby modern apartment complex, which director Merzak Allouache immediately compares with a local cemetery. Omar's only prized possession is his tape recorder, which he carries everywhere and plays constantly, even in the small bedroom he shares with his sister and her grimy children.

•

One night Omar is robbed, and the tape recorder is stolen, so his burly friend Moh finds him a replacement. The new machine has a used tape inside, a recording by a woman who is as lonely and unsatisfied as Omar himself. He plays the tape over and over, and becomes obsessed with the idea of meeting her. This story of unrequited love provides the film with its only real plot, but it is not nearly as compelling as the portraits of Omar, his friends, and their workaday world.

"Your life is rather dull," a machine

tells Omar, when he pays it to tell his fortune. For relief, he goes to the movies (where we see a fascinating film clip from an Indian musical), attends variety shows, and goes to weddings to hear the music (Abdelkader Chaou, a singer seen performing several times, has a lovely face and a haunting self-assurance). He visits gaming tables and watches soccer. He also hangs around with his buddies, an unusually diverse-looking bunch who share little more than their communal squalor. Few of Omar's friends look healthy or clean; a couple of them, when they eat, have a way of winding up with food in their hair.

The marvelous thing about "Omar Gatlato," though, is that it is in no way bleak, even though by rights it ought to be. Omar and his friends make the best of what little they have—and figuring out what they do have should be, at least for the American viewer, an interesting and enjoyable challenge. Energetic and colorful, filled with styles and customs that are glimpsed but never explained, this is one of those rare films that gains even more than it loses in translation.

1977 O 2, 67:1

FILM VIEW

VINCENT CANBY

The 'Special' Talents of Loren And Mastroianni

Very early in Ettore Scola's "A Special Day," you feel that things are going to be all right, that the director and his actors know what they're up to. The time is the day in 1938 when Mussolini threw a gigantic rally to honor Hitler on his visit to Rome in celebration of their historic axis. The setting of the film, though, is confined entirely to a modern working-class apartment block of terrifying drabness. The moment I'm thinking of occurs just after Antonietta (Sophia Loren), the barely literate mother of six and prematurely exhausted, has just packed her children and her husband off to the rally. She slops the coffee remains from several cups into one, sits at the littered table and sips the coffee while surveying the incredible kitchen mess. She doesn't anticipate the morning's chores with any pleasure, but she still can enjoy the momentary peace. Suddenly this peace is broken by the cry of the family's pet mynah bird who, though it can talk, always gets her name wrong. There's something very funny and touching and revealing about Antonietta's reaction. She's both annoyed with the bird and aware that to be furious with a bird is a waste of her energies.

Exactly how Miss Loren manages to suggest this so easily I've no idea, but it's just one of the dozens of sequences in the film that are simultaneously mysterious and brilliantly revealing—mysterious because we aren't sure how certain emotional effects are obtained and revealing because of what those effects say about the characters. It's movie acting at its best, though I'm not at all sure anyone can accurately define, in general terms, what great movie acting consists of.

"A Special Day" is a very good, though something less than great, film that is an acting tour de force for Miss Loren and Marcello Mastroianni, who plays the unlikely role of a suicidal homosexual, just fired from his announcing job on the state-sponsored radio station. Gabriele (Mastroianni) is an intelligent, literate fellow who responds to Antonietta's no-nonsense approach to everyday matters and to her natural warmth, though he's appalled by her hero-worship of Mussolini (she keeps a scrapbook on the dictator's life) and by the way she parrots the wisdom of Mussolini without question ("Genius is strictly masculine. . . .").

A Special Day" is essentially a two-character film in which, in the space of a few hours, Antonietta and Gabriele meet, become friends, fight, reconcile and, toward the end, make love in a gesture that will not change either of their lives outwardly (Gabriele is not thus "saved" from his homosexuality) but will profoundly alter their view of life and themselves.

Scola, who collaborated on the screenplay as well as directed the film, has provided the stars with an intelligent script but I can't imagine any other two players who could have turned this essentially somber tale into an experience of such good humor. When I say good humor, I don't refer to what goes on within the film, but to the effect of seeing Miss Loren and Mastroianni take off with their material in ways that not only illuminate the characters but also give us a chance to marvel at what they are doing as actors, something more often experienced in the theater or at the opera, where performers are in repertory, than in the movie house.

• • •

Oddly, I think, this is something that happened much more often in the era of mass-produced movies. When the same stars appeared in three or four films a year we came to understand them so well that we could read the variations in their performances to a degree that was impossible with unknown actors. Some of the extraordinary responses that Katharine Hepburn and Spencer Tracy were able to achieve were the result of our having come to know how they played together. It was our familiarity with them in various earlier roles that gave later performances a resonance that was special to them.

This is partially responsible for the fun of watching Miss Loren and Mastroianni in "A Special Day," no matter how sad the tale. They've made eight films together and though only two of those—"Marriage, Italian-Style" and "Yesterday, Today and Tomorrow"—are memorable, they have been able to create special moments even in a turkey like "Sunflower." They work together with a self-assurance that allows each to take risks, which, in "A Special Day," includes a scene in which Miss Loren seduces Mastroianni, something that, I'm sure, could have been unintentionally hilarious had the seducer been anyone of less style and experience than Miss Loren. One watches this sequence breathlessly, much as one waits to hear whether a singer is going to be able to hit the high note, or falter and fake it.

One of the qualities that both Miss Loren and Mastroianni have as performers—and something that, perhaps, all great performers share—is a way of presenting the surface characteristics of a role (the gestures, expressions, language) while also somehow making a comment on those characteristics. It's a dividend. It's why we watch Laurence Olivier doing outrageous things as the sadistic dentist in "Marathon Man" and yet come out of the theater buoyed up and maybe even smiling, not because of what the character did in the film, but for the way Olivier set the character off by, in the case of "Marathon Man," sheer technical effrontery.

• • •

I've a suspicion—still somewhat dim in my mind and incapable of ever being proved—that all great actors, if not essentially comic, are gifted with an appreciation for paradox that is one of the roots of comedy. Olivier has this. So do Ralph Richardson, Marlon Brando, Dustin Hoffman and, I suspect, Robert De Niro. At the peak of her form in a film like "The Little Foxes," Bette Davis was funny—dishonest and stingy and mean, but also funny. One doesn't necessarily laugh, but the awareness of the wit within a performance is one of the pleasures of both the cinema and theater.

Jane Fonda has it, though it's not always apparent in the high melodrama of "Julia," directed by Fred Zinnemann, the film adaptation of the Lillian Hellman story from "Pentimento." It's not obvious in the film's scenes of intrigue, but it is apparent in her scenes with Vanessa Redgrave and especially in her scenes with Jason Robards, who plays Dashiell Hammett to Miss Fonda's Lillian Hellman.

This is defininitely what Miss Loren and Mastroianni have, but it's a quality that often takes a bit of time, a familiarity with the way an actor acts, before one can identify it. Not always. There are debut performances—offhand I think of Audrey Hepburn's in "Roman Holiday"—that are so complete that the performer, sprung on us brand-new, seems to have arrived with the kind of presence and associations it takes other performers years to acquire.

Miss Loren was one of those who had to work long and hard, mostly in a lot of rather ordinary Hollywood films, before she emerged as one of the best actresses and comediennes we have. Vittorio De Sica's "Two Women" is the film that forever separated her from the mob, and so opened our eyes that never again did we look upon her work, even in bad films, as perfunctory.

One of the few fond memories I have of any Cannes Film Festival (where it's an achievement just to get from one screening to another on time) is of the festival of 1961 when "Two Women" was screened in competition.

• • •

In the rarefied atmosphere of the festival "Two Women" was a revelation of truth, but more than that, Miss Loren's performance was astounding. The audience watched the neo-realistic movie with the sort of pleasurable excitement that might have been thought unseemly when connected with the tragic events on the screen. The excitement, though, had to do with what the actress was accomplishing on the screen. Success *is* fun.

When the film was over, a spotlight was thrown onto the box where the actress was sitting. She stood up, wearing a smashing white evening dress and what looked to be the complete stock of Van Cleef and Arpels. The contrast to the drab but heroic peasant woman we'd been watching on the screen was obvious and intentional and, in the fashion of her best performances, exhilaratingly funny. She brought down the house then, and is still doing it. ■

1977 O 2, II:15:1

JULIA, directed by Fred Zinnemann; screenplay by Alvin Sargent, based on the story by Lillian Hellman; produced by Richard Roth; executive producer, Julien Derode; diretor of photography, Douglas Slocombe; music, Georges Delerue; editor, Walter Murch; distributed by 20th Century-Fox. Running time: 118 minutes. At the Cinema 1 Theater, Third Avenue near 60th Street. This film has been rated PG.

Lillian........................Jane Fonda
Julia........................Vanessa Redgrave
Hammett........................Jason Robards
Johann........................Maximilian Schell
Alan........................Hal Holbrook
Dottie........................Rosemary Murphy
Anne Marie........................Meryl Streep
Woman passenger........................Dora Doll
Girl Passenger........................Elizabeth Mortensen
Sammy........................John Glover
Young Julia........................Lisa Pelikan
Young Lillian........................Susan Jones
Grandmother........................Cathleen Nesbitt
Undertaker........................Maurice Denham
Passport officer........................Gerard Buhr
"Hamlet"........................Stefan Gryff
Little Boy........................Phillip Siegel
Woman........................Molly Urquhart
Butler........................Antony Carrick
Woman in Berlin station........................Ann Queensberry
Man in Berlin station........................Edmond Bernard
Fat man........................Jacques David
Woman in greeen hat........................Jacqueline Staup
Vienna concierge........................Hans Verner
Paris concierge........................Christian de Tiliere

By VINCENT CANBY

Friendship is the most difficult of all relationships to define in films that are not caper movies or adventure melodramas, in which action is the emotion, or in romances that lead to sexual fulfillment. Friendship is profound and mysterious. It defies close examination. In a movie, friendship is anticlimactic.

This is the principal difficulty that faced Fred Zinnemann, the director, and Alvin Sargent, who wrote the screenplay, when they came to adapt "Julia," one of the stories from Lillian Hellman's best-selling memoir, "Pentimento."

"Julia' 'is Miss Hellman's moving recollection of her childhood friend who was a rebel in the nursery, an angry recorder (with her Brownie) of the peasant's unfortunate lot when she toured Egypt as an adolescent, and a full-fledged anti-Fascist by the time she was a young woman studying medicine in Vienna when Hitler came to power.

•

"Pentimento" moves back and forth in time and place as we do in good conversation, without self-consciousness, the main thread (and the real urgency) being the need to get some grip on feeling and, possibly, the truth.

Removed from this frame, the story of Julia, a rich young woman with a heedless, title-marrying mother and venal grandparents, becomes an illusive narrative fragment in desperate need of further amplification. Mr. Sargent and Mr. Zinneman have amplified the story with solemn care, in good taste (which is not always desirable), and have come forth with a film that is both well-meaning and on the side of the angels but with the exception of a half-dozen scenes, lifeless.

"Julia," which opened yesterday at the Cinema 1, tells us both too much and not enough. It opens with the mature Lillian Hellman, played by Jane Fonda, her back to the camera, recollecting her friendship with Julia as a little girl, alternating with later recollections of them both before Julia went off to study at Oxford and then Vienna. When Vanessa Redgrave plays the grown-up Julia to Miss Fonda's grown-up Lillian, in their comparatively few scenes together, the movie begins to build some emotional momentum.

•

But this more or less contemporary story, which has to do with Lillian's attempts to help Julia, the freedom fighter in the late 1930's (and particulariy in a good cloak-and-dagger bit when Lillian smuggles $50,000 to Julia in Hitler's Berlin), is constantly interrupted by further flashbacks meant to demonstrate the relationship of the two girls.

Only one film maker I know of (Carlos Saura in his recent "Cousin Angelica") has successfully managed to suggest on film the complex bundle of associations that an adult brings to the memories of childhood. Mr. Saura's way was to have the adult actor play those scenes as if he had wandered into a place where everyone else had been frozen in time. The middle-aged Saura character thus played scenes with parents younger than he was.

This isn't the only way to handle such a problem, but almost anything might be better than the conventionally styled, soft-focus flashbacks that Mr. Zinnemann and Mr. Sargent employ with child actors who look and behave like numbingly literate, talking dolls, always ready to say or do something that has an immediate, weighty relevance to the present. This sort of thing hasn't much to do with good moviemaking and less to do with childhood.

To flesh out the story further, Mr. Sargent has included some sequences dramatizing Miss Hellman's long, tumultuous, sometimes agonizing relationship with Dashiell Hammett, who was her lover, friend and most severe critic. With Jason Robards as Hammett, these scenes are so good and occasionally so tough that one wishes the film were about Hellman and Hammett rather than Lillian and Julia, the meaning of whose friendship mostly escapes the movie.

•

There is a single exception, the meeting between Lillian and Julia in Hitler's Berlin, just after Lillian has successfullly brought the $50,000 through Nazi customs to deliver to the now-crippled but still valiant Julia. Miss Fonda and Miss Redgrave are marvelous and true, and even the small echoes of English speech cadences one hears in Miss Fonda's voice are moving, as if she were in some fashion bowing to her English co-star (though Miss Redgrave's Julia is supposed to be an American).

There are two other memorable moments. In one Maximilian Schell, as a courier sent by Julia to reach Lillian in Paris, seems actually to have reduced himself in size to play a man of physical frailty and immense courage. The other scene, in which Lillian is having dinner with Sammy (John Glover), a gross, drunken friend from her childhood, does more to suggest the social, economic and emotional backgrounds of Lillian and Julia than all of the flashbacks combined. In addition it's very funny.

This may be hair-splitting but I also found the very elegance of the physical production—including the well-upholstered period sets and costumes and automobiles—to be at war with the film's subject. The movie looks soft, which has nothing to do with the Hellman flintiness, guts, self-mockery, wisdom, above all, impatience with cant. As Julia might have said, "Something else is needed."

•

"Julia," which has been rated PG ("Parental Guidance Suggested"), contains some violence but young children will probably fall to sleep long before anything untoward is shown on the screen.

Jane Fonda and Vanessa Redgrave in a scene from "Julia"
Movie moves back and forth through time like good conversation

1977 O 3, 40:1

HOT TOMORROWS, directed by Martin Brest; screenplay by Mr. Brest; photography, Jacques Haitkin; editor, Mr. Brest; music, Friedrich Hollander, Danny Elfman, Joe Primrose, Brad Kay, Duke Ellington, Bubber Miley, Harry Harren, Al Dubin, Fats Waller, James P. Johnson, Clifford Hayes, Tobias & Mencher; Paradise Ballroom sequence performed by the Mystic Knights of the Oingo Boingo; choreographer, Lloyd Gordon; executive producer, Mr. Brest; production company, American Film Institute. At the New York Film Festival, Alice Tully Hall, Broadway at 65th Street. Running time: 72 minutes. This film has not been rated.

Michael........................Ken Lerner
Louis........................Ray Sharkey
Alberict........................Herve Villechaize
Tony........................Victor Argo
Man in mortuary........................George Memmoli
Night embalmer........................Donne Daniels
Tante Ethel........................Dr. Rose Marshall

AND

MY GRANDMOTHER, directed by Kote Mikaberidze; screenplay by Gote Mikaberidze, G. Mdivani and S. Dolidze; photography by A. Polikevich and B. Poznan; music by Oleg Karavaichuk. Made in the Soviet Union in 1929, print courtesy of the Pacific Film Archive. In Russian with English narration. Alice Tully Hall, 65th Street and Broadway. Running time: 65 minutes. This film has not been rated.

WITH: A. Takaishvili, B. Chernova, E. Obanov, A. Khorava and M. Abesadze.

By JANET MASLIN

The best thing about "Hot Tomorrows" is its title, which is so full of promise and urgency but has precious little bearing upon the film at hand. Martin Brest's first feature, which he wrote, produced and directed on a minuscule budget, is a 72-minute black-and-white portrait of a young man who is so artily obsessed with death that he decorates his room with a life-size Grim Reaper.

Michael (Ken Lerner), the young man, is not quite as ghoulish as this might lead one to imagine, and so he has friends. His closest buddy, a Bronx alumnus named Louis (Ray Sharkey), joins him for a night-long adventure in Hollywood one Christmas Eve. The two of them travel to the Paradise Ballroom, which is deserted except for a few carefully chosen oddballs, and then they head for a mortuary, where Michael encounters his first corpse. At the club, an eerie-looking combo in heavy makeup is playing "St. James Infirmary," and en route to the mortuary Michael and Louis hear traffic-fatality predictions on the radio. Nothing in "Hot Tomorrows" happens without its being more than adequately preordained.

•

After Michael finally experiences the close brush with death toward which the film has been ponderously building, he wanders around dumbstruck, finally arriving at a nursing home, where the sight of a group of elderly women only amplifies his grief and arouses his horror. Michael seems an extraordinarily humorless and self-absorbed soul, and Mr. Brest's direction all too effectively echoes his character's insensitivity.

Incidentally, Michael is a writer ("Right now, I'm working on a couple of short stories about my great-aunt and her encounters with death") and a movie buff; one thing that interests him about film is that it offers the opportunity to watch people, like Laurel and Hardy, who are actually dead. "Hot Tomorrows" concludes, in a flash of unexpected originality, with a Busby Berkeley-styled musical number in which the deceased are reunited with the living.

•

On the same bill at the New York Film Festival, is "My Grandmother," a 1929 Russian film that has only recently been recirculated. The title is a colloquial reference to patronage, and the film is about the foibles of various one-dimensional bureaucrats, including a corrupt, hook-nosed production manager who is dismissed and tries to regain his job through favoritism. A Lenin-like party representative, photographed from the ground up so that he looks 10 feet tall, reprimands this bourgeois nogoodnik at the film's end.

"My Grandmother" is most interesting as a compendium of every type of trick photography that could be executed at the time it was made, and for the startling skew angles at which the director, Kote Mikaberidze, places the camera, giving the film a strongly Expressionistic feeling. Also noteworthy is the bureaucrat's wife, who has such pronounced bourgeois leanings that she is seen dancing a Soviet charleston and ordering 40 jars of cold cream at a time.

1977 O 4, 50:1

THE HAPPY HOOKER GOES TO WASHINGTON, produced and directed by William A. Levey; written by Robert Kaufman; director of photography, Robert Caramico; executive producer, Alan Marden; distributed by Cannon Releasing Corporation. At the Loews State, Trans Lux East and other theaters. Running time: 86 minutes. This movie has been rated R.

Xaviera Hollander	Joey Heatherton
Ward Thompson	George Hamilton
Senator Sturges	Ray Walston
Senator Caruso	Jack Carter
Senator Krause	Phil Foster
Senator Rawlings	David White

NOBODY appears to have expended much time or money on "The Happy Hooker Goes to Washington," and there is no perceptible reason why anyone should want to expand any time or money on seeing this movie, which is playing at the Loews State, Trans-Lux East and other theaters.

The plot takes Joey Heatherton, in the guise of former prostitute and sex counselor Xaviera Hollander, before a Senate investigating committee. Under subpoena, she manages to turn the tables by exposing the publicly prudish members of the committee as privately licentious. Spectators at the hearing serve the purpose of the laughtrack in a television sit-com.

"The Happy Hooker Goes to Washington" is the sort of movie that poses as taking an enlightened and liberal attitude toward sex; but while displaying the bare breasts of most of the women involved, it carefully keeps Miss Heatherton clothed and swaddles its men in underpants.

Among other considerable flaws this is a tedious, semi-literate, dim witted, cheap-looking and hypocritcal movie.

LAWRENCE VAN GELDER

1977 O 5, C17:5

Sheik of Aridity

VALENTINO, directed by Ken Russell; written by Mr. Russell and Mardik Martin; photographed by Peter Suschitsky; edited by Stuart Baird; music by Ferde Grofe and Stanley Black; produced by Irwin Winkler and Robert Chartoff; released by United Artists. At the National, Trans Lux East, Trans Lux 85th Street and 34th Street East Theaters. Running time: 128 minutes. This film is rated R.

Rudolph Valentino	Rudolf Nureyev
Nazimova	Leslie Caron
Natasha Rambova	Michelle Phillips
"Fatty's" Girl	Carol Kane
June Mathis	Felicity Kendal
George Ullman	Seymour Cassel
Rory O'Neil	Peter Vaughan
Jesse Lasky	Huntz Hall

By JANET MASLIN

THERE'S ONLY one scene in Ken Russell's "Valentino" that is as viscerally offensive as Mr. Russell, at his best and most headstrong, can be. Midway through the movie, Valentino is arrested and forced to spend the night, in a jail cell where the jailer denies him bathroom privileges and the other prisoners maul him and taunt him about his virility.

This episode is very much in the mode of Mr. Russell's most overpowering moments those that have simultaneously provoked admiration and outrage, but it has no place in an effort as a typically tame as this one. "Valentino" is Mr. Russell's least disturbing movie since "The Boy Friend": That should come as a relief to his distractors and as a slight disappointment to those who respect and appreciate his abrasive energy.

•

To a large extent, the film's relative ordinariness is attributable to Valentino's. For all of his glamour, he was a bland figure, more of a star than he was an actor, and Mr. Russell's best films have been about artists, such as Henri Gaudier-Brzeska in "Savage Messiah" and Tchaikovsky in "The Music Lovers," whose lives were governed by their unruly talent. Valentino's greatest dream was to leave Hollywood and became an orange grower, so there isn't room for the grandiose ambition that animated "Tommy." Valentino's sexuality was nil, at least as far as Mr. Russell's interpretation is concerned, so these is no place for the tortured erotic wrangling that amounts to another Russell specialty.

The most intriguing thing about Valentino, as he appears here, is his old-world notion of manly honor, but even that poses minor problems. When Oliver Reed, as a besieged priest in Mr. Russell's "The Devils," was subjected to public humiliation, he looked properly humiliated. When Rudolf Nureyev, who plays Valentino with a fierce sense of style, is abused or insulted, he looks magnificent. The screenplay represents Valentino as a fairly meek character but, as played by Mr. Nureyev, he seems positively to thrive upon affronts to his dignity.

The best parts of the film are those that pit Valentino against Hollywood, which both he and Mr. Russell seem to see as the biggest affront of them all. Whether he is courting a starlet (Carol Kane) who serves a huge tureen of French fries and ketchup on a silver tray, or dressing up in a Yale sweater and knickers in hopes of being cast as the all-American boy, Valentino is surrounded by (and a party to) the most aggressive kind of vulgarity. The screenplay, by Mr. Russell has no ear for American speech. "Everyday is Halloween in Tinseltown," says one character—twice.

The dialogue is compounded by Mr. Nureyev's uncertain accent (mostly Russian, but he hums a few bars of "O Sole Mio" from time to time). Mr. Nureyev has trouble delivering snappy patter with much conviction, and so do the other European members of the cast. Michele Phillips, suitably steely-eyed as Valentino's conniving wife, Natasha Rambova, often sounds even less authentic than these others.

But Leslie Caron, as Valentino's benefactor Alla Nazimova (there also seems to be a touch of Pola Negri to the role), copes admirably with the script's strangeness by reading her lines more peculiarly than is necessary, shouting and waving her arm all the while. There are a number of excellent small performances here—Carol Kane's dopey chorine, Felicity Kendall's studio liaison, Seymour Cassel's plain-suited shyster—but Miss Carol's is the most enjoyable outlandish of the lot.

•

And Mr. Nureyev's is, of course, the most graceful. It should certainly come as to no surprise that Mr. Nureyev is incapable of making an uninteresting gesture, whether he is daily sipping a vanilla malted out of a champagne glass or reeling dizzily in a boxing ring. More surprising is Mr. Nureyev's malleability, and the apparent effortlessness with which he adapts himself to fit into the film's varied tableaux. He is at his most stunning as he tangoes in a dimly lit nightclub of the film), and fighting for his life in a noisy, crowded area one wall of which hangs a tattered American flag.

These are only two of the better looking sequences in an extremely handsome film, whose look of overripe 20's opulence provides an ironic running commentary upon its characters. Even when Mr. Russell's verbal wit is not up to snuff, his visual jokes are alive and well. As Valentino and Rambova squabble with a studio head (played by Huntz Hall), a ridiculous little western is being filmed in the background. When Valentino attempts to seduce Natasha in his movie-set sheik's tent, the two shed their wraps and then Natasha, as is her wont, begins carping about business matters. But the couple continue to behave so romantically, and so incongruously with their real thoughts, that the scene becomes—well, ravishingly funny.

1977 O 6, C21:1

Rudolf Nureyev, as Valentino, with Christine Carlson
Ken Russell's least disturbing film since "Boy Friend"?

WOMEN, directed by Marta Meszaros; screenplay (Hungarian with English subtitles) by Ildiko Korody, Jozsef Balazs and Geza Beremenyi; photography, Janos Kende; music, Gyorgy Kovacs; production company, Dialog Studio. At the New York Film Festival, Alice Tully Hall, 65th Street and Broadway. Running time: 94 minutes. This film has not been rated.

Mari	Marina Vlady
Juli	Lili Monori
Feri, Mari's husband	Miklos Tolnay
Janos, Juli's husband	Jan Nowicki
Zsuzsi, Juli's daughter	Zsuzsa Czinkoczy

WHEN her mother dies at the beginning of Marta Meszaros's reflective quietly intelligent "Women," Mari (Marina Vlady) is pained but she barely cries. Mari is a big, beautiful, fortyish woman with an air of unnatural serenity and almost no lines on her face, and the film has little interest in explaining how she came to be that way. Instead, it wakes up along with her, in an empathetic and purposefully somnolent style, as Mari's friendship with a younger and less patient woman helps her to realize how much of her life has passed her by.

The important thing about the friendship, as it is presented here, is its galvanizing effect. Juli (Lili Monori) is a high-strung young mother who has left her husband and moved into the workers' hotel managed by Mari, and something about Juli's presence makes the older woman begin to wonder about her own 20-year marriage. Mari's husband is a dull and thoughtless sort—"Now you'll believe me when I say you're far from old," he observes, when his wife confesses she has been kissing another man.

Juli's husband is a handsome young alcoholic, and their affair is still, after several years, too hot to handle. Though their situations may seem opposite, the two wives turn out to have more in common than they at first realize. Whatever their reasons they both assume the same tearful, terribly resigned stare when they make love.

"Women" is set in clean, antiseptically modern places that have a frustrating effect rather then a revealing one; the film deliberately stays within the boundaries of its characters' imaginations, articulating their malaise rather than explaining it. Miss Mészàros's direction is correspondingly stern: The film looks so beautiful, and yet so barren, that the women's deprivation becomes palpable after a while. The characters, settings and script are beautifully integrated, working together to demonstrate that sometimes numbness is the worst kind of pain.

Miss Mészàros's approach has certain limitations, particularly when it comes to the husbands. Janos (Jan Nowicki), married to Juli, is as clearly drawn as she, but Mari's husband Feri (Miklos Tolnay) is one of those soulless male ciphers who can give women's films or fiction a partisan air.

"Women" doesn't have a happy ending; it hardly has an ending at all, just a hint of what the future will be. Both women take a few tentative steps away from their mates, but the breaks are not decisive. Still, Juli is unwilling to visit her husband in an alcoholics' clinic, so Mari goes instead, taking Juli's little daughter. Afterwards, Mari assures Juli that everything is fine. "It isn't," cries the little girl, startlingly. "You all tell lies."

JANET MASLIN

1977 O 6, C21:3

Mistress and Bore

THE LACEMAKER (La Dentelliere), directed by Claude Goretta; screenplay (French with English subtitles) by Mr. Goretta and Pascal Laine, based on the novel by Mr. Laine; director of photography, Jean Boffety; editor, Joele Van Effenterre; music, Pierre Jansen; a coproduction of Citel Films, Action Films and Filmproduktion Janus, distributed by New Yorker Films. Running time: 108 minutes. At the New York Film Festival at Lincoln Center. This film has not been rated.

Beatrice .... Isabelle Huppert
Francois .... Florence Giorgetti
Pomme's mother .... Anne Marie Duringer
Francois's friend .... Renata Schroeter
The painter .... Michel de Re
Francois's mother .... Monique Chaumette
Francois's father .... Jean Obe

By VINCENT CANBY

BEATRICE (Isabelle Huppert), the young heroine of Claude Goretta's new French film, "The Lacemaker," lives at home with her widowed mother and works in a Parisian beauty salon as an apprentice, sweeping up hair, running errands for tips, with the hope of one day be coming a hair stylist.

It's not an especially strong hope. Beatrice doesn't have any passions of her own. She's not cold—she's undiscovered, to herself as well as to others. She's also very pretty in an idealized way, having the sort of looks that are so undefined they accept any interpretation. In an earlier era, she woud have been a D. W. Griffith heroine.

•

In "the Lacemaker," Mr. Goretta's third film (after "The Invitation" and "That Wonderful Crook") to be seen in this country, the Swiss director has made a rather solemnly beautiful film to expose the dark side of what is, essentially, a silly, romantic notion.

"The Lacemaker" will be shown at Alice Tully Hall at Lincoln Center at 9:30 and tomorrow evening at 6:15. It will begin its regular commercial engagement at the Fine Arts Theater Saturday.

The film is the story of Beatrice's inevitably unhappy affair with François (Yves Beneyton), a tall, lanky, decent-mannered university student who wins Beatrice's maidenhead and subsequently comes to realize, with a sinking heart, that she only exists for him, to be around him, to reflect his love.

Beatrice has no ambition, no interest in the world, no identity except as an ideal, an abstraction, someone who, says the film's epilogue, a painter would have made the subject of a genre painting, as a seamstress or a water girl or a lacemaker.

•

Beatrice is a blank canvas, which, as Mr. Goretta seems to be saying, may be fine for painters but leaves something to be desired as the companion of one's life. She seldom talks or expresses any feeling except affection. As François says in frustration at one point, "I don't know what goes on in your mind . . . you never ask questions."

It's not difficult to understand why François decides thay have to split—living with her is like living with a sweet-natured mannequin—a decision she accepts with her usual passivity and that ultimately leads to tragic consequences.

Just what Mr. Goretta is up to here, I'm not sure. As he has shown in his earlier films, he is a director of delicacy who appreciates the odd variation on conventional behavior, the unexpected wisdom within the banal pronouncement.

"The Lacemaker," though it is nicely acted and set, is only interesting and moving in a theoretical way. Miss Huppert is all too believable as a figure of idealized innocence who would drive any ordinary man out of his mind with boredom and then, in a final irony, leave him feeling guilty for not having sufficiently appreciated the rare gift that briefly had been his.

1977 O 6, C21:5

THE LINCOLN CONSPIRACY, directed by James L. Conway; written by Jonathan Cobbler; director of photography, Henning Schellerup; editor, Martin Dreffke; music by Bob Summers; produced by Charles E. Sellier Jr., released in conjunction with a book by David Balsiger and Charles E. Sellier, Jr. by Sunn Classic Pictures. At the Rivoli, 85th Street, Quad Cinema and showcase theaters. Running time: 90 minutes. This film is rated G.

John Wilkes Booth .... Bradford Dillman
Col. Lafayette C. Baker .... John Dehner
Abraham Lincoln .... John Anderson
Narrator .... Brad Crandall
Edwin M. Stanton .... Robert Middleton
Capt. James William Boyd .... James Greene
Sen. John Conness .... Whit Bissell
Sen. Benjamin Wade .... Dick Callinan

By LAWRENCE VAN GELDER

IT IS the contention of "The Lincoln Conspiracy," which opened yesterday at the Rivoli and other theaters, that traditional beliefs about the assassination of Abraham Lincoln are wrong—the result of a high level cover-up.

True, John Wilkes Booth shot and mortally wounded the President. But the movie, whose makers maintain that their thesis is the product of costly new research, depicts Lincoln as the target of another, concurrent conspiracy.

This one involved, among others, Secretary of War Edwin Stanton, Col. Lafayette C. Baker, the head of what today would be the Secret Service; a Senator and a Representative—all united by opposition to Lincoln's emphasis on post-Civil-War unification and their fear that his reconstruction policy would lead to Democratic domination of Congress.

To that end, the movie has it, they decided to remove Lincoln from the scene by kidnapping him. Although Booth was involved in a similar plot, he was regarded as a bungler. Warned off by the Stanton group, he nevertheless proceeded to move against the President; and during his escape, he left behind a diary containing incriminating evidence against some of the Stanton group.

It then became necessary for them to insure that Booth never lived to testify. The movie maintains that a man believed to be Booth was killed; and once word that Booth was dead had been flashed to the public, the Stanton plotters had no recourse but to abandon the hunt and to proceed to frame the individuals they had already seized as Booth's co-conspirators.

The movie says that Booth was ultimately traced to New York, where his trail vanished.

As a movie, "The Lincoln Conspiracy" is a competent enough piece of work. Low-key and tending toward ponderous exposition (it employs both a narrator and a noticeable amount of explanatory dialogue), it can boast a cast of tried and true professionals: Bradford Dillman as the determined but inept Booth; John Dehner as Col. Baker, the prime mover in the events depicted; Robert Middleton, beneath a flowing chinpiece, as Stanton; and John Anderson as Lincoln, radiating compassion and homespun dignity under his makeup.

The trouble with "The Lincoln Conspiracy" is that, as film, it is a one-sided case. Although a documentary source list is provided at the conclusion, "The Lincoln Conspiracy" cannot help but leave anyone seriously interested in the subject wondering about the tangible proofs for the arguments it advances. A book on the subject has been issued in conjunction with the release of the movie, and this may be one case where ten thousand words are worth one picture.

1977 O 6, C22:4

OH, GOD!, directed by Carl Reiner; screenplay by Larry Gelbart; based on the novel by Avery Corman; director of photography, Victor Kemper; edited by Bud Molin; music by Jack Elliott; produced by Jerry Weintraub; distributed by Warner Bros. At Loews State 2 and Cine Theaters. Running time: 104 minutes. This film is rated PG.

God .... George Burns
Jerry Landers .... John Denver
Bobbie Landers .... Teri Garr
Dr. Harmon .... Donald Pleasence
Sam Raven .... Ralph Bellamy
Rev. Willie Williams .... Paul Sorvino
Priest .... Barry Sullivan
Dinah .... Dinah Shore
Rabbi .... Jeff Corey

By JANET MASLIN

"Oh, God!" is either a one-joke movie or a two, depending upon how you feel about John Denver's acting debut. The Lord, in the form of George Burns, chooses a Tarzana, Calif., supermarket manager (Mr. Denver) to spread the message that "what we have down here can work." Mr. Burns, who makes a number of house calls, wears a fishing cap and tennis shoes and says things like "so help me, me" when he is sworn in at a concluding trial sequence. Mr. Denver, when he is asked why the Lord chose him as a messenger, says things like "God only knows—I mean . . ." Though it isn't much of a contest, Mr. Burns readily emerges as the funnier

In all fairness, neither actor has the kind of part that can be played strictly for laughs. Mr. Denver, who is compared by the screenplay with Moses, Jesus, Einstein and Joan of Arc, asks some decidedly unfunny Big Questions: "If you're so involved with us, how can you permit all the *suffering* that goes on in the world?" Mr. Burns doesn't exactly supply the corresponding Big Answers, but he does provide a modicum of spiritual guidance. "You have the strength that comes from knowing," he tells his protégé.

Mr. Burns also makes a lot of wisecracks, which aren't entirely compatible with the movie's underlying sanctimoniousness. God doesn't look forward to Doomsday, Mr. Burns says; there will be "a lot of yelling and screaming, and I don't need that any more than you do."

As directed by Carl Reiner, "Oh, God!" is an uneasy amalgam of inconsistent attitudes, without enough humor or zaniness to divert attention from its questionable premise. But Mr. Burns is amusing even when his material is substandard. And Mr. Denver, though he is unable to convey any emotion more complex than enthusiasm, is obviously trying.

Mr. Reiner has marshaled an impressive supporting cast, including Ralph Bellamy as a trial lawyer and Teri Garr as Mr. Denver's frazzled wife, who lives with him in a cluttered suburban house where all the domestic debris looks brand new. The religious leaders of the world are played by Barry Sullivan, Donald Pleasence, Jeff Corey and Paul Sorvino, but of these only Mr. Sorvino has been given anything to do. He plays an evangelist in white shoes who boasts of having "personally . . . been chosen to render the benediction at this year's Super Bowl."

The film's only other dashes of genuine levity come when Mr. Burns scares up a rainstorm inside Mr. Denver's compact car and when Mr. Denver appears on the "Dinah Shore Show" and tries with the help of a police artist, to come up with God's portrait.

•

"Oh, God!" is rated PG ("Parental Guidance Suggested") because Mr. Burns made a few harmless jokes about Adam and Eve, and because Mr. Denver appears barechested several times. These latter scenes are not likely to be mistaken for erotica.

1977 O 8, 13:1

1900, directed by Bernardo Bertolucci; screenplay by Mr. Bertolucci, Franco Arcalli and Giuseppe Bertolucci; executive producer, Alberto Grimaldi; director of photography, Vittorio Storaro; editor, Franco Arcalli; music, Ennio Morricone; a P.E.A. production, distributed by Paramount Pictures. Running time: 245 minutes (plus intermission). At the New York Film Festival at Lincoln Center. This film has not been rated.

Alfredo .... Burt Lancaster
Giovanni .... Romolo Valli
Eleonora .... Anna-Maria Gherardi
Regina .... Laura Betti
Alfredo (the grandson) .... Robert De Niro
Alfredo as a child .... Paolo Pavesi
Ada .... Dominique Sanda
Leo Dalco .... Sterling Hayden
Olmo Dalco .... Gerard Depardieu
Olmo as a child .... Roberto Maccanti
Anita Foschi .... Stefania Sandrelli
Attila .... Donald Sutherland
Octavio .... Werner Bruhns
Signora Pioppi .... Alida Valli
Sister Desolata .... Francesca Bertini

By VINCENT CANBY

Bernardo Bertolucci's "1900" is a four-hour, five-minute (plus intermission) movie that covers approximately 70 years of Italian social and political history, from 1901, the year Verdi died and peasants were still in bondage to the landowners, to the 1970's, when a capitalist movie producer would put up millions of dollars to make a film such as "1900," which is essentially a Marxist romance. This is progress of a very particular sort.

The film begins beautifully, uproariously, as a realistic, three-generation, the-mansion-and-the-shanties family saga and then slowly congeals into the overblown attitudes of a political pageant, so positive and upbeat it's difficult to believe it comes from a land whose problems are a tiny bit more complex than those of Oz.

Before the family saga becomes a political statement, Mr. Bertolucci ("Last Tango in Paris," "The Conformist," "Before the Revolution") presents us with a series of heavy-breathing and, I'm afraid, unintentionally comic sequences that more or less define current fashions of decadence as seen in movies made by European left-wing intellectuals.

•

Aristocrats, they tell us, are impotent. They loll around, lift fingers only when wrapped around champagne glasses, dance during the daytime, and, when being really wicked, sniff cocaine. The Italian Fascists (one could also read the German Nazis) have more strength, being bourgeois. They torture animals, sodomize little boys, exploit epileptic females and murder children and widows.

Aristocrats and fascists can be nasty, all right, but the sad fact is that, though in movies like this they are no more believable than the politicized peasants, they are more cinematically decorative.

"1900" will be shown twice today at Alice Tully Hall at Lincoln Center, at 2 P.M. and 7:30 P.M. It is scheduled for commercial release in this version (not always happily dubbed into English) later this month or next.

This 245-minute version of "1900" is not to be confused with the 5½-hour version that was shown at the 1976 Cannes festival, nor with the five-hour, 10-minute version that was later released in Europe, nor with the 4½-hour version that Mr. Bertolucci once said was as short as the film could possibly be, before giving his full approval to this even shorter version.

At one point or another, each of these versions has been approved by the young Italian director, who is not only talented and ambitious, but also flexible, so much so that

Robert De Niro in "1900"
Film's shortest version to date

when one looks at the film now one brings to it a certain amount of skepticism. How could a film that he once insisted on showing in its 5½-hour length be cut almost 90 minutes without losing entire sequences? A spokesman for the director insists, however, that nothing of importance has been eliminated.

If this is the case, and I've no reason to doubt the director's representative, it seems to reinforce one's suspicion that as grandly conceived as "1900" was, it has always lacked a guiding vision of real vitality and strength. It's a shapeless mass of film stock containing some brilliant moments and a lot more that are singularly uninspired.

•

Everything of real interest and epic sweep occurs in the film's first half, which introduces us to members of the land-owning Berlinghieri family, headed by the old patriarch Alfredo, robustly played by Burt Lancaster, and the Dalco family, who farm the Berlinghieri estate and whose patriarch is old Leo, played with a kind of severe passion by Sterling Hayden. The stage for the subsequent events is set when Alfredo and Leo each are presented with a grandson born on the same day, the one to grow up to be a dillettantish Robert De Niro and the other to be a passionate union organizer and Marxist, played by Gerard DePardieu.

The early lives of the two young men, their relationships to their families and to each other, are beautifully and movingly detailed, but as the years overtake them, so do Mr. Bertolucci's political purposes overtake the film.

Even in a film that runs more than four hours, Mr. Bertolucci still hasn't the time to give us more than posterlike sequences relating to the rise of unionism and Mussolini's Fascists. People that once were characters become points of view, a conscious decision on the part of the film maker who names his prototypical Fascist, the Berlinghieri estate's foreman, Attila, a role that Donald Sutherland plays in modified Casanova make-up and with such melodramatics he doesn't seem to have heard that Verdi really is dead.

Equally outrageous is Laura Betti as Mr. De Niro's aristocratic cousin who, disappointed in love, throws in her lot with Attila and his blackshirts. The other major role in the film is Dominique Sanda's as Mr. De Niro's high-born French wife, portrayed as an initially hedonistic type who wears clothes magnificently, especially evening dresses and various kinds of fur pieces, but who takes to drink when her husband won't come out firmly against the Fascists.

•

Mr. Lancaster has some fine moments early in the movie, including a tough, shocking but eloquent scene in which the old man comes to realize that he can't have his way with a pretty little peasant girl who says to him matter-of-factly, "You can't milk a bull."

Even the boys who play Mr. De Niro and Mr. Depardieu as children are good. Once the film moves into the 1920's, only Mr. Depardieu's character maintains interest and identity. Mr. De Niro behaves as if he were making up his character as he went along, doing busy, Actors' Studiolike things that suggest he is sending up both the character and the film. It's his first bad performance.

The English dubbing doesn't relieve the feeling that the film has been patched together. Although all of the English-speaking actors have dubbed in their own lines, the dialogue often sounds as it it were an English translation of an Italian libretto. And the voices of the non-English actors are awful. Sometimes you suspect that only one man is playing all the peasants, each of whom sounds like a troll at the bottom of a well.

"1900" is not an uninteresting failure, but being a failure, it looks arrogant. Mr. Bertolucci took risks as great with "Last Tango." I realize that because he succeeded there, the quality that now looks like arrogance is basically not much different from the courage he displayed in the earlier film. That's what happens when you fail.

1977 O 8, 14:1

A PIECE OF THE ACTION, directed by Sidney Poitier; produced by Melville Tucker; screenplay by Charles Blackwell; story by Timothy March; director of photography, Donald M. Morgan; music and lyrics by Curtis Mayfield; songs by Mavis Staples; presented by the First Artists Production Co. Ltd.; distributed by Warner Bros. At the Criterion, 86th Street East and Eastside Cinema. Running time: 135 minutes. This movie has been rated PG.

Manny Durrell .... Sidney Poitier
Dave Anderson .... Bill Cosby
Joshua Burke .... James Earl Jones
Lila French .... Denise Nicholas
Sarah Thomas .... Hope Clarke
Nikki McLean .... Tracy Reed
Bruno .... Titos Vandis
Bea Quitman .... Frances Foster
Ty Shorter .... Jason Evers
Louie .... Marc Lawrence
Nellie Bond .... Ja'net DuBois

By LAWRENCE VAN GELDER

Sidney Poitier has done it again. What he has done again is his hit movie "To Sir, With Love." But he has done it with a difference, an obvious social purpose and a new name: "A Piece of the Action."

This movie, which opened yesterday at the Criterion, 86th Street East and Eastside Cinema theaters is, at heart, a candy-coated training film, four-square in favor of industry, honesty, courtesy, matrimony and culture; dead-set against wasted lives, ignorance, defeatism, sloth, senseless impudence, drugs and organized crime.

The candy-coating consists of a caper plot that enmeshes Mr. Poitier and Bill Cosby as a pair of independent, ingenious and hugely successful thieves with angry and vengeful underworld victims and with crooked and manipulative police.

Set inside the candy-coating is the training film: "To Sir, With Love," recycled for domestic identification and trans-shipped from a school in a London slum to a black-operated community center in a rundown neighborhood in Chicago.

There, Mr. Poitier and Mr. Cosby, each blackmailed by an unknown man who apparently knows enough about their crimes to send them to prison, find themselves reluctant volunteer members of the staff.

•

Mr. Cosby works in the administrative end, where he finds a good deal of amelioration of his plight in the form of Lila French, the center's director, vivaciously portrayed by Denise Nichols. And Mr. Poitier, thanks to a coin flip, finds himself in a familiar classroom.

Here are 30 rambunctious young black men and women for whom he and Mr. Cosby must find jobs although they are clearly less than prime candidates for employment.

Well, Mr. Poitier has been here before. As star and director, he knows precisely what to do with them. He uses them for little performing tours de force—to frighten and wound with their toughness;

Sidney Poitier in "A Piece of the Action."
A candy-coated training film

to amuse with their street talk, their irreverence, their flippancy; to wrench tears with their vulnerability; and, of course, to bend to his will, absorb his lessons about self-esteem and consideration for others and ultimately to serve as illustrations that adversity can be overcome.

•

When all the didacticism threatens to reduce the pace to that of sludge, Mr. Poitier takes advantage of several options: he can concern himself and Mr. Cosby with unraveling the mystery of their blackmailer (it gives away nothing to reveal him to be James Earl Jones, playing a retired policeman whose late wife founded the community center); he can strike a slightly grudging blow for matrimony by arranging for an unexpected visit from the dismayed, religious parents of the woman he has been living with; he can espouse culture by tossing in a dressy night on the town that takes him, Mr. Cosby and their dates to a performance by the Dance Theater of Harlem; or he can stir up suspense by looking in on the Mafia types who are determined to kill him for robbing them.

In short, Mr. Poitier has provided something for just about everyone, including those who might be concerned about the question of all this moralizing coming from a character who is introduced as a criminal.

"A Piece of the Action" is firmly on the side of the angels. It is possible to criticize its lack of originality and its transparent slickness; but these are flaws that must be balanced against its evident craftsmanship, its entertainment and its social conscience.

•

The PG ("Parental Guidance Suggested" rating seems primarily attributable to the street language.

1977 O 8, 14:1

Bunel Work Triumphantly Funny and Wise

By VINCENT CANBY

Every film festival should end with a new film by the incomparable Luis Buñuel, whose latest work, the triumphantly funny and wise "That Obscure Object of Desire," will be shown at Lincoln Center tonight at 8:30 to close the 15th New York Film Festival.

After one has sat through hours and hours of films by directors who don't know when to stop (and some who should never have started), seeing a work of such perfect control and precision has the effect of magically clearing the mind. It restores one's common sense and one's appreciation for the fantastic, and it reminds us of the profound possibilities of film in the hands of someone we now acknowledge to be an authentic master.

•

"That Obscure Object of Desire" is Buñuel's "Don Giovanni." It combines the effervescence and gaiety of "The Discreet Charm of the Bourgeoisie" with the dark wit of "Tristana," and though it continues to explore themes we recognize from these and other Buñuel films, it is something quite other.

Most obviously, I suppose, "That Obscure Object of Desire" is an upside-down romance in which love, Buñuel seems to be telling us, is "a devastating act of subversion." The setting is the easily recognizable contemporary world, but a world that is a half-degree off its axis and fast going to pieces, though everyone displays the fastidious manners of the members of a society that will last forever.

Just beyond the horizon of the film, which is set in Paris and in Seville, chaos reigns. Through newspaper headlines and radio broadcasts we learn that terrorism is rampant. Planes are being hijacked and innocents slaughtered. A mysterious virus is nearing Barcelona and a guerrilla group that calls itself the Revolutionary Army of the Infant Jesus has attempted to assassinate the Archbishop of Sienna. Even the Communists are outraged by the anarchic state of things.

•

Seemingly unruffled by all this (though he is impatient when a booby-trapped automobile in front of his explodes and forces his car to make a detour) is the charming, literate, wealthy Mathieu (Fernando Rey), Buñuel's Don, a French businessman whose life is in perfect order until the day that the beautiful Conchita enters it, dressed as a maid.

Though he has been a widower for seven years, Mathieu is no ordinary lecher. As he tells his brother, the judge (Julien Betheau), Mathieu can count on the fingers of one hand the number of times he has ever made love to a woman whom he didn't love passionately. From the minute he sees Conchita, Mathie is in the throes of an uncontrollable passion.

Conchita, though, is not someone whose measure he can get, and who eludes him even he gets her into bed. Conchita flees his house, only to turn up a few months afterwards traveling through Switzerland with a group of musicians. Later Mathieu makes a deal with Conchita's pious mother to set up Conchita as his mistress. Again she runs away. Each time they meet again, she leads him further into the recesses of his obsession, always promising him the moon (in the form of her virginity), then suddenly changing her mind.

As Mathieu sees her, Conchita is so changeable that Buñuel has cast two lovely new actresses to play her—Carole Bouquet, who looks a little like a young Rita Hayworth, as the coolly enigmatic Conchita, and Angela Molina as the earthy, flamenco-dancing Conchita whom he follows to Seville.

Poor old Mathieu. The night he succeeds in getting Conchita to his country house, where she has promised to be his mistress, the Conchita who goes into the bathroom to change, changes not only her clothes. Miss Bouquet goes in but Miss Molina comes out.

Mathieou huffs, puffs and groans in his agony. He leaves Conchita a dozen times but always is lured back. At one point he persuades her to live with him and to share his bed, though no sexual contact can be made. When the judge asks his brother why he doesn't marry her, Mathieu answers earnestly that if he married her, he would be helpless. At another point, when Mathieu upbraids Conchita for her maddening ways, she answers, "You only want what I refuse. That's not all of me. . . ."

•

Who really loves whom? Though Conchita at first seems to be the classic coquette, she becomes, as the film progresses, the true lover, while Mathieu becomes the coquette, a reversal of roles that is, nevertheless, not to be taken as the last word.

"That Obscure Object of Desire" is beatifully played by its small, impeccably chosen cast, beginning with Mr. Rey who, at this point in his career, is virtually a projection of Buñuel's artistic personality—gentle, polite, self-aware incapable of the superfluous gestures, and driven. Miss Bouquet and Miss Molina are enchanting—I don't think Buñuel has ever before been so successful with neophyte actresses.

There are further delights in the performances of Mr. Bertheau (who played the "worker bishop" in "The Discreet Charm"), of Andre Weber, as Mathieu's all-wise valet, and of Pieral, a dwarf who plays the psychologist to whom Mathieu pours out his sad story on the train from Seville to Paris, which provides the frame for the film.

"That Obscure Object of Desire" is a lot more open-ended and surreal than I've indicated, but these are pleasures that one should discover for oneself. To attempt to interpret them in this sort of review would be as gross as giving away the ending of a whodunit. One particular prop, though, I would suggest that you watch out for. It's an ordinary, but apparently well-stuffed burlap sack that the always-well-groomed Mathieu carries with him.

With an effortlessness matched by no other director today, Buñuel creates a vision of a world as logical as a theorem, as mysterious as a dream, and as funny as a vaudeville gag. I especially like the response of a waiter in a posh restaurant when an insect turns up in Mathieu's martini. "A fly," the waiter exclaims. "I've been after that one for days, and he had to fall into your glass!"

The Cast

THAT OBSCURE OBJECT OF DESIRE (Cet Obscur Object du Desir), directed by Luis Bunuel; screenplay (French with English subtitles) by Mr. Bunuel with Jean-Claude Carriere, suggested by the novel "La Femme et Le Pantin" by Pierre Louys; produced by Serge Silberman; director of photography, Edmond Richard; editor, Helene Plemiannikov; a co-production of Greenwich Film Production (Paris), Les Films Galavie (Paris) and Incine (Madrid). Run-Festival at Lincoln Center. This film has not been rated.
ning time: 100 minutes. At the New York Film Festival at Lincoln Center. This film has not been rated.

Mathieu .... Fernando Rey
Conchita .... Carole Bouquet
Angela Molina
Judge .... Julien Bertheau
Valet .... Andre Weber
Traveler .... Milena Vukotic
Psychologist .... Pieral

1977 O 9, 81:1

FILM VIEW

VINCENT CANBY

'Accessible' Films

As I write this, the 15th New York Film Festival still has one more week to go but by the time you read the piece, the festival will be in its last day. Perhaps, then, it isn't too early to declare a ban of at least six months on any further use of the word "accessible" in connection with movies, especially the movies of people like Marguerite Duras, Werner Herzog, Pier Paolo Pasolini or Robert Bresson.

In suggesting this I'm aware that I've been as guilty as the next person in the too-easy use of the word, but I've suddenly had it up to here. It has to do, I know, with seeing a great many films in a very short time, which takes its toll, but sometimes in fatigue truth reveals itself, an epiphany seen through bloodshot eyes. The point is that to describe a film as accessible is both to damn it with faint praise and to praise it pejoratively. The result: usually meaningless, mostly a sign of the critic's desperation.

When one says that a film is accessible, what is one actually saying? Not that one can get physically at it, though I guess it's possible to arm oneself with a lead pipe and break into the projection booth to carry off the print. Few of us are so obsessed.

What one hopes to mean, I suppose, is that a film makes sense. One can get at its meaning, rather as if one had to break through a thick, cement-like casing to extract the kernel of truth within. But even this is not quite the way it is. A movie doesn't have a shell, or if it does, the shell is as much the movie as any treasure inside.

• • •

All of this is a roundabout way of saying that a film is not only what the moviemaker has made, but what we who look at it are willing to make of it—which is something that varies from person to person, from critic to critic, and there are no absolutes. For one reason or another one person may get great delight out of tearing a Douglas Sirk film apart frame by frame, analyzing each, discovering associations and meanings that lie in it like lucky pennies in a plum pudding. Sirk's films are certainly accessible but I don't care to seek access. Perhaps I will in the future. One's interests and priorities change.

A case in point for me is the work of Marguerite Duras, the French novelist-turned filmmaker who is an indefatigable festival-attender and proselytizer on behalf of the New Film, though I'm not sure she knows what the New Film is. After liking the first film Duras directed, "La Musica," quite a lot, I've sat through a succession of more recent Duras films ("Destroy, She Said," "Nathalie Granger," "India Song") in physical pain as she became increasingly, aggressively minimal. Imagine my surprise, then, when I went to the festival to see her latest effort, "The Truck," more or less as a duty, and found myself, if not on the edge of my seat, then not ready to leave it on some made-up pretext.

The festival program note called "The Truck" Duras's "most accessible" film, though it looks and sounds much like her other movies. The thing was that this time I was ready for it. I was prepared for everything that was *not* going to happen (though about one-third of the audience wasn't, and the swirling movement of people toward the exit after 15 minutes suggested that someone had removed the Alice Tully Hall stopper).

In "The Truck" Miss Duras, a small, slight, middle-aged woman who can probably lift a trailer rig if she puts her mind to it, sits in a room at a table and, with actor Gerard Dépardieu, reads a screenplay for a film that, were it ever made, would be about a small, slight, middle-aged woman who hitches a ride in a truck driven by a young man like Dépardieu. Occasionally, as they read, the film cuts away to shots of a fine, big, sort of Eleanor-blue trailer-truck moving through the banlieus of Paris, sometimes, it seems, in circles. That's all.

The woman is lonely, perhaps slightly nutty. She may or may not hitch these rides every day to be able to have someone to talk to, or she may be on her way to visit a daughter who's just had a baby. It doesn't make any difference if you get on the Duras wavelength, which I was the other night. For the first time. The effect was disturbing, because one couldn't ever be sure about the film-within-the-film, but also invigorating because of its demonstration of Duras playing at being herself, a woman of vitality, immense self-assurance and tireless curiosity about the world, politics, women, men and the artistic process.

But "The Truck," I suspect, is no more or less accessible than any of her other films. It was just that I was ready to fit in with it.

• • •

I was also ready to fit in with "The Devil Probably," the new film by Robert Bresson, the great 70-year-old French director whose movies ("Diary of a Country Priest," "The Trial of Joan of Arc," "La Femme Douce," "Lancelot of the Lake," among others) are always incredibly beautiful in an unreal way and so delicately dry that one can't taste them if one has seen any other movie within the week.

"The Devil Probably" is Bresson's very measured, handsome (François Truffaut calls it "voluptuous") meditation upon a world that's destroying itself, told in the terms of an idealized young man who chooses (in the first reel) to commit suicide rather put up with physical and emotional pollution around him. Bresson pulls his punches somewhat more than usual (he gives us a shot of our old friend from the avant-garde cinema of the 1950's, the Bikini A-bomb, going off) but the movie is also funny—perhaps sardonic is a more accurate word—in ways that seem new to Bresson.

Accessible is what almost everyone at the festival agreed that Werner Herzog's new German film, "Heart of Glass," is not. Though I watched this private allegory (about the citizens of a medieval town who go mad and destroy themselves for the lack of a formula to make a certain kind of ruby-red glass) in as much confusion as everyone else, it did strike me in my restlessness and disappointment (for I've admired so many other Herzog films) that, of course, it wasn't meant to be "understood." Not for one minute. Yet that still didn't make it more interesting. The doomy pronouncements made by its hynotized (that's right) actors seemed terribly juvenile, and no match at all for the magnificent camerawork. Every frame of the film is too beautiful for words, but, in that case, why all the words, and if it's really supposed to be so glum, why all the beauty, which is not, after all, difficult to create if you have a good cameraman? As much as I've liked his other films, I was impatient with this one. Bored.

Shown on the same bill with "Heart of Glass" was "La Soufrière," a marvelous, 30-minute short that Herzog made last year in Guadeloupe when Mount Soufière, the volcano, was threatening to blow its top and take much of the rest of the Caribbean island with it. This simple, extraordinarily fine little film says just about everything that (I think) Herzog was saying in "Heart of Glass" about man's condition on this planet, as well as something about Herzog's priorities: The film concentrates on several people who elected to remain on the threatened island, awaiting death at any minute, and never once cuts away to show the wretched conditions in which thousands and thousands of evacuated islanders were forced to live while Soufrière was carrying on. But then Herzog is a poet, not a social worker.

• • •

Another film that was not supposed to be accessible but was, if one cared to climb down to it, was "Salo, 120 Days of Sodom," the late Pier Paolo Pasolini's adaptation of the Marquis de Sade's "120 Days of Sodom," updated from the 18th-century France of the Bourbons to the 1944 Italy of the puppet Fascist state established at Salo after Mussolini's collapse. Like the Sade novel, the film is a series of round-robin tableaux of every possible sexual perversion, plus coprophilia, necrophilia and explicit torture, all of it simulated, of course. Also simulated is the intelligence that attempts to justify this sort of sensational (sometimes almost vomit-inducing) imagery as a political statement about the ways the power elite uses, humiliates and reduces to mere property its human subjects. That's not good enough.

Nobody would dream of using a word like accessible in connection with a Truffaut film or with a hilarious, robustly made and performed new American comedy like "Handle With Care" (formerly titled "Citizens' Band"), which was written by Paul Brickman and directed by Jonathan Demme, and which was, for me, the revelation of the first 10 days of the festival.

One of the reasons that I don't like the word "accessible" is that it's used exclusively for films that are supposed to be difficult and never in relation to a more or less conventional film whose complete measure often eludes a viewer simply because it is conventional and the surface is so much fun.

Truffaut's "The Man Who Loved Women" is a very funny, lighthearted comedy about a sweet-natured, middle-aged wretch (played by Charles Denner) whose obsession with women is the end of him (the movie opens with his funeral). The Truffaut method is to beguile us with a recollection— an inventory, really—of the hero's relations with womem of all ages, sizes and shapes, most of them boisterously funny, though just behind the humor is the darkness that shadows (and gives dimension to) all of Truffaut's comedies. That rather grim shade is seldom seen, or acknowledged, by most people who look at Truffaut's films. But not because his films are not—can I say it one more time?—accessible, but because people don't look.

"Handle With Care" is as much about the pollution of our world as Bresson's "The Devil Probably," though I doubt many people will have time to notice, since the movie is so consistently funny and because it has the shape of the sort of film that would delight the very lower-middle-class, middle-American people it's about.

It's the uproarious story of a small American city where everybody owns a CB radio and thus lives two lives, the lives that all the rest of us lead and the lives of the personalities they assume over the radio. The movie has a beginning, middle and what almost amounts to a musical-comedy ending, yet in the accuracy of its locale, characters, speech and culture, it's very nearly a profound movie but—and this really is the last time—it's also accessible. ■

1977 O 9, II:15:5

Power at Stake

SCENES FROM THE CLASS STRUGGLE IN PORTUGAL, a documentary feature by Robert Kramer and Philip Spinelli; produced by David and Barbara Stone; distributed by Third World Newsreel. Running time 85 minutes. At the Whitney Museum of American Art, Madison Avenue at 75th Street.

By VINCENT CANBY

SCENES from the Class Struggle in Portugal," the new documentary feature at the Whitney Museum of American Art, may be of more cinematic than political interest here, having been directed (with Philip Spinelli) by Robert Kramer, the young man who made two impressive fiction films ("Ice" and "The Edge") dealing with America's militant left in the late 1960's and early 70's.

In Portugal, where nearly 50 years of a fascist dictatorship was overthrown in 1974, Mr. Kramer found the sort of revolutionary struggle in progress that "Ice" and "The Edge" predict (so far, fruitlessly) for the United States. There was something extremely invigorating going in Portugal, but also—this film seems to say without being entirely aware of it—something that wasn't following the neat plans of the theoreticians.

•

In Portugal, where the film is being distributed as a kind of teaching tool in factories, on farms and in neighborhoods, the title is "Will the Revolution Triumph?" The American title better describes the movie's content for those of us who aren't knowledgeable about the power blocs struggling for control in Portugal.

It is a film of isolated scenes—interviews, newsreel footage, demonstrations, parades—all designed to present the case for one of the most militant of Portugal's political parties, the Proletarian Revolutionary Party, with no attempt to hide the film makers' biases. If one doesn't share the film makers' particular Marxist way of looking at the world, much of what the two narrators (one man, one woman) tell us is likely to be received with skepticism, though their analyses of Portugal's past seem sound enough.

•

"Scenes from the Class Struggle" means to inform, not to entertain. Even so, it's a handsome film to look at, a collage of footage in color, in black-and-white and in monochromes. Its tone is meant to be as high and firm as the clenched fist of the Communist salute, but the final effect of the pictures we are shown is one of chaos, confusion, of people being polarized into political positions they don't even understand.

1977 O 13, C21:5

Easy on the Villains

BREAKING WITH OLD IDEAS; produced by the People's Republic of China; in color; in Chinese with English substities; distributed by October Films. Made in 1975. At the Film Forum, 15 Vandam Street, through Sunday and next Thursday through next Sunday. Running time: 120 minutes. This film has not been rated.

By JANET MASLIN

THERE IS a heated confrontation near the end of "Breaking With Old Ideas," a 1975 feature made in China and now at the Film Forum, that is as familiar in tone as it is foreign in substance. One night, the students at a rural branch of the Communist Labor College are worrying about the next day's big exam when they receive word that insects are devouring the rice crop. Should they keep on studying, like good little crypto-bourgeois bookworms, or should they take practical action?

One student leader, a pretty young woman who never seems to stop frowning, makes an impassioned plea for the latter option. In this situation, she insists, fumigation would be in accordance with the teachings of Chairman Mao. With that, the group is won over, and the sequence ends happily: Everyone marches out to the fields and commences spraying.

A scene from the 1975 Chinese feature, "Breaking With Old Ideas"

"Breaking With Old Ideas," reported to be the first Chinese feature released here commercially, is fascinating in its often-successful efforts to combine didacticism with entertainment. In order to explain the Party's attitude toward education—an attitude that has been substantially altered since this film was made, by the way—the film tells the story of Principal Lung, who in 1958 is appointed head of an agricultural college in a mountainous region. Lung believes in Mao's notion that education should be freely available to everyone, and that it is important for students to acquire both practical and political knowledge, "to become both Red and expert."

But some of the older, stuffier faculty members resist the changes Lung institutes, upholding their older, stuffier ideas about entrance exams and course requirements. They teach Lung's all-peasant student body about the functions of a horse's tail instead of how to cure a sick water-buffalo. They don't entirely renounce the elitism of Confucius. They aren't even smart enough to schedule their lessons on seedlings for crop-planting time.

One of the more amusing things about the film is the way it treats its villains. These reactionary teachers scheme and connive like the wickedest of fiends, but a film about the joys of enlightenment can't advocate revenge without seeming small-minded. So at the finale these soreheads publicly confess to the error of their ways, and the students forgive them. Then Mao sends a letter telling the students they were right all along, and everyone cheers euphorically.

Shot in fading color and translated rather strangely at times ("'How did you get here so quickly?' 'I came at great-leap-forward speed'"), "Breaking With Old Ideas" is a lot more warm and animated than it may sound. The characters are sketched broadly, without much human detail, and en masse they tend to shout things in unison, like the students at Billy Jack's Freedom School. But their fervor is so palpable, and their earnestness so affecting, that there is almost as much liveliness and drama here as there is propaganda.

1977 O 14, C10:3

'Desperate Living' Sordid Without Much Point

DESPERATE LIVING, written, directed and filmed by John Waters; sets by Vincent Peranio; costumes and makeup by Van Smith; director of photography, Thomas Loizeaux. At the D. W. Griffith Theater, 59th Street and Second Avenue, and at the Quad Cinema, 13th Street between Fifth Avenue and Avenue of the Americas. Running time: 100 minutes. This film has not been rated.

Muffy St. Jacques .... Liz Renay
Peggy Gravel .... Mink Stole
Mole McHenry .... Susan Lowe
Queen Carlotta .... Edith Massey
Grizelda Brown .... Jean Hill

You could look far and wide to find a more pointlessly ugly movie than John Waters's "Desperate Living," but why would you bother? This one more than takes the cake, and regurgitates it in close-up. The graphic sex scenes are enough to make absolutely anyone swear off amour.

Mr. Waters's point, such as it is, is that there is high humor to be found among low life. He emphasizes this almost as deftly as he sends up bourgeois manners—and he does *that* by showing, in the credits sequence, somebody eating a cooked rat off a fancily set dinner table.

JANET MASLIN

1977 O 15, 19:1

ROLLING THUNDER, directed by John Flynn; screenplay by Paul Schrader and Heywood Gould, based on a story by Mr. Schrader; produced by Norman T. Herman; executive producer, Lawrence Gordon; director of photography, Jordan Croneweth; editor, Frank P. Keller; music, Barry De Vorzon; distributed by American International Pictures. Running time: 99 minutes. At the Cinerama 1 Theater, Broadway at 47th Street, and other theaters. This film has been rated R.

Maj. Charles Rane .... William Devane
Johnny Vohden .... Tommy Lee Jones
Linda Forchet .... Linda Haynes
Texan .... James Best
Maxwell .... Dabney Coleman
Janet .... Lisa Richards
Automatic Slim .... Luke Askew
Cliff .... Lawrason Driscoll
Lopez .... James Victor
Candy .... Cassie Yates
Mark .... Jordan Gerler
Sister .... Jane Abbott

By VINCENT CANBY

After spending eight years in a Vietcong prison camp, Maj. Charles Rane (William Devane) returns home to a small town in Texas to be greeeted as a hero with a Cadillac convertible and couple thousand dollars in silver dollars (donated by a supermarket), one for each day of his imprisonment, plus one for luck. He accepts the car and the money in much the same manner as he accepts his wife's news that she's fallen in love with another man—impassively.

Nothing seems to move Charlie, though he cares for his young son and he is something of a physical fitness nut. He tells himself that it's as if he'd died when he was captured. One survives years of torture, he says, if "you learn to love the rope—that's how you beat them."

•

Charlie, as written in the screenplay by Paul Schrader and Heywood Gould, and as acted by Mr. Devane, is such a tough, complicated, explosive character that one keeps wishing that "Rolling Thunder," the film that contains him, were a match for him. It isn't. The movie, which opened yesterday at the Cincerama I and other theaters, has some good things, but in the way it has been directed by John Flynn it moves so easily and sort of foolishly toward its violent climax that all the tension within Charlie has long since escaped the film.

"Rolling Thunder," written in 1973, a year after Mr. Schrader wrote the screenplay for "Taxi Driver," gives evidence of having once been something much more complex than the neo-"Death Wish" this film is. There are a number of similarities between Charlie, the seemingly cool, unnervingly collected vet of "Rolling Thunder," and the psychotic Travis Bickle of "Taxi Driver." Within each is a small vial of nitroglycerine ready to go off.

The event that detonates Charlie is a brutal holdup in which a gang of thugs invades his house looking for his silver dollars. Not knowing Charlie's secret for survival, they torture him. They grind up his right hand in the garbage disposal unit, then murder his wife, his son and, they think, Charlie.

The manner in which Charlie, now equipped with a metal claw for a hand, goes about tracking down the murderers is such a model of efficiency—and he seems so cheerful about the task—that the complicated, seething character of the film's opening sequences appears to have become not much more interesting than the fellow played by Charles Bronson in "Death Wish."

•

William Devane as Maj. Charles Rane
A tough, complicated and explosive character.

I can't believe that it was Mr. Schrader's idea merely to have Charlie reliving his Vietnam duty (and, anyway, Charlie was a flier, not a ground soldier) when he sets up the bloody series of executions that conclude the movie. This, however, seems to be the point. Something is missing, but what it is, I'm not sure.

Though "Rolling Thunder" appears to have been made primarily for what is loosely called "the action market," which will take violence, blood and gore over sex any day, it has a nice feeling for the way small-town America looks and sounds and it has several excellent performances.

In addition to Mr. Devane's, there are those of Linda Haynes, as a young blond cocktail waitress who manages simultaneously to look beautiful and slightly ravaged (something that it took Ava Gardner years to achieve), and Tommy Lee Jones, as a fellow who shared Charlie's time in the P.O.W. camp and effectively suggests a man who, though he pretends to be like anyone else, now lives in a small closet in the back of his soul. Like Charlie, he is haunted but ever-alert—and armed to the teeth.

1977 O 15, 20:1

FILM VIEW

VINCENT CANBY

Triumph and Flop

Little things keep interrupting Mathieu (Fernando Rey), the charming, urbane, 50-ish French businessman who's the hero of Luis Bunuel's effervescent new comedy, "That Obscure Object of Desire." While Mathieu is in his elegant library in Paris, in the middle of some delicate negotiations with the mother of Conchita, the maddeningly fickle, changeably beautiful, 18-year-old Spanish dancer he wants to make his mistress, there is a sudden, very loud "snap," just offscreen. Mathieu's eyes betray the tiniest flicker of impatience as his ever-ready valet, Martin, enters the room and, most discreetly, without a word, removes the body of the mouse that's just been trapped while Mathieu was talking solemnly of love, respect and financial security.

Some time earlier, when Mathieu was in his limousine en route to the railroad station in Seville, a booby-trapped automobile had exploded in the street ahead, forcing Mathieu's chauffeur to make a detour. In a fancy Paris restaurant a fly plummets into Mathieu's gently stirred, certainly not bruised martini. One serene morning in Seville, Mathieu is strolling in the courtyard of an ancient church. Two black-robed peasant women stop him, one carrying an infant in her arms. The mother pulls back the blanket to show Mathieu her baby—a small, pink-snouted white pig.

One of the aspects of the film that makes "That Obscure Object of Desire" simultaneously so cockeyed funny and so mysterious is the manner in which the outside world keeps impinging on the consciousness of Mathieu, whose only wish is to possess, now and forever, the willful, headstrong Conchita. The object of his obsession is so unknown to Mathieu that Bunuel has two actresses—the serene Carole Bouquet and the equally beautiful but more earthy Angela Molina—alternate in playing the role, though not in any schematic way. The two faces of Conchita simply indicate Mathieu's mounting confusion and frustration as he pursues his love through a contemporary world in which a fly in a martini is scarcely any more or less momentous than the attempted assassination of the Archbishop of Sienna, reportedly the work of a guerrilla group called the Revolutionary Army of the Infant Jesus.

What is the extraordinary Bunuel telling us in "That Obscure Object of Desire," the 77-year-old master's 30th feature since "L'Age D'Or" (1930) and a comedy to match the best of his recent work, including "The Exterminating Angel" and "The Discreet Charm of the Bourgeoisie"? Almost as many things, I suspect, as there are people who see the film, but mainly he is sharing with us a view of life as seen by an artist who's as old as our century and whose creative impulse has not, as usually happens with filmmakers, been dampened by the years. Instead, it has been refined to an easy control and a perfection more often seen in painters and writers than among people who make movies in the furious hustle of the market place.

It was no more than an accident of programming by which the final two films at the recently concluded 15th New York Film Festival were this new masterpiece by Bunuel, which runs a speedy 100 minutes, and Bernardo Bertolucci's semi-controversial, 245-minute epic about 70 years of Italian political and social life told in the stories of three generations of two families, one landowners and the other serfs. "1900," the would-be magnus opus by the 37-year-old Bertolucci, is the grandiose flop of a very young, very talented man who has sought to capture truth by marshalling what looks to be a large portion of the physical resources of the Italian movie industry and employing the best actors of three countries and two continents. Truth, though, is not so cheaply and easily captured.

"1900" is virtually an anthology of various kinds of indecisions. When Bertolucci showed it at the 1976 Cannes Film Festival, it ran almost 5½ hours. When it was subsequently released in Europe, Bertolucci had cut it to five hours and 10 minutes, and it was shown in two parts as if it were two separate films. At one point Bertolucci was editing it down to a 4½-hour version while his producer, Alberto Grimaldi, was trying to peddle his own 3¼-hour version to Paramount Pictures against Bertolucci's protests (as well as those of a number of film critics who signed a petition on behalf of Bertolucci's artistic integrity and the director's civil rights).

I refused to sign that petition, not because I had seen the film or had anything against Bertolucci, whose work I've long admired, but because it seemed to be an intramural fight of the sort that makes the movie business go around (and forever separates it from any identification with the fine arts). After all that fuss the Bertolucci-approved version we are now seeing here runs four hours and five minutes and has been dubbed into a sort of opera-libretto English that numbs the mind in a way that not even four hours of adequate English subtitles would.

"1900," which started off with a budget of something over $3,000,000 and went over $8,000,000, would probably never have seen the light of day, at least in this form, if Bertolucci's previous film hadn't been such a huge financial success. It would have been a tough producer who could deny the director of "Last Tango in Paris" everything he wanted for his next picture, and it would have taken a director of more modesty and self-doubts than Bertolucci apparently has not to believe that he could make the epic he wanted of "1900." The reviews of "Last Tango" and the balance sheets must have been heady reading.

Backed by these reassurances, Bertolucci plowed ahead with his major work that, had it succeeded, might have been a Marxist "War and Peace." As it is, it's a mixed-up, Marxist romance that's soft at the core, full of outrageously operatic touches of the kind that only the late Luchino Visconti ever got away with, and then only once, in "The Damned." It's also full (toward the end) of highly stylized, group-movement choreography that's already been taken to its cinematic dead-end by Hungarian director Miklos Jancso.

"1900" starts off quite nicely and conventionally as the interwoven story of the aristocratic Berlinghieri family and the Dalco family, who are serfs on the Berlinghieris' estates. Two sons born into the families on the same day in 1901 grow up side by side, as friends, competitors and, ultimately, points of view. Alfredo, played by Robert De Niro with a kind of Lower East Side charm that hasn't much to do with the movie he's in, is the Berlinghieri scion, a man with too much taste and humanity to embrace Mussolini's Fascists but not enough guts to fight them. Olmo, played by Gerard Depardieu in the film's only consistently good performance, is the peasant who becomes transformed by his social conscience and a proud, banner-waving, Marxist-psalm-singing revolutionary.

Between these two men is a third, Attila (Donald Sutherland), who isn't a Hun but might as well be, a prototypical Fascist who works for the Berlinghieris as their foreman and who, when he's not insulting the help, is squashing cats with a butt of his head, sodomizing little boys and dropping helpless widows atop spiked fences.

Decadence in Bertolucci movies can be terrifically cinematic and rather perversely beautiful, as he demonstrated in "The Conformist." In "1900" it is virtually set decoration and is so overdone as to be ludicrous.

Until now Bertolucci's fondness for excess has always been part of the method rather than the point. In "1900" it's almost all there is. Even in this four-hour and five-minute version there's too much of everything—too many pretty pictures of broad landscapes, too many scenes of peasants behaving in the hearty, ribald manner that movie peasants affect, too many easy juxtapositions of upper-class decadence and lower-class strength, too much (at the end) red-flag waving that isn't meant to be realistic but impressionistic, though that switch in style comes too late.

In addition to Depardieu's, there are some other good performances, especially by Burt Lancaster as the Berlinghieri patriarch, but the rest are quite bad, including Donald Sutherland (whose role, admittedly, is an impossible one), and Dominique Sanda as De Niro's French wife, a lady who takes to drink because she's turned off by her husband's lack of political bone.

Bertolucci takes over four hours to show us more than we need to know about his characters, more than we want to know about his politics (which is passionate in a theoretical way) but not as much as we might have liked to know about specific political events that mark the 70 years covered by the movie. Though the film spans a lot of time, its view is short and narrow.

• • •

"That Obscure Object of Desire" tells what seems to be a small, rather special story about one man's mad obsession with a woman he can't possess, but Bunuel being Bunuel (a man whose politics, I suspect, are not too different from Bertolucci's), is incapable of limiting himself to the short view. "That Obscure Object of Desire" is not only about sex and manners but politics, religion, physics, you-name-it, about almost everything that touches us in our daily lives. Though his film is a model of efficient narrative, there's hardly a scene in it that doesn't evoke the manifold mysteries that—Bunuel knows—lie just beyond the film-frame.

Though he's now 77 and made his first films when in his twenties, Bunuel did not begin to earn a living from films until he was 47. He's never had a box-office hit to equal that of "Last Tango." Because he came late to commercial movies (in Mexico), he appears to be frugal about the way he shoots, getting as much as possible from every image, with the least waste of motion. This is why—when his films work as "That Obscure Object" does—the images have the effect of exploding in a continuing flow of odd, contradictory associations. They are the bubbles in his champagne. It's ironic that Bunuel, whose age is more than twice Bertolucci's, should make a film that looks so fresh, modern and tough, while Bertolucci's is sentimental, downright old-fashioned. ■

1977 O 16, II:17:1

EQUUS, directed by Sidney Lumet; screenplay by Peter Shaffer, based on his play; produced by Lester Persky and Elliott Kastner; director of photography, Oswald Morris; music, Richard Rodney Bennett; editor, John Victor-Smith; distributed by United Artists. Running time: 138 minutes. At the Trans-Lux East Theater, Third Avenue at 58th Street. This film has been rated R.

Dr. Martin Dysart	Richard Burton
Alan Strang	Peter Firth
Frank Strang	Colin Blakely
Dora Strang	Joan Plowright
Harry Dalton	Harry Andrews
Magistrate Hester Saloman	Eileen Atkins
Jill Mason	Jenny Agutter
Horseman	John Wyman
Margaret Dysart	Kate Reid
Mr. Pearce	Ken James
Miss Raintree	Elva Mai Hoover
Mr. Davies	James Hurdle
Mary	Karen Pearson
Dr. Bennett	David Gardner
Hospital patient	Patrick Brymer

Richard Burton as Dr. Martin Dysart confronting a patient.

Beautifully and sometimes almost grandly acted

By VINCENT CANBY

When "Equus," Peter Shaffer's psychological mystery play, was originally staged on Broadway, I was inclined to credit its great emotional impact to the stunning performances by Anthony Hopkins and Peter Firth and to the spectacular, highly stylized theatrical effects devised by Mr. Shaffer and John Dexter, who directed the production. On stage, "Equus' was a breathtaking experience of light, sound, performance and text, more or less, I thought, in that order of importance. Later, however, when I saw other actors take over the leads, the production suffered hardly at all.

Now, after seeing Sidney Lumet's comparatively realistic film version, it's possible to appreciate Mr. Shaffer's text for what it is—an extraordinarily skillful, passionate inquiry into the entire Freudian method—without being distracted by dazzling theatricality.

My problem, though, doctor, is that as much as I respect Mr. Shaffer's script (and his screenplay), I like being distracted by dazzling theatricality. Indeed, I prefer it.

This new "Equus," which opened yesterday at the Trans-Lux East, is probably about as good as one can get on film. It represents intelligent decisions. It's beautifully, sometimes almost grandly acted, by Richard Burton as the troubled psychiatrist attempting to bring back to sanity a young man who, in a fit of furious passion, has blinded six horses in a riding stable where he worked.

"EQUUS"—Peter Firth, an emotionally disturbed youth, fantasizes about a god-like horse.

Peter Firth repeats his stage role as the boy, with Joan Plowright as his mother, Colin Blakely as his dad, Eileen Atkins as the judge who brings the boy to the doctor's care and Jenny Agutter as the pretty girl who indirectly triggers his furious breakdown. There's not a thoughtless or uninteresting performance in the film.

Mr. Lumet manages to suggest some of the play's theatricality in the up-tempoed pacing of these performances and by retaining the doctor's agonizing monologues as speeches spoken directly to the camera. Yet something is missing—specifically, our need to use our imaginations to fill in the visual and emotional gaps in the stories of Dr. Martin Dysart, the psychiatrist, and Alan Strang, his patient.

•

Although Mr. Shaffer's screenplay does not differ in any marked way from the play, the film seems to exclude us by doing all the work for us. It shows and tells us everything there is to know about the doctor and his patient. In great plays, what happens offstage demands our attention as much as anything that happens on.

In Mr. Lumet's "Equus," there's no such thing as an off-screen space, no privacy that we can invade, in effect, at our own risk. Everything mentioned in the play's text, or recalled through a mimed, re-created moment, happens front and center, on the screen. The movie exhausts us with information. We see the unhappily married doctor with his dentist wife, though everything we have to know about her and their relationship is carefully evoked in dialogue or monologues. The images are redundant.

We are shown young Alan's bedroom at home, a sacred place where he created his private religion devoted to the worship of Equus, the vengeful, demanding horse-god. When Alan takes off on his clandestine midnight rides—his psychosexual communion rites—we watch a naked young man riding a real horse bareback through a real countryside. We are as likely to worry about his catching pneumonia as to wonder about his emotional state.

What once was poetic and mysterious becomes, when seen in this literal detail, banal, anticlimactic.

•

Yet this may well seem like hair-splitting to anyone seeing "Equus" for the first time, for, behind all of this realistic scenery, the play remains intact, and it's a good one. It's the most interesting, most serious appraisal of psychiatry that we've ever had in a commercial film—an appraisal that probably has infuriated quite as many psychiatrists as it has pleased. It's the terrible suspicion of Mr. Shaffer's Dr. Dysart that, by removing Alan Strang's demons, by returning him to "normal" life, he has removed the boy's passion forever, emotionally lobotomized him.

Though the film is held together by the mystery of Alan Strang's behavior, the unraveling of which provides the narrative line, it's Mr. Burton's performance as the psychiatrist that dominates the movie, whether or not you agree with his fears that he cuts from his patients "their portions of individuality." This is the best Burton performance since "Who's Afraid of Virginia Woolf?" He receives excellent support, especially from Mr. Firth, but the film, which is otherwise in the siege of commonplace realism, becomes bigger than life in the presence of this self-mocking, troubled, still-searching miracle-worker.

1977 O 17, 39:1

Statistics Plus

ANGEL CITY; produced, directed, edited, timed and written by Jon Jost; photography by Jon Jost and Robert Schoenhut. At the Whitney Museum, Madison Avenue and 75th Street. Running time: 74 minutes. This film has not been rated.
WITH Robert Giaudini, Winifred Golden, Pierce del Rue, Kathleen Kramer, Mark Brown.

By JANET MASLIN

THE BIRTH RATE, the death rate, the mean annual temperature and the number of tons of zinc produced each day: These are among the most valuable tidbits of information about Los Angeles to be gathered from "Angel City," a feature by Jon Jost included as part of the Whitney Museum's New American Filmmakers Series.

Mr. Jost's film means to reveal a deeper kind of truth about its subject, to be sure; the statistics are only a very small part of the show. But so many of Mr. Jost's other images are deliberately ambiguous and without real satirical sting that after a while the brevity and clarity of cold hard fact—become most attractive.

•

The film combines a Chandleresque detective story, told in a tone hovering indecisively between myth and parody, with other kinds of footage meant to convey the nature of the city. There is also descriptive voice-over narration of a quasi-poetic nature ("Exploding . . . imploding . . . a matrix insidious . . . deceptive . . . dangerous"). One of the more interesting images is that of a giant red lipstick being amorously applied to a giant mouth, while an off-screen voice reads a cool, contrasting news item about the advertising campaign for the film "Lipstick."

Mr. Jost likes to present objects in contexts that alter their meanings, but he soon exhausts the possibilities of such methods. His depiction of Los Angeles as a ghostly, vaguely sinister example of what happens when capitalism runs amuck is old news at best, and his very lengthy takes and garrulous performers tend to dull ideas rather than amplify them.

1977 O 19, C17:2

The Singles Scene

LOOKING FOR MR. GOODBAR, directed by Richard Brooks; screenplay by Mr. Brooks, based on the novel by Judith Rossner; produced by Freddie Fields; director of photography, William A. Fraker; editor, George Grenville; music, Artie Kane; distributed by Paramount Pictures. Running time: 136 minutes. At Loews State I, Broadway at 45th Street, and Loews Tower East, Third Avenue near 72d Street. This film has been rated R.

Theresa . . . . . Diane Keaton
Katherine . . . . . Tuesday Weld
James . . . . . William Atherton
Mr. Dunn . . . . . Richard Kiley
Tony . . . . . Richard Gere
Martin . . . . . Alan Feinstein
Gary . . . . . Tom Berenger
Mrs. Dunn . . . . . Priscilla Poinier
Brigid . . . . . Laurie Prange
Barney . . . . . Joel Fabiani
Black Cat . . . . . Julius Harris
George . . . . . Richard Bright
Cap Jackson . . . . . Levar Burton
Mrs. Jackson . . . . . Marilyn Coleman
Marvella . . . . . Carole Mallory
Principal . . . . . Mary Ann Mallis
Teacher . . . . . Jolene Dellenbach
Teacher . . . . . Louie Fant
Bartender . . . . . Eddie Garrett
Arthur . . . . . Alexander Courtney
Surgeon . . . . . Brian Dennehy
Doctor . . . . . Richard Venture
Patrick . . . . . Richard Burke
Rafe . . . . . Robert Fields
Father Timothy . . . . . Richard O'Brien
Chuck . . . . . Tony Hawkins
Rhoda . . . . . Caren Kaye

By VINCENT CANBY

"LOOKING for Mr. Goodbar," Richard Brooks's film version of Judith Rossner's novel, is about a lonely woman who hangs around singles bars and one night takes home a stranger who, after sex, stabs her to death because she won't let him sleep till morning. At least, that's what I think it's about because I doubt very much if Mr. Brooks would have made the movie if the girl had been just as arbitrarily murdered on the street at 10 A.M. by a psychopath who didn't like the color of her pantyhose.

•

In her book, Miss Rossner frames this story with the murder, a device that has the effect of making the novel itself an exploration of the circumstances that brought its heroine to such an end. Though the book, which was based on a real-life case, was such a best-seller that I can hardly believe anyone will be going to see the movie without being aware of its plot, Mr. Brooks lops off this frame, thus to pretend to discover the sad fate of Theresa Dunn.

This may turn out to be the cinema year's most ingenuous decision, though it's only one of several taken by Mr. Brooks in the interests of transforming into something glossy what might have been a truly grubby, urban horror story.

Another major mistake is presenting us with a Theresa Dunn in the person of the splendidly beautiful, intelligent, funny Diane Keaton, who is virtually the only reason to see "Looking for Mr. Goodbar," which is, I admit, something of a contradiction, unless you're sex-and-violence starved.

Miss Keaton, who continues to grow as an actress and film presence, is worth paying attention to in bits and pieces of the movie, whether she's trading arch banter with a potential pickup in a barroom as she studies her copy of "The Godfather," or teaching a class of deaf children, her occupation by day, or making breathless, abandoned love with a stranger. She's too good to waste on the sort of material the movie provides, which is artificial without in anyway qualifying as a miracle fabric.

Miss Rossner's novel is very much a New York novel. It moves around the city—from the Bronx to Brooklyn to Greenwich Village, and up and down the avenues, during the day and late at night—in such a way that the city becomes an always visible if silent conspirator in Theresa's tragic fate.

The city in Mr. Brooks's film is never identified. At times it looks a bit like Chicago, then Los Angeles, sometimes New York, thus to become Nowhere, U.S.A. Even the city's singles bars and disco scenes are unconvincing. There are moments when Theresa appears to be entering a Village strip joint, the sort that caters to conventioneers, only to find, right inside, a place not unlike Maxwell's Plum. Nothing fits.

This is also true of Theresa's case-history that Mr. Brooks laboriously details for us in flashbacks that are meant to be jazzy but look as if someone were flipping a television dial.

Diane Keaton falls in love with Alan Feinstein, a professor she works for, in "Looking for Mr. Goodbar." Miss Keaton is "virtually the only reason to see it."

Theresa, we are told, comes from lower-middle-class Irish-American family whose mom never opens her mouth, and whose older sister (Tuesday Weld) is an unhappy swinger.

Worse for Theresa, though, was a siege of polio that left her lame as a child and then, at a crucial time in her life, in a corrective plaster cast for a year. She is mortified by a genteel scar on her back, which actually looks no worse than a mark that might be left by a wicker chair, though we are asked to believe it contributes to her furious pursuit of anonymous sex instead of lasting relationships. With Miss Keaton playing the part, this seems like arrant nonsense.

•

Contributing effective supporting performances are Miss Weld; William Atherton, as a good young Catholic man Theresa should love, but doesn't; Alan Feinstein, as the English professor who first seduces her, and Tom Berenger, as the part-time homosexual who murders her. Especially good is Richard Gere as Tony, the maniac, switchblade-toting stud who's none too bright and beats her up on occasion, but is apparently the answer to Theresa's wildest dreams.

"Looking for Mr. Goodbar," which is R-rated for good reason, opened yesterday at Loews State 1 and Loews Tower East Theaters.

1977 O 20, C19:1

VOLCANO: AN INQUIRY INTO THE LIFE OF MALCOLM LOWRY, a documentary written and directed by Donald Brittain with John Kramer; director of photography, Douglas Kiefer; edited by John Kramer; music by Alain Clavier; produced by the National Film Board of Canada; words of Malcolm Lowry are spoken by Richard Burton. At the Cinema III Theater, 5yth Street and Fifth Avenue. Running time: 100 minutes. This film has not been rated.

By JANET MASLIN

WRITERS ARE notoriously poor subjects for biographical study. If the writer's life warrants close scrutiny at all, chances are that he or she was articulate enough to have dealt with the most interesting facets already, and that few biographers will be canny enough to develop a perspective more valuable than the author's. Malcolm Lowry is a case in point: Mr. Lowry captured a far more vivid sense of his own demons in "Under the Volcano," his one great novel, than the one evidenced by a new film biography entitled "Volcano: An Inquiry Into the Life of Malcolm Lowry."

•

The film, made by Donald Brittain with John Kramer and showing at Cinema III, documents Mr. Lowry's life in a curious manner. Key events, such as the 1957 inquest that deemed his having choked drunkenly on his own vomit as "death by misadventure," are re-enacted for the camera, but they are staged too vaguely to have much impact, and too literally to cast any new light. To illustrate the fact that Mr. Lowry's house burned down, for example, the camera simply lingers over footage of another modern-day house on fire. To show that his book was successful, the camera whisks across rows of shelves filled with paperback copies.

As the film often indicates, Mr. Lowry was a difficult character, an alcoholic so desperate that he would drink after-shave lotion when nothing more palatable was at hand. He was a hard man for even his friends and family to love, but his talents were extraordinary enough to make people forgive him his drunken excesses.

The film attempts to suggest the scope of Mr. Lowry's writing, mostly through unidentified voice-over passages read eloquently by Richard Burton, but it in no way makes the genius seem as palpable as the unpleasantness. What remains is the portrait of a tragic and disagreeable man with many patient, all-forgiving friends.

Mr. Brittain has made other biographical films, about people as diverse as Leonard Cohen and Henry Ford 2d, and he has also worked as a police reporter. His experience in the latter field is apparent in the thoroughness with which he reels off details of limited consequence: an old schoolmaster of Mr. Lowry's recalls that the boy slouched in class, and Mr. Brittain's narration adds that Mr. Lowry had small hands, was chronically constipated, and had a physique that made him a figure of fun on bath night among the other boys at school.

Mr. Brittain's attention to fact, combined with his obvious desire to lend the film an impressionistic air, produces a strange sort of sloppiness. Chronology is sometimes sketchy, and many of the numerous people interviewed in the film go unidentified. Often this doesn't matter, but it does pose problems at times. "He chose to live as he did, and he produced 'Under the Volcano,'" says one man. "I chose to live differently, and I didn't produce anything much." "Well, that's not true," insists another voice off-screen. Maybe not, but how can we be sure if the man we're watching hasn't been properly introduced?

"Volcano" presupposes a certain knowledge of Mr. Lowry's work on the part of the viewer, but it isn't really a film for Lowry scholars: there are few photos of the man here, little new information, and no insights not already provided by his work. Some of the interviews, notably one with Margerie Lowry, the author's widow, are quite moving at times, and the images of Mr. Lowry at his most grotesque are stark and mesmerizing. But a viewer who knew nothing about Mr. Lowry at the outset might come away wondering at the disparity between the caliber of the man's work and the wretchedness of his life. Mr. Brittain's "Inquiry" never satisfactorily addresses his single most important issue.

1977 O 20, C19:4

THE DEMISE OF FATHER MOURET, (LA FAUTE DE l'ABBE MOURET), directed by Georges Franju; screenplay (French with English subtitles) by Jean Ferry and Mr. Franju, based on the novel by Emile Zola; produced by Vera Belmont; director of photography, Marcel Fradatai; music, Jean Wiener; distributed by Images Film Library. Running time: 90 minutes. At the Renoir Cinema, 100 Seventh Avenue South. This film has not been rated.

Serge Mouret	Francis Huster
Albine	Gillian Hills
Archangias	Andre Lancombe
La Teuse	Margo Lion
Bambaousse	Lucien Barjon
Jeanbernat	Hugo Fausto Tozzi
Dr. Pascal	Tino Carroro

By VINCENT CANBY

EMILE ZOLA'S "La Faute de L'Abbé Mouret," written in 1875, is not, as far as I can learn, in print in English at the moment, but if it were, I doubt that the title would be "The Demise of Father Mouret." This is what the American distributors are calling Georges Franju's 1970 French film adaptation that opened yesterday at the Renoir Cinema.

Most often "faute" is translated as "mistake," "shortcoming," "defect," and, I suppose, if the word were pushed, it could even mean "sin." To freight it with the finality of "demise" is really too much. It seems to be just another in a series of wrong decisions that began with Mr. Franju's desire to make the movie, which is a sort of fairy-tale version of the Adam and Eve story updated to the France of the Second Empire.

Mr. Franju is not a well-known film maker in this country, perhaps because he is at his best when he is being what most critics think of as frivolous, though he's not a frivolous man. His fine horror film, "Eyes Without a Face," received few reviews when it opened here in a badly English-dubbed version in the mid-60's, though his more solemn, ambitious films, "Thérèse Desqueyroux" and "Thomas the Imposter" have been reviewed, if not ecstatically.

•

"Judex," Mr. Franju's homage to Louis Feuillade, the creator of the great French silent serials "Fantômas" and "Les Vampires," simply baffled everyone not sharing the Franju opinion of Feuillade.

"The Demise of Father Mouret" is not likely to win him new friends, though I've no doubt that the film may be faithful to the novel, which I haven't read, and to Zola, whose occasional flights into a kind of naturalized romanticism haven't worn well.

"The Demise of Father Mouret" is a mixture of social realism and Walt Disney, about a delicate young French priest, Father Mouret (Francis Huster), who elects to take a parish in the provinces where the peasants have long since embraced every sin there is. The priest himself successfully sublimates his own lustful thoughts in prayer until one day he meets a strange young woman, Albine (Gillian Hills), who lives with her atheistic uncle in the remains of old chateau set in the middle of a an old chateau set in the middle of a magic garden.

Well, one thing leads to another and poor Father Mouret loses his memory, long enough to lose himself to worldly pleasures in the garden with Albine, who, like Eve, tempts the man, though in this case the author is clearly in favor of apple-eating. Things go very badly for the couple. The priest returns to his church and Albine commits suicide in a way that is unique in my movie-going memory: She smothers herself to death with calla lilies.

The actors are steadfastly unconvincing. The one interesting character in the film is an old lady we meet only after her death—someone, we're told in shocked tones, who, during the Revolution, posed naked as a living-statue of Reason.

1977 O 21, C10:3

DAMNATION ALLEY, directed by Jack Smight; screenplay by Alan Sharp and Lukus Heller; from the novel by Roger Zelazny; director of photography, Harry Stradling Jr.; music by Jerry Goldsmith; film editor, Frank J. Urioste; produced by Jerome M. Zeitman and Paul Maslansky; released by 20th Century-Fox. At Showcase theaters. Running time: 91 minutes. This film is rated PG.

Tanner	Jan-Michael Vincent
Denton	George Peppard
Janice	Dominique Sanda
Keegan	Paul Winfield
Billy	Jackie Earle Haley

Foreign powers blow up all of North America in "Damnation Alley," a movie to make anyone wish the foreign powers had made Hollywood the first town to go. After the holocaust, all that remains is George Peppard, Paul Winfield, Jan-Michael Vincent, Dominique Sanda and Jackie Earle Haley, plus a few dusty slot machines in Las Vegas and a landscape that looks as if it's been photographed through a used coffee filter.

There are also hordes of giant cockroaches, and the first thing they do is eat Mr. Winfield, the only cast member who shows signs of being ready to give even a passable performance.

The only real value of "Damnation Alley" is educational: This is the movie to see if you don't understand what was so wonderful about the special effects in, say, "Star Wars." Here, the sky features streaks of red and blue light that make it look like a giant Rya rug, and it actually moves in relation to the equally phony-looking landscape.

JANET MASLIN

•

"Damnation Alley" is rated PG (Parental Guidance Suggested"), probably because it contains some very gory footage of actors being gnawed to death by giant insects.

1977 O 22, 14:6

Short and Long of It

RAPID EYE MOVEMENT, A program of short animated films by Loring Doyle, Vincent Collins, Dennis Pies, Paul Glabicki, Paul Driessen, Joan Freeman, Jeff Carpenter, Joyce Borenstein, Margaret B. Doogan, Barbara Bottner, Richard Baily, John Brister, Kathy Rose and Ulrich Kretzschmar. At the Film Forum, 15 Vandam Street, between Seventh Avenue South and Avenue of the Americas. Running time: 79 minutes. This film has not been rated.

By JANET MASLIN

ANIMATORS have more freedom than most other kinds of filmmakers, and "Rapid Eye Movement," a program of 14 animated shorts, celebrates that freedom. The films vary dramatically, in length (the longest runs 13 minutes, the briefest a minute and a half), and in technique, to provide a lively cross-section of the effects that animation can produce. Some of the films are first-rate and others most emphatically are not, but quality is almost beside the point; the exciting thing about this program is its variety.

The best films here are the hardest to describe, because they use animation to create images and sensations not readily found in other art forms.

Dennis Pies's "Sonoma" begins in charcoal gray, as a line drawing that gradually, very delicately, begins to give birth to hints of color. The drawing evolves unpredictably, its movement impervious to any commonplace logic; it bears so little relationship to rational thought that it feels like truly unbridled fantasy.

Paul Glabicki's "Dream 733," on the other hand, is such a ponderous compilation of spacemen, ray-guns, electronic wheeps and ancient statuary that it never comes close to achieving a similarly liberating mood.

•

"An Old Box," by Paul Driessen, hovers somewhere in between; it narrates an uninteresting Christmas fable, but Mr. Driessen's spatial sense is much more novel than his storytelling, because he is continually erasing and then re-inventing parts of the frame to enhance his drawings' movement.

Joan Freeman's "Toilette" uses stop-motion animation to show a clay woman trying on various outfits before her mirror, then shuffling back to bed in despair. In a similar vein, and by no means as witty, is Barbara Bottner's "Later That Night," in which a woman imagines that her breasts are biceps.

•

Also noteworthy are John Brister's clever "Mandarin Oranges," a kind of ballet featuring real oranges in Chinese hats, and the title film, an impressive 13-minute look at a dark, sinister world of pointless relationships and cocktail-party chitchat. Its protagonist of sorts is a hip-looking young man with a cool manner and poker-chip eyes.

"Rapid Eye Movement" will be shown at the Film Forum on two consecutive weekends, Oct. 27-30 and Nov. 3-6, at 7:45 each evening.

1977 O 28, C13:4

ALICIA, a documentary feature in Spanish with English subtitles; directed by Eduardo Manet; produced by the Instituto Cubano del Arte e Industria Cinematograficos; distributed by Tricontinental Film Center. Running time: 75 minutes. At the Renoir Cinema, 100 Seventh Avenue South. This film has not been rated.

WITH Alicia Alonso, Azari Plisetski, Jose Pares, Josefine Mendez, Mirta Pla, Aurora Bosh, Loipa Araujo, Roberto Rodriguez, Alberto Mendez, Hugo Guffanti, Coferino Barrios, Nidia Rochepkina, Joaquin Banegas.

By VINCENT CANBY

"ALICIA," the documentary feature that opened yesterday at the Renoir Cinema, celebrates one of Cuba's greatest living national treasures, Alicia Alonso, the ballerina who first gained fame in this country in the 1940's and who, since the Castro revolution, has served as the principal dancer and artistic director of Ballet Nacional de Cuba.

The film, produced last year by the Cuban Film Institute, is no great shakes as movie-making, but because its star is both its subject and its style, it doesn't make much difference. Most of "Alicia" is devoted to ballet footage, including excerpts from "Giselle," "Swan Lake" and what appears to be almost all of "Carmen," which may not be the most interesting ballet in the world but which is extremely photogenic in this production.

Most of this dance footage was made in 1967 when the Cuban Film Institute recorded Miss Alonso's entire repertory, though "Carmen" was photographed last year. All of it is in CinemaScope, the very wide-screen process that allows the camera to remain at a neutral middle distance so that we can see the figures of the dancers in relation to the spaces through which they move. There are occasional cuts to close-ups of faces or feet, but they are fewer and less distracting than in most ballet films one sees.

The dance footage is punctuated from time to time by montages of still photographs that give us a once-over-lightly version of the ballerina's childhood in Cuba and her early days in New York. There also are snippets from an interview with Miss Alonso today. These are appealing (as she talks about her fight against the blindness threatened by a detached retina) without being particularly revealing, though her passionate identification with the revolution is always emphasized.

•

Miss Alonso's buoyant personality can't easily be hidden behind banal questions and English subtitles, however. And it fills up the screen when she dances, particularly in "Giselle" and "Black Swan" sequences with Azari Plisetski as her partner.

Most remarkable are the heat and light she creates as Carmen, one of the few sequences shot in full color. In repose, talking directly to the camera, Miss Alonso makes no effort to hide the years (she'll reportedly be 56 this December), but her Carmen is as ageless as the femme-fatale myth on which it's based. She's breathtaking.

1977 O 28, C13:4

Failed Aspirations

VOYAGE TO GRAND TARTARIE, directed by Jean-Charles Tacchella; screenplay (French with English subtitles) by Mr. Tacchella; director of photography, M. Andre du Breuil; music, Gerard Anfosso; produced by MK2 Productions and V. M. Productions; distributed by New Line Cinema. Running time: 100 minutes. At D. W. Griffith Cinema, 59th Street near Second Avenue, and Quad Cinema, 13th Street near Avenue of the Americas. Opens today at Embassy 72d Street Theater, on Broadway. This film has not been rated.

Alexis	Jean-Luc Bideau
Daphne	Micheline Lanctot
Sports champion	Lou Castel
Orlane	Catherine Verlor
Pamela	Catherine Laborde
Pamela's husband	Fulbert Janin
Nelly	Sybil Maas

By VINCENT CANBY

"VOYAGE TO GRAND Tartarie" is brought to us by Jean-Charles Tacchella, the director who hadn't yet brought to us "Cousin, Cousine" when he made "Grand Tartarie," his first feature, a comedy of such consistent mirthlessness and accidental cruelty you might believe them to be his method.

Although I'm an admirer of "Cousin, Cousine," which became one of the most successful foreign-language movies we've had in years, I can see some associations between its rather casual treatment of other people's feelings and the total self-absorption that Mr. Tacchella displays in "Voyage to Grand Tartarie," which opened yesterday at the D. W. Griffith and Quad Cinemas, a social satire made with a heavy hand and small mind.

•

Only someone dangerously sure of his own talents would think he could make—as Mr. Tacchella has described "Grand Tartarie"—a film that is a "farcical trip through our society" as well a "satire of films which make fun of contemporary society." If Mr. Tacchella were a shipbuilder, you might expect him to put sails on a submarine.

"Voyage to Grand Tartarie," a title that is supposed to suggest a trip through hell, is set in a landscape that is meant to be a surreal projection of a France in the grip of social and political revolution, environmental pollution and emotional alienation.

The journey is undertaken by Alexis (Jean-Luc Bideau) after his pretty young wife is arbitrarily shot down by a maniac in a cowboy suit as she comes out of a supermarket. Alexis, one is asked to believe, feels so much grief he expresses none at all. He withdraws his money from the bank, packs one shirt in a suitcase, and climbs in to his car with the intention of committing suicide when his money runs out.

Micheline Lanctôt in "Voyage to Grand Tartarie": a comedy of consistent mirthlessness and accidental cruelty.

Unfortunately he has too many whimsical adventures ever to carry out his plan. With a completely deadpan expression, Alexis alternately observes the idiocies around him and participates in them. It's a lunatic world, Mr. Tacchella tells us over and over again, a mysterious place where a businessman works so hard he has to take sleep cures twice a year, where people carry guns to and from work, where everyone's on strike, where water is about to be rationed and where nothing is so awful at home but that news of a war in Kenya doesn't make things seem better.

•

Alexis's life becomes a kind of elongated movie serial, a point that is emphasized by his reading "Fantomas" adventures in moments of repose. He has a couple of desultory affairs along the way, including one with a young woman played by Micheline Lanctot, who has a very pretty face but is otherwise so husky-voiced and androgynous I began to wonder if she could possibly be a boy. This suspicion was further increased by Mr. Tacchella's decision—which I ultimately took to be just another failed joke—to shoot several scenes featuring Mr. Bideau in the nude while the actresses remain prudishly clothed from the neck down.

Mr. Tacchella has no knack whatsoever for the cinema of the absurd. Images that are intended to strike us as revealing and ridiculous simply look like mistakes, things that should have been left on the cutting-room floor but weren't—a little girl cheerfully burying a cat alive, or a woman shining the shoes of her husband while he hangs by his neck from a tree. Only Luis Buñuel has the tact and the wit to deal successfully in such expressions of rage.

•

The movie is such a mess it even fractures the talents of Mr. Bideau, the Swiss actor who has proven himself in such films as "La Salamandre," "The Invitation" and "Jonah Who Will Be 25 in the Year 2000." In this film, he behaves like a zombie.

"Grand Tartarie" is not completely incapable of creating some sense of wonder, if only the wonder that the man who made his debut with a movie of so many failed aspirations could have gone on to make "Cousin, Cousine," a small, beautifully acted love story, simultaneously tough and lyric, which never overreaches itself in the juvenile ways of his first endeavor.

1977 N 4, C6:4

Sweet, Green Fire

PETE'S DRAGON; directed by Don Chaffey; produced by Ron Miller and Jerome Courtland; screenplay by Malcolm Marmorstein, based on a story by Seton I. Miller and S. S. Field; director of photography, Frank Phillips; music and lyrics by Al Kasha and Joel Hirschhorn; music supervised, arranged and conducted by Irwin Kostal; choreography by Onna White; animation director, Don Bluth; Elliott created by Ken Anderson. At the Radio City Music Hall, 49th Street and Avenue of the Americas. Running time: 134 minutes. This film has been rated G.

Nora .... Helen Reddy
Pete .... Sean Marshall
Lampie .... Mickey Rooney
Hoagy .... Red Buttons
Lena Gogan .... Shelley Winters
Dr. Terminus .... Jim Dale
The Mayor .... Jim Backus
Mark .... Charles Tyner
The voice of Elliott .... Charlie Callas

By JANET MASLIN

DID YOU EVER see an elephant fly? You did? Well, then, how about a chubby green dragon who trots across live-action landscapes with animated aplomb, and who can casually turn himself into a cloud of blue vapor? "Pete's Dragon," which opened yesterday at the Radio City Music Hall, is the most energetic and enjoyable Disney movie in a long while.

Pete is a rather strenuously cute little boy played by Sean Marshall, and Elliott is his fire-breathing, often invisible friend. Together, they run away from the filthy, snaggle-toothed Gogans (Mama Gogan is Shelley Winters), who have bought Pete from an orphanage for $50 and change and mean to keep him. Pete and Elliott wind up in Passamaquoddy, a Maine town that looks remarkably like a California movie set, with a populace that includes Jim Backus as the bumbling mayor, Mickey Rooney as the tippling lighthouse-keeper, Helen Reddy as the lighthouse-keeper's wonderful daughter, and Jim Dale and Red Buttons as a pair of half-funny, half-dastardly medicine salesmen. Lots of things happen to Pete and Elliott there, and every time anything happens, someone is sure to sing about it.

•

Directed by Disney veteran Don Chaffey, "Pete's Dragon" is full of performers who nicely detract attention from one another's weaknesses. Sean Marshall doesn't sing well, but Helen Reddy does, so she often accompanies his vocals. Miss Reddy is serviceable but undistinguished as an actress—she has a tendency to behave as if she were a very bright light bulb in a very small lamp—but she so often finds herself in the company of Messrs. Rooney, Dale or Buttons that her scenes work well.

Onna White's choreography is charmingly ragtag, especially when it comes to the Gogans, and the score by Al Kasha and Joel Hirschhorn (whose lesser credits include "The Towering Inferno" and "The Poseidon Adventure") has some sunny moments. At two hours and 14 minutes, the movie is a lot longer than it needs to be. On the other hand, Elliott (whose beeps and bomps and chomping sounds are supplied by Charlie Callas) is very sweet and emotive, and you don't often see children's musicals as ambitious as this one any more.

Kids may love it, but adults will find themselves wondering about a thing or two. Granted, a movie starring a green dragon invites a few jokes about characters' seeing things that aren't there; even so, there is an awful lot of drinking in the script, and the film treats alcohol carelessly enough to give one pause. Also, there is something disconcerting about the musical number in which Miss Reddy and a chorus of children proclaim that "There's room for everyone in this world." Passamaquoddy counts a handful of blacks among its population, but the children in that scene appear to be exclusively white.

1977 N 4, C6:1

1900, directed by Bernardo Bertolucci; screenplay by Mr. Bertolucci, Franco Arcalli and Giuseppe Bertolucci; executive producer, Alberto Grimaldi; director of photography, Vittorio Storaro; editor, Franco Arcalli; music, Ennio Morricone; a P.E.A. production, distributed by Paramount Pictures. Running time: 245 minutes (plus intermission). At the Festival Theater. This film is rated X.

Alfredo .... Burt Lancaster
Giovanni .... Romolo Valli
Eleonora .... Anna-Maria Gherardi
Regina .... Laura Betti
Alfredo (the grandson) .... Robert De Niro
Alfredo as a child .... Paolo Pavesi
Ada .... Dominique Sanda
Leo Dalco .... Sterling Hayden
Olmo Dalco .... Gerard Depardieu
Olmo as a child .... Roberto Maccanti
Anita Foschi .... Stefania Sandrelli
Attila .... Donald Sutherland
Octavio .... Werner Bruhns
Signora Pioppi .... Alida Valli
Sister Desolata .... Francesca Bertini

"1900" was shown at the 1977 New York Film Festival. The following excerpts are from Vincent Canby's review, which appeared Oct. 8. The film ***opens today at the Festival Theater.***

Bernardo Bertolucci's "1900" is a four-hour, five-minute (plus intermission) movie that covers approximately 70 years of Italian social and political history, from 1901, the year Verdi died and peasants were still in bondage to the landowners, to the 1970's, when a capitalist movie producer would put up millions of dollars to make a film such as "1900," which is essentially a Marxist romance. This is progress of a very particular sort.

The film begins beautifully, uproariously, as a realistic, three-generation, the-mansion-and-the-shanties family saga and then slowly congeals into the overblown attitudes of a political pageant, so positive and upbeat it's difficult to believe it comes from a land whose problems are a tiny bit more complex than those of Oz.

Before the family saga becomes a political statement, Mr. Bertolucci ("Last Tango in Paris," "The Conformist," "Before the Revolution") presents us with a series of unintentionally comic sequences that more or less define current fashions of decadence as seen in movies made by European left-wing intellectuals.

Aristocrats, they tell us, are impotent. They loll around, lift fingers only when wrapped around champagne glasses, dance during the daytime, and when being really wicked, sniff cocaine. The Italian Fascists have more strength, being bourgeois. They torture animals, sodomize little boys, exploit epileptic females and murder children and widows.

This 245-minute English-dubbed version of "1900" is not to be confused with the 5½-hour version that was shown at the 1976 Cannes festival, or with the five-hour, 10-minute version that was later released in Europe, or with the 4½-hour version that Mr. Bertolucci once said was as short as the film could possibly be, before giving his full approval to this even shorter version.

At one point or another, each of these versions has been approved by the young Italian director, who is not only talented and ambitious, but also flexible, so much so that when one looks at the film now one brings to it a certain amount of skepticism. How could a film that he once insisted on showing in its 5½-hour length be cut almost 90 minutes without losing entire sequences?

One suspects that as grandly conceived as "1900" was, it has always lacked a guiding vision of real vitality and strength. It's a shapeless mass of film stock containing some brilliant moments and a lot more that are singularly uninspired.

Everything of real interest and epic sweep occurs in the film's first half, which introduces us to members of the land-owning Berlinghieri family, headed by the old patriarch Alfredo, robustly played by Burt Lancaster, and the Dalco family, who farm the Berlinghieri estate and whose patriarch is old Leo, played with a kind of severe passion by Sterling Hayden. The stage for the subsequent events is set when Alfredo and Leo each are presented with a grandson born on the same day, the one to grow up to be a dilettantish Robert De Niro and the other to be a passionate union organizer and Marxist, played by Gerard Depardieu.

The early lives of the two young men, their relationships to their families and to each other, are beautifully and movingly detailed, but as the years overtake them, so do Mr. Bertolucci's political purposes overtake the film.

Even in a film that runs more than four hours, Mr. Bertolucci still hasn't the time to give us more than poster-like sequences relating to the rise of unionism and Mussolini's Fascists. People that once were characters become points of view, a conscious decision on the part of the film maker who names his prototypical Fascist, the Berlinghieri estate's foreman, Attila, a role that Donald Sutherland plays in modified Casanova makeup and with such melodramatics he doesn't seem to have heard that Verdi really is dead.

Equally outrageous is Laura Betti as Mr. De Niro's aristocratic cousin who, disappointed in love, throws in her lot with Attila and his blackshirts. The other major role in the film is Dominique Sanda's as Mr. De Niro's high-born French wife, portrayed as an initially hedonistic type who wears clothes magnificently, especially evening dresses and various kinds of fur pieces, but who takes up drink when her husband won't come out firmly against the Fascists.

Mr. Lancaster has some fine moments early in the movie, including a tough, shocking but eloquent scene in which the old man comes to realize that he can't have his way with a pretty little peasant girl who says to him matter-of-factly, "You can't milk a bull."

Even the boys who play Mr. De Niro and Mr. Depardieu as children are good. Once the film moves into the 1920's, only Mr. Depardieu's character maintains interest and identity. Mr. De Niro behaves as if he were making up his character as he went along, doing busy, Actors' Studiolike things that suggest he is sending up both the character and the film. It's his first bad perfomance.

The English dubbing doesn't relieve the feeling that the film has been patched together. Although all of the English-speaking actors have dubbed in their own lines, the dialogue often

Sean Marshall as Pete chats with Elliott the dragon in Disney's "Pete's Dragon"
The most energetic and enjoyable Disney movie in a long while

sounds as if it were an English translation of an Italian libretto. And the voices of the non-English actors are awful. Sometimes you suspect that only one man is playing all the peasants, each of whom sounds like a troll at the bottom of a well.

"1900" is not an uninteresting failure, but being a failure, it looks arrogant. Mr. Bertolucci took risks as great with "Last Tango." I realize that because he succeeded there, the quality that now looks like arrogance is basically not much different from the courage he displayed in the earlier film. That's what happens when you fail.

1977 N4, C11:1

HEROES, directed by Jeremy Paul Kagan; screenplay by James Carabatsos; produced by David Foster and Lawrence Turman; director of photography, Frank Stanley; music, Jack Nitzsche; editor, Patrick Kennedy; distributed by Universal Pictures. Running time: 119 minutes. At the Rivoli Theater, Broadway and 49th Street, and other theaters. This film has been rated PG.

Jack Dunne .... Henry Winkler
Carol Bell .... Sally Field
Ken Boyd .... Harrison Ford
Bus driver .... Val Avery
Jane Adcox .... Olivia Cole
Dr. Elias .... Hector Elias
Gus .... Dennis Burkley
Chef .... Tony Burton
Peanuts .... Michael Cavanaugh
Bus depot manager .... Helen Craig
Mr. Monro .... John P. Finnegan
Mrs. Monro .... Betty McGuire

Henry Winkler
An aggressively cute performance

By VINCENT CANBY

"Heroes," co-starring Henry (The Fonz) Winkler and Sally (The Flying Nun) Field, brings to the motion-picture theater all of the magic of commercial television except canned laughter. Well, no truly rotten movie is perfect.

"Heroes" is about Jack Dunne (Mr. Winkler), a demented Vietnam veteran of repulsive winsomeness, a fellow who attempts to demonstrate the proposition that certified nuts have an exclusive franchise on truth and beauty. When we first meet Jack, skylarking around Times Square, he tries to interrupt a recruiting officer who's about to sign up six enlistees. However, Jack simply winds up back at the veterans' hospital, where he's been an off-and-on patient for five years.

•

"Heroes" is the story of Jack's flight from the hospital and his cross-country bus trip toward California, where he plans to start a worm farm. Jack is meant to be a lovable eccentric or, as one of the other characters says of him, a person who's "got rainbow, honey." It's the latter quality that apparently appeals to Carol (Miss Field), another lovable eccentric, a young woman who is taking a bus trip to Kansas City, Mo., so she can have time "to think." Instead, she falls in love with Jack.

"Heroes," which was written by James Carabatsos and directed by Jeremy Paul Kagan, who directed Mr. Winkler in the television film "Katherine," is something more than just a bad film. It's a frighteningly bad film because it could well be the definitive theatrical motion picture of the future.

Like the medium that spawned the talents who made it, "Heroes" deals in concepts made so simple that their meanings would be obvious to the dimmest minds. Gestures and emotions are foreshortened, truncated. Watching Mr. Winkler and Miss Fields "act" is suddenly to understand what television may eventually do to movies. Actors in television series and often in television movies simply don't have time to develop or discover characters. They must be entirely visible from the first minute they're on.

One result is the sort of performance that Mr. Winkler gives in this film. It's one that seems to be aggressively cute not because he's appealing, but because the will to please is so naked and the mannerisms are so unconnected to life. Television is creating a school of acting made up entirely of signals that evoke emotions less often than they label them.

I can imagine some not-too-distant time when we'll all sit around our home screens watching—and becoming emotionally involved with—comedies and dramas that show not people, but transistorized robots of the sort the Disney people have developed. They'd simplify casting, eliminate the union problem and would offer numerous merchandising possibilities.

Merchandising is something else that "Heroes" deals in. By blaming Jack Dunne's emotional problems on his traumatic Vietnam experience, the movie somehow denies the true horrors of that war while purveying bitterness for easy, supposedly painless entertainment.

Harrison Ford, who may be one of the most-seen movie actors of the day because of his role in "Star Wars," is effective in a supporting role too small to make the picture worth seeing.

•

"Heroes," which has been rated PG ("Parental Guidance suggested", contains some mildly vulgar language, but is otherwise almost prudish enough to be shown on television on Saturday morning.

1977 N 5, 13:1

FIRST LOVE, directed by Joan Darling; screenplay by Jane Stanton Hitchcock and David Freeman, based on "Sentimental Education" by Harold Brodkey; film editor, Frank Morriss; director of photography, Bobby Byrne; music by John Barry; produced by Lawrence Turman and David Foster; released by Paramount Pictures. At the Baronet Theater, Third Avenue and 60th Street, and the Little Carnegie Theater, 57th Street east of Seventh Avenue. Running time: 92 minutes. This film is rated R.

William Katt
Deserves to be seen

Elgin .... William Katt
Caroline .... Susan Dey
David .... John Heard
Shelley .... Beverly D'Angelo
John March .... Robert Loggia

By JANET MASLIN

"I think it's loathsome that we sleep together. I feel like a you-know-what," says a character named Caroline to her college sweetheart, Elgin, in "Sentimental Education," the 1950's short story by Harold Brodkey on which "First Love" is very loosely based. The film, written by Jane Stanton Hitchcock and directed by Joan Darling, is a 70's update with a vengeance.

We seem hardly to have met the two young lovers when Elgin begins asking Caroline about her orgasms, and Caroline chides him, not at all pleasantly, about those postcoital moments when "you're no good to me anymore." If "First Love" is to be believed—and there's no good reason why it should be—then these days romance is a much uglier and hard-boiled business than it ever used to be.

•

The title promises warmth and a tentative, trembling sense of discovery, but this simply isn't that kind of movie. Elgin (William Katt) a handsome and reserved college student who is looking for the real thing, becomes smitten with Caroline (Susan Dey), a fellow student who appears to have been through the real thing more times than she can count. Caroline is involved with an older, married man when Elgin falls for her, and this apparently has something to do with Caroline's father, who committed suicide in her dollhouse (it was a roomy dollhouse) when she was small. This, and a would-be contemporary air of sexual overkill, is perhaps supposed to explain why Caroline is a heartless and abrasive tease who resorts to wisecracks at even the most intimate moments. It doesn't.

Miss Darling (who directed the first episodes of "Mary Hartman, Mary Hartman"), by not bothering to cast much light on Caroline's nasty nature, shows herself to be as peculiarly misogynistic as such other women directors as Elaine May (in "The Heartbreak Kid") and Lina Wertmuller (especially in "Swept Away"). The two main female characters in "First Love" are Caroline and the predatory, rather pathetic Shelley (Beverly D'Angelo), and they both pounce avariciously upon Mr. Katt, who seems passive and rather saintly under pressure. ("You can't handle a real woman—you want us all to be shy violets" shrieks Shelley, after Elgin rejects her grabby advances.) Both Miss Hitchcock's script and Miss Darling's directing suggest that he is far too good for either lover.

•

Though Miss Darling brings not the slightest whit of tenderness or understanding to the love scenes, the movie is not without its gentle touches. It opens with slow-motion, idyllic-looking footage of Mr. Katt playing soccer alone, and it includes a lush, very prominent score. In fact, when Mr. Katt and Miss Dey have their first sexual encounter, they are accompanied by a Paul Williams ballad.

However, the music is so overbearing that it says nothing about intimacy, but a lot about Miss Darling's fear of being alone with her characters, or of leaving anything at all to the audience's imagination. As a director, she seems comfortable only with smart remarks or with scenes that hammer home every last nuance. "When you know this room, you'll know me," says Miss Dey, leading Mr. Katt through her childhood bedroom. The pictures on the wall might as well have dialogue balloons.

Miss Dey's Caroline is flippant and unconvincing. But the good news is that Mr. Katt's performance far transcends the chilliness of its surroundings. His Elgin is bursting with hope and urgency even when Miss Dey does nothing to warrant his enthusiasm, and in his rosy optimism there are hints of what might, in more sympathetic hands, have been. Even so, Mr. Katt's work is passionate and resourceful, and it deserves to be seen.

1977 N 5, 13:1

WHICH WAY IS UP? directed by Michael Schultz; screenplay by Carl Gottlieb and Cecil Brown, adapted from "The Seduction of Mimi" by Lina Wertmuller; produced by Steve Krantz; director of photography, John A. Alonzo; music, Paul Riser and Mark Davis; editor, Danford B. Greene; distributed by Universal Pictures. Running time: 94 minutes. At Loew's State 2, Broadway at 45th Street, and Loew's Cine, Third Avenue near 86th Street. This film has been rated R.

Leroy Jones .... Richard Pryor
Vanetta .... Lonette McKee
Annie Mae .... Margaret Avery
Mr. Mann .... Morgan Woodward
Sister Sarah .... Marilyn Coleman
Thelma .... BeBe Drake-Hooks
Janelle .... Gloria Edwards
Jose Reyes .... Ernesto Hernandez
Sugar .... DeWayne Jessie
Henry .... Morgan Roberts
Estrella Reyes .... Diane Rodriguez
The Boss .... Dolph Sweet
Tour Guide .... Timothy Thomerson
Chuy Estrada .... Danny Valdez
Ramon Juarez .... Luis Valdez

"Which Way Is Up?" is a haphazard, contradictory sort of movie, an adaption of Lina Wertmuller's Italian comedy, "The Seduction of Mimi," transplanted from Sicily to Southern California, with Richard Pryor as a cowardly, lecherous orange picker, a role modeled after the Sicilian peasant played by Giancarlo Giannini in "Mimi."

The transplant is a failure. Being black has very little do with being Sicilian. Thus when the screenplay attaches Sicilian cultural responses to its black characters, the effect seems more like an idiosyncrasy than a revelation of time, place and people.

•

Though "Which Way Is Up?" is a cultural mess, it's also very funny in bits and pieces that turn up like specialty acts in a musical show, but they allow Mr. Pryor to display his gift for manic, thoroughly rude comedy. He's one of the few actors I've seen who manages to be funny—sometimes outrageously so—while giving every impression of being furious with his audience and removed from his material. This distance from his characters, however, allows him to play black stereotypes in a way that sends up the stereotypes while getting every last laugh from them.

The screenplay, written by Carl Gottlieb and Cecil Brown, follows the general outlines of the Italian film, though Miss Wertmuller's concerns with social, sexual and political power have been reduced to virtually nothing.

This is the story of Leroy Jones (Mr. Pryor), an orange picker who accidentally becomes a union hero, and leaves his wife and family at home while he seeks work in Los Angeles. In the city Leroy finds himself a new woman, starts a second family, and eventually sells out to the capitalists.

•

Miss Wertmuller's original story keeps intruding on "Which Way Is Up?" at inopportune moments that force its characters to behave in arbitrary, out-of-character ways. It's as if Michael Schultz, the director, and the writers every now and then remembered they'd bought the rights to a very funny Italian film and thought they'd better get something for their money.

Mr. Schultz ("Greased Lightning," "Car Wash," "Cooley High") is a lively director without being a very stylish or controlled one. "Which Way Is Up?" belongs to that school of film making that holds that the zoom lens is the greatest invention since sound and that a film without nonstop music on its soundtrack would be as archaic as a silent movie.

He is, however, exceedingly good with actors. Mr. Pryor, in a class by himself, plays not only Leroy Jones, but Leroy's angry, foul-mouthed old father and a third role, that of the local preacher, a psalm-singing hypocrite of the sort that Flip Wilson really does better.

The women in his life are charmingly, sometimes hilariously done by Lonette McKee (as his mistress), Margaret Avery (as his wife) and Marilyn Coleman (as the preacher's lusty wife). I also liked the movie's personification of capitalism, a man called Mr. Mann, a role played by Morgan Woodward in makeup that suggests a fellow who has made a fortune out of selling Kentucky-fried chicken to the underprivileged.

VINCENT CANBY

1977 N 5, 13:1

How Can Such A Good Film Be Such a Flop?

VINCENT CANBY

One of the funniest, wittiest, most refreshing, most American—in short, one of the *best*—films of the year is about to sink out of sight into that great American peat bog reserved for flop movies. The picture is Jonathan Demme's uproarious comedy, "Handle With Care," a title that suggests absolutely nothing (except other meaningless titles on the order of "Too Hot to Handle" or "Hard to Handle") and thus is far worse than the film's original title, "Citizen's Band," which was dropped after the film played a few test dates and did no business.

The case of "Handle With Care" is worth careful attention at this time when American films are becoming more and more expensive, the profits as well as the losses ever bigger, producers increasingly desperate and opinion about movies so polarized that 95 percent of the public fights its way to get in to see five percent of the available films. It's a sick situation all around.

The case of "Handle With Care" has something for everybody, including those members of the public who still believe that critics can make or break a movie. It proves that we obviously can't. It should also remind us critics that when one persists in finding each week (or, at least, each month) a new masterpiece, or a movie that will change America's cultural landscape, or one that will forever alter our perception of the universe, or even one of incomparable genius, artistry, beauty and wisdom, the public begins to turn off. It's not difficult to understand why. As a friend of mine once said when a movie ad promised him two hours of sheer pleasure, "I'd better not go. Fifteen seconds is all I can stand at one time."

However, the failure of "Handle With Care" in New York has been so complete, so thorough, so utter, beginning with it first week at the Little Carnegie Theater (where it opened immediately after its highly successful showing at the New York Film Festival, and closed this past Friday) that it would be difficult to blame any one thing for a flop of such dimensions. What went wrong?

Everything, apparently, except the movie.

Like all good movies, "Handle With Care" works with marvelous skill on several levels simultaneously. As written by Paul Brickman, whose only other screen credit is "The Bad News Bears in Breaking Training," and directed by Mr. Demme, who has been making exploitation films like "Caged Heat" and "Crazy Mama," "Handle With Care" gracefully straddles the county line that separates small-town, hot-rod melodramas from the kind of small-town comedies that Preston Sturges once made. It manages to preserve a sort of sugar-coated, B-picture optimism about the world in which it's set, while using characters of such invigorating idiosyncracy that they come very close to being complex as well as comic. Among other things, it has a heroine, played by Candy Clark, who is no less intent on expressing her sexuality than poor, doomed Theresa Dunn of "Looking for Mr. Goodbar." Though the Candy Clark character in "Handle With Care" creates a certain amount of havoc among the men in her life, nobody must be arbitrarily murdered for her sins and the young woman does, in fact, wind up with the fellow of her choice, in a conventional clinch.

The setting of the film is a small American town in what looks to be California. Every now and then one spies a palm tree. More important, it's the essential middle-American small town where, though everybody may not actually know one another, they probably know *of* each other. They eat fast-foods that require only defrosting (as opposed to slow foods that need to be cooked), watch television non-stop, take high-school sports seriously and, one suspects, have one automobile per capita.

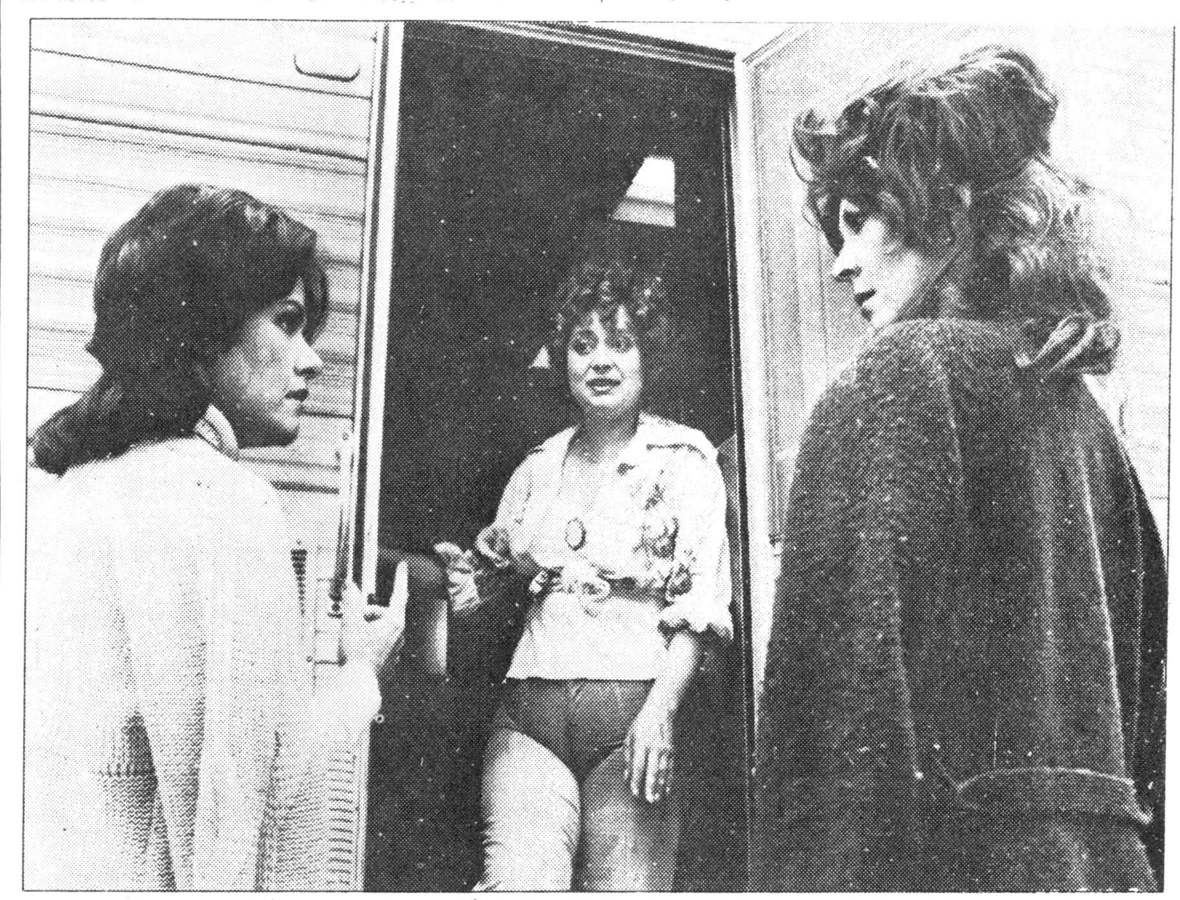

Marcia Rodd and Ann Wedgeworth, newly acquainted wives of the same truckdriver, meet his sweetheart, Alix Elias, center, in "Handle With Care."

The town is also in the grip of the Citizen's Band radio mania. Everybody has his own CB radio—the local bigot who is sure the country is about to be overrun by Commies and degenerates, a nice little old lady, a small boy, a shy young man who uses his kit to exchange erotic talk with a woman he doesn't know, truckers, the local hooker, cops, do-gooders. All day long, every day, everyone is talking into the air, cluttering it with the electronic equivalents of empty beer cans and candy wrappers, assuming in these transmissions call-name identities such as Spider, Papa Thermodyne, Chrome Angel, Hot Coffee, Smilin' Jack and God.

"Everybody in this town," says Spider (Paul Le Mat), a decent-spirited young man who attempts to police the CB chaos, "is somebody they're not supposed to be,"

Among the persons who are dissembling most flamboyantly is Chrome Angel (Charles Napier), a bluff, good-hearted, bigamous truck driver who is successful until he has an accident and his two wives happen to meet on a bus while coming to see him. In one of the film's nicest sequences the two women, after discovering the secret in a mutual exchange of family photographs, and after having the obligatory hysterics, settle down to wonder if they must now be somehow related.

Mr. Napier and Marcia Rodd and Ann Wedgeworth, who play his unhappy wives, as well as Alix Elias, who plays the trucker's girlfriend, are as rambunctiously, seriously funny as any actors I've seen in any American film this year. Mr. Le Mat is also extremely good in a role that is, technically, that of the film's hero, though there's something slightly bent about Spider who, by trade, is a mechanic. He's a handsome young man, well-meaning, an enthusiastic CBer himself. He's also emotionally attached, to a pathetic degree, to his gung-ho brother, a basketball coach who has fled the family home (which is in a junkyard), and to his rum-soaked old father, who won't talk to Spider, only to his invisible cronies out in CB land. Spider is a very eccentric hero to find in such a movie—a fellow who is well on his way to being an Oedipal mess until saved by the love of a woman who's not as good as she should be.

I don't want to overload "Handle With Care" with analysis, though both Mr. Demme and Mr. Brickman, who have immense affection for their characters, knew exactly what they were doing when they made the film—it has one of the best written scripts I've seen in a long time. "Hande With Care" is virtually an homage to B-pictures, but one that never slips into facetiousness or camp. With all this going for it, as well as with the good reviews, you'd think it would have become the sleeper of the year, but no. When I went back to see it at the Little Carnegie Theater on a recent Friday afternoon, there were five people in the theater and they looked as if they were neighborhood types or people who had come in to find a place to sit down.

"Handle With Care" has had a curious history. The distributor originally opened the film out West last May in what the trade calls "a multiple opening," that is, in a number of theaters on the same day, thus to cover a lot of theaters with a single advertising-promotion campaign. At that time the film was called "Citizen's Band" and the ad-promotion emphasis was placed on CB-radio tie-ins. But nobody came to see it, even though it received appreciative reviews. CB-radio fans are not interested in movies—they are too busy talking.

The film was withdrawn from release, then accepted by the New York Film Festival, at which time its title was changed to "Handle With Care." This was an attempt to disassociate the film from its CB-radio connections and, I suppose, to suggest a comedy. But "Handle With Care" unfortunately means nothing much of anything. Even with the good reviews, the business at the Little Carnegie was dismal.

I can't imagine that the ads helped much. These simply showed a box with the label "Handle With Care" painted across it. Handle *what* with care? You'd never find out from the ad copy, but though the accompanying quotes from the critics were enthusiastic, nothing suggested the buoyant nature of the movie.

To further complicate matters, word got out after the two festival showings that the producer had decided to lop off the film's final sequence. This is a funny, quite nutty marriage ceremony in which the bride and groom, riding in separate automobiles, are married by a preacher riding in a third car. Just why this sequence was cut, I don't know. It was very much a part of what the film was all about. It only lasted a few minutes, so length could not have been the point. Taste? If so, the producer didn't understand the film.

Though I don't think the cutting of the sequence seriously damages the movie, the word that something has been tampered with must eventually put off the public who would have liked to see what the critics saw. It was a bad decision.

I'm not sure that "Handle With Care" would have done better without reports of that cut, or with a different advertising campaign. It's a cinch, though, that it could hardly have done worse.

Whom should we blame? The critics, for having oversold too many movies in the past? The ad men, for not having caught the flavor of the movie? The producer, for having messed around with what was already a very good thing? Maybe we could even blame Mr. Demme and Mr. Brickman for having made a movie that was too good. In this case, I'm convinced, it was the public that flopped. ■

1977 N 6, II:13:1

MR. KLEIN, directed by Joseph Losey; screenplay (French with English subtitles) by Franco Solinas; produced by Raymond Danon; executive producer, Ralph Baum; director of photography, Gerry Fisher; music, Egisto Macchi and Pierre Porte; a Basil Film presentation, distributed by Quartet Films. Running time: 122 minutes. At the 68th Street Playhouse. This film has not been rated.

Mr. Klein	Alain Delon
Florence	Jeanne Moreau
Pierre	Michel Lonsdale
Janine	Juliet Berto
Concierge	Suzanne Flon
Nicole	Francine Berge
Vendeur	Jean Bouise
Mr. Charles	Massimo Girotti

By VINCENT CANBY

If a movie could be said to be immaculately groomed, Joseph Losey's work would qualify. No matter what it's about or where it's set or even whether it's any good (and Mr. Losey has made some that weren't), a Losey film is as much fun to wander through as the lobby of a great, stylish hotel, say the Ritz in Paris. One is aware of order, caste, manners and, very often, the power of money, which has as much to do with the way his films look as subject matter.

At his best, in films like "The Servant" and "Accident" (both of which were written by Harold Pinter) and the almost diffident "The Assassination of Trotsky," Mr. Losey entertains the mind and the eye as well as one's innate appreciation of snobbism. At his worst, as in "The Romantic Englishwoman" or "Figures in a Landscape," the director reveals a total lack of humor put in the service of pretentiousness.

Alain Delon
Has traveled a lot but his baggage is empty.

His newest film falls somewhere between these two extremes.

"Mr. Klein," which opened yesterday at the 68th Street Playhouse, is a cool, elegantly dressed movie that at first appears to take a dim view of moral opportunism, almost as if it were a breach of good manners, like wearing Mickey Mouse cufflinks with a dinner jacket. It's the story of the dandyish Robert Klein (Alain Delon), a successful upper-class entrepreneur whose life in the Nazi-occupied Paris of 1942 is probably not much different than it was before the war, except that he doesn't hesitate to deal in objets d'art being sold by Jewish refugees desperate for cash.

Klein's settled existence (a handsome house, high-toned friends, a sexy mistress he more or less confines to bed) is suddenly broken one morning when he finds at his door a copy of the local Jewish newspaper, addressed to him and apparently sent to him on more than a 13-week trial-subscription basis. The Roman Catholic, Alsatian-born Klein has nothing against Jews—he sympathizes with his Jewish clients—but it could be terribly inconvenient if the authorities came to believe that he himself was Jewish.

The screenplay by Franco Solinas, the Italian writer who collaborated with Gillo Pontecorvo on "Battle of Algiers" and "Burn," and with Costa-Gavras on "State of Siege," is a metaphorical mystery melodrama, which is a phrase that usually makes my heart sink. When a mystery melodrama is described as metaphorical, it often means that the writer and the director feel free of the obligation to tell us what actually was going on. This isn't quite the case with "Mr. Klein," but you might say that it satisfies only on a metaphorical level, and that isn't enough.

As Klein sets about to unravel the mystery of the newspaper subscription, he discovers what appears to be a plot to destroy him by another Robert Klein, who apparently bears some resemblance to him and who is a Jewish member of the Resistance. Klein's friends think he may be losing his mind. The police, to whom he reports the story of the other Klein, believe that as a Jew he is trying to throw them off his track with a confusion of Kleins.

While doing his own legwork, Klein comes across odd, conflicting profiles of the other Klein. The fellow lives in a rat-infested flat maintained by a crazy concierge. Yet he also is apparently the lover of the aristocratic mistress of a magnificent chateau, a woman who may or may not be Jewish herself and whose grande salle shows naked places where paintings once were hung.

This lady, a cameo role played by Jeanne Moreau with the fine, throwaway arrogance of the very rich, describes the missing Klein as "a snake in hibernation until a better season." Where does he live? She answers with the address of the real Klein.

Some of this cat-and-mouse game is extremely effective, until one realizes that Mr. Losey and Mr. Solinas are not as interested in the workings of the plot as in matters of identity and obsession, which lead eventually to a conclusion I didn't for a minute believe.

There's a major problem with Alain Delon's Mr. Klein, who is neither interesting nor mysterious enough to hold a film like this together. When Mr. Delon was younger, he didn't have to do anything—his good looks spoke for him.

It may be that the role is not great, or that it asks an actor to bring to it too much that's missing in the script. Mr. Delon is not aging especially well. Other actors with careers as long as his acquire, over the years, a lot of useful baggage in the form of associations to earlier performances. Mr. Delon has traveled a lot but his baggage is empty.

Though there's a hole in the center of the canvas, "Mr. Klein" is a seductive picture to watch, splendidly visual, witty, concerned with ideas that are fashionable without being at all disturbing.

1977 N 7, 45:1

Happy—and Gone

THE ONA PEOPLE: LIFE AND DEATH IN TIERRA DEL FUEGO, a documentary directed and edited by Anne Chapman and Ana Montes de Gonzalez; director of photography, Jorge Preloran. Running time: 55 minutes.
and
THE BELL RANG TO AN EMPTY SKY, a short film by William Farley; narration by Dennis Banks. Running time: 5 minutes, at the Whitney Museum of American Art, Madison Avenue and 75th Street.

By JANET MASLIN

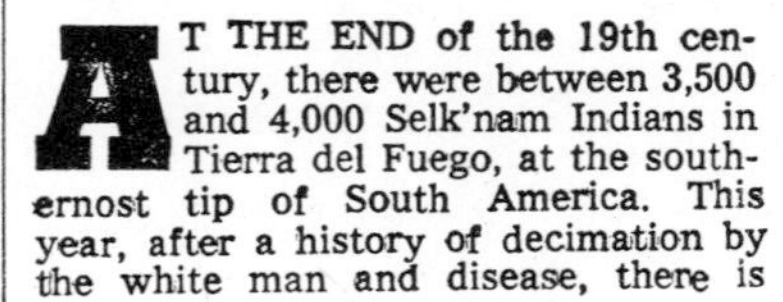

AT THE END of the 19th century, there were between 3,500 and 4,000 Selk'nam Indians in Tierra del Fuego, at the southernost tip of South America. This year, after a history of decimation by the white man and disease, there is only one. "The Ona People: Life and Death in Tierra Del Fuego" shows her wandering rather dazedly through the streets of Buenos Aires on her first trip to that city, peering into store windows and marveling at strange animals in the zoo.

The woman, called Angela, grew up as one of the Selk'nam, commonly called the Ona people, at a time when the tribe still hunted and roamed; they lived by such a viable set of laws that its last survivors never quite understood what sin was. "If one lives as one should, where is sin?" one old man wondered.

•

The film makers, Anne Chapman and Ana Montes de Gonzalez, began interviewing the last of the Selk'nam in the mid-60's and have gracefully combined interview footage with color scenes of Tierra del Fuego and haunting old photographs of the Indians as they once lived. The Selk'nam appear to have been a handsome people and a happy one, and the film ably suggests what their life must have been like.

"The Ona People," part of the Whitney Museum's New American Filmmakers Series, presents a powerful subject, but the film's methods are less effective than they might be. Miss Chapman, who reads much of the narration, speaks in flat, measured, nearly dispassionate tones. But since there is no irony to the text she reads, her voice becomes numbing, even when she describes the most brutal and heartbreaking events. The film simply isn't pointed enough to rely on narration this low-key.

•

Also on the bill is the very short "The Bell Rang to an Empty Sky," by William Farley, a crisp and effective comment on America's treatment of its Indians that combines an Indian's tale of injustice, images of money being minted and the story of the crack in the Liberty Bell.

1977 N 9, C19:5

Nuclear Documentaries

MORE NUCLEAR POWER STATIONS, a documentary directed by Per Mannstaedt; photographed by Teit Jorgensen; a Flip Film Production (Denmark); distributed by Green Mountain Post Films. Running time: 50 minutes.
THE LAST RESORT, a documentary directed and edited by Daniel Keller; written by Mr. Keller and Harvey Wasserman; produced by Green Mountain Post Films; executive producer, Charles Light; narration by Cecilia Tucinsky; distributed by Green Mountain Post Films. Running time: 60 minutes. Both at the Film Forum, 15 Vandam Street.

By JANET MASLIN

Lionel Delevingne

A scene from Daniel Keller's documentary "The Last Resort" at the Film Forum.

THERE is a lot to be learned from the Film Forum's double bill on atomic power, and not all of it is about the subject at hand. The fortuitous pairing of "The Last Resort," Dan Keller's documentary about the contested plan to build an atomic power plant in Seabrook, N.H., and "More Nuclear Power Stations," a Danish film that examines the inner workings of an atomic plant outside Hamburg, teaches an interesting lesson about how to win an argument —and how to lose one.

It's hard to imagine anyone's condoning the proliferation of atomic plants after viewing "More Nuclear Power Stations," a 1975 Danish film by Per Mannstaedt that coolly examines an utterly ghastly situation. The camera tours through a power station, and a calm-voiced narrator explains the procedures being shown. We watch workers donning their radioactivity-proof gear to perform repairs, and watch them being gone over afterwards with geiger counters, to make sure they haven't received more than the allegedly safe dosage. As the narrator assures us, accidents occur only once in a long while.

The most horrifying segment has to do with atomic waste. The techniques for storing it seem even more elaborate than those used in generating power in the first place; the waste must be carefully guarded, since it remains radioactive for centuries. Sometimes it is stored under water, and sometimes underground. There is not supposed ever to be any leakage and, as a matter of fact, there only rarely is.

Then there's the plutonium waste: the narrator explains soothingly that only a few hundred pounds disappear mysteriously every year. It takes about ten pounds to build an atomic device of one's own.

With its elaborate technology and its workers in grimly futuristic safety outfits, "Another Nuclear Power Station" looks like science fiction without the romance. This is an extraordinarily tough and persuasive film, one that makes its point through the use of cold, hard facts rather than rhetoric. As such, it provides a wonderfully instructive contrast to Dan Keller's more impassioned, and much less convincing, "The Last Resort."

Mr. Keller's film is about the events that led up to the arrest of about 2,000 people who protested the building of an atomic plant in a small, beachfront town—although Mr. Keller rather inexplicably ends the film before the arrests took place, and makes no reference to them at all. Instead, Mr. Keller concentrates on the demonstrators' feeling of solidarity, and on the townspeople's reaction to the proposed plant. The film is rather good in this latter department, particularly when it talks about the tax burden the power plant will create, and when it shows interviews with a police chief's wife who opposes the plant and the chief himself, who doesn't think he ought to take sides.

But Mr. Keller also manages to trivialize a very important subject by almost reflexively playing up the event's joyful side. We hear speakers advocating other, not altogether related causes at a rally, and we hear protest songs, both while they are being performed and over footage of people marching. By emphasizing the music and the fun, Mr. Keller inadvertently creates the impression that this, instead of being a serious occasion, is a smaller Woodstock.

Mr. Keller's film is at its most revealing when it shows long-haired demonstrators trying to argue with the local police. The demonstrations at Seabrook were largely peaceful and, indeed, many of the police seemed sympathetic to the anti-atomic plant cause. And the demonstrators were armed with the most compelling evidence that the plant would impair the welfare of the town. But we see at least one young man using his knowledge as a weapon rather than a tool, completely alienating a policeman who reacts to the protester's manner rather than to his cause. This demonstrator seems to think style more important than substance—and so, at times, does Mr. Keller.

1977 N 11, C12:1

FILM VIEW

VINCENT CANBY

Movie Actors Should Not 'Teleperform'

People in movies are seldom convincing as packers of suitcases and in bad movies they are ridiculous: a man opens a bureau drawer, pulls out a shirt and a pair of socks that have never been worn, drops them into a Gladstone bag, and that's that. For the next few weeks or months or years,

Sally Field and Henry Winkler—TV's "Flying Nun" and "The Fonz"—star in "Heroes." "The film makes one apprehensive about the future of movies."

the character, looking forever spruce, changes clothes at will, coming up with variations of costume that would be beyond the capacity of a steamer trunk.

In real life the packing of a suitcase is not something one does casually. It involves a series of interlocking decisions based on itinerary, length of trip, season of the year, maximum weight allowance, reading habits and other value judgments and, most important, the general condition of the suitcase (is this the trip on which it's going to split?). Even when the job is carefully done, is there anyone among us who hasn't at some point arrived at his destination to find that an essential prop has been left behind? Unless it's part of the plot, a man in a movie never has this problem. Also, unless the movie is a comedy, his suitcase never threatens to pull his arm from its socket, to leave him with blisters on both hands or to throw his back out of gear.

Though I cannot substantiate the following statement with any immediate facts, I have the definite impression that suitcase-packing in movies these days has reached a new low, and I suspect that television is to blame. Have you ever seen one of Charley's Angels pay an airline overweight? Unconvincing suitcase-packing is obviously no big deal but the way in which the manners, techniques and personalities of television are beginning to shape theatrical motion pictures—to make them smaller, busier and blander—must give us pause.

• • •

The first great wave of television directors who made their way to theatrical films—Arthur Penn, Sidney Lumet, George Roy Hill, Franklin Schaffner, John Frankenheimer—adapted themselves to the older medium. Even while they brought to Hollywood some of the frenetic tensions that were virtually a method of working in television when major shows were done live, these directors couldn't wait to exploit the cinema resources that then separated movies from television. The kind of imperial crane-shots and deep-focus vistas that are the marks of a Franklin Schaffner film like "Patton" would have been out of the question in any live TV production. For Mr. Schaffner and the others, movies were a whole new thing.

Today the exact opposite is true—possibly because these TV people have grown up using film and tape. The television directors who are now switching to the big screen can't wait to reduce its dimensions, to make movies that look as much as possible like the sitcoms and so-called "television movies" that are being relentlessly ground out for the tube.

What is this "look"?

First, it is an overpowering blandness, the sort that John Denver exudes in Carl Reiner's "Oh, God!," a sketch-like comedy about God (George Burns) and a supermarket manager (Mr. Denver). Bland has always been big in television, probably because the principal function of almost any TV show is to entertain without disturbing, to occupy the eye without troubling it, to soothe without leaving a hangover. Perry Como, Dick Clark, Andy Williams and even Dean Martin haven't endured as long as they have by sending rockets into their audiences.

Though Mr. Reiner once made a very funny theatrical film, "Where's Poppa?," his principal experience has been in television, and television sets the style of "Oh, God!" It has the rhythm of a variety show in which the sequence of sketches is of no great importance. The colors are just a little too bright and the characters are seen in (though they don't appear to inhabit) suburban houses with kitchens in which you can't believe anyone has ever opened a can of frozen orange-juice concentrate.

There's another aspect to this "look" that's all over a frivolously rotten comedy-drama called "Heroes," which stars Henry "The Fonz" Winkler, as a picturesquely disturbed Vietnam veteran, and Sally "The Flying Nun" Field as the picturesquely mixed-up young woman he meets on a transcontinental bus.

"Heroes," which was directed by Jeremy Paul Kagan, who directd Mr. Winkler in the TV film, "Katherine," is an almost perfect example of what I fear may become the standard theatrical film of our television-dominated future. It's not simply that the performances of the two stars are the sort one sees in 30-minute sitcoms where everything must be laid on the line as quickly as possible, nor that the two stars, by the frequency of their appearances on TV, are now TV icons of which there are maybe a half-dozen principal models (though I certainly don't agree with a friend of mine who says that Miss Field is simply a Mary Tyler Moore someone has stepped on).

I suspect both Mr. Winkler and Miss Field are not only capable but possibly talented actors when given the chance of acting instead of what might be called teleperforming. To teleperform is to use a set of simplified mannerisms that express TV's five basic emotions—joy (ear-to-ear grin), anger (furrowed brow), hope (a slightly less than ear-to-ear grin), hurt/surprise (dropped jaw), ecstasy (running). (These are not the only emotions that can be expressed by teleperforming. Combining hope with hurt/surprise, for example, may approximate anxiety, and if you add these to ecstasy, you've got something very much like blind panic.) One doesn't respond to the emotion of a teleperformance as often as one reads it, as if it were a series of traffic signals.

The television roots of "Heroes" are apparent in both large and small matters. There's a brief sequence in which Miss Field calls on one of the crazy Vietnam veteran's friends and finds, instead, the friend's abandoned wife, who is black. This is fine as far as it goes, but the role has been cast and played in a manner that says less about a woman who's been abandoned by a drifting husband (also traumatized by the war?) than it says about the bland manner in which television thinks that blacks must be presented for a positive image. Olivia Cole, who plays the unhappy wife, is so stately, serene, regal and collected (and altogether unreal) that as she walks around her model home, you might think she was really the mistress of a maison of haute couture in Paris.

"Heroes" makes one apprehensive about the future of movies in other, more important ways, though. Television movies, because of the nature of the medium that presents them, are as carefully composed to accommodate the commercial breaks as they are to entertain, and some of the ways in which they entertain are the tricks they employ to get us across the breaks. The films are paced in bits and pieces, which is why theatrical films with fragmented narratives sometimes play even better on television than they do in theaters.

• • •

As a result of their television backgrounds, many of these new directors and writers seem incapable of putting together films that not only sustain narrative interest but build it to some kind of climax. Instead, like "Heroes" and like another new film, Michael Schultz's "Which Way Is Up?," the new Richard Pryor comedy, the movies begin, fool around horizontally, and then end. You begin to wonder if these films would seem better, less brainless, if one could watch them in their full glory, that is, complete with commercial and station breaks.

Instead of real dramatic movement, TV shows can get by—in a way theatrical films seldom can any more—by physical movement. A large part of TV's police shows appears to be shots of people getting into or out of their cars, driving away from or arriving at destinations, with a bit of necessary exposition squeezed into a shot inside the car as it's en route.

"Heroes" opens with Henry Winkler doing a lot of busy, extremely cute things around Times Square. Not only does Henry run frequently, but when the film-proper gets going, he's riding buses or automobiles. He *is* moving but the picture never gets any place until the last reel, when it must end.

"Which Way Is Up?," a failed attempt to transplant "The Seduction of Mimi," Lina Wertmuller's Italian comedy about sex, politics and Sicily to Southern California, is a lot less painless to watch than "Heroes," but then it stars Richard Pryor, who is a very, very funny actor even though he's no Giancarlo Giannini.

• • •

Like "Heroes," however, "Which Way Is Up? " doesn't discover its narrative and then build on it. Rather, it sort of moves through its story as if walking through someone's cluttered backyard. What happens—the events of the narrative—seem to be impediments to the real business of the film, which is to give Mr. Pryor the opportunity to perform a series of sometimes hilarious sketches, as, of course, he does on television.

The director and his writers, Carl Gottlieb and Cecil Brown, use the Wertmuller original only in the most superficial ways, and occasionally make their Southern California black characters behave as if they were supposed to be Sicilian, which is very odd to watch, indeed.

The producers who make these films, of course, may well know what they're doing. It must be assumed that the people who go to see them are mostly the same people who watch television, whose attention spans are limited, and who have sensibilities attuned to movies that deal almost entirely in the kind of immediate sensation provided by the zoom lens and non-stop soundtrack music. Will these films succeed at the box office? I'm not sure. I don't know why anyone would want to pay a theater's stiff admission price to see a movie in which the characters walk around with empty suitcases. They can stay home and see the same thing free. ■

1977 N 13, II:15:1

Effervescence and Dark Wit Imbue Delightful Work

Ornament of Film Festival Opens at Columbia 2

"That Obscure Object of Desire" ("Cet Obscur Object du Désir") was shown at the 1977 New York Film Festival. The following excerpts are from Vincent Canby's review, which appeared Oct. 9. The film opened Saturday at the Columbia 2 Theater.

Every film festival should end with a new film by the incomparable Luis Buñel, whose latest work, the triumphantly funny and wise "That Obscure Object of Desire," is a work of such perfect control and precision that it has the effect of magically clearing the mind. It restores one's common sense and one's appreciation for the fantastic.

"That Obscure Object of Desire" is Buñuel's "Don Giovanni." It combines the effervescence and gaiety of "The Discreet Charm of the Bourgeoisie" with the dark wit of "Tristana," and though it continues to explore themes we recognize from these and other Buñuel films, it is something quite other.

Most obviously, I suppose, "That Obscure Object of Desire" is an upside-down romance in which love, Buñuel seems to be telling us, is a "devastating act of subversion." The setting is the easily recognizable contemporary world, but a world that is a half-degree off its axis and fast going to pieces, though everyone displays the fastidious manners of the members of a society that will last forever.

The Cast

THAT OBSCURE OBJECT OF DESIRE (Cet Obscur Object du Desir), directed by Luis Bunuel; screenplay (French with English subtitles) by Mr. Bunuel with Jean-Claude Carriere, suggested by the novel "La Femme et le Pantin" by Pierre Louys; produced by Serge Silberman; director of photography, Edmond Richard; editor, Helene Plemiannikov; a co-production of Greenwich Film Production (Paris), Les Films Galavie (Paris) and Incine (Madrid). Running time: 100 minutes. This film as rated R. At the Columbia 2 Theater, Second Avenue and 64th Street; released by First Artists.

Mathieu .... Fernando Rey
Conchita .... Carole Bouquet
Angela Molina
Judge .... Julien Bertheau
Valet .... Andre Weber
Traveler .... Milena Vukotic
Psychologist .... Pieral

Just beyond the horizon of the film, which is set in Paris and in Seville, chaos reigns. Through newspaper headlines and radio broadcasts we learn that terrorism is rampant. Planes are being hijacked and innocents slaughtered. A mysterious virus is nearing Barcelona and a guerrilla group that calls itself the Revolutionary Army of the Infant Jesus has attempted to assassinate the Archbishop of Siena. Even the Communists are outraged by the anarchic state of things.

Seemingly unruffled by all this (though he is impatient when a booby-trapped automobile in front of his explodes and forces his car to make a detour) is the charming, literate, wealthy Mathieu (Fernando Rey), Buñuel's Don, a French businessman whose life is in perfect order until the day that the beautiful Conchita enters it, dressed as a maid.

Though he has been a widower for seven years, Mathieu is no ordinary lecher. As he tells his brother, the judge (Julien Brethau), Mathieu can count on the fingers of one hand the number of times he has ever made love to a woman whom he didn't love passionately. From the minute he sees

Angela Molina and Fernando Rey in Luis Bunuel's film "That Obscure Object of Desire" at Columbia II

Conchita, Mathieu is in the throes of an uncontrollable passion.

Conchita, though, is not someone whose measure he can get, and eludes him even when he gets her into bed. Conchita flees his house, only to turn up a few months afterwards traveling through Switzerland with a group of musicians. Later Mathieu makes a deal with Conchita's pious mother to set up Conchita as his mistress. Again she runs away. Each time they meet again, she leads him further into the recesses of his obsession, always promising him the moon (in the form of her virginity), then suddenly changing her mind.

As Mathieu sees her. Conchita is so

changeable that Buñuel has cast two lovely new actresses to play her—Carole Bouquet, who looks a little like a young Rita Hayworth, as the coolly enigmatic Conchita, and Angela Molina as the earthy, flamenco-dancing Conchita.

Poor old Mathieu. The night he succeeds in getting Conchita to his country house, where she has promised to be his mistress, the Conchita who goes into the bathroom to change, changes not only her clothes. Miss Bouquet goes in but Miss Molina comes out.

Mathieu huffs, puffs and groans in his agony. He leaves Conchita a dozen times but always is lured back. At one point he persuades her to live with him and to share his bed, though no sexual contact can be made. When the judge asks his brother why he doesn't marry her, Mathieu answers earnestly that if he married her, he would be helpless. At another point, when Mathieu upbraids Conchita for her maddening ways, she answers, "You only want what I refuse. That's not all of me. . . ."

Who really loves whom? Though Conchita at first seems to be the classic coquette, she becomes, as the film progresses, the true lover, while Mathieu becomes the coquette, a reversal of roles that is, nevertheless, not to be taken as the last word.

"That Obscure Object of Desire" is beautifully played by its small, impeccably chosen cast, beginning with Mr. Rey who, at this point in his career, is virtually a projection of Buñuel's artistic personality—gentle, polite, self-aware, incapable of the superfluous gestures, and driven. Miss Bouquet and Miss Molina are enchanting—I don't think Buñuel has ever before been so successful with neophyte actresses.

There are further delights in the performances of Mr. Bertheau (who played the "worker bishop" in "The Discreet Charm"), of Andre Weber, as Mathieu's all-wise valet and of Pieral, a dwarf who plays the psychologist to whom Mathieu pours out his sad story on the train from Seville to Paris, which provides the frame for the film.

"That Obscure Object of Desire" is a lot more open-ended and surreal than I've indicated, but these are pleasures that one should discover for oneself.

With an effortlessness matched by no other director today, Buñuel creates a vision of a world as logical as a theorem, as mysterious as a dream, and as funny as a vaudeville gag.

1977 N 14, 42:1

Shirley MacLaine, left, and Anne Bancroft in "The Turning Point"
They are among the film's principal assets

THE TURNING POINT, directed by Herbert Ross; screenplay by Arthur Laurents; produced by Mr. Ross and Mr. Laurents; executive producer, Nora Kaye; music adapted and conducted by John Lanchbery; director of photography, Robert Surtees; editor, William Reynolds; distributed by 20th Century-Fox. Running time: 118 minutes. At the Coronet Theater, Third Avenue and 59th Street. This film has been rated PG.

Emma .... Anne Bancroft
Deedee .... Shirley MacLaine
Yuri .... Mikhail Baryshnikov
Emilia .... Leslie Towne
Wayne .... Tom Skerritt
Adelaide .... Martha Scott
Sevilla .... Antoinette Sibley
Dahkarova .... Alexandra Danilova
Carolyn .... Starr Danias
Carter .... Marshall Thompson
Michael .... James Mitchell
Freddie .... Scott Douglas
Arnold .... Daniel Levans
Peter .... Jurgen Schneider
Rosie .... Anthony Zerbe
Ethan .... Phillip Saunders
Janina .... Lisa Lucas
Florence .... Saax Bradbury
Sandra .... Hilda Morales
Barney .... Donald Petrie
Billy Joe .... James Crittenden

Also guest appearances by Lucette Aldous, Fernando Bujones, Richard Cragun, Suzanne Farrell, Marcia Haydee, Peter Martins, Clark Tippet, Marianna Tcherkassky, Martine Van Hamel and Charles Ward.

By VINCENT CANBY

The story to date: 20 years ago Deedee abandoned her ambitions to become a star of the American Ballet Theater and, instead, moved to Oklahoma City with her husband, Wayne, with whom she opened a fabulously successful ballet school, raised three fabulously sweet children, moved into a split-level house and acquired a fabulously long station wagon. Deedee chose love—unlike her best friend, Emma, who chose success and became Ballet Theater's prima ballerina.

As our movie, which is called "The Turning Point," opens, Deedee and Emma are reunited when Ballet Theater comes to Oklahoma City. Old hopes are rekindled for, as all of us know, an old hope never dies in fiction of this sort, no matter how many tears are pumped on it. Emma, who gets 19 curtain calls and has "everything" envies Deedee, while Deedee, the one who got pregnant, still dreams of stardom. Wil lthey ever find peace and fulfillment—these two women who now recall their—how shall I put it?—turning points?

To ask that question is to know the worst about this entertaining new movie, an old-fashioned backstage musical transplanted to the world of ballet by three people who not only know it but also love it, sentimental cliches and all.

"The Turning Point," which opened last night at special performances at the Coronet and Baronet Theaters, begins its regular commercial engagement at the Coronet today. It's the work of Herbert Ross, the director; Arthur Laurents, the screenwriter, and Nora Kaye (Mrs. Ross), the former ballerina who is its executive producer. Their curious, collective achievement is in having found so much vitality in the sort of movie that demands that its audiences weep with sympathy for characters who have all they ever wanted but simply don't realize it yet.

Among the film's principal assets are Shirley MacLaine, looking very pretty and almost matronly, but not quite, as the sharp-tongued, intelligent, deep-down furious homemaker, Deedee; and Anne Bancroft as the driven ballerina, Emma, a woman of ravaged beauty and whose frail frame could possibly lift a freight car if she willed it.

The intensity of their lifelong friendship, and rivalry, is carefully and sometimes hilariously detailed as "The Turning Point" follows Deedee's daughter, Emilia, charmingly played by Leslie Browne, her mother and her little brother to New York, where Emilia joins Ballet Theater's school. It's not giving away too much to report that the girl's almost instantaneous success means that one day in the not too distant future she will be replacing her beloved godmother, Emma, as the A.B.T.'s major attraction.

These are more or less the bones of the film, which are hardly bare, what with Emma's having to face the reality of time's passage, and Deedee's having to come to terms with her missed opportunities. Could she have danced the lead in "Anna Karenina" 20 years ago? Probably not, though from what we see of Emma in the role, it's mostly walking through steam.

There are also the emotional crises faced in New York by Emilia, who has an unhappy affair with a young Soviet dancer named Yuri, a role played with cheerful ease by Mikhail Baryshnikov, the young Soviet dancer who chose success in the West several years ago.

As Emilia learns that the love of a young Soviet ballet dancer is not forever—which is just as well when one has her eye on the top of the bill—and as Emma and Deedee are wrestling, once physically in a very funny and moving scene, with their doubts, "The Turning Point" gives us excerpts from more than a dozen ballets that feature, in addition to Mr. Baryshnikov and Miss Browne, the stars and the corps de ballet of Ballet Theater.

The manner in which Mr. Ross handles these sequences defines the choice that he made when planning "The Turning Point." That is, he chose to create a backstage film about the ballet rather than a ballet film. The excerpts are lovely but often so brief that not even an obnoxious child would have time to become bored. Because this is a film about people and not dance, the film spends as much time showing us the dancers' faces and reaction shots of people in the audience as it does showing us the complete figures of the dancers in motion. The method is that of show-biz not art.

Show-biz is also apparent in the tone of Mr. Laurents's screenplay, which delights not only in backstage sentiment but also backstage bitchiness with, I'm told, all sorts of references to people living and dead. Though "The Turning Point" does show us that ballet is an extremely difficult, physically demanding art, the film's concentration on its female characters tends, if only by accident, to confirm the oldest ballet cliché of them all—that ballet is, in this country anyway, women's work.

All of the men in the film exist as little more than dance partners or as props for the drama. This is partly the result of the focus of the movie in which Miss MacLaine and Miss Bancroft give such powerhouse performances and only Mr. Baryshnikov is allowed to be a man of any substance.

The others, including Tom Skerritt, who plays Miss MacLaine's blandly decent husband, are background figures. Such a comment, I realize, could also be made about any number of Bette Davis, Joan Crawford or Greer Garson movies of long ago.

"The Turning Point" is entertaining, not for discovering new material, but for treating old material with style and romantic feeling that, in this day and age, seem remarkably unafraid.

•

"The Turning Point," which has been rated PG ("Parental Guidance Suggested"), contains some mildly vulgar language and one nude love scene that is tó tastefully and genteelly done, perhaps because it is actually the last scene in a ballet.

1977 N 15, 54:1

Shades of 1950's

CLOSE ENCOUNTERS OF THE THIRD KIND, directed and written by Steven Spielberg; produced by Julia Phillips and Michael Phillips; music, John Williams; director of photography, Vilmos Zsigmond; visual effects coordinator, Douglas Rrumbull; editor, Mike Kahn; distributed by Columbia Pictures. Running time: 137 minutes. At the Ziegfeld Theater, 54th Street west of the Avenue of the Americas. This film has been rated PG.

Roy Neary .... Richard Dreyfuss
Claude Lacombe .... Francois Truffaut
Ronnie Neary .... Teri Garr
Jillian Guiler .... Melinda Dillon
Barry Guiler .... Cary Guffey
David Laughlin .... Bob Balaban
Robert .... Lance Hendriksen
Wild Bill .... Warren Kemmerling
Farmer .... Roberts Blossom
Jean Claude .... Phillip Dodds
Brad Neary .... Shawn Bishop
Sylvia Neary .... Adienne Campbell
Toby Neary .... Justin Dreyfuss
Team Leader .... Merrill Connally
Major Benchley .... George Dicenzo

By VINCENT CANBY

IN THE 1950'S, the decade in which we fought the Korean War, witnessed the rise and fall of Senator Joseph R. McCarthy and fretted (along with Mort Sahl) about the atomic bomb's falling into the hands of Princess Grace, and Prince Rainier, science-fiction films enjoyed a new, lively popularity largely by feeding on our wildest nightmares. We watched movies in which planets fought wars with each other, worlds threatened to collide and a huge malignant carrot, a vegetable with a higher form of intelligence, landed at the North Pole.

A favorite theme was the invasion of earth by alien creatures who, 9 times out of 10, were up to no good. The unholy immigrants in "The Invasion of the Body Snatchers" attempted to usurp earth by catching the souls of the incumbents in giant peapods, receptacles that suggested the work of an early Jasper Johns.

Melinda Dillon is frightened as her son, Cary Guffey, is mysteriously drawn to a UFO in "Close Encounters."

Sometimes the visitors were motivated by a territorial imperative—they were running out of air back home or there were no more materials for beer cans. Often the creatures were simply making mischief, though occasionally they expressed benign intentions. From Krypton came Superman to play the role of a supercharged savior whose work would never be done.

Klaatu, the impeccably space-suited, English-accented visitor in "The Day the Earth Stood Still," wanted earthlings to stop fooling around and live in peace. The implied threat of Klaatu's "Or else . . ." might have struck some of us as galactal neo-fascism, but that was to read the film deeper than it was meant to go.

•

Steven Spielberg's giant, spectacular "Close Encounters of the Third Kind," which opened at the Ziegfeld Theater yesterday, is the best—the most elaborate—1950's science fiction movie ever made, a work that borrows its narrative shape and its concerns from those earlier films, but enhances them with what looks like the latest developments in movie and space technology. If, indeed, we are not alone, it would be fun to believe that the creatures who may one day visit us are of the order that Mr. Spielberg has conceived—with, I should add, a certain amount of courage and an entirely straight face.

Mr. Spielberg's tongue is not in his cheek, as was George Lucas's when he made "Star Wars," the funniest, farthest-out kid-trip of this decade to date. "Star Wars" is virtually an anthology of all sorts of children's literature. "Close Encounters" is science fiction that means us to say, "this is the way it could be," though we don't for a minute forget that we're watching a movie almost entirely related to other movies—the ones that Mr. Spielberg, who's just 30 years old, grew up with, rather than a movie with its own poetic vision, like Stanley Kubrick's "2001."

As he has demonstrated in "The Sugarland Express" and especially in "Jaws," Mr. Spielberg is at his best as a movie craftsman, someone who seems to know by instinct (and after millions of hours of movie-watching) how best to put together any two pieces of film for maximum effect. He's serious about this—sensation as an end in itself, an interest that defines better than anything else his generation as moviegoers, music lovers and moviemakers.

"Close Encounters" is most stunning when it is dealing in visual and aural sensations that might be described as being in the 70's Disco Style. The unidentified flying objects that both terrorize and enchant the citizens of Muncie, Ind., early in the film, when the night sky is suddenly filled with blinking lights and several brilliantly colored shapes, each of which looks like a Portuguese man-of-war, make up an extraordinary psychedelic light show.

The disco manner is further suggested in the movie's use of sound, an almost nonstop confusion of voices, languages, technical jargon, weather, vehicles and (I sometimes suspect) gibberish, often so noisy that you can't hear yourself think.

•

Though "Close Encounters" is strictly a product of the 70's in its dress and manners, its heart is in the 50's. This is apparent from the first scene, when a squadron of World War II fighter planes, missing on a training mission more than 30 years earlier, suddenly turn up intact, as good as new, in the Mexican desert. In classic sci-fi manner, Mr. Spielberg's screenplay then cuts from this general introduction to the "mystery" to encounters with the mystery by individual folks in Muncie, homespun types like you and me who draw us into the adventure.

Mr. Spielberg's homespun types are mostly serviceable characters like Roy Neary, a blue-collar worker whose life is changed the night he spots the U.F.O.'s over Muncie. As do many of the others who shared his experience, Roy is obsessed by the memory, though his wife and three children think he is nuts. Another person similarly obsessed is a young mother, played by Melinda Dillon, whose 4-year-old son appears to be in some kind of psychic connection with the U.F.O's.

Following this initial, quite magnificent display of the movie technicians' special-effects wizardry, "Close Encounters" settles down to cross-cutting between scenes of Roy's seemingly lunatic efforts to find the U.F.O.s again, and the efforts being made by an international team of scientists who are preparing themselves for the second coming (of the U.F.O.s).

The film's two most arresting personalities are the 4-year-old Indiana boy (played with marvelous lack of self-consciousness by Cary Guffey), who gets to take a trip into space, and the French scientist who is the chief of the international U.F.O. team. As this fellow, François Truffaut, making his acting debut in an American film, gives "Close Encounters" a kind of prophetic center and dramatic weight it would otherwise lack.

•

Mr. Spielberg's usually uncanny cinematic instincts fail him from time to time in the extended central section of the film. He attempts to give "Close Encounters" a substructure of both scientific and theological importance. That might have been fascinating if I'd had a chance to understand it. Since I didn't, it came across as rather high-toned mad-doctor stuff.

There's also a sequence set on a hillside in India with the French scientist and his team of experts that seems to have been rather badly staged. It's a mess, perhaps in the confusion of an expensive movie location trip.

The final 30 to 40 minutes of the film, however, are what it's all about—and they are breathtaking: the close encounter of the third kind in which the earthlings and the alien creatures come together on a secret landing field in Wyoming. This sequence, as beautiful as anything I've seen since "2001," has been deliberately designed to suggest a religious experience of the first kind. Whether or not you believe it, this climax involves the imagination in surprising, moving ways. This is a day in which the earth might have stood still.

Mr. Spielberg tempts fate (and the value of Columbia Pictures' stock) by briefly introducing us to the alien creatures, and it's the measure of his success that no one giggles. Is "Close Encounters" better or worse than "Star Wars"?—that's the boring question this morning. It's neither one. It's different, an achievement on its own.

1977 N 17, C19:1

Nonstop Mayhem

THUNDER AND LIGHTNING, directed by Corey Allen, screenplay by William Hiortsberg; produced by Roger Corman; editor, Anthony Redman; music, Andy Stein; director of photography, James Pergola; distributed by 20th Century-Fox. Running time: 95 minutes. At the Victoria Theater, Broadway at 46th Street, and other theaters. This film has been rated PG.

Harley Thomas .... David Carradine
Nancy Sue Hunnicutt .... Kate Jackson
Ralph Jr. Hunnicutt .... Roger C. Carmel
Hobe Carpenter .... Sterling Holloway
Rudi Volpone .... Ed Barth
Bubba .... Ron Feinberg
Jake Summers .... George Murdock
Taylor .... Pat Cranshaw
Jim Bob .... Charles Napier
Mrs. Hunnicutt .... Hope Pomerance
Rainey .... Malcolm Jones

"THUNDER and Lightning," which opened yesterday at the Victoria and neighborhood theaters, is a buoyantly slapdash comedy about bootleggers in the Everglades. Although the movie appears to have been photographed almost entirely on Florida location and although its cast includes some good actors, David Carradine, Kate Jackson, and Sterling Holloway. "Thunder and Lightning" is less like a live-action movie than a 95-minute Bugs Bunny cartoon—which is one of the nicest things about it.

Mr. Carradine plays an independent-minded young bootlegger, a fellow who wears an earring in his left ear and who swaggers with just a little more self-assurance than his charm allows. Miss Jackson, one of the better comedians to come out of television, is his friend, the daughter of the syndicate-backed bootlegger who is Mr. Carradine's nemesis.

•

The movie begins with a chase involving swamp buggies, and later shifts to various makes and models of automobiles. There's hardly a moment in the movie when someone's not being pursued by, or in pursuit of someone else. It's painless, sometimes funny, good-natured, as well as extremely pro-life. As in a Bugs Bunny work, no one is permanently damaged by the nonstop mayhem. This is no big deal, I suppose, though as soon as one realizes this is its method, watching the movie becomes a benignly peaceful experience.

Roger Corman, sometimes known as the King of the Bees—B-pictures—who has given early employment to such directors as Francis Ford Coppola, Peter Bogdanovich and Jonathan Demme, produced "Thunder and Lightning." It was directed by Corey Allen and written by William Hjortsberg; we may well be hearing from them again.

•

"Thunder and Lightning," which has been rated PG ("Parental Guidance Suggested"), contains some vulgar language and a lot of action but no real violence.

VINCENT CANBY

1977 N 17, C22:3

Chilly as Death

THE CONFESSIONS OF AMANS, directed, produced and edited by Gregory Nava; screenplay by Mr. Nava and Anna Thomas; distributed by Bauer International. Running time: 90 minutes. At the Renoir Cinema, 100 Seventh Avenue South. This film has not been rated.

Amans .... William Bryan
Absolom .... Michael St. John
Anne .... Susannah Macmillan
Petrus .... Richard Gardner
Arnolfo .... Leon Liberman
Nicholas .... Feliciano Ituero Bravo

"THE CONFESSIONS OF AMANS," a story of tragic love set in medieval Spain, is a most unusual movie—so rigorously disciplined and composed it looks as if it were the work of someone who is nearing the end of a career and has long since abandoned the tricks of a trivial trade.

Instead, it is the first feature of 28-year-old Gregory Nava, an American of Basque-Mexican parentage who studied at the film school of the University of California at Los Angeles. Using professional actors, costumes that once appeared in "El Cid" and a lot of the castles of ancient Segovia, Mr. Nava made "The Confessions of Amans" in Spain on a budget of about $20,000, including a grant from the American Film Institute. Like all successful film makers, Mr. Nava apparently has an artistic sensibility matched by an ability to promote himself and get things done.

"The Confessions of Amans" is a beautiful, muted film of the kind that takes some getting used to. People seldom raise their voices or lose control of themselves. Passion is expressed discreetly in glances or in the holding of hands.

I've no idea whether this is the way life was in medieval Spain, but this is the way it seems to have been to us today. We're so far removed that we can't quite make out the feelings, only the looks on the faces, the gestures, the etiquette. Interiors are almost as barren as the lovely, lonely landscapes, as if the people who once inhabited them had died long ago or moved to the city. The movie has the manner of something slowly freezing in time, which is as chilly as death.

This, I assume, is exactly the manner Mr. Nava sought. It also explains the curious neo-Bressonian distance from which we observe the story of Amans, a poor young philosophy scholar, and Anne, the young wife of the lord of the castle where Amans is employed as the tutor. Amans and Anne, whose love has no happy end, are parts of the medieval landscape.

It's difficult to judge actors in this sort of film, in which every performance appears to be as much the composition of the director as his choice of the color for a costume. The actors are English stage performers who speak the mostly jargon-free dialogue in accents that have no immediate association to any particular time or place.

Mr. Nava produced, directed, photographed and edited the movie, and wrote the screenplay in collaboration with Anna Thomas, another U.C.L.A. graduate.

VINCENT CANBY

1977 N 18, C10:5

Hands Get Bitten

WHY DOES HERR R. RUN AMOK? Directed by Rainer Werner Fassbinder nad Michael Fengler; screen play (in German with English subtitles) by Mr. Fassbinder and Mr. Fengler; director of photography, Dietrich Lohmann; editors, Franz Walsch and Mr. Fengler; music, Christian Anders; distributed by New Yorker Films. Running time: 88 minutes. At the Cinema Studio, Broadway at 67th Street. This film has not been rated.

Herr R. .... Kurt Raab
Herr R's Wife .... Lilith Ungerer
Their Son .... Amadeus Fengler
The Boss .... Franz Maron
Colleagues of Herr R. ....
Harry Baer, Peter Holand, Lilo Pempeit
Schoolfriend .... Hanna Schygulla
Father .... Mr. Sterr
Mother .... Mrs. Sterr

By VINCENT CANBY

IN THAT BODY of grisly-comic literature devoted to worms-that-turn, to Mr. Milquetoasts who suddenly sour, to nice family men who quietly take axes to their innocent families, "Why does Herr R. Run Amok?" is one of the scariest as well as one of the funniest works of all.

The film, which was made in 1969, is an almost perfect example of the early cinema of Rainer Werner Fassbinder—though I suppose the reason it wasn't included in the New Yorker Theater's Fassbinder retrospective last spring and summer is that it's not technically a Fassbinder film. That is, it was codirected by Mr. Fassbinder and Michael Fengler in the days when the members of the Fassbinder theater and film company thought of their work as communal endeavors. This was the first and last time Mr. Fassbinder let that happen. Such communism, fine for ants, is difficult in the arts.

•

In terms of the chronology of the Fassbinder films we've seen here this year, "Why Does Herr R. Run Amok?" comes immediately after "Katzelmacher" and "Gods of The Plague" and just before "Beware the Holy Whore" (1970), which was all about the difficulties of making a film on which no one had any real authority. Mr. Fassbinder is not a film maker to let an unhappy experience go to waste.

If the making of "Why Does Herr R. Run Amok?" with Mr. Fengler was an unhappy experience, it doesn't show in the completed movie, which is as spare, blunt and sardonic as anything that Mr. Fassbinder has ever done by himself. It's also a revealing demonstration of how the style of a Fassbinder film becomes its subject.

The story is simply told: Herr R. (Kurt Raab), a paunchy, mild-mannered fellow, works by day as a draftsman in a small architectural firm. He functions as the master of T-squares, straight-edges and nonleaky pens. At night he is the proper husband to his wife (Lilith Ungerer) and the proper father to young Amadeus (Amadeus Fengler). Together they watch television, plan for the promotion Herr R. hopes to get, and say all the proper things to his boring parents, with whom they talk about television, eating and money.

•

One night while Herr R.'s wife and a neighbor are discussing to the point of exhaustion the subject of ski clothes as Herr R. is trying to watch television, he gets up from his chair and methodically sets about expressing his irritation, using a large blunt instrument.

Why does Herr R. run amok? He is bored, but because he has no safety valve of impatience, he explodes. Similarly bored is the camera that observes Herr R.'s life and times.

The camera has a habit of more or less settling down—as if it were someone vastly overweight filling up a chair. It watches what goes on with no special interest, but it hasn't the strength to move. The camera often can't be bothered to turn to focus on a person who's talking off-screen, knowing that if it waits long enough someone within its range will talk.

•

As Herr R.'s work is completely absorbed by petty details that seem to have no importance in themselves, so is the film composed of a series of small scenes of crushing banality. Much of the dialogue sounds improvised, and like a lot of improvisation, it sometimes is unexpectedly funny and sometimes goes on too long, which is also an aspect of Herr R.'s existence.

In addition to Mr. Raab, who is grossly appealing in the title role, the cast includes such other Fassbinder regulars as Hanna Schygulla (in a tiny but funny role), and Lilo Pempeit (the mother of Effi Briest) as one of Herr R.'s office associates, a gray, spinsterish-looking woman who giggles a lot.

"Why Does Herr R. Run Amok?" is short, bitter film. It's full of sneers for the same German affluence that has made Mr. Fassbinder's extraordinary film career possible, but that's the way with many artists these days. They must bite the hands as long as they feed them.

1977 N 18, C15:1

SUMMERDOG, directed by John Clayton; screenplay by George and Sherry LaFollette-Zabriskie; cinematography, Bil Godsey; editor, Julie Tanser; music, Michael Gibson; produced by Mr. Clayton; a Film Foundry Production; presented by Salisbury Associates. Running time: 90 minutes. At the Guild Theater, 33 West 50th Street. This film has been rated G.

Peter Norman .... James Congdon
Carol Norman .... Elizabeth Eisenman
Adam Norman .... Oliver Zabriskie
Becky Norman .... Tavia Zabriskie
Caleb Grimes .... Don Rutledge
Mrs. Baleeka .... Estelle Harris
Mr. Baleeka .... Tony Capra

By JANET MASLIN

Don't bring your children to see "Summerdog" unless you either own a hound or are prepared to pick one up on the way home. This is yet another shaggy-dog movie with a plot that hinges on the physical, moral and intellectual superiority of the family pet. Hobo, the dog of the title, isn't Lassie by a long shot, nor is he even Benji. But he is so much smarter and more appealing than either his owners or their enemies that the film amounts to one long advertisement for canine companionship.

Mom (Elizabeth Eisenman), Dad (James Congdon) and their two perfect blond children (Oliver and Tavia Zabriskie) live in an unspecified city that incorporates both a small-town air and large chunks of Central Park, but they have decided to spend their summer vacation in the country. They rent a sweet little cottage, and Dad tries to write there. "I'm afraid the words aren't flowing too well today," he complains at one point.

Mom grows radishes. Dad: "It's hard to believe they were just little tiny dried-up seeds a couple of weeks ago." Mom: "It's kind of magical, isn't it?"

And the kids find Hobo, whose paw has gotten caught in a bear trap set by Old Caleb, a grizzled neighbor. "Do you think Caleb Grimes is really a bad person or just someone who can't cope with today's world?" Mom inquires.

Everyone falls in love with Hobo, but the family can't bring him home: The landlord won't allow pets, and they simply can't afford to move. After a lot of fuss and intrigue, the problem is solved, and a song praising Hobo is sung. Needless to say, he gets to stay.

"Summerdog" is so unimaginatively made, and so full of noisily exaggerated acting of the "More Parks Sausages, Mom!" school, that it should be of only slight interest to older children and of no interest to adults—unless they can keep busy with puzzling out the plot's fine points, like the matter of how a family too strapped to move can magically rent a summer house without subletting their treasured apartment.

However, there are a few isolated scenes here that a preview audience of small children found screamingly funny. One such episode involved a dozen people chasing madly down a circular staircase, with Hobo at the fore. Another featured a mouse, who appeared in the summer house and gave Mom a good scare.

1977 N 19, 12:1

SEMI-TOUGH, directed by Michael Ritchie; screenplay by Walter Bernstein, based on the novel by Dan Jenkins; produced by David Merrick; director of photography, Charles Rosher Jr.; editor, Richard A. Harris; music, Jerry Fielding; distributed by United Artsts. Runnng time: 108 minutes. At the Crierion Theater, Broadway at 45th Street, and Baronet Theaer, Third Avenue at 59th Street. This film has been rated R.

Billy Clyde Puckett .... Burt Reynolds
Shake Tiller .... Kris Kristofferson
Barbara Jane Bookman .... Jill Clayburgh
Big Ed Bookman .... Robert Preston
Friedrich Bismark .... Bert Convy
Puddin .... Roger E. Mosley
Clara Pelf .... Lotte Lenya
Phillip Hooper .... Richard Masur
Dreamer Tatum .... Carl Weathers
T. J Lambert .... Brian Dennehy
Earlene .... Mary Jo Catlett
Jose Manning .... Joe Kapp
Vlada .... Ron Silver
McNair .... Jim McKrell
Interpreter .... Peter Bromilow
Coach Parks .... Norm Alden
Minister .... Fred Stuthman
Dressmaker .... Janet Brandt
Fitter .... William Wolf
Stewardess .... Jenifer Shaw
Puddin Jr. .... Kevin Furry
Puddin's Wife .... Ava Roberts

By VINCENT CANBY

"Semi-Tough," Dan Jenkins's best-selling comic novel about big-league professional football, has been slimmed down, beefed up and reworked to make a funny film that is as much satire as parody, as much about our time as it is about some of our more bizarre culture heroes.

The movie, which opened yesterday at the Criterion and Baronet Theaters, takes us on a sort of "Through the Looking Glass" journey into the Sunday afternoon television screen and beyond, into the lives of Billy Clyde Puckett (Burt Reynolds) and Shake Tiller (Kris Kristofferson), prostars whose names are part of the film's comic method, and Barbara Jane Bookman (Jill Clayburgh), the pretty but failure-prone daughter of the owner of their ball club. Barbara Jane shares a platonic friendship with the two players as well as their Miami Beach penthouse apartment, a gaudy nest that looks as if it had been decorated by the people who did our Ziegfeld Theater.

•

Other "characters" who move in and out of the film are Big Ed Bookman (Robert Preston), Barbara Jane's father, a hot-tempered tycoon with a fondness for patriotic songs (Gene Autry records); Friedrich Bismark (Bert Convy), the hustling head of a terrifically successful "energy training" course called BEAT, and Clara Pelf (Lotte Lenya), a ferocious chiropractor who calls what she does "pelfing."

Walter Bernstein, who wrote the screenplay, and Michael Ritchie, the director, haven't been success-

Jill Clayburgh
Charming

ful in giving dramatic structure to the episodic novel, but they do succeed in restraining a terrible tendency toward cuteness, not an easy thing to do in a comedy in which all men are recognized as just overgrown boys.

With this film Mr. Ritchie ("The Bad News Bears," "Smile," "Downhill Racer") reinforces his reputation as one of those rare directors who is able to look at Middle America critically without being especially outraged or even surprised.

Mostly he is amused, not as someone who sets himself apart from the scene, but as a man who recognizes his own place in it. He may wish it were other than it is, but he doesn't rage that it isn't. He's a humanist fascinated by the manners and mores of a society in which everything, from food to mental health, has been merchandized for the take-out trade.

"Semi-Tough" is not a movie that forces a lot of plot on you. It's under way for some time before you begin to grasp what is meant to be the story—the thing that is supposed to pull you along. This is about the rivalry that suddenly springs up between the self-assured Billy Clyde, a role that effectively uses Mr. Reynolds's television talk show personality, and Shake Tiller, a fellow who is a pared-down, very hesitant version of Mr. Kristofferson's identity as a musician-singer. At the center of the quarrel is Barbara Jane.

If the film's various sketch-pieces were not so funny, "Semi-Tough" would not have any story at all. As it is, we go along with it for the three leading players, who are good company, and for the wit that, though random, is consistent. For a film about football, "Semi-Tough" spends comparatively little time on the field and makes no serious attempt to trap our interest in questions about winning or losing.

•

Winning or losing is not the concern of the film, which knows that there are always new seasons to improve old records. The film isn't even too concerned about whether Barbara Jane marries Billy Joe or Shake Tiller. Its interest is in the overall scene—in the shambles of her wedding ceremonies, a very nice sequence that begins as we overhear the minister and Friedrich Bismark, the mental-health tycoon, standing at the altar solemnly discussing tax shelters.

Miss Clayburgh, who's been asked to play zany heroines in "Gable and Lombard" and "The Silver Streak" by people who failed to provide her with material, has much better luck this time. She's charming.

"Semi-Tough" pokes fun in rambling fashion, but it is vulgar in intelligent ways and almost always amusing in its perceptions of befuddled people who are perfectly healthy but often convinced they're not.

1977 N 19, 12:1

"SEMI-TOUGH"—Teammates Brian Dennehy, Burt Reynolds and Kris Kristofferson rowdily rejoice in their gridiron triumph in Michael Ritchie's film of the Dan Jenkins novel.

FILM VIEW

VINCENT CANBY

Rediscovering the Secrets That Made Hollywood Corn Grow

Steven Spielberg, who will be 30 next month, grew up on movies and never had a serious intention of doing anything except making movies, which he now does. Herbert Ross, 50, moved into films sideways. He started as a dancer in Broadway musicals, later became a choreographer for both the musical theater and the ballet, switched to films (where he staged the dances for "Funny Girl") and eventually became an extremely successful movie director ("Play It Again, Sam," "The Seven-Per-Cent Solution," among others). Though the two men are separated by their backgrounds as much as by their generations, it is significant that in his new film each man has rediscovered secrets that once made Hollywood corn the world's most popular entertainment.

Mr. Spielberg's science-fiction epic, "Close Encounters of the Third Kind," a movie so expensive (around $18,000,000) that it could do fiscal damage to its studio (Columbia) if it should flop, is more closely related to sci-fi movies of the 1950's like "The Day the Earth Stood Still" and "The War of the Worlds" than it is to rather more sublime work on the order of Stanley Kubrick's "2001:A Space Odyssey" or George Lucas's "Star Wars." Yet, though it lacks the poetic vision of "2001" and the witty innocence of "Star Wars," "Close Encounters" is such a dazzling display of certain movie modes and technology that it comes close to apotheosizing a movie genre of the second kind.

"Close Encounters" makes no attempt to be anything but the science-fiction it is, and it succeeds by doing this better, more thoroughly, than anyone else has done to date.

Mr. Ross's "The Turning Point," which is described as having been conceived jointly by him, his wife, Nora Kaye, and Arthur Laurents, who wrote the screenplay, is the sort of movie you're likely to hate yourself in the morning for having liked so much the night before. But don't throw yourself out a window. A lot of equally strong types will have liked it quite as much as you and they won't feel any guilt whatsoever.

• • •

Although "The Turning Point" is set in the somewhat rare world of the ballet, it's essentially an old-fashioned, backstage musical that contains every backstage musical cliche I can think of except two—the shot of a Variety headline announcing some small plot point and a close-up of a review in which a critic raves about the chorus girl who has become a star overnight.

As Mr. Spielberg has done with "Close Encounters," Mr. Ross and his associates have followed a familiar formula as if it were a sacred text, but they have added so much humor, feeling and visual beauty that one hardly realizes the movie is knee-deep in the kind of sentimentality that once lubricated such vehicles as "Forty-Second Street," "Footlight Parade," "Give My Regards to Broadway" and "Torch Song."

Not long ago I was worrying about Hollywood's half-hearted attempts to be hip that result more often than not in movies that are neither hip nor genuinely committed to the values they seem to admire. A perfect example this season has been Sydney Pollack's "Bobby Deerfield," which looks as if it were an effort to remake "Love Story" with characters as chilly and disengaged as the tormented souls who wandered across Michelangelo Antonioni's landscapes in the 1960's. "Bobby Deerfield" is a multimillion-dollar contradiction in terms. Corn is corn and any effort to upgrade it by changing the rules of the genre, or by adding elements from other, very different, kinds of movies, denies the audiences for whom the movie originally was intended.

Mr. Spielberg, a movie nut who appears to relate everything in his life to movies, has made no such mistake with "Close Encounters of the Third Kind," the best 1950's science-fiction film I've ever seen, not because it's different in any genre-breaking way, but because it's classier and far more intelligent.

The screenplay, which he wrote, begins in the classic science-fiction manner of "Jaws" (which borrowed its shape from science-fiction no matter how you classify the film): Somewhere in the Mexican desert there has been discovered a squadron of World War II American fighter planes that disappeared on a training flight without trace more than 30 years ago. The planes are in perfect shape. They look as if they'd just landed. A group of scientists who arrive on the scene are told by an addled old Mexican that "last night the sun came up and sang to me." Good heavens, is the man mad?

Cut to a small town in Indiana where even more bizarre things are going on. First a mysterious blackout (night is absolutely essential to this sort of science-fiction since extraterrestrial visitors define themselves by the quality and quantity of their lights, which simply wouldn't be seen during the day). Not only is there a blackout but also curious things happen to Coke cans (they pop open unaided), while electric appliances and toys come to life. A small boy, played by 4-year-old Cary Guffey, one of the film's most charming assets, awakens to find his bedroom a carnival of animated playthings— marching soldiers, blinking robots, miniature cars scooting about with their sirens going. He is delighted. It's Christmas in July.

The child is one of the first to see the unidentified flying objects that sweep over Indiana that night, and one of the first to accept them totally. Another is a blue-collar worker, played by Richard Dreyfuss, a fellow who watches a magnificent UFO display and finds himself the next morning with half his face burned, as if he'd spent a day at the beach lying on one side. It's the curious reaction shared by everyone who has seen this brilliant, midnight light show (which looks as if the sky were filled with dozens of furiously active Portuguese man-of-war jelly fish) that no one worries about the burns. No one thinks he might have been subjected to some form of radiation. Instead, everyone feels peculiarly blessed.

• • •

As the film and its ads tell us, close encounters of the first kind are sightings of UFOs. Those of the second kind are physical evidence of UFOs, and of the third kind are contacts with the alien beings.

The movie is exactly what its title promises, with the contact between the earthlings and the space visitors taking up the final 40 minutes of the film, a sequence of spectacular beauty (and special effects wizardry), about which it isn't fair to say too much except that Mr. Spielberg has had the courage to show us his extraterrestrial creatures in a stunningly effective climactic moment and we don't laugh. Otherwise, he has stayed pretty close to the genre-variation that holds that the creatures from outer space will be not only far more intelligent than we are, but so benign as to be virtually perfect. God, you suspect, may not be just the cocaptain of this mission. He may be the captain as well.

The movie, which begins magnificently and ends in glory, has a middle section that seems to go on and on, when characters tend to say things like "What is happening here?" or "I know it sounds crazy, but . . ." This, unfortunately, gives one time to seek out contradictions within the movie's own mythology. Why do the visitors' space ships cause blackouts over Indiana but don't even interfere with hand-held walkie-talkies at the Wyoming meeting place, where the movie concludes? One also wonders whether Mr. Spielberg means to tell us something by the physical appearance of the little boy whom we meet very early in the film, and who is kidnapped for a brief flight into the heavens by the visitors for a brief flight into the heavens. The child recalls not only the foetus-creature we saw floating in space at the end of "2001," but also Mr. Spielberg's extraterrestrial creatures.

"Close Encounters" has no characters of real interest, but it does have two arresting personalities—the little boy and the French scientist who is in charge of what appears to be a united earth effort to make contact with the visitors. This man, as played by Francois Truffaut, mostly in French through an English translator, is someone of such compelling wisdom and understanding that he seems as much prophet as scientist. I suspect that part of this effect must be the result of our knowing who the actor is. In our world artists and scientists are the only prophets who remain.

Because of Mr. Truffaut's presence, and because Mr. Spielberg has such an optimistic view of this close encounter, the film is not the cold panorama of space ships, gadgetry and special effects that most science fiction films become. Nor is it cerebral in any way. It's a big, noisy, meticulously realized adventure. It is also great fun.

• • •

The lady who narrates the radio commercial for "The Turning Point" sounds exactly as I remember Helen Trent, the long-suffering queen of radio soaps. In a voice so smooth it seems to come out of a cold-cream jar, she tells us that "The Turning Point" is about "choices—security or stardom, success or love." She isn't kidding. "The Turning Point" is the story of Deedee (Shirley MacLaine) who, 20 years before, elected to marry and have children rather than remain with the ballet, and of Emma (Anne Bancroft), who stayed on to become the great, lonely prima ballerina Deedee thinks she should have been. It's also the story of Deedee's daughter, Emilia (Leslie Browne), who chooses the career her mother abandoned. Less that four months out of Oklahoma City, Emilia is well on her way to the stardom that Emma will soon have to sacrifice. Smile through your tears, folks.

There's no way to describe what goes on in "The Turning Point" without making it sound ridiculous—yet it's a most entertaining movie in which almost everything works. It may be because the world of the ballet, like that of the theater, really is corny, where people say "Oh I wish I knew who I was!" and mean it, where they must make certain decisions that the rest of us will never get close to. Stars are not made overnight—non-pros know that—but they can be discovered suddenly, and it seems as if it were overnight. Age takes its toll in the ballet as dramatically as in any other branch of show business, and the egos are as overwhelming as the potential triumphs and the disappointments. None of these things are left out of the Laurents screenplay, which is decorated at regular intervals by fleeting glimpses of a number of ballets. These are treated pretty much the way Louis B. Mayer used to spoon-feed us the opera excerpts in old Mario Lanza and Kathryn Grayson movies: just enough to give peons the idea without seriously testing any peon's threshold of boredom. The movie leaves us wanting more rather than less, which is, I suppose, a virtue.

"The Turning Point" has some other, much less equivocal virtues, particularly the performance of Miss MacLaine. It's her best in years, perhaps of her career—strong, intelligent, and as funny as it is moving. Miss Bancroft's role requires that she say some of the script's worst lines, but when she and Miss MacLaine are on the screen together, in the movie's finest sequences, there's genuine life. As the two old friends who envy, loathe and love each other, they work together beautifully and contribute a penultimate scene that is almost great.

Mikhail Baryshnikov, the Russian ballet dancer who defected to Western stardom several years ago, and Leslie Browne, of the New York City Ballet, make very attractive debut performances as film actors who also appear to dance splendidly. I say "appear" because "The Turning Point," being a "serious" drama, can never keep its eyes on the stage very long at any one time. It is always cutting away for reaction shots of the smiling or weeping people off-stage, as if it didn't trust our judgment.

The filmmakers have used the stars and the corps de ballet of the American Ballet Theater very effectively and, I'm told, Mr. Laurents has borrowed the lives of some real ballet people for his characters, so that to those who know, the movie is full of inside jokes. The real inside joke is that you don't have to be privy to any inside information to be entertained by "The Turning Point." Louis B. Mayer would have loved it as he loved his mother's chicken soup. The old-fashioned ways survive. ■

1977 N 20, II:15:1

IPHIGENIA, directed by Michael Cacoyannis; screenplay (in Greek with English subtitles) by Mr. Cacoyannis, based on "Iphigenia in Aulis" by Euripides; executive producer, Yannoula Wakefield; director of photography, Georges Arvantis; music, Mikis Theodorakis; editors, Mr. Cacoyannis and Takis Yannopoulos; a Greek Film Center production, distributed by Cinema 5. Running time: 130 minutes. At the Plaza Theater, 58th Street west of Fifth Avenue. This film has not been rated.

Clytemnestra	Irene Papas
Agamemnon	Costa Kazakos
Menelaus	Costa Carras
Iphigenia	Tatiana Papamoskou
Ulysses	Christos Tsangas
Achilles	Panos Michalopoulos
Servant	Angelos Yannoulis
Calchas	Dimitri Aronis
Orestes	Georges Vourvahakis
Nurse	Irene Koumarianou
Messenger	Georges Economou

By VINCENT CANBY

Because Euripides (480-406 B.C.) was Greek and Michael Cacoyannis (1922-) is Greek, there is a tendency to applaud Mr. Cacoyannis's thoroughly ponderous attempts to make the ancient Euripidean tragedies comprehensible to contemporary movie audiences. We are asked to believe that the playwright and the film maker share some sort of deep cultural bond, as if they'd been in the same class at Athens High. Good old Mike and Rip — the Mutt and Jeff of the Acropolis.

The bond may well be there, but it isn't apparent in the films Mr. Cacoyannis has made to date — "Electra" (1962), "The Trojan Women" (1971), which was a big-budget production with an international cast that spoke various kinds of English, and now "Iphigenia," a Greek-language version of the last Euripides tragedy, "Iphigenia in Aulis."

•

Like "The Trojan Women," "Iphigenia in Aulis" is a bitter reflection on the war that Athens had been waging against Sparta since 431 B.C., and that Athens would lose in 404 B.C. with the complete destruction of her defenses. When it was written in 407 B.C., "Iphigenia" was a topical play in which the playwright substituted Troy for Sparta. Even though Euripides was then in exile, he wasn't foolish enough to believe that such an attack on state policy would get very far if staged frontally.

"Iphigenia" is not a conventional tragedy. There are no easily recognized heroes in the way Euripides dramatized the story of the Trojan War. As Euripides tells it,

Costa Kazakos, playing Agamemnon, about to sacrifice Tatiana Papamoskou, who plays the title role in the film "Iphigenia."

Agamemnon, the leader of the Greek forces waiting to sail against Troy, agrees to sacrifice his eldest daughter, Iphigenia, to please the gods and insure victory. To this end, he has Iphigenia come to the camp in Aulis on the pretext that she's going to marry Achilles. Instead, she is to die, a bit of flimflammery that outrages Clytemnestra, not because she cares about her daughter that much but because she fears how much she will suffer the loss of a daughter.

There's not a truly noble person in the entire play, not even the doomed Iphigenia who, though she goes bravely to her death, goes as a deluded child for all the wrong reasons.

Euripides's method in "Iphigenia" is oblique — nobody ever means everything that is said. This undercurrent of furious irony is something that is completely lost in Mr. Cacoyannis's "Iphigenia," whose characters have been so simplified as to become tragic stereotypes. It's not that the text has been tampered with but the manner in which it's played and set.

Irene Papas, with her magnificent profile intact and her eyebrows in full bloom, plays Clytemnestra as if she were Mother Earth and not the complicated, selfish, conniving bitch she should be. Miss Papas's Clytemnestra asks for sympathy, as does the Agamemnon of Costa Kazakos, though he also manages to convince us of the contradictory desires that have been his undoing. Iphigenia is played by Tatiana Papamoskou, a tall, skinny, doe-eyed 12-year-old who looks as if she might grow up to be a terrific Dior model, which has nothing to do with ancient Greece or Euripides.

•

In "Iphigenia," as in "The Trojan Women," Mr. Cacoyannis employs all sorts of comparatively snappy film techniques—the hand-held camera, the zoom lens, and the subjective camera by which we look out through the eyes of the character—to make us believe that we are there. It never works and can't work. We're not meant to get inside these characters, but to stand aside and observe the spectacle as a single, headlong ritual.

Mr. Cacoyannis's fondness for photographing these densely packed, poetic melodramas in scenic, real-life landscapes distracts from the text and demolishes the actors, whose grandly theatrical mannerisms look silly in sets as big as all outdoors. People in the movie tend to run in a half-crouch, the way a stage actor runs when he wants to indicate a sprint even though he's covering no more than 10 feet of stage space.

The film is not without its own paradox: The best thing in it is all wrong. This is a pre-credit sequence in which we are shown the state and condition of the Greek forces in Aulis as they await orders to sail to Troy. We see their boredom as they lie about the beaches, their ships idle, their rations low, their anger accumulating. The sequence has a lazy, eerie kind of beauty, but it should be the preface for a big, overblown historical pageant like "The Fall of the Roman Empire," not "Iphigenia," which has no need of anything more than its action and the extraordinary text.

1977 N 21, 33:1

ANOTHER MAN, ANOTHER CHANCE; written and directed by Claude Lelouch; produced by Alexandre Mnouchkine and Georges Dancigers; directors of photography, Jacques Lefrancois and Stanley Cortez; Music by Francis Lai; casting by Mike Fenton and Jane Feinberg. At the Cinerama Theater, 47th Street and Broadway; the Trans-Lux 85th Street Theater, 85th Street and Madison Avenue; the Columbia I Theater, Second Avenue and 64th Street. Running Time: 129 minutes. This film has been rated PG.

David Williams .... James Caan
Jeannne Leroy .... Genevieve Bujold
Francis Leroy .... Francis Huster
Mary .... Jennifer Warren
Debbie/Alice .... Susan Tyrrell

By JANET MASLIN

SHE (GENEVIEVE BUJOLD) is a French baker's daughter who leaves her battered homeland at the end of the Franco-Prussian war and travels by sea to America, where she and her husband, a photographer, board a wagon train and head for the Old West. En route, a Polish woman prophesies that she will be widowed and never see France again. Both things turn out to be true.

And he (James Caan), he is a veterinarian. One day, he returns home and, after greeting his dogs and cattle, discovers that his pretty young wife has been raped and murdered. He is heartbroken for a few years, but gradually he begins to recover. This is most fortunate, since he and she are by now living in the same frontier town, and fate is ready to throw them together. At the very end of Claude Lelouch's "Another Man, Another Chance," they fall in love.

The plot sounds like vintage James Michener, give or take a couple of generations, and indeed it has the makings of a good yarn. However, Mr. Lelouch proves to be less interested in telling his story than in tippy-toeing around its edges. There is abundant cross-cutting, between images as disparate as the veterinarian's giving a local schoolteacher a friendly squeeze and a breadline in wartime France.

•

There are filters so yellowy that the sky turns green. Most maddeningly of all, there is incessant hand-held camerawork in sequences that don't warrant it: One of Mr. Lelouch's favorite tricks is to track the camera for a while, hold it only half-still as a conversation takes place, and then track some more. The viewer is likely to feel seasick long before Miss Bujold makes her ocean voyage.

It would be unfair to accuse Mr. Lelouch of pretentiousness, since more often than not one is bound to be uncertain about just what he is pretending to do. The opening bars of Beethoven's Fifth Symphony, for instance, punctuate many scenes for no apparent reason. "If I can't joke about death, what can I joke about?" asks one rather bewildering character. And the film begins with a modern-day sequence in which Mr. Caan, playing one of his own descendants, is hired to photograph an ad man's vision of what the Old West must have been like.

•

This involves a Cadillac, four horses and several women in pioneer garb, and Mr. Caan complains that it's silly. More to the point, the whole sequence is silly, especially since neither the photographer nor the present is referred to again.

By the second half of the film, though, Mr. Lelouch has either cleaned up his act or lost his power to annoy. The story begins to take flight when Miss Bujold and Mr. Caan finally meet, and the rest of it is told in a reasonably straightforward manner.

The performances are helpful even when Mr. Lelouch is not. The film is so poorly and inconsistently dubbed into English that the actors often seem to be shouting from across a large, empty room, but Miss Bujold nevertheless creates a feeling of intimacy. Her peculiarly childlike prettiness becomes ever more interesting as time gives her an incongruously haggard look.

•

Mr. Caan has had few roles that show him off to proper advantage, accentuating his playfulness and physicality. Here, he struts about manfully and says things like "Over my dead body—you got it?" But he also radiates an easy charm, and his ruggedness helps keep Mr. Lelouch's sepia-toned tableaux from turning to utter mush.

Jennifer Warren and Francis Huster are quite memorable as the ill-fated first spouses; so is Susan Tyrrell, in a less successful way. Miss Tyrrell is Mr. Lelouch's rather bizarre choice for the role of the good-natured schoolmarm with whom Miss Bujold leaves her daughter and Mr. Caan his son. Even in her most innocuous moods, Miss Tyrrell never quite seems like the sort of person with whom one ought to park small children.

•

"Another Man, Another Chance" is rated PG ("Parental Guidance Suggested"). It contains a nasty rape scene, though not a graphic one, and another sequence that makes childbearing look like the scariest thing in the world.

1977 N 24, C17:1

"ANOTHER MAN, ANOTHER CHANCE"—James Caan, an American widower, gets acquainted with Genevieve Bujold, a French widow.

Provocative German

IT'S NOT THE HOMOSEXUAL . . . ., directed and written by Rosa Von Praunheim. Running time: 65 minutes. **AUDIENCE RESPONSE TO: "IT'S NOT THE HOMOSEXUAL . . . .,"** a documentary by Mr. Von Praunheim. Running time: 30 minutes. Both films distributed by the Serious Business Company. At the Film Forum, 15 Vandam Street.

By VINCENT CANBY

"IT'S NOT THE HOMOSEXUAL Who Is Perverse, but the Situation in Which He Lives," is a militantly Marxist call for an end to homosexual oppression, made by a young German film maker who has taken the nom de cinema of Rosa Von Praunheim. The 65-minute movie, which was shown in the Museum of Modern Art's Cineprobe series in 1972, opened yesterday at the Film Forum on a bill with a 30-minute film, "Audience Response to 'It's Not the Homosexual . . . .'" which is just what the title says, a record of (mostly angry) viewers' responses to the Von Praunheim film after screenings in New York.

In "It's Not the Homosexual . . . ." Mr. Von Praunheim uses the highly stylized mannerisms of epic theater to tell the story of poor Daniel, an innocent young country boy who comes to Berlin, has his first homosexual affair and then devotes himself to various kinds of homosexual pursuits with increasing desperation and lack of satisfaction. Mr. Von Praunheim's treatment of homosexual stereotypes does not endear him to many homosexual liberationists, who, like many other revolutionaries, want artists to promote positive rather than negative images.

It is apparent, though, that the point of the Von Praunheim attack is to provoke homosexual liberationsts to seek not tolerance, but self-awareness and then acceptance so that they can, in turn, play some useful role in changing society at large. The director's sometimes grotesque, macabre images and voice-over narration (in English) are merciless in the way they ridicule the elaborate role-playing affected by certain kinds of homosexuals and the narcissism that, he says, serve to confirm the values of a sick, outdated bourgeois society.

Though Mr. Von Praunheim is clearly a film maker of imagination and talent, the content of his film is so loaded that it makes all other comments superfluous. The program will play at the Film Forum tonight through Sunday at 7:47 and next week at the same hour, Thursday through Sunday.

1977 N 25, C10:3

Simon Says

THE GOODBYE GIRL, directed by Herbert Ross; screenplay by Neil Simon; produced by Ray Stark; director of photography, David M. Walsh; editor, John F. Burnett; music scored and adapted by Dave Grusin; a Raster production, distributed by Warner Brothers. Running time: 110 minutes. At Loews Tower East Theater, Third Avenue near 72d Street. This film has been rated PG.

Elliot Garfield	Richard Dreyfuss
Paula McFadden	Marsha Mason
Lucy McFadden	Quinn Cummings
Mark	Paul Benedict
Donna	Barbara Rhoades
Mrs. Crosby	Theresa Merritt
Linda	Marilyn Sokol

By VINCENT CANBY

IF ONE COULD ENTER the mind of Neil Simon, I have the feeling it would be like attending a convention of standup comedians—everyone busy topping everyone else, not really listening to anything that's being said except to identify the key word that will be the springboard into the next snappy retort, then the next and the next. Exhuasting without being much fun.

Which is more or less the way I feel about Mr. Simon's newest work, the original screenplay for "The Goodbye Girl," a movie that has the form of a romantic comedy but which is so relentlessly wisecracked that it finally has the very curious effect of seeming to be rude to its own characters.

•

The people in "The Goodbye Girl" are very nice indeed, at least when we first meet them. They are a desperately cheerful young woman named Paula (Marsha Mason), a former Broadway hoofer who has a precocious 10-year-old daughter named Lucy (Quinn Cummings) and terrible luck with men, and Elliot Garfield (Richard Dreyfuss), a maniacally egocentric young Chicago actor who's come to New York to star in an Off Off Broadway production of "Richard III."

Paula and Elliot loathe each other at first sight, for good reason. Paula's former lover has just sneaked off to Italy after having sublet to Elliot the apartment in which Paula and Lucy are living. Paula and Lucy refuse to give up the premises and Elliot refuses to acknowledge the right of their occupancy. After thus meeting cute, they compromise, deciding to share the flat while keeping their respective distances.

"The Goodbye Girl," which opened yesterday at Loews Tower East Theater, may be the perfect American comedy for an age in which opportunism is not only an acceptable way of getting ahead in the world, but also a fashionable style of conversation, patterned largely, I suspect, on the manners of television talk-show guests who trample one another for the camera's attention. It's as if Zsa Zsa Gabor had become our Euphues.

•

The courtship of Paula and Elliot is conducted mostly in terms of outrage, insult and misunderstanding. They don't talk to each other—they compete for the last word. A lot of this, especially early in the film, is quite funny, but eventually it overtakes the characters and the situations so that, to keep the comedy moving, Mr. Simon himself appears to take over, making the characters say and do uncharacteristic things to get the laugh.

Thus Paula, who has done her share of sleeping around, must behave as if she were both jealous and morally outraged when Elliot brings home an actress-friend to rehearse one evening. We also are asked to believe that Elliot, who is essentially sane though ambitious, would go along with a ridiculously silly production of "Richard III" in which the title character is conceived as a Billy DeWolfe drag-queen.

The thing that always confuses my reactions to Mr. Simon's more outrageous inventions—such as the nutty "Richard III" production here—is that many of them are funny by themselves, but they don't fit easily together. Mr. Simon doesn't hesitate to sentimentalize little Lucy, played with eerie self-assurance by Miss Cummings, while stuffing her mouth with lines that would do justice to Groucho Marx.

In certain situations, Mr. Simon's insults and wisecracks work naturally, as in "The Sunshine Boys," about the two old vaudevillians who hate each other while being mutually dependent. It was also very comic in "The Odd Couple," whose two heroes were really early sketches for the Sunshine Boys. His gift for parody was marvelously apparent in "Murder by Death." However, something essential seems to be missing when he attempts to write with feeling about men and women. As he views the war between the sexes, it's a contest of unisex gag writers.

•

Herbert Ross, this year's "hot" director (what with "The Turning Point" already out and Mr. Simon's new play, "Chapter Two," about to open), who is a man of wit and humane concerns, appears to have put his talent so totally in the service of the Simon script that I have no idea what his contributions to the movie may be. Miss Mason and Mr. Dreyfuss are enthusiastic farceurs who manage to keep their wits about them even when they are doing absurd things. Miss Mason's Paula is especially funny in her early scenes with her daughter when she creates a genuinely comic portrait of a woman who has prepared herself for every possible treachery except the one that turns up.

•

"The Goodbye Girl," which has been rated PG Parental Guidance Suggested"), contains some mildly vulgar language but is otherwise no more or less offensive than a singing commercial that is insidious because it is more clever than most.

1977 D 1, C17:1

Marsha Mason and Richard Dreyfuss in "The Goodbye Girl"

Behind the Screens

THE CINEMA ACCORDING TO BERTOLUCCI, a documentary directed by Giuseppe Bertolucci; screenplay (Italian and English with English subtitles) by Mr. Bertolucci; photography, Tonino Nardi; editing, Mr. Bertolucci; produced by Ovidio Assonitis; released by Bauer International. At the Jean Renoir Cinema, 100 Seventh Avenue South. Running time: 70 minutes. This film has no rating.

WITH: Bernardo Bertolucci, Vittorio Storaro, Giuseppe Bertolucci; Robert De Niro, Gerard Depardieu, Dominique Sanda, Burt Lancaster, Donald Sutherland, Sterling Hayden, Stefania Sandrelli, Laura Betti and Alida Valli.

A scene from "The Cinema According to Bertolucci" at Jean Renoir Cinema

By JANET MASLIN

"IF I SAY 'CINEMA' what comes to mind?" asks an interviewer on the set of Bernardo Bertolucci's "1900." "Cold," answers the actress Stefania Sandrelli, who has been waiting around to complete an outdoor shot too long. "Actor?" the interviewer parries. "Cold," she again replies. "Director?" "Hot." "Money?" "Cold." "Woman?" "I don't know."

"The Cinema According to Bertolucci," which is on view at the Jean Renoir Cinema, should be of interest only to those viewers who find the above exchange illuminating. An unfortunate illustration of sibling rivalry in action, it is an attempt by Giuseppe Bertolucci, Bernardo's brother, to turn the making of his brother's epic into an occasion for examining the meaning of the cinema.

•

Though it is possible that he is marginally successful along these lines, viewers who don't understand Italian will never know for sure. The English subtitles translate only about half of what is being said, and they are scandalously inaccurate. The star of Bernardo's film, glimpsed here only in passing, is introduced as "Bob DeNero."

Those snatches of dialogue that are translated are usually incomplete. For example, Bernardo, who strides about commandingly wearing a variety of rakish hats and mufflers, announces that "tracking is my life's obsession," and goes on to elaborate, but the titles ignore the rest of his answer. On the other hand, when Gérard Depardieu observes that he likes "making good films and being happy," it's probably just as well that the translator disregards the remainder of what he has to say.

The only parts of the film that are adequately translated are those episodes involving a wandering peasant who engages some of the extras in ponderous discussions about the injustices of capitalism. It's too bad the peasant has so little opportunity to grill the makers of this multimillion-dollar movie on the same points.

Mr. Bertolucci's camerawork is adequate, but it's no match for his brother's, even if one makes allowances for their disparate budgets, and for the fact that Giuseppe must often shoot from vantage points behind Bernardo's crew. The only authentically lively episode here is a brief one: An extra dressed as a simple, humble peasant explains that he learned about rock-and-roll from Elvis Presley movies, and then launches into a frantic, most incongruous version of "Tutti Frutti."

1977 D 2, C9:3

FILM VIEW

VINCENT CANBY

What's So Good About 'Goodbye Girl'?

"Long-time no-see," said Stanley, my film producer friend, as I joined him at table Number One at Sardi's. It was four o'clock in the afternoon, so there wasn't much competition for the privileged position. The place was empty. "You long-time no make movie," I said, "so we long-time no-see." Stanley's new movie had just opened and I hadn't much liked it, so this meeting was, I felt, the least I could do, a chance to let Stanley blow off steam,.to tell me how wrong I was and how much he respected me and my right to disagree while reserving his right to think that I was an idiot.

"As a matter of fact," said Stanley, "you don't look very well. You look tired. You need a vacation. A long vacation. I wish you'd gone on vacation last week." He laughed. It was Stanley's way of joking. Because Stanley's movie had received fine reviews from almost everyone and had broken the opening day's box-office record at an East Side theater, Stanley wasn't distraught, but he was troubled. Stanley doesn't expect mostly fine reviews. He expects unanimous raves. When I once asked him what he wanted from life, he put it quite simply: "Everything."

Stanley was in a benign mood, though, which is something he feels he can afford when he breaks a box-office record.

"I'm not going to talk about my movie," he said. "I'm probably biased. No . . . . I'll put it more strongly. I *am* biased. But that's water over the bridge. What I really don't understand, however, is your review of 'The Goodbye Girl.' My God, here's the funniest, most heartwarming movie of the year, even if I didn't make it myself, and you hated it!"

"I didn't hate it," I said, finding myself on the defensive as I often do when Stanley suddenly shifts subjects in mid-paragraph.

"Do you enjoy writing nasty reviews," he asked, "kicking a guy just because he's up? Just because everybody else likes it? Is that how you assert yourself?"

"No," I said. "As a matter of fact, I really don't enjoy writing unfavorable reviews. Very few critics do. Among other reasons, they're harder to write. You have to be more careful. When I write an unfavorable review, I have to pay attention or I hear myself talking in the voice of Mary Jane Harovski."

"Mary Jane Harovski?" said Stanley. "Whom does she write for?"

"Nobody," I said. "When I was eight, Mary Jane Harovski was 10. She lived down the street from us. She had gray hair that she wore in a bun—at least, that's the way I remember her."

"You were in love with her," said Stanley.

"No," I said, "more like intimidated, even though I could beat her up when I had to. The thing was, there was nothing that Mary Jane Harovski didn't know. She knew the rules for everything from hide-and-seek, sardines and kick-the-can to contract bridge. She could spell 'accommodate,' multiply by twelves, go to movies on school nights and tie half-hitches. She was indispensable."

"In short," said Stanley, "she was intolerable."

"Exactly," I said. "It was only years later that I realized that she had no more idea how to multiply by twelves than I did and that the half-hitches she tied were granny knots. Mary Jane Harovski was a fraud. She fooled us all that time by just being decisive."

"So," said Stanley, "what does this gray-haired, 10-year-old phantom have to do with Neil Simon and 'The Goodbye Girl'?"

"Everything," I said. "Whenever I start to write a review of something about which I have very mixed feelings, I hear the voice of Mary Jane over my shoulder urging me to be more decisive, even more outraged, than I feel. Mary Jane wasn't elected president of the Summit Street Zorros by using words like 'perhaps,' 'maybe' and 'on the other hand.' She qualified nothing, not even the praise she occasionally bestowed on others.

"For my part," I continued, "I find myself qualifying everything connected with a Neil Simon comedy, even my enjoyment with the gags I laugh at."

"You're still furious with Mary Jane," said Stanley, no stranger to couch therapy.

"No," I said, "more like disappointed with Neil Simon, and that is tiring. The thing is that I'm baffled and, I suppose, intimidated by the fact that I have such mixed reactions about someone who's so immensely popular. I don't dislike Neil Simon. I liked 'The Odd Couple,' especially on Broadway, and I was truly enthusiastic about 'The Heartbreak Kid,' which he adapted for the movies from a story by Bruce Jay Friedman and which Elaine May directed, and 'The Sunshine Boys,' the movie, directed by Herbert Ross, with those two great performances by Walter Matthau and George Burns. In 'The Sunshine Boys' Simon's gifts for sentimentality and show-offy show-busy dialogue were in keeping with the story of two ancient vaudevillians. About halfway through 'The Goodbye Girl,' I found myself tuned out. It was just silly."

"That was what they said about Moliere," said Stanley. "I read that somewhere."

" 'The Goodbye Girl,' " I said, "seems to me to be an almost perfect example of Simon's way of creating nice, attractive, slightly eccentric characters early on and then abandoning them—sacrificing them, really—for the cheap laugh."

For those who haven't seen the film, I suppose I should explain that "The Goodbye Girl" is about a pretty, 30-ish Broadway hoofer named Paula (Marsha Mason), her wise-beyond-her-years little daughter, Lucy (Quinn Cummings) and the nutty, self-absorbed Chicago actor, Elliot Garfield (Richard Dreyfuss) who, through a mix-up, comes to share their New York flat.

When we first meet them, they seem to be extremely appealing people. Paula, just having been abandoned by an ambitious, two-timing movie actor who has scrammed to Italy, is particularly appealing, trying to make ends meet and to keep one step ahead of little Lucy, the sort of child who knows the title and number of performances of every Broadway show produced in the last 10 years. Elliot, too, is amusing company, intensely ambitious but also, apparently, quite aware of how self-absorbed he is and how he must appear to others.

"I liked the characters," I said to Stanley, "and I liked the performances, but then Simon, with the complete cooperation of Herbert Ross, the director, makes the comedy work by having everyone behave in ways that are either nasty or unbelievably ludicrous.

"There's the matter of the Off Off Broadway show that Elliot is involved in, a production of 'Richard III,' in which he is required to play Richard as a ridiculously mincing, lisping homosexual, which would be funny in a comedy satirizing Off Off Broadway, perhaps, when someone might say seriously, 'It wasn't the hump that crippled Richard, it was society,' but it doesn't fit with the characters Simon has created. The fellow played by Richard Dreyfuss would walk out of that 'Richard' on the first day of rehearsal.

"There's also the troubling character that Simon has written for Paula. Though Miss Mason comes across as a warm, intelligent, proud woman, the character of Paula becomes increasingly trivial and silly as the movie progresses. She's desperate to hang onto her lover as much because he is a meal ticket as anything else. Then, too, the child, who is

Marsha Mason, a mugging victim, is comforted by Richard Dreyfuss in Neil Simon's new comedy, "The Goodbye Girl."

precocious in perfectly acceptable ways at the beginning of the movie, slowly evolves into one of those founts of wisdom that any sane adult would immediately put up for adoption, given half a chance."

"You just don't like children," said Stanley.

"I don't like elderly children," I said. "That does go back to Mary Jane."

"Well," said Stanley, "you can't say Simon doesn't write funny lines."

"I could," I said, "but I won't. My problem with Simon's dialogue is that I find it exhausting. It's less witty than competitive. I feel all his characters are less interested in each other than in topping each other's last line. Even the men and women who are supposed to love each other. Listening to them is like eavesdropping on a poker game at the Beverly Hillcrest Country Club. About halfway through 'The Goodbye Girl,' the characters disappear and the only voice you hear is Simon's."

"But it's still funny," said Stanley. "What do you want?"

"I keep wanting something better."

"How would Mary Jane Harovski put it?"

"She could put it either way but she either way would be decisive: 'Neil Simon is the funniest man writing for the English-speaking theater today,' or 'Neil Simon's tiny gift is for the rootless contemporary wisecrack.' She wouldn't equivocate."

There was a pause.

Stanley: "Do you have any further thoughts about Neil Simon?"

"No." ■

1977 D 4, II:13:1

Doubleheader

NOMADIC LIVES, a program of two films: "Clown White," directed by John Walker, with Bruce Elliot as Keno. Running time: 47 minutes. "Nomadic Lives," directed and written by Mark Obenhaus, with Marcia Jean Kurtz and James Carrington. Running time: 60 minutes. At the Film Forum, 15 Vandam Street.

By VINCENT CANBY

NARRATIVE FILMS of less than feature length are not often programmed either by television, where time slots are filled with series material, or by theaters, whose managers prefer to supplement their features with refreshment breaks or with industrial films of the sort that explore the romance of synthetic fibers.

Short narrative films have no place to put down roots. It is appropriate, then, that "Nomadic Lives" should be the collective title of the Film Forum's new program devoted to two less-than-feature-length movies, Mark Obenhaus's 60-minute "Nomadic Lives" and John Walker's 47-minute "Clown White."

Watching them one begins to realize why such films are so rare—they are immensely difficult to bring off successfully. Like "Clown White," they may be too long to be decisive or, like "Nomadic Lives," not long enough to be as fully developed as the material deserves.

•

Having expressed these reservations, I should quickly point out that Mr. Obenhaus's "Nomadic Lives" has some things to recommend it, including its two leading performers, Marcia Jean Kurtz, a highly gifted actress who has the advantage of not looking like any other actress you've ever seen, and James Carrington, who looks like dozens of other handsome actors but who manages to find the idiosyncrasies of what might be called a type.

They play Gretchen and Wesley, a young go-go dancer and a quick-sketch artist who share a New Jersey trailer-home and, in the course of the movie, appear to be coming apart in mutual boredom. Of the two, Gretchen is especially funny and appealing. Trudging through the early morning mess in her trailer, Gretchen looks like a skinny, disgruntled City College dropout. In her fancy wig, false eyelashes and go-go costume, she's a reasonable facsimile of a would-be hooker.

As Miss Kurtz and Mr. Carrington fight, reconcile and fight again, they create two almost prototypical characters of today's aimless, affluent society. Yet having presented us with characters, the movie does nothing with them. Mr. Obenhaus, who made this film on a joint commission from French and German television interests, has a feeling for time, place and people. The next thing is make a movie with them.

•

"Clown White" depends less on character than on the local color of rural Texas. Part of it appears to have been staged for the movie, part of it photographed as a straight documentary. The film records the travels of a one-man Texas traveling show featuring Keno (Bruce Elliot), a young stocky fellow who puts on white-face make-up, funny hats and does stand-up routines for schoolchildren. As Mr. Walker shows us, Keno's life is a dreary succession of less-than-riotous performances, followed by lonely nights in sleazy motels.

"Clown White" is Mr. Walker's first film and looks it. The material is raw unrefined, suggesting no particular feeling or point of view, which is not the same as presenting us with life as it is. A movie without a point of view tends to make its subject look distant and small, as if seen through the wrong end of a telescope, and thus unimportant.

"Nomadic Lives," which opened at the Film Forum yesterday, will be seen there tonight through Sunday at 7:45 and at the same time next week Thursday through Sunday.

1977 D 9, C12:4

FILM VIEW

VINCENT CANBY

NO ROOM FOR LAUGHTER OR LOVE

f all the national film movements that have surfaced in Europe since the end of World War II, none has exhibited the consistent ferocity of the half-dozen young German directors whose work now more or less defines—for us on this side of the Atlantic—the long-awaited renaissance of

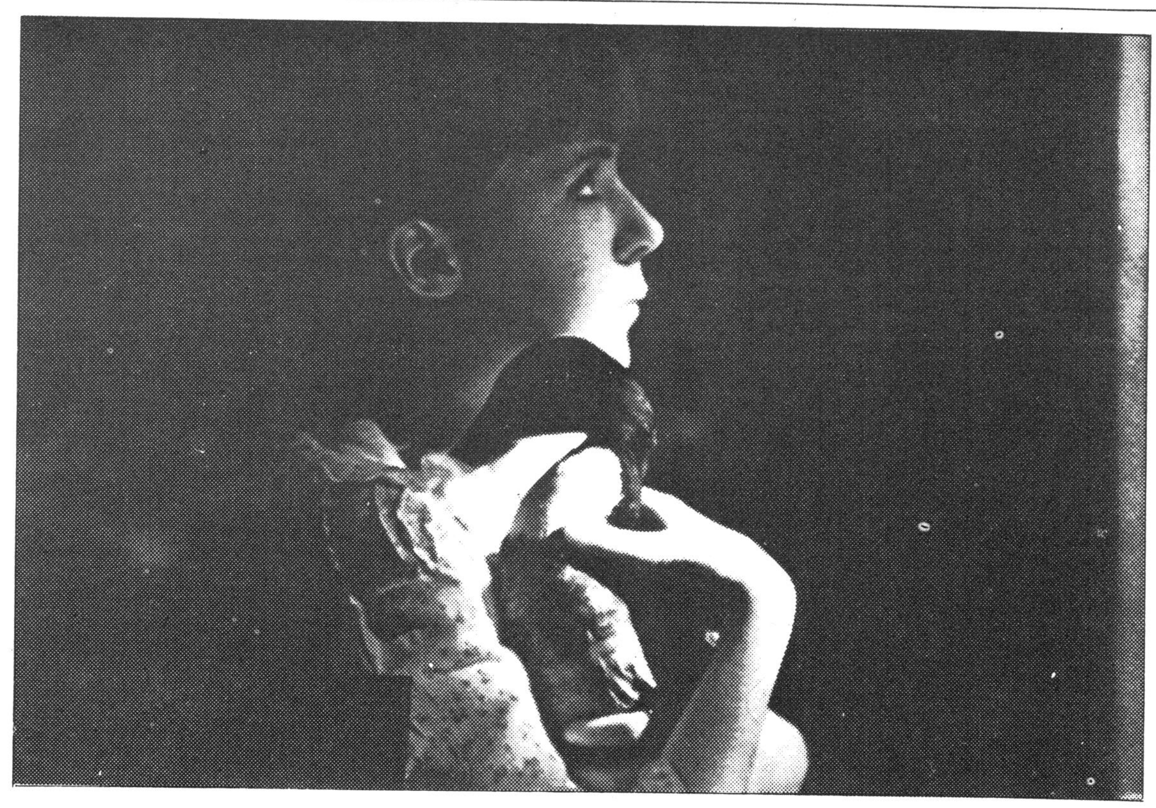

Geissendorfer's "Wild Duck"—"a painless introduction to today's German cinema."

the German film. "It's a very different kind of renaissance from any others we've seen in movies. For one thing, none of the young Germans has made much of a dent at theater box offices at home or abroad. It's not simply that they don't feed on popular support; they seem to go out of their way to spurn it, as if such success would be a sign of artistic failure or moral weakness. Though these directors—Rainer Werner Fassbinder, Werner Herzog, Wim Wenders, Volker Schlondorff, among others—have as their only easily defined common denominator the humanist's outrage with the quality of life in West Germany today, their revolutionary zeal tends to make their work elitist, either incomprehensible to mass movie audiences or too harsh and rigorous for people who still consider films as a means of escape. Perhaps in no other country today is there such a gulf between the artist and his public.

These impressions are prompted by the recent German film retrospective at the Cinema Studio and by experience limited almost entirely to the films themselves. The impressions are particular, isolated, virtually virginal.

Trying to get a fix on the state of German film art—and on the state of Germany—from the vantage point of New York is like studying a star 2,000 light-years away. One can't be sure that the star we're seeing still exists. When we describe the star, we're talking history. Distance is time frozen, and in the case of Germany it's frozen in wildly differing attitudes, pleasant and unpleasant, idiotic and profoundly disturbing, depending on the information received. On any New York neighborhood street, Germany is a series of parked Volkswagens, which seem to be every third car on New York's Upper West Side. On our radios Germany is tourism commercials such as the one featuring the woman with the sexy voice who tells us in a manner that is meant to be disarming, "I can't help it . . . I'm falling in love again . . . I can't help it!" But after she tells us she's falling in love again with Germany, with the mountains and the villages and the cities and the museums and especially with the people (because "they're so nice and friendly and so many speak English"), my thoughts have a way of turning to Auschwitz or to the activities of the Baader-Meinhof gang. This is not, I suspect, what the ad agency intended.

My impressions, of course, are inevitably influenced as much by the era in which I was born and grew up (between the two wars with Germany) as by the films I've been seeing and find, for the most part, fascinating and original, sometimes mystifying and often very scary.

Insofar as the work of a half dozen directors of very different natures can be lumped together for convenient analysis, the new German film is unsentimental, occasionally cruel, largely loveless and, though often witty, hardly ever funny. Offhand, I can think of only two German films, Herzog's "Stroszek" and Alexander Kluge's "Strongman Ferdinand," that have made me laugh out loud. Briefly. They are very different from the films that have characterized the sudden coming of age of film talents in other countries.

The great Italian neorealists—Rossellini, Fellini (in his early films), Visconti—burst upon the postwar international scene like prisoners suddenly released not from the darkness of dungeons but from the boredom of bureaucratic waiting rooms, their social and political concerns exalted by the exuberance they felt on being at long-last free. Though they acknowledged the existence of evil, they recognized the possibility of heroism. Lindsay Anderson, Tony Richardson, Karel Reisz and the other English directors of the late 50's were angry and young, and they were intensely serious about what they were doing to a class system that was as emotionally inhibiting as it was economically and socially, but the films they made were often mercilessly funny. Francois Truffaut, Jean-Luc Godard, Claude Chabrol and the other members of France's New Wave were (at the beginning, anyway) reacting not to society-at-large but to society-at-small, to the tradition of what they called "quality" filmmaking, which, they felt, had stifled the French cinema and imposed a set of fake standards upon directors. Even so, one way and another, conventional love made their films go round.

• • •

It's extremely dangerous to speculate about the factors that have shaped the interests, needs and talents of the members of the new German cinema, though a few generalizations can be made. They all belong to the post-Hitler generation, even those who were born before the war. They grew up carrying the burden of a guilt that was not necessarily theirs, either resenting it or, in fleeting moments, embracing it, while being witness to an economic recovery that had the appearance (to them) of turning back the clock at least part of the way. In Fassbinder's films like "Mother Kusters Goes to Heaven" and "Why Does Herr R. Run Amok?" the voracious appetite of the consuming capitalistic society is the Final Solution for the human spirit.

Though the affluence of postwar Germany has made possible the emergence of the new German cinema, the numbing effect of this affluence is probably the one thing on which the new German filmmakers could agree. Fassbinder is scathing in his criticism, though he makes films about it with the enthusiasm of a spoiled little rich boy seeing how far he can go before he gets his knuckles rapped. Fassbinder is also fascinated by the power games played by the decadents, by their

Fassbinder's "Effi Briest"—"preoccupied with power and society"

dress, decor and manners, things that give his films a Manichean quality that puts many people off. It's as if he weren't serious. He is, but he's still young enough (early 30's) to feel that he doesn't have to wear his heart on his sleeve. That's for the bourgeoisie, and you can't trust them.

• • •

Equally serious is Werner Herzog, perhaps the most accomplished and most lyrical of the young German directors, a man who sometimes cloaks his humane concerns in parables so personal that he seems to have reached the absolute dead-end of cinema, which, too, could be interpreted as a comment on the society that bred him. His newest film, "Heart of Glass," now at the Cinema Studio, is to me incomprehensible if beautiful. "Fata Morgana" is a feature-length lament for the world in terms of a documentary about the disintegration of the Sahara Desert. Most of us worry that Kansas may be turning into a desert. Herzog worries about preserving the desert—he's one step ahead of us.

In his best films Herzog's severe visions are made to seem terrifying and extraordinarily lovely, as in "Aguirre, The Wrath of God," about the mad Spanish conquistador, and especially in "Stroszek," the story of three misfit German immigrants in northern Wisconsin, which comes as close to being a heartwarming comedy as any member of the new German cinema has made.

• • •

There have been other comedies but none that would make the heart leap up, even an inch. Alexander Kluge's "Strongman Ferdinand" takes a lot of fast satirical swipes at German society through a tale about a fellow who almost destroys society by being such a stickler for the order that preserves it. Fassbinder's one attempt to make us laugh, "Satan's Brew," was an elephantine failure in which a typical recurring sight gag was the appearance of the beautiful Margit Carstensen wearing moles all over her face. Humor is not the strong point of any of the German directors. Passion—controlled and disciplined to an eerie degree—is. One sometimes feels these filmmakers are hanging onto their sanity by their finger tips.

This is the feeling one takes away from Wim Wenders's remarkable film adaptation of Peter Handke's "The Goalie's Anxiety at the Penalty Kick," perhaps the most effective screen realization of a novel of social and emotional disorientation ever made, and to a lesser extent from his "The American Friend," a stunningly beautiful mystery film that seems to want to be conventional. "The American Friend" often looks and sounds like a mystery film but the continuity is such a mess we forget the mystery and contemplate instead the peculiarly ambiguous relationship between two very different sorts of men, an American con artist and a German picture-frame maker, which is the film's heart. Says Wenders, life is a joke that, if we're lucky, we recognize.

Volker Schlondorff appears to be an especially solemn filmmaker if only because his movies lack the dazzle and impudence of Fassbinder, the metaphysical concerns of Herzog and the almost drugged, icy calm of Wenders. Unlike Fassbinder, Herzog and Wenders, Schlondorff never seems to discover anything in the course of his films that he hasn't planned in advance. There are no surprises for him and few for us. He constructs movies the way a writer might sketch the points to be covered in an editorial against the North Atlantic Treaty Organization.

Yet his films aren't silly. "Young Torless" is a passionate, angry contemplation of Prussian militarism in the form of a story about life in a pre-World War I boys' boarding school. "The Lost Honor of Katharina Blum," an adaptation of Heinrich Boll's novel, is a furious attack on yellow journalism (and the society that supports it). Of all the new German directors, Schlondorff is the only one who has attempted to interest himself in feminist subjects.

Two other directors aren't as easily identified with the main trends of the new German cinema but they belong in the group because of their talent and discipline. One is Jean-Marie Straub, whose minimalist cinema is impossible to sit through except when he is focussing our attention on music, as in "The Chronicle of Anna Magdalena Bach" and in his screen record of Schoenberg's "Moses and Aaron" (when, of course, the effect is not minimal at all but glorious). The other director is Hans W. Geissendorfer, whose stylish vampire film, "Jonathan," was seen here five years ago, and who more recently directed the extremely intelligent, German-language screen version of "The Wild Duck," starring Bruno Ganz (of "The American Friend") and Jean Seberg.

•

Though Geissendorfer's two films would provide an easy, completely painless introduction to today's German cinema, they would not be especially typical of a movement whose members seem to have approached the abyss, looked over the side and drawn back, at least temporarily. To obtain a more accurate impression of what's going on, I'd advise starting out with any (or all) of the films mentioned above, plus two more by Fassbinder. One is "Katzelmacher," an early work adapted by Fassbinder from his own one-act play, about a group of lazy lower-middle-class lay-abouts who couple less often for fun than for profit, who indulge their racial prejudices (against a Greek migrant worker) much as they play pinball machines—to pass the time. It's beautifully acted by the Fassbinder stock company and staged by the director as formally as if it were a minuet. Also, "Effi Briest," Fassbinder's elegant adaptation of the Theodor Fontane novel, which, though set in the 1890's, is as preoccupied with power and society as any of his films with contemporary settings.

One should also make a point of seeing two extraordinary short films by Herzog, "The Great Ecstasy of the Sculptor Steiner," about a champion ski jumper whose obsession threatens to be the end of him, and "La Soufrière," about an old man on the Caribbean island of Guadeloupe who refused to leave his shack a year ago when the volcano, Soufrière, was expected to blow its top. This film is not only about the people who refused to flee but also about the thousands who did. It is typical of the manner in which Herzog works in this film that though we never see one of the refugees, their absence and that of civilization are as dramatically felt as the poetic resignation of the people who stayed. ■

1977 D 11, II:15:1

PHANTOM BARON, directed by Serge de Poligny; dialogue by Jean Cocteau (French with English subtitles); screenplay by Mr. Cocteau and Mr. De Poligny; editor, Jean Feyte; cinematographter, Roger Hubert; produced by Consortium de Productions de Films; released by Raymond Rohauer; at the Bleecker Street Cinema, 144 Bleecker Street. Running time: 100 minutes. This film is not rated.

Baron Carol	Jean Cocteau
Herve	Alain Cuny
Elfy	Odette Joyeux
Anne	Jany Holt
Alberic	Claude Samval

By JANET MASLIN

"The Phantom Baron" is a fairy tale that *ends* with the words "once upon a time," but that's the least of its eccentricities. Written by Jean Cocteau, and nominally directed by Serge de Poligny (Cocteau is known to have directed parts of the film himself), it combines the structure of an ordinary fable with the nebulous spirit of a sweet dream. Characters who are fully identified remain perplexingly unknowable, and no situation is ever quite what it seems to be. Yet Cocteau's screenplay is drawn with such delicacy that the film's warmth and generosity override its cool fascination with sleight-of-hand.

•

In this 1943 production, now having its New York theatrical premiere at the Bleecker Street Cinema, the baron of the title is played by Cocteau himself. He vanishes mysteriously in his own chateau, leaving behind a very knowing-looking black cat. His family, including a countess and her young daughter and stepdaughter, come to live on the estate, which is photographed in shadow and on a tilt, and which is made to look as haunted as an estate can possibly be. The girls immediately befriend a young servant boy, Herve.

Years later, they both begin to fall in love with him. However, they are also a little bit in love with the dashing soldier Alberic, (Claude Samval), whose confident manner makes Herve (Alain Cuny) seem especially withdrawn by comparison. The young women seem somewhat alike at first, but the heiress Elfy (Odette Joyeux) gradually reveals herself to be more frivolous than the lovely and generous Anne (Jany Holt).

The actors swirl in and out of

Jack Nisberg

Jean Cocteau
His screenplay is drawn with delicacy.

character, and the romantic alignments shift subtly and often, until the circumstances surrounding the baron's mysterious death are explained. It seems he deliberately sealed himself inside a cellar (his death was "somewhat Egyptian," someone remarks), and left behind a will that untangles the plot's many questions of identity. His legacy should be one of clarity, but the film's concluding note is more one of wise and joyful acceptance, and of long-delayed understanding of the way things have always been.

•

There is a thin, almost satirical wit to the stylized opening of the story, but it is not until later that a mood of maturity is established, and the more breathless segment of the story begins. The loveliest scene, an extravagantly romantic one, shows a dream shared by Anna and Herve, he carrying her across a misty "Wuthering Heights"-style landscape and she in a white gown with a long flowing veil. The ecstasy of the moment is unequaled by anything else here, but it is so extravagantly lovely that its radiance goes a long way.

1977 D 12, 52:1

Screen: Puzzling 'Heart of Glass'

"Heart of Glass," which was shown at the New York Film Festival, was reviewed on Oct. 1 by Janet Maslin. Following are excerpts from the review. The picture opened yesterday at Cinema Studio, 1966 Broadway, at 66th Street.

"Heart of Glass" has an undeniable loveliness, but it is almost entirely indecipherable. Werner Herzog hypnotized an entire cast to film this parable about a medieval town that has thrived by producing ruby-colored glass, until the only man who knows the formula dies. After that, the town goes mad trying to recapture its lost glory.

The film is much less accessible than Mr. Herzog's best work, and often it is downright obscure. The actors' trance is contagious, though, and that has both its soporific qualities and its advantages. The film contains some genuinely mesmerizing moments, as when the town seer, whose words have made little sense previously, suddenly begins to predict an alarmingly recognizable future.

At times the script reads like a collection of nonsequiturs."Do you want our people to eat oatmeal bread again, that gives them headaches?" asks one character. "Rats will bite your earlobes," someone swears.

The film is unflaggingly meticulous—every trace of red anywhere, even on the head of a goose, is clearly planned. But even its color scheme, though easy enough to notice, is hard to fathom.

1977 D 12, 49:3

Cliche That Touches

SATURDAY NIGHT FEVER, directed by John Badham; screenplay by Norman Wexler, based on a story by Nik Cohn; director of photography, Ralf D. Bode; editor, David Rawlins; musical numbers staged and choreographed by Lester Wilson; additional music and adaptation by David Shire; original music by Barry Robin and Maurice Gibb; produced by Robert Stigwood; released by Paramount Pictures. At Loews State 1, Broadway and 45th Street; Loews Cine, Third Avenue at 86th Street and 34th Street East, east of Third Avenue. Running time: 119 minutes. This film is classified R.

Tony Manero.............................John Travolta
Stephanie.........................Karen Lynn Gorney
Bobby C.................................Barry Miller
Joey....................................Joseph Call
Double J...................................Paul Pape
Annette.................................Donna Pescow

By JANET MASLIN

TONY IS A HANDSOME, big-hearted guy with a lot more style than he knows what to do with. His job in a paint store doesn't call for much élan, but Tony supplies that anyway, charming the customers and strutting gamely down the street as he makes his deliveries. His room at home is dreary and his family even more so, but Tony has done what he can with Farrah and Rocky and Pacino posters to give the place a little class. Even so, things can get him down—but just when they do, another week is over and it's time to hit the local disco. On the weekend, and on the dance floor, Tony is king.

Tony's whole life, as somebody else in "Saturday Night Fever" manages to point out, is "a cliché." But John Travolta is so earnestly in tune with the character that Tony becomes even more touching than he is familiar and a source of fierce, desperate excitement. The movie, which spends mercifully little time trying to explain Tony, has a violent energy very like his own.

•

This is best demonstrated during the dancing sequences, which take up much of the film's time. Tony is depicted as being better than most, but also one of many; everyone in the 2001 Odyssey disco in Bay Ridge, Brooklyn, seems possessed of a similar short-term vitality and pride. Their dancing is fluid, but it's also strictly, almost militaristically choreographed; people who stake everything on style can't afford to be sloppy, or even genuinely boisterous. Though the dancing is set to a blaring, contemporary score and often photographed in a red glow, the movie owes a lot more to "West Side Story" than it does to "Mean Streets."

Mr. Travolta dances with a fine arrogance that follows naturally from the rest of his performance, and he has one solo number that stops the show. But John Badham, who previously directed another stylish, street-smart movie, "The Bingo Long Travelling All-Stars and Motor Kings," isn't always content to let the simple energy of the music or the performances suffice. Too often, he cuts distractingly in the middle of a routine, and his efforts to aggrandize characters by shooting them at angles or from below are superfluous. If these kids weren't flamboyant enough on their own, no amount of camera tricks could cover for them.

•

"Saturday Night Fever," which opens today at several theaters, begins to flag when, after an initial hour filled with high spirits and jubilant music, it settles down to tell its story; the effect is so deflating that it's almost as though another Monday has rolled around and it's time to get back to work.

It seems that Tony's friends, who are a lively but uninteresting lot are so dead-ended that they're beginning to make him worry about his own future. And Stephanie (Karen Lynn Gorney), who has a job in Manhattan, is such a braggart that she has begun to give him notions of upward mobility.

Ten minutes into the movie, you can be sure that its ending will be at least partly upbeat and that whatever happens will be blunt. But that is still no preparation for all the gruesome tricks Norman Wexler's screenplay uses to get Tony out of Brooklyn.

Surely there are some people who make decisions without needing to be spurred on by a serious family trauma, an exceedingly ugly sexual episode and a friend's leap off the Verrazano Bridge. Tony, from what we've seen of him, is too proud and sensitive to need this much disillusionment to get him moving, but the screenplay has a way of indirectly insulting the character by coddling him far more than he would ever coddle himself.

•

Mr. Travolta is deft and vibrant, and he never condescends to the character, not even in a scene that has Tony and Stephanie arguing about whose "Romeo and Juliet" it is, Zeffirelli's or Shakespeare's. (They also try to identify Sir Laurence Olivier, and then remember that he's the guy who sells cameras on television.) Miss Gorney uses a much thicker accent and many more mispronunciations, and too often she is transparent in playing dumb. Donna Pescow, as one of the many local girls whom Tony could have but doesn't want, stays much more comfortably within the boundaries of her role.

Among the movie's most influential principals—although they never appear on screen—are the Bee Gees, who provided the most important parts of its score. It could be argued that the Bee Gees have been turning out the kinds of jaunty, formulaic disco hits that punctuate the movie for so long that they've lost any trace of originality. But it could also be argued that the group now has this kind of music down to a science, and that originality is not exactly a key ingredient in the disco mystique. In any case, at its best, the music moves with a real spring in its step, and the movie does too.

John Travolta in Bay Ridge in "Saturday Night Fever"
Desperate excitement and violent energy

1977 D 16, C10:1

TELEFON, directed by Don Siegel; screenplay by Peter Hyams and Stirling Silliphant, based on the novel by Walter Wager; produced by James B. Harris; music, Lalo Schifrin; director of photography, Michael Butler; editor, Douglas Stewart; distributed by United Artists. Running time: 100 minutes. At the Rivoli Theater, Broadway at 49th Street; Loew's 83d Street Theater, Broadway at 83d Street; Loew's Orpheum, 86th Street near Third Avenue, and other theaters. This film has been rated PG.

Grigori Borzov ....Charles Bronson
Barbara ....Lee Remick
Nicolai Dalchimsky ....Donald Pleasence
Dorothy Putterman ....Tyne Daly
Col. Malchenko ....Alan Badel
Gen. Strelsky ....Patrick Magee
Marie Wills ....Sheree North
Harley Sandburg ....Frank Marth
Emma Stark ....Helen Page Camp
Doug Stark ....Roy Jenson
Mrs. Hassler ....Jacqueline Scott
Carl Hassler ....Ed Bakey
Harry Bascom ....John Mitchum
Father Stuart Diller ....Iggie Wolfington
Mrs. Maloney ....Kathleen O'Malley
Lt. Alexandrov ....Ake Lindman
Dalchimsky's mother ....Ansa Konen

By VINCENT CANBY

There are a lot of things working against Don Siegel's "Telefon," including its title, which as easily suggests one of Jerry Lewis's marathon television specials as it does the material with which skillets are lined so that eggs won't stick. "Telefon," of course, has to do with neither.

It's the Russian code name for a sabotage plan so unbelievable that the actors, when they must explain it to us in the course of the film, actually seem to be embarrassed. They know that we know that they know that it's tall-tale-time in the Kremlin—shared knowledge that has the effect of disarming solemn criticism and inviting us to succumb to the breathless nonsense as co-conspirators.

The Peter Hyams-Sterling Silliphant screenplay, based on the novel by Walter Wager, is a sort of post-Cold War update of one of John Frankenheimer's best films, "The Manchurian Candidate," though it's nowhere near as stylish. As people in such movies are inclined to say at key moments, the situation, briefly, is this:

•

During the height of the Cold War, the Soviets hypnotized and programmed about 50 agents who then were sent to the United States to lead lives as ordinary Americans, though they were, in fact, ticking time bombs. Should someone come along and whisper in their ears a few lines from Robert Frost's "Stopping by a Woods on a Snowy Evening," they'd be triggered into action to carry out a series of suicidal sabotage missions. The agents, we are told, were programmed to believe they were true-blue Americans of the sort, one assumes, who wouldn't be caught dead at poetry readings.

This plan, we are told further (and not so briefly), was junked with détente, though the agents remained in place. Thus, today, when a nutty, unreconstructed Stalinist, played by Donald Pleasence as if on leave from Charendon, decides to wreck détente by setting off these time bombs, something must be done.

In some ways, I suppose, "Telefon" is almost heart-warming. The film, which opened yesterday at the Rivoli and other theaters, is the story of how the peace-loving members of the Soviet Secret Police and the Central Intelligence Agency work together (without always knowing it) to capture the mad Stalinist and defuse the agents.

The man who does this is a dour, dedicated Soviet operative with a photographic memory, a fellow named Grigori Borzov, a role that Charles Bronson plays not much differently from the way he plays anything else, but which I now find I can respond to. Mr. Bronson is a movie actor of the old school. He doesn't seem to act (though that is what he's doing) as much as he inhabits a film with his particular, massive presence, giving the film much-needed ballast. Without him, "Telefon" would fly up to the ceiling and just hang there.

As his resident contact in America, Lee Remick is as likely a Soviet spy as Janet Leigh was once a Soviet pilot (Von Sternberg's "Jet Pilot"), but she's pretty and game and very cheery company, even with the screenplay's failed attempts at breezy dialogue.

•

"Telefon" is one of those movies that can't sit still. It moves from Moscow to Denver to Washington to Moscow to Los Angeles like a spy with the fidgets. While it's rather fun anticipating what disguise Mr. Pleasence is next going to turn up in (I think I favor his blond toupee and sneakers), some of the other supporting actors are more difficult to take. Patrick Magee plays a Soviet intelligence chief as if he were in a revue sketch, and the people who play C.I.A. types look so bland and empty you may suspect that they, too, have been hypnotized by the KGB.

Mr. Siegel ("Dirty Harry") is not a director whose light touch is always sure, though "Two Mules for Sister Sara" and "Charley Varrick" were very entertaining. He needs good screenplays and room in which to build action sequences. Though there are action sequences in "Telefon," they are never sustained, and the screenplay only occasionally comes up with witty substitutes for the missing plausibility. However, to describe "Telefon" as synthetic is to take it more seriously than it's taken by anyone connected with it.

•

"Telefon" has been rated PG ("Parental Guidance Suggested"). It has isolated moments of explosive action and some blood, but nothing that would shock a child or a Soviet censor.

1977 D17, 20:1

FILM VIEW

VINCENT CANBY

Why 'Smokey And the Bandit' Is Making A Killing

Something curious is happening to country movies. Like country music, they are becoming a big, respectable if still largely unpublicized business. In recent years "Macon County Line" has earned $10,000,000. "Dirty Mary Crazy Larry" brought in $14,700,000, while "Walking Tall," the film based on the life of the late Tennessee sheriff, Buford T. Pusser, has earned $17,000,000 and its first sequel (there have been two) $11,000,000. Now, according to Variety, "Smokey and the Bandit" has brought in close to $36,000,000 in domestic rentals since its release in May.

What? You've never heard of "Smokey and the Bandit"? It's not the sort of movie that's talked about at cocktail parties. Yet it did play at Radio City Music Hall and it does star Burt Reynolds, one of the few major actors who crosses over between country movies and conventionally acceptable films. More important, perhaps, "Smokey and the Bandit" would appear to be the second most popular American film of the year, topped only by "Star Wars," which is topping everything, including "Jaws," "The Godfather," "The Sound of Music" and "The Birth of a Nation." Some attention should be paid.

• • •

More than fancier, big-budget movies that receive front-cover treatment in the news magazines and are widely publicized on TV talk shows, country movies tell us about the state of mind of a large part of our union. They are the movies supported—often exclusively—by people who live in the rural South, Southwest and Middle West, people who see most of their movies in drive-ins and respond, I suspect, to the nonstop action (which is often just movement), to the colorful, heightened vulgarity of the language and who feel most at home in the country movie's principal setting: the automobile. Because a country movie is seldom three or even two years in the making, it appears to be more closely in touch with its audience than more ambitious films. The country movie aims to please and will bust a gut doing it.

"Smokey and the Bandit" is not your average country movie but it, and a new country movie, "Thunder and Lightning," which is about Florida moonshiners, are virtually quintessential in that everything of importance takes place either in/on a vehicle or in the immediate vicinity of one. When Will Rogers predicted that America would be the first nation to ride to the poorhouse in an automobile, he wasn't reckoning on the shock absorbers built into the time-payment system. No one can go broke as long as there is a single friendly finance company to keep the faith. Country movies like "Smokey and The Bandit" and "Thunder and Lightning" evoke something much more profound than economic theories. They show us that America is the first nation to find heaven on the highway. Heaven is no longer a destination. It's something experienced en route.

"Smokey and the Bandit" and "Thunder and Lightning" are, among other things, a good deal of benign if brainless fun, something that represents a dramatic change in mood from most of the post-"Easy Rider" country movies. Though I realize that "Easy Rider" wasn't strictly a country movie, the country it called attention to—Southern, rural, bigoted, fatal to all self-styled free spirits—provided landscapes for the majority of the country movies that came after, including "Macon County Line," "Jackson County Jail" and "Dirty Mary Crazy Larry." These movies merchandized violence and arbitrary death as basic ingredients of the American system. A bloody massacre was as obligatory at the end as the fadeout clinch had once been in comedies of the 30's and 40's.

The ads for "Easy Rider" told us that "a man went looking for America and found it wasn't there." If that film's fuzziness could be read for political meanings, "Easy Rider" was left-wing in ways that corresponded to the antiwar, anti-Nixon sentiments of the late 60's and early 70's.

In "Smokey and the Bandit" Burt Reynolds, playing a locally legendary truck driver, a fellow whose CB name is Bandit, accepts an $80,000 bet to drive from Georgia to Texas and back in 28 hours, a 1,800-mile round trip, to fetch 400 cases of Coors beer that can't be legally distributed east of Texas. "Smokey (the CB'ers nickname for the police) and the Bandit"—the account of this mostly uproarious trip—is about a man who goes looking for beer and finds an America that is a barrel of laughs. He also finds a sweet, quirky young woman (nicely played by Sally Field), a bride-to-be fleeing from the church in all her veils, who becomes his life's highway companion. The movie is one long, seldom interrupted chase.

So too is "Thunder and Lightning," about an honorably independent Everglades bootlegger, played by David Carradine, his girl friend (Kate Jackson) and his girl friend's father (Roger C. Carmel) who spend a large part of the movie pursuing (in order to destroy) a truckload of poisoned moonshine while they, in turn, are pursued by a pair of bungling Mafia types.

The landscapes that the characters in "Smokey and the Bandit" and "Thunder and Lightning" pass through never change, no matter how many miles are covered, yet it's a radically different rural America from the one discovered by Dennis Hopper and Peter Fonda in "Easy Rider." There still are red-neck cops all over the place and they still are bigoted, like the one in "Smokey" played by Jackie Gleason with a series of Edgar Kennedy-like slow-burns, but now the villains have been defused. They are joke-cops, forever destined to be outwitted, led astray, out-maneuvered, out-driven and at the climax—in the unkindest cut of all—to have their vehicles mangled or their tires shot out from under them, which, of course, renders a man impotent when man and machine are recognized as one.

Why should "Smokey and the Bandit" become a box office hit of such huge proportions when other, more or less similar country movies haven't done anywhere near as well? It may be that Burt Reynolds in this sort of film is box office while Burt Reynolds in the over-produced, under-thought-out "Lucky Lady" is not. Though his performance as the Bandit is not much different in character from the one he gave in "Lucky Lady," the surroundings suit him better. As in his new "Semi-Tough," the surroundings are down-home and in them he gives an easy, relaxed, genially self-assured performance that never upstages the film.

There also is evidence of a certain wit in the material, written by James Lee Barret, Charles Silver and Alan Mandel, and directed by Hal Needham. If I heard the dialogue correctly, some of it is almost surreal, as when one man says to another of Bandit's trailer-rig, which has a huge, sylvan landscape on the side, "Any guy who'd paint his truck like that would go to a minister's funeral in feathers." Or, as Bandit says to a woman who has curlers in her hair, "They make me think you're listening to a radio station in Savannah." People in these movies are seldom at a loss for words, and the words in "Smokey" are often funny.

Even more significant, perhaps, is that nobody in either "Smokey and the Bandit" or in "Thunder and Lightning" ever gets killed or even permanently damaged in epic fist fights or on the highway, though cars are smashed up continually and no one ever thinks twice about passing another car on a blind curve or on a hill. In "Smokey and the Bandit" the top of the automobile Jackie Gleason is driving, with his idiot son at his side, is sheered off but are the two men decapitated? No. Only inconvenienced and made ridiculous.

Today's country movies depict a land quite as far removed from reality as the universe of Bugs Bunny, a place where none of the familiar physical laws (especially gravity) holds true to the extent that consequences must be fatal. I suppose that such extravagant optimism can be interpreted as a shift toward the right. As politics they may be naive, but as movies they are a welcome change from the movies of mayhem and murder of the post-"Easy Rider" years. Those films were just as naive but, being gloomy, they tended to intimidate audiences into taking them seriously. ■

1977 D 18, II:13:5

Gene Wilder and Carol Kane in scene from "The World's Greatest Lover"
As satisfying as cloud-watching

THE WORLD'S GREATEST LOVER, directed, written and produced by Gene Wilder; co-producer and production designer, Terence Marsh; co-producer and supervising film editor, Chris Greenbury; music, John Morris; director of photography, Gerald Hirschfield; editor, Anthony A. Pellegrino; distributed by 20th Century-Fox. Running time: 89 minutes. At the Beekman Theater, Second Avenue at 65th Street; Paramount Theater, Broadway at 61st Street, and Murray Hill Theater, 34th Street near Third Avenue. This film has been rated PG.

Rudy Valentine	Gene Wilder
Annie	Carol Kane
Zitz	Dom De Luise
Hotel manager	Fritz Feld
Cousin Buddy	Cousin Buddy
Maid	Hannah Dean
Anne Calassandro	Candice Azzara
Uncle Harry	Carl Ballantine
Rudolph Valentino	Matt Collins
Mr. Kipper	Lou Cutell
Room clerk	James Gleason
Director	Ronny Graham
Barber	Michael Huddleston
Aunt Tillie	Florence Sundstrom

By VINCENT CANBY

There's a scene in "A Boy Named Charlie Brown," the 1969 feature film based on the Peanuts characters, in which Lucy, Linus and Charlie Brown are lying on their backs, freely associating as they watch the clouds roll by. Charlie Brown sees horsies and duckies in the clouds. Linus can make out the stoning of St. Stephen "and, down in one corner, the profile of Thomas Eakins, the 19th-century American portrait painter." Lucy, though she's as much at ease as she ever manages to be, is reminded only of wads of cotton. One feels sorry for poor Lucy, her appreciation of fantasy severely limited by an awareness that she is life's umpire.

A comedy like Gene Wilder's "The World's Greatest Lover" is not for the Lucies of this world. Rather it's for people whose spirits more or less match those of Mr. Wilder, an imaginative fellow who tries to control his madness and, when he fails, comes forth with a movie. First there was "Sherlock Holmes's Smarter Brother" and now "The World's Greatest Lover"—movies in what may be described as the "melbrooks" manner in honor of Mr. Wilder's occasional collaborator and the director of his funniest performance (in "Young Frankenstein").

•

Watching "The World's Greatest Lover" is about as cheerful and satisfying a substitute for cloud-watching as I can imagine. It's also frequently side-splitting and, when it's not causing physical damage, so full of intelligent associations that it would hold the attention of someone with interests as varied as those of Linus.

"The World's Greatest Lover" was produced, written and directed by Mr. Wilder, who also plays the title role, that of an ambitious but desperately neurotic Milwaukee baker who, in 1926, sets out to become the new Rudolph Valentino.

Rudy Valentine is not at first glance—or second or even third—a likely prospect. His face looks like a coconut on which someone has drawn a pair of blue eyes and pasted a Harpo wig. Then, too, in moments of stress he's inclined to invert the words of a sentence or, worse, to stick out his tongue, a gesture that's misunderstood in public places.

Though Rudy is maniacally ambitious, he's very insecure, a failing that is not helped by his sweet but equally nutty wife Annie (Carol Kane), who writes mash notes to the real Rudolph Valentino, or by the sort of people he meets on the road to the top. These include a classically crazy hotel manager (Fritz Feld), a hyperventilating Hollywood studio chief (Dom De Luise), and assorted, mostly anonymous lunatics who would give fatal pause to anyone less self-absorbed than Rudy.

In an end credit card, Mr. Wilder thanks Federico Fellini for his encouragement in making "The World's Greatest Lover," thus acknowledging the inspiration he received from Fellini's 1950 comedy, "The White Sheik," which is also about naifs and the magic world of moviemaking, though an entirely different kind of film from the one that Mr. Wilder has made. Fellini's characters are rooted in a recognizable place and time. Mr. Wilder's live in the marvelous cloud-cuckooland of movie comedy where characters are defined by the routines and gags they survive.

"The World's Greatest Lover" has a story line, meaning that it makes narrative sense, but it moves forward through more or less accidental set-pieces, such as a hilarious sequence on the train carrying Rudy and Annie to Hollywood when Rudy, through no real fault of his own, finds himself feigning passion for an old man in a blanket.

Do Rudy and Annie love each other? Their private lives are completely spelled out in another sequence in which Rudy attempts to teach Annie how to make love with the help of a manual called "Sex by the Numbers": "Are we doing 3?" asks Annie. "You're doing 3," says Rudy, "I'm doing 8."

•

For a comedy of this kind, "The World's Greatest Lover" is uncommonly handsome, the period sets and costumes having a lot of the fantasy quality of a stylish Broadway musical. There are also moments when the film's action seems to have been choreographed, which suggests the flow of a musical as well as the movements of old-time slapstick farce. Thus even when one isn't laughing, one is beguiled.

Like Mel Brooks, Mr. Wilder always surrounds himself with fine actors. Dom De Luise and certainly the venerable Fritz Feld are known quantities, as is Ronny Graham, who is splendidly funny as a harried movie director. Miss Kane, though, is something of a revelation as a comedian—whether she is being stubborn, dim, sexy, plain or, sometimes, very, very beautiful.

•

"The World's Greatest Lover," which has been rated PG ("Parental Guidance Suggested"), contains some suggestive material that is less offensive than the copy on most perfume ads.

1977 D 19, 44:1

MOVIES TRY TO GET A HANDLE ON OUR TIMES

By JANET MASLIN

Has Richard Dreyfuss become a romantic leading man? On the evidence of "The Goodbye Girl," the answer is yes indeed. But the real question, to anyone who thinks that leading men must measure up to any fixed standards of glamour, is why.

Certainly Mr. Dreyfuss's breakthrough as a heartthrob would make perfect sense if he were tall, dark and dazzlingly handsome, but, as it happens, he is not. Mr. Dreyfuss is on the short side, a bit pudgy, and not what one might normally characterize as a looker. But he is also, in "The Goodbye Girl," warm, funny, understanding and eminently reasonable, able to be accommodating in even the most trying situations.

These days, attributes like his may be in far greater demand than the toughness and unyielding masculine self-sufficiency that used to be so stylish. These are confusing times, and characters like the one Mr. Dreyfuss plays are to be very much appreciated for the tenderness and clarity they can provide.

•

"Julia" and "The Turning Point" are both movies about friendship under fire, but it would be difficult to imagine two more opposite ways of handling the subject. The camaraderie of "Julia" is noble and flawless, astonishingly so: Seldom have two more admirable women loved each other so selflessly on the screen.

When in one scene the young Lillian (Jane Fonda) goes to visit

Shirley MacLaine, left, and Anne Bancroft in "The Turning Point"
They play two reunited friends who renew old rivalries

her cherished Julia (Vanessa Redgrave) while the latter is at the university. Lillian asks about the curriculum and Julia replies coolly that she's studying relativity. Can Julia possibly understand that stuff, Lillian wants to know? Julia says that of course she can, and shrugs. Lillian just stares at her in awe.

The women in "The Turning Point" are a lot less wonderful. When the two friends and dancers are reunited after a long separation, during which Emma (Anne Bancroft) has become a prima ballerina while Deedee (Shirley MacLaine) has raised a family and run a ballet academy, their old rivalry flares up almost immediately.

For all her fine manners and regal bearing, Emma is the ruthless and somewhat patronizing one; Deedee, for her part, is envious and sulky, yet unable to vent her frustration. Sometimes she tries, but only ineffectually: "Why is it that the problems of people like you seem so much more important than the problems of people like me? It's obvious—you're more important." Deedee says that only half glibly. When Emma begins her reply with "Well, if I am..." it's clear that she's too self-absorbed to notice.

But when Deedee is finally moved to action by Emma's efforts to outdo her as a mother, this feud-cum-friendship produces one of the most resonant and moving sequences any film has offered in a long while. The two women finally fight, first verbally and then physically, until they collapse in tears and embraces. At times like these, "The Turning Point" shows signs of unexpected wisdom: It understands that close friends are people who know each other so well that, for all the love that binds them, they can't help disliking each other a little bit, too.

"Julia," for all its excessively good intentions, has nothing more interesting to say about real friendship than "Butch Cassidy and the Sundance Kid" did. But "The Turning Point," though it is sometimes as soggy as "Julia" is dry, treats the subject with warmth, intelligence and uncommon courage.

•

On the other hand, the back-slapping cronies of "Semi-Tough" scarcely seem to have been even introduced when the movie begins, even though the screenplay insists that Shake (Kris Kristofferson) and Billy Clyde (Burt Reynolds) have been roommates and pals for quite some time. Though there's nothing directly objectionable about the nonchalance with which their relationship is drawn, it does prefigure a disturbing stoniness about the rest of this shapeless and often rather mean-spirited movie.

There is an incomprehensibly ugly moment here, one of several, that shows Billy Clyde and his teammates scorning the advances of a pathetic, unattractive woman in a bar. A while later, Billy Clyde is feeling sufficiently sorry for himself to invite this same woman up to his room—although he is greatly embarrassed when another player catches him in the act. In any case, he is at his nastiest and most mocking as he allows the woman to seduce him.

We know that Billy Clyde is upset, because his best friend and the woman they both love have just vanished into the sunset (or, more precisely, into a neighboring room at the same hotel). And we know that Billy Clyde is a hard-boiled guy. But we don't know enough to make full sense of the situation and so Billy Clyde, who is supposed to be wholly sympathetic, suddenly becomes a difficult character to like.

The director, Michael Ritchie, has made satirical movies ("Smile") and more serious ones ("The Candidate"), but he has not yet developed a talent for integrating the two moods. "Smile" ran into terrible trouble when Bruce Dern, playing a dead-serious (and hence very zany) beauty-pageant impresario, suddenly began to have real troubles with his family. In the same movie, Barbara Feldon was shot by her husband, but the scene was played so aimlessly that it was hard to know whether to laugh or cry; as a result, audiences tended to do neither. This wasn't madcap, it was merely messy.

"Semi-Tough" has the same trouble, and to an even greater degree. Mr. Ritchie's love scenes are so flippantly staged that this may be the least romantic movie about a romantic triangle ever made; on the other hand, the movie's various send-ups of self-help movements demand to be taken at least semiseriously, because of the presence of the principals. The three main characters are drawn with just enough conviction to make one at least wonder why they involve themselves in such apparent silliness.

After all, they can't merely be attending "BEAT" seminars for laughs: first of all, Mr. Ritchie doesn't make the sessions funny, and second of all, pure cynicism would be as noxious here as it is in Billy Clyde's hotel room. But Mr. Ritchie is either unwilling or unable to explain, and he places himself in an especially hot spot by alternately treating his stars as principal players and then, in the satirical scenes, almost as extras. Any audience grows tired of laughing at characters it hasn't had a chance to understand.

•

Sure, they can make Marthe Keller look shorter than Al Pacino, and sure, they can make Burt Reynolds or Kris Kristofferson look as if he had the waistline of Scarlett O'Hara. They were even able, only a few short months ago, to make "Valentino's" Michele Phillips and Rudolf Nureyev look as though they liked each other. But sometimes the artists responsible for movie posters can work their magic in more bothersome or, at the very least, more mysterious ways.

When "The Heartbreak Kid" opened several years ago, for example, the first posters for the move more or less depicted Cybill Shepherd as she really is: tall, big-boned, seductive-looking and not particularly buxom. But a few weeks later, something very strange began to happen underneath Miss Shepherd's letter sweater. Her figure blossomed, in a way that grown women's figures don't naturally do, until—shades of Raquel Welch!—it began to seem as though the movie were being marketed on the strength of an artificially inflated physique alone.

Poster-art aficionados know that this sort of thing happens to movie queens all the time. And keen-eyed adwatchers may have noticed that it is beginning to happen to Genevieve Bujold, whose shirt from "Another Man, Another Chance" has not only begun to fill out but has also turned from off-white to green.

But even though the facts of the matter are easy to document, the underlying logic remains elusive. If these women aren't thought to be attractive in their natural state, how did they get to be movie stars in the first place? If they *are* attractive, why fiddle around with a good thing? Are there really filmgoers who make their decisions about what to see based on such criteria—and, if so, don't they know there's a special part of town, and a whole movie sub-industry, that caters lavishly to their tastes? Even in this age of no-nonsense pantyhose, truth in packaging still has a long way to go.

1977 D 20, 44:1

Artistry Demystified

THE CHILDREN OF THEATER STREET, a documentary on the Kirov School directed by Robert Dornhelm; written by Beth Gutcheon; director of photography, Karl Kofler; produced and co-directed by Earle Mack; narrated by Princess Grace of Monaco; released by Peppercorn-Wormser. At the Cinema Studio, Broadway and 66th Street. Running time: 90 minutes. This film has not been rated.
WITH: Angelina Armeiskaya, Lena Vorozova,, Alec Timoushin, Michaela Cerna, Galina Messenzeva and Konstantine Zaklinsky

By JANET MASLIN

ONE of the many ballet teachers interviewed in "The Children of Theater Street" is a man who, in his youth, once saw Nijinsky. The great dancer was a student at the time, and the man being interviewed recalls how different he seemed from the others; he could leap into the air and stay aloft much longer than seemed physically possible. The man remembers, though, that Nijinsky's own teacher saw things another way. The teacher was less impressed by talent and grandeur than he was by the fact that Nijinsky never landed in time to the music.

"The Children of Theater Street," a documentary about the famed Kirov ballet school in Leningrad, is made in a spirit of which this teacher would doubtless approve. It is earnest, plodding and thoroughly earthbound, a fine illustration of how easy it is to demystify artistry by trying too hard to understand it.

We watch young students auditioning for admission to the school, and we see older ones rehearsing for their all-important graduation performance. We are casually introduced to many of their teachers. And we are told endlessy, by a narrative script read in a genteel monotone by Princess Grace of Monaco, that these children must study long and hard to achieve a level of success that will always fall short of perfection. But we are never allowed much individual insight into anyone; the film shifts its attention too erratically and often to allow any of the dancers' struggles or triumphs much meaning. This is less a sustained study than it is a series of glimpses through keyholes.

For a film about people who have dedicated their lives to the single-minded pursuit of one goal, "The Children of Theater Street" meanders to a surprising degree. Just when the director, Robert Dornhelm, seems about to single out a particular student or aspect of life at the school, the narration will make a point about dance in the 19th century and then change that subject, too. Details, when they are offered, are far from revealing: All we are told about one stocky older woman who plays the piano at dance classes is that she has been wandering the halls of the school for ages, carrying her sheet music and her purse.

The film pays particular attention to several of the students, and there is an 11-year-old girl named Angelina who takes one's breath away. With a long neck, sloe eyes and an expression of exquisite serenity, she already dances more beautifully than many of the older children we see; there's something magical about the way she always catches the eye, even in a crowd. The scenes that feature Angelina are both the loveliest here and the least successful; a spirit like hers is precisely what the film is so ill-equipped to capture.

1977 D 21, C15:4

THE GAUNTLET, directed by Clint Eastwood; screenplay by Michael Butler and Dennis Shryack; produced by Robert Daley; director of photography, Rexford Metz; editors, Ferris Webster and Joel Cox, music, Jerry Fielding; a Malpaso production, distributed by Warner Brothers. Running time: 111 minutes. At the Columbia I Theater, Second Avenue at 65th Street, and National Theater, Broadway at 43d Street. This film has been rated R.

Ben Shockley .... Clint Eastwood
Gus Mally .... Sondra Locke
Josephson .... Pat Hingle
Blakelock .... William Prince
Constable .... Bill McKinney
Feyderspiel .... Michael Cavanaugh
Waitress .... Carole Cook
Jail matron .... Mara Corday
Bookie .... Douglas McGrath
Desk sergeant .... Jeff Morris

By VINCENT CANBY

IN "THE GAUNTLET," his new film as both director and star, Clint Eastwood plays a detective in Phoenix who is described as a drunk and an incompetent. It is, you see, a character role. So, too, is that of Sondra Locke, the pretty, fresh-faced actress who made her debut in "The

Sondra Locke

Heart Is a Lonely Hunter." Miss Locke plays a Las Vegas hooker who graduated from Finch College. "The schoolgirl look is very popular right now," someone says by way of explanation.

Explanations aren't really necessary. "The Gauntlet" has nothing to do with reality and everything to do with Clint Eastwood fiction, which is always about a Force (Mr. Eastwood) that sets things straight in a crooked world.

"The Gauntlet," which opened yesterday at the Columbia I and National Theaters, is about the rigors faced by Mr. Eastwood's detective when he attempts to return the hooker from Las Vegas to Phoenix to testify at a mob trial. Along the way the detective and the girl establish a revivifying relationship (he will give up his Jack Daniel's if she gives up her johns), though the movie is more concerned with the mob's efforts to prevent them from completing their trip.

•

There are escapes in ambulances, gunfights in speeding automobiles, a helicopter attack, a ride on a stolen motorcycle and, for the climax, a sequence in which a bus, armored like the Monitor, runs a police gantlet through downtown Phoenix to reach City Hall.

It is a movie without a single thought in its head, but its action sequences are so ferociously staged that it's impossible not to pay attention most of the time. It's not simply that the film is noisy. It has a kind of violent grace, as when a house, which has been bombarded by the heavy artillery of the police, quietly gives up and collapses into fine rubble.

Michael Butler and Dennis Shryack wrote the screenplay, which exists to accommodate the mayhem much in the way that the book for a Broadway musical supports the songs. Mr. Eastwood's talent is his style, unhurried and self-assured, that of a man who goes through life looking down onto the bald spots of others. Miss Locke is not only pretty, but also occasionally genuinely funny.

In supporting roles, Pat Hingle has nothing much to do and as Mr. Eastwood's fussy, nannylike cop-friend, and William Prince models some very dapper haberdashery as the mob's highly placed contact within the Phoenix Police Department.

1977 D 22, C11:5

The Cast

PADRE PADRONE, directed by Paolo and Vittoria Taviani; screenplay (Italian with English subtitles) by Paolo and Vittorio Taviani; story outline from "Padre Padrone by Gavino Ledda; photography, Mario Masini; music, Egisto Macchi; editing, Roberto Perpignani; produced by Giuliani G. de Negri; released by Cinema V. At the Cinema 2 Theater, Third Avenue and 60th Street. Running time: 114 minutes.

Gavino's Father .... Omero Antonutti
Gavino .... Saverio Marconi
Gavino's Mother .... Marcella Michelangeli
Gavino as a Child .... Fabrizio Forte
Servant-Shepherd .... Marino Cenna
Sebastiano .... Stanko Molnar
Cesare .... Nanni Moretti

"Padre Padrone," which was shown at the New York Film Festival, was reviewed on Sept. 25 by Janet Maslin. Following are excerpts from the review. The picture opened yesterday at the Cinema 2 Theater, Third Avenue and 60th Street.

By JANET MASLIN

Paolo and Vittorio Taviani, the two brothers who wrote and directed "Padre Padrone," say they first got the idea for their film from a newspaper clipping—about a shepherd who had lived in almost complete isolation in the hills of Sardinia until he turned 20, then went on to become a professor of linguistics and write a book about his experience.

When the brothers learned more about the man's story, they began to perceive him not as an unsocialized innocent à la Truffaut's "The Wild Child" or Herzog's "The Mystery of Kasper Hauser," but rather as a more conventional figure whose character was shaped through his battle with a single huge impediment. The obstacle in "Padre Padrone" is not the shepherd's estrangement, or even his monumental loneliness, but rather his terrifying and tyrannical father.

The film's beginning, and its most stirring segment, presents a 6-year-old boy being taken out of school and sent off to tend a flock on a desolate, ruggedly beautiful mountainside. His father, who beats young Gavino with objects as stridently symbolic as a stick and a dead snake, inducts the boy into his new way of life in the cruelest manner possible.

There are isolated instances of the father's tenderness, when he shares his perceptions of nature with his son and when he realizes, after the boy bursts into tears and then faints from fright and exhaustion, that the torture has gone far enough. But most of the father's behavior borders on sadism, despite the economic necessity in which it is rooted. So the father remains as inconsistent and irrational to the viewer as he might seem to a small child.

Years later, when Gavino begins bridling under his father's authority and angling for a chance to escape, his battle is fought along more familiar lines and his father seems a less formidable adversary. Gavino enlists in the army and travels to the Italian mainland, where he begins to educate himself and delight in the precise meaning of words. The title which means "My Father, My Master," also refers to Gavino's sheer exultation in the nuances of his new vocabulary.

By the time Gavino returns to Sardinia, his father has begun to seem smaller, pettier, a bit more pathetic in his stubbornness. Gavino finally wins his freedom, but at a terrible cost: He is forced to witness the spectacle of his father's defeat and humiliation.

•

"Padre Padrone" is stirringly affirmative. It's also a bit simple: The patriarchal behavior of Gavino's father is so readily accepted as an unfathomable given constant that the film never offers much insight into the man or the culture that fostered him. Intriguingly aberrant behavior is chalked up to tradition, and thus robbed of some of its ferocity. But the film is vivid and very moving, coarse but seldom blunt, and filled with raw landscapes that underscore the naturalness and inevitability of the father-son rituals it depicts.

The Taviani brotheres have made other films, but this is the first of their efforts to receive wide international exposure and acclaim. "Padre Padrone," which was the grand prize winner at Cannes this year, should serve less as a debut than as an introduction.

1977 D 24, 12:1

THE CHOIRBOYS, directed by Robert Aldrich; screenplay by Christopher Knopf, based on the novel by Joseph Wambaugh; produced by Merv Adelson and Lee Rich; executive producers, Pietro and Mario Bregni and Mark Damon; director of photography, Joseph Biroc; music, Frank De Vol; editors, Maury Winetrobe, William Martin and Irving Rosenblum; a Lorimar/Airone production, distributed by Universal Pictures. Running time: 119 minutes. At the Cinerama Two, Broadway near 47th Street, and other theaters. This film has been rated R.

Spermwhale Whalen .... Charles Durning
Calvin Motts .... Louis Gossett Jr.
Baxter Slate .... Perry King
Francis Tanaguchi .... Clyde Kusatsu
Spencer Van Moot .... Stephen Macht
Roscoe Rules .... Tim McIntire
Dean Proust .... Randy Quaid
Cheech Sartino .... Chuck Sacci
Sam Lyles .... Don Stroud
Harold Bloomguard .... James Woods
Sgt. Dominic Scuzzi .... Burt Young
Deputy Chief Riggs .... Robert Webber
Fanny Forbes .... Jeanie Bell
Kimberly Lyles .... Blair Brown
Cra Lee Tingle .... Michele Carey
Sgt. Nick Yanov .... Charles Haid
Hod Carrier .... Joe Kapp
Hadley .... Barbara Rhodes
Capt. Drobeck .... Jim Davis
Foxy/Gina .... Phyllis Davis
Luther Quigley .... Jack DeLeon
Lieut. Grimsley .... George Di Cenzo
Lieut. Finque .... David Spielberg
Pete Zoony .... Vick Tayback
Alexander Blaney .... Michael Wills

By VINCENT CANBY

"The Choirboys," which opened yesterday at the Cinerama Two and other theaters, is Robert Aldrich's screen adaptation of Joseph Wambaugh's best-selling novel about the private panics of a bunch of Los Angeles cops of assorted eccentricities. After dealing day and night with the city's flotsam, Mr. Wambaugh tells us, these policemen, neither brighter nor more sensitive than any other group of men, survive only with the help of booze and pills and a see-through cynicism that is worn as if it were plastic raingear.

Mr. Wambaugh's episodic novel is tough and funny and comes alive with the unexpected details

Burt Young
Funny and spirited

of a forlorn truth. The movie, which Mr. Aldrich directed from a screenplay by Christopher Knopf, is cheap and nasty without having any redeeming vulgarity and absolutely no conviction of truth. What went wrong?

The material seems to be the sort that would perfectly suit Mr. Aldrich ("The Dirty Dozen," "The Grissom Gang," "Ulzana's Raid"), a man whose darker humors match those of the novelist, yet there's little evidence of that here. Further, the movie is such a stylistic and narrative mess one suspects it was originally shot to be one of those six-hour "television novels" and then cut down to its present two-hour running time for a theatrical play-off.

•

Though it's the kind of film that's designed for people who don't read much, it can be followed only by someone who has some familiarity with the book. However, anyone who liked the book will probably be appalled by the movie. Which is about as close as "The Choirboys" ever gets to "Catch 22."

The title, for those who came in late, is derived from the impromptu, late-night, booze-and-broads blow-outs that Mr. Wambaugh's cops hold in L.A.'s MacArthur Park after getting off duty. The sessions, which the cops call choir practice, are epic benders that have the effect of decompressing the men's psyches. They sing, fight, get sick, play cruel practical jokes on one another and, eventually, return to the surface of the earth.

•

In Mr. Wambaugh's novel, the reader is able to understand the manic intensity of the choirboys at these parties, having been given some idea of the grubby violence of their working lives. The film attempts to treat their working lives mostly in comic terms, even though what happens is not especially comic, so that their off-duty behavior has no more meaning than would the off-duty behavior of a bunch of loutish television repairmen.

Among the actors in the huge cast, some of the more prominent are Charles Durning, as the father-

figure cop; Perry King, as an Ivy League sort, who turns out to be fatally effete; Tim McIntire, a redneck, bigoted sadist; Randy Quaid, as "the kid," and Burt Young, who is funny and spirited as the vice-squad chief whom everyone mistakes for the station-house janitor.

1977 D 24, 8:5

HIGH ANXIETY, directed and produced by Mel Brooks; screenplay by Mr. Brooks, Ron Clark, Rudy De Luca and Barry Levinson; director of photography, Paul Lohmann; music, John Morris; editor, John C. Howard; a Crossbow production, distributed by 20th Century-Fox. Running time: 92 minutes. At the Sutton Theater, 57th Street, east of Third Avenue. This film has been rated PG.

Richard H. Thorndyke .... Mel Brooks
Victoria Brisbane .... Madeline Kahn
Nurse Diesel .... Cloris Leachman
Dr. Charles Montague .... Harvey Korman
Brophy .... Ron Carey
Professor Lilloiman .... Howard Morris
Dr. Wentworth .... Dick Van Patten
Desk clerk .... Jack Riley
Cocker spaniel .... Charlie Callas
Zachary Cartwright .... Ron Clark
Killer .... Rudy De Luca
Bellboy .... Barry Levinson
Norton .... Lee Delano
Dr. Baxter .... Richard Stahl
Dr. Eckhardt .... Darrell Zwerling
Piano player .... Murphy Dunne
Man who is shot .... Al Hopson
Flasher .... Bob Ridgely
Arthur Brisbane .... Albert J. Whitlock

By VINCENT CANBY

Dr. Richard H. Thorndyke, the Nobel Prize-winning psychiatrist, could be the quintessential Alfred Hitchcock hero. His is unmarried but available. He dresses immaculately in dark suits with vests. He wears his Phi Beta Kappa key on a fine gold chain and neatly spears his understated tie with a gold pin that also keeps his shirt collar tucked in. More importantly, he has an elegant flaw. Dr. Richard H. Thorndyke, newly appointed head of Los Angeles's posh ($12,000 a month for room and board) Psycho-Neurotic Institute for the Very, Very Nervous, suffers from high anxiety, which is like vertigo, only worse.

One could easily mistake Dr. Richard H. Thorndyke for the hero of a film like "The Man Who Knew Too Much" or "Vertigo" except for one thing. He has the cowardly man's restless glance as he keeps track of the terrain and of all the ways to make a quick exit. The explanation is simple. The actor playing the role is Jimmy Stewart compacted to the volatile proportions of Mel Brooks in Mr. Brooks's funny, brainy, film-buff comedy, "High Anxiety," which opened yesterday at the Sutton Theater.

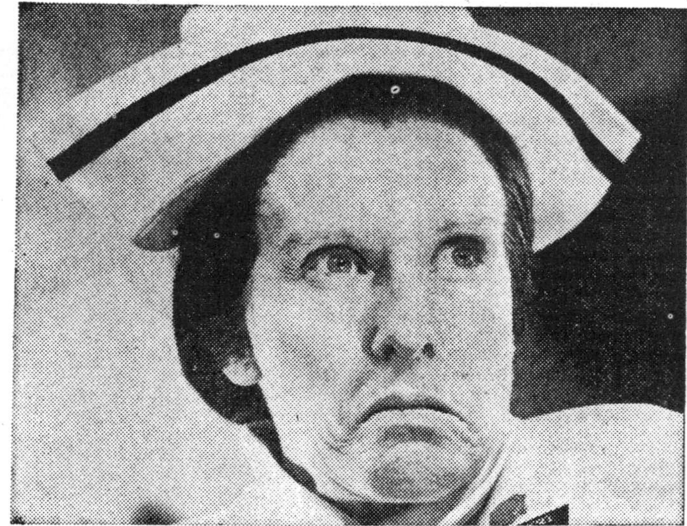

Cloris Leachman in a scene from "High Anxiety"
A thin-lipped sadistic Florence Nightingale

In a way that seems sneaky only because he has been so successful at the box office (and popularity must always be suspect), Mr. Brooks is extending the boundaries of parody in contemporary films. In "Blazing Saddles" he brought anarchy to the Wild West and in "Silent Movie" he demonstrated his affection for slapstick comedy with approximately 258 variations on the pratfall and the pie-in-the-face. "Young Frankenstein," his best film to date, cheerfully recalled everything we remember most fondly about 1930's horror films in general and James Whale's "Frankenstein" in particular.

"High Anxiety," Mr. Brooks's homage to the extraordinary career of Alfred iHitchcock, is as witty and as disciplined as "Young Frankenstein," though it has one built-in problem: Hitchcock himself is a very funny man. His films, even at their most terrifying and most suspenseful, are full of jokes shared with the audience. Being so self-aware, Hitchcock's films deny an easy purchase to the parodist, especially one who admires his subject the way Mr. Brooks does. There's nothing to send up, really. There are only characters' scenes, manners and gestures to be remembered with affection.

In "High Anxiety," the story of the flawed Dr. Richard H. Thorndyke's coming to terms with his neurosis, Mr. Brooks remembers all sorts of Hitchcock films, including "The Lodger," "Rebecca," "Psycho," "Vertigo" and "The Birds," and a lot of the film's fun is sharing his affection. That the enjoyment tends to be cerebral is confirmed. I think, by the fact that it's a movie that is almost as funny to hear about as to see.

What will people feel about the film if they don't know Hitchcock from Hawks? After watching five- and 10-year-old children, who'd never heard of "Frankenstein," collapsing with laughter at "Young Frankenstein," I suspect it won't make any difference at all. There's an infectiously funny rhythm to a Brooks film to which even the unenlightened can respond.

As the afflicted Dr. Thorndyke, Mr. Brooks plays it so very, very straight that just the memory of one of his famous leers is funny, as when he arrives at his post and meets Nurse Diesel (Cloris Leachman), a thin-lipped, sadistic Florence Nightingale who has the slightest hint of a mustache and breasts that seem borrowed from Brunhilde. Among the other people with whom he must deal, there are the dapper but masochistically bent Dr. Montague (Harvey Korman), kindly old Professor Lillolman (Howard Morris) and especially the glamorous San Francisco socialite, Victoria Brisbane, played by Madeline Kahn, a woman who can be gloriously funny simply by attempting to control an upper lip. She's a cocktail waitress's loving concept of "the real Kim Novak."

The screenplay, written by Mr. Brooks with Ron Clark, Rudy De Luca and Barry Levinson, all of whom make cameo appearances in the film with gusto, deals in Hitchcockesque skullduggery set at the Psycho-Neurotic Institute and at a doctors' convention in San Francisco where, one way and another, the doctor gets to the bottom of the mysterious incidents at his sanitarium.

Miss Leachman and Mr. Korman have great fun as the villains, as does Ron Carey, who, early in the movie, dutifully introduces himself to Dr. Thorndyke as "your driver and sidekick." Mr. Brooks also has succeeded in making the movie look like a Hitchcock production, even to dolly shots of a kind one seldom sees in movies any more.

•

"High Anxiety," which has been rated PG "parental guidance suggested"-, includes a few vulgar gestures and words of the sort that, to children, have Shavian impact.

1977 D 26, 34:1

'Annie Hall' Picked as Best of '77 By National Film Critics Society

The National Society of Film Critics yesterday selected "Annie Hall," the comedy starring, directed and co-written by Woody Allen, as the best film of 1977. The group, whose membership comprises 29 critics from New York and other cities, named Luis Bunuel's "That Obscure Object of Desire" and Steven Spielberg's "Close Encounters of the Third Kind" as second and third choices.

Unless a contender wins a majority of votes on the first ballot, each member votes for three selections, awarding three, two and one points, respectively. Second-and third-place winners are announced in each category. "Annie Hall," which was chosen as the best film, with 43 points, was followed by "That Obscure Object of Desire," with 27 points, and "Close Encounters of the Third Kind," with 21.

Diane Keaton received the best actress citation for "Annie Hall," with 50 points. The closest runners-up were Shelley Duvall, with 26 points for "3 Women," and Jane Fonda, with 14 points for "Julia." Neither Miss Keaton's performance in "Looking for Mr. Goodbar" nor Miss Fonda's in "Fun With Dick and Jane" was cited.

Art Carney a Winner

The screenplay for "Annie Hall," written by Mr. Allen and Marshall Brickman, was also cited as the year's best. The screenplay category was the only one in which a winner was chosen on the first ballot, with 16 of the 26 critics selecting "Annie Hall."

The group's choice for best director was Mr. Buñuel, with 31 points. In second place was Mr. Spielberg, with 25 points. Mr. Allen, with 24 points, was third.

Art Carney, with 25 points, was named best actor for "The Late Show." John Gielgud, in "Providence," was second with 19 points. There was a tie for third, at 13 points, between John Travolta of "Saturday Night Fever" and Fernando Rey of "That Obscure Object of Desire."

Ann Wedgeworth was named best supporting actress for "Handle With Care," receiving 25 points. Marcia Rodd, also of "Handle With Care," was second with 22 points. Sissy Spacek received 20 points for her performance in "3 Women."

Edward Fox, who appeared in "A Bridge Too Far," was named best supporting actor, with 29 points. Runners-up were Bill Macy of "The Late Show," with 23 points and, tied for third place, David Hemmings of "Islands in the Stream" and Maximilian Schell of "Julia," each with 21 points.

The group judged the best cinematography to have been Thomas Mauch's, in the German film "Aguirre, the Wrath of God," which was directed by Werner Herzog. In second, with 21 points to the 30 points for "Aguirre," was Vittorio Storaro's cinematography for Bernardo Bertolucci's "1900." Third choice, with 20 points, was Robby Müller's cinematography for another German film, "The American Friend," which was directed by Wim Wender.

1977 D 20, 45:1

Woody Allen and Diane Keaton in "Annie Hall"
Choice of the National Society of Film Critics as the best film of 1977

Critics' Circle Picks 'Annie Hall'

By JANET MASLIN

"ANNIE HALL" was chosen the best film of 1977 by the New York Film Critics' Circle yesterday. The Woody Allen comedy was selected over Luis Buñuel's "That Obscure Object of Desire," in second place, and Steven Spielberg's "Close Encounters of the Third Kind," in third. The critics' group has 26 members, 25 of whom took part in the voting.

Mr. Allen's script for "Annie Hall," co-written by Marshall Brickman, was named best screenplay, in the group's only first-ballot choice. Mr. Allen was also cited as best director, ahead of Mr. Buñuel and Mr. Spielberg. Diane Keaton was named best actress for her performance in "Annie Hall." Second choice for best actress was Shelley Duvall, who appeared in "3 Women." Third choice was Miss Keaton again, this time for "Looking for Mr. Goodbar."

Like the National Society of Film Critics, which also cited "Annie Hall" as best picture, last Monday, the New York Film Critics' Circle allows its members one vote each on a first ballot. Then, if no majority winner is chosen, each member makes three choices and awards them three, two or one point.

Gielgud Best Actor

"Annie Hall" received 46 points in the best-picture category, as opposed to 28 for "That Obscure Object of Desire" and 12 for "Close Encounters of the Third Kind." Mr. Allen received 35 points, as opposed to 33 for Mr. Buñuel and 16 for Mr. Spielberg. Miss Keaton received 34 points for her "Annie Hall" performance and 25 points for "Looking for Mr. Goodbar." Miss Duvall was voted 27 points for "3 Women."

John Gielgud was named best actor for his performance in "Providence," with 37 points. Fernando Rey was second choice with 31 points for "That Obscure Object of Desire." John Travolta was also cited, with 25 points, for his performance in "Saturday Night Fever."

Sissy Spacek was named best supporting actress for her performance in "3 Women," with 31 points. "She's going to be very interested to find out she was playing a supporting role," one group member was heard to comment. The other two actresses named for supporting performances were Vanessa Redgrave, who had the title role in "Julia," with 25 points, and Donna Pescow of "Saturday Night Fever," with 22 points.

Edward Fox Not Named

Maximilian Schell was named best supporting actor for his role in "Julia," with 30 points. Bill Macy was second choice, with 17 points, for his performance in "The Late Show," and David Hemmings was cited third, with 14 points, for "Islands in the Stream."

Although the memberships of the National Society of Film Critics and the New York Film Critics Circle overlap considerably, and although the former group named Edward Fox of "A Bridge Too Far" as best supporting actor on Monday, he received not a single vote at yesterday's meeting.

The awards will be presented at a party at Sardi's on Jan. 29. The group's only other business, at a meeting in the offices of the Newspaper Guild of New York, 133 West 44th Street, was a motion to admit radio and television critics to its ranks, which presently include only writers from newspapers and magazines. The motion was defeated.

1977 D 22, C12:2

FILM VIEW

VINCENT CANBY

This Was the Year Comedy Was King

Going over the list of the 10 best films of the year—those 10 that moved or amused me most or that altered my perceptions of things—I've been surprised to see how many of them are comedies. Seven out of 10. That's an unusually high percentage, especially for a year in which I don't remember having laughed all that much, and for a decade in which people seem to be saying with increasingly boring frequency, "What I'd like to see is a good comedy, but they don't make them any more." They do make them, but today's comedies don't necessarily look or sound the way they used to. I'm not talking about "Star Wars," which I regard as much a comedy as a charming sci-fi fantasy. I'm talking about movies like "Annie Hall" and "The Late Show" and "Stroszek," movies that are essentially somber but which contain characters who are comic, who possess unexpected reserves of the kind of gallantry and courage that make bearable, if not comprehensible, the contradictions of life. Woody Allen's Alvy Singer is very funny and very appealing even when he's not being entirely nice. He's also heroic in a typically Woody way, hanging onto life while he's aware that he must eventually fail in a universe that is mysteriously, relentlessly expanding. Alvy Singer keeps going. So does Art Carney's aging gumshoe in "The Late Show," although he has a game leg and is convinced that the world is populated exclusively by chislers and certified nuts. A conviction like that is a terrible burden.

It's not been a great year for American films, though five of this year's 10 best are American, which is about par for the course. There are only four in the follow-up, which, if I remember correctly, is usually dominated by the work of Americans. Whether this is really indicative of what's happening in American films or simply an accident dependent upon the year's release schedules, I've no idea. Time will tell, but only some time in the future.

Because it's so unusual, I should also report that this year there were no bitter interior debates about which films should or shouldn't make the list. It was easy, which, I suppose, is simply another indication that we weren't exactly overwhelmed with films of superior quality during this calendar year. That's no reflection on the films that are on the list. The gap is widening between movies of true interest and those that fade from memory in an instant.

• • •

The following, then, are the 10 best films of 1977, listed in alphabetical order:

"Annie Hall." Since America is the home of the stand-up comic, soyburgers, drive-in banking and sex therapy by-the-hour, it's only fitting that our Ingmar Bergman should be a talent as immediately in touch with our mass-produced, instant insecurities as Woody Allen. "Annie Hall" is Woody's "Scenes from a Marriage," a hilarious and moving analysis of a love affair between two neurotics so perfectly matched that disaster is inevitable. As writer (with Marshall Brickman), director and star, Woody has never more completely realized himself while also obtaining from Diane Keaton the performance of a career.

"Close Encounters of the Third Kind." Steven Spielberg apotheosizes the science-fiction film of the 1950's in this handsome, cheerful epic of special effects and good news about some extra-terrestrial visitors who come not to terrify but—is it possible?—to redeem. The movie has a fine cast—Francois Truffaut, Carey Guffey (a remarkably unaffected little four-year-old), Richard Dreyfuss and Melinda Dillon—and extraordinary contributions by the technicians, but it's as much a one-man movie (Mr. Spielberg's) as is anything by Chaplin. It is his dream come true.

"Effi Briest." Of the seven or eight or nine films we've seen this year by Rainer Werner Fassbinder, to whom the New Yorker Theater devoted a retrospective, "Effi Briest" is my favorite, although it's not—on its surface—typical of the work of this young German phenomenon. I like it, I think, because it shows just how prodigiously talented Mr. Fassbinder is, being able to move from the Godard-like, neo-Brechtian films of his early period (1969-70) to the more expansive work of his middle period (1970-) when he made this adaptation of Theodore Fontane's 1894 novel. "Effi Briest" deals neither with movie myths ("The American Soldier") nor with the contemporary low-lifes ("Katzelmacher") that seemed to describe all of the early Fassbinder movies. It's a beautiful, ironic, intentionally literary-sounding film-of-manners about the decline and fall of a sweet, foolish young woman who has no comprehension of the system whose rules she breaks. Hanna Schygulla, an actress of enchanting versatility, plays the title role with such delicacy one has to check the records to make sure she's the same actress who has been so extraordinarily good as various strumpets and feather-brained shop girls in other Fassbinder films.

"The Goalie's Anxiety at the Penalty Kick." This early (1971) film by Wim Wenders, another young German director, was first shown here at the Museum of Modern Art in 1972 and only this year received a theatrical engagement. Mr. Wenders's adaptation of the Peter Handke novel is a cool, composed, spellbinding drama about disorientation and madness, a nearly perfect example of the New Movie, if there ever is to be such a thing.

"Handle With Care." This is the American movie we've all been waiting for—and one that hardly anyone went to see when it finally arrived. First released under the title of "Citizen's Band," when it failed, then retitled "Handle With Care" and shown with great success at the New York Film Festival, the film subsequently failed all over again. It's now being given a third lease on life and may well catch on. It certainly should. It's as funny and witty and alive as any commercial American film in a long time, and acted with verve by a cast that includes Paul Le Mat, Candy Clark, Bruce McGill, Roberts Blossom, Charles Napier, Ann Wedgeworth, Marcia Rodd and Alix Elias, all of whom should be remembered in our prayers, along with Jonathan Demme, the director, and Paul Brickman, who wrote the screenplay.

"The Late Show." Robert Altman, who once made his own homage to the private-eye film ("The Long Goodbye") produced "The Late Show," a very different but equally entertaining homage. It was written and directed by Robert Benton and stars two incomparable actors, Art Carney, who plays the crochety, lonely L.A. detective, and Lily Tomlin as the loony one-time actress ("I couldn't play the Hollywood game") who persuades the detective to take on one last case, a caper involving her kidnapped cat. With a facility that amazes me, Mr. Benton has made a movie that evokes all the pleasures we once received from Sam Spade-Philip Marlowe fiction, yet one that never is anachronistic. It's a remarkably accomplished work.

"The Man Who Loved Women." Francois Truffaut loves women but somewhere deep in his subconscious he must feel a rat for not loving them more but better. "The Man Who Loved Women" is the sophisticated, supremely humane story of Bertrand Morane (Charles Denner), a fellow whose life is obsessed by women—by the ones he had, is having or wants to have. It's a fatal chase (the movie is told in flashbacks from his funeral), involving a number of marvelous actresses (including Brigitte Fossey, Leslie Caron and Nelly Borgeaud) and some darker observations on men and women, parents and children, sex and love.

"Star Wars." What can you say about a movie that has been seen by more people in San Francisco (I think this is what I read) than the city has residents? It's more than popular. It's a way of life, and it couldn't happen to a nicer movie. George Lucas ("American Graffiti"), who both wrote and directed "Star Wars," has transferred to film a lot of the wonder, delight, magic and mystery of the fiction we all read as children. "Star Wars" is a live-action comic-strip that never makes fun of its material while being consistently fun and often funny. It may say something about the age we live in that the film's three most popular characters are a villain named Darth Vader and two Laurel and Hardy-like robots, See-Threepio and Artoo-Deetoo. Then again, it may not. Did the popularity of the Cowardly Lion throw any light on World War I?

"Stroszek." A film by another immensely gifted young German director, Werner Herzog. "Stroszek," which Mr. Herzog describes as a ballad, is the tale of three mismatched German friends, all losers, who set out from Berlin for the New World and wind up in a small town in northern Wisconsin in the middle of winter. Things couldn't go worse for them. Eva (Eva Mattes) starts hooking again, while old Scheitz (Clemens Scheitz) and Stroszek (Bruno S.) turn to a life of feeble crime. It sounds sad and it is sad, but it's also exuberantly funny at times, and the uncomplicated honesty we see in the eyes of Bruno S. recalls some primal definition of the Good Man. If you've seen no other films by Mr. Herzog ("The Mystery of Kaspar Hauser," "Aguirre, The Wrath of God," "Heart of Glass"), this is the one you should see first.

"That Obscure Object of Desire." At the age of 77, Luis Buñuel is not growing older, only more precise in his style and more impatient with the windy rhetoric of conventional filmmaking. "That Obscure Object of Desire" is a dozen different movies atop one another, so successfully fused that we can see only one at a time. It's the story of Mathieu, a rich, cultivated, aristocratic Frenchman (Fernando Rey), and his consuming obsession for a Spanish girl who is so mysterious to him that she is played by two actresses (Carole Bouquet and Angela Molina). The movie is a civilized chase through a world where civil order, like Mathieu's sanity, is being put to the test by terrorism and deadly new diseases. "That Obscure Object of Desire" ranks with "The Discreet Charm of the Bourgeoisie" and "Tristana" as one of the supreme works of this master's late career.

• • •

The 10 runners-up, in no special order of preference, are "A Special Day," Ettore Scola's comedy-drama that comes to brilliant life in the performances of Sophia Loren and Marcello Mastroianni; "Cousin Angelica," Carlos Saura's moving meditation upon Spain's civil war in the form of a middle-aged man's journey to the home of his childhood; "That Wonderful Crook," a sweet and bitter Swiss comedy, directed by Claude Goretta, about a nice young man (Gérard Départdieu) who becomes a bank robber to meet the payroll for his father's small furniture factory; "Three Women," Robert Altman's not-always-coherent but very moving comedy about two women, comically and touchingly played by Shelley Duvall and Sissy Spacek; "Aguirre, The Wrath of God," a movie of barely describable beauty, filmed in Peru and Brazil by Werner Herzog, about the mad Spanish conquistadore who decided to carve out his own empire in the Amazon jungle and wound up, according to Mr. Herzog, reigning over a raft of insubordinate monkeys.

Also, "From Noon Till Three," a most unusual comedy-satire about Americn myth-making procedures, written and directed by Frank D. Gilroy, starring Charles Bronson as a second-rate western outlaw who becomes a national hero through the love of a good crazy woman, played by Jill Ireland (Mrs. Bronson); "Katzelmacher," Rainer Werner Fassbinder's highly articulate adaptation of his own one-act play about a bunch of totally inarticulate, nasty young people who hang out together and victimize a Greek immigrant worker, to pass the time and assert their own identities; "Let Joy Reign Supreme," a magnificently set, costumed and acted (by Philippe Noiret) period comedy about Philippe d'Orleans, the regent for Louis XV; "Short Eyes," Miguel Pinero's eloquent screen adaptaion of his prison play, directed by Robert M. Young and acted with manic intensity by Bruce Davison, Shawn Elliott and Joseph Carberry, among others; and "High Anxiety," this year's Mel Brooks comedy, a loving, knowledgeable and often hilarious tribute to the work of Alfred Hitchcock, with Mr. Brooks, Cloris Leachman, Madeline Kahn and Harvey Korman doing terrible things to each other and generally making the world a happier place to be. ■

1977 D 25, II:1:1

'Annie Hall' Wins 4 Academy Awards

Woody Allen and Diane Keaton in "Annie Hall"
Best picture, best director and best actress

By ALJEAN HARMETZ
Special to The New York Times

LOS ANGELES, Tuesday, April 4— Woody Allen's "Annie Hall," was named best picture of the year and took three other prizes as the Hollywood film industry staged the 50th anniversary award ceremonies of the Academy of Motion Picture Arts and Sciences.

Diane Keaton, who played the title role in "Annie Hall," was named best actress, and Richard Dreyfuss was named best actor for his role in "The Goodbye Girl."

Mr. Allen won Oscars for directing and screenplay as his "Annie Hall" swept four of the major awards, beating out "Star Wars," which was limited to six lesser categories, including original musical score for the ubiquitous theme.

The awards for best supporting actor and actress went to Jason Robards and Vanessa Redgrave for their roles in "Julia."

Several hundred members of the militant Jewish Defense League picketed the Los Angeles Music Center, where the ceremonies were held, because of Miss Redgrave's involvement in a documentary, "The Palestinians," which the league has denounced as an anti-Jewish propaganda effort.

Mr. Allen shared the Oscar for original screenplay with Marshall Brickman. Mr. Allen's double victory, while unusual, was not unprecedented. Joseph Mankiewicz did it with "All About Eve" in 1950. Mr. Allen did not appear at the ceremonies.

In presenting the writing awards, the triple Academy Award-winning playwright Paddy Chayefsky, chastised Miss Redgrave's statement when she received her award for supporting actress. "I'm sick and tired of people exploiting the occasion of the Academy Awards for the propagation of their own political propaganda," Mr. Chayefsky said. "I would like to suggest to Miss Redgrave that her winning an Academy Award is not a pivotal moment in history, does not require a proclamation, and a simple thank you would suffice."

Miss Redgrave would have been the clear favorite for her part as the almost inhumanly dedicated Julia of Lillian Hellman's memoir "Pentimento" except for the controversy that swirled around her artistic and financial involvement in the documentary film "The Palestinians.

Although many Jewish members of the film industry quickly supported Miss Redgrave's right to her political opinions, it was widely thought that the controversy had damaged her chances for the supporting-actress award.

Political Statement

Miss Redgrave's acceptance speech was a fiery and impassioned political statement. Addressing the audience, she said: "You should be very proud that in the last few weeks you stood firm and you refused to be intimidated by the threats of a small bunch of Zionist hoodlums whose behavior is an insult to the stature of Jews all over the world and to their great and heroic record of struggle against Fascism and oppression. I salute that record and I salute all of you for having stood firm and dealt the final blow against that period when Nixon and McCarthy launched a worldwide witch hunt against those who tried to express in their lives and their work the truths that they believed in."

Holding her Oscar aloft in triumph, she ended, "I salute you and I thank you and I pledge to you that I'll continue to fight against anti-Semitism and Fascism." Although she ended her speech to thundering applause, there was an outbreak of booing with the words "Zionist hoodlums."

Under a 50-Foot Balloon

Outside, beneath a 50-foot-high vinyl-coated nylon Oscar that swayed on top of the Los Angeles Music Center last night, members of the Jewish Defense League and a smaller number of supporters of the Palestine Liberation Organization—who were demonstrating in behalf of Miss Redgrave—were kept apart by lines of police and special security officers.

There was a brief moment of violence when three men wearing Nazi uniforms were jumped by three Jewish Defense League partisans. According to one Los Angeles Police Department report, two of the Nazis were taken to a hospital, and two of the Jewish Defense League members had been arrested.

Associated Press

Woody Allen, whose "Annie Hall" won four Academy Awards, playing clarinet last night during his regular Monday evening stint with jazz group at Michael's Pub in Manhattan.

Jason Robards made it two Oscars in a row as best supporting actor for his performance as the mystery writer Dashiell Hammett in "Julia." Mr. Robards's victory was expected, because the Hollywood grapevine had established him as the favorite in that category. Despite this, he was not present at the ceremony and had delegated no one to pick up the Oscar for him. Mr. Robards won last year for his role as Benjamin C. Bradlee, chief editor of The Washington Post, in "All the President's Men."

The surprising victor for foreign-language film was France's "Madame Ross," starring Simone Signoret as an elderly Jewish woman, a former prostitute, and dealing with her relationship with an Arab boy. The two best-known and most widely distributed films in that category were the Italian "A Special Day," starring a nominee for best actor, Marcello Mastroianni, and Luis Buñel's "That Obscure Object of Desire." Last year's foreign-language category produced an equal surprise when "Black and White in Color" defeated "Seven Beauties" and "Cousin, Cousine."

Both documentary film awards went to inspirational films. John Korty's "Who Are the DeBolts? And Where Did They Get 19 Kids?" about a family of handicapped adpoted children won for feature-length, and "Gravity Is My Enemy," about a quadriplegic painter took the short-documentary Oscar.

Except for the award to Miss Redgrave, the early awards presented were minor or technical ones. Frank E. Warner received an Oscar for special achievement in sound-effects editing for "Close Encounters of the Third Kind," while "Star Wars" kept pace with a special award to Benjamin Burtt Jr. for creating the robot voices in that film.

A Feverish Music Controversy

Mr. Allen, who was involved in four awards as writer, actor and director, played his regular Monday night stint at clarinet in a Dixieland jazz band at Michael's Pub at 211 East 55th Street. The Pub's hatcheck woman, Noreen Smith, described the atmosphere as "restless and milling—but not a big crowd for Monday night; they're here to see him."

Mr. Allen left the establishment at 12:15 A.M., before the awards he was up for were announced, making his way with some embarrassment through

Richard Dreyfuss
Best actor

Jason Robards
Best supporting actor

Associated Press

Vanessa Redgrave making her statement as she accepted Oscar for Supporting Actress for "Julia."

a crowd of photographers and running through a next-door lobby to a waiting car dressed in a combat jacket and plaid shirt.

In addition to the controversy over Miss Redgrave, two other organizations publicly protested the ceremonies. yesterday, Robert Stigwood, producer of "Saturday Night Fever," sent a telegram to the academy's board of governors expressing his anger "at the total exclusion of the Bee Gees and their original music for 'Saturday Night Fever' from any and all music nominations."

Last Wednesday, Panavision boycotted the presentation of technical awards. Panavision rejected a Class II award for its Panaflex camera and insisted that the camera was worthy of a Class I award, Robert Gottschalk, president of Panavision, said the main reason for the refusal was that only one cameraman was among the 36 members of the scientific and technical awards committee during the awards voting.

The awards show itself was a return to the opulence and glamour of years past after the deliberately austere show produced last year by William Friedkin, director of "The Exorcist." It opened with a lavish production number starring Debbie Reynolds and 30 dancers. The number, "Look How Far We've Come," spotlighted 37 former Oscar winners in acting, directing, writing, cinematography, music and costume design.

Sentiments Evoked

The loudest applause of the evening and a standing ovation went to Margaret Booth, who was given a special Oscar for her 62 years as a film editor. She started her career as a negative-film cutter for D.W. Griffith and, most recently, was supervising editor on "The Goodbye Girl."

Among the other special awards were the Gene Hersholt Humanitarian Award to the actor Charlton Heston and the Irving G. Thalberg Award—given for the body of a producer's work—to Walter Mirisch, producer of "West Side Story," "Fiddler on the Roof" and "In the Heat of the Night."

"Star Wars" swept most of the early awards, winning for art direction, sound, costume design, visual effects, film editing and original score.

The award for best original song went, as expected, to Joseph Brooks for "You Light Up My Life," the most popular song in the country for several months. The Oscar was only the last of many awards for the song, which has also received a Grammy and a Golden Globe. The award was presented by Fred Astaire, who was also greeted with a standing ovation.

For the 15th time, Bob Hope was master of ceremonies. He was the sole M.C. as he had been in eight previous years. It was the first time sincet 1967 that the show has had only one M.C. "We felt that for Oscar's 50th birthday, Bob Hope should be host," Howard Koch, president of the academy, said.

The program was seen on ABC-TV and was being broadcast in 51 countries, live and on tape.

Other awards included:

Short Subjects (Live)

"I'll Find A Way," National Film Board of Canada. Beverly Shaffer and Yuki Yoshida, producers.

Documentary Film (Features)

"Who Are the DeBolts? And Where Did They Get Nineteen Kids?" Korty Films and Charles M. Schulz Creative Associates, in association with Sanrio Films. John Korty, Dan McCann and Warren L. Lockhart, producers.

Visual Effects

"Star Wars," John Stears, John Dykstra, Richard Edlund, Grant McCune and Robert Blalack.

Short Subjects (Animated)

"Sand Castle," National Film Board of Canada. Co Hoedeman, producer.

Documentary (Short Subjects)

"Gravity Is My Enemy," a John Joseph Production. John Joseph and Jan Stussy, producers.

Original Music Score

"Star Wars," John Williams.

Costume Design

John Mollo for "Star Wars."

1978 Ap 4, 24:1

The New York Times Film Reviews 1978

Monster Search

SASQUATCH Directed by Ed Ragozzini; a John Fabian Production; photography and editing by John Fabian and Bill Farmer; sound recording by Steve Winitzky; costumes and make-up, Woody Crocker. Released by North American Film Enterprises Inc. Running time: 102 minutes. At the Embassy 46th Street Theater, 46th Street and Broadway. This film has been rated G.
Chuck Evans .... George Lauris
Hank Parshall .... Steve Boergadine
Barney Snipe .... Jim Bradford
Josh Bigsby .... Ken Kenzle
Dr. Paul Markham .... William Emmons
Techka Blackhawk .... Joe Morello

By JANET MASLIN

"SASQUATCH" is the kind of pseudoscientific silliness that manages to discredit itself entirely, thanks to an approach that might best be labeled simulated-verité. It begins with some hyperbole about Bigfoot, a.k.a. Sasquatch, who would allegedly be the most important anthropological find of our time if anyone could bag him. Then it turns up some "authentic" footage of the creature that has been examined and pronounced The Real Thing by "scientists." After that, we even see a computer making a composite sketch of Bigfoot, based in part on this very same footage, and are expected to marvel at the similarity between the two images.

•

But the movie then disintegrates into a long and tedious account of an expedition to track the monster through the Pacific Northwest to his lair, and the search-party personnel are so appallingly actorish that they throw any semblance of seriousness to the winds.

In addition to Josh, an old mountain man who whistles "Swanee River" and is accompanied by his faihful mule, there are also a bumbling cook who is kidded about his culinary skills but is always praised for his coffee. There are a skeptical reporter from New York City, a dog tracker, an Indian guide, "one of the most distinguished anthropologists in the world," and an expedition leader who puffs thoughtfully on his pipe and speaks alternately of the beauty of nature and the gravity of this mission.

There is also Sasquatch himself, a pointy-headed fellow in a Kong suit, who is seen throwing papier-Mâché boulders a few times and whose presence is often represented by "Jaws"-type music and rustling branches. Sasquatch isn't on camera long and, of course, he isn't captured. But this expedition, we are told, "will provide volumes of information to stimulate more-extensive exploration."

•

Actually, the only interest in the Bigfoot phenomenon that "Sasquatch" is likely to generate will be in Hollywood, if by some outlandish fluke the movie becomes a hit. This seems unlikely, unless the market for poorly shot nature footage—the movie is padded with endless shots of furry little scamps twitching playfully for the camera—is more sizable than seems possible. Indeed, the animal shots are so repetitive that, when the print at the first show at the Embassy 46th Street Theater inadvertently included two versions of the same reel, it took a benumbed audience quite a while to realize it was watching the same grizzly bear scuffle all over again.

Jim Bradford in "Sasquatch."

1978 Ja 12, C14:3

Tolstoyan Parable

DERSU UZALA, directed by Akira Kurosawa; screenplay by Mr. Kurosawa and Yuri Nagibin, based on a story by Vladimir Arseniev; photographed by Asakadru Nakai, Yuri Gantman and Fyodor Dobronavov; a Soviet-Japanese co-production, in Russian with English subtitles. Running time: 137 minutes. At the Baronet Theater, Third Avenue and 59th Street.
Dersu Uzala .... Maxim Munzzuk

"Dersu Uzala" was shown at the 1976 New York Film Festival. The following review by Richard Eder appeared Oct. 5, 1976. The film opens today at the Baronet Theater, Third Avenue and 59th Street.

WHEN Akira Kurosawa, the gifted Japanese director, takes the unusual step of making a movie in co-production with the Soviet film industry, and when the first half is delicate and haunting and the second half is numb and ponderous, it is hard not to jump to conclusions about who did what.

In any event, "Dersu Uzala," which opens today at the Baronet Theater, seems to be not so much co-produced as partitioned. Unequally.

Essentially, "Dersu Uzala" is a Tolstoyan parable about the encounter of the blind and deaf power of civilization with the perceiving and magical helplessness of nature. Set in the Asian forests of Imperial Russia around the turn of the century, it tells of the relationship between a military mapping expedition and an old Tungus trapper who acts as its guide.

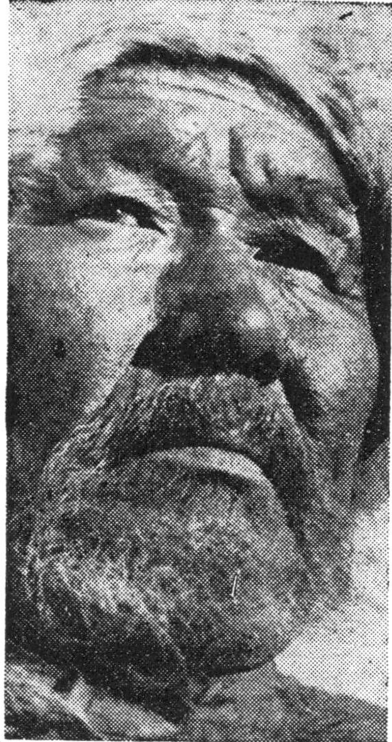

Maxim Munzzuk in "Dersu Uzala"

The soldiers sit in the winter forest at night, uncomfortable, alien, scared. There is a rustle in the bushes and, mastering the temptation to flee, they grab the intruder. He is Dersu, a short, stocky, aging tribesman. He sits by the fire with them, and when a log crackles he speaks sharply to it.

"Fire is a man," he tells them. "Water is a man, too." The captain, a sensitive intermediary between the brutal confidence of the soldier-surveyors and the mystical trapper, hires him as guide. In a series of episodes, told flatly and some with obviousness, but with accumulating force, we see Dersu, through the captain's eyes, reveal his total communication with the world he lives in.

Seeing footprints, he knows that men have been by two days before, and that they are Chinese. Seeing trees with the bark off, he predicts that they will find a shelter, and they do. When the party is about to leave the shelter, he insists on repairing the roof first: for anyone else who may come along.

Dersu, marvelously played by Maxim Munzzuk, a Soviet Asian, draws his wisdom from his complete openness to the natural world. The openness means vulnerability as well. The captain, whose relation to the old man is a growing reverence, discovers him one night, broken with grief by the fire. He is remembering his family, dead of smallpox; and he has no barriers against remembered pain—it is as real as a tree falling upon him.

In the climactic scene of this first part, Dersu and the captain go out to chart a frozen lake. Kurosawa films the cold as it has rarely, if ever, been filmed. It is a visible, red-eyed enemy, visibly terrifying. The two are lost and Dersu, seeing death, is in total fear. The captain has his civilized schooling to constrain him; he also has a compass. When the compass fails, though, Dersu saves them both.

Then this beautiful first part recedes. The detachment prepares to return to the city. Dersu declines the captain's offer to come with them. He would die in the city, he says, but as he trudges off through the snow we see he is older and is simply following his own road to death. The soldiers march down a railroad track, singing; Dersu reach the top of a hill. Just before he crosses, he turns and waves. "Dersu!" the captain cries. "Captain!" Dersu calls back.

It is complete, or should be. If "Dersu Uzala" ended there it would be an odd marvel. But it goes on, repeating the cycle. The captain returns some years later, this time in the summer. He meets Dersu, who displays his powers once more, but with diminishing effect. He has grown too old for the forest; finally he goes to the city with the captain, can't adapt to it, and returns to the forest for the last time.

The episodes in this second part go on endlessly, loosely, obviously. They lack the revelations of the winter scenes and they do little but belabor at length the points already made. They wreck the film's balance and make its achievements dull.

1978 Ja 13, C10:1

Guzman Documentary

THE BATTLE OF CHILE, a documentary directed by Patricio Guzman; in Spanish with English subtitles and English narration; director of photography, Jorge Muller; editor, Pedro Chaskel; production manager, Federico Elton; produced in 1973-1976 by the Equipo Tercer Ano with the collaboration of the Cuban Film Institute and Chris Marker; distributed by Tricontinental Film Center. Running time: 191 minutes. At the Film Forum, 15 Vandam Street. This film has not been rated.

By VINCENT CANBY

"THE Battle of Chile," which opened yesterday at the Film Forum, is an admittedly biased, pro-revolutionary film that raises more questions than it can easily answer. Though it is fabricated of facts, it seems to skirt issues. It is monotonous and long, but it is an important, profoundly disturbing work. It makes one wonder if there is such a thing as a truly revolutionary film form, or if revolution exists only in the eye of the beholder.

The film is a three-hour-and-10-minute, two-part documentary on the last months of the democratically elected, pro-Marxist regime of Chilean President Salvador Allende Gossens, who reportedly committed suicide during the right-wing military coup that overturned his Government in September 1973. The film was directed by Patricio Guzmán, a young Chilean, and assembled in Cuba by him and his Chile-

The late Chilean President Salvador Allende in the documentary, "The Battle of Chile," at the Film Forum: an epic and a profoundly disturbing work.

an associates from some 20 hours of footage smuggled out of Chile after the coup. "The Battle of Chile" is not an easy film to watch, not because the events it details are so sorrowful, so inevitable, which they are, but because the film itself is so studiously impersonal.

•

Mr. Guzmán has done nothing less than photograph the conflicting forces of contemporary history and found, when he emerged from the darkroom, that the forces of contemporary history are so faceless there's very little to distinguish one side from the other. The only thing that gives point and direction to "The Battle of Chile" is Mr. Guzmán's Marxist interpretation of the events, but this interpretation—relying, as it does, on the age-old conflict between proletariat and bourgeoisie as well as on the exploitation of a poor nation by a rich one—doesn't do full justice to the Chilean tragedy as we know it to be.

The country we see in this film looks like a playground for mischievous gods, the result, I suspect, of the director's conscious decision not to appeal to bourgeois sentimentality. The film is virtually one long, unbroken montage composed of scenes of mass demonstrations, either pro- or anti-Allende, of people chanting slogans or marching with banners that contain slogans, of press conferences, of union meetings, of rallies of every description. Everyone is anonymous, even the subject of periodic man-in-the-street interviews.

•

The effect is to depersonalize history to such an extent that even the documented interventions in Chilean internal affairs by agencies of the United States is made to seem remote, a tide of history, something for which no one need take personal responsibility. I doubt that this is the way Mr. Guzmán intended his film to be taken, and, indeed, I doubt that is the film's effect in other parts of the world where simply the mention of the Central Intelligence Agency is enough to cause cold sweats. Revolutionary films cannot be all things to all people.

I assume that the filmmakers must regard the late Dr. Allende as some kind of hero, though, because we see him here only as part of an official background, not as a character but as a personage, in newsreels on state occasions, even he remains remote. And because he was not a very imposing man physically, the movie appears to make him a less dynamic, heroic figure than he really was.

•

In "The Battle of Chile," President Allende appears to be a sort of weightless symbol, whether surrounded by aides or as the central figure at mass rallies, where he was adored. His fate, the film seems to say without wanting to, was as much the result of the failure of his supporters to inform and protect him as it was the victory of the enemies who conspired against him.

No matter how one reacts to "The Battle of Chile," it is undeniably an epic. It is also depressing in the way it keeps trying to make complex events seem simple. There's a scary moment at a pro-Allende rally where the thousands of assembled workers are instructed, "Jump if you are not a fascist." Just about everybody starts bobbing up and down on cue, as if that, after all, was what the battle of Chile was all about.

The film will be shown at the Film Forum tonight through Sunday at 7:45 and repeated there next week, Thursday through Sunday, at the same time.

1978 Ja 13, C7:1

THE DUELLISTS, directed by Ridley Scott; screenplay by Gerald Vaughan-Hughes, based on Joseph Conrad's story "The Duel;" director of photography, Frank Tidy; editor, Pamela Power; music by Howard Blake; produced by David Puttnam; released by Paramount Pictures. Running time: 101 minutes. This film has been rated PG. At the Fine Arts Theater, 58th Street between Park and Lexington Avenue.

D'Hubert	Keith Carradine
Feraud	Harvey Keitel
Fouche	Albert Finney
Colonel Reynard	Edward Fox
Adele	Cristina Raines
General Treillard	Robert Stephens
Jacquin	Tom Conti
Second Major	John McNenery
Laura	Diana Quick
Lecourbe	Alun Armstrong
Tall Second	Maurice Colbourne
Maid	Gay Hamilton
Leonie	Meg Wynn Owen
Mme. de Lionne	Jenny Runacre
Chevalier	Alan Webb

By VINCENT CANBY

"The Duellists," the first major film to open here this year, may well remain one of the most dazzling visual experiences throughout all of 1978. The movie, set during the Napoleonic Wars, uses its beauty much in the way that other movies use soundtrack music, to set mood, to complement scenes and even to contradict them. Sometimes it's almost too much, yet the camerawork, which is by Frank Tidy, provides the Baroque style by which the movie operates on our senses, making the eccentric drama at first compelling and ultimately breathtaking.

"The Duellists," which opened yesterday at the Fine Arts Theater, is an adaptation of a Joseph Conrad story, "The Duel," which I haven't read. It's the first feature film by Ridley Scott, a young English director whose previous experience appears to have been entirely in the making of television commercials (though this doesn't show) and it was written by Gerald Vaughan-Hughes, whose work is also unfamiliar to me. However they collaborated, the result is a film that satisfies not because it sweeps us off our feet, knocks us into the aisles, provides us with visions of infinity or definitions of God, but because it is precise, intelligent, civilized, and because it never for a moment mistakes its narrative purpose.

•

This is to recount the bizarre story of how the life of a young French officer named Armand D'Hubert (Keith Carradine) comes to be dominated by the obsession of a fellow officer, Gabriel Feraud (Harvey Keitel), who believes that D'Hubert has somehow impugned his honor. It begins in Strasbourg in 1801, the year Napoleon comes to power, and continues for the next 15 years, throughout the Emperor's rise, fall and brief comeback as the two men accidentally meet in the course of various campaigns, each meeting culminating in a duel that D'Hubert cannot gracefully deny.

Though Feraud is clearly mad, there is no way that D'Hubert can avoid the challenges within the code of honor that defines the professional life of each. At Strasbourg, they fight with sabers, at Augsburg with what looks almost like broadswords. Once they meet on horseback. Another time pistols are the weapons. Every time they meet, each pares a little more off the other. It's as if they were whittling each other down to the bone, though the ending, which is a perfect short-story ending, makes it apparent that Feraud's obsession has had the effect of tempering the spiritual strength of the other man.

•

I assume that it's to the credit of Mr. Scott, the director, that after we once get over the shock of seeing Mr. Keitel and Mr. Carradine in the uniforms of Napoleonic Hussars, we never again see anything anachronistic about these two most contemporary of American actors in such strange surroundings. They are splendid and are never once upstaged by such high-powered English acting talent as Albert Finney, Alan Webb, Robert Stephens, John McEnery, Meg Wynn Owen, Edward Fox and Jenny Runacre, who appear in supporting roles. Cristina Raines, a young American actress ("The Sentinel"), is charming in the small but important part of Mr. Carradine's young wife.

Harvey Keitel
Never once upstaged

What one carries away from the film, though, is a memory of almost indescribable beauty, of landscapes at dawn, of overcrowded, murky interiors, of underlit hallways and brilliantly sunlit gardens. It's not a frivolous prettiness, but an evocation of time and place through images that are virtually tactile, and which give real urgency to this curious tale. It's marvelous.

•

"The Duellists," which has been rated PG ("Parental Guidance Suggested"), contains a half-dozen duelling scenes of explicitness as well as grace. They are bloody and brutal and absolutely essential to the point of the film.

1978 Ja 14, 10:1

OPERATION THUNDERBOLT, directed by Menahem Golan; screenplay by Clarke Reynolds; director of photography, Adam Greenberg; editor, Dov Henig; music, Dov Seltzer; produced by Mr. Golan and Yoram Globus; released by Cinema Shares International Distribution Corporation. At the Guild Theater, 33 West 50th Street. Running time: 126 minutes. This film has not been rated.

Boese	Klaus Kinsky
Halima	Sybil Danning
Jabbar	Yitzhak Neeman
Jonathan	Yehoram Gaon
Shuki	Assaf Dayan
Air Force Commander	Ori Levy

By JANET MASLIN

Maybe what's missing is the surprise, or the fear, or the suddenness. Maybe the real-life story is simply too exciing to be improved upon. Maybe no film makers of appreciable talent have been tempted to try. But, whatever the reason, there has not yet been a compelling or even serviceable movie treatment of the Israeli rescue raid at Entebbe, even though the event had more of a cinematic feeling than most of the stories one finds on the screen.

Thus far, there have been two inept and sluggish television movies spun out of the episode; now there is "Operation Thunderbolt" at the Guild Theater, a dull and propagandistic Israeli-made feature that is in some ways the least successful version of all.

"They look like Arabs! I don't trust them!" cries a little boy aboard an Air France jetliner, and it turns out he's right to worry about the passengers across the aisle. Their fruitcakes are full of hand grenades and, sure enough, they hijack the plane. Their comrades are a shrill German woman (Sybil Danning) who might better have been cast in "Ilsa, She-Wolf of the SS," and a "mad-looking German man, played by Klaus Kinsky, who looks even wilder-eyed here than he did in "Aguirre, the Wrath of God."

•

The terrorists are seen embracing Arab leaders at a brief stopover, and in Uganda they wind up in telephone contact with Yassir Arafat of the Palestine Liberation Organization. The tattooed forearm of one passenger, a concentration-camp survivor, is shown in close-up, not once, but twice in a row. When the hostages are divided into Jewish and non-Jewish groups, a little boy cries "Mommy, Mommy, why aren't they calling us?" "Because we're not Jewish, darling," she replies. "What's Jewish?" he wants to know, and because there is no direct reply, the segregation process is allowed to serve as an answer.

Even Idi Amin, acted buffoonishly by Mack Heath, is heard to complain about the terrorists' sorting out the passengers. It scares him, he says: "You'll make the Jews mad, and when the Jews get mad, the whole world gets mad."

•

There's no reason to expect the movie to deal gingerly with the terrorists. But the real German (played by Mr. Kinsky) was reported to have shown signs of uncertainty and guilt during the ordeal, and the fact that he might have mowed down many of the hostages at the last moment but chose not to lend a not of unexpected humanity to the drama. In the movie, however, the man is nothing more than a cardboard villian, and his death is a real crowd-pleaser. "Kill him!" cried one woman, at a preview of the film. "Scum!" shouted another.

Aside from the fact that it is at times disturbingly inflammatory, "Operation Thunderbolt" is objectionable on another score: This is yet another disaster movie that can't manage its mob scenes. There are too many passengers for one director, Menahem Golan, to differentiate gracefully among them, so he opts for stereotypes and turns the group into an uninterestingly familiar one. Also, the film makers' unwillingness to elaborate on the details of the Israelis' crackerjack strategy robs the event of its most exciting and unexplored aspect.

1978 Ja 17, 41:1

THE BEST WAY, directed by Claude Miller; screenplay (French with English subtitles) by Mr. Miller and Luc Beraud; original story by Mr. Miller; director of photography, Bruno Nuytten; editor, Jean-Bernard Bonis; music, Alain Jomy; producers, Mag Bodard and Jean-Francois Davy; a Filmoblic Production. Running time: 85 minutes. This film has not been rated. At the Cinema Studio, Broadway and 66th Street.

Marc .... Patrick Dewaere
Philippe .... Patrick Bouchitey
Chantal .... Christine Pascal
Camp director .... Claude Pieplu
Deloux .... Michel Blanc
Gerard .... Marc Chapiteau
Leni .... Michel Such
Herve .... Frank D'Ascanio
Young boy with glasses .... Nathan Miller
Children of the Saint-Saturnin Studio

By VINCENT CANBY

"The Best Way," the French film that opened Sunday at the Cinema Studio, is the first feature film by Claude Miller, who has had extensive experience in France as an assistant director and as a production director for such people as Jacques Demy, Jean-Luc Godard and François Truffaut. This film, which was released in Paris in 1976, comes to us accompanied by high praise from Mr. Truffaut, who, I assume, was acting in his role as old friend and collaborator and not as critic.

"The Best Way" is a very small, very earnest movie that has almost everything going for it except a life of its own. It's nicely acted and intelligently composed, but it has no soul that would give it a particular identity. It has the vacant look of a movie made by someone who wanted to make a movie first and then later cast around for a subject.

•

The chosen subject is the relationship between two young men who are counselors at a boys' summer camp near Paris. Marc (Patrick Dewaere) is a strutting, athletic fellow, while Phillippe (Patrick Bouchitey) is, as they used to say before gay liberation, "sensitive." He teaches theater and in the evening he prefers to watch Ingmar Bergman movies on the telly instead of playing poker with the others.

One night Marc blunders into Phillippe's room to discover his friend in the full make-up, wig and dress of a drag queen. Instead of telling the others, Marc simply torments Philippe with the possibility that he might snitch.

Mr. Dewaere (the co-star of "Going Places") and Mr. Bouchitey have some trouble making their roles work since Mr. Miller, who also wrote the screenplay (with Luc Beraud) appears to change the characters at will in the course of the movie. Philippe, we are given to believe, isn't necessarily a homosexual or even a transvestite. He is quite literally, "sensitive," which isn't quite enough to explain the nonsense of his beloved dress. And, of course, it's the revelation of this kind of movie that the macho Marc has —well—"tendencies" toward Phillippe that frighten him.

•

The movie has the air of a 40's problem play recycled—though not very effectively—for the 70's. There is, at its center, no problem, only a lot of perfectly capable acting by the two stars and by Claude Pieplu, as the head of the summer camp, and Christine Pascal, as the young woman who loves Philippe, secrets and all.

"The Best Way" is also one of the first movies I've seen in a long time that can't even be convincing in creating a sense of place. This summer camp has less routine than one of those third-rate public schools in the literature of Evelyn Waugh, and it's never anywhere near as funny.

1978 Ja 17, 41:4

Random Moments

LIFE AND OTHER ANXIETIES, directed by Ed Pincus and Steven Ascher; director of photography, Mr. Pincus; sound, Mr. Ascher; editors, Mr. Pincus, Mr. Ascher and Gary Greenstein. Running time: 90 minutes. At the Whitney Museum of American Art, Madison Avenue at 75th Street.

By VINCENT CANBY

IN HIS OPEN-ENDED autobiographical films called "Diaries, Notebooks and Sketches," Jonas Mekas says at one point that he's been told he should be searching for understanding. "Instead," he says, "I celebrate what I see." The Mekas films recall old friends, lazy afternoons, family reunions, solitude, bull sessions, impromptu parties, moments of sadness and moments of no importance whatsoever.

Steven Ascher, left, and Ed Pincus: Trying to give life meaning in a diary about a friend and some strangers.

Celebration is a kind of understanding for Mr. Mekas, whose sensibility informs every frame of his films. Though the events are impromptu, there's never any doubt about the film maker's relation to them. We share his vision.

In "Life and Other Anxieties," which opened yesterday at the Whitney Museum of American Art, the film makers Ed Pincus and Steven Ascher attempt to take the diary-film form one step further. A portion of the film—the most moving and disturbing portion—is a record of some of the last thoughts and wishes of the film makers' friend, David Hancock, 30 years old, himself a film maker, who was dying of cancer of the liver and asked Mr. Pincus and Mr. Ascher to share this time with him.

We see Mr. Hancock one summer afternoon as he sits on a New England hillside with his wife and attempts to put his affairs in order. We see him talking to his doctor, saying that he wishes to avoid drugs to ease any pain. "I want to be able to be a human being with my wife and family." We see him later, in bed in the living room of the half-finished house he was building for his family, wasting away but trying to keep a grip on things. Suddenly, at his funeral, we feel his absence as acutely as do his friends and family.

On the soundtrack Mr. Pincus tells us, "I tried to give David's life meaning, but none came . . . . What more can I say?"

Mr. Pincus need not have worried. Meaning is not something to be presented to a life as an award for its having been lived. These scenes of the last months of his friend's life are meaning enough, full of courage and concern and love

They are somewhat far afield from the rest of "Life and Other Anxieties," in which Mr. Pincus and Mr. Ascher, having traveled from New England to Minneapolis, photograph strangers, more or less at random, as they go about the business of their daily live. We see a young woman applying for a job, listen to the repartee at a "toastmasters' debate." We watch a little boy playing in the snow, then a sweet-natured black nurse as she tends the empty-eyed shell of a woman said to be 105. Dozens of people—faces of various shapes and colors—cross the screen and disappear, some to make brief reappearances, but most to exit without leaving emotional trace. Mr. Pincus calls this "an experiemnt in filming total strangers" and an attempt to "bestow the ordinary with a sense of heroism," though it doesn't quite work out that way.

The camera is an arrogant sort of instrument that has to be kept in control. When Mr. Pincus and Mr. Ascher are dealing with their dying friend, the camera responds to them and to him, capturing the pathos not only of a brave man's facing his terminal illness but also of his children playing heedlessly (as they should) nearby, of friends coping as best they can, of life going on.

In the Minneapolis sections of the film, one has the impression that the camera is more important than the people being photographed. Somehow one feels that people have become its fuel, to be used up as the camera moves on to others, and to others after that. The camera doesn't automatically refine raw material into art. In this case, it appears to consume it, mostly, I suspect, because the feelings of the film makers, so apparent in the earlier section of the film, are here undefined. There is little sense of heroism and, after the death of Mr. Hancock, survival of this sort seems paltry.

1978 Ja 18, C14:5

On Business And Pleasure

By JANET MASLIN

"Mado" runs two hours and 10 minutes and feels interminable, but

"MADO"—Ottavia Piccolo, in the title role, shares a moment with Michel Piccoli, who plays her middle-aged lover, in the French film directed by Claude Sautet.

it still seems like only half a movie. Director Claude Sautet, a man able to devote his full attention to the tiniest of issues, takes pains to explain those things he shows us, but the movie has no guiding spirit or identifiable raison d'être. Nothing about it really commands the attention.

Mado, (Ottavia Piccolo) the young woman of the title, is sullen and indecipherable, so it's just as well that her importance to the film is relatively slight. She has two groups of acquaintances, working-class kids and older, prosperous businessmen, and we are made to understand that she hires herself out to members of the latter group because members of the former are out of work. Mado only sleeps around enough to support herself, and she doesn't buy anything she doesn't need; also, she doesn't behave this way for pleasure, because she doesn't like anybody. This isn't sex, it's economic reality.

One of Mado's well-heeled admirers is Simon. (Michel Piccoli) a wealthy land developer, and it's Simon and his business that most of the film is about. Much of the plot centers around a real-estate deal, and there is a certain amount to be surmised from watching the businessmen's manners and mores. Soon enough, though, the inherent excitement of the real-estate deal begins to pall, and all that remain are vague but somehow familiar observations about the bourgeoisie.

•

Every now and then, Mado reappears to hammer home some comparison between free spirits and captive ones. In one scene, for example, Simon tries to make some coffee but is annoyed to learn that he can't operate his fancy new coffee machine. Then Mado leans over and gives the thing a twist, and it works perfectly. Sacre bleu!

The performances by Piccoli, Charles Denner (as one of Mado's beaux) and Romy Schneider (as an alcoholic in love with Piccoli) are unexpectedly moving, especially since one seldom knows why any of these characters is behaving as he or she behaves. Mr. Piccoli's role is terribly ill-defined, but he manages to give a general impression of concern.

Mr. Sautet's ending for the film is much more interesting than the slush that precedes it. Mado's two groups of friends begin to resemble one another, and to drift together, until they all wind up making an expedition to look over an important parcel of building lots (for the businessmen) and a ramshackle old farm (for the hippies). Then the party heads home, but a rainstorm and a traffic jam induce them all to leave the main road. They wind up knee-deep in mud in the countryside and it is there that everyone does something or other to reflect his or her true nature. The whole episode has the feeling of a failed Robert Altman movie as seen through a very thick fog.

1978 Ja 21, 26:1

Rolling Thunder

RENALDO AND CLARA, directed and written by Bob Dylan; edited by Mr. Dylan and Howard Alk; photography by David Myers, Paul Goldsmith, Mr. Alk and Michael Levine; music by Mr. Dylan, Ronee Blakley, Joan Baez, Roger McGuinn and Jacques Levy, Allen Ginsberg and others; produced by Lombard Street Films; distributed by Circuit Films. At The Festival, 57th Street at Fifth Aveune; The New Yorker, Broadway and 88th Street and The Waverly, Third Street and Sixth Avenue, Theaters. Running time: 292 minutes. This film is rated R.

Renaldo .... Bob Dylan
Clara .... Sara Dylan
The Woman In White .... Joan Baez
Bob Dylan .... Ronnie Hawkins
Mrs. Dylan .... Ronee Blakley
Longheno de Castro .... Jack Elliott
Lafkezio .... Harry Dean Stanton
The Masked Tortilla .... Bob Neuwirth
Helena .... Helena Kallianiotes
The Father .... Allen Ginsberg
David Blue .... David Blue
Roger McGuinn .... Roger McGuinn
Security Guard .... Mick Ronson
Sister of Mercy .... Anne Waldman

By JANET MASLIN

THERE'S an insolence about "Renaldo and Clara," the four-hour film written and directed by Bob Dylan and featuring members of his Rolling Thunder Revue, that is not easily ignored. Mr. Dylan, who has a way of insinuating that any viewer who doesn't grasp the full richness of his work must be intellectually deficient or guilty of some failure of nerve, has seen fit to produce a film that no one is likely to find altogether comprehensible. Yet for anyone even marginally interested in Mr. Dylan—and for anyone willing to accept the idea that his evasiveness, however exasperating, is a crucial aspect of his finest work — "Renaldo and Clara" holds the attention at least as effectively as it tries the patience.

No knowledge of Mr. Dylan or his history is supposed to be central to an understanding of the film, but it nevertheless trades heavily upon his past. The singer David Blue, playing himself, talks about the artistic climate of Greenwich Village when Mr. Dylan first arrived there, and Joan Baez is rather coyly cast as Mr. Dylan's former lover. Mr. Dylan, even more coyly, is cast as someone other than himself, a very vague figure named Renaldo.

•

As an actor, Mr. Dylan specializes in giving the simultaneous impressions that he isn't really interested in acting, and that he is always acting anyway. Renaldo is thus virtually useless as a character, but his alleged presence in the film does help call attention to Mr. Dylan's obsessive camouflaging of his feelings, a tendency that produces the film's only intelligible conceit. There are only two central characters in the film, a man and a woman, yet their identities are splintered and then parceled out to a dozen different actors.

The woman is most frequently played by Sara Dylan, who is now Mr. Dylan's ex-wife, but aspects of her can also be seen in Miss Baez, Ronee Blakley and Helena Kallianiotes. Mr. Dylan, Ronnie Hawkins and Rob Stoner are among the actors who stand in for the man. The two lovers, apparently about to become ex-lovers, are irremediably locked in battle, but the device of fluctuating identities prevents them from ever confronting each other face to face.

•

"RENALDO AND CLARA"—Bob Dylan performs in his new film, which he also wrote, directed and produced. It will

This technique, not unlike one used by Robert Altman in "Images," is potentially an intriguing one, but Mr. Dylan's love of mystery prevails over his exhibitionism, with disappointing results. Most of the actors here seem to be playing either Mr. or Mrs. Dylan, and all of them slavishly do the director's bidding. But Mr. Dylan's instructiveness, to his actors and to his audience, is incomplete. "Renaldo and Clara" is so personal it borders on being obscure, yet it remains surprisingly deficient in personality. The figure who dominates the film is a man in hiding.

Mr. Dylan hs always been elusive; that's no mean part of his charm. But his best work, like the "Blood on the Tracks" album released a couple of years ago, has derived its momentum from alternating currents of passion and restraint, from conflicting impulses to repress and to reveal. "Renaldo and Clara" addresses this apparent contradiction so passively, even cold-bloodedly, that it seldom has the urgency it needs. The film is full of connections to be made and riddles to be solved, but it approaches these things so dispassionately that the viewer has little choice but to follow suit.

Even though Mr. Dylan makes it clear that he in no way wanted to make a concert film, the footage of him in performance provides not only the film's most electrifying moments but also its most emblematic ones. On the Rolling Thunder tour, Mr. Dylan performed in whiteface, and he is photographed here in tight closeup, singing so ferociously that his sweat melts the makeup; the film's sense of a person at war with a mask is never more riveting than when the camera studies Mr. Dylan's face as he sings. Every detail of these shots is resonant, from the fiery look in Mr. Dylan's eyes to the fresh flowers that someone has apparently been hired to tuck into his hatbrim, just before each show.

The film contains more than its share of dead weight, but it is seldom genuinely dull. On the credit side, there are a great many isolated images that have an independent vitality, from the sight of Joan Baez, looking unexpectedly dreamy in a white gown, to the spectacle of Allen Ginsberg, introduced as "without a doubt a very interesting and clever personality," reading his poetry to a bewildered band of middle-aged ladies.

•

It's a pity that the editing of the film, which is credited to Mr. Dylan and Howard Alk, pays so little heed to consistency. Following a pattern of linear thought is clearly not one of the film's concerns, but maintaining a constant degree of intensity should have been; this way, by carelessly commingling very complex and suggestive episodes with very flat and simple ones, the editing continually throws an already befuddled viewer even further off balance. Interludes like the culminating meeting of Mr. Dylan, Mrs. Dylan and Miss Baez, at once quite rarefied and in an atmosphere that is amusingly mundane, and an exceedingly one-note segment devoted to Hurricane Carter, are so incompatible that they simply don't belong in the same movie.

1978 Ja 26, C18:1

BIGTIME, directed by Andrew Georgias; music by Smokey Robinson; produced by Christipher Joy, Leon Isaac, Andrew Georgias and Louis Gross; distributed by Big Time Company Ltd. At the National and other theaters. Running time: 90 minutes. This film is rated PG.

WITH: Christipher Joy, Tobar Mayo, Jayne Kennedy, Art Evans and Roger E. Mosley.

THEY DON'T COME much more small-time than "Bigtime," a harmless but also brainless comedy about an insurance swindler who can't do anything right. Eddie Jones, played with an ear-to-ear grin by Christipher Joy, specializes in throwing himself in front of cars and then collecting damages. But he does this so uninterestingly that the screenplay must also throw in pizza-guzzling Mafiosi, a hot $100,000, a love interest who looks and sounds as if she ought to have a wind-up knob between her shoulder blades and a lot of white folks who are venal enough to make Eddie look positively heroic by comparison.

The only character of any interest is the mob's white-suited "Negro Representative," an amusingly incompetent Superfly type played nicely by Roger E. Mosley, the actor who starred in "Leadbelly."

The best that can be said for the soundtrack, which is by Smokey Robinson, is that it's genial and innocuous and at least it isn't disco.

•

"Bigtime" is rated PG ("Parental Guidance Suggested"), perhaps because Mr. Joy ogles a couple of buxom women and perhaps because of a few lines that are only marginally risqué.

JANET MASLIN

1978 Ja 26, C19:4

Made in Exile

THE SERPENT'S EGG, directed by Ingmar Bergman; screenplay by Mr. Bergman; produced by Dino De Laurentis; executive producer, Horst Wendlandt; director of photography, Sven Nykvist; music, Rolf Wilhelm; editor, Petra von Oelffen; distributed by Paramount Pictures. Running time: 119 minutes. At the Coronet Theater, Third Avenue near 59th Street. This film has been rated R.

Manuela Rosenberg .... Liv Ullmann
Abel Rosenberg .... David Carradine
Inspector Bauer .... Gert Froebe
Hans Vergerus .... Heinz Bennent
Musician .... Glynn Turman
Priest .... James Whitmore
Mr. Rosenberg .... Toni Berger
Student .... Christian Berkel
Mrs. Hemse .... Paula Bräend
Mrs. Rosenberg .... Edna Bruenell
Cabaret comedian .... Paul Buerks
Woman with baby .... Gaby Dohm
Cupid .... Emil Feist

By VINCENT CANBY

BERLIN, NOV. 3-11, is a city without sunlight. Mostly it rains. It snows occasionally but it's the kind of snow that is already gray by the time it reaches the cobblestones. Everything is damp, chilled. No winter coats anywhere. People cling to one another for warmth, but there is none. In effect, life is over in Ingmar Bergman's new film, "The Serpent's Egg." What we witness are involuntary twitches, the glazing of eyeballs—the onset of rigor mortis.

"The Serpent's Egg" is the darkest, most barren Bergman film since "Shame," and the windiest, most banal since "The Touch," full of dark portents that he treats as if they were his privileged information, as if they hadn't been in the public domain for nearly four decades. The film, which opens today at the Coronet, is dispossessed Bergman, Bergman in exile from his native Sweden whose serene political-social landscape has always highlighted the particular terrors of Bergman characters.

•

"The Serpent's Egg" is the first film to be made by Bergman after he voluntarily left Sweden to take up residence in Germany following his brush with the Swedish authorities. This information may not be relevant, but it might help to explain the peculiar sense of screenplay, a melodrama that never quite makes any connection to the characters within it.

The film, which takes place in Berlin in the week in 1923 when Hitler failed in his first attempt to take power, has the form of a mystery and some of the elements of rudimentary science-fiction, though, with hindsight, we (and Bergman) know it to be science-fact.

The two principal characters are Abel Rosenberg (David Carradine), an American trapeze artist stranded in Berlin after his partner-brother has had a minor accident, and Abel's sister-in-law, Manuela (Liv Ullmann), who is separated from Abel's brother. In the film's opening sequence Abel returns to his hotel room to find that his brother has committed suicide for no apparent reason, leaving behind a barely legible note warning of people "being poisoned."

•

In the succeeding days, Abel, who is a somewhat more mysterious character than Bergman may have intended, appears on the edge of an hysteria that has its origins in events that occurred before the start of the movie, as well as in the current events he participates in. Manuela, so beautiful and sweet-natured that we wonder why she and her late husband split up, sings and dances in a sleazy cabaret by night and works from 9 A.M. to 3 P.M. several days a week in a whorehouse.

While the city is apparently coming apart through apathy and inflation, Abel is losing his grip on reality. One morning he is picked up by a friendly, though menacing, police inspector (Gert Froebe) who suspects him of being implicated in his brother's death as well as in the unexplained deaths of a half-dozen other people he has known. Is Abel going out of his mind? If you know your standard mystery movie, you know he is not, but the explanations that Bergman finally gives us aren't worthy of the mysteries he has tantalized us with.

It is Bergman's point that Abel and Manuela, in this week in which they attempt to survive in Berlin, witness the "nesting" of the serpent's egg, the embryo that 10 years later will hatch Hitler, the Nazis, the holocaust, World War II and all the evils we know eventually to have come forth.

The audience, unfortunately, is way ahead of the movie's political forecast, which might not be fatal if Bergman's characters provided any particular insights, or interest. They don't.

As played by Mr. Carradine, Abel Rosenberg is a wounded creature even before his brother's suicide. He may be surprised to experience anti-Semitism for the first time, but his surprise isn't enough to give the experience dramatic weight in the film.

•

Miss Ullmann's Manuela is an extremely ladylike cabaret singer and part-time whore, and there is something perfunctory about the jazzy cabaret sequences shot in lewd colors and featuring performers in bizarre costumes and makeup. Decadence of this sort is the easiest thing in the world to capture on film, second only to the kind of suspense that can be generated by a horse race in a movie—any movie.

Bergman's villain, a mad scientist played by Heinz Bennent, is a B-movie creature. He's so rotten he almost seems to be an old friend, though he talks rather better than most villains as he describes the terrible things that will soon come to pass.

•

Is this all there is to "The Serpent's Egg?" it seems to be, but there are

Liv Ullmann and David Carradine in Ingmar Bergman's "The Serpent's Egg"
A melodrama that never quite makes any connection to the characters within it

indications that despair is really the film's theme, though this despair is made compelling on only a couple of occasions. The opening of the film with the brother's suicide is one of the most sorrowful sequences Bergman has ever done. There's also a fine, ghoulish sequence in which the drunken Abel breaks the window of a Berlin bakery shop, as if to make himself the object of the wrath that German Jews feel toward all Nazis.

Mostly, "The Serpent's Egg" is a movie of beautifully photographed weather and handsome period sets and costumes that encase characters who remain as anonymous as the bodies in a morgue. It's dead.

1978 Ja 27, C8:1

Two by Red Grooms

FAT FEET, directed by Red Grooms; produced by Mr. Grooms and Yvonne Anderson; running time: 20 minutes. RUCKUS MANHATTAN, a documentary by David Saunders, Mr. Grooms, Peter Hutton and the Ruckus Construction Company; running time: 61 minutes. Both films distributed by Film Makers' Cooperative. At the Film Forum, 15 Vandam Street.

LOTS OF PEOPLE have conquered Manhattan for short periods of time but perhaps only Red Grooms, the artist, has conquered it more or less permanently by making it funny, unthreatening, invigorating and completely comprehensible without denying its vitality. This is the dominant note of "Ruckus Manhattan," the extraordinary walk-in, see-through, sit-on, look-up-at sculptured (and painted, nailed, pasted, riveted, etc.) construction that was shown here in 1975-1976.

•

"Ruckus Manhattan" is also the name of the documentary film made by Mr. Grooms and his associates as they went about their work like a lunatic crew of Santa Claus and helpers. The film, as well as a 20-minute Grooms short, "Fat Feet," opened yesterday at the Film Forum, where it will be shown tonight through Sunday at 7:45 and at the same time next week, Thursday through Sunday.

"Ruckus Manhattan," the movie, is almost as much fun as the completed construction, a collection of colorfully woozy mock-ups and miniatures of some of Manhattan's foremost attractions, including its citizens, from the Brooklyn Bridge and Staten Island Ferry to its subways, porn parlors, Times Square and the World Trade Center. The movie records in the speeded-up style of a Keystone Kops comedy the frantic activity that followed Mr. Grooms's original inspiration, which was clearly that of a happy, well-adjusted, extremely witty man.

"Fat Feet," which Mr. Grooms made in 1966, is a day in the life of the same city, a movie that combines animation, live action and cartoon techniques in a way that recalls the work of the greatest movie magician of them all, George Melies. The Grooms Manhattan is an interlocking series of fires, holdups, get-aways, a place where a hungry rat can swallow a cat. It's ebullient and cheerful and about as far away from intimations of urban despair as you can get without moving to Idaho.

VINCENT CANBY

1978 Ja 27, C18:5

FILM VIEW

VINCENT CANBY

Bergman's Baffling 'Serpent's Egg'

Having produced in comparatively quick succession in the past seven years five films that may well be masterpieces—"The Passion of Anna," "Cries and Whispers," "Scenes from a Marriage," "The Magic Flute" and "Face to Face"—Ingmar Bergman has earned the right to fall short of our expectations of him, to force us to wonder if, perhaps, we are somehow failing him rather than the other way around. His new film, "The Serpent's Egg," looks to be so obviously wrong-headed—too explicit when one longs for mystery, too oblique when one needs a few direct answers—that it seems inconceivable that a man of Bergman's genius did not know exactly what he was doing. If so, we owe it to him to find out.

"The Serpent's Egg" was filmed in Germany where Bergman settled two years ago in his self-imposed exile from Sweden following his Kafkaesque brush with the Swedish tax authorities. His screenplay, which he was working on long before he left his homeland (or knew that he had any intention of leaving), is about dispossession, the literal, geographic dispossession of people trying to survive in an alien land, something that has appeared in earlier Bergman films as an emotional dispossession, of the kind that haunted Jenny, the psychiatrist played by Liv Ullmann in "Face to Face."

Beause it's the first movie Bergman has produced outside Sweden, a country whose past and present have illuminated every film he's ever made, I anticipate that one popular way to explain the strangeness of "The Serpent's Egg" will be to blame it all on the filmmaker's uncertain state of mind when he set about to shoot the picture. His judgment was thrown off by the new surroundings, some will say. He felt that he had to mark his new territory immediately by making a film there, whether he was ready or not, to reassert his identity as an artist. Perhaps. Others may well put the blame on the English-language screenplay, as many (including myself) were inclined to do in the case of "The Touch," his 1971 film that co-starred Elliott Gould, Bibi Andersson and Max von Sydow.

The quality of the language in "The Touch" reduced Bergman's metaphysical musings to the level of Mary Hartman's prose. Yet, Bergman can write fine, spare, incisive English, as anyone who read "Cries and Whispers" in The New Yorker knows, and there's nothing wrong with the language in "The Serpent's Egg." What's troublesome—to be most gentle about it—is its field of vision. "The Serpent's Egg" appears to be a tale of nothing less than apocalyptic hindsight, a warning of dreadful events to happen 40 years ago, a prediction of dire things that already have occurred.

• • •

The setting is Berlin and the time is specific, from Nov. 3 to Nov. 11 in 1923, the week in which Hitler made his aborted attempt to take power and was himself packed off to prison. It is Bergman's metaphor that in this week was nested "the serpent's egg" from which, 10 years later, was hatched the Third Reich and the holocaust that followed.

Bergman's two principal characters are Abel Rosenberg (David Carradine), an American acrobat stranded in Berlin following the injury of the brother with whom he did his high-wire act, and Abel's former sister-in-law, Manuela (Liv Ullmann), once a member of the act, now a cabaret "artiste" whose nationality is never made clear, though she's certainly not German.

At the start of the film Abel and Manuela, who apparently have been fond of each other in the past but nothing more, are brought together by the suicide of Abel's brother, who was Manuela's ex-husband. The self-murder, as well as a suicide note that seems to make no sense, baffle Abel and Manuela, but it somehow fits the despair of a time and place where, in Bergman's words, "there is no future." Inflation is running rampant. The democratic government is powerless to act in decisive fashion. New political groups are born every day. Right-wing newspapers editorialize on the dangers of Bolshevism, of "circumcized Asiatics" who threaten the middle class with rape and murder and worse—the destruction of private property.

For reasons that initially appear to be arbitrary, Abel is pursued by a philisophical police inspector (Gert Frobe) who believes that Abel is somehow implicated not only in his brother's suicide but also in the mysterious deaths of a half-dozen other people who, in one way and another, have been associated with him. Another character who materializes out of this chaos is a mysterious, patently evil scientist named Hans Vergerus (Heinz Bennent), whom the Philadelphia-born Abel knew as a boy (they both vacationed in Amalfi, the script tells us rather lamely) and who turns up in the present as a sometime suitor of Manuela.

"The Serpent's Egg" begins with a cry of despair of a pitch it never again attains—when Abel returns to the shabby Berlin hotel room to find his brother sitting up in bed, his mouth hanging open, his head framed by recently blown-out brains. As played by Mr. Carradine, Abel is a camera that can barely contain its images. He has one of those fine, sensitive-tough faces that seems to be a perfect Bergman instrument in the early sections of the films when, by his enigmatic responses, we are drawn into the vortex of a mystery. Yet, as the mystery begins to dissipate, the movie has the effect of leaving Mr. Carradine stranded without a character. We know that he is Jewish, though he's never thought much about it, and that at the start of the film he is an alcoholic though, until recently, he has been one of the world's great aerialists.

Equally mysterious is the character of Manuela, whose name is far more suggestive and exotic than the woman Liv Ullmann plays, a rather classy type to find performing in a supposedly decadent cabaret (decadent, we know, because she wears a green wig, lots of blue eye shadow, exposed black garters and sings naughty, neo-"Blue Angel" songs). Yet, being Liv Ullmann and coming to us bearing associations to her extraordinary performances in "Scenes from a Marriage" and "Face to Face," she is never terribly convincing as the third-rate singer and part-time whore. It's not because she seems too fine-grained and intelligent, too ladylike, but because the movie gives her hardly anything to work with.

• • •

I have no doubt that Bergman has made exactly the sort of movie he intended, but it's my suspicion that the movie he intended is not the kind of movie he does best. Everything that interests Bergman most (on the evidence of his most satisfying films) would appear to have happened before "The Serpent's Egg" begins. I know that critics have no business telling any artist what he should have done, but what interests me most about "The Serpent's Egg" is the drama by which Abel and Manela get to where they are at the film's opening.

What sort of high-wire act did Abel, Manuela and Abel's brother do? Why did Manuela and her husband split? What was the relationship between Abel and Manuela when they were touring the world as circus stars? Why has Abel gone to pieces, as he apparently has when we first meet him? What really is the relationship between Manuela and the evil Hans Vergerus, whom Bergman presents to us as a kind of prototypical apologist for the Nazi Superman ideology? In "The Serpent's Egg," Bergman has Manuela say of Hans that she felt sorry for him, which I take to be a true statement and is the only indication that this obvious monster might be a man. Bergman never sees fit to explore any of these questions in the course of "The Serpent's Egg," though he ends the film by giving us rather more of a vision than we need of the future horrors that have been projected from the events he has shown us.

As I wrote that last paragraph, it suddenly occurred to me that the questions I raised may be just the questions that Bergman wants raised, and that it's the series of unanswered questions that makes the film succeed to the extent that it does. In this case, though, it seems to me he asks us to fill in more than we can be reasonably expected to.

"The Serpent's Egg" is not a failure. There's never any doubt about the Bergman sensibility and the weight of the intelligence brought to bear on the options taken. Yet, this awareness is haunted, troubled. The film begins by calling forth timeless despair and evolves gradually into particular melodrama that is less convincing, less meaningful, less fun and less evocative of its period than the nightmare worlds of Fritz Lang's Dr. Mabuse movies. ■

1978 Ja 29, II:17:1

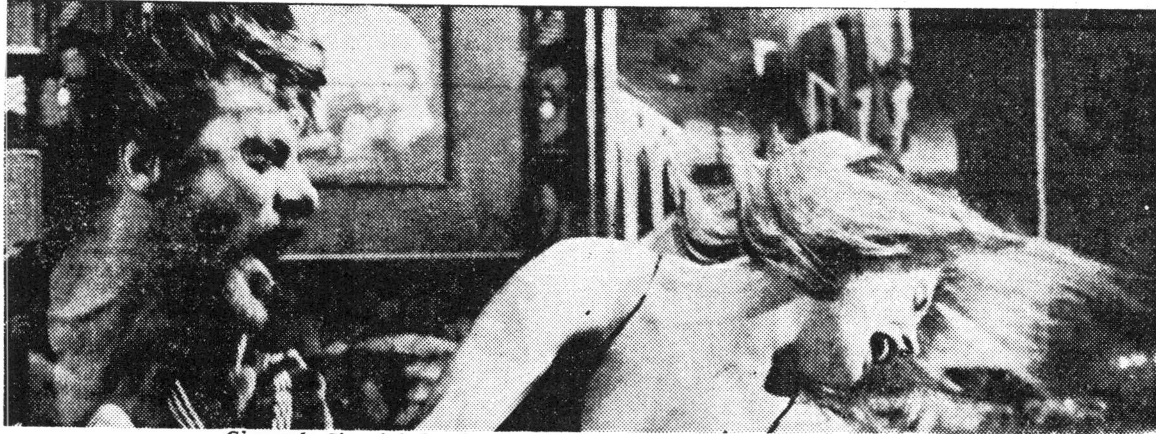

Giancarlo Giannini slapping Candice Bergen in Lina Wertmuller's new film
A movie that uses too many words to say very little

THE END OF THE WORLD IN OUR USUAL BED IN A NIGHT FULL OF RAIN, directed and written by Lina Wertmuller; executive producer, Harry Colombo; produced by Gil Shiva; director of photography, Giuseppe Rotunno; editor, Franco Fraticelli; music, G. B. Pergolesi and Roberto De Simone; distributed by Warner Bros. Running time' 104 minutes. At Loews Tower East, Third Avenue near 72d Street. This film has been rated R.

Paolo .... Giancarlo Giannini
Lizzy .... Candice Bergen
Chorus: Anne Byrne, Flora Carabella, Alice Colombo, Michel Tucker, Lucio Amelio, Agnese De Dunoto, Anny Papa, Massimo Wertmuller.

By VINCENT CANBY

"THE END of the World in Our Usual Bed in a Night Full of Rain," the title of Lina Wertmuller's new film, her first in English, is more or less a pictograph of a movie that uses too many words to say very little, at least very little that hasn't been said before with more wit and ebullience, often by the Italian director herself.

The subject is once again sex and politics, which in "The Seduction of Mimi" and "Swept Away," two of Miss Wertmuller's funniest films, erupted all over the place as the natural consequences of ordinary—though far from commonplace—heterosexual relations.

In Miss Wertmuller's little red book, men are capitalists and women the proletariats. Sex is a projection of the class struggle and romantic love is the foundation for an economic system that creates co-conspirators of masters and slaves, of lovers and those loved. What has made her films so surprising and moving and comic, perhaps even counterrevolutionary, until now, is the peculiar way in which contradictory class roles can become hilariously and naturally confused within a single character.

•

The Communist deckhand in "Swept Away," the fellow played by Giancarlo Giannini, is as outrageously self-interested as a 19th-century railroad baron once he takes command of his woman on a desert island. The title character in "The Seduction of Mimi," another Communist played by Mr. Giannini, is seduced, abandoned and seduced again by love. The most appealing Wertmuller characters are earnest, sincere, sometimes none-too-bright, full of awareness about others and absolutely blind about themselves.

This gult is what makes them figures of essential comedy. Pasqualino (Mr. Giannini), the third-rate Neapolitan hood who chooses survival above honor in "Seven Beauties," is comic not because of what he does, but because of the great value he puts on things the rest of us have been taught are worthless. We don't feel superior to him. We can recognize similar patterns in ourselves.

Unfortunately, there are no surprises, no feelings of recognition, no real contradictions at work in "The End of the World," which opened yesterday at Loews Tower East and which Miss Wertmuller apparently considers her most political film. That may be, though I doubt that any movie as essentially lifeless as this one can be political in the sense that it might move one to specific action.

"The End of the World" is about Paolo (Mr. Giannini), a Communist journalist, a thinking male chauvinist, and his American wife, Lizzy (Candice Bergen), a feminist and a professional photographer, whose marriage is coming apart in the course of the film for reasons that could surprise only someone who's been out of the universe for the last 20 years.

The setting is a magnificent Roman apartment on a rainy night that, through hints that march through the movie like painted elephants, could be the beginning of Armageddon. A television commentator speaks ominously of floods that are without precedent, of an upper atmosphere that's been worn out through air pollution down below.

Lizzy represents not only liberated woman, but also the entire New World, which hasn't realized its potential. Paolo is the Old World intellectual who recognizes his defects and is powerless to correct them. Lizzy and Paolo aren't people. They are personalized shopping carts overloaded with large, economy-sized, precooked ideas.

In a series of flashbacks, Miss Wertmuller fills us in on the meeting, courtship and marriage of Lizzy and Paolo, a series of scenes that becomes increasingly humorless as we approach the present night and its anticlimax—when Lizzy accuses Paolo of making love as if he were taking a walk before going to sleep. In his turn, Paolo accuses Lizzy of wanting to abandon the home. He: "You blame me for what you haven't done." She: "You're right—that's why I have to go."

"The End of the World" is virtually a two-character movie, though there's a hideous chorus made up of Lizzy and Paolo's friends who appear from time to time to make facetious comments about the married couple.

The movie isn't witty and it's seldom funny, partly because Lizzy and Paolo are forever saying things Miss Wertmuller seems to agree with, but Miss Wertmuller is not Shaw. As a political philosopher, she'd be great at a cocktail party. There are no self-delusions in the characters. We are meant to attend to their clichés as if hearing them for the first time. There's nothing to discover in this movie, which hasn't evolved as a human comedy, from its characters, but from points of view for which characters have been created.

Miss Bergen's is the least attractive, since the dialogue Miss Wertmuller has given her leans heavily on desperate sarcasm. Most of the time Mr. Giannini replays his familiar Italian male-chauvinist-pig character, which doesn't quite fit here because he is supposed to be an intelligent, knowing man. Neither actor is helped by Miss Wertmuller's addiction to tight close-ups that have the effect of exposing the film's emptiness.

There is one very funny sequence near the beginning of the film, when Lizzy makes a shambles of a solemn religious procession by coming to the aid of a woman who's being beaten up by a boyfriend, but the rest of the movie is made tolerable only by the sets, including a beautiful 14th-century monastery and the huge, old-fashioned apartment where Lizzy and Paolo live. "The End of the World" appears not to have been written and directed, but furnished by a classy interior decorator.

1978 Ja 30, C15:1

Five in Vietnam

BOYS IN COMPANY C, directed by Sidney J. Furie; written by Rick Natkin and Mr. Furie; director of photography, Godfrey A. Godar; film editors, Michael Berman, Frank J. Uriosle, Alan Pattillo and James Benson; music by Jaime Mendoza-Nava; produced by Andre Morgan; released by Columbia Pictures. At Loews State 2, Orpheum, Bay and other theaters. Running time: 126 minutes. This film is rated R.

Tyrone Washington .... Stan Shaw
Billy Ray Pike .... Andrew Stevens
Alvin Foster .... James Canning
Vinnie Fazio .... Michael Lembeck
Dave Bisbee .... Craig Wasson
Captain Collins .... Scott Hylands
Lieutenant Archer .... James Whitmore Jr.
Sergeant Curry .... Nobie Willimgham

By JANET MASLIN

ACCORDING to a recent ad, "The Boys in Company C" are "the craziest group of men this country ever sent off to war." Here's why: Dave Bisbee is a hippie who says, when he is drafted into the Marines, "I guess that's my karma coming out," and who is seldom without his guitar. Vinnie Fazio is a fast-talking ladies' man from Brooklyn. Alvin Foster is a sensitive type, and he keeps the journal upon which the movie is supposedly based. Billy Ray Pike is an even more sensitive type, because he worries about having left his young sweetheart pregnant and later winds up hooked on drugs in Vietnam. And Tyrone Washington is a former ghetto dope dealer who turns out to have astounding leadership abilities, plus the soul of a philosopher and a heart of gold.

Stan Shaw

"You may want to forget the war, but you'll never forget the Boys in Company C," this same ad continues. One reason you won't forget them is that they're already so familiar. In fact, they are so stereotypical, and hence so constricted, that they don't seem to have any feelings of consequence about what they do or what happens to them. This amounts to a failure to take any stand on Vietnam, something that a more slapdash movie might be able to pass off as mere irresponsibility. But "The Boys in Company C" is, in every other respect, as calculating as can be. As a film about heroism, it is chiefly remarkable for its gutlessness.

•

The mood is a carefully balanced one: sure, there are mines in the rice paddies and there's murder in the air, but there is also a spirit of cute camaraderie. In addition, there are a madcap ballgame finale out of "M*A*S*H," tidy where-are-they-now? closing credits out of "American Graffiti," and an odd clarity of purpose that, under the war's confusing circumstances, is out of the blue.

The movie is so determined to create instant heroes that it must have its instant villains too; in this case, there are corrupt South Vietnamese officials and excessively gung-ho Marine officers to be blamed. Less visible, but also under indictment, are drugs, the Vietcong and American racism. But there's no real evidence of the troubled American political climate of 1967, which is when the story takes place. As far as the screenplay is concerned, this might as well be World War II.

An opening sequence, which typifies the film's teasing tactics, introduces the five protagonists and establishes them as wildly different from one another, then robs them of all eccentricities as soon as they hop into uniform and have their heads shaved. Next thing we know, they're in boot camp, being told things like "You see that guy next to you? You think he's a $%/& or a *)%/ or a &!!/)? I don't care, cause he's gonna save your $%/$%&!* life some day!" Next thing after that, the boys have shaped up and shipped out, each one retaining only one-note remnants of his original nature.

The cast is made up of new young actors, all of whose performances are eclipsed by the cheap ironies of the screenplay (recruit accidentally discovering a body bag: "Hey, I got it, you sleep in it! It's a lightweight sleeping bag!") and by the banality of their roles. The wise guy, Vinnie Fazio, is particularly grating, but the actor who plays him (Michael Lembeck) seems to be doing exactly what's expected of him. James Whitmore Jr., who plays a reasonable officer to Scott Hylands's fanatic, gives the only performance with even a trace of the unexpected. But the actor likely to make the biggest splash is Stan Shaw. As the black recruit, Mr. Shaw is handsome and more than competent, and the character he plays is wonderful in a way that only movie characters can ever be.

In fact, it's hard to recall anyone on the screen who has demonstrated such unremitting nobility, such unmitigated righteousness, in recent years. And it's hard to imagine a less appropriate occasion on which those qualities might reappear.

1978 F 2, C15:5

Snooping in the O.R.

COMA, directed by Michael Chrichton; screenplay by Dr. Crichton, based on the novel by Robin Cook; produced by Martin Erlichman; music, Jerry Goldsmith; director of photography, Victor J. Kemper; editor, David Bretherton; distributed by United Artists. Running time: 112 minutes. At the Criterion Theater, Broadway near 44th Street; Plaza Theater, 58th Street east of Madison, and Murray Hill Theater, 34th Street near Third Avenue. This film has been rated PG.

Dr. Susan Wheeler	Genevieve Bujold
Dr. Mark Bellows	Michael Douglas
Mrs. Emerson	Elizabeth Ashley
Dr. George	Rip Torn
Dr. George Harris	Richard Widmark
Nancy Greenly	Lois Chiles
Dr. Morelind	Harry Rhodes
Computer Technician	Gary Barton
Kelly	Frank Downing
Jim	Richard Doyle
Dr. Marcus	Alan Haufrect
Vince	Lance Le Gault
Chief Resident	Michael MacRae
Nurse	Betty McGuire
Sean Murphy	Tom Selleck
Dr. Goodman	Charles Siebert
Lab Technician	William Wintersole

By VINCENT CANBY

"COMA" is a hospital thriller that has the manner of a cool, brisk night nurse. It does what must be done and moves on before you can really see what it looks like. The film, adapted and directed by Michael Crichton, himself a doctor, is based on the best-selling novel by Robin Cook, who is also a doctor. It's the kind of story that, after you've seen "Coma," you might suspect a couple of waggish surgeons of having cooked up in the operating room while removing a brain tumor.

One can only hope the surgeons would be more efficient in cleaning up after the brain tumor than they've been in tidying up the plausibility questions that remain after the movie. Plausibility is not always important, but in a film as bereft of distinctive style and wit as "Coma," it helps to believe in something. It can even help if one is offended. The aftereffect of "Coma" is a catlike yawn ,benign and bored.

The movie is about the Nancy Drew-like adventure faced by pretty, plucky Dr. Susan Wheeler (Genevieve Bujold), a resident surgeon at Boston Memorial Hospital, after her best friend suffers irreparable brain damage in the course of a minor operation. Against the advice of her lover, handsome, hearty Dr. Mark Bellows (Michael Douglas), a young surgeon on the make for money and position, pretty, plucky Dr. Susan Wheeler initiates her own investigation and discovers that in the last year, something like a dozen other patients, all young and in good health, have met similar fates.

It soon becomes apparent to pretty, plucky Dr. Susan Wheeler that there is a conspiracy afoot. All of the fatal operations have been performed in the very same operating room, a fact that handsome, hearty Dr. Mark Bellows dismisses as the merest coincidence. Even gruff, kindly old Dr. George Harris (Richard Widmark), the hospital's avuncular head, refuses to listen to her suspicions. What can a pretty, plucky girl do?

Well, the last thing she ever thinks about in this movie is going to the police. Instead, like Nancy Drew, she snoops around alone in the hospital basement and up its air shafts. She receives a promise of vital information from a hospital maintenance engineer and then is a witness to his not quite accidential electrocution. Still pretty plucky Dr. Susan Wheeler pushes on and on, tempting fate and, more dangerously, our patience.

In his first film as a director, "Westworld," Mr. Crichton made very efficient use of some Disneyland-like robots. "Coma" is the kind of movie that turns real-life actors into robot-like functions of the story. Miss Bujold, Mr. Douglas and Mr. Widmark, as well as Rip Torn, Elizabeth Ashley and a stunningly beautiful actress named Lois Chiles, are as mechanical as dolls whose expressions are controlled by a computer's console.

•

"Coma," which has been rated PG ("Parental Guidance Suggested"), contains some mildly vulgar language and some fleeting nudity in a sequence in which a lot of bodies, which are in a state of suspended animation, appear to be sleeping in fancy, Danish-modern hammocks.

1978 F 2, C15:1

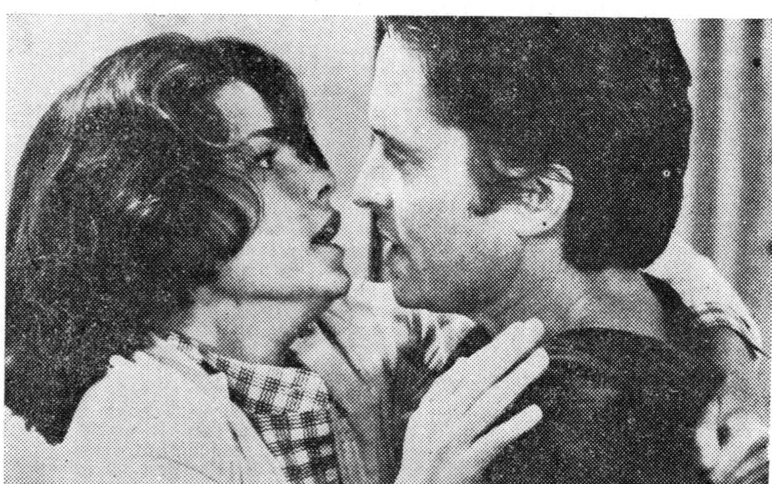

Genevieve Bujold and Michael Douglas in the film

From 'Out There'

STARSHIP INVASIONS, directed and written by Ed Hunt; director of photography, Mark Irwin; music by Gil Melle; film editors, Millie Moore and Ruth Hope; produced by Norman Glick, Mr. Hunt and Ken Gord; released by Warner Bros. At the Cinerama, Lyric, UA East 85th Street, 83d Street Triplex and other theaters. Running time: 89 minutes. This film is rated PG.

Professor Duncan	Robert Vaughn
Captain Rameses	Christopher Lee
Anaxi	Daniel Pilon
Phi	Tiiu Leek
Betty	Helen Shaver
Malcolm	Henry Ramer
Gezeth	Victoria Johnson
Dorothy	Doreen Lipson

"STARSHIP INVASIONS" appears to have been made early enough to borrow from "Stars Wars" but too soon to borrow more than a vague U.F.O. angle from "Close Encounters of the Third Kind," on a budget that might better have been used to supply hot dogs for a small picnic. The flying saucers look like hubcaps, the spacelings' bodysuits are baggy and the Christopher Lee part isn't even properly played by Christopher Lee.

Mr. Lee does appear in the film, playing an extraterrestrial from a planet whose sun is about to explode, and he scouts Earth as a possible new home for his dislocated people. But Mr. Lee's people do not speak, except in voice-over; this, plus some black costumes with pointy hoods, is supposed to indicate that they come from somewhere other than B-movieville. Wherever they're from, they should have stayed there.

Information about the earthlings is scanty, and it all seems to come from magazine covers. Professor Duncan, played wearily by Robert Vaughn, is evidently a Very Famous U.F.O. Expert, because we glimpse his picture on the cover of People magazine one day. And the star wars, which are cheesily staged and should be of no interest even to the most avid science-fiction buffs, generate a mysterious wave of despondency on earth. "Suicide Epidemic!" screams a fake cover of Time, which depicts a bleeding wrist. As the subhead adds, "Will There Be a Tomorrow?"

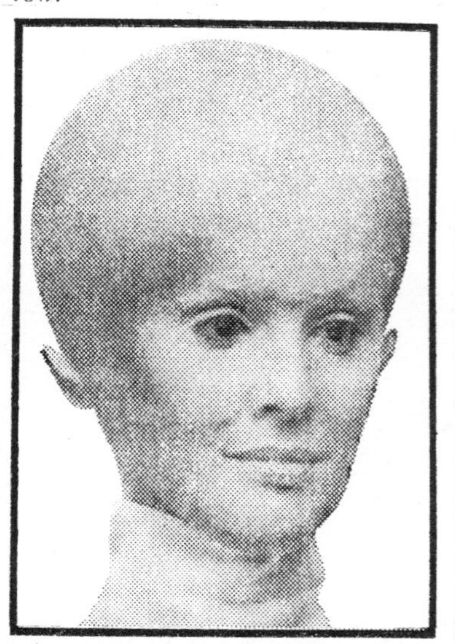

Tiiu Leek as Phi in "Starship Invasions"

"Starship Invasions" is full of outmoded plexiglass props that look as though they've been remaindered at Bloomingdale's, and cardboard sets that are painfully underdecorated. The movie's only truly futuristic touches are in its exterior shots, which are so grainy they make the air look even muddier than it actually is.

"Starship Invasions" is rated PG ("Parental Guidance Suggested") because one scene features a recreation center stocked with cuties from outer space. No recreation takes place and, in any event, the cuties aren't all that cute.

JANET MASLIN

1978 F 3, C10:1

En Route to Stardom

THE ONE AND ONLY, directed by Carl Reiner; screenplay by Steve Gordon; produced by Steve Gordon and David V. Picker; executive producer, Robert Halmi; director of photography, Victor J. Kemper; editor, Bud Molin; music, Patrick Williams, a First Artists production, distributed by Paramount Pictures. Running time: 98 minutes. At Loews State 1 Theater, Broadway near 45th Street; Loews Cine Theater, Third Avenue near 86th Street, and the 34th Street East Theater, near Second Avenue. This film has been rated PG.

Andy Schmidt	Henry Winkler
Mary Crawford	Kim Darby
Sidney Seltzer	Gene Saks
Mr. Crawford	William Daniels
Hector Moses	Harold Gould
Milton Miller	Herve Villechaize
Mrs. Crawford	Polly Holliday
Announcer	Bill Baldwin
Little Andy	Anthony Battaglia
Arnold, the king	Ed Begley Jr.
Sherman	Brandon Cruz
Agatha Franklin	Lucy Lee Flippin

By VINCENT CANBY

THERE is one very funny moment in Carl Reiner's "The One and Only," which otherwise stars Henry Winkler as an egocentric, young, would-be actor who wants to become a Broadway star in the 1950's.

The funny moment stars Hervé Villechaize, whom you probably remember as the evil midget in "The Man With the Golden Gun." This time Mr. Villechaize, who is 3 feet 11 inches tall, plays a good guy, or at least as good a guy as his character's licentiousness allows.

Milton (Mr. Villechaize) is a part-time wrestler and a full-time Romeo and, in the one and only funny moment in the new movie, he is mysteriously smitten with a timid, square, middle-aged, Midwestern housewife. She sits primly on a sofa, hands in lap, attending to her husband's clichés. Milton sits next to her, smiling up at her in a way intended to be sweet but actually the expression of rampant sexuality. He inches closer to her. She inches away. Suddenly he slips his tiny wicked hand onto her lap. She screams and—that more or less is that.

What? That doesn't sound especially funny? Well, it is funny and in the context of the rest of "The One and Only," it's something of a privileged moment. Mr. Villechaize is a remarkably gifted comic actor who just happens to be smaller than most. He has a fine appreciation for the ridiculous and possesses a slack-jawed leer that would tone up any French farce.

He also tones up "The One and Only," which opens today at three theaters. "The One and Only" is a far cry from French farce and any other kind of farce, being instead an attempt to make a heart-warming comedy about a fellow who, in the film's own terms, is an arrogant boob.

When we first meet Mr. Winkler's Andy Schmidt, he seems to be a comparatively elderly undergraduate at a midwestern university where he successfully courts another undergraduate, a woman named Mary Crawford (Kim

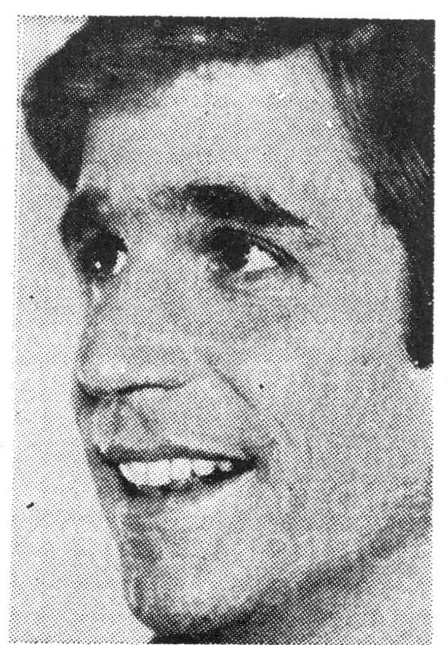

Henry Winkler in "The One and Only"

Darby), who looks old enough to be a tenured professor of physics, by talking to celery stalks, singing (badly) in public places and telling her how great he is.

Some forms of egotism can be extremely funny—I think especially of Oscar Jaffe's in "Twentieth Century"—if only because we know that the egotism, though infinitely elastic, is a fragile skin enclosing a gigantic inferiority complex. At any moment it might pop. There are no such self-deceptions and no dangers in "The One and Only." Mr. Winkler's Andy Schmidt is all brass, which means, I assume, that we are meant to like him for what he appears to be, which is noisy and untalented.

Mr. Reiner, who once directed a hilariously vulgar film called "Where's Poppa," subsequently found God (and great popular success) with "Oh, God." "The One and Only" is more of that sort of safe, schmalzy comedy, but fatally lacking the presence of someone like the great George Burns.

Steve Gordon's screenplay, which shows us how Andy Schmidt accidentally becomes a professional wrestling star called the Lover, a sort of combination of Gorgeous George and Liberace, plays with bad taste but never really lets it triumph, which was one of the reasons why "Where's Poppa" succeeded. "The One and Only" makes some mildly bigoted homosexual jokes, but even these can be supported as part of the picture of a bygone era.

Mr. Winkler's performance alternates between the coy and the cute, which is monotonous and never as endearing as Mr. Villechaize's random leers. Miss Darby seems miscast and Gene Saks is nicely rude as the foul-mouthed fellow who promotes Andy Schmidt to sleazy stardom.

•

"The One and Only," which has been rated PG ("Parental Guidance Suggested"), talks dirty but its heart is as pure as a biodegradable detergent.

1978 F 3, C10:4

A Youthful Addict

A HERO AIN'T NOTHIN' BUT A SANDWICH, directed by Ralph Nelson; screenplay, based on her novel, by Alice Childress; director of photography, Frank Stanley; music by Tom McIntosh; film editor, Fred Chulack; produced by Robert B. Radnitz; released by New World Pictures. At the Embassy I and Columbia I Theaters. Running time: 105 minutes. This film is rated PG.

Sweets .... Cicely Tyson
Butler .... Paul Winfield
Benjie .... Larry B. Scott
Mrs. Bell .... Helen Martin
Nigeria .... Glynn Turman
Cohen .... David Groh
Tiger .... Kevin Hooks
Jimmy Lee .... Kenneth (Joey) Green
Doctor .... Harold Sylvester

By JANET MASLIN

WHEN WE FIRST meet Benjie (Larry B. Scott), a 13-year-old boy who lives in the Watts ghetto, he appears to be a happy child. Even though he's poor, his father has long since left his mother (Cicely Tyson) and his mother's lover (Paul Winfield) is a formidable disciplinarian, Benjie's spirits are still high.

In no time at all, though, Benjie has become a heroin addict, a development for which the screenplay lays too much groundwork and Ralph Nelson's soft-pedaling direction lays none at all. This is a tragic tale told by film makers who don't seem able to believe that such things are really possible.

•

As its title perhaps indicates, "A Hero Ain't Nothin' But a Sandwich," which opens today at the Embassy I and Columbia I Theaters, is a movie that spells out everything but never manages to be entirely lucid. The boy's drug problem is hashed over endlessly, and it takes enough up-and-down turns to sustain a full-length movie, but neither its cause nor its resolution is well enough defined to make the story plausible. However, Mr. Scott is a winning young actor, able to charm and fast-talk his way through the fuzziest situations.

Although Mr. Winfield and Miss Tyson have performed together often, they are not, at least in this instance, an ideally matched pair. Mr. Winfield, as a maintenance man struggling valiantly to provide the boy with a surrogate father, is tough and persuasive, so much so that it's hard to see why Benjie can't take more comfort in his presence. Miss Tyson, on the other hand, is paper-thin; the boy's mother might just have well been played by Donna Reed.

•

One measure of Mr. Nelson's confused approach to his material is the sequence that shows Benjie undergoing drug withdrawal at a clinic; Mr. Nelson's montage of sepia-toned stills, prettily scored, clashes crazily with the tortured expressions on the boy's face.

Another measure is the film's presentation of George Washington Carver Junior High School, where the only two teachers we meet are the harshly opposite Cohen (David Groh) and Nigeria (Glynn Turman). Nigeria is shown to be a smart, stimulating teacher of black history; he is also shown to be a headstrong and slightly unreasonable character who has managed, a little puzzlingly, to raise the best-adjusted son in town. Mr. Winfield seems so much more helpful a role model, even as a stepfather, that it's hard to understand why the boys' fates should diverge so drastically.

•

"A Hero Ain't Nothin' But a Sandwich" is rated PG ("Parental Guidance Suggested") because of its subject and because it contains a good deal of harsh language.

1978 F 3, C10:1

Larry B. Scott in "A Hero Ain't Nothin' But A Sandwich"
A winning actor who charms his way through the fuzziest of situations

FILM VIEW

VINCENT CANBY

Second Thoughts

Painters, poets, novelists and filmmakers should avoid talking publicly about their work until some future date when they (and we) have had time to get some distance from it. It's too easy for the reporter or critic to strangle the artist with the artist's own words tied in a slip-knot. It's of some value, I suppose, to know what the artist intended in his work, and to know what he thinks he has brought off. Yet, quite often the artist is the last person to listen to. Not always, but frequently enough to make self-analysis a dangerous endeavor.

Lina Wertmuller, the sometimes brilliant Italian director ("The Seduction of Mimi," "Love and Anarchy," "Swept Away," etc.), is a case in point. Several years ago when her controversial "Seven Beauties" opened here, Miss Wertmuller traveled to New York, where, in a series of non-stop interviews, she successfully sabotaged her supporters (myself included) and confirmed the worst suspicions of her detractors by giving us interpretations of the movie that had little or nothing to do with what most of us had seen. Said one friend of mine: "No wonder it's all mixed up. Even she doesn't know what it's about." To which I answered, obviously: If a movie works, it doesn't make any difference whether or not the director is right.

Miss Wertmuller has been at it again. Here last week for the opening of "The End of the World in Our Usual Bed on a Night Full of Rain," her first movie in English, Miss Wertmuller was talking with enthusiasm and at such length and so articulately about the movie that (to vary an old Hollywood joke) it seems Warner Brothers might do better to scrap the movie and distribute the director.

"The End of the World," which the director calls "the most political movie I ever made," is also the most banal, most humorless, most schematic movie she's ever done. Is there some connection between her describing the movie as political and my finding it such a pretentious bore? Not really. We're simply not seeing the same movie.

Unlike her earlier films, which have had firm political substructures relating to the social and psychological behavior of characters, "The End of the World" is all surface movement and interior decoration. In effect, she asks us to believe what is said, not to pay attention to how it's said.

The movie is about the failing marriage of Paolo (Giancarlo Giannini), an Italian Communist journalist, and Lizzy (Candice Bergen), an American feminist who once made her living as a professional photographer. In the comfort of their beautiful Rome apartment, and in the course of one long rainy night (which Miss Wertmuller tells us in interviews could refer to the Bible's Great Flood and the end of the world), Paolo and Lizzy re-live their meeting, courtship and marriage. The sum and substance of this is that she's dissatisfied with her role as wife and mother and he's dissatisfied with her longings to have her own career again, as well as to make love with someone who is no longer automatic about the process. From these quite conventional dissatisfactions, which plagued marriages long before the birth of Karl Marx and certainly long, long before the invention of the term "male chauvinist pig," Miss Wertmuller asks us to regard her movie as some kind of political statement.

The movie *contains* political statements, in its dialogue, but it doesn't *demonstrate* any particular political truths that couldn't be written on the wrapper around a piece of bubble gum. A political movie is not necessarily one that contains a lot of random thoughts about politics. A political movie may well be about football or big game hunting, as long as it demonstrates in some fashion the mechanics of power, the meaning of choices, and the individual's relationship to some larger community. Miss Wertmuller's "The Seduction of Mimi," "Swept Away" and "Seven Beauties" are political movies, though the first two appear to be mostly about the war between men and women. "The End of the World" is about people who spout a lot of political jargon (in very awkward English) and then disappear completely from memory, like people at cocktail parties.

I was also interested to read in Miss Wertmuller's interviews about the importance to her new film of the photographs on the walls of the apartment where Lizzy and Paolo live with Paolo's elderly aunt, who appears in the movie rather late and as something of a surprise. We see these photographs in closeup behind the opening credits—a series of still shots of anonymous soldiers in anonymous wars, of anonymous family members in anonymous decades. They are, she says, "a history of Italy."

Though there's no reference in the film to their origins, Miss Wertmuller told one interviewer that the photographs are the work of the husband of Paolo's aunt, who was a famous photographer, and of the father of the husband, who was also a famous photographer.

Good grief! How could we have missed that information —except for the fact that it isn't in the movie!

Much of the English dialogue that the director has imposed on her two stars is facetious, sarcastic, arch or numbingly serious. Paolo and Lizzy are never at a loss for a familiar word or phrase; yet—and this is the difference between living dialogue and dead—they can't even seem to swear with ease. Invectives fail them.

Travel note: the handsome, old building featured in the early scenes of the film is a 14th-century Carthusian monastery in Padula, Calabria. It's worth a side-trip the next time you're in southern Italy.

• • •

Critics aren't the only people who make unforgivable mistakes, as I did some weeks ago when I attributed the co-authorship of the screenplay of "Smokey and the Bandit" (which I liked) to Charles Silver when the man's name is really Charles Shyer. Not even the people who make up movie advertisements are infallible, as was all too evident for a week or so in the advertisements for Ingmar bergman's new film, "The Serpent's Egg." Said the copy in the early version of the advertisements that featured a picture of Liv Ullmann looking startlingly like Alice Ghostley: "Berlin. The Thirties. . . ." The film takes place in Berlin, but in the twenties.

Beauty in movies is often suspect, if only because almost anybody is capable of taking pretty pictures, given equipment of a certain standard and the right images. The important thing is the relation of the beauty to the film. Sometimes it's a cosmetic that hides the blemishes. Sometimes, as in "Barry Lyndon," it's one of the fundamental expressions of the movie.

In Ridley Scott's new English film, "The Duellists," based on a Joseph Conrad novella, the breathtaking beauty of the landscapes provides the film with its style as much as does the prose of a writer. The elegant, bizarre story is about two French officers, one a decent, intelligent sort of fellow (Keith Carradine), the other (Harvey Keitel) a man obsessed with an old-fashioned sense of honor, who go through the Napoleonic wars fighting a series of increasingly furious and foolish duels. It's a fascinating narrative, precisely and economically told, about events so strange they seem as remote as the moon, yet also splendidly heroic—because of the dazzling camerawork (by Frank Tidy).

• • •

As has been said many times before, the problem with a long movie is that you can't flip through it as you might a long book, to see whether or not you want to read it all. You have to adjust yourself to the movie, give in to it, cry "Uncle!" It's worth noting that while almost everything else in our daily lives is becoming shorter, faster, less of a fuss, movies are getting longer than ever. Bernardo Bertolucci's original cut of "1900" ran 5½ hours. Bob Dylan's contemplation of self (I haven't seen it yet, so I'm being vague), "Renaldo and Clara," runs approximately four hours.

Now Joris Ivens, the Dutch-born documentary filmmaker ("The Spanish Earth") who's in his 80th year, has just completed a 12-hour film about Red China called "How Yukong Moved the Mountains," which will be shown in installments at the Museum of Modern Art and the Donnell Library on seven consecutive Tuesdays starting Feb. 7. The Ivens film is actually seven features and five shorts, with a total running time of one-half a day.

I haven't seen this yet either, but I wonder what non-film critics will do about it. The problem with films of such staggering length is that they suddenly force the members of the public, even film aficionados, to weigh each possible film experience against a whole range of other activities. Moviegoing becomes a rigorous, demanding, merciless activity. Is 12 hours of Joris Ivens on Red China worth more than, say, reading "The Possessed," listening to all of Beethoven's and all of Brahms's symphonies at one sitting, or seeing "Star Wars" six times? Think about it. ■

1978 F 5, II:15:1

Latvia, 1919-20

COUP DE GRACE, directed by Volker Schlondorff; screenplay (French and German with English subtitles) by Genevieve Dormann, Margarethe von Trotta and Jutta Bruckner, based on the novel by Marguerite Yourcenar; produced by Eberhard Junkersdorf; music, Stanley Myers; director of photography, Igor Luther; a Franco-German co-production by Argos Films, distributed by Cinema V. Running time: 96 minutes. At the Cinema Studio, Broadway at 65th Street. This film has not been rated.

Sophie .... Margarethe von Trotta
Erich .... Matthias Habich
Konrad .... Rudiger Kirschstein
Volkmar .... Matthieu Carriere
Tante Praskovia .... Valeska Gert
Dr. Paul Rugen .... Marc Eyraud
Franz von Aland .... Frederik Zichy
Chopin .... Bruno Thost
Borschikoff .... Henry Van Lyck

By VINCENT CANBY

THE TIME is winter, 1919-20, shortly after the end of World War I. The setting is that Baltic territory where the Allies, for a while represented by troops of the defeated Kaiser, waged a desultory campaign against the Bolsheviks who had come to power in Russia. That war, too, was already over but the people fighting it hadn't been told. As the war became increasingly fragmented, the battles became increasingly violent, bitter and personal.

On one of the great Latvian estates near Riga, still comparatively serene in spite of food shortages, disease and defections to the Red cause, the last act is played out as the kind of domestic drama that comes perilously close to farce. No one quite understands what's happening, but then when they do, they continue to pursue doom not as duty but as conscious choice.

•

Volker Schlondorff's "Coup de Grace," adapted from Marguerite Yourcenar's 1939 novel (published here in 1957), has the form of a violent nightmare now dimly remembered. The film is the recollection of a Prussian officer who participated in specific events from which all pain has long since vanished. What is now remembered is the series of curious occurrences that, in hindsight, appear to have been inevitable.

Margarethe von Trotta
Plays a handsome, strong-willed aristocrat in film

"Coup de Grace," which opened yesterday at the Cinema Studio, is an extremely studied, sorrowful movie, photographed in a fine, chilly black and white that has the important effect of removing the story even further away from our emotions. We don't respond to it viscerally. We contemplate it with a certain amount of detachment, which, in this movie era of fast-cutting and obligatory shock, is almost refreshing.

I'm not quite sure that I know exactly what Mr. Schlondorff ("Young Torless," "The Lost Honor of Katharina

Blum," etc.) and his wife, Margarethe von Trotta, who collaborated on the screenplay and has the leading role, see as the point of the movie, though it's a vivid and haunting experience.

•

The film is, I suppose, a kind of parable about the collapse of one order and the survival of another. It's the story of Sophie (Miss von Trotta), a handsome, strong-willed aristocrat, her younger brother Konrad (Rudiger Kirschstein), and Erich (Matthias Habich), the Prussian officer who commands the White garrison at their country house. Sophie loves Erich, Erich loves (apparently from afar) Konrad, and Konrad, having not much passion for anything, exists passively, to be supported by those around him.

Though Sophie loves Erich, her sympathies are with the Reds, a political commitment she doesn't act upon until she learns about Erich's feelings for Konrad. As the campaign against the Bolsheviks collapses, only Erich the true Prussian, maintains some sense of purpose. Life at the great house falls into disorder. The crazy old aunt, who talks French and wears horrendous makeup, presides at formal dinners as artillery shells land in the garden. When the Bolsheviks triumph, only Erich survives to muse—in voice-over narration—about the depth of Sophie's love and fury.

Does Erich survive to support the later rise of Adolf Hitler? "Coup de Grace" remains at such a distance from its characters that one must make all sorts of assumptions about them, which is the reason it is disturbing without being entirely satisfying.

"Coup de Grace" raises many questions that it refuses to answer in any easy fashion, which is just the opposite of Mr. Schlondorff's "The Lost Honor of Katharina Blum," a film that had an answer for everything. Since I'm suspicious of answers in art, I much prefer this new film.

1978 F 6, C15:5

Bring Bread and Pate

BLUE COUNTRY, directed by Jean-Charles Tacchella; screenplay (French with English subtitles) by Mr. Tacchella; photography, Edmond Sechan; music by Gerard Anfosso; executive producer, Alain Poire for Gaumont International; released by Quartet Films, Inc.; a Murray Walter Inc. Presentation. At the 68th Street Playhouse, at Third Avenue. Running time: 104 minutes. This film has not been rated.

Louise ..... Brigitte Fossey
Mathias ..... Jacques Serres
Zoe ..... Ginette Garcin
Moise ..... Armand Meffre
Manon ..... Ginette Mathieu
Fernand ..... Roger Crouzet

By JANET MASLIN

ON THE EVIDENCE of "Cousin, Cousine" and now "Blue Country," Jean-Charles Tacchella's specialty is the madcap crowd scene. By gathering together a band of zanies on an appropriately festive occasion, Mr. Tacchella can tickle his audiences with a disjointed, determinedly fluffy-headed brand of comedy. He can also, by allocating one or two piquant remarks to each character and never allowing anyone to conduct a sustained conversation, create the impression that this is merriment with a message.

•

Mr. Tacchella's messages, upon close inspection, don't amount to much: He offers endless variations on the notions that people must do what makes them happiest, that they don't always live up to their dreams and that they must be forgiven their foibles. But the thematic banality of his films in no way compromises Mr. Tacchella's most useful talent, which is for sleight-of-hand. In "Blue Country," he once again manages to suggest that the lightweight mood of his films bespeaks an inner seriousness. Mr. Tacchella's peculiarly circular gift is for lending ephemeralness and insubstantiality the appearance of virtues.

In "Blue Country," the obligatory zanies meet in a rural setting, a breathtakingly beautiful French valley populated by a happy mixture of peasants and ex-Parisians. The peasants have more children than they can keep track of, and long for the luxuries of city living; the Parisians like to bake bread, speak knowingly of their newly acquired goats and talk of the landscape in terms of Corot or Cézanne ("No wonder peasants don't buy paintings!" one unreconstructed bourgeoise exclaims).

The valley's populace meets gaily and often for communal dinners so appetizing that viewers headed for the 68th Street Playhouse, where the film has opened, would be well advised to arm themselves with bread and paté. At least half of "Blue Country's" appeal is based on its sheer pastoral pleasantness, and on the gusto with which its principals indulge their appetites.

As in "Cousin, Cousine," there is a romantic subplot that seems strangely tangential to the film's predominant hustle and bustle. Louise (Brigitte Fossey), an ex-Parisian, meets Mathias (Jacques Serres), a country bachelor, and both are so fiercely independent that they vow not to fall in love. Fall in love they do, though, very picturesquely, and each makes a few sacrifices to accommodate the other. But they never move in together, even after 10 years of courtship, which is the film's rather lumbering way of reminding us that they have retained that fierce independence.

Here, as before, Mr. Tacchella seems unable to integrate the romance with all the brouhaha, and it's the romance that suffers. Miss Fossey is unflaggingly radiant and Mr. Serres attractively stalwart, yet the director seems unaccountably uneasy when his screenplay leaves him alone with these two very agreeable lovers.

•

"Blue Country" is less structurally coherent than "Cousin, Cousine," and its delightful eccentrics seem a little more contrived in their delightfulness. Both films are likely to appeal to the same audience, though—to viewers who ascribe a certain Gallic cachet to films with the consistency of cotton candy, and who approach with utter fearlessness the prospect of being charmed to death.

1978 F 6, C19:3

Introducing Violence

FILM/FICTIONS, a series of short films: **IGOR ORIG,** by Michael Harvey, 9 minutes; **IN A TRAIN STATION,** by James Pasternak, 14 minutes; **THE WAYFARER,** by Mr. Pasternak, 25 minutes; **DEAD LETTER,** by Mr. Harvey, 20 minutes. At the Whitney Museum of American Art, Madison Avenue and 75th Street.

By JANET MASLIN

WATCHING "Film/Fictions," a new series of short films at the Whitney, is rather like seeing double, since each of the two directors represented has more or less made the same film twice. One of them, Michael Harvey, is much more justified in repeating himself than J. D. Pasternak, the other.

All four films are supposed to be about the intrusion of violence and madness into everyday life, but Mr. Harvey's efforts have a nicely incongruous, almost lackadaisical air. In both "Igor Orig" and the superior "Dead Letter," a man is confined to a room, where he discusses with the camera some crime that seems already to have been committed.

The man in the latter film, played with exaggerated sang-froid by David Warrilow, paces about a jail cell in a variety of dressing gowns, chatting about things like the time his mother knitted a sweater for his pet canary. His mother neglected to knit sleeves, and the bird was so adversely affected by this, he explains, that it died of distress.

•

The urbanity of Mr. Harvey's work is far preferable to the portentousness of Mr. Pasternak's. Two films by Mr. Pasternak, both adaptations of stories by Robert Coover, pit together two seemingly peaceful, actually antagonistic characters in desolate, windy settings. In each case, one character carries a weapon and, in each case, he uses it, gruesomely but to no avail. Both films begin and end on a note of cosmic tiresomeness.

"In a Train Station" takes place just where you imagine it would, as a middle-aged man (Sully Boyar), carrying dinner and a pocketknife, becomes inexplicably hysterical as he talks with the stationmaster. Then another man rushes in, and the first two cut his throat. After that, the stationmaster resets the clock to the time the middle-aged man first walken in, and everything ends as it began.

•

In "The Wayfarer" a silent hobo stands by the side of a highway, and his presence so enrages and frustrates a state trooper that the trooper, who also becomes inexplicably hysterical, shoots him. A chorus of average Joes in automobiles watches this silently, then cheers as the hobo's blood begins to flow.

Mr. Pasternak has no gift for making the spareness of such a story resonate, and his visual sense allows for only the uncomfortable intimacy of the close shot or the belabored angst of the long view. His eye for verisimilitude is such that the trooper, otherwise convincingly played by Gerrit Graham, makes no bones about having very untrooperlike long hair tucked up inside his helmet.

1978 F 8, C14:5

The Assembly Line

BLUE COLLAR, directed by Paul Schrader; screenplay by Paul Schrader and Leonard Schrader, suggested by source material by Sydney A. Glass; executive producer, Robin French; produced by Ron Guest; director of photography, Bobby Byrne; music, Jack Nitzsche; editor, Tom Rolf; a T.A.T. Communications production, distributed by Universal Pictures. Running time: 110 minutes. At the Rivoli Theater, Broadway near 50th Street, Trans-Lux East Theater, Third Avenue at 58th Street, and 86th Street East Theater, 86th Street near Third Avenue. This film has been rated R.

Zeke ..... Richard Pryor
Jerry ..... Harvey Keitel
Smokey ..... Yaphet Kotto
Bobby Joe ..... Ed Begley Jr.
Eddie Johnson ..... Harry Bellaver
Jenkens ..... George Memmoli
Arlene Bartowskl ..... Lucy Saroyan
Clarence Hill ..... Lane Smith
John Burrows ..... Cliff De Young
Dog Miller ..... Borah Silver
Caroline Brown ..... Chip Fields
Hank ..... Harry Northup
I.R.S. man ..... Leonard Gaines
"Sumabitch" ..... Milton Selzer
Barney ..... Sammy Warren
Charlie T. Hernandez ..... Jimmy Martinez
Superintendent ..... Jerry Dahlmann
Unshaven thug ..... Denny Arnold
Blond thug ..... Rock Riddle

By VINCENT CANBY

"BLUE COLLAR," directed by Paul Schrader and written by him and his brother Leonard, is a film about which you are likely to have very mixed feelings. It is a sort of poor man's "On the Waterfront," a movie that simply — often primitively — describes corruption in a Detroit auto workers' local without ever making the corruption a matter of conscience. Corruption is there. It exists. It's part of the system.

This emphasis on inevitability, which is one step away from complete passivity, may be the essential difference between a certain kind of pop culture today and that of the mid-50's when Elia Kazan made his furious, idealized film about crooked locals on New York piers. The Kazan film dramatized one man's fight against corruption and made a hero of a fellow brave enough to testify before a crime commission.

At the end of "Blue Collar" we see a man more or less cornered into turning state's evidence. His testimony probably won't do any good. The movie even implies that his decision to testify may make him an unwitting tool of the system. His fate isn't especially tragic. It's a pop tune with a big beat.

•

At least, this is the way I reacted to "Blue Collar," which opens today at three theaters. "Blue Collar" is the first film to be directed by Mr. Schrader, who was one of Hollywood's hottest young writers even before the appearance of "The Yakuza," his first screenplay to be filmed. Since then he has been represented by "Taxi Driver," "Obsession" and "Rolling Thunder," all movies containing a lot of highly cinematic violence and a certain amount of intellectual confusion. Is "Blue Collar" an action film or a meditation upon the American Dream? I suspect it wants to be both though it's not very serious at being either.

The movie is at its best in describing the quality of the day-to-day life of its three leading characters—Zeke (Richard Pryor), Jerry (Harvey Keitel) and Smokey (Yaphet Kotto), friends who work together on the assembly line at the automobile plant. Zeke, who is married, is irrepressibly rude and in debt to the Internal Revenue Service for claiming six children instead of his actual three. Jerry, also married, also is in debt and works two jobs to make ends meet. Smokey is the sophisticated one. An ex-con and a bachelor, he throws parties that he imagines Playboy would admire. All three work nonstop to afford the material comforts they've been told they deserve. Each in his own way is a very angry man.

Where "Blue Collar" starts to go awry is in its melodramatic plotting that has the three friends attempting to rob their union headquarters. Instead of a large amount of cash, they finda a ledger that records the details of the union's loan-sharking activities. When they attempt to use this information as blackmail, the results are predictably disastrous—for the friends and for the movie that otherwise shows us a kind of existence seldom accurately depicted on the screen.

•

Everything in the characters' private lives looks right, from the pictures on the walls (and stuck into the corners of mirrors), to their color television sets, plastic slipcovers and bowling costumes. You suspect that each item was bought yesterday on time and will be worn out tomarrow before the payments are completed.

Richard Pryor and Harvey Keitel in Paul Schrader's film "Blue Collar"
The center of the film is Pryor, who makes use of the wit and fury that distinguish his straight comedy routines

The performances are excellent. Mr. Keitel's Jerry is all itchy ignorance, baffled by the circumstances in which he finds himself to do the right thing but having no idea of what that is. Mr. Kotto's Smokey appears to be as much a matter of his sheer presence as it is of his cool, self-assured performance.

The center of the film, however, is Mr. Pryor who, in "Blue Collar," has a role that for the first time makes use of the wit and fury that distinguish his straight comedy routines. It's a sneakily funny performance right up to the film's angry, freeze-frame ending, which, by this time is a mannerism that almost any film could do without.

Mr. Schrader's decision to use that freeze-frame calls attention to the phoniness that haunts the film at other moments. The scene in which a fussy I.R.S. man calls on Mr. Pryor is funny, but do I.R.S. men often make house calls at night? If the television programs that Mr. Keitel's family watches are always black programs, how did something like "Rhoda" become so popular? I'd even question whether the Keitel character, given the probable prejudices of a man in his position, would have two blacks as his only friends.

The movie, which is so accurate in other ways, manipulates life to create the sort of idealized, color-balanced reality we are force-fed by television.

1978 F 10, C5:4

LANDSCAPE AFTER BATTLE, directed by Andrzej Wajda; screenplay (Polish with English subtitles) by Mr. Wajda and Andrzej Brzozowski, adapted from the stories of Tadeusz Borowski; director of photography, Zygmunt Samosiuk; music, Zygmunt Konieczny; produced by the Polish Corporation for Film Production; distributed by New Yorker Films. Running time: 110 minutes. At the Film Forum, 15 Vandam Street. This film has not been rated.

Tadeusz .... Daniel Olbrychski
Nina .... Stanislawa Celinska

ANDRZEJ WAJDA'S 1970 Polish film, "Landscape After Battle," is a movie whose sorrow is sealed off by its beautiful images if behind thick, protective glass. We see the sorrow—its expressions and movements—but it's so special that it seems silent and remote. How can anyone who was not in the Holocaust begin to comprehend it? Even to attempt to understand it seems an impertinence, as if this would be an invasion of an especially privileged privacy.

"Landscape After Battle" is based on the autobiographical stories of Tadeusz Borowski, the Polish writer who, having survived Auschwitz and Dachau and the postwar displaced-persons camps, committed suicide in 1951 at the age of 29. That knowledge gives particular poignancy to the Wajda film, which is about a young poet named Tadeusz who goes through this landscape trying to convince himself of the validity of the advice he gives a Jewish girl he loves: "To love, one must forget."

Mr. Borowski could not forget, which is why his stories, published here by Penguin in a collection called "This Way to the Gas, Ladies and Gentlemen," comprise one of the most measured, calm and harrowing books about the Holocaust you're ever likely to read. Mr. Borowski was an extraordinary writer. Mr. Wajda, who made "Ashes and Diamonds" and "Kanal," can be an extraordinary film maker, but his style is more lyric and contemplative than the writer's, which is to the film's advantage.

"Landscape After Battle" is Mr. Wajda's recollection of an idealized Borowski, played with a kind of sweet cynicism by Daniel Olbrychski as a handsome young man who wears spectacles—Mr. Wajda seem to belong to that school of film makers that still feels that writers must be identified by the glasses they put on, take off and drop. This is the only unworthy note in the movie, which is a series of vignettes that follows Tadeusz from the day his camp is liberated until he decides to strike out from a benignly mismanaged displaced-persons camp to return to Poland.

Because Tadeusz is obsessed with a sense of homeland, which has less to do with conventional nationalism than with mythic roots, there is throughout the film the unstated irony contained in our awareness of what eventually happened to Tadeusz.

The landscape of the title is postwar Europe, whose mood is caught in the film's opening sequence, when Mr. Wajda shows us how the prisoners of a concentration camp, at first jubilant with their freedom, come to realize at the end of that first day that they have no place to go but back to the camp.

"Landscape After Battle" has no dominant story line. Some of its sequences may mystify those of us not familiar with Polish history or with the spheres of influence that were allocated after the war. Yet it's so beautifully composed, so elegiacal, it compels attention and will be likely to stay in the memory for a very long time. I've no idea why it's taken almost eight years for such a special work to reach us.

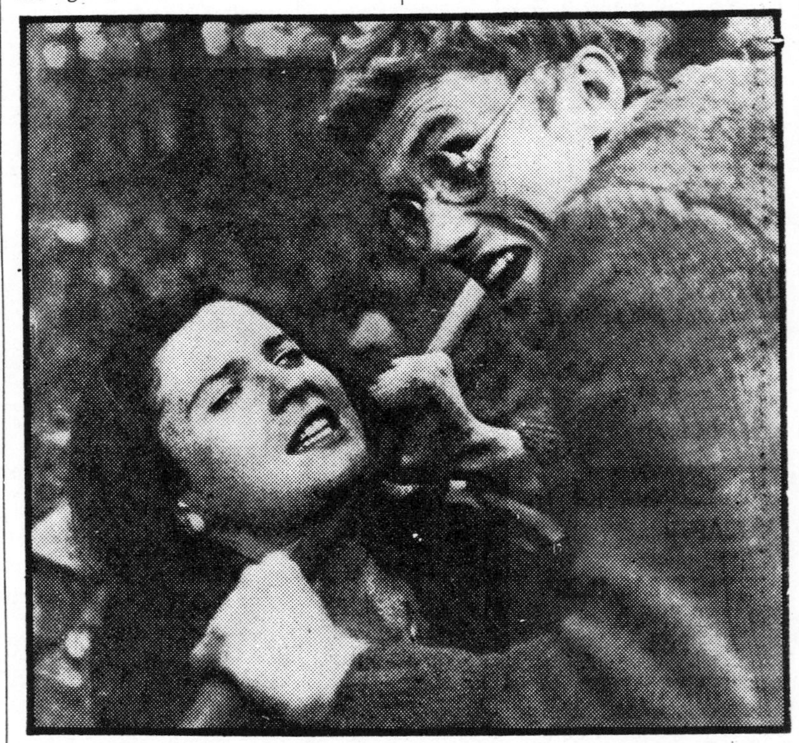

Stanislawa Celinska and Daniel Olbrychski in "Landscape After Battle"
It will likely stay in the memory for a very long time

The film opened yesterday at the Film Forum, where it will be shown tonight through Sunday at 7:45, and again next week, Thursday through Sunday, at the same time.

VINCENT CANBY

1978 F 10, C8:5

Cars, Sex Money and 'The Betsy'

By JANET MASLIN

MEET the Hardeman family, the oversexed czars of Detroit's most Harold Robbinsy auto empire. They're They're all descended from Loren Hardeman Sr., a rough-and-tumble First Tycoon played by rough-and-tumble Laurence Olivier. This Hardeman, a.k.a. "No. 1," is about 90 years old now, but he is often described as "amazing . . . for his age." Loren Hardeman Jr. (Paul Rudd) was a no-good weakling, so they don't talk much about him any more. They talk even less about his beautiful wife, Sally (Katharine Ross), who used to fool around with her father-in-law. On her wedding night, Sally caught No. 1 fooling around with Roxanne, a French maid, and the spectacle gave her ideas. "I've wanted it to be like that ever since — just once," Sally whispered.

Loren 3d (Robert Duvall), who saw quite a primal scene in his day, is a mean-tempered fellow who hates being called Loren 3d. He likes playing a savage game of squash, running the family business, and forsaking his glum wife Alicia (Jane Alexander) for his high-toned English mistress, Lady Bobby (Lesley-Anne Down).

But Lady Bobby is not exactly what you'd call a one-man woman, and so she inevitably winds up in the arms of Angelo Perino (Tommy Lee Jones), the hot-blooded Italian racing driver and automotive designer who is in No. 1's employ. Just before she flings herself at Angelo, they drink a toast.

Lady Bobby: "To fast cars, and the men who race them."

Angelo: "To their women, who wait and worry."

Last in line is nubile young Betsy (Kathleen Beller), whose poolside love scene with this same Angelo will get a huge hand, and an even huger giggle, if you go to see "The Betsy" with a properly punchy crowd. Betsy has the movie's finest line, which she delivers while lying on a lounge chair: "I knew it would be like this," she coos. "You're a beautivul child," Angelo coos in reply. "No Mr. Perino, I'm a beautiful *woman*," she corrects him. "It's my 21st birthday, remember?"

The Hardeman's have their incest, their infidelity, their homosexuality and all the rest, and they have another problem so awful that no one ever talks about it: The Betsy, which is

Robert Duvall, Laurence Olivier and Kathleen Beller in "The Betsy"

THE BETSY, directed by Daniel Petrie; screenplay by Walter Bernstein and William Bast, based on the novel by Harold Robbins; director of photography, Mario Tosi; editor, Rita Roland; music, John Barry; produced by Robert R. Weston; released by Allied Artists Corporation. At the National, 43d Street and Seventh Avenue and other theaters. Running time: 125 minutes. This film has been rated R.

Loren Hardeman Sr. .... Laurence Olivier
Loren Hardeman 3d .... Robert Duvall
Sally Hardeman .... Katharine Ross
Angelo Perino .... Tommy Lee Jones
Alicia Hardeman .... Jane Alexander
Lady Bobby Ayres .... Lesley-Anne Down
Jacke Weinstein .... Joseph Wiseman
Betsy Hardeman .... Kathleen Beller
Dan Weyman .... Edward Herrmann
Loren Hardeman Jr. .... Paul Rudd

being designed by Angelo in great-granddaughter's honor, is going to be *a cheap car*. Trouble is people don't go to see big-budget adaptations of Harold Robbins stories to find out about cutting costs and getting better mileage; they want to know about luxury and limousines and what Lady Bobby does in her spare time. How can a movie about the invention of something like a Pinto have much of a gloss?

"The Betsy" careens recklessly from the 1930's to the 70's and back again, from Hardeman generation to Hardeman generation, in a vain effort to generate the illusion of a storyline. Laurence Olivier doesn't change much over 40 years, and he never seems to have the unscrupulousness of a real magnate, but that hardly matters: What he does have are a roguish Scots accent, a lot of lines like "I'll be hornswoggled," and a twinkle in his eye, as befits the material.

There are some good performances here (such as Edward Herrmann's, as a corporate yes-man, Mr. Duvall's and Miss Alexander's), and some terrible ones (Miss Ross is deadly serious, and just awful). But only Olivier manages to play his role and wink at it simultaneously, and his is surely the most sensible approach.

For the most part, the director, Daniel Petrie, has a classier cast than he knows what to do with. He also has at his disposal an unwieldy script and the worst set of costumes to be seen in a movie in years. (All the men wear ill-fitting suits, even the zillionaires, and Betsy's yellow ballgown for her birthday party is a lollapalooza. Mr. Petrie, who also directed "Lifeguard" and the television movie "Sybil," regularly dissolves his love scenes into shots of city skylines, and he treats the Hardemans with a reverence they in no way warrant.

Mr. Petrie was in no danger of making a good movie out of "The Betsy," but he might easily have made a funnier or more enjoyable smarmy one. Without much of a plot, "The Betsy" often sags, and a movie this frivolous has no business being dull.

1978 F 10, C5:1

EVERY FILM HAS A MOMENT OF COMMITMENT

VINCENT CANBY

WHETHER one is flying to Paris or taking the tube to Hoboken, there's always a moment at mid-trip that is the point of no return, when the pilot must choose whether to go back or be forever committed to the destination. Something of the same sort happens when one is watching a movie, but it's more mysterious and unpredictable than any ordinary halfway mark, and the decision that is made (when a decision must be made) is always negative. This point-of-no-return in a movie may come in the first five minutes or the last five or at any point in between; though, usually, the longer one watches a film the more one becomes committed to it. Time has been invested. Interest accrues. The most dangerous moments in any movie are those shortly after take-off.

• • •

In Lina Wertmuller's new film, "The End of the World in Our Usual Bed in a Night Full of Rain," it happens at approximately the time that in any trans-Atlantic flight the pilot would have turned off the No Smoking sign. The movie opens with a brief introductory scene in which we meet the two principal characters, Paolo (Giancarlo Giannini), a Communist journalist, and his wife Lizzy (Candice Bergen) in their Rome apartment. This precedes a flashback to their meeting some years before in southern Italy, a briefly funny scene in which Lizzy disrupts a solemn religious procession and Paolo must rescue her.

So far, so good. Paolo and Lizzy seek sanctuary in the ruins of a grand old monastery where they immediately start insulting each other about their politics. Their politics? Exactly, though they don't know each other and, besides, the angry mob outside threatens to break in at any moment to carry off Lizzy to wherever angry mobs carry off ugly Americans in southern Italy.

One's reaction is a defensive, "Now wait a minute . . . ." Paolo and Lizzy seem to be rather decent people. At least they are played by very attractive actors; yet, they carry on like two people who've been on a collision course for 20 years. It's not just that they talk about matters that most strangers wouldn't talk about until they'd had a couple of glasses of wine, but that their style is rancidly unreal, childishly vulgar. As the scene goes on and on and on, one begins to tune out on Lizzy and Paolo and Miss Wertmuller and the movie: If that's where they're going, I'll get off here.

In "The One and Only," Carl Reiner's new comedy about a would-be actor (Henry Winkler) who accidentally becomes a pro-wrestling star in the 1950's, the point of no return comes a little later, but not much. To set the scene for the movie that follows, "The One and Only" has a prologue in which we meet the Winkler character at age six or seven, when, as the impossibly spoiled child of boobish parents, he does a dreadfully self-assured, show-bizzy and not entirely unfunny imitation of Al Jolson singing "Mammy," to the great discomfort of his other relatives and friends. Then there's a quick cut to the grown-up kid, now played by Mr. Winkler himself, at college and behaving in the same outlandishly egocentric fashion that we saw in the child. There's a slight difference, though. Now, apparently, almost everybody finds this pushy fellow pricelessly funny—other students and especially the girl he loves, played by Kim Darby. Clearly the movie's point of view is asserting itself. We, too, are meant to find this guy as appealing and as heart-warming as the movie does. If you don't, as I didn't, you may want to head for an emergency exit.

"Coma" is better. This hospital thriller, directed and adapted by Michael Crichton from Robin Cook's best-selling novel, has much more going for it, including the fact that both Mr. Crichton and Mr. Cook are doctors and know how hospitals operate. In addition, Mr. Crichton is a good, clean writer who understands popular entertainment as written fiction ("The Andromeda Strain") and as movie fiction ("Westworld").

• • •

"Coma" is essentially a jeopardy melodrama about an intelligent young resident surgeon (Genevieve Bujold) who finds her sanity threatened and then her life when she begins to suspect (correctly) that someone is systematically murdering patients who come to her Boston hospital for ordinarily minor, generally riskless operations. The movie sets up the situation very efficiently, but about one-third of the way in, it starts to test our patience, first by making everyone other than Miss Bujold a suspect and then by forcing her to behave with the kind of pluck that could be hiding a death wish. Never once does she think of going to the cops.

• • •

There's one realistic moment near the middle of the film that is so good that it recoups some of the movie's silliness; that is, when Miss Bujold, shoe-less, is climbing a ladder inside an air shaft and finds that the miracle fabric of her pantyhose makes for slippery footing. She must stop and, at some physical risk, remove them. That's the sort of honestly surprising detail that "Coma" otherwise lacks. One stays with the movie until the end, but with increasing disappointment.

"Saturday Night Fever" is very easy to stick with until the end, if only because of the music by the Bee Gees and one's curiosity about John Travolta, who is not at all bad. Even when it turns melodramatic, it never takes itself too seriously, and some of its family scenes are first-class, slice-of-life stuff. Yet, there's a bad moment quite early on that prompts one to wonder just how John Badham, the director, and Norman Wexler, who wrote the screenplay, feel about their characters. This is when Mr. Travolta and Karen Lee Gorney, who plays his Bay Ridge girlfriend, argue about whether "Romeo and Juliet" is Shakespeare's work or Zeffirelli's. It's funny, but in a way that suggests the filmmakers are patronizing their characters and, by extension, their audiences.

It's one thing for a filmmaker to keep his distance from his characters and the events he depicts on the screen, thus forcing us to make our own connections, to assume our own points of view. This, indeed, is the dominant method of what can be called the New Movie as made by Robert Altman ("Nashville," "Buffalo Bill and the Indians," "3 Women"), Martin Scorsese ("Mean Streets," "Taxi Driver"), Terrence Malick ("Badlands") and so many European directors, including Rainer Werner Fassbinder, Wim Wenders and Volker Schlondorff, whose current film, "Coup de Grace," though not perfect, is a good example of the studied coolness of the New Movie.

The point-of-no-return scenes in "The End of the World," "The One and Only," "Coma" and "Saturday Night Fever" suggest not that the people who made the films are expressing any kind of detachment but that they are inconsistent and/or have underrated the intelligence of their audiences.

Miss Wertmüller is so eager to score what she thinks to be political points that she asks us to attend to cardboard characters who have no artistic function except to speak her lines, which are presented to us straight, without irony. "The One and Only," which employs the simplified comic manners of television, asks us to like the egocentric, would-be actor not because he demonstrates any kind of self-awareness or wit or humanity but because he is played by Henry Winkler, whom we all are supposed to know anyway from the weekly visits he makes to our living rooms. One might say the movie exploits Mr. Winkler, though it's obvious he's an enthusiastic party to that exploitation. "Coma" asks us not only to suspend disbelief for the duration of the film but to pretend that we haven't seen and thoroughly enjoyed dozens of other movies in which we were amply rewarded for disbelief's suspension. Mr. Crichton asks too much of us without being prepared to surprise us.

"Saturday Night Fever" presents another kind of question: How are we supposed to respond to a character (the fellow played by Mr. Travolta) when we're told he doesn't know the difference between Shakespeare and Zeffirelli? I, for one, simply don't believe it. "Saturday Night Fever" is cheating in search of a laugh. The movie's music and the Travolta performance have enough energy and drive to carry us over this rough patch, but the inclusion of the gag is still a serious mistake. If it had been a less entertaining movie until that moment, I would have been tempted to make a U-turn and head back for the lobby. ■

1978 F 12, II:15:1

Detritus of War

COMING HOME, directed by Hal Ashby; screenplay by Waldo Salt and Robert C. Jones, based on a story by Nancy Dowd; produced by Jerome Hellman; director of photography, Haskell Wexler; editor, Don Zimmerman; distributed by United Artists. Running time: 127 minutes. At the Cinema One Theater, Third Avenue near 60th Street. This film has been rated R.

Sally Hyde	Jane Fonda
Luke Martin	Jon Voight
Capt. Bob Hyde	Bruce Dern
Sgt. Dink Mobley	Robert Ginty
Viola Munson	Penelope Milford
Bill Munson	Robert Carradine
Virgil Hunt	Willie Tyler
Beany	Ron Amador
Ken	Ken Augustine
Corney	Cornelius H. Austin Jr.
Rick	Richard Blanchard
Bozo	Louis Carello
Bob	Robert Murdock
Pepe	Eddie Ramirez
Curtis	Curtis Waddy
Doc	J. J. Britt
Jim	James Williams
Chris	Chris Sweeden
John	John Sweeden
Kevin	Kevin K. Lewis
Wil	Wil Friedman
Nurse	Peggy Underwood
Aide	Claudie Watson
Nurse Degroot	Tresa Hughes
Corrine	Olivia Cole
Pee Wee	Charles Cyphers
Dr. Lincoln	Bruce French
Fleta Wilson	Mary Jackson
Jason	Jim Pelt
Pat	Richard Lawson

By VINCENT CANBY

A GROUP of young men in various stages of casual dress is playing pool. The single overhead light leaves deep shadows on the perimeter of the game to create a feeling of isolation and conspiracy. A man moves to the table, makes his shot, pulls back. As they play, the men argue about Vietnam. Someone says that if he had it all to do over again, he would. He believes in defending his country, he says. The others hoot with laughter. A second man sneers at the first fellow, though he understands the desperate need to justify what happened.

The men, each of whom is in a wheelchair or on a cot, are paraplegics, the visible detritus of the invisible war. Now isolated in the ward of a California veterans' hospital, they conspire to come to terms with numbed bodies and memories composed of non-sequiturs.

Thus begins Hal Ashby's "Coming Home," Hollywood's most solemn and serious attempt yet to deal with the Vietnam experience in a commercial fiction film, which may well be an impossibility, at least the way Mr. Ashby and his associates have gone at the job.

"Coming Home," which opened yesterday at the Cinema One, starts beautifully. As long as it observes the behavior of its troubled veterans, including the manic fury of one young man who finds himself falling in love with a hospital volunteer, the film has a kind of terse, tough documentary truth But "Coming Home" is not really about paraplegia or the emotional chaos left behind by the Vietnam War. At first, it touches on these things and uses them (sometimes very movingly), and then slowly, disastrously, it reveals its true identity as a three-sided love story about two Vietnam veterans and the one woman who loves them both.

It's a fiction problem of the sort that prompts the dopiest of romantic resolutions, which also has the effect of transforming "Coming Home" into what used to be called a "woman's picture." Consider, dear reader, what poor Jane should do. Should she stay with the man to whom she's legally bound, but who's clearly a neurotic mess since he came home, even though he wasn't much better before he left? Or should she follow her heart with the other vet who, though paralyzed from the waist down, has taught her the joy of orgasms and who shares her newly raised political consciousness?

Jane is Jane Fonda, who plays the pivotal role of Sally Hyde and who, we are told, was the principal mover behind this film's production. The other major roles are played by Bruce Dern, as Sally's husband, a Marine captain who goes to Vietnam as a gung-ho type and returns a mentally shattered man, and by Jon Voight, as the paraplegic vet, the best role Mr. Voight has had in years, even when the movie more or less washes away from under him.

The trouble seems to be that "Coming Home" wants to be all things to as wide an audience as possible. It wants to condemn war. It wants to be a love story. It wants to record the kind of polarization that Vietnam prompted in people like Sally who, otherwise, would never have come to any political commitment whatsoever. It looks like a house whose plans were drawn up to incorporate the favorite idea of each member of the family. Too many things have been tacked onto the main structure.

Though the screenplay is credited to Waldo Salt and Robert C. Jones, based on a story by Nancy Dowd (who wrote the quite remarkable screenplay for "Slap Shot"), other people reportedly made a lot of suggestions that went into the final work. This results in moments of arbitrary, patently phony plot twists and in subsidiary characters who inhabit the film as if they were décor, like the suicidal veteran (Robert Carradine) who hangs out in the paraplegic ward though his problems are obviously mental.

Mr. Dern's role is a sort of modified version of the nut he played in "Black Sunday," though Miss Fonda and Mr. Voight are immensely appealing in the film's opening sequences, before they are required to do and say things that are gross and heavy-minded.

What's worse, though, is the general tone of Mr. Ashby's direction, which puts great store by period (1968) detail that is intrusive even when it's accurate. The soundtrack is a nonstop collection of yesterday's song hits (Beatles, Rolling Stones and so on), not one of which is allowed to pass without making some drearily obvious or ironic comment on the action on the screen. Mr. Ashby has poured music over the movie like a chilld with a fondness for maple syrup on his pancakes.

Jane Fonda as she appears in "Coming Home."

"Coming Home" is soggy with sound, just as, eventually, it becomes soggy with good if unrealized intentions

1978 F 16, C20:1

Stately Power Struggle

CEDDO, directed and written (in Wolof with English subtitles; by Ousmane Sembene; director of photography, Georges Caristan; editor, Florence Eymon; music, Manu Dibango; distributed by New Yorker Films. Running time: 120 minutes. At the New Yorker Theater, Broadway near 89th Street. This film has not been rated.

Princess Dior	Tabara Ndiaye
Madir Fatim Fall	Moutapha Yade
The kidnapper	Ismaila Diagne
The Imam	Goure
The king	Makoura Dia
Jaraaf	Oumar Gueye
Prince Biram	Mamadou Dioum
Saxewar	Nar Modou Sene
Diogomay	Ousmane Camara
A Ceddo renamed Ibrahima	Ousmane Sembene

By VINCENT CANBY

AT HIS most engaging, as in films like "Xala" and Mandabi," Ousmane Sembene, the talented Senegalese writer-director, is a sophisticated social satirist who considers the follies of his countrymen with the humanistic appreciation of a Jean Renoir. His heroes are often fools or slightly cracked, self-deluding imitations of the recently departed French colonials. Whatever they are, the Sembene landscape they inhabit is always the same whether urban or rural—a land where one culture has been all but squashed by another, yet refuses to die.

Mr. Sembene's newest film, "Ceddo," which opened yesterday at the New Yorker Theater, is also about cultural continuity and the threat of displacement, but with a major difference. "Ceddo" is a folk tale presented as the kind of pageant you might see enacted at some geographic location made famous by history and now surrounded by souvenir stands. It's not cheap or gaudy, but it's an intensely solemn, slightly awkward procession of handsomely costumed scenes designed to pass on a lot of information

A character in "Ceddo," Ousmane Sembène's film from Senegal
The manner is cool, reserved, almost stately

as quickly and efficiently as possible.

Set in some indefinite time (mostly the late 19th century with bits and pieces of the mid-20th century in it as well), it's the sad, formally told tale of what happens to life in a small rural village after the king becomes a convert to Islam and invites a Muslim teacher, the Imam, into his circle of advisers. As goes the king, so go the nobles. The little Roman Catholic church is quickly abandoned. Only the Ceddo, or common people, who earlier resisted Rome, refuse to follow the king.

In the ensuing power struggle, the Ceddo kidnap the king's daughter to force him to meet their demands. The film is composed of meetings of state, of parleys between opposing factions, of trials or strength and cleverness between the loyalists and the rebels, always conducted according to time-honored traditions. Then the ambitious Imam steps in and, through deceit and murder, effectively wipes out an entire people.

This is more or less the content of "Ceddo," though the manner is reserved, cool, almost stately. There are no characterizations in the film, only rather grand impersonations. Most of "Ceddo" has been photographed in the sort of medium-long shot from which one might observe an outdoor theatrical. Only twice, in fantasy sequences, does Mr. Sembene allow himself the imaginative film maker's freedom to distort history to achieve some kind of dramatic truth. The rest is picturesque.

It is interesting to note that "Ceddo," which takes a very dim view of the Muslim influence in Senegal, has been banned in that country though not, reportedly, because of any religious sensitivity, but because Mr. Sembene insists on spelling "ceddo" with two d's while the Senegalese Government insists it be spelled with one.

1978 F 17, C8:3

BEYOND AND BACK, directed by James L. Conway; produced by Charles E. Sellier Jr.; written by Stephen Lord, based in part on the book by Ralph Wilkerson; narrated by Brad Crandall; released by Sunn Classic Pictures Inc. Running time: 93 minutes. At the RKO Cinerama and neighborhood theaters. This film has been rated G.

Narrator....Brad Crandall
Plato....Vern Adix
Louisa May Alcott....Shelley Osterich
Mrs. Houdini....Beverly Rowland

By JANET MASLIN

"Did Harry Houdini really manage to contact his wife from the world beyond, and if so, where was he?" What are "the 14 elements common to the experience related by all those who seem to have died and seen beyond?" When Louisa May Alcott and two relatives claimed that they had seen a little cloud of vapor floating up to heaven when Louisa's sister died, "could all three of them have seen the same optical illusion?" Was Dr. Duncan MacDougal barking up the wrong tree when he found empirical proof that a dog has no soul—or that a person does, and it weighs three-quarters of an ounce? Do you know real malarkey when you hear it? What would you consider a fair price for the Brooklyn Bridge?

"Beyond and Back," a G-rated documentary about "the death experience," poses most of the above questions. It laves the viewer equipped to answer only the last two.

"Would *you* like to see what it's like to enter that region between life and death?" asks the film's bearded narrator, a serious-looking fellow with glasses, a three-piece suit and a big empty desk in an office lined with hardcover books. "No!" shouted the audience at the RKO Cinerama theater, where "Beyond and Back" was being shown very much out of focus yesterday afternoon.

•

The narrator continued, undaunted. When we go, we will apparently see our own bodies from afar, through a wobbly lens that makes them look as if they were under water. We will see rays of turquoise light. A divine being will beckon to us, and he will be wearing a long white robe with red trimming. Our lives will flash before our eyes, and we will hear oohing and aahing and music of the spheres. Our departed friends and loved ones will welcome us. They will all be smiling, and they will all be blond.

1978 F 18, 13:3

FILM VIEW

VINCENT CANBY

Hollywood Focuses on Vietnam at Last

In "Letter to Jane," a short (45-minute), 1972 film-discourse by Jean-Luc Godard and his former partner, Jean-Pierre Gorin, the two movie makers examined a newspaper photograph of Jane Fonda talking to a group of North Vietnamese civilians. As they zeroed in on particular details of the photograph—a close-up of the eyes, a gesture of the hands—Godard and Gorin ridiculed Miss Fonda's apparent sympathy, the fundamental motives of her visit to North Vietnam and even her ability to express any meaningful commitment to what Godard and Gorin saw to be the anti-imperialist cause, which they espoused with a passion that was virtually elitest. When "Letter to Jane" was shown at the 1972 New York Film Festival, audiences erupted first with laughter and then walked out in anger and boredom.

"Letter to Jane" really is an impossible film. Its dialectics are devious, and it is rude and cruel to Miss Fonda, who had just starred in Godard and Gorin's Maoist "Tout Va Bien," a movie that no other American actress of that time would have touched with her ex-agent. According to Godard and Gorin, Miss Fonda symbolized the impotence of the well-meaning, do-gooding bourgeoisie. Their point in "Letter to Jane," repeated in other films: It's impossible to fight a corrupt system, or even to demonstrate any real opposition to it, by using the tools of that system, including its accepted values and the responses those values elicit automatically.

Godard and Gorin put themselves above not only sentimentality but also sentiment. They went on to make a series of so-called revolutionary films that spoke to increasingly smaller audiences until, at last, Godard and Gorin were not even speaking to each other.

• • •

Now that the Vietnam disaster seems to be behind us, Hollywood, with its usual timeliness, is discovering the horrors of the war that, in the war's own time, only the hawkish John Wayne had the courage to use as material for a commercial movie, his ludicrously gung-ho "The Green Berets." Today Vietnam is being discovered by mass-entertainment movie makers but in ways that make me wonder whether Godard and Gorin might not, after all, have been right. Is it inevitable that commercial movies must trivialize intense feelings and complex ideas because of the nature of a system that must appeal to as many people as possible? I don't think so, but the way Hollywood film makers—even the high-minded ones—have treated Vietnam to date has not been terribly promising. With the exception of Peter Davis's ambitious documentary "Hearts and Minds," there have been no films to come within an eon of our written literature—Michael Herr's spell-binding "Dispatches," reportage that simultaneously evokes the particular nature of the Vietnam War and discovers its hidden associations with even "popular" wars, David Halberstam's "The Best and the Brightest," or a novel like Robert Stone's "Dog Soldiers," which itself is being made into a film. So far, film makers have shaped the Vietnam experience to fit their needs, being either incapable or afraid of meeting it on its own terms. Most of the time, Vietnam is simply a convenient excuse, something to be trotted out to explain someone's bizarre behavior.

This is the sum and substance of Vietnam as seen in "Heroes," a movie that is meant to be a heart-warming

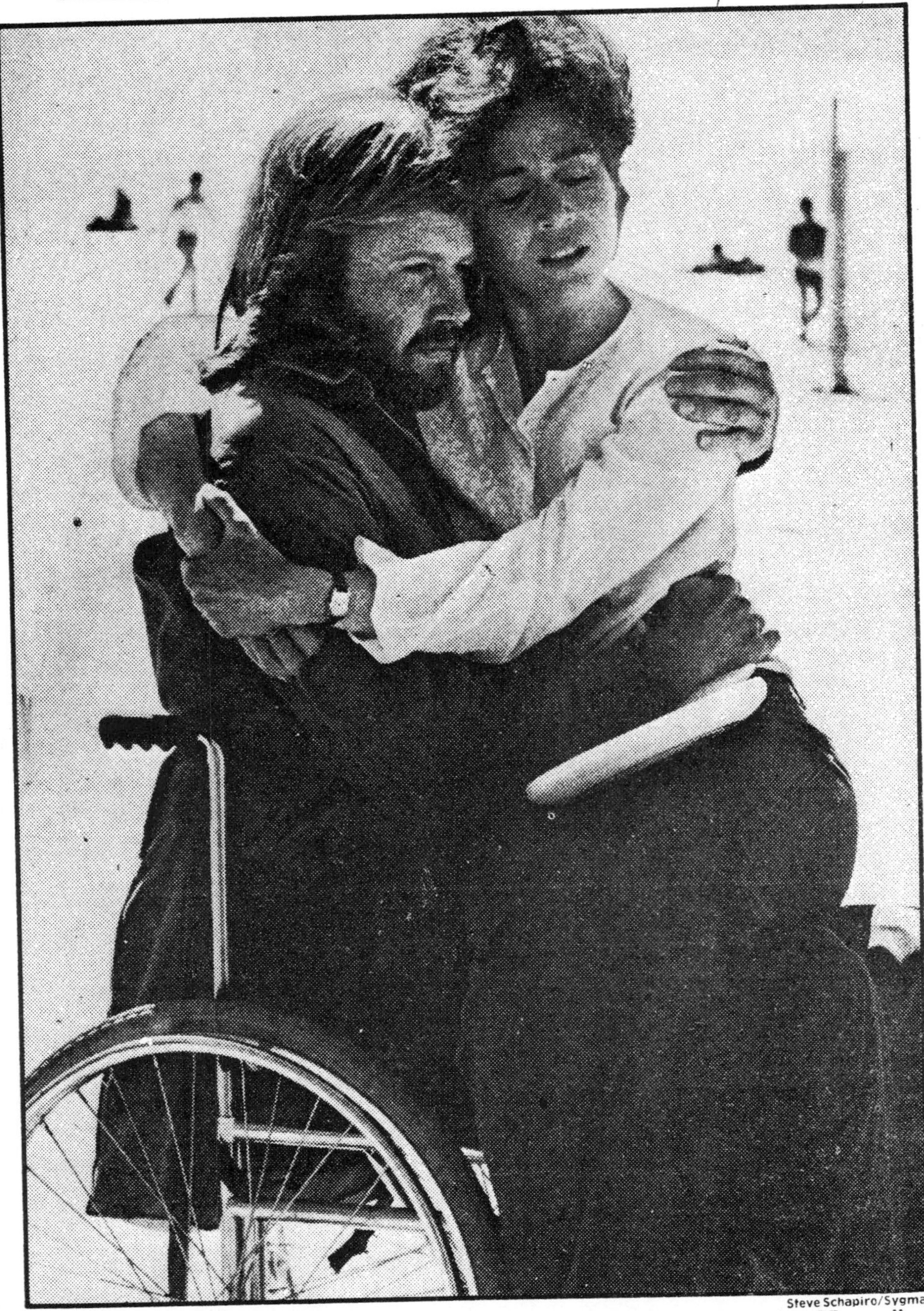

Steve Schapiro/Sygma

Jon Voight, as a paraplegic Vietnam veteran, and Jane Fonda in "Coming Home."

comedy about a lovable, traumatized veteran, played by Henry Winkler, who saw his buddies "buy it" over there. Mr. Winkler goes through most of "Heroes" being so aggressively adorable and eccentric, making a play for the adorable, eccentric Sally Field on a trans-continental bus, that near the end, when his eccentricities are blamed on Vietnam (which we see in splintery flashbacks) it seems as if the reels for two different movies have been mixed up. If the movie had been made 10 years ago, Winkler's emotional problems might as easily have been blamed on an unhappy Boy Scout picnic where two of his buddies died of ptomaine.

"Heroes" has about as much to say about Vietnam, and its place in American lives, as it has to say about spoiled potato salad—which is nothing.

Maybe I'm being too critical. It may be that even using Vietnam as an excuse is some sort of progress, though I doubt it. Paul Schrader, the screen writer recently turned director (with the new film, "Blue Collar"), made reference in his "Taxi Driver" screenplay to the fact that Travis Bickle, the psychotic character played by Robert De Niro, had learned how to handle guns in Vietnam. I suppose, too, that the apparently cathartic effect of Travis's bloody rampage at the film's end may be Schrader's comment about Vietnam and the American psyche, though I can't be sure. But if it is, I don't believe it for a minute.

Mr. Schrader made more direct reference to Vietnam in the screenplay for another film, "Rolling Thunder," in which William Devane plays a former prisoner-of-war of the North Vietnamese, a fellow who returns home to find his wife in love with another guy and, shortly afterwards, witnesses the murders of his wife and son by petty hoods who also leave him for dead (after grinding up Devane's right hand in a garbage disposal unit). Most of "Rolling Thunder" has to do with Devane's cool, careful search for the murderers whom he systematically destroys, on camera with much realism of splattered blood. If the Devane character had never been to Vietnam, if he hadn't learned to survive in a p.o.w. camp, would he have been able to plan and carry out the execution of these fellows so efficiently? I suppose that's what "Rolling Thunder" is saying, but it's very iffy, and it doesn't do much to explain the anti-social behavior of the guys who stuck Devane's hand in the garbage disposal unit in the first place. What was their problem? Vietnam is a convenience, like an unhappy childhood for the alcoholic.

• • •

In Robert Aldrich's film version of "The Choirboys," as in Joseph Wambaugh's novel from which the film was adapted, Vietnam turns up as a sort of prologue to the film's main events, to explain the friendship of two men who later are seen as part of the team of neurotic, hard-drinking, supposedly wacky Los Angeles policemen. "The Choirboys" has nothing to do with Vietnam and doesn't pretend to. I find it interesting, however, that a subject that once dared not be mentioned in a film, now is so easily used as part of conventional exposition. The casual way in which movie makers now make use of Vietnam implies that the Vietnam War has always been there in our movies, even though we never saw it.

"The Boys in Company C," directed by Sidney J. Furie and written by him and Rick Natkin, is a fairly clumsy movie; yet, it makes no bones about being about the war in Vietnam, particularly as experienced by the Marines of Company C. The problem is—as has been noted elsewhere—the Vietnam War we see in this film, from the opening sequences in boot camp until the end on a bloody battle field, looks amazingly like the war as dramatized in any number of World War II movies. As I watched "The Boys in Company C," I kept being reminded of the kind of boys-will-be-boys high jinks, followed by the quick maturation process, that I remember from something like "Battle Cry."

• • •

There is a difference, however, and it's a major one, and that is the film's pervasive if not entirely believeable pessimism. The men in this film quickly come to realize that this war is rotten, that it will have no decisive end, and that in the name of freedom all sorts of atrocities are being committed. This would be strong stuff in a commercial American movie if the tone of "The Boys in Company C" weren't alternately so sentimental and so heroic. The movie recognizes that the Vietnam experience was particular for the American fighting men; yet, it seems incapable of saying that in terms that don't automatically cancel the message. "The Boys in Company C" is a war comedy that wears an unconvincing long face.

The most ambitious, pious attempt to date to deal with the Vietnam War in a commercial American fiction film is "Coming Home," a film that was apparently made largely because of the interest and perseverance of Jane Fonda. Wouldn't it be pleasant if it were the stunning, no-holds-barred Vietnam drama we've all been waiting for? Wouldn't it be nice to think that Jean-Luc Godard and Jean-Pierre Gorin were wrong, and to know that it is possible to make a movie within the system that cracks the system? "Coming Home" is not that movie. Like many well-born things, it starts out very well and ends a fine old mess. It's not stretching things too far to report that "Coming Home," which is the story of a revivifying love affair of a paraplegic Vietnam veteran (Jon Voight) and the wife (Miss Fonda) of a Marine officer (Bruce Dern) serving in Vietnam, is really about the wife's first fully satisfying orgasm. This she experiences in the company of the paraplegic vet, which may or may not be meant as a kind of irony, but then the Voight character is militantly anti-war (sexy?) and, though paralyzed, in touch with himself. The gung-ho husband, on the other hand, is full of repressions. He's out of touch—impotent and confused. "Coming Home" is more about Freud, perhaps, than about the war.

Without knowing much about how the film was made, I suspect from the looks of it that too many people got in on the act of creation. The screenplay is credited to Waldo Salt and Robert C. Jones, based on a story by Nancy Dowd, who wrote the excellent screenplay for "Slap Shot." It was directed by Hal Ashby ("Bound for Glory," "Shampoo," etc.) photographed by Haskell Wexler, and the first 45 minutes of it, which detail the beginning of the affair between Miss Fonda and Voight in a veterans' hospital are superb—moving, tough, surprising and often funny.

Then something happens and the movie seems to go off in all directions at once. It's as if the writers, the director and the cameraman all decided that the movie had to be more explicit in its anger about the war, as if what we'd already seen wasn't going to be convincing enough. The film has two suicides (one too many for anything except Shakespeare). It flies to Hong Kong for a short interlude (the most unnecessary location trip any film has taken in years), and the central triangle is resolved with a sequence that should get an appalled laugh from any movie historian.

Miss Fonda and Voight are immensely appealing, even when the movie is dissolving around them in the confusion of everybody's good intentions. The pseudo-hip style of the movie is not appealing at all—lots of halo-white photography and soundtrack music composed of sixties hits that won't shut up commenting upon the action on the screen. To the extent that "Coming Home" talks about the war and dramatizes a lot of feelings associated with Vietnam, it rates a B-plus for effort, but it's ideas are totally confused and its manner of smug self-importance barely tolerable after the first hour.

To put it another way, "Coming Home" almost makes me want to go back and look at "Letter to Jane" again. ■

1978 F 19, II:1:3

BLACK AT YALE: A FILM DIARY, directed, produced and edited by Warrington Hudlin; directors of photography, Mr. Hudlin and Robert Slattery. Running time: 50 minutes.
I COULD HEAR YOU ALL THE WAY DOWN THE HALL, directed, written and edited by Robert Gardner; director of photography, Collis Davis. Running time: 15 minutes.
At the Whitney Museum of American Art, Madison Avenue at 75th Street.

FILMS by two young black film makers make up the new program that opened yesterday at the Whitney Museum of American Art — Warrington Hudlin's 50-minute "Black at Yale: A Film Diary," and Robert Gardner's 15-minute "I Could Hear You All the Way Down the Hall."

"I Could Hear You," about the adventures of a group of young students when the teacher leaves the classroom, is casual, warm and disarmingly funny, even when the quality of the soundtrack leaves something to be desired.

"Black at Yale" is sober reportage on black student life at the Ivy League institution, mostly as reported in two interviews. In the first, an articulate English major tells about his feeling of discrimination from the other students, who are no longer politically active, and the white students who, to his amusement, seem to be afraid of him.

The second student isn't, technically, a student. He's a young man from Philadelphia who, one day, decided he wanted to study philosophy at Yale and so hitchhiked to New Haven, where he began to attend classes without going through the formalities of matriculation. The film maker appears not to make a judgment on the fellow who, when we first see him, seems wildly sincere. By the end, though, one suspects there may be a lot of the con artist about him.

Mr. Hudlin approaches his subjects directly, without condescension, never imposing his own ideas on them. The result is a good, straightforward record of some particular experiences. "Black at Yale" is a film limited only by the resources of money and time available to the director. One would like more of it.

VINCENT CANBY

1978 F 22, C22:5

CELINE AND JULIE GO BOATING (Celine et Julie Vont en Bateau), directed by Jacques Rivette; screenplay (French with English subtitles) by Mr. Rivette, Eduardo di Gregorio, Juliet Berto, Dominique Labourier, Bulle Ogier and Marie-France Pisier; photography, Jacques Renard and Michel Cenet; editors, Nicole Lubtchansky and Chris Tullio-Allan; music, Jean Marie Senia; executive producer, Barbet Schroeder; production companies, Les Films du Losange/Les Films 7/Renn Productions/SAGA/SIMAR/V.M. Productions/Action Films/Les Film Christian Fechner; released by New Yorker Films. At the Cinema Studio, Broadway and 66th Street. Running time: 193 minutes. This film is not rated.

Celine .... Juliet Berto
Julie .... Dominique Labourier
Camille .... Bulle Ogier
Sophie .... Marie-France Pisier
Olivier .... Barbet Schroeder
Guilou .... Philippe Clevenot

"Céline and Julie Go Boating" was shown at the 1974 New York Film Festival. The following review, written by Nora Sayre on Oct. 8, 1974, has been excerpted. The film opens today at the Cinema Studio, Broadway and 66th Street.

THE riddles and delusions of Jacques Rivette's "Céline and Julie Go Boating" are much more accessible than the enigmas of his "Out One/Spectre." "Céline," the later movie, has the dotty logic of dreams, and the characters' rational solemnity while talking nonsense does succeed in evoking Lewis Carroll.

There's a beguiling opening, as Juliet Berto (Céline) dashes past Dominique Labourier—Julie, a librarian who's reading on a park bench—dropping her possessions and conveying the desperate haste of the White Rabbit. A droll chase ensues; eventually, the two young women meet and become flirtatious friends—it's not clear if there's a sexual relationship, although the possibility is suggested.

•

Céline—a professional magician—is also a true spellcaster. Inventing a story about a mystifying household, she soon inspires her friend to visit the site of her fantasies. Proustian flashbacks, set off by bits of candy or memory potions, enable both of them to review various events within the house; thus, they become spectators of a film within a film, and they can even rerun the footage as though they were using a Moviola.

Inside the house, two women compete over a widower who had promised his dying wife that (for the sake of their child) he would never remarry—a scenario that indirectly alludes to Henry James's "The Other House" (which was itself influenced by "Hedda Gabler" and several other of Ibsen's plays). These imaginary beings are stagey in their manner, rather like zombies oozing with grandeur. Bulle Ogier manages to be aggressively ethereal in what almost seems to be a spoof on a bad Ophelia. Finally, Céline and Julie participate in the drama; they take turns playing a nurse, while rehearsing and forgetting their lines, messing up the dialogue and signaling wildly to the other characters like incompetent amateur actresses.

•

Miss Berto, as a defiant, ruthless clown, simply runs away with this movie. She brings an intense concentration to everything she does, and also excels at horseplay. At times, she shows an extraordinary resemblance to Jeanne Moreau—minus a couple of decades—but she's in no way derivative. Miss Labourier was clearly cast and directed as a contrast for Miss Berto, but her more pedestrian part lacks the agility and wit that Miss Berto scatters all over the screen.

Céline and Julie complain that their interior film is full of holes, like a Swiss cheese—and of course that's what Mr. Rivette intended for his own 3¼-hour feature. When this movie sags, it becomes a series of skits, but the best parts do achieve the spontaneity and impudent freshness that this director relishes.

1978 F 24, C10:3

RIDDLES OF THE SPHINX; written and directed by Laura Mulvey and Peter Wollen; produced by the British Film Institute; cinematography by Diane Tammes; editing by Carola Klein and Larry Sider; music by Mike Ratledge; sound by Mr. Sider. With Dinah Stabb as Louise. At the Film Forum, 15 Vandam Street, through Saturday and March 2 to 5, 7:45 PM. Running time: 92 minutes. This film has not been rated.

By JANET MASLIN

In "Riddles of the Sphinx," Laura Mulvey, a feminist and film critic, and Peter Wollen, author of "Signs and Meaning in the Cinema," reduce the story of a housewife's radicalization to a set of 13 360-degree pan shots. (The film plays part of this week and next at the Film Forum.)

"The point," write the co-directors in a set of accompanying program notes, "is not so much to distance the spectator from the narrative, but to split his/her interest and tension between the story line and the workings of the camera (and soundtrack)." But with all his/her work done by the film makers, the poor spectator will be hard pressed to function as an interested observer. A technique this ironclad loses its power to provoke.

Some of the early 360-degree shots—one around the woman's kitchen, and another that circles the inside of her house as her husband packs and leaves—are coolly effective. But the latter part of the film is so hamstrung by this format that it becomes numbing. Aside from the 13 pans, there are shots of Miss Mulvey pondering the story of the Sphinx and Oedipus, extreme close-ups of the Sphinx to establish that film is indeed a grainy medium, and other equally overbearing episodes. None of this is genuinely challenging, and none of it comes alive.

1978 F 24, C14:5

FILM VIEW

VINCENT CANBY

Don't Panic, But We're Short Of Prototypes

Watching Daniel Petrie's giggly, not unamusing film version of "The Betsy," Harold Robbins's breathless novel about four generations of a Detroit auto family who may or may not resemble the Fords, the Dodges or the Chryslers (were there ever any Pontiacs who weren't Indians?), I was suddenly panicked by the fear that we might soon run out of the real-life prototypes that inspire such fiction. They are going fast and the supply is not inexhaustible. So far Mr. Robbins has already had his way with characters apparently suggested by Howard Hughes ("The Carpetbaggers"), Porfirio Rubirosa ("The Adventurers") and Hugh Heffner/Larry Flynt ("Dreams Die First"), among others. He even helped himself to the late Jacqueline Susann in his "The Lonely Lady," a rather ungentlemanly thing to do, all things considered, since Miss Susann was a colleague in the same big business of the literary hustle, recycling the public-domain reputations of such people as James Aubrey, Doris Duke, Judy Garland, Jacqueline Onassis and, only heaven knows now, who else, plotting her human comedies as if she were Grant attempting to encircle Richmond (mostly with the same results).

Unfortunately for us, Mr. Robbins and Miss Susann haven't been the only ones working this side of the street. There have been highly publicized tell-all novels by the likes of Rona Barrett, who wrote "The Lovomaniacs," about a Frank Sinatra-type of singer, a character who also turned up in another novel called "The King." And Joyce Haber is the author of another, supposedly, a-clef Hollywood novel called "The Users," which is not to be confused with the new Robert Ackworth novel called "The Takers" ("a sprawling, colorful saga of the Golden Age of the motion picture, the rise and fall of a major studio, and the sensuous, tormented lives of its three biggest stars").

• • •

Life would certainly be a dreary place if not without these novels then without the prose that accompanies their publication. Consider the ad copy for Judith Krantz's new work: "The story of a woman who wanted absolutely everything. And got it. The super-rich, the super-beautiful, the super-powerful .... these are the people who fill the world of 'Scruples': the most titillating, name-dropping, gossipy, can't-put-it-down novel of this decade." Today everybody is getting into the act. Eugenia Sheppard and Earl Blackwell, heretofore well-known for hanging-on elsewhere, are now authors. Their novel: "Crystal Clear," which, according to its publishers, "takes you inside the glamorous, closely-guarded world where the super-celebrities of business, fashion and show business meet. . . ."

Apparently unfazed by this competition is Sidney Sheldon, who hit the jackpot with "The Other Side of Midnight," a hilariously awful novel about a very rich Greek shipping tycoon that was made into an equally awful, but not as funny, movie. Mr. Sheldon is now represented on the best-seller list by "Bloodline"—"with the world as its stage and a heroine you'll never forget .... a tale of love and suspense that leads from New York to London, Paris, Zurich and Rome," which was more or less the itinerary of the characters who cruised so helplessly to power, riches, fame and disaster through "The Other Side of Midnight."

Not all of these novels will soon become motion pictures—major or otherwise. All that restless, jet-setting tourism from Rome to Paris, from London to New York, from Hollywood to Palm Beach, makes them very expensive to produce, and, as the people who financed the movie versions of "The Adventurers" and "The Love Machine" found out, a novel that is a best-seller in hardback as well as in paperback does not automatically become a hugely profitable picture. The public, with a daintiness of feeling that should boggle the mind, may not know anything about junk movies, but it knows which ones it wants to see.

• • •

From the number of people who were paying $4 a head to see "The Betsy" at the National Theater on Times Square one afternoon last week, the public clearly knows it wants to see "The Betsy." What makes "The Betsy" apparently different from, say, "Once Is Not Enough" is not easy to see. It's like candling eggs. The similarities, though, are obvious to the naked eye.

"The Betsy" darts back and forth between the boardrooms of Detroit and the bedrooms of various members of the powerful, staggeringly rich Hardeman family, who include among their clan not one but two ruthless tycoons; one sensitive scion who may or may not be a transvestite (the film, which pretends to pull no punches in other areas, goes terribly discreet on this point); one incestuous daughter-in-law (if sleeping with one's father-in-law can be considered incest instead of just poor form); one suicide that is witnessed by the suicide's young son, who then runs to tell mummy and finds her in bed with the wrong man; a beautiful, titled English woman with the morals (as Robbins or Sheldon or Susann might say) of an alley cat; a young, reckless, power-driven (metaphorically speaking) racing driver; and a sweet, pretty young heiress who is deflowered by the racing driver on the night of her 21st birthday in a scene that ends as follows:

She: "I always knew it would be like this, from the moment I first saw you."

He: "You're a beautiful child."

She: "I'm a beautiful *woman*. It's my 21st birthday, remember?"

"The Betsy" has its share of fairly graphic though unflaggingly lyric sex scenes. As often as not, its characters travel around in private helicopters and Lear jets, and they deal in sums of money that can only be compared to New York City's indebtedness. At one point, a father presents his son with a wedding gift of company stock that, the father says proudly, is worth somewhere between $25 million and $27 million, (depending on the price per share at the close of that day's market, I suppose). All their houses look like San Simeon.

Yet—as in all other junk movies of this sort—the most important thing is neither the possession of money nor the exercise of various sexual options. It is, rather, the accumulation and the exercise of power, not for any special purpose other than having it and being able to use it as wantonly as anyone might wish. It's this demonstration of power, I suspect, as much as the escapist settings and the shopgirl's idea of upper-crust living, that makes this fiction so endlessly appealing to the reading public.

• • •

I've really no idea what the public may be seeing in "The Betsy" that it didn't see in "The Adventurers," though I know what I see that makes this marshmallow bigger and more pleasantly gummy than any of the others I've mentioned. It's Laurence Olivier, who plays the patriarch of the Hardeman family and who gives one of the wildest, wittiest, most low-down comic performances of his long career, a demonstration that recalls bits and pieces of some of his greatest accomplishments, including Richard III and George Hurstwood (in "Carrie").

His is not the usual "cameo" part that often attracts big-star names to this kind of not-quite-all-star movie fiction. Olivier is on the screen throughout the movie, starting off as a shrewd, wheelchair-based old man of almost 90 and then, in the course of various flashbacks, turning up as the character in his 40's and in his 50's. Make-up and a certain judicious use of camera filters help these transformations, but at the heart of them is the magnificent actor's intelligence that discovers the unexpected truth in everything that Olivier does.

Not once does Olivier appear to condescend to the movie, which under the circumstance, he would have had every right to do. He doesn't pretend to be discovering the interior life of the character, which would certainly be the last thing that Harold Robbins wanted or that Robbins could have brought off. Olivier's performance is all show, all surface mannerisms that are the cinematic equivalent to the kind of prose that Robbins writes and which Walter Bernstein and William Bast, who did the screenplay, have preserved with nuttily reverential fidelity.

It would be difficult for anyone in good conscience to recommend "The Betsy" without adding so many qualifications that the recommendation would have to come out reading like a lease. I can't. Yet, let it be said that Laurence Olivier remains a performer of infinite delight and surprise no matter what the peculiar circumstances and no matter what accent he chooses to use. In "The Betsy," the accent might be described as modified Middle West, an accent that I associate with Darryl F. Zanuck.

On second thought, I realized that the fear I expressed earlier that our pop novelists might run out of prototypes for their romans à clef was an artificial panic. It was induced in part by whiffing the exhaust fumes from marijuana smokers who now make New York movie-going something of a trip, when one doesn't move away. ■

1978 F 26, II:17:1

Indivisible

DONA FLOR AND HER TWO HUSBANDS, directed by Bruno Barreto; screenplay (Portuguese with English subtitles) by Mr. Barreto, based on the novel by Jorge Amado; director of photography, Maurilo Salles; editor, Raimundo Higino; music, Chico Buarque; produced by Luiz Carlos Barreto, Newton Rique and Cia Serrador; distribution by Carnival Films. At the Paris Theater, 58th Street west of Fifth Avenue. Running time: 105 minutes. This film is not rated.

Dona Flor .... Sonia Braga
Vadinho .... Jose Wilker
Teodoro .... Mauro Mendonca
Rozilda .... Dinorah Brillanti
Mirandao .... Nelson Xavier
Carlinhos .... Arthur Costa Filho
Cazuza .... Rui Rezende
Arigof .... Mario Gusmao

By JANET MASLIN

DONA FLOR'S first husband is dead, but that's just as well, since he was a grievous no-goodnik in his lifetime. He was a gambler, a wise guy and a womanizer, and he beat his pretty young wife shamelessly, pacifying her with the occasional moonlight serenade or nice gesture. Once he took her out to a fancy nightclub, where he bought her champagne and caviar and didn't even pinch the waitress.

Apparently, this man's only noteworthy talent was for lovemaking, and "Dona Flor and Her Two Husbands," at the Paris Theater, devotes more than enough screen time to that aspect of the marriage. And Dona Flor's second husband, a dopey druggist who drops a medicine bottle the first time he sees the pretty widow, is a sorry successor. So Dona Flor mopes and broods and smiles wanly, until one day her prayers are answered. Husband Number One is such a devil that he manages to come back, sans clothing, and pay his wife amorous visits while Husband Number Two isn't looking. Even if Husband Number Two *were* looking he wouldn't catch on, because he is slow-witted anyway and because death has conveniently rendered Husband Number One invisible.

This story, adapted from the novel by the Brazilian author Jorge Amado, would seem to have the makings of a bawdy "Topper," and indeed the film's final 20 minutes make reasonably amusing use of the dead man's return. But Bruno Barreto, who directed the film, devotes far more time to setting up the situation than he finally does to exploiting it, and the early part of the film has a dangerously uncertain tone. Dona Flor's life looks terrible, yet this is not a didactic film or even a particularly satirical one, so there's little to be learned from her plight.

There are various glimpses of Bahia and its customs, circa the 1940's, but

Sonia Braga
Plays the title role

the only interesting bit of local color is Dona Flor's recipe for crabmeat casserole. Dona Flor teaches a class in gourmet cooking: Husband Number One liked to sit in on the class and, by the by, fondle the students.

Sonia Braga, a Brazilian model and actress who plays Dona Flor, is called upon alternately to frown and to engage in various soft-core shenanigans. She is adequate to these demands, but her role is really little more than that of the butt of a family dirty joke.

1978 F 27, C18:2

SEBASTIANE, directed by Derek Jarman and Paul Humfress; screenplay (Latin with English subtitles) by James Whaley and Mr. Jarman; director of photography, Peter Middleton; editor, Mr. Humfress; music, Brian Eno; produced by Howard Malin and Mr. Whaley; released by Libra Films. At the Quad 3 Cinema 3, 13th Street between Fifth and Sixth Avenues. Running time: 83 minutes. This film is rated X.

Sebastian	Leonardo Treviglio
Severus	Barney James
Maximus	Neil Kennedy
Justin	Richard Warwick
Claudius	Donald Dunham

By JANET MASLIN

BEFORE you take any budding little linguists in the family to see "Sebastiane," think it over. Yes, this is the first feature film ever made in Latin, and yes, it deals with the life of a saint. But what is the tanned, well-muscled male cast intoning about in such a serious-sounding tongue? Piles. Insects. St. Sebastian's famous masochism. And the contents of one another's very skimpy loincloths.

"Sebastiane," a soft-core gay porno epic, is prettily photographed by Peter Middleton and rather languidly directed by two Englishmen, Derek Jarman and Paul Humfress (Mr. Jarman, the set designer for Ken Russell's "The Devils," reflects a bit of Mr. Russell's extravagance but none of his wit). The film includes footage of the martyrdom of St. Sebastian, whose nude body is punctured by arrows in some remarkable places.

1978 Mr 2, C14:1

Oliver Reed, left, as Miles Hendon, and Mark Lester as the pauper in film "Crossed Swords."

Shades of Twain

CROSSED SWORDS, directed by Richard Fleischer; original screenplay by Berta Dominguez D. and Pierre Spengler, based on the novel "The Prince and the Pauper" by Mark Twain; final screenplay by George MacDonald Fraser; director of photography, Jack Cardiff; music, Maurice Jarre; editor, Ernest Walter; produced by Pierre Spengler; an Alexander and Ilya Salkind Production; released by Warner Bros. At Radio City Music Hall. Running time: 113 minutes. This film is rated PG.

Miles Hendon	Oliver Reed
Edith	Raquel Welch
Tom Canty/Prince Edward	Mark Lester
John Canty	Ernest Borgnine
The Ruffler	George C. Scott
Norfolk	Rex Harrison
Hugh Hendon	David Hemmings
Henry VIII	Charlton Heston

By VINCENT CANBY

"CROSSED SWORDS" has many things going for it. It's based on Mark Twain's classic, "The Prince and the Pauper," about the mad mix-up that ensues when a 10-year-old London beggar boy and his look-alike, Prince Edward, the son of Henry VIII, change places, the one to stand the court on its ear, the other to learn the bitter facts of life in Tudor England.

The movie contains some stunning views of English palaces and countrysides, a lot of swordplay and its fair share of grandly fruity lines, such as the one spoken when Henry (Charlton Heston) finds the pauper hiding in his garden and steps on the boy's back. The boy cries out, "What?" bellows Henry. "Is the weight of England too heavy for you? I've carried it for these 5 and 30 years!"

•

When I was two-and-eight, I loved this kind of dialogue, though I was puzzled. Why did kings always say, 'these 5 and 30 years"? Why not "these 10 and 25 years," or even "these 17 and 18 years"? No matter—style was the thing.

Style is not something that "Crossed Swords" is exactly burdened with, though the movie comes to life every time Rex Harrison, as the fastidious, wiley, Roman Catholic Duke of Norfolk, makes his amused way across the screen, or when George C. Scott turns up briefly, but hilariously, as a snaggle-toothed bandit chief named the Ruffler, an ex-monk with a tendency to talk as if all speech were a Gregorian chant.

The most notable thing about the film—and something that might guarantee its place in the history books—has nothing to do with the esthetics of popular cinema, but with the fact it opens today at Radio City Music Hall and will probably be the last movie to play that most extraordinary of all picture palaces. The hall may well survive, but not as we've known it for the last 45 years.

•

"Crossed Swords" is not an inappropriate choice to receive this distinction. Though it is rated PG, it recalls the kind of romantic-adventure fiction that distinguished one of Hollywood's several golden ages and that served well the patrons of the Music Hall. I emphasize, however, that "Crossed Swords" only recalls those earlier times. It doesn't re-create them. It's a far cry from the sort of 1930's movie that starred Errol Flynn and presented great character actors such as Henry Stephenson, Halliwell Hobbes, Claude Rains and Montagu Love, who made the 1937 version of "The Prince and The Pauper" so entertaining.

"Crossed Swords" is vastly more elaborate and more expensive than that film, but it doesn't have its simplicity of spirit or even its know-how. Instead of the young Mauch brothers, the identical twins who played the title role, it has an 18-year-old Mark Lester, who was such a steadfast little Oliver in "Oliver" 10 years ago, as both the prince and the pauper.

I suppose the argument is that an older pair of heroes will attract a more sophisticated audience to "Crossed Swords," but Mr. Lester, now so long of limb as well as of tooth, simply looks silly in the roles. The readings are still those of a child actor and do not fit his physique. It's a comment on the age in which we live to be required to say of an 18-year-old actor: he hasn't aged especially well.

•

As Miles Hendon, the soldier-of-fortune who befriends the prince on his travels around the kingdom, Oliver Reed makes every attempt to overwhelm the part and the movie. Mr. Reed's intensity as an actor is intended, I assume, to come across as character conviction, but the result is a kind of scary, humorless self-absorption. There's no sense of fun in the performance.

There's somewhat more fun in the performance of Raquel Welch, as the woman Miles Hendon loves, if only because it's fun to see her in such costume spectacles as she exposes a perfectly straight face and a lot of well-tanned cleavage. Ernest Borgnine plays the pauper's vicious old dad as if Fatso Judson (of "From Here to Eternity") had awakened in Tudor London, which is not at all bad. There is also an attractive supporting performance by Lalla Ward as the self-possessed, opinionated little princess who later became Elizabeth I.

Though the screenplay by George MacDonald Fraser seems to dawdle a lot, the direction of Richard Fleischer is much of the time paralyzed with indecision. Is "Crossed Swords" supposed to be funny or is it supposed to be an all-out adventure? The Old London sets are splendid, but the atmosphere is as tepid and unconvincing as that of a road-company operetta. When Mr. Fleischer cross-cuts between two lines of action, he has a unique way of cutting suspense in half instead of doubling it.

There aren't so many costume films that one can easily dismiss "Crossed Swords." Yet one keeps wanting it to be better than it ever could be, given these circumstances.

•

"Crossed Swords," which has been rated PG ("parental guidance suggested"), includes some rough-and-tumble fight scenes, but nothing as blood-curdling as an average child's everyday nightmare.

1978 Mr 2, C14:1

FINGERS, directed and written by James Toback; director of photography, Mike Chapman; produced by George Barrie; presented by Brut Productions Inc. At the Cinema 2, 60th Street and Third Avenue. Running time: 91 minutes. This film is rated R.

Jimmy Angelelli	Harvey Keitel
Carol	Tisa Farrow
Dreems	Jim Brown
Ben	Michael V. Gazzo
Mother	Marian Seldes
Christa	Carole Francis

Tisa Farrow and Harvey Keitel in James Toback's "Fingers" at the Cinema II
A stiff style of direction that's heavy on the hocus-pocus and low on insight

By JANET MASLIN

JIMMY ANGELELLI, the hypersensitive hero of "Fingers," which opened yesterday at Cinema 2, is a man who has no frieends and who doesn't deserve any. For one thing, Jimmy is too busy pacing, brooding, pouncing, snarling and having inexplicable conniptions to have time for much of a social life. For another, he isn't the sort of fellow who'll allow anyone to get very close to him.

We know this, and a lot of other things about Jimmy, courtesy of his portable tape deck, which he carries with him everywhere (because it puts up a kind of wall between him and the rest of the world), and which he uses to play both classical music and 50's rock-and-roll (Jimmy's is a divided nature). He even turns on the machine in restaurants, in scenes that mean to establish him as a desperately insecure figure but instead make him out to be a public nuisance.

"Fingers" marks the directional debut of the screenwriter James Toback ("The Gambler"), who exhibits a fatal fascination with Jimmy's every petulant quirk. Mr. Toback, having created a character whose intrinsic charm plus 50 cents would only barely get him onto the subway, seems incapable of putting his hero in any kind of dramatic perspective, and he is apparently unwilling to explore him in terms more intimate than those of an introductory psychology course. Jimmy's mother was a musician and his father is a boorish gangster; his mother resents him bitterly and his father wishes he'd strangled him in his crib. No wonder the kid's got a headache.

Many of Jimmy's troubles revolve around sex, to which he devotes himself far too selflessly, according to his doctor (if this isn't the only movie to show someone having his prostate examined, it ought to be). Jimmy is obsessively entangled with a strange, elusive, mysterious girl (Tisa Farrow) who is so spitefully uncommunicative that one begins wanting, in the spirit of the movie, to give her a good belt. Jimmy's machismo—he tries to castrate a rival, thinks women are sexier without birth control—is enough to make Tarzan blush.

Mr. Toback favors a stiff, staccato, nervous style of direction that's heavy on the hocus-pocus and low on verisimilitude or insight. Aiming for a mood of nightmarish abstraction, he borders all too often on jumpy incompetence. Although the film's production credits are impressive—the cinematographer from "Taxi Driver," the production designer from "Three Days of the Condor," the costume designer for "Next Stop, Greenwich Village"—and suggest that the film ought to have a good feeling for New York, it contains moments of surprising amateurishness. The sets look uninhabitable and the sound mixing is particularly appalling: A phone in the back of a restaurant rings at top volume, and the music sounds equally scratchy whether it's coming from a tape deck or a concert piano.

Perhaps this should have been the movie to establish Harvey Keitel as a leading man of depth and versatility, but Mr. Keitel's performance as Jimmy only underscores Mr. Toback's skittishness. The screenplay draws Jimmy's character in such rudimentary terms that Mr. Keitel might have breathed a little healthy confusion into the role by playing against it. Instead, he does little more than illustrate Mr. Toback's points with a textbook tidiness, turning each scene into a virtual exercise. The part of Jimmy on which Mr. Keitel concentrates most avidly is, you guessed it, his fingers, whether Jimmy is working as a loan collector in his father's employ or a pianist in his mother's shadow. Not since Captain Queeg have a character's hands done so much restless wiggling and tapping.

Mr. Keitel, as always, gives an impression of earnestness and dedication, but everyone else in the film appears to be in a big hurry to get to his or her lunch date. Miss Farrow is lovely to watch, but she gives a performance of such low wattage she barely seems plugged in; Marian Seldes and Michael V. Gazzo, as Jimmy's parents, suggest that Mr. Toback doesn't believe there's any such thing as overacting.

Jim Brown, as the only real sex object in the movie (he's the only character who doesn't wear underwear), has the film's most memorably silly moment, in which he smacks two women's heads together because they don't want to kiss each other. This episode, intended as a kind of taunt to Jimmy, is only one of many things in the film that only Mr. Toback could, or would want to, understand.

1978 Mr 3, C9:1

AN UNMARRIED WOMAN, directed and written by Paul Mazursky; produced by Mr. Mazursky and Tony Ray; director of photography, Arthur Ornitz; editor, Stuart H. Pappe; music, Bill Conti; distributed by 20th Century Fox. Running time: 124 minutes. At the Beekman Theater, 65th Street and Second Avenue; Paramount Theater, Broadway at 61st Street, and Murray Hill Theater, 34th Street near Third Avenue.

Erica	Jill Clayburgh
Saul	Alan Bates
Martin	Michael Murphy
Charlie	Cliff Gorman
Sue	Pat Quinn
Elaine	Kelly Bishop
Patti	Lisa Lucas
Jeanette	Linda Miller
Bob	Andrew Duncan
Dr. Jacobs	Daniel Seltzer
Phil	Matthew Arkin
Tanya	Penelope Russianoff
Jean	Novella Nelson
Edward	Raymond J. Barry
Herb Rowan	Ivan Karp
Claire	Jill Eikenberry
Fred	Michael Tucker
Cabby	Chico Martinez
Hal	Paul Mazursky
Sophie	Donna Perich
Man at party	Vincent Schiavelli

By VINCENT CANBY

What would you do if, after 15 years of what has seemed to be a happy marriage, you're walking down the street with your husband, making plans to rent a house on Fire Island for the summer, when he stops, looks suddenly bereft, and breaks into the sobs of childhood as he says he wants out? He confesses that he has another woman, another life he wants to go to, and he feels so miserable about everything he's shocked when you don't sympathize.

In Paul Mazursky's new comedy, "An Unmarried Woman," about America's dangerously mobile, just-this-side-of-rootless middle class, Erica (Jill Clayburgh) gets bloody mad. She stalks off alone down the street, throws up in a trash basket and, when she at last lets the news sink in, starts to cry in fury, surprise, hurt and fear.

•

As Miss Clayburgh plays this scene, one has a vision of all the immutable things that can be destroyed in less than a minute, from landscapes and ships and reputations to perfect marriages. The scene is beautifully written by Mr. Mazursky. It is high comedy of a sharp, bitter kind, and Michael Murphy is fine as the weasel husband named Martin, but Miss Clayburgh is nothing less than extraordinary in

Sobbing, Michael Murphy tells Jill Clayburgh he wants to end their marriage in scene from "An Unmarried Woman"

what is the performance of the year to date. In her we see intelligence battling feeling—reason backed against the wall by pushy needs.

In the succeeding weeks, Erica begins to cope. Daily routine helps. She has her job in a SoHo art gallery. She has her teen-age daughter and her women friends, some of whom are in worse shape than she is. One night she gets out of bed and systematically throws out Martin's shaving gear, golf clubs and Adidas sneakers. For a while Erica also has a woman therapist who makes her feel better by appearing serenely understanding (and a tiny bit smug) as she repeats to Erica truisms that can be very comforting to the deeply distressed.

"An Unmarried Woman," which opens today at the Beekman, Paramount and Murray Hill Theaters, is Mr. Mazursky's most ambitious movie so far, and the first film to put Miss Clayburgh's talents to full use. She was charming in "Semi-Tough," but otherwise she's had to wade around in things such as "The Silver Streak" and "Gable and Lombard," pretending that mud puddles are swimming pools.

Mr. Mazursky has written a marvelous role for the actress, so I suppose it's not unfair of him to depend on her to carry the movie, which is ultimately not as tough and funny and critical as it is in individual moments. Because Mr. Mazursky has such a sharp eye for the essential props of a certain kind of American life, and because he has an ear for the way people talk, one expects him to be a more merciless social satirist than he has any intention of being.

In his best films, "Blume in Love" and "Harry and Tonto," as in the supposedly elegiacal "Next Stop Greenwich Village," he inevitably chooses the sentimental over the satiric, which one could defend as his right if he weren't so effective in portraying the essential foolishness of a plastic society. It's as if he couldn't restrain his affection for people and thing that, as he shows them to us, aren't worth it. Specific scenes in "An Unmarried Woman" come across in sharp focus, but the overall view is as soft and fuzzy as something photographed through gauze.

This is especially apparent in the new film after he has introduced us to Erica and her "problem," and after we witness her first desperate, comic attempts to liberate herself sexually with an egocentric Village painter, nicely played by Cliff Gorman). Erica doesn't flounder for long. She meets Mr. Right in the form of an English artist (Alan Bates), who's so manly, wise, affectionate and dependable that he seems to be out of "The Sleeping Beauty."

The final quarter of the movie gives the impression not of having been written, directed and acted, but of a tone poem that's been scored with slushy music and paced with swoony camera shots, thus to suggest an alternate title, "An Unmarried Man and A Woman."

The way the film evolves should not be a complete surprise, I suppose, because in the earlier sequences one is always aware of the sort of romantic method by which scenes must begin with images as seen through mirrors, a device that is even more boring than the freeze-frame, which he also uses.

Mr. Mazursky is a writer-director of such real abilities that we've the right to demand that he be better. He's fine with his actors (though Mr. Bates's role is no challenge to an exceptional actor) and he has the potential of a great satirist. It's as if he were afraid to let himself go because he wouldn't please enough people. He attempts to soothe when he should scratch.

1978 Mr 5, 52:1

"FURTIVOS"—Jose Luis Borau plays a corrupt provincial governor in a film that he produced and directed as well.

FURTIVOS, directed by Jose Luis Borau; screenplay (Spanish with English subtitles) by Manuel Gutierrez and Mr. Borau; director of photography, Luis Cuadrado; editing, Ana Romero; music, Vainica Doble; produced by Mr. Borau; distributed by Empresa Cinema International, Inc. At the Cinema Studio, Broadway and 66th Street. Running time: 88 minutes. This film has no rating.

Martina .... Lola Gaos
Angel .... Ovidi Montllor
Milagros .... Alicia Sanchez
Priest .... Ismael Merlo
Governor .... Jose Luis Borau
Cuqui .... Felipe Solano

By JANET MASLIN

There is a familiar-sounding romantic triangle in "Furtivos," involving a man, his sweetheart and his terribly chagrined old mother, but the Spanish director José Luis Borau chooses to present the situation in an exceedingly unfamiliar way.

The mother lives quietly in an isolated cottage, where the woods are full of wolves and the provincial governor makes special visits just to sample her stew. But when her sad-eyed son comes home, madly in love with a thirtyish-looking woman who says she is a reform-school runaway, the mother's life is disrupted.

In fact, the son is so bent on making his lover feel at home that one night he drags his mother from her own bed, screaming, so that he and his paramour can cuddle in comfort. The mother is so vexed by this, and so without effective recourse, that she stalks out to one of her wolf traps and takes out her rage on a hapless creature that has the ill fortune to be caught there.

•

This episode takes place in the evening but many of the eeriest moments in "Furtivos," at the Cinema Studio, are set in brilliant sunlight and sparkle with disconcertingly deadpan humor; it's no wonder that the film has been advertised as a favorite of Luis Buñuel.

Mr. Borau, whose work has apparently been both popular and controversial in Spain (though it is new to American audiences), has a talent for shifting things ever so slightly askew, without sacrificing the air of oppressive normality that gives his best scenes a subversive vitality. In his most sharply successful moments, Mr. Borau manages to get things so wrong that they seem just right.

So when the governor makes one of his periodic stew stops at this rude cottage in the forest, he brings a little chandelier as a bread-and-butter present. And when the runaway interrupts her truffle-gathering and dismisses her pig so she can seduce the sad-eyed son (now her sad-eyed husband) in the forest, who should appear on a motorcycle but her former boyfriend, a desperado who has come to find her.

The newlyweds just stand there, as the desperado circles around and around and never quite seems to notice them. Rather than being irritated by the interruption, they seem quite impressed, even mystified, by the outlaw's peculiar timing.

•

There is a marvelous spirit of mischief to Mr. Borau's work, and an unusual delicacy to his gift for making things seem daintily unhinged; the most enduring image presented by this handsome, impressively single-minded movie is that of an exquisitely serene autumnal forest with countless animal traps beneath the leaves.

Mr. Borau, who begins the film with Franco's statement that "Spain is a peaceful forest," is better able to suggest subversion visually than he is through more pointedly political plot elements, such as the reformatory, the renegade, or the sad-eyed man's illegal poaching of the governor's game. And, in fact, the boldness of such ingredients tends to overwhelm the understated rebelliousness at which the film otherwise hints so ably.

"The climate of oppression that the film means to dramatize is important, but what makes Mr. Borau's American debut particularly auspicious is not his film's subject but its muted, idiosyncratic and altogether clear-eyed madness.

1978 Mr 7, 44:6

Bergman-Inspired

A LITTLE NIGHT MUSIC, directed by Harold Prince; screenplay by Hugh Wheeler, based on his book for the musical play suggested by Ingmar Bergman's "Smiles of a Summer Night"; music and lyrics by Stephen Sondheim; executive producer, Heins Lazek; produced by Elliott Kastner; edited by John Jympson; director of photography, Arthur Ibbetson; distributed by New World Pictures. Running time: 124 minutes. At the Columbia 1 Theater, Second Avenue at 64th Street. This film has been rated PG.

Desiree Armfeldt .... Elizabeth Taylor
Charlotte Mittelheim .... Diana Rigg
Frederick Egerman .... Len Cariou
Anne Egerman .... Lesley-Anne Down
Mme. Armfeldt .... Hermione Gingold
Carl-Magnus Mittelheim .... Lawrence Guittard
Erich Egerman .... Christopher Guard
Fredericka Armfeldt .... Chloe Franks
Kurt .... Heinz Marecek
Petra .... Lesley Dunlop
Conductor .... Jonathan Tunick
Franz .... Hubert Tscheppe

By VINCENT CANBY

INGMAR BERGMAN'S "Smiles of a Summer Night" is, next to his film version of "The Magic Flute," the most charming, most buoyant movie he's ever made. "A Little Night Music," the Broadway musical adaptation of the Bergman film, directed by Harold Prince, with music and lyrics by Stephen Sondheim at his best, sent one out of the theater feeling in top form.

It's something more than a shock, then, that the film adaptation of the Broadway show not only fails to raise the spirits; it also tramples on them. The more kindly disposed will leave the theater depressed. a lot of others may be in a rage. Though it's possible to fail with intelligence and grace, the movie, which opens today at Columbia 1, pursues disaster in the manner of someone who, with mindless self-confidence, saws off the limb he's sittin on.

•

Perhaps the movie's worst sin is to make the critic feel he must play the role of the piously aggrieved scoutmaster, who has to say a lot of boring, obvious things—in this case about the difference between the stage and movies. These are things that Mr. Prince, who also directed the movie, and Hugh Wheeler, who wrote the screenplay from his own Broadway book, certainly know from experience that is more practical than most critics will ever have. The way they have made the movie, it looks like a publicly posted suicide pact. Such a succession of mistakes can't be accidental.

The Broadway show, like the Bergman film, is a wickedly lyric rondel, a romantic, turn-of-the-century masquerade about three mismatched couples who, in the course of a limpid summer night, on a magnificent country estate, more or less stumble into perfect happiness.

They are a beautiful, worldly actress of certain years (Elizabeth Taylor), her lover, a foolish hussar (Laurence Guittard), the hussar's jealous wife (Diana Rigg), the wife's school friend (Lesley-Ann Down), whose much older husband (Len Cariou) loves the actress and whose stepson (Christopher Guard) loves his stepmother.

Looking on are the actress's ancient mother (Hermione Gingold), herself once a famous courtesan, and the actress's daughter (Chloe Franks), plus one lively, pretty maid (Lesley Dunlop), without whom no farce can be complete.

•

The sum and substance of the show are not the characters but Mr. Sondheim's music and lyrics. They describe the awful and funny torments of hearts that rule minds of the size and consistency of baby peas. It's not exactly a problem play. It's Mozartean comedy in which stylized settings, costumes and even lighting create a world of sweet timelessness.

Having elected to transform the Sondheim show into a film, Mr. Prince appears to have made every decision that could sabotage the music and the lyrics. He has cast the film with people who don't sing very well and then staged almost every number in such

"A LITTLE NIGHT MUSIC"—Elizabeth Taylor and Len Cariou (left) co-star with Diana Rigg and Laurence Guittard in Stephen Sondheim's musical.

a way that we can't respond to the lyrics.

He often photographs the singers in those blandly uninformative close-ups that force us to consider hairlines, necklines and lip-sync techniques.

•

Mr. Sondheim's marvelous two-and three-part songs, in which characters, often in different settings, share their sentiments, work on the stage since the characters are enclosed by the same proscenium. In the movie, which is set in elegant but realistic locations, these numbers require all sorts of busy cross-cutting that upstages the music, which becomes as effectively fragmented as the images.

It is, of course, possible to hear the songs, but in this movie it seems like work. "Send in the Clowns" will survive Miss Taylor's game way with a lyric, and so will "You Must Meet My Wife" (Miss Taylor and Mr. Cariou), but "A Little Night Music" shouldn't be a matter of survival. It should be ebullient and fun. It isn't. It often seems to be mean-tempered.

There's no reason why Miss Taylor should be photographed so unflatteringly (unless she gave the orders), or that Lesley-Ann Down and Diana Rigg should appear at times in flesh colors of grayish-green (at least in the print I saw).

Someone should also have had the decency to blip out a word in one of the lyrics that gets a cruel laugh in the way it refers to Miss Taylor, who is an actress of more wit and character than "A Little Night Music" ever allows.

So are Miss Down and Miss Rigg, though they, and Miss Taylor and Mr. Cariou do have one very funny scene. It's a dinner table scene in which everything goes wrong and no one is required to sing.

•

Of the actors, Mr. Cariou is the only one who registers as a character. The others are animated mannequins. Hermione Gingold, re-creating her Broadway role, gets short shrift from the film, which even nips off her last scene, though that may be just as well. It's become increasingly apparent that less of Miss Gingold is more—and sometimes too much.

•

"A Little Night Music," which has been rated PG ("Parental Guidance Suggested"), contains a couple of love scenes that are less heated than furious in the way of farce.

1978 Mr 8, C17:4

At Home With Ibsen

A DOLL'S HOUSE, directed by Joseph Losey; screenplay by David Mercer from Michael Meyer's English translation of Henrik Ibsen's play; director of photography, Gerry Fisher; editor, Reggie Beck; music by Michel Legrand; art director, Eileen Diss; costume designer, John Furniss; makeup, Bob Lawrence; produced by Mr. Losey; a World Films Services presentation; released by Tomorrow Entertainment Inc. At the Thalia Theater. Running time: 103 minutes. This film has not been rated.

Nora .... Jane Fonda
Torvald .... David Warner
Dr. Rank .... Trevor Howard
Kristine Linde .... Delphine Seyrig
Krogstad .... Edward Fox

"A Doll's House" was shown at the 1973 New York Film Festival. It was also shown on ABC-TV Dec. 23, 1973. The following are excerpts from the review written by Nora Sayre and published in The Times on Oct. 2, 1973. The film opens today at the Thalia Theater, 95th Street and Broadway, and will play through next Tuesday.

DAVID MERCER'S adaptation of the Ibsen play, directed by Joseph Losey, has been fattened with feeble lines and even short scenes that the old genius didn't write. Also, some passages, such as Kristine Linde's reunion with Krogstad and Nora's tarantella, have been intercut. So the dramatic momentum is butchered. Although we can sympathize with a film maker's urge to escape one single indoor setting, and it's always nice to have an excuse for shots of snow—especially if you can sling in a sleigh or two—most of these tricks merely weaken a tightly written play.

Though the Losey film is ferociously flawed, I recommend it for Jane Fonda's performance. Beforehand, it seemed fair to wonder if she could personify someone from the past; her voice, inflections, and ways of moving have always seemed totally contemporary. But once again she proves herself to be one of our finest actresses, and she's at home in the 1870's, a creature of that period as much as of ours.

Dancing or laughing or worrying, eating macaroons, skating or suffering, Miss Fonda brings an emotional range to the part—here is the ringing gaiety and the energy that the role demands. She can also be innocent without seeming stupid or silly—which is a traditional bear trap in this play.

Actresses in tight-laced 19th-century waistlines often tend to wear their hands on their hips.

But Miss Fonda does it with a difference: even her liveliest gestures are tempered by constricting clothes. However, she flirts at a minimum, though she wheedles well when she has to. Still, it's regrettable that the movie omits her impulse to seductively show her stockings to Dr. Rank; the absence of that telling detail leaves a gap like a yanked tooth.

•

Gradually and subtly, however, we are given a portrait of Nora as a political prisoner—one who hasn't ever tasted the air outside the walls. And Miss Fonda is such a sensitive actress that we can even see the ideas taking root—as when it occurs to her to try to milk money from Dr. Rank (Trevor Howard, very good), and when she quietly makes the moment-to-moment discovery that her marriage is worthless, that the time for departure has come.

David Warner as Torvald and Edward Fox as Krogstad both overact, and Delphine Seyrig walks through the role of Kristine as though she yearns to be back in a luxuriant comedy by Truffaut or Buñuel. Thus, many of Ibsen's intentions have been squelched or stomped on—apart from one magnificent piece of casting.

1978 Mr 8, C24:5

Earning a Day's Pay

WORKING: LET THE SPIRIT MOVE by Bill Gray; **ROSI,** by Rachel Wohl; **SIGNS** by Rhoden Streeter and Tony Ganz; **JERRY'S** by Tom Palazzolo; **PART OF YOUR LOVING** by Tony de Nonno; **STUDS TERKEL: AT HOME ON THE AIR** by Alan Jacobs and Nick Egleson. Total running time: 86 minutes. At the Film Forum, 15 Vandam Street.

By JANET MASLIN

THE six short films in the "Working" program at the Film Forum show people with widely varying degrees of self-consciousness about what they do.

Rosi, the subject of a nine-minute study by Rachel Wohl, is a fisherwoman who contemplates her art, her toil and especially her sexual frustration with such uninviting self-absorption that even the unusual nature of her job begins to seem ordinary.

•

On the other hand, Ben Togati is a Brooklyn baker who, in Tony de Nonno's "Part of Your Loving," approaches his morning's dough with the hands of a wizard and the soul of a poet.

"The color tells you when the bread smile, when the bread is happy, when the bread is full of grace," says Ben, as he models what look like the loveliest loaves in the world. For those whose interest in "Part of Your Loving" goes beyond Mr. de Nonno's deft and impressive film making, the closing shots of the exterior of Ben's shop show his phone number in large, clear letters. The sign also says that he delivers.

Ben is the only worker in the program who describes his daily routine with unusual felicity, but some of the others speak with a simplicity and pragmatism that come from years on the job. "Signs," by Rhoden Streeter and Tony Ganz, has an interview with billboard painters who fondly recall the trouble it took to get all the little indentations right on a huge painting of a golf ball, or vegetable platter so well crafted that "everything was like a real good-lookin' vegetable up there."

The best films in this group are so utterly respectful of and interested in the minutest details of their subjects' occupations that they require no manipulative technique on the film makers' parts, and no abstraction. Accordingly, "Signs" is slightly marred by a speeded-up segment that, while efficiently showing how billboards are painted, also places a slightly comic construction on tasks that the workers take absolutely seriously.

•

"Let the Spirit Move," one of two longer films in the group, touches revealingly on the restorative, even uplifting qualities of an absorbing job. Grover Lee Moss, a Southern evangelist and faith healer who ran off and left his constituency just before Bill Gray's film was completed, says he was a sex offender, a mental patient and a white man who used to beat up blacks for sport, until he began to preach two years earlier; now, he says, he has a black wife and, 500 faith cures under his belt.

Mr. Moss is loquacious but subdued as he's being interviewed, but when he begins pacing about and praising the Lord for his congregation, his eyes gleam and his whole body comes alive. He takes center stage with such power and conviction that he might as well be Elvis Presley.

"Studs Terkel: At Home on the Air," by Alan Jacobs and Nick Egleson, is, at 27 minutes, the longest film on the bill; it's also the most obviously contemplative one, and in some ways the least appropriate. Mr. Terkel is seen preparing his radio broadcasts, doing interviews, talking casually and receiving an award.

The film means to represent him as a worker and an expert on working, an approach that yields a fractured portrait rather than a fluid one. It also introduces an element of explicit outspokenness that seems quite unnecessary in a program that speaks so eloquently for itself.

1978 Mr 9, C18:4

"GRAY LADY DOWN"—Charlton Heston barks orders to Ronny Cox and Stephen McHattie as their nuclear sub runs into trouble.

Gray Lady Down

GRAY LADY DOWN, directed by David Greene; screenplay by James Whittaker and Howard Sackler, from an adaptation by Frank P. Rosenberg, based on the novel, "Event 1000," by David Lavallee; produced by Walter Mirisch; director of photography, Stevan Larner; editor, Robert Swink; music, Jerry Fielding; a Mirisch Corporation presentation, distributed by Universal Pictures. Running time: 111 minutes. At the Cinerama 2 Theater, Broadway at 47th Street, and other theaters. This film has been rated R.

Capt. Paul Blanchard	Charlton Heston
Captain Gates	David Carradine
Captain Bennett	Stacy Keach
Mickey	Ned Beatty
Murphy	Stephen McHattie
Commander Samuelson	Ronny Cox
Fowler	Dorian Harewood
Vickie	Rosemary Forsyth
Page	Hilly Hicks
Admiral Barnes	Charles Cioffi
Waters	William Jordan
Harkness	Jack Rader
Caruso	Antony Ponzini

By VINCENT CANBY

"GRAY LADY DOWN," which opens today at the Cinerama 2 and other theaters, is this year's model of your standard peacetime submarine melodrama which is not about a confrontation between navies but about one with the element through which the submarine moves.

In the first scene of "Gray Lady Down," the nuclear-powered United States Navy submarine Neptune surfaces in a fog off Cape Cod and is immediately rammed by a Norwegian freighter. The damaged Neptune sinks to a precarious position on a sea shelf 1,400 feet below, and for the next 100 or so minutes we are asked to wonder whether Charlton Heston, the skipper, and his ethnically balanced crew are going to be saved.

The fact that "Gray Lady Down" was made with the enthusiastic cooperation of the Navy may give you a clue. The Navy seldom looks on the dark side of things, especially itself. "Gray Lady Down" has about it a sort of capitalistic sunniness, best summed up when, just after the wounded sub has come to rest on the ocean bottom, a scared sailor says, "Thank God." Says Chuck Heston, "Thank God and General Dynamics."

The movie also takes care to reassure us that even though the tremendous sea pressure may eventually crush the ship's hull. There's absolutely no danger that the ship's nuclear power-pack will pollute the seas. In a world where all is change, it's reassuring to know that one thing will last forever.

"Gray Lady Down" is somewhat less enduring, though it seems endless. It's been composed with its crises so evenly spaced that you ache for a station break bracketed by commercials. Will that bulkhead hold? Mercy me, it's starting to leak! The oxygen supply is giving out. Will Captain Bennett (Stacy Keach), the man in charge of the rescue (and an old friend of Chuck's), get the undersea rescue vessel to the doomed sub before the crew has the fatal vapors? Do you doubt it?

The people who appear in movies like that don't act. They display various cuts of resolve and steadfastness as if they were male models. The Navy is so particular about the men it lets into the sub service, you may also rest assured that when the Neptune's executive officer, played by Ronny Cox, has a brief, neurotic temper tantrum, he will recoup his reputation by making the sacrifice sometimes called supreme. David Carradine attempts—and fails—to give some individuality to his role, that of a idiosyncratic officer who has invented an experimental undersea craft.

The screenplay, which is terrible, was directed by David Greene, who directed the first segment of "Roots" and other television shows. Considering the material, he seems to be an efficient fellow.

1978 Mr 10, C14:4

SUMMER PARADISE, directed by Gunnel Lindblom; script (Swedish with English subtitles) by Ulla Isaksson and Miss Lindblom, based on a novel by Miss Isaksson; director of photography, Tony Forsberg; editor, Siv Lundgren; music, Georg Riedel; produced by Ingmar Bergman for Cinematograph AB/Swedish Film Institute/Svensk Filmindustri; a Cinema 5 Release. At Cinema 3, 59th Street and Fifth Avenue. Running time: 113 minutes. This film has not been rated.

Katha	Birgitte Valberg
Emma	Sif Ruud
Annika	Margaretha Bystrom
Sassa	Agnetta Ekmanner
Saga	Inga Landgre
Ingrid	Solveig Ternstrom
Alma	Dagny Lind
Wilhelm	Holger Lowenadler

By JANET MASLIN

The weather is perfect, the wild flowers are in bloom, and the old house is so spacious that everyone has his or her own prettily wallpapered room, but all is not right in the film "Summer Paradise"—or at least it's not supposed to be. The middle-class extended family that spends its yearly vacations at this idyllic retreat is meant to seem much too complacent for its own good and for anyone else's.

As the director Gunnel Lindblom sees it, the ills of the world don't intrude enough to spoil these merry Swedes' good time, and whenever anyone has a bad dream, Grandma, who is a physician, merely prescribes sleeping pills. The family takes its greatest satisfactions in the lake, the flowerbeds and the freshly baked bread.

•

Naturally enough, there are a few termites in the woodwork: The women are lonely, the men are weaklings, and the children are growing up without proper supervision. These things are pointed out by great-grandpa and by grandma's social-worker friend, older people who are wise enough to realize that subsequent generations have gotten further and further out of line. "It's a disgrace to be a human being today, woman," says the social worker at last, in a rather blunt and unconvinicing moment of pique.

Miss Lindblom, an actress who worked with Ingmar Bergman in films such as "The Seventh Seal" and "Wild Strawberries," fills "Summer Paradise" with hints of trouble and indications that a great deal is being swept under the rug. However, she never manages to suggest that the family genuinely gives a hoot about any of this, and the film's glimpses of bourgeois guilt are singularly unaffecting. When unrest finally does burst forth at the end of the story, it comes as a bolt out of the much-too-blue sky.

Miss Lindblom's point may very well be that people who live life too comfortably aren't even capable of intelligent or moving regret, but that's a poor premise on which to construct a drama; she winds up with two hours' worth of ripples in the water and not a single wave.

She also has a tendency to undercut her own points through overemphasis: A lower class mother and son, very conspicuous brunettes in a sea of blondes, are treated with wildly exaggerated rudeness by the others. When, at the end of the film, the little boy sits dejectedly on the lawn, Miss Lindblom photographs him in the foreground of a larger shot, then makes the point in the closeup, and then in even closer closeup than that.

Miss Lindblom gets some vivid characterizations out of a distinguished Swedish cast, and she is particularly successful in presenting scenes between lovers with an equal appreciation of male and female sensuality.

But there is no sense of real darkness beneath the film's patently artificial light, and the viewer is finally swamped by those very same middle-class amenities that Miss Lindblom means to deplore. One does wind up feeling sick to death of nice-looking people with nicely manageable problems, but that's apparently only half of what Miss Lindblom had in mind.

1978 Mr 12, 60:4

FILM VIEW

VINCENT CANBY

Who Keeps House in Those Women's Films?

"Housework is really very boring," a friend of mine once said in what amounted to a long-delayed consciousness breakthrough. Housework is boring, but somebody has to do it unless you can adapt to living in garbage. One of the repeated criticisms made by women seeking to raise the consciousness of movie makers not long ago was that most roles offered to actresses were of women as adjuncts to men—wives, mistresses, whores, home-makers, sex objects, dishwashing machines. Now that we've apparently entered an era when women in movies can be seen having careers ("The Turning Point," "Julia") and friendships ("Julia" and "3 Women"), giving expression to sexual needs ("Coming Home," "Looking for Mr. Goodbar," "The End of the World in Our Usual Bed on a Night Full of Rain"), or making serious decisions about living as themselves, without men as emotional crutches ("An Unmarried Woman"), I keep wondering who's doing the housework for them.

There's a sequence early in "The Turning Point" when we're aware that the housewife, played by Shirley MacLaine, has been making preparations to entertain a group of old friends at home. She's been cooking. She has curlers in her hair. She's harried. Yet shortly after that introduction, Shirley goes to New York where I'm not even sure she makes her own bed.

In "Julia," Jane Fonda's Lillian Hellman puffs wildly away on cigarettes while writing what Dashiell Hammett finally calls "a great play." Though we never see them washing a dish, Lillian and Dash don't appear to live in filth. We're not told but it seems likely that they have a local girl who comes in twice a week to sweep up and empty the ash trays.

In "Coming Home," Jane Fonda cooks one meal but never even rinses a pot. When Shelley Duvall and Sissy Spacek prepare a meal in "3 Women," we understand it's a rather unusual event. Most of the time they eat from containers of prepared food or at lunch counters and restaurants.

In "The End of the World in Our Usual Bed etc.," Candice Bergen mopes about not having her own career anymore. She feels unrealized, bored. No wonder. From the looks of her, Candice does no housework and has even less interest in cooking. How have she and her husband survived this last decade? Somewhere in their vast, beautiful Rome apartment there is a nice, faithful, wise, efficient, even-tempered slave who, though never seen, is most likely a woman. She would be the sort of unliberated woman who actually enjoys washing, ironing, mending, baby-sitting, cooking and general cleaning up so that heroines of movies like this have the time and energy to fret about their sad lots in life.

Behind each unhappy woman in today's liberated woman's movie there are, I suspect, at least 10 unliberated women doing the chores. It's something like the elaborate support system needed to keep a single soldier fighting at the front.

I don't really believe that these films should spell out in detail the ways in which the households of their heroines are maintained. I overstress one point to make another, that something seems to be lacking in each of these new women's pictures.

In "The Turning Point," "3 Women" and "Looking for Mr. Goodbar," the missing factor is a man of any substance. This, I realize, is also the problem with films about macho males and nitwit, sex-pot females—something that women have been objecting to for years, often with good reason—but the injustice isn't corrected by simply reversing the roles. "Julia" has a substantial male figure in the person of Jason Robards as Dashiell Hammett, but because the movie is not about him, he's off-screen most of the time. Jon Voight gives a terrific performance as the paraplegic Vietnam vet in "Coming Home," though the movie has less to do with him or the war than it has to do with the quality of Jane Fonda's orgasms. "The End of the World in Our Usual Bed etc." lacks any characters whatsoever.

• • •

To call Paul Mazursky's "An Unmarried Woman" the best American movie of the year to date is less to praise it than it is to call attention to the disappointing nature of everything else that's opened since Jan. 1. Nineteen seventy-eight is not a very good year so far. Ingmar Bergman's "The Serpent's Egg" is a mistake to be indulged. Lina Wertmuller's "The End of the World in Our Usual Bed etc." is a disaster. Paul Schrader's "Blue Collar" is not an important movie. James Toback's debut as a movie director, "Fingers,' is a lightweight, unintentionally comic, furiously inept "Son of Taxi Driver." Which leaves "An Unmarried Woman."

First the good news: Jill Clayburgh is superb as Erica, a bright, intelligent, pretty New York wife/mother in her 30's, who is suddenly told by her husband Martin (Michael Murphy) that he wants a divorce to marry another woman.

When "An Unmarried Woman" opens, Martin is at that itchy time of life. If Erica had been looking for signs that all was not well, she might have seen them. One morning when they're out jogging together along the East River, Martin has an unexpected tantrum after stepping into dog droppings and, to make a point that remains his secret, throws his expensive jogging shoe into the river. On another occasion, he tells her wanly, as if remembering a long-gone career as a high school football star, "You remember how I was always a 'take-over' guy? Well . . ." "Well?" she asks. "Well," he says, "now I'm tired . . . ."

The film, written and directed by Mr. Mazursky, whose credits include "Next Stop, Greenwich Village," "Harry and Tonto," "Blume in Love" and "Bob and Carol and Ted and Alice," is the story of Erica's valiant and ultimately successful attempt to come to terms with her life as an unmarried woman. She gets help from her teen-age daughter, her friends, her job in a Soho art gallery and finally from a new man, an English artist played by Alan Bates.

In individual moments, "An Unmarried Woman" is comic, cutting, accurate and moving in ways that are completely surprising. Mr. Mazursky has a particular knack for catching the humor and pathos of people who, in one sort of circumstance or another, often an emotional extremity, do the wrong thing, usually by talking too much. There was that very funny encounter between Dyan Cannon and the psychiatrist in "Bob and Carol," when the patient, after being tongue-tied during most of the 50-minute hour, became suddenly articulate as she was being ushered out and wouldn't shut up. The single most memorable sequence in "Next Stop, Greenwich Village" is the one in which an arrogant actor wilfully destroys an audition by displaying an arrogance that is suicidal.

In "An Unmarried Woman," there's a ruefully funny sequence when Erica, after debating with herself, decides to go to bed for the first time with a man who isn't her husband. The fellow, a painter played by Cliff Gorman, has been passing himself off to Erica for years as a sort of Village Don Juan. When they get to his loft, however, he won't stop talking. It's left to Erica to make the first move.

Miss Clayburgh, Mr. Murphy, Mr. Gorman and Mr. Bates (whose role is ham-on-white) are fine. The movie so easily captures the nearly rootless, fad-prone quality of certain kinds of well-off New Yorkers that one comes to resent Mr. Mazursky's affection for them. He romanticizes and sentimentalizes them, even while he is recording the silly jargon in which they "relate" much of the time.

• • •

For a movie that appears to have had its origins in Mr. Mazursky's wish to make a film about women in particular circumstances, instead of about a particular character with a life all her own, "An Unmarried Woman" works remarkably well. Yet, he glosses over crucial details. His characters here would seem to be Jewish in their backgrounds, though the people we see have no connections to any special culture, which could well be one of the factors that lead to their problems. Erica and Martin and their friends have liberated themselves into limbo, but this is never acknowledged.

In addition, I have trouble connecting Erica with her four woman friends, who come across as civilized harpies. Instead of being the friends of someone as intelligent as Erica, they seem to be types picked out of a wide range of the director's acquaintances. I even somewhat resent the fact that the artist Mr. Bates plays is presented as someone of fame and success, though the paintings we see recall fashions of 25 years ago.

I also find the end of the film mystifying, considering the romantic style the movie has adopted to dramatize Erica's hugely satisfying affair with the English painter. The end is illogical, dictated by the dogma of liberated women who really don't want to have a man around. It makes less emotional sense than political.

Finally, I've been saving my toughest question to the last: Who is Erica's cleaning woman and how much does she charge? We don't see her, of course, but Erica's apartment is spotless. The cleaning woman is obviously reliable and loves what she does. She makes Erica's freedom possible. ■

1978 Mr 12, II:15:1

New Mazursky

By JANET MASLIN

PAUL MAZURSKY'S ambitions are so singular that in the past it has been foolhardy to compare a film of his with anything except another Mazursky film. But "An Unmarried Woman," which is far enough ahead of its time to be his most groundbreaking effort, is also more conventional than much of his best work has been. For the first time, he has departed from the comic ambiguity that has thus far been so essential to his style.

Mr. Mazursky, who somehow manages to turn out crisp comedies of manners in an age when behavior is at its fuzziest, likes to approach his characters with a keenly satirical eye, then temper his observations with a remarkable even-handedness and generosity; in his best films, people manage to seem silliest when their intentions are most sincere. Mr. Mazursky's most endearing characters are full of self-importance and deep uncertainty, developing and discarding trendy new attitudes as if they were trying on Nehru jackets and their day-to-day predicaments are so disarmingly muddled that neither the viewer nor the director can effectively take sides. Mr. Mazursky's best movies, like "Blume In Love" and "Bob and Carol and Ted and Alice," are full of warmth and bemused affection, and much of what makes them so provocative is the director's never quite revealing where his sympathies lie.

But in "An Unmarried Woman," he, for the first time, chooses to play with a stacked deck. Even though the movie makes half-hearted stabs at understanding the two men who figure most prominently in the life of Erica, the heroine of the title, this remains Erica's side of the story all the way. We don't know much about her husband, except that he's the kind of fellow who'll vow to stop smoking with a cigarette in his mouth, and who'll throw away a soiled sneaker instead of cleaning it, just as he lets his marriage fall apart without struggling to save it. Besides, if this man is cad enough to desert a demonstrably perfect wife, we can't much like him anyway.

The lover Erica subsequently takes, made out by Mr. Mazursky's screenplay to be the world's most eligible bachelor and played with impenetrable charm by Alan Bates, is so darn wonderful that an audience can't care much about him either. He's rich, he's handsome, he's divorced and desirable, and the worst thing likely to happen to him is that Erica may decide not to go steady with him after all. Mr. Bates approaches the role with a captivating but slightly inappropriate self-assurance, creating the impression that even if Erica gets away, he'll easily manage.

So who is there left to care about? Erica and Erica alone, even though—for all Mr. Mazursky's obvious compassion, and for all the vibrance and buoyancy of Jill Clayburgh's performance—she remains one of Mr. Mazursky's most uncomplicated characters. Erica's sturdiness and resilience are commendable qualities, but they simply don't mesh with the rest of the movie.

Mr. Mazursky deliberately skips past some of the most painful elements of any marital breakup (e.g. the obligatory scenes of packing, fighting, pleading and weeping). Indeed, he goes out of his way to show Erica and her husband sharing their daily routine, taking comfort in each other's company, and enjoying an active sex life. The danger signs are there—in the couple's fancily arid apartment, and in moments of monotony—but they're small, and they don't fully account for the breakup. Mr. Mazursky is particularly clever in showing the way things can go wrong for no good reasons, and in approaching his characters' problems as superficially as they themselves do. He doesn't try to understand them any better than they understand themselves, and he makes the kind of allowances you might expect from an old friend. One of the most likable things about Mr. Mazursky's movies is his acknowledging the bewildering way in which unimportant-sounding problems cause such real pain.

The trouble with Erica is that, for all the upset in her life, she seems quite able to make do without a directorial helping hand. In fact, Erica is so much braver and nobler than anyone else in her neighborhood that she begins to seem the product of a man's post-feminist guilty conscience.

Even with this very contemporary cramp in his style, Mr. Mazursky remains an enormously appealing and original director, one whose perceptions always manage to hit home. But it's a shame to find someone who's most dazzling when he's neutral, or even naughty, bending over backward to be nice.

•

One of the jokes in "An Unmarried Woman" seems to have some bearing on Paul Schrader, screenwriter of "Taxi Driver" and co-writer and director of "Blue Collar." Two couples (one of the men is played by Mr. Mazursky) on a double date in a Chinese restaurant are talking about movies, and somebody mentions a hot film that's forthcoming, about an embittered Vietnam veteran who goes home to the Middle West and shots 300 persons. The couples then argue about whether this film is actually new, or whether they've already seen it too many times.

Mr. Schrader's specialty is supposed to be movies of this sort, movies of erupting violence and bottled-up madness and wildly overstated machismo. And Mr. Schrader's reputation, as a former film critic who used to have a license plate reading "OZU" (in homage to the great Japanese director), might make it seem that if he weren't being bloody he would be a terrible bore. Many of the notices on "Blue Collar" make it sound like a dreary, schematic, utterly humorless treatise on the plight of the working class in a hopelessly racist society.

"Blue Collar" does have its points to make, and they are serious points indeed, but the movie never forgets to entertain. Mr. Schrader proves himself to have a surprisingly light touch and an impressive talent for getting the best from actors, such as Richard Pryor, Harvey Keitel, Yaphet Kotto and Cliff De Young, who are good to begin with. "Blue Collar" has none of the patented Schrader fanaticism; instead, it flows quickly and easily, on a current of friendliness that Mr. Schrader develops expertly and then destroys in accordance with the film's overall scheme.

Mr. Schrader turns out to be a much livelier director than any student of his screenplays or criticism might have expected, and his film is at least as much a character study as it is a political tract. The ads for the film do nothing to suggest that it has its enjoyable side, but audiences seem to be getting the message just the same. "Blue Collar's" grosses have been picking up slowly but surely—thanks, evidently, to word of mouth.

•

Three of the nicest-looking movies in town are Jean-Claude Tacchella's "Blue Country," Michael Winner's remake of "The Big Sleep" and Lina Wertmüller's "A Night Full of Rain." However, none of these films is about anything particularly agreeable: their

Paul Mazursky directing Jill Clayburgh during shooting of a scene from the movie "An Unmarried Woman"

subjects are, respectively, the senselessness of marriage, the endless corruption of the human race, and the contemptible sexist decadence of a man who lives in a too-nice apartment with his too-nice, too-beautiful, too-miserable wife.

This kind of disparity between a movie's subject and its appearance—did the Depression really have to look so gorgeous in "Bound for Glory?"—usually amounts to a major drawback. But when a movie is in enough trouble otherwise, excessive glamour can have its advantages. In each of these films, there comes a moment of release about midway through, a moment when one realizes that the movie's real message is so unfathomable, and so uninteresting, that one might as well sit back and enjoy the scenery.

•

This may sound like a sloppy directorial technique, but it can be quite a successful one; Lina Wertmüller has produced some of her biggest hits this way. There are still unsuspecting filmgoers who thought Miss Wertmüller's "Swept Away" was little more than the story of a pretty woman and a handsome man, both scantily clad and marooned on a beautiful desert island —even though Miss Wertmüller has taken great pains to explain that the woman was actually a man, the man was actually a woman, and the love story was actually a parable about capitalist and sexist oppression

Likewise, there are people foolish enough to have mistaken "The Seduction of Mimi" for an amusing sex comedy with only marginally important political overtones. And there may even be those who don't understand what Miss Wertmüller is really saying in "A Night Full of Rain," who merely enjoy watching Candice Bergen and Giancarlo Giannini kiss and wrestle and get drenched in a concluding downpour.

Maybe this is a terrible failing on the part of the audience. On the other hand, if the point of a movie is so unobtrusive it can go virtually unnoticed, maybe it's best to look and not listen after all.

1978 Mr 13, C17:1

Psyching a Spy

THE FURY, directed by Brian De Palma; screenplay by John Farris, based on his novel; produced by Frank Yablans; executive producer, Ron Preissman; director of photography, Richard H. Kline; music, John Williams; editor, Paul Hirsch; distributed by 20th Century-Fox. Running time: 118 minutes. At the National Theater, Broadway at 44th Street, Cine Theater, Third Avenue at 86th Street, and other theaters. This film has been rated R.

Peter .... Kirk Douglas
Childress .... John Cassavetes
Hester .... Carrie Snodgress
Dr. Jim McKeever .... Charles Durning
Gillian .... Amy Irving
Susan Charles .... Fiona Lewis
Robin .... Andrew Stevens
Dr. Ellen Lindstrom .... Carol Rossen
Kristen .... Rutanya Alda
Mrs. Bellaver .... Joyce Easton
Raymond .... William Finley
Vivian Nuckells .... Jane Lambert
Blackfish .... Sam Laws
Robertson .... J. Patrick McNamara
Mrs. Callahan .... Alice Nunn
LaRue .... Melody Thomas
Cheryl .... Hilary Thompson
Lander .... Patrick Billingsley
Greene .... J. P. Bumstead

By VINCENT CANBY

"TELEPATHY," someone says solemnly in "The Fury" is a timeless form of communication to which Woody Allen (were he around) might add with equal solemnity, "and far cheaper than Western Union."

"The Fury," which opens today at the National, Cine and other theaters, was directed by Brian De Palma in what appears to have been an all-out effort to transform the small-scale, Grand Guignol comedy of his "Carrie" into an international horror/spy/occult mind-blower of a movie. He didn't concentrate hard enough, though. "The Fury" is bigger than "Carrie," more elaborate, much more expensive and far sillier. Let's face it—it's the De Palma "1900"—a movie that somehow got out of hand.

Kirk Douglas and Amy Irving in "The Fury."

It's also, in fits and starts, the kind of mindless fun that only a horror movie that so seriously pretends to be about the mind can be. Mr. De Palma seems to have been less interested in the overall movie than in pulling off a couple of spectacular set-pieces, which he does. He leaves the rest of "The Fury" to take care of itself.

The John Farris screenplay, though based on a published novel, has the air of something that hasn't been thought clearly through, or at least thought through to the point where basic plot questions don't distract us from enjoying a line like, "I'm just a receiver and Robin sends me pictures."

The girl who says this is one of the two doomed young people who possess the power, like that of the heroine of "Carrie," to move objects through force of will. They also are able to communicate, telepathically, to share memories with someone unknown, to detonate things and to bring on cerebral hemorrhages at random. The film's pathology is as confused as the story, so one spends most of "The Fury" impatiently anticipating the next demonstration of something that one keeps hoping will be unspeakable but never is.

•

In particular, "The Fury" is about Peter Sanza (Kirk Douglas), an American superagent whose son, a fellow with psychic powers, is abducted from an Israeli beach by one of Peter's colleagues, apparently for the exclusive use of the United States Government.

For most of the film, Peter searches vainly for the young man (why he had to be abducted is never made clear), the trail eventually taking him to Chicago and to a mysterious "institute" where the psychically gifted are studied. There Peter finds not his son, but a young woman named Gillian (Amy Irving) who is in thought communication with the son.

The story is too witless to bear more scrutiny than that. The things that keep one sitting through "The Fury" when one's mind knows better are the occasional action sequences (including a fine, funny automobile chase through Chicago) and the special effects that finally bring the movie to an end that recalls "Zabriski Point," on a more personal level.

When a screenplay is so bad, there truly isn't much that actors can do except behave themselves, which is more or less what happens. In addition to Mr. Douglas and Miss Irving, the most prominent members of the cast are John Cassavetes as the Government kidnapper, Andrew Stevens (Stella's boy) as the son, and Charles Durning as the head of the mysterious institute.

•

The most peculiar thing about the movie is why Carrie Snodgress, who retired after receiving an Oscar nomination for "Diary of a Mad Housewife," should have elected to use it as her comeback film. It's a nothing role—that of a psychiatric instructor who helps Mr. Douglas locate his son. She's efficient and so invisible it's as if she never left home.

1978 Mr 15, C19:1

Showroom Piece

THE BIG SLEEP, directed by Michael Winner; screenplay by Mr. Winner, from the novel by Raymond Chandler; director of photography, Robert Paynter; editor, Freddie Wilson; produced by Elliott Kastner and Mr. Winner; released by United Artists. Running time: 100 minutes. At the Criterion, Broadway at 45th Street; Trans-Lux East, Third Avenue and 58th Street; R.K.O. 86th Street Twin I, at Lexington Avenue; Bay Cinema, Second Avenue and 32d Street, and other theaters. This film has been rated R.

Philip Marlowe .... Robert Mitchum
Charlotte Sternwood .... Sarah Miles
Lash Canino .... Richard Boone
Camilla Sternwood .... Candy Clark
Agnes Lozelle .... Joan Collins
Joe Brody .... Edward Fox
Inspector Carson .... John Mills
General Sternwood .... James Stewart
Eddie Mars .... Oliver Reed
Norris .... Harry Andrews

HOWARD HAWKS directed the 1946 version of "The Big Sleep" in black and white, so it's conceivable that Mr. Hawks didn't furnish Philip Marlowe's bedroom with color-coordinated sheets and blankets merely because he wasn't able to. However, it's also conceivable that Mr. Hawks chose deliberately to depict Marlowe as something other than an immaculately appointed fellow with a decorating flair. Michael Winner's new film version of the Raymond Chandler novel concentrates so heavily on the dapper side of Marlowe that it makes the first version look like an unmade bed—which may be what it was meant to look like, after all.

There are no shadows in this senselessly gaudy remake; there isn't much nighttime, either, and there isn't any rain. There isn't any Los Angeles, because Mr. Winner, pretending to switch the story's setting to London for no intelligible reason, seems actually to have transferred it to a succession of furniture-store showrooms. Not a single prop looks used, not even the dainty china cups out of which Marlowe drinks his morning coffee.

The name of Lew Grade, the British entrepreneur who "presents" this new version—he has also sponsored "The Cassandra Crossing" and "Voyage of the Damned"—has come to denote too many stars and not enough savvy. Sure enough, "The Big Sleep" is overloaded with big names, and in this case the net effect of an all-star cast is to make an already confusing mystery even harder to follow.

•

Oliver Reed is hilariously foppish as the gangster Eddie Mars, and Richard Boone is almost as delightful a villain here as he as in "The Shootist." But Joan Collins, Edward Fox, John Mills and even James Stewart get lost in the shuffle, reeling off plot details that will seem confusing to anyone who hasn't seen Mr. Hawks's version or read Mr. Chandler's, and numbingly familiar to anyone who has.

As the insinuatingly sensual Charlotte Sternwood, in a role first played by Lauren Bacall, Sarah Miles is at least twice as lewd as the screenplay requires her to be, and nowhere near as electrifying. Candy Clark, as Miss Miles's mad younger sister, winds up in desperate trouble. Under Mr. Winner's dependably off-base direction, Miss Clark skips and giggles and foams at the mouth, frantically overplaying the most unsalvageable kook role of her kook-ridden career. It would be lovely to find her playing someone who made sense once in a while.

Mr. Winner, who wrote the screenplay as well as directed it, approaches Mr. Chandler's material with the same depth and delicacy he brought to "Death Wish." It's hard to imagine a director less suited to the subtleties of this kind of story, but then subtleties aren't anything Mr. Winner even tries for. Instead of struggling with the seediness implicit in this story's layer upon of layer of corruption, Mr. Winner substitutes a high-priced vulgarity that wipes out every last touch of evil. The villains in this version aren't wicked, and they aren't even particularly villainous. They just manage to do everything in stultifyingly bad taste.

If Robert Mitchum seemed to be an effective Marlowe in the 1975 "Farewell, My Lovely," that had as much to do with Dick Richards's carefully evocative direction as it did with the actor's performance.

Mr. Mitchum's world-weariness and his unflappable calm simply don't, on their own, add up to the suspicious, swaggering style that the character and the overall movie require. Taking the strong, silent route once again, Mr. Mitchum gives a performance meant to blend in with the kind of lurid and evocative backdrop Mr. Richards's film provided. But Mr. Winner strips away the neon colors, the 40's costumes and the pulp-novel paraphernalia, substituting sunny skies and a lot of green lawn. With only that to work against, the best Mr. Mitchum can do, figuratively speaking, is to play croquet.

JANET MASLIN

1978 Mr 15, C19:1

HOUSE CALLS, directed by Howard Zieff; screenplay by Max Shulman, Julius J. Epstein, Alan Mandel and Charles Shyer; story by Mr. Shulman and Mr. Epstein; director of photography, David M. Walsh; film editor, Edward Warschilka; produced by Alex Winitsky and Arlene Sellers; released by Universal Pictures. At Loews Tower East, Third Avenue at 72d Street. Running time: 96 minutes. This film is rated PG.

Dr. Charley Nichols .... Walter Matthau
Ann Atkinson .... Glenda Jackson
Dr. Amos Willoughby .... Art Carney
Dr. Norman Solomon .... Richard Benjamin
Ellen Grady .... Candice Azzara
Irwin Owett .... Dick O'Neill
Pogostin .... Thayer David
T.V. Moderator .... Anthony Holland
Mrs. De Voto .... Reva Rose

By JANET MASLIN

WANTED: Personable actress, mid-30's or older, to play a wry divorcée with romantic leanings, a consumer advocate who gets most of her information from Reader's Digest, and avid reader of nothing but best sellers, and perhaps the first movie heroine to make her living by baking since Mildred Pierce. Divorcée will meet and fall for a surgeon, now an eligible widower, to be played by a gruff, lovable actor who never stands up straight. Eventually, they will jog together and romp in the sand. Presumably, this will be love.

If all of this makes perfect sense to you, consider the fact that the sweethearts of "House Calls" are played by Glenda Jackson and Walter Matthau, an odd couple if ever there was one. Mr. Matthau is no problem: He has been gruff but lovable before, and he never stands up straight anyway.

But Mr. Matthau and Miss Jackson don't particularly set off fireworks together, and Miss Jackson is way too steely to play the kind of woman who'd sit up all night watching the candles burn down if Dr. Right didn't arrive for dinner on schedule, or who would hope to bag that special guy by whipping up that special cheesecake.

•

Howard Zieff, who also directed "Slither" and the frequently funny "Hearts of the West," swivels nervously among enough plot points for three and a half different movies. One of them, the love story, could be "Pete 'n' Tillie"—in fact, it already has been. The second thread is about the workings of a poorly administered hospital, run by a sneakily senile doctor (played by Art Carney) with an amusingly selective memory.

The third and most interesting element has to do with the indignities to which the young submit the middle-aged (Mr. Matthau, after attending a rock concert with a nurse he's dating, has to sit in a beanbag chair in her apartment), and to which the middle-aged submit the old.

The half movie is an affectionate comedy about a married man who begins to regard himself as a ladykiller when he becomes a bachelor again, and perhaps it should have been a whole movie. But Mr. Matthau's career as a swinger is cut short soon after Miss Jackson blazes a trail to his heart by way of his stomach.

•

Mr. Zieff, who directed commercials before he came to movies, is as crisp and economical with brief comic vignettes as he is overwhelmed by the demands of a sustained plot; "House Calls" continuously juggles fast, flashy jokes with nagging inconsistencies. The early portion of the movie is quite promising, especially since—because the doctor meets the divorcée when the rewires her broken jaw, and she doesn't get to talk until later on—it takes a while to realize how seriously Miss Jackson has been miscast.

•

Once it becomes apparent that this droll, tough-minded actress is playing a tomato who wants little more from life than a few trash novels and a jogging partner, confusion set in.

"House Calls" tries to seem stern and modern in establishing the divorcée's independence, and her superiority to the bimbos the doctor regularly courts, but it turns too sentimental too soon. One minute these lovers are talking good, solid horse sense about their ralationship; the next minute they're mired in mush.

Mr. Zieff seems never to have determined what sort of romance he wanted to show, and as a result the movie is constantly contradicting itself.

•

Mr. Matthau, Miss Jackson and Mr. Carney are as pleasant and plausible as a jumpy screenplay and Mr. Zieff's wandering directorial attention will allow Richard Benjamin is less unctuous here than he's been in years, and Candice Azzara, in something like a Judy Holliday role, offers the kind of quick caricature that Mr. Zieff often uses to fill his movies with types rather than people.

Among the questions the film inadvertently raises are: How does Mr. Matthau manage to charm a rich widow into reconsidering her lawsuit against the hospital merely by mentioning Brooklyn? Has there ever been a clumsier seduction scene than the the main one presented here? And how come Mr. Matthau, after Miss Jackson steals his clothes and hides them in her freezer, manages to find in her closet a boa-trimmed bathrobe that fits him better than it fits her.

•

"House Calls" is rated PG ("Parental Guidance Suggested") because Mr. Matthau spends part of the movie as a swinger and because he and Miss Jackson evidently become more than good friends.

1978 Mr 15, C19:5

The Big Race

CASEY'S SHADOW, directed by Martin Ritt; screenplay by Carol Sobieski, based on a short story by John McPhee; produced by Ray Stark; director of photography, John A. Alonzo; executive producer, Michael Levee; music, Patrick Williams; editor, Sidney Levin; a Rastar production, distributed by Columbia Pictures. Running time: 115 minutes. At the Loews State 2 Theater, Broadway at 45th Street, and the Baronet Theater, Third Avenue near 59th Street. This film has been rated PG.

Lloyd Bourdelle .... Walter Matthau
Sarah Blue .... Alexis Smith
Mike Marsh .... Robert Webber
Tom Patterson .... Murray Hamilton
Buddy Bourdelle .... Andrew A. Rubin
Randy Bourdelle .... Stephan Burns
Kelly Marsh .... Susan Myers
Casey Bourdelle .... Michael Hershewe
Calvin Lebec .... Harry Caesar
Jimmy Judson .... Joel Fluellen
Dr. Williamson .... Whit Bissell
Donovan .... Jimmy Halty
Dr. Pitt .... William Pitt
Dean .... Dean Turpitt
Old Cajun .... Sanders Delhomme
Lenny .... Richard Thompson
Indian .... Galbert Wanoskia
Old Man .... William Karn

By VINCENT CANBY

"CASEY'S SHADOW" is not exactly an offbeat horse movie, but it is so decently tempered and its principal characters so surprising at important moments that, in the world of horse movies it seems rare indeed. Having said that, I should admit I've never been a particular fan of movies about horses, not since I was very young and a pony I was feeding made a serious if unsuccessful attempt to take a few fingers too. I've nothing against horses, but I let them go their way while I go mine.

•

"Casey's Shadow," which opens today at the Loews State 2 and Baronet Theaters, is much more reliable than your average, mean-spirited pony. It's about a splendidly fast 2-year-old quarter horse named Casey's Shadow, about the big race (the All-American Futurity at Ruidoso, N. M.) he is expected to win, and about the little boy named Casey who loves him. It's also about Lloyd Bourdelle (Walter Matthau), Casey's dad, a kindly, tobacco-chewing slob who trains quarter horses on a run-down Louisiana farm, and about Casey's oldest brother Buddy (Andrew A. Rubin), who acts as an assistant trainer and as the conscience of the family, in the absence of a mother who has fled for what appear to have been good reasons. Among other things, they're born losers.

•

With the exception of a tendency to overorchestrate the movie in the manner of television commercials, Martin Ritt, the director, has made such an easygoing, understated film, one of such good feelings, that it seems almost rude to fault it for clichés—such as the big race—it cannot avoid, though it attempts to play them down. In the case of the race, this is done by showing us the race entirely in slow motion, which has the odd, not entirely unpleasant, effect of completely dissipating the tension.

•

More important to the total effect of the film are the performances, especially those of Mr. Matthau, who plays the father with an unusual mixture of intelligence and comic wilfullness; Alexis Smith, as a rich, very classy owner of quarter horses, a person with both scruples and humor, and Mr. Rubin, as the son who must forever pick up after his father.

•

The principal supporting roles are handled by Stephan Burns, as the Bourdelle son who doubles as the family jockey; Michael Hershewe, as Casey, the youngest son who has the tough job of attempting to be both lovable and, on occasion, stupid, and Murray Hamilton and Robert Webber, who are as close to villains as the film contains.

The screenplay by Carol Sobieski, based on a John McPhee story, manages to touch almost all of the bases one expects in a horse movie, but it does so without condescension. The screenplay even has the temerity to suggest that the racing of 2-year-old quarter horses, whose leg bones have not yet matured, may be a much more cruel sport than anyone in the film, with the exception of a veterinarian, cares to acknowledge. I'm not sure this is true but it's nice to know that Ray Stark, the producer, has taken the matter under consideration.

•

"Casey's Shadow," which has been rated PG ("Parental Guidance Suggested"), contains an explicitly photographed foaling sequence, which might be perfectly harmless facts-of-life material except that the mare dies in the process. It thus may raise more questions in the minds of the very young than it answers.

1978 Mr 17, C11:3

Walter Matthau in "Casey's Shadow": mixture of intelligence and comic willfulness.

Brooklyn Rocks

AMERICAN HOT WAX, directed by Floyd Mutrux; screenplay by John Kaye, story by Mr. Kaye and Art Linson; director of photography, William A. Fraker; edited by Melvin Shapiro and Ronald J. Fagan; music, Kenny Vance; produced by Mr. Linson; released by Paramount Pictures. At Loews State I, Broadway and 45th Street and Loews Orpheum, 86th Street at Third Avenue, and 34th Street East, near Second Avenue. Running time: 90 minutes. This film has been rated PG.

Alan Freed .... Tim McIntire
Sheryl .... Fran Drescher
Mookie .... Jay Leno
Teen-age Louise .... Laraine Newman
The Chesterfields .... Carl Earl Weaver, Al Chalk, Sam Harkness and Arnold McCuller
Lennie Richfield .... Jeff Altman
Artie Moress .... Moosie Drier
Chuck Berry .... Himself
Jerry Lee Lewis .... Himself
Screamin' Jay Hawkins .... Himself

By JANET MASLIN

THERE'S the seed of an interesting movie inside "American Hot Wax," but it never gets a chance to sprout. The picturesque aspects of the 50's reach way beyond cinch belts and finny Cadillacs, and the flap surrounding the birth of rock-and-roll is evidence that style can be as important as substance in initiating social change. But "American Hot Wax," which has a plot so thin you could thread a needle with it, chooses to see the era strictly in terms of the B-movie melodramas it produced.

"Look," says the disk jockey Alan Freed, as the police try to muscle in on a concert he is sponsoring, "you can close the show. You can stop me. But you never can stop rock-and-roll, don't you know that?" Of course they know it, and we know it, too—as the title of one song performed at this same concert puts it, "Rock-and-Roll Is Here to Stay." The suspenseful elements of the movie, and its stabs at poignancy, are strictly old news.

Alan Freed, played gently and reservedly by Tim McIntire, is less the movie's focus than its storm center. Freed, who pointedly applied the name "rock-and-roll" to what had once been called "race music," and who regularly played records other white disk jockeys were afraid to go near, is never clearly established as a renegade, a fan, a fanatic or even a character.

Instead, he's merely someone who marches from his crowded office through his bustling lobby and out to his encircled limousine, giving the camera a chance to glimpse the throngs of fans and musical aspirants who dogged his footsteps. The flurry of activity looks exciting for a while, but sooner or later an audience is bound to grow accustomed to the clutter, and

Tim McIntire, who portrays Alan Freed

unhappily aware that the movie has nowhere to go.

Art Linson, who also produced "Car Wash," seems to subscribe to the notion that a completely amorphous movie can be a lively movie if everyone just keeps on jiving along and the viewer is never given a chance to think. So "Car Wash" was sloppy, and "American Hot Wax"—which also manages to seem strangely anachronistic in applying disco-movie methods to the 50's—is even sloppier.

The plot holes are as big as potholes, particularly when it comes to Mr. Freed's payola problems, and to his ambitions as an entrepreneur (in one scene, we watch him trying to buy a huge, very-California mansion that's supposed to be just outside of New York, but we never find out why he wants it or whether the sale is actually made).

Mr. Freed's office is full of eager young singers who audition for him, some of them singing songs that were already hits in 1959, when the movie is set—are these the people who went on to have the hit records, or are they merely imitating the most popular numbers of the day? Why are some hits attributed to the people who actually sang them, and others attributed to fictitious singers? Is Laraine Newman, of "Saturday Night Live," really plausible as an enormously gifted young songwriter, the kind of girl who later grew up to become Carole King?

The movie's cast includes some of the world's oldest teen-agers, like Chuck Berry and Jerry Lee Lewis, old favorites who unfortunately perform their material as if they had been performing it for 20 years. (They have been.) It also includes the record producer Richard Perry, featured in a rousing little sequence that shows him making up the arrangement for "Come and Go With Me" right there in the studio, just by adding the proper set of dom-dom-dom-dom-dom's.

And there is a wonderful, unexpectedly delicate scene between Freed and a young boy (Moosie Drier), who is president of the Buddy Holly fan club and who begins to cry as he tries to explain to Freed's listeners why he loved the late Holly so much. On this boy's face, there is more passion, more hopefulness, more understanding of what rock-and-roll meant to those who were most powerfully influenced by it than there is anywhere else in the movie.

Some of the music is expertly rendered, particularly by the four black male singers who play a fictitious group called The Chesterfields, and some of the concert numbers, like one by three women in spangled turquoise dresses, make a strongly evocative visual impression. A feeling of nostalgia does come through, powerfully at times. But there should have been a lot more to "American Hot Wax" than memories.

1978 Mr 17, C13:3

STRAIGHT TIME, directed by Ulu Grosbard; screenplay by Alvin Sargent, Edward Bunker and Jeffrey Boam, based on Mr. Bunker's novel, "No Beast So Fierce"; produced by Stanley Beck and Tim Zinnemann; director of photography, Owen Roizman; editor, Sam O'Steen and Randy Roberts; music, David Shire; executive producer, Howard B. Pine; a First Artists presentation, distributed by Warner Brothers. Running time: 114 minutes. At the Coronet Theater, Third Avenue at 59th Street. This flim has been rated R.

Max Dembo .... Dustin Hoffman
Jenny Mercer .... Theresa Russell
Jerry Schue .... Harry Dean Stanton
Willy Darin .... Gary Busey
Earl Frank .... M. Emmet Walsh
Manny .... Sandy Baron
Selma Darin .... Kathy Bates
Mickey .... Edward Bunker
Salesman No. 1 .... Stuart I. Berton
Salesman No. 2 .... Barry Cahill
Carlos .... Corey Rand
Manager .... James Ray
Cafe owner .... Fran Ryan
Carol Schue .... Rita Taggart

By VINCENT CANBY

"Max," says the parole officer, "I think you have a serious attitude problem." Just how serious is the dramatic substance of "Straight Time," the grimly witty account of the decline of Max Dembo (Dustin Hoffman), an ex-con (six years for armed robbery) who would say that he pursues success though he measures his life in small failures and the treacheries of others. He knows the world is crooked and he behaves accordingly. Like millions of other people who live on the right side of the law, Max never questions the system. He simply tries to beat it in his own half-baked way.

Max is the sort of fellow who automatically lies when someone asks him how much rent he pays. It would make no difference if he told the truth, but Max has to keep in practice. The only time he can look someone in the eye with ease is when he stares, through the slits in a face mask—during a holdup.

Max is shrewd, self-absorbed, tough in superficial ways, and doomed. He defines the meaning of recidivism. In real life you wouldn't trust him to hang up your coat. In "Straight Time," in the person of Dustin Hoffman, he's a fascinating character, made romantic only to the extent that an actor of such stature invests him with importance that is otherwise denied. Max is strictly small-time.

•

Even though "Straight Time," which opens today at the Coronet Theater, has been tailored to Max's dimensions it's not a small-time movie. Ulu Grosbard, the director, and Alvin Sargent, Edward Bunker and Jeffrey Boam, who wrote the screenplay, have succeeded in making an uncommonly interesting film about a fellow whose significance is entirely negative. It's almost as if the real subject of the movie were all the things Max isn't.

This may be to invest "Straight Time" with more purpose than was ever intended, but it is such a leanly constructed, vividly staged film that one seeks to justify the way it compels the attention. The first words we hear in the movie are those of the guards as Max is getting out of prison—"Open the gates"—while the rest of the film is the detailed case history of a man doing his unconscious best to get back in.

Dustin Hoffman
Makes Max a fascinating character

The movie makes no attempt to explain Max. It simply says that this is the way he is. It requires us to fill in the gaps, and it's the measure of the film that we want to. In the meantime, we watch as Max has his early run-ins with his Los Angeles parole officer, a sadistic, patronizing redneck, marvelously well-played by M. Emmet Walsh, and accept as inevitable his return to life as a holdup man.

The film's most surprising and involving sequences are the series of heists that Max carries out, at first solo, then in the company of an old associate, a fellow named Jerry Schue (Harry Dean Stanton), an ex-con, now a paint contractor apparently happily married, who is going out of his mind with the boredom of a settled life that involves a backyard swimming pool and barbecue pit.

"Straight Time" makes a concession to convention in the casting of Theresa Russell as the young woman who has a brief affair with Max. Miss Russell, who was so good in "The Last Tycoon," is an extremely appealing actress, with a kind of contemporary authority, but she looks so classy, so understated-chic, that she suggests an upper-class girl whose path would cross Max's only at the beach, or maybe at a singles bar. The two really belong in different movies.

The film is beautifully acted by everyone, but especially by Mr. Hoffman, Mr. Walsh, Mr. Stanton and Gary Busey, who plays a junkie friend of Max who cops out at the last minute of a crucial job. "Straight Time" is not a movie to raise the spirits. It is so cool it would leave a chill were it not done with such precision and control that we remain fascinated by a rat, in spite of ourselves.

1978 Mr 18, 14:1

MADAME ROSA, directed by Moishe Mizrahi; screenplay (French with English subtitles) by Mr. Mizrahi, based on the book by Emile Aiar; executive producers, Raymond Danon, Roland Girard and Jean Bolvary; music, Philippe Sarde; director of photography, Nestor Almendros; a Libra Film production, distributed by Atlantic Releasing Corp. Running time: 105 minutes. At the Plaza Theater, 58th Street east of Madison Avenue. This film has not been rated.

Madame Rosa .... Simone Signoret
Dr. Katz .... Claude Dauphin
Momo .... Sammy Ben Youb
Hamil .... Gabriel Jabbour
Nadine .... Michal Bat Adam
Ramon .... Costa Gavras
Madame Lola .... Stella Anicette
Kadir Youssef .... Mohammed Zineth

By VINCENT CANBY

Israeli films, even the best, are specialized entertainments for most American audiences. They tend to deal in sentiment of an intensity that strikes us as almost rude. In our popular literature, as defined by the sitcoms of television, we take close family relationships for granted and move on to other matters: Will dad allow the kids to go on that camping trip? Otherwise, we treat family relationships as subjects for psychoanalytical scrutiny because we know that nothing—certainly not love—can be trusted to be exactly what it seems. Just beyond one's love of mom is the raging desire to carry her off to the nearest honeymoon motel.

In Israeli films, family relationships are fundamental and secure, even if the film happens to be about changing attitudes toward them. One result is that Israeli films often seem too simple and sunny for sophisticated American audiences. What we fail to detect in the intensity of these feelings is an element that is far from sentimental, but is, rather, dark, obsessive—the need to establish continuity in the face of chaos.

•

These thoughts are prompted by "Madame Rosa," which is not an Israeli film at all. It is, in fact, France's nominee for the Oscar as the best foreign-language film of 1977, but it was directed (beautifully) by Moishe Mizrahi, the Egyptian-born Israeli director best known in this country for his Israeli films, "I Love You, Rosa" and "The House on Chelouche Street."

Though it's not an Israeli movie, "Madame Rosa" makes profoundly moving the kind of emotions that have earlier been involved rather than effectively demonstrated by Mr. Mizrahi in even "The House on Chelouche Street." "Madame Rosa," which opens today at the Plaza Theater, is sweet and tough in conventional ways, but it also acknowledges something you don't often see except in the films of directors like Renoir and Truffaut, that the greatest courage may often be the will to go on, to continue, in the conviction that there is nothing but darkness beyond.

Such a character is Madame Rosa, born and raised a French Jew, self-described agnostic, a once-gaudy whore who was the toast of a few streets of Paris, but who has been inactive since her release from Auschwitz at the end of World War II. To make ends meet, Madame Rosa now runs a kind of makeshift boarding house in her cramped, sixth-floor flat in Paris's Belleville quarter, a working-class district where Algerians, black Africans, Jews and gentiles live in a harmony dictated by necessity. Her boarders are the off-spring of her friends and former associates in "the life," some of whom take their parental duties as seriously as busy film stars who make it a point to see their children once a week, while others leave them and vanish.

As played by Simone Signoret, Madame Rosa is a tremendous character, an overwhelming mountain of worn-out flesh whose arteries are hardening, whose ankles are weak, and whose lungs are less dependable than a couple of ancient innertubes. Madame Rosa is tired. She's in the process of dying and she's afraid, not because of what comes after death—she's tough enough to face that, except sometimes in the middle of the night—but because of what will happen to her last boarder,

Simone Signoret in the title role

a solemn, old-for-his-years, Arab boy named Momo (Samy Ben Youb).

Momo is one of her abandoned boarders. As, little by little, the other children are picked up by their mothers and placed in other refuges, Momo stays on because he has no place else to go. He's both attached to Madame Rosa and furious. One day he steals a dog from a pet shop, cares for it lovingly and then, in an act he can't explain, sells the dog to a passerby and drops the 500 francs thus earned into the sewer. Madame Rosa thinks he may be losing his mind. Actually he's passing through puberty.

"Madame Rosa," which Mr. Mizrahi has adapted from the 1975 Prix Goncourt novel by Emile Ajar, is a story of love and especially of mutual need and appreciation that will, I suppose, be read as some kind of parable about the Near East, though that is to freight it with a kind of political significance it doesn't have to depend on. It's a clear-eyed, often very funny film about two brave, complex, immensely appealing characters as they discover resources within themselves that are as surprising to them as to us.

•

Miss Signoret has her best role in years, one that uses the extraordinary physical presence she has become without exploiting it. As Momo, Samy Ben Youb — slight, large-eyed, solemn — matches her performance perfectly. Claude Dauphin has several very effective moments as Madame Rosa's old doctor, a fellow who is understandably somewhat shocked when Momo, with the best of intentions and the most careful tact, tries to talk the doctor in putting the old lady out of her misery. Costa Gavras, the director of "Z" and other films, makes a sort of token appearance as the father of the family Momo will probably move in with.

There are sentimental moments in "Madame Rosa," but they are the shadows, not the substance, of a very good, very firm movie.

1978 Mr 19, 54:5

FILM VIEW

VINCENT CANBY

'Fingers' Is Strictly From Desperation

One of the oldest ploys of movie advertising is the one that insists that you'll either love the film or hate it. In the case of "Fingers," the ads read: "Some will love it. Others will be angered by it. Everyone will be stunned by it." Fearing the worst (indifference) the copywriters do their utmost to create polarized views. They are ever-hopeful, like the would-be celebrity who says, "I don't care what they say about me as long as they spell my name right."

Because "Fingers" seems to be creating a lot more discussion than it deserves, I feel that by writing about it, as I'm about to do, I've somehow been hooked by the ad, though my reaction to it when I came out of the screening room was a mildly amused, "How did he—James Toback—ever hustle up the money to make it?" On the basis of his one previous screenplay (for Karel Reisz's "The Gambler"), which had the excitement and insight of a sticky-fingered comparative-literature student's first term paper, and certainly on the basis of his screenplay for "Fingers" itself, something more than apparent talent was involved. "Fingers" is to the films of Martin Scorsese and Paul Schrader—films that "Fingers" seems to ape—what that long list of failed "youth" pictures ("The Strawberry Statement," "Getting Straight," "RPM" and "The Magic Garden of Stanley Sweetheart") was to "Easy Rider." A spin-off. Mr. Scorsese and Mr. Schrader, even when their films are less than great, are original talents. Their obsessions with religion, sex, violence, guilt and the general quality of American life are matched by their knowledge of cinema. They know what the camera can and cannot do. Mr. Toback's obsession is much simpler. He wants very much to make a movie. Any movie. He wants to see his na e in lights. But it's as if he hadn't spent much time thinking about what kind of movie he'd like to make or even much about how movies are made, that is, what makes them different from the literary models he evokes, much like an aggressively talkative but none too sensitive comp-lit student. "The Gambler" was out of Dostoyevsky. "Fingers" is out of desperation.

"Fingers" wants to be An Urban Movie of Our Time, about sex and violence and the contradictory demands of family, when family bonds are disintegrating. Specifically, it's about Jimmy (Harvey Keitel), a character created out of old whole-cloth, the musically talented son of a Mafia hoodlum (Michael V. Gazzo), who is Italian, and a concert-pianist mom (Marian Seldes), who is Jewish and who is, for reasons never explained (perhaps because she's sensitive), locked up in a funny farm.

When the movie opens, the camera catches Jimmy in a long-shot, down the length of his fashionable East Side studio apartment, as he ecstatically plays a little Bach cantata, which, we learn later, he is preparing for an audition with an important concert impresario. As Jimmy feels himself increasingly swept up in Bach, responding to the music as if on the point of sexual fulfillment, the camera approaches him slowly, taking so long that one feels the only way for the scene to be concluded is to show us that Jimmy is, in fact, seated at a player-piano. But no. Jimmy/Harvey is really playing—which is just the first of a series of anti-climaxes that dog the movie with the persistence of a humorless flat-foot.

• • •

Jimmy, Mr. Toback would have us believe, burns with something more than a hard, gem-like flame—with the fury of a blow-torch. Music is his life. When he's not fingering Bach on his baby grand, he is walking about the city carring, as his security blanket, a portable tape deck on which he plays the rock-and-roll classics of the 1950's so loudly he offends everyone. Jimmy is supposed to be one of those impossible nuts whose passions are too much for him— and perhaps even for one movie—to contain. He's meant to be a series of successive emotional revelations, explosions really; though, as the intense Mr. Keitel plays him, the intended explosions are an anthology of peculiar, quirky mannerisms that not only don't go off, they don't add up to much more than an actor's monthly exercises. They're little, peculiar, "phfffts"—firecrackers heard at a great distance.

This may not be the actor's fault. One assumes that if the film had had some guiding theme, the performance would not seem so busy and, finally, so superfluous.

The plot that Mr. Toback has hatched for this character has to do with two underworld "collections" Jimmy's dad wants carried out just before Jimmy's big audition with the concert impresario. There's also the subplot, though I suspect the subplot contains the most compelling reason "Fingers" was made. This subplot is about an illusive (actually dopey) girl Jimmy picks up, a fey sculptor (Tisa Farrow) who inhabits a SoHo loft she looks ill-at-ease in and who carries on with a black gangster named—are you ready?—Dreems, played by Jim Brown, who, though he's going thick around the middle, is clearly the movie's principal sex object.

Without building any momentum whatsoever, the movie darts among its various plot threads like a cat who wants to play, but can't stick at one thread long enough to have any fun: Jimmy makes one collection successfully, from the owner of a pizza parlor. He goes to have his prostate gland examined (the doc says he's straining himself). He practices for his audition. He calls on Tisa. They have sex, quite as speedily as two pigeons. He seduces one young woman (the friend of a gangster he wants to anger and humiliate) while both are standing up in the women's room of a health club. He is invited by Dreems to participate in a sex party for four and refuses, preferring to watch. Dreems is impatient when the second girl in the party won't kiss Tisa. Dreems knocks the two women's heads together. Whack! Jimmy goes home and weeps. Which leads—as June follows December—to a climactic fist-and-gun-fight sequence with lots and lots of blood. Is it too much? No. It's not enough. It's about as close to nothing as can be created out of random feelings.

Perhaps not entirely random. The key to the film, I suspect, is a book Mr. Toback wrote some years ago called "Jim," about his association with Jim Brown when Mr. Toback went to Hollywood on an assignment from Esquire to write a piece about the actor/football star. Instead of doing the piece, Mr. Toback became so fascinated by Mr. Brown, and fascinated by that fascination, that he moved in with Mr. Brown and wrote the book. "Jim" is an appalling and fascinating mixture of self-analysis, hero-worship and incredible self-importance, the climax of which is a scene in which Mr. Brown, Mr. Toback and two women recently picked up, repair to Mr. Brown's bedroom for sex. The author, ever ready to tell all, describes in detail how he adjusted to the bounces on the other side of the bed to time his needs to coincide with Mr. Brown's.

As might be expected, "Jim" says a lot less about Jim Brown than "The Autobiography of Alice B. Toklas" says about Alice, but Mr. Toback is not Gertrude Stein. The picture that emerges from "Jim" is of a groupie with an irrespressible gift for gab, a guy so busy seeing himself in relation to an admired object that the real world becomes pure fantasy.

• • •

Even though Jim Brown/Dreems enters "Fingers" as a peripheral character, it's quickly apparent that the movie, whose scenes are badly framed and often clumsily staged, exists as a testament to the feelings that Mr. Toback has toward Mr. Brown. The movie suddenly has a focal point. Mr. Brown physically dwarfs Mr. Keitel (the artist's surrogate) who, after Mr. Brown's appearance on the scene, becomes a kind of pathetic joke, not because the director-writer doesn't take him seriously but because he does.

This era of new, highly subjective journalism has produced some remarkable literature, including Norman Mailer's "Armies of the Night," Tom Wicker's "A Time to Die" and Michael Herr's "Dispatches," and a great deal of junk on the order of Tennessee Williams's "Memoirs." Some books, like "Memoirs," are not very well written, while others, like "Jim," are not very well written about subjects of no great import to anyone except the author's friends.

Such a film is "Fingers," whose twitchy principal performance, peculiar mixture of milieus and final violence, plus the moviemaker's frankness about such things as prostate exams, give it kind of bogus chic, but it's a groupie's movie. You don't have to love it or be angered by it. You may only be depressed. ■

1978 Mr 19, II:19:1

THE CONFESSIONS OF WINIFRED WAGNER, a documentary feature directed and produced by Hans-Jurgen Syberberg; in German with English subtitles; director of photography, Dietrich Lohmann; distributed by Bauer International. Running time: 104 minutes. At the Film Forum, 15 Vandam Street. This film has not been rated.

IF YOU STILL have doubts about the ability of the motion-picture camera to reveal the profound complexities and contradictions within the human character, you shouldn't miss "The Confessions of Winifred Wagner," the 104-minute, German, with English subtitles, documentary that opens today at the Film Forum.

The film has been edited from five hours of footage made three years ago in a series of interviews with Winifred Wagner, then 78, the English-born daughter-in-law of Richard and Cosima Wagner, the widow of Siegfried, for decades the keeper of the Wagner flame at Bayreuth and, today, still loyal to the memory of her dear friend Hitler, nicknamed Wolf.

The documentary is the work of Hans-Jurgen Syberberg, who was helped in obtaining the interview by the intercession of Gottfried Wagner, the son of the Bayreuth festival's current director, Wolfgang, and the grandson of Winifred. The method of the film is so self-effacing as to be no method at all, a series of close-ups and medium close-ups of this extraordinary, shrewd, amazingly vigorous old woman as she answers questions put to her by the film maker.

•

"The Confessions of Winifred Wagner" is ironically titled in that Winifred Wagner tells everything but confesses nothing. With the kind of candor that is so aggressive that it puts her listeners on the defensive, she talks about her early meetings with Hitler, and of their shared love of the music of Richard Wagner that became the basis of a friendship that lasted from 1922 until Hitler's death in 1945.

She also talks about family squabbles, about her early decision to put her husband and his work with the Bayreuth Festival ahead of her children —"There were always people to take care of them"—about great musicians she's known, about the rise of National Socialism and the devastating war; but always what fascinates us is the manner in which she resolutely refuses to turn her back on Hitler.

Winifred Wagner professes to believe that she was always "unpolitical," that the Hitler she knew was a kind and gentle man, and, when she is pressed, that he really wasn't responsible for the Final Solution. Both she and Hitler, she says rather airily, were sad about the bombing of London, but by that time she considered herself to be completely German. There were no feelings of divided loyalties.

•

"The Confessions of Winifred Wagner" is much more than the self-serving memoir it might initially appear to be, largely because Winifred Wagner is too honest in her own way to be concerned with the minor disturbances of reputation. What we see on the screen is one manifestation of a singular family, as well as of an entire European cultural tradition, captured simply, cleanly, by a film maker who understands that by deferring to its subject, the camera is most often victorious.

"The Confessions of Winifred Wagner," will be shown at the Film Forum tonight through Sunday at 7:45 P.M., and repeated there next week, Thursday through Sunday, at the same time.

1978 Mr 23, C16:5

THE OTHER SIDE OF THE MOUNTAIN, PART II, directed by Larry Peerce; screenplay by Douglas Day Stewart; produced by Edward S. Feldman; director of photography, Ric Waite; music, Lee Holdridge; editors, Eve Newman and Walter Hannemann; a Filmways production, distributed by Universal Pictures. Running time: 97 minutes. At the Guild Theater, 50th Street east of the Avenue of the Americas, and other theaters. This film has been rated PG.

Jill Kinmont	Marilyn Hassett
John Boothe	Timothy Bottoms
June Kinmont	Nan Martin
Audra-Jo	Belinda J. Montgomery
Linda	Gretchen Corbett
Bill Kinmont	William Bryant
Mr. Boothe	James A. Bottoms
Mrs. Boothe	June Dayton
Roy Boothe	Curtis Credel
Beverly Boothe	Carole Tru Foster
Mel	Charles Frank
Doctor in Los Angeles	George Petrie

By VINCENT CANBY

AT THE END of "The Other Side of the Mountain," the 1975 movie based on the life of Jill Kinmont, Jill (Marilyn Hassett), the radiantly pretty championship skier who'd been paralyzed in a downhill accident, was coping quite beautifully with her paraplegia, with the loss of her fiancé in a plane accident and with the loss of her father—heart attack, I think. She was finding a new life as a teacher.

At the start of "The Other Side of the Mountain, Part II," which opens at the Guild and other theaters today, Jill Kinmont, still played by Miss Hassett, continues not simply to cope, but to achieve. Very early on she's named Los Angeles's Woman of the Year and almost immediately meets and falls in love with handsome, sensitive John Boothe (Timothy Bottoms), a long-distance trucker who comes from her hometown of Bishop, Calif.

The fact that a lot of us already know that in real life Miss Kinmont and Mr. Boothe got married creates certain difficulties for Douglas Day Stewart, who wrote the screenplay for this sequel to the extremely popular first film. The problem with "Part II" is that there is no problem.

The ones that Mr. Stewart has attempted to dramatize are lugubriously unbelievable. Jill supposedly thinks of herself as a bad-luck charm—"everyone I've ever loved has died"—and so she puts off John. Then she tries to convince us that though they love each other, they are incompatible. "He's not interested in anything I am," she says, "not books or plays or concerts," though the Jill we see is hardly a culture-nut.

The first film, directed by Larry Peerce, who also directed the spinoff, was a slickly prefabricated bathtub of movie sentimentality, at the heart of which was a gallant young woman facing real handicaps. "Part II' is really a 30-minute postscript to that story, blown up to feature-length by artificial plot problems and so many flashbacks to the first movie that the second becomes a sort of reverse trailer, a coming attraction for something that's already gone.

All of the characters are so relentlessly genial that the movie comes to look like the smile on a billboard. I suppose that some interest is generated by our curiosity about the sexual lives of paraplegics, but this subject is so discreetly attended to that it seems to be another one of the film's nonproblems.

Mr. Peerce's direction suggests a certain amount of desperation. You can almost hear him asking, "What can I do to make things interesting?" Sometimes characters talk to each other's backs, but mostly they just look cheery. In moments of emotional crescendo, he puts his camera on a helicopter so that it can slowly pull away from the scene in a grand manner that may or may not indicate God is taking care of things.

•

"The Other Side of the Mountain, Part II," which has been rated PG ("Parental Guidance Suggested"), indicates that before their marriage Miss Kinmont and Mr. Boothe went off on a trial honeymoon, during which they sometimes shared the some bed.

1978 Mr 24, C12:1

NEAR AND FAR AWAY, directed by Marianne Ahrne; screenplay (Swedish with English subtitles) by Miss Ahrne and Bertrand Hurault; director of photography, Hans Welin; film editor, Miss Ahrne; produced by the Swedish Film Institute. At the Cinema Studio, Broadway and 66th Street. Running time: 97 minutes. This film has not been rated.

Mania	Lilga Kovanko
The Mute	Robert Farrant
Annicka	Annicka Kronberg
Jaeger	Helge Skoog
Stenius	Jan Erik Lindqist
Bente	Bodil Martensson
Scanian	Bengt C W Carlsson

By JANET MASLIN

PSYCHIATRISTS are the villains of "Near and Far Away" and, as depicted by the Swedish director and co-scenarist Marianne Ahrne, they're sitting ducks. As Mania, an earnest student who works in a mental hospital, becomes more and more attached to a handsome, mute young man on her ward, her superiors notice only that there's a case of countertransference under way. Mania is gentle and loving, full of understanding and wonder, and her teachers are, by comparison, a bunch of cold, careerist dunderheads who think they can help anguished patients by prescribing sleeping pills. Small wonder, then, that the handsome young man would rather make eyes at Mania than talk to anyone else.

The film, which opens today at the Cinema Studio, is ambiguous about the reasons for the young man's silence, but he seems to have made a conscious decision to stop speaking, rather than having fallen victim to some mysterious ailment. His lover, whom Mania goes to visit—and of whom she is very commendably not jealous—suggests that the young man has chosen to explore the world within rather than the world without, and that sometimes actual words only get in the way of true knowledge.

Mania, who has never had the good sense to change her name to anything less redolent, never emerges as more than a cardboard figure, and Lilga Kovanko plays her with a great deal of warmth but not much variety. Robert Farrant, as the mute, is sometimes afforded the camera's intensive scrutiny, sometimes used only as Mania's foil; he is often compelling, but always a little more elusive than the screenplay demands.

The other actors function more as props than as characters. The story's two doctors, played by Helge Skoog and Jan Erik Lindqvist, exist only to espouse rigid attitudes and behave with improbable insensitivity, and Annicka Kronberg, playing Mania's temporary roommate, is merely someone for the heroine to talk to. Owe Stefanson, as an inmate whose specialty is demanding cigarettes from strangers who have already *given* him cigarettes, seems at least as interesting and troubled as the mute, but Mania is considerably less interested in befriending this much less attractive fellow.

Miss Ahrne's film is carefully made and elegantly photographed, but it flows much too smoothly from one prettily austere setting to another, with no texture to catch the eye and no loose ends to hold the interest. Events proceed according to a schedule that is apparent 15 minutes into the film, and there are no real surprises in store.

1978 Mr 24, C12:5

WORD IS OUT, a documentary film by Mariposa Film Group: Peter Adair, Nancy Adair, Veronica Selver, Andrew Brown, Robert Epstein and Lucy Massie Phenix; produced by Peter Adair. At the Eastside Cinema, Third Avenue between 55th and 56th Streets. Running time: 124 minutes. This film has not been rated.

By JANET MASLIN

Most of the 26 homosexual men and women interviewed in "Word Is Out" are photographed at home, and a couple of their homes look alike. A curvaceous blond woman, with teased hair and bright blue eyeshadow and little earrings, sits flanked by photographs of her children in a suburban living room; another woman, who seems to be a man until she identifies herself as a mother, appears in a similar setting. As it later turns out, these two people are ensconced on the very same sofa, and they have been lovers for nine years, ever since they were introduced by their neighborhood Avon lady.

One of the most appealing things about this graceful, funny and often very moving documentary, now at the Eastside Cinema, is its altogether disarming presentation of material that might have invited prejudice or misunderstanding; in this case, what could have been a titillating revelation is artfully molded into nothing more than a wry and tender little surprise. "Word Is Out," made by the Mariposa Film Group, is comfortably constructed and quite informative, but what really carries the film is its casual seductiveness. Even filmgoers who imagine they'd rather sit through root canal work than find out what it's like to be homosexual may wind up unexpectedly captivated by the film's friendly, even-handed approach to a potentially divisive subject.

•

"Word Is Out" is at times extremely romantic, full of people gently reminiscing about what it was like to fall in love for the first time. And, as befits its romantic spirit (and its obvious desire to appeal to filmgoers of all sexual persuasions), the movie leaves sex to the imagination. One woman, who stridently announces herself to be a black lesbian (and who sits before a stained-glass window bearing a combined feminist and black power logo), simply talks about the way she gradually found herself looking forward to lunch dates with a particular woman friend much more enthusiastically than she awaited her dates with men in the evening.

A man wistfully describes an adolescent crush that blossomed into a 10-year love affair. And another man, a student, remembers being so thrilled by someone who brushed against his knee as they watched Part Three of Kenneth Clark's "Civilisation" series that he eagerly dashed back to catch Parts Four and Five.

The film's most stirring sequence involves a young man who dated the same girl for years but never felt adequate to the situation. Then he had

John Burnside and Harry Hay discuss their lives in "Word Is Out."

a quick homosexual experience; still, the earth failed to move. Finally, he met a man he could really care about. "When I was in high school, I thought I was one of those cold people who could never love anybody," he says quietly. "And when I fell in love with this guy, it meant so much to me. It meant I was a real person . . . I was using a part of myself that I never felt before . . . and the best part, too." At a preview screening of "Word Is Out," there wasn't a dry eye in the house after that particular revelation.

Much of the film is laced with humor: a hefty comedienne recalls joining the WAC's, marching into the mess hall and hearing cries of "Good god, Elizabeth, here comes another one!" One fellow in makeup and a nose ring complains that "toy stores are sexist, so you have to buy the Ken doll and then go over to Barbie's department to get a tutu."

•

Most of the interviewees are quite appealing, but a few of them aren't, and that's one of the film's most refreshing aspects. One man, an actor who endlessly congratulates himself for being "weird," would be a bit grating under any circumstances. The film simply presents him as part of a very broad spectrum, and the lack of any insistence upon gay supremacy or solidarity leaves the viewer quite free to draw his or her own conclusions.

The people presented here range from their 20's to their 70's, from being almost overbearingly articulate to communicating mostly through facial gestures, from being extroverted and affectionate to feeling isolated and private. The one thing they seem to have in common—something that makes the film particularly attractive—is a kind of confidence and certainty, the ability to speak matter-of-factly and behave with firm conviction.

1978 Mr 26, 40:1

FILM VIEW

VINCENT CANBY

Singing the Praises Of Some Unsung Players

In Dustin Hoffman's new film, "Straight Time," there's a scene in which Mr. Hoffman, who plays an edgy, self-destructive ex-con, is in an automobile on a Los Angeles freeway with his parole officer, a portly, alternately sadistic and patronizing slob. The scene slowly builds to a smashing climax in which the ex-con seizes control of the car, pulls it over to the side of the road and leaves the parole officer, his pants pulled down around the ankles, handcuffed to a fence. It's a funny, scarifying scene, breathlessly staged. It's emotionally satisfying for the way in which the underdog—the ex-con—turns the tables on his tormentor and it owes a great deal to Ulu Grosbard, the director, as well as to Mr. Hoffman, whose performance makes an otherwise downbeat film sometimes exhilarating.

It also owes a great deal to someone you've probably never heard of until now, H. Emmet Walsh, who plays the parole officer with the kind of thorough, idiosyncratic tackiness that extends even to his choice of rings—a large, garish, probably fake turquoise on his right middle finger, the stone a sickly blue that almost, but not quite, matches his blue sport shirt.

Every now and then we should stop to take stock of some of the extraordinary contributions being made to current movies—some good, some not so good—by people like Mr. Walsh, for whom there's seldom space enough in a daily newspaper's film reviews to do full justice. In many ways, the lives of supporting actors are charmed. They're seldom blamed for a movie's failure, but unless they have a show-stopping scene, one to equal Richard Widmark's murder of the little old lady years ago in "Kiss of Death," they tend to be appreciated in anonymity. There are right now more than a half-dozen such performances that deserve attention and make attendance at a number of films a lot less dreary than one might be led to expect.

• • •

Though their lives may be charmed, and though they can sometimes light up worthless movies, supporting actors are as much at the mercy of their material as stars. Ned Beatty, one of our best and most tireless supporting actors ("Network," "All the President's Men," "Nashville," etc.) has a fairly fat role in the inept submarine film, "Gray Lady Down," but the movie is of such blandness that it virtually wipes him out. He remains invisible. Brian De Palma's gaudy, ultimately ridiculous thriller, "The Fury," has an excellent cast including Carrie Snodgrass, Charles Durning and Amy Irving, but the film is so concerned with its busy pyrotechnics that it absorbs performances as if it were blotting paper. The one person I remember vividly from "The Fury" is an actress named Fiona Lewis, whose stunning beauty is the only thing in the movie that can match the stunning special effects.

A good movie makes use of its supporting and character actors and actresses without overwhelming them or letting them run off with the picture. Ideally, they are no more or less important than any of the other elements that make up a movie.

Such is the case with Mr. Walsh in "Straight Time." He is so effective that the movie misses his departure from the scene, but then the movie is so effective that it doesn't suffer from the loss of his presence. Such was not the case in the first film I remember seeing him in, Elaine May's "Mickey and Nickey," when he played the Los Angeles bus driver who has a tricky encounter with the manic character played by John Cassavetes. The rest of the film has receded into the gray gloom, but I still vividly recall that particular bus ride.

• • •

It is, I suppose, a reflection of the interest and care of a film's director, producer and casting director that good supporting performances seldom come singly. If a film has one good character actor, it's likely to have several. "Handle With Care" was composed almost entirely of superior character performances. Though "Straight Time" is dominated by the performance of Dustin Hoffman, who is himself as much a character actor as a star, there are several other performances that also contribute to the film's impact, most notably that of Harry Dean Stanton.

Mr. Stanton, lean (almost to the point of being cadaverous), with a face that, in repose, could be contemporary America's Everyman (in debt up to his eyeballs but still unworried), plays an old friend of Mr. Hoffman's, a fellow who has gone straight as a paint contractor and is now happily married, living in a comfortable suburban house that is complete with a backyard swimming pool and barbecue pit. He is, in short, going out of his mind with boredom and leaps at the chance to join the Hoffman character in a renewed life of petty crime.

Mr. Stanton has been around for some time, in films like "The Missouri Breaks," "Rancho DeLuxe," "92 in the Shade," but he has never been better than he is in "Straight Time," nor has he ever had a film that better utilized his particular, quick-to-register talents. Its his mysterious gift to be able to make everything he does seem immediately authentic.

• • •

Another actor worth noting in "Straight Time" is Gary Busey, a tall, strapping, long-haired young man who is startlingly good as a weak-willed junkie who wants to do the right thing and never will. Seen in the principal woman's role in the same film is Theresa Russell, a very classy looking young woman who suggests a cross between Lauren Bacall and Cybill Shepherd, which is not at all bad. Miss Russell, who made a very effective film debut as Cecilia Brady, the studio chief's daughter in "The Last Tycoon," scores a small triumph in "Straight Time" by being absolutely believable in a role that isn't. Unless she takes the vows, we'll be seeing a lot more of her.

Because Jill Clayburgh has been getting most of the attention for her tour de force in Paul Mazursky's "An Unmarried Woman," critics have tended to brush over Michael Murphy's exceptionally complex performance as the husband whose emotional problems set in motion the events that make possible the Clayburgh character's eventual liberation. Mr. Murphy, whose looks suggest the kind of 1930's leading man played by Dennis O'Keefe, has been quietly accumulating a series of remarkable character performances that more often than not have been overshadowed by someone else's triumph.

In "The Front," in which he played the fellow for whom Woody Allen fronted, it was Woody's performance. In "Nashville," in which he played the hustling advance man for the never-seen political candidate, it was Robert Altman's American Dream of a movie. In "An Unmarried Woman." it's Miss Clayburgh's performance, though without Mr. Murphy I doubt that the film would seem anywhere near as complicated as it does.

As I read the Murphy performance, the husband in "An Unmarried Woman" is not the rat that most other people take him so readily to be. Nor is he so weak-willed. The easy intimacy and humor of the film's opening scenes give the lie to that. He's a fellow who has quite as many problems as his wife, but it's the character's bad luck that the film is about the wife, not the husband. One of the most profoundly comic scenes that Mr. Mazursky has ever written, and which is acted to perfection by Mr. Murphy and Miss Clayburgh, is the scene in which the tearful husband finally tells his wife that he wants to leave her and, in his self-absorption, is completely surprised when she becomes furious instead of comforting him in *his* grief.

• • •

It's no surprise that Walter Matthau gives a brilliantly funny, beautifully thought out performance in "Casey's Shadow," this year's horse-movie. We expect Mr. Matthau to surprise us, which is, I suppose, something of a burden for him. He's fine as the Cajun farmer who breeds quarter-horses for racing and dreams of winning "the big one." The real surprises in the film, which was directed by Martin Ritt, are two first-rate performances that the movie probably could have survived without, but which give "Casey's Shadow" an extra measure of quality.

The first is that of Alexis Smith, whom I last saw on the silver screen under howlingly funny circumstances ("Jacqueline Susann's Once Is Not Enough"). In "Casey's Shadow," she has a comparatively small role, that of a very rich woman who breeds and races quarter-horses and wants very much to own the title character, the quarter-horse of the century, we are led to believe. Neither as played by Miss Smith nor as written is this woman your standard rich-bitch character. She has the self-assurance that pots of old money give, but she also is a woman of humor and feeling, always in command and accustomed to being in charge without having to throw her weight around. The performance is a detail that gives the film stature.

So, too, is the performance by an actor I don't remember seeing before, Andrew A. Rubin, a tall, slim, dark-haired young man who plays the oldest of Mr. Matthau's three sons, a fellow who may be a good deal more interesting than the movie has time to explore. In competition with Mr. Matthau's performance and with those of the actors who play the other two sons (one cute, one pretty), Mr. Rubin's performance seems self-effacing, which it is. It is also rooted in anger and touched with hopelessness, which is exactly what the character is supposed to be. If you like "Casey's Shadow," Mr. Rubin's performance will be one of the reasons.

You don't have to like a movie, though, to appreciate and respond to the work of the character people. If you should possibly find yourself trapped inside the theater that's showing the Henry Winkler comedy, "The One and Only," directed by Carl Reiner, relax and enjoy the contributions of Gene Saks, who plays a riotously foul-mouthed promotor of professional wrestlers, and of Hervé Villechaize, the 3-foot-10-inch midget, who plays a would-be actor who doubles as a pro-wrestler and wins bouts by doing unspeakable things because they're in such easy reach.

It's not been a great season for American movies so far, but these people have been among the compensations. The least we can do is attach the faces to the names and then remember them. ■

1978 Mr 26, II:17:1

'Sylphide' Opens Beacon's Ballet Film Series

By ANNA KISSELGOFF

The Beacon Theater opens what it calls the First Ballet Film Festival today with an unusual, potentially controversial, film version of the 19th-century Romantic ballet "La Sylphide."

The three-week series will alternate five different programs. If some of the ballets on camera have been seen in New York before, most of the actual films have not.

The "Sylphide," for instance, is a Paris Opéra Ballet production that attempts to go back to the original 1832 French version, although the production consistently presented in the United States has been the 1836 version from Denmark by August Bournonville.

Tomorrow, the Beacon will present two films made by a West German television producer shortly after the New York City Ballet's 1972 Stravinsky Festival, one of which is George Balanchine's "Pulcinella" from that festival. The other is the City Ballet in Mr. Balanchine's "Liebeslieder Walzer." Thursday brings in Alicia Alonso's "Giselle" with the National Ballet of Cuba. The 1964 film, starring Miss Alonso, was seen at a gala for the New York Public Library's Dance Collection but has not had general release in New York.

The other two films are a 1967 view of the Bolshoi Ballet and the previously distributed and very successful filmed version of Rudolf Nureyev's production of "Don Quixote" for the Australian Ballet.

Meanwhile, we have "La Sylphide," starring Ghislaine Thesmar and Michael Denard, both of whom will appear live on stage at the theater tonight in a precurtain pas de deux. Miss Thesmar's husband, the choreographer Pierre Lacotte, first tried to reconstruct the original "Sylphide" in a production for French television in 1971. Presumably this is the same film. In 1972, the Paris Opéra Ballet transferred the production to its stage.

If we are to believe the rather inaccurate handout provided by the Beacon, Mr. Lacotte discovered a long-lost notation of some of the original choreography by Philippe Taglioni and much of the original score by Jean Schneitzhoeffer in an attic belonging to a godchild of the son of Marie Taglioni, who created the title role March 12, 1832 in Paris. Because modern audiences have been familiar only with totally new choreographic versions or the 1836 Bournonville recension with a score by the Danish composer Hermann Lowenskjold, Mr. Lacotte's attempted reconstruction is, of course, of great interest.

Alas. It is so stylistically and dramatically out of kilter with what we know about Romantic ballet in general and "La Sylphide" in particular that it is difficult to have confidence in the authenticity of the choreography itself.

The story and the structure are identical to the Bournonville version—the Taglioni version survived into Petipa's day in Russia. In this film version, James, a Scottish farmer, is still torn between his fiancée, Effie (Laurance Nerval), and the sylphide, a woodland spirit.

Yet here, so wrongly, the sylph is made to appear no different from the mortals around her. The crucial distinction, that she wears toe shoes while Effie and her friends do not, is not maintained. All are on pointe.

Repeatedly, James gathers her in his arms and partners her while the dramatic point is that she must die at the human's touch. In Act I, a strangely modern pas de trois, in full Antony Tudor psychological style, shows James interchangeably partnering the two women in his life.

Stylistically, of course, 19th-century Romantic ballerinas could not turn so quickly on their toes or keep their legs up so high. Nor did the man have such bravura dancing. What Mr. Lacotte has done is not try to replicate authentic style, but possibly to give us some of Taglioni's choreography. His Sylphide certainly darts around much more than her Bournonville counterpart, and she works harder, too. This film is worth seeing for every balletomane precisely because it is so wrong-headed.

1978 Mr 28, 50:4

Sunny and 16

THE FIRST TIME, directed by Claude Berri; screenplay (French with English subtitles) by Mr. Berri; produced by Raymond Danon; director of photography, Jean Cesar Chiabaut; editor, Dominique Daudon; music, Rene Urtreger; distributed by EDP Films. Running time: 85 minutes. At the Columbbia 2 Theater, Second Avenue at 64th Street. This film has not been rated.

Claude	Alain Cohen
Claude's father	Charles Denner
Claude's mother	Zorica Lozic
Arlette	Delphine Levy
Rene	Claude Lubicki
Bernard	Philippe Teboul
Sammy	Jerome Loeb
Loulou	Bruno Rosenker
Carole	Daniele Schneider
Bernadette	Maryse Raymond
Irene	Carine Riviere
Nathalie	Daniele Minazzoli
Robert	Roland Blanche
Cousin Leon	Joel Moskowitz

By VINCENT CANBY

BENEATH the rather sunny 16-year-old exterior of Claude Langmann (Alain Cohen), there are raging the lusts of a rather sunny, 16-year-old boy who has made do, until now, with girlie magazines, saucy novels by such as Boris Vians ("I Spit on Your Grave") and the occasional attentions of a slow-witted male cousin named Leon. "I'd have preferred a girl cousin," Claude tells us matter-of-factly on the soundtrack, "but I didn't have any choice."

There is nothing wrong with Claude that time and heterosexual experience won't see him safely through, which is the subject of "The First Time," Claude Berri's latest comic memoir about growing up healthy, bright, sensitive and generally happy, to become eventually Claude Berri, the successful, funny and infinitely generous French film maker.

•

"The First Time" picks up the story of the same Claude, also played by Mr. Cohen, in Mr. Berri's first film, "The Two of Us" (1968), about the film maker's experiences during the German occupation, when he was a little boy and was sent from Paris to live in the country with a crusty, wheezing old anti-Semite, played by Michael Simon.

Mr. Berri's use of autobiographical material, as well as his continuing relationship with Mr. Cohen as his surrogate screen self, inevitably recalls François Truffaut's Antoine Doinel films in which Jean-Pierre Léaud, as Antoine, has gown before our eyes from adolescence to manhood. There is a major difference between the work of the two directors, though. Mr. Truffaut's comedies are illuminated by a kind of madness, an awareness of ultimate despair. They are the work of the permanent outsider, someone who will never feel quite at home in the bourgeois society he thinks he admires.

Mr. Berri's films, including "Marry Me, Marry Me," which is the story of

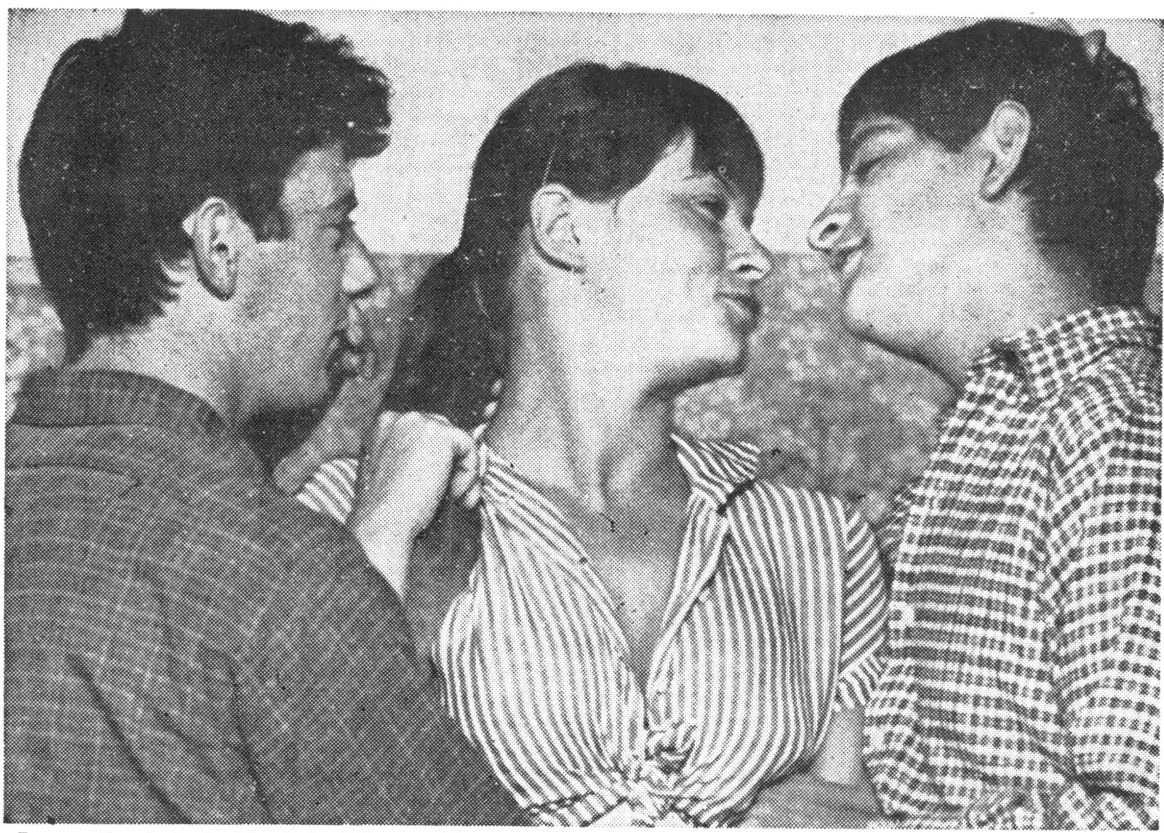

Jerom Loeb, left, Daniele Minazzoli and Alain Cohen in "First Time"
The film has the air of pure fantasy

Claude as a young man, are obviously the work of someone who feels completely at home, a fellow whose family ties are emotionally secure in ways that will forever elude the poor, obsessed Antoine.

"The First Time," which opens today at the Columbia 2 Theater, is all about sex — about Claude's disastrous first encounter with a woman for pay, then about his more successful encounters with girls his own age — yet the mood is so gentle, so understanding, so optimistic, the film has the air of pure fantasy. This may be exactly what the director and writer intended, yet I prefer Mr. Berri in a somewhat less benign frame of mind, as he was in "Male of the Century," in which Claude had grown into an impossibly arrogant — and hilarious — male chauvinist.

Though Mr. Cohen is comically serious and charming as the young Claude, Charles Denner, who plays his furrier-father, gives the film its real substance. The straight, no-nonsense relationship between the father and the son is the nicest thing about the movie. Also it's often funnier, in that it is more surprising, than the catalogue of Claude's encounters with women.

•

These are clever and, considering the unsuccessful nature of some, amazingly serene. It's as if, in looking back, Mr. Berri cannot bring himself to fake melodramatic crises when he —and we—know that, after all, everything turned out all right.

1978 Mr 29, C24:3

Admirer of Actor

SEPTEMBER 30, 1955, directed by James Bridges; screenplay by Mr. Bridges; produced by Jerry Weintraub; director of photography, Gordon Wilis; music, Leonard Rosenman; editor, Jeff Gourson; distributed by Universal Pictures. Running time: 101 minutes. At the Cinema II Theater, Third Avenue near 60th Street. This film has been rated PG.

Jimmy J	Richard Thomas
Melba Lou	Susan Tyrrell
Charlotte	Deborah Benson
Billie Jean	Lisa Blount
Hanley	Thomas Hulce
Frank	Dennis Quaid
Pat	Mary Kai Clark
Eurgene	Dennis Christopher
Jimmy J's mother	Collin Wilcox
Coach Haynes	Ben Fuhrman
Edgar	Mike Farris
Radio annonucer	Tom Bonner
Band director	Glen Irby
Dickie	Bryan Scott
Charlotte's father	Bush Satterfield
Charlotte's mother	Katherine Satterfield
Nurse	Betty Harford
Aunt Ethel	Ouida White
Mr. Brown	James Dombek

By VINCENT CANBY

WE SEEM to be in the grip of a whole new batch of movies that are as much meditations on the meaning of various aspects of American popular culture as they are demonstrations of that culture—"Saturday Night Fever," 'American Hot Wax," "Handle With Care" now James Bridges's funny, solemn, dead-on-accurate "September 30, 1955."

The film, which opens today at the Cinema II, is all about the sturm und drang precipitated on that day, nearly 23 years ago, in one small Arkansas college town when word is received that James Dean has been killed in a car crash in California.

Actually the town takes the news rather well. "After all," says one typical young woman, "he was *only* a movie star." But for Jimmy J. (Richard Thomas), the death means the loss of someone whose only released film, "East of Eden," defined his own amorphous personality and still unfulfilled life. For a few hours Jimmy J. goes to pieces in the manner he imagines James Dean might have, given the same more or less tacky circumstances.

Like Mr. Bridges's "The Paper Chase," the new film is full of affection and carefully observed detail of place and period. But also like the earlier film it lacks the edge of satire that can make the difference between a good film and a great one, between a film that is somehow in thrall to its sentiments instead of being in charge of them.

Mr. Bridges likes Jimmy J. so much that he sees more in him than many of the rest of us probably can. Is it because he knows that at the end of the film, after Jimmy J. goes roaring off to California on his James Dean-like motorcycle, Jimmy J. will grow up to be a writer and director of movies, like Mr. Bridges? If so, he knows more than I do.

My conviction from the film is that Jimmy J. will land in Hollywood, work at odd jobs and, eventually, settle down as the manager of a supermarket. It is thus apparent that I find the film's implications sadder and more depressing than Mr. Bridges, who, I assume, is drawing on his own life and knows what's going to happen next.

"September 30, 1955" was filmed in Arkansas and even has the look of a movie of the 50's, when film makers were starting to go on location in the interests of accuracy. It is beautifully cast and acted with self-absorbed intensity by a number of young performers who are very, very funny, especially by Deborah Benson, as the college's pretty, square, homecoming queen, a girl who loves Jimmy J. a lot, but who loves conventional behavior even more, and by Lisa Blount, as Jimmy J.'s ex-girlfriend, someone who shares his nutty adoration of James Dean and who must pay a high price to grow up.

The problem with "September 30, 1955" is that Jimmy J. never does grow up. Essentially he is a figure of comedy, a fellow desperate for direction and out of touch with reality.

Mr. Bridges and Mr. Thomas, who was John-Boy on TV's "The Waltons" for so many years, insist on treating him as a figure of magic and mystery, as if he were a poet in his own right. To model one's life on that of a movie star to the extent that Jimmy J. does suggests arrested development — though it does say something important (and scary) about the influence of what are sometimes called the popular arts.

It is the latter that makes "September 30, 1955" so interesting, as well as the ways in which Mr. Bridges recalls—comically—Jimmy J.'s attempts to relate the humdrum events of his life with those of the melodramatic movie fiction he so admires. Jimmy J. himself is a cipher to me but the movie around him is extremely stylish, even to the manner in which it takes on in modified form—the shape of juve-

Richard Thomas in James Bridges's "September 30, 1955" at Cinema II
Funny, solemn, dead-on-accurate

nile-delinquent films of the 50's. Mr. Bridges is a sophisticated. knowing film maker, but I wish he had built his movie around a tougher, more knowing character we might have believed in.

•

"September 30, 1955," which has been rated PG ("Parental Guidance Suggested"), contains some mildly obscene language.

1978 Mr 31, C13:3

Robert Clouse also directed "Enter the Dragon" and "Black Belt Jones," which makes him sound as if he ought to know a thing or two about action footage. Here, however, Mr. Clouse proves himself capable of showing a car being driven through a houseboat and into a canal without generating any excitement at all. The same thing holds true for the film's final demolition scene, which involves a bulldozer, a greenhouse and a very large number of innocent mums and roses.

The film's only real selling point is the abundance of fresh flowers that begin to figure into the drug-smuggling plot during the last half-hour. Mr. Clouse can't make a chase through a flower market look any more thrilling than a stroll in a garden might be, but the flowers are nicely photographed and prettily arranged. And, after all, it's springtime.

1978 Mr 31, C13:3

Guns and Flowers

THE AMSTERDAM KILL, directed by Robert Clouse; screenplay by Mr. Clouse and Gregory Teifer, from a story by Mr. Teifer; director of photography, Alan Hume; film editors, Allan Holzman and Gina Brown; music by Hal Schaefer; produced by Andre Morgan; released by Columbia Pictures. At Loews State 2, Broadway and 45th Street, and other theaters. Running time: 89 minutes. This film is rated R.

Quinlan .... Robert Mitchum
Odums .... Bradford Dillman
Ridgeway .... Richard Egan
Knight .... Leslie Nielsen
Chung Wei .... Keye Luke
Jimmy Wong .... George Cheung
Assassin .... Chan Sing

By JANET MASLIN

THERE'S a Chinese drug-smuggling ring operating out of Amsterdam, and an American narcotics agent seems to be the kingpin. It might be Leslie Nielsen; it might be Bradford Dillman; it might be Richard Egan. For all the difference the fine points of the plot make in "The Amsterdam Kill," it might even be your old Aunt Betty. All that matters is the body count, which is impressive enough to have given a film without sex scenes an R rating. There are so many shootings, and so many hapless victims, that one thug even barges into a kitchen by mistake, machine-gunning a helpless chicken.

"The Amsterdam Kill," which opens today at a number of neighborhood theaters, has all the weariness of a genre movie but none of the comfortable familiarity. In a misguided attempt to appeal to an international audience, the film flits from London to Hong Kong to Amsterdam; one key scene takes place, for no clear reason, at a horse show in Utrecht. One important Chinese character wears tweeds, plaids and a watchchain on his waistcoat. There are so many shots of airports and train terminals that it begins to seem as if one has purchased a Eurail pass rather than a movie ticket. The film is so intent on taking place everywhere that its nervous geography becomes terribly jarring.

•

Robert Mitchum plays a good cop who's been disgraced, but who is still good, the only honest man in a cesspool of international corruption, a disillusioned fellow who can still rise to a challenge if the stakes are high enough . . . oh, you know the type. Mr. Mitchum knows the type, too, so intimately that he manages to lend unexpected weight and dignity to moments of no consequence at all. This is the flimsiest movie Mr. Mitchum has made in some time, but for that very reason his performance is particularly arresting.

Most of his dialogue sounds like dialogue, and Mr. Mitchum delivers both the punchy lines ("Let's go stick our finger in somebody's eye") and the implausible ones with the cool, dependable air of a man who's only following orders. But there's something impressive about the imperturbability with which he marches through the most potentially embarrassing situations.

•

FILM VIEW

VINCENT CANBY

Measuring the Year's Films

The man with the tape recorder stopped by the office for his quarterly report. He wasted no time with preliminaries.

Q: You look depressed. Have you just seen a heartwarming movie?

A: How'd you guess? "The Other Side of the Mountain, Part 2," the follow-up film about Jill Kinmont, the paralyzed skier, but that's not the problem. Under ordinary circumstances I can absorb movies so heartwarming they'd make your feet sweat, but not this year. These circumstances don't seem especially ordinary. On second thought, maybe they're too ordinary.

Q: Can you explain?

A: I suppose it's just an accident of timing, not important as a trend or anything, but it does seem true that the movies that have been released so far this year have ranged mostly from the awful to the failed, to the disappointing, to the not-so-hot, all the way up to the pretty good.

Q: Which is not very high up?

A: No. Last year by this time we'd already seen Robert Benton's "The Late Show," which is the kind of movie one could really get excited about. We'd had two good commercial movies, "Slap Shot" and "Fun With Dick and Jane," and though "Fellini's Casanova" was a difficult movie to appreciate, it seemed to represent a failure of choices, not of inspiration, which we've seen this year with Ingmar Bergman's "The Serpent's Egg" and Lina Wertmuller's "The End of the World in Our Usual Bed on a Night Full of Rain."

Q: Are you sure it's not you who's failing, rather than the movies?

A: Quite.

Q: I mean to say that critics have good days and bad, just like everyone else.

A: Whoever put that idea into your head?

Q: I have a friend who has taken a course in Film.

A: The only bad day a critic has is the day he can't write. Otherwise he's infallible.

Q: You're kidding?

A: Yes. What can you say about a season when the two best movies are films about which you have serious reservations? "An Unmarried Woman" is as good as we've had, but that's principally because of Jill Clayburgh. And I liked "Straight Time" very much, even though it's an extremely chilly movie about a loser of the second rank. It's a beautifully made movie, but it's not one that I can't wait to see again right away.

Q: Have there ever been such movies?

A: Of course. "That Obscure Object of Desire," "Annie Hall," "Handle With Care," "Nashville," "The Magic Flute." Let me put it this way: The only current American films I feel I might like to see again, at this very minute, are "Saturday Night Fever," which actually came out last year, because the music has that nice, soporific beat, and "The Betsy," to see Laurence Olivier exercising his talent in the way that a dancer might when practicing his leaps. Watching him is an exhilarating experience.

Q: You haven't mentioned "Coming Home."

A: No.

Q: Well?

A: Watching it is like watching the water drain out of a bathtub. It starts off full and at the end it's empty. The only things that remain are the memories of some extremely affecting scenes with the paraplegics at the beginning and the early scenes between Jane Fonda and Jon Voight. Considering what most of the other new films are like, "Coming Home" is not all that bad, but it should be better, which, I think, is the theme for the first quarter. Just about everything should have been better.

Q: Such as . . .

A: Paul Schrader's "Blue Collar," which makes a certain claim for our support because it attempts to deal seriously with the life and lot of the American blue-collar worker. It's also of some historical interest in the way it reflects—accurately, I think—the ultimate cynicism of so many Americans about whom it might be said by their bosses, "They never had it so good." The movie is aware that something important is missing from their lives, yet it trips over its own melodrama. The performances by Richard Pryor, Harvey Keitel and Yaphet Kotto are fine. Still, it should have been better.

• • •

Q: What about . . ?

A: . . . I know what you're going to say . . .

Q: Brian De Palma?

A: I knew you'd ask.

Q: He's crying all the way to the bank.

A: If he's crying, it must be because he's allergic to money. I understand he's doing very well critically as well as financially.

Q: But you have mixed feelings about "The Fury"?

A: I wouldn't say they were mixed, more like self-righteously disappointed. I liked him better when he was poor and, when measured against Hollywood's yardstick, he was a failure. I still remember most fondly "Greetings," "Hi, Mom" and "Sisters." "The Fury," with all of it nonsense about telepathy and its solemnly silly plot, is absurd without succeeding as Cinema of the Absurd.

Q: I understand that De Palma feels that people who worry about the plot simply aren't with it. Plots are old hat. Who worries about the plots of comic-strips?

A: I do. I often fret about them.

Q: Everything in "The Fury" is an excuse for his big set-pieces—the crazy car chase around Chicago, the telekinetic assassination at the fun house, and, finally, the two murders that conclude the movie.

A: Perhaps my point is that everything else really doesn't work as an excuse. Everything else really detracts from those big scenes, which De Palma and his special-effects people do very well. Those scenes would be truly breathtaking if the connectives made any sense, or any sense of nonsense. Technically his big scenes are superb, but as I watch them, I'm so aware of all the work that's gone into them—especially in that grand finale—that I find them less funny than exhausting. Which, I must say, is just the reverse of the reaction I have when Hitchcock pulls off a good one, as, for example, he did repeatedly throughout "The Birds." Hitchcock gives one a feeling of flying. "The Fury" makes me feel as if I were hitchhiking across New Jersey.

• • •

Q: Now for some quick, off-the-top-of-your-head opinions.

A: Shoot.

Q: "Casey's Shadow," the film about Walter Matthau, a small boy and a superb quarter-horse named Casey's Shadow?

A: A nice movie—one you want to feed sugar to.

Q: "Madame Rosa" with Simone Signoret?

A: You don't have to be Jewish etcetera etcetera . . .

Q: "A Little Night Music"?

A: Only for close friends and members of the families of those involved.

Q: "The Confessions of Winifred Wagner," the feature film made from five hours of German TV interviews with the 78-year-old daughter-in-law of Richard Wagner?

A: One of the few don't-miss movies so far this year. Actually, it's hardly a film. The critic in the Village Voice called it right when he described it as a "talking head" movie, since it's composed of a series of close-ups and medium close-ups of the old lady talking about her life, her long and close friendship with Hitler, her support of National Socialism, her almost complete indifference to the Holocaust. It's a really scary and fascinating experience.

Q: I take it you liked this film?
A: Yes.

Q: Should it have been better?
A: Of course. It should have been longer.

Q: Are you being difficult?
A: I certainly hope so. ■

1978 Ap 2, II:13:5

Through Violet's Eyes

PRETTY BABY, directed and produced by Louis Malle; screenplay by Polly Platt, based on a story by Miss Platt and Mr. Malle; director of photography, Sven Nykvist; supervising editor, Suzanne Baron; editor, Suzanne Fenn; music, Jerry Wexler; distributed by Paramount Pictures. Running time: 109 minutes. At the Coronet Theater, Third Avenue near 59th Street. This film has been rated R.

Violet .... Brooke Shields
Bellocq .... Keith Carradine
Hattie .... Susan Sarandon
Nell .... Frances Faye
Professor .... Antonio Fargas
Red Top .... Matthew Anton
Frieda .... Diana Scarwid
Josephine .... Barbara Steele
Flora .... Seret Scott
Gussie .... Cheryl Markowitz
Fanny .... Susan Manskey
Agnes .... Laura Zimmerman
Odette .... Miz Mary
Highpockets .... Gerrit Graham
Mama Mosebery .... Mae Mercer
Alfred Fuller .... Don Hood
Ola Mae .... Pat Perkins
Nonny .... Von Eric Perkins
Justine .... Sasha Holliday
Antonia .... Lisa Shames
Harry .... Henry Braden
Senator .... Philip H. Sizeler
Violet's First Customer .... Don K. Lutenbacher

By VINCENT CANBY

IN a high panoramic shot we look over the roofs of a city at night. The opening title card tells is it's Storyville, New Orleans, 1917. From the far distance we hear a steamboat's whistle, followed by a few notes on a blues trumpet. The mood is of impending loss, of the kind of bone-deep loneliness that is particular to the middle of the night.

There's a sudden cut to the rapt face of a little girl. Just off-screen there are moans that could be either of pain or of ecstasy. Violet, the child, watches with both terror and excitement as her mother gives birth. The mother screams. The midwife gives reassuring instructions, and downstairs the nightly parties go on.

•

The setting is Nell's place, one of the fancier brothels in the New Orleans tenderloin, and the bed might be the same one where Violet herself was born 12 years before, the daughter of Hattie, one of Nell's best "girls," and of a father no longer known. Like her new half brother, Violet is what used to be called a "trick baby."

In this fashion Louis Malle takes us inside the hermetic world of "Pretty Baby," an almost incredibly romantic, autumnally beautiful movie that looks at life in a Storyville whorehouse with the unsurprised curiosity and boredom of a child who's never known anything else. Mr. Malle, the French director ("The Lovers," "Murmur of the Heart" and "Lacombe, Lucien"), has made some controversial films in his time but none, I suspect, that is likely to upset convention quite as much as this one—and mostly for the wrong reasons.

Though the setting is a whorehouse, and the lens through which we see everything is Violet, who, in the course of the film, herself becomes one of Nell's chief attractions, "Pretty Baby" is neither about child prostitution nor is it pornographic.

The film, which opens today at the Coronet, is about the last days of Storyville, just before the New Orleans city fathers bowed to the reformers and closed down one of the most notorious redlight districts in the country. It is also a sad, essentially tender memoir about Violet's brief liaison and marriage with an obsessed photographer named Bellocq, a character based —but very loosely—on Ernest J. Bellocq, the physically misshapen, hydrocephallic photographer whose portraits of Storyville whores are now recognized as the work of a unique artist.

Mr. Malle and Polly Platt, with whom he collaborated on the screenplay, have largely avoided judgmental attitudes by looking out at the world through Violet's eyes. They've also softened the contours of what was probably very sordid history by making a film of dazzling physical beauty. Sven Nykvist's camera is as obsessed as Bellocq's with texture, light, shade, line, expression.

When one realizes that Keith Carradine's Bellocq is actually the center of the film, "Pretty Baby" becomes a parable about art and life, about the artist who makes the mistake of falling in love with his subject, a creature who, is, in effect, his own creation. Mr. Carradine gives a haunting and haunted performance, as someone sentenced by his obsession always to be observer and interpreter, never a full participant.

I've no idea whether or not Brooke Shields, the breathtakingly beautiful 12-year-old model who plays Violet, can act in any real sense, but Mr. Malle uses her brilliantly. As Gloria Swanson said of silent stars in "Sunset Boulevard," "We had faces then," and Miss Shields has a face that here transcends the need to act.

She is, in quick succession, willful and funny, sly and stupid. At one minute she's a child with her first doll. Next she is grotesque in full makeup as she repeats by rote lines meant to excite a customer—"Why, I can feel the steam inside me, right through my dress!"—or pathetic as she excitedly awaits the outcome of a whorehouse auction, the highest bidder to win her favors.

The consistent coolness of Mr. Malle's view prevents the movie from seeming to be exploitative. There is one key shot that, I think, defines this method, when, during the auction for Violet, the camera stays on the not quite impassive face of "the Professor" (Antonio Fargas), the black pianist who entertains Nell's drawing-room guests. As Mr. Fargas listens to the bids, we have, for just a fraction of a moment, a glimpse of what all this means in terms of life in the outside world, which is infinitely sad but far, far removed.

•

Both Mr. Fargas and Susan Sarandon, who plays Violet's mother, give fully realized performances but Frances Faye, who plays old Nell, the madam, is so bad that you can't believe it's not intentional. Has her dialogue been postsynchronized? It has that disconnected sound. Miss Faye seems properly tough, but it's a toughness of another era. Toward the end of the film, too, the narrative continuity seems to go astray. Have key scenes been cut to assure the film's Rating?

These, though, are niggling questions to ask of something that is in every other way the most imaginative, most intelligent and most original film of the year to date.

1978 Ap 5, C21:1

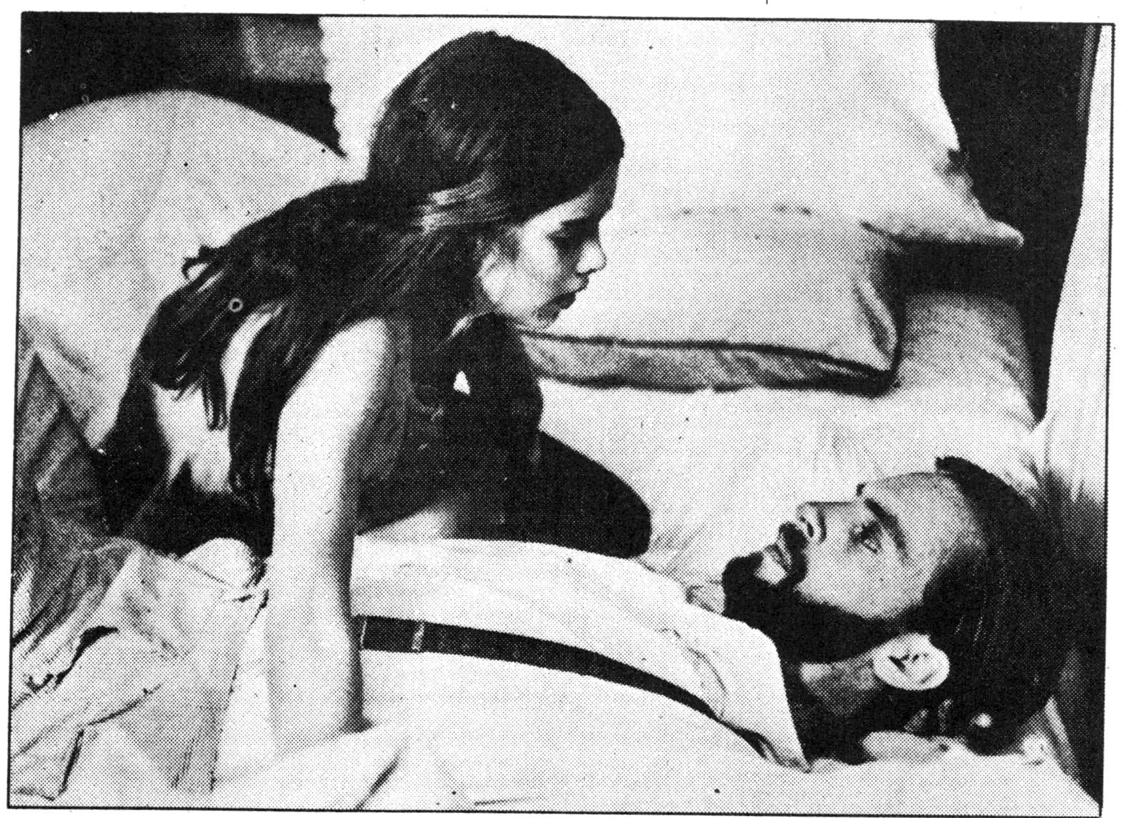

"PRETTY BABY"—Brooke Shields and Keith Carradine co-star in Louis Malle's film set in Storyville, the red light district of New Orleans, during the early 1900's.

A Poetic Parable

CALM PREVAILS OVER THE COUNTRY, directed by Peter Lilienthal; screenplay (German with English subtitles) by Antonio Skarmeta and Mr. Lilienthal; director of photography, Robby Muller; distributed by New York Films. Running time: 100 minutes. At the Film Forum, 15 Vandam Street. This film has not been rated.

Grandfather Parra .... Charles Vanel

By VINCENT CANBY

PETER LILIENTHAL'S "Calm Prevails Over the Country" is a German film made in Portugal about the gradual destruction of democracy in a South American country that resembles both Uruguay, where the German-born film maker lived for 20 years, and Chile. It's an intensely interesting film, very measured and clear at the beginning, full of the precisely observed details of daily life that in movies are the equivalent to life's small talk, and then, quite suddenly, a poetic parable of implications that extend beyond the political.

The film will be shown at the Film Forum tonight through Sunday at 7:45 and repeated there next week Thursday through Sunday at the same time. Though "Calm Prevails" is not especially difficult, it makes no concessions to popular tastes and is thus a practically perfect presentation for the Film Forum, the most consistently successful showcase for offbeat films in New York.

•

The film's central character is a remarkably resilient, intelligent old man, the owner of a small hotel in the capital city. This fellow, played with serene self-assurance by Charles Vanel, the veteran French actor who was 83 when the film was made three years ago, has lived long enough to have survived all sorts of political weather.

At first he observes with passing interest the first signs of the state's suppression of the opposition. It doesn't immediately touch him. Then he's aware of the arrest of the children and grandchildren of friends. Finally his own grandchildren disappear.

In the film's final sequence, there are no more able-bodied men left in the city. The old man makes some sandwiches, pays a young boy to take him to the city prison, where, after shouting a few vigorous denunciations of fascism to the guards, he enters the walls to rejoin his community.

•

It should not spoil the film to be told its shape. In fact, I think it can increase one's appreciation for the manner in which the director works, beginning with the humdrum and escalating to moments that have the spirit of pure fantasy.

Mr. Lilienthal's control of particular episodes sometimes is uncertain. An extended sequence about a jailbreak is total confusion in narrative terms. There's also a problem in that several of the younger men in the cast look so much alike that one can't always be sure who is supposed to be doing what or why.

Mr. Vanel, though, is superb. It's very moving to see this fine old star, whom I first remember in Clouzot's "Wages of Fear," lending the weight of his presence and his experience to such a venture.

1978 Ap 6, C18:4

Hunger and Mushrooms

THE LAST SURVIVOR, directed by Ruggero Deodato; screenplay by Tito Cardi, Gianfranco Clerici and Renzo Genta; a Giorgio Carlo Rossi Production; released by United Producers. At the Embassy 46th Street Theater, at Broadway and other theaters. Running time: 83 minutes. This film has been rated R.

Robert Harper ..... Massimo Foschi
Palen ..... Me-Me Lau
Rolf ..... Ivan Rassimov
Swan ..... Judy Rosly

By JANET MASLIN

BEWARE of action movies in which, only 15 minuts into the proceedings, somebody shouts "We're saved Rolf! I see the plane [ship] [campsite] [S.W.A.T. team] right over there!" You can bet your buttons they aren't safe at all, and that something unpleasant is in the wind. In "The Last Survivor," a small planeload of Italians, whose speech is dubbed unconvincingly into British, gets lost on an island inhabited by Stone Age holdovers. Of course, these natives are restless.

They're hungry, too. This viewer headed for the hills not long after she watched the locals, a ittle crude even by Stone Age standards, gnawing on a set of human arms and legs, which had presumably belonged to somebody else until only lately. "Scene of cannibalism photographed from real life," a subtitle said.

When last seen, the survivor of the title had lost his friends in a variety of messy ways, then wolfed down a mushroom that made him think trees could spin. Just before he grew dizzy and vomited green goo, the Stone Age natives had him surrounded. That left them about an hour of screen time to poke him with homemade implements and otherwise educate him in their Stone Age ways.

1978 Ap 6, C18:4

Ghost of Garcia Lorca

TO AN UNKNOWN GOD (A un Dios Desconocido), directed by Jaime Chavarri; screenplay (Spanish with English subtitles) by Elias Querejeta and Mr. Chavarri , based on a script by Francisco J. Lucio; produced by Mr. Querejeta; director of photography, Teo Escamilla; editor, Pablo G. Del Amo; music, Luis de Pablo. Running time: 95 minutes. At the New Directors/New Films seris at the Museum of Modern Art, 53d Street west of Fifth Avenue.

Jose ..... Hector Alterio
Miguel ..... Javier Elorriaga
Adela ..... Maria Rosa Salgado
Clara ..... Rosa Valenty
Soledad ..... Angela Molina
Soledad (grown up) ..... Margarita Mas
Mercedes ..... Mercedes San Pietro
Pedro ..... Jose Joaquin Boza
Ana ..... Mirta Miller
Julio ..... Jose Pagan
Jorge ..... Emilio Siegrist

By VINCENT CANBY

"TO AN UNKNOWN GOD" ("A un Dios Desconocido"), the second feature film by Jaime Chavarri, the Spanish director, is a handsome, densely packed, evocative movie that makes a lot of rather stern demands upon anyone who sees it. It's the sort of thing one should prepare for, like an uncut "Hamlet," a full-length "Die Meistersinger" or a "Blood Wedding" in Spanish.

The film, which will be shown at the Museum of Modern Art today at 8:30 P.M. and on Monday at 6 P.M., is one of three that today begins the annual New Directors/New Films series at the museum. The series is jointly presented by the museum's department of film and the Lincoln Center Film Society.

Like the recent films of Carlos Saura and Victor Erice, "To an Unknown God" recalls the legacy of nearly 40 years of the Franco dictatorship but it does this in terms that are so special, so private, that one attends the film as if it were a meeting of cabalists. The movie is full of secret signs and mysterious associations. Over it all hangs the ghost of Federico García Lorca, the Spanish poet and playwright who was murdered in 1936 by the Falangists who despised his homosexuality as much as his left-wing politics.

Though most of the film is the contemporary memoir of a middle-aged, homosexual magician named José (Hector Alterio), the film opens in Granada in 1936 when José as a small boy, was seduced by an older boy who was living in the elegant old house where García Lorca's murder, this opening secunfamiliar with the circumstances of García Lorca murder, this opening section makes no sense whatsoever. As it is, one never is exactly sure who José's young male lover is, or what his connection is to the famous guest, who is seen once in a long, shot, much as Christ is sometimes glimpsed in Biblical epics.

José appears to be a successful magician, at least in bookings, but his life is fastidiously lonely. Though his somewhat younger lover, Miguel (Javier Elorriaga), a worker on behalf of radical causes, is open-hearted and generous, José devotes himself to the memo-

Angela Molina and Emilio Siegrist in Jaime Chavarri's "To an Unknown God"

ry of his lost youth. At one point he returns to Granada for a reconciliation with a woman who, like José is obsessed by the memory of García Lorca as well as by the memory of the boy, now dead, whom they both loved.

For some peculiar reason, English subtitles, which adequately translate most of the film's Spanish dialogue, are denied us in two key sequences in which José as he's going to bed, plays a tape containing (I think) José himself speaking García Lorca's poetry. Perhaps Mr. Chavarri thinks it would be sacrilege to translate the poet's lines as mere subtitles. In any case we are denied key information and must make out as best we can by recognizing, on the tape, references to "Valt Vitmann" and the Spanish words meaning "sleep," "dream" and "death."

Because of its Spanish origin, "To an Unknown God" has astonished a number of European critics for its frank, unhysterical treatment of homosexuality, but the truth is that Mr. Chavarri's particular preoccupations result in a movie that seems as self-interested, even arrogant, as poor, lonely José. "To an Unknown God" is lovely to look at, highly cultivated and poised, and very, very difficult to get to know.

1978 Ap 7, C7:1

From Limb to Limbo

JANE IS JANE FOREVER (Jane Bleibt Jane), directed and written (German with English subtitles) by Walter Bockmayer and Rolf Buhrmann; director of photography, Peter Mertin; editor, Inge Gielow; music, David Bowie, Asha Putli, Mandingo and Syomu Yamahia; produced by Mr. Buhrmann for Enten Productions. Running time: 85 minutes. At the New Directors/New Films series at the Museum of Modern Art, 53d Street west of Fifth Avenue.

Johanna Konig ..... Johanna Konig
Eugen ..... Peter Chatel
Tarzan ..... Karl Blomer
Nurse ..... Brigitte Gonsior
Old Ladies Evelyn Hall, Hannelore Lubeck, Anita Riotte

A FAVORITE and rather tiresome assumption of a certain kind of sentimental comedy is that the only sane way to respond to the world is by being crazy. It is the small achievement of Walter Bockmayer and Rolf Buhrmann, who wrote and directed the new German film, "Jane Is Jane Forever" (Jane Bleibt Jane), that they can appreciate lunacy without mistaking it for a state of grace.

"Jane Is Jane Forever" is about a little old lady, Johanna (Johanna Konig), resident of a fairly luxurious home for the elderly, who firmly believes that she is Jane, the long-separated mate to Tarzan, who is pictured on her walls in the persons of Johnny Weissmuller, Gordon Scott and Lex Barker. Her deepest desire: to go back to Tarzan and to Africa, where, she knows, all her problems will vanish.

The film, an entry in the Museum of Modern Art's New Directors/New Films series, will be shown at the museum today at 11 P.M. and again Sunday at 8:30 P.M.

Johanna is something of a burden to the other women at the home. She sets out to re-create the African jungle in her tiny room, filling it with plants, outlawed by the house rules, and taking as her companion a South American parrot named Loretta. One day she contemplates buying a python, but thinks better of it as she watches it digesting a small white mouse.

The thing about Johanna that sets her apart is not her delusion but her awareness that it is a delusion, which is of no importance to her in view of the satisfactions of being crazy. Though Miss Konig, who really looks too young to be senile, has a tendency to play the character for charm, the movie itself is comparatively austere. It contemplates Johanna without tears as if accepting something as inevitable as death, the film's real subject.

"Jane Is Jane Forever" is a small, sharp movie, sometimes funny but more often decently understanding in the manner of someone who appreciates the privacy of another's terminal illness. Like the newspaper reporter (Peter Chatel) who befriends Johanna, and who accepts her fantasies without ridiculing her, the movie never patronizes its subject.

VINCENT CANBY

1978 Ap 7, C7:5

Creators at Work

NORTH STAR: MARK DI SUVERO, directed by Francois de Menil; written by Barbara Rose; photographed by Mr. de Menil; music by Philip Glass; edited by Paul Justman and Lana Jokel; produced by Mr. de Menil; Miss Rose and Parrot Productions Ltd. Running time: 54 minutes.

ROGER CORMAN: HOLLYWOOD'S WILD ANGEL, produced and directed by Christian Blackwood; narration written by Richard Koszarski; edited by Harvey Greenstein and Mr. Blackwood. Running time, 54 minutes.

At the Museum of Modern Arts New Directors/New Films series.

By JANET MASLIN

"IN THIS FILM, we are combining the myth of Romeo and Juliet with high-speed car action and a plea for international weapons control in our time," says a young director, hard at work on a 10-day wonder for Roger Corman. Mr. Corman is the man whose New World Pictures gave work to directors like Martin Scorsese and Francis Ford Coppola before anyone else would hire them; even now, after having distributed films by Ingmar Bergman and François Truffaut, he is still widely regarded as the king of the action quickie.

"Roger Corman: Hollywood's Wild Angel" chooses to examine Mr. Corman and his work obliquely, compiling laughably lurid film clips with brief revealing looks at some of Mr. Corman's protégés, who have been forced by New World's tight budgets and breakneck pacing to take a fairly cavalier attitude toward the esthetic possibilities of the cinema. As one of them puts it, "The toughest thing about directing is getting up in the morning."

•

Although Mr. Corman is briefly interviewed here his employees' recollections of his advice are a good deal more telling than anything he says himself. Jonathan Demme, who made films like "Caged Heat" for New World before directing "Handle With Care," explains that Mr. Corman likes to annotate each script he reads, scribbling things like "breast nudity possible here?"

Another Corman protégé remembers a tidbit that proved invaluable: Try not to stand up when you don't have to, Mr. Corman told him. And don't stop to congratulate your crew after each shot is completed. If chewing the fat takes a minute each time, and you knock off 30 shots in a day, you can save yourself all of half an hour that way.

Christian Blackwood, who directed this profile as part of the Museum of Modern Art's New Films/New Directors series, has assembled an amusing series of excerpts and trailers ("The Student Nurses—enter their course!"). He has also lined up interviews with some of Mr. Corman's best-known and most personable protégés, among them Mr. Demme, Paul Barthel, Allan Arkush, Joe Dante, David Carradine, Ron Howard, Peter Fonda and Mr. Scorsese.

Also on hand are a number of actors and actresses who aren't likely to work again anywhere, ever. Mr. Corman doesn't seem to care who his directors hire, as long as the performers can drive, scream, bleed, make horrible jokes and work for peanuts.

In view of its subject, and of Mr. Corman's oft-repeated emphasis on speed and economy, Mr. Blackwood's generally frisky film goes slacker than it should at times. And it does seem a shame that after Mr. Blackwood cites Mr. Corman's prescient qualities and paints him as a man with his hand on the pulse of America's youth, the film never grills this entrepreneur about the current zeitgeist. A film about a man so clearly ahead of his time ought to explore his notion of the mood of the moment.

•

The sculptor subject of "Mark di Suvero: North Star," a film by François de Menil that shares the same bill, should have been a good match for Mr. Corman: Both men are playful, economical and quite purposeful about what they do. But Mr. di Suvero's work, huge metal sculptures, however eloquent they may seem when photographed from various angles and accompanied by Philip Glass's pulsating electronic score, loses something in scope and grandeur when captured on the screen. And Mr. di Suvero's observations about his work tend to undermine rather than amplify.

Mr. di Suvero is clearly a man of enormous charm and vitality, but his conversation is every bit as vague as his work is streamlined. And Mr. de Menil's direction takes the sculptor's fuzziest observations at face value. "The artist has to reject whatever society is doing around him in order to become an artist," Mr. di Suvero says. And: "The United States is guilty of something like Chile—that's incredible."

"Do any of your sculptures make a political statement?" Mr. di Suvero is asked. He cites one called "Mother Peace," explaining that "if you really look carefully at it, it works in many different ways." Later, the art critic Barbara Rose asks, in an insinuatingly intimate, Rona Barrett-like tone, whether Mr. di Suvero is afraid he's crazy. "C'mon, I'm afraid I'm too sane," is his predictable reply.

•

Mr. di Suvero's works are seen in many different settings, from bleak, industrial-looking cities to the Tuileries. However, the question of what relationship a large, outdoor work of art ought to have to setting is sniffed at rather than addressed. A few French people are shown to have mixed opinions about a huge sculpture in a public garden, and one American art commissioner sadly but smugly notes the general public's inability to understand contemporary avant-garde art.

Footage of the 1975 opening of the Whitney Museum's di Suvero retrospective is much more revealing of what art loses in translation on its way to an audience, as well-dressed first-nighters view the show with an elitism fiercely incompatible with the work and all it stands for. The film's most piquant moment shows a woman reclining playfully on one of Mr. di Suvero's mobile pieces, drawling that it might be fun to have something just like this at the summer place in the Hamptons.

1978 Ap 7, C8:5

THE BAKER'S BREAD (Das Brot des Backers), directed by Erwin Keusch; screenplay (in German with English subtitles) by Mr. Keusch; photography, Dietrich Lohmann; editing, Lilo Kroger; music, Condor; produced in West Germany of Artus Film/Prokino/ZDF. Running time: 122 minutes. At the New Directors/New Films series at the Museum of Modert Art, 53d Street west of Fifth Avenue.

Werner .... Bernd Tauber
Georg Baum .... Gunter Lamprecht
Mrs Baum .... Maria Lucca
Gisela .... Silvia Reize
Margot .... Anita Lochner
Kurt .... Menfred Seipold
Rudi .... Gerhard Acktun
Georg .... Krystian Martinek
Peter .... Ronald Nitschke

By JANET MASLIN

"The Baker's Bread" is as small-scale and modest as the West German village in which its story takes place. At the film's beginning, a young man arrives in town to begin his apprenticeship with a local baker, whose durable, family-run business is being threatened by the prosperity of a nearby supermarket and the prospect of a new shopping center. From then on, we watch the baker and his assistants worry about automation and begin to question the economic system that has made their kind of craftsmanship obsolete. We also watch the young newcomer evolve into a family member of sorts, and then become the gruff, blustery, lovable boss's right-hand man.

Erwin Keusch, whose low-keyed but often compelling film is being shown as part of the Museum of Modern Art's New Films/New Directions series, occasionally jeopardizes the engaging plainness of his story to bring one character or another to the figurative podium, so that the obligatory speeches about the evils of modernization can be made. But for the most part the film proceeds as swiftly as a day in the bakery might go. Mr. Keusch's gift for being most communicative when his film seems to be saying the least is nothing to sneeze at, and his work is effective in eccentric, nicely unexpected ways.

•

Mr. Keusch is the son of a baker; if you didn't know that before seeing his film, you would surely surmise it from the loving attentiveness with which he sketches bakery life. This is an absolutely spellbinding movie for anyone who likes watching dough rise, and even those who prefer to be on the eating end of the baking process may enjoy learning a thing or two. Werner Bernd Tauber, the assistant, graduates during the course of the movie from simple kneading and sifting to inventing his own recipes. The camera doesn't dwell unnecessarily on his handiwork, but it follows his progress closely, as he takes ever-increasing pride in his work.

Another baker, Kurt (Manfred Siepold), is meanwhile seen in the background, knotting pretzels in a split-second and performing other similarly magical feats. Mr. Siepold is a handsome fellow and a good actor, but if he doesn't actually bake for a living, it's a shame.

•

When he isn't working or dragging himself out of bed hours before dawn, young Werner is pitching woo, but this aspect of his hero's life leaves Mr. Keusch strangely ill-at-ease. One affair, with a rich girl Werner meets when he delivers her birthday cake, seems present in the film solely to make a point about the class system, and the portion of the story that involves her has the feeling of an unexpected and unwelcome lecture. When Werner falls in love for real, the baking and spooning episodes are so clumsily integrated that the romance once again seems tacked-on.

In another episode, a most disturbing one, Werner is pounced upon by a very attractive older woman who works in the shop. After they spend one night together, he becomes unaccountably hurtful and rude; she, even more unaccountably, decides life without Werner just isn't worth living. At times like this, Mr. Keusch's presentation of his young hero as a man of few words becomes problematic, and his trick of cutting away from tender moments almost before they happen makes his story hard to follow.

"The Baker's Bread" is being billed as a West German comedy, but viewers expecting belly laughs would be well advised to try to recall the last West German film they deemed even remotely amusing. In this case, lets just say that nobody dies, all ends reasonably well and—here's the funny part—the bakery crew one day confounds the manager of the supermarket by buying up all his breakfast rolls.

1978 Ap 8, 16:1

MOTHER AND DAUGHTER (Maternale); directed by Giovanna Gagliardo; screenplay (Italian with English subtitles) by Giovanna Gagliardo; photography, Giuseppe Lanci; music, Stelvio Cipriani; editing, Roberto Perpigani; produced by La Rai-Radiotelevision Italianna, Cooperative A.A.T.A., and Pantheon I Film. Running time: 90 minutes. At the New Directors/New Films series at the Museum of Modern Art, 53d Street west of Fifth Avenue.

The Mother .... Carla Gravina
Aunt Lucia .... Anna Maria Gherardi
The Father .... Marino Mase
Teresa, the Maid .... Francesca Muzio
Carla, the Daughter .... Benedetta Fantoli
Francesco, the Son .... Francesco Fantoli
The German Officer .... Lajos Balaszovits
The Professor .... Umberto Silva

As "Mother and Daughter" begins, a wealthy Italian family is seen eating breakfast in an outdoor setting, smoothing exquisite-looking honey over perfect toast. The villa is spectacular, and the sunlight is dazzling; the maid tending to everyone's tiniest need is young and pretty, and she seems to enjoy being a maid. In the garden, flowers bloom and birds chirp, and at table, father complains jovially that mother never remembers to serve grapes. Just then, the teen-age son reaches over and plucks a bunch of grapes out of a bowl, tossing them playfully at his sister. So there isn't any trouble in paradise, after all.

"Hah!" director Giovanna Gagliardo means to say. All this wonderfulness is merely a sham. The beautiful mother (Carla Gravina), who wears pearls to chop carrots in her elegant kitchen, has absolutely nothing of consequence to do. So she pads about the palazzo in a near-stupor, occasionally stopping to prepare an elaborate meal.

Though the mother expresses little, she is actually engaged in an age-old struggle with her young daughter, whom the mother would like to keep dependent forever. We know this because the daughter is symbolically crippled, walking gingerly with a cane that has a silver handle.

The film, which is part of the New Directors-New Films series at the Museum of Modern Art, more or less takes place on one day. But the daughter is sometimes crippled and sometimes not, sometimes an adolescent and sometimes a child; figments of the mother's memory or imagination wander in at will.

"Mother and Daughter" never lets a scene go by quietly when an intrusive blast of directorial technique will do, and so it becomes impossible for the viewer to care a fig about either the sleepwalking mother or her half-imaginary child. Miss Gagliardo's insights into the mother-daughter struggle are so slight, and her direction so overbearing, that the results suggest what might happen if an infantry unit were called in to kill a bat.

As a director, Miss Gagliardo is distressingly insensitive to the relationship between style and purpose. As an interior director, however, she is formidable. The film is gorgeously photographed, from sunny beginning to profoundly uneventful ending, and everything in the villa is bright and gleaming and just-so. One need only imagine that the setting is Beverly Hills rather than Italy, and that instead of listlessly chopping vegetables the mother is giving a few passionless flicks to her Cuisinart, to imagine just how ineffectual this numbingly glamorous parable really is. JANET MASLIN

1978 Ap 8, 18:1

BAROCCO, directed by Andre Techine; screenplay (French with English subtitles) by Mr. Techine and Marylin Goldin; produced by Andre Genoves; executive producer, Alain Sarde; director of photography, Bruno Nyutten; music, Philippe Sarde; editor, Claudine Merlin; A Films La Boetie-Sarah Films production. Running time: 102 minutes. At the New Directors/New Films series at the Museum of Modern Art, 53d Street west of Fifth Avenue.

Laure .... Isabelle Adiani
Samson .... Gerard Depardieu
Nelly .... Marie-France Pisier
Walt .... Jean-Claude Briarly
Jules .... Claude Brasseur
Gauthier .... Julien Guiomar
Antoinette .... Helene Surgere

By VINCENT CANBY

Behind the opening credits of "Barocco," André Téchiné's second feature to be shown in New York (his first was "French Provincial"), we see a series of distorted close-ups of such exotic fauna as crocodiles, giant snakes and horned lizards so ancient they might have witnessed creation—images designed to make the flesh crawl with primal fears.

It's something of a disappointment, then, that when the film begins, we are in a neon-bright, busy, commercial European city. It's actually Amsterdam, though

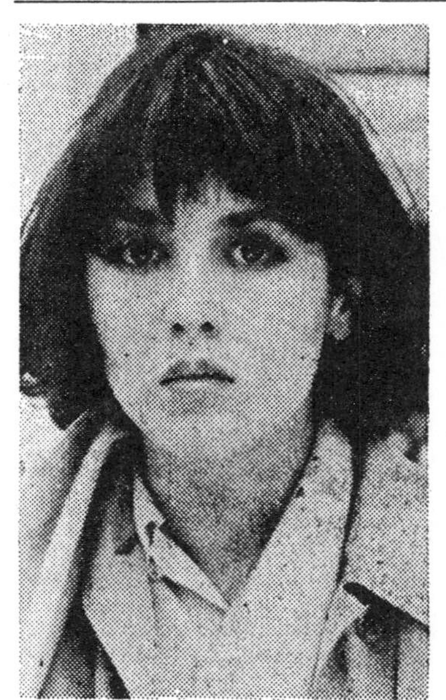

Isabelle Adjani in "Barocco"
A tale of murder and blackmail.

the film never specifically says so, which is one of the smaller affectations of this would-be thriller that cares less about the fundamental mechanics of murder, blackmail and physical intimidation than it does about such weighty subjects as redemption and resurrection.

"Barocco" will be shown at the Museum of Modern Art tonight at 11 in the annual New Directors/New Films series, and again tomorrow evening at 6.

•

Mr. Téchiné, who was born in 1943, belongs to a second generation of French film critics associated with 'Cahiers du Cinema who followed François Truffaut, Claude Chabrol and others from criticism into film-making. On the basis of both "French Provincial," which was about nothing less than the rise and fall of the French bourgeoisie, and now "Barocco," Mr. Téchiné remains more of a theorist than an artist.

His films have a way of starting off very well and then slowly congealing into stiff, intellectualized attitudes that have less to do with art than with its interpretation. Only Mr. Chabrol, at the top of his form, and Wim Wenders, in his recent "The American Friend," successfully manage to fuse the two disciplines.

"Barocco" means to be baroque, but it's about as baroque as a pedant's laundry list. It's a schematic tale of murder and blackmail during a municipal election. Its focal point is a nice dumb-lug of a boxer, played by Gérard Depardieu, who is paid a handsome fee to say he had a homosexual affair with one of the candidates, and the boxer's girl, played by Isabelle Adjani, who originally persuaded the boxer to take the bribe so that they could flee to more exotic climates.

•

Something goes wrong, however, and the boxer is murdered and Miss Adjani finds herself falling in love with the hood who murdered her lover. This is easy to understand. The hood is also played by Mr. Dépardieu, though "Barócco" would have us believe that the girl's love redeems the murderer and, in effect, resurrects him. Nonsense. The miracle is in the casting.

"Barocco" is a very classy looking movie, with lots of fancy camerawork in lots of fancy, ultramodern settings. In addition to Mr. Dépardieu and Miss Adjani, the cast includes such superior performers as Marie-France Pisier, who has some funny moments as a hooker, Jean-Claude Briarly, and Claude Brasseur. They are most attractive, lively people, but their material is dead.

1978 Ap 8, 18:1

RABBIT TEST, directed by Joan Rivers; written by Miss Rivers and Jay Redack; director of photography, Lucien Ballard; edited by Stanford C. Allen; music by Mike Post and Pete Carpenter; produced by Edgar Rosenberg; a Laugh or Die production in association with Mel Simon Productions Inc.; released by Avco Embassy Pictures. At Loews State I, Broadway and 45th Street, and Loews Orpheum, 86th Street and Third Avenue. Running time: 84 minutes. This film has been rated PG.

Lionel .... Billy Crystal
Segoynia .... Joan Prather
Danny .... Alex Rocco
Mrs. Carpenter .... Doris Roberts
Interviewer .... Margaret Adachi
Sobbing Sailor .... Adam Anderson
African Chief .... John Andersonjo
Second Newscaster .... Edward Ansara

As Woody Allen's career demonstrates, there's no good reason why a stand-up comic with a nervous, staccato delivery can't adapt that style to fit the demands of a feature-length film, provided that the comedy stems from a consistent, genuinely funny point of view. Joan Rivers's nightclub routines abound with the same kind of self-deprecation and misanthropy in which Mr. Allen used to specialize, and her premise for "Rabbit Test"—what would happen if a man became pregnant?—sounds like it might be good for an hour-and-a-half's worth of bunny fluff.

But like entirely too many comics before her, Miss Rivers has turned to directing without paying much heed to whether a whole movie constructed from one-liners is worth even the sum of its parts. In her case, it's not—and the one-liners weren't all that sparkling to begin with.

When it winds up on television, which is where a movie this visually crude belonged in the first place, "Rabbit Test" may improve slightly: Constant commercial interruptions may help distract attention from the movie's continuity problems, which are severe. And the coarseness of its comedy may not seem so insufferable to an audience willing to sit still for "Laverne and Shirley."

Miss Rivers's jokes mostly have to do with racial stereotypes and the essential revoltingness of pregnancy, but a few of them are funny just the same. However, as a director, Miss Rivers is forever sandbagging her own scenes, throwing away a good chuckle in a sequence that desperately needs a punch line, or wasting something fairly subtle right after a broad, dopey joke about a urine sample. Whenever one does laugh, it's in spite of the movie, rather than because of it.

At mechanically regular intervals, a variety of veteran performers wander by for wasted cameos—the cast includes George Gobel, Imogene Coca, Richard Deacon, Paul Lynde, Sheree North, Tom Poston and a lot of other players who are almost always funnier than they are here. Too many of them mimic Miss Rivers's breathless delivery, and in some cases—like Alex Rocco's—the dialogue is so speedy it becomes almost inaudible.

As for the world's first pregnant man, played by Billy Crystal, his predicament turns out to be a lot less curious than it sounds. Miss Rivers makes almost nothing of the role-reversal possibilities her premise suggests, and Mr. Crystal manages to convey neither astonishment nor acceptance of the impossible. He just becomes pregnant and has a baby, and that's the end of that. It's a lot easier to entertain the notion of a pregnant man than it is to understand why anyone would choose to end an alleged comedy with such a lead balloon.

•

"Rabbit Test," which has been rated PG ("Parental Guidance Suggested"), contains a number of bathroom jokes, mostly of an infantile nature.

JANET MASLIN

1978 Ap 9, 53:1

Malle's 'Pretty Baby'

VINCENT CANBY

Because the popular cinema has profited so long and so well from its own, denatured kind of romanticism, as represented by everything from Joan Crawford's early shopgirl films and Johnny Weissmuller's Tarzan adventures to something as recently lachrymose as "Love Story," it's not

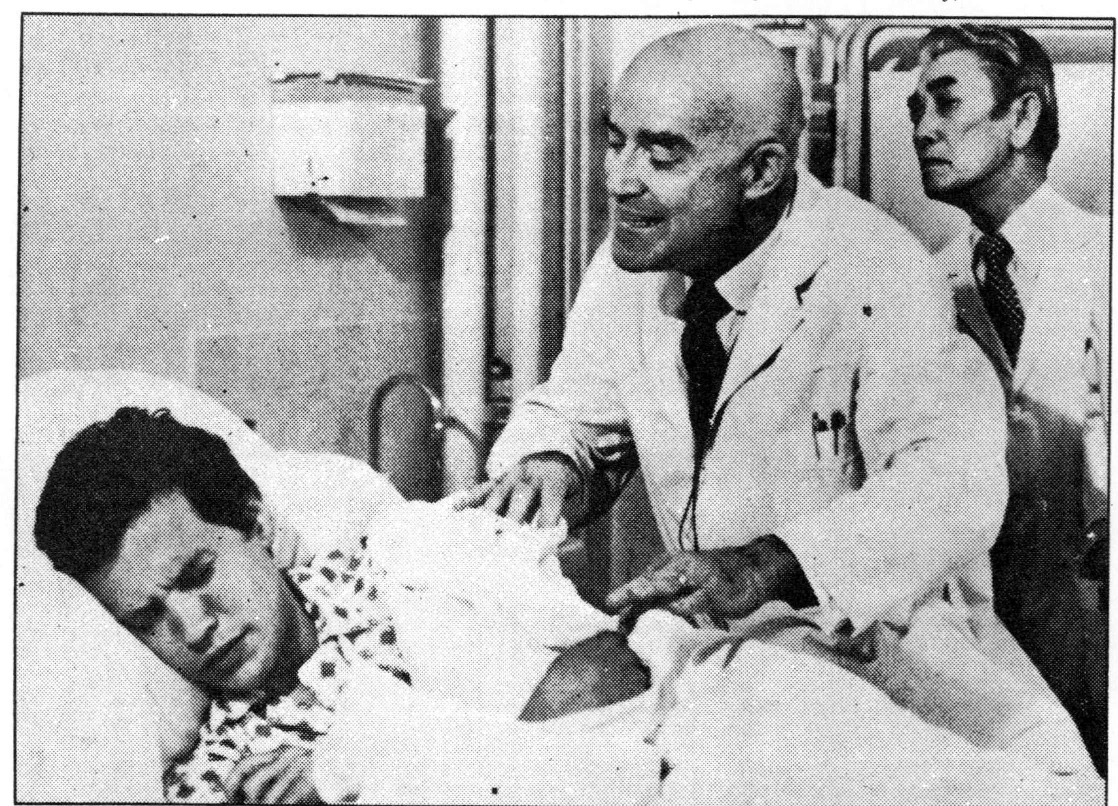

"RABBIT TEST"—Keene Curtis leads a team of doctors examining Billy Crystal as the world's first pregnant man.

always easy to identify as romantic the perversities that keep reappearing in the films of Louis Malle. The French director makes no attempt to disguise a style that is visually dazzling. It's simply that his subjects are bent from conventional shape, most dramatically in his new, splendid, perhaps most romantic film, "Pretty Baby," which is about a 12-year-old prostitute in the New Orleans tenderloin of 1917. Romantic? Thoroughly, but it's also haunting and sad and uninhibited and wise.

Romantic is not often a nice thing to call a movie. It's a put-down. It usually means a silly, optimistic, out-of-touch movie that glides over the true consequences of reality for the purpose of providing some little escape for us wretched folk, who must watch the stars above from the mud below. Lost are the associations to the romanticism of the 18th and 19th centuries, which was a reaction to the pieties of reason and rationalism. The usual motion-picture romanticism isn't as much a reaction to reason as it is a total ignorance of it. Instead of liberating the senses, it anesthetizes them.

More than any other filmmaker today, Mr. Malle has worked to redirect romanticism in movies, to define it as a way of looking at the world that doesn't necessarily deny reality but transcends it. The romanticism in Mr. Malle's movies may afford escape, but, more importantly, it forces us to reexamine all sorts of popular attitudes. In doing this, his films quite often have seemed to be shocking, none more so (at least, in its day) than "The Lovers," which, in the early 60's, was shown in almost as many American courtrooms as theaters.

"The Lovers," which made Jeanne Moreau an international star, seems awfully tame to us now. It's also about as romantic a tale of the liberating effects of sexual congress as anyone has concocted since D. H. Lawrence told us about Lady Chatterley's adventures. Yet, its romanticism was so charged by the explicit details of the love scenes that the film's romantic nature was mostly overlooked by the people who saw it. Audiences weren't as interested in the effects of love as they were in who did what to whom and how. So were local censor boards, and, as a result, "The Lovers" is remembered less often as the hugely romantic movie it is than as one of the early films that fought the good fight and made possible the almost total freedom of the screen in the 70's.

Mr. Malle is not, I suspect, someone who goes around looking for good causes to defend, but his sensibility is such that he refuses to accept as correct manners and morals that have become convention. Just because there are a lot of persuasive physiological and psychological arguments to be made against incest—I feel he might have said—doesn't necessarily mean that *all incest* must be evil, and so he set about to make the extremely cheerful romantic comedy "La Souffle au Coeur" ("Murmur of the Heart"), which is about nothing more or less than a teen-age boy who scores with his mother.

Does the boy commit suicide? Does mom rush off to a convent or, at least, seek out the advice of a family-guidance counselor? Of course not. In Mr. Malle's romantic view, each goes his separate way, somewhat wiser and more secure for the experience. I don't think that anyone seeing "La Souffle au Coeur" could interpret it as propaganda on behalf of incest. In its high-spirited fashion, though, it defuses our fears of the thought of it. By being rational about a taboo subject, Mr. Malle becomes a romantic.

• • •

An argument can be made, I think, that he was even being romantic in the feature-length documentary he made several years ago about the lives of the workers in a Citroen automobile assembly plant. Like all Malle films, "Humain, Trop Humain" is stunning to look at. It is almost too beautiful, as if the beauty were an editorial comment. Yet, the film is surprisingly unconventional. It dares question the dearly held, liberal idea that mass production's assembly-line procedures would turn workers into robots. The film goes beyond suggesting that the industrial revolution, in the 20th century, has created a new kind of middle class (about which the director might have some not-so-flattering things to say) to make us see the ways in which factory routine may well provide a new kind of emotional/spiritual continuity in lives in which religion is no longer such a stabilizing factor. "Humain, Trop Humain" certainly does not say this so bluntly, but the movie is so free of the usual cant that it prods us into seeking new conclusions, into making romantic leaps of mind.

Sometimes the leaps may be too great—we land nowhere, as is the case with his 1975 surreal comedy, "Black Moon," another staggeringly beautiful movie (photographed by Sven Nykvist, who also did "Pretty Baby") which is so private as to be unintelligible to the rest of us. Only a romantic of immense self-confidence would attempt what Mr. Malle does in "Black Moon"—to make his own version of "Alice in Wonderland." His Wonderland is a nightmare world where there's a deadly war being fought between men and women, where animals talk, where grass groans when stepped on, and where, unfortunately for us, the sense to be made of nonsense is not especially fun.

"Lacombe, Lucien" (1974), one of the finest Malle films, does not immediately seem to testify to the Malle romanticism. The story, about a French farm boy who more or less drifts into collaboration with the Nazis just as the war is ending, is basically social history, though the Malle approach is almost serenely poetic. The romanticism is there—in the way the landscapes are seen, in the delicacy with which the director treats his none-too-bright hero, and especially in the curious relationship that grows up between the young neo-Nazi and a pretty Jewish refugee, a relationship climaxed in the most unabashedly lyric of love scenes just before the boy faces his sad but not entirely unreasonable fate.

Of all of Mr. Malle's films, "Pretty Baby" is likely to cause the most controversy and the most self-righteous outrage, not only because it resolutely refuses to moralize but also because the overall mood of this whorehouse film is so tender. The director and Polly Platt, who collaborated with him on the screenplay, have had the nerve to make a movie that displays not only prostitution but especially a prepubescent prostitute at a time when the exploitation of children in commercial pornography is under intense public scrutiny.

"Pretty Baby" is not *about* child prostitution, and it certainly does not promote it, though it will have tough going answering those critics who think that by not making New Orleans whoredom, circa 1917, look more squalid, sleazy and disease-ridden, the film is, by default, one of the last, truly unspeakable social ills, as well as a totally inaccurate picture of history. I've no doubt that the movie will delight a lot of Humbert Humberts among us, though I don't know that it will create any new ones. However, these are questions for the social critic. Art has no obligations to historical accuracy, if there ever is any such thing.

"Pretty Baby" is a lyrically romantic memoir of a young photographer named Bellocq, whose obsession is photographing the whores in the fancy houses of New Orleans red-light district, Storyville, just before the district was closed down. Though Bellocq is based on a real character, E. J. Bellocq, in life a misshapen man who suffered from hydrocephalus, he is played in the movie by handsome Keith Carradine as the quintessential artist. In "Pretty Baby," Bellocq makes the mistake of falling in love with his subject who, because she is his subject, is someone of his own creation. That she is a child simply extends the lost nature of his love—she is emotionally out of his reach. In effect, she doesn't exist.

Because "Pretty Baby" shows us the way that life at Madame Nell's looks to 12-year-old Violet (Brooke Shields), it is never judgmental. It is the only life that Violet, who was born there, has ever known. Nights are lively, but mornings and afternoons tend to be boring because everybody is sleeping off the night before or busy sorting linen, cleaning floors, cooking and making preparations for the new night's activities. When the time comes to join the profession, Violet agrees enthusiastically. It's her way of growing up.

Though the movie is told from Violet's point of view, it is less about her than it is about Bellocq and his art, and about the tragic mistake of confusing life with art. I use the word tragic very loosely since the film is not really tragic at all. It is sad, autumnal, inevitable. Bellocq's loss of Violet (through the happiest of circumstances, if one is worried about her) is the only way the movie could end.

Bellocq, marvelously well played by Mr. Carradine, who is very toned-down from the actor we've seen in "Nashville," "Welcome to L.A." and his other recent films, is the most interesting, most convincing portrait-of-an-artist we've had in films since Alec Guinness's Gulley Jimson in "The Horse's Mouth." This isn't to say that the artist is totally revealed or explained—he isn't—only that we glimpse something of what drives him and something of the fleeting satisfaction of his art.

•

One of the film's most moving moments: Bellocq is busy in the backyard of Madame Nell's preparing to make some portraits of Violet's mother, Hattie (Susan Sarandon). Hattie lounges in a large chair, wearing a white gown, her hair hanging in loose curls, the sun backlighting the foliage around her. Says Bellocq with excitement as he adjusts her pose, "You are very beautiful and . . ," (he returns to his camera) ". . . I am very happy right now." It's the measure of the film's achievement that we believe the artist in Bellocq even though we may not understand him.

With "Pretty Baby," Louis Malle gives to the popular cinema his most sustained vision of romanticism—poetic, perverse, mysterious and liberating. It makes most of the other films we've seen this year look as drab and unimaginative as a series of tax returns. ■

1978 Ap 9, II:17:1

RUNNING FENCE, a documentary film by David Maysles, Charlotte Zwerin and Albert Maysles; camera, Robert Elfstrom, Donald Lenzer, Stephen Lighthill and Richard Pearce; music arranged and conducted by Jim Dickinson; distributed by Maysles Films, Inc. At the Whitney Museum of American Art, Madison Avenue and 75th Street. Running time: 58 minutes.

By JANET MASLIN

As befits a documentary about a work of conceptual art, "Running Fence" has as much to do with the reception that greeted Christo's construction of a 22-mile fence as it does with the fence itself. Early footage of community meetings in northern California's Marin and Sonoma Counties, where the fence was temporarily erected, indicates opinion in the area was sharply divided, and tempers ran high.

One woman feared that allowing Christo to build the fence—which he planned to remove two weeks later—would open the region up to "carnivals, rock concerts, motorcycle races, whatever." One man was heard to mutter, "I bet he can't even paint a picture—he's an idiot."

•

A friendly looking older woman compared the project to a well-cooked meal: "Sometimes I go to a lot of work to prepare a masterpiece, and what happens? It gets eaten up." Later, in a local cafe, one waitress explained that the completed fence wasn't "pretty in the sense of pretty, but it looks different, and it's kinda nifty."

Directed by Albert Maysles, David Maysles and Charlotte Zwerin, the film records the most intriguing reaction of all, that of a herd of sheep seen running beside the fence on a silent, misty morning. The sheep dash towards the barrier so impetuously that they seem about to collide with it; watching them, one can't help wondering what they make of this unexpected obstruction on familiar terrain.

The fence is extravagantly lovely, standing 18 feet high and made of a gleaming white fabric that ripples in the wind, but do sheep really care about such considerations? Who can say? In any case, these particular sheep finally find the opening that has been left for them and blithely pass through, as a rancher looks on with a wonderfully knowing expression.

There is a great deal of shouting and arguing in "Running Fence," but the hubbub is punctuated by wordless interludes like this one, brief sequences that suggest both the large issues and the tiny ones suggested by Christo's undertaking. Very deliberately, the film never explains either Christo or his intentions. But it demonstrates, wordlessly and at times almost magically, that what he hoped to accomplish was very like what he attained.

Christo's Running Fence project, shown here in its planning, construction and completed stages, is about as ideal a subject as any documentary film maker could hope to find.

•

Every participant in the process seems keenly aware of and vastly amused by his or her own role, and the camera becomes a welcome, openly acknowledged witness. The particular artfulness of the Haysles brothers and Miss Zwerin lies in their having taken the film beyond the golden opportunity Christo and his fence provided, and into the realm of keen, unerringly even-handed acuity. "Running Fence" presents its material clearly and impartially, yet it establishes and sustains a distinct point of view. The directors' influence is palpable, yet never meddlesome.

"Running Fence," which is being shown at the Whitney Museum, is 58 minutes long—an ideal length, but a commercially unwieldy one, unless the film later turns up on television or on a double bill. In any case, for all the books and posters Christo's exhilarating and audacious project will spawn, this is the next best thing to having been there.

1978 Ap 11, 44:4

Stockholm Saga

THE BUS, directed by Bay Okan; screenplay (Turkish with English subtitles) by Mr. Okan; director of photography, Gunash Karabuda; editors, Mr. Okan and Jean-Louis Misar; music, Omar Zultu, Pierre Favre and Leon Francioli; produced by Helios Films. Running time: 87 minutes. At the New Directors/New Films series at the Museum of Modern Art, 53d Street west of Fifth Avenue.

First man on bus .... Bay Okan
The homosexual .... Bjorn Gedda
Second man on bus .... Tuncel Kurtiz
Third man on bus .... Aras Oren
Fourth man on bus .... Nuri Sezer
Speaker .... Leif Ahrle
The driver .... Ogur Arlas
Fifth man on bus .... Hasan Gul
Sixth man on bus .... Sumer Isgor
Seventh man on bus .... Unal Nurkan
Eighth man on bus .... Nadir Sutemen
Ninth man on bus .... Yuksel Topcugurler
Playgirl .... Tissou Bjorkman
Playboy .... Pontus Platin

By VINCENT CANBY

"THE BUS," a Turkish-Swiss coproduction filmed mostly in Sweden, is as sincere as a public-service ad on behalf of clean air but somewhat less engrossing. The film, which was written, directed and produced by Bay Okan, a leading Turkish actor who also stars in it, will be shown in the New Directors/New Films series at the Museum of Modern Art today at 6 P.M. and again on Friday at 9:30 P.M.

"The Bus" is about a group of Turkish workers who are swindled by a compatriot who smuggles them into Sweden, takes their money and then leaves them sitting in their bus in the middle of Stockholm.

For three days they remain in the bus, the curtains drawn, suspecting the worst. At night they sneak out to go to a nearby lavatory, forage for food and explore the cruel city.

One fellow is picked up by a homosexual and goes mad, as if that were the natural order of events. All are hungry and not one of them is more articulate than a Labrador retriever. Though it's a sad story, Mr. Okan never makes it seem especially moving, maybe because his pretentions as a film artist get in his way.

•

He has a fondness for starting scenes by having the image swim into focus, as if someone were awakening with a hangover. The camera is fascinated by the usual oddities and ugliness of urban living and by horizontal panshots, which make you feel as if your eyeballs had come loose. Mr. Okan himself plays the immigrant worker who goes to spectacular pieces. The only other easily indentifiable role, that of the swindling bus driver, a fellow who in turn is swindled himself, is played by Ogur Arlas. The performances are not great.

The film is meant, I suspect, to be are so dense, so naïve and so faceless tion of the innocent, but the workers are so dense, so naïve and so faceless that it seems more to be an indictment of native ignorance.

1978 Ap 12, C19:4

Fading Fiefdom

TORRE BELA, directed by Thomas Harlan; in Portuguese with English subtitles; photography, Russell Parker; editors, Roberto Perpignani, Claudio Cutry and Giorgio De Vincenzo; produced by Luisa Orioli, Alexandre Duly for S.C.I. (Cinematografica Italiana, Rome)/New Times United Film Workers (Lisbon). At the Museum of Modern Art, 11 West 53d Street, New Directors/New Films Series. Running time: 115 minutes.

By JANET MASLIN

THE DUKE who appears at the beginning of "Torre Bela" may not be the nicest guy in town, but he's the most interesting interviewee. Casting his eyes shiftily, choosing his words carefully and then stammering, the Duke talks about his methods for managing his huge estate in Portugal; the estate employs only a handful of people year-round and hires extra workers as they are needed.

The Duke is photographed in black and white, made to appear even sicklier and more unattractive than he probably is, and Thomas Harlan, the director, occasionally lets the image fade to black while the Duke is talking, to emphasize a particularly improbable remark. For instance, when the Duke explains patiently that "there's not a problem, there's plenty of work around here," the camera simply closes its eye.

•

As it turns out, the local peasants are sick and tired of the Duke's rather limited outlook. The rest of "Torre Bela" is about their ousting him from his fiefdom and beginning to till his land communally.

Although Mr. Harlan's film, which is part of the New FilmsNew Directors series at the Museum of Modern Art, is essentially a documentary, it sometimes has the ring of ungainly melodrama. The camera's place in the proceedings is never clearly established, but the presence of a film crew has an evident effect on the peasants, as they conduct a great number of chaotic meetings and rallies. A few people's conversation begins to sound like awkward expository dialogue, along the lines of "Oh, yes, 1974—that was the year Uncle Luis got run over by a tractor."

Even worse, certain key peasants begin to realize that the camera, which swivels about to capture speeches at group meetings, will naturally gravitate toward whoever shouts the loudest. This inevitably leads both to poorly organized meetings and a lot of noise.

•

"Torre Bela" devotes too much time to shapeless squabbling, but it includes three memorable episodes, the first one the interview with the Duke. Another shows the peasants, after having commandeered the Duke's villa, opening every drawer and examining his personal artifacts; some behave playfully, others seem deeply embarrassed.

Another sequence captures an argument between an irate farmer and the leader of the newly formed cooperative, a dispute about a hoe. The group bought the hoe from this farmer, paying him a fair price of 100 escudos; now it belongs not just to him, but to everyone. That's all well and good with the farmer, but he still doesn't understand why he doesn't have a hoe any more.

1978 Ap 12, C22:5

Life on the Couch

THE MEDUSA TOUCH, directed by Jack Gold; screenplay by John Briley, based on the novel by Peter Van Greenaway; produced by Anne V. Coates and Mr. Gold; executive producer, Arnon Milchan; music, Michael J. Lewis; director of photography, Arthur Ibbetson; editor, Ian Crafford; distributed by Warner Brothers. Running time: 110 minutes. At the Loews State 2 Theater, Broadway at 45th Street, and other theaters. This film has been rated PG.

Morlar .... Richard Burton
Brunel .... Lino Ventura
Zonfeld .... Lee Remick
Asst. Commissioner .... Harry Andrews
Barrister .... Alan Badel
Patricia .... Marie-Christine Barrault
Parrish .... Jeremy Brett
Fortune teller .... Michael Hordern
Dr. Johnson .... Gordon Jackson
Publisher .... Derek Jacobi
Pennington .... Robert Lang

"THE MEDUSA TOUCH," the English suspense melodrama that opens today at the Loews State 2 and other theaters, is about a man who goes to see a psychiatrist not because he thinks the world is too much for him, but because he thinks he's too much for the world. The fellow, who's named Morlar and is played gloomily by Richard Burton, possesses telekinetic powers to make those of the characters in "The Fury" look frail indeed. On the merest whim he can, by simply willing it, cause a 747 to crash, ruin a moon-landing and shake a thousand-year-old Gothic cathedral to its cornerstones.

The movie was directed by Jack Gold from a screenplay by John Briley and it's fuzzy on a number of key issues that possibly could have made it fun, had they been sharper. Morlar is neither an evil character nor is he pathetic in the manner of someone who has a terminal illness. We see him as if he had some sort of antisocial disease, which, coupled with his bad temper, makes him unpleasant to have around.

•

Lino Ventura, the veteran French star, plays the detective called in to investigate a near-fatal attack on Morlar, and Lee Remick plays the psychiatrist who relates much of Morlar's life, which we see in flashbacks.

Mr. Gold, who directed "The Bofors Gun" some years ago, displays a gift for comedy in some of the sequences, especially when we see how Morlar, as a 10-year-old, got rid of his mum and dad while picnicking on the white cliffs of Dover, but there's not a single really scary shock-effect in the entire film. Among the good actors who assist Mr. Burton, Mr. Ventura and Miss Remick, are Harry Andrews, Michael Hordern and Marie-Christine Barrault ("Cousin, Cousine"). A job is a job.

•

"The Medusa Touch," which has been rated PG ("Parental Guidance Suggested"), includes some vulgar language and, at the end, a not-very-convincing disaster.

VINCENT CANBY

1978 Ap 14, C9:1

Misadventures Galore

JOSEPH ANDREWS, directed by Tony Richardson; screenplay by Allan Scott and Chris Bryant; screen story by Mr. Richardson, based on the novel by Henry Fielding; produced by Neil Hartley; director of photography, David Watkin; music; John Addison; editor, Thom Noble; a Woodfall Film production, distributed by Paramount Pictures. Running time: 99 minutes. At the Festival Theater, 57th Street near Fifth Avenue, and other theaters. This film has been rated R.

Lady Booby .... Ann-Margret
Joseph Andrews .... Peter Firth
Parson Adams .... Michael Hordern
Mrs. Slipslop .... Beryl Reid
Pedlar .... Jim Dale
Fanny .... Natalie Ogle
Sir Thomas Booby .... Peter Bull
Wicked Squire .... Kenneth Cranham
Pamela .... Karen Dotrice
Mr. Booby .... James Villiers
Gaffar Andrews .... Norman Rossington
Gammar Andrews .... Patsy Rowlands
Beau Didapper .... Murray Melvin
Mr. Wilson .... Ronald Pickup
Mrs. Wilson .... Penelope Wilton
Lady Tattle .... Peggy Ashcroft
Lady Tittle .... Pauline Jameson
Parson Trulliber .... Bernard Bresslaw
Mrs. Trulliber .... Sheila Burrell
Mr. Tow-wouse .... Timothy West
Mrs. Tow-wouse .... Wendy Craig
Betty .... Vanessa Millard
Doctor .... John Gielgud
Squire Weston .... Hugh Griffith
Postilion .... Altie Lynch
Coach Driver .... Dan Meaden
Lawyer in coach .... Gerald Cross
Gypsy .... Jenny Runacre

By VINCENT CANBY

HAVING had such a smashing financial and critical success with his screen version of Henry Fielding's "Tom Jones," Tony Richardson was, one suspects, a bit reluctant to make a film based on "Joseph Andrews," Fielding's second greatest novel, a work that originated as Fielding's answer to what he saw as

Peter Firth and Ann-Margret in Tony Richardson's "Joseph Andrews"
One of the few movies around now that truly lifts the spirits

the hypocritical pieties of Samuel Richardson's "Pamela."

In the mid-18th century, "Pamela" enjoyed the kind of success that today is had only by the work of Victoria Holt and those other Gothic novelists who continue to sell the idea that virtue is its own reward, often accompanied by a large fortune.

In "Pamela," which was published in 1740, Richardson told the inspiring tale of Pamela Andrews, a serving girl who tenaciously held onto her virginity until her employer, the rich Mr. Booby, came across with a marriage license. Several years later, Mr. Fielding turned this story wildly upside down in a novel about Pamela's brother, Joseph, a serving boy who is as innocent as his sister but not nearly as calculating, who must fight off all sorts of lewd advances and whose triumph is one of true virtue rather than greed.

•

Not wanting to appear to be repeating himself, Mr. Richardson waited nearly 15 years before turning to "Joseph Andrews." The funny, stylish, infinitely cheerful film, which opens today at the Festival and other theaters, is well worth the wait. "Joseph Andrews" is not a sequel to "Tom Jones" in any literal sense, though it shares with that earlier movie its 18-century period and its exuberant high spirits.

In addition "Joseph Andrews" contains more great (and more greatly funny) character performances than any film I've seen in years. It's one of the few movies around now that truly lifts the spirits, not only because it is so good-humored but also because the humor is laced with so much wit and wisdom.

Peter Firth, who was nominated for an Oscar for his performance in "Equus," is marvelously earnest and innocent in the title role. He is the calm eye that is the center of a hurricane of extraordinary characters who tumble around him in all sorts of adventures involving mistaken identities, coincidental meetings on country lanes, stolen babies, lust, true love, gypsies, highwaymen, evil squires, urban corruption and rural pleasures.

Foremost in this cast of characters is the single-mindedly lecherous Lady Booby, Joseph's employer, played by Ann-Margret at the top of her magnificent form, a lady who goes after the unsuspecting Joseph with something of the purpose of a warped missionary. She looks great and she is enchantingly funny, but so is almost everyone else in a cast so big I really don't know where to begin, since I'm sure to leave out someone important. It's one of those films in which even the smaller roles are as beautifully and as memorably done as the larger ones.

There is, for example, John Gielgud's brief and hilarious appearance as the doctor who is called in at one point to minister to Joseph's wounds but who examines, instead, a corpse, taking some while to realize that the patient is, in fact, "no more." There are also Beryl Reid as Mrs. Slipslop, Lady Booby's servant, a battered, flirtatious crone with the manners of a truck driver attempting to be dainty; the incomparable Michael Hordern as Parson Adams, the well-meaning clergyman who defends Joseph at all costs; Natalie Ogle, as Fanny, Joseph's virginal true love, and Karen Dotrice, who is most comic as the prissy and successful Pamela Andrews.

•

There is in the entire film just one shot that I wish someone had cut out, but I won't describe it since it may go unnoticed by others. The film is otherwise an almost perfect blending of beauty, romance and adventure, of landscapes too lovely to believe alternating with the kind of gritty period detail that prompts one character to say of a street jam in the resort city of Batti, "The only things that move here are the bowels of the horses."

Mr. Richardson, as the director, and Allan Scott and Chris Bryant, who wrote the screenplay, based on Mr. Richardson's screen story, have captured the particular, very special charm of Mr. Fielding's narrative style, which never holds onto one adventure for a second too long. Thus Joseph's escapades open, one out of the other, with the effortlessness of a dream. Even the flashbacks, which we see through what seems to be a fish-eye lens, move the narrative forward at a breakneck pace that never falters.

The movie year, which has not been great so far, looks a great deal richer today.

1978 Ap 14, C9:1

Tyranny and Growth

PAULE PAULANDER, directed by Reinhard Hauff; script (German with English subtitles) by Burkhard Driest and Wolf-Dietrich Bruckner; photography, Jurgen Jurges; editor, Ines Regnier; a Bioskop-Film Munich/WDR (West German TV) co-production. Running time: 95 minutes.

Paule ..... Manfred Reiss
Elfi ..... Angelika Kulessa
Father ..... Manfred Gnoth
Mother ..... Katharina Tuschen
Heinrich ..... Heinz Hurlander
Trossbert ..... Klaus Hellmold

THE MAIN ACTOR (DIE HAUPTDARSTELLER), directed by Reinhard Hauff; script (German with English subtitles) by Christel Buschmann and Mr. Hauff; produced by Eberhard Junkersdorf; photography, Frank Bruhne; music, Klaus Doldinger; editor, Stefanie Wilke; a Bioskop-Film, Munich/WDR (West German TV, Cologne) co-production. Running time: 88 minutes. At the Museum of Modern Art, 11 West 53d Street, New Directors/ New Films Series.

Father ..... Mario Adorf
Max, the filmmaker ..... Vadim Glowna
Pepe ..... Michael Schweiger
Reporter ..... Hans Brenner

THE title character in both of these films is a dark-haired youth of 15, slim, silent, finished with school, seemingly not very bright, and suffering under a father's tyrannical rule.

In "Paule Paulander," the father is a pig farmer; in "The Main Actor," the proprietor of a rural junkyard. Reinhard Hauff, the director, in other words, seems to have scoured West Germany for unlovely settings, not picturesque villages and valleys or bright and bustling towns. The country is flat, the people coarse, the color photography dim. In short, we are mired in the "realism" into which young film makers are apt to stumble while seeking a shortcut to Parnassus. Or in this instance to the Museum of Modern Art, where the two films will be shown at 6 P.M. today and at 8:30 P.M. tomorrow as part of the New Directors/New Films series.

•

The climax of "Paule Paulander" occurs when an outbreak of swine fever—not to be confused with swine flu—ruins the father and brings on an emotional breakdown. The youth knocks away the rifle that his father is threatening him with and clubs him briskly with a shovel. Leaving the stubborn old fellow moaning on a pile of dying piglets, he abandons the acres that his family has tilled for 300 years to seek his fortunes in the big city.

In "The Main Actor" the youth is recruited to play the starring role in a film within a film, an unsparing quasi-documentary look into the horrors of rural life, as seen from the perspective of the film's director, who seems to be a socialist of some sort and it is hinted, a homosexual.

•

Tired of dismantling old Volkswagens, encouraged by his father's kicks and cuffs, this youth abandons the junkyard. He follows the director to what may be the same city, possibly Cologne, where he turns out to be no happier.

Mr. Hauff has made the mistake of stating his intentions in a credo distributed at the screening of the films

Michael Schweiger in a scene from Reinhard Hauff's "The Main Actor."

instead of fulfilling them on the screen. For artistic ideological reasons that he fails to make entirely clear in the statement, he has amateur actors in "Paule Paulander" and professionals in "The Main Actor." Both perform at about the same level of plodding inadequacy, with the edge, perhaps, going to the amateurs.

TOM BUCKLEY

1978 Ap 14, C12:1

A Gilded Cage

A WOMAN OF PARIS, written, produced and directed by Charles Chaplin; photography, Rollie Totherch and Jack Wilson; editorial direction, Monta Bell; distributed by Kino International Corporation Inc. At the Cinema Studio, Broadway and 66th Street. Running time: 83 minutes. This film is not rated.

Marie St. Clair ..... Edna Purviance
Pierre Revel ..... Adolphe Meniou
John Millet ..... Carl Miller
His mother ..... Lydia Knott
His father ..... Charles French
Marie's father ..... Clarence Geldert
Fifi and Paulette..... Betty Morrissey and Malvina Polo

By JANET MASLIN

MARIE ST. CLAIR, the heroine of Charles Chaplin's radiantly beautiful "A Woman of Paris," is, at the film's beginning, locked inside her bedroom by her foul-tempered father. That same evening, after she has escaped by climbing out a window, her father reverses the trick and locks her out. A year later, fate has whisked Marie away from her simple country home and off to "the magic city of Paris, where fortune is fickle and a woman gambles with life." There, she is imprisoned, once again, but this time the cage is gilded and then some: Marie has become the expensively kept mistress of a very rich, very dapper, eternally bemused man. Almost obscenely wealthy by now, Marie isn't always happy, but she wasn't always happy as a simple country girl, either. Fate, as Mr. Chaplin understands it, works in endlessly ironic and enormously touching ways.

The wisdom of "A Woman of Paris," which was first released in 1923 but often feels as if it were made just yesterday, really does seem boundless; so do the affection and generosity with which Mr. Chaplin presents his characters. The film, described by him in an introductory note from Mr. Chaplin as "the first serious drama written and directed by myself," has nothing of the Little Tramp about it, although the director does appear in a tiny cameo role as a railway porter. Consequently, it was

Adolphe Menjou and Edna Purviance in "A Woman of Paris" (1923), written and directed by Charlie Chaplin, at the Cinema Studio.
An uninterrupted series of perfect vignettes

a commercial failure in its day. After that, it stayed out of circulation for more than 50 years, until Mr. Chaplin prepared a new score and allowed the film to be screened at the Museum of Modern Art two years ago. Since then, the film has had the reputation of a lost masterpiece, and it more than lives up to its renown.

•

The tale of a pampered woman who learns the hard way to value simplicity and honesty may not seem like big news, but Mr. Chaplin used that premise to string together an uninterrupted series of perfect vignettes. One of the best of these involves Marie (Edna Purviance), her lover Pierre Revel (Adolphe Menjou) and some pearls he long ago bestowed upon his mistress. Marie defiantly tells Pierre that she is leaving him to marry her provincial sweetheart, because all she really wants from life are a few children and the love of a good man. To prove her point, she rips off the necklace and flings it out a window. But when she looks out to find a hobo discovering the jewels, she races into the street and grabs them back. She is followed by a little dog, which appears just long enough to suggest a certain side of Marie's nature and is never seen again.

•

Although "A Woman of Paris," which opens today at the Cinema Studio, is a drama in many respects, it is at times extremely funny; Mr. Chaplin gets some wonderfully witty milage out of the incongruity of upper-class pretensions and the bestial side of anyone's nature. The film's most dazzling sustained sequence takes place in a posh restaurant, where Marie and Pierre dine elegantly on champagne and truffles. As a title explains, "Note: truffles rooted up from the soil by hogs—a delicacy for pigs and gentlemen." The moment is wry, but not satirical, thanks both to Mr. Chaplin's complex sympathies and the enormously alluring performances of Miss Purviance and Mr. Menjou. Mr. Chaplin never forgets that the most effective way of sending up a life of ease involves exaggerating, not deflating, its sense of easiness.

•

The stirring tableau that ends the film's Parisian segment ideally exemplifies Mr. Chaplin's care, compassion and economy. Marie, having re-encountered her country lover after she began putting on airs, commissioned him to paint her portrait in an elegant white gown. Instead, he chose to depict her in a simple, dark dress he remembered her wearing before.

Long after the portrait is completed, Marie happens to be wearing the white outfit on a night that ends in tragedy, and destiny leads her to a spot directly beneath the dark portrait, where she weeps so honestly that an enemy is moved to spare her life. Nothing could be less melodramatic than the manner in which Mr. Chaplin presents this small epiphany. And nothing could be more rich with the eternal promise of redemption.

1978 Ap 14, C13:1

SCENIC ROUTE, directed and produced by Mark Rappaport; director of photography, Fred Murphy; screenplay by Mr. Rappaport; produced in cooperation with ZDF (German Television). Running time: 76 minutes. At the New Directors/New Films series at the Museum of Modern Art, 53d Street west of Fifth Avenue.

Estelle ....Randy Danson
Lena ....Marilyn Jones
Paul ....Kevin Wade

By VINCENT CANBY

Having now seen several films of Mark Rappaport, including "Local Color" and his newest work, "Scenic Route," I can say definitely that they are an acquired taste. There's nothing really wrong with them if you're willing to supply your own critical system that justifies the film maker's dead-panned pursuit of the banal. This, though, is decadence of the least rewarding kind. It's flavorless bubble gum.

"Scenic Route" is a series of facetious tableaux about two sisters who sometimes love the same man and speak endless clichés that, I think, are meant to be funny. The difficulty is that Mr. Rappaport's film-making manners are quite as foolish and empty-headed as his characters' affections. The result is a film not about boredom, but one that uses boredom as its environment.

"Scenic Route" will be shown at the Museum of Modern Art's New Directors/New Films series today at 6 P.M. and on Monday at 8:30 P.M. "Local Color" was shown at the 1977 New Directors/New Films series, which makes me wonder at what point we can expect a "new director" to turn into an old one, thus to become ineligible to occupy space in this annual series presented jointly by the Film Society of Lincoln Center and the museum's department of film.

1978 Ap 15, 14:2

FOUL PLAY (Przepraszam Czzy Tu Bija?), directed by Marek Piwowski; screenplay (Polish with English subtitles) by Mr. Piwowski; photography, Witold Stock; music, Potr Figiel; produced by the Polish Corporation for Film Production Silesia. Running time: 88 minutes. At the Museum of Modern Art, 11 West 53d Street, New Directors/New Films Series.

Inspector Milde ....Jerzy Kulej
Inspector Gorny ....Jan Szozepanski
Belus ....Zdzislaw Richter
Student ....Ryszard Faron
WITH: Wiodzimierz Stepinskim, Bogdan Kowalczyk, etc.

"Foul Play," the Polish *policier* being shown tonight and Wednesday evening in the New Directors/New Films series at the Museum of Modern Art, spends a good deal of its seemingly interminable 88 minutes plodding up to a worthwhile question:

Are police entrapment tactics ever justified?

In this instance, the question arises because—logic aside—a smug punk named Belus has deliberately drawn police attention to himself in the course of testing recruits for a robbery of cash receipts at a huge Warsaw department store.

•

Having posed the question, "Foul Play," directed by Marek Piwowski, proceeds not to answer it. Burdened by its amateur actors and an occasionally hazy narrative line, "Foul Play" leaves little for Western audiences familiar, say, with "Topkapi" or "Rififi" to savor besides the realization that some of the seedier parts of swinging London of the 1960's may be alive and well in Warsaw in the 70's.

Mr. Piwowski, who is described as having a background in documentary films, seems more adept at dealing with places than people and more competent to derive from the movies that have inspired "Foul Play" than to equal or transcend them.

With its major idea unexplored, with its moral position unoccupied, with its characters given more surface than substance and with its sludgy pacing, "Foul Play" cannot command much interest in the outcome of the effort to foil the holdup.

The result, then, is a thriller without thrills.

LAWRENCE VAN GELDER

1978 Ap 16, 60:3

'Far Road,' Japan Film, At Museum

THE style and subject of "The Far Road," a Japanese entry in the Museum of Modern Art's New Directors/New Films series, are nicely consonant. The film's story, which spans 30 years and follows the life of a railroad worker and his family, is of course deeply concerned with the effects of modernization upon postwar Japan.

Accordingly, the film's direction incorporates standard elements of both Japanese and Western film technique. "The Far Road" is the first feature film directed by Sachiko Hidari, who also plays the railway worker's wife, and it is often quite successful in mingling incompatible scenes and ingredients without generating a sense of clashing moods.

•

For instance, an opening episode shows the railway worker (Ichizo Takinogami) and his wife traveling by train to attend a ceremony, during which the worker will be awarded a medal for his many years of service. His wife, donning a kimono for the first time in ages, is nervous and shy, and the other wives in the audience look similarly ill at ease. Meanwhile, the few young children in the crowd wear Western clothes and squirm with boredom. These different generations seem every bit as bewildered as they are divided.

After the ceremony, the whole family is shown back home, carousing over dinner and drinking beer. Then it turns out that the couple's stunning daughter (Yoshie Shimo) has brought her suitor home for the first time, an act that enrages her father beyond all reason. In his day, he howls, marriages were arranged by families and that was that. The daughter is frightened by his outburst, and sorry to have defied his wishes. But, saddened as she is by the episode, she just doesn't understand it.

•

Miss Hidari's film, which was sponsored by the Japanese National Railway Workers' Union, is full of change and upheaval, but it has an uneventful feeling. The railway scenes lend themselves to lovely blue-gray winter tableaux, as the smoke from the trains blends with falling snow, and the troubled history of the worker's family is of interest at times. But by and large "The Far Road" introduces a director of evident promise whose talents are more impressive than the material upon which she has concentrated them.

JANET MASLIN

1978 Ap 17, C20:3

CHUQUIAGO, directed by Antonio Eguino; screenplay (Aymara and Spanish with English subtitles) by Oscar Soria; directors of photography, Mr. Eguino and Julio Lencina; editors, Deborah Shaffer and Susane Fenn; a Ukamau production. Running time: 87 minutes. At the New Directors/New Films series at the Museum of Modern Art, 53d Street west of Fifth Avenue.

Isico ....Nestor Yulra
Johnny ....Edmundo Villarreol
Carlos ....David Santalla
Patricia ....Tatiana Aponte

By VINCENT CANBY

This year's New Directors/New Films series, under the joint sponsorship of the Film Society of Lincoln Center and the film department of the

Museum of Modern Art, has not been much cause for celebration until now, with the showing of "Chuquiago." Antonio Eguino's fine Bolivian feature will be seen at the museum today at 6 P.M. and tomorrow at 8:30 P.M., to close the series.

"Chuquiago," the Indian name for the capital city that the Spaniards named La Paz, appears to be such an even-tempered film that one is well into it before recognizing the fury with which it is charged. Its dominant expression is of inscrutable calm, much the way Indians look to those of us who don't know them.

"Chuquiago" is the second feature to be directed by Mr. Eguino, who began his career as a still photographer and then became a motion-picture cameraman. The movie displays the ease of someone far more experienced, however. Its themes of rootlessness and casual corruption are the connectives for the four separate though overlapping stories that present us with a cross section of contemporary Bolivian society.

•

The film opens when Isico (Nestor Yujra), a young Indian boy, is brought into La Paz and apprenticed by his parents to an old woman who works in the peasant marketplace. Isico, without particular direction except the need to eat and sleep, drifts into the life of a street boy, probably to become, one day, much like the drunken Indians who torment him as he moves about the city.

In the second story, Johnny (Edmundo Villarreol) is an upwardly mobile Indian teen-ager, the son of hard-working parents whose Indian ways now embarrass him. Johnny drops out of school and into a life of petty crime, is conned by an agency that promises to find him work in the United States and is last seen running, though no one is chasing him.

The film's third episode is both funny and scathing. It's about Carlos (David Santalla), a vain, middle-aged fellow who works in government office where bureaucracy has been raised to a kind of art. Carlos is well on his way to joining the middle class. He has five children, debts up to his ears and parrots the government political line, though he seems to have been a committed radical in his younger years. His aspirations now have to do mostly with appliances and being able to spend Friday nights on the town with his friends.

•

The last episode is about a pretty, intelligent university student, Patricia (Tatiana Aponte), who takes one brave last stand against her conservative parents, loses the fight and winds up willingly accepting marriage with a young man who promises to be just like her father—and possibly worse.

Though each narrative is essentially bleak, the film makes its points with such humane wit that it's far from depressing experience. Mr. Eguino's achievement can be measured in the superb performances he has drawn from his actors, both professional and amateur, and in the remarkable economy with which he evokes an entire cultural and economic system in four briefly touched-on lives.

"Chuquiago" is a spare, vividly impressive work.

1978 Ap 18, 44:6

Charles and Catherine Scorsese, parents of Martin
"They take pride in their boy's success."

Five at the Forum

ITALIANAMERICAN, by Martin Scorcese, 45 minutes ALBUM by Linda Heller, 5 minutes HAPPY BIRTHDAY LENNY by Lenny Lipton, 8 minutes HOME MOVIE by Jan Oxenberg, 12 minutes. A VISIT TO INDIANA by Curt McDowell, 11 minutes. At the Film Forum, 15 Vandam Street.

By JANET MASLIN

WE KNOW Martin Scorsese is in his parents' dining room because we can see his dinner plate, which he has evidently emptied, and because his hand occasionally reaches across the table to spear some salad. We also know he's on the premises because his parents, whose recollections of Scorsese family lore take up most of the 45-minute running time of "Italianamerican," at one point begin worrying about whether one of their famous son's teeth looks funny. But for the most part, Scorsese the Director prefers to keep Scorsese the Son safely off camera, and his parents prefer to behave as if they had just made the acquaintance of a very charming stranger.

By deliberately attempting to limit his own influence, Mr. Scorsese backhandedly turns himself into the film's most important figure. His parents are a bit nervous, and they clearly aren't behaving the way they ordinarily might; to heighten the formality with which they present themselves. Mr. Scorsese invites them to tell stories they've told a hundred times before. but their carefully chosen words and expansive smiles speak volumes about the pride they take in their boy's success, and the momentousness they attach to his work. It's delightful to see how flattered they are by their Marty's making them a part of his professional life.

"Italianamerican" concentrates mostly on keeping up appearances, but there are occasional lapses and digressions, all of them welcome. Mr. Scorsese, sending his mother into the kitchen to make spaghetti sauce for the camera, uses a tone that would make a drill sergeant sound like the Easter Bunny by comparison. Later, the film's closing credits include Mrs. Scorsese's recipe.

Of the five films on the Film Forum's "Scorsese's Italianamerican & Other Family Portraits," Mr. Scorsese's is the only one made in a spirit of affection.

"Album," an animated short by Linda Heller, concentrates on parental repressiveness, but Miss Heller's animation is so sweetly whimsical that the sting is minimal.

Equally successful, and equally fish-eyed, is Lenny Lipton's "Happy Birthday Lenny." Footage of an apartment, presumably the director's, is interspersed with shots of lush tropical foliage and birds flying free. All the while, a woman sobs nonstop about her son's not being tidy enough, and about the various sacrifices she has made. The credits don't specify whose voice we're hearing, but if she isn't Mama Lipton, she must be the greatest actress in the world.

Jan Oxenberg's "Home Movie" shows a group of lesbians merrily playing football, and Miss Oxenberg uses childhood films of herself, somewhat unpleasantly, to reinforce ideas about herself that came later in life, rather than to explore the attitudes that were evident years ago.

"A Visit to Indiana," by Curt McDowell, uses the strangely self-destructive technique of combining rough, almost unwatchable footage of an Indiana family with a sardonic voice-over conversation. The dialogue is funny, but it distracts attention from footage that is already hard to follow, and the prevailing spirit is so sarcastic it turns sour.

1978 Ap 20, C17:3

The Devil in Person

THE CHOSEN, directed by Alberto De Martino; screenplay by Sergio Donati, Mr. De Martino and Michael Robson; music by Ennio Morricone; produced by Edmondo Amati; presented by Samuel Z. Arkoff; released by American International Pictures. At the Forum Theater, Broadway at 46th Street and other theaters. Running time: 105 minutes. This film is classified R.

Robert Caine .... Kirk Douglas
Angel .... Simon Ward
Sarah Golan .... Agostina Belli
Griffith .... Anthony Quayle
Eva Caine .... Virginia McKenna
Meyer .... Alexander Knox
Prime Minister .... Ivo Garrani
Harbin .... Spiro Focas
Young Arab .... Massimo Foschi
Priest .... Adolfo Celi
Charrier .... Romolo Valli

By VINCENT CANBY

IRK DOUGLAS, who has a weird son, a fellow with telekinetic powers, in "The Fury," has a son who is even more weird in "The Chosen," a nasty Italo-English coproduction about diabolism.

In "The Chosen," the young man, who is played by Simon Ward, is actually the devil who has apparently come to earth to build faulty atomic power plants. That, at least, is all I can make of the plot, which was put together by three people and then directed by Alberto De Martino, who seems to have studied "The Omen" the way other directors might study "Potemkin" and "Freaks."

"The Chosen" sincerely flatters "The Omen" with such special effects as assorted cuttings and stabbings, the sight of a man as the top of his head is chopped off and of another who seems to be sliced in two. The Book of Revelation, which was called "Revelations" in "The Omen" and is in the public domain, is cited as the source material.

The film opened yesterday at a number of theaters in the neighborhoods and on Broadway at the Forum, where the program was supplemented by a short called "The Diamond—A Miracle of Nature," distributed by the Diamond Information Center, and by trailers for "Jennifer," "Here Come the Tigers," "The Incredible Melting Man" and "Youngblood."

At one point I thought my foot had gone to sleep but it was only that my shoe was temporarily stuck to the floor by gum discarded by an earlier patron.

1978 Ap 20, C21:3

Out of Sight

I WANNA HOLD YOUR HAND, directed by Robert Zemeckis; written by Robert Zemeckis and Bob Gale; director of photography, Donald M. Morgan; film editor, Frank Morriss; produced by Tamara Asseyev and Alex Rose. At the Rivoli, Broadway and 49th Street, and other theaters. Running time: 104 minutes. This film is rated PG.

Pam Mitchell .... Nancy Allen
Tony Smerko .... Bobby Di Cicco
Larry Dubois .... Marc McClure
Janis Goldman .... Susan Kendall Newman
Grace Corrigan .... Theresa Saldana
Rosie Petrofsky .... Wendie Jo Sperber
Richard (Ringo) Klaus .... Eddie Deezen
Peter Plimpton .... Christian Juttner
Ed Sullivan .... Will Jordan
Peter's Father .... Read Morgan
Al .... Claude Earl Jones
Eddie .... James Houghton
Neil .... Michael Hewitson

By JANET MASLIN

THE GIMMICK behind "I Wanna Hold Your Hand" is the fact that you never actually see the Beatles; the genius of the film is the fact that you never miss them. Their likenesses turn up everywhere, plastered on record jackets and tacked on doors and walls, and their music is continually in the air.

At the end of the movie, which revolves around the group's first appearance on "The Ed Sullivan Show," the sneakiness with which the neophyte director Robert Zemeckis skirts the issue is positively dazzling. The Beatles are both there and not there, and the paradox hardly even matters. This movie is about the fans and their hysteria, and so it's the shouts that count.

•

The premise of the screenplay, by Mr. Zemeckis and Bob Gale, might have lent itself to a wittier and less broad treatment, but "I Wanna Hold Your Hand" plays it safe, quite successfully. If there's a tray full of food within camera range, rest assured that somebody will knock it over. If a stuck-in-the - elevator - on-the-eve-of-an-important-event routine presents itself, rest assured that its staging will be tried and true.

However, Mr. Zemeckis's taste in routines of this sort is very sound, and midway through the movie he begins

Theresa Saldana as a Beatles fan in "I Wanna Hold Your Hand"

juggling them with such speed and dexterity that perhaps he belongs on the Sullivan program, along with such memorable acts—whose names are dropped here by Will Jordan, doing his Sullivan imitation—as "Topo Gigio, the Little Italian Mouse."

In addition to Mr. Zemeckis's impressive new hand with old tricks, the film's assets include the fortuitous ambience of Beatlemania. In an atmosphere rife with weeping and screaming, a climate in which one fan can sweetly announce that she hopes Cynthia Lennon will die in a plane crash so that she can marry John, anything goes. Some routines work a lot better than others, but the whole film sparkles with a boisterous lunacy that's perfectly in keeping with the frenzy of the fans.

•

Of course, such infectious high spirits don't come without calculation: This is a film that's quite meticulous about its innocence. Nobody gets hurt, and the jokes stay clean. The principals are typecast straight out of anyone's high-school year-book: Best Looking (Nancy Allen), Best Personality (Wendie Jo Sperber), Most Earnest (Susan Kendall Newman), Class Weirdo (Eddie Deezen), Class Creep (Marc McClure), Town Tough Guy (Bobby Di Cicco) and Most Likely to Succeed No Matter Whose Arm She Has to Break to Do It (Theresa Saldana).

The bad guys are stock characters, too: grownups. With a wicked, wicked smile, one hotel chambermaid shakes a dark dustmop out a hotel window and snickers while the fans—who know a mopton haircut when they see one—go wild. When the adorably unhinged Miss Sperber, who looks like a slackjawed baby elephant in stretch pants, bowls over a little old lady, it's an old lady who has had the audacity to badmouth the Beatles. When one boy's father refuses to give the kid his Sullivan tickets unless his son gets rid of his Beatle haircut, Mr. Zemeckis makes the barbershop look like Death Row.

When the adults in the film aren't being nasty, they're stupid, hilariously so. "How do I know which one's Ringo?" asks one technician in the control room for the Sullivan program. "He's the one who plays guitar another replies. "What guitar? There's three guitars," is the reply, while a title reading "John—Sorry, Girls, He's Married" flashes on one monitor screen.

And then there is Miss Allen's fiancé, a stiff in the plastic furniture-cover business, who tells her proudly that "in a couple of hours you're gonna be Mrs. Eddie Lupus." They plan to elope, but fate has some other, wonderfully funny adventures in store for Miss Allen, who winds up doing even lewder things to one of the Beatles' bass guitars than she did to John Travolta in "Carrie."

Miss Allen, who manages to seem years younger here than she did in "Carrie" does some of her best acting with her legs, squirming and flopping about with girlish glee as she finds herself delivered, quite by accident, into the Beatles' actual hotel suite. Nobody else is around, and Miss Allen spends a few delightful moments savoring every last cigarette butt. Needless to say, when the Beatles arrive she never sees them. She hides under a bed, catches one glimpse of their boots and passes out in ecstasy.

•

"I Wanna Hold Your Hand," which is at the Rivoli and other theaters, is an A-plus B-movie, but it's a B-movie just the same. The fine points aren't fine, the clothes and makeup are anachronistic at times, the plot falters crazily in places, and a final car chase through the streets of New York very clearly takes place in California. The teen-agers appear to range in age from 16 to 30, and one Beatle voice has an oddly American accent.

Miss Newman, daughter of Paul Newman, plays a completely implausible Beatle-hater, a lover of folk music who would never have been caught wearing makeup in 1964, even though she has lipstick on here. When she complains about the Beatles in a record store, the proprietor sneers something unpleasant about "Jane" Baez, but that's nonsense: "Jane" sold plenty of records in her day, too.

•

"I Wanna Hold Your Hand," which is rated PG (Parental Guidance Suggested), include one sequence involving a prostitute. However, the woman is merely seen rubbing mustard on her client's cranium.

1978 Ap 21, C11:1

Swiss Laundry

THE SILVER BEARS, directed by Ivan Passer; screenplay by Peter Stone, based on the novel by Paul E. Erdman; produced by Alex Winitsky and Arlene Sellers; music, Claude Bolling; director of photography, Anthony Richmond; editor, Bernard Gribble; distributed by Columbia Pictures. Running time: 113 minutes. At the RKO 86th Street Theater, 86th Street near Lexington Avenue, and other theaters. This film has ben rated PG.

Doc Fletcher	Michael Caine
Debbie Luckman	Cybill Shepherd
Prince di Siracusa	Louis Jourdan
Shireen Firdausi	Stephane Audran
Agha Firdausi	David Warner
Donald Luckman	Tom Smothers
Joe Fiore	Martin Balsam
Albert Fiore	Jay Leno
Marvin Skinner	Tony Mascia
Charles Cook	Charles Gray
Henry Foreman	Joss Ackland
Nick Topping	Jeremy Clyde

By VINCENT CANBY

IVAN PASSER'S "Silver Bears" is a chilly, cheerless comedy about the machinations of a Las Vegas syndicate chief and his associates who buy their own Swiss bank to launder illegal profits and, in the process, become enmeshed in a swindle involving the world's silver market, some secret silver mines in Iran and a greedy California bank.

Peter Stone's screenplay is based on a novel by Paul Erdman, the author of the current novel "The Crash of '79" and himself no stranger to the arcane methods of Swiss-based wheeling-and-dealing. I suspect that Mr. Passer means the film to be a comedy about Western decadence, though "Silver Bears," in failing in the flat-footed way it does, becomes, instead, an example of it.

•

It looks very much like the sort of picture made primarily to fulfill the obligations of an international movie deal designed to be somebody's tax write-off, a project that profits no one except the people who appear to lose money on it. This, I emphasize, is speculation based on the sloppiness of the film as art and on the extravagances of the production as a whole.

The cast is headed by some very good actors, lots of boringly picturesque Swiss scenery and a number of exotic locales, including marketplaces in Morocco, which substitutes for Iran and where, apparently, poverty is pretty.

Among the people who appear in the film are Michael Caine and Martin Balsam, who aren't diminished by the experience, and Cybill Shepherd and Stephane Audran (two of the screen's most glorious faces), and Louis Jourdan, David Warner and Tom Smothers. All of the roles are ridiculous, though poor pacing, foolish lines, unnecessary connective scenes and badly matched shots within scenes also work against them. I hope everyone was well paid.

The film opens today at the RKO 86th Street Theater and other theaters.

•

"Silver Bears" which has been rated PG ["Parental Guidance Suggested"), includes some fleeting shots of nude old men, a couple of even more fleeting shots of a not-quite-nude young woman and some mildly vulgar dialogue.

1978 Ap 21, C14:2

FILM VIEW

VINCENT CANBY

A 'Lost' Chaplin Masterpiece

When "A Woman of Paris" was originally released in 1923, the fans of Charlie Chaplin reacted as if they'd been the target of some kind of gigantic swindle. Here was a Chaplin film without Charlie, which seemed as obvious a contradiction-in-terms as an egg salad sandwich without egg. An introductory title card in which Chaplin described the film as "the first serious drama written and directed by myself" was not of much help. The 1923 public could not conceive of a Chaplin film without the Tramp at its center. His talent was his physical presence. Although the reviews were generally enthusiastic—the anonymous Times critic called Charlie a "director par excellence"—the public was buying none of it, or at least very little of it, with the result that Chaplin put the film away until another day, which, it's now happily apparent, is today.

With a music score composed by Charlie, who also reedited the film from its "almost" two-hour running time down to the present 83 minutes (among other things, he removed what the Times writer had called "a picturesque prologue"), "A Woman of Paris" is once again available to the general public, and this time, I trust, we won't fail him.

The film is not only a treasure in itself—witty, sophisticated and often beautifully funny, though it means to be "serious," as Chaplin says—it's also a rare opportunity to see what Chaplin is like as a filmmaker when he is not contemplating his own image. "A Woman of Paris" is immensely entertaining, but, more important, it's an inside report on the essential Chaplin talent that, in the films in which he is also a star, seems so closely bound to the performer's personality we can't easily tell where one starts and the other leaves off.

In this respect, "A Woman of Paris" is much more revealing than "A Countess From Hong Kong," another Chaplin comedy without Charlie and a film I happen to be very fond of, though it's always clear that the movie is an attempt to reprise a kind of comedy that doesn't easily fit its stars (Marlon Brando and Sophia Loren) or the time in which it was made (1967). "A Countess From Hong Kong" is talent recollected at the end of a career. "A Woman of Paris" is the work of that talent at the peak of its vigor.

• • •

In "My Autobiography," Chaplin tells about the origins of "A Woman of Paris": For sometime he'd been looking for a suitable property for Edna Purviance, his leading lady in a number of shorts and in the features "The Kid" and "The Pilgrim." First he had been seriously considering a film version of "The Trojan Women," but that, as the accountant in

Charlie soon realized, would be too expensive. He later thought of a movie about Empress Josephine, which would have been even more expensive, but he pursued this project anyway, perhaps because if Edna Purviance, one of the earlier women in his life, were Josephine, he, Charlie, would have to be recognized as Napoleon. Indeed, Charlie eventually abandoned the Josephine idea because, as he later remembered, "the further we delved into the life of Josephine, the more Napoleon got in the way." The Josephine project was shelved and Charlie went ahead with "A Woman of Paris," based on a story Peggy Hopkins Joyce told him about her relationship with a wealthy French publisher.

In "A Woman of Paris," the wealthy French publisher becomes Pierre Revel (Adolphe Menjou), the richest bachelor in Paris "whose whims," according to a title card, "have made and ruined many a woman's career." The Peggy Hopkins Joyce character is Marie St. Clair (Miss Purviance), a beautiful, not-so-innocent small-town girl who, after being jilted by her true love, goes off to Paris to become one of the city's most celebrated demimondaines, the mistress to Pierre Revel.

In the context of such Chaplin films as "The Kid," "The Gold Rush" and "The Circus," which were made before and after "A Woman of Paris," the latter seems at first to be a very worldly movie, much closer to the kind of life Chaplin knew first-hand than the Tramp comedies in which he was recording his metaphysical autobiography. I emphasize "at first" because the Tramp comedies are, upon close inspection, much less sentimental than they originally appear to be. The Tramp lives outside society to show it up, and though he's inclined to get dewy-eyed and speechless in the company of the beautiful girl he's worshiped from afar, there's something quite perverse about his romantic vision of women. Idealizing them is a backhanded way of calling attention to the ways in which most women fall short.

Though Charlie insisted that "A Woman of Paris" was his first "serious drama," it is comedy of a very rich sort, a highly moral tale that teaches that the wages of naïveté is death, while the wages of sin may well be a better understanding of the true values of living.

In "My Autobiography," Chaplin explains that one of the reasons that prompted him to search for a vehicle for Miss Purviance was the fact she was becoming more and more "matronly" in her appearance, and thus her days were numbered as a suitable leading lady to him. There are times in "A Woman of Paris" when Miss Purviance does display a sort of seminal Margaret Dumont look (which may have as much to do with the costumes of the period as with her figure), but she's such a beauty and the character so surprising that the movie becomes almost a testimonial to her. (Though "A Woman of Paris" was the last major role played by Miss Purviance for Chaplin, she remained on his payroll until her death from cancer in 1956.)

• • •

Chaplin called "A Woman of Paris" "a Drama of Fate," but it's more accurate to call it a comedy of manners in which fate steps in at opportune moments. It's also one of the most economical narratives Chaplin ever wrote. After Marie St. Claire is jilted by her lover and she takes off, alone, for Paris, all we are given is a title card to let us know that "one year later in Paris, where fortune is fickle and a woman gambles for her life," Marie has become the toast of the town. We don't need to know how she became connected with Pierre Revel. What's important, as Chaplin knew, is what that connection meant to her. It's one of the joys of the film that Marie is no victim. She takes to the life of luxury (and sin) with ease, and with her eyes wide open.

In one of the film's loveliest moments, Marie learns that Pierre is going to marry a suitably rich society girl, having been told by friends who expect her to throw a tantrum or, at least, a small fit. Instead Marie laughs it off. When she's alone, she's a bit depressed, but there are no fits. Marie is tough, in the best sense, intelligent and unsentimental, as is Pierre, who is not the lecher of cliché. He's realistic, self-centered, but he's also generous, good-humored and amused by the kind of role-playing of which both he and Marie are guilty.

There's a charming sequence in which Marie swears that she wants to break off from Pierre to become a wife and mother by marrying her priggish former suitor, suddenly transformed into a Parisian artist. Marie stamps her pretty foot, tears a string of pearls from around her neck and flings it triumphantly out the window into the street. Her point is well made until she sees a tramp come along, pocket the pearls and wander away. Marie is no dope. As Pierre breaks up with laughter, she goes tearing after the tramp to retrieve the pearls.

"A Woman of Paris" doesn't malign virtue, but the way Chaplin sees it, virtue is, more often than not, the refuge for the weak of knee. Jean (Carl Miller), the poor artist whom Marie thinks she loves, is a well-meaning twit, dominated by his mother and by the memory of a mean-spirited father, for whom Jean and his mother are still in deep mourning more than a year after his death.

As usual, Chaplin uses hardly any close-ups in "A Woman of Paris," and though he doesn't have the advantage of a deep-focus lens, he makes delightful use of medium and long shots in which we often see two or more characters interacting. In the film's funniest scene, Marie is on a massage table listening to two friends, Fifi and Paulette, talk about her problems with Pierre. We don't see Marie's face, only those of Fifi on one side, Paulette on the other and, in the center, that of the formidable masseuse, whose expression is a wickedly pointed comment on the chatter going on around her.

"A Woman of Paris" is simply composed, as are all Chaplin films, but as beautifully, wittily set, costumed, photographed and edited as any of the early Lubitsch films. Though it's hardly autobiographical, except for the presence of Miss Purviance, who is, in effect, the memory of a Chaplin romance, it is a record of Chaplin's thinking about life of a sort that's touched upon only obliquely in his other comedies, most notably in his two-reel classic "The Idle Class." One does not truly know the work of Chaplin until one has had the good fortune to see this rediscovered masterpiece. ■

1978 Ap 23, II:1:4

Twinkle, Twinkle

DEAR DETECTIVE, directed by Phillippe De Broca; screenplay (French with English subtitles) by Mr. De Broca and Michel Audiard, based on the novel, "Le Frelon," by Jean-Paul Rouland and Claude Olivier; produced by Alexandre Mnouchkine; music, Georges Delerue; director of photography, Jean-Paul Schwartz; editor, Francoise Javet; a Les Films Ariane-Mondex Films production, distributed by Cinema 5. Running time: 105 minutes. At the Sutton Theater, 57th Street east of Third Avenue. This film has not been rated.

Lise Tanquerelle	Annie Girardot
Antoine Lemercier	Philippe Noiret
Christine Vallier	Catherine Alric
Mr. Charmilie	Hubert Deschamps
Simone	Paulette Dubost
Inspector Dumas	Roger Dumas
Director of Criminal Division	Raymond Gerome
Commissioner Beretti	Guy Marchand
Suzanne	Simone Renant
Alexandre Mignonac	Georges Wilson
Catherine Tanquerelle	Armelle Pourriche
Cassard	Czarmiak

By VINCENT CANBY

ANTOINE LEMERCIER (Philippe Noiret) is a professor of Greek at the Sorbonne. He is portly, fond of good food, middle-aged and a confirmed bachelor with a deep if wandering interest in pretty women as playthings. He also has a twinkle in his eye. Lise Tanquerelle (Ann Girardot) is a pretty divorcée, with a pretty young daughter, a pretty, youngish mother and a pretty youngish aunt, and they all live together in a pretty sylvan cottage that seems to be in the center of a very pretty Paris. Lise, who is a detective with the Paris police, also has a twinkle in her eye.

•

If Philippe De Broca's "Dear Detective" does nothing else (and it doesn't), it proves that so much prettiness can be poisonous and that two twinkles are one too many for any movie not intended to make the viewer throw up.

"Dear Detective," which opens today at the Sutton Theater, tries too hard to be pleasant. It has the manner of someone who grovels at one's feet. One's first reaction is not to smile but to kick—which is the way I've felt about all of Mr. De Broca's recent films. There's nothing inherently wrong with pleasant movies except when they are as relentlessly phony as his have been.

•

"Dear Detective" pretends to be a comedy sympathetic to a liberated woman, the female detective, but it attempts to get most of its laughs by such things as having her worry about her hair, chase a suspected murderer with curlers still in place and deal with the professor's outrage when he learns she's a cop.

Though Miss Girardot and Mr. Noiret have given fine performances in the past, neither has a single redeeming moment in this failed farce. Even glorious Notre Dame Cathedral, which the characters frequently drive, run or walk past, looks as if it had been baked in a bad pâtisserie.

1978 Ap 24, C16:6

Montreal Commune

THE RUBBER GUN, directed by Allan Moyle; screenplay by Steve Lack, Allan Moyle and John Laing; photography, Frank Vitale and Jim Lawrence; music; Lewis Furey; edited by Mr. Laing; produced by Mr. Moyle and Mr. Lack; distributed by Edward Schuman and Gabriel Katzka. At the Little Carnegie, 57th Street near Seventh Avenue. Running time: 86 minutes. This film has not been rated.

With: Steve Lack, Pierre Robert, Pam Holmes-Robert, Peter Brawley, Rainbow Holmes, Pam Merchant, Bob Sontag and Allan Moyle.

By JANET MASLIN

"THE RUBBER GUN" is being advertised as "a strange movie, and it certainly is that: It's a drama that feels like a documentary, a series of episodes that at first seem entirely disconnected, a story so steeped in drug culture that it's hard to tell the characters' lucid moments from their idle mutterings. Strangest of all, "The Rubber Gun" is a movie that can be enjoyed even when it isn't understandable.

The director, Allan Moyle, whose film was part of the Museum of Modern Art's New Directors/New Films series last year (it opens today at the Little Carnegie), is as careful to set and sharpen the film's mood as he is reluctant to explain it. His methods are irritating at first, but they are ultimately quite memorable.

•

A prologue to the film introduces the principals, whose real names and screen names are the same, and presents them as Montreal's hippest bunch of drug-smugglers, members of a band that the narrator would very much like to infiltrate. This narrator, played by Mr.

Steve Lack

His delivery is successful

Moyle, is a shy sociologist, and his motives at first seem purely professional. But as the film progresses, he becomes more and more enmeshed in, and compromised by, what he sees.

The central figure in the communal family Mr. Moyle so admires is an artist, glamourpuss and father hen named Steve Lack. Mr. Lack, who wrote the screenplay with Mr. Moyle and John Laing, and who co-produced the movie, presents himself as a young, high-adrenaline jokester, and his delivery is successful enough to make even the slangy or half-audible lines sound funny.

•

But Mr. Lack also has his serious side, a side that is concerned with the commune's disintegration. The film means to use this family's breakup as a way of encapsulating the end of an era, and that's too tall an order. But it does succeed in careening unexpectedly from drug-haze episodes to important clashes of ethics and temperament, and Mr. Moyle's direction never turns maudlin or cute.

Instead, his style suggests the probing and grittinss of John Cassavetes's films. Mr. Moyle's work is less passionate than Mr. Cassavetes's, but also a bit more crisp. In both cases, for every glowing moment there are a fair share of flat ones. And the technique is often much more overpowering than the material to which it is applied.

1978 Ap 24, C17:5

"F.I.S.T."—Sylvester Stallone is an organizer in a drama about the rise of American labor unions in the 1930's.

F.I.S.T., directed and produced by Norman Jewison; screenplay by Joe Eszterhas and Sylvester Stallone, based on a story by Mr. Eszterhas; executive producer, Gene Corman; director of photography, Laszlo Kovacs; music, Bill Conti; supervising film editor, Tony Gibbs; editor, Graeme Clifford; distributed by United Artists. Running time: 146 minutes. At the Cinerama 1 and 2 Theaters, Broadway at 47th Street; Eastside Cimema, Third Avenue at 55th Street; 86th Street East Theater, 86th Street east of Third Avenue, and other theaters. This film has been raled PG.

Johnny Kovak	Sylvester Stallone
Senator Andrew Madison	Rod Steiger
Max Graham	Peter Boyle
Anna Zerinkas	Melinda Dillon
Abe Belkin	David Huffman
Babe Milano	Tony Lo Bianco
Vince Doyle	Kevin Conway
Molly Story	Cassie Yates
Arthur St. Claire	Peter Donat
Win Talbot	Henry Wilcoxon
Gant	John Lehne
Mike Monahan	Richard Herd
Tom Higgins	Tony Mockus
Mrs. Zerinkas	Elena Karam
Bernie Marr	Ken Kercheval
David Roberts	Robert Lipton
Angel	Joe Tornatore
Frank Vasko	Brian Dennehy
Lincoln	Frank McRae
Jocko	Patrick Hughes
Andrews	James Karen
Mrs. Kovak	Rozsika Halmos
Mishka	John Bleifer
Phil Talbot	Stuart Gillard
Russell Langley	Earl Montgomery
Jugovich	Charles Gradi
Zigi	Hugo Bolba
Priest	Alphonse Skerl
Mrs. Vasko	Nada Rowand
Congressman	Robert Courtleigh
Milano's attorney	Barry Atwater
Kovak's attorney	Judson Pratt

By VINCENT CANBY

OF ALL THE STORIES of organized labor, the most fascinating—perhaps because it seems the most American—has been the rise to power and affluence of the corruption-riddled International Brotherhood of American Teamsters, whose one-time president, James Hoffa, disappeared in 1975 and is now presumed to have been the victim of a one-way ride ordered by his sometime gangland associates.

Using material freely drawn from the Hoffa story, as well as from the recent history of the United Mine Workers of America, the director Norman Jewison has made "F.I.S.T.," a pop epic that covers 30 crucial years in the life of the fictitious Federation of Inter-State Truckers, from feeble beginnings to its emergence as an organization as powerful and corrupt as any of the industries it did business with.

•

"F.I.S.T.," which opens today at the Cinerama 1 and 2 and at other theaters, doesn't run especially deep but it runs long and, more important, it runs wide. It presents in the form of a diorama the story of F.I.S.T. from its origins in idealism and compromise, through its early successes, to the point in the late 1950's when a Senate committee, much like the one headed by the late Senator John L. McClellan, brought the nation's attention to bear on the union's extraordinary wealth, to the quixotic way in which that wealth was administered, and to its widespread underworld connections.

Specialists in the history of the Teamsters may not be particularly pleased with "F.I.S.T." Being movie fiction aimed at the mass market, it sets its early scenes in the depressed 30's, with all of the poor-boy clichés so dear to hearts of movie makers. The central character, that of Johnny Kovak, is played by Sylvester Stallone with a combination of brute power and arrogance that are convincing, but with little of the shrewdness, charm and murderous cynicism that made Jimmy Hoffa so successful and such popular copy for so many years. Mr. Stallone's Johnny Kovak is a rat who's all heart.

•

Yet once "F.I.S.T." disposes of the obligatory exposition that is the opening section of the picture, it becomes a compelling demonstration of a kind of power manipulation that is as integral to big capital as it is to big labor. The movie, which pictures the Depression in the golden glow of something sweetly remembered (as did "Bound for Glory"), becomes increasingly tough as it gains momentum and, at the end, genuinely tragic, not because of the fate of Johnny Kovak but because of the social and political implications. If this system doesn't work, which one will?

The screenplay, written by Joe Eszterhas and Mr. Stallone, based on a story by Mr. Eszterhas, is not great. There is, for example, a key scene early-on, in which we are supposed to be witness to the manner by which Johnny Kovak mesmerizes the union brotherhood, yet the speech itself simply isn't very rousing. We may not believe the way Johnny works his way to the top, yet the machinations by which he consolidates his power and exercises it brings the movie to real life.

•

"F.I.S.T." is a big movie that benefits more from the accumulation of small, ordinary detail than from any particular wit or inspiration of vision. It's also played with great conviction by its huge cast.There's never any doubt that Mr. Stallone is the star, but the other actors Mr. Jewison has collected are not overwhelmed by the Stallone mannerisms.

Chief among these are Melinda Dillon as the Lithuanian sewing-machine girl Johnny Kovak courts and marries; David Huffman as his boyhood friend, a fellow who shares Johnny's rise to the top but refuses to compromise; Tony Lo Bianco as the mobster who makes Johnny's earlier successes possible and who stays around to collect his debts; Kevin Conway as another boyhood friend who provides Johnny with his introduction to the mob, and Peter Boyle as the crooked F.I.S.T. president Johnny eventually succeeds.

They're all excellent. Even Rod Steiger, whose recent performances have not been memorable, makes us pay attention to the crusading senator whose mission to expose crooked union practices may or may not be for the highest of motives. The vanity is always visible.

Like "Fiddler on The Roof," "Jesus Christ Superstar" and "Rollerball," Mr. Jewison's last three films, "F.I.S.T." is a massive, essentially shapeless film, but because it's about a terrifically interesting, complicated subject, shapeliness doesn't seem especially important. There's not a moment in it to compare with the intensity of feelings contained in such documentaries as "Union Maids" and "Harlan County, U.S.A.," yet it's encouraging to hear Hollywood talking about such things at a time when play-it-safe is virtually industry policy.

•

"F.I.S.T.," which has been rated PG ("Parental Guidance Suggested"), contains some vividly accurate scenes of labor violence and some mildly vulgar language.

1978 Ap 26, C15:1

Final Fling

THE LAST WALTZ, directed by Martin Scorsese; directors of photography, Michael Chapman, Laszlo Kovacs, Vilmos Zsigmond, David Myers, Bobby Byrne, Michael Watkins and Hiro Narita; editors, Yeu-Bun Yee and Jan Roblee; music by the Band and others; produced by Robbie Robertson; released by the United Artists Corporation. At the Ziegfeld Theater, Avenue of the Americas and 54th Street. Running time: 120 minutes. This film is rated PG.

WITH: Bob Dylan, Joni Mitchell, Neil Diamond Emmylou Harris, Neil Young, Van Morrison, Ron Wood, Muddy Waters, Eric Clapton, the Staples, Ringo Starr, Dr. John and the Band.

By JANET MASLIN

MARTIN SCORSESE had the makings of a better-than-average concert movie at his disposal when he made "The Last Waltz," but the film is full of evidence that Mr. Scorsese had something more ambitious in mind. One exquisitely edited sequence of the Band performing "The Weight," filmed on a soundstage by cameras that sway and rotate with the music, infuses the interaction of a rock band with more joy and lyricism than any other rock film has ever approached. A guest appearance at the concert by the singer

Howard Rosenberg

"THE LAST WALTZ"—Bob Dylan (left) sings with Robbie Robertson in a documentary about the final concert of The Band in 1976.

Van Morrison, now paunchy and balding but triumphantly galvanizing just the same, makes for a moment rich with both euphoria and regret.

•

Mr. Scorsese's decision to train his cameras more closely on the musicians' faces than on their instruments leads to an unexpected examination of the physical and emotional costliness of their craft, and of the element of acting that's an integral part of any kind of live performance. Indeed, Mr. Scorsese manages to turn Rick Danko, the Band's bassist, into a veritable double for one of the director's favorite actors, Robert De Niro.

"The Last Waltz," which opens today at the Ziegfeld Theater, is Mr. Scorsese's record of a 1976 Thanksgiving concert given by the Band—and several of their most famous friends, like Joni Mitchell, Neil Young, Muddy Waters, Eric Clapton and Bob Dylan—to mark the group's farewell to live performing.

However definite the show's raison d'être may have been, though, its spirit remains strangely ambiguous. Members of the Band, interviewed by Mr. Scorsese afterward in footage that is interspersed among the songs, speak about the performance almost noncommittally, and their offhandedness is contagious.

•

If this wasn't a particularly sad or celebratory occasion for them, it can't mean much to the viewer either, unless the one approaches the film with a full set of memories of the principals in better days. A peculiarly myopic view of the aging process is also required, if one is to find "The Last Waltz" unusually stirring. The life of a rock star may be more draining than the life of a Maytag repairman, but when the film tries to milk too much from every last sign of wear and tear, it comes dangerously close to self-importance and self-pity.

One of the Band's most fascinating idiosyncrasies has always been its combination of a strong group identity with the virtual anonymity of individual members. The group identity has also been powerfully visual, reinforced by album-cover photographs that make the musicians out to be woodsy and austere, so deliberately antiquated looking that they summon up an impression of simpler times.

•

"The Last Waltz" takes pains to introduce them as individuals, in interviews that are slack at times but occasionally very winning. Other group members explain, for instance, that in their early days the bashful organist Garth Hudson demanded $10 a week from each of them, ostensibly for music lessons. Only later, they realized that the classically trained Mr. Hudson was too embarrassed to tell his family he was working as a rock-and-roller, and was instead claiming to have found a few teaching jobs.

The interviews are uneven, but their function is to amplify. On the other hand, the setting for the concert—an elegant stage backed by drapes and candelabra — is mightily incongruous with the Band's group identity, and the mismatch is more disruptive than illuminating. A guest appearance by the very Las Vegasy Neil Diamond, one of whose albums was recently produced by the Band's leader, Robbie Robertson, is so jarring and unwelcome that the movie takes minutes to recover. And Mr. Scorsese's efforts to stir up a distinct visual style for the film, a style that might somehow have compensated for the curious lack of sentiment that marks all but the film's final half-hour, are so half-hearted and sporadic they become almost maddening.

•

Just think of the rich visual eloquence with which Mr. Scorsese was able to invest a simple Checker cab in "Taxi Driver," and just notice that all he supplies here are a waltzing couple behind the credits and some smoke clouds. Given that, you can't help realizing that for all its impressive musical accomplishments, "The Last Waltz" is a great lost opportunity. There is a dazzling array of talent on display here, and the film surely has its memorable moments. But it articulates so little of the end-of-an-era feeling it hints at—and some of Mr. Scorsese's accomplishments have been so stunning—that it's impossible to view "The Last Waltz" as anything but an also-ran.

1978 Ap 26, C15:4

'Gentleman Tramp'

THE GENTLEMAN TRAMP, directed, written and edited by Richard Patterson; produced by Bert Schneider; music, Charles Chaplin; additional photography, Nestor Almendros; a Tinc Productions Corporation production, distributed by Marvin Films. Running time: 80 minutes. At the New Yorker Theater, Broadway at 89th Street, and other theaters. This film has been rated G.
Narrators: Walter Matthau, Laurence Olivier, Jack Lemmon.

"THE GENTLEMAN TRAMP," opening today at the New Yorker and other theaters, is an authorized documentary devoted to the life of Charlie Chaplin. The film, which was made sometime before the great man's death last year, carries the information that "every frame, from rough cut to final version, has been checked and approved personally by Charles Chaplin." Like all authorized biographies, it's somewhat too pious for its own good humor.

The film was directed, written and edited by Richard Patterson, who worked with Peter Bogdanovich on the 1972 Oscar salute to Chaplin, footage of which is the true climax of the picture. Most of the film is devoted to scenes (many splendid ones) taken from 17 Chaplin comedies, including "City Lights," "The Gold Rush," "Modern Times" and "The Kid."

•

There's an attempt to recapitulate highlights of Chaplin's life—both good times and bad—with newsreel footage, as well as with still photographs, some of which are accompanied by lofty quotations from Chaplin's book, "My Autobiography." The quotations, read by Laurence Olivier, come off worse on film than they do on the printed page: "In Philadelphia I discovered Emerson," says Chaplin, meaning, I suppose, Ralph Waldo. As in "My Autobiography," there's also a good deal of name—or photograph—dropping, to prove that Charlie hobnobbed with swells of his time, including Lloyd George, Winston Churchill and George Bernard Shaw.

Some of the film is dreadful, as when we hear a gossip-columnist, who sounds like Hedda Hopper, as she attacks Charlie, but a lot of the comedy footage is still fun, even if out of context. The nicest moments, though, are the home movies in which we see the elderly Charlie and his wife, Oona. They seem to have been a truly happy couple.

VINCENT CANBY

1978 Ap 26, C16:5

THE SEA GYPSIES, written and directed by Stewart Raffill; director of photography, Thomas McHugh; edited by Dan Greer, R. Hansel Brown and Art Stafford; music by Fred Steiner; produced by Joseph C. Raffill; distributed by Warner Bros. At Radio City Music Hall, Avenue of the Americas and 50th Street. Running time: 101 minutes. This film is classified G.

Travis .... Robert Logan
Kelly .... Mikki Jamison-Olsen
Courtney .... Heather Rattray
Jesse .... Clon Damitri Patterson
Samantha .... Shannon Saylor

Robert Logan

By JANET MASLIN

THE first fun filled minutes of "The Sea Gypsies," the latest attraction at the Radio City Music Hall, are enough to fill anyone with nameless dread. Television news crews flock to a Seattle marina, to interview a handsome young widower who plans to sail his yacht around the world, accompanied by his two cute blond daughters, their cute tawny mutt, Mushroom, and (unbenownst to anyone but all 6,000 of us in the audience) a cute young black stowaway named Jesse.

•

Just before sailing time, who should arrive on deck but a cute female magazine reporter, who has been assigned to go along on the journey in place of an (undoubtedly) cute male reporter who has conveniently broken his leg. Is there any doubt as to how this will end? Can anyone seriously question the likelihood of Dad's falling in love with the reporter? Isn't it a sure thing that everyone will live happily ever after, off the profits from the movie sale of the best-selling book Step-Mom will write about the cruise?

Miraculously, "The Sea Gypsies" turns into smooth sailing, and a very agreeable children's film, not long after the yacht pulls prettily out of the harbor. The obligatory storm sinks the boat, and the family is marooned somewhere on the Alaskan coast, amidst caribou, sea lions, and some of the loveliest snow-capped mountains in the world.

Since it is summertime, the elements don't pose any severe problems for this Seattle Family Robinson, and so they can sleep in a lean-to and bask in the sunshine. Foraging for food is a more difficult matter. Question: How can a Dad kill a caribou or a musk ox with only a homemade spear for a weapon? Answer: He can't, in a family movie like this one. The best he can do is come close enough to slaughter something, look into its limpid brown eyes, melt into a puddle of sympathy and then go out and catch fish, whose eyes aren't nearly so compelling. Parents who plan to take small children to see the film should note that G rating notwithstanding, the one sequence in which Dad does actually hunt some meat ends with the carcass's being torn apart, in close-up by a pack of wolves.

•

The scenery is spectacular, the Alaskan birds and animals are well photographed, and the film's various lessons in survival are memorable and well worth learning. After a while, one develops an unexpected fondness not only for the principals but also for their pelican, Pinocchio, and for the pet sea lion who goes "arf-arf-arf" in moments of merriment.

And the acting, while unexceptional, is more than competent. Mikki Jamison-Olsen is perky and agreeable as the reporter, and Robert Logan is a good-humored Dad; together, they're a fun couple. Shannon Saylor, as the younger daughter, is so precious she makes the sea lion look like Greta Garbo. But Heather Rattray, as the older daughter, and Cjon Damitri Patterson, as the stowaway, are spirited, personable child actors with a mercifully clear understanding that less is generally more.

1978 Ap 27, C18:5

Sight and Sound

THE FOREIGNER, written, produced and directed by Amos Poe; screenplay by Mr. Poe and Eric Mitchell; director of photography, Chirine El Khadem; editing, Michael Penland, Mr. Poe and Johanna Heer; music by Ivan Kral; an Amos Poe Visions Release. At the Whitney Museum of American Art, Madison Avenue and 75th Street. Running time: 95 minutes.

Max Menace .... Eric Mitchell
Fili Harlow .... Patti Astor
Dee Trick .... Deborah Harry
Zazu Weather .... Terens Severine
Doll .... Anya Phillips
Shake .... Duncan Hannah
Forbag .... David Forshtay
The German .... Ana Marton

By TOM BUCKLEY

"I DON'T deserve this," the title character of "The Foreigner" is heard to say as he reclines in numb despair on his bed at the Chelsea Hotel. It is a thought likely to be shared by whatever audiences are attracted to the film, which is being shown through Sunday as part of the New American Filmmakers Series at the Whitney Museum.

"The Foreigner" deals with the "punk" sensibility as manifested at CBGB, the rock nightclub on the Bowery; the streets and lofts of SoHo and the leather bars of the West Village.

The subject is not without interest, although punk seems to have lost some of its spark in the six months or so since the film was made. The trouble is that no one in the cast, which includes a couple of comely young women, has the least idea of how to act, the story is infantile and the photography, sound and editing are primitive in a way that stopped being amusing 10 years ago.

"The Foreigner" was written, produced and directed by Amos Poe, with the assistance, as a screen credit coyly notes, of a $5,000 personal loan from the Merchants Bank of New York. It seems incredible that a museum that is exhibiting Saul Steinberg on the third floor should be showing the cinematic equivalent of kindergarten scribbles on the second.

1978 Ap 27, C21:3

FM, directed by John A. Alonzo; written by Ezra Sacks; director of photography, David Myers; edited by Jeff Gourson; title song by Steely Dan; produced by Rand Holston; released by Universal Pictures. At the Criterion Theater, Broadway at 45th Street and the 86th Street Twin 2, at Lexington Avenue. Running time: 110 minutes. This film is rated PG.

Jeff Dugan .... Michael Brandon
Mother .... Eileen Brennan
Doc Holiday .... Alex Karras
Prince .... Cleavon Little
Eric Swan .... Martin Mull
Laura Coe .... Cassie Yates
Carl Billings .... Norman Lloyd
Bobby Douglas .... Jay Fenichel
Lieutenant Reach .... James Keach

"FM"—Cleavon Little portrays a late-night disk jockey at a present-day rock radio station in the musical at the Criterion and RKO 86th Street Twin.

By JANET MASLIN

THE CROWDS are massed beneath the windows, chanting their support for the strikers inside. The strikers are the staff of Los Angeles's hippest radio station, and they are standing up against corporate hypocrisy, standing up for hipsters everywhere, telling the Establishment where it can get off. The throngs are so fired with admiration that they are on the verge of rioting, when suddenly the much-beloved station manager, Jeff Dugan (Michael Brandon), makes a plea for sanity and brotherhood. The strikers will give up, he says sadly. But, he promises, "we'll give you what you want and if we can't do it here, we'll do it someplace else."

"No you won't!" croaks someone in the audience. The someone proves to be the station's curmudgeonly old owner, and he has been so moved by his staff's honesty, integrity and general panache that he is now willing to let them do everything just as they please. Good vibes will prevail, and the profits will be damned. And so ends the sort of episode that one might have thought went out with Day-Glo paint and strobe lights.

•

"FM," which opens today at the Criterion and 86th Street Twin 2 Theaters, turns into a preposterously self-serving variation on 1960's themes. It also falls into another grand tradition, that of the 70's movie-in-search-of-a-Jello-mold. These days evidently, it is possible to bankroll a film merely by suggesting a suitably hang-loose environment: car wash, hippie newspaper office, hippie radio station, country music town, high school, drugstore, musty old attic, whatever.

If this sort of thing were only being done by the George Lucases and Robert Altmans of this world, it might amount to something. But since "American Graffiti" and "Nashville," none of the bungled movies in this newly amorphous spirit have significantly broken ground.

Instead, they wind up double-dealing, keeping up contemporary appearances with loud rock soundtracks while falling back on the hoariest movie devices. "FM" at various times compares —not at all favorably—with "Mr. Smith Goes to Washington," a wide variety of soap operas, "Network" and "The Mary Tyler Moore Show."

•

The film's premise has to do with the corporate co-option of hip enterprise. QSKY, a popular station evidently owned by a conglomerate, is under pressure to play more commercials and turn a bigger profit, and the station's personnel feel too responsible to their audience to let these changes take place without a fight. The problem is certainly a real one, for rock radio stations everywhere. But Ezra Sacks's screenplay manages, by taking this crisis so very, very seriously, not to take it seriously at all.

One bone of contention, for instance, involves the staff's unwillingness to broadcast rock jingles advertising the new "fun" Army, jingles that turn up on real radio stations everywhere.

Instead of sending up these ads gently or letting them work as automatic self-parody, Mr. Sacks insists on calling in the troops, quite literally, and machine-gunning a potentially stinging episode to death. His script introduces a giggling, unhinged, pot-smoking Army officer who merrily suggests that perhaps we went to Vietnam just to commandeer their marijuana supply.

•

John A. Alonzo, the former cinematographer who directed the film, is still very much a cinematographer; he specializes in up-to-the-minute, very Robert Altman-ish, slow, pull-back shots that are slightly, piquantly out of kilter. The look of the film is convincing, and its soundtrack very well-chosen. The hair and costumes are particularly effective, rich with an amusingly studied casualness that seems apt. Mr. Alonzo has also assembled a number of gifted satirical actors to play the station's superstars. But his direction is so frequently slack, and Mr. Sacks's script so frequently dopey, that the players seldom have enough to do.

Eileen Brennan plays the station's night-shift seductress, and her very tone of voice is enough to bring on a hoot or two. Mr. Sacks, however, gives her nothing more interesting to work with than the character's growing weariness with rock-and-roll. Michael Brandon, who was so appealing as the young groom in "Lovers and Other Strangers," delivers the script's jiviest lines in a seductively deadpan style. Martin Mull, who is more or less playing Ted Knight, has some very funny moments, one of them a wonderful pantomime battle with Mr. Brandon, a battle so full of earnest sensitivity and psycho-hooey that Mr. Mull ends up tearfully sucking his thumb.

•

"FM," which is rated PG ("Parental Guidance Suggested"), is full of buxom, imbecilic women just dying to fling themselves at the station's superstars. Mr. Mull manages to catch most of them.

1978 Ap 28, C12:1

Bad Vibrations

THE MANITOU, directed by William Girdler; screenplay by Mr. Girdler, Jon Cedar and Tom Pope, based on the novel "The Manitou" by Graham Masterton; editor, Bub Asman; director of photography, Michael Hugo; produced by Mr. Girdler; released by Avco Embassy Pictures. At Loews State 2, Broadway and 45th Street and Orpheum, 86th Street at Third Avenue, and other theaters. Running time: 104 minutes. This film is rated PG.

Harry Erskine .... Tony Curtis
Singing Rock .... Michael Ansara
Karen Tandy .... Susan Strasberg
Amalie Crusoe .... Stella Stevens
Dr. Jack Hughes .... Jon Cedar
Mrs. Karmann .... Ann Sothern
Dr. Ernest Snow .... Burgess Meredith
Dr. Robert McEvoy .... Paul Mantee

THAT lump on Susan Strasberg's back in "The Manitou" isn't benign. It isn't malignant, either. Worse. It turns out to be the rapidly growing fetus of an Indian medicine man who lived 400 years ago. How come? Don't ask.

Surgeons try excision instead of exorcism only to have their scalpels turn in their hands. When they focus a laser on the enlarging protuberance, the beam goes out of control and burns holes all over the operating room.

So, despite all the efforts of medical science, the medicine man is reborn, hideously deformed by the X-rays used in the diagnosis. Hunched over Miss Strasberg's corpse, he begins tuning up his malefic vibrations, and San Francisco, where the story takes place, begins to tremble again. The city and, for all we know, the world, seems to be on the verge of destruction until . . .

The conflict in "The Manitou," which opens today at Loews State 2, the Orpheum and other theaters, isn't so much between good and evil Indian spirits as it is between seasoned performers, among them Tony Curtis, Stella Stevens, Burgess Meredith, Michael Ansara and Miss Strasberg, and an absurd penny-dreadful script and a cheapjack production. It's another knockoff in the cycle of supernatural horror films that began with "The Exorcist."

Regrettably, "The Manitou" is also the film epitaph of William Girdler, the producer, director and co-author of the screenplay. Mr. Girdler, who had

had a hand in several other movies aimed at the drive-in trade, was killed last January at the age of 30 in a helicopter crash in the Philippines while scouting locations for his next production.

"The Manitou" is rated PG ("Parental Guidance Suggested"), probably because of its generally disagreeable subject matter. TOM BUCKLEY

1978 Ap 28, C12:5

FILM VIEW

JANET MASLIN

The Rock Era Seen as History

The movies are currently offering a crash course in the history of rock and roll. In the beginning, according to "American Hot Wax," rock was the music of teen-age rebellion, and adults were scandalized. By the mid-1960's, as "I Wanna Hold Your Hand" would have it, rock was capable of generating full-scale teen hysteria, and those adults who objected were literally bowled over. By 1976, on the evidence of "The Last Waltz," the adults were the musicians themselves, well into their 30's and looking quite the worse for wear. "The Last Waltz," according to one of its more muddled and unconvincingly optimistic principals, marks "the beginning of the beginning of the end of the beginning."

There have been rock movies for as long as there has been rock music, but these latest efforts mark a significant departure. For the first time, Hollywood has begun to regard rock as a fit subject for historical scrutiny or perhaps even a thing of the past. Concert films of yesteryear, even when they aspired to a kind of time-capsule durability ("Woodstock") or attempted to read meaning into the events they recorded ("Gimme Shelter"), were much too caught up in the immediacy of the moment to take a long view. Films that followed rock stars both on and off stage, like Richard Lester's Beatle films or "Elvis on Tour," had an understandable stake in emphasizing the vitality and freshness of their subjects. "Tommy," filmed several years after The Who's rock opera was released, made every effort to update the music instead of merely to accompany it. The thrill behind dramatic films that rely heavily on their soundtracks to create a mood, like "Superfly" or the current "Saturday Night Fever," comes from the exhilarating hipness of their absolute contemporaneity.

"American Graffiti" may have had a nostalgic spirit and a nonstop score of hits from the early 60's, but even that film never really treated rock as a closed subject. The particularly haunting scene near the movie's end, in which Richard Dreyfuss finally locates the disk jockey who has been spinning out all these records, depends less on the particular songs of that era than it does upon the magical powers of music in general. The scene's subject may ostensibly be rock, but its spirit is straight out of "The Wizard of Oz."

"American Hot Wax" never aspires to any such air of timelessness. Instead, it tries to make the rock of the late 50's inseparable from all sorts of period details and from a spirit of rebelliousness that is by now so outmoded that it cries out for some kind of ironic commentary. The movie never provides it. The setting is New York and the year is 1959, but this might as well be ancient Athens, considering the distance director Floyd Mutrux puts between his story and modern times.

• • •

The trotting out of veteran rockers Chuck Berry and Jerry Lee Lewis, for a concert at the film's end, only compounds the movie's moroseness and detachment. The film offers no real hints that the upheaval of the late 50's might have created a climate in which an even more exciting and sophisticated music would later blossom. Instead, it merely suggests—and the glimpses of Mr. Berry and Mr. Lewis confirm—that everyone simply got older.

Set almost 20 years later, Martin Scorsese's "The Last Waltz" is just as glum about the aging process and just as content to let an audience's memories do the work that is ordinarily a director's. Neither of these films would be entirely intelligible to a Martian without a radio: "American Hot Wax" simply assumes its audience understands what the 60's and 70's would bring, and "The Last Waltz" aspires to a poignancy that will make sense only to viewers who know and care about the principals and their pasts.

The occasion for "The Last Waltz" was a 1976 Thanksgiving concert in San Francisco, which marked The Band's decision to stop performing after 16 years on the road. The Band hasn't broken up—they still make records, separately and together—and the film's interview footage doesn't show them looking or sounding terribly saddened by the change. Yet, they don't seem to be in a celebratory mood, either. In fact, they hardly seem moved at all.

• • •

Still, some of the guest performers at the show, like Van Morrison, Eric Clapton and Muddy Waters, seem genuinely invigorated by the occasion. And the finale, in which an all-star lineup of aging rock stars sing the saddest song Bob Dylan ever wrote, "Forever Young," is deeply stirring. But for the most part, "The Last Waltz" feels less like a celebration than a resigned shrug. The concert itself seems to have had no particular guiding spirit, and Mr. Scorsese's filming of it—except for some special sequences, shot after the show—never lends the event a governing style.

So what comes through most clearly is a sense of the performers' weariness, an acknowledgment that even the most exuberant singing and playing here mark triumphs of mind over matter. The music's physical and emotional costliness is made by Mr. Scorsese to seem so great that the film implies rock's end is upon us. This is sad, in the way that any ending is sad, and it's happy too, because veteran rockers like The Band have chosen to quit while they're ahead. But it's also self-pitying and somewhat banal, if you care to put it in perspective. After all, plumbers get old, too.

•

The next few months promise a spate of rock films that may well be able not only to put rock in perspective but also have an appeal that's independent of it—"Grease," "The Buddy Holly Story," "Sgt. Pepper's Lonely Hearts Club Band" and "FM" are on their way. But so far, only "I Wanna Hold Your Hand" has accomplished what ought to be child's play: the feat of using rock as a pretext for making a movie anyone might enjoy.

"I Wanna Hold Your Hand" is so jubilantly in keeping with the spirit of Beatlemania that it manages both to capture and to capitalize on the rock frenzy **of the mid-60's. The premise of the movie, which is about a bunch of kids who'll practically kill to get into their heroes' hotel on the day the Beatles first appeared on the Ed Sullivan show, would work with or without the Beatles as a focal point. And Robert Zemeckis's direction—ingenious but also conservative—takes pains to avoid in-jokes, rock at the headache level, or the kind of teenage idiocy that might make an older audience wish it were home in bed.**

Mr. Zemeckis's casting is particularly ingenious, since his best performers—the uproariously oafish Wendie Jo Sperber, and the very pretty, satirically demure Nancy Allen—are both buoyantly youthful and gifted beyond their years. They'll go far, and so will "I Wanna Hold Your Hand." Wherever they go, they won't really have needed the Beatles to get there. ■

ALWAYS FOR PLEASURE, directed, produced, filmed and edited by Les Blank; 58 minutes; THE BLACK INDIANS OF NEW ORLEANS, by Maurice M. Martinez, 33 minutes. At the Whitney Museum of American Art, Madison Avenue and 75th Street.

The black Mardi Gras organizations of New Orleans are the principal subject of the two films that will be shown from today through Sunday as part of the New American Filmmakers series at the Whitney Museum.

The longer and more ambitious is "Always for Pleasure," by Les Blank, a Berkeley filmmaker who has previously chronicled the lives of Cajuns in rural Louisiana, blacks in Texas and Chicanos in Chicago.

•

Because Mr. Blank appears to have no point of view beyond the rubric, "Life Is for the Living," his 58-minute film tends to be structureless and finally tedious. There are endless shots of happy blacks, less footage of happy whites on St. Patrick's Day in the crescent city, the obligatory interview with an old jazz-man at Preservation Hall, where the lifeless, out-of-tune playing is an embarrassment, a fellow explaining how he cooks crawfish, towboats puffing on the Mississippi, and of course, a long look at the carnival organizations themselves.

The 33-minute "The Black Indians of New Orleans" is by Maurice M. Martinez, a member of the faculty at Hunter College, and its approach is more disciplined than coherent. It focuses on two organizations, the Yellow Pocahontas and the White Eagles, their leaders, and their preparations for their parades. Unlike "Life Is for the Living," it also provides a brief historical context in a narration.

Why these black equivalents of the white "krewes" have all adopted Indian names and feathered and beaded costumes is, by the way, a matter of conjecture. One is that long in the past there was a certain intermarriage between the blacks and the Indian tribes of the hinterland.

TOM BUCKLEY

1978 My 2, 42:3

Fun and Philandering

WE WILL ALL MEET IN PARADISE (NOUS IRONS TOUS AU PARADIS), directed by Yves Robert; screenplay (French with English subtitles) by Jean-Loup Dabadie; based on a story by Jean-Loup Dabadie and Mr. Robert; music, Vladimir Cosma; a La Gueville-Gaumont International Co-Production, a First Artists Release. At the Columbia I Theater, Second Avenue and 64th Street. Running time: 110 minutes. This film is rated PG.

Etienne .... Jean Rochefort
Daniel .... Claude Brasseur
Simon .... Guy Bedos
Bouly .... Victor Lanoux
Marthe .... Daniele Delorme
Mouchy .... Marthe Villalonga
Bastion .... Daniel Gelin

By JANET MASLIN

E WILL ALL Meet in Paradise," the director Yves Robert's follow-up to "Pardon Mon Affaire," has the unmistakable air of a sequel—not because it seems like the continuation of a story, but because it doesn't seem like a story at all. Four fun-loving philanderers are up to a variety of boyish tricks, and the film apportions equal time to each of them, with no predominant plot thread or guiding principle. The characters are entertaining, and so are many of their adventures, but the film has all the structural solidarity of a dandelion in seed stage: it's pretty, airy, and just on the verge of blowing away.

The terribly solemn Etienne, played by Jean Rochefort just as Peter Sellers would have played him, does a "Pink Panther" ineffectual-snoop routine, trying to figure out whether his wife (Daniele Delorme) really is "a faithful, happy example of the French woman, who is the envy of tourists the world over." Loutish, lustful Bouly (Victor Lanoux) keeps busy supporting his wife, his mistress, and a lot of interchangeable-looking children.

•

Daniel (Claude Brasseur) may be on the verge of entering into a marriage of convenience with a wealthy older woman, but when he looks out a window and whistles "Not bad!" the object of his attention is—much to his heterosexual cronies' disappointment — a handsome young soldier. And Simon (Guy Bedos), a doctor who is the ultimate mama's boy, makes love to his female patients behind the X-ray machine.

The film's funniest sequences involve this foursome's ill-advised purchase of a country home, a fist-fight they conduct wearing earmuffs on a tennis court, and a bully's single-handedly demolishing an entire car, whch happens to have Mr. Rochefort inside it at the time. Mr. Bedos's dealings with his mother are also most amusing. Mr. Robert has a dry wit, a sure hand and, figuratively speaking, an old hat: His is a lightly likable, essentially familiar brand of comedy, designed to elicit a few mild chuckles and an occasional ooh-la-la.

Mr. Robert also attempts good-humored social satire at times, but his work is a good deal more tepid in this department. Mr. Robert's notion that the foibles of the French bourgeoisie are silly but lovable is a profoundly uninteresting one.

It should be noted that "We Will All Meet in Paradise" bears a distinct resemblance to "My Friends," an Italian film released two years ago, also about the adventures of four fun-loving philanderers. "My Friends" was uproariously funny, and deftly satirical and "We Will All Meet in Paradise" doesn't hold a candle to it.

1978 My 3, C18:5

Intense Shorts

MAYA DEREN RETROSPECTIVE: MESHES OF THE AFTERNOON, made with Alexander Hammid, 14 minutes; **AT LAND,** 15 minutes; **A STUDY IN CHOREOGRAPHY FOR CAMERA,** made with Talley Beatty, 4 minutes; **OUT-TAKES FROM: A STUDY IN CHOREOGRAPHY FOR CAMERA** 15 minutes; **RITUAL IN TRANSFIGURED TIME,** 15 minutes; **MEDITATION ON VIOLENCE,** 12 minutes; **THE VERY EYE OF NIGHT,** 15 minutes; distributed by Grove Press Films (excluding Out-Takes), at the Film Forum, 15 Vandam Street May 4-7 and 11-14.

THE FEW FILMS directed by the late Maya Deren are extremely short—ranging from 4 to 15 minutes—and they cannot be watched with anything less than the utmost concentration. Miss Deren, a pioneer avant-garde figure who did most of her work in the late 1940's, invested every last object and gesture in her films with strong symbolic meaning, and her work requires the same kind of painstaking scrutiny one might ordinarily bring to a painting. The Film Forum's Deren retrospective, which will be shown tonight through Sunday and again from May 11 to May 14, lasts only an hour and a half, but the relentless intensity of the program makes it exhausting.

•

Aside from the draining effect Miss Deren's films have when shown together, there are other good reasons for taking her efforts in small doses. She tended to repeat herself somewhat, in both her extreme attentiveness to the voluptuous possibilities of the human body and in her predilection for shifting characters back and forth between natural, primitive-looking locales and abstract, "socialized" settings. Typically, "At Land" begins alternating an image of Miss Deren crawling along a beach with one of her wriggling across the table at a dinner party.

Miss Deren figured as physically and seductively as she could in most of her films, but "A Study in Choreography for Camera" concentrates entirely on the dancer Talley Beatty, who leaped through a forest, a living room and a museum. The completed film runs only four minutes, and it is followed on the program by 15 minutes of out-takes, extra footage of Mr. Beatty that Miss Deren shot and stored away.

•

This unused material would be illuminating if one had the time or the inclination to study it closely, and it would certainly cast more light upon Miss Deren's decision processes if the finished film were shown again, afterward. Scheduled as they are, though, the out-takes merely overwhelm the film itself, and they serve to limit the potential audience for this program to only the most serious students of the avant-garde cinema.

JANET MASLIN

1978 My 4, C16:1

Saturnine Pellagra

THE INCREDIBLE MELTING MAN, written and directed by William Sachs; film editor, James Besnears; director of photography, Willy Curtis; produced by Samuel W. Gelfman; released by American International. At the Victoria, Broadway and 46th Street and other theaters. Running time: 86 minutes. This film is rated R.

The Incredible Melting Man .... Alex Rebar
Dr. Ted Nelson .... Burr DeBenning
General Perry .... Myron Healey
Sheriff Blake .... Michael Alldredge
Judy Nelson .... Ann Sweeny
Dr. Loring .... Lisle Wilson

THERE'S a powerful temptation to say that you never thaw a movie as foolish as "The Incredible Melting Man," but the fact is that each spring brings similar releases to fill the need of drive-in operators for something cheap to put on the screen for the kids in the cars to ignore or laugh at.

This one, which opened yesterday at several theaters, is about an astronaut who contracts a disease during a trip to Saturn that causes his flesh to melt like wax unless he gets an all-meat diet. The problem is that prime steak or the whitest veal won't do. Only human flesh has the nutrients necessary to control this interplanetary pellagra.

Alex Rebar in the title role heads the cast of unknowns. William Sachs, writing and directing his first feature film, shows no aptitude in either department. The real puzzle is not how the movie got made but why, on a brilliantly sunny day, a dozen adults including a dignified man in a white turban, presumably spent $3.50 to see it at the Victoria, a shabby house with uncomfortable seats, still filthy with the debris left by the previous day's audiences.

TOM BUCKLEY

1978 My 4, C16:1

Politics and Religion

THE LAST SUPPER, directed by Tomas Gutierrez Alea; screenplay (Spanish with English subtitles) by Tomas Gonzalez, Maria Eugenia Haya and Mr. Alea; produced by Santiago Llapur and Camilo Vives; director of photography, Mario Garcia Joya; editor, Nelson Rodriguez; music, Leo Brouwer; a Cuban Film Institute production, distributed by Tri-continental Film Center. Running time: 110 minutes. At the 68th Street Playhouse, Third Avenue at 68th Street. This film has not been rated.

The Count .... Nelson Villagra
WITH: Silvano Rey, Luns Alberto Garcia, Jose Antonio Rodriguez, Samuel Claxton and Mario Balmaseda.

By VINCENT CANBY

THE time is the late 18th century Holy Week—and the place—a huge, isolated Cuban sugar plantation owned by a Spanish count from Havana who appears to represent the best of the ruling aristocracy. The Count is middle-aged and has the gaunt look of someone who suffers spiritually, as well as from intestinal disorders. He does not take lightly the responsibilities of power. He is as much concerned for the souls of his slaves as he is for their physical fitness.

When his overseer, a brutishly practical man named Manuel, punishes a returned runaway by slicing off the slave's ear, the Count feels the victim's pain. The Count doesn't question the system, of course. Instead, he devotes himself to making it work. To this end he invites 12 slaves, picked at random, to join him for dinner on Maundy Thursday, in effect to re-enact the Last Supper that Jesus shared with his disciples the night before his crucifixion.

•

"The Last Supper," a new Cuban film by Tomas Gutierrez Alea, the director whose "Memories of Underdevelopment" was one of the critical hits of 1973, is a fine, cool, almost detached political parable told entirely in religious terms. In this way it recalls the kind of contradictions that made "Memories of Underdevelopment" so fascinating, and that are, for Mr. Alea, virtually a stylistic method.

Though "Memories" looks at the Cuban revolution through the eyes of a middle-class intellectual who can't bring himself to participate, the film itself is passionately committed. "The Last Supper" is about death resurrection, not only about the death and resurrection of freedom, but also of repression.

Like the earlier film, it seems to say more than one ever expects to hear in popular revolutionary literature, where ideas and feelings are supposed to be recognized and accommodated by even the dimmest minds.

"The Last Supper," which opens today at the 68th Street Playhouse, is not an easy film. It has something of the haunted, guilt-ridden manner of the Count, the character who dominates the film and who remains forever mysterious. It's not, I think, that the director or Nelson Villagra, who plays the Count, withhold information. It is, rather, that the truth of human behavior can never be more than action observed. The rest is speculation.

The film's centerpiece is the extraordinary last supper presided over by the Count, who begins by washing and kissing the feet of the 12 slaves while each, in turn, giggles and panics at the lunatic behavior of the master. In the course of the meal, as the wine flows, the Count attempts to instruct the slaves in Christian mythology and dogma.

"Sorrow," he says, "is the only thing we can give God with joy"—everything else belongs to God anyway. The slaves find this concept confusing, while all, except one former cannibal, are amused at the thought of consuming the body and blood of Jesus in the form of bread and wine.

A scene from "The Last Supper," a Cuban film directed by Tomas Alea
A fine, cool, almost detached political parable

Before the supper has ended, the Count, now thoroughly drunk and in a mood to be pals with the help, has freed one slave and promised no work the next day, Good Friday. When those promises are not honored, the rebellion that breaks out results in the crucifixion of a most unlikely son-of-God and in his resurrection in the person of the Count himself. His wrath is not that of a disappointed God, but of a property owner.

•

My program notes, unfortunately, identify only the actor who plays the Count, but the film has several other memorable performances. There is the man who plays the priest at the sugar mill, a boyish-looking fellow who attempts to meet the needs of the Count and the slaves and fails everyone. There are also the actor who plays the runaway slave, a man who becomes a symbol for eventual revolutionary victory, and the old, old black man who plays the briefly freed slave.

Except for the occasional use of the hand-held camera, which is so intrusive as to seem self-congratulatory, "The Last Supper" has been beautifully photographed in color by Mario Garcia Joya, who also shot the black-and-white "Memories of Underdevelopment." The colors are mostly the colors of depressed rural areas—lots of tobacco browns and the yellows of feeble candlelight. The skies are blue, but they are oppressive, and the greens suggest a landscape of weeds.

1978 My 5, C6:5

CAT AND MOUSE, written, directed and produced by Claude Lelouch; French with English subtitles; photography by Jean Collomb; music by Francis Lai; a Robert A. McNeil Presentation, distributed by Quartet Films. At the Cinema I Theater, Third Avenue and 60th Street. Running time: 107 minutes. This film has been rated PG.

Madame Richard .... Michele Morgan
Inspector Lechat .... Serge Reggiani
His Assistant .... Philippe Leotard
Monsieur Richard .... Jean-Pierre Aumont
Valerie .... Valerie Lagrange

By JANET MASLIN

The title of Claude Lelouch's pretty and personable new murder mystery, "Cat and Mouse," is a play on the name of the story's main character, a police inspector called Lechat. It also refers to the brand of gamesmanship Mr. Lelouch uses—this time to unusually good effect—to keep an audience on its toes. "Cat and Mouse" is populated by characters with fertile imaginations, so the film depicts quite a few incidents that prove, on close inspection, not to have taken place. In this same spirit, Mr. Lelouch keeps his camera continually pacing and peering, until it begins finding clues that aren't really clues at all.

An unseen man, a minor figure in the story, always directs his visitors to a drawerful of identical-looking cigars in his humidor, ominously reciting the same line: "Take any one, they're quite correct." A peculiar jewel theft turns out to have been part of another movie someone was watching at the time of the actual crime. A married woman is seen visiting her lover, whose back is toward the camera; it turns out that Mr. Lelouch has shot the scene this way not out of any particular discretion, but because the whole episode is being described by a gossip-mongering, unreliable witness. The film reeks of that staple ingredient of any good-humored tale of intrigue, the red herring.

•

In the past, Mr. Lelouch has often applied his full powers of obfuscation to more dramatic or romantic material, fudging the fine line between fantasy and reality at moments when it needs to be drawn most clearly. Here, though, these same stylistic idiosyncrasies are so appropriately applied that they take on a whole new dimension of wit.

"Cat and Mouse" isn't primarily a comedy, but it continually sends up the conventions of mystery fiction, and also parodies a great many movie-making gimmicks. The jewel-robbery scene, the one that is actually part of another film, is shot exactly as if it were part of this one. Mr. Lelouch takes great pains to trick his audience, and an even greater delight in the camera's power to deceive.

Serge Reggiani as a detective in "Cat and Mouse."

The plot revolves around the death of a wealthy businessman (Jean-Pierre Aumont), the questionable innocence of his bereaved wife (Michele Morgan) and the genial snooping of Detective Lechat (Serge Reggiani). Its dénouement is complicated in the extreme, rich with the unflagging niceness that is so formidable a part of Mr. Lelouch's mystique. Even the lesser characters, such as the couple's sneaky-looking servants or the dead man's pornographic-star mistress, are so likable that it's hard to imagine any of them as cold-blooded killers.

The solution to the mystery isn't clever enough to rank Mr. Lelouch's script with the work of Conan Doyle, but it does manage to satisfy the demands of logic without compromising the film's essentially benign view of human nature. For a murder mystery, that's a great deal more difficult and impressive than it may sound.

Mr. Lelouch always uses handsome, friendly-looking actors to reinforce his films' feeling of warmth, but this time he has really outdone himself in the realm of clever casting. In 1975, when "Cat and Mouse" was made, Miss Morgan hadn't been in a film in years, and was perhaps still identified in most viewers' minds with her earlier, more glamorous roles. Mr. Lelouch cast her as a serene, implacably elegant matron of about 50, and chose the rumpled, redoubtable Mr. Reggiani—a wonderful character actor who had also been out of view for a while—to play the detective who both suspects and admires her.

The teaming of Miss Morgan and Mr. Reggiani gives the film an ironic recogniton of class boundaries and a delight at the ease with which they can sometimes be crossed; in addition, it provides great deal of romantic spark. Their performances are top-notch, and they make a fine couple.

•

However, they don't spend a great deal of time ogether Miss Morgan is most often seen at home, on one of the most spectacular estates suburban Paris has to offer. Mr. Reggiani is usually seen with his assistant, an equally rumpled, younger fellow played by the estimable Phlippe Leotard. Together with two women friends and one of the worst-trained police dogs in movie history, they are often shown eating, drinking and emphatically illustrating that a policeman's lot need not be an unhappy one. The unlikely domestic troubles revolving around Mr. Reggiani produce some of the film's most amusing and memorable vignettes.

Occasionally, Mr. Lelouch's methods backfire. A brief flashback to the death of a young man in an auto accident, prettily shot and scored by Francis Lai, has the ill-chosen rosiness that mars some of Mr. Lelouch's other films. And an episode showing the two detectives racing through traffic, meant to be dizzying, goes on so long that it has the desired effect and then some.

Luckily, lapses like these are infrequent. Besides, in a backhanded way, they're useful: They recall the preciousness that has been so tiresome in some of the director's other films, and that is so commendably absent this time. In addition to being one of his best and most ingenious films, "Cat and Mouse" is the closest Mr. Lelouch has come to producing his patented glow with enough discipline and economy to attract moviegoers of all persuasions, not just the romantics in the crowd. Those who are not charter members of Mr. Lelouch's fan club ought to find "Cat and Mouse" a specially nice surprise.

•

"Cat and Mouse," which is rated PG (Parental Guidance Suggested"), features one very innocuous-looking shooting and a plot involving a young prostitute, a pornographic-movie star and a few extramarital love affairs.

1978 My 7, 70:3

FILM VIEW

JANET MASLIN

When Thrillers Fizzle

On transcontinental flights, certain airlines now train closed-circuit cameras on the cockpit during takeoff and landing, broadcasting the pilot's every maneuver to a truly captive audience. The idea behind this innovation is presumably to reassure the passengers, but it is self-defeating. After all, most of us have been conditioned by the movies to regard pilot-at-the-controls scenes as menacing. They signal that a mid-air collision with a UFO is only seconds away. That Charlton Heston will try his level best to make a successful crash-landing. That skyjackers are about to commandeer the life vests. That we will all be given mouth-to-mouth resuscitation by Karen Black.

Even more insensitive than the airlines, to the strong subliminal effects that such loaded images have on an audience, are the directors of a couple of current thrillers. Often, there's a distinct difference between what a particular object or gesture or camera movement is supposed to mean and what it actually suggests. A director who doesn't make use of this disparity has no business turning out thrillers; on the other hand, a director who can successfully exploit the hidden meaning of a scene is in a position to make truly terrifying mischief. Do you think, for example, that a hospital setting ought to suggest safety and efficiency and the miracles of modern medicine? That's not what Michael Crichton uses it for in "Coma," any more than Alfred Hitchcock used a clear blue sky and pretty wheat field to signal serenity during his famous crop-dusting chase in "North by Northwest."

Movies full of cheap thrills—the kind with "chainsaw" in the title—are on the wane these days. But a subtler yet equally inept type of thriller is very much in vogue. Unfortunately, the only real shocks behind expensive, stylish-looking suspense films like Brian de Palma's "The Fury" and Michael Winner's remake of "The Big Sleep" come from the director's startling obliviousness to the responses their films produce. When Mr. Winner decided to set "The Big Sleep" amidst new, expensive-looking furniture and under sunny English skies, he managed to invest a supposedly murky mystery with all the menace of a Macy's white sale.

As Mel Brooks satirically demonstrates in "High Anxiety," by letting an outdoor camera move slowly toward a window until it crashes through a pane of glass, there are times when directorial cleverness can call too much attention to itself. Brian de Palma, who will never shoot a scene simply when there's a chance to try an inappropriate camera trick, is as expert at imitating Hitchcock's most inspired techniques as he is uncertain about how to use them. With "The Fury," he seems once again to be senselessly showing off. This would be fine, or at least it would be tolerable, if Mr. De Palma's fancy footwork were not so often at odds with the literal content of his scenes. At the beginning of "The Fury," for instance, Mr. De Palma slowly, ominously pans the camera from side to side while Kirk Douglas and John Cassavetes conduct a joking, seemingly unimportant conversation. As it turns out, a lot of vital plot information is being conveyed quite casually; so, perhaps the director means to hint to his audience that more is happening than meets the ear.

• • •

Later in the film, Mr. De Palma is up to the same old trick: the camera moves slowly, ominously from side to side while Amy Irving and Carrie Snodgress eat ice cream sundaes. This time, though, the small talk is genuinely small; so, what is the camera asking us to notice? Is there Clorox in the whipped cream? Has someone been given the wrong flavor by mistake? Or is this simply artiness for artiness's sake?

Mr. De Palma's endless emphasizing of his technical skill takes its toll on "The Fury's" already weak plot. One critic has argued that Mr. De Palma's technique is so impressive that his movies don't need to make sense. Yet, when logic is thrown as heedlessly to the winds as it is in "The Fury," an audience can become too confused even to follow the action, much less find it exciting. The two telekinetic teen-agers in the film have such vaguely defined magical powers that one never really knows, when either one of them winds up in trouble, whether he or she is equipped to escape. The girl, played by Miss Irving, can sometimes read minds; yet, she asks questions to which she ought to know the answers. The boy, played by Andrew Stevens, is capable of hanging in midair at will; yet, he dies falling off a roof.

Mr. De Palma has a way of sacrificing anything and anybody—even the few sympathetic figures in his films—for the sake of a good stunt. For example, the messy murder of the boy's doctor and lover (played by Fiona Lewis) makes for one of the film's most spectacular special effects. But the quarrel that leads up to the killing is very clearly just a set-up for the murder; it is silly, implausible and—worst of all—slow. When you care as little about logic as Mr. De Palma seemingly does, it's a fatal mistake to give an audience time to scratch its head in befuddlement.

Even for audiences who don't care to swallow the human organ-smuggling premise behind "Coma," Michael Crichton's crisp, unobtrusive direction is bound to seem more effective than Mr. De Palma's hocus-pocus approach. Mr. Crichton's film plays brilliantly upon the way clean, well-lighted hospital settings leave most people utterly panic-stricken. But the fact that his heroine (Genevieve Bujold) is a doctor, presumably someone who doesn't find the hospital ambiance disturbing, allows his audience a safe entree into this frightening world. Mr. Crichton gives the formula an additional clever twist by placing his heroine in jeopardy at the hands of other doctors: An audience can easily identify with her fear and also be glad for the medical expertise that may save her, instead of disliking her for the bloodless or snooty qualities some people associate with doctors.

"Coma" has a first-rate suspense plot, but what keeps the movie continually surprising is the way it constantly plays upon the qualities that make doctors different from most people. While being pursued by a thug, Miss Bujold, trapped in a freezer full of corpses for dissection in an anatomy lab, is perfectly prepared to treat these cadavers the way another kind of trapped heroine might treat the furniture in a drawing room. Mr. Crichton stages his chase sequence very conventionally, without calling attention to the special scariness of a med-school lab. That's precisely why the episode is so thrilling; because Miss Bujold isn't unusually terrified by the setting, the audience is allowed to enjoy a vicarious sense of detachment and bravery.

"Coma" is at its most bloodcurdling in an early operat-ing-room sequence, but not for the reasons one might imagine. Mr. Crichton must be perfectly aware that operation scenes, like cockpit scenes, never turn up in movies unless something is about to go wrong. Accordingly, he doesn't fill the screen with worried doctors, erratic bleeps on the monitoring instruments and frantic nurses hurriedly handing over scalpels. Instead, he shows the doctors joking, chatting, poking at their unconscious patient and generally expressing no particular concern for the welfare of someone whose life hangs in the balance.

Wouldn't anyone in a "Coma" audience expect to be fussed over during an operation the way patients in movies ordinarily are? Mr. Crichton's suggestion that a place one associates with elaborate concern may actually be rife with indifference is a lot more chilling than the medical scenes movies usually offer. Indeed, this is the kind of turnabout that makes for genuine terror. ■

1978 My 7, II:17:1

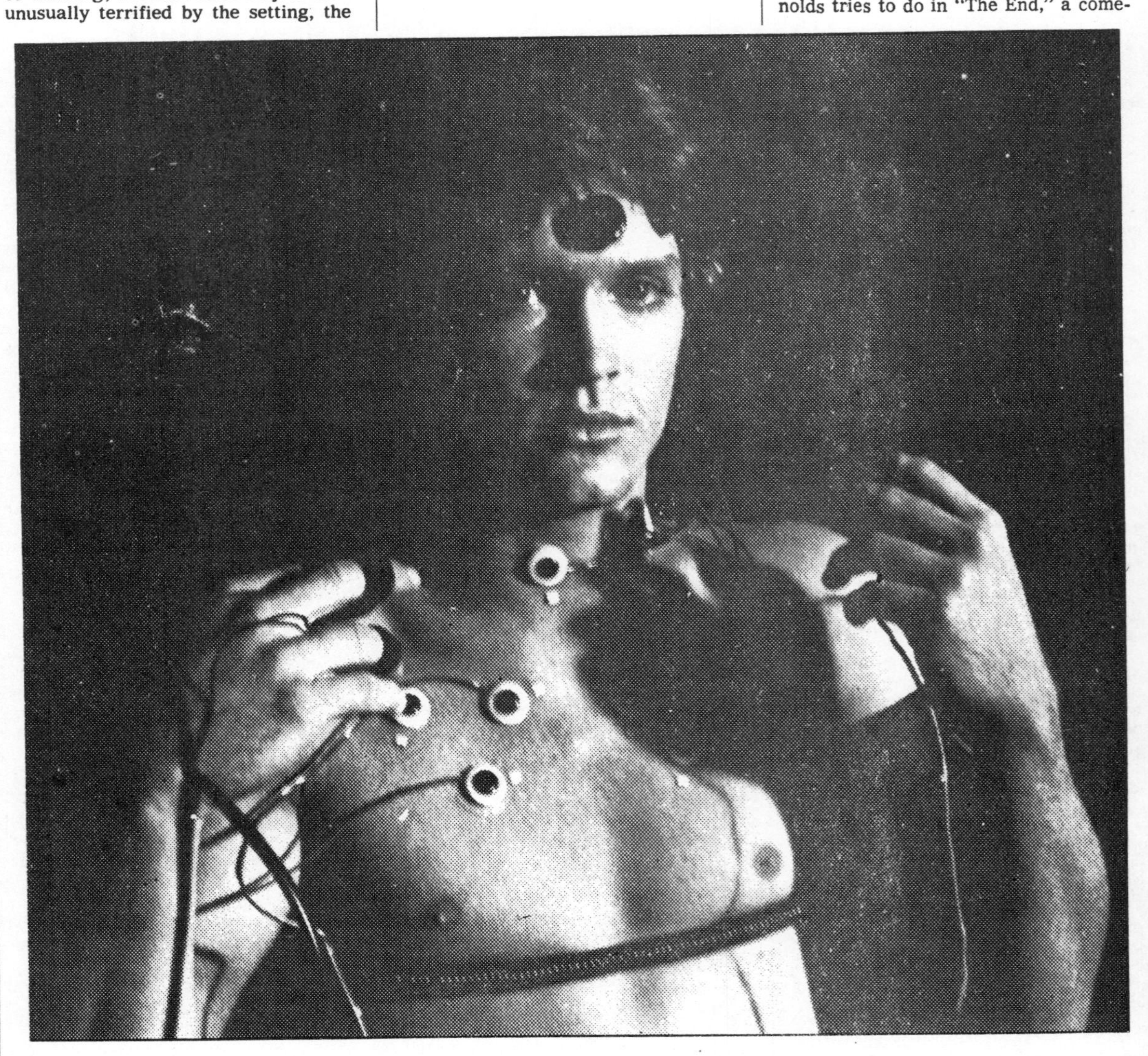

Andrew Stevens in Brian de Palma's "The Fury"—"Logic is thrown to the winds."

Director and Star

THE END, directed by Burt Reynolds; screenplay by Jerry Belson; produced by Lawrence Gordon; executive producer, Hank Moonjean; editor, Donn Camberu; director of photography, Bobby Byrne; music, Paul Williams; distributed by United Artists. Running time: 100 minutes. At the Baronet Theater, Third Avenue near 59th Street. This film has been rated R.

Wendell Sonny Lawson....Burt Reynolds
Marlon Borunki....Dom DeLuise
Mary Ellen....Sally Field
Dr. Waldo Kling....Strother Martin
Marty Lieberman....David Steinberg
Jessica....Joanna Woodward
Dr. Samuel Krugman....Norman Fell
Maureen Lawson....Myra Loy
Julie Lawson....Kristy McNichol
Ben Lawson....Pat O'Brien
The Priest....Robby Benson
Dr. Maneet....Carl Reiner
Receptionist....Louise Letourneau
Hearse driver....Bill Ewing
Limousine driver....Robert Rothwell
Hospital orderly....Harry Caesar
Pacemake patient....James Best
Latin lover....Peter Gonzales
Girl dancer....Connie Fleming
Ballet teacher....Janice Carroll
Whistling lunatic....Ken Johnson

By VINCENT CANBY

"THE END," which was directed by Burt Reynolds, who also stars in it, is like being with good friends at a party where nothing goes right. The food doesn't arrive. The ice runs out. A couch catches fire and, outside in the street, the Department of Water Supply is making a noisy, after-hours dig to locate a broken main. Instead of calling the whole thing off, the host tries to cope.

This is pretty much what Mr. Reynolds tries to do in "The End," a come-

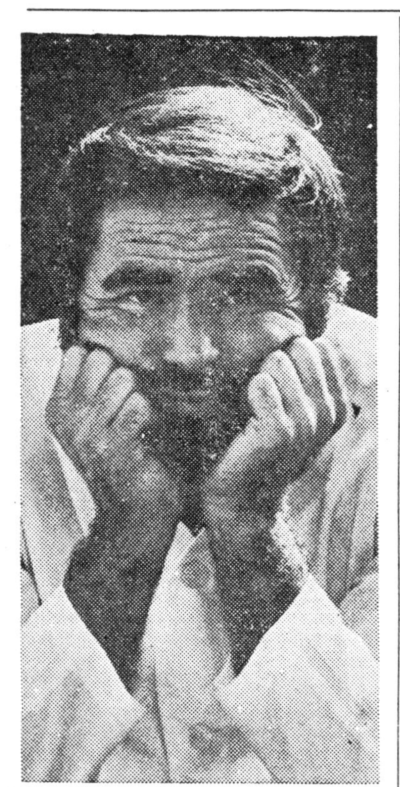

Burt Reynolds

dy about a cheerful, completely unreliable Los Angeles real-estate promoter who learns he has a fatal blood disease and takes the news badly. Mr. Reynolds tries to cope but the party seldom results in much more than physical and emotional exhaustion.

•

The beginning of "The End," which opens today at the Baronet, more or less defines everything that's wrong with the movie that follows. Wendell Sonny Lawson (Mr. Reynolds), who has a measure of fame for having been his own television huckster, is in his doctor's office receiving the fatal news.

The camera doesn't show us the two men in the same shot. Mostly we get close-ups of Wendell, who overacts so broadly that we know the film's mood is comic even though neither he nor the doctor (Norman Fell) are funny. Wendell becomes enraged. He cries. The doctor, who has a cold, doses himself with nasal spray and offers feeble hope ("Perhaps some doctor, somewhere, in some little lab will find a cure. . . .")

The scene wants to be funny. It tells us it's trying to be funny, but you sense mounting desperation, which is suddenly made manifest when, for no apparent reason, the director begins to photograph the star through the tropical fish tank that tones up the doctor's office. There's no logic to this shot. It's another way of shooting a scene that is not going anywhere anyway.

•

Thereafter Wendell Sonny Lawson undertakes a frantic search for sympathy and a practical, painless way out. He visits his elderly parents (Myrna Loy and Pat O'Brien), who are nice but too self-absorbed to notice that he has absconded with all their sleeping pills. His ex-wife (Joanne Woodward) loathes him for good reason, though she would seem to be as bad a bargain as Wendell in any marriage.

His best friend (David Steinberg) simply agrees that suicide is the wisest course, while his girlfriend (Sally Field), a sweet slob who lives in a clutter of cats and unwashed dishes, cries a lot and, after they've made love, admits that she didn't have an orgasm —but then she never does.

It is difficult to believe that Jerry Belson, who wrote the screenplay for "The End" (as he did for the successfully satiric "Smile"), didn't have more in mind about the barren lives of these people than what we see on the screen. This is half-heartedly satiric material that's been directed by Mr. Reynolds as if it were broad, knock-about comedy sometimes and, at other times, as if it were meant to evoke pathos, which it never does.

•

With the right direction, Mr. Reynolds has shown himself to be an accomplished comedian as in "Semi-Tough," but the actor here is betrayed by the director who doesn't appear to know which way the camera should be pointed.

The movie isn't totally unfunny. Wendell has an amusing encounter early on with Bobby Benson, who plays a Catholic priest so young and naïve that all he can say is "wow" when Wendell attempts to confess. Carl Reiner has a nice, very brief bit as a "death therapist," But the film's only sustained comedy is supplied by the incomparable Dom DeLuise as a schizophrenic murderer who befriends the desperate Wendell. Mr. DeLuise's characterization amounts to a solo nightclub performance and, like many a nightclub performance, it doesn't really go anywhere, it just runs out of material.

The film's most serious shortcoming is Mr. Reynolds's apparent inability to direct himself in relation to the other actors. He's not rude to them. He doesn't upstage them. He has an excellent supporting cast and he obviously relishes their talents, but he has no concept of where he, as actor as well as director, stands as boss. He's simply overwhelmed.

1978 My 10, C21:1

IT LIVES AGAIN, directed, written and produced by Larry Cohen; music, Bernard Herrmann; musical adaptation and additional music by Laurie Johnson; director of photography, Fenton Hamilton; editors, Curt Burch, Louis Friedman and Carol O'Blath; distributed by Warner Bros. Running time: 92 minutes. At the National Theater, Broadway near 43d Street, and other theaters. This film has been rated R.

Eugene Scott .... Frederic Forrest
Jody Scott .... Kathleen Lloyd
Frank Davis .... John P. Ryan
Mr. Mallory .... John Marley
Dr. Perry .... Andrew Duggan
Dr. Forest .... Eddie Constantine
Detective Lieutenant Perkins .... James Dixon

"IT LIVES AGAIN," which opens today at the National and other theaters, is Larry Cohen's sequel to the financially successful horror film he made last year, "It's Alive," in which a newborn baby laid waste a large part of Greater Los Angeles.

Shot for shot, performance for performance, non-scare for non-scare, "It Lives Again" surpasses the tackiness of the original, perhaps because the new work has three monster-babies instead of one.

The cast includes venerable Eddie Constantine, the American-born-and-bred French film star, as a doctor who walks as if he were wearing a cement corset. The other actors have less assurance than porn performers attempting to play a scene of straight dramatic exposition. Being fully clothed, they don't know where to look or move. Mr. Cohen wrote, directed and produced the film, which, most of the time, has the manner of something improvised in blind panic. VINCENT CANBY

1978 My 10, C21:1

Anthony Quinn and Jacqueline Bisset in "The Greek Tycoon"
The film is as witless as it is gutless

Two Jacquelines

THE GREEK TYCOON, directed by J. Lee Thompson; produced by Allen Klein and Ely Landau; screenplay by Mort Fine; photography by Tony Richmond; music composed and orchestrated by Stanley Myers; a Universal release. At the Loews State II, Loews Cine and 34th Street East theaters. Running time: 106 minutes. This film is rated R.

Theo Tomasis .... Anthony Quinn
Liz Cassidy .... Jacqueline Bisset
Spyros Tomasis .... Raf Vallone
Nico Tomasis .... Edward Albert
Simi Tomasis .... Camilla Sparv
Sophia Matalas .... Marilu Tolo
Michael Russell .... Charles Durning
Paola Scotti .... Luciana Paluzzi
John Cassidy .... Robin Clarke
Nancy Cassidy .... Kathryn Leigh Scott
Robert Keith .... Roland Culver
Doctor .... Tony Jay
Servant .... John Bennett
Helena .... Katharine Schofield
Lady Allison .... Joan Benham
Angela .... Linda Thorson
Tahlib .... Guy Deghy
Magda .... Jill Melford
Mia .... Lucy Gutteridge

By VINCENT CANBY

"THE GREEK TYCOON" recalls a sort of newspaper journalism you don't see much anymore—the Sunday supplement recapitulation of a famous murder, divorce or other scandal, put together, from morgue clips, and filled out by the writer with breathless speculation about what really might have happened and what really might have been said, always with more exclamation points than are absolutely necessary. It's the literature of vultures who have no interest in tearing into something of the first freshness.

In case you haven't seen the ads, which tell all, the film is the something-less-than-passionate love story of the beautiful young widow of an assassinated United States President and an aging Greek promoter who owns oil tankers, airlines and islands and dreams of becoming President of Greece, which would be decidedly odd since his real-life model traveled on an Argentine passport.

Cast in the leading roles are Jacqueline Bisset, who bears a striking resemblance to Jacqueline Kennedy Onassis, but, at this date, is younger and more beautiful, and Anthony Quinn, who sort of looks like the late Aristotle Onassis, though he's a much bigger man and according to all reports about Mr. Onassis, possesses much less charm.

•

Some of the other characters who pop up like animated mannequins are a former British prime minister, who looks as if he'd like to look like a bulldog; the Greek tycoon's noisy, publicity-loving mistress; his first wife, who commits suicide under what may or may not be mysterious circumstances; the late President of the United States himself, played by James Franciscus, and his brother (the Attorney General) and sister-in-law.

The movie wastes no time attempting to create a fictional equivalent to the Camelot that was the Kennedy era, giving us only a fast montage that includes a reference to a glittering White House dinner party where Neil Diamond entertained and "Greg and Véronique Peck" headed the guest list. If Mort Fine, who wrote the original screenplay, had shown any point of view elsewhere in the script, you might think this was meant to be funny. However, the film is as witless as it is gutless.

Most of it is devoted to the courtship and marriage of Liz Cassidy (Miss Bisset) and Theo Tomasis (Mr. Quinn), about whom the writer and J. Lee Thompson, the director, would like to have it both ways. They portray Liz as being deeply in love with both her husbands (in succession) but having a teeny tiny weakness for shopping, and Theo as a brilliant international pirate with a heart of gold, a fellow who loves Liz but loves what she represents even more.

Though at 106 minutes the film seems as long as "The Other Side of Midnight," which ran 160 minutes, "The Greek Tycoon" is only truly intolerable when it attempts to be serious, as when Mr. Quinn talks with supposed feeling about his humble peasant origins or deals lovingly with his son and heir, played by Edward Albert. But then it's not even fun when it's wrestling with its gossipy subject at a skin-deep level, perhaps because our fantasies outrun those of the moviemakers. Played straight, though the laughs are built-in, is the sequence about the notorious wedding contract, which guarantees the bride $10 million for every year she remains married to the Greek. This prompts Liz to recoil in disgust ("It's horrible—writing it all down!"), while Theo explains patiently that it's simply an old Greek custom.

•

The performances are uniformly awful, which is a record not easily matched by any movie not made by

Larry ("It Lives Again") Cohen. Miss Bisset is great to look at, but "The Greek Tycoon" is the sort of movie in which a fine-looking woman can be upstaged by a boat. This is the magnificent yacht, owned in real life by William Levitt, which doubles as Theo Tomasis's La Belle Simone.

"The Greek Tycoon," which opens today at Loews State II and other theaters, is fiction divided against itself. It would make no sense if we hadn't read the headlines and gossip columns, to titillate us.

1978 My 12, C10:5

JENNIFER; directed by Brice Mack; produced by Steve Krantz; story by Mr. Krantz; screenplay by Kay Cousins Johnson; director of photography, Ivy Goodnoff; edited by Duane Hartzell; music supervised by Jerry Styner. Released by American International Pictures. At the Forum Theater, Broadway and 47th Street. Running time: 90 minutes. This film has been rated PG:

Jennifer Baylor .... Lisa Pelikan
Jeff Reed .... Bert Convy
Mrs. Calley .... Nina Foch
Sandra Tremayne .... Amy Johnston
Senator Tremayne .... John Gavin
Luke Baylor .... Jeff Corey
Miss Tooker .... Florida Friebus

By JANET MASLIN

Say, have you heard the one about the shy, strange-looking high school girl who lives with her religious-nut parent and is tormented by her wealthier classmates, until she uses her telekinetic powers to knock 'em dead? "Jennifer" is a hand-me-down version of "Carrie," from which it borrows all of the above, plus a shower scene, final scare and a couple of costumes that look just like Sissy Spacek's. If it doesn't copy the precise ending of "Carrie," the reasons appear to have been financial rather than esthetic ones. Instead of marshaling an entire special-effects department to help Jennifer (Lisa Pelikan) trash her hometown, the film merely shows her summoning up "the vengeance of the viper." After that, giant snakes appear. They bite all the right people.

B-movie knock-offs ordinarily tend toward campiness, but "Carrie" is a hard act to follow in that department. So "Jennifer" is every bit as sane and solemn as "Carrie" was outlandish. The class consciousness "Carrie" hinted at is more pronounced here: Jennifer's vicious archenemy (Amy Johnston) is the daughter of a senator played by John Gavin, with her own Mercedes for joy riding and assorted B's, G's and YSL's placed prominently on her clothing. Lest anyone miss the point, she also knows Warren Beatty, has dated John Travolta and smokes her cigarettes from a holder.

All things considered, "Jennifer" could be a whole lot worse. The cast, which includes Nina Foch, Jeff Corey, Florida Friebus and Bert Convy, is more reputable than the material might warrant, and while Miss Pelikan is not Sissy Spacek by a long shot, she does have a suitably spooky look in her eye.

1978 My 13, 14:3

THE TEACHER, director by Octavio Cortazar; screenplay (Spanish with English subtitles) by Luis R. Noguera, based on a story by Mr. Cortazar; director of Photography, Pablo Martinez; editor, Roberto Bravo; music, Sergio Vilier; a Cuban Film Institute production, distributed by Tricontinuental Film Center. Running lime: 113 minutes. At the Beacon Theater, Broadway at 74th Street. This film has not been rated.

WITH Patricio Wood, Salvador Wood, Rene de la Cruz, Luis Alberto Ramirez, Luis Rielo, Mario Balmaseda.

By VINCENT CANBY

Six years and two months late, the first New York festival of Cuban Films starts tonight at the Beacon Theater, with the local premiere of "The Teacher," an example of the kind of determinedly upbeat movie making that is as common in a revolutionary society today as it once was in pre-World War II Hollywood.

During the festival, which begins continuous performances at the Beacon on Tuesday, eight new Cuban films, including "The Teacher," will be shown three times each before the event ends next Sunday.

Tricontinental Film Center is the sponsor of the event, as it was in March 1972, when attempts to hold a Cuban film festival in this country were aborted by agents of the United States Treasury Department, who seized the prints of the films for possible violation of the Trading With the Enemy Act. Two films that had been scheduled to be shown in that festival—"Memories of Underdevelopment" and "Lucia"—were successfully released in this country later.

"The Teacher," made last year, is the first narrative feature by Octavio Cortazar. It's set in early 1961 and is about the adventures of a 15-year-old Havana boy, Mario, who goes as a student-teacher into the remote Zapata swamps as a member of President Fidel Castro's Conrado Benitez Brigade, whose mission was to eliminate illiteracy. In the course of his mission, Mario not only teaches the peasants to read but also learns to overcome his own various fears (of spiders, rats, death), participates in the successful repulsion of the Bay of Pigs invaders and learns how to chop down trees, make charcoal, shoot wild boars and catch alligators.

Part political parable, part discreet love story, part melodrama, part nature movie, "The Teacher" has something for everyone in its home market. For us, it makes Cuba look like a gigantic camp. No scene passes without someone's heartily clapping someone else on the back. It is nicely acted and set but is much less interesting as cinema than as a interim report on what the Cuban Government and Cuban film makers think they can contribute to the revolution's success.

For a glimpse of much more provocative kind of Cuban film making today, one should see "The Last Supper," now at the 68th Street Playhouse. It's the work of Tomas Gutierrez Alea, whose "Memories of Underdevelopment" is one of the best films to come from any country in the last 10 years.

1978 My 14, 48:3

NUNZIO, directed by Paul Williams; produced by Jennings Lang; screenplay by James Andronica; music by Lalo Schifrin; at the Cinema II Theater, Third Avenue and 60th Street. Running time: 85 minutes. This film is rated PG.

Nunzio .... David Proval
Jamesie .... James Andronica
Mrs. Sabatino .... Morgana King
Michele .... Tovah Feldshuh
Jo Jo .... Vincent Russo
Carol .... Maria Smith
Bobby .... Jamie Aba
Angelo .... Joe Spinell
Maryann .... Theresa Saldana
Georgie .... Glenn Scarpelli
Priest .... Joseph Sullivan

By JANET MASLIN

Like "Rocky," "Nunzio" is a movie that tells you what to feel and then twists your arm anyway, just to make sure you're still paying attention. The resemblance ends there, since "Rocky" was miraculously able to pull off a ploy that, in "Nunzio," is merely exasperating. It's not for nothing that the ads for the film show its title apparently scrawled in crayon; this is a blunt manipulative movie full of strong-arm tactics, with a central point that is made, then reiterated, and then endlessly underscored. There aren't any fine points to "Nunzio," nor are there any true background details. If the director, Paul Williams, wants something to be noticed, he simply shoots it in close-up.

The title character is a 31-year-old man with the mind—and the innocence, and the goodness of heart and so on—of a child. As played by David Proval, the excellent actor who appeared as the bartender in "Mean Streets," Nunzio is part Rocky, part Superman and part David Berkowitz, a wide-eyed, unnervingly uncommunicative eccentric. On those few occasions when the film allows the character to mesh with his surroundings or behave comfortably, Mr. Proval brings an eerie accuracy to the character's lumbering movements, his strange habit of repeating phrases over and over, his fierce concentration on tasks that would strike anyone else as easy, and his childish eye for unusual details.

•

However, neither Nunzio nor the audience is ever allowed much room to breath. When the character is alone, he is almost always seen doing something attention-getting, like dressing up in a cape and sweat-shirt with a great big "N" across the chest. When he is with the others, Mr. Williams never focuses the scene sharply enough to suggest either how Nunzio accommodates himself to others or how his friends and family feel when they aren't humoring him.

None of the film's supporting characters seem to have lives that extend beyond the confines of the screenplay. The gang of Brooklyn toughs who pick on Nunzio are occasionally seen talking among themselves, but their conversation invariably looks and sounds as if it is being conducted for the camera's benefit. It becomes impossible to believe that soft-spoken, ineffectual Nunzio figures as influentially in the lives of half the population of Brooklyn as the screenplay insists he does.

James Andronica, who wrote the script and appears in the large role of Nunzio's brother, overwrites in the same way that he overacts. Mr. Andronica, a muscular actor who combines a toughness strongly reminiscent of Harvey Keitel's with extreme effusiveness, alternates fits of weeping or hugging with elaborate shows of forcefulness. Either way, the hey-ma-look-at-me aspects of his performance are distracting and, even worse, commonplace.

Some of the other players, particularly Mr. Proval, work hard to elevate "Nunzio" from the ranks of run-of-the-mill Italian family melodramas. But Mr. Andronica's mannerisms are so stereotypically attached to that genre, and his script is so much a case of a situation's masquerading as an actual story, that they overwhelm the film's few half-hearted bids for originality.

"Nunzio" is either for audiences who've never seen an Italian family on screen before, or for viewers who need to be convinced that the retarded are somtimes capable of doing wonderful things, and that they therefore ought to be treated with respect.

•

"Nunzio" is rated PG ("Parental Guidance Suggested") because of a sex scene that has been trimmed, presumably to avoid an R rating. As a result, the scene no longer makes sense.

1978 My 14, 49:1

FILM VIEW

VINCENT CANBY

'F.I.S.T.' Delivers

The thing we call the American Dream—the possibility of achieving a better life—is probably not much different from anybody else's dream. What distinguishes the dream of our era, though, is not the ease of achievement but the fleetness of the vision itself. No sooner wished for than done, then, if not lost, turned into a nightmare. In these speeded up times, the American Dream sometimes looks like an American synthetic, as disposable as Saran Wrap but not nearly as durable. Cycles that once took several generations can now be got through in several years. From shirtsleeves to shirtsleeves in one Administration.

This seems to be the sorrowing theme of Norman Jewison's "F.I.S.T.," a massive, sometimes clumsy and oversimplifed but ultimately very moving melodrama about the rise and fall of a powerful union leader whose history bears a strong resemblance to that of James Hoffa, the one-time boss of the International Brotherhood of American Teamsters. Like Jimmy Hoffa, the hero of "F.I.S.T.," Johnny Kovak (Sylvester Stallone), starts from virtually nothing and then, through shrewdness, energy and strong-arm tactics, builds his Federation of Inter-State Truckers into the most powerful single union in the country, only to be undone by the underworld associates who helped make the dream possible.

There have been plenty of movies in the past that have idealized the union ethic—the romance of communal action—everything from Michael Curtiz's "Black Fury" to Hal Ashby's "Bound for Glory," and probably even more that have capitalized on union corruption, including "On the Waterfront," "Godfather II" and the recent "Blue Collar." The special feature of "F.I.S.T.," which was written by Joe Eszterhas and Mr. Stallone, is its attempt to tell an entire union story, from humble beginnings to the kind of power that matches that of the Federal government. It's not a subject that fits easily on a movie screen. Films don't carry footnotes to explain fine points. Contradictory motives and compromised ideals are difficult to dramatize—they tend to confuse storylines if presented effectively or simply to be misunderstood. Because Mr. Stallone brings to "F.I.S.T." the mannerisms of the lug-with-the-big-heart that so delighted audiences in "Rocky," the character of Johnny Kovak never seems as cunning or brutally cynical as we have every right to expect this union leader to be. He's just a nice guy who makes a few small compromises at the beginning of his career and lives to regret them. Otherwise he's a prince. The center of "F.I.S.T." is a rock of sponge rubber.

• • •

Yet, "F.I.S.T." is a fascinating film. I might even say courageous except that suggests movies should be graded for moral uplift, which I don't believe. Its story of 30-some years in the life of a potentially great union is a particularly American kind of epic. It embraces everything that 20th-century America seemed to promise its citizens, especially those who arrived from Europe immediately after World War I, measured against actual experience, all touched with the disillusion that is commonly associated with the post-Watergate years though it has been alive and ubiquitous since the late 1950's.

The dramatic structure of "F.I.S.T." is awkward, necessarily, since a major point of the movie is the evolution of the union over the years and the ways in which it becomes corrupted, not only by power but by the strategies by which it attained its power. In the case of the Federation of Inter-State Truckers these strategies involve close ties with Mafia people, who, in return for providing muscle in the early days of the union's organization (a method pictured as the only way the union could fight the bosses on their own terms), received the cooperation of the union in the smooth operation of various rackets.

The first half of the film, set in the depressed 1930's, details the early hardships experienced by Johnny Kovak and his best friend, Abe Belkin (David Huffman), as they more or less stumble into union organization as a way of life. Like the two brothers played by Jimmy Cagney and Donald Woods in "Public Enemy," Johnny and Abe represent, respectively, opportunism and idealism, Johnny always ready to justify means by ends, while Abe, for rather a longer time than is quite believable, retains his scruples.

Warner Brothers and director William Wellman told the same kind of story much more efficiently in "Public Enemy" in 1931, though this groundwork, including a furious strike that is crucial in the union's history and to its eventual success, is stunning screen material and vital to the vastly more interesting second half of the movie.

This is set in the late 1950's, when the union has become fat and powerful with its own fancy glass-and-steel high-rise headquarters in Washington and even with its own internal problems. One of these is a secret company owned by the wife of the union president (Peter Boyle) that makes healthy and completely illicit profits from the sale of union momentos to the locals.

"F.I.S.T." is beautifully acted by all except one member of its large cast, but it really comes alive only when it reveals the specific machinations by which union hierarchy wheels and deals in power. There's a funny and scary sequence at a Miami Beach union convention and another that attempts (successfully, I think) to explain some of the ways in which F.I.S.T.'s huge pension fund was used to bail out its friends in the mob.

Rod Steiger, whose screen roles have been something less than great recently, is fine in the small but key role of a crusading United States Senator who is out to expose F.I.S.T., much in the manner employed by the late Senator John L. McClellan, when the Senator was investigating the Teamsters in the 1950's. Mr. Steiger's Senator is both arrogant and sincere, self-assured and desperate, a fellow (you can believe) who's not unaware of an upcoming election.

Though her role is a small one, Melinda Dillon looks and sounds absolutely right as the Lithuanian girl Johnny Kovak courts and marries, a young woman who puts great store by proper behavior as she understands proper behavior in the New Land. Elena Karam is very moving as her mother, a role that is hardly more than a cameo. The other notable performances are those of Tony Lo Bianco, as a mob chief, Peter Boyle and Mr. Huffman.

Mr. Stallone is not, I think, a very interesting actor, an opinion that was very much in the minority when I expressed it in connection with his performance in "Rocky." He has the physical presense to carry the character of Johnny Kovak but none of the charm or wit. Even the narcissism of his barbell physique works against our believing that he could truly feel any passion for the rights of the union brotherhood.

One question that nags as one watches "F.I.S.T." is how much of the film is fiction and how much is history. Since so many of the early experiences of Johnny Kovak parallel those of Jimmy Hoffa (Johnny grows up in Cleveland, Hoffa grew up in Detroit; both men began as handlers in food produce warehouses), one wants to know whether or not the rest of their histories coincide to the same degree.

If "F.I.S.T." were a profound examination of the human spirit rather than the topical social/political melodrama it is, these questions would be beside the point. They are to the point, however, when the film depends to a great extent on our awareness of recent Teamster history.

These questions nag but they don't invalidate the movie's importance as it raises other questions about the entire American experience, which may still be called the American experiment. Is corruption built into the system? That would seem to be one of the points being made by Mr. Jewison here. Put it another way: The life cycles of everything in our 20th-century civilization, including those of our unions, have been so accelerated that birth, life and death have become almost a single, simultaneous action. ■

1978 My 14, II:17:1

Civilized Impotency

THE CHESS PLAYERS, directed by Satyajit Ray; screenplay (In English and Hindi with English subtitles by Mr. Ray; produced by Siresh Jindal; director of photography, Soumendu Roy; music, Mr. Ray; editor, Dulal Dutta; a Devki Chitra production, distributed by Creative Films International. Running time: 135 minutes. At the Little Carnegie, 57th Street, east of 7th Avenue. This film was not been rated.

General Outram .... Richard Attenborough
Mirza Saijad Ali .... Sanieev Kumar
Mir Roshan Ali .... Saeed Jaffrey
Mirza's Wife .... Shabana Azmi
Mawah Wajid Ali Shah .... Amzad Khan
Adviser .... Tom Alter

By VINCENT CANBY

IT IS 1856 in the beautiful city of Lucknow, the capital of Oudh, one of the last independent states in the north of India. "The King," the narrator tells us, "didn't much like to rule but he was proud of his crown," an elaborate, jewel-encrusted headdress that had been publicly exhibited in London. Instead of ruling, the King prefers to compose poems and songs and to while away his time with his wives.

The British East India Company is preparing to gobble up Oudh, but to do this legally, it must persuade the King to sign a new treaty of what's euphemistically called friendship.

•

While all this is going on, two friends, wealthy Lucknow noblemen named Mirza and Mir, carry on a nonstop chess tournament. There are no stakes other than their egos. The two men are obsessed with the game to such an extent that one of them has no time for his lovely young wife (Shabana Azmi), while the other is the last person in Lucknow that his wife has made him a cuckold.

"The Chess Players," Satyajt Ray's new film that opens today at the Little Carnegie, is social satire of a sort that is so graceful, so polite, so balanced and in such good taste, that it virtually amounts to a shrug: This is the way it was, Mr. Ray seems to be saying. So be it.

Though it is often witty, "The Chess Players" lacks the passion that guides the intelligence and can make urgent the most remote of problems. More

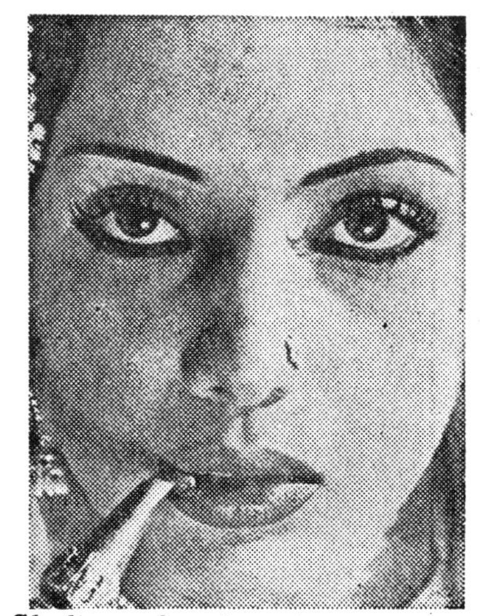

Shabana Azmi

than anything else, I suppose, it is stately. Watching it is like being witness to a formal ceremony. One admires the costumes, the perfectly picked-up cues, the elegance of the principals, the complicated footwork, the manner in which an entire civilization has been encapsulated in a few particular gestures. Yet one is always a little ahead of the film. It's unable to surprise us.

Some of this must be the intention of Mr. Ray. He's not trying to keep us on the edge of our seats but to make us contemplate a bit of history, not because of any special parallels to our own times but because it has to do with the birth-life-death rhythm of all civilizations. He's not outraged. Sometimes he's amused; most often he's meditative, and unless you respond to this mood, the movie is so overly polite you may want to shout a rude word.

"The Chess Players" becomes epigrannatic in form as it cuts among its three arenas of action, which are the equivalent to plot lines. There is the nonstop chess game and the minor irritations that must be faced by the two friends played by Sanjeev Kumar and Saeed Jaffrey—who was so good as the sly Indian guide in "The Man Who Would Be King."

Then there are the scenes in the British resident's office in which Richard Attenborough, as the resident, talks, very intelligently, about British policy in India, and the scenes in the palace where we watch the King at play and, finally, as he comes to the realization that he's been checkmated and that the best he can do is to retire with honor.

•

The film is not without feelings, but they are muted, reined-in. There's resignation everywhere, even in the line, "The Indians invented the game but the British changed the rules," and especially at the end when the two chess players, having escaped from Lucknow for a day of uninterrupted chess-playing in the country, wonder whether they should return to the city, now occupied by British troops. "If we can't cope with our wives," one of the chess players says to the other, "how can we cope with the British Army?"

Actually it's a funny line, and it's meant to be, but it also reflects the civilian impotency that is the film's subtext.

1978 My 17, C17:5

Wrath of God

WERNER HERZOG: NEW DOCUMENTARIES. HOW MUCH WOOD WOULD A WOODCHUCK CHUCK: Observations on a New Language, 45 minutes; **LA SOUFRIERE,** 30 minutes, both in English; distributed by New Yorker Films. At the Film Forum, 15 Vandam Street. Through Sunday, and Thursday to May 28.

By JANET MASLIN

ONE of the best films in town this weekend is also one of the shortest: "La Soufrière," a 30-minute masterpiece by Werner Herzog that was arguably the best thing to be shown at last fall's New York Film Festival. In the summer of 1976, Mr Herzog read a newspaper article predicting a volcanic eruption on the tropical island of Guadeloupe. A day and a half later he and two cameramen had arrived on the spot all the way from Germany, ready—and peculiarly eager—to photograph the end of the world.

What they found were the deserted city of Basse-Terre, packs of starving dogs, snakes that had been frightened out of the mountains and then drowned in the sea, billowing clouds of noxious gas, and an exquisitely unearthly silence.

"La Soufrière," named for the volcano—which never erupted, although there had been every indication that it would—is Mr. Herzog's brave and unforgettable vision of the wrath of God, informed by the peculiarly ironic logic of catastrophe. At the turn of the century, when a volcano erupted on the nearby island of Martinique, Mr. Herzog explains, the sole survivor was the island's wickedest criminal, because he had been imprisoned underground.

Provocative, contemplative and very beautiful, "La Soufrière" will be shown this weekend and next at the Film Forum, from Thursday through Sunday each time. On the same bill is a later short Herzog film, made for German television, entitled "How Much Wood Would a Woodchuck Chuck: Observation on a New Language." The film is a documentary account of the World Championship contest for livestock auctioneers, conducted in the Amish country of Pennsylvania. The title comes from a tongue-twister that one of the contestants uses to practice.

Since the auctioneers' language is unintelligible to anyone save potential cattle buyers, the film becomes a study of gestures, a chance to view the contestants' near-fanatical animation in abstract terms. The auctioneers' absolute dedication to an unfathomable craft has the kind of freakishness that has often fascinated Herzog in the past, and here he once again examines odd behavior with distance and clarity. This is a much slighter film than "La Soufrière," but it is still a work of considerable interest.

1978 My 18, C18:3

THANK GOD IT'S FRIDAY, directed by Robert Klane; screenplay by Barry Armyan Bernstein; executive producer, Neil Bogart; produced by Rob Cohen; director of photography, James Crabe; editor Richard Halsey; music by various artists and composers; a Motown-Casablanca production, distributed by Columbia Pictures. Running time: 100 minutes. At the Criterion Theater, Broadway near 44th Street, and other theaters. This film has been rated PG.

Frannie .... Valerie Landsburg
Jeannie .... Terri Nunn
Marv Gomez .... Chick Vennera
Nicole Sims .... Donna Summer
Bobby Speed .... Ray Vitte
Dave .... Mark Lonow
Sue .... Andrea Howard
Tony .... Jeff Goldblum
Maddy .... Robin Menker
Jennifer .... Debra Winger
Ken .... John Friedrich
Carl .... Paul Jabara
Jackie .... Marya Small
Gus .... Chuck Sacci
Shirley .... Hilary Beane
Floyd .... DeWayne Jessie
The Commodores .... Themselves

By VINCENT CANBY

"THANK GOD It's Friday" has the form of a disco movie, but it's really a record album with live-action liner notes featuring a dozen young actors, most of whom are quite nice and, as yet, unknown, and a few who are better known but not as impressive as the new people.

The setting is the Zoo, a Los Angeles discotheque, and everything in the movie happens either in or around the Zoo in the space of a few hours on a Friday night.

A young couple, married five years, rediscovers their love. Miss Plain-Jane finds romance. The womanizing owner meets his comeuppance. A dance-crazy Mexican-American wins the big contest, and an unknown singer, played by Donna Summer, in her film debut, begins her climb to stardom. Miss Summer, whose wigs are as elaborate as Diana Ross's, is competition for the superb Miss Ross in no department other than hair.

The film, which opens today at the Criterion and other theaters, was directed by Robert Klane (who wrote the novel on which "Where's Poppa?" was based) and written by Barry Armyan Bernstein in the breathless, multinarrative manner of "Car Wash," which gives one the impression that a good deal is happening even when the movie is standing still.

Among the actors who fare best are Chick Vennera, as the Mexican-American fellow who has the film's only good number, an exuberant disco dance on the tops of the cars in the Zoo's parking lot; Ray Vitte, who was in "Car Wash," as the Zoo's manic disk jockey; Valerie Landsburg and Terri Nunn, as two extremely underage patrons, and Jeff Goldblum, who played the rock critic in "Between the Lines," as the Zoo's pushy manager.

The Commodores come on to play themselves in the finale, which is not much different from any other part of the movie. The dècor of the Zoo is suitably garish and looks dangerously flammable. I would have felt easier while watching the movie if I'd known where the exits were.

•

There is nothing in the way of explicit sex or nudity in "Thank God It's Friday," which has been rated PG ("Parental Guidance Suggested"), though the language is sometimes vulgar and there is one sequence involving the use of various kinds of drugs, uppers and downers, that is supposed to be funny but isn't.

1978 My 19, C8:3

FILM VIEW

VINCENT CANBY

How Does 'The Greek Tycoon' Get Away With It?

The full-page ad is dominated by an illustration that shows the head of a familiar-looking woman who wears large dark glasses and seems vaguely miffed. Cheek by jowl is the face of a dark-skinned, gray-haired man, also familiar-looking, also in dark glasses, who seems to be comforting the woman, though one has the impression they might be on a private yacht the size of Crete. Below them we see a montage of smaller images that call to mind high-life in high places—a speedboat, an ocean-going yacht, beautiful women in evening dresses or bikinis, the ruins of a Greek temple on the top of a Greek hill and, in the lower left-hand corner, the White House with, standing in front of it, two beautiful people in beach gear.

"She was the most famous woman in the world," says the ad. "He was a peasant, a pirate, a shark. What he couldn't buy with money he stole with charm."

As movie ads go, this one is actually pretty good. It tells us what the movie is about, which is exactly what we see in the images—pretty settings, virtually non-stop traveling, and a beautiful woman, who has connections to the White House, and a swarthy older man, both of whom fancy the same kind of huge dark glasses that protect their eyes from the glare and are guaranteed to attract the attention of the three people in the world who don't already know who they are.

• • •

If "The Greek Tycoon" had one-tenth as much style and imagination as it has chutzpah, it would be the "Citizen Kane" of junk movies, which it isn't. Still, this kind of chutzpah is not to be sneezed at. Such gall must be saluted if not admired. How, one is bound to ask, do they get away with making a movie that so freely helps itself to the lives of Mrs. Jacqueline Kennedy Onassis and her late husband, Aristotle Onassis, with supporting characters modeled on the late Robert F. Kennedy, his widow Ethel, the late President John F. Kennedy, Winston Churchill, Maria Callas and others? Even though the Onassis character is called Theo Tomasis and the character who stands for Mrs. Onassis is called Liz Cassidy Tomasis, and even though all the Kennedys are named Cassidy, there's obviously no doubt about who is who. If there were any doubt, the people who made the film would have to count themselves failures, which, in this tiny respect, they're not.

How do they get away with it? The answer, I suspect, is quite simple. People who live in the public eye would have a difficult time proving invasion of privacy, and though there

Associated Press

Aristotle Onassis (top) weds Jacqueline Kennedy in 1968; Anthony Quinn and Jacqueline Bisset re-enact the scene.

may be other grounds on which the film could have been stopped, it's easier and cheaper to let it go by without providing it with the kind of publicity that any lawsuit would present the producers.

All fiction is, to a greater or lesser extent, a spin-off of history, but the screenplay that Mort Fine has written for "The Greek Tycoon" fails even that minor test. In its extremely few lively moments, it recapitulates facts culled from the gossip columns, but though it's not fact, really, neither is it fiction. It's an overdressed plot outline.

Though "The Greek Tycoon" gives short and rather nasty shrift to the Kennedy family, I suppose it could be argued that *any* movie in which the Kennedys are supporting characters to the Onassises would automatically have to be regarded as nasty. After all, the Kennedys were the stars of an era, not the comic relief. Yet, "The Greek Tycoon" doesn't pretend to be about the Kennedys. Rather, it presents us with a picture—wittingly or not—of one of the greatest non-love stories of our generation: the courtship of the widow of an assassinated United States President by one of the richest men in the world, a Greek who owns oil tankers, airlines and islands and who may or may not indulge in a bit of blackmail to see a business deal successfully concluded.

With a face that is absolutely straight, perhaps for legal reasons as well as for lack of literary skill, "The Greek Tycoon" characterizes Liz Cassidy (Jacqueline Bisset) as a woman who loves her President-husband deeply but who doesn't hesitate to run off on a Greek island vacation after her baby is still-born, leaving the President to make out as best he can in the White House.

The movie, I think, wants us to take Liz seriously, though it sometimes is hard put to succeed. When, early in the film, Liz announces she is going to Greece whether the President (James Franciscus) likes it or not, he explodes. "Don't you know who you are? You're the wife of the President of the United States!" Liz: "Oh, for God's sake, James, I know who I am . . . and I need a change." They clinch and vow undying love.

"The Greek Tycoon," which is dreadfully acted by everyone (though Miss Bisset and a huge yacht are stunning to contemplate), never has the courage to deal in anything more than hearsay. Watching it I kept wondering what Gore Vidal might have wrought had he got his mitts onto the screenplay. But then, I guess, the movie never could have been made. Which, on second thought, wouldn't have been a major loss of anything except the salaries collected by the people who worked on the picture.

• • •

"The Greek Tycoon" is of interest, however, for being a film that plagiarizes real lives more outrageously than any other film in recent memory, and though plagiarism isn't nice, it isn't this that is worrisome but the fact that so little is done with the stolen goods. Which is more or less the way I felt when I saw "F.I.S.T."—fiction that uses the life of the missing (and presumed murdered) Jimmy Hoffa and Hoffa's wheeling-and-dealing as president of the International Brotherhood of American Teamsters. It's a waste of fascinating material.

Taking their cue from Harold Robbins, who has made a mini-industry writing fiction based on the lives of actual persons, Allen Klein and Ely Landau, who produced "The Greek Tycoon," J. Lee Thompson, who directed it, and Mr. Fine, the writer, have succeeded in reducing a big subject to the size of a story that wouldn't test the capacities of a comic book. There are, of course, comic-book aspects to the lives of the originals, especially in the power they possessed and which, to us, seems comparable to Superman's. Someone might argue that the originals weren't especially interesting, which may well be true, but that shouldn't hobble the imagination of the artist. Fiction isn't photography, though you can get that idea from "The Greek Tycoon." Fiction offers the freedom to speculate, which is why it's so liberating to write and to read. The impulse behind fiction is the attempt to impose order on chaos.

The problem with works like "The Greek Tycoon," "F.I.S.T.," "The Betsy" and "The Carpetbaggers" is that the speculation isn't good enough. It's second-rate, predictable, sentimental. There is no impulse to make sense out of things, only to use and exploit the superficial order that can be seen in the pattern of events already lived. These works don't expand the imagination. Sometimes they fulfill the imagination, but, more often, they shrink it.

The only recent *films à clef* that have done justice both to fact and fiction have been those of Costa-Gavras, especially "State of Seige," his fictionalized account of the kidnapping and murder in Uruguay in 1970 of Dan A. Mitrone, who was an official with the United States Agency for International Development. Costa-Gavras succeeds where the others fail because he has a point of view about his subject, whether one agrees with it or not. He's not merely out to recycle the known, but to speculate about causes and effects, about personalities, even about the unknown.

I've no doubt that "The Greek Tycoon" will make a bundle, but be forewarned. Though it's only 106 minutes long, it's a numbing experience, like being forced to read the collected works of Louella Parsons. ■

1978 My 21, II:17:1

Jingle Jangle

IF EVER I SEE YOU AGAIN, directed and produced by Joe Brooks; screenplay by Mr. Brooks and Martin Davidson; director of photography, Adam Holdender; music by Mr. Brooks; edited by Rick Shaine; released by Columbia Pictures. At Loews Tower East, 72d Street and Third Avenue. Running time: 105 minutes. This film has been rated PG.

Bobby Morrison .... Joe Brooks
Jennifer Crly .... Shelley Hack
Mario Marino .... Jimmy Breslin
Steve Warner .... Jerry Keller
David Miller .... Kenny Karen
Lawrence Lawrence .... George Plimpton

By JANET MASLIN

WHAT sort of scenery comes to mind when you dream about falling in love? Are you the kind of romantic who envisions purple sunsets, walks along the beach, orange sunsets, more walks along the beach, horseback rides *à deux*, sailboat rides *à deux*, and ice cream cones *à deux*, all accompanied by a dangerously overworked string section? If so, "If Ever I See You Again," which opens today at Loews Tower East, would like very, very much to be your kind of movie. However, as the film itself readily acknowledges, in song and story and encounter-group jargon, wishes don't always come true.

On the outside, "If Ever I See You Again" is the treacly stuff-and-nonsense of which greeting cards are made. On the inside, though, something quite different is going on.

The story is about Bobby Morrison (Joe Brooks), a composer of jingles who has, in the words of one of his friends, "made the big time." He's rich, he's in demand, he uses a huge photograph of himself to adorn what he would undoubtedly call his work space, and he has been profiled in TV Guide. However, there's one thing Bobby lacks: Jennifer Corly (Shelley Hack), a college sweetheart who jilted him 12 years ago.

•

This episode has taken just enough wind out of Bobby's capacious sails to make him vow to track Jennifer down, a decision that smacks at least as much of revenge as it does of romance. The main thing Bobby wants, he half-jokes, is to know that Jennifer has seen that TV Guide story about him.

His wish is more than granted: not only is Jennifer gorgeous, easy to find and conveniently unattached, but she has also read the article and loved it all by herself. Even better, she admits to Bobby that the fellow she preferred to him years ago is now a dress manufacturer of no particular renown. "Oh, I love it, I love it!" Bobby gloats, very unbecomingly.

As played by Mr. Brooks, Bobby is an ambitious egomaniac whose immodesty knows no bounds, and this makes him something less than the ideal leading man. As played by Miss Hack, Jennifer is just one more model with a monotone.

•

Miss Hack, perhaps best known as the star of Revlon's "Charlie" ads, made a previous movie appearance in "Annie Hall," as half of a beautiful couple Woody Allen approaches in the street. Mr. Allen asks them how they manage to look so radiant, and Miss Hack replies, in essence, that maybe it's because they haven't a thought in either of their heads. Here, in a role that has her gazingly either adoringly or sadly at Mr. Brooks and saying things like "I'm not a forever person," she generates much the same mood.

The only redeeming feature of her performance is the way in which, whenever she is called on to do anything silly, Mr. Brooks promptly does something sillier. For example, after Miss Hack watches Mr. Brooks conducting an orchestra in a recording studio, she cries out. "It's unbelievable! Unbelievable!" Replies Mr. Brooks, with a completely unconvincing display of bashfulness: "It's what I do for a living."

Actually, what the real Mr. Brooks did for a living before he wrote, produced, scored and starred in "If Ever I See You Again" was exactly what the character Bobby Morrison does: compose enormously popular commercials. The hit song from his first film, "You Light Up My Life," was an illustration of the overlap between pop and commercial music at a time when Top-40 radio had become particularly tepid.

This time, Mr. Brooks has tried to one-up himself by filling the screen with the visual imagery of television commercials as well as with their sounds. When an airplane is shown taking off for California, accompanied by one of Mr. Brooks's songs, it truly seems to be flying the friendly skies of United.

Early in the film, there is enough turnabout and self-mockery to suggest that the director is aiming for something halfway between caricature and salesmanship. But his send-ups of the advertising business quickly turn nasty, and it becomes all too apparent that Mr. Brooks is both extremely talented and contemptuous of his own gifts.

It's easy to see why he was so resoundingly well suited to his former line of work, but as a film director he has not yet progressed beyond the visual monotony of most television direction, nor does he risk much in his pacing. The film is entirely without dramatic highs or lows.

Mr. Brooks's title song this time sounds much too much like his title song last time, but his real gaffe is a song called "California," which includes a syrupy lyric about how "the winds called Santa Ana make you feel that you belong." The Santa Ana winds, as they have been vividly described by Joan Didion and other Californian writers, are a nightmare. Mr. Brooks's peppy presentation of them can't help but make one wonder what was really in those soft drinks and fun foods he used to help sell, in his earlier, more appropriate incarnation.

•

"I Ever I See You Again" is rated PG ("Parental Guidance Suggested"). It includes a love scene between Mr. Brooks and Miss Hack that is strictly soft-focus, in every way.

1978 My 24, C19:5

Ghetto Melodrama

YOUNGBLOOD, directed by Noel Nosseck; written by Paul Carter Harrison; director of photography, Robbie Greenberg, editor, Frank Morriss; produced by Nick Grillo and Alan Riche; released by American International Pictures. At the Forum Theater, Broadway at 46th Street, and other theaters. Running time: 90 minutes. This film is rated R.

Rommel .... Lawrence-Hilton Jacobs
Youngblood .... Bryan O'Dell
Sybil .... Ren Woods
Hustler .... Tony Allen
Corelli .... Vince Cannon
Junkie .... Art Evans
Basketball Pusher .... Jeff Hollis
Reggie .... Dave Pendleton
Bummie .... Ron Trice
Joan .... Sheila Willis
Geronimo .... Ralph Farquhar
Durango .... Herbert Rice
Chaka .... Lionel Smith
Skeeter-Jeeter .... Maurcie Sneed
Mrs. Gordon .... Ann Weldon
School Principal .... Isabel Cooley
Bodyguard .... Bernie Weissman

By VINCENT CANBY

“OUNGBLOOD," the low-budget melodrama that opened yesterday at the Forum and other theaters,

Lawrence Hilton-Jacobs

effectively trivializes a lot of problems without offering in return anything in the way of entertainment, which is what movies like this are supposed to deal in.

•

Written by Paul Carter Harrison and directed by Noel Nosseck, whose bland achievements suggest they learned their trades in television, the film is about a troubled high school student nicknamed Youngblood (Bryan O'Dell) and his attempts to adjust to black ghetto life by joining a youth gang. The gang is really not so young since its leader, a fellow named Rommel (Lawrence-Hilton Jacobs of "Cooley High"), is a married Vietnam vet coping with the horrors of civilian life.

"Youngblood" tries to walk down both sides of the street at the same time. The gang is depicted as not above murder and other forms of antisocial behavior, though it becomes as righteous as a Sunday school group when one gang member dies of a dose of a bad drug. Most of the film is about the gang's attempts to bust the narcotics racket, which is complicated by the fact that Youngblood's older brother is a chief pusher.

•

The performances seem less bad than thin. There isn't much in the way of material to work with. Instead, the actors display all these loose-jointed, no-longer-hip mannerisms that, one suspects, they've learned from watching dozens of other movies exactly like this one.

1978 My 25, C16:5

The Bears Are Back

HERE COME THE TIGERS, directed by Sean S. Cunningham; written by Arch McCoy; director of photography, Barry Abrams; editor, Stephen Miner; music by Harry Manfredini; produced by Mr. Cunningham and Mr. Miner; released by American International Pictures. At the Embassy 46th Street Theater. Running time: 95 minutes. This film is rated PG.

Eddie Burke .... Richard Lincoln
Burt Honneger .... James Zvanut
Betty Burke .... Samantha Grey
Felix the Umpire .... Manny Lieberman
Kreeger .... William Caldwell
Aesop .... Fred Lincoln

By JANET MASLIN

FILM stock were carbon paper, the fourteenth or fifteenth copy of "The Bad News Bears" might resemble "Here Come the Tigers," a low-budget Little League epic of no particular zest or stamina. Once again, a team of cute little no-accounts is coached toward victory by an older fellow from the neighborhood, even though the kids curse better than they play. Once again, success comes only after the team adds a couple of unlikely new players, in this case a karate-champ batter and a deaf pitcher.

•

There are new touches, too, none of them helpful. The coach, played by Richard Lincoln, has a warm, understanding smile that just won't quit, even when it ought to. The kid's shout things like "Cram it!" and complain about one another's flatulence a lot, but for the most part they're pretty subdued; the adults. on the other hand, overact like crazy.

And even though a Little League movie might be the last place you'd expect to find a sad song accompanying a wistful-walk-along-the-beach scene, there is one here, to mark a particularly tender moment between a boy and his coach.

On the evidence of this film and

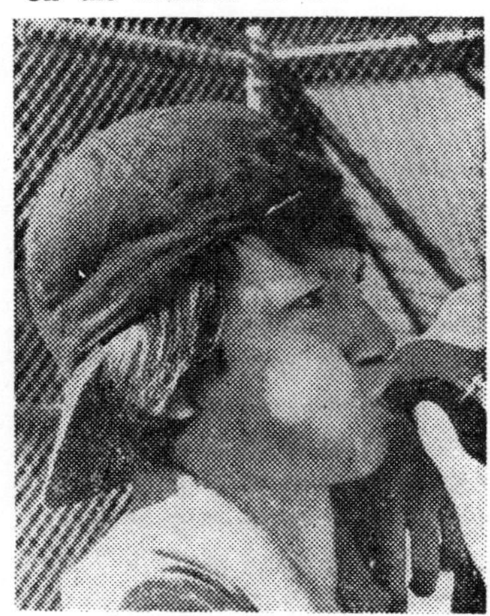

David Schmalholz

others, like the "Exorcist"-based "Abby" and the current "Jennifer," American International Pictures seems to believe that there's money to be made on the film equivalent of elevator music, on toned-down versions of guaranteed hits. That may be true, but as the only person to see the film's 11 A.M. show at the Guild Theater, where it opened yesterday, I have reason to have my doubts.

"Here Come the Tigers" was shot in Westport, Conn. Nevertheless, it could easily have been called "The Bad News Bears Go to Queens."

•

'Here Come The Tigers" is rated PG ("Parent Guidance Suggested") because it contains a certain amount of half-hearted profanity. It's much less gamy than the film on which it has been modeled.

1978 My 25, C16:5

Artist Considered

PIROSMANI, directed by Georgy Shengelaya; screenplay (Russian with English subtitles) by Mr. Shengelaya and Eriom Akhvlediani; director of photography, Konstantin Apryatin; editor, M. Karalashvili; music V. Kukhianidze; produced by Gruzia Film Studio. Running time: 85 minutes. At the Cinema Studio, 66th Street and Broadway.

Niko Pirosmanashvili .... Avtandil Varazi

"Pirosmani" was shown at the 1975 Museum of Modern Art's New Directors/New Films series. The following review was written by Vincent Canby and was published in The Times on April 5, 1975. The film opens today at the Cinema Studio, 66th Street and Broadway.

Niko Pirosmanashvili, the Georgian primitive painter, is the subject of the Russian film "Pirosmani" at the Cinema Studio.

"PIROSMANI" is a fine, firm, gentle consideration of the life and work of the Georgian primitive painter Niko Pirosmanashvili, who was born in 1862 and died in 1919, an alcoholism and poverty victim.

I use the word "consideration" instead of biography because the movie is not interested in factual details. Rather it attempts to reconstruct the feelings experienced by the alternately determined and tortured artist as reflected in his work—straightforward portraits of village elders, scenes of wedding celebrations, idyllic pastoral scenes, functional, four-feet-on-the-ground pictures of cows used to identify a dairy shop.

A lot of "Pirosmani" re-creates the special look of the Pirosmanashvili paintings. One is often conscious of foreshortened perspectives and of the texture of things that someone untutored might find difficult or boring to paint — large expanses of wooden floors, of earth of no special marked color. Pirosmanashvili, like other primitives, delighted more in small details fastidiously reproduced, which is something the film does in the photography and in the narrative structure.

Georgy Shengelaya, the 38-year-old Georgian director whose second feature this is, makes no attempt to analyze or explain the artist in conventional ways. Instead the film seems to glide across the artist's life seeing odd though not-so-random details, some more psychologically important than others. It has the manner of the artist whose attention at his own wedding was sidetracked by the look of his wife's hands, the shape of the fingers outlined against the cloth of her dress. He sees some things with rare clarity, and reacts to them, while other matters, including his poverty and alcoholism, are ignored as if invisible.

"Pirosmani" is one of the few films I've ever seen that respects the mystery of the creative process and sidesteps melodrama. The manner of the film is detached, almost shy, like the artist himself as played by Avtandil Varazi.

Mr. Shengelaya attempts to show us the world as seen by the painter, though he never presumes to go inside the artist's mind to the extent of making connections between things seen and actions taken.

As a result, we, in the audience, have to form our own connections, which in the long run, makes "Pirosmani" much more moving and involving than films that give us too much information and reduce the artist to the dimensions of case-history.

1978 My 26, C8:5

A Rediscovery

A GEISHA (Gionbayashi), directed by Kenji Mizoguchi; screenplay (Japanese with English subtitles) by Yoshikata Yoda, based on a story by Matsutaro Kawaguchi; director of photography, Kazuo Miyagawa; music, Ichiro Saito; editor, Mitsuzo Miyata; a Daiei production, distributed by New Yorker Films. Running time: 87 minutes. At the Film Forum, 15 Vandam Street. This film has not been rated.

Miyoharu .... Michiyo Korgure
Eiko .... Ayako Wakao
Kusuda .... Seizaburo Kawazu
Okimi .... Chieko Naniwa
Sawamoto .... Eitaro Shindo
Kanzaki .... Mikio Koshiba
Saeki .... Ichiro Sugai
Ogawa .... Haruo Tanaka

By VINCENT CANBY

TO the extent that any Japanese film directors can be well known in this country, Akira Kurosawa and Yasujiro Ozu have made it. Yet Kenji Mitzoguchi, who died in 1958 and who may well be one of the greatest film makers of all time, remains relatively obscure, even to those audiences for whom such obscurity is usually a certification of honor.

Kurosawa had the luck to make a couple of films that found comparatively large American audiences ("Rashomon," "Seven Samurai") while Ozu, though not as well known as Kurosawa, became something of a small fashion early in the decade with the release of many of his later films.

To date, fewer than 10 Mizoguchi works have received commercial engagements in New York, and though each has been critically acclaimed, especially "Ugetsu," "Sansho The Bailiff" and "Utamaro and His Five Women," there's never been a continuing Mizoguchi audience. Every time we receive a new-old Mizoguchi, he must be rediscovered.

Mizoguchi's "A Geisha," which is having its New York theatrical premiere today at the Film Forum, was made in 1953. Unlike most of the other Mizoguchis we've seen here, it is set in its own time, 1953, in Kyoto, though it shares with the director's period films the quality of being incredibly beautiful without being particularly, foolishly pretty.

The story is about the friendship of two women, Miyoharu (Michiyo Korgure), an older geisha bound by a tradition that no longer holds, and Eiko (Ayako Wakao), a 16-year-old girl whom Miyoharu agrees to sponsor and train as a geisha after the death of Eiko's mother, a former geisha who'd been Miyoharu's friend. Though Mizoguchi's film makes only two quick trips outside Kyoto's tea houses and geisha houses, the film is as much about the social revolution taking place in 1953 occupied Japan as it is about the emotional relationship between the two women.

From the beginning, it's apparent that the young Eiko is not going to

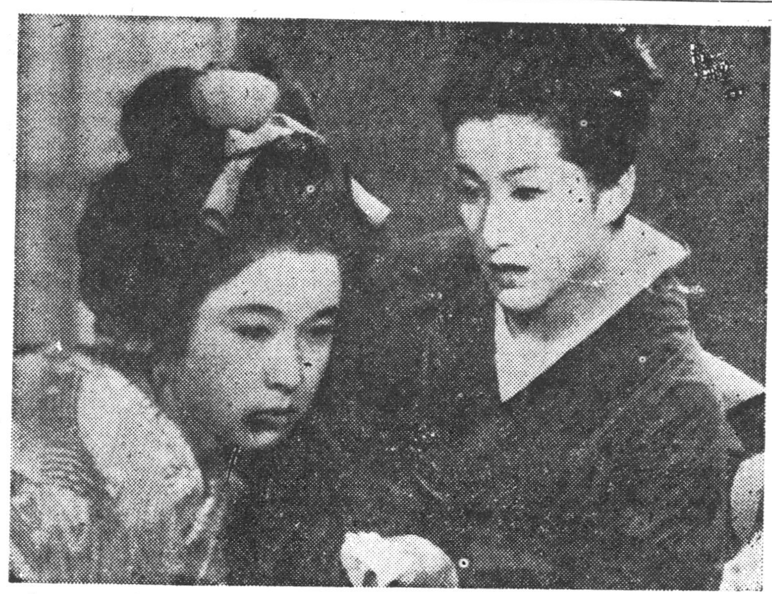

A scene from Kenji Mizoguchi's "A Geisha"

be a conventional, subservient geisha. After a class in which the teacher has told her pupils that the geisha is a work of art, like Noh drama and the tea ceremony, Eiko wonders whether the new Japanese constitution doesn't guarantee a geisha the right to say no to a patron. The other young women giggle, but Eiko is serious.

•

It's evidence of the system of balances that always operate in a Mizoguchi film that as Eiko is wondering about the geisha's constitutional rights, the geisha's role is being corrupted. In postwar Japan, the geisha, who had once been a highly skilled entertainer, was being called upon with increasing frequency to perform the duties of the not necessarily skilled prostitute.

It's a trend that the older Miyoharu resists, more or less passively, while Eiko does battle. When her would-be patron takes the two women on a trip to Tokyo, Eiko refuses to perform the duties she does in the teahouse. "I serve at parties," she says, "I'm a lady."

This doesn't put off the man. He makes a lunge at her, wrestles her to the floor, plants a big kiss on her mouth, to which Eiko responds by biting his lip so badly the fellow has to be hospitalized. Because of the scandal, the two women are blackballed by all of Kyoto's teahouses. Miyoharu is confused, worried, though she doesn't blame the younger woman. Says Eiko, in effect, "If that's what being a geisha means, then I don't want it."

The charm of "A Geisha" is the compassionate but completely unsentimental way it regards the two women's friendship, as well as the manner in which this friendship changes and deepens as their responsibilities, each to the other, are acknowledged. Miyoharu is much the more interesting of the two, but it is the younger Eiko who is more often right.

Though the landscape of the film is restricted to a small, rather exotic quarter in Kyoto, "A Geisha" is far from esoteric. The scope is narrow and the focus is deep.

The two actresses who dominate the film are splendid, as are several other performers, especially Chieko Naniwa, who plays the not unkind but money-minded doyenne of Kyoto's geishas, and Eitaro Shindo, who plays Eiko's father.

"A Geisha" is actually a remake, being based on a film Mr. Mizoguchi made in 1936 that, to my knowledge, has never been released here, yet the 1953 version is far from being dated. One can say that the best, most intelligent film about women to be seen here in the last 12 months was a film made 25 years ago.

"A Geisha" will be screened at the Film Forum tonight through Sunday at 7:45 and next Thursday through Sunday at the same time.

1978 Je 1, C15:4

Mother's Fault

LASERBLAST, directed by Michael Rae; written by Franne Schacht and Frank Ray Perilli; produced by Charles Band; released by Aquarius Films. At the Embassy 46th Street, Lyric and other theaters. Running time: 85 minutes. This film is rated PG.

Billy Duncan .... Kim Milford
Cathy Farley .... Cheryl Smith
Tony Craig .... Gianni Russo
Sheriff .... Ron Masak
Pete Ungar .... Dennis Burkley
Jesse Jeep .... Barry Cutler
Chuck Boran .... Mike Bobenko
Froggy .... Eddie Deezen
Colonel Farley .... Keenan Wynn
Dr. Melon .... Roddy McDowall

By JANET MASLIN

A YOUNG MAN staggers out into the desert, wearing greenish-white makeup with black circles around his eyes and sporting a dangerous-looking gadget on his right arm. With the gadget, he begins blowing up cactuses. Just then, a spaceship arrives, and out step wo animated clay creaures, with long necks and pretty dark eyes, of the approximate vintage of Godzilla or Rodan. They nod and clap each oher on the back with their three-fingered tentacles. "Gleep," one remarks, approvingly.

At first, this turns out to be a dream the young man is having later on in "Laserblast." It turns out to be actually happening. Never mind the fine points: All that matters is that we understand why the fellow is so given over to violent fantasies, and we do. It's his mother's fault. His mother, a swelte blonde who looks younger than he does, appears to be either a jet-setter or a stewardess, and she is neglecting her boy. Just as the film begins, she leaves town, announcing she's headed for Acapulco. "Mama, you've already been to Acapulco. How many times are you going to go?" the boy whines. "Till they stop asking me, sweetheart," Mom replies, with a pretty little frown.

Soon enough, the kid has gone to seed, and developed a big green sore on his chest, too. He blows up a dozen cars and—rather amusingly—one "Star Wars" poster, using what the poster for "Laserblast" refers to as "The Force." This is a simple bit of equipment that could easily have become "The Toy" if the film seemed destined for hitdom. But it doesn't.

Kim Milford, as the fellow whose fangs get longer every time he goes on a shooting spree, is a dull actor, but the cast also includes Gianni Russo, doing a very curious Clint Eastwood imitation, and Eddie Deezen, as the town creep. Mr. Deezen was very funny in the late, lamented "I Wanna Hold Your Hand," as all 15 or 20 persons who saw that film at the Rivoli can attest.

"Laserblast" is playing at the Embassy 46th Street, where one man in the audience began yelling "Sex! Sex! Sex!" and "Meatball!" during the 11 A.M. show. The ushers conferred worriedly about this for a while. Much to the movie's credit, it eventually quieted him down.

•

"Laserblast" is rated PG ("Parental Guidance Suggested"). It contains very brief nudity, one mild-mannered sex scene and a lot of explosions.

1978 Je 1, C20:4

CAPRICORN ONE, directed and written by Peter Hyams; produced by Paul N. Lazarus 3d; director of photography, Bill Butler; music, Jerry Goldsmith; editor, James Mitchell; a Lew Grade presentation for Associated General Films, distributed by Warner Bros. Running time: 127 minutes. At the Rivoli Theater, Broadway at 50th Street, and other theaters. This film has been rated PG.

Robert Caulfield .... Elliott Gould
Judy Drinkwater .... Karen Black
Albain .... Telly Savalas
Charles Brubaker .... James Brolin
Kay Brubaker .... Brenda Vaccaro
Peter Willis .... Sam Waterston
John Walker .... O. J. Simpson
Dr. James Kelloway .... Hal Holbrook
Hollis Peaker .... David Huddleston
Walter Loughlin .... David Doyle
Betty Walker .... Denise Nicholas
Elliot Whitter .... Robert Walden
Sharon Willis .... Lee Bryant
Capsule Communicator .... Alan Fudge

By VINCENT CANBY

DAWN. Various shots of a huge missile on the launching pad at Cape Canaveral, Fla. Cut to spectators watching from several miles away. Cut to the Houston Mission Control Center—you've seen it dozens of times on television and in the movies. Real or fake, it always looks the same—people intensely busy as they monitor complex computers, television screens flash incomprehensible data, and scientists drink coffee from paper cups. On the soundtrack we hear the voice of a radio announcer give the solemn details of what was eaten at breakfast by the three astronauts who begin their journey to Mars this day.

The sequence lasts perhaps 10 minutes, and it's very promising. It's funny. It's accurate in all those banalities we know and love. Then, however, "Capricorn One," an expensive stylistically bankrupt suspense melodrama, gets down to its real narrative.

This is the story of a United States Mars landing, faked by apparently several hundred thousand employees of the National Aeronautics and Space Administration, because the mission's life-support system is faulty, but to scratch the mission would mean the end of the nation's space program. Or so says Hal Holbrook, who plays the mission's director, as he tries to convince us—as well as the mission's three astronauts, who've been removed from their space capsule at the last minute—that the plot we're about to see is not a piece of cheesecloth.

Plots of movies like "Capricorn One," which was written and directed by Peter Hyams, don't have to be flameproof, and they don't even have to carry water, only a tiny bit of conviction and, more important, wit. In addition to its overture, "Capricorn One" has two decent sequences—a runaway-car interlude, which has been done much more funnily by people like Buster Keaton and W. C. Fields, and a final chase involving two wicked helicopters and a nice, old-fashioned biplane, the sort of machine that is to aircraft what Labrador retrievers are to dogs. Lovable and always reliable.

The stuff that comes in between is humorless comic-strip stuff about a conspiracy so widespread that you finally realize that the only people in the country who don't know about it are the three astronauts, a minor space employee, one unreliable television reporter, an eccentric crop-duster, owner of the lovable biplane, and the members of their immediate families.

Such complicity reduces the problems for the screenwriter so that, as Mr. Hyams does, he can have the good guys arbitrarily confounded by the bad for as long as it is convenient. No explanations are needed.

At movies like this I tend to regress. I'm once again 16 years old when I was quick to point out to adults all those contradictions they'd learned to ignore. For example, how are the three astronauts spirited away from Cape Canaveral in a jet while at least a million people in the immediate vicinity are watching? Why is a medallion, used by one of the astronauts to slip the hinge in their desert prison, later

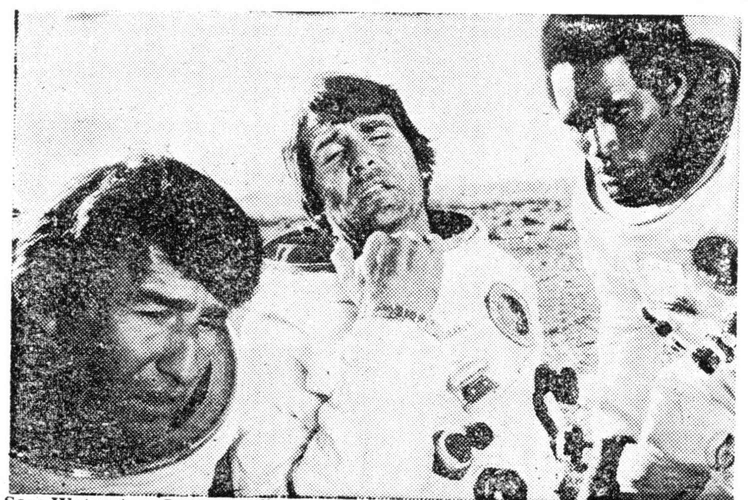

Sam Waterston, James Brolin and O. J. Simpson in "Capricorn One"
To scratch the mission would mean the end of the nation's space program

found by the nosy reporter some yards away on the Mars television "set," which has been used to fake the television coverage of the Mars landing? Why . . . but does anyone care?

I don't, which is unusual because I am, by nature, ready to disbelieve everything from religious prophesies to time schedules printed in movie ads.

The cast for this nonsense includes Elliott Gould, as the reporter, the fellow who stumbles on what someone must call "the story of the century;" Karen Black, as his sometime girlfriend; James Brolin, Sam Waterston and O. J. Simpson, as the astronauts, whose lives are endangered in inverse relation to the billing they receive; Brenda Vaccaro, as Mr. Brolin's wife; Telly Savalas, as the crop-duster, and David Huddleston, as a United States Senator. If I didn't know they were actors I might suspect they'd originated on a drawing board.

It should be noted, I think, that "Capricorn One" is another "presentation" by Britain's tireless show-business entrepreneur Lew Grade, who has recently given us such other exercises in conspiracy as "The Domino Principle," "The Cassandra Crossing" and "Voyage of the Damned," all entertainments of a strikingly similar, mingy order.

•

"Capricorn One," which has been rated PG ("Parental Guidance Suggested",) has some mildly vulgar language, but it offends only common sense. Its a G-rated movie in disguise.

1978 Je 2, C8:1

FILM VIEW

VINCENT CANBY

Eight Films In Search Of an Auteur

The 1978 film festival season is now officially open. Cannes, which has just ended, begins the season that includes festivals in Tashkent, Cracow, Cork, Zagreb, Karlovy Vary, Trieste, Taormina, Locarno, San Sebastian, Thessalonika, Cairo, New York, Sorrento, Barcelona, Teheran, New Delhi, London and Jerusalem. That's to name only a few—there are more, almost as many festivals as there are films. Well, not quite, but it seems that way. Based on the reports from the Cannes festival, it also seems as if the same films, or at least the same *kinds* of films, keep reappearing, festival after festival, year after year. Déjà vu is a system of cinema esthetics.

With this in mind, I've prepared a tentative program for this year's New York Film Festival, based on nothing more than intuition and a certain familiarity with the tastes (and the syntax) of the people who choose the pictures.

"The Eagle Flies on Friday" (U.S.A., 1978). Opening night selection. This spellbinding political thriller, a work of mesmerizing intensity, offers conclusive proof that Peter Hyams ("Capricorn One") must at last be recognized as one of Hollywood's most talented and original directors in the tradition of Hitchcock, Ulmer, Aldrich, Fleischer and Alan J. Pakula. At once absurd and convincing, Hyams posits the idea that Richard M. Nixon doesn't exist and, indeed, has never existed. The person we "know" as Nixon is, instead, an innocent, bookish, Whittier, Calif., pharmacist whose personality has been purloined by conspirators and whose life is suddenly endangered when he wins a TV set in a raffle and recognizes a newsreel image of himself as the former President. The film combines sheer nerve, physical beauty, pride, humor, grace under pressure and suspense that involve the C.I.A., the F.B.I., the I.R.S. and the K.G.B. With Burt Lancaster, Richard Widmark, Edward Albert and, in a stunningly effective cameo, Candice Bergen as "Pat." No one who is or ever has been an American citizen can afford to miss it.

• • •

"Cherry Blossom Petals in the Vacuum Cleaner" (Japan, 1953). A Festival Retrospective Selection. Sometimes confused with "Late Winter," "Cherry Blossom Petals in the Vacuum Cleaner" is one of the least known yet most charming of the late Yasujiro Ozu's early *tsuma-mono* or wife films, about an upper-middle-class marriage that was arranged in the old-fashioned way and is now falling gently apart. Exquisitely acted by Shin Saburi as the husband and Michiyo Kogura as the wife, the film juxtaposes subdued high comedy and ineffable sadness to create a work of art that is both immensely sophisticated and innocent (almost shockingly). Worth the price of admission alone is a six-minute sequence in which Yuharu Atsuta's camera focuses on the unmoving silhouette of Saburi as his wife (off-screen) empties her new Sunbeam canister. Though the mood is serene, the sequence is informed (and even contradicted) by an eroticism that von Sternberg might have appreciated.

"Les Rendezvous Echoués" (Unkept Appointments) (France, 1978). "Unkept Appointments" is likely to be Marguerite Duras's break-through movie, being at the same time an existential thriller, a comedy about a liberated woman in a world still dominated by men, an agonized scream of partial despair and a meditation upon the French motorist's total dependence upon oil imports. A beautiful woman (Jeanne Moreau) is seen reflected in the door of a shiny new motor car. Is it a Porsche, a Renault, a Citroen, a Toyota? We never know. On the soundtrack, three voices are heard—Moreau's, Duras's and Gerard Depardieu's (though neither he nor Duras appear). Sometimes their words seem at cross purposes. Sometimes they recall the events that apparently led up to a suicide, or perhaps it was murder. Occasionally, one of the women sings a lullaby. The male voice becomes tender. The two women appear to respond, then mercilessly berate the man and, through him, all men. The film is simultaneously an anthology of ideas that have occurred to Duras at one time or another and a lively dissertation on the meaning and possibilities of film.

• • •

"Family Affections" (Greece, 1978). Nothing less than a tour de force for all concerned is "Family Affections," Jules Dassin's most mature, most courageous work—Sophocles' "Oedipus Rex" set in the contemporary Greece of supertankers, superfortunes and superpassions. Dassin's casting of Melina Mercouri as the modern-day Oedipus is a super-risk that brought the Cannes audience repeatedly to its cheering feet. Here at last is a role big enough for Mercouri to get her teeth into. She is magnificent, as are Irene Pappas as her wife/mother and Keith Carradine as an ambiguous goatherd. Dassin fuses text with image, sex with politics, love with hate, ecstasy with guilt to create a searing canvas that respects classical tradition while tearing at its very foundations.

"The Cow-Hide Mysteries" (U.S.A, 1978). Rainer Werner Fassbinder's first American film (and the third feature he's finished this year) dissects the love/sex lives of four not-so-young New York City "leather freaks"—Nonnie (Mimsy Farmer), Paul (Peter Chatel), Greta (Irm Herman) and Texas (Paul America) who share shifting alliances and a posh upper East Side town house where even the pinball machines are upholstered in cow-hide. Though there are a number of sexually explict scenes and one sadomasochistic episode that is for strong-stomached adults only, Fassbinder's militant anarchism should be taken with a grain of salt. It's as if Douglas Sirk had decided to make "Our Lady of the Flowers" with Jane Wyman and Rock Hudson. Nothing fits at first, but eventually everything does. Here is a wryly knowledgeable, human comedy in the form of a metaphor that evokes Armageddon. Splendid.

• • •

"Zone de Feu" (Belt of Fire) (France, 1978). Full of brawling vitality and bursting with visual and erotic excitement, this newest film by Polish-born Walerian Borowczyk, the giften *enfant terrible* of soft-core porn ("Immoral Tales," etc.) is a lusty comedy about the legendary Gilles de Rais, prototype for Bluebeard. Though the real-life Gilles de Rais (1404-1440) generally favored the kidnapping and murder of young boys, Borowczyk presents us with a Bluebeard whose tastes run more to nubile maidens on the order of the extraordinary Paloma Picasso, who has clearly reached the age of consent. The film is a riot of color, decor and female flesh and sometimes simply a riot, period. Michel Piccoli, as the lecherous nobleman, pursues his prey in an uproariously bumbling manner that recalls the comedy of the late Bert Lahr at his best. The film was shot on a shoe-string and looks it, which is the director's way of reminding us we are watching a very cheap film. In the Borowczyk vision, seedy is sublime.

• • •

"Sidewalk in the Rain" (Hungary,

1978). "Sidewalk in the Rain" is Marta Meszaros's best film since "Women," which was her best film since "Adoption." Like those films, it is about the friendship between an older and a younger woman, and about the conflicting demands made by children, husbands, the home, the state, washing dishes and pursuing careers (one is a telephone operator, the other a forewoman in a textile plant). The older woman considers taking a lover. The younger wants to study civil engineering. Ultimately, each abandons her dream in the awareness that being a woman is not a condition from which one escapes, but, rather, a condition to be embraced, like life. Meszaros finds poetry in every austere image of black, white and gray.

"Le Touriste" (The Tourist) (France, 1978). French critic Georges Heinz-Poulenc makes a smashing debut as a fully developed film auteur with this metaphysical comedy about a pair of identical twins, both played by Gerard Depardieu. Drawing freely from old movies ("A Stolen Life," "The Corsican Brothers" and even "Devotion"), Heinz-Poulenc wittily complicates the old formula by having the twins not only look alike but behave in exactly the same fashion, even to speaking the same lines, often in unison, with the obvious results of utter (and comic) confusion. Depardieu gives two masterful prformances, at once crude and lyric, tough and innocent, as the brothers who themselves are not sure which is which! Can anyone ever again explore the question of identity with a straight face? ■

1978 Je 4, II:13:1

"SERVANT AND MISTRESS"—Victor Lanoux and Andrea Ferreol are master and servant forced into a role reversal.

Love and Money

SERVANT AND MISTRESS, directed by Bruno Gantillon; screenplay (French with English subtitles) by Frantz-Andre Burguet and Dominique Fabre; executive producer, Gilbert de Goldsmidt; director of photography, Szabo; editor, George Kloiz; music, Jean-Marie Benjamin; a production of Madeleine Films and Shangrila Productions, distributed by New Line Cinema. Runnnig time: 90 minutes. At the Columbia Two Theater, Second Avenue at 64th Street. This film has not been rated.

Jerome	Victor Lanoux
Maria	Andrea Ferreol
Christine	Evelyne Buyle
Charles	Gabriel Cattand
Dancer	David Pontremoli
Chef	Jean Rougerie

By VINCENT CANBY

FOR years Maria (Andrea Ferreol) has been the faithful cook/housekeeper/domestic to a wealthy fertilizer dealer who lives outside Paris. When the old fellow dies, his nephew Jerome (Victor Lanoux), who used to play childhood games with Maria, returns to collect his legacy. Imagine his surprise when he learns that the legacy—the house, the Rolls-Royce, the fortune, everything—has been left to the servant. Maria, a maid who always wanted to be a lady, agrees that Jerome may stay on in the mansion on her terms, that is, if he becomes **her** servant.

Thus begins, more or less, "Servant and Mistress," a first feature film by Bruno Gantillon, a French director with a good deal of style but not much on his mind. The film opens today at the Columbia II.

•

"Servant and Mistress" might possibly have been a funny film, but Mr. Gantillon takes his fancy sado-masochism quite seriously. Jerome hangs around the mansion accepting the various humiliations that Maria heaps on him. He serves her breakfast in bed. He washes the floors. He picks up purposely dropped napkins and observes her having sex with another man, all in the fond hope that one day she'll tire of the game and revert to their earlier relationship.

But—are you really ready for this?—he begins to fall in love with her. However, poor Maria, who dearly loves Jerome, knows she can never be a real lady (or, at least, I think that's what her conclusion is), and so these escalating humiliations must come to a sad, freeze-frame ending.

•

"Servant and Mistress" is the sort of deadly earnest, crashingly irrelevant romantic melodrama that the French are inclined to take much more seriously than we do, perhaps because they recognize in its artificialities a relationship to a kind of French boulevard comedy that's never been very popular here. "Servant and Mistress" is not comedy by any means, but it has more to do with manners than with ideas, characters, life or even sex.

Miss Ferreol ("La Grande Bouffe") and Mr. Lanoux ("Cousin, Cousine"), both of whom are in much more trim shape than they were in those earlier films, are performers of wit whenever the screenplay allows, which isn't often. Mostly they move through the movie like Siamese fighting fish in water that's begun to freeze. They are elegant but sluggish.

1978 Je 7, C19:5

Angles of Love

A WOMAN AT HER WINDOW, directed by Pierre Granier-Deferre; screenplay (French with English subtitles) by Jorge Semprun and Mr. Granier-Deferre, based on the novel by Pierre Drieu La Rochelle; produced by Albina Du Boisrouvray; director of photography,, Aldo Tonti; music, Carlo Rustichelli; editor, Jean Ravel; a co-production of Albina Productions (Paris), Rizzoli Film (Rome) and Cinema 77 (Berlin), distributed by Cinema Shares International. Running time: 114 minutes. At the Festival Theater, 57th Street near Fifth Avenue. This film has not been rated.

Margot	Romy Schneider
Raoul	Philippe Noiret
Michel	Victor Lanoux
Rico	Umberto Orsini
Dora	Delia Boccardo
Avghi	Martine Brochard
Primoukis	Gastone Moschin
Von Pahlen	Carl Mohner
Stahlbaum	Joachim Hansen

By VINCENT CANBY

THE place is Greece and the year is 1936. We see three people photographed on a cliff against a magnificent panorama of arid mountains. The air is so clear it seems to have been dry-cleaned. Margot (Romy Schneider) is beautiful and dreamily serene, like someone who's been smoking marijuana. Raoul (Philippe Noiret) is shaped like a bowling pin and ill-tempered, but he's impeccably dressed. Michel (Victor Lanoux) is handsome, self-assured and patronizing in the manner of a man with a higher calling.

Though they stand far enough apart to be playing catch, they talk about history, politics and literature as earnestly as three people huddled around a tiny cafe table.

Michel is a Greek Communist on the run from his country's new Fascist Government. Raoul, a French capitalist, is in love with Margot, and Margot, who is married to Rico (not in this scene), an Italian diplomat, is in the process of falling in love with Michel.

•

Thus starts "A Woman at Her Window," a French political melodrama with heavily romantic overtones written by Jorge Semprun, the Spanish-born French writer who has done much, much better things ("La Guerre Est Finie," "Z," "State of Siege"), and directed by Pierre Granier-Deferre, who has done one somewhat better thing that I know of (Georges Simenon's "The Cat").

The film, which opens today at the Festival Theater, is a muddle of big ideas, mysticism and cinematic posing. It's the story of how Margot—rich and so completely wrinkle-free it's eerie—is redeemed from her life of idleness by a chance meeting wih Michel, who climbs into her first-floor Athens window one night when fleeing the police (hence tha poetic title).

Margot's husband, Rico (Umberto Orsini), is a perfectly nice, attractive fellow. He has a sense of humor. He's kind. He cares about her, but for reasons never explained adequately, theirs is a marriage in what once used to be termed "name only." They are good friends but he has his mistresses and she's kept busy being the toast of Athens.

•

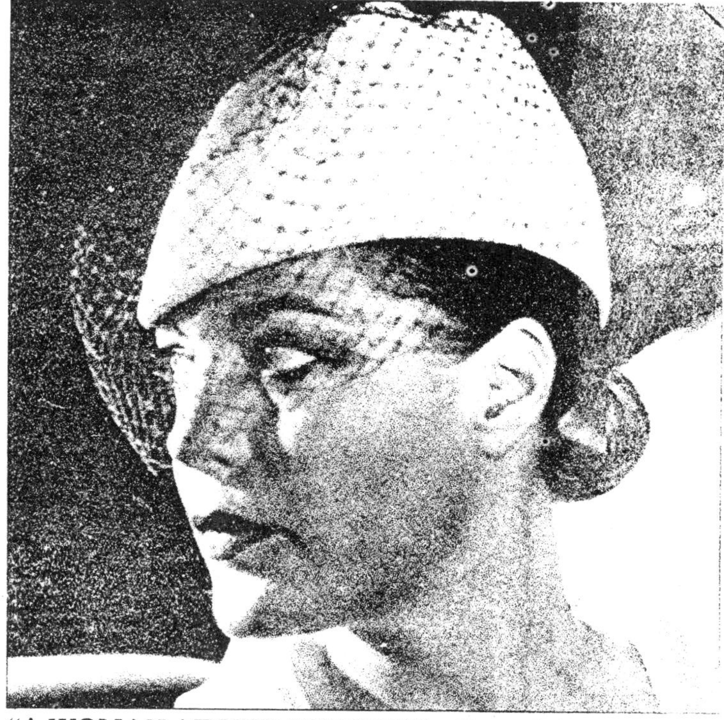

"A WOMAN AT HER WINDOW"—Romy Schneider's life is changed by the abrupt arrival of a political fugitive (the ubiquitous Victor Lanoux).

As you might guess, the time in which the film is set is important. The old European order is collapsing into two opposing camps on the eve of first the Spanish Civil War and then World War II. Margot's redemption—her love for the Communist organizer and, through him, commitment to the radical Left—is, I suspect, supposed to tell us something about the inexorable movement of civilizations, about history.

Mostly, though, it tells us how easily a bored woman can be swept off her feet even when the language of love is hack work. Surveying the ruins of an ancient temple, Michel says, "We build for men, not gods," and Margot goes absolutely limp. When Margot has the temerity to wonder aloud why she loves him, Michel answers in complete confidence, "There's something in me greater than myself."

"A Woman at Her Window" jumps around in time for no apparent reason other than to simulate the building of suspense. Part of the film has to do with the faithful Raoul and Rico's helping Margot to get Michel safely out of Greece, but there also are jumps forward to 1945 and then to 1967, when Miss Schneider turns up as her own daughter.

•

Even with all of this hopping around the most interesting things in Mr. Semprun's screenplay inevitably happen off-screen. It's left to messengers of one sort and another to tell us exactly how Michel escaped, how Margot eventually joined him, how they became very important in resistance movements, and how Rico at last sickened of working for Mussolini and sought exile in France.

There's a lot of pretty Greek scenery in "A Woman at Her Window" but so little action it could have been a stage piece. As I've already indicated, the talk, at least as rendered by the subtitles, is not great, especially when Margot, early in their relationship, comes on to Michel saying in a manner meant to be inviting, "You wanted to know . . . the taste of my mouth?"

Miss Schneider is incapable of registering any emotion except pleasure in her own beauty. Mr. Lanoux also gives the impression of intense self-absorption. Only Mr. Orsini and Mr. Noiret seem real, but the movie is interested in them only as props necessary to the great romance that is the film's hollow center.

1978 Je 8, C14:5

'Born Unto a Jackel'

DAMIEN—OMEN II, directed by Don Taylor; screenplay by Stanley Mann and Michael Hodges, from a story by Harvey Bernhard based on characters created by David Seltzer; produced by Mr. Bernhard; co-producer, Charles Orme; director of photography, Bill Butler; music, Jerry Goldsmith; editor, Robert Brown Jr.; distributed by 20th Century-Fox. Running time: 110 minutes. At the National Theater, Broadway at 43d Street, and other theaters. This film has been rated R.

Richard Thorn....William Holden
Ann Thorn....Lee Grant
Damien Thorn....Jonathan Scott-Taylor
Paul Buher....Robert Foxworth
Charles Warren....Nicholas Pryor
Bill Atherton....Lew Ayres
Aunt Marion....Sylvia Sidney
Sergeant Neff....Lance Hendriksen
Joan Hart....Elizabeth Shepherd
Mark Thorn....Lucas Donat
Pasarian....Alan Arbus
Murray....Fritz Ford
Dr. Kane....Meshach Taylor
Teddy....John J. Newcombe
Butler....John Charles Burns
Colonel....Paul Cook
Jane....Diane Daniels
Teacher....Robert E. Ingham
Minister....William B. Fosser

By VINCENT CANBY

WHEN we took our leave of him at the end of "The Omen," Damien, the cherubic-looking Antichrist, come to earth to claim his rights, was 6 years old and in attendance at the state funeral of his father and mother, the recently deceased United States Ambassador to the Court of St. James's and Mrs. Thorn. Holding the hand of the President throughout the ceremony, Damien did not fidget. Apparently fidgets are not something to which a child "born unto a jackal" is subject.

At the start of "Damien—Omen II," the inevitable sequel, we leap seven years into the future when Damien, now 13 and played by round-faced Jonathan Scott-Taylor, is living near Chicago with his uncle, Richard Thorn (William Holden), Richard's wife, Ann (Lee Grant), and his cousin Mark (Lucas Donat) in the sort of suburban splendor that only multimillions can buy in the Middle West: a 50-year-old, mock French chateau and more liveried servants than you're likely to find at Buckingham Palace.

To all outward appearances Damien is, if not *the* Antichrist, then at least *an* Antichrist. He rarely smiles, and when he does it's a sneer. He's rude to his ancient aunt. He smokes cigarettes if he can get them and, when crossed by a schoolmate, all he has to do is stare to send the other kid into convulsions. Yet nobody recognizes him for what he is, not even Damien himself.

It's left to a sergeant at the military school attended by Damien and Mark to pass the word on to Damien. The sergeant is one of the Devil's helpers who miraculously appear from time to time to help Damien (and the movie's plot) along.

•

"The time is coming," says the sergeant sternly, "for you to put away childish things and face up to who you are."

Those of us who endured "The Omen" know what the sergeant means: "You're too old to go around murdering mummies and daddies and nannies. Act your age."

One way and another Damien does, and "Damien—Omen II" is the open-ended record of this particular—what should I call it?—rite of passage. Before Damien is finished this time, there have been approximately a dozen new victims, a couple of whom have succumbed to what appear to be internal disorders while others have been sliced in half, stabbed, burned, impaled, gassed, pecked (by a nasty crow) and, in the film's most inspired moment of cinematic nonsense, drowned beneath the clear ice of a Wisconsin lake.

Perhaps my resistance has given out but I must say that "Damien—Omen II," though it's as foolish as the first film, is rather more fun to watch and sometimes very stylish-looking. Much of the movie was shot in and around Chicago, which, in winter, with its extraordinary architecture, must be one of the handsomest of American cities—so handsome, in fact, that the moviemakers haven't hesitated to let Chicago's railroad yards double for those in New York when the need arises.

•

"Damien" does have some trouble getting its seasons straight. Though the story covers approximately nine months, the leaves on the trees suggest a perpetual autumn with occasional bouts of winter.

The winter scenes, filmed in Wisconsin, are spectacularly beautiful, and work in a subliminal way to make us accept the not uncomic absurdities of the screenplay, written by Stanley Mann and Michael Hodges. Because Mr. Hodges began as the film's director, but was later replaced by Don Taylor ("The Island of Dr. Moreau," "Tom Sawyer"), I've no idea who is responsible for the movie's classy look.

A cast of good actors helps, of course. Mr. Holden and Miss Grant play it straight, with nice assistance from Mr. Scott-Taylor, Mr. Donat, Sylvia Sidney, Lew Aires and several actors new to me, Robert Foxworth, Elizabeth Shepherd and Lance Hendriksen.

I'd hate to have anyone go off to see "Damien" with the idea that it's going to be some sort of transcendental experience. It's a joke, but as such jokes go, it's much funnier than "The Fury," and quite as shrewd in its Grand Guignol special effects.

1978 Je 9, C6:5

William Holden and Lee Grant in "Damien-Omen II"
As foolish as the first film, but rather more fun to watch

BONJOUR AMOUR, directed by Roger Andrieux; screenplay (French with English subtitles) by Mr. Andrieux and Jean Marie Besnard; produced by Catherine Winter and Gisele Rebillon; music, Maxime Le Forestier; director of photography, Ramon Saurez; editor, Kenout Peltier; a Sofracima production, distributed by Atlantic Releasing Corporation. Running time: 90 minutes. At the Cinema 2, Third Avenue near 6th Street. This film has not been rated.

Marc....Pascal Meynier
Martine....Guilhaine Dubos
Marc's father....Michel Galabru
Mark's mother....Alix Mahieux
Martine's mother....Francoise Prevost
Christian....Bruno Raffaeli

By VINCENT CANBY

If you can't wait to see another French film about first love, then rush over to the Cinema 2 where "Bonjour Amour" opens today. It might not be there long.

The film is about Marc (Pascal Meynier), a boy of unspecified teen age, and the sweet, presumably older 17-year-old shopgirl, Martine (Guilhaine Dubos), with whom he shares first love's joys, sorrows, discoveries and other clichés, until they are separated by his boorish, lower middle-class parents.

There's nothing stunningly wrong with the movie except a lack of apparent talent, which is as fatal to a movie about first love as it would be in the counterfeiting of $20 bills. Roger Andrieux, the director, obviously means the film, called "L'Amour en Herbe" (Budding Love) in France, to be tender and sensitive. It is, instead, trivial and humorless. Watching it is like waiting for a subway with nothing to read.

The performances are adequate, though Mr. Meynier appears to be not only very young but slightly stunted. Everybody in the movie seems to be bigger than he is.

1978 Je 11, 61:5

FILM VIEW

VINCENT CANBY

Films To Break—or Make Summer Doldrums

Everybody has his own definition of a "summer movie." To some it's the sort of movie that you might expect to see in a drive-in—soft-core sex 'n violence or maybe soft-core sex 'n comedy. To others, a summer movie is one that doesn't make you think, as if the mind has to stay in the city while you go to the shore. If it's true that more people tend to go to movies in the summer than at any other time of year, then most movies are summer movies, since most people see them then. A summer movie is a movie that's experienced in summer—that's all—whether it's Mizoguchi's "A Geisha" or Michael Rae's "Laserblast."

The following is a consumer guide for the early-departing vacationist. It's compiled with the full awareness that people on vacation have a particularly high tolerance for nonsense they wouldn't be caught dead watching at home: "Oh, what the hell, we're on vacation. Why not?"

I haven't included in the guide movies about which I've recently written in this space: such films as "Pretty Baby," which one should see whatever the circumstances; "F.I.S.T.," which I like though it's hardly perfect, and "The Greek Tycoon," which, I've no doubt, will be the major hit of the vacation season since it's exactly the sort of throwaway movie one lunges for when one is far from home. If "The Greek Tycoon" were a book, you could spill Coppertone all over it and no one would care less. It's also completely biodegradable. Within a few months it will have been reabsorbed into the earth where it will begin its long dark crawl back to the surface as some elemental substance from which, next time, bubble gum may be manufactured.

Neither have I included in this guide comments on "Jaws 2," "Damien—Omen II" or "Grease." Custom frowns on the reviewing of films that haven't yet been seen. Drat!

"Capricorn One." Trade predictions are that this may be one of the summer's big ones. All I can say is that it's livelier than "The Domino Principle," a piece of wilted lettuce also "presented" by England's indomitable show-biz knight, Sir Lew Grade. "Capricorn One," written and directed by Peter Hyams, is poppycock without wit, meaning popcorn without butter. It's a suspense melodrama about the attempts of NASA to fake a manned Mars probe when the head of the mission realizes the equipment is faulty. He fears doing the obvious—scratching the mission—because Congress and the President might then withdraw all funds from the space program. The movie has nothing to do with science-fiction and everything to do with earth-bound melodrama as a sloppy reporter (Elliott Gould) tries to get the "real" story and as the three astronauts (James Brolin, Sam Waterston and O.J. Simpson), sequestered at a remote desert air base, try to escape to tell the world the awful truth. Telly Savalas and Karen Black make token appearances and Hal Holbrook plays a very benign sort of villain, the evil fellow who masterminds the fakery and isn't above murder to keep a secret shared by several hundred thousand other NASA people. Tolerable only if seen at the last show on a hot Saturday night in Nantucket with a convivial crowd.

"The Chess Players." Satyajit Ray's elegant, understated contemplation of the forces at work when in 1856 the British decided to take control of Oudh, the last of the independent kingdoms in the north of India. The film is satire of a very gentle, polite nature, though if you know Ray's work, you'll know that it runs deep. Unless you're spending your vacation in the heart of Manhattan, or in Berkeley or in Delhi, you may not get the chance to contemplate making a decision to see "The Chess Players." If you do, remember you have to be in the right mood. You have to rev down to its pace, which is somewhat slower than that of Prissy when Scarlett sent her off to fetch the doctor.

"Dear Detective." Philippe De Broca's valentine to valentines is about a supposedly intelligent, effective detective (Annie Girardot) who worries a lot about her clothes and her hair and wonders why her male colleagues in the Paris police patronize her as a mindless sex-object. It's also about a lovable middle-aged professor (Philippe Noiret), a confirmed bachelor with an eye for a pretty leg, who falls in love with her and is aghast and furious when he finds out that she's a detective. Mercy! "Dear Detective" is cute in the manner of an elderly midget dressed up to look like a child—it's unconvincing. Even its well-meaning optimism is out of date. You can bet that if De Broca ever gets around to the story of Sodom and Gomorrah, Lot's wife, when she looks back, will turn into a pretty, red-and-white striped candy cane.

"The End." In the very first scene, Burt Reynolds, who is the star as well as the director, is in a doctor's office being told that he has a terminal disease. "Oh, my God," he wails, "like Ali McGraw in 'Love Story.' " That's a promising line, but neither the actor nor the director know how to make it as funny as it wants to be. The entire movie is this way. Reynolds mugs very hard but he never can convince us that (1) he's dying,nor (2) this is a serious comedy. Reynolds's attempts to do something off-beat are appealing even when the results are not successful, and he has had the good taste to surround himself with some actors who are very nice, very good or very funny, including Myrna Loy, Pat O'Brien, Sally Field, Joanne Woodward, Robby Benson, Carl Reiner and Dom DeLouise, who almost pulls it all together by showing us that schizophrenia can be hilarious, at least in his case.

"House Calls." This has been around some time but I suspect it will be around a lot longer still. It's not the greatest comedy ever made, but Walter Matthau and Glenda Jackson are attractive and they're very funny when they're giving each other a tough time, and very, very funny when director Howard Zeif lets them slip in a little slapstick, as when they try to discover if it's possible to make love in a bed when each party keeps one foot on the floor (a reference to an early Production Code rule. The film is at its best, though, when it is dealing with life in a dreadful hospital run by a senile doctor played by the great Art Carney. At the annual meeting the old fellow reports that Dr. Debakey can't make the big hospital dinner but that they've snared a Hertz representative who'll talk to the staff about "the benefits of car-leasing." It's a very pleasant movie, one of the few around.

• • •

"Joseph Andrews." This is the year's most cheerful movie to date, and probably the most neglected movie of the decade. Why it should be overlooked is difficult to fathom. Tony Richardson's adaptation of the gloriously convoluted, wise and comic Henry Fielding novel is a trip of succeeding highs. It's beautifully acted by almost every fine actor in England (Michael Hordern, Beryl Reid, Peggy Ashcroft, John Gielgud, among others), as well as by young Peter Firth in the title role, and by Ann-Margret as the lecherous Lady Booby, whose husband, Lord Booby, expires in the bath at Bath. In addition to being so much fun, it's splendid to look at.

"Thank God It's Friday." This month's disco film should be avoided unless you really don't want to go back to see "Saturday Night Fever" for the second (third, fourth or fifth) time. All the action takes place in one night in a Los Angeles discothèque called The Zoo, where the dozen main characters come together, dance, have unimportant adventures, and then move on. The Zoo looks like a fire-trap. The characters aren't very interesting, though the actors aren't bad at all. The music is terrible and non-stop. This movie was[illegible] photographed. It was pressed—by Motown and Casablanca Records, who co-produced it. ■

1978 Je 11, II:21:1

A Loving Look

THE POPOVICH BROTHERS OF SOUTH CHICAGO, a documentary film made by Jill Godmilow in collaboration with Ethel Raim and Martin Koenig of the Balkan Arts Center; director of photography, Tom Hurwitz. Running time: 60 minutes.
SONOMA, an animated film by Dennies Pies. Running time: nine minutes. At the Whitney Museum of American Art, Madison Avenue at 75th Street.

THE POPOVICH Brothers of South Chicago," a 60-minute documentary about the small but fiercely close-knit Serbian community in this country, heads the week's new film program opening today at the Whitney Museum of American Art.

The film is the work of Jill Godmilow, who co-produced and co-directed "Antonia: A Portrait of the Woman" with Judy Collins, and was commissioned by the Balkan Arts Center. It's a loving examination of Serbian customs, family ties and especially Serbian music, as represented by the Popovich Brothers, who played and sang for their countrymen around America for more than 50 years.

Also on the Whitney bill is Dennis Pies's short, beautiful, animated film, "Sonoma," an expressionist recollection of what seem to be landscapes, seascapes and times of day executed in pencil and vivid watercolors.

VINCENT CANBY

1978 Je 13, C5:1

Meg Foster

By JANET MASLIN

A DIFFERENT STORY, directed by Paul Aaron; produced by Alan Belkin; screenplay by Henry Olek; music by David Frank; director of photography, Philip Lathrop; editor, Lynn McCallon; a Peterson Company presentation, released by Avco Embassy Pictures. At the Baronet Theater, 993 Third Avenue. Running time: 107 minutes. This film is rated R.

Albert	Perry King
Stella	Meg Foster
Phyllis	Valerie Curtin
Sills	Peter Donat
Mr. Cooke	Richard Bull
Mrs. Cooke	Barbara Collentine
Ned	Guerin Barry
Roger	Doug Higgins
Chris	Lisa James
Sam	Eugene Butler
Chastity	Linda Carpenter

THE lovers in "A Different Story," which opened at the Baronet Theater yesterday, don't meet cute, they meet adorable. Stella (Meg Foster) a realestate sales representative who seems to deal exclusively in mansions, first encounters Albert (Perry King) because he is the chauffeur and Boy Friday of one of her homosexual male clients. Later, after Albert's lover has found a new driver, Stella is showing another palazzo and finds Albert camping in it. She invites him to stay on the sofa of her comfortable apartment.

He stays for good, and soon the comfortable mess is no more. Because Albert is a homosexual, you see, he likes to cook, vacuum, fluff pillows and hang up Stella's clothes.

The Gay Activists' Alliance has circulated a letter expressing alarm about "A Different Story," and, indeed, the group has a point.

•

Albert, thinking himself very clever, tells Stella at dinner one night "Yes I have, several and not particularly," in answer to three questions he anticipates her asking. ("Have I ever been with a woman, how many, and did I like it?") But Stella turns out to be a lesbian, so she isn't nearly as shocked by this as Albert expects her to be. Albert and Stella don't appear to remain homosexual for long: they marry, have a baby, buy a Mercedes, move into a big house with too much wallpaper, and squabble just as other couples do.

The movie's use of their homosexuality is indeed exploitative, insensitive, and offensive in a variety of ways. Even worse, it is unconvincing. For all of Mr. King's mincing, preening and complaining about how Miss Foster's tardiness has made him scorch their dinner, Albert's homosexuality is nothing but a gimmick, something for the screenplay to coax him out of. Mr. King makes Albert so unattractive that it's hard to care about his taking the cure.

•

Mr. King is much worse than the movie, which is no mean accomplishment Miss Foster is much better, with an aggressive vitality that lets her upstage Mr. King at every turn. But her talents are continually undercut by the direction of Paul Aaron, who makes the kind of debut that ought to be a swan song. Mr. Aaron's ineptitude knows no bounds, especially when it comes to blasting an insufferable score, ending scenes at uninteresting moments, and making the film's chronology completely obscure. After a while, the only way to mark time is by counting Albert's divine little dinners.

The film's notion of reversing sex roles is not without comic potential. But there's something quite ugly about its manner of accepting sexual stereotypes in the first place, just for the sake of shuffling them around.

1978 Je 14, C20:4

Fantasy of the 50's

GREASE, directed by Randal Kleiser; screenplay Bronte Woodward, adapted by Allan Carr from the Broadway musical by Jim Jacobs and Warren Casey; produced by Robert Stigwood and Mr. Carr; dances and musical sequences staged and choreographed by Patricia Birch; music supervision Bill Oakes; director of photography, Bill Butler; editor, John F. Burnett; distributed by Paramount Pictures. Running time: 110 minutes. At Loews State 2, Broadway at 45th Street, and other theaters. This film has been rated PG.

Danny	John Travolta
Sandy	Olivia Newton-John
Rizzo	Stockard Channing
Kenickie	Jeff Conway
Frenchy	Didi Conn
Principal McGee	Eve Arden
Teen Angel	Frankie Avalon
Vi	Joan Blondell
Vince Fontaine	Edd Byrnes
Coach Calhoun	Sid Caesar
Mrs. Murdock	Alice Ghostley
Blanche	Dody Goodman
Johnny Casino and the Gamblers	Sha-Na-Na
Jan	Jamie Donnelly
Marty	Dinah Manoff
Doody	Barry Pearl
Sonny	Michael Tucci
Putzie	Kelly Ward
Patty Simcox	Susan Buckner
Eugene	Eddie Deezen
Tom Chisum	Lorenzo Lamas
Leo	Dennis C. Stewart
Cha Cha	Annette Charles
Mr. Rudie	Dick Patterson
Nurse Wilkins	Fannie Flagg
Mr. Lynch	Darrell Zwerling
Waitress	Ellen Travolta

By VINCENT CANBY

"GREASE," the film version of the still-running Broadway musical show, is not really the 1950's teen-age movie musical it thinks it is, but a contemporary fantasy about a 1950's teenage musical—a larger, funnier, wittier and more imaginative-than-Hollywood movie with a life that is all its own. It uses the Eisenhower era — the characters, costumes, gestures and, particularly, the music—to create a time and place that have less to do with any real 50's than with a kind of show business that is both timeless and old-fashioned, both sentimental and wise. The movie, which opens today at Loews State 2 and other theaters, is also terrific fun.

Olivia Newton-John and John Travolta in "Grease"
Its sensibility is tied to a free-wheeling, well-informed, high-spirited present

Because I seem to be one of the few persons who has never seen the Broadway show, I'm not sure how the movie differs from the original, yet it's apparent that the film's score, which is one of the best things about the production, has been liberally supplemented by new material and new-old material, including "Love Is a Many Splendored Thing," which has never before sounded so marvelously, soaringly inane.

Somewhat in the manner of "Close Encounters of the Third Kind," which recalls the science-fiction films of the 50's in a manner more elegant and more benign than anything that was ever made then, "Grease" is a multimillion-dollar evocation of the B-picture quickies that Sam Katzman used to turn out in the 50's ("Don't Knock the Rock," 1957) and that American International carried to the sea in the 1960's ("Beach Party," 1963).

•

The gang at old Rydell High, which is the universe of "Grease," is unlike any high school class you've ever seen except in the movies. For one thing, they're all rather long in the tooth to be playing kids who'd hang around malt shops. For another, they are loaded with the kind of talent and exuberance you don't often find very far from a musical stage. They not only portray characters but effectively make comments on them.

Olivia Newton-John, the recording star in her American film debut, is simultaneously very funny and utterly charming as the film's ingénue, a demure, virginal Sandra Dee-type. She possesses true screen presence as well as a sweet, sure singing voice, while the Sandra Dee I remember had a voice that seemed to have been manufactured in Universal's speech-and-special-effects department.

John Travolta, as Miss Newton-John's costar, a not-so-malevolent gang-leader, is better than he was in "Saturday Night Fever." I'm still not sure if he's a great actor, but he's a fine performer with the kind of energy and humor that are brought to life by the musical numbers.

Stockard Channing, as the high school's tramp who has a dirty mouth and a heart of gold, would (if it were possible) stop the show twice, once with a party put-on of poor Olivia ("Look at Me, I'm Sandra Dee") and another when she attempts, in song, to explain why it's more honorable to be loose than uptight ("There Are Worse Things I Could Do").

The film's producers, Robert Stigwood and Allen Carr, and director, Randel Kleiser (whose first theatrical feature this is), have also supplemented the cast of comparative youngsters with a whole crowd of actors we associate with the 50's, and who seem here to have survived with barely a visible dent.

Eve Arden, a fixture of the 50's as Our Miss Brooks, plays Rydell High's unflappable principal; Sid Caesar is the football coach; Edd Byrnes comes on briefly as the lecherous host of a teenage TV show that decides to spotlight Rydell in a network program; Joan Blondell is the harassed waitress at the corner soda fountain, and, maybe funniest of all, is Frankie Avalon, who appears in a dream sequence to counsel an unhappy student ("Beauty School Dropout").

Bronte Woodward has adapted the Broadway book by Jim Jacobs and Warren Casey, who also wrote the show's original score, in such a way that the plot serves the purpose of the music without needlessly interfering with it.

It's to the director's credit that the musical numbers slip in and out of reality mostly with hugely comic effect. The highlights of the stage show include the upbeat rock number, "We Go Together," and the rueful "Summer Nights," both sung by Mr. Travolta and Miss Newton-John, but the hit of the film is probably a breathless new number, "You're the One That I Want," written by John Farrar and beautifully choreographed by Patricia Birch.

Because there haven't been that many movie musicals recently, it doesn't mean much to say that "Grease" is the best we've had in years. I'm also afraid that people who (like me) have no special fondness for the 50's might be put off by the film's time and place. Let me emphasize, then, that "Grease" stands outside the traditions it mimics. Its sensibility is not tied to the past but to a free-wheeling, well informed, high-spirited present.

•

"Grease," which has been rated PG ("Parental Guidance Suggested") has some language that would never have been heard even on Broadway in the 50's, and though it deals with teen-age lust quite frankly, it's heart is always pure.

1978 Je 16, C10:1

The Great White Redux

JAWS 2, directed by Jeannot Szwarc; screenplay by Carl Gottlieb and Howard Sackler, based on characters created by Peter Benchley; produced by Richard D. Zanuck and David Brown; director of photography, Michael Butler; editor, Neil Travis; music, John Williams; a Zanuck/Brown production, distributed by Universal Pictures. Running time: 120 minutes. At the Cinerama 1 and 2 Theaters, Broadway at 47th Street, and other theaters. This film has been rated PG.

Brody	Roy Scheider
Ellen Brody	Lorraine Gary
Mayor Vaughan	Murray Hamilton
Peterson	Joseph Mascolo
Hendricks	Jeffrey Kramer
Dr. Elkins	Collin Wilcox
Tina	Ann Dusenberry
Mike	Mark Gruner
Andrews	Barry Coe
Old lady	Susan French
Andy	Gary Springer
Jackie	Donna Wilkes
Ed	Gary Dubin
Polo	John Dukakis
Timmy	G. Thomas Dunlop
Larry	David Elliott
Sean	Marc Gilpin
Doug	Keith Gordon
Lucy	Cynthia Grover
Patrick	Ben Marley
Marge	Martha Swatek
Bob	Billy Van Zandt
Brooke	Gigi Vorgan

UNTIL great white sharks learn how to fly or use automatic weapons or develop their powers of telekinesis, it would seem that "Jaws 2" has pretty much exhausted the cinematic possibilities of sharks as man-eating monsters.

Watching the new film, which opens at the Cinerama 1 and 2 and other theaters today and is, of course, a spin-off from the phenomenally successful 1975 movie, one quickly realizes that there's only a fixed amount of excitement that can be generated by the sight of a $2 million mechanical shark upsetting sailboats, nipping the legs of swimmers or even swallowing victims whole, without even a burp.

One also longs for the talent and discipline of Steven Spielberg, who directed the original film and knows how to use a motion picture camera, something that is not at all evident in the work of Jeannot Szwarc, the young man who directed "Jaws 2." The screenplay, based on some of Peter Benchley's original characters, is something of an impediment, being about nothing at all except another batch of shark attacks that upset life at Amity, which is supposed to be a Long Island resort community though it often resembles Florida.

A worried, ill-tempered-looking Roy Scheider reprises his role as the Amity police chief, along with Lorraine Gary as his wife and Murray Hamilton as Amity's smarmy, always-wrong mayor. Most of the rest of the cast are teen-agers, young men and young women, all of whom look enough alike as to make it virtually impossible to remember which kid has been gobbled up in what sequence. Not that it matters much.

Some of the action sequences have been well staged, but they've been dropped into the film so indiscriminately that "Jaws 2" never builds to a particular climax. It simply drones on and on and on, like a television movie.

Someone also made a mistake in showing us so much of the mechanical shark so early in the film. One of the canny decisions in "Jaws" was the withholding of such visual information until near the end, by which time suspense had overwhelmed logic to such an extent that our imaginations were in league with the movie makers'. The shark in "Jaws 2" looks like something one might ride at Disneyland.

•

"Jaws 2," which has been rated PG ("Parental Guidance Suggested"), contains some mildly vulgar language and a number of scenes showing children in jeopardy, but the violence is mostly implied and bloodless.

VINCENT CANBY

1978 Je 16, C10:5

FILM VIEW

VINCENT CANBY

On Keeping The Scenery In Its Place

One of the most obvious pleasures in watching movies is responding to a film's sense of place, which is more than just the way a place looks, though that too is important. I remember some years ago when, for the first time, I arrived in Cairo by air. As we circled the city we could see the Citadel and the old quarter on the east bank of the Nile, while, on the other side of the river, just beyond the line where the city suddenly stops and the desert begins, we could see the Sphinx and the pyramids at Giza. I had the feeling that I'd been through all this before, but it wasn't déjà-vu. It was Cinerama. To be more exact, "This Is Cinerama." The first Cinerama feature had included a spectacular flight over Cairo that gave the audience not only a breathtaking view but an awareness of where each major landmark stood in relation to the others. The film, in fact, was more efficient than the airplane I was in, since it was necessary, in the plane, to dart from one side of the cabin to the other while the Cinerama view, shot from the pilot's cabin, set everything before us in one vast panorama.

All moviemaking is a kind of cartography, laying out not only landscapes but relationships, at various times of day, in all sorts of climates and particular weather conditions. But moviemaking at its best should do more than simply chart a location or capture a scenic likeness, which is something I'm sure that most moviemakers know though they don't always have the time or the imagination to act on it. In the best films geographic locations are so integrated with the other production components that one doesn't pay much attention to them. They are as much a part of a total performance as the actor, the director or the screenplay. Everything interacts. It's only in movies of something less than a transcendental nature that we're likely to be aware of just how this works.

Take "Damien—Omen II," the inevitable sequel that carries the career of the Antichrist-hero of "The Omen" seven years further along. It's a movie that should, by all rights, be tired. The writers, Stanley Mann and Michael Hodges (who also directed part of the movie, though Don Taylor receives the screen credit), haven't tampered with the formula set forth in David Seltzer's screenplay for the original film. Damien (Jonathan Scott-Taylor), now 13, continues his campaign to take over the world, principally by murdering, in one fashion or another, anyone who gets in his way.

Something quite special has been added to the sequel, however, and it is, of all things, the city of Chicago and its skyline, changed during the long reign of the late Mayor Daley.

In "Damien—Omen II," the round-faced little Antichrist has become the ward of his uncle, a multi-millionaire tycoon, played by William Holden, a fellow whose multi-national conglomerate, called Thorn Industries, could serve as a practical operating concern for any devil obsessed with world domination.

The home office for Thorn Industries is in Chicago, formerly the world's Hog Butcher, which, as we see it in "Damien," is an eerily under-populated, wintery landscape—the background for some of the most beautiful and / or nervy modern architecture in America, particularly the Hancock Building and the Prudential Life Building, monuments to Mammon. It's only fitting that when the heads of Thorn Industries (which, I assume, Damien will inherit in the already planned "Omen III") gather to talk business in their executive suites, we, in the audience, are always aware that the world is at their feet. We can see it there, in the hazy distance, 60 or 70 stories below, as if it were the Devil's acreage waiting to be reclaimed.

I'm not sure how much of this "look" of "Damien" is the result of conscious decision or of happy accident. However it came to be, it helps to persuade us to go along with what otherwise is a standard exercise in demonology. The actors (William Holden, Lee Grant, Sylvia Sidney, Lew Ayres and the rest) are quite efficient and help, of course, but the film, which is about the last days of the rich and powerful, communicates this most effectively in its striking images. Though "Damien" is supposed to span a number of months in the feverish life of the young Antichrist, it appears to be stuck in the perpetual dank of autumn and the chill of winter.

• • •

Perhaps because it's not easy to fake snow and ice in this day and age of cinema sophistication, two of the movie's best sequences are set in visually spectacular winter exteriors. One, in which we watch a fellow drown lazily beneath the clear ice of a Wisconsin lake, is as good as any shock sequence of its kind I've ever seen. The other, the murder of a nice, fresh-faced teen-age boy (by a telepathically induced brain hemorrhage), takes place deep in a snow-blanketed Wisconsin forest, which, though it gives the impression of peace and beauty, is also scary. The quiet is not friendly. Snow has a way of muffling all sounds, including cries for help.

When moviemakers go out into the world to shoot their pictures, they must seek something more than realism or the trip is a waste.

Though Philippe De Broca's "Dear Detective," a comedy about a woman detective (Annie Girardot) on the Paris police force and the male chauvinist (Philippe Noiret) who loves her, is pretty cloying stuff, De Broca effectively transforms the Paris we all know and love into a candy-box city. The real Paris is mostly gray but it's a gray that contains dozens of colors that can be perceived best only in retrospect. Such a city wouldn't serve the frivolous purposes of "Dear Detective." The colors must be perceived here and now, which is what the director and his cameraman achieve.

The Paris in "Dear Detective" is not like any Paris you've seen. The film was shot in the city's streets and on its quais but it's a fictitious place that suits De Broca's fiction, whether you like it or not—sunny, smogless, full of squeaky-clean colors, primary and pastel.

One of the inevitable results of moviemakers' fondness for location shooting has been the creation of a whole new set of cinema clichés. One of the smaller triumphs of Paul Mazursky's "An Unmarried Woman" was Mazursky's managing to make an entire movie in New York without having his characters spend any time in Central Park. Nor did they ever stroll along the Brooklyn Heights promenade, walk through Times Square or discover colorful derelicts so dear to the heart of second-rate directors. Instead we saw them entirely in terms of the Upper East Side and Soho where their apartment, jobs and interests would naturally keep them.

Location shooting creates temptations that demand strict discipline. The odd, unexpected character or building or street corner found in the course of production may seem great at the time, but it also has a way of cluttering up any film that's been carefully conceived in advance. In this connection I think of Federico Fellini, a director whose feeling for place probably is as acute as any filmmaker's today. Yet Fellini, who began by making his films entirely on location, has in recent years been working almost exclusively in studio sets. Though his films have become more fantastic, his feeling for place has not changed. It's only that the vision is different, and, in a studio, Fellini is God. He is responsible for weather, light, sound.

Fellini learned by experience that the reality of a location, transferred to film, is not necessarily truth, which may explain why the increasing number of films set in southern California and photographed on location there—films like "The End," "Thank God It's Friday" and even "House Calls"—have hardly any geographic identity at all. ■

1978 Je 18, II:17:4

'Roo in the Ring

MATILDA, directed by Daniel Mann; screenplay by Albert S. Ruddy and Timothy Galfas, based on the book by Paul Gallico; executive producer, Richard R. St. Johns; producer, Mr. Ruddy; director of photography, Jack Woolf; editor, Allan A Jacobs; music Jerrold Immel; distributed by American International Pictures. Running time: 103 minutes. At Radio City Music Hall, 50th Street and the Avenue of the Americas. This film has been rated G.

Bernie Bonnelli .... Elliott Gould
Duke Parkhurst .... Robert Mitchum
Uncle Nono .... Harry Guardino
Billy Baker .... Clive Revill
Kathleen Smith .... Karen Carlson
Pinky Schwab .... Lionel Stander
Gordon Baum .... Art Metrano
Wild Bill Wildman .... Roy Clark

By VINCENT CANBY

"MATILDA," which opens today at Radio City Music Hall, is a comedy about a male kangaroo named Matilda who is the chief contender for the heavyweight boxing championship of the world.

The cast is headed by Elliott Gould, as the vaudeville promotor who gives Matilda his start; Clive Revill, as a former British flyweight boxer who owns Matilda and loves him like a son, and Robert Mitchum, as a sports columnist who manipulates the news he covers and, at the end, becomes the managing editor of the New York Post.

According to the film's production notes, the role of Matilda is played both by a kangaoo named Whammo and by someone named Gary Morgan in a kangaroo suit that reportedly cost $30,000 but fits as if it had been ordered by seamail from Hong Kong. Matilda looks like the neighborhood practical joker on his way to a costume party, so I assume that it's Mr. Morgan we see on the screen most of the time.

Paul Gallico wrote the novel on which Albert S. Ruddy and Timothy Galfas based their screenplay, which was directed by Daniel Mann with a total lack of spontaneity and with the groveling desire to please you might associate with a door-to-door salesman.

The movie is chock-a-block with uncomic jokes and facetious inspirations, including Lionel Stander as a short-tempered boxing promoter, and several scenes showing two inept Mafia "soldiers" trying to kidnap Matilda and then to cut off his tail. Harry Guardino, a good actor, plays the Mafia chief with no great charm.

Mr. Mitchum sort of lazes his way through the movie, knowing that he's bigger than it is. Mr. Gould seems to want to disassociate himself from the picture by watching the other actors as if astonished by the fools they are making of themselves. He's right, of course, but since he's in the movie, he looks a bit foolish, too. Mr. Revill, another able actor, plays Matilda's owner in a manner that recalls David Wayne's leprechaun period, which may not be something that all of us want to recall at this very minute.

"Matilda" is a movie that's in even worse shape than the Music Hall. It's future is decidedly iffy.

1978 Je 22, C19:6

"THE CHEAP DETECTIVE"—Marsha Mason threatens Peter Falk in the private-eye parody by Neil Simon.

THE CHEAP DETECTIVE, directed by Robert Moore; screenplay by Neil Simon; produced by Ray Stark; director of photography, John A. Alonzo; music, Patrick Williams; editors, Sidney Levin and Michael A. Stevenson; a Columbia/EMI presentation, distributed by Columbia Pictures. Running time: 98 minutes. At the Coronet Theater, Third Avenue near 59th Street, Little Carnegie Theater, 57th Street east of Seventh Avenue and other theaters. This film has been rated PG.

Lou Peckinpaugh .... Peter Falk
Jezebel Dezire .... Ann-Margaret
Betty DeBoop .... Eileen Brennan
Erza Dezire .... Sid Caesar
Bess .... Stockard Channing
Marcel .... James Coco
Pepe Damascus .... Dom DeLuise
Marlene DuChard .... Louise Fletcher
Jasper Blubber .... John Houseman
Mrs. Montenegro .... Madeline Kahn
Paul DuChard .... Fernando Lamas
Georgia Merkle .... Marsha Mason
Hoppy .... Phil Silvers
Sgt. Rizzuto .... Abe Vigoda
Boy .... Paul Williams
Colonel Schlissel .... Nicol Williamson
Butler .... Emory Bass
Sgt. Crosseti .... Carmine Caridi
Schnell .... James Cromwell
Tinker .... Scatman Crothers
Captain .... David Ogden Stiers
Lt. DiMaggio .... Vic Tayback
Hat Check Girl .... Carole Wells
Qvicker .... John Calvin

By VINCENT CANBY

IN 1853, 12 Albanian fishermen conquered China, Mongolia and Tibet—one souvenir of that extraordinary moment of history being a set of diamond eggs, each the size and shape of a Grade A, extra-large, brown chicken egg. In pursuit of this prize, more than a dozen persons converge on San Francisco in 1939 to cross and double-cross one another in "The Cheap Detective," Neil Simon's funny, affectionate recollection of "The Maltese Falcon," with substantial references to "Casablanca" and more than a passing interest in "The Big Sleep."

From that description you might suspect either that "The Cheap Detective" takes in more territory than can easily be evoked by one picture or that it's very thin material to sustain an entire feature-length film. Either way you may be right. "The Cheap Detective," which was directed by Robert Moore and produced by Ray Stark (Mr. Simon's collaborators on "Murder by Death"), belongs to a very special subcategory of motion picture comedy whose rules, which have the tensile strength of hot fudge, are what you want to make them.

Like Mel Brooks's "High Anxiety," which was a fond overview of the career of Alfred Hitchcock, "The Cheap Detective" is not the parody of ridicule that is most readily appreciated, but a cheerful remembrance of old movies that are as substantial today as they ever were. From time to time, "The Cheap Detective" seizes and wickedly shakes a remembered moment of outrageous foolishness or sentimentality, but, mostly, watching it is like being with a group of friends as they recall their favorite moviegoing experiences. It's not as a movie that it's so much fun, but as a multimillion-dollar, all-star parlor game.

Starting with Peter Falk, who gives a fine, feature-length, utterly straight-faced imitation of Humphrey Bogart as a Frisco private-eye named Lou Peckinpaugh, most of the players are superbly funny. They include Ingrid Bergman in "Casablanca" (described by her husband as "a brave, beautiful, extremely boring woman"); Marsha Mason as the Gladys George character from "The Maltese Falcon," perhaps the only woman in San Francisco who knows how to find an all-night dress shop specializing in widow's weeds; Madeline Kahn as the mysterious Mary Astor character, also from "The Maltese Falcon," and John Houseman (wearing something that is less a suit than a special effect), Dom DeLuise and Paul Williams, as, respectively, characters who would once have been played by Sydney Greenstreet, Peter Lorre and Elisha Cook Jr.

Then, too, there are Nicol Williamson, as the Nazi colonel whose mission is to prevent the Free French patriot (Fernando Lamas) from opening a French restaurant in Oakland; Sid Caesar (in a fright-wig) and Ann-Margret (in virtually nothing) as mysterious Rumanians; James Coco as a cafe impresario, and Stockard Channing as Lou Peckinpaugh's ever-faithful though never-to-be unfulfilled Girl Friday.

Phil Silvers is also in the movie but he's on and off the screen so quickly that I don't really remember him. The one place where the recollections go awry is in the casting of Eileen Brennan as the Lauren Bacall figure. Miss Brennan is an able comedienne but next to the original she is small, limited. She never once recalls the amalgam of larger-than-life sexuality, intelligence, self-mockery, and class that was (and is) the unique Bacall screen presence.

"The Cheap Detective," which opens today at the Coronet, Little Carnegie and other theaters, is more difficult to review than to talk over, as one might last night's dinner party. One wants to ignore the lapses in taste and wit as well as the lack of coherence. No particular comic point is made by setting the film in 1939, which is a year before there ever was a Free French movement, and though the movie tries very hard to reproduce the "studio" look of the 40's, that look is overwhelmed by vivid color photography.

More important, though, are the inspirations—large and small—that do work beautifully, such as Lou Peckinpaugh's undershirt, to which is still attached every laundry marker it ever knew. I also admire Mr. Simon's variations on 1940's movie dialogue, whether snappy (reports a detective to his superior, "We got four bodies, three as cold as yesterday's toast and one ready to pop up") or solemn ("Paul is an obstinate man. Even with a bullet in his head, his mind is made up"). And, there is no way seriously to object to a movie that has as one of its principal locations a seedy hotel called the Crusaders, which, on its first floor, houses the St. John the Divine Bar.

•

"The Cheap Detective," which has been rated PG ("Parental Guidance Suggested"), contains some mildly vulgar language. The film's violence is in the nature of slapstick comedy.

1978 Je 23, C8:1

FILM VIEW

VINCENT CANBY

Having Fun With the 50's

Movie musicals have their own quite unpredictable logic, which has little to do with reason and everything to do with emotional commitment. This truism bears repeating as we stand (sit, lie down or maybe snooze) on the brink of a new era of movie musicals ("The Wiz," "Hair," "Sergeant Pepper's Lonely Hearts Club Band," "A Chorus Line," "Annie"), most of which, like the just-opened "Grease," are based on successful Broadway shows. Movie musicals have their ups and downs, one of the problems being that we've not always been able to tell that we were in some kind of Golden Age of movie musicals when we actually were. I can't remember critics in the late 40's or 50's throwing hats in the air or dancing in the streets because of all the great musicals that were then coming out of Hollywood, most of them (like "Seven Brides for Seven Brothers" from M-G-M), many directed by Vincente Minnelli ("The Pirate," "Gigi," "An American in Paris"), often written by Betty Comden and Adolph Green ("On The Town," "Singin' in the Rain," "It's Always Fair Weather") and at least once, for classic results, written by Comden and Green and directed by Minnelli ("The Band Wagon").

Not many of us realized that we were having it so good until, in the late 50's and 60's, we started having it so bad. Not that there weren't great musicals still being written, including "My Fair Lady," "West Side Story" and "Fiddler on The Roof," but, increasingly, musical shows were becoming solemn, literate, meaningful, which is essentially a contradiction in terms, like a solemn, literate, meaningful showgirl. A sense of fun, of irreverence and of irrepressible vulgarity was being lost or painted over, disguised. The tremendous success of the treacly movie version of "The Sound of Music" virtually doomed movie musicals for all time, prompting the production of a whole rash of even more expensive, much less accomplished musical films like "Dr. Dolittle," "Star," "Paint Your Wagon" and "On A Clear Day," which came close to bankrupting their studios. Musicals, which had never been very big in the foreign market, also began to die at home. Curtains, it seemed.

• • •

A major problem was that the music being written for Broadway shows, the major source of the supply for musical movies, was beginning to have less and less to do with the popular music people were listening and dancing to. Broadway show music remained more or less frozen in the timeless 50's, ignoring the tremendous influences of country-and-western, soul and rock on the public. With the exception of a few shows like "Hair" (1967), with music by Galt MacDermot, and "Promises, Promises" (1968), with music by Burt Bacharach, Broadway shows gave us music that, even at its best, seemed to have little connection to the world outside where the Beatles were running rampant.

I'm not sure Broadway is much better today than it was then, though the situation has clearly improved. An interesting case in point is "Grease," the Jim Jacobs-Warren Casey paean to the 1950's, to duck-tailed haircuts, proms, making out, James Dean mannerisms and, especially, to rock and roll. The show, which opened in 1972 and is still running at the Royale Theater, seems to have evolved into the biggest must-see hit of the decade among members of a generation that hadn't yet been born in the 50's.

However, the kids who were crowding into the Royale lobby the other night when I was there (for the first time) were not reliving anything lost in time but discovering another aspect of a present in the form of the "Grease" music, which provides a kind of Darwinian link between the Stone Age of swing and today's disco beat.

I must say that I didn't drop into the Royale by accident. Two days before I'd seen the exuberant, all-stops-out screen version, which stars John Travolta and Olivia Newton-John as the (respectively) duck-tailed and bobby-soxed high school sweethearts, and I was on a research trip. The film, though it retains most of the best and funniest of the original rock score, also includes some Golden Oldies ("Hound Dog Man," "Love Is a Many Splendored Thing," "Blue Moon" and "Rock 'n Roll Is Here To Stay") as well as several smashing new numbers—the title song, written by Barry Gibb, and "You're the One That I Want," written by John Farrar, both of which are closer to the disco sound than to rock and roll, and Louis St. Louis's "Sandy" (lyrics by Scott J. Simon), which apparently replaces the Broadway show's "Alone At A Drive-in Movie" and is one of the film's wittier inspirations. It's a lament sung by Danny (Travolta), the leader of the T-Bird gang, when Sandy (Miss Newton-John) has gotten huffy because he's made a pass at her. The song's introduction (if memory serves): "Stranded at the drive-in/ Branded a fool/What will they say about me/Monday at school?" As much as anything in the original score, the number captures the tone of sweetness mixed with mockery that makes the show so winning.

Not having seen the Broadway show before I saw the film, and having few fond memories of the 50's as they really were, I responded to the film version of "Grease" with what apparently was a lot less reason than most of my colleagues, some of whom did everything except complain that high-school kids in the 50's didn't sing their hearts out in places like cafeterias and garages.

• • •

In the great if tacky tradition of B-picture musicals of the 50's and 60's, the high-school students of "Grease" seem to have been cast rather than enrolled. Some of them are old enough to be their own parents. Though we can see that the film's principal setting, Rydell High, is obviously in sunny southern California, almost everybody in the movie talks with a nightclub comedian's idea of a Brooklyn accent. If one insists on being logical while watching the movie, one must assume that there has been a mass migration—comparable to the Oakies' flight in "The Grapes of Wrath"—from Bay Ridge to the San Fernando Valley shortly before "Grease" opens. Even worse, the show's original rock score has been diluted—updated—in key places by the introduction of the disco beat that paid off so handsomely for Robert Stigwood, co-producer of "Grease" with Allen Carr, in his "Saturday Night Fever."

All these things are very true, yet "Grease" is nothing but fun. It's pop entertainment of an extremely clever, energetic sort, sung and danced with style by its two stars, Travolta and Miss Newton-John; by Stockard Channing, as Rydell High's easiest mark who, when she sings about her lust ("There Are Worse Things I Could Do") is taking a moral position; by newcomers Jeff Conaway (as Travolta's sidekick) and Didi Conn (who drops out of Rydell only to fail at beauty school), and by such real-life Golden Oldies as Eve Arden, Sid Caesar, Joan Blondell, Frankie Avalon, Edd Byrnes, Alice Ghostley and Dody Goodman.

"Grease," which was directed by Randal Kleiser (his first theatrical feature), is not a movie that one can easily defend with reason. If one doesn't immediately respond to its energy, to its music and to the comic conventions of this kind of movie musical, and if one insists that movie teenagers must be less than 25 in real life, then it's a movie to be avoided as if it were one of television's Saturday morning cartoon shows.

Otherwise, go. ■

1978 Je 25, II:17:1

HEAVEN CAN WAIT, directed by Warren Beatty and Buck Henry; screenplay by Elaine May and Mr. Beatty, based on a play by Harry Segall; produced by Mr. Beatty; executive producers, Howard W. Koch Jr. and Charles H. Maguires; director of photography, William A. Fraker; editors, Robert C. Jones and Don Zimmerman; music, Dave Grusin; distributed by Paramount Pictures. Running time: 101 minutes. At the Loews State 2 Theater, Broadway at 45th Street, and other theaters. This film has been rated PG.

Joe Pendleton .... Warren Beatty
Betty Logan .... Julie Christie
Mr. Jordan .... James Mason
Max Corkle .... Jack Warden
Tony Abbott .... Charles Grodin
Julia Farnsworth .... Dyan Cannon
The Escort .... Buck Henry
Krim .... Vincent Gardenia
Sisk .... Joseph Maher
Bentley .... Hamilton Camp

"HEAVEN CAN WAIT"—Warren Beatty and Julie Christie become lovers when he's granted a heavenly reprieve.

Everett .... Arthur Malet
Corinne .... Stephanie Faracy
Lavinia .... Jeannie Linero
Gardener .... Harry D. K. Wong
Security Guard .... George J. Manos
Peters .... Larry Block
Conway .... Frank Campanella
Tomarken .... Bill Sorrells
TV Interviewer .... Dick Enberg
Head Coach .... Dolph Sweet
General Manager .... R. G. Armstrong
Trainer .... Ed V. Peck
Former Owner .... John Randolph

By VINCENT CANBY

THERE is something eerily disconnected about "Heaven Can Wait." It may be because in a time of comparative peace, immortality — at least in its life-after-death form — doesn't hold the fascination for us that it does when there's a war going on, as there was in 1941 when "Here Comes Mr. Jordan" was released and became such a hit. Or perhaps we are somewhat more sophisticated today (though I doubt it) and comedies about heavenly messengers and what is, in effect, a very casual kind of transubstantiation seem essentially silly.

Whatever the reason, "Heaven Can Wait," Warren Beatty's remake of "Here Comes Mr. Jordan," gives the impression of being a swinging 1978 romantic comedy struggling to free itself from the body of the 1941 film. Most of the time it remains locked in, embraced by the unyielding requirements of its elaborate, facetious plot gimmick.

This, as in "Here Comes Mr. Jordan," which also was based on a play titled "Heaven Can Wait," is about a professional athlete, a star quarterback with the Los Angles Rams, who is accidentally gathered by a heavenly messenger before his time has come. When the mistake is realized, the athlete, named Joe Pendleton (Mr. Beatty), is escorted back to earth to find a suitable body to inherit so that Joe can go on to play in the Super Bowl. That, unfortunately, is just the beginning, though it takes so much screen time to tell that the audience is always ahead of it.

The surprise is that "Heaven Can Wait" is as much fun as it is when it has to waste so much energy in the service of a gimmick that we would now endure only in a pilot film for a projected television series titled "I Dream of Joey."

The movie, which opens today at Loews State 2 and other theaters, is a hybrid of no great style but of a good deal of charm and with a marvelous cast headed by Julie Christie, Jack Warden, Dyan Cannon, Buck Henry, James Mason and Mr. Beatty, who stars in the film, produced it, co-directed it (with Mr. Henry) and cowrote the screenplay (with Elaine May).

Only time and innate modesty, I assume, prevented him from acting as his own assistant producer.

Though updated from the 40's, the May-Beatty screenplay seems to follow closely the earlier film, written by Sidney Buchman and Seton I. Miller, yet only Harry Segall, the author of the play, is given screen credit. Some of the film's best moments, however, are random inspirations of dialogue and bits of business that recall the tone of Miss May at the peak of her comic form.

The film's funniest characters are not played by Mr. Beatty or Julie Christie (as the spunky English girl Joe Pendleton falls in love with). They are Joe's wife (when he is in the body of a wealthy nut named Farnsworth) and her lover, a pair of scheming, would-be murderers of the sort Miss May showed such fondness for in "A New Leaf." The characters are well written and beautifully played by Dyan Cannon and Charles Grodin.

I suspect that no one but Miss May (and possibly Buck Henry) would envision a scene in which one of the murderers, expecting at any minute to be discovered, says to his accomplice when the police are about to enter the drawing room, "Pick up 'The Fountainhead' and pretend to be reading."

•

The film's associations to time are nothing if not eclectic. Memories of "Here Comes Mr. Jordan" evoke the 1930's and early 40's. "The Fountainhead" suggests the late 40's and early 50's. The Rams and pro football are very much of today, while the very funny populist speech that Joe Pendleton delivers (in the body of Mr. Farnsworth to a board of directors' meeting) recalls Frank Capra's comedies of the mid-30's. All of which may lead you to believe — correctly — that "Heaven Can Wait" hasn't much personality of its own.

Instead it has a kind of earnest cheerfulness that is sometimes most winning. Mr. Beatty and Miss Christie are performers who bring to their roles the easy sort of gravity that establishes characters of import, no matter how simply they are drawn in the script. Neither James Mason as Mr. Jordan, the fellow in charge of recently gathered souls, nor Mr. Henry, as the messenger who botched his first job, have much to do, but they are presences we recognize. In a much more colorful part, that of Joe Pendleton's trainer, Jack Warden must bridge the gap between the film's sentimental impulses and its lunatic comedy, and he succeeds with ease.

All of these people, though, are upstaged by a plot that keeps butting into the movie just as it's building some comic momentum. There's nothing worse than a pushy narrative.

•

"Heaven Can Wait," which has been rated PG ("Parental Guidance Suggested"), contains some language that, I suppose, could be called grown-up if not adult, but there is nothing else in the movie to disturb the smallest mind.

1978 Je 28, C17:1

Truckers and Women

CONVOY, directed by Sam Peckinpah; screenplay and story by B.W.L. Norton, based on the song by C.W. McCall; produced by Robert M. Sherman; executive producers, Michael Deeley and Harry Spikings; director of photography, Harry Stradling Jr.; supervising film editor, Graeme Clifford; editors, John Wright and Garth Craven; music, Chip Davis; distributed by United Artists. Running time: 111 minutes. At the Criterion Theater, Broadway near 44th Street, and other theaters. This film has been rated PG.

Rubber Duck .... Kris Kristofferson
Melissa .... Ali MacGraw
Lyle Wallace .... Ernest Borgnine
Peg Pen .... Burt Young
Widow Woman .... Madge Sinclair
Spider Mike .... Franklyn Ajaye
Chuck Arnoldi .... Brian Davies
Governor Haskins .... Seymour Cassel
Violet .... Cassie Yates
Hamilton .... Walter Kelley
Big Nasty .... J.D. Kane
Pack Rat .... Billy E. Hughes
White Rat .... Whitey Hughes
Old Iguana .... Bill Foster
Lizard Tongue .... Thomas Huff
Chief Stacey .... Love Tom Bush
Reverend Sloane .... Donald R. Fritts

"CONVOY," which opens today at the Criterion and other theaters, is Sam Peckinpah's multimillion-dollar "B" picture, the sort of movie about men who drive trailer trucks, and the women who love them, which has been made before much less expensively and much more entertainingly by directors with no aspirations to be artists. "Convoy" is a bad joke that backfires on the director. He has neither the guts to play the movie straight as melodrama nor the sense of humor to turn it into a kind of "Smokey and the Bandit" comedy.

The movie is a big, costly, phony exercise in myth-making, machismo, romance-of-the-open-road nonsense and incredible self-indulgence. It takes its large cast of good actors and makes a fool of each one of them, including Kris Kristofferson, who plays a trucker whose CB radio handle is Rubber Duck, a fellow so laid-back he seems horizontal even when walking upright, and Ali MacGraw, who, for reasons that remain forever obscure, has had her hair clipped like Maria's in "For Whom the Bell Tolls."

•

Miss MacGraw is supposed to be a classy society photographer, a woman of intelligence and realized sexuality, but the effect of the haircut is to make Mr. Kristofferson's girlfriend look like an exceedingly pretty boy.

This may well be one of Mr. Peckinpah's more knowing sexist gags, but because the movie is so muddled or nasty in every other way, I don't feel like trying to decipher the point. To transform a naturally beautiful woman into a figure of such androgyny seems, at best, short-sighted; at worst, it's mean-spirited.

That may be to credit "Convoy" with more consistent purpose than it has. The screenplay by B.W.L. Norton, based on C.W. McCall's song about a showdown between a group of independent truckers and the law, attempts to be both funny and serious. It asks us to admire the free spirit of the truckers who own their own rigs, who love their trucks as cowboys used to love their horses, and who represent — or so we are told — a vanishing breed of Americans whose backbone made this country great.

I could buy that in earlier Peckinpah movies like "The Wild Bunch," "The Ballad of Cable Hogue" and "Junior Bonner," but here the director is sending himself up but not in any healthy, good-humored way. There is a feeling of desperation about "Convoy."

•

It's like finding Mr. Peckinpah as the star of a carnival sideshow. There is still talent evident, but the backbone has rotted away. Here's a fellow, you feel, with no pride, no scruples, who'd sell his grandmother for 5 percent of the gross.

The movie has the form of one long, occasionally interrupted chase as the independent truckers, objecting to unrealistic speed limits and corrupt highway cops, flee across Arizona to New Mexico. There are roadside-diner brawls filmed in slow-motion, a couple of spectacular traffic violations and a lot of scenery so pretty it would tone up any post card.

The supporting cast includes Ernest Borgnine as a vicious, bigoted cop; Burt Young, as a trucker who hauls pigs and fancies himself a ladies' man; Seymour Cassel, as an opportunistic and foolish state Governor, and Madge Sinclair, as a woman trucker who is black and who, maybe significantly, is the only trucker to have a major accident in the course of the film.

•

"Convoy," which has been rated PG ("Parental Guidance Suggested"), contains some coarse language and mildly suggestive sex scenes.

VINCENT CANBY

1978 Je 28, C17:2

"CONVOY"—Reporter Ali MacGraw causes problems for trucker Kris Kristofferson.

Feline Marvel

THE CAT FROM OUTER SPACE, directed by Norman Tokar; written by Ted Key; director of photography, Charles F. Wheeler; film editor, Cotton Warburton; music, Lalo Schifrin; produced by Ron Miller; distributed by Buena Vista Distribution Company Inc. At the Rivoli and other theaters. Running time: 103 minutes. This film is rated G.

Frank	Ken Berry
Liz	Sandy Duncan
General Stilton	Harry Morgan
Mr. Stallwood	Roddy McDowall
Link	McLean Stevenson
Earnest Ernie	Jesse White
Dr. Wenger	Alan Young
Dr. Heffel	Hans Conried
Sgt. Duffy	Ronnie Schell
Capt. Anderson	James Hampton
Col. Woodruff	Howard T. Platt
Mr. Olympus	William Prince

THE opening scenes of "The Cat From Outer Space," which opens in New York today at the Rivoli and other theaters, are a moderately amusing parody of "Close Encounters of the Third Kind." Deep-focus photography, flashes of light in the night, unearthly roaring and wailing, chickens squawking, a puzzled farmer with a shotgun and a Labrador retriever that sniffs the air and insouciantly returns to the house.

However, we don't have to wait until the end of the film to see the visitor from another galaxy. It won't be giving anything away to say that it turns out to be a quite ordinary-looking male cat wearing a crystal collar.

•

In Disney movies of another era, the collar would simply have been described as magical, like Cinderella's glass slipper. Nowadays it is necessary to say that the collar focuses highly developed telepathic powers. Anyhow, it enables the cat to open doors and windows, to levitate his friends, to freeze his enemies in their tracks, control remote events and, of course, to speak English and probably the language of every other country in which the film is exhibited.

Naturally, the Pentagon wants the cat, who goes by the name of Jake. So does a mysterious and unquestionably villainous figure, who knows that the collar would give him control not merely of the world, as a stooge suggests, but of the universe. All Jake wants to do, at first, is to repair his comfortable little spaceship and get back to pussycat heaven, but then he falls in love.

The complications begin amusingly enough, but tend to become tiresome and predictable well before the movie is over. Even so, "The Cat From Outer Space," is likely to keep the under-14's amused, at least if supplemented by plenty of popcorn.

The human players, led by Ken Berry, as a scientist who befriends Jake; Sandy Duncan as his colleague, friend and the owner of the feline femme fatale; McLean Stevenson, as a scientist who drinks beer and gambles, which are relatively serious failings in a Disney film, and Harry Morgan as a short-tempered general, all perform creditably.

Jake, a 15-month-old Abyssinian making his screen debut, gets the best of it in front of the camera, however. He should hire out between films as a watch cat. No one could steal a scene from him, at any rate.

TOM BUCKLEY

1978 Je 30, C10:3

FILM VIEW

VINCENT CANBY

Moviemakers Everywhere Are Putting Safety First

Critics, I realize, have a habit of saying that this year is worse than last year and the future looks gloomy and wouldn't it be nice to be able to return to some earlier golden age? These were pretty much the thoughts expressed the other night among some of my colleagues, with each person, in turn, qualifying his pessimisim, wondering aloud if, perhaps, this was a perpetual delusion. Or might we be jaded, since we do see more films than anyone else in his right mind would see? Might—heaven forfend—we be getting old? Might our sour reaction to so many 1978 movies simply be a sublimated desire to put a stop-payment order on time?

Possibly, but I don't think so, not after laughing in the wrong places in the new Sam Peckinpah film "Convoy," and feeling vaguely short-changed by Warren Beatty's "Heaven Can Wait," and certainly not after going into the files to compare the first six months of this year with the first six months of 1977. All is not well. Among other things, the film critics of The New York Times reviewed 131 films in the first half of 1977 against 117 in the first half of 1978. That's not a huge difference, but it's indicative, I suspect, of what's happening. When there are more films, the odds increase that there will be better films.

More important, by this time last year, there had already been released in New York three of the five American films that would eventually wind up on the year's 10-best list —Woody Allen's "Annie Hall," George Lucas's "Star Wars" and Robert Benton's "The Late Show." This year I've seen only one American film that I'm sure will make the 10-best list, "Pretty Baby," and that one, of course, was directed by Louis Malle, who is French. The only two other candidates for the list are Tony Richardson's "Joseph Andrews," which is English, and Charlie Chaplin's "A Woman of Paris," which was made in 1923.

It's definitely *not* been a good year.

Some other facts: During the first half of 1977 New Yorker Films treated us to a stunning retrospective of the films of Werner Rainer Fassbinder, one of which, "Effi Briest," made the 10-best list, and several others of which could have, but didn't, including "Katzelmacher." We also had the New York theatrical premiere of Wim Wenders's "The Goalie's Anxiety at the Penalty Kick" (another one of the 10-best).

It was a good time for foreign films in general in 1977, what with the openings of Claude Goretta's "That Wonderful Crook" and Carlos Saura's "Cria" and "Cousin Angelica." True, "Fellini's Casanova" was not successful, but the film was not a failure of talent or intelligence; rather Fellini was so brilliantly self-absorbed that he was virtually incapable of communicating with anyone else. That film may one day be rediscovered.

Aside from Moishe Mizrahi's Oscar-winning "Madame Rosa," Ridley Scott's "The Duellists" and Satyajit Ray's "The Chess Players," even this year's foreign films have been dismally poor. Ingmar Bergman's "The Serpent's Egg" and Lina Wertmuller's "The End of the world in Our Usual Bed in a Night Full of Rain" were major misadventures. Among the minor ones were a continuing flow of French films on the order of "Servant and Mistress," "A Woman at Her Window," "Bonjour Amour," "We Will All Meet in Paradise," "Borocco" and "Dear Detective"—works that suggest that the French film industry is once again being ruled by a "tradition of quality," which is what the New Wave directors originally rebelled against. It's a measure of our year to date in French films that a comedy by Claude Lelouch ("Cat and Mouse") appears to be a hit.

Is this dearth of vital films simply an accident of timing and of release schedules or do we have here evidence that film making, worldwide, is entering an ice age? Some further observations:

Though the first half of 1977 had its fair share of junk movies ("The Other Side of Midnight," "The Deep," "Heretic: The Exorcist 2," etc.), it also had a number of commercial pictures that displayed the kind of wit or concern or style or energy that can make writing about movies invigorating. I think of the Burt Reynolds's "road" movie, "Smokey and The Bandit," of Joan Micklin Silver's "Between the Lines," of George Roy Hill's "Slap Shot," of "Fun With Dick and Jane" and Robert Altman's "3 Women," with its beautiful performances by Shelley Duvall and Sissy Spacek.

This year's pop movies have been mostly junk, while the more ambitious productions, such as "An Unmarried Woman" and "Coming Home," have been, on balance, merely pop. The issues that "An Unmarried Woman" and "Coming Home" pretended to be about (female identity, Vietnam, politics) became the props for romantic drama of a not very arresting sort, though each film is ultimately saved by the superior quality of the actors (Jill Clayburgh and Michael Murphy in "An Unmarried Woman" and Jon Voight and Jane Fonda in "Coming Home").

So far this year we have a list of junk movies as long as your arm, starting with such sequels as "Jaws 2," "The Other Side of the Mountain, 2" and "Damien, The Omen 2," and including "Capricorn One," "The Greek Tycoon," "Gray Lady Down," Michael Winner's remake of "The Big Sleep," and all those movies ("The Medusa Touch," "The Chosen," "Fury," etc.) about people with telekinetic powers, our decade's comparatively new genre that has become equivalent to the monster movies of the 1930's.

• • •

Sam Peckinpah's latest film, "Convoy," may be the quintessential junk movie for the first half of this year, being a hilariously inept attempt to combine two well-known Peckinpah concerns (doomed individualism, machismo) and a currently popular film form (the "road" comedy). Peckinpah tries unsuccessfully to make us believe he takes lightly his story about the last of the independent truckers, but the movie winds up as self-parody. Though the film has some handsome, carefully staged action sequences, its machismo seems as phony as a three-dollar bill and its attempts to make us sympathize with those tough, gallant truckers (who every day must come to terms with an unfair speed limit) is only slightly less ludicrous than the problem posed by "Lifeguard": What can a man do when he finds himself over-the-hill in his chosen profession at 32?

There have been some entertaining, not insulting popular movies this year ("House Calls," "F.I.S.T.," "Straight Time" and "The Betsy," principally because of Laurence Olivier) but the best of these seem to be less concerned with original thoughts, feelings and attitudes about life than with other times and movies ("Grease," "The Cheap Detective," "Heaven Can Wait").

As much as I enjoyed "The Cheap Detective," in which writer Neil Simon, director Robert Moore and some of Hollywood's most accomplished comedians (Peter Falk, Louise Fletcher, Ann-Margret, Marsha Mason, etc.) recall the best of Humphrey Bogart, there remains something essentially non-essential about a movie so utterly dependent on our knowledge of its source material ("The Maltese Falcon," "Casablanca" and "The Big Sleep").

Watching "Heaven Can Wait," which has nothing to do with the 1943 Ernest Lubitsch classic of the same name but is, rather, a remake of "Here Comes Mr. Jordan," (1941), I kept wishing that all of the people involved (Warren Beatty and Buck Henry, as co-directors and actors, Julie Christie, Dyan Cannon, Charles Grodin, and writer Elaine May) had devoted their time and money to an original project.

"Heaven Can Wait" has a number of raffishly funny and charming moments, but Beatty and Miss May, who wrote the screenplay, have stuck more closely to the original than is good for them in the movie. Trapped inside their version of the 1941 film is a witty, hip 1978 movie screaming to get out. Every time it seems about to do just that, the film must pay attention to the lumbering mechanics of a plot that now seems arch and facetious.

On the evidence of the films we've seen in the first half of this year, it's apparent that a new spirit of conservatism is governing filmmakers, not just in this country but elsewhere in the world, especially in France. Such conservatism—attempting to play movie making safe—is a direct, inevitable effect of the rising costs of production and the ever-increasing gap between the astronomical profits of the hit films and the total losses of the failures. Re-makes are supposedly safe (if the original was a big enough hit). Sequels are usually safe (if the budget doesn't go over a predetermined figure). Action films are safe (much of the time).

• • •

I doubt that either Paul Mazursky ("An Unmaried Woman") or Hal Ashby ("Coming Home") set out to make "safe" films, but with one thing and another, each film lacks the abrasive qualities that might have made it seem a particular endeavor. They're soft, soothing.

The possible problem, and one for which there is no easy answer, is that film is a mass entertainment medium that has lost its constituency, which now is television's. There are still millions of people who may go to the movies in any one week, but then they may not. They certainly no longer go automatically. This puts the producer of any movie in the peculiar position of a host who sends out invitations for a dinner party and receives no R.S.V.P.s. He has absolutely no way of knowing how many people are going to show up. He may have a full table, or perhaps no one will appear. It's not a situation to inspire the cook to come forth with something unique. No baked Alaska. Far from it. Serve hotdogs and those that aren't eaten can be put back into the fridge.

There are good reasons to be gloomy. ■

1978 Jl 2, II:1:1

Unharried Director

FACES OF LOVE, directed by Michel Soutter; script (French with English subtitles) and dialogues by Mr. Soutter; editing by Albert Jurgenson; photography by Renato Berta; music by Arie Dzierlatka; executive producers, Yves Peyrot and Yves Gasser; released by New Yorker Films. At the Cinema Studio, Broadway and 66th Street. Running time: 90 minutes. This film has not been rated.

Victor .... Jean-Louis Trintignant
Julie .... Delphine Seyrig
Cecilia .... Lea Massari
Esther .... Valerie Mairesse
Jean Vallee .... Roger Jendly
The Russian Teacher .... Gabriel Arout
The Young Mute France Lambiotte ....

By VINCENT CANBY

IF ONE movie can ever be considered less essential than another, then "Faces of Love," a serenely windy, empty-headed movie about art, love, death and table manners, is probably the least essential film you're likely to come upon this summer. It adds less to one's sum total of experience than, say, "Jaws 2," which at least teaches one about the care and operation of plastic sharks.

"Faces of Love," a Swiss film that opens today at the Cinema Studio, is the story of a monumentally unharried film director named Victor (Jean-Louis Trintignant) who comes to the lovely, old-fashioned resort-hotel at Bex, Switzerland, to scout locations for a screen adaptation of Chekhov's "The Three Sisters." Apparently having access to an unlimited budget and all the time in the world, Victor is accompanied on this trip not by his producer or his production manager but by the three actresses who'll star in his movie.

They are Julie (Delphine Seyrig), Victor's ex-wife, who'll play Olga; Cecilia (Lea Massari), an Italian actress who'll play Masha, and Esther (Valerie Mairesse), who'll play the young Irina.

Though we share with Victor his dream about Chekhov's funeral, early in the film, and though he has studied Russian in preparation for the film, we quickly learn that he is only making the movie in order to be near Julie, whom he still loves. Julie may still love him but she is hooked on pills and fearful of getting old, yet like so many women in movies who fear the ravages of age, she is magnificent looking.

As the camera swoops around the largely empty landscape, Victor, Julie, Cecilia and Esther swoop around each other, reciting large, fatuous speeches about art, life and the meaning of being a woman. Victor dallies with Esther and I think (though it's done so discreetly I can't be sure) Julie dallies with Cecilia. In any case, Julie becomes increasingly bad-tempered and, in the dining room one night, stabs poor Cecilia's hand with a knife. Being actors — people of high spirits and hot temperaments — nobody makes a fuss about the stabbing, however.

•

Mr. Trintignant, Miss Seyrig, Miss Massari and Miss Mairesse ("One Sings, The Other Doesn't") are intelligent performers but here they all act so high-toned and elegant you might suspect they'd been sniffing airplane glue. They seem to be totally out of it, which is more or less what the movie is.

Valerie Mairesse and Delphine Seyrig in Michel Soutter's "Faces of Love"
Probably the least essential film you're likely to come upon this summer.

"Faces of Love" is the kind of film that, in desperation, people often describe as civilized, but it's civilized in the manner of an haute couture fashion show. It moves with stately grace. It's pretty to look at and, at heart, it's as self-absorbed and frivolous as a manniquin. It's not only about art-as-pretense. It is numbingly pretentious.

"Faces of Love" is the third feature film to be directed and written by Michel Soutter, a Swiss colleague of Alain Tanner and Claude Goretta, but his first to be released here. Though Mr. Soutter invokes the theater of Chekhov, even to the quoting of lines from "The Three Sisters," it doesn't give dimension to his own work. At its least offensive it's simply name-dropping. More often, however, it makes us wish that we were someplace else, maybe even watching a first-class production of "The Three Sisters."

1978 Jl 7, C8:1

High-Toned Manny

THE MOUSE AND HIS CHILD, directed by Fred Wolf and Chuck Swenson; screenplay by Carol MonPere, from the novel by Russell Hoban; music by Roger Kellaway; animators, Fred Wolf, Charles Swenson, Dave Brain, Vince Davis, Gary Mooney, Mike Sanger, Lu Guarnier, Willie Pyle and Frank Zamboni; animation camera, Wally Bullock; distributed by Sanrio. At the Guild, 33 West 50th Street and other theaters. Running time: 83 minutes. This film has been rated G.

Manny the Rat .... Peter Ustinov
Euterpe .... Cloris Leachman
The Seal .... Sally Kellerman
The Frog .... Andy Devine
The Mouse .... Alan Barzman
The Mouse Child .... Marcy Swenson
Iggy .... Neville Brand
The Clock and Hawk .... Regis Cordic
The Elephant .... Joan Gerber
Muskrat .... Bob Holt
The Starling and Teller .... Maitzi Morgan
Crow .... Frank Nelson
Crow .... Cliff Norton
C. Serpentina .... Cliff Osmond
Paper People .... Iris Rainer
Jack in the Box .... Bob Ridgely
Bluejay and the Paper People Charles Woolf ....

By JANET MASLIN

THE trouble with "The Mouse and His Child," a particularly elegant children's film opening today at the Guild Theater, is that it isn't really meant for children. The title characters, who are linked hand-in-hand and activated by a wind-up key in the father's back, begin life in a toy store. But a long and complicated series of adventures lead them to witness beatings, slavery, warfare, an electrocution and a very bad experimental play. They also have occasion to explore the idea of infinity, think about what it means to be self-winding and generally ponder the philosophical condition of Toyhood.

As expertly as this animated film has been directed (by Fred Wolf and Chuck Swenson), scored (by Roger Kellaway and Gene Lees) and, especially, written (by Carol MonPere, who adapted Russell Hoban's novel), 83 minutes is a long time for an adult to think about mice. And for children, many of the bleak, gray, rat-ridden settings may seem at least as scary as they are whimsical.

•

Violence and destruction are often made to appear harmless enough in the world of animated films, a world in which characters can be squashed by boulders or run over by trucks and then trot away with nary a scratch. But here, the comic relief comes in the form of grown-up witticisms a young child won't necessarily understand. And the darkish backdrops, though artfully rendered, generate a cumulative gloom.

Manny the Rat, the villain of the piece, has the wickedest front teeth in the garbage dump, over which he presides. He also has the voice of Peter Ustinov, all flourishes and rolling r's, to make him the most high-toned blackguard this side of Captain Hook. And the supporting cast, including a big green bird with theatrical pretensions (whose lines are spoken by Cloris Leachman) and a frog dressed as a giant white glove (played by Andy Devine), is correspondingly clever. A great deal of talent has gone into the making of a movie that may never find its audience — or may not have any audience to find.

1978 Jl 7, C8:5

FILM VIEW

VINCENT CANBY

Let's Hear It For the Belly Laugh

In the role of Warren Beatty's greedy, hysterical, murderous wife in "Heaven Can Wait," Dyan Cannon is the most revivifying comic spectacle of the current movie season. Miss Cannon — slim and long as a shoelace and beautiful in the way of a woman who uses every artifice and then, from time to time, says to hell with it — is no newcomer, but each time she appears her funny, furrowed-brow intensity is a surprise. She was very appealing as the dim-witted wife in "Bob and Carol and Ted and Alice," and, in "The Last of Sheila," she was a tonic as the bitchy talent agent who could say "I loathe my luggage" as if she really meant it. She has a particular gift for discovering the humor in characters who are totally self-absorbed and have no idea they are funny, which may be why she was so successful in her direction of 'Number One," a short film about very small kids whose self-absorption matches that of the people Miss Cannon plays so well.

In addition to being the best single thing in "Heaven Can Wait," Miss Cannon restores to this season's cinema something that I thought was becoming extinct — the belly laugh.

I suppose I should define my term, which won't be easy.

The belly laugh has many of the characteristics of a long, purifying sneeze, being, in effect, a series of small laughs that suddenly interconnect, as mysteriously as information that's been fed into a computer, to produce a response that is larger than the sum of its parts. Belly laughs are primitive. They don't add to one's dignity. One can't easily hold a teacup and belly laugh. The cup will rattle on the saucer and the tea will probably spill. Belly laughs leave one wide open to the cool if not openly hostile responses of others not similarly seized. "What is it?" they ask, as if one had started to speak in tongues, a reaction that frequently has the effect of making the belly laugh bigger and more unreasonable than it should be.

• • •

We've had a number of good comedies in recent years, but very few that contained belly laughs. Woody Allen always comes through with several in any one picture, from the bank hold-up in "Take The Money and Run" ("This is a gub," says Virgil's written message to the teller) to the scene in last year's "Annie Hall" when the lobsters get loose in the kitchen and threaten to take up permanent residence behind the refrigerator.

Real belly laughs are comparatively rare in movies, however. Try to think of 20 in a hurry and you may have difficulty. You have to ransack film history. You will remember the good movies as well as some you only recall for their one belly laugh, like "Sitting Pretty," which stays in my mind for that one explosive moment when Clifton Webb, fed up to here with a baby's willfulness, picks up a bowl of oatmeal and pours it over the surprised child's head.

Some others at random: the scene early in Howard Hawks's screen version of "Twentieth Century" when John Barrymore, as the mad Broadway director, decides that the only way he can get the response he wants from Carole Lombard, as the tyro actress, is to jab her with a dangerously long hat pin;

Or the scene in Billy Wilder's "Some Like It Hot" when Marilyn Monroe crawls into Jack Lemmon's upper berth for some "girl talk";

Or the classic stateroom sequence from the Marx Brothers' "A Night at The Opera";

Or Charlie Chaplin's getting caught in the mesh of the giant gears in "Modern Times";

Or W.C. Fields in his role as a shopkeeper trying vainly to protect a display of lightbulbs from the cane of the crotchety, deaf-and-blind Mr. Muckle in "It's A Gift." This is a comedy sequence that builds (as only Fields knew how to build them) to the crucial point where the old man finally leaves the store and starts to cross a busy street. Says Fields sweetly, "Be careful, Mr. Muckle, honey," hoping (again vainly) that Mr. Muckle will be immediately run over;

Or the sequence in last year's "The World's Greatest Lover" in which we can hear but not see Gene Wilder and his wife, Carol Kane, in a canopied bed as they attempt to make their love life more interesting by following the directions in a book titled "Sex By The Numbers." Says Miss Kane, "Are we doing 'three'?" Wilder: "You're doing 'three.' I'm doing 'eight'."

When watching television—the late-night talk shows and especially the situation comedies—I often have the depressing feeling that belly laughs are being phased out of our civilization, to be replaced by titters that build to giggles that build not to the belly laugh but to applause. Applause, for heaven's sake!

We have become truly alienated when our automatic response to something outrageously comic is to clap our hands, not because it's funny but to show our appreciation for the effort no matter how far removed we are from the endeavor. It's as if we held laughter to be some kind of emotional commitment we simply cannot afford. Possibly this may be the natural reaction to a kind of comedy, particular to television, in which the stand-up comedian on the talk show or the actor in the sitcom always presents himself as being just slightly removed from his material. There's no belief.

The belly laugh is rooted in belief, in commitment, in allegiance to the craziest, most improbable of circumstances, which is why so many belly laughs are assocaited with slapstick comedy. The physical mayhem we see in slapstick comedy is a perfect reflection of emotional mess. When Stan Laurel and Oliver Hardy attempt to move a grand piano, we laugh at all the dreadful things that happen because there's such a gap between the intensity of their efforts — between their good will — and what they ultimately accomplish.

People who are completely committed to whatever nonsense they're up to tend always to be better (funnier) comic characters than those who are self-aware, unless they have dialogue written by Wilde or Shaw. Self-awareness is as much of a drag in a film like "Heaven Can Wait" as it would be in a Tom & Jerry cartoon. Indeed, the characters in "Heaven Can Wait" played by Miss Cannon and by Charles Grodin, who appears as her paramour and her accomplice in the attempted murders of her husband, are essentially cartoon characters, which, in a film like this, is all to the good.

"Heaven Can Wait," a remake of the 1941 "Here Comes Mr. Jordan," is much more fun as a slapstick cartoon about furious ineptitude than it is as a romantic fantasy about eternal love, dying too soon, heavenly messengers, etc. The film sort of wilts when Miss Cannon and Mr. Grodin aren't on the screen, but when they are on the screen, it acquires a very funny lunatic life. You couldn't meet two more transparent villains, which is why their efforts in homicide are so comic.

The Grodin character, affecting a nonchalance that is skin-deep, constantly having to soothe the frayed nerves of his over-wrought mistress, makes an ideal mate for Miss Cannon's faint-of-heart Lady Macbeth. Elaine May, who wrote the screenplay with Mr. Beatty, has given the pair some fine lines. I shall long cherish the exchange in which Mr. Grodin attempts, desperately, to explain to Mr. Beatty why Miss Cannon has screamed when she saw Mr. Beatty on entering an elegant drawing room. (She has assumed, of course, that he is dead, since she just murdered him.)

Mr. Grodin (blandly): "She saw a mouse."
Mr. Beatty: "In here?"
Mr. Grodin: "No . . . before . . . outside, but she *relives* it."

It's obviously a wild improvisation, but then you can believe that the character created by Miss Cannon is the sort whose mind would go back to relive such non-essential terrors. She's marvelous. ■

1978 Jl 9, II:13:4

Alberto Sordi in "Viva Italia!"

VIVA ITALIA!, directed by Mario Monicelli, Dino Risi and Ettore Scola; story and screenplay (Italian with English subtitles) by Age-Scarpelle, Ruggero Maccari and Bernardino Zapponi; cinematographer, Tonino Delli Colli; editor, Alberto Gallitti; music by Armando Trovaloli; produced by Pio Angeletti and Adriano De Michell. At the Paris Theater, 58th Street and Fifth Avenue. Running time: 87 minutes. This film has no rating.
WITH: Vittorio Gassman, Ornella Muti, Alberto Sordi and Ugo Tognazzi.

By VINCENT CANBY

"Viva Italia!" is a cheerful attempt to revive the sort of European sketch film ("Love at Twenty," "Yesterday, Today and Tomorrow," "Boccaccio 70") that was so popular in the 50's and 60's but slipped out of style (and public favor) in the 70's, as much because of the availability of the half-hour television drama as because the quality of the sketch films themselves declined.

"Viva Italia!" isn't likely to turn back any clocks, but it is so good-humored and, on balance, so entertaining that one feels like wishing it well. Of the film's nine episodes, four are very, very good and two are quite nice. The other three can be sat through without too much pain.

The Italian movie, which opens today at the Paris, is the work of three directors — Dino Risi, Mario Monicelli and Ettore Scola — who, for reasons of modesty or maybe friendship, have declined to identify their individual contributions. It may be just as well. Of the three, only Mr. Scola ("We All Loved Each Other So Much," "A Special Day") has had any success here recently. Neither Mr. Risi ("The Easy Life," "The Priest's Wife") nor Mr. Monicelli ("The Organizer," "My Friends") has a distinctive style that would make it easy for anyone not a psychic to attach the director to his sketch.

•

The three film makers, however, do share an amused, appreciative, sometimes jaundiced view of Italian life that fuses the parts into a charming entity. It's not by chance that each of the film's best sketches has a particularly national identity, if not as the Italians really are, then as Italians like to see themselves, especially in the persons of three of the country's finest actors, Vittorio Gassman, Alberto Sordi and Ugo Tognazzi.

The three throw-away pieces are stateless, jokey stories that could as easily be French, Japanese or American.

Largely because of their material, Mr. Gassman and Mr. Sordi dominate the movie, with Mr. Sordi starring in three of the four best sketches. The actor, whom you may remember in the early Fellini classic, "The White Sheik," is supremely funny as a lecherous Papal aristocrat who, on his way to a dreaded family dinner, attempts to help a pedestrian who's been run over. Never has a noble been so ineffectually obliging.

•

The rich fellow, a cartoon character of the sort Peter Sellers loves to play, drives an ancient Rolls-Royce that he describes as his "itinerant living room" (because the back seat is so handy for casual assignations). He also suspects (happily) that everyone he meets is either on his way to an orgy or going home from one, and he fusses constantly about "the Lefevre schism," which he fears is the only thing his family will be able to talk about. He is, of course, oblivious to the death rattles of the injured pedestrian beside him.

Mr. Sordi is also marvelous in the concluding sketch, a funeral that turns into a Fellini-esque celebration, and in the movie's most effectively moving episode, which is about a middle-aged son (Mr. Sordi) who cons his old mother (beautifully played by Emilia Fabi) into a freezingly efficient home for the elderly.

•

Mr. Gassman has great fun with the role of a Cardinal of the church who, by force of his oratory (and such theatrical props as candles, bells and liturgical music), more or less neutralizes the reform-minded, socialist spirit of the members of a working-class parish, and as a waiter in one of those simple, rustic country restaurants that's become popular with the jet set. This sketch features a magnificent kitchen brawl between the waiter and his lover, the chef (Mr. Tognazzi) during which shoes get left in the minestrone, one combatant's toupé is replaced by a large squid and a cigar goes into the stew. It's the kind of mayhem to warm any very small child's heart.

The movie pretty much comes to a halt in a sketch about an Arab terrorist and an airline stewardess, in another sketch about a fellow whose wife has been kidnapped, and in one about a couple of actors being interviewed in connection with a porn film. None of them, though, is very long.

1978 Jl 9, 41:4

Case of Amnesia

REPLAY, directed by Michel Drach; screenplay (French with English subtitles) by Pierre Uytterhoeven and Mr. Drach, based on a book by Dominique St. Alban; photography by Etienne Szabo; music by Jacques Monty and Jean Louis d'Onorio; edited by Francoise Bonnot; a Gaumont Films Presentation distributed by Quartet Films. At the 68th Street Playhouse, at Third Avenue. Running time: 96 minutes. This film has not been rated.

Cecile	Marie-Jose Nat
Francois	Victor Lanoux
Josepha	Anne Lonnberg
Bruno	Vania Vilers
Man on Train	Philippe March
Dr. Mercier	Marc Evraud
Taxi Driver	Albert Dray
Man in Apartment	Roland Blanche

By JANET MASLIN

THERE is a taxi driver character in "Replay," and oh! what a terrible time he has. His passenger is a high-strung sophisticate with no definite destination in mind, and with a tendency to leap frantically out of the cab without warning, forgetting all about paying her fare. "Left? Right?" asks the driver. The woman replies that she doesn't care. She is too desperate, too agonized to care, and the movie's premise depends upon the notion that hers is an interesting condition. This poor, exasperated cabbie has ample reason to think otherwise, though. So will poor, exasperated you.

It seems that there has been a slow-motion automobile accident, one that landed Cecile (Marie-Jose Nat) in the hospital, swathed in bandages but with her mascara intact. When she awakens from her coma, she does not recognize François, her husband (Victor Lanoux). He, realizing that his wife has total amnesia, lumbers out to the hospital corridor and stares off into space. And she, understanding the extent of her predicament, begins to cry. She does this very photogenically, standing with her back against a wall and photographed in profile, wearing a black negligee. One arm is flung across her chronically furrowed brow.

All too early in "Replay," the director Michel Drach, establishes himself as a man of problematically refined tastes. Miss Nat's search for her true identity leads her to pretty sites all over Paris, and wherever she flees, she manages to do most of her running in the same ensemble of leather skirt and fur-trimmed coat, with a pair of shoes to match.

It's certainly possible to make an effective romantic thriller while worrying about nice shots and just the right outfits, but Mr. Drach simply isn't the man for the job. When he wants to show that Cecile, who thinks she has run away from François, is actually being pursued by him, Mr. Drach positions the two of them on a beautiful, rain-drenched street, with Cecile walking briskly and François following alongside in his car. This is lovely to look at, but — since the street is otherwise deserted, and Cecile takes no notice of the car at her elbow — it does give one pause about the plot.

•

Perhaps the convoluted story line is unimportant, since "Replay" is, au fond, a tale of amour. But Mr. Drach, in attempting to interweave two highly compatible genres, manages to make Cecile and François's love affair play second fiddle to the secret of Cecile's past. And the secret, when it is at long last revealed, merely serves to place everyone in a very unflattering light. This is hardly necessary, since Mr. Lanoux has been vaguely boorish throughout, and Miss Nat (who is actually Mrs. Drach) has been nothing but tiresome in her hysteria.

Mr. Drach's premise, from a book by Dominique St. Alban, is not without intriguing possibilities, but the director's attention to cosmetic details is at odds with the sense of estrangement and rediscovery that is pivotal to the tale. And his heroine's amnesia, which ought to be the film's most compelling element, is simply one more gimmick in a movie that's overloaded with them.

1978 Jl 10, C16:1

BREAD AND CHOCOLATE, directed by Franco Brusati; screenplay (Italian with English subtitles) by Mr. Brusati, Iaia Fiastri and Nino Manfredi, based on a story by Mr. Brusati; director of photography, Luciano Tovoli; edited by Mario Morra; music by Daniel Patrucci; a World Northal Corporation. At the Baronet Theater, Third Avenue between 58th and 59th Streets. Running time: 111 minutes. This film has not been rated.

Nino .... Nino Manfredi
Elena .... Anna Karina
Italian Industralist .... Johnny Dorelli
Commis .... Paolo Turco
Old Man .... Ugo d'Alessio
Grigory .... Federico Scrobogna
The Turk .... Gianfranco Barra
Police Inspector .... Giorgio Cerioni
Renzo .... Max Delys
Rudiger .... Francesco D'Adda
Boegli .... Geoffrey Copplestone
Maitre .... Umberto Raho
The Blonde .... Nelide Giammarco
Sporting Swiss .... Manfred Freyberger

By VINCENT CANBY

WE COULD be in Elysium where it's always summer. We watch a boat with a pair of lovers laze its way across sun-bleached water. On shore, a family prepares to picnic on grass whose greeness is absolute. Nearby we see some friends stand self-consciously for a group photograph. The chamber music that scores this idyll is real. It's being supplied by a tense-looking quartet that sits on camp chairs and civilizes the landscape with sound.

Everything is perfect until the arrival of an outsider. He is tall and well-built but, close up, he looks most peculiar. His face is aged but his hair is remarkably full and youthfully brown. There is something so unblemished about his skin, so dramatically dark about his eyebrows and mustache, he could be wearing make-up or — and this is the thought that occurred to me — he might possibly be dead. Is he the new arrival in Elysium who's not yet had time to unpack?

The fellow sits down to listen to the music while he eats a sandwich. When he takes a bite, the chamber music group abruptly stops playing. The leader stares at him in disapproval. They can't play if he's going to eat in that fashion. He is clearly a fellow who's never given much thought to his manner of munching.

This sequence, which opens Franco Brusati's new Italian film, "Bread and Chocolate," is filled with mystery and a good deal of wit. Nino (Nino Manfredi), the fellow who has so rudely interrupted the concert on the lawn, has not died and gone to heaven, but he has wandered into a setting almost as unreal, at least to him.

Nino, an immigrant worker from southern Italy, has made himself comfortable on the lawn of an elegant Swiss resort hotel where, most of the day and much of the night, he works as a temporary waiter. The hotel guests are people who travel through life first-class. Nino is forever steerage.

•

In "Bread and Chocolate," which opens today at the Baronet, Nino aspires to move upward in a world of rigidly fixed rules. The film is the picaresque tale of his attempts to fit into the life of a place that speaks a different language (German) and tolerates him only as long as he accepts the crumbs left on tables by a voraciously consuming, casually unfeeling society. The Swiss bourgeoisie loathe the invaders from the south.

In one of the moments of clarity that the screenwriters impose on Nino from time to time (for our edification if not his), Nino says, in effect, there is bound to be friction when you have two million Italian workers in a nation of five million people.

"Bread and Chocolate," which was written by Mr. Brusati, Mr. Manfredi and Iaia Fiastri, means for us to accept Nino as a tragicomic hero as he wanders, like a lead-footed Candide, into one hard-luck situation after another. He is wrongly accused of a child's sex murder (actually committed by a priest, who makes no effort to hide his guilt). He's later dischargedd from the hotel because he has urinated in the street in broad daylight.

•

A millionaire Italian banker, who recognizes Nino's homesickness and befriends him, turns out to be an embezzler who loses all Nino's savings. In the film's most bizarre episode, Nino is

Anna Karina

taken in by a group of Italian immigrants who run an illicit chicken-plucking business. They live in a chicken coop and, so the movie indicates in a sequence that desperately needs the humor and discipline of Luis Buñuel, are quite happily turning into chickens.

Through all this, Nino maintains a muddled optimism of the sort that has the effect of patronizing a character rather than illuminating it. Nino is patronized not only by the Swiss but also by the people who made the film.

Neither Mr. Brusati nor Mr. Manfredi possesses the kind of overview of man and his society that would fuse the various comic and melodramatic episodes into a consistent whole. Instead of being shocking or moving or funny, their movie is sentimental.

Mr. Manfredi, like his makeup, is much too obvious and mechanical an actor to be able to sneak up on us with something unexpected. Every scene is a confrontation between us and Mr. Manfredi's busy, pushy performance, which negates the character he plays and calls attention, instead, to the actor behind it.

The script is not great. It wants to have several characters for the price of one. When it suits the convenience of the authors, Nino assumes a sort of bargain-basement, Chaplinesque innocence. At other times he must behave as one who is basically dim-witted. Then, too, he's a fellow who can question the gods.

Innocence, especially, is being hustled here. The film reaches a low point in a drag show put on by Nino and two friends at the Italian workers' barracks. I think we are meant to be touched by the condition of these virtually stateless persons, but they have so much in the way of costumes, makeup and lighting that you might be reminded of an act at Reno Sweeney.

Anna Karina has the film's few genuine moments as a young Greek woman, a teacher, who has come to Switzerland to make her fortune and who, briefly, is infatuated by Nino. There are many moments of promise — as when Nino attempts to pass for German by dying his hair blond — but Mr. Brusati and Mr. Manfredi, having had their inspiration, make no decent theatrical use of it. They are all too knowing as film makers, but not especially interesting ones.

1978 Jl 14, C14:1

Earthbound Spacelings

RETURN FROM WITCH MOUNTAIN, directed by John Hough; written by Malcolm Marmorstein, based on characters created by Alexander Key; director of photography, Frank Phillips; music, Lalo Schrifrin; editor, Bob Bring; produced by Ron Miller and Jerome Courtland; distributed by Buena Vista Co. Inc. At The Coliseum, 181st Street and Broadway and other theaters. Running time: 94 minutes. This film is rated G.

Letha .... Bette Davis
Victor .... Christopher Lee
Tia .... Kim Richards
Tony .... Ike Eisenmann

By JANET MASLIN

IF I WERE 10 again, I don't think I'd mind the fact that the space vehicle featured in the opening of "Return From Witch Mountain"looks like a flying pith helmet, or that the subsequent special effects are equally tinny.

On the other hand, I think I'd very much enjoy watching telekinetically gifted kids from another planet applying their special powers to such earthbound situations as car chases (when another vehicle gets in the way, they lift it) and fight scenes (they vanquish enemies with the flip of a flying garbage can). On balance, I think I'd be even more tickled by this Disney movie's abundance of mischief than tired by its emphasis on good, clean, freckle-faced fun.

Two young spacelings, a cute boy and an adorable girl, are transported from Witch Mountain to the Rose Bowl, where their Space Uncle instructs them to "have a lot of fun" and "never energize unless it's absolutely necessary."

They plan only an ordinary, Disneyland kind of visit to Los Angeles ("I can't wait to see the museums and go to all the concerts!" the girl exclaims).

But soon they are separated, and involved in all sorts of intrigue: Tia (Kim Richards) has been adopted by a harmless, good-hearted, perfectly interracial gang called the Earthquakes, and Tony (Ike Eisenmann) has been captured by Christopher Lee and Bette Davis, who play the gruesome twosome of the piece. Mr. Lee and Miss Davis mean to incorporate poor Tony into their plan to take over the entire world.

Tony is brainwashed by the villains, and Tia sets out to rescue him, aided only by the Earthquakes and a very smart goat.

Tia has been so nicely brought up, on whatever planet she came from in "Escape to Witch Mountain," this film's predecessor, that she is forever thanking people, even — as when the goat does her a good turn — when it isn't exactly necessary. But her search for Tony affords the film some authentically hilarious moments, especially when the goat takes a taxi ride, and during an elaborate sequence in which the siblings wreak havoc with an Old West exhibit at a museum.

The two young principals are serviceable, but not nearly as lively as some of their co-stars — Christian Juttner, as the tallest Earthquake, steals virtually every scene he doesn't share with Miss Davis or Mr. Lee.

The material makes negligible demands upon the latter pair, but they manage to be agreeably wicked throughout. Mr. Lee's particular vice is supposed to be wild ambition; we know this because he dresses much more elegantly than the average megalomanic might. And Miss Davis's weakness is her greed, which she amply demonstrates with a series of dry asides.

John Hough's direction, ungainly at its best, is occasionally downright cruel. Shooting snub-nosed kids from a low camera angle is not a very nice thing to do, and neither is shooting Miss Davis in close-up when her heavy makeup seems designed for long shots. She's supposed to look frightening much of the time, but there's such a thing as gallantry, too.

1978 Jl 14, C14:5

Innings and Outings

THE BAD NEWS BEARS GO TO JAPAN, directed by John Berry; written by Bill Lancaster; directors of photography, Gene Polito and Kozo Okazaki; editor, Richard A. Harris; music by Robert Kruger; produced by Michael Ritchie; released by Paramount Pictures. At the Guild, 50th Street and Rockefeller Plaza, and other theaters. Running time; 92 minutes. This film is rated PG.

Marvin Lazar .... Tony Curtis
Kelly Leak .... Jackie Earle Haley
E. R. W Tillyard 3d .... Matthew Douglas Anton
Ahmad Rahim .... Erin Blunt
Miguel Agilar .... George Gonzales
Jimmy Feldman .... Brett Marx
Rudy Stein .... David Pollock
Toby Whitewood .... David Stambaugh
Mike Engleberg .... Jeffrey Louis Starr
Mustapha Rahim .... Scoody Thornton
Abe Bernstein .... Abraham Unger
Coach Shimizu .... Tomisaburo Wakayama
Antonio Inoki .... Antonio Inoki
Arika .... Hatsune Ishibara
Dick Button .... Dick Button
Louie The Gambler .... Lonny Chapman
Regis Philbin .... Regis Philbin
Network Director .... George Wyner
Pennywall .... Hugh Gillin
Southerner .... Robert Sorrells
Referee .... Tak Kubota
Network Man No. 3 .... Dick McGarvin
Network Man No. 4 .... James Staley
Usher .... Michael Yama
Mean Bones Beaudine .... Clarence Barnes
Network Man No. 5 .... Dennis Freeman
Madam .... Kyoko Fuji
Stunt Double .... Hector Guerrero
Waitress .... Marjorie Jackson
Moderator .... Bob Kino
Fight Announcer .... Yangi Kitadani
Mean Bones's Manager .... Gene LeBell
Page Boy .... Jerry Maren
Director's Aide .... Ginger Martin
Manager .... Dean A. Okinaka
Band Leader .... Daniel Sasaki
Network Man No. 2 .... Tim P. Sullivan
Interpreter .... Victor Toyota
Network Man No. 1 .... Don Watters
Eddie of Network .... Jerry Ziesmer

"THE BAD NEWS BEARS Go to Japan" is the third in the comedy series about the California baseball team with the pint-sized players who have dirty mouths and hearts of driven mush. The title tells only part of the story.

The Bad News Bears, who last time out won their big game in the Houston Astrodome, do go to Japan and they do play some baseball, but most of the time they and their schlock promoter (Tony Curtis) are searching for material worthy of their raffish talents. The film is a demonstration of the kind of desperation experienced by people trying to make something out of a voyage to nowhere.

Though this film was written by Bill Lancaster, who wrote the original "Bad News Bears," produced by Michael Ritchie, who directed the first film, and directed by John Berry, who helped to make "Claudine" such a lark, "The Bad News Bears Go to Japan" has the appearance of a movie made by people who didn't know how, or who didn't care, or who possibly turned over their responsibilities to Japanese Airlines and the Japanese Tourist Bureau, whose principal interests are prominent among the screen images.

•

Mr. Curtis plays a seedy agent named Marvin Lazar, a character who seems to be a comic valentine to Irving (Swifty) Lazar, one of Hollywood's most successful agents and most active legends. Marvin, after conning the Bears into going to Japan to make his fortune, is himself conned and conquered by the Bears who persuade him to go straight, which is just about the only road left open to a fellow whose credit cards have all been ceremoniously cut in two. When given a chance by the material, Mr. Curtis projects a picture of second-rate hucksterism that is all the more funny for being so blatantly rude and transparent.

Of the original Bears remaining in the new movie, Jackie Earle Haley is perhaps best remembered as the little Bear who seemed old for his size and years but now, with his years and growth in size, he seems only a little old to be hanging around the Bears. A most attractive newcomer is 6-year-old Scoody Thornton, a small, incurably optimistic boy who persists in sticking up for Marvin when all the other Bears know him to be the failed scoundrel he is.

A Japanese star, Tomisaburo Wakayama, plays the taciturn coach of the Japanese team and Dick Button appears in a comic cameo as himself as he describes a televised karate match entirely in figure-skating terms.

"The Bad News Bears," which opens today at neighborhood theaters, isn't the sort of bad movie that angers you. It's sad in the way of something that's been abandoned. It deserved better from the people involved.

•

"The Bad News Bears Go to Japan," which has been rated PG ("parental guidance suggested"), contains most of the mildly vulgar language that was so popular in the first two "Bears" films.

VINCENT CANBY

1978 Jl 14, C15:3

Scoody Thornton is one of this year's Bears and Tony Curtis this year's coach in "The Bad News Bears Go to Japan."

Plus Ça Change

LET'S FACE IT, C'EST LA VIE, directed by Samy Pavel; a French film with English subtitles; a Kashfi/Sera for K.S.P. Entertainment Corp. Production. At the Festival Theater, Fifth Avenue and 57th Street. Running time: 98 minutes. This film has not been rated.

Anne .... Martine Kelly
Pierre .... Richard Leduc
Yves .... Neils Arestrup
Laurent .... Gino Da Ronch

A WOMAN stands at a railway station, dressed as a kind of cut-rate Victoria Holt heroine, in a floor-length white suit and huge, outlandish hat. Then two men approach and look the woman over from head to toe. She goes home with them, to a cottage by the sea in Brittany, and there is so much leering and smirking and pregnant pausing that it looks as if we're on the verge of witnessing something smutty. The photography is grainy and amateurish, and the music the kind of thing you hear in supermarkets, just to heighten the intimations of soft-core porn.

One hour and a lot of idle chitchat later, it turns out that "Let's Face It, C'est La Vie" isn't leading up to anything lewd. Instead, this is merely the story of how Anne (Martine Kelly) goes to visit her former lover, Pierre (Richard Leduc), only to discover that the new object of Pierre's affections is a sullen, disagreeable fellow named Yves (Neils Arestrup). When she learns what Pierre and Yves have been up to, Anne demonstrates that tolerance is not her strong suit by throwing a fit. "Of course you charm a lot of people, especially at the hairdresser's," she shrieks. And "Michelangelo, Freud, all of them — I'm fed up with them!"

•

Yves does his best to smooth matters over. "Do you know what Pierre is?" he asks. "He's a totally normal human being who's not completely at ease with himself, which can make him very uptight. Do you understand?" Anne doesn't, and to demonstrate the point she falls into a state of arty catatonia. Pierre and Yves are left with the chore of dressing her up in the white outfit again and wheeling her back to the train station.

The coda to the film — or "the final Proustian twist," as the production notes have it — finds Anne arriving at a train station to meet Pierre many years later. This time, Anne is done up as something like a high-fashion flamenco dancer, and Pierre is accompanied by a crew of gypsy violinists.

What's a nice theater like the Festival doing with a movie like this? Once upon a time, a French film wasn't worth distributing in New York unless it met certain basic standards of quality, but this is one more distressing bit of proof that times have changed. A movie this poorly acted, cheesily shot, small-minded and pea-brained can't fairly be compared with even the less successful French commercial efforts that have cropped up here lately, like "Replay" or "We Will All Meet in Paradise"; whatever shortcomings those films may have, they employ gifted actors and are easy on the eye. "Let's Face It, C'est La Vie" has nothing to recommend it save perhaps the language barrier, which lends even the worse nonsense a certain je ne sais quoi.

JANET MASLIN

1978 Jl 14, C16:4

'The Swarm,' By Allen, Flies Onto Screens

By JANET MASLIN

Some day, African killer bees may wind up having the last buzz on us, but for the time being they simply aren't scary, at least not in Irwin Allen's "The Swarm." When Mr. Allen films large numbers of bees from afar, they look like clouds of nutmeg or, sometimes, like peculiarly chunky smog; up close, they suggest a naturalist's documentary about habits of the hive. A couple of times, Mr. Allen offers gigantic blowups of the bugs, in hopes of generating a "Towering Antennae" effect, but still the bees don't look as if they'd hurt a fly. Mr. Allen might just as well have devoted his talents to man-eating goldfish, poodles on the rampage or carniverous canaries.

"Oh, my God — bees, bees, millions of bees!" cries a helicopter pilot, who, needless to say, is not long for this world. The horde is headed for a sweet little town where the movie theater is playing "The Towering Inferno," Mr. Allen's previous exercise in pre-fab pandemonium, and where the local drugstore must do land-office business selling hair spray to the schoolmis-

Richard Widmark

tress, played by Olivia de Havilland. Once they arrive, the bees slaughter everybody they can get their stingers on.

Mr. Allen stands to gain a great deal from the bloodthirstiness of his swarm, but there isn't much in it for the bees. We see a few bee's-eye point-of-view shots of innocent picnickers and the like, but their motives are never made clear. Are they out to avenge themselves on mankind? Michael Caine, playing the entomologist of the piece, hazards a guess or two, but nothing he says is helpful to Richard Widmark, as a general on Bee Patrol. "I always credit my enemy, no matter what he may be, with equal intelligence," Mr. Widmark grimly observes. Because the military's first 10 or 12 schemes to outsmart the little devils are unsuccessful, Mr. Widmark's assessment sounds very fair.

•

It could be argued that "The Swarm" is the surprise comedy hit of the season, what with Katharine Ross as a doctor, Mr. Allen's cutting to something noisy every time he doesn't know how to end a scene and exchanges like this one, as an attempt to poison the pests goes kerflooey:

Entomologist Caine: "They're not touching the pellets. They seem to sense it's something that will kill them."

Rival scientist Richard Chamberlain (worriedly): "They're brighter than I thought."

Distinguished senior scientist Henry Fonda (knowingly): "They always are."

There ought to be a word for what actors do in movies like this one; in fact, there probably is. In any case, players like Mr. Fonda and Mr. Caine manage to cooperate with the material without seeming compromised by it. Mr. Caine can apparently do anything, except give a bad performance.

There are no black principals in the large, all-star cast. There are frequent references to "the war against the Africans," by which the characters, of course, mean their battle with the bees. Nevertheless, it's a very unfortunate bit of phrasing.

1978 Jl 15, 8:3

Killer bees have it in for Olivia de Havilland in "The Swarm."

The New Masculine Hero

By PAUL STARR

In what may be an emerging genre in the movies — the post-feminist romance — there appears a character who expresses in his personality and relations with the heroine a new ideal of masculinity. He might be described as the emotionally competent hero. Alan Bates plays him in "An Unmarried Woman"; Jon Voight plays him in "Coming Home." He is the man to whom women turn as they try to change their own lives: someone who is strong and affectionate, capable of intimacy, unthreatened by commitment, masculine without being dominating.

Compared to the archetypal, old-fashioned hero exemplified by John Wayne or Gary Cooper or Cary Grant, the current figure of romantic imagination is less wooden, more emotionally articulate. Unlike the intensely emotional heroes that Marlon Brando and James Dean portrayed in the fifties, he is at ease with himself; he's more mature and less troubled. Nor is he the kind of anti-hero played by Dustin Hoffman or Jack Nicholson in movies of the last decade — small, estranged, in Nicholson's case often cynical and debauched. The hero in the post-feminist romance, although not overpowering, is a firm and clear-headed fellow, possessed of a calm intensity of feeling, a capacity for un-neurotic expressiveness.

Kris Kristofferson, in Martin Scorsese's 1975 film "Alice Doesn't Live Here Anymore," played what now seems like the prototype for this role. Calm, peaceable and warmly attentive, Kristofferson — as the rancher who gains Alice's affections — embodied the sort of nonviolent sexuality and relaxed intimacy also communicated by Alan Bates as the artist Saul Kaplan, who wins the heroine's affections in "An Unmarried Woman," and by Jon Voight as the wounded veteran Luke Martin, who wins the heroine'e affections in "Coming Home."

Indeed, these three film — "Alice," "An Unmarried Woman" and "Coming Home" — share remarkable similarities. In each there is a first husband who is clean-cut, aggressive, tense, self-absorbed, handsome but utterly unresponsive to his wife. He departs early in each film: Alice's husband (Billy Green Bush) dies in a truck accident; in "An Unmarried Woman," Erica's husband (Michael Murphy) leaves her for another woman; in "Coming Home," Sally's husband (Bruce Dern) is sent to Vietnam. Then Alice (Ellen Burstyn) and Erica (Jill Clayburgh) and Sally (Jane Fonda), who have shown signs of muted unhappiness, are forced to reconstruct their lives. In the course of doing so, they meet the new man — played by Kristofferson, Bates or Voight — who in each case is less conventional in his style of life, more relaxed, more immediately "there" than the husband.

"Alice" and "An Unmarried Woman" have been widely received as films about changes in women's consciousness, and "Coming Home" is generally labeled an "anti-war" film. Yet all three are as much about changing ideals of male character, represented by the contrast between the first husband and the new man and dramatized by the passage that the women in the films make between them. Just a few years ago, at a time when the movies were dominated by buddy relationships of the Newman-Redford type, vigilante violence, the disaster cult, and a pervasive sense of moral rot, Pauline Kael could write in an essay titled "On the Future of the Movies" that "nobody understands what contemporary heroes or heroines should be, or how they should relate to each other." That is no longer as true as it was then. For although these new films can be rather sanctimonious about their own implicit values, they do point toward a recovery from nihilism and an attempt to put relations between men and women on some reasonable foundation. Part of that effort is a rethinking of male personality.

•

As if to highlight the difference between the old and new images of manliness, the films show two contrasting scenes of the husband and the lover with the heroine — the first a moment of coercion, the second a moment of tenderness. In the first, the husband, consumed by his own sexual urges, virtually relieves himself on his wife, while she passively accepts what amounts to little better than a rape. Later in the film, with the new man, she is passionate and responsive, and her body comes alive with energy. The contrast is especially graphic in "Coming Home," where Luke, though paralyzed, is able to give Sally more satisfaction than her virile husband. Sally and her husband, on the eve of his departure for Vietnam, make no eye contact as they make love; he turns down the light and grapples above her in search of his own satisfactions, while her eyes stare off somewhere else. On her first night with Luke, he insists the light be kept on. "I want to see you," he

Paul Starr, assistant professor of sociology at Harvard, is the author of "The Discarded Army: Veterans After Vietnam."

tells Sally, and he lavishes attention over her in what is plainly a statement about what it takes — and what it doesn't take — to be a good lover.

The two men in each film present a study in contrasting appearances. It can hardly be an accident that in all three movies the first husband is clean-shaven, while the new man has a rough beard. (It's probably no accident, either, that the husbands all have very American names — Don, Bob and Marty — while the names of the new men are more Biblical — David, Luke and Saul.) Kristofferson, Bates and Voight all look a bit ragged and furry in these pictures; the beards make their faces seem soft and round rather than angular. (A beard may also call attention to the more sensual, soft and oral quality of their relations with the women, as opposed to the husband's sometimes violent and more narrowly genital preoccupations.) Their more irregular appearance also highlights their more irregular style of life. The husband in each case is an employee of some kind — a truck driver in "Alice," an Army captain in "Coming Home," a stockbroker in "An Unmarried Woman." By contrast, none of the new men holds down a regular nine-to-five job — Kristofferson plays a rancher, Voight a recuperating veteran, Bates an artist. While the first husbands are preoccupied with the anxieties about work and competition, the new men are less hurried, more easygoing, more playful. They have a sense of humor. They are good with children.

The new man is not simply, as he might have been in a novel of a few decades ago — a lustier, more Dionysian lover, set against a weak and sexually repressed but socially respectable husband. That is an old opposition, out of D. H. Lawrence, belonging to an earlier period of revolt against ideals of Victorian gentility, when (it was said) an "effeminate" civilization had corrupted manliness. The husband in these new films is virile enough, even athletic. (In yet another curious correspondence, the opening frames of "Coming Home" and "An Unmaried Woman" show Bruce Dern and Michael Murphy out jogging, which sugests not only that they are fit, but that they are quite self-conscious about keeping in shape.) The husbands' problem isn't impotence: He can respond physically, but he can't respond emotionally. The new man is more responsive, softer, in some ways more domestic.

Ideals of male identity go through periods when they become more "masculine" or more "feminine." (Here I use the terms to stand for the various qualities conventionally associated with each one, such as physical strength and emotional self-control with masculinity and nurturance and compassion with feminity.) Whereas earlier in this century we were in a "masculinizing" period — of which Lawrence and Hemingway and the cult of the "real man" were an expression — today we are in a period when masculinity is being softened. Superficially, this was apparent in the long hair and unisex clothing of the 1960's, but it now goes deeper. Feminism and economic independence have encouraged women to make greater emotional demands of men not to put up with the distant self-absorption of the competitive male primarily involved with his career. These new characters on screen embody many of the qualities of responsiveness and intimacy now sought by women. They are the idealized response to a real change in social life.

•

The husbands in the films are representatives of the old order, and treated accordingly. At their worst (which they often are), they are selfish pigs; at their best, they are merely pathetic or foolish. The wives are presented as victims, innocent of whatever has gone wrong in their marriages. (That part of the story may be missing here goes without saying.) The films examine the emotional struggles of the women, not the men, although it's clear in "An Unmarried Woman" and "Coming Home" that the husbands are in the throes of some desperate uneasiness. But they evoke little more than pity. Whatever they are suffering, they keep to themselves — indeed, their inability to articulate their anxieties is itself part of their character. Michael Murphy, who is more expressive than the other husbands, attempts to give some complexity to his part in "An Unmarried Woman," and, interestingly enough, he recently told Janet Maslin in an interview, "I'd love to have played that guy in 'Coming Home,' the Bruce Dern part, because if you can bring some sympathy to those characters and not make them just these obnoxious jerks, there's a nice kind of ambivalence about it." But the films are ultimately firm in their verdict on these characters: They are the badmen of the tale and they meet a sad and just retribution.

The new men, to be sure, might not satisfy a radical feminist either. Saul Kaplan makes it clear to Erica that painting comes first in his life, and Luke tells Sally that nothing has been on his mind more than sex. Still, these new lovers are gentler and more sensitive than the husbands, and they are clearly meant to be counter-images of comparatively unchauvinistic men. If anything, they seem too good to be real: Only Jon Voight, of the three actors, portrays a character with some inner tension. The others do not have to struggle to be what they are. They're the stuff of romantic fantasy, only now the fantasies have been adjusted in light of the changing relations between men and women.

•

The more troubling issue for some feminists, who would like to see women making it on their own, is why in "Alice" and "An Unmarried Woman" Kris Kristofferson and Alan Bates show up at all. By having the heroines meet their fair princes, even though they are princes of a new masculinity, the films avoid some of the issues they initially promise to raise. But without the new men, the movies would not only lose the element of romantic fantasy that makes them more widely appealing, but also fail to develop the positive side of their implicit critique of masculinity.

Of course, the emotionally competent hero is by no means a dominant figure in the movies, any more than he is in real life. In her recent book, "Big Bad Wolves," a history of masculinity in the American cinema, Joan Mellen argues that the male in the 1970's — epitomized for her by actors like Clint Eastwood and Charles Bronson — has become even more violent and brutal than he was before. Perhaps there are more heroes in the Eastwood-Bronson mold than of the sort played by Kristofferson, Bates and Voight. Yet regardless of the numbers, the new, softer image of masculinity seems to represent what is distinctive and significant in recent films, and I expect we will see more of the post-feminist hero because the old strong, silent type no longer seems adequate as a lover — or as a person. ■

1978 Jl 16, II:1:1

Long-Delayed Sequel

INTERNATIONAL VELVET, directed, written and producaed by Bryan Forbes; suggested by the novel "National Velvet" by Enid Bagnold; director of photography, Tony Imi; music by Francis Lai; editor, Timothy Gee; released by United Artists. At the Guild, 33 West 50th Street, the Trans Lux East, Third Avenue and 58th Street and other theaters. Running time: 126 minutes. This film is sated PG.

Sarah Brown .... Tatum O'Neal
John Seaton .... Christopher Plummer
Captain Johnson .... Anthony Hopkins
Velvet Brown .... Nanette Newman
Pilot .... Peter Barkworth
Mr. Curtis .... Dinsdale Landen
Beth .... Sarah Bullen
Scott Saunders .... Jeffrey Byron
Tim .... Richard Warwick
Wilson .... Daniel Abineri
Roger .... Jason White
Mike .... Martin Neil
Howard .... Douglas Reith
Policeman .... Dennis Blanch
Team Doctor .... Norman Wooland
TV Interviewer .... Susan Jameson
Alice .... Brenda Cowling
Commentators .... James Smilie, David Tate

By VINCENT CANBY

"INTERNATIONAL VELVET," Bryan Forbes's sequel to Clarence Brown's classic 1944 film, "National Velvet," is a racking experience for any reasonably self-possessed adult, continuously pulling the viewer between a sneer and a tear.

The film, which opens today at the Guild and other theaters, exploits without shame, wit or subtlety our sympathy for misunderstood children, for animals, for pluck, progress, perseverance and, especially, for against-all-odds success.

The photography is so lyrical you may feel airsick by the end, while the soundtrack score by Francis Lai should be labeled with a skull and crossbones. After listening to this music for more than two hours, you get an idea of what it would have been like to be in Pompeii that fatal day had Vesuvius been full of butterscotch instead of lava.

Yet "International Velvet" has more than its share of moments, almost all of them centering on the performance of the eerily talented, immensely appealing Tatum O'Neal, who was 14 years old when the film was made and, for the purposes of Mr. Forbes's fiction, ages (if that's the right word) from 10 to 18 in the course of the movie. She just may be a superlative actress. It's not easy to tell yet, though she seems to possess the sort of infinitely adaptable personality that film directors dream of. Her face, still in process of being formed, reflects degrees of feeling that transform the child into someone beyond identifiable age. She's unique.

The movie is something else. Mr. Forbes's screenplay picks up the character played by Elizabeth Taylor in "National Velvet" about 25 years later (though the movie is very fast and loose with time), when the girl, now played by Nanette Newman (Mrs. Bryan Forbes), becomes the guardian of her orphaned niece, Sarah Brown (Miss O'Neal).

The niece, a very large 10-year-old who's been raised in Arizona, arrives in England with a chip on her shoulder that can be removed only by an obsessive interest in horses and by the love and understanding of her aunt and Christopher Plummer, the writer Miss Newman lives with.

Whereas Velvet won her nickname by winning the Grand National steeplechase as a girl, Sarah becomes International Velvet by being the youngest member of the British Olympic riding team.

As domestic drama, "International Velvet" is facetious and coy and just about unbearable. Miss Newman and Mr. Plummer have silly roles that they play with a kind of provincial sophistication, which may be what the director wanted (since nothing in this film is uncalculated). As a movie about a girl, her horse and the big race, "International Velvet" sneaks up on you in unexpectedly moving ways.

The steeplechase sequences are superb and the film has a first-class performance by Anthony Hopkins as the tough, no-nonsense trainer of the Olympic riding team. Mr. Hopkins is an actor of such crisp intelligence that he seems to be in a movie completely removed from the sentimental romantic drama inhabited by Miss Newman and Mr. Plummer. It's to Miss O'Neal's credit that she moves from one to the other not only without visible strain but with (dare I say womanly?) ease.

1978 Jl 19, C15:1

Jumping Hybrid

FOUL PLAY, written and directed by Colin Higgins; director of photography, David M. Walsh; film editor, Pembroke Herring; produced by Thomas L. Miller and Edward K. Milkis; released by Paramount Pictures. At the Cinema 3, 59th Street and Fifth Avenue and the Forum, Broadway and 46th Street. Running time: 116 minutes. This film is rated PG.

Gloria .... Goldie Hawn
Tony .... Chevy Chase
Hennesey .... Burgess Meredith
Gerda .... Rachel Roberts
Archbishop Thorncrest .... Eugene Roche
Stanley Tibbets .... Dudley Moore
Stella .... Marilyn Sokol
Fergie .... Brian Dennehey
Stiltskin .... Marc Lawrence
Theater Manager .... Chuck McCann
MacKuen .... Billy Barty
Scarface .... Don Calfa
Scott .... Bruce Solomon
Sandy .... Cooper Huckabee
Mrs. Venus .... Pat Ast
Mrs. Russel .... Frances Bay
House Manager .... Lou Cutell
Albino .... WAilliam Frankfather
Captain Coleman .... John Hancock
Sally .... Barbara Sammeth
Elsie .... QueenieSmith
Ethel .... Hope Summers
Mrs. Monk .... Irene Tedrow
Turk .... Ion Teodorescu
Sylvia .... Janet Wood

By JANET MASLIN

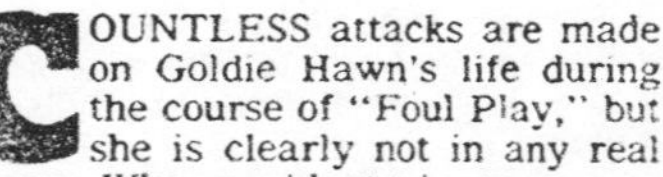

COUNTLESS attacks are made on Goldie Hawn's life during the course of "Foul Play," but she is clearly not in any real danger. When a midget tries to menace her, for instance, she simply picks up a broom and chases him around her apartment, eventually knocking him out a window. Later, feeling sorry about the incident, she goes to visit the poor traumatized midget in a hospital, and behaves so sweetly and contritely that she gives him an even worse scare.

In another scene, when a thug makes the mistake of catching Miss Hawn by surprise, she greets him with the most adorably indignant little shriek the movies have witnessed in years. Miss Hawn often looks frightened, as befits the complicated suspense plot of "Foul Play," but she even more often looks tremulously furious, and that's her secret weapon. Gloria, the librarian Miss Hawn plays here, may be so disarmingly dense she can't spot trouble brewing on the horizon, but once it arrives she's never too out-to-lunch to lose her temper. And her anger, imbued with all the quivering, outraged self-righteousness Miss Hawn can muster, is enough

Goldie Hawn

to make the most hardened villain or moviegoer melt.

If Miss Hawn does a wide-eyed dead-pan through most of the film, her co-star, Chevy Chase, is correspondingly cool. "Enjoy your dinner, there's nothing to worry about," says Mr. Chase's detective character reassuringly, having just crashed his car through the front window of a restaurant. "Be careful, it's very slippery here," he warns Miss Hawn, as he escorts her to the houseboat that serves as his lair. No one familiar with Mr. Chase's career on television's "Saturday Night Live" need wonder which of them is about to fall into the drink.

Miss Hawn and Mr. Chase meet very early in the film, looking bright and funny and all set to make beautiful music together. Accordingly, it's quite a surprise when "Foul Play" turns out to be more like a thriller than a comedy, and when neither performer is given much opportunity to cut loose. "Foul Play" is a slick, attractive, enjoyable movie with all the earmarks of a hit. But as "House Calls" did a few months ago, it starts out promising genuine wit and originality only to fall back on more familiar tactics after a half-hour or so. If either film had a less winning opening, perhaps it wouldn't leave a vague aftertaste of disappointment.

•

Colin Higgins, who wrote and directed "Foul Play," has aimed for the same kind of thriller-comedy-romance hybrid he attempted in writing "Silver Streak," and this time he's much more successful. Parts of the film, like a few aerial shots at the beginning, that mean to recall Hitchcock do, and there are enough good scares to keep things jumping. Still, Mr. Higgins isn't a facile enough juggler to keep the film's diverse elements from colliding at times. The finale, with two lovers flanked by two corpses, surrounded by the cast of "The Mikado" and cheered on by a religious leader, is bewildering at the very least.

Mr. Higgins's penchant for mixing visual elegance with coarse gags is equally ill-advised, especially because it makes him work the gags so hard. Dudley Moore, as a swinging single Miss Hawn unwittingly picks up in a bar, would have been a great deal funnier had Mr. Higgins decorated his bachelor pad with only half the sex-aid devices in the world, instead of all of them. Indeed, the soundtrack from "Saturday Night Fever," which Mr. Moore slaps on the turntable the moment Miss Hawn walks in, would probably have been enough. Here and elsewhere, Mr. Higgins would have done well to demonstrate more confidence in both his actors and his audience.

1978 Jl 19, C15:2

For the Pun of It

REVENGE OF THE PINK PANTHER, directed by Blake Edwards; screenplay by Frank Waldman, Ron Clark and Mr. Edwards; story by Mr. Edwards; director of photography, Ernie Day; music, Henry Mancini; animation, Depatie-Freleng; produced by Mr. Edwards; released by United Artists. At the Ziegfeld Theater, Avenue of the Americas and 54th Street. Running time: 99 minutes. This film is rated PG.

Clouseau ... Peter Sellers
Dreyfus ... Herbert Lom
Simone ... Dyan Cannon
Douvier ... Robert Webber
Cato ... Burt Kwouk
Scallini ... Paul Stewart
Marchione ... Robert Loggia
August Balls ... Graham Stark
François ... André Maranne
Claude Russo ... Sue Lloyd
Guy Algo ... Tony Beckley
Tanya ... Valerie Leon

"THE REVENGE of the Pink Panther," the fifth in the series of Inspector Clouzot comedies by Blake Edwards, the writer and director, and Peter Sellers, the star, drives a wooden stake through the heart of reason.

If you have the Clouzot habit, as I have, there's very little that Mr. Edwards and Mr. Sellers could do that would make you find the movie disappointing, or not up to their own standards, or slow in spots, or, unfortunately, not as much fun as "The Pink Panther Strikes Again," "The Return of the Pink Panther," "A Shot in the Dark" or "The Pink Panther."

Such comments are pointless when one has come to the realization that the "Panther" films are not separate entities but one continuing, effervescent saga about man (Inspector Clouzot) and his deficiencies.

Clouzot rides (walks, stumbles, falls, trips) again in "The Revenge of the Pink Panther," which opens today at the Ziegfeld and other theaters, and which provides Clouzot with all sorts of marvelously transparent excuses for physical bungling and for interfering with the progress of what he calls "loowa" and order.

Once more on hand to complement and support Mr. Sellers are Burt Kwouk as Cato, his reliably unreliable, karate-chopping manservant, and the inestimably funny Herbert Lom as Chief Inspector Dreyfus, Clouzot's former superior who's been driven mad by Clouzot's internationally acclaimed triumphs.

Robert Webber plays it more or less straight as Clouzot's latest arch-enemy, an American business tycoon who deals in heroin. Most important of all, Dyan Cannon is around to play what might be called a flawed femme fatale, a person who, like Clouzot, has a tendency to bend — successfully — all the laws of nature. They are most winning sleuths, especially when, disguised as Chinese coolies, they register at a fancy Hong Kong hotel as Mr. and Mrs. Low Key.

Horrendous puns, slapstick gags and disguises are the material of the comedy that, for no particular purpose that I can think of, has Clouzot, at one point and another, masquerade as a woman, a peg-legged sailor who carries an inflatable rubber parrot on his shoulder, and as Toulouse-Lautrec, a masquerade that prompts someone to say in admiration, "Now you can work both the Left Bank and Montmartre in anonymity!"

"The Revenge of the Pink Panther," which has been rated PG ("Parental Guidance Suggested"), contains one or two suggestive sequences that will go over the head of anyone less than three feet tall and 9 years of age.

VINCENT CANBY

1978 Jl 19, C15:5

Peter Sellers disguised as a Swedish herring fisherman

Tale of Rock Star

THE BUDDY HOLLY STORY, directed by Steve Rash; screenplay by Robert Gittler, story by Mr. Rash and Fred Bauer; director of photography, Stevan Larner; film editor, David Blewitt; music director, Joe Renzetti; produced by Fred Bauer; released by Columbia Pictures. At the Criterion, Broadway and 44th Street, and other theaters. Running time: 99 minutes. This film is rated PG.

Buddy Holly ... Gary Busey
Jesse ... Don Stroud
Ray Bob ... Charles Martin Smith
Riley Randolph ... Bill Jordan
Maria Elena Holly ... Maria Richwine
Ross Turner ... Conrad Janis
Eddie Foster ... Albert Popwell
Jenny Lou ... Amyu Johnston
Mr. Wilson ... Jim Beach
T. J. ... John F. Goff
Madman Mancuso ... Fred Travalena
Sol Zuckerman ... Dick O'Neil
Luther ... Stymie Beard
Emcee (Buffalo) ... M. G. Kelly
Sam Cooke ... Paul Mooney
Tyrone ... Freeman King
Mrs. Santiago ... Gloria Irricari
Richie Valens ... Gilbert Melgar
The Big Bopper ... Gailard Sartain
Dion ... George Simonelli
Mr. Holly ... Arch Johnson
Mrs. Holly ... Neva Patterson

By VINCENT CANBY

THERE are a lot of actors in "The Buddy Holly Story" — some of them very nice — but the movie is really a one-man show. It's Gary Busey's galvanizing solo performance that gives meaning to an otherwise shapeless and bland feature-length film about the American rock-and-roll star who was killed in a plane crash in 1959.

The film, which opens today at the Criterion and other theaters, was made with the cooperation of Holly's widow, Maria Elena Holly, and may be a demonstration of why keepers of the flame are not the best people to have around when you're making a movie

"The Buddy Holly Story" has a story of sorts, but it's a B-picture plot with all of the crises and villains discreetly removed, about the virtually unimpeded rise to the top, within three years, of a nice, gawky kid from Lubbock, Tex., who could express himself only through his music.

•

Buddy Holly was not Wolfgang Amadeus Mozart. What he expresses are not the contradictory impulses of a society of rare sophistication, but the pounding lusts and comic heartbreaks of people who have trouble dealing with any gratification not instant.

It may be argued that the film, written by Robert Gittler and directed by Steve Rash, reflects the essential simplicity of Holly's music, but that, I think, is to confuse simplicity with lack of technique, which is the manner of the film. Holly's music — including the dozen songs ("That'll Be the Day," "Well Alright," "Every Day," among others) that are reprised in the movie — is not especially complex but it expresses a kind of youthful vitality that has nothing much to do with the conventions of dopey movie making.

•

Which brings us to Mr. Busey, who's already been seen in "The Last American Hero," "Thunderbolt and Lightfoot" and, most recently, in "Straight Time," as Dustin Hoffman's junkie pal. Mr. Busey, tall and slightly awkward, a fellow whose teeth appear to have been grown and not styled, has the look of middle America all over him. He's also capable of making articulate a character who remains inarticulate except in his music. He's not only an actor who possesses a center of gravity — of intelligence — but he's also a pop musician (professional name: Teddy Jack Eddy) who understands the mysterious (to the rest of us) transformation that takes place during a performance.

•

Don Stroud and Charles Martin Smith ("American Grafitti") are effective and functional as Buddy Holly's two hometown pals who accompany him to stardom. Maria Richwine plays the Puerto Rican girl he marries, Gloria Irricari is her skeptical, watchful aunt (who doesn't trust musicians), and Paul Mooney, Gilbert Melgar and George Simonelli show up as some of

Gary Busey, who stars in the title role of "The Buddy Holly Story": *A movie that comes alive only during the musical sequences performed by Mr. Busey.*

the other rock stars (Sam Cooke, Richie Valens and Dion) whose careers crossed that of Holly.

Although "The Buddy Holly Story" can't be classified as a musical, it's a movie that comes alive only during the musical sequences, and these sequences, featuring Mr. Busey's transformed country-boy, are so good, so full of energy, they turn the material that frames them into wood.

•

"The Buddy Holly Story," which has been rated PG ("parental guidance suggested"), contains some mildly vulgar language.

1978 Jl 21, C14:1

Many Forms Involved

SGT. PEPPER'S LONELY HEARTS CLUB BAND, directed by Michael Schultz; written by Henry Edwards; director of photography, Owen Roizman; music by John Lennon, Paul McCartney and George Harrison; edited by Christopher Holmes; produced by Robert Stigwood; released by Universal Pictures. At the Rivoli, Broadway and 49th Street, the Plaza, 58th Street near Madison, 34th Street East, near Second Avenue and other theaters.

Billy Shears	Peter Frampton
Mark Henderson	Barry Gibb
Dave Henderson	Robin Gibb
Bob Henderson	Maurice Gibb
Mean Mr. Mustard	Paul Nicholas
Dougie Shears	Paul Nicholas
B. D. Brockhurst	Donald Pleasence
Strawberry Fields	Sandy Farina
Lucy	Dianne Steinberg
Dr. Maxwell Edison	Steve Martin
Future Villain	Aerosmith
Father Sun	Alice Cooper
Benefit Performers	Earth, Wind & Fire
Sgt. Pepper	Billy Preston
Mr. Kite	George Burns

By JANET MASLIN

IS IT A film? Is it a record album? Is it a poster, or a T-shirt, or a specially embossed frisbee? "Sgt. Pepper's Lonely Hearts Club Band" is the ultimate multimedia mishmash, so diversified that it doesn't fully exist in any one medium at all. This isn't a movie, it's a business deal set to music.

There are three brief sequences good enough to put the rest of the picture to shame. Steve Martin, cackling his completely unhinged rendition of "Maxwell's Silver Hammer," is a reminder that the film is otherwise humorless. Billy Preston, doing a flashy, rousing dance to the tune of "Get Back," makes the other hoofers look sadly two-left-feet. And Aerosmith, singing a piercing rock version of "Come Together," bring a taste of the 60's to a movie dead-set on both exploiting and soft-pedaling that era.

•

The point behind turning Peter Frampton and the Bee Gees into the Beatlesque band of the title was, presumably, to lure both young rock fans and members of the rocking chair set. But the plan has its drawbacks.

However much of a fan rave Mr. Frampton may be, he's a musician, not a movie star, and even a plot that merely requires him to look sad, peppy or joyful from time to time is more than he can manage.

In the role of Mr. Frampton's brother, Paul Nicholas, the actor who played nasty Cousin Kevin in "Tommy," provides a particularly unhelpful contrast, since he is every bit as lively as the singer is stiff. Still, Mr. Frampton looks like Marlon Brando beside the even more wooden Brothers Gibb.

•

Even if the Bee Gees aren't natural-born cutups, their principal job here is to perform a number of Beatles songs, mostly from the title album and "Abbey Road."

This sounds as if it ought to be child's play, in view of arrangements and production by George Martin (who worked with the Beatles in the first place), and considering the uncanny way the Bee Gees first rose to popularity by perfecting a Beatlish sound. However, the brothers have since risen to even greater popularity doing something different, so different that their newest fans may be dismayed to find not a whit of disco in the movie's soundtrack. And their Beatle numbers vary dramatically in quality, depending upon the nature of the particular song.

"Nowhere Man" suits them beautifully, for instance. But a less pretty number requiring zest and a strong lead singer — such as the title song, or "With a Little Help From My Friends," both sung with Mr. Frampton — merely makes them sound short on character. The Bee Gees's special gift for elaborate musical teamwork is often undercut by songs that cry out for individual personalities. Accordingly, Robin Gibb's bluesy solo on "Oh! Darling" is a sweet and surprising exception.

•

The musical numbers are strung together so mindlessly that the movie has the feel of an interminable variety show. Characters are named, invented or introduced to one another simply to provide excuses for the various songs.

This reaches a pinnacle of idiocy when a character named Strawberry Fields (Sandy Farina) sings "Strawberry Fields Forever" to her beau, Billy Shears (Mr. Frampton), who has been knocked unconscious. "Living is easy with eyes closed/Misunderstanding all you see," Strawberry sings, prettily but for absolutely no good reason. Even worse, when the screenplay has Strawberry killed (temporarily) so that a few sad songs can be sung, Mr. Frampton is obliged to croon "Golden Slumbers" to a woman in a see-through coffin.

The movie may have been conceived in a spirit of merriment, but watching it feels like playing shuffleboard at the absolute insistence of a bossy shipboard social director. When whimsy gets to be this overbearing, it simply isn't whimsy any more.

•

"Sgt. Pepper's Lonely Hearts Club Band" is rated PG ("Parental Guidance Suggested"). Its most risque moments, having to do with the morals and drug habits of people in the record business, are among its few funny ones.

1978 Jl 21, C16:1

George Burns joins Peter Frampton and the Bee Gees in a scene from "Sgt. Pepper's Lonely Hearts Club Band": an interminable variety show.

FILM VIEW

VINCENT CANBY

'The Swarm'— A Bumbling 'B'

It's not easy to resist it. "The Swarm," this year's funniest if only big-budget group-jeopardy movie, stars people like Olivia de Havilland, Henry Fonda, Richard Widmark, Fred MacMurray and Michael Caine. It's about a swarm of African killer bees who, in the space of 24 hours, terrorize a large part of the American Southwest. The bees attack picnickers at their peanut-butter sandwiches, then helicopters, and, for an encore, the personnel at an underground missile silo. They cause the explosion of an atomic power plant, whose fail-safe system hasn't been programmed for killer bees (which results in the death of 32,000 people in one town alone) and, for a climax, threaten the complete destruction of Houston.

For a movie with such an enormous body count, "The Swarm" is surprisingly benign. It wouldn't frighten a flower. The bees' victims scream and thrash around a lot, and though they expire with speed, the deaths are bloodless. The victims of these bees don't even swell up in any unsightly way.

Further, "The Swarm" is chock-full of the kind of dialogue that warms the cockles of any movie buff's heart. "General, every minute now is precious," says the scientist (Caine) to the General (Widmark) who, thank heavens, doesn't listen. "Sometimes we have to choose the lesser of two evils," says the General to the scientist as the military threaten to defoliate most of Texas in what will obviously be a doomed attempt to thwart malignant nature. And when the scientist finally comes up with a solution we know will work (not only because it's good-guy Caine who has discovered it, but because the movie is now running close to two hours in length), this inevitable exchange: "Then you're saying . . . ." "That's right!"

• • •

"The Swarm" also provides us with an instant overview of who is still who in Hollywood. There is the incomparable pro-of-pros, Henry Fonda, looking his age and still great, saying nonsensical lines with the grace and clarity of an actor who now brings more to any movie than any movie can possibly bring to him. There are also Fred MacMurray, looking cosmeticized, as he did for all those years he starred in TV's "My Three Sons," and Olivia de Havilland, a little plumper but still as pretty as she was 40 years ago, playing a school teacher with the sort of Melanie Hamilton-sweetness that once, with good reason, drove Scarlett O'Hara up the wall.

Jose Ferrer comes on briefly as the chief of the atomic energy plant, a fellow who has barely enough time to tell us how safe his operation is before the whole place goes up in a mushroom cloud, and Bradford Dillman plays what is, in effect, the spear carrier in movies of this sort. He's the General's loyal, stiff-backed aide, the kind of officer who never questions an order. Mostly, though, there is Richard Widmark, playing the conservative, unbending, right-wing general that has become, for him, a sinecure.

"The Swarm" seems innocent, and I suppose it is. Although bees do sting and in swarms are scary, they aren't scary in a photogenic way. The people we see being attacked look more like people fighting an inconvenient gnat invasion of a lawn party. Yet the movie is not entirely innocent.

It's not that Irwin Allen has committed any conscious sin. I suspect that he really didn't know any better. How else to explain what seem to be the repeated references in the course of the film to "the Africans," meaning the bees, as in "the Africans are coming"? Because there's not a single black actor in the movie, at least not in a featured role, the references to "the Africans" begin to take on a hilariously ominous meaning after a while. The suspense in "The Swarm" is such that one's mind wanders, which gave me time to consider whether Allen and his screenwriter, Stirling Silliphant, hadn't hidden within their live-action cartoon a prophecy in the shape of a metaphor about a forthcoming race war.

I doubt it, but the idea, once planted, grows during the course of the movie.

More sinister, though, is what "The Swarm" represents in terms of contemporary film making, for it is nothing less than the ultimate apotheosis of yesterday's B-movie. It's the fondly remembered low-budget horror film of the sort exemplified by movies like "Them" (about giant mutant ants) and "The Naked Jungle" (about man-eating soldier ants) upgraded in terms of financial investment, stars, care in production and intensity of promotion to the status of A-movie.

I don't suppose we should be surprised. Allen, the producer of such spectacular (and financially successful) melodramas as "The Poseidon Adventure" and "The Towering Inferno," has been working toward this goal for some time. However, those two films were so much harmless fun, and so technically elaborate, that their essential nature didn't make much difference. Also, there were a lot of other movies of different sorts to choose from when they were released. In the context of today's increasingly vapid commercial film production, the glorified B-movie has become the style-setter, and Mr. Allen ("Voyage to the Bottom of the Sea," "Five Weeks in a Balloon") our decade's Samuel Goldwyn.

Three of the most successful films of the last 12 months share these roots with "The Swarm"—George Lucas's "Star Wars," Steven Spielberg's "Close Encounters of The Third Kind" and the screen version of "Grease." Yet as Lucas, Spielberg and the people who put "Grease" together transcended the tacky, B-picture genres they recall with affection and imagination, Allen merely reproduces the tacky genre while spending a great deal of money doing it. There's not a frame of film, not a twist of plot, not a line of dialogue, not a performance in "The Swarm" that suggests real appreciation for film history, only a slavish desire to imitate it. That's not enough.

•

One of the subsidiary amusements of "The Swarm" is watching Michael Caine survive the silliness with his dignity intact, though how he does it I'm not at all sure. He's a fine, slippery sort of actor who can inhabit a bad movie without actually seeming to be in it. This is quite different from the effect that Henry Fonda has under such circumstances. Fonda never disassociates himself from "The Swarm." He gives the performance that's required, adding to it (there's no way he couldn't) the Fonda presence, which is everything we have come to see in a Fonda performance over the decades.

Caine's technique, I suppose, is a kind of sophisticated cool. In the surroundings of "The Swarm," of course, he stands out anyway by being so unmistakably English. Yet he also survived the recent "The Silver Bears," a muddled comedy about a bunch of swindlers, which had a completely international cast. His secret may well be nothing more than a quality that registers as innate intelligence, which works for him as well in his good movies ("Sleuth," "The Man Who Would Be King") as it does in the rotten ones. He knows that we know that he knows exactly what he's doing. In this case, making (I hope) a pot of money. ■

1978 Jl 23, II:13:4

Daffy Deltas

NATIONAL LAMPOON'S ANIMAL HOUSE, directed by John Landis; written by Harold Ramis, Douglas Kenney and Chris Miller; director of photography, Charles Correll; edited by George Folsey Jr.; music by Elmer Bernstein; produced by Matty Simmons and Ivan Reitman; released by Universal Pictures. At the Astor Plaza, Broadway and 44th Street and other theaters. Running time: 107 minutes. This film is rated R.

Larry Kroger .... Thomas Hulce
Kent Dorfman .... Stephen Furst
Doug Neidermeyer .... Mark Metcalf
Mandy Pepperidge .... Mary Louise Weller
Babs Jansen .... Martha Smith
Greg Marmalard .... James Daughton
Chip Diller .... Kevin Bacon
John Blutarsky .... John Belushi
Katy .... Karen Allen
Robert Hoover .... James Widdoes
Eric Stratton .... Tim Matheson
Daniel Simpson Day .... Bruce McGill
Dave Jennings .... Donald Sutherland
Dean Vernon Wormer .... John Vernon
Mayor Carmine DePasto .... Cesare Danova
Marion Wormer .... Verna Bloom
Clorette DePasto .... Sarah Holcomb
Otis Day .... DeWayne Jessie
Shelly .... Lisa Baur

By JANET MASLIN

IT'S Rush Week of 1962 at Faber College, where "Knowledge Is Good" was the founder's most memorable witticism. The classiest fraternity on campus — the one to which the editor of the Daily Bavarian belongs — is wowing potential pledges with an elaborate show of gentility and a pianist who can play "Tammy." But right next door, at the eyesore that is the Delta House, something a little less civilized is going on.

The Deltas are the kind of guys who bash beer cans against their foreheads, wheel their dates home in shopping carts and think they know the words to "Louie, Louie," which they will sing in off-key unison at less than the slightest provocation. Needless to say, they will not be having a very good year. The brother who racks up a 1.2 grade point average will be the brightest of the bunch, and the house Romeo will be reduced to gearing his visits to a nearby girls' school to the obituary notices. Pretending to be the grieving fiancé of a dead coed is evidently a successful, if pitiable, gambit.

"National Lampoon's Animal House" is by no means one long howl, but it's often very funny, with gags that are effective in a dependable, all-purpose way. The movie works hard to supply something for the broadest possible audience, instead of aiming only at the viewer who'd like to watch John Belushi — as the Delta who knows the fewest words of more than one syllable — eating Jell-O with his fingers.

"Animal House" is too cheerfully sleazy to be termed tame, but the film makers have been smart enough to leaven each gross-out with an element of innocent fun. Even the action-packed finale amounts to nothing more dangerous than the spectacle of all heck breaking loose.

Except for Mr. Belushi, who mugs like crazy and spills a wide variety of substances all over himself, the actors tend to be as clean-cut and dopey as the movie's setting. Tim Matheson is a particularly self-congratulatory Joe College who whistles "Peter and the Wolf" as he loiters in a women's dorm; Stephen Furst does some very successful scene-stealing as the house blimp.

And Thomas Hulce is appropriately dim playing the first guy in the frat to be offered a reefer, by the obligatory hyper-hip English professor (Donald Sutherland, in a throwaway role). "O.K., so that means our whole solar system could be one tiny atom in the fingernail of some other giant being," Mr. Hulce postulates, while under the influence. Then he breaks out in uncontrollable giggles.

At its best, in moments like this, the movie isn't strictly satirical, because it doesn't need to be. The film makers have simply supplied the appropriate panty-girdles, crew-neck sweaters, frat-house initiation rites and rituals of the toga party, and let all that idiocy speak — very eloquently, and with a lot of comic fervor — for itself.

1978 Jl 28, C7:3

John Belushi on the attack in "National Lampoon's Animal House": *Often very funny, with gags that are effective in a dependable, all-purpose way."*

Isabelle Adjani and Ryan O'Neal in Walter Hill's "The Driver": *"Singularly unexciting and uninvolving, though it does have its laughs."*

No Names, Please!

THE DRIVER, written and directad by Walter Hill; director of photography, Philip Lathrop; edited by Tina Hirsch and Robert K. Lambert; music by Michael Small; produced by Lawrence Gordon; released by Twentieth Century-Fox Film Corporation. At the National, 44th Street and Broadway and other theaters. Running time: 90 minutes. This film is rated R.

The Driver	Ryan O'Neal
The Detective	Bruce Dern
The Player	Isabelle Adjani
The Connection	Ronee Blakley
Red Plainclothesman	Matt Clark
Gold Plainclothesman	Felice Orlandi
Glasses	Joseph Walsh
Teeth	Rudy Ramos
Exchange Man	Denny Macko
The Kid	Frank Bruno
Fingers	Will Walker
Split	Sandy Brown Wyeth
Frizzy	Tara King
Floorman	Richard Carey
Card Player	Fidel Corona
Boardman	Victor Gilmour
Blue Mask	Nick Dimitri
Green Mask	Bob Minor
Patron	Angelo Lamonea
Patron	Patrick Burns
Patron	Karen Kleiman
Passenger	Thomas Myers
Passenger	Bill McConnell
Commuter	Peter Jason
Commuter	William Hasley
Uniformed Cop	Allan Graf

By VINCENT CANBY

HE drives getaway cars, so he's called The Driver. The man who's obsessed with catching The Driver is a member of the police force. He's called The Detective. The young woman who's hired by The Driver to be his alibi when The Detective attempts to frame The Driver is called The Player, probably because when we first see her she's in a gambling casino, playing five-card stud.

There are a lot of other people in "The Driver" (hereafter referred to as The Movie), including phantoms with names like The Connection, Red Plainclothesman, Gold Plainclothesman, Glasses, Teeth and The Kid.

The movie, which opens today at neighborhood theaters, was written and directed by Walter Hill, who once wrote and directed a good movie, "Hard Times," with Charles Bronson. This one is not good. It is Awful Movie. It is Pretentious Movie. It is Silly Movie. It talks just like this.

According to the program notes, Mr. Hill thinks he is getting at "the muscle, the sinew, the tissue, the very nerve center of a getaway driver." It doesn't work, though. By stripping away the individual idiosyncracies, Mr. Hill simply lays bare The Cliché, and The Cliché is Horrendous, if sometimes horrendously funny.

Ryan O'Neal plays The Driver, who is supposed to be to getaway driving what Matisse was to scissors and colored paper. Not so. The Driver always does too much. He's too fancy. He's to getaway driving what Edgar Guest was to poetry. He doesn't know when to stop. Truly.

He couldn't put his car into a parking lot without attracting the attention of the sleepiest traffic cop. All those screaming accelerations, those two-wheel turns and those brake-slammings have less to do with effective getting away than with random self-expresssion. Having no role to act, Mr. O'Neal seems bewildered.

•

As The Detective, Bruce Dern snarls a lot, more or less repeating the rabbit-toothed psychotic he played in "Black Sunday" and "Coming Home," an unreliable fellow full of distress and possibly an upset stomach. Isabel Adjani, in her first (and possibly last) American film (Hollywood doesn't like a loser) is The Player, a beautiful young woman who means to be mysterious but more often may remind you of the trick-turning Barnard girls in Woody Allen's classic sketch, "The Whore of Mensa."

She wears her mouth turned down at both ends and generally affects the world-weary manner of a jaded comp-lit student who's been through it all — Cather, Hemingway, Fitzgerald, Dos Passos, Irwin Shaw and Harold Robbins.

For a movie in which there are so many chases, The Movie is singularly unexciting and uninvolving, though it does have its laughs.

•

I'm fascinated by Mr. Hill's way of emphasizing the peak emotional moment in a scene by having one character talk intently to the back of another character's head. And he must mean us to break up when Miss Adjani, trying to sneak into a busy railroad station to fetch a satchel full of stolen loot, appears wearing a black costume of such arresting style she'd stop the music at Studio 54.

Ronee Blakely, nominated for an Oscar after her fine performance in "Nashville," appears to no particular purpose in the throwaway role of The Connection, The Driver's business agent. She's not great.

1978 Jl 28, C8:3

Buddyhood of Surfing

BIG WEDNESDAY, directed by John Milius; written by Mr. Milius and Dennis Aaberg; director of photography, Bruce Surtees; edited by Robert L. Wolfe and Tim O'Meara; music by Basil Poledouris; produced by Buzz Feitshans; distributed by Warner Bros. At the Cinerama 2, Broadway and 47th Street, and other theaters. Running time: 125 minutes. This film is rated PG.

Matt	Jan-Michael Vincent
Jack	William Katt
Leroy	Gary Busey
Sally	Patti D'Arbanville
Peggy Gordon	Lee Purcell
Bear	Sam Melville

IT wasn't very long ago that John Milius's expensive, ambitious "Big Wednesday" was one of the more widely touted movies on the horizon, so what's it doing sneaking into Flagship theaters for only a week-long run? The honorable thing, that's what. "Big Wednesday" isn't even a tiny fraction of what it was once cracked up to be.

The surprise is not that Mr. Milius has made such a resoundingly awful film, but rather that he's made a bland one. Mr. Milius's reputation, after all, rests at least as heavily on his well-publicized walk-softly-and-carry-an-elephantgun world view as it does on his several screenplays and his direction of "Dillinger" and "The Wind and the Lion." So one might have supposed that "Big Wednesday," his epic about surfing and buddyhood, would have boasted at least enough trigger-happy machismo to make it controversial.

True, "radical" is something of a dirty word in the screenplay Mr. Milius co-wrote with Dennis Aaberg. And Jan-Michael Vincent, as one of the three legendary surfers a narrator describes as "the big names, the kings, our own royalty," has a strident hippie-baiting scene during the segment of the film that's set in 1968. Mr. Vincent, outraged to find that his favorite hangout now serves organic food instead of cheeseburgers, and that a waiter in a butterfly-patterned undershirt keeps calling him "brother," douses the incense on his table with water and cautions the waiter to turn down the music.

This, plus a scene that shows the three surfers quietly watching the Watts riots on television, is about as much of a nod "Big Wednesday" cares to give the real world.

But it's not just the film's rapt attention to wave patterns that makes it so emphatically all wet. Mr. Milius's three adventurers, whom we watch over the course of 12 years and still never get to know, have an unbecoming horror of growing up, not just of growing old. "It's really different here," gushes a girl from Chicago who is just becoming initiated to the glories of beach life in L.A. "Back home, being young was just something you'd do until you grew up. Here . . . it's everything!"

Being young means different things to our three respective heroes. For Leroy (Gary Busey), it's a chance to experience the joys of painting his torso with what looks like barbecue sauce and then trying to crawl into an oven. For Jack (William Katt), it's going to Vietnam for three years and then coming home expecting an old girlfriend to be a current girlfriend, even though he hasn't kept in close enough touch with her to find out she's now married. For Matt (Mr. Vincent), it means saying everying he needs to say through very careful flexing of the neck and the nostrils.

For all of them, being young means acquiring a kind of oral history of wavesmanship from a senior surfer named Bear. Bear tells his biggest, saddest story at a party early in the film, after everyone has finished pouring beer on everyone else's head. He

William Katt, Jan-Michael Vincent, Gary Busey in John Milius's "Big Wednesday": *"It isn't even a fraction of what it was once cracked up to be."*

tells his much too solemn audience about a time when "the water was hittin' the cliffs and splashin' 100 feet high — it was like the end of the world." A surfer disappeared that day, and "they never found his body — they just found little pieces of his board."

•

The movie often seems even more uneventful than material like this need make it, and Mr. Milius's attention to his actors focuses more closely on their pectorals than on their performances. He encourages such stiffness in his players that Barbara Hale, for instance, is quite unconvincing as Mr. Katt's mother. This is a faux pas of no mean eminence; after all, Miss Hale actually *is* Mr. Katt's mother.

The score for the film includes a number of hit songs from the early 60's, which makes the absence of any "surf music" of that period worth noting. Surely the Beach Boys or Jan and Dean were just as deeply in love with the sport as Mr. Milius, and for them, too, it had connotations of masculine daring. However, it also had a spirit of fun. And there's no room for real levity or pleasure in Mr. Milius's grim, dispirited and too often incoherent scheme of things.

"Big Wednesday" is rated PG ("Parental Guidance Suggested") apparently because its characters' pranks tend to be violent, and their language slightly rough.

JANET MASLIN

1978 Jl 28, C14:1

FILM VIEW

VINCENT CANBY

It Isn't Always the Star Who Carries the Film

Actors — God bless them. So far it's not been a great season for films but there have been compensations in a number of recent performances whose delights are real not only because they often are so unexpected. I mean, did you ever think you'd find Fernando Lamas being funny — intentionally? Well, in "The Cheap Detective," Neil Simon's feature-length spoof of "The Maltese Falcon" and some other Humphrey Bogart movies, Mr. Lamas is a model of straight-faced nonsense as he plays a dedicated Free French patriot whose mission during World War II is to open a French restaurant in Oakland. Mr. Lamas doesn't have to do much except look vaguely sorrowful, as if he'd just misplaced an entire nation, which is what he does to evoke in an instant the character played by Paul Henried in "Casablanca." His is not the most spectacular performance in "The Cheap Detective" but it is witty and aware and it gives resonance to the Simon comedy.

"The Cheap Detective," an entertaining parlor game of a movie, has virtually an all-star cast but two other contributions that must not be overlooked are those of Ann-Margret and Louise Fletcher. Ann-Margret is hardly an unknown comic quantity by this time. She's been raising the caret-count of all sorts of forgettable films for years, including Stanley Kramer's hilariously wrong-headed, well-meaning campus-revolution caper, "R.P.M." However, until Mike Nichols put her in "Carnal Knowledge" it wasn't apparent that she could do more than survive mediocre material. She could also illuminate material of substance. With her marvelously fake-classy English accent, she's one of the joys of Tony Richardson's "Joseph Andrews," while in "The Cheap Detective," playing a character named Jezebel Dezire, she comes across as a woman who has earned her letter-sweater as a femme fatale and isn't about to let anyone forget it. The comic secret: a kind of indefatigable sexiness. Ann-Margret simply will not rest.

• • •

The surprise of "The Cheap Detective," though, is Louise Fletcher, who won an Oscar for her performance in "One Flew Over The Cuckoo's Nest" but who has not, until now, been a threat to anyone's funnybone. In "The Cheap Detective" she does something that I never thought I'd live to see. She sends up Ingrid Bergman and all of those noble, brave, passionate, beautiful, self-denying heroines Miss Bergman has ever played, and she does it in a way that I would hope even Miss Bergman would find funny.

The comic conception, of course, is Neil Simon's. He has looked behind the mask of the goddess and discovered a lady who takes herself somewhat too seriously ("I'm very busy now," she says irritably, "I'm trying to run an underground") and, horror of horrors, is also a latent interior decorator. At one point when Miss Fletcher and the Bogart character, played by Peter Falk, are dreaming of the life they will never have together, she makes it clear that while he is anticipating romantic bliss, she is contemplating redoing his apartment in chintz. Miss Fletcher's steely resolve is terrifically engaging, and never for a moment betrayed by even a flicker of an eyelash.

"The Bad News Bears Go to Japan" is not a movie to see unless you're trapped on a trans-Atlantic flight and have gone through all available reading matter, including the timetables. Still, it's not without certain cinematic and historical interest since it more or less confirms Tony Curtis's new status as a first-rate character actor. Mr. Curtis is not so old that he has to play character roles, but I suspect that he is enjoying the possibilities of a wider range of roles, formally initiated with his fine performance as the impotent actor in "The Last Tycoon."

In "The Bad News Bears" he plays a fast-talking but remarkably unsuccessful Hollywood talent agent named Marvin Lazar, the fellow who latches onto the baseball team that calls itself the Bad News Bears, in the hopes of making his fortune on their trip to Japan. As played by Mr. Curtis, who must know Hollywood talent agents of every conceivable stripe, Marvin Lazar is a character of classic seediness and unreliability, someone who perhaps deserves an entire film to himself. Mr. Curtis doesn't have this film to himself. He has to share the screen with a bunch of foul-mouthed, scene-stealing kids, including one small, meltingly funny and serious black boy (Scoody Thornton), but he's ahead of everyone else by a mile. Some time has passed since his days as Universal's most hardworking juvenile but that time has been good to Mr. Curtis. His actor's intelligence has deepened while his energy is undiminished.

Mr. Curtis is not only the star of "The Bad News Bears Go to Japan," he's all there is to it. This is not the case of some other noteworthy performances of the season.

The personalities and talents of Peter Sellers and writer-director Blake Edwards pretty much define the course of "The Revenge of The Pink Panther," the fifth in their series of comedies about the magnificently flat-footed, bird-brained Paris detective, Inspector Clouzot. I've no doubt that Mr. Sellers and Mr. Edwards could make a funny Clouzot film with Sellers playing all the roles (which, knowing Mr. Sellers's innate modesty, I'm sure is an idea he's already entertained). That might be a mistake, however, if only for the fact that it would deprive us of the pleasures of Herbert Lom's contributions to the lunacy of the "Pink Panther" series.

As Chief Inspector Dreyfus, Clouzot's once-reasonable superior, Mr. Lom brings to these films a degree of mania that is in perfect contrast to the easy, totally misplaced self-assurance with which Clouzot goes about his bungling business. In the course of these films, Mr. Lom's Chief Inspector Dreyfus has evolved from essentially a straight-man into a first-rate comic character who, in "The Revenge of The Pink Panther," has one of the best scenes in the entire film. This is a memorial service for Clouzot at which the hardly grief-stricken Dreyfus must deliver a fulsome eulogy for his (everyone thinks) recently incinerated colleague; the act sends Dreyfus into paroxysms of hysterical laughter that are, of course, interpreted as the expressions of unrestrained grief.

• • •

Fourteen-year-old Tatum O'Neal, playing a girl who ages from 10 to 18 during the film, is very much the star of "International Velvet," Bryan Forbes's sequel to "National Velvet," and she is very, very good — straight-forward, direct, sometimes sweet and sometimes astonishingly grave. Yet the movie itself is so loaded with the tricks of cinema sentimentality the film seems hardly worthy of her performance. That is, until the appearance of Anthony Hopkins, who plays the tough, hard-driving trainer of the Olympic riding team to which Tatum aspires.

Mr. Hopkins contributes not only his own crisply efficient screen personality but also what sounds like his own dialogue. Mr. Forbes wrote the entire screenplay but I find it difficult to understand why approximately half the movie sounds like an eau de cologne ad and the rest of the language sounds so reasonably intelligent, brisk and to the point. It's a schism like this that makes one suspect — wrongly, in most cases — that actors have written their own dialogue. The answer in this case, I'm sure, is that Mr. Forbes wrote a better adventure melodrama than he did a love story, and he had the great good fortune to have an actor of Mr. Hopkins's talents in the film's better half.

Gary Busey has been around for some time, getting good, solid reviews in films like "The Last American Hero," "Thunderbolt and Lightfoot," "A Star Is Born" (as Kris Kristofferson's road manager) and, most recently, in "Straight Time," as Dustin Hoffman's junkie pal whose chicken-heart precipitates the tragic ending. Compared to his latest film, "The Buddy Holly Story," all of these earlier works are landmarks in movie history.

"The Buddy Holly Story," the life of the American rock and roll star who was killed in a 1959 plane crash, has the predictable shape and the skimpy look of an old B-picture, but it's the picture that will make Gary Busey a star. The movie isn't great but Mr. Busey's performance — much of it on stage, as he performs Holly's music with a somewhat reduced (from real life) group of two called The Crickets — is tremendous, full of drive, eccentric life and the sort of idiosyncracy that creates a screen personality the public will remember. "The Buddy Holly Story" should be Mr. Busey's breakthrough movie.

"Viva Italia," a nine-part sketch film from Italy, was directed by Dino Risi, Ettore Scola and Mario Monicelli, and stars Vittorio Gassman, Alberto Sordi and Ugo Tognazzi. Not all of the sketches are equally good but some are superb and Mr. Sordi is splendid. Yet the image you're likely to take away from the film, and maybe even be haunted by, is that of a small, resolute, wise old lady as, against her will, she accepts her fate and enters the dreadful retirement home to which he son and off-screen daughter-in-law have abandoned her.

The actual drop comes at the end of what the old lady had been led to believe would be a nice day in the country with her son. They've stopped for coffee and sodas. They've admired the foliage. The son, though trying always to be patient, lets it be known that he still resents the way his mother favored his brother. The old lady protests, but at a distance. It all seems so long ago, and if this son is a bit of an ass, he has done well in the world. That's the way things are.

The old lady is played by Emilia Fabi in a performance that might well be the breakthrough movie in her career if she still cared about such things. I doubt that she does, but it helps make "Viva Italia" one of the few memorable movie experiences of the summer to date. ■

1978 Jl 30, II:13:1

Culture Shock

INTERIORS, written and directed by Woody Allen; director of photography, Gordon Willis; edited by Ralph Rosenblum; produced by Charles H. Joffe; released by United Artists. At the Baronet Theater, Third Avenue and 59th Street. Running time: 99 minutes. This film is not rated.

Flyn .... Kristin Griffith
Joey .... Marybeth Hurt
Frederick .... Richard Jordan
Renata .... Diane Keaton
Arthur .... E.G. Marshall
Eve .... Geraldine Page
Pearl .... Maureen Stapleton
Mike .... Sam Waterston

By VINCENT CANBY

TO describe "Interiors" as Woody Allen's first serious drama is to stress the irrelevant. Mostly, though, it's to overlook the earnestness of all his comedies, from "Take the Money and Run" to "Annie Hall," as well as the upside-down gravity of his familiar comic locutions that shrink Large Subjects to takeout size. "There is no question that there is an unseen world," he once wrote in a trenchant essay titled "Examining Psychic Phenomena." "The problem is, how far is it from midtown and how late is it open?"

All of Mr. Allen's films have been serious to a certain degree, and they have been getting seriouser and seriouser as he has developed into one of America's most original, most personal, most audacious writer-directors. "Annie Hall" is a comedy of rare spirit, and it's as serious as any American film made in the last decade.

•

Rather than describe "Interiors" as his first serious drama, I think it's more precise to say that it's the first Woody Allen film that doesn't care to be funny. That's something else entirely.

"Interiors," which opens today at the Baronet, is a culture shock. Not to be prepared for it is to embark on a Miami Beach vacation having just taken a total immersion course in 17th-century English literature.

"Interiors" looks beautiful. It has been photographed by Gordon Willis in cool colors that suggest civilization's precarious control of natural forces.

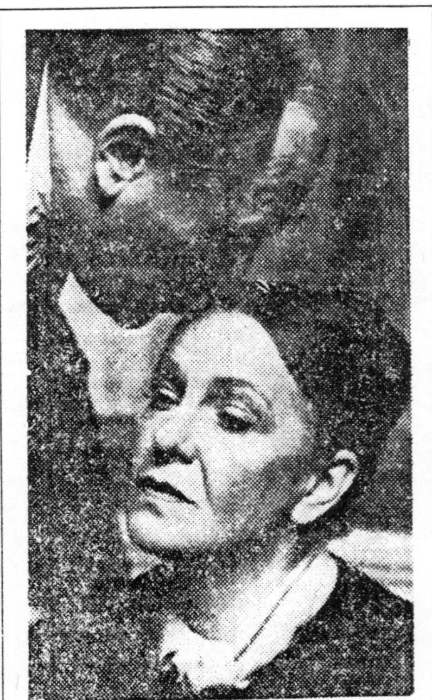

E.G. Marshall and Geraldine Page in "Interiors."

Woody himself is nowhere to be seen. It actually looks very much like an Ingmar Bergman film, and even sounds like one — the specific flatness of the Allen dialogue, its fondness for the jargon of the analysand, being the spoken equivalent to the not always inspired but perfectly functional English subtitles for Mr. Bergman's Swedish dialogue.

There is even something foreign about the members of the middle-class New York family who are the center of the drama. They seem as socially disconnected from the world around them as they are emotionally and psychically disconnected from themselves and from one another. It's not simply that the movie concentrates so intensely on its characters, but that there are virtually no other people in sight. We do see people passing in the street, in corridors, in cars on highways, and we see, one time each, a small child and a Protestant minister, but it still seems as if the family inhabited its own empty, very spooky universe.

"Interiors" is not inaptly titled. From the opening sequence, a series of shots looking out at the sea from the sparely furnished rooms of a large, handsome Long Island beach house, it's apparent that we are to be given a film about emotional drain, unfulfilled longings and vaguely defined fears — things that are never easy to describe and always difficult to dramatize. Mr. Allen's characters are in the furious grip of making do. They are seized — and sometimes overcome — by the need to accommodate the commonplace.

They are Renata (Diane Keaton), the eldest daughter who is identified as a successful poet, and her husband Frederick (Richard Jordan), who is an unsuccessful novelist; Joey (Marybeth Hurt), the youngest daughter, a failed artist and actress who'd like to write and who lives on scratchy terms with a film maker named Mike (Sam Waterston); Flyn (Kristin Griffith), the middle daughter, a successful actress who makes dopey television films; Eve (Geraldine Page), the mother of the girls, an interior decorator and a woman who remains on the edge of despair because her longtime marriage to Arthur (E.G. Marshall), a very rich lawyer, is coming apart, and Pearl (Maureen Stapleton), the buxom, warmhearted widow Arthur now wants to marry.

My problem with "Interiors" is that although I admire the performances and isolated moments, as well as the techniques and the sheer, headlong courage of this great, comic, film-making philosopher, I haven't any real idea what the film is up to. It's almost as if Mr. Allen had set out to make someone else's movie, say a film in the manner of Mr. Bergman, without having any grasp of the material, or first-hand, gut feelings about the characters. They seem like other people's characters, known only through other people's art.

Could it possibly be that "Interiors" is really a Brooklyn Jewish boy's fantasy about middle-class American Protestantism? But I'm not even sure whether the family in the movie is Protestant, Catholic or Jewish. They could be anything because they are placed in no identifiable social context, something that Mr. Bergman never has had to worry about (until "The Serpent's Egg") because he has always dealt with the terrors of a thoroughly homogenized society.

Miss Page, looking a bit like a youthful Louise Nevelson with mink-lashed eyes, is marvelous — erratically kind, impossibly demanding, pathetic in her loneliness and desperate in her anger. Miss Stapleton beautifully projects the tone and feelings of a sweet, robust, coarse woman who is never, never ridiculous. Mr. Marshall is also fine as the husband whose desperation matches his wife's, though it is disciplined by purpose. The other roles are more difficult to judge because the material is so nebulous.

Miss Hurt is very appealing as the youngest daughter who hates her mother and, thus, goes out of her way to convince herself she doesn't. Her feelings of creative impotence are also understandable, but I don't know what we are meant to feel for her when she writes in her diary, "Today I couldn't help experiencing a few nostalgic memories." She suddenly sounds like one of those humorless college types — a young woman who aspires to talk beyond her degree — that appear so frequently in Mr. Allen's written literature.

•

Mr. Waterston's role doesn't make any outrageous demands on him, but Mr. Jordan's unsuccessful novelist — as written — is very much the bearded, hard-drinking, tough-talking novelist that's been a Hollywood cliché since movies began to talk. He just writes for higher-toned periodicals (The New York Review of Books).

The most difficult role is Miss Keaton's. It's probably impossible to write or act convincingly a character who's supposed to be a successful poet. Just what constitutes success for a poet? Being published in The New Yorker? Winning famous awards (never mentioned in the film)? Not combing your hair and still looking great? Being miserable? From the dialogue and insights Mr. Allen gives her, Renata sounds as if she might really be quite a bad poet, at least when she goes on about being "hyper-aware of her body."

Though the movie looks beautiful, the elegant style occasionally works against it, showing it up. This happens in a striking close-up of Miss Keaton, sitting alone on a photogenically windswept ocean beach as she is supposed to be thinking sensitive poet-type thoughts. Yet the image is empty. It's not the actress. It's not the director, whose close-ups of Miss Keaton in

Diane Keaton, left, Kristin Griffith, center, and Marybeth Hurt in a scene from the film

"Annie Hall" burst with love, pride and affection. The movie that contains the image fails to invest it with any associations whatsoever.

1978 Ag 2, C15:1

Jaded Pooch

THE MAGIC OF LASSIE, directed by Don Chaffey; screenplay by Jean Holloway, Robert B. Sherman and Richard M. Sherman; story and music by Robert B. Sherman and Richard M. Sherman; produced by Bonita Granville Wrather and William Beaudine Jr.; released by Lassie Productions Inc. At Radio City Music Hall, 50th Street and Avenue of the Americas. Running time: 90 minutes. This film is rated G.
WITH: James Stewart, Mickey Rooney, Alice Faye, Pernell Roberts, Stephanie Zimbalist, Michael Sharrett, Lane Davies and Mike Mazurki.

By JANET MASLIN

"THE MAGIC OF LASSIE," the latest ill-advised lulu at the Radio City Music Hall, begins with a song. James Stewart, playing the newest of Lassie's kindly old grandpas, leads two children in a number about "that hometown feelin' " and how wonderful life's simple virtues are. But in a movie in which the local grocery is a supermarket, the old-timey furniture is straight out of a Sears catalogue and the "bricks" by the hearth look like wallpaper, this kind of sentimentality is genuinely distressing. If anything, "The Magic of Lassie" is a testament to the creeping modernization of just about everything worthwhile. Even Lassie, who used to be just a smart, good-hearted and very, very clean dog, has developed the jaded manner of a veteran movie star.

The ostensible villain of the piece is an evil zillionaire (Pernell Roberts), who means to steal Lassie, rename her "Heatherbelle," and annex Grandpa's land to his own vineyards. These lackluster ambitions give rise to a lackluster plot, but never mind — the real heavies are offscreen, creating a monster of a score. The songs, written by Robert B. Sherman and Richard N. Sherman, and sung by either Debby or Pat Boone, are not to be wished upon even that most cloying of creatures, the show-biz dog.

•

It's a well-known fact that Lassie, now a direct male descendant of the original male collie (female collies supposedly have less photogenic coats), has some very special talents. He/she has sixth, seventh and eighth senses when it comes to returning home or retrieving lost children and kittens. And he/she can understand remarks made in English, replying with a hearty "Bark, bark!" from time to time.

But until now, Lassie's gift for breaking into song (via voiceovers) had been largely unexploited. No more: This time, as Lassie wanders forlornly along a railroad track, Miss Boone supplies Lassie-ish thoughts in the background. Sample lyric: "I'm gonna get free by and by/ I'm gonna get my patch of the sky."

•

Then there are the numbers attributed to the little boy who has loved and (temporarily) lost his magical pet: "Lassie, my Lassie, I don't know why/ But Lassie, I can't say goodbye." And, most reprehensible of all, there is the episode in which Lassie, having of course run away from his/her wicked new master, stumbles across the entire Mike Curb congregation in a country field, just as they happen to be rehearsing a big banjo number.

To whom is all this a worse insult — the dog lover, the music lover, the child forced to sit through the film by a well-meaning relative, or the optimist who thought the Music Hall's reprieve might amount to something? Whatever your sentiments, the point is best argued at home.

1978 Ag 3, C15:1

EYES OF LAURA MARS, directed by Irvin Kershner; screenplay by John Carpenter and David Zelag Goodman; story by John Carpenter; director of photography, Victor J. Kemper; film editor, Michael Kahn; musical supervisor, Dr. Charles A. Koppelman; costumes designed by Theoni V. Alredge; gallery photographs by Helmut Newton; special photographic consultant, Rebecca Blake; produced by Jon Peters; released by Columbia Pictures. At the Coronet, Third Avenue and 59th Street and Lowe's State One, Broadway and 45th Street. Running time: 103 minutes. This film is rated R.

Laura Mars .... Faye Dunaway
John Neville .... Tommmy Lee Jones
Tommy Ludlow .... Brad Dourif
Donald Phelps .... René Auberjonois
Michael Reisler .... Raul Julia
Sal Volpe .... Frank Adonis
Michele .... Lisa Taylor
Lulu .... Darlanne Fluegel
Elaine Cassell .... Rose Gregorio

By JANET MASLIN

DEAD men in evening clothes; supine women guarded by sleek, ferocious dogs; upside-down corpses wearing garter-belts, with their hair and makeup in exquisite disarray — these are the tricks of Laura Mars's trade, the hallmarks that have established her as the New York fashion photographer who out-kinks them all. However, not everyone is a fan. Someone has gotten the notion that there's evil in Laura's work, he/she/it has decided to wipe out the photographer plus all her super-hyper-ultra chi-chi friends.

So far, very good indeed — especially because the "Eyes of Laura Mars" audience is given ample opportunity to share the killer's pique. Laura (Faye Dunaway), being much too self-involved an artiste to worry about the implications of her work, merely thinks of herself as someone who gives "an account of the times in which I'm living," times rife with "moral, spiritual and emotional murder."

•

Questions about the exploitative aspects of her art merely prompt Laura to snap, "Look, does anyone have anything *positive* to ask?" The models she works with are even more trendily blase.

These models are almost certainly being set up, deliciously, during the early parts of the film. They giggle, chew bubble gum, have pet teddy bears, don't seem to know when they're wearing clothes and when they aren't, and date rich idiots when they aren't making eyes at one another.

When Laura's whole crew is hauled into a police station for questioning, one of the girls is irate at being treated like a hooker, even though she's more than dressed for the part. Another merely complains of being bored.

•

A couple of Laura's shooting sessions, staged with a delightful blend of nonchalance and depravity, epitomize the wickedly satirical edge of this lively, high-toned thriller.

While two cars are aflame in Columbus Circle, and models in lingerie and fur coats prettily smack each other around, Laura, bless her creative little heart, is all business, solemnly snapping away in a Theoni Aldredge creation. Occasional cuts to spectators in the street make it clear that Laura may well have just arrived from the planet for which she is named, as far as workaday Joe or Joan America is concerned.

However, right in the middle of the session Laura has a psychic flash,

Faye Dunaway and Tommy Lee Jones in "Eyes of Laura Mars": *Cleverness that manifests itself in superlative casting and drily controlled direction.*

something that neither she nor the movie needs.

•

Laura can witness killings taking place across town, but only from the unseen killer's point of view — the better to forestall a surprise ending that is altogether dumbfounding (with the emphasis on dumb). These flashes leave her understandably frantic, but Laura has already been established as too much of an amoral flake to arouse much sympathy in her lady-in-distress capacity.

But forget the faltering finale, and never mind about a score that, although it includes Barbra Streisand's smashing rendition of the theme song, also makes the killer's forays even more ominously heralded than Bruce the Shark's.

It's the cleverness of "Eyes of Laura Mars" that counts, cleverness that manifests itself in superlative casting, drily controlled direction from Irvin Kershner, and spectacular settings that turn New York into the kind of eerie, lavish dreamland that could exist only in the idle noodlings of the very, very hip.

•

René Auberjonois brings his full supply of comic prissiness to the role of Miss Mars's principal artistic whatchamatcallit, and Raul Julia makes her ex-husband a brooding loon, hence a good suspect.

The best supporting performance comes from Brad Dourif (who played the young suicide in "One Flew Over The Cuckoo's Nest"), as an ex-con who epitomizes both the movie's taste for voyeurism and its essential seediness. Mr. Dourif, whose bedraggled appearance and half-unhinged manner make it hard to believe he would ever have been hired to carry Miss Mars's lens caps, has been given the job of chauffeur by Mr. Auberjonois, for shady reasons we will never know.

Mr. Dourif's awe and fear at what he witnesses during the course of a typical Mars day is the keenest commentary the movie has to offer. His tiniest gestures are noteworthy.

Miss Dunaway is perfect for her role, but it's beginning to look like the only role she cares to play.

•

Hysterical jitters, countered by fits of extreme hauteur or assertiveness, have constituted so many of her recent performances that it's hard to remember what else she can do. In any case, high-minded artistic fluttering — the kind Diane Keaton attempts in "Interiors" — comes so naturally to Miss Dunaway that Tommy Lee Jones, as a down-to-earth, soothing cop, is not just a good foil but an indispensable one. Without his stabilizing presence, the movie might well have turned into a "Network" set in the netherworld.

A footnote: Miss Dunaway has lately had to play some of the worst-written love scenes on the block, and "Laura Mars" gives her another clinker of this ilk. When she and Mr. Jones embrace at long last, she says "It's terrifying." He says "It's beautiful." She was right the first time.

1978 Ag 4, C10:1

Moviemaking Fun

HOOPER, directed by Hal Needham; screenplay by Thomas Rickman and Bill Kerby, story by Walt Green and Walter S. Herndon; director of photography, Bobby Byrne; edited by Donn Cambern; music by Bill Justis; produced by Hank Mooniean; released by Warner Bros. Inc. At the Cinerama Theater, Broadway and 47th Street and other theaters. Running time: 97 minutes. This film is rated PG.

Burt Reynolds and Sally Field in "Hooper": *Mr. Reynolds had made a movie to please fans of all persuasions, and to please them a great deal."*

Sonny Hooper	Burt Reynolds
Ski	Jan-Michael Vincent
Gwen	Sally Field
Jocko	Brian Keith
Max Berns	John Marley
Cully	James Best
Adam	Adam West
Tony	Alfie Wise
Roger Deal	Robert Klein

"SMOKEY AND THE BANDIT," the Burt Reynolds movie that "Hooper" both follows up and improves upon, was a nationwide blockbuster and a washout in New York. The audience for "Hooper" won't be so neatly divided, and it may even be just as big. Mr. Reynolds is one of the most effortlessly appealing movie stars around, but consolidating his following has always been a problem: There are fans who like to watch him tearing up the highway, and there are fans who enjoy his delightfully flippant self-mockery, with all the covert thoughtfulness it implies. This time, Mr. Reynolds has made a movie to please fans of all persuasions, and to please them a great deal.

The title character, whom Mr. Reynolds plays, is the greatest Hollywood stuntman of his generation. Accordingly, he is sandwiched between the battered, ex-greatest stuntman of the previous generation (Brian Keith) and a fancy young newcomer (Jan-Michael Vincent) eager to give the old boys a run for their money. Watching Mr. Vincent dive off a skyscraper, Hooper and a friend remark, with a characteristic blend of malice and merriment, "Well, we probably could've done that when we were his age — 'cept they didn't have buildings that high."

Hooper, who is working as stunt coordinator on a movie called "The Spy Who Laughed at Danger," sees retirement in the cards. So does his doctor: "If you were a horse, I'd shoot you," the doctor remarks, looking over the latest demolition job Hooper has done on his vertebrae. The presence of young, handsome and vigorous Mr. Vincent suggests the limitations time will impose on both Hooper's career as a glutton for punishment and Mr. Reynolds's as a matinee idol.

•

But the film, while pensive enough to hint at these things, isn't so morose that it cares to dwell on them. It's far more interested in demonstrating — very convincingly — that making a movie can be more fun than almost anything else in the world.

Mr. Reynolds and Hal Needham, who directed "Smokey and the Bandit," use the film-set milieu to generate some lovely in-jokes. At one point, Hooper is shown entertaining guests at a party with a reel of his favorite stunts, including some of Mr. Reynolds's own whitewater work in "Deliverance." The guests are fast asleep.

And then there is the highly unpopular director of the spy film, played with wonderfully humorless self-importance by Robert Klein. Concocting a finale that involves cars crashing into people in wheelchairs, buildings collapsing, explosions everywhere and a spectacular automobile jump across a river, the director is peeved to hear that his crew may not be able to execute all this. "I don't care, I want it!" he whines. "It's the ending I want. It's the statement I want to make." Later, when the elaborate scene is set up, Mr. Klein pronounces it to have "a nice grayness, like 'La Strada.'"

In another scene, Mr. Klein shrieks something about movies being "pieces of time." For anyone unfamiliar with the title of Peter Bogdanovich's book of critical essays, let's just say that Mr. Reynolds has got even for "Nickelodeon" and "At Long Last Love."

•

There is genuine humor and tenderness in Mr. Reynolds's romantic episodes with Sally Field, who plays Mr. Keith's very patient daughter, and there is real vitality in the large-scale action sequences. Also, Mr. Reynolds's generosity is particularly impressive. It's heartening to watch as scene-stealing an actor as Mr. Reynolds work this hard to make himself an ensemble player, just one of the boys.

•

"Hooper" is rated PG ("Parental Guidance Suggested"), largely because of the innocuous cussing that constitutes part of the stuntmen's camaraderie. JANET MASLIN

1978 Ag 4, C11:1

David Niven and Helen Hayes in the Walt Disney Production "Candleshoe."

Dickensian Disney

CANDLESHOE, directed by Norman Tokar; screenplay by David Swift and Rosemary Anne Sisson, based on the book "Christmas at Candleshoe" by Michael Innes; director of photography, Paul Beeson; film editor, Peter Boita; music by Ron Goodwin; produced by Ron Miller; released by Buena Vista. At the Coliseum, 181st Street and Broadway and other theaters. Running time: 90 minutes. This film is rated G.

Priory	David Niven
Lady St. Edmund	Helen Hayes
Casey	Jodie Foster
Bundage	Leo McKern
Cluny	Veronica Quilligan
Peter	Ian Sharrock
Anna	Sarah Tamakuni
Bobby	David Samuels
Jenkins	John Alderson
Mrs. McCress	Mildred Shay
Mr. McCress	Michael Balfour
Mr. Thresher	Sydney Bromley
Train Guard	Michael Segal
Grimsworthy	Vivian Pickles

IF this were a world of perfect logic, the arrival today in neighborhood theaters of "Candleshoe," the latest Walt Disney production, would be an occasion of calculable joy not among children but among the elderly.

For "Candleshoe," with its beguiling English countryside settings, languid pace, defanged Dickensian villains, compassionate butler, down-at-the-heels nobility, hidden treasure and orphaned children engaged in a plot to outwit swindlers, keep up appearances and save the old manor from foreclosure, is the fiction of a bygone era.

The chords it sounds, with its evocation of a world of stately homes, formal gardens, family heirlooms, titled women, eccentric ancestors, perfect servants, tea parties, steam engines and classic motorcars can resonate within an older generation in a way they never can among children whose cultural touchstones are more likely to run the gamut from Big Bird to The Hulk to John Travolta and the Bee Gees.

•

The values "Candleshoe" espouses — kindness, consideration, good manners, sacrifice for the sake of others, pluck in the face of odds — were, too, the overt moral currency of a society that long antedates Watergate, Koreagate and the Me Generation.

So entering the world of "Candleshoe," which is based on the Michael Innes novel, "Christmas at Candleshoe," is like taking a trip in a time machine. Within the terms of its plot, Jodie Foster, a delinquent foster child up to no good in the streets of Los Angeles, is whisked off to a Tudor mansion in Warwickshire, a journey that seems more a vault across generations than across distance.

There, ostensibly in league with a blustering villain inspired by Dickens and played by Leo McKern, she is to try to pass herself off as the long-missing marchioness, heir to the estate; and she is to endeavor to find a hidden treasure, whose existence is known only to McKern and Vivian Pickles, who portrays his sister, a servant discharged from Candleshoe.

•

And who should be the kindly current mistress of Candleshoe? Why none other than Helen Hayes, who has taken in a few orphans from the overcrowded local children's home. And who should be the perfect butler, the feisty Scottish gardener, the tippling chauffeur and the old colonel who takes tea with old Lady Gwendolyn? Not four people, but one — David Niven, doffing and donning wigs and mustaches and eyebrows and various articles of clothing in league with the orphans to keep Lady Gwendolyn from knowing that time and the taxman have reduced her circumstances to a point of peril.

The cast is beyond reproach. In this summer when Hollywood seems to have concluded that box-office magic lies in setting its best young actresses down in England, Miss Foster as Casey Brown easily keeps pace with Tatum O'Neal as Sarah Brown (could they be related?) in "International Velvet." Miss Hayes, Mr. Niven, Mr. McKern and Miss Pickles comport themselves with their customary professionalism.

There's a new Walt Disney movie in town. Kids, take grandma.

LAWRENCE VAN GELDER

1978 Ag 4, C12:1

A Double Debut

CORVETTE SUMMER, directed by Matthew Robbins; screenplay by Hal Barwood and Matthew Robbins; director of photography, Frank Stanley; editor, Amy Jones; music by Craig Safan; produced by Hal Barwood; A Metro-Goldwyn-Mayer production; released by United Artists. At the Trans Lux East, Third Avenue and 58th Street, and other theaters. Running time: 106 minutes. This film is rated PG.

Kenneth W. Dantley ..... Mark Hamill
Vanessa ..... Annie Potts
Ed McGrath ..... Eugene Roche
Wayne Lowry ..... Kim Milford
School Principal ..... Richard McKenzie
Police Public Relations ..... William Bryant
Gil ..... Philip Bruns
Kootz ..... Danny Bonaduce

THERE isn't a line in "Corvette Summer" that doesn't read better than it plays. It's not just that Hal Barwood and Matthew Robbins, who make their respective producing and directing debuts, are best known as the screenwriting team responsible for "The Sugarland Express," "MacArthur" and "Bingo Long"; it's that they overstage scenes in a way they'd never dream of overwriting them.

The central portion of "Corvette Summmer," set in Las Vegas with an "Alice in Wonderland" air, has a visual zaniness that meshes effectively with the script. But for the most part, the movie takes a slender, boyish conceit — of the sort that is suddenly so popular among Hollywood's current batch of boy wonders — and invests it with silliness rather than whimsy.

Mark Hamill pursues a stolen sports car in "Corvette Summer"
Conceived in a sophisticated spirit and then clumsily translated

Ostensibly, this is the story of a boy (Mark Hamill) and his car (a lovingly customized Corvette). In fact, it is the picaresque saga of a crazy, hopeless search, once the car is stolen and the boy sets out to recover it.

The premise is not unlike that of "The Sugarland Express," in which a mother embarked on a long journey to recover her child, traveling across a landscape that seemed increasingly mad as the trip wore on. But Mr. Barwood and Mr. Robbins brought a wisdom to that earlier script that they deliberately eschew here, in the interests of a brand of juvenilia that simply doesn't suit them.

•

"Hal and I really aren't into cars, but we felt the Corvette was the perfect symbol for our story and our hero," Mr. Robbins is quoted as saying in production notes for the film. That's the trouble, right there: The movie seems to have been conceived in a fairly sophisticated spirit and then clumsily translated into kiddie-ese.

Mr. Hamill, who had just the right insistent innocence for "Star Wars," is this time obliged to affect a naïveté that would be unconvincing in a tiny child. Annie Potts, as a would-be call girl he meets along his way, has Goldie Hawn's loopiness without the charm.

Miss Potts may well be a gifted comedienne, but Mr. Robbins never lets her relax enough for the talent to show. Too often, he strains his actors' enthusiasm to the breaking point.

Still, the middle of the movie is appealing, for anyone who can tolerate a mirthlessly nutty beginning and an ungainly shoot-'em-up finale. In Las Vegas, the half-mad buoyancy of Mr. Hamill's search for a four-wheeled Holy Grail finds an appropriately sunbaked setting, and Mr. Robbins's direction tackles pop culture with a gusto that resembles his hero's. It's a pity that the segment of the film that finally achieves a cockeyed conviction is so short-lived.

JANET MASLIN

1978 Ag 4, C13:3

FILM VIEW

VINCENT CANBY

Woody Allen: Risking It Without Laughs

With the possible exception of Mark Twain, there have been very few first-rate comic writers who have been as much appreciated in their own day as they have been later. Only recently have the early comic novels of Evelyn Waugh been recognized as the works of art they are, while "Brideshead Revisited," originally hailed as being far more serious than "Decline and Fall," "Vile Bodies" and "A Handful of Dust," now seems comparatively fat, overwrought if not overwritten. "The Importance of Being Earnest" is one of the greatest plays written in the English language in the last hundred years, and though it was a huge success at the time it was originally produced, few people dared to acknowledge its profound brilliance. Oscar Wilde, after all, made jokes about his genius.

Humor, although an extra dimension of awareness and another perspective on human experience, is always suspect, even to those who deal in it, perhaps because it's spontaneous and because it tends to disappear under analysis. That may be why one of our most perceptive humorists, Woody Allen, has now turned to "serious drama" in his new film "Interiors." Although Woody has been promising us a serious drama for some time, "Interiors" comes as a surprise.

I emphasize the word surprise. "Interiors" is something you have to adjust to. It's a disappointment to me, I admit, but it's a failure only if you insist that Woody forever make spin-offs of his earlier comedies. By talent, prodigious energy and singularly fortunate economic circumstances, Mr. Allen is entitled the freedom to push into new areas of filmmaking, and "Interiors" is nothing if not a new area of filmmaking for him. It's an intelligent, beautifully composed and acted movie about the anxieties and panics that he has previously coped with comically, by shouting the names of those fears in the dark, thus to make them disappear. It's peopled by characters ravaged by doubts and self-delusions of the sort he ordinarily finds so funny, but "Interiors" is not funny, and because it's not funny, something vital seems to be missing. It's as if we can only hear one-half of a two-way conversation. The characters are so humorless, so solemn, they could have been lobotomized.

They pass through the rooms of their lives like underwater divers wearing old-fashioned, heavy-booted diving suits with helmets that look like steel-reinforced fishbowls. Nothing comes easy to them, be it a smile or the jargon of the analysand. Every step requires special effort and concentration. Though the movements are graceful, they suggest exhaustion. The characters in Woody's science-fiction comedy, "Sleeper," possessed the buoyancy of helium-filled balloons. Like the inhabitants of a very small planet, they bounced as they walked. The characters in "Interiors" are waterlogged with angst.

They include Renata (Diane Keaton), a beautiful, very intense young woman who writes poetry that's published in The New Yorker and who is in analysis, and her two sisters, Flyn (Kristin Griffith), the youngest of the three, a successful television actress who resembles a miniaturized Dyan Cannon, and Joey (Marybeth Hurt), who is very sweet and as intense as Renata but who is driven by a furious unfulfilled need to be — as she puts it more than once — "creative."

Joey makes life difficult for Mike (Sam Waterston), the filmmaker she lives with, by complaining about her inability to create ("What happens to those who can't create when they're overwhelmed with feelings?"). Renata, in turn, bugs her husband, Frederick (Richard Jordan), by being all too creative, while he, a writer of novels that get published but don't sell, is reduced to writing mean-spirited reviews for The New York Review of Books. "Sometimes," Frederick says in dispair, after writing a particularly nasty review of a friend's book, "my anger frightens me."

The family circle is completed by their parents: Eve (Geraldine Page), an apparently fashionable but emotionally unreliable interior decorator who tends to say things like "I thought we had agreed the paler tones would make a warmer statement," and Arthur (E.G. Marshall), a successful lawyer who, mild-mannered and kind as he is, upsets the equilibrium by announcing one morning at breakfast that he wants a separation, which becomes a prelude to a second marriage. The most vital and believable character in the entire film is Arthur's intended, Pearl, a good-hearted, none-too-bright widow played with enormous humanity and humor by Maureen Stapleton.

Because in his writings ("Getting Even" and "Without Feathers") and in his earlier films Mr. Allen has developed into a superb social satirist as well as parodist, it's difficult to watch much of "Interiors" — and especially to listen to it — without anticipating and hoping for the perspective of the Woody Allen humor. "What happens to those who can't create when they're overwhelmed with feelings?" is something that the endearing Annie Hall might say, perfectly aware that as she's asked the question, she's answered it. Because nobody in "Interiors" is especially gifted with such insights, they are not only not very endearing but also so dense that it's hard to believe that any of them could write even an unsuccessful novel, much less a successful poem.

They go at each other with vocabularies learned on the couch. "Why do you keep pushing me away?" Joey asks Renata at one point, although Renata hasn't actually pushed her away but simply avoided what she knows would be an unpleasant scene.

Though it took great courage to make "Interiors," given Woody's comic reputation, the movie he's made seems inhibited, something done with one hand tied behind his back, which is not to say that the film doesn't have its fine moments. A scene in which Arthur pleads with his middle daughter to show some kindness to her new stepmother is full of unexpected anguish that is very real. Arthur and Pearl's wedding reception, with only his daughters and their men in attendance, is both bleak and funny in a seemingly spontaneous way that is missing from most of the rest of the movie.

Two sequences with Miss Page are among the memorable things of this film season — the one in which the camera catches her confused reactions as her husband cooly announces his plans for a separation, and the other, which is virtually a subliminal shot, showing the actress in three-quarters profile, sitting in a darkened room, sipping white wine and watching a Christian revivalist on television. This is one way the world can end.

It's no accident, I think, that the greatest filmmakers are often the most prolific. I think immediately of the early Godard and the current Altman and Truffaut. Woody Allen now belongs in this group, and of this group I can't think of another filmmaker who has taken a risk comparable to that taken by Woody with "Interiors." It's not a success in itself, but it's of incomparable value to our knowledge of him and what he's up to. Among other things, "Interiors" must demonstrate for us, once and for all, just how close to Woody's skin have been all those marvelous nuts of his earlier films, from Virgil Starkwell in "Take the Money and Run" to Alvy Singer in "Annie Hall." He's always taken them with utmost seriousness, as he does the characters in "Interiors." The only difference is that now there's no laughter to confuse us. ■

1978 Ag 6, II:1:5

Due to a strike, *The New York Times* was not published from August 10 through November 5. The following reviews are reprinted from *The New York Times News Service.*

NEA, directed by Nelly Kaplan; scenario and adaptation by Nelly Kaplan and Jean Chapot; director of photography, Andreas Winding; edited by Helene Plemiannikov and Catherine Dubeau. Released by Libra. Running time: 101 minutes. This film is rated R.

Axel Thorpe	Samy Frey
Sybil Ashby	Ann Zacharias
Helen Ashby	Micheline Presle
Judith Ashby	Francoise Brion
Philip Ashby	Heinz Bennent
Anne	Ingrid Caven
Benito	Robert Freitag
Florence	Chantal Bronner
Raphael	Martin Provost

By HAROLD C. SCHONBERG

The subtitle of Nelly Kaplan's new French film, "Nea," which opens Friday in New York, is "A New Woman." Miss Kaplan is an Argentine-born film director who has worked in Paris since 1954, and whose documentaries on Picasso, Gustave Moreau and Andre Masson have attracted a good deal of attention. So did her first film, "A Very Curious Girl," which was released last year.

That film was a study of youth in revolt, and so is "Nea," Miss Kaplan is quoted as saying that Sybille Ashby, the heroine of "Nea, expresses her own feelings of revolt. Sybille "must be radical, otherwise you're shot.... Sybille represents those who do not feel guilty, the equals of the other half of humanity. Woman is a totality. My totality."

So it will come as no surprise that "Nea," which incidentally is the title of a pornographic book written by Sybille, is one of those currently fashionable films that looks at the plight of contemporary woman in a male society.

Let's take a peek at this young lady who is Miss Kaplan's heroine.

Sybille is a 16-year old kleptomaniac, an arsonist, a voyeur, a liar, a rotten spoiled kid in a rich family, a pornographer, a venomous little bitch who frames a man for rape.

But we're supposed to identify with her, even admire her, because she's in "revolt," because she is the "victim" of all that is bad in today's male society with its hypocritical values, and also because she is the victim of an unhappy family life.

But this is sloppy thinking and, as it turns out, also bad art. To take a rich, spoiled, unlovely, emotionally rotten young woman and make her the symbol of a worldwide movement (Women's Lib) makes as much sense as casting Yasir Arafat as a romantic lead. It may be that Miss Kaplan wants us to see Sybille as a young person standing up to the inequities of present-day society. But what emerges in this film is a mean, petty, sullen, untalented girl with very little to recommend her.

At the end, Sybille and her lover are reunited in one of the more unlikely sequences of a cynical film, and there is some unconscious humor here. Sybille may be in revolt, but that is not going to deprive her of the good things in life. Before she and her lover drift down a river, presumably to a happy life together, she thoughtfully takes with her close to $1 million in cash from the earnings of her pornographic novel.

This film is not for the kiddies. There are some very explicit sexual scenes. These are as phony and calculated as the rest of the film. There are good performances by Ann Zacharias as Sybille, Samy Frey as her lover, Micheline Presle, Francoise Brion and Heinz Bennent. Miss Zacharias, a 22-year old Swedish actress, is a radiant beauty who deserves better material. Even she looks uncomfortable at times at the antics that Miss Kaplan has asked her do.

1978 Ag 19

GIRLFRIENDS, produced and directed by Claudia Weill; screenplay by Vicki Polon, based on a story by Claudia Weill and Vicki Polon; co-producer, Jan Saunders; director of photography, Fred Murphy; music by Michael Small; art director, Patrizia von Brandenstein; edited by Suzanne Pettit. Released by Warner Bros. Running time: 87 minutes. This film is rated PG.

Susan Weinblatt	Melanie Mayron
Anne Munroe	Anita Skinner
Rabbi Gold	Eli Wallach
Eric	Christopher Guest
Martin	Bob Balaban
Julie	Gina Rogak
Ceil	Amy Wright
Beatrice	Viveca Lindfors
Abe	Mike Kellin

By HAROLD C. SCHONBERG

The girlfriends are named Susan Weinblatt and Anne Munroe, and they live in New York. Susan is Jewish, very much so, and as often as not there is "Fiddler on the Roof" kind of music when she appears on the stage. That's so you will not forget. Anne is Gentile, a SOI DISANT poet, ambitious but not very talented. For her we get a sort of neo-baroque music. They share a flat together, but soon Anne goes off to marriage and a child. Susan goes on living alone.

Nothing much happens in "Girlfriends." Nothing much is supposed to happen. "Girlfriends," the first feature film of Claudia Weill, now playing here, is a study of loneliness and alienation. Susan is a photographer trying to make it. She works with a rabbi on bar mitzvahs and weddings, but she is an artist and she desperately wants recognition, exposure, a show, anything. So she knocks on doors, hoping, hoping, hoping.

She is a sensitive girl who needs affection and love. But God has not been kind to her; she is not very attractive, and male eyes do not turn when she walks down the street. Even her girlfriend, with a new life of her own, drifts away. Other people appear and vanish. She has an affair; it is not very satisfactory. She finally gets a show. Even that, the great moment of her life, has aphids in the roses; happiness and Susan Weinblatt do not go together.

It's all very sad and, at its core, rather sentimental. But Claudia Weill keeps the film from degenerating into pathos. Any big city is full of sad, unfulfilled girls who lead desperately lonely and frightened lives. Miss Weill does not belabor the point, though every now and then she takes a cheap shot at the audience's emotions. For the most part, however, this is a slice-of-life cinema, realistically acted and filmed, with a good deal of charm under the quiet desperation.

Most of the charm comes from Melanie Mayron as Susan. With her halo of frizzled hair, her marvelously intelligent and expressive face, her blundering coping with life, her hesitant and repressed gestures, comes a total characterization. The young lady is a brilliant actress.

But everybody in the cast is also good. Anita Skinner as Anne has temperament and a character of her own. Eli Wallach is an urbane rabbi who befriends Susan and has one or two decidedly unrabbinical ideas about her. Christopher Guest as Eric comes into Susan's life as a lover, and then they break up. It's a man's world. At the end he turns up; perhaps they will get together again. Perhaps not. In the short role of a gallery owner, Viveca Lindfors turns in the sharp characterization expected from so fine an actress. In its quiet way, "Girlfriends" is an appealing film, done with unusual expertise and sympathy.

1978 Ag 19

HAZEL'S PEOPLE, written and directed by Charles Davis, based on the novel by Merle Good; produced by Burt Martin; director of photography, Stan Martin; music composed by Bill Loose; lyrics by Robert Fillies; costumes by Phyllis Good; sound by Robert Janus; edited by Erwin Dumbrille. Released by A People's Place. Running time: 105 minutes. This film is rated PG.

Anna Witmer	Geraldine Page
Eli	Pat Hingle
Eric	Graham Beckel
Hazel	Rachel Thomas
Jim Witmer	Steve Weaver
Rufus	Elvin Byler
Sarah	Noreen Huber
Ben	John Miller
Menno Witmer	Luke Sickle

By HAROLD C. SCHONBERG

Set a hippie type from New York into the Mennonite region of Pennsylvania. Pretty idea, no? The clash of two cultures, mutual suspicion and hostility, the soil versus the city, conservatism versus liberalism.

All this is explored in "Hazel's People," which opens Thursday at the New Yorker Theater. It is slowly, slowly explored, so that everybody will get the message. It has high inspirational moments, with wise, homespun philosophy, and it tries to be fair to all sides. The result is a perfectly dreadful film.

Presumably the idea behind "Hazel's People" is to show that in an imperfect world there is bound to be injustice. The simple, God-fearing Mennonites are anything but angels; the snake of intolerance crawls in that particular Eden, too. Two polarities are set up, and at the end one proves stronger than the other. Hippie and Mennonites learn from each other, but it is the hippie who turns out to be the better human being and the better Christian. Off he goes to fight for justice, wiser from his experience.

The trouble with "Hazel's People," among many other things, is the way the situations are set up. The conversion of the hippie is as hard to believe as it is to take. Motivations are simply scrapped for the sake of the story line. Soon the film degenerates into a stort of Disney Americana extravaganza, in which the all-American boy, now shorn of his hippie locks, smiles dimpled smiles and walks around looking worried and sensitive.

Despite the good intentions of the film, it cannot be taken seriously. Characters are one-dimensional throughout, symbols rather than real people. The responsibility can be placed on Charles Davis, who directed the film and wrote the screenplay based on Merle Good's novel, "Happy as the Grass Was Green."

This is Davis's first major film, and he has not been able to rise above stereotypes. Even the musical background is stereotyped, with a theme song blaring forth the Message.

There are some good actors and actresses in the film, notably Geraldine Page as the mother. She spends most of her time looking sad and wistful. Pat Hingle as the minister is so sturdy, so Rock-of-Gibraltar in his faith, so understanding of man's foibles, so utterly good, that you want to throttle him.

The leading role of the hippie is taken by Graham Beckel, a personable youngster who has an impossible role. There is no room for subtleties in this film, and all he can do is try to bring a modicum of dignity to the part, which he does when the direction allows him to do so. Steve Weaver, Elvin Eyler, Noreen Huber, John Miller and Luke Sickle turn in fine performances as assorted Mennonites. But it's all in a lost cause.

1978 Ag 24

WHO'LL STOP THE RAIN, directed by Karel Reisz; screenplay by Judieth Rascoe and Robert Stone, based on Mr. Stone's *Dog Soldiers;* produced by Herb Jaffe and Gabriel Katzka; director of photography, Richard H. Kline; music by Laurence Rosenthal; production designer, Dale Hennesy; set designer, Dianne Wager; costume designer, Wiliam Theiss. Released by United Artists. Running time: 126 minutes. This film is rated R.

Ray Hicks .... Nick Nolte
Marge Converse .... Tuesday Weld
John Converse .... Michael Moriarty
Antheil .... Anthony Zerbe
Danskin .... Richard Masur
Smitty .... Ray Sharkey
Charmian .... Gail Strickland
Eddie Peace .... Charles Haid
Bender .... David Opatoshu
Angel .... Joaquin Mattinez
Gerald .... James Cranna
Jody .... Timothy Blake
Janey .... Shelby Balik
Edna .... Jean Howell
Galindez .... Jose Carlos Ruiz
Alex .... John Durren
Hippie .... Bobby Kosser
Marine Driver .... Wings Hauser
Marine .... Jonathan Banks
Blinded Man .... Michael Bair
Soldier .... Derrel Maury
Mother .... Jan Burrell
Father .... Stuart Wilson
Helicopter Pilot .... James Gavin
Radio Operator .... Bill Cross

By HAROLD C. SCHONBERG

It's an unpleasant bunch of characters in "Who'll Stop the Rain," which opened Aug. 25 here. The hero is an ex-marine who has smuggled in a kilo of heroin from Vietnam and is determined to handle the sale by himself. The heroine is a dope addict. There is a pair of sadistic goons determined to get their hands on the goods. There is the husband of the heroine, a sensitive schnook who initiates the smuggling plan in the first place. There is a bent FBI official, who orders life taken with the nod of his head.

Probably "Who'll Stop the Rain" intended to give an idea of the drug generation during the Vietnam war. But what this rather incoherent film really is all about is superman. The hero even reads Nietzsche. He is a tremendous hunk of man, a killer animal in the jungle, as fierce as a tiger, as suspicious as one, as quick in his reflexes. As such he is an archetypal figure. Like all archetypes, he does not have to be explained, though he does spout something about being tired of being pushed around by inferior men. Nietzsche would have approved.

The film starts in Vietnam, where a reporter makes a deal to get the heroin into the United States. He asks his friend Ray Hicks—the role played by Nolte—to smuggle it in on his ship. Hicks does so, only to walk into a trap. He and his friend have been set up. It's rather confusing; the film never explains just why the frame took place, and it ends up a clumsy device to start the chase sequences. Hicks grabs his friend's wife and starts running, with the goons just behind.

There's not much convincing characterization in "Who'll Stop the Rain," and some of the plot elements do not hang together. The entire film is an excuse to encompass near-mythic elements in one figure—the superman who is willing to take anybody on despite the odds. It is not exactly a new concept. John Wayne has been doing it for years. The difference here is that the hero, not on the side of the angels, is a reflection of an entirely different set of standards. Today's moral values have shifted, and in some circles it is considered admirable to be on the wrong side of society. As Ray Hicks is. As his friend John Converse is—though at the very end John displays redeeming social values.

There is nothing wrong with the acting. Nolte does his job with a great deal of physical panache, and this film might well make him a star. Michael Moriarty as his friend John starts out as a weakling who finds himself a man, and even has a bit of puckish humor under great stress. He is an excellent actor. Anthony Zerbe is smooth and deadly as can be as the mysterious FBI man; and his two venomous sidekicks, Richard Masur and Ray Sharkey, have juicy parts that they play with relish. Their type of character can be encountered in any number of films along this line, but that does not detract from the real skill they bring to the roles of Danskin and Smitty. Only Tuesday Weld as Marge Converse is a bit weak; her projection is rather negative, her movements too carefully studied. "Who'll Stop the Rain" is no great shakes and it breaks no new paths, but if it's action you're after, the film will sweep you along.

1978 Ag 26

The Opium Wars

By HAROLD C. SCHONBERG

In recent years, the People's Republic of China has made virtually no films. Material shown in the movie houses in China are generally propaganda films about the evil West that are made in North Korea. Thus it is of unusual interest that a Chinese film made only a few years ago has just opened at the Guild Theater here. It never was shown in its own country. Chiang Ching, the wife of Chairman Mao, suppressed it for ideological reasons.

The film is named "Lin Tse-hsu," after the leading character, and it is subtitled "The Opium Wars."

Naturally, it is all propaganda; the film is in color, but its characters are black and white. The heroes, those who want to rid China of the opium trade about 150 years ago, are all impossibly noble, heroic and honest, with penetrating eyes looking into the future vision of a New China. The villains, to a man, are evil, slinking cowards, wiped out by the gallantry of the Chinese workers, peasants and soldiers.

This is not a good film, alas. Technically it is poor, with washed-out color and badly handled transitions. The plot has the usual stereotyped situations. Toward the end, there are some battle scenes that go back to D.W. Griffith and Eisenstein, though entirely without the realism and genius of "Birth of a Nation" or "Potemkin." The stagings are too clumsy, the confrontations too pat and the Chinese have a very funny idea of British soldiers on the march in the 1840's.

At least there is one very good actor in Lin Tse-hsu. Cao Tan, described as China's most important film star, acts the hero with a quality of strength and dignity that transcends the wretched material. A product of an old tradition, he uses wonderfully stylized gestures that have pronounced mimetic elements and his face is capable of extraordinary shades of expression. Everybody else in the cast suggests a poster, but not Chao.

The dialogue, of course, is in Chinese. There are subtitles in English. The music combines Russian Socialist Realism of the Khachaturian sort with more traditional pentatonic Chinese melodies. There are some pretty views of Canton, where most of the action takes place and the camera even takes us into the Emperor's room in the Forbidden City. Bad as the film is, it is exotic and does have curiosity value, like a two-headed calf.

1978 Ag 29

DAYS OF HEAVEN, written and directed by Terrence Malick; produced by Bert and Harold Brackman; director of photography, Nester Almendros; additional photography by Haskell Wexler; music composed and conducted by Ennio Morricone; art director, Jack Fisk; costumes by Patricia Norris; edited by Billy Weber. Released by Paramount Pictures. Running time: 92 minutes. This film is rated PG.

Bill .... Richard Gere
Abby .... Brooke Adams
The Farmer .... Sam Shepard
Linda .... Linda Manz
The Farm Foreman .... Robert Wilke
Linda's Friend .... Jackie Shultis
Mill Foreman .... Stuart Margolin
Harvest Hand .... Tim Scott
Dancer .... Gene Bell
Fiddler .... Doug Kershaw
Vaudeville Leader .... Richard Libertini
Vaudeville Wrestler .... Frenchie Lemond
Vaudeville Dancer .... Sahbra Markus
Accountant .... Bob Wilson
Headmistress .... Muriel Jolliffe
Preacher .... John Wilkinson
Farm Worker .... King Cole

By HAROLD C. SCHONBERG

Some years ago Terrence Malick produced, wrote and directed "Badlands," a film that created a certain stir. Now comes "Days of Heaven," which opened here. It stars Richard Gere, Brooke Adams, Sam Shepard and Linda Manz; it obviously has cost a lot of money; it is full of elegant and striking photography; and it is an intolerably artsy, artificial film.

At the beginning, it is as though this is going to be a film about European immigrants in the early days of President Wilson's presidency. Then it switches to the Texas Panhandle, where the buffalo roam and the deer and the antelope still play. Migrant workers, fleeing the big cities, help reap the wheat harvest of young, wealthy farmer. There are all kinds of special effects, including a plague of locusts and a prairie fire. There is a romance, in which the girlfriend of a young worker, who poses as his sister, marries the farmer. What results is jealousy and murder.

But "Days of Heaven" never really makes up its mind what it wants to be. It ends up something between a Texas pastoral and "Cavalleria Rusticana." Back of what basically is a conventional plot is all kinds of fancy, self-conscious cineaste techniques. The film proceeds in short takes: people seldom say more than two or three connected sentences. It might be described as the mosaic school of film-making as the camera and the action hop around, concentrating on a bit here, a bit there.

A young girl named Linda Manz — and a talented young lady she is—has a prominent part of the action. The voice-over that constantly runs through the film is hers; she comments on the action, something in the manner of a Greek chorus. The photography, beautiful as some of it is, is as self-conscious as the rest of the film. People are carefully arranged, frames are carefully composed; there are more silhouettes than in an old nickelodeon.

Anyway, the old cars, and the biplane and triplane in an airplane sequence are fun.

A competent group of actors tries to deal with the farrago. Richard Gere, looking as though the genes of the young Gregory Peck and Montgomery Clift have gotten mixed up, gives a sturdy performance as Bill, even if he is too sophisticated to give the impression of a migrant worker.

Sam Shepard has the part of the farmer. He is the well-known playwright, the author of such interesting works as "Mad Dog Blues" and "Operation Sidewinder." This appears to be his first acting assignment in a film. He has a tall, rangy figure, a broodingly intense quality, and his work comes as a welcome surprise.

Brooke Adams, as Abby, the hero's girlfriend, is not a conventionally pretty girl. She has something better: an elfin quality, a wonderfully expressive face, an ability to project. But the one who really steals the show is little Miss Manz, in her first film. She comes from New York is 17, looks 16, acts in an unselfconscious manner, and nonchalantly takes in stride any crazy hop made by the football of life. She will have a big future. The minor roles in "Days of Heaven" are in good hands. But nobody can really overcome the nature of the material.

1978 S 14

NO TIME FOR BREAKFAST, directed by Jean-Louis Bertucelli; screenplay, originally titled *Docteur Françoise Gailland,* by Andre G. Brunelin and Jean-Louis Bertucelli, based on the book *Un Cri* by Noëlle Loriot; produced by Yves Gasser; director of photography, Claude Renoir; music by Catherine Lara, arranged by Del Newman; edited by François Ceppi. Released in Paris by Filmedis; distributed in the U.S. by Daniel Bourla Film Enterprises. Running time: 100 minutes. This film is not rated.

François Gailland . . . . . Annie Girardot
Daniel Letesier . . . . . Jean-Pierre Cassel
Gerard Gailland . . . . . François Perrier
Elisabeth Gailland . . . . . Isabelle Huppert
Julien Gailland . . . . . William Coryn
Genevieve Lienard . . . . . Suzanne Flon
Fabrienne Cristelle . . . . . Anouc Fergac
Regis Chabret . . . . . Michel Subor
Helene Varese . . . . . Josephine Chaplin
Jean Rivemale . . . . . Andre Falcon
Raymonde . . . . . Jacqueline Doyen
Françoise's mother . . . . . Margolion
Dr. Sexoux ("Lulu") . . . . . Jacques Richard

By CHRISTOPHER LEHMANN-HAUPT

There's no disputing it: Annie Girardot is marvelous in Jean-Louis Bertucelli's new film, "No Time for Breakfast," which opened here Friday. As Docteur Francoise Gailland—which, incidentally, is the original French title of the film, far more apt than the farcically tinted one under which it has been released in this country—she projects at least a dozen dimensions of humanity as she makes her hospital rounds, steals a night off to spend with her lover, tries to soothe her troubled teenage son and daughter, and meshes the gears of her frantic life with those of her stolid bourgeois husband.

And, of course, her story—based on "Un Cri," the memoirs of a French cancer-research specialist—is irresistably touching. It is as if a grown-up had re-imagined "Love Story" and filmed it in the colors of reality instead of a hazy sentiment. The cancerous growth that develops in Dr. Gailland's lung is not gratuitous: she smokes too much; she exists in a perpetual state of crisis trying to reconcile her professional life and her private one.

Even in the face of Susan Sontag's denials, it is hard not to see her illness as a metaphor of something rotten in her state—perhaps the hypocrisy of her keeping up appearances, which so infuriates her children.

But neither an outstanding acting performance nor sure-fire pathos is enough by itself to sustain a film. What makes "No Time for Breakfast" consistently effective is the way Bertucelli has knit together the last obvious elements of the movie—how he exploits the cold and ominous machinery of the modern hospital, for instance, (there is a wrenching scene in which the drone of a life-signs monitor announces the death of an old lady), or the finesse with which he works mirrors into the story without ever trampling us with their age-old significance as symbols of appearance. (Jullien, Dr. Gailland's fawn-like son actually steals a mirror, and gets in trouble with the police for it, at the height of his disaffection with his parents' marital arrangement, and we are none the worse off for the incident's obviousness as a symbol).

I don't care that "No Time for Breakfast" can ultimately be construed as a critique of the woman who tries to have a profession as well as a family. I don't even mind that it seems in the end to pump somewhat thoughtlessly for the virtues of bourgeois marriage. (In the penultimate shot of the film, we see Gerard Gailland standing loyally by as his wife is wheeled away for surgery). "No Time for Breakfast" has the final simple effect of putting life and death in clear perspective, and at a time when phony optimism seems to be riding high in the film industry, it is a relief to see an affirmative statement made in the shadow of tragedy.

1978 S 16

A WEDDING, produced and directed by Robert Altman; screenplay by John Considine, Patricia Resnick, Allan Nicholls and Robert Altman, from a story by Robert Altman and John Considine; executive producer, Tommy Thompson; director of photography, Charles Rosher; edited by Tony Lombardo; sound by Jim Bourgeois and Jim Stuebe. Released by 20th Century-Fox. Running time: 125 minutes. This film is rated PG.

Tulip Brenner . . . . . Carol Burnett
Snooks Brenner . . . . . Paul Dooley
Muffin Brenner . . . . . Amy Stryker
Buffy Brenner . . . . . Mia Farrow
Nettie Sloan . . . . . Lillian Gish
Regina Corelli . . . . . Nina Van Pallandt
Luigi Corelli . . . . . Vittorio Gassman
Dino Corelli . . . . . Desi Arnaz, Jr.
Antoinette Goddard . . . . . Dina Merrill
Mackenzie Goddard . . . . . Pat McCormick
Dr. Jules Meecham . . . . . Howard Duff
Bishop Martin . . . . . John Cromwell
Rita Billingsworth . . . . . Geraldine Chaplin
Jeff Kuykendall . . . . . John Considine
Florence Farmer . . . . . Lauren Hutton
Ingrid Hellstrom . . . . . Viveca Lindfors

By WALTER KERR

You have to be able to count to get through Robert Altman's "A Wedding." So do the 48 characters (not including musicians and children) who drift in and out of corners, bathrooms, sickrooms and cellars during the reception following the ceremony.

Viveca Lindfors, for instance, appears briefly as a drunken caterer whose hair seems to have been set in a wind tunnel, and one of the last things she says as she floats away through the French windows is: "'Death' is a four-letter word." This leaves the woman to whom she's been speaking baffled enough to begin counting letters in the empty air, just to make sure how death IS spelled. It also establishes the comic level of the occasion, up to a point.

Later in the film, and much more importantly, simple mathematics reaches out to engulf the bride and bridegroom and all their kin. The bridegroom (Desi Arnaz Jr.) is accused of having impregnated his bride's sister (Mia Farrow), and the father of the two girls is understandably, if rather thick headedly, incensed. Arnaz acknowledges that he's slept with Miss Farrow but points out, in somewhat ungentlemanly self-defense, that so has every other member of the military academy he attended.

The father promptly turns upon his four-month pregnant offspring to ask if this is so, and if so, how many? Now Miss Farrow, who seems to have been rendered speechless by her extensive experience, nods and begins to count on her fingers. The fingers of two hands aren't quite enough, however, whereupon she borrows two more hands from a woman conveniently nearby. You may begin to see the problem.

If you don't, you'll cotton to it soon enough as you try to keep track of (a) those 48 people who aren't characters at all, but caught-in-passing character fragments, and (b) their private pecadillos. The pecadillos—which constitute the gallows-humor underside of a glitteringly conducted ceremony—run the gamut, rather: drug addiction, lesbianism, suspected homosexuality, nymphomania, infidelity, assault and battery, and a desperate inability to locate the bathroom.

You may also wish to keep tabs on the number of times writer-director Altman and his colleagues have done the same thing over again in their determination to establish an atmosphere that is grisly and gala at once. Lillian Gish appears as the matriarch of the bridegroom's family, lying ill in an upstairs room.

Miss Gish and another veteran performer, John Cromwell, are very nearly the only members of the film's cast who seem able to take care of themselves, establishing firm—and in Cromwell's case—funny identities. But Miss Gish doesn't have long to make herself indelible; she dies before the wedding party assembles, and her doctor goes to extreme lengths to keep news of her demise from family and friends.

Which means that one after another various daughters, caterers and even Cromwell himself—who plays a tired and querulous bishop heartily sick of bestowing blessings—must go to Miss Gish's chamber and carry on conversations with her corpse.

One daughter does become concerned enough to ask how Miss Gish's temperature is; the doctor replies that is is somewhat below normal, but that this is usual in the circumstances. The others either assume she's playing possum or talk so much themselves that they don't notice a body turning slowly to stone.

It's not just that these seem pall through repetition, they're not funny to begin with. The humor is, of course, meant to be macabre, as is much that surrounds these awkward vigils. But Altman has failed to find a mix of moods that will justify the alternation of wedding-reception cliches, ambiguous gags and sudden garishness. It's as though he had gone atmospherically tone-deaf and produced near cacophony, where a subtle dissonance was wanted.

By the time the brouhaha over Miss Farrow's pregnancy is followed by a long shot of a blazing gasoline truck with the honeymooners' car pinned and burning beneath the wreckage, I found a genuinely unpleasant knot tightening in my stomach. Not because I'd become interested in the people involved, but because the violent bid for shock was so flamboyantly out of kilter with the foolishness that had directly preceded it. Nerve ends can rebel when you're asked for the wrong response—or because you can give no response at all. (I might add that the sequence is a cheat, and there's no way to absorb it retroactively).

I don't think there's any faulting the shredded performances: Carol Burnett, Geraldine Chaplin, Howard Duff, Vittorio Gassman, Dina Merrill, Lauren Hutton and a dozen others do decently what is required of them. But the film doesn't know how to balance out its serio-comic shift of style, and having the doctor mutter that "It's like the last days of Hitler" squares nothing. The trumpet sounds that accompany the handsomely photographed wedding may have a hint of doomsday about them; but any mourning in which we indulge must be for the half-hearted, two-headed film itself.

1978 S 23

GO TELL THE SPARTANS, directed by Ten Post; screenplay by Wendell Mayes, based on the novel *Incident at Muc Wa* by Daniel Ford; produced by Allan F. Bodoh and Mitchell Cannold; executive producer, Michael Leone; director of photography, Harry Stradling; music composed and conducted by Dick Halligan; art director, Jack Senter; edited by Millie Moore. Released by Avco Embassy Pictures. Running time: 114 minutes. This film is rated R.

Major Asa Barker . . . . . Burt Lancaster
Cpl. Stephen Courcey . . . . . Craig Wasson
Sgt. Oleonowski . . . . . Jonathan Goldsmith
Capt. Al Olivetti . . . . . Marc Singer
Lt. Raymond Hamilton . . . . . Joe Unger
Cpl. Abraham Lincoln . . . . . Dennis Howard
Lt. Finley Wattsberg . . . . . David Clennon
Cowboy . . . . . Evan Kim
Cpl. Ackley . . . . . John Megna
Signalman Toffer . . . . . Hilly Hicks
Gen. Harnitz . . . . . Dolph Sweet
Col. Minh . . . . . Clyde Kasatsu
Capt. Oldman . . . . . James Hong
Butterfly . . . . . Denice Kumagai
One Eyed Charlie . . . . . Tad Horino
Minh's Interpreter . . . . . Phong Diep
Minh's Aide-de-Camp . . . . . Ralph Brannen
Capt. Schlitz . . . . . Mark Carlton

By HILTON KRAMER

Ten years ago, at the height of the anti-war movement in this county, who would have thought it possible for Hollywood to produce an entertaining, old-fashioned combat movie about the war in Vietnam—a movie, moreover, in which Americans are depicted as perfectly decent and honorable, if sometimes confused, and pretty darned brave, too? Yet this is exactly what we have now in "Go Tell the Spartans," in which Burt Lancaster stars as a cynical, attractive wordly wise army major on a "sucker's tour" of duty in Vietnam in 1964. In both its action and its ideology, and in its sentimentality, it could easily be mistaken for a movie about World War II, with the Vietcong substituting for the hateful "Japs" of yesteryear.

The movie does contain a lot of "dirty" language of a sort we were never allowed to hear in combat adventure films about World War II. And there is also a pathetic, doomed character who takes drugs. But otherwise, both the director, Ted Post, and the writer of the film Wendell Mayes, have marshalled all the old war-movie cliches in making "Go Tell the Spartans," and they turn out to have quite a lot of dramatic life in them still.

This is essentially a movie about a platoon on a "routine" mission that turns into an unexpected disaster. First, the main characters—new arrivals at headquarters in Penang—are interviewed one at a time by the crusty Major Barker (Burt Lancaster) and the younger, equally cynical but more ambitious Capt. Olivetti (Marc Singer). There is the war-weary Sgt. Oleonowski (Jonathan Goldsmith), the innocent, gutless 2nd Lt. Hamilton (Joe Unger), the intelligent, sensitive draftee, Cpl. Courcey (Craig Wasson), and so on. It is all as stagey as the first act of a drawing-room comedy, but it serves to introduce the flaws and virtues of the men who will shortly go into combat with the Vietcong, and it certainly holds our interest.

Then the suspense accelerates as the mission to secure a garrison at Muc Wa gets underway. Of course the young Lt. Hamilton turns out to be a hopeless incompetent, and the war-weary Sgt. Oleonowski takes over. The South Vietnamese mercenaries, under the command of these American "advisers," turn out, after an initial period of suspicion, to be good guys—both brave and loyal, and shrewder than the Americans in judging the villainy of their Communist adversaries.

Even the American general, played by Dolph Sweet, who at first gives our admirable Major Barker such a hard time, turns out to have a heart of gold.

It is the combat action that is riveting in the film, and it is the tests of character under the pressure of combat that provide it with its human interest. The real hero of the mission is the draftee—very well acted, with a kind of bewildered idealism, by the new Craig Wasson—and it is his example that lures the cynical Major Barker into a heroic final action of his own. We are left in no doubt that war is hell—and also the real test of manhood.

Burt Lancaster does his usual professional turn as Major Barker, playing more or less the character that Burt Lancaster has played in many movies—a man of power, authority and manly grace just vulnerable enough to be appealing. But all the actors here—virtually unknowns except for Lancaster—turn in persuasive performances within the limits of Wendell Mayes's cliche-ridden script.

The script does contain one novelty, however—a verbal and quite funny description by Major Barker of a sexual escapade allegedly witnessed by the President of the United States. Both this and the "dirty" language account, I suppose, for the film's

"R" rating. But otherwise, "Go Tell the Spartans" is a movie that returns us to the normalcy of the war-movie world in which "we" are still the good guys.

The title, incidentally, is a reference to Herodotus's account of the heroism of the Battle of Thermopylae, and it is not used ironically.

1978 S 23

BLOODBROTHERS, directed by Robert Mulligan; screenplay by Walter Newman, based on the novel by Richard Price; produced by Stephan Friedman; director of photography, Robert Surtees; music by Elmer Bernstein; production designer, Gene Callahan; edited by Shelly Kahn. Released by Warner Bros. Running time: 116 minutes. This film is rated R.

Chubby de Coco....Paul Sorvino
Tommy de Coco....Tony Lo Bianco
Stony de Coco....Richard Gere
Marie....Lelia Goldoni
Phyllis....Yvonne Wilder
Banion....Kenneth McMillan
Dr. Harris....Floyd Levine
Annette....Marilu Henner
Albert....Michael Hershewe
Cheri....Kristine DeBell
Mrs. Pitts....Pauline Myers
Sylvia....Gloria Leroy
Paulie....Bruce French
Malfie....Peter Iacangelo
Butler....Kim Milford
Mott....Robert Englund
Jackie....Raymond Singer
Jackie's Mother....Lila Teigh
Blackie....Eddie Jones
Artie....Danny Aiello

By HAROLD C. SCHONBERG

Ordinary people is what "Bloodbrothers" is all about. Jes' folks: New York hardhats, tough, violent in temper, profane in language, hard-drinking, women-chasing, wife-cheating, anti-intellectual, wrapped up in work and family. Especially family.

"Bloodbrothers" is about an Italian clan in the Bronx. There are two married brothers, both construction electricians. One is childless. The other has two sensitive kids and an hysterical wife. What are two sensitive kids doing in a place like this? We find out.

But it takes two rather dull hours to find out. "Bloodbrothers," which opened Thursday, attempts to be a slice-of-life verismo. It even makes a timid pass at a social message. "The more bloodbrothers you have," says the sensitive boy to a group of underprivileged children, "the better off you are." The film tries to tell us that the old order giveth way: that the new generation cannot—must not—live by outmoded rules of behavior.

Unfortunately the message ends up as trite as the film itself. "Bloodbrothers" is mostly stereotypes, right down to our old friend, the whore with a heart of gold.

The trouble with "Bloodbrothers" is that it attempts to have it both ways. On the one hand, it tries to work up sympathy for the two brothers who represent the emptiness of unfulfilled life, and who have to find their outlet in alcohol and whores. On the other hand, it spends a great deal of time knocking them down. The idea presumably is to show that, like all humans, they are neither all bad nor all good, but as presented in this film, they are all bad, those hollow men, and the film simply fails to make its points in any convincing manner.

It is not because of trying. Robert mulligan, whose "To Kill a Mockingbird" scored a success some years ago, is the director. He has left absolutely nothing to the imagination, apparently figuring that the mental age of the American filmgoer is in the vicinity of absolute zero. So he spells everything out, no word over three letters.

Everything is carefully manipulated in what amounts to a series of family vignettes, all aimed at underscoring a theme that was obvious to begin with. At basis, "Bloodbrothers" is terribly sentimental, with several unabashed tear-jerking episodes. One of them, in which the hardhats throw a party for a crippled saloon owner, just might make you gag. The film is full of these cheap assaults on the emotions.

There is a notable bit of miscasting, too, in Richard Gere as Stony DeCoco, the sensitive son. By no freak of genetics could he have come from the lines of his parents. Here is a fine young actor with immense charm, but he is not believable in this role. He has to cope with too many artificial and predictable situations, and not even he can overcome the simplistic contrived qualities of the role and of the picture.

Anyway, the camera work is fine, and there are some good performances. In addition to Gere, there are Paul Sorvino as Chubby DeCoco, the childless brother, and Tony Lo Bianco as Tommy De Coco. Both give dynamic characterizations. Sorvino, built like Ernest Borgnine, obviously studied that fine actor's work and provided, in addition, sensitivity of his own.

1978 S 29

PERCEVAL, screenplay adapted and directed by Eric Rohmer, based on the novel by Chrétien de Troyes; executive producer, Barbet Schroeder; photography by Nester Almendros; music by Guy Robert; art direction by Jean-Pierre Kohut-Svelko; production manager, Margaret Menegoz; costumes by Jacques Schmidt; sound by Jean-Pierre Ruh. Released by Gaumont/New Yorker Films. Running time: 137 minutes. This film is not rated.

Perceval....Fabrice Luchini
Gawain....Andre Dussolier
Blanchefleur....Arielle Dombasle
The Fisher King....Michel Etchverry
King Arthur....Marc Eyraud
Queen Guenievre....Marie-Christine Barrault
Perceval's mother....Pascale de Boysson
The Damsel in the Tent....Clementine Amouroux
The Proud Lord of the Heat..Jacques le Carpentier
The Red Knight....Antoine Baud
The Damsel who laughs....Jocelyne Boisseau
Kay....Gerard Falconetti
The Fool....Alain Serve
Yvonet....Daniel Tarrare
Gornemant of Gohort....Raoul Billerey
Anguingueron....Sylvain Levignac
Clamadien of the Isles....Guy Delorme
The Hideous Damsel....Coco Ducados
Sagremor....Gilles Raab
Guingambresol....Jean Boissery
Thiebaut of Tintaguel....Claude Jaeger
Thiebaut's elder daughter...Frederique Cerbonnet
The Damsel with the small sleeves....Anne-Laure Meury
The King of Escavalon....Frederic Norbert
The King's sister....Christine Lietot
The Hermit....Hubert Gignoux

By CHRISTOPHER LEHMANN-HAUPT

The archetypal Percival calls to mind violence and reverence—Percival brandishing a sword and Percival contemplating the Holy Grail. But neither of these images is apt to French director Eric Rohmer's "Perceval," (eg) a film adaptation of Chretien de Troyes's 12th-century Arthurian romance, which opens Sunday at the Cinema Studio after two showings at the New York Film Festival.

Although Rohmer's Perceval (the French spelling of Percival) does his fair share of sword-brandishing and Grail-Watching, as Fabrice Luchini plays the role, the image one carries away from the film is of Perceval gazing dumbfounded, eyes round, mouth agape, as he focuses the fierce energy of his naivete in yet another direction.

For Rohmer has chosen to develop the comic aspect of Perceval's character, which he insists lies buried in the original medieval French version. And when Rohmer, in an interview on the film, compares Perceval with Buster Keaton, he isn't kidding.

Rohmer's Perceval is the fellow who listens so hard to instructions that he gets everything wrong. At the beginning of his story, when he announces his plans to go forth in search of knighthood, his mother advises him always to go to the aid of ladies in distress, for which he should expect to be rewarded with at least a kiss and a ring. Perceval listens hard, gets it wrong, and demands of the first damsel he meets on his journey the immediate presentation of said kiss and ring, thus putting her in deep distress when her lover returns and punishes her for her apparent generosity.

At the end of the film, when his uncle tells Perceval that his greatest sin is to have forsaken his mother, for which he should let repentance "flood his heart," Perceval again listens hard and then imagines a re-enactment of Christ's Passion with himself in the central role. It is the difference in the scale of these two misconstructions of advice that measures the growth of the hero's character throughout the movie.

Actually Perceval is not the only one I can remember gaping during the film. I have an image of myself staring, too, for this is not a film that absorbs and transports you, but rather one that makes you highly conscious that you are watching cinema. I don't know what contributes to this awarenss most—the slow development of the story; the stylized acting; the intentionally artificial sets, the charming habit the players have of narrating their actions as they undertake them, or the presence of a chorus that fills in parts of the narrative with 12-century chants and accompanies itself on medieval instruments—but it is not at all a bad thing.

Because the film is beautiful to watch, whether you concentrate on the appealing faces and expressions of the actors or on the composition of the scenes, which are like an unfolding series of medieval illuminated-manuscript pages reconceived by the Dutch painter Vermeer. The film is longish—137 minutes—and I could easily have watched it another hour.

1978 O 5

THE BOYS FROM BRAZIL, directed by Franklin J. Schaffner; screenplay by Heywood Gould, based on the novel by Ira Levin; produced by Martin Richards and Stanley O'toole; executive producer, Robert Fryer; director of photography, Henri Decae; music by Jerry Goldsmith; art director, Peter Lamont; production designer, Gil Parrondo; edited by Robert E. Swink. Released by 20th Century-Fox. Running Time: 124 minutes. This film is rated R.

Dr. Josef Mengele....Gregory Peck
Ezra Lieberman....Laurence Olivier
Eduard Seibert....James Mason
Esther Lieberman....Lilli Palmer
Frieda Maloney....Uta Hagen
Barry Kohler....Steven Guttenberg
Sidney Beynon....Denholm Elliott
Mrs. Doring....Rosemary Harris
Henry Wheelock....John Dehner
David Bennett....John Rubinstein
Mrs. Curry....Anne Meara
Jack Curry/Simon Harrington/Erich Doring/ Bobby Wheelock....Jeremy Black
Strasser....David Hurst
Professor Bruckner....Bruno Ganz
Mundt....Walter Gotell
Mr. Harrington....Michael Gough
Lofquist....Wolfgang Preiss
Fassler....Joachim Hansen
Hessen....Guy Dumont
Trausteiner....Carl Duering
Nancy....Linda Hayden
Doring....Richard Marner
Gunther....Georg Marischka
Farnbach....Günter Meisner
Mrs. Harrington....Prunella Scales
Ismael....Raul Faustino Saldanha
Kleist....Jurgen Anderson
Schmidt....David Brandon
Gertrud....Monica Gearson
Schwimmer....Wolf Kahler
Stroop....Mervyn Nelson
Berthe....Gerti Gordon

By HAROLD C. SCHONBERG

In "The Marathon Man" Laurence Olivier was a bad, bad Nazi. In "The Boys from Brazil," just released, Olivier is a good, good Jew, a Simon Weisenthal type who has dedicated his life to tracking down Nazi war criminals. Poor (but beautifully, expensively and oh, so impeccably dressed), working alone except for his sister, he flies all over the world to track down clues.

"The Boys from Brazil" is all about ex-Nazis and a monstrous plot that has science-fiction elements. It will be revealing no great secrets, especially to those who have read the Ira Levin book on which the film is based, to state that a mad Nazi doctor now living in Paraguay, has succeeded in cloning little Hitlers. The idea is not as far-fetched as it sounds; recent developments in this sector of science have been agitating the community and scaring a large number of people.

So given the germ of fact, we have sort of a cancer of a film. Yet some cancers can be cured, and "The Boys from Brazil" at least has a happy ending, after a harrowing finale in which the Nazi doctor, played by Gregory Peck, is killed by slavering Dobermans. The ending is supposed to be ironical; man is killed by the very monster he creates.

Of its kind, "The Boys from Brazil" is a good job. It is slickly devised entertainment, professionally shot, gaining momentum as it goes, full of tense situations and constant suspense. Thank goodness, it never tries to be arty, contenting itself with telling a story and nothing else. The ending, however, is a little pat, and nobody is going to believe that the meek little Jew can survive his encounter with the burly Nazi, who in addition is backed by a gun.

Gregory Peck and Laurence Olivier do most of the work in this film. Peck employs a guttural German accent and walks around with a mean face and squinty eyes. He's a Nazi, isn't he? He never really has been a very good actor, has he? Olivier, that suavest of artists, is marvelous as the Jew, and everybody else in the film is hugely competent, especially young Jeremy Black as the cloned youth. He will bring a chill or two to your inner thermostat. Lilli Palmer has one of those oh-so-understanding roles as the Jewish investigator's sister, and Uta Hagen does some conventional snarling as an ex-Nazi. She's great, even if her material is not. James Mason, in a surprisingly small role, exudes menacing authority as one of the Nazis in high position. "The Boys from Brazil" is one of those films where you get a bag of popcorn and settle back to a make-believe world. Check your brains outside, and you'll have good time.

1978 O 6

GOIN' SOUTH, directed by Jack Nicholson; screenplay by John Herman Shaner, Al Ramrus, Charles Shyer and Alan Mandel; story by Mr. Shaner and Mr. Ramrus; produced by Harry Gittes and Harold Schneider; director of photography, Nester Almendros; music by Van Dyke Parks and Perry Botkin, Jr.; production designer, Toby Carr Rafelson; costumes by William Ware Theiss. Released by Paramount Pictures. Running time: 118 minutes. This film is rated PG.

Henry Moon....Jack Nicholson
Julia Tate....Mary Steenburgen
Towfield....Christopher Lloyd
Hector....John Belushi
Hermine....Veronica Cartwright
Sheriff Kyle....Richard Bradford
Big Abe....Jeff Morris
Hog....Donny DeVito
Coofan....Tracy Walter
Polty....Gerald H. Reynolds
Mrs. Anderson....Luana Anders
Mr. Anderson....George W. Smith
Mrs. Haber....Lucy Lee Flippen
Mr. Haber....Ed Begley, Jr.
Mrs. Warren....Maureen Byrnes
Mr. Warren....B. J. Merholz
Parson Weems....Britt Leach
Florence....Georgia Schmidt
Spinster I....Barbara Ann Walters
Spinster II....Anne Ramsey
Spinster III....Marsha Ferri
Parasol Lady....Lin Shaye
Bartender....Don McGovern
Hangman....Dennis Fimple
Painted Lady....Anne T. Marshall
Painted Lady....Anita Terrian
Drunk....Robert L. Wilson
Stage Driver....Carlton Risdon
Stuntwoman....May R. Boss
Stuntman....Loren Janes
Mrs. Standard....Nancy Coan Kaclik
Farmer Standard....R. L. Armstrong

By MICHAEL WILLIAMS

Jack Nicholson's extraordinary versatility as an actor is as firmly established by now as a sparrow in a wren house. In commenting on his range, Nicholson himself once observed that if he were ever cast as Adolf Hitler, he would proably make him a "likable person." Certainly, in "Goin' South," his first film since "One Flew Over the Cuckoo's Nest," Nicholson makes a likable person of Henry Moon, a scruffy Texas outlaw with incredibly dirty fingernails, no change of clothes, and one lofty ambition: to buy a bar in Mexico and be its "padrone."

Even in an inconsequential film, which "Goin' South" ultimately is, Nicholson moves into his character with riveting energy and conviction. The film also represents the actor's second effort at directing (his first was the 1971 picture "Drive, He Said," in which he did not have a part), and for the first third or so "Goin' South" bounces along with a tight antic sense of nonsense.

It is Longhorn, Texas, 1866, a dusty backwater on the Mexican border—lynching capital of the county. There are no square-jawed heroes of noble cowponies in sight, in fact, almost everyone here has dirty fingernails, bad teeth and a look of robust dopiness. The local kindergarten class; the lawmen (represented, in fiendishly funny performances, by Christopher Lloyd and John Belushi) are corrupt, and a noble cowpony is observed keeling over after a long run, unable to go that customary extra mile.

Henry Moon (Nicholson) appears in this place to be hanged for an unspecified combination of horse rustling and bank robbing. He is saved from the gallows by an ordinance, in effect since the end of the Civil War, that gives a convicted criminal his freedom if a single woman with property agrees to marry him.

Moon's angel of mercy is played by Mary Steenburgen, a strapping young woman with the unconventional beauty of a Modigliani portrait (who in real life was discovered by Nicholson when she was working as a waitress at the Magic Pan on East 57th Street). As they ride off together to her cabin in the hills, "Goin' South" goes into a terminal slump, scuttled by Miss Steenburgen's inability to give her character life or motives and by a script that becomes a predictable romantic comedy, merely clocking such matters as how long it will take for Moon to be allowed to bed down in the house instead of the barn.

Miss Steenburgen, of course, is up against strong stuff, but on this outing, she shows less expressiveness than Charlie McCarthy did, and the director has settled for posing her self-consciously, though attractively, in front of the camera.

Nestor Almendros, who has done luscious work for Francois Truffaut, Eric Rohmer and Terrance Malick—notable in the recently released "Days of Heaven" — is the man behind the camera. There's not a lot to be done with the painted set except move the camera along briskly, but the location shots are spectacular as usual, and there is a quality to the lighting on the faces in the film that is almost painterly.

But, finally, "Goin' South" suffers from an insufficiency of concentration in several areas, most importantly script and direction. Nicholson's performance is what has to carry the film, and it's too heavy a load, even for him.

19768 O 6

WHO IS KILLING THE GREAT CHEFS OF EUROPE? directed by Ted Kotcheff; screenplay by Peter Stone, based on *Someone Is Killing the Great Chefs of Europe* by Nan and Juan Lyons; produced by William Aldrich; executive producers, Merv Adelson and Lee Rich; photography by John Alcott; music by Henry Mancini. Released by Warner Bros. Running time: 112 minutes. This film is rated PG.

Robby .... George Segal
Natasha .... Jacqueline Bisset
Max .... Robert Morley
Kohner .... Jean-Pierre Cassel
Moulineau .... Philippe Noiret
Grandvilliers .... Jean Rochefort
Ravello .... Juigi Proietti
Fausto Zoppi .... Stefano Satta Flores
Beecham .... Madge Ryan
Blodgett .... Frank Windsor
St. Claire .... Peter Sallis
Doyle .... Tim Barlow
Doctor Deere .... John Lemesurier
Cantrell .... Joss Ackland
Salpetre .... Jean Gavin
Saint-Juste .... Daniel Emilfork
Massenet .... Jacques Marin
Chappenmain .... Jacques Balutin
Brissac .... Jean Paredes
Soong .... Michael Chow
Blonde .... Anita Graham
Skeffington .... Nicholas Ball
Bussingbill .... David Cook
Couterman .... Nigel Havers
Actor .... John Carlisle
Actress .... Sheila Ruskin
Director .... Kenneth Fortescue
Assistant Director .... Strewan Rodger

By WALTER KERR

The big question: Just how should Jacqueline Bisset react when she discovers that the chef she just might have spent the night with is not only dead as a mackerel but floating about, mouth open wide, in a fish tank? The attractive and intelligent Miss Bisset is confronted with this problem in the new Ted Kotcheff film, "Who is Killing the Great Chefs of Europe?," and for all her obvious skill, she can't find an answer to it. The camera gives her every opportunity, lingering long and lovingly on the contours of her shapely, normally expressive face, but it can't really catch an honest reaction because Miss Bisset doesn't dare have one.

The film, you see, is an uneasy mix — like a salad dressing, the ingredients of which haven't quite agreed to come together — of broad comedy and murder rampant. If the actress, coming across a body seriously overcooked in an oven or yet another body dangling from a meat hook, reacts with real terror, she'll be spoiling the comedy. And if she reacts lightly, or whimsically, or in some way with less horror than the shocking surprise demands, she'll be undercutting the suspense. So there's nothing for her to do but open her eyes wide, make a small oval of her mouth, and simply freeze her noncommittal expression until the camera goes away again. It's no solution, of course, but I don't suppose there is one. The problem is built in from the film's special credits—shot against some very handsome place-settings — to its finish in a marriage ceremony with vows to never substitute margarine for butter.

Director Kotcheff and screenwriter Peter Stone simply haven't decided on an emphasis for their two-ton film. Obviously it's possible to combine merriment with mayhem; it's been done often enough. But one vein or the other — the suspense or the gagging — has got to be dominant if we're to know how to respond, and so ride along. Miss Bisset plays a celebrated American cook who specializes in desserts — bombes especially — and that does turn out to be a pun. When three of Europe's chefs are roasted, drowned, or crushed like pressed duck — each is killed according to his best-known dish—and we realize that Miss Bisset is next in line for destruction, are we supposed to feel any apprehension for the pretty thing? How much does it matter if George Segal, her former husband and continuing lover, gets there in time to save her?

It doesn't, much, because we've stopped believing in the detective-story nonsense, way back. The fun and games of outright farce have got in the way too often, not by dominating the thrills of the chase but by dampening them. The knockabout eruptions aren't sly enough, for one thing. They seem, in the beginning, as though they are going to be sly whenever Robert Morley's about. Morley appears as a magazine editor who not only rates restaurant dishes across the continent but also eats them. When the camera catches him below the belt, he looks like a dirigible floating away from its mooring. It is when he's told by his doctor he must either diet or die soon that the chain of killings begins. And Morley's defense of his bulk as a carefully created masterpiece, with every crease in his body a work of culinary art, is amusing for starters. He would no doubt remain amusing — with his hyperthyroid eyes blazing like a perpetual sunrise — if he weren't so quickly embroiled in so much primitive pie-throwing.

Not literally pie-throwing, though eventually everyone winds up in a deluge of multi-colored whipped cream. There's an early battle in the kitchen in which meat, vegetables and bread loaves are hurled aimlessly about without ever hitting an actual joke, and it pretty much sets the comic level of the enterprise. A police chief sits down to a hearty meal while waiting for the body directly behind him to be removed, a Parisian chef wonders whether it would be better to be killed or passed over as unimportant, what seem to be sex sounds—heavy breathing and all that — turn out to be food sounds, gourmets deriving their passion from a platter. The humor isn't strong enough to take over, and the film winds up with no more than a half-hearted grin on its face.

Segal in particular plays half-heartedly, and his romance with Miss Bisset stops and starts as though the film's motor were on the verge of stalling. What suspense is left comes entirely from Henry Mancini's studiously ominous musical score, and I'm afraid you're going to have to settle for some very handsome shots of Venice in the misty off-season. And there's Miss Bisset just to look at. "Who Is Killing the Great Chefs of Europe?" isn't the sort of mismatch that makes you angry; it just makes you sorry. A more decisive hand at the controls could have brought the combination off.

1978 O 6

VIOLETTE, directed by Claude Chabrol; screenplay by Odile Barski, Hervé Bromberger and Frédéric Grendel; adaptation and dialogue by Odile Barski, based on the book by Jean-Marie Fitère; music by Pierre Jansen; photography by Jean Rabier; art direction by Jacques Brizzio; director of production, Roger Morand; costumes by Pierre Nourry. Released by Gaumont/New Yorker Films. Running time: 123 minutes. This film is not rated.

Violette Nozière .... Isabelle Huppert
Germaine Nozière (Violette's mother) .... Stéphane Audran
Baptiste Nozière (Violette's father) .... Jean Carmet
Jean Dabin .... Jean-François Garreaud
Maddy .... Lisa Langlois
The Judge .... Guy Hoffman
Andre de Pinguet .... Bernard Lajarrige
Violette's cellmate .... Bernadette Lafont
Mr. Emile .... Jean Dalmain
Dr. Deron .... Jean-Pierre Coffe
Zoé (maid) .... Zoé Chaveau
Mr. Mayeul .... François Maistre
Frist Student .... François-Eric Gendron
Black Musician .... Gregory Germain
Boy in Café .... Dominique Zardi
Inspector Champs-de-Mars .... Jean-François Dupas
Commissioner Guilleaume .... Henri-Jacques Huet
Willy .... Maurice Vaudaux
Camus .... Fabrice Luchini

By HILTON KRAMER

From the very first moments of the new Claude Chabrol film, "Violette," we are held spellbound by a combination of stunning artistry and brute suspense that never relaxes its grip until the final frame two hours later. This is an enthralling movie, virtually certain to become a classic, and in the performance of the title role it establishes Isabelle Huppert as one of the most enchanting actresses currently to be seen on the screen.

The story is based on a sensational murder case that caused a great stir in France in the 1930s. At the age of 18, Violette Noziere was put on trial for the murder of her father and the attempted murder of her mother. She was found guilty, and sentenced to death. (Later the sentence was changed to life imprisonment). The time was 1933, and Violette Noziere became a heroine of the Left and a particular object of veneration by the Surrealists, who proclaimed her a symbol of liberation from "burgeois" morals. Paul Eluard wrote a poem about her called "Violette Noziere's Complaint."

What had emerged in the course of the trial was a tale sordid enough to have been invented by Georges Simenon or James Cain. Violette Noziere had lived a double life. In the cramped tenement apartment she shared with her conventional, lower-class parents, she was a model of schoolgirl innocence—the very picture of a demure virgin unpracticed in the ways of the world. Unknown to her family, however, she was also living the loose life of a near-prostitute, on the prowl for men wherever she could find them.

In the course of this secret life, Violette acquired a ne'er-do-well lover for whom she began to steal from her parents. Eventually she plotted their murder in the hope of satisfying her lover's demands. Her mother survived, however, and sought retribution for her husband's murder.

From this once famous case Chabrol has fashioned an extraordinary movie that manages to make Violette a compelling character, utterly obsessed by the wayward appetites that govern her every action. Yet Chabrol does not for a moment subscribe to the misplaced political pieties once used to justify—and indeed, glorify—Violette's crime. He remains fascinated but detached, and in fact mocks this political response to her case as much as he ridicules the public's shameless absorption in the horror of the crime. About the motive of the murder he is completely clear-eyed, seeing it as plainly criminal. What really interests him is the character of the criminal and the special fate she had created for herself.

Where Chabrol excels in "Violette" is not only in the recreation of this curiously dour, obsessed character but in rendering the contrasting milieux in which she moves. The cramped flat in which Violette lives with her parents, without the least privacy or freedom, is itself a kind of prison from which her nocturnal escapades are a temporary liberation. (The first image we see on the screen is of iron bars—the gate to the building in which Violette lives with her parents, but also a forecast of the prison to which she will be condemned).

Yet the cafes where she picks up her men, and the seedy hotel room to which she takes them, are almost as confining as her parents' flat. There is nothing of glamour or romance in Violette's secret life, but simply other forms of bondage. Only in prison does she find release, and a kind of freedom.

The Paris that we glimpse in this film—Paris in the 1930s—is very beautiful, but it is not dwelt on. The drama is mainly indoors, in the flat, the cafe and the hotel room, and we are made to feel the pressure of their claustral atmosphere tightening its hold until the final denouement. Interestingly, there is only one moment of real passion in the film, and it comes not in the love scenes or the murder but at the moment when Violette, having poisoned her parents and thinking them both dead, sits down to the dinner they were about to share and consumes it with an animal fury. It is a brief but chilling scene—utterly unforgettable.

In this, as in everything else she is called upon to do in this film, Isabelle Huppert shows herself to be a superb actress, able to convey in every gesture, in every utterance and facial expression, that special combination of passivity and violence that is the essential mark of Violette's personality. So persuasive is her performance of this role that even in those moments when she is most nakedly wicked, she continues to puzzle and even enchant us with her air of innocence and indifference.

But then, all the principals are superb in this film—Stephane Audran, who plays the mother; Jean Carmet, who plays the father; and Jean-Francois Garreaud, who plays the gutless lover who holds Violette in his power. It is the kind of film in which we feel the director totally in control of every detail and nuance, from the look of the bed in the seedy hotel room to the look in the eyes of Violette's mother when she awakens to her daughter's criminal act, and are yet caught up completely in the suspense of the action. "Violette" is a triumph for Chabrol, and may be the best film he has yet made.

"Violette," which closes the New York Film Festival Sunday night, starts its regular commercial run Monday.

1978 O 7

MIDNIGHT EXPRESS, directed by Alan Parker; screenplay by Oliver Stone, based on the true story of Billy Hayes from the book by Billy Hayes and William Hoffer; produced by Alan Marshall and David Puttnam; executive producer, Peter Guber; music by Giorgio Moroder; art director, Evan Hercules; production manager, Garth Thomas. Released by Columbia Pictures. Running time: 123 minutes. This film is rated R.

Billy Hayes .... Brad Davis
Susan .... Irene Miracle
Tex .... Bo Hopkins
Rifki .... Paolo Bonacelli
Hamidou .... Paul Smith
Jimmy Booth .... Randy Quaid
Erich .... Norbert Weisser
Max .... John Hurt
Mr. Hayes .... Mike Kellin
Yesil .... Franco Diogene
Stanley Daniels .... Michael Ensign
Chief Judge .... Gigi Ballista
Prosector .... Kevork Malikyan
Ahmet .... Peter Jeffrey

By CHRISTOPHER LEHMANN-HAUPT

Maybe it was the overwrought sound track that made me suspicious of "Midnight Express," which concerns a young American named Billy Hayes who gets arrested and thrown in prison by the Turks for trying to board a home-bound plane in Istanbul with two kilos of hashish taped to his body. Or perhaps it was the excessive violence of the film, which depicts a sadistic crew of Turkish guards beating up the prisoners at every slight provocation. Or perhaps it was the portrait painted of Turkey as a uniformly evil society, peopled by lying lawyers, incompetent policemen, brutal prison guards, and corrupt bureaucrats.

Something, in any case, made me disbelieve "Midnight Express"—so named after the universal prison expression for a means of escape—and sent me to read the book on which the movie is based, written by the real Billy Hayes with the help of a professional writer, shortly after his dramatic escape from prison and Turkey in the fall of 1975. And sure enough, the story that Billy tells here is very different from the version presented in the movie. Billy's suffering is not nearly so pronounced; he even admits some benefits of his experience. The Turks are not presented as uniformly evil; some of the guards and prisoners are even quite pleasant and friendly.

Instead of waging what verges on a Holy War against the people of Turkey, ("A nation of pigs," he calls them at one point in the film), Billy is angry only at the people he feels are mistreating him. Altogether, what we get in the book is the memoir of a misguided young man who makes a bad mistake, gets caught in the mills of a foreign bureaucracy (the situation was exacerbated by the Nixon administration's ban on opium poppy growing, which had angered Turkish farmers and prompted their government to retaliate by being extra tough on Americans caught smuggling), suffers a prison experience that could have happened anywhere in the world, and then effects an exciting escape when the opportunity presents itself.

Of course, some of the changes that the movie makes are necessary for dramatic foreshortening. But what purpose is served by taking an incident which is casually mentioned in the book as a scuffle between one of Billy's fellow prisoners and a money-hoarding trusty, and transforming it into a scene of horrifying violence in which Billy goes berserk, beats the trusty nearly to death, bites out the trusty's tongue, then throws back his head and screams an insane cry of triumph that the sound tract segues into a muezzin's chant off-camera, an aural pun which has the effect of simultaneously degrading a ritual prayer-call to a barbaric cry, and suggesting that Billy, in his act of barbarism, has become a Turk? Are such violence and racism really necessary for dramatic impact? I have no idea if the people who made the film, most of whom are English, have altered Billy Hayes's story thus out of simple stupidity or because of some unexplained grudge against the Turkish people. I only wish to report the effect of the film was to make me reject its contents and go elsewhere in search of the truth.

1978 0 8

Theater and Film

By HAROLD C. SCHONBERG

When the new Harold Clurman Theater at 412 West 42nd Street opens Monday night, it will present a play and a film. The play is Eugene Ionesco's "The Lesson," which has to do with the madness of today's society. The film, "The California Reich," echoes that theme. It is a look at the Nazi movement in California, "The California Reich" is a documentary film that does no preaching in itself. But the message comes through: hate, hate, hate.

This is the first film from the two young directors, Walter F. Parkes and Keith F. Critchlow. With the full permission of the California Nazis, who want to get their message across, the camera focuses on their faces while they talk about their dreams and aspirations, most of which involve killing "niggers and Jews" and setting up a structured society for the white race. It would be pitiful were the ideology not so malevolent and dangerous.

Perhaps the directors have slanted the film, though somehow one doubts it. Everything rings true. The typical Nazi shown here is middleclass, alienated, full of fears and prejudices, as maladjusted as a fish on a bicycle. Their lives are empty, and they now have found something to cling to, something that makes them feel superior, something that gives them a mission.

None of this will come as any great secret. But to move into the homes and the lives of the Nazi families is a scary experience. The film shows them at work and play, indoctrinating their children, marching in demonstrations (some of them obviously scared stiff), living their dream life.

One of the kids who comes in for special attention is a sensitive, good-looking youngster not yet in his teens. The boy has talent; he can draw and he is an embryo writer. But he ends up parroting the hate message of his parents — reluctantly at first, then with increasing fervor.

Allen Vincent comes in for special attention. He is the leader of the San Francisco unit of the National Socialist White People's Party — a man who has spent a good part of his life in reformatories and jails. Vincent does not hide his criminal record. He considers himself "a victim" of society, and he blames his troubles on the fact that he had been lonely most of his life. He is porcine and inarticulate, but he no longer is lonely. He has his friends and he has a vision.

So does the U.S. Army staff sergeant who comes alive and glows when he thinks of Dachau and Auschwitz.

1978 O 17

THE WIZ, directed by Sidney Lumet; screenplay by Joel Schumacher, based on the play *The Wiz,* book by William F. Brown, the original story *The Wonderful Wizard of Oz* by L. Frank Baum; produced by Rob Cohen; executive producer, Ken Harper; director of photography, Oswald Morris; music and lyrics by Charlie Smalls, music adapted and supervised by Quincy Jones; production design and costumes by Tony Walton, choreography by Louis Johnson; film editor, Dede Allen; special make-up designed by Stan Winston. Released by Universal Studios. Running time: 133 minutes. This film is rated G.

Dorothy .... Diana Ross
Scarecrow .... Michael Jackson
Tinman .... Nipsey Russell
Lion .... Ted Ross
Evillene .... Mabel King
Aunt Em .... Theresa Merritt
Miss One .... Thelma Carpenter
Glinda the Good .... Lena Horne
The Wiz .... Richard Pryor

By MICHAELA WILLIAMS

It looks as if, for the moment, anyway, *"The Wiz"* is the most expensive movie musical ever made. Thirty million dollars, it's said to have cost. For this mountainous sum Universal has produced a film that combines the best and worst of what money can buy.

In moving the successful stage production of *"The Wiz"* to the screen, the director, Sidney Lumet, decided on some fundamental changes. Dorothy, the little girl from Kansas who was swept off to Oz by a tornado in L. Frank Baum's original story, has become a 24-year-old black kindergarten teacher from Harlem who has never been south of 125th Street. She is swept off to Oz—which, in the movie, is played brilliantly by Manhattan—by a funnel-shaped special effect that materializes out of a snow storm.

In Oz, Dorothy meets up with variations of the usual complement; the Scarecrow, who here is dressed in plastic garbage bags and stuffed with trash; the Tin Man, who is unearthed at a Coney Island amusement park; and the Cowardly Lion, discovered hiding out under one of the granite egrets in front of the New York Public Library.

Together, they all ease on down the yellow-brick road in search of Emerald City and the all-powerful Wiz. This yellow-brick road, though, looks as if it's made of enough yellow linoleum to pave every kitchen in Kansas, and Emerald City turns out to be the World Trade Center, entered by crossing the Brooklyn Bridge.

But adjustments in the story line are not the problem; in fact, they are for the most part quite ingenious. The problem is that a major adjustment seems to have been made to allow for the casting of superstar singer Diana Ross as Dorothy, and while her presence will probably help at the box office, she is wrong for the part ten ways from Sunday. Aside from the fact that Miss Ross is a less-than-girlish 34-year-old she seems unable to find facial expressions appropriate to the action. Mainly she looks tragic, as if she is about to burst into tears. It is a sort of relief, then, when she does get to burst into tears in her final song, and the camera closes in on her and lets us watch every drop splash to her chest.

Of the other stars in the cast, Nipsey Russell as the Tin Man makes the best impression. Lena Horne does a campy number as the good witch Glinda, swathed in blue tulle and shot at an angle that adds heroic dimension to her teeth and nostrils. Richard Pryor does a short, manic turn as the man behind the Wiz Mask. But most of the scenes that involve the Wiz are also the major production numbers, and the extravagance of them overshadows his significance as a poseur.

And there are real, old-fashioned production numbers, with the camera looking on from a great distance at what appear to be hundreds of people in extraordinary costumes. Several of these are just too long, particularly a sequence in Munchkinland shot at the New York State Pavilion on the old World's Fair Grounds. And one, a rich and funny piece in the wicked witch Evillene's Sweatshop, seems to represent the immigrant European experience rather than the black American one.

Nevertheless, these scenes are spectacular, and even adults who are not Diana Ross fans should enjoy watching them and estimating where the $30 million went. Children and Diana Ross fans will probably think every penny was well spent.

1978 O 26

COMES A HORSEMAN, directed by Alan J. Pakula; screenplay by Dennis Lynton Clark; produced by Gene Kirkwood and Dan Paulson; executive producers, Robert Chartoff and Irwin Winkler; director of photography, Gordon Willis; music composed and conducted by Michael Small; production designer, George Jenkins. Released by United Artists. Running time: 119 minutes. This film is rated PG.

Frank .... James Caan
Ella .... Jane Fonda
Ewing .... Jason Robards
Neil Atkinson .... George Grizzard
Dodger .... Richard Farnsworth
Julie Blocker .... Jim Davis
Billy Joe Meynert .... Mark Harmon
Hoverton .... Macon McCalman
George Bascomb .... Basil Hoffman
Ralph Cole .... James Kline
Kroegh .... James Keach
Cattle Buyer .... Clifford A. Pellow

By CHRISTOPHER LEHMANN-HAUPT

The details may be new but the story is old in Alan J. Pakula's new film "Comes a Horseman." This time it's an oilman (George Grizzard) and a cattle-baron (Jason Robards) against a couple of small ranchers (Jane Fonda and James Caan), all contending over a lush piece of Montana real estate at the end of World War II. And as usual, though it never comes out that way in real life, the little people win. But it might as well be the cattlemen against the sheep-herders, or the homesteaders against the ranchers, or any of a dozen rivalries that have been fought since the western was first stamped on our collective unconscious.

Which is swell with me. What one looks for in horse operas is not fresh stories, but villains to hate, heroes to cheer, and a fistfight or two through which to vent our aggressions. "Comes a Horseman" scores well enough in some of these basic departments. Jason Robards, in the role of Ewing, a cattle-baron who is trying with one hand to fend off progress and with the other to drive Jane Fonda off her plot of ground, is particularly detestable with his mien of watery-eyed inscrutability. And I enjoyed the expression of sleepy resignation that comes over James Caan's face just before he slams an empty beer mug down on a tormentor's hand and dispatches two of Ewing's harrassing henchmen with his fists.

Also, Richard Farnsworth gives a touching performance as old Dodger, the dying cowhand who works for Jane Fonda until James Caan comes along and convinces her to share her burdens with an equal. And cinematographer Gordon Willis, whose affection for dark landscapes and shadowy rooms was a virtue in such films as "The Godfather, Parts I and II" and Woody Allen's "Interiors" turns a few of the potentially conventional big-sky backdrops in "Horsemen" into landscapes of subtle evocativeness.

But unfortunately, these few bright spots do little to dispel the film's shortcomings, most of which have the effect of unnecessarily drawing attention to the movie's technique. For the first half hour it is so difficult to tell what the story is about we begin to look for messages that aren't there. The characters mumble so in their effort to be authentic western types that one is tempted to ask if the theme of the film isn't incoherence, which of course, it isn't. The most incidental sound effects are so loud and insistent that we wonder if the clinking silverware and the scraping chairs aren't trying to tell us something, which, of course, they aren't.

And even after the plot suddenly lurches into lucidity, we are treated to a scene or two where only the background music conveys what is about to happen — as if the film were actually about background music — as well as to a climax in which everybody starts moving in slow motion, as if they had all been inundated by invisible treacle.

I don't know if these irritations are to be blamed on Pakula's directorial affectations, which were just as evident and pointless in two of his earlier films, "Klute" and "The Parallax View" (though not in "All the President's Men" so far as I can recall); or if "Comes a Horseman" is simply unhappy with being nothing but a western. Whatever the explanation, the effect is disconcerting. What would have been enjoyable enough on its own terms tries to be something more. As a result, it comes across as a good deal less.

1978 N 2

A DREAM OF PASSION, produced, written and directed by Jules Dassin; director of photography, George Arvanitis; music by Iannis Markopoulous; sets and costumes by Dionysis Fotopoulos; edited by George Klotz. Released by Avco Embassy Pictures. Running time: 110 minutes. This film is rated R.

Maya/Medea	Melina Mercouri
Brenda	Ellen Burstyn
Kostas	Andreas Voutsinas
Maria	Despo Diamantidou
Dimitris/Jason	Dimitris Papamichael
Edward	Yannis Voglis
Ronny	Phedon Georgitsis
Margaret	Betty Valassi
Stathis	Andreas Filippides
Bible Student	Kostas Arzoglou
Diana	Irene Emirza
Manos	Pano Papaioannou
Kreon	Manos Katrakis
Lighting Man	Nios Galiatsos
Soundman	Savvas Axiotis
BBC Script	Litsa Vaidou
Attendant	Olympia Papadouka
Emma	Anna Thomaidou
Editor	Freddie Germanos
Shopkeeper	Stefanos Vlachos
Dr. Pavlidis	Alexix Solomos

By ANATOLE BROYARD

"A Dream of Passion" opens with the camera ranging portentously over a succession of stones, as if to warn the audience that the film will be hard going, and indeed it is. In modern times, the Medea myth seems to be an occasion for actresses to throw off all restraint and to invent gestures that have not yet occurred to anyone else. Melina Mercouri scrubs the gritty floor of an open-air theater with her palm. She screws herself into various Gordian knots of grief, plays cat's cradle with her hands, contrives to make her enormous eyes go bloodshot, experiments with cross-grained contraposto postures, and more.

She emits animal cries and Sarah Vaughan-like wails, spits staccatos and generally has a marvelous time while her Greek chorous flutters around her humming like flies. Perhaps the Theater of the Absurd has been elbowed off the stage by the theater of the self.

Playing a famous Greek actress who has returned to her homeland to do "Medea," Miss Mercouri is accused by her director of injecting too much femininism, too much irony, into her rendering of the part. This is an eternal woman, he says, not the passing fancy of politics.

As it so happens, there is an American woman in jail nearby for having killed her three children in order to revenge herself on her unfaithful husband. Truth is as strange as fiction. Miss Mercouri visits the American woman, first as a publicity stunt, then in a rather omnivorous identification with her.

Ellen Burstyn, a sensible-looking woman who seems designed to remind us of moderate emotions, has a thankless part as the American murderess. While Miss Mercouri is allowed so many dimensions that it is difficult to know which extravagance she is portraying at any given time. Miss Burstyn is squeezed into the cramped psyche of a Bible-quoting maniac.

While Miss Mercouri tears Greek to tatters, Miss Burstyn, casting her pupils into the corners of her eyes, is obliged to sing-song the Bible. Dilated, unfocused eyes and a vengeful smile are her paltry allotments.

Miss Mercouri fattens like a cannibal on the American woman's case. She weeps over an early abortion, mourns her childlessness, understands why her husband is impotent, why she can't respond to her latest young lover. She sees her whole life, her career, as a sacrificial revenge against men for not having loved her as much as she feels she deserves.

There is a certain virtuosity of ham in her performance, which trembles on the edge of parody. She is such a vehement-looking woman. The structure of her face—eyes and mouth too large, bones too prominent—is rather like an anatomical diagram of drama.

The direction of "A Dream of Passion," by Jules Dassin, who is married to Miss Mercouri, suggests that he is an uxorious husband.

1978 N 3

WATERSHIP DOWN, produced, written and directed by Martin Rosen, based on the novel by Richard Adams; director of animation, Tony Guy; music composed by Angela Morley and Malcolm Williamson; edited by Terry Rawlings. Released by Avco Embassy Pictures. Running time: 87 minutes. This film is rated PG.

Hazel	John Hurt
Fiver	Richard Briers
Bigwig	Michael Graham-Cox
Captain Holly	John Bennett
Blackberry	Simon Cadell
Pipkin	Roy Kinnear
Dandelion	Richard O'Callaghan
Silver	Terrence Rigby
Chief Rabbit	Sir Ralph Richardson
Cowslip	Denholm Elliott
Kehaar	Zero Mostel
Clover	Mary Maddox
Hyzenthlay	Hannah Gordon
Cat	Lyn Farleigh
General Woundwort	Harry Andrews
Campion	Nigel Hawthorne
Blackavar	Clifton Jones
Narrator	Michael Hordern
Black Rabbit	Jose Acklond

By HAROLD C. SCHONBERG

No need describing "Watership Down," the best-selling book about rabbits by Richard Adams. For several years Martin Rosen, an American literary agent who turned film producer (Ken Russell's "Women in Love"), has been working on an animated film about Fiver, Bigwig, Woundwort and the other creatures who eventually find happiness in a lagomorphic paradise. The film, made in England under British auspices, opened Friday in New York.

Before the credits arrive, there is a sequence explaining how rabbits came to be what they are. It has points of interest. The animated drawings break the mold a bit: the rabbits are stylized, the predatory animals look like something out of Dubuffet. Will the Disney mold be broken?

Not after the film proper starts. From there on, the drawings are representational and the backgrounds sentimental. King Walt still reigns. In line, color and technique, "Watership Down" is an epigone of the Disney Studios.

That is true in more ways than one. The plotting also has a Disney philosophy. There is the figure of innocence opposed to the figure of evil (Pinocchio and the fox; Snow White and her stepmother; the Jungle Boy and the tiger). There is the comic figure (Dopey; Jiminy Cricket; the Snake in "Jungle Book"). There is the inevitable triumph of goodness over evil.

In most of the full-length Disney features, the comic figure is usually the most appealing and interesting of all, and so it is in "Watership Down." It is the seagull, Kehaar, who supplies whatever fun there is. His voice, with ripe Scandinavian accent, belongs to the late Zero Mostel, who sounds as though he must have had a wonderful time. Elsewhere one can hear the voices of Sir Ralph Richardson (Chief Rabbit), John Hurt of "Midnight Express" (Hazel) and other fine actors.

There is nothing objectionable in "Watership Down" (except the stereotyped music). But neither is there anything striking or original. The animations are smooth, however; there is an uncomplicated story line, and kids should love it. The full-length animated film is a medium that has hardly been explored (there are, of course, many animated short films — especially from Czechoslovakia — that do not follow the Disney formula). One of these days a real artist is going to show how it can be done. Suggested story, which already has a great built-in score: Ravel's "L'Enfant et les Sortileges."

1978 N 3

SLAVE OF LOVE, directed by Nikita Mikhalkov; screenplay by Friedrich Gorenstein and Andrie Mikhalkov-Konchalovsky; director of photography, Parel Lebeshev; music by Eduard Artemiev; set designers, A. Adabashyan and A. Samulekin; sound by V. Bobrovsky. Released by Cinema 5. Running time: 94 minutes. This film is not rated.

Olga	Elena Solovey
Victor	Rodion Nakhapetov
Kalyagin	Alexander Kalyagin
Yuzhakov	Oleg Basilashivili
Fedotov	Konstantin Grigoryev

This Soviet film, which opened on Aug. 14, is, on one level, a sweet, affectionate look at the early days of film-making, with all of its melodrama and improvisation and idiotic plots. On another level, it is a celebration of the new Bolshevism just after the 1917 Revolution. The film traces the development of a woman from a spoiled, giddy leading lady to the opening of her eyes to the ideals of the Communist revolution. This is a handsome, beautifully photographed film, and it has a fine group of actors. But be warned that basically it is nothing less than our old friend Socialist Realism, celebrating in a rather one-dimensional way the heroism of the early defenders of the faith. *HAROLD C. SCHONBERG*

1978 N 6

Women

This bleakly existential study in pessimism, which opened Sept. 6, is a sensitive and powerful film that raises many questions and proposes no answers. It was made in Hungary by Marta Meszaros, and it tells the story of four unhappy, frustrated people. Their marriages are going badly, and the two women become closer and closer. Perhaps a lesbian relationship is suggested, though here, as elsewhere in the film, nothing is explicitly stated. The film has to do with the plight of people — good people, in their way — **who cannot cope with life, perhaps because life has no meaning. The acting is splendid, with leading roles taken by Marina Vlady, Lili Monori, Miklos Tolnay and Jan Nowicki.**

HAROLD C. SCHONBERG

1978 N 6

Death on the Nile

This new Agatha Christie movie, which opened Sept. 29, is a big expensive, star-studded bore in which a lot of famous talent is permitted — no, encouraged — to do a series of campy turns on their own worst mannerisms. Peter Ustinov plays the legendary Hercule Poirot, but whether he is parodying Agatha Christie or only himself, it would be difficult to say. Bette Davis's performance as a wreck of a wealthy old dowager is the purest parody of Bette Davis by herself. Others contibuting to the tedium are Mia Farrow, David Niven, Angela Lansbury, Maggie Smith and Jack Warden. But the real heroes of this film are the costume designer, Anthony Powell, and the makeup man, Freddie Williamson. Their artful creations keep us wondering what extravagant things will turn up next, and thus provide the only suspense there is in this so-called murder mystery. *HILTON KRAMER*

1978 N 6

SOMEBODY KILLED HER HUSBAND, directed by Lamont Johnson; screenplay by Reginald Rose; produced by Martin Poll; directors of photography, Andrew Laszlo and Ralf D. Bode; music composed and adapted by Alex North; song, "Love Keeps Getting Stronger Every Day," music by Neil Sedaka, lyrics by Howard Greenfield. Released by Columbia Pictures. Running time: 97 minutes. This film is rated PG.

Jenny Moore	Farrah Fawcett-Majors
Jerry Green	Jeff Bridges
Ernest Van Santen	John Wood
Audrey Van Santen	Tammy Grimes
Hubert Little	John Glover
Helene	Patricia Elliott
Flora	Mary McCarty
Preston Moore	Laurence Guittard
Benjamin	Vincent Robert Santa Lucia
Frank Danziger	Beeson Carroll

Farah Fawcett-Majors's first major film, which opened Sept. 29 at the Rivoli and neighborhood theaters, is no cause for America to rejoice. It is a film of amiable idiocy, in which Miss Fawcett-Majors and Jeff Bridges wisecrack their way through a series of murders in New York. It seems that they accidentally meet, fall in love at first sight, find her dead husband on their hands, and have to clear themselves. Which they do, in Macy's basement amid relics of the Thanksgiving Day Parade. End of plot.

HAROLD C. SCHONBERG

1978 N 6

THE BIG FIX, directed by Jeremy Paul Kagan; screenplay by Roger L. Simon, based on his novel; produced by Carl Borack and Richard Dreyfuss; director of photography, Frank Stanley; music by Bill Conti; production designer, Robert F. Boyle; costumes by Edith Head; edited by Patrick Kennedy. Released by Universal Studios. Running time: 108 minutes. This film is rated PG.

Moses Wine .... Richard Dreyfuss
Lila .... Susan Anspach
Suzanne .... Bonnie Bedelia
Sam Sebastian .... John Lithgow
Alora .... Ofelia Medina
Spitzler .... Nicolas Coster
Eppis .... F. Murray Abraham
Oscar Procari, Sr. .... Fritz Weaver

In this film, which opened Oct. 6, Richard Dreyfuss plays a private eye who has dropped out of law school because the law has dropped out too. Susan Anspach plays his old flame from their activist days in Berkeley. Mr. Dreyfuss is a good actor. Miss Anspach is warm and attractive, in spite of the attempts of the makeup man to make her look tawdry. Only a compulsive moviegoer could disentangle the plot of "The Big Fix." It ends reassuringly, however.

HAROLD C. SCHONBERG

1978 N 6

AUTUMN SONATA, a film by Ingmar Bergman; director of photography, Sven Nykvist. Released in the U.S. by New World Pictures. Running time: 97 minutes. This film is rated PG.

Charlotte .... Ingrid Bergman
Eva .... Liv Ullmann
Helena .... Lena Nyman
Viktor .... Halvar Björk
Leonardo .... Georg Lokkeberg
The Professor .... Knut Wigert
The Nurse .... Eva Von Hanno
Josef .... Erland Josephson
Eva as a Child .... Linn Ullmann
Uncle Otto .... Arne Bang-Hansen

Any Ingmar Bergman film is an event, and his new "Autumn Sonata," which opened Oct. 8 at the Baronet, is a special event in that it brings together those two wonderful women of the theater, Ingrid Bergman and Liv Ullman. Miss Bergman plays a concert pianist in the autumn of her life, and Miss Ullman is her tormented daughter. "Autumn Sonata" is a psychodrama about the love-hate relationship of mother and daughter, about the egocentricity of a concert artist, about the inability to communicate, about the immutability of any person's basic character. It raises questions but gives no answers. Ingmar Bergman is the supreme realist, and he knows that in life there are no easy answers. He also knows more than any film-maker today about the boiling torment under the surface of the most placid exterior. Ingrid Bergman, looking older and even more beautiful, is superb as the pianist, and Liv Ullmann is positively searing as her repressed daughter.

HAROLD C. SCHONBERG

1978 N 6

CARAVANS, directed by James Fargo; screenplay by Nancy Voyles Crawford, Thomas A. McMahon and Lorraine Williams, based upon the book by James A. Michener; produced by Elmo Williams; photographed by Douglas Slocombe; music composed and conducted by Mike Batt; art directors, Ted Tester, Peter Williams and Peter James; edited by Richard Marden; costumes by Renie Conley. Released by Universal Studios. Running time: 127 minutes. This film is rated PG.

Zulfigar .... Anthony Quinn
Mark Miller .... Michael Sarrazin
Ellen Jasper .... Jennifer O'Neill
Sardar Khan .... Christopher Lee
Crandall .... Joseph Cotten
Nazrullah .... Behrooz Vosoughi
Richardson .... Barry Sullivan
Dr. Smythe .... Jeremy Kemp
Maftoon .... Mohammad Kahnemoui
Shkkur .... Mohammad Ali Keshavarz

Films like "Caravans" make one wonder if the Radio City Music Hall deserves to be saved. It opened there Nov. 2, all grisly two hours of this fake epic. It has a fabricated plot, based on the James Michener novel, it has bad acting, it has unbelievably inane dialogue, and it has every cliché in the books, including an ending with the caravan silhouetted against the sunset. Even so reliable an actor as Anthony Quinn looks idiotic; he displays his macho by grunts and mutters, and occasionally there is a peculiar look on his face that suggests what he really thinks of all this nonsense. Michael Sarrazin and Jennifer O'Neill are the romantic leads; neither can act very well, and they fully deserve each other.

HAROLD C. SCHONBERG

1978 N 6

Wooden Handed

MAGIC, directed by Richard Attenborough, screenplay by William Goldman, based on his novel; produced by Joseph E. Levine and Richard P. Levine; music by Jerry Goldsmith; released by 20th Century-Fox. At the Gramercy, Beekman, Paramount and National. Running time 106 minutes. This film is rated R.

Corky .... Anthony Hopkins
Peggy Ann Snow .... Ann-Margret
Ben Greene .... Burgess Meredith
Duke .... Ed Lauter
Fats .... Anthony Hopkins
Merlin .... E.J. Andre
Cab Driver .... Jerry Houser
Todson .... David Ogden Stiers
Sadie .... Lillian Randolph
Club M.C. .... Joe Lowry
Laughing Lady .... Beverly Sanders
Maitre d'hotel .... I.W. Klein
Captain .... Stephen Hart
Doorman .... Patrick MCullough
Father .... Bob Hackman
Mother .... Mary Munday
Corky's Brother .... Scott Garrett
Young Corky .... Brad Beesley
Minister .... Michael Harte

By VINCENT CANBY

"MAGIC" looks like the year's most earnest effort to underestimate the intelligence of the public. The film, directed by Richard Attenborough and adapted by William Goldman from his own novel, is a no-frills, no-imagination reworking of the story about the ventriloquist who is taken over by his dummy. This is a fable you may fondly remember from the 1946 English film "Dead of Night," or from the later, very stylish "Alfred Hitchcock Presents" television show.

Among other things, the word "magic" should evoke the sleight-of-hand by which one's attention is skillfully diverted from seeing what is taking place — which is precisely what "Magic" lacks. Unless you resolutely make yourself stare at the theater's exit sign, it's impossible not to see the wheels moving around inside this small, cumbersome movie.

•

It's the sort of entertainment in which the most bizarre spectacle is the casting of that fine English actor, Anthony Hopkins, as a failed Catskill magician who suddenly hits the big time

Anthony Hopkins

when he adds ventriloquism to his act. Equally fanciful is the casting of the irrepressible Ann-Margret — a personality for whom Las Vegas would have had to be invented had it not already existed — as the frumpy, off-season proprietor of a run-down Catskill camp, a woman whose love for the ventriloquist precipitates the movie's not-so-dread climax.

The only actor in the cast who seems comfortable is Burgess Meredith, who plays a high-powered agent. He is unfortunately murdered early on when the ventriloquist suspects that the agent suspects that the ventriloquist has an unhealthy dependency on his foul-mouthed dummy. Would such suspicions be grounds for anything more than harsh words or, perhaps, advice? Not in any other movie, but "Magic" is even more desperate than its characters.

Mr. Hopkins is too good an actor to be completely lost in this nonsense, but the best he can do is convince us of his intentions, to represent a timid soul in need of his dummy's identity. We believe none of it for a minute, partly because Mr. Goldman's screenplay spends too much time on irrelevant details, including flashbacks and jumps forward that neither inform nor amuse but simply look trendy in the dated fashion of that word.

Mr. Attenborough ("A Bridge Too Far," "Oh, What a Lovely War") once made an effectively eerie film called "Seance on a Wet Afternoon." "Magic" is neither eerie nor effective. It is, however, very heavy of hand.

1978 N 8, C17:2

SLOW DANCING IN THE BIG CITY, directed by John G. Avildsen; written by Barra Grant; director of photography, Ralf Bode; music by Bill Conti; produced by Michael Levee and Mr. Avildsen; released by United Artists. At the Cinema I Theater, Third Avenue and 60th Street. This film is rated PG.

Lou Freidlander .... Paul Sorvino
Sarah Gantz .... Anne Ditchburn
David .... Nicolas Coster
Franny .... Anita Dangler
Roger .... Hector Jaime Mercado
Christopher .... Theao Penghlis
Barbara .... Linda Selman
Marty .... G. Adam Gifford
Diane .... Tara Mitton
George .... Dick Carballo
Dr. Foster .... Jack Ramage
T.C. .... Daniel Faraldo
Punk .... Brenda Joy Kaplan
Fabrizio .... Dick Boccelli
Ribbi .... Danielle Brisebois
Stage Manager .... Peter Marklin
Dance Troupe .... The Manhattan Dance Company

By JANET MASLIN

HE hero of "Slow Dancing in the Big City" looks like a plain, ordinary big lug, but in fact he's a well-known lug-about-town whose very name — Lou Friedlander — is enough to make people ooh and aah and hope to catch his eye. Lou, played by Paul Sorvino, is a Very Famous Columnist for The Daily News, and his specialties are overworking metaphors and writing about the little guy.

The more upbeat the little guy, the better — not for nothing is Lou's column advertised as "The Heart of the Apple." As the movie begins, Lou is hard at work on the tale of a man who tried to jump off the Brooklyn Bridge and the Eskimo named Comet who saved him. As Lou puts it, "Who says Eskimos are a dying breed?"

•

If you're planning to watch "Slow Dancing in the Big City" with the kind of beatific optimism Lou lavishes on all his subjects, then you'd better suppose — from the facts that he works in his underwear, has a desk littered with beer cans and calls a lovesick cleaning woman his "muse" — that Lou is one great talent as well as one great guy.

And you'll have to, as Lou himself might put it, turn the other cheek when the long arm of coincidence plants Sarah, an exotic hothouse flower of a dancer, in the relatively barren soil of Lou's brownstone. In other words, don't be surprised when this gorgeous, rich creature moves from her own palatial setup into a dreary cubbyhole across the hall from Lou.

The script, chock-full of coincidences just this unlikely, has Sarah shrug about the grubbiness of the place and explain that she'll brighten it up when she brings a few things over. Sure enough, she later arrives with her parakeet, who has a clever name and lives in a very decorative cage.

When John Avildsen was removed as the director of "Saturday Night Fever," there were complaints that he had been trying to recreate his prior triumph by turning that film into a dancing "Rocky." This time, having hung onto his dream and come up with a "Rocky" in toe shoes, Mr. Avildsen demonstrates the same kind of pluck and endurance his characters have — Lou, Sarah, Rocky or even Orville (Mr.) Wright, the parakeet. So Rocky talked to turtles? So Lou and Sarah hope that one day Orville will be set free, to spread his wings and find his piece of the sky.

•

Sarah is the Rocky-ette of the piece, because she has just one great performance in her, and she must sweat and strain to go the distance. But Sarah, as played by Anne Ditchburn, the Canadian dancer, is so beautiful that she doesn't have to say much about this, especially because Lou is on hand to supply the sentiment. "I tellya, if we can beat the odds in New York, we can do anything — walk on the moon, kiss the stars, turn the garbage into roses," Lou enthuses, the first time he takes Sarah to dinner. "You're a poet," she replies. "You're beautiful," says he, bending forward to kiss her hand.

Sarah's high-tone background is just evident enough to give the film a touch of class struggle, the better to establish that the Lou-Sarah romance is star-crossed while aiming the dance sequences at the "Turning Point" crowd. But Mr. Sorvino and Miss Ditchburn are so obviously mismatched that their incompatibility hardly needs special emphasis.

Mr. Sorvino is perfectly plausible as a newsman. But when the screenplay finally rules out the possibility that Sarah merely regards him as a pal, it does him in. Miss Ditchburn, making her acting debut, is so glamorous and mystifyingly odd that she recalls the young Audrey Hepburn, but she, too, is sabotaged by the script. One character describes Sarah as "a natural spellbinder . . . she tries not to be — that only makes things worse." This is not a helpful thing to say about a woman who never goes anywhere without the perfect strip of antique lace tied just-so, to flatter her perfect forehead.

Clearly, Mr. Avildsen had better luck with "Rocky" than he's had this time, even though the material is similar enough to make comparisons inevitable. The formula's failure on its current go-round is a good deal less baffling than its first flush of success.

"Slow Dancing in the Big City" is rated PG ("Parental Guidance Suggested"). The featured romance is pointedly sexless, but there is some strong language elsewhere in the film, particularly in a subplot about street kids. And Miss Ditchburn's rehearsal outfits have a way of slipping off her shoulders.

1978 N 8, C24:3

Wayne Rogers

ONCE IN PARIS, produced, written and directed by Frank D. Gilroy; music composed and conducted by Mitch Leigh; director of photography, Claude Saunier; co-producers, Manny Fuchs and Gerard Croce; production managers, Gerard Croce and François X. Moullin. At the 68th Street Playhouse. Running time: 100 minutes.

Michael Moore	Wayne Rogers
Susan Townsend	Gayle Hunnicutt
Jean-Paul Barbet	Jack Lenoir
Marcel Thery	Phillippe March

By VINCENT CANBY

THOUGH its hero, a high-powered screenwriter, travels by Concorde, Frank D. Gilroy's "Once in Paris" appears to be a tale out of the comparatively naïve, propeller-driven 1950's rather than the more jaded, jet-propelled 1970's, the period when it's all supposed to take place. The movie, which opens today at the 68th Street Playhouse, is a sweet-natured, gentle comedy about a happily married, almost incredibly innocent American who, while on a script-fixing assignment in Paris (which he has never seen before), has the kind of picturesque adventure that, I suspect, was much more believable when Paris was a week (or at least a day) away from New York, instead of a mere three and one-half hours.

"Once in Paris" is obviously a labor of a great deal of love, which is also what the film is all about. Mr. Gilroy, the Pulitzer Prize-winning playwright ("The Subject Was Roses") and film writer-director ("Desperate Characters," "From Noon Till Three"), produced as well as wrote and directed "Once in Paris." In addition, he is apparently tending to the film's distribution himself. After his stylish and witty "From Noon Till Three" (one of the few Charles Bronson movies not to make a fortune) was more or less dismissed by its distributor, he wants, as he has reportedly said, to make his own mistakes.

"Once in Paris" is not a mistake, but it's too innocent and too without guile for its own good. Like its writer-hero, Michael Moore, played by Wayne Rogers (of the "M*A*S*H" and "City of Angels" television series), "Once in Paris" discovers movie clichés with a sense of wonderment we seldom share. Though Michael may never have been to Paris before, most of the rest of us have, if only in the movies.

The first thing that happens to Michael is that he is taken in hand by a colorful native, whom such movies present as a tour guide or a taxi driver or a panhandler but always as a figure of comic wisdom. In this case the native is a pushy, know-it-all chauffeur named Jean-Paul, played by Jack Lenoir, a French actor of singularly little charm. Next, Michael meets Susan, the woman every man dreams of meeting in Paris while on temporary leave of domestic obligations. As played by Gayle Hunnicutt, Susan is smashing — an Englishwoman of beauty, intelligence and, best of all (thinks Michael), no wish for permanent attachments.

In the mornings Michael and Susan take care of their career duties — she has "an interest in a department store" somewhere. In the afternoons they go sightseeing — the Eiffel Tower, Arc de Triomphe, Tuileries gardens, the flower markets, etc. There are also picnics on the grass, cozy meals at undiscovered restaurants, glimpses of the city at dawn from the Trocadero and, in between, love, love, love.

Mr. Rogers has a good, substantial, amused screen personality that is of great benefit to the film, and he and Miss Hunnicutt make an appealing couple. If Mr. Lenoir is less successful, it may be that the character is essentially off-putting. Small, ragged, adolescent hustlers in bombed-out cities are, if not socially acceptable, then understandable. Middle-aged fellows playing the same game are sometimes called pimps.

That may be to take "Once in Paris" more seriously than Mr. Gilroy ever intended. The film means to be a romantic lark, but this lark seldom becomes airborne.

1978 N 9, C21:4

Armand Assante, Lee Canalito and Sylvester Stallone in "Paradise Alley"
"Rocky" warmed over and then thrown out.

PARADISE ALLEY, written and directed by Sylvester Stallone; produced by John F. Roach; director of photography, Laszlo Kovacs; music by Bill Conti; art director, Deborah Beaudet; set decorations by Jerry Adams. Released by Universal Studios. Running time: 108 minutes. This film is rated PG. At the Rivoli, 49th Street and Broadway.

Cosmo Carboni	Sylvester Stallone
Victor	Lee Canalito
Lenny	Armand Assante
Big Glory	Frank McRae
Annie	Anne Archer
Stitch	Kevin Conway
Franky the Thumper	Terry Funk
Bunchie	Joyce Ingalls
Burp	Joe Spinell
Susan Chow	Aimee Eccles

By VINCENT CANBY

SYLVESTER STALLONE needs help. If he continues to write, direct and star in movies like "Paradise Alley," the career that only really began with "Rocky" may turn out to have been an extremely brief dream. He won't be going the course.

"Paradise Alley," which opens at three theaters today, is a phony, attitudinizing, self-indulgent mess, a multi-million-dollar B (for boring) picture with the ear of a cauliflower, the heart of a hustler and the soul of a used-car salesman. It's so gross it's almost funny but, by not being funny, it makes one even more impatient than is absolutely necessary.

If there had been just a tiny bit of wit involved, or a consistent point of view, or genuine feeling, "Paradise Alley" might have been an engaging throwback to the true B pictures of yesteryear. As it is, it's "Rocky" warmed over and then thrown out.

Mr. Stallone's screenplay is set in New York's Hell's Kitchen in 1946, though it often looks like the Lower East Side in 1933 and San Francisco's Barbary Coast in 1890. In any case we get the idea it's a place people want to escape from — to go uptown or downtown, as the geography might have it.

There are three brothers, Italian-Americans, trying to make a go of things. Cosmo (Mr. Stallone), the middle brother, wears a gold earring and his hair long, which he says are his trademarks. Cosmo is the con artist. Lenny (Armand Assante), the oldest brother, was wounded in World War II, and walks with a slight limp. Lenny works in an embalming parlor and is, in the language of such fiction, bitter at the world. Though the work is quiet and steady, there's no great future in embalming. The youngest brother, Victor (Lee Canalito), is a huge, immensely strong but gentle fellow, not unlike Lenny in "Of Mice and Men."

In dramatizing the story of how Lenny and Cosmo attempt to promote Victor as a saloon wrestler to finance their way out of Hell's Kitchen, Mr. Stallone, the writer and director, introduces an assortment of eccentric and sentimental characters who seem to have been borrowed from other people's fiction. They include a small-time Irish hood, nicely played by Kevin Conway, who appeared with Mr. Stallone in "F.I.S.T.," and Frank McRae, as a down-and-out black wrestler, the only actor in the movie with a decently funny and appealing scene.

The women in the brothers' lives are a lovely, virtuous redhead (Anne Archer), who works in a dime-a-dance hall; a faithful whore (Joyce Ingalls) and a terrifically literate Chinese-American (Aimee Eccles) who cares about Victor enough to read him passages from the dictionary at night. She wants to improve his brain.

The movie sort of coasts along from one predictable confrontation to another, bending characters to suit the plot, until the climactic wrestling bout on Christmas night when poor Victor must fight for a $9,000 purse.

Mr. Stallone is no more interesting as a director than he is as an actor, nor does he have much sense of self-preservation. In "Paradise Alley," bracketed by Mr. Canalito, who makes him look the size of Mickey Rooney, and by Mr. Assante, who gives indications of being a good actor, he becomes virtually invisible. Which isn't entirely bad.

•

"Paradise Alley," which has been rated PG ("Parental Guidance Suggested"), includes some scenes of violence in the wrestling arena and some mildly vulgar language.

1978 N 10, C14:1

African Big Horn

THE WILD GEESE, directed by Andrew V. McLaglen; screenplay by Reginald Rose; produced by Euan Lloyd; based on the novel by Daniel Carney; director of photography, Jack Hildyard; music by Roy Budd; production designer, Syd Cain; costume supervisor, Else Fennell. Released by Allied Artists. At Loews State I, 45th Street and Broadway, and the RKO 86th Street. Running time: 135 minutes. This film is rated R.

Colonel Allen Faulkner	Richard Burton
Shawn Fynn	Roger Moore
Rafer Janders	Richard Harris
Peter Coetzee	Hardy Kruger
Sir Edward Matherson	Stewart Granger
R.S.M. Sandy Young	Jack Watson
President Limbani	Winston Ntshona
Jesse	John Kani
The Priest	Frank Finlay
Witty	Kenneth Griffith
Balfour	Barry Foster
Mr. Martin	Jeff Corey
Jock	Ronald Fraser

By JANET MASLIN

A movie that makes it impossible to tell whether Richard Burton's eyes are blue, green, pale gray or puce is a movie that has not been photographed properly. "The Wild Geese," which opened yesterday at Loews State and other theaters, is just as bewildering about the shade of Richard Harris's hair, which looks chartreuse. Those parts of the film that are set in London appear to have been staged indoors.

Richard Burton

even if they weren't, in a makeshift studio lit with one or two fluorescent bulbs. The African sequences are so dim and grainy that they seem to be taking place inside a tea bag.

Reginald Rose's screenplay may not provide the definitive account of mercenary soldiers in present-day Africa, but it deserved better treatment than this. Mr. Rose, whose credits include "The Defenders" television series and "Twelve Angry Men," is an old-fashioned scenarist mindful of such old-fashioned niceties as pacing, clarity and economy. And his story gives each supporting character a memorable establishing line or two while still moving along at a brisk clip. There's actually quite an effective war movie lurking behind the unsightly facade of "The Wild Geese."

•

The plot concerns a band of seasoned mercenaries hired by a wealthy British industrialist (Stewart Granger) to execute a mission in Africa. This tiny army, recruited by Mr. Burton, Mr. Harris and Roger Moore, is being sent to kidnap an African leader (Winston Ntshona) who has long been held prisoner and is believed by his followers to be dead. At the time the story starts, it suits Mr. Granger and his copper-mining interests to restore this leader to the public eye.

But rich industrialists' interests have a way of changing. Things go swimmingly for Mr. Burton and his colorful, high-priced recruits until Mr. Granger decides, about an hour and a half into the story, to make a change in his plans. At this point, the faint-hearted would be well-advised to take themselves elsewhere, because the rest of the film is devoted to sickening, wholesale slaughter. There's no sex and not much profanity in "The Wild Geese," but the film has an R rating. Let that serve as the warning it's supposed to be.

Until "The Wild Geese" begins devoting itself solely to violence, it's well-suited to a general audience; that makes the change of mood particularly unfortunate. Andrew V. McLaglen, best known as the director of John Wayne's lesser westerns, spends the early part of the film alternating long shots with abrupt close-ups that don't match, but the caliber of the cast and the sparkle of the screenplay are enough to hold one's attention.

Later, Mr. McLaglen does greater damage when he begins treating hordes of African soldiers, who outnumber the mercenaries about 600 to 1, as if they were Indians at Little Big Horn. "The Wild Geese" is not about to address itself to the complexities of contemporary Africa — that becomes clear when the political hostage says "If we have no future together, white man, we have no future," and quickly moves on to a less inflammatory subject. But it's a shame the film makers managed to travel so far without capturing even the faintest flavor of their story's exotic backdrop.

1978 N 11, 15:1

FILM VIEW

JANET MASLIN

'Interiors'— The Dark Side Of 'Annie Hall'

The exteriors in Woody Allen's "Interiors," which has recently moved into neighborhood theaters throughout the metropolitan area, are all-important. Not since Robert Altman combined pink, yellow and a nebulous notion of the feminine mystique in "3 Women" has an American director worked so hard — using meticulously chosen costumes, airtight compositions and a strict color scheme — to establish a film's seriousness in such unmistakable terms. Unlike Mr. Altman, though, Mr. Allen isn't substituting pretentiousness where precision ought to be. And, notwithstanding flashes of angst-ridden dialogue in a Swedish mode, he hasn't imitated an Ingmar Bergman film. Rather, Mr. Allen has used careful, stylized solemnity to find his way into areas where comedy just won't go.

If "Annie Hall" was this era's "nervous romance," "Interiors" is its genteel nightmare. And the disintegrating adult family the film examines is — like the uneasy, indecisive lovers in Mr. Allen's last film — as recognizably contemporary as it is new to the screen. The couple played by E. G. Marshall and Geraldine Page have three grown daughters, one scatterbrained and the others painfully preoccupied with painfully banal problems, but it's the parents' crisis that is pivotal. The husband has decided to leave his wife, after 30-odd years of seemingly satisfactory marriage, in an age when such drastic changes need not — and often cannot — be accounted for.

If the wife were as spunky and resilient as Jill Clayburgh in "An Unmarried Woman," and if she were about to stumble onto a Mr. Wonderful along the lines of Alan Bates, hers might be a manageable predicament. But Mr. Allen's bereft wife, called Eve, is 15 or 20 years older, alternately furious and mortified to find herself suddenly without resources. As played by Miss Page, whose performance not only carries the movie but takes one's breath away, Eve has been turned, by grief and rage and sheer surprise, into an impossible burden to everyone who's ever loved her. She's both a lost cause and a holy terror.

For all of the psycho-jargon and soul-searching the film's other characters bring to bear upon their troubles, Eve's state remains frighteningly difficult for her family to describe, let alone understand. And, perhaps because Eve's collapse is so central and yet so baffling, "Interiors" creates a sharp distinction between the quality of what the audience sees and what it hears. All three daughters talk too much and say too little, fumbling and complaining, yet there is a deep serenity to the pale settings in which Mr. Allen has them speak, and a haunting delicacy to the way he frames and composes each scene. The refined, rarefied look of the film is a function of Eve, who is an interior decorator with a deep faith in the efficacy of beige. More important, it's an indication that "Interiors" is more of a still-life, a portrait, than it is a story.

A good deal happens during the course of the film; nothing really changes. Mr. Allen, in the same spirit of overcautiousness with which he spells out certain things too clearly in the screenplay, begins the film with a stark, arty flashback, as if to suggest that time has marched on eventfully. In fact, even the most turbulent scenes in the film are more descriptive than they are dramatic, as characters live out destinies that have been unmistakable from the start. Mr. Allen is at his most eloquent with a series of silent tableaux that invest the most important events in his characters' lives with the stillness of hindsight, of retrospection. A woman in black, lying alone, attempting suicide in a pale, perfect room — the moment is terrible, but the shot is as serenely beautiful as a Vermeer. A dramatic life-saving effort on a beach is composed so studiedly that the symbolic import of one character's red robe makes as strong an impression as the episode's outcome. Mr. Allen arranges figures, furniture and events with an eye toward clarity and simplicity. Doing so, he attempts — with visual intelligence and a stirring generosity — to counteract the characters' own helplessness and confusion about their lives.

• • •

Mr. Allen's using the camera to distill scenes rather than aggrandize them places "Interiors" in sharp opposition to something like "3 Women," where Mr. Altman's stunning imagery had a momentousness quite disconnected from the explicit content of the screenplay. "3 Women" had the look of a movie about something very, very important, but upon close inspection its ambitions were no more clear or consequential than the kind of "statement" Mr. Allen's Eve talks about making when she puts the right vase on the right table. "Interiors" takes the opposite route, achieving a heightened realism by building meticulously upon the banal.

There was an inkling of "Interiors" in "Annie Hall," however delightfully diverting that film's humor may have been. A gifted costume designer, a brilliant cinematographer and a leading lady with striking fashion sense helped obscure the originality of Mr. Allen's own directorial eye, but "Annie Hall" has a visual style that's as memorable as its story. More important, "Annie Hall" hinted at a fascination with the kind of WASP gentility that permeates "Interiors." Alvy Singer, the character Mr. Allen played, had no trouble making fun of the culture gap between himself and Annie; the sequence in which he visited her family cut right to the bone. But to the extent that the film made it understandable, Alvy's losing Annie had to do with his Pygmalion tendencies, and with his inattentiveness to her real nature. The regretful ending of "Annie Hall" carried the hint that Alvy's indifference to Annie's background had done him in. The family in "Interiors" could so easily have produced a daughter like Annie that the solemnity of the new film almost has the ring of a belated apology.

• • •

And at times, Mr. Allen approaches his somber, joyless family with all the trepidation Alvy felt as he listened to the Halls' dinner-table conversation. "Interiors" does have the mark of a foreign film at times, but not because it emulates Ingmar Bergman — Mr. Allen's concern with family life is different enough from Mr. Bergman's preoccupation with affairs between men and women to make comparisons beside the point. It's Mr. Allen's tentativeness about the tiny niceties of his characters' lives that gives parts of the film a far-away feeling. Having dined with them only once, he may not fully understand their table manners.

But if their gentility is at times unconvincing in its fine details, its poisonous quality is what Mr. Allen means to make use of, and he uses it very ably. The ostensibly rebellious outsider, played by Sam Waterston, is pointedly dressed in the family's wheat-and-oatmeal color scheme. The usually severe father wears a soft, comfortable-looking sweater as he asks his most recalcitrant daughter to do something she finds deeply unpleasant, if not impossible. The oldest sister is a sadist and a liar, but she always manages to do her damage politely.

These aren't laughing matters. How brave Mr. Allen is in taking them seriously. And how impressive he is in understanding them so well. ■

1978 N 12, II:23:1

KILLER OF SHEEP, by Charles Burnett. Principal performers are Henry G. Sanders, Kaycee Moore, Charles Bracy, and Angela Burnett. At the Whitney Museum of American Art, 945 Madison Avenue. Running time: 87 minutes.

By JANET MASLIN

"KILLER OF SHEEP," which opens today at the Whitney Museum, is a film to make one mindful of the difference between genuinely abstract art and iciness for its own sake. The program notes say that Charles Burnett, the director, thinks the idea of the film "is to try to recreate a situation without reducing life to a simple plot," but his film has just enough of a story to make it taxing.

The action, which of course is hardly supposed to be action at all, revolves around a black man whose only measure of prosperity is the fact that he's well enough off to give things to the Salvation Army. He is remote and depressed. His wife is bored and sexually frustrated, and she's depressed, too.

He has two children, whom we see eating breakfast and scratching and walking around the neighborhood. He has a lot of young and reasonably attractive male friends who live with grotesquely bloated women; sometimes the men get together and fix cars, or worry. The central character works in a slaughterhouse, hence the none-too-apt title.

•

To all this monotony and alienation Mr. Burnett brings an estrangement of his own. The film consists of loosely linked glimpses of the characters' lives, punctuated by occasional cuts to the slaughterhouse. It is acted by nonprofessionals, who call attention to the falseness of many of the situations. It is beautifully photographed in black and white, and very spare.

The dialogue, which is read with either insufficient or excessive emphasis by the nonactors, is often buried under a soundtrack of vintage blues, making it doubly hard to follow. Even the slaughter of the sheep is numbingly uneventful.

That may be Mr. Burnett's very point, but he makes it so studiedly that the character's estrangement from his surroundings overlaps too conveniently with the director's arty detachment from his material.

And for all its air of starkness, "Killer of Sheep" is more often arid than it is genuinely economical. Mr. Burnett obviously has a keen eye for tiny moments — the way a child pulls up a sock, the way a man's hands move on machinery — but he doesn't demonstrate the kind of coherence that might give them larger meaning.

1978 N 14, C10:5

Animated Mythology

THE LORD OF THE RINGS, directed by Ralph Bakshi; based on the novels of J.R.R. Tolkien; produced by Saul Zaentz; screenplay by Chris Conkling and Peter S. Beagle; music by Leonard Rosenman. A Fantasy Films presentation released by United Artists. Running time: 133 minutes; at the Ziegfeld Theater, 54th Street east of Seventh Avenue. This movie is rated PG.

By VINCENT CANBY

RALPH BAKSHI ("Fritz The Cat," "Heavy Traffic" and so on) is probably the wittiest, most original animator now working in American theatrical films, and his big, busy, very long screen adaptation of the late J.R.R. Tolkien's trilogy, "The Lord of the Rings," is both numbing and impressive.

The Wizard Gandalf in "The Lord of the Rings"

Yet it would be difficult to recommend this movie to anyone not wholly absorbed by the uses of motion-picture animation or to anyone not familiar with Tolkien's home-made mythology, which borrows liberally from various Norse myths, the Eddas, the Nibelungs and maybe even Beatrix Potter. In the way of grand opera sung in Urdu, "The Lord of the Rings" is likely to be total confusion to someone who doesn't speak the language.

•

In 1956, Edmund Wilson said it very well in The Nation when he described Tolkien's trilogy as "essentially a children's book which has somehow got out of hand." To be exact, it's out of hand by half a million words plus indexes, appendixes, footnotes and maps.

The three books, set in the mythological past of Middle Earth, recount an epic battle between good and evil, between heaven and hell, when the dark powers, in order to rule the world, attempt to recover a magic ring that has fallen into the possession of a heroic hobbit named Frodo. The cast of characters includes wizards (good and bad), dragons, men, elves, dwarfs, goblins and, of course, hobbits, which are sort of superdwarfs. Hobbits are smaller than the dwarfs of conventional fairy tales but they are jollier, heartier, cuter, braver and in general much more difficult to stomach than Sneezy, Sleepy, Doc, Dopey and the rest of that crowd.

W.H. Auden and other pro-Tolkien critics have found in "The Lord of the Rings" comparisons to Milton, Dante and other epic-makers, and they may be right. I must admit that since I reached voting age I haven't been as fascinated by confrontations between good and evil (with the exception of "Star Wars," which was funny) as I've been by attempts to cope with what Grace Paley identified as "the little disturbances of man." Until I can understand how Con Ed operates, heaven (and hell) can wait.

•

The movie, which opens today at the Ziegfeld Theater, includes material from the first two books of the trilogy, "The Fellowship of the Ring" and "The Two Towers," and ends more or less in mid-crisis (after more than two hours) with the screen message, "Here concludes the first part of the history of the War of the Ring." It's not a movie for the child (or adult) who has yet to conquer his need for instant gratification. Mr. Bakshi is, I'm told, already working on the second part utilizing the third book, "The Return of the Ring." You are thus warned to have some kind of explanation ready for your child when the movie ends without actually ending. If the child is my age, watch out that he doesn't rip up a seat.

The major fault of the screenplay by Chris Conkling and Peter S. Beagle is that the film attempts to cover too much ground too quickly, packing in more incomprehensible exposition in the first 15 minutes than you'd get in a year of "All My Children." I know one 12-year-old Tolkien scholar, who otherwise thoroughly approved of the movie, who was disappointed because a lot of the events of the books had been "simplified" in the movie. This comment prompted a certain amount of awe among a small group of adults who'd had difficulty following the simplified material.

After some introductory information about the origin of the magic ring, the film settles down to attend to the adventures of the hobbit named Frodo as he attempts to return the ring to Mount Doom, in the land of Modor, where the ring was cast and can be destroyed, in this way to keep it out of the clutches of the evil Sauron. Frodo's companions on his quest include a wise wizard named Gandalf; a faithful, comic servant named Sam, and other assorted types with such names as Aragorn, Boromir, Merry and Pippin. There are terrible goblins called orcs, and one very skinny, ugly, unreliable, obsequious, completely winning creature named Smeagol, who is a gollum.

•

As in all his films, Mr. Bakshi attempts to go beyond the limits of movie animation as we know it. Before he and his staff began the actual animation, he shot most of his script with live actors in Spain (where else?) and used this material as a guide for the animators. Some of this original material appears to have been incorporated into the finished production, though it has the look of video tape that has been electronically altered to give it an unworldly, unfilmlike quality. Sometimes this is most effective; at other times it simply looks like badly developed film stock. Still, the film is visually compelling even when murk overtakes the narrative.

If Tolkien was not above quoting the mythology of others, Mr. Bakshi appears to have had his own fun quoting such films as "2001," "Ivan the Terrible," "Henry V" and "Snow White and the Seven Dwarfs." His hobbits look very much like Disney dwarfs, though somewhat more introspective, and not once does anyone waste time wishing on a star. The War of the Ring is serious business, and the movie seldom makes light of it, which is something parents should keep in mind.

•

"The Lord of the Rings," which is rated PG ("Parental Guidance Suggested"), contains much fantastic material that could frighten very small children or confuse those less susceptible to nightmares.

1978 N 15, C21:1

Far Out

MESSAGE FROM SPACE, directed by Kinji Fukasaku; produced by Banjiro Uemura, Yoshinori Watanabe, Tan Takaiwa; created by Shotaro Ishimori, Masahiro Noda, Hiroo Matsuda, Kinji Fukasaku; screenplay by Hiroo Matsuda; director of photography, Toro Nakajima; music composed by Ken-Ichiro Morioka; music performed by Columbia Symphony Orchestra (Japan). Released by United Artists. Running time: 105 minutes. At Loews State I and 86th Street East. This movie is rated PG.

General Garuda .... Vic Morrow
Hans .... Sonny Chiba
Aaron .... Philip Casnoff
Meia .... Peggy Lee Brennan
Esmeralida .... Sue Shiomi
Noguchi .... Tetsuro Tamba
Rockseia XII .... Mikio Narita
Urocco .... Makoto Sato
Shiro .... Hiroyuki Sanada
Robot Beba 2 .... Isamu Shimuzu
Jack .... Masazumi Okabe
Kamesasa .... Noburo Mitani
Dark .... Hideyo Amamoto
Kido .... Junkichi Orimoto
Lazari .... Harumi Sone

By JANET MASLIN

NOTHING looks right in "Message From Space," a Japanese science-fiction film that's so terrible it has a certain comic integrity. The meteors resemble intergalactic lint, and the earth, as seen from afar, is a big, blue volleyball with eczema. The spacewalk special effects are straight out of "Peter Pan."

The beleaguered people of the planet Jillucia wear wreaths of plastic leaves around their foreheads and travel in a vehicle that looks like the Flying Dutchman with a battery pack. The surface of Jillucia is made up of big gray hunks of papier-mâché. The spaceships are so obviously miniatures that it becomes fun to imagine what would have happened if a real live mouse had wandered into the frame. The mouse would have looked like Rodan.

However, the plot of "Message From Space," which opens today at Loews State and 86th Street East theaters, is pleasantly indecipherable, and the screenplay seems to have passed through a food processor with a sense of humor. Wicked old crone describing the mountains near her home: "And then there is the wolves who roam about very hungry at this time of year." Madcap heiress with spunk, explaining why she has decided to follow the Jillucians to their new planet after the old one has been demolished: "Because I feel my life would have some purpose there."

If you were spinning your television dial at 1 A.M. and happened upon "Message From Space," you would undoubtedly consider it as lively as it is preposterous, a real find; whether you would stay tuned for an hour and three quarters is another matter. On the big screen, it's worth recommending to anyone who won't mind a movie that looks as though it costs less than his or her ticket. And, for archivists with an interest in the all-time worsts, here is a "Star Wars" knockoff that looks less like the original than most television commercials for new cars. Here is a tale of intergalactic intrigue that revolves around magical walnuts. Here is a real contender.

•

"Message From Space" is rated PG ("Parental Guidance Suggested"). It is no more violent than "Star Wars," which also carried a PG rating. And its action scenes are a good deal more confusing.

1978 N 17, C9:1

FILM VIEW

VINCENT CANBY

What's So Funny About Potheads and Toga Parties?

Sometimes the only way to find out what's happening in the national soul is to read Variety, the show-business weekly. Variety wastes little time predicting trends; it's too busy reporting events, mostly in terms of business, which, as every good trade paper knows, has been the one true art of this nation since its founding. If you happened to see the Nov. 8 issue of Variety, you might have been startled to read that in October, which was an unusually big month for movies in this country, two films accounted for 23 percent of all the money spent at theater box offices. The films: "National Lampoon's Animal House" and Cheech Marin and Tommy Chong's "Up in Smoke."

Following "Animal House" and "Up in Smoke" in order of their box-office receipts were such classy endeavors as "Death on the Nile," "The Boys from Brazil," "Who Is Killing the Great Chefs of Europe?," "The Big Fix," "Midnight Express," "Foul Play," "A Wedding," "Going South," "Interiors" and "Grease." Not even in the running, apparently, was the much publicized Farrah Fawcett-Majors film, "Somebody Killed Her Husband." Great teeth, it seems, aren't selling tickets this season.

• • •

My first reaction to the news about "Animal House" and "Up in Smoke" was one of surprise, though something less than the shock of one friend who suggested that this must be, at long last, the bitter end we've all been predicting since the disappearance of the five-cent Hershey bar. I'm not by nature an optimist, but I am contrary. The vision of Armageddon, I thought, might be premature, at least on the basis of this evidence. "Think of it this way," I said, "it could be worse. What if the two most successful movies in October had been 'The Greek Tycoon' and 'The Eyes of Laura Mars,' or 'The Magic of Lassie' and 'Dear Detective,' or 'The Fury' and 'Capricorn One'?"

My friend was not convinced, nor was I, though I did find it increasingly interesting that "Animal House" had come out of left field in July and had already become more popular (according to the Variety charts) than "Jaws 2," "Hooper" and "Coming Home," and was on the brink of beating Warren Beatty's multi-million-dollar salvage operation that might have been called "Raise the Titanic" but was actually titled "Heaven Can Wait."

There is simply no respect — and that is, of course, the key to the whole matter.

• • •

I'd seen a portion of "Animal House" some time ago, before its hit status was known, but all I knew about "Up in Smoke" was the information contained in the ads — that is, that "It will make you feel very funny!" and that it starred a pair of comedians who had some success several years ago with comedy recordings. Having now seen the film, I'm still not sure which is Cheech Marin and which is Tommy Chong, though it is possible to understand its huge success, which, I suspect, is not as broad as the receipts would indicate but, rather, the result of a lot of repeat trade, like the success of "Star Wars."

To one who is uncommitted to the marijuana culture and who is unfamiliar with the work of Cheech and Chong, "Up in Smoke" is a genially slapdash, sometimes winning live-action cartoon about a pair of aging pot-heads whose lives revolve around the acquisition of and smoking of dope, and then the recovery from the effects, which frequently include headaches, smashed automobiles and brushes with the cops who, as personified by a manic Stacy Keach, are uniformly dim-witted.

The movie's insistence upon the giddy, essentially innocent highs to be had from marijuana is more than a little reminiscent of the way booze used to be treated in two-reel comedies, when one whiff of alcohol was enough to send Charlie Chase or Stan Laurel or some other naif into a fine delirium that promised chaos for the sober (straight) world he inhabited.

There are several genuinely funny moments in "Up in Smoke," such as the scene in which Stacy Keach and his associates mistakenly bust a station wagon full of nuns they think are smuggling several billion dollars worth of grass across the Mexican border. The film also contains a wonderfully tacky love-boat of a car (is it owned by Cheech or Chong?). With seats upholstered in some fluffy, baby-blue miracle fiber and tassles hanging from the ceiling, the vehicle looks very much like a motorized lampshade.

• • •

More important for the overall comic effect of the movie, though, is its appreciation of sloppiness in speech, dress, hygiene, traffic regulations and what used to be called, in grade school, general deportment. In their sleepy, unshaven way, Cheech and Chong constitute a visual affront to the straight world just by walking down Main Street. It's a revolution without danger, however, because, as the movie's popularity shows, this particular revolution has already been won. The true eccentrics are no longer Cheech and Chong but the clean-shaven nitwits, like the cops in "Up in Smoke," who persist in their attempts to uphold repressive traditions. It is one of the film's comic points that Cheech and Chong represent the American ideal of freedom. Says Stacy Keach's furious narcotics agent at one point, "The buying and selling of dope is one of the last vestiges of free enterprise in this country!"

Irreverance is also what "National Lampoon's Animal House" is all about, but it demonstrates irreverance with a style that makes "Up in Smoke" look like a failed 8-mm. production. This is not to say that "Animal House" is great shakes as movie-making. It's the only movie I can remember seeing that I think I could have edited better than whoever did it, and I'm not even very good at changing typewriter ribbons.

"Animal House" is cinematically sloppy — I've now seen the film twice and I still can't separate some of the people. There always seem to be two characters who look much alike to represent a single type. It's full of supposedly comic scenes that have no adequate punch lines to end them, and some of the cross-cutting seems to have been done during a blackout. Yet the movie's fondness for sloth, mess, vulgarity, non-conformism (circa 1962, of course), as demonstrated by the members of an epically disorganized college fraternity, is frequently very, very funny.

The targets of its humor (gung-ho fraternities, neatness, Nixon, chastity, sobriety, Vietnam, patriotism, ceramics) are not exactly sacred at this point, but the gusto of the movie is undeniably appealing. So too are the performers, including John Belushi, Stephen Furst, Tim Matheson and Bruce McGill, as four of the more typical brothers in the slob-fraternity; Mark Metcalf, Mary Louise Weller, Martha Smith and James Doughton, who stand for all that's stuffy and hypocritical in this small, limited world, and Karen Allen, who plays the one sane person in the entire film without once appearing to be aware of that extraordinary distinction.

The success of "Animal House" and "Up in Smoke" is rather easier understood after the fact than before. Among other things, "Animal House" calls attention to a sentimentality not previously acknowledged in a movie like "American Graffitti." I suspect too that some portion of the movie-going public is a lot more bored with orderliness — with the formulas — of conventional comedies and dramas in theaters and on television than has been recognized heretofore. Both "Animal House" and "Up in Smoke" manage to suggest the sublime, if sometimes infantile, joys of chaos and disorder without seriously questioning the system that contains them. They are, ultimately, very soothing movies. ■

1978 N 19, II:17:1

Hollywood Flimflam

MOVIE MOVIE, produced and directed by Stanley Donen; written by Larry Gelbart and Sheldon Keller; executive producer, Martin Starger; music by Ralph Burns; costume designer, Patty Norris. Released by Warner Bros. At the Sutton Theater. Running time: 105 minutes. This movie is rated PG.

Gloves Malloy....George C. Scott
Betsy McGuire....Trish Van Devere
Peanuts....Red Buttons
Vince Marlowe....Eli Wallach
Joey Popchik....Harry Hamlin
Troubles Moran....Ann Reinking
Mama Popchik....Jocelyn Brando
Pop Popchik....Michael Kidd
Angie Popchik....Kathleen Beller
Johnny Danko....Barry Bostwick
Dr. Blaine....Art Carney

By VINCENT CANBY

"THESE hands," says Joey Popchik, the delivery boy who wants to become a lawyer, "are for reading books." But fate and the Great American Depression interfere. Joey's kid sister, Angie, is going blind. "It's okay, Joey," Angie says, "I've seen a lot already, I'll remember."

The only way Angie can be cured is to go to Vienna for an operation that will cost $25,000, which comes to approximately $12,500 an eye, as one observer carefully calculates. Where to get the money? Joey must put aside his books and become a prizefighter. Thus begins the event-crammed, dopily herioc plot of "Dynamite Hands," the first half of Stanley Donen's sweet, hilarious, very witty recollection of the sort of movie programs that came off the Hollywood assembly lines in the 1930's.

•

In addition to "Dynamite Hands," "Movie Movie" includes a breathless trailer for a movie about World War I flying aces, "Zero Hour," "war at its best!" and, as the top feature on the program, "Baxter's Beauties of 1933," a full-color — "Dynamite Hands" is in black-and white — triumphantly nutty backstage musical that Warner Baxter, Ruby Keeler, Dick Powell and Ginger Rogers might well have made. Instead, we have the great good fortune to have George C. Scott, Trish Van Devere, Art Carney, Red Buttons, Eli Wallach, Barry Bostwick and Rebecca York. These actors, many of whom also appear in "Dynamite Hands," represent one of the happiest poolings of resources since Balaban met Katz.

"Movie Movie," opening today at the Sutton Theater, was written by Larry Gelbart, who was responsible for "Sly Fox," Mr. Scott's most recent Broadway hit, and Sheldon Keller. It seems so effortlessly funny that I suspect that the real intelligence and discipline that guide the project will be overlooked.

Mr. Gelbart and Mr. Keller not only appreciate the comic uses of the mixed metaphor — one that is driven into the ground to the bursting point — but, more importantly, they have recreated the efficiency and manic, upbeat innocence of those Depression pictures. This has to do with more than screen styles — wacky montages and attention-getting wipes and fades, which anyone can imitate.

The movie's spirits are high even when its eyes are filled with tears. The film makers genuinely like their models. When Joey Popchik says, "How do you get two cents back on a heart," after he realizes he's been played for a sucker by a hardboiled nightclub singer, the writers are recollecting movie manners to which we still respond. People in 30's movies never talked quite this fruitily so consistently. The point is that this is the way we enjoy remembering them, to remind us, perhaps wrongly, that we've grown up.

Mr. Donen's production is his most

Rebecca York and George C. Scott in "Movie Movie"

buoyant film since "Singin' in the Rain," and goes a long way toward erasing the memory of things like "Lucky Lady," "The Little Prince" and "Staircase." For the most part, the timing is as precisely right as in one of those rare Broadway musicals in which everything works perfectly. Nothing is held too long. When we anticipate a gag, it is funnier simply because we do anticipate it, and then it is frequently topped.

The performers are marvelous. Mr. Bostwick (of Broadway's "The Robber Bridegroom") is a standout as the mild-mannered bookkeeper who, in the nick of time, turns out to be a singer, dancer and composer of hit songs in "Baxter's Beauties." Miss York is most comically earnest in the Ruby Keeler role in the same film, with terrific support from Barbara Harris, who plays the Ginger Rogers-Glenda Farrell part.

The newcomers who light up "Dynamite Hands" include Harry Hamlin, in the William Holden-John Garfield role; Ann Reinking as "Troubles" Moran, the nightclub singer with the rhinestone heart, and Kathleen Beller, as the poor girl with the mysterious eyesight problems. Messrs. Carney, Wallach and Buttons show up in each film, as well as in the "Zero Hour" trailer. They appear to have had a picnic, which they share.

Mr. Scott and Miss Van Devere are superb in both "Dynamite Hands" and "Baxter's Beauties." In the first, she is Joey Popchik's bespectacled librarian-sweetheart, only temporarily eclipsed by the acquisitive "Troubles" Moran, and in the second, she's the big Broadway actress whose drinking problem allows the chorus girl to become an overnight star. It's high praise to say Miss Van Devere is as funny and appealing as she was in "Where's Poppa?"

Mr. Scott is such a powerful actor that it's always a surprise he can be so wickedly funny when he puts his mind to it. It's more than a physical transformation, which anyone can accomplish with a bit of makeup. There's a change in his center of gravity. As "Gloves" Malloy, the trainer who grooms Joey Popchik for the title bout, he is a model for all slightly too colorful, unbearably wise and sentimental old character actors. In "Baxter's Beauties" he is the grandly stylish "Spats" Baxter, the legendary Broadway producer whose only real problem is that he has been struck down by something called Spencer's Disease, another mysterious ailment without many symptoms, but which seems to strike people in show business quite regularly. All of which is why "Spats" has to get his last show on in a hurry and make sure that it's a hit.

The appearance of "Movie Movie" at this point in a dreary season restores my confidence in the joys to be had from Hollywood flimflamming at its elegant best.

•

"Movie Movie," which has been rated PG ("Parental Guidance Suggested"), contains a couple of benignly funny double entendres that are probably out of the reach of any child who could be shocked by them.

1978 N 22, C9:1

Trysting Annually

SAME TIME, NEXT YEAR, directed by Robert Mulligan; produced by Walter Mirisch and Morton Gottlieb; screenplay by Bernard Slade; based on the stage play by Mr. Slade. Music by Marvin Hamlisch. Released by Universal Studios. At the Cinema I. Running time: 119 minutes. This movie is rated PG.

Doris....Ellen Burstyn
George....Alan Alda
Chalmers....Ivan Bonar
Waiter....Bernie Kuby
Second Waiter....Cosmo Sardo
Pilot 1....David Northcutt
Pilot 2....William Cantrel

By JANET MASLIN

THERE'S a big stumbling block in Bernard Slade's play "Same Time, Next Year," and the movie version trips and goes flying. What keeps these two lovers — who meet accidentally in a romantic little inn and then keep on meeting there, one night annually, for 20-odd years — eternally interested in each other? How do they manage to stay so gaga and still live peacefully with their spouses? How do they forget each other so conveniently when each anniversary tryst is over? At the best, this premise is full of terribly sad implications for the characters and their everyday lives. At worst, it stops an audience dead by calling constant attention to the play's falseness.

If "Same Time, Next Year," which opens today at Cinema I, were a success as a comedy, this patently phony pretext wouldn't necessarily hurt; indeed; its very outlandishness might become part of the joke. But Mr. Slade's screenplay isn't often funny, and it's full of momentous events that can't be laughed away.

During the half-dozen encounters that make up the story, there are a birth, some deaths, two guilty consciences and countless marital problems to be contended with. For instance, when we see them in 1966, George (Alan Alda) is a straitlaced businessman, and Doris (Ellen Burstyn) a very premature hippie. They have begun to have a domestic quarrel about Barry Goldwater when George blurts out that his son was killed in Vietnam; this is supposed to both melt Doris (it does) and explain the drastic change in George. It's hard to say which is more noxious, Mr. Slade's wringing a cheap tear out of his audience or his burdening a cardboard character with real grief.

As directed by Robert Mulligan, who has careened about 180 degrees away from his last film, the screamy and high-strung "Bloodbrothers," "Same Time, Next Year" is both less and more than it could have been. By moving the action outdoors once in a while, or into the inn's restaurant, Mr. Mulligan loses the element of claustrophobia that might have taken an audience's mind off the screenplay's troubles. But he substitutes the serenity of a California coastal setting, and gives the film a visual glamour that is mercifully distracting. Mr. Mulligan seems to have been more interested in sprucing up the material than in preserving its absolute integrity, and under the circumstances, his approach makes sense.

What sells "Same Time, Next Year" on stage, and what keeps the movie halfway afloat, is the chance it gives George and Doris to change with the times. Not much happens to George, relatively speaking. He evolves from young Lothario to stodgy executive to know-it-all analysand, and always stays something of a straight man to Doris. She, on the other hand, changes from ingénue to sexpot to pregnant frump to successful businesswoman with a logic that has more to do with costuming than with character. These shifts have such slight bearing on one another that the story becomes little more than a series of blackout sketches. But the scenes' very incongruity is funnier than any one episode is individually, and clearly the actors have a lot to play with.

Mr. Alda isn't terribly playful, and he reads every line as if it were part of a joke, which only accentuates the flatness of the script. Miss Burstyn, on the other hand, is the eternal coquette, even when — in the latter part of the film — she begins looking like Betty Ford. Her gestures vary absolutely from scene to scene, yet she brings so much sweetness to Doris's various incarnations that the character very nearly comes to life. Miss Burstyn never tries to make sense of the role, and she often undercuts what little sense there is; her 24-year-old Doris, for instance, is so demure it's impossible to believe she ever succumbed to George's charms in the first place. But she gives the role a warmth and grace that become quite an adequate substitute for reason.

•

"Same Time, Next Year" is rated PG ("Parental Guidance Suggested") thanks to the intimations of tawdriness in the characters' annual hotel-room reunions.

1978 N 22, C9:5

Worth About 150 Goats

THE WEDDING CAMELS, produced and directed by David and Judith MacDougall. An anthropological feature on the Turkana people of Kenya. In Turkana with English subtitles. Running time: 109 minutes. At the Film Forum, 15 Vandam Street. This film is not rated.

One of the performers in "The Wedding Camels."

By JANET MASLIN

A FEW days before the ceremony, the bride is all smiles, but at the wedding she's a nervous wreck. The women wear much too much jewelry. The bride's mother has worn herself out sewing the bridal outfit and gossiping about what others wore at other weddings, while the father of the bride has kept an eagle eye on the gifts. An aunt has been in charge of the hospitality extended to the new in-laws, and she has plotted this with a vengeance. When a hostess wows her guests, the aunt explains, "They say, 'She is good — let us marry her daughter so we'll always be treated like this.'"

Anything unusual here? Certainly not. But bear in mind that the guests and family members seen in "The Wedding Camels," a funny, informative and thoroughly delightful documentary that will have a limited run beginning tonight at the Film Forum, are members of a seminomadic tribe in Kenya that habitually swaps its young women for cattle. The bride we are watching turns out to be worth about 150 goats.

These people wear ornaments in their chins and very little to cover the rest of them, and they spend a remarkable portion of their waking hours just squatting peacefully on the ground. But when it comes time to thrash out family problems or haggle over the bridal livestock, they suddenly don't seem to be so primitive. When the bride's sweet but confused-looking father discovers that he hasn't gotten enough camels in the bargain to pacify his wife or her sisters, and sheepishly doles out his own camels just to quiet them down, his embarrassment has a universally comic appeal.

The Turkana people, who appear in the film and speak their own language — there are subtitles — have allowed David and Judith MacDougall extraordinary access to the quarrels and customs that surround this wedding. Still, they have their complaints about the film makers. "There's just one thing I dislike about these people — they don't marry our daughters," the bride's father complains, glancing balefully at the camera.

Through the MacDougalls' resourceful direction and their brisk, well-organized editing, this one social occasion becomes indicative of what the general life of the tribe is like. The trouble with the cattle-trading arrangement for brides, it turns out, is that because the herds are tended by girls, a family can wind up with more animals than it can manage if too many daughters marry. The family's peculiarly businesslike, unsentimental attitude toward its frightened young daughter is explained thusly: "Our daughters are not ours, they are born to be given out. It is the wives of our sons who care for us in our old age."

There is a great deal of hardship in what we see of the Turkana people's lives. Everyone except the bridegroom's sneaky nephew is angularly handsome, but noone carries an ounce of fat; the cattle negotiations are a desperate economic necessity as well as a matter of pride. But the camera also captures these people's foxy intelligence, and their dry humor. When the aging bridegroom told his other wives he wanted to marry this young girl, the senior wife explains, they all insisted on having a look at her. "We've seen better," they declared. But they agreed to lend their old goat of a husband a few extra animals anyway, to clinch the deal, if marrying a teen-ager would make him happy.

1978 N 23, C19:1

To Near-Bankruptcy

IF IT FITS, a documentary film by John Marshall and Mark Erder; part of the New American Filmmakers Series at the Whitney Museum of American Art. Running time: 60 minutes.

By VINCENT CANBY

"ANYONE who wants to work hard can still get ahead in this country," says Lewis Burton, the fire chief of Haverhill, Mass., and the successful candidate for the office of mayor in 1976. In the context of "If It Fits," John K. Marshall's anthropological documentary now at the Whitney Museum of American Art, these words are whistling in the wind.

"If It Fits" takes its shape from that mayoral campaign, following Mr. Burton and the incumbent mayor, George Katsaros, as each goes stumping outside supermarkets, on street corners, at ethnic picnics and in debates where the real issues seem to be beyond both of them. Yet the film has less to do with electioneering and politics than it does with time and tide, with social and economic changes that have reduced a once prosperous American manufacturing community to near-bankruptcy.

Haverhill's story is hardly unique. Until World War II, "the Queen Slipper City," as its boosters called Haverhill, was one of the most important shoemaking cities in the state. After the war, as the shoe companies departed, seeking cheaper labor in the South and West, the city's self-assurance was severely tried. Unemployment increased, taxes and municipal spending rose, and no new industries moved in to fill the void.

"If It Fits" records desperation in the faces, voices, plans, promises and ultimately, complete confusion not only of the candidates, but also of the union leaders, manufacturers, suppliers and workers who, like Mr. Burton, invoke their faith in the American system with clichés that don't provide answers.

"If It Fits," a cool, unsurprised sort of movie, offers no answers either. It doesn't mean to. It calls attention to history, which may be the best way to solve the kind of problems now faced by Haverhill and hundreds of other American cities.

1978 N 30, C18:4

From Pirandello Novel

THE VOYAGE, directed by Vittorio de Sica; screenplay by Diego Fabbri, Massimo Franciosa and Luisa Montagnana; produced by Carlo Ponti; director of photography, Ennio Guarnieri; music composed by Manuel de Sica; editor, Kim Arcalli; released by United Artists. At the Thalia theater, Broadway and 95th Street. Running time: 102 minutes.

Adriana de Mauro .... Sophia Loren
Cesare Braggi .... Richard Burton
Antonio Braggi .... Ian Bannen
Signora de Mauro .... Barbara Pilavin
Simona .... Annabella Incontrera
Nandino .... Paolo Lena
Doctor Mascione .... Renato Pinciroli
Notary Salierno .... Daniele Vargas
Rinaldo .... Ettore Geri
Clementina .... Olga Romanelli
Doctor Carlini .... Richard Mangano
Doctor de Paolo .... Barrie Simmons
Notory's Clerk .... Franco Lauriano

By VINCENT CANBY

IN common with many other great men, Vittorio de Sica, the Italian film maker who died four years ago, had a chronic weakness that was as disorienting to him as a whiff of booze can be to the alcoholic. Mr. De Sica, the social critic ("The Bicycle Thief") with an immense talent for comedy as both an actor ("It Started in Naples") and as a director ("Marriage Italian-Style"), was from time to time subject to fits of teary sentimentality that upset his balance and completely dissolved his judgment.

As a sentimentalist Mr. De Sica never went on a bender by himself. He surrounded himself with friends, as if the making of these ponderously romantic movies were really occasions of great conviviality. Perhaps they were, though it never shows in the completed pictures.

•

Think of the laughably long-faced "A Place for Lovers," in which the magnificently structured Faye Dunaway succumbed to Marcello Mastroianni and death (in that order) in some of the most beautiful scenery in the world, from a disease never identified except for the lack of horrid symptoms.

In "Sunflower" he persuaded Mr. Mastroianni and the exuberant Sophia Loren to play out a woeful tale about a plucky little peasant woman who hitchhikes her way to the Soviet Union after World War II to search for her reportedly lost-in-action soldier-husband. Does she find him? Does Naples have a bay?

That "The Voyage," which Mr. De Sica made the year before he died, is only now reaching us is not difficult to understand. The film, which opens today at the Thalia Theater, has the manner of something out of sync with itself and the world around it.

•

I'm not referring to the sound of the English-dubbed dialogue, which isn't great (though the film's three stars, Miss Loren, Richard Burton and Ian Bannen, are speaking their own lines), but to other aspects of the film that are even more important.

"The Voyage," based on a Luigi Pirandello novel I do not know, is set in Sicily in the years just before World War I and is another unnamed-fatal-disease picture.

It's the unusually unconvincing story of Cesare Braggi (Mr. Burton), the scion of rich landed gentry, his younger brother Antonio (Mr. Bannen), and the beautiful young seamstress Adriana (Miss Loren) whom Cesare loves but whose hand he presents to Antonio in accordance with the wishes expressed in their father's will.

Nothing in the movie fits. The casting of two extremely English actors as Sicilian aristocrats need not have been ludicrous — one of the best performances Burt Lancaster ever gave was in Luchino Visconti's "The Leopard."

•

But even if Mr. Burton and Mr. Bannen had been Italian they would have been wrong for the movie. They are too old and their temperaments do not suit the cinematic landscape. Miss Loren's age is not right but, worse, she has no role.

The movie, now at least four years

Ian Bannen and Sophia Loren in De Sica's "The Voyage" at the Thalia
Has the manner of something out of sync with itself and the world around it

old, may have been edited somewhere along the line — I do not know — but the evidence on view at the Thalia suggests there never was a role for this most intelligent, inventive, seductive, profoundly surprising of actresses.

"The Voyage" consists of a lot of pretty sets and costumes, much period detail (an early automobile with unreliable brakes is a key plot device), some comically irrelevant references to world events (like that nasty shooting in Sarajevo), while the two lovers refuse to acknowledge their passion until a major obstacle to that passion falls off the side of a mountain.

Movies like "The Voyage" couldn't be made without falls off mountains, nor without the sort of heart trouble Adriana suffers without too much inconvenience until it's time for the film to end. Then it's gulp, over and out.

The English-language screenplay, which, I assume, is faithful to the Italian one written by Diego Fabbri, Massimo Franciosa and Luisa Montagnana, is chock full of the kind of lines you haven'y heard since Andrew and Virgina Stone penned their screen version of "Song of Norway."

Some are funny ("Who was that, dear?" "That was the maestro Puccini") but most are simply out of touch with the feelings and emotions the movie should be dealing in.

1978 D 1, C9:1

FILM VIEW

VINCENT CANBY

Beguiling Actors, Old and New

The films haven't been great this season but there have been a number of performances that have made them seem worthwhile in this something less than best of all possible worlds. I'm thinking of what is virtually a brand-new Ingrid Bergman in Ingmar Bergman's handsome though patchy exercise in familial self-analysis, "Autumn Sonata"; Laurence Olivier as the Nazi-hunter in Franklin J. Schaffner's "The Boys from Brazil"; Bette Davis, Peter Ustinov and their travelling companions in "Death on the Nile"; Richard Farnsworth's small but very affecting performance in "Comes A Horseman," which is billed as a Western but looks like a documentary on the weather; George C. Scott, Trish Van Devere and a group of new-to-movies actors in Stanley Donen's "Movie Movie," and Isabelle Huppert as the beautiful, mysterious teenager with armored emotions in Claude Chabrol's "Violette."

All acting is difficult to analyze, and film performances n ay well be beyond rational explanation except by someone who is plugged directly into heaven. What we see as a performance on the screen has been filtered through so many layers of technology, and has been shaped by so many decisions made by others, that I can understand it when an actor says the finished performance is as much a surprise to him as to the members of the ticket-buying public. Then, too, there are differerent kinds of performance — the Olivier kind, whose roots and methods are clearly of the theater, and the Isabelle Huppert kind, which, though it obviously involves the performer's intelligence and craft, also is the result of the way she looks to the camera and the way Chabrol uses those looks. Miss Huppert's bone structure is as important to "Violette" as anything she says or does, which makes this sort of actor extremely vulnerable in films.

Witness what happened to Isabelle Adjani in her first American film, "The Driver." Wrestling with a language that was not her own, Miss Adjani behaved like someone under sedation. The lines were spoken with difficulty. Her movements appeared to have been over-rehearsed. There was never any sense of freedom or spontaneity. Yet these were some of the very same mannerisms that made her performance in François Truffaut's "The Story of Adele H." seem so remarkable. In the Truffaut film Miss Adjani was playing a woman in the process of being consumed by her obsession. The self-consciousness we saw was a symptom of an interior life we were meant to guess at. In "The Driver" it simply looked like bad acting, though the actress had brought the same abilities to both films.

• • •

"Autumn Sonata" is about as gloomy — and potentially as arid — a film as one might imagine. It's essentially two extended confrontation scenes between a tough, talented, ambitious concert pianist (Miss Bergman) and her furious, self-pitying daughter (Liv Ullmann), whose chief talent is nursing a hatred of the mother who abandoned her. Because the film ends with at least the bare possibility of a reconciliation, it seems that the writer-director wanted us to feel for the two women equally. Yet the daughter is someone of such limited emotional resources, and the mother so complicated in moving, contradictory ways, that one's attention throughout the film is riveted by Miss Bergman, who has never before had a role to match this one.

This is not to underrate her Hollywood career — the great star of "Saratoga Trunk," "Gaslight," "Casablanca" and "Notorious" — or her later work with Roberto Rossellini and Jean Renoir. The earlier films represent a different kind of movie acting, a kind for which she was beautifully suited. Those films — even Rossellini's "Stromboli" — either demanded star-turns that utilized the actress's familiar professional personality, or asked for the complete subjugation of the actress to the director and the material. It is a paradox that Ingmar Bergman, one of the strongest of directors, should have provided Miss Bergman with a role that has the effect of revealing the complete woman for the first time.

Watching Miss Bergman in this film, as she complains about her back, or counts her money, or tries to conceal her boredom with second-rate Chopin, becomes an exhilirating experience. Here is an actress we've never seen before. "Autumn Sonata" is not something to warm the heart, but it provides the kind of excitement one only experiences when recognizing a new talent.

• • •

Watching Laurence Olivier in "The Boys from Brazil" is almost as much fun, though for slightly different reasons. Olivier almost always surprises us, even when he makes mistakes, as he did when he played his Othello with a Calypso beat and attempted to upgrade Big Daddy's vulgarity in the television adaptation of "Cat on a Hot Tin Roof." Having recently set out to build his bank account, Olivier has been lending his presense to the kind of pop films he seldom had time for earlier in his career, not in cameo roles but in demanding, full-length performances.

His performance as the obsessed hunter of long-lost Nazis in "The Boys from Brazil" is a constant delight. By letting us see the physical frailty of the man, he emphasizes his character's tenacity and strength. Olivier's performance is also shaded by perceptions that have the effect of comedy, even when the events are far from comic. It is acting of a rare sort that more than matches his mad Nazi dentist in "Marathon Man" and the sybaritic, shrewd old automobile tycoon in "The Betsy." The latter featured one of Olivier's extra-special, heavy-on-the-seasoning accents (a seeming blend of Scots, English and Middle American West) of the sort that makes every Olivier performance a kind of linguistic pousse-cafe.

"The Boys from Brazil," based on Ira Levin's novel about the cloning of 90-some Adolf Hitlers, is fairly silly material, but the movie is not quite as silly as you may have been led to believe. It's too easy to poke fun at Gregory Peck's stately impersonation of a Nazi bent on populating the world with a bunch of mini-Hitlers, but the movie has been otherwise very carefully directed by Schaffner and, in addition to Olivier, features James Mason and Lilli Palmer, fine actors who are never around often enough.

Almost everybody in "Death on the Nile" is a star doing the obligatory star-turn, which is exactly what's required of a movie based on one of Agatha Christie's more durable, genteel whodunits. It's handsome, ageless nonsense in which set and costume designers are as important as director and writer, and the stars most important of all. Like the Nile in the dry season, the movie flows very, very gently, but this allows us to appreciate the turns, as when Mr. Ustinov says, "Perhaps you could shed some light on all this . . . ?" or when Miss Davis pronounces the film's ending: "This place is beginning to resemble a mortuary." That line isn't exactly Shavian but the way she bites into it, separating subject from predicate, putting the emphasis on the unexpected word, in effect not speaking the sentence but parsing it, is to be reassured that one of our most remarkable talents is still in top form.

• • •

"Movie Movie" is about movies that Hollywood was making in the early thirties, just about the time that Bette Davis was gathering force. It's two movies in one — "Dynamite Hands," a black-and-white urban melodrama about a poor but honest delivery boy who must put aside his law studies to become a boxer, and pay for the operation in Vienna that will cure his sister's mysterious eye ailment, and "Baxter's Beauties of 1933," a full-color backstage musical that, with light heart, sends up the conventions of "Footlight Parade" and the Golddigger movies.

"Movie Movie," wittily written by Larry Gelbart and Sheldon Keller, also contains a trailer for a Richard Arlen-type of World War I meller called "Zero Hour," and a terribly facetious introduction by George Burns, something that was apparently added to make sure we would know that what we were about to see was a comedy. Among the principal pleasures of "Movie Movie" are the comic performances of George C. Scott, as the gruff, wise, sentimental trainer in "Dynamite Hands" and as the Broadway producer named Spats Baxter in "Baxter's Beauties," and Trish Van Devere, who plays the young boxer's loyal girlfriend in the first and a tempermental Broadway star in the second. By bringing a laser-beam intensity to bear on this material, both Scott and Miss Van Devere come close to transforming parody into farce.

The film also introduces us to some new performers who, I trust, are headed for big things. They include Barry Bostwick, a singer-dancer-comedian of great energy and humor; Rebecca York, who plays the Ruby Keeler role as if she were born in her tap shoes; Harry Hamlin, as the young boxer, and Kathleen Beller, who is exceedingly funny in the tiny role of the boxer's astigmatic sister.

Richard Farnsworth, a former stunt man turned actor, is the one defensible reason to sit through Alan J. Pakula's pretentious, cliché-ridden "Comes A Horseman," at least until that point when Farnsworth dies. This is not giving away any plot since it's apparent from the time he makes his entrance that this character, a sort of latter-day Gabby Hayes, is doomed by the script. It's never a question of whether he'll die, only how, and the how turns out to be pretty tacky. Jane Fonda, James Caan and Jason Robards are required to carry the burden of this movie about cattle barons, oil-hungry speculators and land, but the film's class is Farnsworth's. He has a magically compelling film presence that lights up a movie that is otherwise so dark (photographically) you almost need a flashlight to see it. ■

1978 D 3, II:13:1

New faces: Richard Farnsworth (left) "is the one defensible reason to sit through 'Comes a Horseman,' " while Rebecca York and Barry Bostwick of "Movie Movie" are "headed for big things."

Film: SoHo Samples

By JANET MASLIN

"THE Best of Ann Arbor 1978," a program of 10 independently made shorts from the Ann Arbor (Mich.) Film Festival, is yet another feather in the Film Forum's projector — that is, another bit of evidence that this small SoHo theater dependably screens some of the best, most imaginatively chosen films in town. This time, the selections are short, well-matched, whimsical and funny, and most of them have some satirical bearing on movies of other kinds. One of them, "Hardware Wars," is such an ingenious parody that it has already been a substantial success across the country.

"Hardware Wars," an $8,000, 13-minute, surprisingly complete send-up of "Star Wars," is the work of a San Franciscan named Ernie Fosselius; Mr. Fosselius is now making something called "Swamp Gas," subtitled "We Are Not Alone, but We Might as Well Be." Why was his version of "Star Wars" — "filmed on location in space," the closing credits will have you know — so inexpensive to make? Well, a lot of money was saved by substituting household appliances for intergalactic paraphernalia. Instead of a starship blasting death rays, for instance, Mr. Fosselius offers wide-angle shots of an iron, flying through the sky and spraying steam. When the ship pulls into a space station, we see a waffle iron with its doors swinging open; when a strange planet appears on the spaceship's monitors, it looks just like a brand-new volleyball. The Princess has crullers on either side of her head, instead of rolled braids. The small robot is a vacuum cleaner. The lightsword battle is fought with flashlights. The whole thing is one long howl.

Nothing else on the program is quite this hilarious, but there are other films just as charming. "Cold Cows," by Franklin Miller, trains a camera on some unhappy-looking cattle in raw, rainy weather for two minutes, occasionally cutting to titles that read: "Cold cows waiting it out . . . only last year they toured Europe . . . loved Paris . . . stopped over in Egypt . . . saw the Pyramids . . . tropical evenings . . . gentle breezes . . . such memories . . . and now this." "Hit-a-sin Rain," another very short film, by Howard Hoffman and Ann Goodman, shows a pair of animated hands acting out a game of charades. The answer, which sounds very much like the title, is the name of a much-celebrated film about a newspaper tycoon who once owned a sled.

●

The zaniest film on the bill is surely Norman E. Magden's "Banana I," in which a young man lectures the audience on rules of etiquette pertaining to the fruit in question. "There's big ones and there's little ones. I think I said that already, but I cannot overstress that point," he explains. And: "It's very important that you don't overreact to the banana, that you treat them with respect."

In Jim Anderson's "Canada Mini Notes," the technique of animating by riffling consecutive drawings on a pad of paper is taken to unreasonable extremes: there are pages equipped with kazoos, pages on fire, pages with somebody's nose sticking through them, and so on.

In Mike Haller's "Bruce and His Things," a man gives us a guided tour of his room, rattling on about his theory of shopping and his opal collection and his sofa made of buffalo tusks. "It behooves you, when you own things like this, to know about them," he explains, as if that explained anything.

Sara Petty's "Furies" is a nice foray into Art Deco animation, and Philip Dauber's "Spaceborne" is a compilation of remarkable lunar footage, all of it from NASA. The one relative bore in the group is Tim Shepard's "China Dog," which has a self-importance that might work better in less sprightly, less effervescent company.

1978 D 7, C17:3

Allen Gorwitz, Peter Falk, Paul Sorvino and Kevin O'Connor in William Friedkin's film "The Brink's Job."

Dream Caper

THE BRINK'S JOB, directed by William Friedkin, produced by Ralph Serpe; screenplay by Walon Green; book by Noel Behn; director of photography, A Norman Leigh; production designer, Dean Tavoularis; film editors, Bud Smith and Robert K. Lambert; music composed by Richard R. Bennett; released by Universal Studios. At the Criterion and Gemini I. Running time: 118 minutes. This film is rated PG.

Tony Pino .... Peter Falk
Joe McGinnis .... Peter Boyle
Vinnie Costa .... Allen Goorwitz
Specs O'Keefe .... Warren Oates
Mary Pino .... Gena Rowlands
Jazz Maffie .... Paul Sorvino
J. Edgar Hoover .... Sheldon Leonard
Sandy Richardson .... Gerard Murphy
Stanley (Gus) Gusciora .... Kevin O'Connor

By VINCENT CANBY

EVERYBODY has his fantasy — the untended candy store, the pay-telephone that offers free calls to Paris, the breakaway bikini and, of course, easy access to the vault of your favorite bank. The seven men who successfully robbed the Brink's armored car company in Boston of more than $2.7 million in January 1950 realized their dream. And, to judge from the continued interest in the caper, they realized the dreams of a lot of other people

For one brief instant, the Brink's bandits — small-time hoods who lucked into what was called "the crime of the century" — wallowed in money, greenbacks, the kind we carry in our wallets, nothing as esoteric as stocks or bonds or letters of credit. They were up to their ears in the real thing. After that, it was one long hangover. For most of them it wasn't much fun, but it was worth that moment of glorious, physical possession.

•

This is the approach of William Friedkin's "The Brink's Job," which attempts to take a lighthearted view of the robbery, but is only involving when it plays these events more or less straight, something that the 1955 Tony Curtis film, "Six Bridges to Cross," failed to do.

"The Brink's Job," opening today at the Criterion and Gemini I Theaters, covers a lot more years than any caper movie has any right to do — from the late 1930's to the late 50's — in order to explain the backgrounds of the hoods involved. However, because the characters are so one-dimensional, it seems a waste of the movie's time and ours.

It's the kind of movie in which each actor registers just about all he has to work with in any one scene. Essentially they are cartoon types. There is the leader of the gang, a sentimental petty thief named Tony Pino (Peter Falk), who loves his wife, Mary (Gena Rowlands), and pursues his dream to success only because he's too stupid to know better.

•

The other gang members are played by Allen Goorwitz (whom we used to know as Allen Garfield), as Tony's almost fatally clumsy brother-in-law; Peter Boyle, as a short-tempered, mean-spirited Irishman; Paul Sorvino, as a bookie and the one member of the crew who seems capable of spelling his own name correctly; Warren Oates, as a battle-fatigued explosives expert who is not so expert when the chips are down, and Kevin O'Connor and Gerard Murphy as the soldiers of the company.

The film, which was written by Walon Green, adapted from a novel by Noel Behn, is neither especially comic nor — and this is surprising, considering Mr. Friedkin's success with "The French Connection" — suspenseful. As in his last film, "Sorcerer," Mr. Friedkin seems bent on supplying us with more sociological information than is entirely necessary, whereas more information about the heist itself would have been welcome. For example, were the Brink's people really as casual about security as they are shown to be in this film?

•

The movie looks very handsome and rather bigger and more expensive than the story actually warrants, except, of course, for the cash we see on screen. The performances are intelligent without being particularly believable or fun. One continually has the impression that Mr. Falk, Mr. Goorwitz and Miss Rowlands are playing down to roles that aren't good enough for them. Mr. Boyle's role is one that he could telephone in by this time. Mr. Sorvino plays it as it comes, which is without fuss but without tremendous conviction. Only Mr. Oates has anything to do as the probably psychologically disturbed war veteran, and he's not around very long.

"The Brink's Job" doesn't do justice to our fantasy, which is, I suppose, only a misdemeanor.

1978 D 8, C13:1

Napoleon's Numbskull

THE ADVENTURES OF GERARD (1970), directed by Jerzy Skolimowski; produced by Henry E. Lester and Gene Gutowski; screenplay by H.A.L. Craig; adapted from the "Brigadier Gerard" stories by Sir Arthur Conan Doyle; music composed and conducted by Riz Ortolani; director of photography, Witold Sobocinski. Released by United Artists. At the Thalia, 95th Street and Broadway. This film has not been rated.
WITH: Peter McEnery, Eli Wallach, Claudia Cardinale and Jack Hawkins.

By JANET MASLIN

IT'S not hard to figure out why "The Adventures of Gerard," directed in 1970 by Jerzy Skolimowski, is only now having its United States premiere. Mr. Skolimowski has made some estimable films, most notably the beautiful and baffling "Deep End," but he has attracted only a smallish following so far.

This is a slight, relatively uncharacteristic historical farce, of the type that went out of vogue about the time that its leading lady, Claudia Cardinale, did. Still, "The Adventures of Gerard" is part of the Thalia's admirable effort to bring to light previously unreleased films by good directors of modest renown. And although it's not likely to win Mr. Skolimowski any new admirers, this is a sufficiently lively and peculiar artifact to be of interest to his avid devotees.

•

The plot, taken from Sir Arthur Conan Doyle's relatively obscure "Brigadier Gerard" stories, has to do with a bumbling incompetent who figures nonsensically in Napoleon's conquest of Spain. Napoleon, played very amusingly by Eli Wallach, commissions one of his officers, Brigadier Gerard, played not at all amusingly by Peter McEnery, to serve as a decoy messenger, never intending that he will reach his destination. But arrive he does, perhaps because the most formidable opponent Spain sends his way is Miss Cardinale. After a series of duels and close shaves and escapades, Gerard wins a medal from Napoleon, and everyone is happy.

Mr. Skolimowski presents this material with garden-variety forced merriment, the kind of thing that Richard Lester rendered obsolete with his cheerfully messy "Musketeer" movies. But he brings an appetite for the bizarre to a couple of slow-motion torture sequences, and to one lovingly shot episode that involves falling food. The cinematography is zesty and a little overripe; so is Miss Cardinale.

On the same bill at the Thalia is "King, Queen, Knave," Mr. Skolimowski's 1972 adaptation of the Nabokov novel, starring David Niven and Gina Lollobrigida.

1978 D 8, C30:1

Invasion of Privacy

DOSSIER 51, (in French with subtitles, and English) directed by Michel Deville; screenplay, Michel Deville and Gilles Perrault; adapted from the novel by Gilles Perrault; director of photography, Claude Lecomte; editor, Raymonde Guyot; music, Franz Schubert (taken from the Arpeggione Sonata); producer, Philippe Dussart; and production companies, Elefilm (Paris), Société Française de Production (Paris), and Maran Film (Munich); released by Gaumont/New Yorker Films. At the 8th Street Playhouse and Cinema Studio 1, Broadway and 66th Street. Running time: 108 minutes. This film has not been rated.

Dominique Auphal .... François Marthouret
Liliane Auphal .... Claude Marcault
Philippe Lescarre .... Philippe Rouleau
Marguerite Marie .... Nathalie Juvet
Sylvie Mouriat .... Françoise Beliard
Cleaning woman .... Jenny Cleve
Esculape 1 .... Roger Planchon

Roger Planchon in a scene from the film "Dossier 51."

By VINCENT CANBY

MICHEL DEVILLE's new French film, "Dossier 51," is the sort of movie that's more interesting to talk about than to sit through. Its method is more intellectual than emotional or dramatic, which is not to say that it's as profound as it is arid. The movie, which was shown at this year's New York Film Festival, opens today at the 8th Street Playhouse and the newly partitioned Cinema Studio 1.

"Dossier 51" is an adaptation by Mr. Deville and Gilles Perrault of Mr. Perrault's novel about the activities of an unidentified intelligence agency as it seeks a possible candidate to infiltrate an international trade organization. The agency, which could be the Central Intelligence Agency or some such group, picks on a young French diplomat and then, with the help of just about every surveillance device developed by man, studies its fellow to find ways in which he might possibly be blackmailed. He is followed, as is his wife, and his wife's lover; his apartment is bugged, as is his wife's lover's apartment; his activities are filmed whenever feasible; his friends, family and servants are questioned, and sometimes sexually seduced; his childhood is examined and analyzed for character defects until, at last, the agency gets the goods on the poor man.

•

In an attempt to dramatize this terrifying invasion of privacy, Mr. Deville has sought out a cinematic equivalent to the method of Mr. Perrault's novel, which told the story through official reports and memorandums that kept the subject of the investigation at several removes from the reader. Mr. Deville does more or less the same thing, composing the movie entirely of secret films, tape recordings, written and oral reports of agents who write and talk in the jargon of their trade.

The idea is more sound in theory than in practice, because it's virtually impossible to see any difference between what are supposed to be secret films and the visualized verbal reports that are presented to us. Mr. Deville's intention that this method will somehow implicate all of us in the audience as voyeurs overlooks the fact that all movies effectively implicate the members of the audience as voyeurs. It's one of the ways in which fiction works.

"Dossier 51" thus is more cinematically tricky than psychologically shocking. It's not only that we're all fairly well aware of the awful possibilities of electronic surveillance and the uses to which it may be put — Francis Ford Coppola's "The Conversation" dramatized this nightmare far more eerily — but that Mr. Deville's agents (unseen except in mirrors or films-within-the-film) are so clever and resourceful that there's never any suspense in the movie. It's a butterfly hunt. We don't especially care about the victim, about the agents, or even about their methods, which, unfortunately, no longer have the power to astonish.

There are further technical problems. Actors playing directly to the subjective camera tend to become extremely self-conscious. The method of the movie never allows us or them to forget the camera. There is a single dramatic scene in the entire film, when an undercover agent interview's 51's (code name for the victim) mother and she spills the beans about her son's true parentage and some sad details about her own life. Françoise Lugagne, who plays the mother, creates the one living character in the film, but Mr. Deville, apparently knowing that he had a good thing going here, allows the scene to go on so long that it finally undercuts not only Miss Lugagne, but everything else in the picture.

The movie takes a small boy's delight in the jargon and syntax of the spy trade. People, things and operations are all called by their code names (Jupiter, Minerva, 51, 52, 52B, Zephyr, Dead Leaves, etc.) to such an extent that one wishes one had been equipped with a lexicon on entering the theater. Much of the film is in French with English subtitles, but the soundtrack narration and the conversation of the unseen agents are presented in an English that sounds as if it had been written and recorded by Martians.

1978 D 13, C21:1

On St. Stephen's Day

RAIN AND SHINE, (In Hungarian with English subtitles), directed by Ferenc Andras; screenplay, Mr. Andras, Geza Beremenyi and Akos Kertesz; photography, Lajos Koltai; production company, Hunnia Studio (Budapest); released by New Yorker Films. At Cinema Studio 2, Broadway and 66th Street. Running time: 98 minutes. This film has not been rated.

Kaltar Sr.	Imre Sarlai
Istvan Kaltar	Lajos Szabo
Mrs. Kaltar	Erzsi Pasztor
Pityu	Zolton Biro
Marika	Maria Fesus
Jolan	Ildiko Pecsi
Vetro	Konstantin Anatol
Mrs. Vetro	Eva Spanyik
Daughter	Zsuzsa Szakacs

"RAIN AND SHINE," Ferenc Andras's Hungarian film that opens today at the new Cinema Studio 2, recalls the humanist comedies that, briefly, came out of Czechoslovakia in the late 60's, before Soviet intervention effectively ended the "Prague Spring." I emphasize that "Rain and Shine" only recalls those films, including the comedies of Milos Forman and Ivan Passer; it doesn't equal either their artistry or their vision, which transcended social and political concerns.

"Rain and Shine" is sweet, decent and essentially very, very safe. It's a gently satiric view of contemporary Hungarian manners as demonstrated during a daylong confrontation between crudely pragmatic country folk and their more sophisticated city cousins on Aug. 20, St. Stephen's Day, the name-day of Hungary's first King and patron saint.

•

Though Mr. Andras, who collaborated on the script as well as directed the film, attempts to make this confrontation particular, he succeeds only intermittently. His heart is clearly on the side of the host-family, buoyant farmers, who are close to nature, know how to cook and eat and deal with the soil, as opposed to the visitors, who have ulcers, prattle on about "serious" (symphonic) music and use body deodorants. This satire is skin deep.

Some of the performances are noteworthy, especially those of Imre Sarlai as the ancient grandfather, a man who has outlived several political regimes and remains benignly unsurprised by any turn of events, and Erzsi Pasztor, as a farmer's wife, a woman whose compulsion to work from sunup to sundown hides disappointments and suggests a depth of feeling expressed nowhere else in the movie.

VINCENT CANBY

1978 D 13, C21:2

2 Hit Films Without Gimmicks

By JANET MASLIN

WHY are "Midnight Express" and "Bread and Chocolate," two movies without stars or gimmicks or other obvious selling points, among this season's most durable hits? Both of these films depict the plights of characters stranded in hostile surroundings, and each reduces the situation to simple, almost storybook terms. Each presents disturbing problems in a manner that is ultimately soothing, alarmingly so. Each depends heavily upon crudely drawn racial or national stereotypes for its dramatic impetus. Too often, each approaches its audience the way someone wielding an electric prod might approach a steer.

Certainly "Bread and Chocolate" is the more easygoing of the two. The main character is an impoverished Italian waiter trying to make a living in Switzerland, and much attention is paid to the sharp contrast between his swarthiness and the blond, Teutonic looks of his clientele. Life for this waiter is tough, and the film follows him from one unlucky break to the next, but — amazingly — the man never voices an ugly sentiment or loses his temper. He is poor, but he doesn't especially resent the rich, no matter how badly they treat him. He is keenly aware of the differences between himself and the Swiss, but his anger develops into self-hatred rather than racism. The waiter's two rivals, at work and in romantic matters, are presented as no less sweet or downtrodden than he.

Small wonder, then, that "Bread and Chocolate" concludes with a list of awards given the film by religious groups and juries at out-of-the-way film festivals. A movie that appears to examine racial prejudice and economic injustice and still manages to remain prettily wistful is bound to be a crowd-pleaser. But audiences are so charmed by the overabundant goodness on display in "Bread and Chocolate" that they're *too* charmed — some crowds respond to a chicken-coop sequence, which constitutes the only note of real bitterness in the film, as if it were just as fluffy and funny as the rest.

•

You can say this much for "Midnight Express": nothing fluffy or funny here.

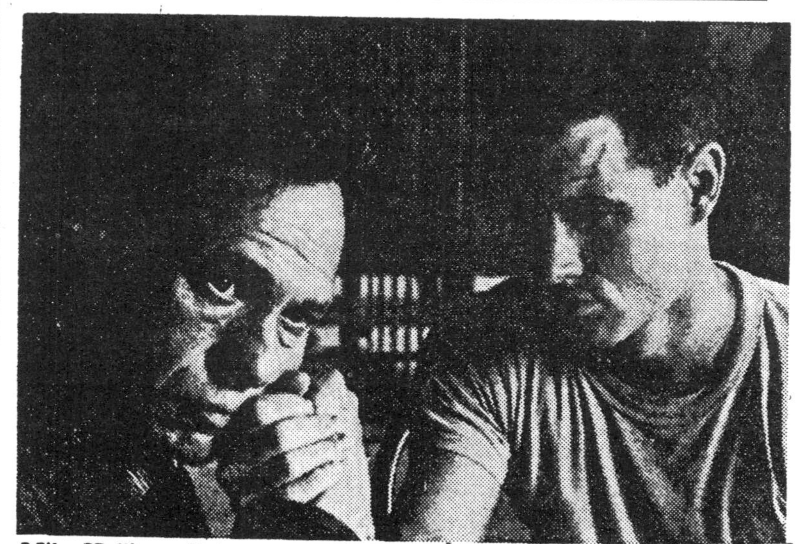

Mike Kellin as father and Brad Davis as his son, in film

From the moment that nice young Billy Hayes is thrown into a Turkish prison, where the guards are greasy nose-pickers and the prisoners are covered with blue-gray grime, it's clear that the rest of the movie will be no picnic. Sure enough, what follow are beatings and atrocities and Billy's altogether grotesque tirades against the Turks. ("I hate you. I hate your cities and I hate your people. You're all pigs.")

When a film savages its audience as relentlessly as "Midnight Express" does, it's bound to strike some viewers as powerful and authentic; the most commonly heard praise of this opus has to do with its purporting to lay bare the horrors of prison life. But its real allure has to do with the conveniently changeable morality that director Alan Parker brings to bear on Billy and his predicament.

When Billy, played whinily by Brad Davis, is arrested for smuggling hashish at the film's beginning, it's just an unlucky accident — he isn't a narcotics pusher, he only means to sell it to his friends. When Billy bites off the tongue of a fellow prisoner who is an informer, Mr. Parker's delirious, ecstatic direction of the scene suggests that Billy has at last succumbed to extraordinary pressures, and that he's in no way responsible for the act. But when Billy finally kills one of his captors and makes his escape, it's a triumph of the human spirit; his sanity reasserts itself just in time for the grand finale.

So "Midnight Express" offers its audience the vicarious thrill of sharing Billy's depravity without making the viewer feel compromised. And when the nastiness is over, the movie becomes reassuring, reminding the crowd that there's order in the world — or steak and ketchup and the Istanbul Hilton, as Billy's father sees it — after all. No wonder this titillating but painless version of a nightmare has its admirers.

1978 D 14, C20:1

Equine Worship

JUST CRAZY ABOUT HORSES, a documentary about horses directed by Tim Lovejoy, Joe Wemple, Victor Kanefsky; cameraman, Peter Stein; additional photography, Colter Watt, Ted Churchill, Mike Levine; assistant cameraman, Phillip Hollahan; edited by Samuel D. Pollard; written and produced by Tim Lovejoy and Joe Wemple; narrated by Tammy Grimes; music composed and performed by Sam Waymon; orchestrated and conducted by Rudy Stevenson; released by Fred Baker Films. At the Guild Theater, Rockefeller Center. Running time: 105 minutes.

"JUST CRAZY ABOUT HORSES" is, as its title implies, less about horses than obsessive horse worship. The documentary, which opens today at the Guild Theater, is a jaundiced valentine from a young film maker to the horse set in which he was raised. It is an absorbing — and horrific — excursion into a world that is unfamiliar to most, whether devoted Central Park canterer or racetrack habitué. Money, breeding and a certain casual arrogance are required. The horses endure.

Tim Lovejoy, who wrote and produced "Just Crazy" with Joe Wemple, has created an episodic collage of events and personalities in this, his first film. Buyers at a thoroughbred auction are urged to ponder the "residual values" in one mare's ovaries and, later, jockeys ride out onto the course to well-bred, almost languid rooting from the stands. The camera sidles into the middle of a crowd of steeplechase groupies, fur coats slung carelessly into car trunks and faces avid with gossip. We stroll into a pre-hunt party at one lavish "place" — for houses are "places" here and dogs are "hounds" who "speak" rather than bark — that was bought, as its owner laughingly recalls, as a "hedge against F.D.R."

•

There are wonderful comic moments. An inarticulate jockey slips into equine body language. A very graphic breeding scene opens with a shot of a stallion teaser, a horse of dubious lineage who is fated only to test a mare's readiness for breeding, and closes with the mated mare being lead away covered delicately in a white sheet. A butler wanders onto a rolling green field to serve a bloody mary to his master and an exquisitely bored dressage rider reveals that "racing in Bombay especially was very popular." A Hepburn sound-alike drawls that she's rooting for a rider because "she's a nice person without masses of money."

We watch an operation performed on a knock-kneed colt, then the camera cuts to a woman confined to a wheelchair after a riding accident, a horse breeder who strapped her crippled body to her horse for one last ride. We meet an equestrian who lives by candlelight in an attempt to re-create the 18th century in his splendid mansion. And the wounded rejects of the horse set are also introduced and their fantasy worlds explored with gentle good taste.

It all becomes a little numbing but

there are sudden compensations: A stallion canters free across a green meadow, a foal totters to its feet a few moments after birth and a tiny would-be rider urges a woolly sheep to a trot. In the film's most affecting scene, a stableman and mare exchange a look of haunting pain as her first foal is delivered stillborn.

•

Peter Stein's grainy photography at first seems only to attest to the film's low-budget status but its softened edges and blurred colors become seductive, a good match for Sam Waymon's easy-going score and Tammy Grimes's amusingly smudge-voiced delivery of the rather breathless script.

"Just Crazy About Horses" is rated PG ("Parental Guidance Suggested") because of scenes of mare breeding and foals being born. Squeamish adults also take note. JENNIFER DUNNING

1978 D 15, C5:5

Blue-Collar Epic

THE DEER HUNTER, directed by Michael Cimino; screenplay by Deric Washburn; story by Michael Cimino, Deric Washburn, Louis Garfinkle, and Quinn K. Redeker; director of photography, Vilmos Zsigmond; production consultant, Joann Carelli; art directors, Ron Hobs and Kim Swados; editor, Peter Zinner; music by Stanley Myers; produced by Barry Spikings, Michael Deeley, Michael Cimino, and John Peverall; released by Universal Studios. At the Coronet Theater, 59th Street and Third Avenue. Running time: 183 minutes. This film is rated R.

Michael .... Robert DeNiro
Stan .... John Cazale
Steven .... John Savage
Nick .... Christopher Walken
Linda .... Meryl Streep
John .... George Dzundza
Axel .... Chuck Aspegren

By VINCENT CANBY

MICHAEL CIMINO's "The Deer Hunter" is a big, awkward, crazily ambitious, sometimes breathtaking motion picture that comes as close to being a popular epic as any movie about this country since "The Godfather." Though he has written a number of screenplays, Mr. Cimino has only directed one other movie (the 1974 box-office hit, "Thunderbolt and Lightfoot"), which makes his present achievement even more impressive. Maybe he just didn't know enough to stop. Instead, he's tried to create a film that is nothing less than an appraisal of American life in the second half of the 20th century.

I don't mean to make "The Deer Hunter" sound like "War and Peace" or even "Gone With the Wind." Its view is limited and its narrative at times sketchy. It's about three young men who have been raised together in a Pennsylvania steel town, work together in its mill, drink, bowl and raise hell together, and then, for no better reason than that the war is there, they go off to fight in Vietnam.

"The Deer Hunter," which opens today at the Coronet, is an update on the national dream, long after World War II, when America's self-confidence peaked, after the Marshall Plan, after Korea, dealing with people who've grown up in the television age and matured in the decade of assassinations and disbelief.

•

The three friends, all of Russian extraction, are Mike (Robert DeNiro), Nick (Christopher Walken) and Steve (John Savage). Mike is the one who calls the tune for his friends. To the extent that any one of them has an interior life, it is Mike, a man who makes a big thing about hunting, about bringing down a deer with one shot. More than one shot apparently isn't fair. As

Meryl Streep in "The Deer Hunter"
Gives a smashing performance

codes go this one is not great, but it is his own.

Nick goes along with Mike, sometimes suspecting that Mike is eccentric, but respecting his eccentricities. Steve is the conventional one, whose marriage (a Russian Orthodox ceremony, followed by a huge, hysterical reception) occupies most of the film's first hour and sets out in rich detail what I take to be one of the movie's principal concerns — what happens to Americans when their rituals have become only quaint reminders of the past rather than life-ordering rules of the present.

Mr. Cimino has described his treatment of the three friends' war experiences as surreal, which is another way of saying that a lot of recent history is elipsized or shaped to fit the needs of the film. What is not surreal is the brutality of the war and its brutalizing effects, scenes that haunt "The Deer Hunter" and give point to the film even as it slips into the wildest sort of melodrama, which Mr. Cimino plays out against the background of the collapse of Saigon and the American withdrawal from Southeast Asia. It's Armageddon with helicopters.

Most particular and most savage is the film's use of Russian roulette as a metaphor for war's waste. It's introduced when the three friends, prisoners of war of the North Vietnamese, are forced by their captors to play Russian roulette with one another. The game crops up again in Saigon where, according to this film, it was played in back-street arenas rather like cockfighting pits, for high-dollar stakes. These sequences are as explicitly bloody as anything you're likely to see in a commercial film. They are so rough, in fact, that they raise the question of whether such vivid portrayals don't become dehumanizing themselves.

More terrifying than the violence — certainly more provocative and moving — is the way each of the soldiers reacts to his war experiences. Not once does anyone question the war or his participation in it. This passivity may be the real horror at the center of American life, and more significant than any number of hope-filled tales about raised political consciousnesses. What are these veterans left with? Feelings of contained befuddlement, a desire to make do and, perhaps, a more profound appreciation for love, friendship and community. The big answers elude them, as do the big questions.

•

Deric Washburn's screenplay, which takes its time in the way of a big novel, provides fine roles for Mr. DeNiro, Mr. Walken and Mr. Savage, each of whom does some of his best work to date. Meryl Streep, who has long been recognized for her fine performances on the New York stage, gives a smashing film performance as the young woman, who, by tacit agreement among the friends, becomes Nick's girl but who stays around long enough to assert herself. In the splendid supporting cast are George Dzundza, Chuck Aspegren, Shirley Stoler and Rutanya Alda. The late John Cazale makes his last film appearance a memorable one as the kind of barroom neurotic who might at any moment go seriously off his rocker.

The film has been stunningly photographed by Vilmos Zsigmond, who provides visually a continuity that is sometimes lacking in the rest of the movie. "The Deer Hunter" is both deeply troubling and troublesome (for the manner in which Mr. Cimino manipulates the narrative), but its feelings for time, place and blue-collar people are genuine, and its vision is that of an original, major new film maker.

1978 D 15, C5:1

Stodgy Love

OLIVER'S STORY, directed by John Korty; screenplay by Erich Segal and John Korty; based on the novel by Erich Segal; director of photography, Arthur Ornitz; "Oliver's Theme" composed by Francis Lai; music score by Lee Holdridge; art director, Robert Gundlach; film editor, Stuart H. Pappe; set decorator, Phil Smith; produced by David V. Picker; released by Paramount Pictures. At the Loews State II, Trans-Lux East, 34th Street East and neighborhood theaters. Running time: 90 minutes. This film is rated PG.

Oliver Barrett .... Ryan O'Neal
Marcie Bonwit .... Candice Bergen
Joanna Stone .... Nicola Pagett
Phil Cavilleri .... Edward Binns
John Hsiang .... Benson Fong
Stephen Simpson .... Charles Haid
Jamie Francis .... Kenneth McMillan
Mr. Barrett .... Ray Milland

By JANET MASLIN

WHO can forget about a 25-year-old girl who died? Not Oliver Barrett 4th, that's for sure. At the beginning of "Oliver's Story," which opens today at Loews State, the Trans-Lux East and Walter Reade 34th Street East, Oliver is sitting in a graveyard mourning his lost Jenny; at the end of the film, he's sitting by the banks of the Charles River doing much the same thing.

The ads for "Oliver's Story" feature a prettily windswept photo of Ryan O'Neal (as Oliver) and Candice Bergen (as Marcie, the new woman in his life), plus the slogan "It takes someone very special to help you forget someone very special." But if you imagine that that indicates the film is about Oliver's falling for Marcie and starting life anew, well, you probably think love means never having to say you're sorry.

In fact, the message of "Oliver's Story" is a decidedly gloomy one: You get just one shot at young love, and after that you're over the hill. The happy-go-lucky Oliver of "Love Story" is gone, replaced by a prematurely middle-aged fellow who grinds away at his job, worries about his family responsibilities and spends some excruciatingly dull sessions with his psychotherapist. ("Nothing happens magically, Oliver," the doctor says on a particularly dreary day. "But just being aware of a problem is beginning to solve it.")

•

When Oliver and Marcie take a whirlwind tour of Hong Kong, they're actually there on a business trip and hardly even enjoying themselves. Over dinner they talk about where they first learned to use chopsticks and how many rolls of film Oliver has used up while touring the city.

At least "Love Story" had a romantic and moderately rebellious worldview, being opposed to parental authority and in favor of angels in the snow. "Oliver's Story" is stodgy through and through, with a hero and heroine who have one good time together jogging through Central Park and never again match the thrill of that moment. Perhaps their detachment and their weary soul-searching and their willingness to get up at 6 A.M. for a good game of tennis are signs of the times. That doesn't make their saga the stuff of which dreams are made.

The screenplay manages to take every possible edge off Erich Segal's novel, even though finding the edges can't have been easy. As written by Mr. Segal and John Korty, who directed it, the script teams Oliver with a WASP department-store heiress whose take-charge attitude eventually gets on his nerves.

•

In Mr. Segal's book, this was supposed to contrast sharply with the memory of Jenny, with her unaffected, lower-class ways, and to remind Oliver of his aristocratic parents, whom he never much liked. In the film, Miss Bergen is only a slight departure from Ali MacGraw, who never seemed all that economically deprived in the first place, so the point is lost. A scene of Mr. Segal's, in which Marcie met Oliver's parents and — unlike Jenny — was a big hit, has been dropped from the movie, as has every other useful parallel with "Love Story."

In fact, all that remains of the first film are Francis Lai's theme song and a little photo of Miss MacGraw on Mr. O'Neal's nighttable, right next to the Excedrin. This is not to suggest that Mr. Korty has moved on in any imaginative way, or that he is above falling back on "Love Story" every time new inspiration eludes him. After Oliver has a fight with Marcie, for instance, Mr. Korty has him drive all the way to Cambridge, just so he can trot briefly and wordlessly past the other film's Harvard Yard settings.

Jenny's father is still around (this time played by Edward Binns instead of John Marley), but he has conveniently forgotten all about his daughter and keeps urging Oliver to go out and have a good time. The Barrett parental estate serves a similarly perfunctory purpose. These evocations are so cold and clumsy that they effectively dispel all vestiges of the first film's highly marketable mood.

•

Mr. Korty has the reputation of a fine independent film maker; his documentary about the DeBolt family, to be shown on television this weekend, won an Academy Award last year. But his direction of "Oliver's Story" is too unsure one moment, too insistent the next, and he has no eye for the glamour that might have been this film's last chance.

Mr. O'Neal is certainly equal to the material, but Mr. Korty doesn't seem to trust him with it; too many montages seem devised to keep the actor from having to talk. Miss Bergen always looks spectacular in close-ups, so why, then, are there so many unflattering long shots of her in unbecoming costumes? And what use has been made of the (highly exploitable) memory of Jenny? The first sequence shows Mr. O'Neal watching her coffin being lowered into the ground, inch by tearjerking inch. But after that, for all his funk, he doesn't often think of her again. Perhaps it's just as well. This is the kind of sequel that could have her turning over in her grave.

•

"Oliver's Story" is rated PG ("Parental Guidance Suggested"), because it contains one brief bedroom scene and because Marcie has inherited much of Jenny's smart-alecky vocabulary.

1978 D 15, C12:1

Super Cast

SUPERMAN, directed by Richard Donner; screenplay by Mario Puzo, David Newman, Leslie Newman and Robert Benton; story by Mario Puzo; creative consultant, Tom Mankiewicz; executive producer, Ilya Salkind; producer, Pierre Spengler; music by John Williams; released by Warner Bros. At Loews Astor Plaza, Loews Orpheum, Murray Hill, and neighborhood theaters. Running time: 142 minutes. This film is rated PG.

Jor-el	Marlon Brando
Lex Luthor	Gene Hackman
Superman/Clark Kent	Christopher Reeve
Otis	Ned Beatty
Perry White	Jackie Cooper
Pa Kent	Glenn Ford
First Elder	Trevor Howard
Lois Lane	Margot Kidder
Non	Jack O'Halloran
Eve Teschmacher	Valerie Perrine
Vond-ah	Maria Schell
General Zod	Terence Stamp
Ma Kent	Phyllis Thaxter
Lara	Susannah York
Young Clark Kent	Jeff East
Jimmy Olsen	Marc McClure
Ursa	Sarah Douglas
Second Elder	Harry Andrews

IN a season in which our motion-picture comic strips have been either heavily mythic ("The Lord of the Rings") or simply pretentious ("Watership Down"), "Superman" is good, clean, simple-minded fun, though it's a movie whose limited appeal is built in. There isn't a thought in this film's head that would be out of place on the side of a box of Wheaties. But to describe as good, clean, simple-minded fun a film on which so much effort, time and talent have been expended is to sound a muted warning.

To enjoy this movie as much as one has a right to expect, one has either to be a Superman nut, the sort of trivia expert who has absorbed all there is to know about the planet Krypton, or to check one's wits at the door, which may be more than a lot of people are prepared to do for longer than two hours.

The Superman comic strip has been carefully, elaborately, sometimes wittily blown up for the big-theater screen, which, though busy, often seems sort of empty. In Christopher Reeve, a young New York stage and television actor who plays Superman and Clark Kent, the mild-mannered newspaper reporter who is Superman's cover, the producers and Richard Donner, the director, have a performer who manages to be both funny and comic-strip heroic without making a fool of himself. Mr. Reeve even looks like something drawn on an easel, being composed entirely of firm lines without a bit of shading. Margot Kidder is also most charming, revealing (is this for the first time?) that Lois Lane is the sort of newspaper reporter who puts two p's in rapist.

The supporting cast is of a caliber one might otherwise expect to see only at fund-raising events for American Indians, the American Film Institute or the March of Dimes. Marlon Brando turns up early in the saga as Superman's dad, Jor-El, who looks rather like George Washington with chrome finish on his hair. Glenn Ford has two scenes as Superman's adopted earth-father.

Gene Hackman, Ned Beatty and Valerie Perrine play the members of the evil trio whose attempts to destroy California (by activating the San Andreas fault) form what might be called the plot. Jackie Cooper plays the harried editor of The Daily Planet, and a number of other major actors, including Terence Stamp, Susannah York, Harry Andrews, Trevor Howard and Maria Schell, play roles so small the actors should wear numbers for immediate identification.

This kind of casting is prodigal but it is an essential element in a film in which extravagance is the dominant style.

The screenplay appears to have been composed by a unisex basketball team — Mario Puzo, who is credited with the original story; David Newman, Leslie Newman (who is the wife of David) and Robert Benton, who in 1966 wrote a Broadway musical about Superman with Mr. Newman. Tom Mankiewicz receives credit as creative consultant, but, because he is a writer, I assume he might also have written a line or two.

There have been a number of published statements by people connected with the film to the effect that the Superman legend has been treated without condescension, not as camp, which is more or less true, though the movie's brightest moments are those very broad ones supplied by Mr. Hackman, Mr. Beatty and Miss Perrine, whose bosom submits to her bodice only with a fight. Their comic moments recall the best of the old Batman television series.

For all intents and purposes Mr. Brando plays it straight, applying to Krypton's most brilliant scientist a neo-English accent and a mock gravity that are funny because he's the actor he is.

The movie does nothing lightly or quickly. After opening credits that are so portentous they could be announcing the discovery of a new mouthwash, the film spends what seems to be an interminable amount of time (approximately an hour) on Krypton explaining the planet's domestic problems (worse than but not as complicated as Iran's) and Superman's heritage, a sequence climaxed by the destruction of Krypton. The rest of the movie proceeds at the panel-by-panel pace of a comic strip, with Superman/Clark Kent's courting of Lois Lane and fighting for "truth, justice and the American way."

The special effects are mostly very good, especially the montages in which we see Superman flying faster than a speeding bullet, saving trains, buses, airplanes (Air Force One) from untimely crashes, or just taking Lois Lane for an evening's spin over New York.

"Superman," which opens today at Loews Astor Plaza and other theaters, doesn't transcend its origins, as "Star Wars" did, but it never means to. For me it's as if somebody had constructed a building as tall as the World Trade Center in the color and shape of a carrot. Rabbits might admire it. They might even write learned critiques about it and find it both an inspiration and a reward, while the rest of us would see nothing but an alarmingly large, imitation carrot.

•

"Superman," which has been rated PG ("parental guidance suggested"), contains two (according to my count) harmless double-entendres.

VINCENT CANBY

Marlon Brando, left, and prisoners of the planet Krypton in "Superman"
A movie whose limited appeal is built in

1978 D 15, C15:1

Warlike Elders

HOMEBODIES, directed by Larry Yust; screenplay by, Larry Yust, Howard Kaminsky, and Bennett Sims; director of photography, Isidore Mankofsky; editor, Peter Parasheles; executive producer, James R. Levitt; producer, Marshall Backlar; released by Avco Embassy Pictures. At the Thalia, Broadway and 95th Street. Running time: 96 minutes. This film is rated PG.

Mr. Blakely	Peter Brocco
Miss Emily	Frances Fuller
Mr. Sandy	William Hansen
Mrs. Loomis	Ruth McDevitt
Mattie	Paula Trueman
Mr. Loomis	Ian Wolfe
Miss Pollack	Linda Marsh
Mr. Crawford	Douglas Fowley

Among the Masai

VISIT TO A CHIEF'S SON, directed by Lamont Johnson; screenplay by Albert Reuben; based on the novel by Robert Halmi; music composed by Francis Lai; cinematography, Ernest Day; film editor, Tom Rolf; produced by Robert Halmi; released by United Artists. At the Thalia Theater, Broadway and 95th Street, today and tomorrow. Running time: 92 minutes. This film has not been rated.

Robert	Richard Mulligan
Nemolok	Johnny Sekka
Kevin	Philip Hodgdon
Kodonyo	Jesse Kinaru
Jock	Jock Anderson
Chief Lomoiro	Chief Lomoiro

WITH: The Masai Tribe of Kenya, East Africa.

BETWEEN the time when Lamont Johnson directed the brilliantly economical "The Last American Hero" and then moved on to direct Margaux Hemingway and Farrah Fawcett-Majors in their screen debuts ("Lipstick" and "Somebody Killed Her Husband," respectively), he made an interesting departure: "Visit to a Chief's Son," a 1974 adventure film set in Africa, among the Masai tribe. Previously unreleased, it opens today at the Thalia on a double bill with "Homebodies," another unreleased film from 1974.

"Visit to a Chief's Son" is based on the experiences of Robert Halmi, who journeyed to Africa as a photographer for Life magazine, wrote a book about his trip, then went on to produce a film about it.

Accordingly, one might suppose the character based on Mr. Halmi would be an attractive and sympathetic one. But no: The anthropologist named Robert who visits Kenya with his adolescent son has surprisingly little respect for or understanding of the natives, and when he and the boy retreat to their own camp they take American-style showers and drink Coca-Cola. Indeed, when the son makes friends with a Masai boy his own age, the first thing young Kevin teaches young Kodoyno is how to shake up a soda bottle and douse somebody with the spray.

With the notable exception of Johnny Sekka, who plays the chief of the title with a welcome cynicism and a winning smile, the non-Masai actors barely hold the screen. But they are upstaged by some remarkable scene-stealers: baby hippos, baby elephants, exotic birds and a lake that seems covered with flamingos, from shore to shore. The rest of the film plays like a relatively transparent pretext for the wildlife footage, but the animal shots are spectacular, and there are a great many of them — more than enough to be worth the price of admission.

The most appealing thing about "Homebodies" is its premise. A band of old people in Cincinnati decide they don't like young people, especially the young people who are trying to evict them from their condemned apartment building, which is being torn down to make room for more skyscrapers.

So they begin defending themselves, disposing of an ill-tempered social worker and a greedy builder and anyone else who gets in their way. Eventually, they declare war on one another, and at this juncture the film loses its quotient of dotty charm. Without their sense of common purpose, they're not a particularly appealing bunch, and in any case Larry Yust, the director, isn't able to hold these two halves of the film together.

"Homebodies" is rated PG ("Parental Guidance Suggested"). It contains some fairly routine violence, plus a scene involving the amputation of a dead man's foot.

JANET MASLIN

1978 D 15, C17:1

UNCLE JOE SHANNON, directed by Joseph Hanwright; written by Burt Young; music by Bill Conti; film editor, Don Zimmerman; production designer, Bill Kenny; director of photography, Bill Butler; executive producer, Gene Kirkwood; produced by Irwin Winkler and Robert Chartoff; released by United Artists. At the Festival Theater, Fifth Avenue and 57th Street. Running time: 115 minutes. This film is rated PG.

Joe Shannon .... Burt Young
Robbie .... Doug McKeon
Margaret .... Madge Sinclair
Goose .... Jason Bernard
Braddock .... Bert Remsen
Dr. Clark .... Allan Rich

By JENNIFER DUNNING

"Uncle Joe Shannon" is about a once-famous jazz musician now lurching through skid row, his trumpet in one hand and a kid with cancer hanging on the other. Uncle Joe does not sell his trumpet to pay for the operation. But that is the film's only surprise. "Uncle Joe Shannon," which opens today at the Festival Theater, leaves no heart-string untugged.

The film was conceived and written by Burt Young, its star, and it is an obvious labor of love. Nominated in 1976 for an Academy Award for his performance as Paulie the butcher in "Rocky," Mr. Young has a deserved reputation as one of the best character actors in films today. He is also the author of a number of television screenplays. But someone else should have taken this one in hand. Mr. Young sinks even himself into a morass of sentimentality.

•

"Uncle Joe" tells the story of a star trumpet player who takes off on a long, fast slide into self destruction after his wife and young son die in a fire. In the process, he acquires a youthful sidekick who is also on the run from life, and together they whip each other back into shape as Christmas rolls inevitably around the corner.

The film is full of odd improbabilities. Uncle Joe keeps his worn possessions, including his son's charred trumpet, in his unlocked room in a fleabag hotel. His trumpet remains at his side, intact, through binges and suicide attempts. A hospital and orphanage are broken into with surprising ease. And, scorned by a group of jazz-club barflys when he is unable to get through a trumpet solo, Uncle Joe has them jiving in the aisles when he swings into a syncopated version of "Jingle Bells."

Mr. Young's own performance stays on a single, beery note throughout, pain registering in his face and trumpet solos (dubbed by Maynard Ferguson) alone. But, in his directorial debut, Joseph C. Hanwright has gotten good performances from Madge Sinclair and Jason Bernard, as Joe's long-suffering friends; from Martin Beck as the wryly wasted hotel proprietor and, in particular, from a remarkable, pudgy little 12-year-old actor named Doug McKeon, who has a welcome, sardonic way with his lines. Bill Butler's cameras capture the slick night surfaces and ruined faces of the street people of Los Angeles so that, clichés in themselves, they have the impact of sudden revelation.

•

For no reason apparent to this viewer, this film was rated PG ("Parental Guidance Suggested").

1978 D 17, 101:3

FILM VIEW

VINCENT CANBY

How True to Fact Must Fiction Be?

Nobody has yet spelled out any hard and fast rules relating to fiction's obligations to historical truth and, I trust, no one ever will. Fiction isn't seamanship, which can be governed by internationally observed rules-of-the-road. All fiction of any merit absorbs history — sometimes with grand self-consciousness, as in "War and Peace," sometimes to create a kind of meta-history, as in Tom Stoppard's "Travesties," and sometimes simply by having been written when it was. "Pride and Prejudice" is hardly a historical novel, but it's as much a record of human events and affairs of the past as is Gibbon's "Decline and Fall."

Where the fiction writer (or filmmaker) is likely to run into the most criticism is in tampering with the present or the recent past.

I remember several years ago when an outraged friend of mine attempted to convince me that Robert Altman's "Nashville," which I liked very much, was a counterfeit movie since the real Nashville was nothing like the one shown in the film. I know nothing about the real Nashville and so I wasn't especially concerned by the authenticity (or lack of it) in the Altman movie. As far as I was concerned, "Nashville" wasn't about Nashville but about a state of mind or, perhaps, a mind of state. Its vision was one that surprised me even as I was recognizing it. If Altman had bent the truth in the cause of some truth greater than that of country-and-western music, so be it. I was on the side of fiction.

This summer, though, watching Altman's "A Wedding," I found myself in much the same frame of mind as my friend who had railed against the liberties taken in "Nashville." Though I have no first-hand knowledge of the country-and-western music business, I do know something about the world of "A Wedding" — including the house where it was photographed — and suddenly, the liberties that Altman took with social history struck me as having fatally compromised his fiction.

I believed not a minute of the movie's confrontation between so-called Old Money and New Money. Today's Old Money (at least in the Middle West) would never find itself in the position of being snubbed the way Altman's family was in this film. If anything, the hint of scandal would have made invitations to the wedding the hottest tickets in town. Money buys its own legitimacy when there's enough of it, particularly when it's been around for a generation or two (which, in the Middle West, can define "Old"). The society that Altman pictured in "A Wedding" seemed to have its roots in "Stella Dallas," not in any world that I'm aware of. A result was that the entire movie became fuzzed up in my mind. I couldn't accept Altman's prerogatives as an artist; I wanted him to have made a different film, one that corresponded to my vision and not to his fiction.

There are some things, of course, that the creator of fiction is not going to do casually. Unless he has some very good reason he's not going to make a movie in which the Titanic sinks in the Indian Ocean, nor one in which Lincoln presides over the Spanish-American War. Usually the mistakes that crop up in movies are simply oversights, one of the most glorious being "Krakatoa, East of Java," which was about the explosion of the volcano that is west of Java.

• • •

The subject of fiction's obligations to history — to known facts — is raised by Michael Cimino's extraordinarily ambitious new film, "The Deer Hunter," which is now playing special engagements in New York and Los Angeles to qualify for the various 1978 film awards, and which will start its regular release in February.

"The Deer Hunter" is a movie with something to offend almost every serious taste, but it's also a movie to admire in spite of its serious lapses in common sense.

It makes use of the Vietnam war, though it's not directly about American involvment in Vietnam. Worse — certainly very risky and unfashionable at the moment — no one in the movie ever questions the morality of that war. It's simply there to be fought automatically, as if it were another rite of passage that had to be lived through by the three young men who are the film's heroes.

Further, the film repeatedly exploits violence through images so graphic they establish new boundaries for the cinema of simulated blood-and-guts, at the same time making one wonder whether this kind of graphic detail isn't a kind of theatrical blackmail. Showing us precisely how a man looks at the instant his brains are being blown out by a bullet is, indeed, a spectacle to elicit strong emotional responses. It also tends to be self-defeating. The shock has a way of disconnecting one from the movie, instead of drawing one further into it.

Yet, with the exception of perhaps a half-dozen speeches that impose on the characters poetic insights that I don't believe, the screenplay (by Deric Washburn, from a story by him, Cimino and others) gives us an unusually poignant, unpatronizing, unromantic view of life in blue-collar America.

The movie opens with a long, magnificently detailed sequence, which lasts approximately an hour and introduces us to the three heroes, who live in a small Pennsylvania industrial city, work in its steel mill and lead lives more or less left over from the Old World traditions of their families. It then shifts to Vietnam, where Cimino shows us how the three men react to imprisonment, torture and, ultimately, freedom.

Because not one of these fellows has a political thought in his head, I suppose that "The Deer Hunter" may be accused of denigrating the political consciousness of the 60's. Yet I don't think it does. That's not the film Cimino was interested in. It's this very lack of awareness that makes "The Deer Hunter" more honestly rueful, sad, provocative and, finally, frightening than any other movie we've yet had about Vietnam, including certainly "Coming Home."

• • •

"The Deer Hunter" is much less about Vietnam than it is about essentially honest people trying to come to terms with lives and times they don't understand or — and this is the ultimate horror — they don't even question.

Awareness, though, is not the issue on which Cimino is likely to be most severely criticized. It's the manner in which he has rearranged various key events in the war to suit the purposes of his fiction, as well as his invention of a torture procedure that is first introduced in the film as a technique favored by the North Vietnamese, who force prisoners of war to play Russian roulette until one man wins. The movie then tells us that this became for the high-rollers of Saigon's back streets a sport comparable in popularity to cockfighting in Latin America.

Russian roulette as a metaphor for United States actions in Vietnam? It's one of those "writer's notions" that sounds good at first, but which the careful writer might well abandon before he used it. It's too good. Too neat. Cimino admits that the Russian roulette idea was his invention, based on no historical evidence whatsoever. In these pages last week he reasoned that in a war like the one we fought in Vietnam, almost anything one could imagine must have happened at one point or another. His film, he said, is not realistic but surreal.

I'm not sure he can get off the hook so easily, especially when the best, most arresting sequences in his film are so compassionately realistic. It's one thing to invent and rearrange the facts of World Wars I and II, and quite another to do that in something still as fresh in minds and memories as Vietnam.

Fiction's primary obligation is to be true to itself, to its own logic, and it's here that "The Deer Hunter" may be faulted even more seriously than for its rearrangement of historical events. The film's penultimate sequence, set in Saigon as the American and South Vietnamese war efforts are collapsing, is very close to ridiculous, giving more responsibility to coincidence than can be borne by any movie that doesn't want to qualify as cheap melodrama.

Having expressed these reservations about the film, I must say I was immensely moved by "The Deer Hunter." No other American film in a very long time has so accurately caught the quality of our lives, the temper of our times and the contradictions built into our culture. The film's feelings for its characters are genuine and even profound, and those characters are magnificently played by the cast headed by Robert De Niro, Christopher Walken, John Savage, the late John Cazale and Meryl Streep, a talented, beautiful actress new to the screen.

Concluding the movie is a sequence that is more audacious than anything that has gone before it: After attending the funeral for the one friend who does not survive Vietnam, the two other young men, their wives, girlfriends and drinking pals gather at their favorite pub to hold an unofficial wake. It is winter. They are cold. They are troubled. They're not sure how they should behave or what they're really feeling. One of the men starts singing "God Bless America." The others join in.

Is Cimino serious? How does he intend us to take this? As irony on his part? Perhaps, but I don't think so. He doesn't condescend to his characters' feelings. He respects them, and if they can express those feelings only in second-rate sentiment, that is the rub. It's one of the more important things the movie is about. They might have sung a hymn, or a school song, or the unsingable "Star Spangled Banner," or even "My Country 'Tis of Thee." Instead they pick Irving Berlin's patriotic pop hit, which is, most likely, on the juke box of that particular tavern. In this sequence, "The Deer Hunter" meets its obligations to both art and history, and it is breathtaking. ■

1978 D 17, II:1:5

Similarly, a late-night dormitory scene involving a number of small boys is shot with such overweening poignancy that it's out of sync with most of the film's airier mood. Mr. Blier has a habit of strong-arming his audience in one scene, and letting his characters drift aimiably in the next. That halting quality was effective enough in "Going Places," but "Get Out Your Handkerchiefs" is a much more substantial and sophisticated effort, in which even the slightest technical clumsiness is notably out of place.

1978 D 18, C15:1

Boyish Adventures

GET OUT YOUR HANDKERCHIEFS ("Preparez Vos Mouchoirs" in French with subtitles), directed and screenplay by Bertrand Blier; photography, Jean Penzer; editor, Claudine Merlin; sound, Jean-Pierre Ruh; music, Georges Delerue; art director, Eric Moulard; production manager, Georges Val; executive producer, Paul Claudon; production companies, Films Ariane and C.A.P.A.C. (Paris), Beiga Films and Soldep (Brussels); released by New Line Cinema. At the Paris, Broadway and 58th Street. Running time: 100 minutes. This film has not been rated.

Raoul	Gerard Depardieu
Stephane	Patrick Dewaere
Solange	Carol Laure
Christian Beloeil	Riton
Neighbor	Michel Serreaul
Mrs. Beloeil	Eleonore Hir
Passerby	Sylvie Joly
Mr. Beloeil	Jean Rougerie

By JANET MASLIN

I HAVE trouble looking at the light side of Bertrand Blier's "Get Out Your Handkerchiefs," a comedy with a heroine who isn't altogether funny. Here is a woman who barely speaks, never thinks, spends most of her time scrubbing and knitting, is completely available (and indifferent) to any man who wants her, and will be happy only when she is at last made pregnant. She has so little will of her own that a 13-year-old boy can persuade her to have sex with him by pointing out that he'll "have to wait five, six years for another chance like this." Arguably, she is an object of mystery. But by the same argument, so is a seashell or a goldfish or an ashtray.

Here, as with his earlier "Going Places," Mr. Blier stops me dead. I never had a clear or reasonable response to that film; I tuned out during a sequence in which two young men petulantly shot a female hairdresser with whom they were both involved, wounding her in the leg, and the woman was such a compliant dimwit that she didn't mind. Compared to that, the scene that showed Jeanne Moreau committing suicide by shooting herself in the genitals was a positive picnic.

Mr. Blier's penchant for depicting behavior like this is certainly daring, but whether it amounts to anything truly provocative is another matter. Genuinely challenging an audience is one thing, and simply upsetting it is something else. At least in my case, Mr. Blier at his most outrageous doesn't elicit much more than fleeting, if heartfelt, indignation.

In fairness, in "Get Out Your Handkerchiefs" he also elicits a great many laughs, and that's certainly more than could be said for "Going Places." This time, the same two actors (Gérard Depardieu and Patrick Dewaere) play the same kind of oversized, irrepressible children, floundering around a woman whose true nature eludes them. She (Carol Laure) is the wife of one of them (Mr. Depardieu) but she's been depressed and uncommunicative for a while. Marriage being whatever it is today, her husband decides she needs another man to cheer her up, and recruits Mr. Dewaere in a restaurant.

Their ostensible pursuit of the wife's

Carol Laure

happiness launches the two men on a series of adventures that makes them seem ever more boyish, until they encounter an adolescent (Riton) who is infinitely wiser and manlier than they. Ever more overshadowed by him, they find their high spirits and their connection with the wife both waning.

Until it takes this fairly solemn turn, the film is an exuberant and highly inventive comedy, filled with the very funny quirks of these characters' lives. The Dewaere character has a collection of every Pocket Book ever printed, and can recite any title if he's given the serial number. The wife quietly knits matching sweaters for half the men in the movie. When Mr. Depardieu first strikes a bargain with Mr. Dewaere, he promises that if Mr. Dewaere accepts the wife as a gift he will become Mr. Depardieu's pal, "and when a man is my pal he can ask for anything." Without the wife, though, "there wouldn't be much to ask me for."

Both of these actors are at once knowing and funny, and their camaraderie can be wonderful to watch; Mr. Depardieu in particular projects an innocence so strenuous it takes on a demonic edge. Miss Laure does an amusing enough deadpan, but she's so opaque her charm eventually wears thin.

•

Riton, the child actor, does a fine job, but there's something disconcerting about his prematurely mournful expression. Mr. Blier's device of setting his boyish adults in opposition to an adult boy has a certain cleverness. But his casting such a dolorous child merely calls too much attention to the patness of this part of the scenario, and to its pretension.

Mysticism Down Under

THE LAST WAVE, directed by Peter Weir; screenplay by Mr. Weir, Tony Morphett and Peter Popescu; director of photography, Russell Boyd; editor, Max Lemon; music, Charles Wain; special effects, Neil Angwin and Monty Fieguth; produced by Hal McElroy and James McElroy; released by World Northal. At the Beekman, Second Avenue and 65th Street, and the Paramount, Broadway and 61st Street. Running time: 106 minutes. This film is rated PG.

David Burton	Richard Chamberlain
Anne Burton	Olivia Hamnett
Chris Lee	Gulpilil
Rev. Burton	Frederick Parslow
Dr. Whitburn	Vivean Gray
Charlie	Nanjiwarra Amagula
Gerry Lee	Walter Amagula
Larry	Roy Bara
Lindsey	Cedric Lalara
Jacko	Morris

By VINCENT CANBY

THE sky is cloudless and brilliantly blue, though one hears ominous thunderclaps in the distance. A few seconds later, hailstones the size of baseballs begin crashing onto the hot, arid, still sunlit landscape. The hail shatters windows, and a small boy, watching the display outside, is brutally slashed.

Far away, the life of a great city is almost brought to a halt by rains that will not stop. Day and night the rains go on. In the middle of the night, David Burton (Richard Chamberlain), a Sydney lawyer, walks into his suburban garden to find that the ground is alive with movement. There are frogs everywhere — all sizes and shapes. Frogs in such number can threaten.

One evening when Burton is driving home in the rain, the speaker of his car radio suddenly erupts with a cascade of water — sound magically given substance. It's as if primeval forces were reasserting their dominion over a world heretofore assumed to be civilized, comprehensible, under reason's control.

•

Thus does Peter Weir, the young Australian director, vividly set the scene for "The Last Wave," an Australian film about matters occult — mental telepathy, thought transference, the reality of dream life.

The film, which opens today at the Beekman and Paramount Theaters, begins so brilliantly and with such promise that it's no real surprise that the closer it gets to its apocalypse, the less effective it becomes. The film's payoff is decidedly small, recalling nothing more esoteric than the discovery of the elephants' graveyard in one of the early Tarzan movies. Yet until we arrive at this breathless anticlimax, "The Last Wave" is a movingly moody shock-film, composed entirely of the kind of variations on mundane behavior and events that are most scary and disorienting because they so closely parallel the normal.

The movie, written by Mr. Weir, Tony Morphett and Peter Popescu, is about the curious chain of events that starts when Burton, a liberal-thinking

Richard Chamberlain in a scene from the film "The Last Wave."

lawyer whose experience has been exclusively in corporation law, finds himself defending five aborigines accused of murdering a sixth in a Sydney alley. The circumstances are unusual. The slain man could have drowned (there's a small amount of water in his lungs and he was found near a mud puddle) or he could have had a heart attack. The coroner isn't sure.

Making matters more difficult for the lawyer is the aborigines' complete indifference to their defense. Only one of them, Chris Lee (Gulpilil), a slight, dark fellow with an impassively cheerful moon-face, will talk to Burton, but this is more unnerving than enlightening since Lee, the lawyer realizes, has for some time been visiting him in his dreams.

The plot that follows makes a great deal of the aborigines' tribal traditions and beliefs, particularly what they call "dreamtime," a nonstop spirit-life that is for the believers more real than the ordinary world.

•

Though the inspiration of Mr. Weir and his associates runs out before the end, "The Last Wave" is an impressive work from a director new to American audiences. He's a man whose ability to find the eerie in the commonplace might please Hitchcock. Mr. Weir got very nice performances from his cast, especially from Mr. Chamberlain, who knows that an actor's obligation in such a film is to play it as small and ordinary as possible, and from Gulpilil. This actor, a full-blooded aborigine, creates a fascinating, self-contained character, the sort of person who has been shown all the mysteries. As a result, he can no longer be surprised or hurt by anything, only mildly amused or disappointed.

1978 D 19, C7:1

Theatrical Montage

QUARRY, an opera in three movements conceived and directed by Meredith Monk; music, Meredith Monk; lighting, Beverly Emmons; costumes, Lanny Harrison; sound, Tony Giovanetti; décor, Ping Chong and Jean-Claude Ribes. At the Harold Clurman Theater, 412 West 42d Street.

Featuring The House: Lanny Harrison, Monica Moseley, Ping Chong, Gail Turner, Coco Pekelis, Daniel Ira Sverdlik, Lee Nagrin, Tone Blevins, Pablo Vela, Mary Schultz, Steve Clorfine and Steve Lockwood.

By JACK ANDERSON

BECAUSE her choreographic works consist of montages of theatrical images, Meredith Monk's style has been called cinematic. Although cinematic theater is not the same as cinema itself, Miss Monk has risked filming her "Quarry," first staged in 1976, and the movie is being shown through Saturday at the Harold Clurman Theater.

Filmed by Amram Nowak Associates at the Brooklyn Academy of Music, "Quarry" is performed by Miss Monk's company, The House, whose members dance, mime, speak dialogue and sing music composed by Miss Monk.

Both movie and stage production concern a sick child, played by Miss Monk. Confined to her bedroom, she is dimly aware of things going on around her. The audience, too, hears what's going on and sees it, as well, for the rooms of the house are indicated by pieces of furniture set in separate pools of light.

•

One meets the child's mother, her sisters and her grandparents, a cultivated elderly couple. There are also two people who resemble an Old Testament prophet and his wife, but one is never certain whether these figures are real or imaginary.

The child tosses restlessly. Everything that happens seems hallucinatory and fragmented. Seldom has childhood fever been more effectively evoked.

But, unlike the child, we can piece the fragments together. The pattern that emerges is disquieting. This family appears to be living during some political crisis. Neighbors vanish mysteriously. The grandparents feel that they are not being allowed to continue their scholarly research. The prophet is alarmed.

•

Although much of "Quarry" is effective on the screen, the filmed version does have weaknesses. The dim lighting makes some images indistinct. Group scenes are either filmed from such a distance that they lack impact or the camera focuses on some aspect of them and obscures their overall design.

As chilling on screen as it was in the theater is the moment when a raucous rally masterminded by the dictator gives way to silence. The scene now seems to be a deportation depot and the silence is broken only by the sounds of people dropping personal belongings on the floor before being sent to some terrible destination.

•

"Quarry" is accompanied at the Harold Clurman by "Mountain Piece," a short silent film by Miss Monk about people moving solemnly on a hillside. Whatever they do, they seem remote. Even in close-up they seem remote, for they keep their eyes closed, and because they never look toward the viewer, they might as well be miles away. This remoteness makes them almost as nonhuman as the grass and stones.

Technically, the film is crude — although, conceivably, Miss Monk may have wanted it to look crude. Yet its images are hard to forget.

1978 D 19, C20:5

EVERY WHICH WAY BUT LOOSE, directed by James Fargo; written by Jeremy Joe Kronsberg; director of photography, Rexford Metz; editors, Ferris Webster and Joel Cox; music supervision, rector, Elayne Ceder; produced by Robert Daley; released by Warner Bros. At Flagship theaters. Running time: 114 minutes. This film has been rated PG.

Philo Beddoe .... Clint Eastwood
Lynn Halsey-Taylor .... Sondra Locke
Orville .... Geoffrey Lewis
Echo .... Beverly D'Angelo
Ma .... Ruth Gordon

By JANET MASLIN

THE bright new star of "Every Which Way but Loose" is an orangutan named Clyde, and he has quite a repertory. He can kiss human actors, smile bashfully and make obscene hand gestures. He can fling up his arms and fall over in a faint, in a game of bang-bang-you're-dead. He can steal scenes even when they aren't worth stealing.

Clyde's many talents notwithstanding, it's alarming to find Clint Eastwood co-starring with an ape. Mr. Eastwood's career since "Dirty Harry" has constituted one long argument for the studio system, for the days before established actors acquired so much control over their own movies that they could work on the flimsiest, most aimless projects with impunity. It's been a long time since Mr. Eastwood made a movie designed for a star.

•

Some of his directorial efforts have been impressive, and his choice of Michael Cimino to direct "Thunderbolt and Lightfoot" certainly indicates that his taste in protégés is shrewd. But his last couple of films have been so lackadaisically plotted, and so haphazardly put together, that they come close to resembling loose strings of blackout sketches with no particular end in sight.

Mr. Eastwood doesn't have the kind of comic agility that would make these episodes individually bright, nor does he tie them together with consistent, tightly coiled characterizations anymore. Far from showing off Mr. Eastwood to flattering advantage, this kind of format virtually eclipses his talents.

"Every Which Way but Loose," which opens today at Flagship theaters, is the slackest and most harebrained of Mr. Eastwood's recent movies. It is overlong and virtually uneventful, even though there are half a dozen cute characters and woolly subplots competing for the viewer's attentions. Ruth Gordon plays Mr. Eastwood's mother, and the cute thing about her is that she curses and owns a shotgun and can't pass her driving test. Sondra Locke plays a country singer with whom Mr. Eastwood is smitten, and if there's anything cute about her at all, it's the fact that she absolutely can't sing.

•

As for the subplots, one has to do with a couple of cops who feel slighted by Mr. Eastwood in a barroom encounter and decide to chase him. Another involves a ne'er-do-well gang of motorcycle hoods who also tangle with Mr. Eastwood and follow him around. A third involves a love affair between Mr. Eastwood's brother and a woman he meets at a fruit stand. A fourth involves Mr. Eastwood's picking fights that his brother can bet on from time to time. No wonder Clyde is the man of the hour.

If "Every Which Way but Loose" gets anywhere at all, it will be on the strength of Mr. Eastwood's considerable charisma, and on the fact that he and Miss Locke work well together even when there's nothing to work on. In "The Enforcer," in which they also co-starred, Mr. Eastwood played a slow-witted cop whom Miss Locke was forever outsmarting, and the departure from his usual tough-guy cynicism was reasonably intriguing. Here, though, the only clearly defined role is Clyde's. The others merely muddle through.

•

"Every Which Way but Loose," which is rated PG ("Parental Guidance Suggested"), contains a certain amount of rough language, mostly from Miss Gordon, and a little libidinous activity, mostly from Clyde.

1978 D 20, C19:3

A Matter of Succession

KING OF THE GYPSIES, directed by and screenplay by Frank Pierson; book by Peter Maas; director of photography Sven Nykvist; edited by Paul Hirsch; music composed by David Grisman; produced by Federico de Laurentiis; released by Paramount Pictures. At Loews State I, Broadway and 45th Street; Loews Ciné, Third Avenue near 86th Street; Bay Cinema, Second Avenue at 32d Street, and at neighborhood theaters. Running time: 112 minutes. This film has been rated R.

King Zharko Stepanowicz .... Sterling Hayden
Queen Rachel .... Shelley Winters
Rose .... Susan Sarandon
Groffo .... Judd Hirsch
Dave .... Eric Roberts
Tita .... Brooke Shields
Sharon .... Annette O'Toole
Persa .... Annie Potts
Spiro Giorgio .... Michael V. Gazzo
Danitza Giorgio .... Antonia Rey

By VINCENT CANBY

THE gypsies should sue. True, it would be something of a con job, since "King of the Gypsies" isn't the worst film of the year. Yet I think the ancient, Romany-speaking tribes could whomp up a good case for their having been maligned by a movie that presents them as an endangered species without once making their plight emotionally arresting or anthropologically important. They've been ripped off. The gypsies themselves would call it a boojo.

Taking as his source material Peter Maas's extensively researched book, which was based on interviews and personal observations and experiences, Frank Pierson has written and directed a melodrama about three generations of gypsies that is all color and no substance. Instead of defining the ways in which their heritage is unique, the movie wants us to believe that gypsies are like every other ethnic group that's been seen in popular movies.

Perhaps they are a bit noisier and more peripatetic, but essentially they are just folks who have their antisocial whims and ways as they drink, dance, celebrate family reunions, love each other one minute and fight to the death the next.

This may be Mr. Pierson's way of dramatizing their humanity, but the effect is mostly the opposite, to trivialize them. "King of the Gypsies" is "The Godfather" played in storefronts.

The movie, which opens today at New York theaters, even sounds like "The Godfather," as when one gypsy accuses another of not having respect. Like a "Godfather" clone, it's also about a war of succession, when the old king of the gypsies, played by Sterling Hayden, his fair skin lathered with make-up, skips the obvious heir to pass his scepter on to a younger, supposedly more capable man.

At the center of the problem, though, is the movie's lack of a point of view toward its subject. Dave, the young gypsy who becomes king when the old king dies, is first introduced as a fellow who wants to escape the gypsy heritage. In his almost tongue-tied way he has asked his grandfather, "Where are the gypsy surgeons? Where are the gypsy astronauts?" From what we see, Dave has a point. We seem to be on the verge of something seminal — the first movie about gypsy liberation!

Eric Roberts makes motion picture debut in this film.

Yet watching this movie, one never has a clear idea whether total integration is something to be wished, so that these mostly illiterate, swindling gypsies might vanish into a homogenized America, or an impulse to be resisted, so that an ancient culture might be preserved. When, at the end, the gypsy king finds himself ruling as before, he's not been trapped by his heritage, but by an act that seems completely uncharacteristic.

From what Mr. Pierson shows us, gypsies and the world in general probably would be better off if integration were successful, but I can't believe we are meant to be quite so cool. Part of the confusion, I suspect, is because the film fails so utterly to make these people's problems at all moving or urgent. Because we don't feel for them, they become minor freaks of time.

As much as the movie exploits gypsies, it also exploits the actors, all of whom have been seen to better advantage in other films. In addition to Mr. Hayden, who acts all over the place and never gets out of the paper bag that is the movie, the cast includes a subdued, very fat Shelley Winters as the old queen of the gypsies; Judd Hirsch as Mr. Hayden's psychotic son who covets the crown and would kill his son for it; Susan Sarandon as the daughter-in-law, a role that permits her the one breast-feeding scene that's become her quota in recent pictures; Brooke Shields as a sweet gypsy girl who looks as if she should wash her face and go back to school at Brearley, and Annette O'Toole as the red-haired WASP whom the young king loves and loses.

Eric Roberts, a handsome young man new to films, plays the gypsy heir and may be a good actor, though here he behaves as if he had studied the cinema of Richard Gere ("Blood Brothers," "Days of Heaven") to perfect a kind-mannered inarticulateness.

The movie has a couple of scenes of blood-letting, which are surprising, since I'd always thought gypsies preferred to get their revenge in ways that didn't leave fingerprints. Sven Nykvist, best known as Ingmar Bergman's cameraman, makes the movie look very pretty even when prettiness is beside the point. As might be expected, the gypsy music never stops, but with Stephane Grappelli on violin, who cares?

1978 D 20, C17:4

Michael Caine and Maggie Smith in "California Suite"
The most agreeably realized Neil Simon film in years and with a dream cast

Things Go Wrong

CALIFORNIA SUITE, directed by Herbert Ross, screenplay by Neil Simon; director of photography, David M. Walsh; film editor, Michael A. Stevenson; music composed by Claude Bolling; produced by Ray Stark; released by Columbia Pictures. At Loews Tower East and the National theaters. Running time: 103 minutes. This film is rated PG.

Bill Warren .... Alan Alda
Sidney Cochran .... Michael Caine
Dr. Willis Panama .... Bill Cosby
Hannah Warren .... Jane Fonda
Marvin Michaels .... Walter Matthau
Millie Michaels .... Elaine May
Dr. Chauncy Gump .... Richard Pryor
Diana Barrie .... Maggie Smith

By VINCENT CANBY

NEIL SIMON deals in the kind of lethal wisecracks — put-downs with dum-dum bullets for centers — that often have a way of destroying the wrong people. In the mouths of unknowing characters they are dangerous weapons, instruments for the sort of accidental suicides that demolish everything in the neighborhood. His wisecracks define a world of mighty desperation in which every confrontation, be it with a lover, a child, a husband, a friend or a taxi driver, becomes a last chance for survival.

When he writes a work in which this desperation is built into the situations Mr. Simon can be both immensely funny and surprisingly moving. Such were "The Heartbreak Kid" and "The Sunshine Boys" and such is his new "California Suite," which opens today at the National and Loews Tower East and is the most agreeably realized Simon film in years.

The screenplay was adapted by Mr. Simon from his four short plays, all set in the Beverly Hills Hotel in Beverly Hills, which were done on Broadway under the collective title of "California Suite" with the same actors tripling in several roles. For the movie Mr. Simon has intercut the stories, now played by eight stars, so that the film simulates the drive and cohesion of a single, seamless comedy.

Despite its title, "California Suite" is anything but a California movie. It's about as far as you can get from the Pacific Ocean if your heart is in New York. Though the locale is California, the sensibility is of New York — rude, fast-paced, uproariously blunt and so insistently contemporary it could have been written tomorrow and (who knows?) out of date the day after.

Here is Mr. Simon in top form, under the direction of Herbert Ross, one of the few directors (in addition to Elaine May) who can cope with the particular demands of material that simultaneously means to be touching and so non-stop clever one sometimes wants to gag him. It all works in "California Suite," not only because the material is superior Simon, but also because the writer and the director have assembled a dream cast.

Chief among these are Maggie Smith, who has her best screen role since "The Prime of Miss Jean Brodie," and Michael Caine, who is seldom acknowledged as the fine actor he is, playing a celebrated English actress and her antique-dealer husband who come to Hollywood for the Oscar ceremony. After having wrestled so long with movie material that offered no real contest, Miss Smith now has a part that makes use of her unique gift for comedy that has its origins in things far from pleasant.

In the film's early scenes she is pricelessly funny, getting ready for her big night in a magnificent display of hope, panic and despair, knowing that she doesn't have a snowball's chance of winning the Oscar, but listening eagerly to even the dimmest person who thinks she has. When, without melodramatic effort, the tale becomes an examination of a marriage that has slipped into compromised intimacy, she and Mr. Caine create characters of unexpected depth and compassion.

•

Jane Fonda and Alan Alda must deliver quintessential Simon dialogue, the sort that can undercut a comic situation of less importance than the one Mr. Simon has provided here. They are a long-divorced couple — he a successful Hollywood writer, she a confirmed New York career woman — who meet in Beverly Hills to discuss the future of their daughter, who has run away from her mother. Miss Fonda is superlative as the glib, semi-intellectual New Yorker whose only way of dealing with desperation is through sarcasm. Mr. Alda, playing it more or less straight, nicely complements her as the sort of man who doesn't have to be told when he's making a fool of himself. With him, that has been a conscious decision.

Walter Matthau and Elaine May play the principals in Mr. Simon's boisterous West Coast version of bedroom farce. He is an aging middle-class businessman, very much the conservative husband, whose one night alone in Los Angeles almost destroys his marriage after his brother presents him with the present of a prepaid hooker. Watching Mr. Matthau, as his wife awaits on the other side of the door, trying to pull pantyhose onto the rubbery form of a very drunk hooker, is one of the more cheerful moments of the entire movie season.

Richard Pryor and Bill Cosby appear as a pair of Chicago doctors who, with their wives, are sharing a vacation of the sort Mr. Simon cherishes. Everything goes wrong, including friendships. This sequence is the film's most frantic and, perhaps because of that, it runs out of breath before the end, but then no comedy can be completely perfect.

•

"California Suite," which has been rated PG ("parental guidance suggested"), contains some mildly racy language and situations.

1978 D 22, C12:1

Symbolic Struggle

THE ASCENT, directed by Larisa Shepitko; screenplay by Yuri Klepikov and Larisa Shepitko, based on a story by Vasil Bykov; photography by Vladimir Chukhnov; sets by Yuri Raksha; a Mosfilm Production, in Russian with English subtitles. At the Thalia Theater, 95th Street and Broadway. Running time: 105 minutes.

WITH: Boris Plotnikov, Vladimir Gostiukhin, Anatoly Solonitsin, Sergei Yakovlev and Ludmilla Pollakova.

The Generation Gap

THE WHITE SHIP, based on a story by Chinghiz Aitmatov; directed by Bolotbek Shamshiev; photography by Manasbek Musayev; sets by Vladimir Donskov; a Kirghizfilm Studio Porduction, in Russian with English subtitles. At the Thalia Theater, 95th Street and Broadway.

WITH: Nurgazi Sudygaliev, Savira Kumushalieva, Asankul Kuttabayev, Orozbek Kutmanaliev and Nazira Mambetova.

By JENNIFER DUNNING

BLACK shapes in an infinity of snow and wind, a knot of men and women stumble from hill to hill, children piled onto weary backs, pots and pans clanking in the vast silence. Two men leave to find food for their friends, on the run from "the Jerries" in wartime Russia. Captured by venal Nazi sympathizers, the two are pushed to psychological limits almost beyond endurance. One holds back his useless scraps of information, but the other betrays his friend and the hapless peasants they have unknowingly incriminated. It is a simple and familiar story that is told by "The Ascent," a 1977 Russian film that opens today at the Thalia in a double bill with "The White Ship," another prize-winning Russian film here receiving its New York premiere.

But, though familiar, this is a fable re-created with an unabashed sense of grandeur as well as deeply touching humanity. Based on a story by Vasil Bykov and directed by Larisa Shepitko, "The Ascent" pits the idealism of the young schoolteacher, Sotnikov, against the driving will to live of his fellow soldier, Rybak. Rybak is a bear of a man who risks his life repeatedly to protect Sotnikov, but he cannot risk it for the good of so vague an entity as his country. It is he who escorts Sotnikov to the gallows. Sniveling, he lags behind his newfound traitor friends, botching a suicide attempt and terrified by the open gate that beckons so ironically at the end. And yet Rybak is never a villain. He is seen with surprising compassion throughout.

Both men have the force and simplicity of symbols. We begin to know them in a deeper sense through their exchanges with the richly nuanced characters with whom they come in contact in an already vivid, shifting landscape scanned with a loving eye for detail. Vladimir Chukhnov's camera moves across stark snow, a remembered summer idyll, a peasant's cluttered shack, a harshly functional police torture room — one can almost smell the disinfectant — and a village square peopled by peasants summoned to the hanging. The carnival atmosphere along the long climb to the gallows, where a band is playing, tells of the ordinariness of evil. Heroes do not die in heroic landscapes.

The performances all have a searing luminosity, particularly those of Boris Plotnikov, as Sotnikov, and Vladimir Gostiukhin, as Rybak.

It is the actors, too, who make "The White Ship" more than a lyrical little folktale. Nurgazi Sudygaliev, the child who plays a dreaming, naughty 7-year-old in this 1977 film, directed by Bolotbek Shamshiev and based on Chinghiz Aitmatov's rendering of Kirghiz legend, must have given the performance of a young lifetime here. He moves with mesmerizing lucidity and lack of artifice through this tale of a boy and his grandfather who nourish themselves on the myths of their people while their family claws its way to self-destruction.

Photographed by Manasbek Musayev, "The White Ship" provides a tantalizing look at the rolling mountains and lush pastures of Soviet-Chinese border country, with occasional glimpses of a sterile modernistic city and mysterious rural shrines to the gods of the past. Like "The Ascent," it is a treat for the eyes and the spirit.

1978 D 22, C12:1

A Very Close Encounter

INVASION OF THE BODY SNATCHERS, directed by Philip Kaufman; screenplay by W.D. Richter, based on the novel "The Body Snatchers" by Jack Finney; director of photography, Michael Chapman; film editor, Douglas Stewart; music by Denny Zeitlin; produced by Robert H. Solo; released by United Artists. At the Rivoli, Gemini I, 86th Street East and neighborhood theaters. Running time: 114 minutes. This film is rated PG.

Matthew Bennell .... Donald Sutherland
Elizabeth Driscoll .... Brooke Adams
Dr. Davis Kibner .... Leonard Nimoy
Nancy Bellicec .... Veronica Cartwright
Jack Bellicec .... Jeff Goldblum
Geoffrey .... Art Hindle
Katherine .... Lelia Goldoni
Running Man .... Kevin McCarthy
Taxi Driver .... Don Siegel

By JANET MASLIN

THERE's a little something extra in virtually every frame of "Invasion of the Body Snatchers," Philip Kaufman's dazzling remake of one of the cleverest of horror classics (and has there ever been a better title for a movie of this sort?). In a shot of someone's office, the camera catches all of one window but just a tiny, ominous corner of another. Two characters go for a friendly drive in a car with a broken windshield. There are too many reflections, outstanding odd details, rays of curiously colored light. The leaves are covered with gelatinous ooze. Whatever the trouble is, it's everywhere.

The trouble, as any horror buff or late-show aficionado well knows, is pod

Donald Sutherland in "Invasion of the Body Snatchers": *Personable, opaque and affecting.*

people. They have arrived "from deep space," according to the ads for the new film (whatever that means, it has a lovely sound). At first they're only spores, but they mean to hatch everywhere — and every time a pod person appears, a human person vanishes. The pod people look just like their human counterparts, but they seldom blink and never smile. Their mission on Earth is never explained, but obviously they're up to no good.

•

In Don Siegel's 1956 version, the story was swift and scary, set forth with a nightmarish economy. But Mr. Kaufman's film, which opens today at the Rivoli and other theaters, is after something different. Mr. Kaufman's direction is so showy, constantly heralding its own ingenuity, that the film operates as both a valentine and a rich, good-hearted joke. Mr. Kaufman entices his audience with a running what-will-he-think-up-next? technique, and each time you begin thinking he's tried every trick in the book, he writes another new chapter.

In its keen, loving attention to beautiful minutiae, "Invasion of the Body Snatchers" recalls Nicolas Roeg's "Don't Look Now"; in its intimations of cool, constant peril, it suggests Alan Pakula's "The Parallax View." (And, like "The Parallax View," Mr. Kaufman's film climaxes on a split-level set, to emphasize a running element of duplicity.) But Mr. Kaufman adds to this an element of comic exaggeration: The creepiness he generates is so crazily ubiquitous it becomes funny.

Accordingly, "Invasion of the Body Snatchers" isn't as frightening as it might be (even though special effects involving the pods and their hairy tendrils are brilliantly unsettling, as is the gruesome moment when one character tries to murder his own half-formed clone). And in the latter half of the film, when the story slows down considerably, Mr. Kaufman's inventiveness begins to seem a bit untethered. The screenplay, by W. D. Richter, remains bright and lively throughout, but the plot just isn't full enough to carry a feature film.

The characters are vivid, and uniformly well-played, and their pre-pod lives are fairly well established. But an hour into the film, once the menace is identified, the few remaining humans begin fleeing for their lives, and after that it's just run, run, run. It hardly helps that they are essentially heading for a dead end, or that in this age of ubiquitous news reports there's not a glimmer of information about what's going on outside San Francisco, no hint as to whether they can possibly be saved. Nor is it useful when Danny Zeitlin's excellent score evolves into an electronic version of "Amazing Grace" very late in the film. This may amount to an epiphany of sorts, but it's no substitute for a dramatically effective ending.

There's a new character in this version, a hip, successful psychiatrist who explains away the legitimate fears of others with a surfeit of self-help jargon. But Leonard Nimoy isn't right for the role; he isn't funny enough. And, besides, in a movie like this it's much too easy to figure out which side he's on.

The problem with Mr. Nimoy's character goes deeper than casting, though. Because Mr. Kaufman generally shoots his extras matter-of-factly, with no clear indication of who's been taken over and who hasn't, the feelings of contemporary urban mistrust that the film plays upon need a focus. And Mr. Nimoy's character, like the doctors in "Rosemary's Baby," is meant to embody the essential unreliability of which one sometimes suspects one's fellows. If there were just one character in "Invasion of the Body Snatchers" who successfully conveyed that kind of menace, the entire film would take place in a more intimate arena, and cut closer to the bone.

Playing a foursome of embattled good guys, Donald Sutherland, Brooke Adams, Jeff Goldblum and Veronica Cartwright are individually impressive and a very smooth ensemble, too. Miss Adams displays animation and intelligence that were far less apparent in "Days of Heaven." Mr. Sutherland is by turns personable and opaque, affecting in a way that he hasn't been since "Klute." Miss Cartwright stays on one's mind even during long intervals when she isn't on the screen. And Mr. Goldblum, who's had similar small roles in a number of movies, at last comes into his own. When it comes to playing nervous hot-heads with maniacal wit, he can't be beat.

•

"Invasion of the Body Snatchers," which is rated PG ("Parental Guidance Suggested"), contains brief nudity and one quick but frightening bloody episode.

1978 D 22, C14:1

Long Delayed Sequel

FORCE 10 FROM NAVARONE, directed by Guy Hamilton; screenplay by Robin Chapman; story by Carl Foreman, based on the novel by Alistair MacLean; director of photograpy, Chris Challis; film editor, Ray Poulton; music composed and conducted by Ron Goodwin; produced by Oliver A. Unger; released by American International Pictures. At the RKO Cinerama on Broadway, the RKO 86th Street and neighborhood theaters. Running time: 118 minutes.

Mallory .... Robert Shaw
Barnsby .... Harrison Ford
Miller .... Edward Fox
Maritza .... Barbara Bach
Lescovar .... Franco Nero
Weaver .... Carl Weathers
Drazac .... Richard Kiel
Reynolds .... Angus MacInnes
Schroeder .... Michael Byrne
Petrovich .... Alan Badel
Rogers .... Christopher Malcolm
Salvone .... Nick Ellsworth
Oberstein .... Jonathan Blake
Bauer .... Michael Sheard

Harrison Ford and Robert Shaw in "Force 10 From Navarone"

"FORCE 10 From Navarone" must be one of the longest-delayed sequels in film history, coming, as it does, 17 years after "The Guns of Navarone." The original was a World War II adventure yarn about British saboteurs assigned to destroy an "impregnable" German position.

A fast-moving, simple-minded script by Carl Foreman, who also produced, and the performances of Gregory Peck, David Niven and Anthony Quinn, brought it considerable box-office success.

Mr. Foreman has also written what is called in the credits the "screen story" for "Force 10," with a screenplay by Robin Chapman.

•

As was the original, it is based on a novel by Alistair Maclean, and continues the adventures of two members of the same suicide squad, here played by Robert Shaw, who died soon after the completion of the film, and Edward Fox, who played the title role in "The Day of the Jackal."

From the Aegean they have moved to the Balkans, where they are seconded to an American Ranger unit, led by Harrison Ford, of "Star Wars," that has been ordered either to destroy a bridge that the Wehrmacht can't do without or not to bother coming back.

There the resemblance between the two films ends. The plot of "Force 10" is banally improbable. Guy Hamilton's direction is sluggish and the camera work, by Chris Challis, makes the least of the picturesque locations in the mountains of Montenegro.

There is, moreover, an unmistakable air of haste and cost-cutting that suggests that most of the production budget went to pay the high-priced stars.

Featured in the cast are Barbara Bach, a beauty miscast as a partisan fighter, Franco Nero, also miscast, as another of the locals, and Carl Weathers as the obligatory black member of the squad.

"Force 10," in passing, considerably romanticizes the activities of the partisans, the irregular troops commanded by Marshal Tito, who has been the freely chosen president of Yugoslavia for 32 years now, and turns the Chetniks, who were linked to the Yugoslavian royalist government in exile in London, into eager Nazi collaborators.

•

This film has been rated PG ("Parental Guidance Suggested"), possibly because of several violent episodes.

TOM BUCKLEY

1978 D 22, C14:1

Historical Speculation

BRASS TARGET, directed by John Hough; screenplay by Alvin Boretz; director of photography, Tony Imi; film editor, David Lane; music by Laurence Rosenthal; produced by Arthur Lewis; released by United Artists. At the Victoria, Trans-Lux 85th Street, Coliseum and Quad III theaters. Running time: 112 minutes. This film is rated PG.

Mara .... Sophia Loren
Major DeLucca .... John Cassavetes
General Patton .... George Kennedy
Colonel Rogers .... Robert Vaughn
Colonel McCauley .... Patrick McGoohan
Colonel Dawson .... Bruce Davison
Colonel Gilchrist .... Edward Herrmann
Shelley/Webber .... Max Von Sydow

IT is the dubious premise of "The Brass Target," a film full of dubiety, that Gen. George S. Patton Jr. was assassinated in Germany in 1945 by a motley crew of United States Army officers in an attempt to hide their theft of $250 million in Nazi gold.

History says that General Patton died in Germany in 1945 following an automobile accident, but Frederick Nolan, who wrote "The Algonquin Project," this film's source material, has connected various unsolved mysteries to make a wobbly case for his conspiracy theory.

As historical speculation goes, it's less interesting than wondering where we might be today if Ford's Theater had been playing "Uncle Tom's Cabin" that fateful night in 1865, instead of "Our American Cousin."

Would Lincoln have attended, or might he have said, "Mary, I just can't sit through it again"?

•

You may elect not to sit through international claptrap like this film, which doesn't measure up even to "The Cassandra Crossing."

"The Brass Target" was shot in Germany and (I assume from the landscape) Switzerland, with a cast headed by John Cassavetes, Sophia Loren, Max Von Sydow, Robert Vaughn, George Kennedy, Bruce Davison and Patrick McGoohan, under the direction of John Hough ("Dirty Mary, Crazy Larry") from a script by Alvin Boretz.

Mr. Cassavetes, as an intelligence officer investigating the theft of the Nazi gold, grimaces a lot, like someone doing anything to stay awake; Miss Loren looks wan; Mr. Von Sydow, Patton's fictitious assassin, looks like a man earning a good salary for a foolish job, and Mr. Kennedy, never a very interesting actor, gives General Patton the personality of a sadistic supervisor at a fat farm. He yells a lot but is immediately forgettable.

Mr. Hough does nothing to improve a bad script. Among his problems is not knowing how to end a scene. Mostly someone just walks out of the frame and he cuts to the person remaining for a reaction shot when no reaction is due.

Sometimes he tries to incite our interest by jumping into the dialogue from the scene to follow. Sometimes he blows a whistle or rings a bell. He's a man of ideas, all of them poor.

•

"The Brass Target," which has been rated PG ("Parental Guidance Suggested"), contains a lot of violence, all of it simulated but random in the way of simple-minded movie-making.

VINCENT CANBY

1978 D 22, C18:1

Pretty Kid, Older Woman

MOMENT BY MOMENT, written and directed by Jane Wagner; director of photography, Phillip Lathrop; film editor, John F. Burnett; music by Lee Holdridge; produced by Robert Stigwood; released by Universal Pictures. At the Coronet Theater. Running time: 105 minutes. This film is rated R.

Trisha	Lily Tomlin
Strip	John Travolta
Naomi	Andra Akers
Stu	Bert Kramer
Peg	Shelley R. Bonus
Stacie	Debra Feuer
Dan Santini	James Luisi
Pharmacist	John O'Leary
Storekeeper	Neil Flanagan
Gas Station Attendant	Jarvais Hudson
Band Leader	Tom Slocum
Hotel Desk Clerk	Michael Consoldane
Bookstore Lady	Jo Jordan
Druggist	Joseph Schwab

"MOMENT BY MOMENT" is this year's California "problem" picture, that is, a movie in which people suffer for reasons that never seem very urgent in settings that, though not particular to California, are emblematic of what we think of as the California culture — elaborate beach houses, imported automobiles (public transportation is nowhere in sight), on throughways that are the main arteries of late 20th-century rootlessness.

The film, which opens today at the Coronet, stars the usually incomparable Lily Tomlin as Trisha, a soon-to-be-divorced woman of 38, and John Travolta as Strip (which is his name as well as what he does), the none-too-bright drifter in his early 20's that she falls in love with.

At the start Trisha is skeptical, being unable to imagine what a pretty kid like him would see in a rich, available, attractive, humorous older woman like her. After Strip's kid-magnetism gets her into bed, Trisha begins to fall in love with him and to see in him what she calls "great potential," though he can't form complete sentences with much ease. When he does form sentences, they are often funny, but they indicate no great potential for anything. "All my friends are undependable," says a gloomy Strip, "except Greg, and he's in jail."

•

Trisha tells Strip he can be anything he wants, and Strip thinks fleetingly that he might like to be a veterinarian or paint billboards. Trisha is depressed, not by Strip's limited ambitions, but by the sudden realization that she has never wanted to be anything. Later she puts into a bottle a message reading simply "What a world," which makes one realize that things are tough all over California.

It's very difficult to understand what Miss Tomlin and Jane Wagner, who wrote and directed the film, wanted to do in "Moment by Moment." As romantic drama it's pretty tepid. That the two stars look enough alike to be brother and sister is no help, and though Miss Wagner's camera comes in for some tactful close-ups of flesh in the love scenes, they are singularly unerotic. One has the impression that these two lovers would prefer to be doing something else.

Then, too, it's impossible to tell what we're to make of Trisha. Mr. Travolta has an easier time of it. Strip is not a terrifically interesting character, but he's a recognizable one, and the actor clearly has a point of view about him. Strip, who dropped out of school when he was 14 and now has no time for education, may luck onto something into the future, but his chances will diminish with age. He has a certain integrity that, instead of giving him direction, actually prevents him from being the successful hustler he was meant to be.

•

This is the character we see in the film, though Miss Wagner and Miss Tomlin apparently want us to believe he is some kind of misunderstood innocent. If we are to believe the character of Trisha, who is supposed to be intelligent, then we can't believe the character of Strip. If we see him for what he is, it's not possible to go along with Trisha, unless Miss Tomlin is sending her up, which I don't think is the case.

Maybe "Moment by Moment" is meant to be a call for sexual liberation — in the way in which it reverses the usual roles of seducer and seduced. I'm not sure. The script doesn't seem to have been thought through to a finish, but there is a further problem with the picture.

In her one-woman Broadway show, "Appearing Nitely," Miss Tomlin, with the help of Miss Wagner, created a series of remarkable characters, memorable misfits, men and women who were out of step with themselves, with other people or with the times. They were sketches, line drawings, fragments so artfully conceived that entire lives came and went in a matter of a few minutes of stage time.

•

It was a curious and fascinating performance since Miss Tomlin herself seemed scarcely to exist. She was a medium to be shaped into somebody else. She's a marvelous monologist and can be a riveting actress, as she showed in "Nashville" and "The Late Show." In "Moment by Moment," in a full-length, comparatively uneccentric role, she is completely miscast. The no-nonsense native intelligence of the real-life performer obscures the character she is trying to play.

Watching her in "Moment by Moment" is to see an actress in the process of preparing a role, while she's still working on its psychological foundation. It's not an uninteresting performance, but it's cold, without shape yet, and it characterizes the movie that contains it.

VINCENT CANBY

1978 D 22, C18:1

Lily Tomlin and John Travolta in "Moment by Moment" at the Coronet
The two stars look enough alike to be brother and sister

FILM VIEW

VINCENT CANBY

Nothing 'Went Wrong'

It was the day after the opening of "Superman," the comic strip-inspired film that reportedly cost four times as much as the Louisiana Territory and is somewhat less big. The reaction to the film was decidedly mixed. "What," asked a friend of mine, "went wrong?" "What went wrong?". I said. "I'm not sure anything went wrong. If they insist on making a movie about Superman, this is probably as good as can be done."

What went wrong, indeed. It's a phrase that should haunt critics, though I know from personal experience that it doesn't. We make our livings pointing out with pain and sorrow everything that has gone wrong. If a movie or a book or a play is truly bad, it's not a very difficult task; one can point in almost any direction and find something that's gone wrong. "Superman" didn't go wrong. To ask what went wrong is to betray one's expectations that somehow, maybe, perhaps, with luck, the original material could be transformed into "The Odyssey." It's also to ask the wrong question.

I have no particular desire to defend "Superman." It's a big, long, elaborate, expensive, mild, essentially foolish film. However, I do wonder about the ways in which our reactions to a movie or a play or a book are shaped by our anticipation of the experience. That anticipation is shaped by a number of things, including advertising and publicity, as well as by what we want to see and what we feel we have a right to see. The reaction to E.L. Doctorow's first play, the recently opened-and-closed "Drinks Before Dinner," is a dramatic example of the manner in which expectations can kill.

Here was the first play by one of our most celebrated and financially successful novelists ("The Book of Daniel," "Ragtime"), in a production directed by Mike Nichols, who has a reputation for formidable success. It should have been fast, funny, fashionably surprising. Instead it was something quite other — not very long but seemingly interminable, with speeches constructed like paragraphs. It wasn't as funny as it was ironic, and we all know that irony after dinner is less welcome than a tray full of stale hors d'oeuvres. To top it off, the production was nearly arrogant in its chic. The clothes, the furniture and the set were very close to being unreal in their extravagance, suggesting Hollywood daydreams of the 30's, not New York life in the 70's. What went wrong?

Nothing, as far as I was concerned. I suspect that the piece was exactly the sort of thing that Doctorow and Nichols wanted to do. If anything went wrong, it was with what we wanted them to put on, which wasn't a play of ideas (some, admittedly, better than others) in which the characters were less important as individuals than as aspects of the same mind. To me, the fast fold of "Drinks Before Dinner" says less about Doctorow's and Nichols's talents than about our ability, and readiness, to accept a highly idiosyncratic work that is valuable as much for being Doctorow's novelist-vision of theater as for what was actually said on stage. Can't we find room in our theater for a production of such marvelous excesses without asking what went wrong?

• • •

Bill Cosby and Sheila Frazier in Neil Simon's "California Suite"—a case where almost everything "went right"

Which brings me back to "Superman," a film as bereft of intelligence as the Doctorow play was overstuffed with it. After the producers decided to make the film, nothing really went wrong with it. Although the figures given for its cost (up to $78 million) scare me, I don't think it can be criticized for not being what it was never meant to be. In saying this I suppose I should admit to a certain bias: even as a child I found the Superman comic strip a bore, as visually exciting as a bowl of cream of wheat and singularly lacking in humor. But then the possibilities for adventure and suspense were severely limited by Superman's superpowers; gods aren't very interesting people.

The film, directed by Richard Donner and written by some of the brightest minds working in movies today, is without particular style, but that simply means it's like the comic strip, which always looked as if it had been drawn by someone who took a cut-rate correspondence course in cartooning. Unlike "Star Wars," which manages to be both juvenile fiction and a commentary on it, "Superman" is simple-minded without being especially innocent. The appearance of all of those stars (Marlon Brando, Gene Hackman, Trevor Howard, Glenn Ford, etc.) somehow belies innocence, revealing, instead, greed.

Christopher Reeve makes a practically perfect Superman/Clark Kent, being a cheerful facimile of the cartoon hero. The film does jazz up the bleakness of the comic strip in two respects. It turns Lois Lane, girl-reporter, into a funny, flesh-and-blood young woman in the person of Margot Kidder, and it brings on the magnificently sculpted Valerie Perrine, who plays the companion to the evil Lex Luthor, to suggest that in the world of Superman not all babies are delivered by spaceship.

The special effects of "Superman" are mostly good, and they're dropped noisily into the movie at regular intervals to wake up those of us who may feel a need to nod off. Having said that, one has said just about everything there is to say about "Superman." What went wrong? Not a thing. The proper question is why they bothered with it in the first place.

Instead of asking what went wrong, it's sometimes possible to ask what went right. This is the pleasant thought that comes to mind with Herbert Ross's slick, very funny film version of Neil Simon's "California Suite." I didn't see the Broadway theater production, but I can't imagine that it could have had more elan than this uproarious film in which Simon's comic gifts are displayed to their best advantage. Instead of presenting these tales of four different couples as four different sketches, Simon and Ross have cut the four stories together in such a way that "California Suite" has the drive of a single, almost seamless comedy.

When Simon attempts to do all-out romantic comedy he has a way of tripping over his tongue. "California Suite" is no less glib than "The Goodbye Girl," but the machine-gun pacing of the jokes works with, not against, the situations in which the characters find themselves. In the film's best moments — those with Maggie Smith and Michael Caine, and Jane Fonda and Alan Alda — the gags become a measure of emotional desperation instead of simply a way of showing off.

Among the things that went right with "California Suite" was the casting, which includes Walter Matthau, Elaine May, Richard Pryor and Bill Cosby. The screenplay is Simon's best since "The Heartbreak Kid," and Ross's direction has never been as unobtrusively right — always on-target, as self-assured in knockabout farce as in the emotionally-charged scenes of truth-telling that are as moving as anything Simon has ever written. ■

1978 D 24, II:11:1

Suburb in the Wild

THE FURTHER ADVENTURES OF THE WILDERNESS FAMILY, PART II. Directed by Frank Zuniga. Produced and written by Arthur Dubs. Director of photography: John Hora. Music by Douglas Lackey and Gene Kauer. Songs performed by Barry Williams. Released by Pacific International Enterprises Inc. At the Embassy, Broadway and 47th Street, and other theaters. This film is rated G.

Skip .... Robert F. Logan
Pat .... Susan Damante Shaw
Jenny .... Heather Rattray
Toby .... Ham Larsen
Boomer .... George (Buck) Flower

BY the time the Wilderness Family gets around to "The Further Adventures of the Wilderness Family, Part II," most of the excitement is behind them. In Part I, this wholesome foursome evidently decided to give up city life, retreated to a spectacular site in the Pacific Northwest, built a log cabin, learned to read by candlelight, and found themselves a couple of pet bears.

As Part II begins, life in the middle of nowhere is very, very calm. Dad splits logs, Mom cooks dinner, and the children — depending on the season — either pick wildflowers or horse around in the snow. Though there's nary a station wagon in sight, the quality of this privileged life is eerily suburban.

•

One hour and a lot of animal shots later, someone on the production end of "Part II," which opened yesterday at the Embassy and other theaters, has decided that songs about snowflakes and footage of the Robinson family on snowshoes don't amount to much of a plot.

So Mom wigs out, complaining that she can't stand bears in the house, and promptly catches pneumonia. The children weather a blizzard. Dad gets stuck in an avalanche. The cabin catches fire while the meanest wolf in the neighborhood — Old Scarface, he's called — is right outside the door. All of this happens in a hurry, and afterward everything is calm once more.

As Dad, Robert F. Logan is a great success, full of reassuring smiles by day and dressed in long underwear by night — so he can leap out of bed in a hurry whenever there's trouble in the smokehouse or the chicken coop.

Mr. Logan is a personable fellow who doesn't mind being upstaged by the odd cougar or raccoon. And he has played this same kind of Dad in a string of family wildlife adventure films, among them the recent and much better "The Sea Gypsies," directed by Stewart Raffill, who also directed the first Wilderness Family film.

But this time, his talent for patiently explaining the wonders of nature, and for providing useful object lessons for children, isn't put to much use. The small details of the Robinsons' daily life would doubtless be of interest to a young audience, but they're never really explained. The big action sequences have a trumped-up feeling, and they're over almost as soon as they begin.

•

The other members of the cast don't make a very convincing family. There are a mother (Susan Damante Shaw), who doesn't really look as if she'd spend one night in a house without carpet; a young son (Ham Larsen), who's too noisily adorable, and an older daughter (Heather Rattray), who's too restrained.

From time to time, the family is visited by a grizzled trader named Boomer, whose favorite words are "heap" and "varmint" and "tarnation." Boomer arrives whenever the plot seems particularly slow, and the sight of the children invariably brings sentimental tears to his eyes. He always outstays his welcome.

JANET MASLIN

1978 D 26, C20:1

A Silent Majority

WE ARE ARAB JEWS IN ISRAEL, directed by Igaal Niddam; a documentary examination of the socio-political implications of Israel's Oriental Jews; in French with English subtitles; distributed by New Yorker Films. Running time: 120 minutes. At the Film Forum, 15 Vandam Street.

By VINCENT CANBY

THE Film Forum, that pocket-sized theater on Vandam Street in the lower reaches of Greenwich Village, continues to offer the most consistently rewarding programs of any film showcase in the city. This year the theater has presented the local theatrical premieres of two of the most interesting films to be seen here in 1978, Kenji Mizoguchi's "A Geisha" (1953) and Andrzej Wajda's "Landscape After the Battle" (1970), both films that could have not survived the economic rigors of conventional New York City first runs.

"We Are Arab Jews in Israel," which opens at the Film Forum today, is not in the same category with those fiction films but it is a provocative, remarkably even-tempered movie, a two-hour documentary about a subject not often explored by the press because of the pressure to cover day-to-day events.

•

The film is the work of Igaal Niddam, a Moroccan Jew and Israeli citizen, at present a resident of Switzerland, who strongly believes that Israel's population of Arab Jews could provide "a natural bridge" leading to an Israeli-Arab understanding.

Though 65 percent of Israel's citizens are so-called Arab Jews, that is, Jews with origins in Arab countries, Mr. Niddam believes they are still a silent majority, inarticulate citizens who, often because of their low economic status, are ignored by the power structure. As a result, says this film, the political policies of the nation are largely determined by Jews whose attachments are to Western Europe and America, people whose cultural sympathies make it impossible for them to understand their Arab neighbors, or to be understood by them.

"We Are Arab Jews in Israel" seems to have been completed last year, before Israeli Premier Menachem Begin and Egyptian President Anwar el-Sadat began their negotiations for an Israeli-Egyptian settlement, though there's nothing in the film to make it seem dated. If anything, it offers clues to the present situation.

•

It is obviously Mr. Niddam's belief that until Israel's Arab Jews find their voice, the present stalemate will continue. This point is eloquently made toward the end of the movie by a young man working on a kibbutz, an Iraqi Jew who also suggests that Zionism, in addition to defining Jewish nationalism, encouraged the previously undeveloped feelings of Arab nationalism. In effect, he says, one is responsible for the other.

•

Mr. Niddam's method is straightforward and direct, without cinematic artifice. "We Are Arab Jews in Israel" deals with highly emotional, extremely complicated issues, but it never attempts to mask the emotion or the complexity, or the film maker's own point of view. The movie will play at the Film Forum tonight through Sunday at 7:45 P.M. and next week, Thursday though Sunday, at the same hour.

1978 D 28, C16:3

FILM VIEW

VINCENT CANBY

Six of the '10-Best' Were American

In a world where everything must eventually pass, the decimal system of priorities may be the last thing to go. As the planet is consumed by flames someone will be compiling the definitive list of the 10 most important events in the history of the world — and there will be one other person around to tell him he's all wet. That last list won't change the course of the apocalypse but it may help to make it seem comprehensible. Which is why we all make lists of the 10 best movies or the 10 best anything; lists don't change history, but they give us a certain perspective.

In looking over the titles of what are the best movies of 1978, I'm struck by what appears to be a lack of any particular trend. Some of the good movies were hits, but so were a number of terrible ones. For example, "Jaws II" and "Damien — Omen II" apparently made mints of money, though "The Swarm," Irwin Allen's group jeopardy movie about bad bees, didn't. Just when you least expect it, the public gets picky.

Several of the the 10 best films are hugely successful at the box office. Several others, I fear, were seen only by me and a couple of bored ushers. Six of the films are American, which would be a fairly high percentage in any year and most surprising this year, when American films, at the time they were being reviewed, seemed so dismal. One of the choices is the work of a man who died in 1958. Perhaps the most buoyant find of the year was Charlie Chaplin's "A Woman of Paris," but that film is ineligible because it was originally released in 1923.

If 1978 can be said to have been memorable in any way, it's because several of our best filmmakers appeared to go to pieces — Ingmar Bergman with his phantasmagoric "The Serpent's Egg" and Lina Wertmuller with her excrutiatingly solemn, far from serious "The End of the World on a Night Full of Rain in Our Usual Bed." Though Robert Altman's "A Wedding" successfully extended the fragmented narrative technique he used in "Nashville," the movie itself failed as comedy, drama, satire or even sociology.

Here, in alphabetical order, are my choices for 1978:

"California Suite." Life in and around the Beverly Hills Hotel, Beverly Hills, Cal., as experienced by five couples in four separate but intercut stories, is a howl, mostly of laughter but also, in two of the tales, of pain. Neil Simon wrote it, Herbert Ross directed it, and it is acted with splendid verve by Maggie Smith, Michael Caine, Jane Fonda, Alan Alda, Walter Matthau, Elaine May, Bill Cosby and Richard Pryor. Here's popular, mass-market movie-making at its slickest.

"Days of Heaven." This handsome, emotionally muted movie about farmers, drifters, migrant workers, lovers and opportunists in the Texas panhandle of 1916 is the second feature by the extraordinarily gifted Terrence Malick, whose first film was "Badlands" (1973). Mr. Malick works so obliquely that it's often difficult to see what he's up to, since his films are so visually stunning one is tempted to think he's interested in superficial prettiness. Far from it. Among other things, "Days of Heaven" is about human isolation in a universe that is neither friendly nor unfriendly, merely indifferent to the transients who, like the characters in this film, spend their lives trying to cope, sometimes with grace. Among the excellent performers are Sam Shepard, Brooke Adams and Linda Manz. Nestor Almendros was the principal cameraman.

"The Deer Hunter." Already named the best film of the year by the New York Film Critics' Circle, "The Deer Hunter," the second film to be directed by Michael Cimino, is about the quality of life in the America that fought the Vietnam war, and lost. The three protagonists, marvelously well played by Robert De Niro, Christopher Walken and John Savage, are the children of first generation Russian-Americans. They work in a Pennsylvania steel mill and when the war comes along, they fight it without question. At its worst "The Deer Hunter" imposes unlikely poetic insights on characters. At its best the film reveals the strengths and weaknesses of a system that pays lip service to an individualism that it cannot easily accommodate. Among the strikingly effective supporting performers are Meryl Streep, George Dzundza and the late John Cazale. Vilmos Zsigmond was the cameraman.

"A Geisha." Kenji Mizoguchi, who died in 1958, made "A Geisha" in 1953 and the movie, which played a limited run here at the Film Forum, remains the best, most intelligent film about women seen here this year. The movie, a remake of one that Mizoguchi made in 1936, is about the friendship of two Kyoto geishas, the younger of whom tries unsuccessfully to upgrade the dignity of the profession as she supposes is guaranteed by Gen. MacArthur's new Japanese constitution. The film is funny and moving, incredibly beautiful without being especially pretty — a major work by a master.

"Movie Movie." Forget the title — it's awful — but the film, Stanley Donen's remembrance of double-features past, is a delight, composed of parodies of two 30's-style pictures: a boxing melodrama called "Dynamite Hands" and a backstage musical, "Baxter's Beauties of 1933," which means it would have come out in 1932. George C. Scott and Trish Van Devere star in both films and receive super support from Barry Bostwick, Barbara Harris, Eli Wallach, Ann Reinking, Rebecca York, Art Carney and Kathleen Beller. The script, which takes particular delight in scrambled language (people are inclined to say things like "I heard it in the papers"), is by Larry Gelbart and Sheldon Keller.

• • •

"Perceval." Eric Rohmer ("My Night at Maud's," "Claire's Knee," etc.) makes movies like no one else and his "Perceval," a comic variation on the Arthurian legend, isn't even much like other Rohmer films except that it shares with them the most highly developed sense of paradox in cinema today. Perceval is played by Fabrice Luchini, a fellow with the blank, self-satisfied look of someone who's already been raised to sainthood. He's an innocent who succeeds by believing everything he's told, taking everybody at his word, and having no awareness of possible defeat. Mr. Rohmer's sets are highly stylized recollections of the work of medieval miniature painters. Everything is tiny, precise, artificial and blindingly beautiful. Nestor Almendros did the camerawork.

"Pretty Baby." Louis Malle's cool, sad movie about the last days of Storyville, New Orleans's famous red light district that was shut down in 1917, and about the curious, for once truly impossible love affair between a 12-year-old whore (Brooke Shields) and a moody, image-obsessed photographer (Keith Carradine), loosely based on the late Ernest J. Bellocq. Polly Platt wrote the screenplay that has the effect of blues remembered, not as they actually sounded but softened, made more romantic and thus less dangerous. Susan Sarandon and Antonio Fargas also have prominent roles. The success of the cinematography by Sven Nykvist is an integral aspect of the movie — Mr. Malle's most original to date.

'Six of the films are American, which is surprising since, at the time they were being reviewed, they seemed so dismal.'

"A Slave of Love." Director Nikita Mikhalkov takes a very lyrical view of history in this Soviet film about a group of self-absorbed actors, writers, directors and producers busily turning out foolish silent movies in southern Russia (circa 1917) while the Bolsheviks desperately try to consolidate their revolution in Moscow. Though the politics are not surprising, the movie is. It's full of rue and wit and quiet courage. "A Slave of Love" owes more to Chekhov than to Marx. There is a deceptive languor in its rhythm. It seems to dawdle, to digress, to fritter away its time, and then suddenly, for reasons not quite beyond the comprehension of its characters, facts must be faced, accountings made. The new Russia that Chekhov anticipated is at hand. An astonishingly fine film.

"Straight Time." A leanly constructed, vividly staged melodrama about a petty crook named Max Dembo (Dustin Hoffman) who defines the meaning of recidivism. Written by Alvin Sargent, Edward Bunker and Jeffrey Boam, and directed by Ulu Grosbad, the film traces the story of Max as if he were a case history in failure. Max is a rat, but a small one; he is more like a large, unreliable mouse. The movie works through a kind of negative attraction. Max is interesting not for what he is but for all the things he isn't. Because "Straight Time" is really a variation on a cops-and-robbers theme, it's not surprising that its most involving sequences are the series of heists Max carries out. Flawless performances by Mr. Hoffman, Harry Dean Stanton, Gary Busey and M. Emmet Walsh.

"Violette." Claude Chabrol makes very good films and some that can be forgotten almost while one is watching them. "Violette" is based on the true story of a sweet young

French girl, Violette Noziere, who, one evening in 1933, with malice aforethought, murdered her father just as he was sitting down to a roast beef dinner. Whether or not she also attempted to murder her mom was open for debate in the trial. Isabelle Huppert plays the beautiful Violette, whom Mr. Chabrol clearly regards as the quintessential bourgeois girl with her eye on the main chance. Her only problem, perhaps, is that she didn't aspire to greater things. Stephane Audran and Jean Carmet appear as her prissy parents. "Violette" ranks with the best work of the director who also gave us "La Femme Infidele," "Le Boucher" and "Les Biches."

• • •

The following 10 films, listed in no special order of importance, cannot honestly be called runners-up, since several of them would never have made the first list no matter what. They are, though, films that deserve special mention for one reason or another:

"The Duellists," Ridley Scott's adaptation of a Conrad novella about the Napoleonic wars and two young officers who go through the campaigns fighting a series of duels with each other, is beautiful and somewhat crazy, even in its casting of Keith Carradine and Harvey Keitel as Frenchmen; "The Buddy Holly Story," an energetic pop biography of the rock-and-roll star, nicely played by Gary Busey; "The Chess Players," Satyajit Ray's graceful, witty comedy about the collapse of the last free Indian state in 1856; "F.I.S.T.," Norman Jewison's history of a fictitious union whose ups and downs recall the real-life Teamsters — not great film making though the material is that of an American epic; "Joseph Andrews," Tony Richardson's riotous and stylish return to the work of Henry Fielding, performed to perfection by every good actor in England and one (Ann-Margret) from the United States.

Also, "An Unmarried Woman," Paul Mazursky's contemplation of life in New York City as it might be lived by a well-to-do, beautiful woman whose husband walks out on her — Jill Clayburgh's performance makes the film; "Landscape After The Battle," Andrzej Wajda's fine, sorrowful Polish film about life in the D.P. camps just after World War II, based on the stories of Tadeusz Borowski; "Death on the Nile," a pretty riverboat of leisurely fun, based on the Agatha Christie whodunit, with (among others) Bette Davis, Maggie Smith, Peter Ustinov and David Niven; "Autumn Sonata," Ingmar Bergman's showcase for Ingrid Bergman and Liv Ullmann, who play mother and daughter in a series of angry confrontation scenes that give bravura acting a good name; and "Interiors," Woody Allen's courageously unfunny examination of family life that, I suspect, is as remote from his experience as the lives of Demetrius and the gladiators — with fine performances by Geraldine Page, Maureen Stapleton and Marybeth Hurt. ■

1978 D 31, II:1:1

Magnum/Lee Gross/Philip Jones Griffiths

Robert De Niro, left, and John Savage in "The Deer Hunter"
Voted best film of the year by the New York critics

Miss Bergman, Jon Voight And 'Deer Hunter' Cited

By JANET MASLIN

"The Deer Hunter" was voted best English-language film of 1978 by the New York Film Critics' Circle yesterday. The group, reinstating a former policy of voting for English and foreign-language films separately, selected the Italian film "Bread and Chocolate" as the year's best import.

Ingrid Bergman was voted best actress for her performance in "Autumn Sonata," and Jon Voight was cited as best actor for "Coming Home." The best director award went to Terrence Malick, for "Days of Heaven."

The group's 26 voting members are allowed one vote each on a first ballot. If no candidate receives a majority of votes, the members list their top three choices, allotting them three points, two points or one point, respectively.

Wins on Third Ballot

This year, there were 29 points for "The Deer Hunter" on a third ballot, with runners-up including "Days of Heaven" (24 points), "An Unmarried Woman" (20 points), "Coming Home" (15 points), "Interiors" (9 points), and "Who'll Stop the Rain?" (8 points).

"Bread and Chocolate" won on the second ballot with 35 points. Other foreign films in the running were "Autumn Sonata" (27 points), "A Slave of Love" (20 points) and "Get Out Your Handkerchiefs" (19 points).

Miss Bergman, with 14 votes, was the only first-ballot winner. In second place was Jill Clayburgh of "An Unmarried Woman," with 4 votes. Jane Fonda received 3 votes for her performance in "Coming Home," and 2 for "Comes a Horseman."

Mr. Voight, voted best actor with 40 points on a second ballot, was followed by Gary Busey of "The Buddy Holly Story" (32 points), Robert De Niro of "The Deer Hunter" (19 points), Nino Manfredi of "Bread and Chocolate" (16 points), and Nick Nolte of "Who'll Stop the Rain?" (13 points).

For the best director award, which Mr. Malick won with 29 points on a fourth ballot, other contenders included Paul Mazursky for "An Unmarried Woman" (20 points), Ingmar Bergman for "Autumn Sonata" (18 points), Michael Cimino for "The Deer Hunter" (17 points), and Bertrand Blier for "Get Out Your Handkerchiefs" (16 points).

Mr. Mazursky won the best screenplay award, with 30 points. Runners-up were the screenplays for "Movie, Movie," "Bread and Chocolate" and "Get Out Your Handkerchiefs," each of which received 21 points. There were 18 points for the screenplay of "Who'll Stop the Rain?" and 15 points for "Interiors."

Maureen Stapleton Named

Maureen Stapleton, of "Interiors," was voted best supporting actress, with 34 points. Next came Maggie Smith, for "California Suite" (26 points), Meryl Streep for "The Deer Hunter" (25 points), and Lisa Lucas, who played Jill Clayburgh's daughter in "An Unmarried Woman" (18 points).

Christopher Walken of "The Deer Hunter" won the group's best supporting actor award, with 35 points. He was followed by Richard Farnsworth of "Comes a Horseman" (24 points) and Barry Bostwick of "Movie, Movie" (23 points).

There were votes cast for 27 different actors in this category, among them Gene Hackman, John Belushi, Charles Grodin, Laurence Olivier and Rex Reed, who has a cameo role in "Superman," and also is a member of the critics' group. "Well, at least I'd come to the party," said Mr. Reed, blushing.

The 43d annual New York Film Critics' awards will be presented in a ceremony at a party to be held at Sardi's late next month.

1978 D 21, C13:1

Burton Berinsky

Ingrid Bergman
Best actress

Jon Voight
Best actor

2 Vietnam Films Cast Aside Ghosts on Way to Oscars

By ALJEAN HARMETZ

Special to The New York Times

LOS ANGELES, April 10 — To win five of the six major Academy Awards last night, "The Deer Hunter" and "Coming Home" had to defeat more than the pictures nominated against them. They had to conquer a number of Hollywood ghosts and truisms. Chief among the phantasms was the movie industry's fear that nobody would go to see a movie about the Vietnam War.

The producers of "The Deer Hunter" were so worried about getting an audience for their $13 million picture that they bullied a rival producer, Allan Carr, into watching a private screening of the film last July. Mr. Carr, an entrepreneur of immense physical proportions whose box-office success in the last few years has more than matched his stout figure, sat all alone in the 1,100-seat theater and sobbed. It was a symbolic foreshadowing for the movie that would win five Academy Awards, including best picture.

Mr. Carr, whose own movie — "Grease" — was well on its way to making $100 million, said: "I probably would never have gone to see 'The Deer Hunter' — or any movie that was three hours long and about Vietnam. But, by the time it was half over, I was so emotionally undone, I was crying. I felt I was seeing a genuine masterpiece. It's not the kind of picture I could make, but I could appreciate it."

'New York Syndrome'

More important, Mr. Carr felt that "The Deer Hunter" was a *salable* masterpiece. He volunteered his services free of charge to devise a marketing strategy for the picture. "Universal kept asking, 'Who will see this movie?' I said, 'If you sell it right, everybody! Intellectuals will go to see it, and so will the Clint Eastwood audience.'"

Mr. Carr persuaded Universal not to release the film, as it had intended, last September. Instead, he orchestrated a limited-run in New York and here at the end of last year. "I wanted to play the picture in New York for one week and take it away. The New York syndrome is that if you can't get into something — a hit play like 'A Chorus Line' — it becomes something special. At every Christmas cocktail party in New York, people would be asking each other if they had been able to get into one of the eight performances of 'The Deer Hunter.' Then we'd bring the picture back when the academy nominations were announced. On a piece of paper that day in July, I wrote '9 to 11 nominations.' It got nine nominations."

Christopher Walken in "The Deer Hunter."
Supporting Actor

Mr. Carr's attempt to convince Universal executives had the unexpected help of Lorraine Gary, the actress and wife of Sid Sheinberg, president of Universal's parent company. "When Lorraine saw the movie," Mr. Sheinberg said, "she didn't, couldn't say a word for an hour afterward. She was fanatical about it."

"Universal," Mr. Carr said, "would hear from me about it in the daytime and from Lorraine about it at night. We persuaded them to treat the movie as a special event."

On the other hand, there was no trouble marketing "Coming Home." The problem was in making it.

Praise Is Showered

It took nearly 10 years for "Coming Home" to get from Nancy Dowd's original script, titled "Buffalo Ghost," to the stage of the Los Angeles Music Center, where an ecstatic Jon Voight and Jane Fonda cradled Oscars for best actor and actress. By that time, according to Miss Dowd, her angry and blistering story, based on her own experiences, had been softened.

Bruce Gilbert, associate producer of "Coming Home," insists that the genesis of the movie was always himself and Miss Fonda, and that Miss Dowd was provided with the characters and asked to write a script. In any case, the film makers felt her script was unworkable. Waldo Salt was brought in as screenwriter, and he added a love affair between Miss Fonda's Army wife and Mr. Voight's paraplegic veteran. Miss Dowd, Mr. Salt and Robert C. Jones won Oscars for her story and their script; but Miss Fonda — who had subsidized the writing of "Buffalo Ghost" — pointedly neglected to thank Miss Dowd, a former friend, while showering praise on Mr. Salt as the first Hollywood heavyweight to believe in the project.

"United Artists," Mike Medavoy, former head of production at the company, said, "decided to take a chance on 'Coming Home' when we were presented with Waldo Salt's script. But it was a big gamble, and everybody knew it. Almost everybody worked for less than their current rate. Jane only took $100,000 and a percentage of the gross *after* break-even. We were also backing Coppola's 'Apocalypse Now,' and we had foreign distribution of 'The Deer Hunter,' and one of our executives said, 'Oh my God, we may be thrown out of the country!'"

Despite the fears of unnamed executive, the country proved itself more ready for Vietnam than Hollywood expected.

Other Winners

The roster of other Oscar winners includes the following:

DIRECTING: Michael Cimino, "The Deer Hunter."
ACTRESS IN A SUPPORTING ROLE: Maggie Smith, "California Suite."
ACTOR IN A SUPPORTING ROLE: Christopher Walken, "The Deer Hunter."
SCREENPLAY BASED ON MATERIAL FROM ANOTHER MEDIUM: Oliver Stone, "Midnight Express."
ART DIRECTION: Paul Sylbert and Edwin O'Donovan, and George Gaines, "Heaven Can Wait."
CINEMATOGRAPHY: Nestor Almendros, "Days of Heaven."
COSTUME DESIGN: Anthony Powell, "Death on the Nile."
FEATURE-LENGTH DOCUMENTARY: "Scared Straight."
SHORT DOCUMENTARY: "The Flight of Gossamer Condor."
FILM EDITING: Peter Zinner, "The Deer Hunter."
FOREIGN LANGUAGE FILM: "Get Out Your Handkerchief."
ORIGINAL SCORE: Georgio Moroder, "Midnight Express."
ADAPTATION SCORE: Joe Renzetti, "The Buddy Holly Story."
ORIGINAL SONG: Paul Jabara, "Last Dance" from "Thank God It's Friday."
ANIMATED SHORT: "Special Delivery."
LIVE-ACTION SHORT: "Teenage Father."
SOUND: Richard Portman, William McCaughey, Aaron Rochin and Darrin Knight for "The Deer Hunter."
SPECIAL VISUAL EFFECTS: "Superman."

United Press International

John Wayne, making his first public appearance since his January cancer operation, presented the award for the best film.

1979 Ap 11, C17:1

How To Use Index

This index covers all the film reviews included in this volume. It is divided into three sections: Titles, Persons, and Corporations.

The Title Index lists each film reviewed by title. The Persons Index lists by name every performer, producer, director, screenwriter, etc. mentioned in the reviews, with the function in parentheses following the name, and the titles of the movies with which the person was connected, in chronological order. The Corporations Index lists all producing, distributing and otherwise participating companies mentioned in the reviews by name, again with the function in parentheses following the name, and the titles of the movies with which they were associated, in chronological order.

Citations in this index are by year, month, day, section of newspaper (if applicable), page and column; for example, 1975 Ja 11, II: 12:1. Since the reviews appear in chronological order, the date is the key locator. The citations also serve to locate the reviews in bound volumes and microfilm editions of The Times.

In the citations, the months are abbreviated as follows:

Ja—January	My—May	S—September
F—February	Je—June	O—October
Mr—March	Jl—July	N—November
Ap—April	Ag—August	D—December

TITLE INDEX

All films reviewed are listed alphabetically by title. Titles are inverted only if they begin with an article ("Doctor Glas" is listed under D, not G; but "The Graduate" is listed under G, not T). Titles beginning with a number are alphabetized as though the number were spelled out. Wherever possible, foreign films are entered under both the English and foreign-language title. Titles given incorrectly in the review appear correctly here. Films reviewed more than once and films with identical titles are given multiple listings.

PERSONS INDEX

All persons included in the credits are listed alphabetically, last name first. Their function in the films is listed after the name in parentheses, such as director, producer, screenwriter, etc. In entries where no such qualifier appears, the person was a performer (actor, actress, singer). A person with multiple functions will have multiple entries; for example, an actor who later turned producer or director will have two listings. A person having two functions in the same film will also have two listings. Functions that are very uncommon or are given imprecisely in the reviews are designated miscellaneous (misc).

Names beginning with Mc are alphabetized as though spelled Mac.

Entries under each name are by title of film, in chronological order.

CORPORATIONS INDEX

All companies mentioned in reviews as involved in the production or distribution of the film or in some other major function connected with it are listed here alphabetically. Company names are not inverted unless they start with a personal surname (for example, J Arthur Rank Organization is listed as Rank, J Arthur, Organization). The function of the company is given in parentheses after the name, abbreviated as follows:

Prod—Producer
Distr—Distributer
Misc—Miscellaneous

Misc is used when the function is uncommon or not precisely defined in the review. A company that has more than one function is given more than one listing; thus a user who has completed scanning a long listing under RKO (Distr) will then find an additional listing under RKO (Prod).

Abbreviations in names are alphabetized as though they were words (RKO as Rko).

Entries under each company name are by title of film, in chronological order.

A

B

C

D

E

F

G

H

I

J

K

L

M

N

O

P

Q

R

S

T

U

V

W

Y

Z

A

B

D

G

H

K

M

Q

R

S

U

V

W

X

Y

Z

A

B

C

T

U

V

W

Z